Y0-ASZ-444

INDIANA HISTORICAL COLLECTIONS
REPRINT

INDIANA LIBRARY AND HISTORICAL BOARD

MRS. FRANK J. SHEEHAN, *President*
CHARLES N. THOMPSON, *Vice President*
WILLIAM M. TAYLOR, *Secretary*
MRS. ELIZABETH CLAYPOOL EARL   WILLIAM P. DEARING
CHRISTOPHER B. COLEMAN, *Director of Historical Bureau*
NELLIE C. ARMSTRONG, *Editor*

COLLECTIONS

OF THE

ILLINOIS STATE HISTORICAL LIBRARY

EDITED BY

THEODORE CALVIN PEASE

UNIVERSITY OF ILLINOIS

VOLUME XXI

INDIANA HISTORICAL COLLECTIONS
REPRINT

ILLINOIS

STATE HISTORICAL LIBRARY

———

BOARD OF TRUSTEES

Otto Leopold Schmidt, *President*
Charles Henry Rammelkamp, *Vice President*
Laurence Marcellus Larson, *Secretary*

———

Georgia L. Osborne, *Librarian*

———

Theodore Calvin Pease, *Editor*

———

ADVISORY COMMISSION

Evarts Boutell Greene
William Edward Dodd
James Alton James
Andrew Cunningham McLaughlin
Edward Carleton Page
Theodore Calvin Pease
Charles Henry Rammelkamp

LAW SERIES

———

THE LAWS OF
INDIANA TERRITORY
1801-1809

———

INDIANA HISTORICAL COLLECTIONS
REPRINT

COLLECTIONS OF THE ILLINOIS STATE HISTORICAL LIBRARY

VOLUME XXI

LAW SERIES

THE LAWS OF
INDIANA TERRITORY
1801-1809

Edited with Introduction by
FRANCIS S. PHILBRICK
Professor of Law, University of Illinois

Published by the Trustees of the
ILLINOIS STATE HISTORICAL LIBRARY
Springfield, Illinois, 1930

Reprinted with Supplementary Indiana Material, by the
HISTORICAL BUREAU
of the
INDIANA LIBRARY AND HISTORICAL DEPARTMENT
Indianapolis
1931

Copyright, 1930

BY

The Illinois State Historical Library

Supplementary Indiana Material Copyright 1931

BY THE

Historical Bureau

OF THE

Indiana Library and Historical Department

Press of
Jeffersons Printing & Stationery Co.
Springfield, Illinois

TABLE OF CONTENTS

ACKNOWLEDGMENTS

The beginning of my work upon the present volume was facilitated by preliminary notes on the materials available for study, generously prepared by Mrs. Marguerite Jenison Pease, then assistant-editor of the *Collections* of the Illinois State Historical Library. To the courtesies of Mr. Charles L. Biederwolf, clerk of the Supreme Court of Indiana, custodian of the manuscript *Order Book* of the General Court of Indiana Territory, and to Mr. Charles E. Edwards, librarian of the Indiana Law Library, I owe thanks for the opportunity to study that interesting record. Mr. J. C. Bocquet, chief deputy circuit clerk of St. Clair County, has shown me every kindness in facilitating my examination of records preserved at Belleville. With particular pleasure I offer thanks to Mr. William Lister, clerk, and Mr. Frank Albrecht, deputy clerk, of the circuit court at Chester, for unstinted kindnesses in forwarding my studies of the records preserved in their office. To various other officials of archives and libraries I am indebted for lesser favors. My obligation to Miss Ernestine Jenison and to Miss Mildred Eversole, also of the editorial staff of the Library, is immeasurable, for they have verified every citation and every statement of fact other than those based upon manuscript sources, and their extremely critical and conscientious scrutiny of the manuscript has saved me from dozens of errors. Most grateful acknowledgments are due to the Chicago Historical Society for access to their set of originals of the Indiana Laws in repeated collations of the present text. Finally, the text of the statutes printed in this volume has been prepared by Mr. Pease, the general editor of the *Collections* of which it forms a part; and to him I am also grateful for several suggestions and corrections, although he has left me almost wholly to my own devices. It is perhaps unnecessary to say that upon myself rests sole responsibility for such errors of fact, interpretation, and judgment as may still be discovered in my Introduction.

F. S. **P.**

THE LAWS OF
INDIANA TERRITORY

SPECIAL INTRODUCTION

INTRODUCTION

The date which separates the administration of the Indiana Territory from that of the Northwest Territory points to no great change, aside from a short-time loss of representative government, even in the administrative history of the western counties; much less to any change in social practices or opinions significant in the life of the Illinois country. Alike before as after the local governments functioned, the courts were active, and relations with the central government—though attenuated—were realities. Few new personalities appear. The problems of general concern remain primarily the same—the division and redivision of the unwieldy mass of the old territory, thereby bringing government nearer home; the readjustment of political machinery to make it more acceptable to those who ran it; and the stimulus of immigration with cheap land, bond labor, and the attractions of representative government under an increasingly liberalized franchise. Variations in political opinion and in the ambitions of individuals give to old problems a somewhat altered guise and shifting emphasis. There is no further change. Before discussing the statutes of the period, the organization of the courts, and the actual administration of justice, it therefore seems desirable to review the political agitation that was roused by the questions just indicated in the years with which the present volume is concerned.

Though the Northwest Territory seethed with the animosities of Federalists and Republicans and to some degree with variant opinions regarding all the problems mentioned, there was no possibility, under the autocratic governmental system of the nonrepresentative stage ("first grade"), for a test of opinion. The meeting of the first legislature[1] under the "second grade" gave the op-

[1] It met on September 16 (organized September 23), 1799. W. H. Smith, *St. Clair Papers*, 2: 439 n., 477 n.

portunity. By a majority of one vote over the supporters of Arthur
St. Clair, son of the Governor, it elected William Henry Harrison
to represent the territory in Congress. Governor St. Clair was
filled with distrust of the "indigent and ignorant people" of the
western counties who were clamoring for a new state. Harrison's
political affiliations at this time seem somewhat obscure,[2] but it is
evident that he was elected by those unfriendly to the Governor,
and that he sympathized with the unrest that pervaded the territory. His victory was that of those who favored a less centralized
judicial system, a consequent division of the Northwest Territory,
and a land law more favorable to unmoneyed immigrants.

Promptly in the next session of Congress he secured a committee to consider alterations in the judicial establishment.[3] Two
weeks later he secured another committee to report upon improvements in the land system. Consideration of the first bill ended in
its recommitment to the committee with instructions to report on
the expediency of dividing the territory. The second bill, after
elaborate consideration,[4] became an act which provided for the
sale of land in tracts of whole or half sections at two dollars per
acre, with generous provisions (later repented) for payment over
four years, foreclosure by sale instead of absolute forfeiture in
case of final default, and the opening of land offices in the territory. The other bill was replaced by one for the division of the

[1] Appointed secretary of the Northwest Territory, in succession to
Winthrop Sargent, July 6, 1798, just after resigning his captaincy in the
army. D. B. Goebel, *William Henry Harrison* (*Indiana Historical Collections*, 14), 37, 38, 40. He married in 1795 a daughter of Judge Symmes,
of the General Court of the territory. Elected delegate to Congress October
3, 1799 (L. Esarey, *A History of Indiana from its Exploration to 1920*,
1: 150; compare *St. Clair Papers*, 2: 499 n.). He was then 26 years
of age. See for details of his life the biography by Mrs. Goebel, published
in 1926.

[2] *St. Clair Papers*, 2: 482 (letter of December 1799 to James Ross);
J. P. Dunn, *Indiana; a Redemption from Slavery*, 280; Goebel, *Harrison*,
42-43.

[3] December 6, 1799. For full proceedings see *Annals*, 6 Congress, 1
session, pp. (H. R.) 193, 197-198, 245, 507. The bill title shows that the
object was to reform the *Superior* courts.

[4] December 24, 1799. For full proceedings see *Annals*, 6 Congress, 1
session, pp. (H. R.) 207, 209-210, 211, 375, 376, 425-426, 527, 537-538, 625-
626, 650-651, 652, 681, 683, 691, 701; (Sen.) 149, 164, 165, 167, 168, 173,
174; (the act of May 10, 1800) 1515-1522.

territory, passed after equally thorough consideration,[1] to go into effect on July 4, 1800. The western half became Indiana Territory (1800-1809), and Vincennes became the capital.

Even Governor St. Clair acknowledged that the territory was of unmanageable size; his opposition to division took the form of suggesting boundaries that raised political and sectional difficulties[2] —which also appeared in the debates of Congress.[3]

The arguments which induced division were based upon the unwieldy size of the territory—a thousand by seven hundred miles; its division by great areas of wilderness, held by the Indians; the large population of the western half (Harrison made the claim of 15,000!); the great inconveniences which the size of the territory presented in the administration of justice and in the transaction of business with the capital (Cincinnati)—the local situations being "too dissimilar to admit of being one Government, either to enact equal laws or to provide for the execution of them"; and the removal of many families into upper Louisiana.[4] These arguments

[1] For proceedings: *Annals*, 6 Congress, 1 session, pp. (H. R.) 583, 632-633, 635, 649, 676, 679, 683, 684, 691, 698-699, 700; (Sen.) 147, 148, 161, 163, 167-168, 168-169, 173; (the act of May 7, 1800), 1498-1500. Also *United States Statutes at Large*, 6 Congress, 1 session, ch. 41. Committee report of March 3, 1800, in *American State Papers: Miscellaneous* 1: 206-207.

[2] Letter of St. Clair to Harrison, February 17, 1800 (while the above bills were under discussion in Congress)—"To render the territory manageable, it would require to be divided into three districts." W. H. Harrison, *Governors Messages and Letters. Messages and Letters of William Henry Harrison*, (Indiana Historical Collections, 7), 11. *St. Clair Papers*, 2: 481-483 (letter of December 1799 to James Ross); 489 (letter of February 17, 1800, to Harrison); 570; see Dunn, *Indiana*, 279. A division was acceptable to St. Clair if so made as to preserve federalist control of his (the eastern) half, and postpone its attainment of statehood—which would end his governorship. He could easily see that he had no future in elective offices. But his opponents were, of course, likewise influenced by personal considerations, including land investments. See Goebel, *Harrison*, 42, 48.

[3] The Senate forced the adoption of a line that left temporarily in the Northwest Territory—until its eastern division should become a state (Ohio)—the relatively well-settled Gore, which was economically dependent upon Cincinnati and objected to the remoteness of Vincennes. St. Clair's view was that "almost any division into two parts which could be made would ruin Cincinnati" (see *supra*, n. 2). Then the seat of government, it could not remain so unless a threefold division were adopted; Harrison had to meet this source of opposition in the debate. *Annals*, 6 Congress, 1 session, 507, 698-699.

[4] *Annals*, 6 Congress, 1 session, 649, 699.

were sound, but it is evident that they could serve equally well, as they subsequently did, for a second division of the territory.

The new territory included three counties: St. Clair and Randolph in the Illinois country and Knox[1] to the eastward. The last included—along with practically all of present-day Indiana, half of Michigan, and part of Wisconsin—more than half of Illinois as then organized. A reorganization of boundaries in 1801 left within Knox only a strip along the eastern boundary, and threw seven-eighths of the present state into St. Clair.[2]

Save for the French villages, a few weak "colonies" of American frontiersmen, and occasional isolated adventurers, the two western counties were an empty wilderness. Peoria—where hundreds of transient traders, voyageurs, and Indians met (as at Mackinac and Prairie du Chien) at certain seasons of the year[3]—was outside all county boundaries until 1801.[4]

There was hardly a single distinctively American settlement except at and about New Design in the American Bottom. Every-

[1] St. Clair was organized April 27, 1790. *St. Clair Papers*, 2: 165 n., for the proclamation. Randolph was organized out of the southern end of St. Clair County by proclamation of October 5, 1795. *Ibid.*, 2: 345 n. Knox was organized June 20, 1790. *Ibid.*, 2: 166 n.

[2] See maps at the end of this volume from L. L. Emmerson, *Counties of Illinois, Their Origin and Evolution* (State document, January 1, 1920) pp. 17, 19, 21, 23. For the proclamation of 1801 (and 1803, altering the line between St. Clair and Randolph—apparently a gerrymander) see J. Gibson, "Executive Journal of Indiana Territory 1800-1816," in Indiana Historical Society, *Publications*, 3: pt. 3, pp. 98, 117-118.

[3] J. Reynolds, *The Pioneer History of Illinois* (Fergus ed.), 151, 235. Governor St. Clair wrote from Cahokia in the spring of 1790 that the village was very weak (his reference is perhaps to Kaskaskia), "as it always is at this season, the greatest part of the young men being absent on voyages, either to New Orleans or Michilimackinac." *St. Clair Papers*, 2: 137.

[4] It was not included within the boundaries fixed by the treaty with the Kaskaskia Indians. Chas. C. Royce, "Indian Land Cessions," in Bureau of American Ethnology, 18th *Annual Report*, pt. 2, 1899, p. 664; treaty in C. J. Kappler, "Indian Affairs, Laws and Treaties," in *Senate Documents*, No. 452, 57 Congress, 1 session, 2: 49-50; *American State Papers: Public Lands*, 1: 285). Nevertheless George Rogers Clark had assumed Virginia's jurisdiction, appointing as commandant Jean Baptiste Mayet (*ibid.*, 138), and Governor St. Clair did the same. He reappointed Mayet, and the instructions (and title) evidently indicate a realization that he was continuing the traditional paternalism of French administration beyond the limits of organized government. Mayet was, among other things, "to see that justice was done, relieve distress, as far as practicable, and see that the inhabitants did not act imprudently." June, 1790—*ibid.*, 167 n., 176.

where else the French were greatly preponderant; their weights and measures were standard in trade and in the courts; their customs dominated social life. Since 1763 many of them had migrated to Louisiana, but a trickle of American immigration from the southern states, east and west, had replaced them and was becoming by 1800 a stream manifestly destined soon to overflow and fill in the whole of the Illinois country. As Governor Reynolds puts it, about 1805 "the country commenced to have frontiers. Before that, inside and outside of the American settlements were all frontiers."[1] A belt of territory less than a hundred miles long and twenty wide embraced all the settlements of the territory up to 1809. The population in 1800 was about 2,500, equally concentrated around Cahokia and Kaskaskia.[2] Distances which for frontier modes of travel were immense separated all these settlements. Even from Kaskaskia to Cahokia was some fifty miles; thence to Peoria, almost two hundred more; to Prairie du Chien, five; across the prairies to Vincennes, at least a hundred and fifty. From Kaskaskia southeastwardly to the Ohio, and northeastwardly to the Wabash, there was probably not one home; a road, hardly usable by other than single horses, ran to each.[3]

[1] Reynolds, *Pioneer History*, 358.

[2] About 100 in Peoria. C. W. Alvord, *Illinois Country*, 407-408; Dunn, *Indiana*, 295-296; and Esarey, *History*, 1: 155, 179, analyze the census data of 1800. Secretary Gibson's summary (Ind. Hist. Soc. *Pub.*, 3: pt. 3, p. 83) showed 4,875 inhabitants in the whole territory. Robert Morrison, who took the census in 1801, estimated the population of St. Clair and Randolph in 1805 at 4,311. Ind. Hist. Soc. *Pub.*, 2: 506. In 1809, when Illinois Territory was created, the estimate was 11,000. The U. S. census of 1810 reported a total population in the two counties of 12,282 (4,854 free whites in St. Clair, 6,647 in Randolph). *Annals*, 10 Congress. 2 session, 973; *Amer. State Papers: Misc.*, 1: 946. In 1800 the census (Gibson's summary, *supra*) reported no slaves in St. Clair County, 28 in Knox in and near Vincennes, 107 in Randolph (60 in Prairie du Rocher, 47 in Kaskaskia). The census of 1810 reported 40 slaves in St. Clair, 128 in Randolph; also 113 free persons, not white and excluding Indians not taxed (mainly, therefore, one would suppose free blacks), in St. Clair and 500 in Randolph. Compare *post*, xlviii, n. 3; li, n. 1; cxxxvii.

[3] The proslavery "convention" petition of 1806 says of the country between Illinois and Vincennes: "dreary beyond description, not a single human dwelling is to be found in this whole region"—see *post*, xxxix, n. 2. The same statement is made in the anti-Harrison petition of 1808 cited *post*, xlvii, n. 1. Governor Reynolds makes the same statement of 1811, when he rode over this route: *My Own Times*, 122. On the road to Golconda or Shawneetown, Reynolds, *Pioneer History*, 298; *My Own Times*, 46, 63; to Vincennes, *Pioneer History*, 293; *My Own Times*, 111.

Apparently one ran also from Vincennes to Cahokia.[1] Such roads could serve only the immigrant, and the occasional traveler whom litigation or other business forced upon long journeys; industry required none, and agriculture none except the local roads in the Mississippi settlements.[2]

The system of government provided by the Ordinance of 1787 for the Northwest Territory was made applicable to Indiana Territory, save that the transition to the second stage should take place, without regard to actual population, whenever the governor should receive "satisfactory evidence" that a majority of the voters ("free-holders") desired the change. In the first stage the people had no direct voice in government, either local or general. The legislative power which, by transition to the second stage, the people of the older territory had just gained for themselves was held by the governor and the judges of the territorial court; and their power was only to "adopt" such "laws of the original States" as fitted the circumstances of the territory.

Harrison was appointed governor, and John Gibson[3]—revolutionary soldier, frontiersman, Indian-captive,-kinsman and -trader—secretary of the new territory. St. Clair, long as he lived on the frontier, never for a moment impresses one as belonging to it; much less his assistant, Secretary Winthrop Sargent. But John Gibson was quintessentially of the frontier; and Harrison, whatever his early associations with Virginia's aristocracy, and though perhaps rather by virtue of political finesse than of any change in the man, fitted extraordinarily well into the west. Harrison had less administrative training than, and was far inferior in general ability and force to, St. Clair;[4] and Gibson, though apparently of fair education, was certainly inferior in that respect to Harrison.

---

[1] The mail route from Vincennes to Kaskaskia was discontinued, and one to Cahokia added, in 1805. *Annals,* 8 Congress, 2 session, 1174, 1692, 1693.

[2] For Illinois roads, Reynolds, *Pioneer History,* 281, 299.

[3] He served throughout the territorial period of Indiana, 1800-1816. See Harrison, *Messages,* 1: 316 n. for details.

[4] See the friendly critical estimate by Jacob Burnet, who knew him well, *Notes on the Early Settlement of the North-Western Territory,* 374-383, especially 378, 380; also Reynolds, *Pioneer History,* 155. Readers of the *St. Clair Papers* will note therein abundant evidences of his very exceptional talents and good sense.

He was a plain, blunt, honest man, who did quiet and apparently acceptable service in a number of offices. He was not the kind of man to be without opinions or to hold them lightly, but he kept free of party quarrels, with which no trace connects him.[1]

William Clarke, Henry Vander Burgh, and John Griffin were the first judges of the territorial court. In general culture, or at least in general schooling, they were certainly inferior to the judges of the older territory. They were also clearly inferior in legal schooling;[2] but as any man of talent could readily have acquired in solitary study the equivalent of the training afforded by the best law schools of the time their inferiority in this respect was probably unimportant. Of Clarke nothing is definitely known beyond his name, and his early death, whatever may have been his legal qualifications, precluded any record of them. Vander Burgh was a New Yorker who removed to Vincennes soon after service in the Revolutionary army. If he had had any legal training it was apparently unknown to his associates. On circuit, and in serving under special commission in courts of jail delivery, he seems to

[1] W. W. Woollen, *Biographical and Historical Sketches of Early Indiana,* 11-20. Harrison, in recommending him to Jefferson (October 18, 1808) for his third nomination, wrote: "He is far from being a very expert Secretary, but he is a very honest man which is much better." Harrison, *Messages,* 1: 315. See *post,* xviii, n. 2.

[2] See T. C. Pease, *The Laws of the Northwest Territory 1788-1800* (*Illinois Historical Collections,* 17), xvii-xviii, xxii, on Parsons, Varnum and Symmes; the latter, however, had not been chief-justice of New Jersey, but only associate-justice, 1777-1783, B. W. Bond (ed.), *The Correspondence of John Cleves Symmes, Founder of the Miami Purchase,* 6; Pease, *op. cit.,* xxiii on Turner. In his arguments with the judges St. Clair (who, in addition to an excellent general education, had had experience as county judge, recorder, and clerk in Pennsylvania—*ibid.,* xvii—certainly appears to good advantage, and he held their professional knowledge in low esteem; it would seem deservedly so. To be sure he referred to Parsons and Varnum as "men who had some eminence in the profession of the law"—legislative address to their successors, Symmes and Turner, in *St. Clair Papers,* 2: 334, 357. But he wrote later, with reference to the question of securing "some person of competent abilities" as attorney-general of the territory (at a salary of $300 or $400): "I am not a lawyer, but should it happen that a Governor may have been bred to that profession, still I think he ought to have a responsible law counselor, and it is a misfortune that some of our judges (all of them, in fact) are in the same predicament with myself. Even Judge Symmes, though he has been upon the supreme bench in Jersey, was not, I believe, a professional man when called to it"—letter of May 9, 1793, to Edmund Randolph, *St. Clair Papers,* 2: 314; cp. 164, 339, 374.

have done much of the work of the General Court in the western counties.[1] Little tangible evidence remains of his ultimate professional attainments, but his services seem to have been satisfactory. Judge Griffin was a Virginian, of some elegant accomplishments and fond of social pleasures, a man of no great force, and an intriguer. It is uncertain whether he ever studied law. He made no mark in the history of Indiana Territory; indeed had little opportunity, for in 1806 he was appointed to the court of the territory of Michigan.[2]

Some of the men added later to the court were of distinctly high quality both in general culture and legal ability. Thomas Terry Davis, who succeeded Clarke, served both on the territorial court and later as chancellor until his death in 1807. He had held public office in Kentucky and represented that state in Congress before his removal to Indiana Territory. His advancement may be attributed primarily to Harrison's friendship, for there is no other evidence of his talents or attainments.[3] Both Waller Taylor, who succeeded Griffin, and Benjamin Parke, who followed Davis on the court, served until Indiana became a state, and had later careers of great distinction. Taylor, a trained lawyer, had served in the Virginia legislature, and was later one of Indiana's first United States senators.[4] Parke had been for four years attorney-general, a representative in the first legislature, and three years delegate of the territory in Congress before his appointment to the court. After Indiana became a state he served for a year as a state circuit judge, and thereafter as the federal district judge for Indiana until his death. He was a cultured gentleman, and a lawyer of talent, probity, industry, and conscience. Not only in the law but also in the cause of education his services to the state were outstanding.[5]

The first chancellor (preceding Davis), John Badollet, was a Swiss, a friend from boyhood on through life of Gallatin, who induced him to remove from Switzerland to this country in 1786;

[1] See *post,* app. notes 2, 3. Vander Burgh is the only member of whose services on circuit, records remain in the Illinois country.

[2] *Post,* app. n. 4.

[3] *Post,* app. n. 5.

[4] *Post,* app. n. 6.

[5] *Post,* app. n. 7.

but though we may certainly assume that he possessed superior
qualities little is known concerning him. Apparently he never
studied law.[1] The first attorney-general of the territory, preceding Parke, was John Rice Jones;[2] and the third (and last of the
period considered in this volume) was Thomas Randolph. John
Rice Jones, who played a very prominent part in the legal and
political history of the time, was a Welshman who came to America
after studying (it is said) at Oxford. He was practicing law in
Philadelphia when he had barely attained his majority, and located
at Vincennes in 1786. For a quarter of a century—first in Vincennes, then for a dozen years in the Illinois country, then again
at Vincennes—he was a leading lawyer of the territory. The Revised Statutes of 1807 are known by his name. In St. Clair County,
of which (as well as of St. Louis, Missouri) he was the first
resident attorney, his fluent command of French added to his success and usefulness. By order of one of the St. Clair courts in
1792 he translated into French the laws of the territory, "for the
use of the Judges, who do not understand English."[3] He stood
high for some years in Harrison's confidence and regard, but an
enmity subsequently arose between them which thwarted the full
satisfaction of his ambitions, and he abandoned definitively Indiana
for the Illinois country in 1808, when it was clear that the latter
(largely owing to him) would soon be an independent territory.[4]
Still later he removed to Louisiana Territory, and became a member of the Supreme Court of Missouri. His talents were not less
unusual than his education, and were combined with a personality
of power and distinction. Thomas Randolph[5] was a Virginian
and graduate of William and Mary, who had studied law and

---

[1] *Post,* app. n. 8.

[2] *Post,* app. n. 10.

[3] Bateman and Selby, *Hist. of St. Clair County,* 699 (quoting the
record, of 1792). He was to deposit the translation "with the clerk of the
district," and to receive $100 for his work. See the protest of the French
judges in 1787 against the election to the Kaskaskia court of American
colleagues; they could not discuss the issues together, and there was no
translator capable of explaining the issues and the Virginia statutes. C. W.
Alvord: *Kaskaskia Records* (*I. H. C.,* 5), 405-407; *Cahokia Records* (*I. H.
C.,* 2), cxxxiv-cxxxv.

[4] See the discussion of this in the biographical note on Jones, *post,* app.
n. 10.

[5] *Post,* app. n. 11.

served in the Virginia Assembly. With Davis and Taylor, fellow Virginians and close companions of Harrison, he played a briefly important part politically, but his merits as a lawyer do not appear.

Although men of good family, education, and talent have never been rarities on the frontier, the above group must nevertheless be regarded as remarkable.

Under the government of the first grade provided for the Northwest Territory, made applicable to Indiana Territory under the first grade, all power, legislative, executive and judicial, was concentrated in the governor and judges, and in its employment they were responsible only to the federal government. Notwithstanding that the liberal guaranties of personal and property rights embodied in the Ordinance[1] insured the inhabitants against abuses in the exercise of this power, they could not long remain content with its existence. In particular, the objections to centralized appointive power (by the national government of all the superior executive and judicial officers, and by the governor of all subordinate officers "necessary for the preservation of the peace and good order" of the territory) became in the Illinois counties a source of discontent steadily accentuated—at least to a small group of men who dominated the Illinois country.

The political spirit of the governing authorities was therefore of great importance. Secretary Gibson's conception of the relation between government and governed amusingly reveals a simpleminded soldier:[2] "There are always some contrary people in all walks of life who are hard to manage . . . When the Govern-

---

[1] Note the bill of rights in the Ordinance—Pease, *Laws* (*I. H. C.*, 17), 127-128. The impropriety of leaving the construction of the laws to the judges who enacted them was evident; it was excused on the ground of "necessity"—doubtless, financial: *St. Clair Papers, 2*: 365.

[2] Letter of May 22, 1807 to Capt. W. Hargrave, on ranger service—to be sure when Indian hostilities were feared. "Anyone who refuses to stay in the fort when ordered, arrest them and send them to this post [Vincennes], under guard." W. M. Cockrum, *Pioneer History of Indiana*, 207. Of course when courts were weak there was much truth in Gibson's view. So William St. Clair had written of the Illinois country in 1793. "Our militia in this country is in a wretched state . . . There has not been a review these eighteen months past, so that it would appear we have no organized government whatever. Our courts are in a deplorable state; no order is kept in the interior, and many times not held." *St. Clair Papers, 2*: 317.

ment does all that it can to protect its people they must and shall obey the rules. This territory is under no law that can force obedience but the Military and all of its subjects must obey the governing rule or be sent out of it"! Harrison was too politically minded to entertain views of such autocratic spice. Harrison's practice showed that he approved the provision of the Virginia act of 1778, creating the County of Illinois, which had provided for the popular election of county officers.[1] His biographer declares that whenever it could be done with propriety he appointed to office "such persons as were recommended by a majority of the people." And when a judicial appointment proved unpopular he addressed the citizens and "stated that the people should have the choice of all the officers who were generally elected by popular suffrage in the states, although the ordinance for the government of the territories, vested the appointing power in the governor alone. He was, notwithstanding, willing to receive and consider all petitions presented to him, relative to any kind of appointment; yet in cases of judges and officers of that character, after hearing all that could be said on the subject, he would reserve the ultimate decision to himself." We find the Randolph Court of Quarter Sessions recommending men for appointment to that body, and he met their desires.[2] Governor St. Clair had refused to countenance even suggestions regarding judicial office.[3] With similar pliancy he avoided the quarrels over county creations which had given St. Clair such trouble.[4] As for the old dispute as to what might be

[1] W. W. Hening, *Statutes at Large of Virginia*, 9: 552.

[2] Case in Clark County, 1809. M. Dawson, *Historical Narrative of the Civil and Military Services of Major-General William H. Harrison*, 172. The Randolph Court recommended James Morrison, Thomas Todd, and John Beaird for their court and the Common Pleas. *Court Record 1802-06*, p. 8, September 1802. He appointed Beaird.

[3] See *St. Clair Papers*, 2: 371.

[4] Their creation involved much the same problems as a division of the territory; and in view of their vast size there was physically little difference. This explains St. Clair's troubles: see Burnet, *Notes*, 321-323, 496; *St. Clair Papers*, 1: 214; and, concerning the creation of Wayne County in 1796—of which the present state of Michigan was then part—*ibid.*, 2: 404 *et seq.* His obstinate insistence upon his powers contrasts with Harrison's address to the first legislature (1805): "From the construction which I have put upon the ordinance of congress, the erection of new counties will rest with the legislature. It is a power, however, which ought to be cautiously used, as the advantages produced by it are often illusive or partial, whilst the expense is certain and general." Dawson, *Harrison*, 74.

done under the power to "adopt . . . laws of the original states,"[1] here again he avoided all controversy and incurred practically no criticism. But though Harrison undoubtedly greatly checked by his democratic practice the demand for transition to the second grade—and in such practice, while expressive of his inherent democracy, he was clearly partly actuated by political caution— he could do no more than delay it. He originally opposed it because it might hamper him with a legislature lost to the Federalists; or lost in some combination of members upon the new issues taking form in the territory, whose effect upon the political balance was still incalculable. His partisans, therefore, regarded the Illinois movement as an "intrigue" against the Governor.[2] Similarly, after he had forced transition to the second grade, having decided that it would increase his political safety, he opposed division— certainly upon a balance of benefits and losses, but certainly also including in these the possible loss of the legislature to the antislavery party of the eastern counties when the proslavery party of the Illinois country had withdrawn,[3] and doubtless also the consequent shrinkage in his appointive power. His success in maintaining his office (1800-1812) despite these great changes is significant of his political acumen.

Agitation for transition to representative government began in 1801 in the Illinois counties. It was preceded by, and associated with, petitions in favor of slavery. A petition for the suspension of Article six of the Ordinance of 1787 (which declared that "there shall be neither slavery nor involuntary servitude in the said territory, otherwise than in punishment of crimes") was sent to Congress in 1796 by John Edgar, William Morrison, William St. Clair, and John Dumoulin; but though claiming to speak for the people of Randolph and St. Clair they showed no authority. In October, 1800, however, a similar petition was forwarded by

[1] Compare Pease, *Laws* (*I. H. C.*, 17), xx-xxii, xxiv-xxx, 124.
[2] Dunn, *Indiana,* 322; H. J. Webster, "William Henry Harrison's Administration of Indiana Territory," Ind. Hist. Soc. *Pub.*, 4: 203. Benjamin Parke, letter of September 5, 1808, in Woollen, *Sketches,* 3 *et seq.*
[3] Dunn, *Indiana,* 322; Webster, Ind. Hist. Soc. *Pub.*, 4: 203-204.

270 inhabitants, most of them French.[1] Both asked that the introduction of slaves be permitted from other states, they to remain in bondage during life, but their children born in the territory, to become freed at certain ages. It was John Edgar and Robert Morrison who stirred in 1801 this demand for transition to the second grade of government. It was claimed that nine-tenths of the inhabitants approved their petitions, which a great part had signed.[2]

This indicated a great change from the earlier attitude of the French population. Royalists by tradition, Federalists by tendency, content with the paternalistic administration vouchsafed their ancestors, they were equally content with the centralized rule of governor and judges. They had resented the burdens[3] and had seemed indifferent to the supposed virtues of popular government. It has been emphasized in explanation of their change that under the second grade Congress would no longer have a veto upon their laws. Dunn's explanation[4] has also been generally accepted: that the change was induced by the hope of insuring their slave-holding interests through the efforts of a delegate in Congress. This was, indeed, illogical—for if Congress would not upon peti-

[1] Army officers who wished to bring slaves into the territory had sent two petitions to the legislature of the Northwest Territory in 1799. For petition of January 12, 1796—*Amer. State Papers: Pub. Lands,* 1: 68-70; *Annals,* 4 Congress, 1 session, 1171 (or Ind. Hist. Soc. *Pub.,* 2: 447-452); comment in Dunn, *Indiana,* 283-288. On those of 1799, Dunn, 288-293. For that of October 1, 1800: Ind. Hist. Soc. *Pub.,* 2: 455-461; *Annals,* 6 Congress, 735; comment, Dunn, *op. cit.,* 297-299. Among the signers were John Rice Jones, John Edgar, William and Robert Morrison, Robert McMahon (who signed twice), George Fisher, "Bte" Barbeau (doubtless "J. Bte," i. e. Jean Baptiste Barbau), James Dunn, and William Kelly of Randolph; Shadrach Bond [Sr.], "Js" (doubtless "Jn," i. e. Jean) Dumoulin, J. F. Perrey, John Hay, John Hays, William Arundel, and George Atchison (who signed twice) of St. Clair. The transcriptions of names as made for Dunn, evidently by some one unfamiliar with the Illinois family names, contain many errors. The names of various judges of both counties are absent.
[2] J. Edgar to St. Clair, April 11, 1801. *St. Clair Papers,* 2: 533.
[3] Dunn, *Indiana,* 271. This is the traditional view, which can be supported by the opinions of Judge Symmes, General Harmar and John Edgar. See quotations, *post,* ccxvi. Inhabitants of Vincennes, chiefly French, petitioned Congress for a restoration of government of the first grade in the Northwest Territory. *St. Clair Papers,* 2: 489.
[4] *Indiana,* 299; Webster, Ind. Hist. Soc. *Pub.,* 4: 198, 203. Mrs. Goebel's view—*Harrison,* 76, 78, 80—is in accord with the writer's; *post,* liv.

tion annul Article six how should a delegate persuade it? But since hope despises logic, the hope was clung to until events proved its emptiness. As for the other explanation, at least as regards slavery there had been evidence that not much protection was to be expected from the territorial judges.[1] And in fact the later change to legislative government proved fruitful; for though representation in a legislature, without preponderant population, could not guarantee security, it actually did enable the western counties to gain their main ends by compromise territorial enactments. Of some importance, also, was the imminence in 1801 of the great acquisition of Indian lands which was consummated in the following year,[2] for cheap land meant—it was believed—immigration and taxes; and the second stage could be had so soon as the people could be induced to risk its expense. And finally, since we know that in earlier years the big land speculators of the Illinois country had stimulated the fears roused by Article six of the Ordinance among the French slaveholders, inducing many to abandon their Illinois lands and remove into Louisiana,[3] it is at least possible that they were now again stimulating their fears for personal—though this time political—ends.

Harrison's partisans attributed to Robert Morrison the ambition to become the first delegate of a new territory. The opponents of the movement urged the stagnation of immigration, the unlikelihood of Indian cessions, the added expense of a government of the second grade.[4] This last became the decisive argu-

---

[1] "All the Supreme Judges of the Northwest Territory were men of pronounced anti-slavery sentiments." L. Monks, *Courts and Lawyers of Indiana*, 1: 13. Compare *post*, cxli-cxliii.

[2] The land westward of the Wabash watershed and between the Kaskaskia River and the Illinois was acquired in 1803, that between the Illinois and Wisconsin rivers in 1804, that east of the Wabash watershed in 1805. See on the Illinois cessions: Harrison (letter December 22, 1808 from Jefferson), *Messages,* 1: 322; Royce, "Indian Land Cessions," 656-657, 664-665; Kappler, "Indian Affairs Laws and Treaties," 2: 65, 74. Indiana cessions: *Amer. State Papers: Pub. Lands,* 3: 461; map in *Indiana Magazine of History,* 12: 5.

[3] *Post,* lxxv, n. 2. This does not necessarily assume that they could fail to realize, after the United States acquired Louisiana, that they would there still be under the same government, and with treaty guarantees less strong than those of 1763. They would be part of a population where slavery was stronger, political protection more likely.

[4] B. Parke, *ante,* xx, n. 2.

ment; Harrison stressed it in an open letter to the people[1] and the movement was defeated.

In 1803, after the acquisition of Louisiana, the Illinois separatists conceived the plan of joinder to that territory. The treaty with France, it is true, did no more than guarantee their "property" to the inhabitants of that colony, as the treaty of 1763 had done for the inhabitants of the Illinois country. But the prior laws of the colony continued in force, of course, by virtue of the principles of international usage; and this was expressly provided in the fundamental American legislation, beginning with the act of 1804, which organized the District of Louisiana. Aside, therefore, from the compact theory of the Ordinance (and Congress had in fact by mere legislation altered some of its provisions), there could be no doubt that annexation would have freed the Illinois country from the antislavery clause of that instrument; and at the same time a public opinion more unifiedly proslavery than that of the Indiana Territory would have given security against later alterations. It is therefore remarkable indeed that the reasons advanced in the petitions for joinder to the French territory were exclusively political, without so much as a reference to slavery.[2] Though shar-

[1] Equally prominent in the later struggle in Michigan: *Michigan Pioneer and Historical Collections*, 8: 596; *Ind. Mag. of Hist.*, 4: 141. Strangely enough this argument is not even mentioned in such abstracts of debates upon the division of 1800 as are preserved in the *Annals*. See also Dunn, *Indiana*, 301; Goebel, *Harrison*, 76. Parke (Woollen, *Sketches*, 4) says that some estimates of the expense ran from $12,000 to $15,000. His own estimate (p. 6) was $3,500 as a maximum.

[2] For the treaty with France (Art. III), F. N. Thorpe, *Federal and State Constitutions*, 3: 1360; the act of March 26, 1804, creating the District of Louisiana (§ 13), *ibid.*, 1369—declaring the continuance of prior law until modified. The reasons of the petitioners are stated in the *Annals*—8 Congress, 1 session, 489 (October 26, 1803), 555, 623; 8 Congress, 2 session, 1659-1660—as being "certain inconveniences and embarrassments" to which the petitioners were "subjected, in consequence of their connexion, under the same Government, with the eastern extremity of the said Territory." Photostatic copies, from the original manuscripts in the files of the House of Representatives, are in the Illinois Historical Survey. Mrs. Goebel's citation (*Harrison*, 83 n.) may indicate that only one memorial is now preserved. There were two: the one she cites referred to the committee on November 9, 1803, signed by 80 inhabitants, primarily of Randolph County but in part from St. Clair; and another, signed by 122 inhabitants, primarily of St. Clair County but in part from Randolph. The second was tabled on October 26, referred on November 3, the report tabled on November 24; the first was referred to the same committee on November 9, the report tabled on November 24. The two petitions were almost, if not quite, iden-

ing the "universal satisfaction and . . . joy inexpressible" felt "throughout the Western Country" over the annexation of Louisiana, the memorialists saw only a "gloomy and discouraging situation" for the Illinois counties if left unconnected with a contiguous territory of luxuriant soil, with settlements "united by reciprocal interests," enjoying "the benefits to be derived from a good government," and so much greater in population. Unfortunately, their argument against a continued connection with the eastern counties of Indiana was mainly based upon their superiority in population! —which, were government of the second grade to be adopted, would entitle them to four representatives out of seven and three councillors out of five, so that "the interests of this part of the Territory would lay entirely at their mercy." They deemed "obvious" the evils to be apprehended from this source. The location of the capital at Vincennes concentrated there the interests of the officers of government, "directing the whole force of the influence attached to their high situations . . . to the exclusive aggrandizement of their chosen place of residence." The Illinois country was "connected in no one respect by a reciprocity of interests" with the eastern counties, but its union with Louisiana would be "rendered firm by the combination of mutual and reciprocal interests and of a mutual confidence." The memorial was a fair summary of the arguments of the divisionists—which in reality simply boiled down to a desire for self-government. The committee of Congress to which these petitions were referred, regarded the inconveniences suffered by the memorialists from their isolated situation as merely transient and "common to all infant settlements," and discovered no evidence of an ascendancy of the eastern counties "other than is consistent with the fundamental principles of a republican system of Government." They found no evidence that "an uncommon or an ungenerous exercise of the power of such majority has taken place—nor that an unusual influence has attached itself to the seat of Government in said Territory—but that the evils stated by said Memorialists are ideal." A union with

---

tical. Mrs. Goebel's statement that the petition "stated that a strong partiality was shown in appointments" (*Harrison*, 83) is inaccurate: neither petition contains any such statement, or implication.

Louisiana they thought would be highly injurious, different as were the past laws and local attachments of the two territories. The reasons offered by the petitioners were certainly not their real reasons. As the problem of land titles was not yet in the field of politics, nor that of taxation, personal ambitions, possibly reën-forced by hopes for slavery, must have been the chief excitants to such designs.[1]

The slavery factor was, of course, always present in the back-ground. There was at this same time some agitation simply for detachment from Indiana Territory,[2] and in this slavery doubtless played a part. Harrison had opposed division, in part, for political and personal reasons already referred to. It is evident that by concessions to the proslavery party of the Illinois country it might have been possible to weaken their pressure for division. It seems not unreasonable to assume that the calling of the Vincennes con-vention in 1802 (December), to consider the legalizaton of slave immigration, must have been associated in Harrison's mind with the idea that by recognizing one demand of the malcontents he might control the other. But the proslavery party had gained nothing by the appeal of this convention to Congress.

In another way, however, the Illinois country (though against the determined opposition of the supposed Illinois party) made a great advance; namely in securing representative government. Since Harrison had defeated this in 1801 conditions had greatly altered. With the admission of Ohio to statehood the populous Gore had been reannexed to Indiana Territory. Harrison had begun the extraordinary activity which in three years cleared of Indian titles a fourth of the area of the present state of Indiana. The opening of land offices at Vincennes and Kaskaskia in 1804 promised a rapid growth of population. Accordingly Harrison

---

[1] Judge Parke says: "Edgar was to be the Governor and R. Morrison the secretary, and all the posse were to be amply provided for in this new arrangement." See *ante*, xx, n. 2. Alvord, speaking of the Edgar-Morrison "party," apparently even before 1803, truly says: "Besides the demand for the introduction of slavery, their platform had two planks: opposition to the territorial administration, and Illinois for Illinoisians"—*Illinois Country*, 423.

[2] Woollen, *Sketches*, 5.

ordered the election which determined transition to representative government.[1]

Edgar and Robert Morrison now opposed in 1804 what they had advocated in 1801.[2] Harrison himself,—who had equally changed, but perhaps with better reason—Judge Parke, Henry Hurst (clerk of the General Court), James Johnson (judge of the Knox Common Pleas), General Washington Johnston (a prominent lawyer of the territory), Francis Vigo, and John Rice Jones were notably active in the eastern counties in favor of the change. Harrison attributed the opposition in the western counties to the fear of the land speculators that a legislature would impose a land tax. Harrison's comments upon land speculators were always unfriendly, but there is ample evidence that the underlying reason was political.[3]

The total vote on the question of transition to the second stage was but 400 (249 in the eastern counties, 142 from Randolph and St. Clair), with a majority of 138, almost wholly in Knox, in favor of the change. It was approved in Randolph by a vote of 40 to 21, but disapproved in St. Clair by one of 22 to 59. This was assuredly no indication of enthusiasm for representative government, either as an end in itself or as a step toward slavery, even in the Illinois country. Doubtless the indecision there was due to the reasons, already pointed out, that popular government

[1] *Ante,* xxii, n. 2. *Annals,* 8 Congress, 1 session, 1286. Proclamation August 4, election September 11, 1804—*Messages,* 1: 106.
[2] Parke (Woollen, *Sketches,* 7) says they were its bitterest opponents.
[3] In a letter to Jefferson November 20, 1805 (in *Messages,* 1: 175), when Shadrach Bond Sr., and John Francis Perrey, judges of the St. Clair Common Pleas and Quarter Sessions, had been nominated for appointment to the Legislative Council, he wrote: "I know nothing against his [Perrey's] character excepting that he has been pretty deeply engaged in purchasing the land claims in the Illinois Country—Both these gentlemen were unfortunately opposed to our going into the second grade of Government—Mr. Bonds opposition was very extraordinary & unexpected—the greatest efforts were however made by the land Jobbers to gain him over to their interests—& those gentry (some of whom own upwards of 100,000 acres of land) frightened at the Idea of having a land tax did not hesitate to spread any falsehood that was likely to defeat the Measure." The virtue of this letter disappears, however, when one notes that Jefferson had earlier instructed him (April 28, 1805, *ibid.,* 127) that "land-jobbers are undesirable." See app. n. 10 as to Jones. Vigo was one of the largest land operators in the Vincennes district, but before this time his claims had passed into other hands (sources cited *post,* lxxxvi, n. 1). In a letter of 1802 he spoke of

was bound to be expensive; and, moreover, the actual gains to democratic government in transition to the second grade were, in fact, extremely slight. As Salmon P. Chase said, "The judges were thenceforth to be confined to purely judicial functions. The governor was to retain his appointing power, his general executive authority, and to have an absolute negative upon all legislative acts. It is difficult to perceive any very strong reasons for preferring this form of government to that originally instituted. It is true, the people elected persons of their own choice to make laws, and were now to be represented by a delegate in the national congress, and, so far, there was something gained. But the governor now had an absolute negative, which he had not before, and here was something lost. The power of the governor, under the new order, was more absolute than under the old. Dependent upon the people for nothing, and responsible to them in no respect, he was subject to no control, but that of a public opinion, which might be disregarded with impunity." On the other hand its value as a step toward slavery was highly speculative. How far this was realized, just what part slavery played in the election, it is difficult to determine, or even to estimate. As Mr. Esarey says, "the only possible significance" of the vote was "that the distant counties opposed and the near ones favored." One must remember that many voters lived far from the county seats, and though three days were ordinarily allowed for elections only one was allowed for this. Alvord concludes that "there is evidence that the whole affair was hurried to completion by the governor in order to confuse his adversaries." On the other hand, Dearborn County's votes (twenty-six) were cast unanimously in the negative, admittedly for anti-slavery reasons; and, so far as it goes this sustains Dunn, who somewhat unconvincingly emphasizes the slavery factor in the actual election. And though Mr. Esarey has criticised the over-emphasis of slavery by Dunn he agrees with him that "a ma-

"those speculators who infest our country"—*Messages,* 1: 36. It is quite clear that Harrison always directed to Jefferson opinions calculated to please the latter; see the correspondence in the *Messages, passim.* Jefferson's practical political philosophy rested upon confidence in a class of small landholders (see C. A. Beard, *Economic Origins of Jeffersonian Democracy,* ch. 14, and pp. 328, 342, 347, 358; compare 25, 125, 157).

jority of the people thought that the repeal of the section of the Ordinance forbidding slavery would largely increase immigration." Harrison wrote that "in all our elections the contest lay between those who were in favor of adopting the second grade of government and the admission of negroes and those who were opposed to these measures."[1] This is, however, certainly inaccurate with respect to the earlier attitude of Harrison himself, of John Edgar, and of Robert Morrison, at least. It is evidently too simple a formula.

At all events, whatever else the election might mean, the statute positively required its interpretation with respect to the question whether representative government was "the wish of a majority of the freeholders." Harrison accepted the vote as the "satisfactory evidence" of such desire which the law required. On December 5, 1804, he proclaimed the establishment of the new régime.[2]

Admit the charge that Harrison fixed the election date so as to preclude the participation of Wayne County therein—still, as that county was absolutely certain to become within a few months an independent territory, his action would seem only justice. Admit that days were allowed ordinarily for elections, and only one for this election;[3] still, proponents and opponents had equal opportunity. Moreover, Harrison justifiably referred, in his message to the first legislature, to "the long and protracted investigation" which preceded the adoption of the measure. "Yet"—as one of his defenders complained only four years later—"it has been stated ten

[1] Salmon P. Chase (editor), *The Statutes of Ohio and of the Northwestern Territory, adopted or enacted from 1788 to 1833 inclusive*, 27-28; Esarey, *History*, 1: 161, 173; Alvord, *Illinois Country*, 424; Dunn, *Indiana*, 321-322; Mr. Webster follows Dunn—Ind. Hist. Soc. *Pub.*, 4: 203; letter to Jefferson, June 18, 1805—quoted by Webster, *loc. cit.*, 205-206; *Ind. History Bulletin*, February, 1924.

[2] Gibson, *Exec. Journal*, 125.

[3] For the boundaries of Wayne fixed by proclamation of January 14, 1803, Harrison, *Messages*, 1: 68. See the proceedings in Congress, *Annals*, 8 Congress, 1 session (Sen.) 16, 26, 29-30 (report of October 27, 1803), 73-74, 75, 78, 211, 212; (H. R.) 645, 699, 1589 (report of December 29, 1803), 941, 1040-1041, 1041-1042. Also 8 Congress, 2 session (Sen.) 20, 21, 23-24, 25, 26, 31, 32; (H. R.) 862, 869, 871-872; (act of January 11, 1805), 1659. The counties bore the cost of the election. *Post*, 140. Doubtless Harrison said he was saving them expense.

thousand times . . . that the Governor thrust the people of the Territory into the second grade against their will."[1] This was the cry of the Edgar-Morrison faction, and in this judgment the leading historians of Indiana have concurred.[2]

The remaining period, 1805-1809, before Illinois became independent was certainly not one of "small causes and mean reasons." They were filled with problems of slavery, territorial division, the clearing of land titles, and the encouragement of immigration. It would be difficult to find another five years in our state history crowded with issues so important.

These issues, in view of Harrison's original opposition to adoption of the second grade, and the fact that he had power to convene, prorogue, and dissolve the Assembly and held an absolute veto, might well have been expected to cause many difficulties. Nevertheless the mechanism of government in the representative stage worked smoothly. St. Clair's unhappy insistence upon his veto power, and a strong hint from the first Legislative Council, were enough to save Harrison from repeating in that regard the errors of his predecessor.[3] With equal tact he avoided unwel-

---

[1] Woollen, *Sketches,* 9; Harrison, *Messages,* 1: 152. Elections were set for January 3. But on January 11 Wayne County became the Territory of Michigan. As the Ordinance required a minimum of seven representatives, and as one was lost with Wayne County and another through the invalidity of the St. Clair election, Harrison proclaimed (April 18, 1805, *Exec. Journal,* 127) a new election in St. Clair for *two* representatives.

[2] Dunn, *Indiana,* 324; Esarey, in Harrison, *Messages,* 1: 106 n.; the charge was emphasized in two Illinois petitions prepared in 1805, Dunn, "Slavery Petitions and Papers," Ind. Hist. Soc. *Pub.,* 2: 486-487, 499. In the former (signed by 354 persons—*post,* xxxviii, n. 2) they declared: (1) that Harrison acted upon an application which, they believed, had been confined to inhabitants of Knox; (2) that "the elections in the counties of Randolph and St. Clair were but very partially attended; a majority, however, of those freeholders who did attend, gave their suffrages against the measure . . . From this mode of procedure, incompetent to the object contemplated, from this slight and partial expression of the public sentiments upon this important subject, the *executive* was *satisfied* that there was a *majority of the freeholders in the territory* in favor of entering into the second grade of government" (sarcasm of the original). The second point treats the Illinois country as a unit, ignoring the variant county votes; justifiably. As to the first, the entry in the *Executive Journal* (124), reads, simply: "Sundry petitions have been received by the Governor from persons Styling themselves Freeholders of the Indiana Territory," etc.

[3] Judges Symmes and Turner protested against St. Clair's use of a veto, the power not being expressly mentioned in the Ordinance—*St. Clair*

come uses of his power of prorogation. "The Territorial form of government"—said he—"possesses some traits which are not altogether reconcilable with republican principles." And again, a few days later, more placatingly still: "It has ever been my wish . . . to conceal those rougher features of our constitution which are so justly offensive to republican delicacy, and which nothing but the infancy of our political state renders tolerable." As so often happens, however, if one analyzes Harrison's virtues, so here one suspects politics. For both of these conciliatory declarations were made after the separation of Illinois had left Harrison on the defensive.[1] He did veto laws in 1808, and in consequence thereof the Assembly instructed the delegate of the territory in Congress to procure a repeal of the absolute veto power, as also of the powers to prorogue and dissolve the Assembly, giving him only the powers held by the President of the United States.[2] A bill was offered to eliminate the powers of proroguing or dissolving the Assembly—leaving the veto still absolute—but was indefinitely postponed.[3]

A tilt with the Assembly, on its face rather amusing than important, over a vacancy in the Council, was the only case of friction. It marked, in fact, the beginning of Harrison's political decline, for he was defeated by the same combination of antislavery opponents of the eastern counties and prodivision enemies of the Illinois country which were soon to force the division of

[1] The first in his annual message to the third General Assembly, October 17, 1809; the second to the irregular Assembly of October 21—*Messages,* 1: 381, 385.

[2] *Ibid.,* 1: 319, 320. Mr. Webster, Ind. Hist. Soc. *Pub.,* 4: 243-244, quotes the official journal; the petition (of October 11, 1808) is not in print, but a photostatic copy of the original MS in the House files is in the Illinois Historical Survey. Compare *post,* xxxii-iii and xxxiii, n. 1, on the other points of the petition. In the attack on Harrison in the petition of the Edgar faction of 1807-1808 one charge indicates that he vetoed other bills than those here cited—*post,* clxviii. And cp. Webster, Ind. Hist. Soc. *Pub.,* 4: 238.

[3] For the proceedings in Congress: *Annals,* 10 Congress, 1 session, 1619, 1648; 2 session, 487, 492-494, 501-510.

Papers, 2: 365. Of thirty-seven acts passed by the General Assembly in 1799 St. Clair vetoed eleven, of which six related to new counties (*ante,* xix, n. 4). See the comments in Burnet, *Notes,* 376. For the Council's hint to Harrison see his *Messages,* 1: 160.

the territory and leave Harrison at the mercy of the antislavery counties.[1]

John Hay, Shadrach Bond "Sr.," and his nephew, Shadrach Bond "Jr.," successively represented St. Clair County, and Pierre Menard and George Fisher represented Randolph, in the Legislative Council. George Fisher and Rice Jones (son of John Rice Jones) were the successive representatives of Randolph, and William Biggs with Shadrach Bond Jr., and later (vice Bond) with John Messinger,[2] were those of St. Clair, in the House of Representatives. Some of these legislators, like their fellows in other branches of the government, were men of very good ability. Some had large business interests. In view of the small salaries[3] received it is rather surprising that practically all officers of the territory must fairly be counted among its leading citizens.

The property qualifications required by the Ordinance for voting or holding elective office (a freehold in fifty and a fee-simple in 200 acres, respectively) might seem easily satisfied. It would have been unreasonable, however, among men to whom land had so long seemed like the air, to expect conceptions of definite "title." In truth such was the state of land titles that the actual enforcement of such qualifications would have proved quite impracticable. No election, certainly, could have been held for years in the Illinois counties, and many high offices would have been

---

[1] See Harrison, *Messages,* 1: 311, 312-315, and discussion in Goebel, *Harrison,* 83-88.

[2] For John Hay and the two Bonds see *post,* app. notes 17, 18, 19. On Fisher and Menard, *post,* app. notes 22, 23. See *post,* app. n. 24, for biography of Jones and the political events connected with his death. On Biggs and Messinger, *post,* app. notes 20, 21.

[3] For salaries of legislators and subordinate executive officers see index. The federal salaries of 1802 were: governor's $2,000, secretary's $750, judges' $800. By act of 1807 the salary of territorial judges was set at $1,200, and by another that of secretaries was made $1,000. *Amer. State Papers: Misc.* 1: 305; *Annals,* 10 Congress, 1 session, (H. R.) 816, 920, 950, (Sen.) 33, 34, 38, 43. Congress had created in 1786 a northern and a southern district for the administration of Indian affairs; and St. Clair was the first superintendent of the northern (all north of the Ohio and west of the Hudson) following 1790. The responsibility was divided among the various territorial governors beginning in 1802; Harrison thenceforth signing himself "Superintendent of Indian Affairs" and "Commissioner Plenipotentiary of the United States." Alvord, *Illinois Country,* 412-413. Harrison received $800 as Superintendent of Indian affairs and $6 per diem when acting as Commissioner in negotiating treaties. He collected no li-

vacant.[1] A demand for wider suffrage began under the first grade, and this was one of the petitions of the Vincennes convention. A committee of Congress reported adversely in 1803; but another recommended in 1804 manhood suffrage, subject only to payment of a territorial tax before election. A third committee recommended in 1806 (the territorial legislature having meanwhile petitioned for an extension) the abrogation of all property qualifications whatsoever.[2] This seemed too liberal. By an act of 1808 the right to vote for representatives in the General Assembly was given to every free white male adult who should have been for one year a citizen of the United States and resident of the territory, and who should have "a legal or equitable title" to fifty acres of land, or who might "become" a purchaser from the United States of fifty acres, or should hold in his own right a town lot worth $100.[3] This same year both houses of the legislature petitioned

---

[1] Pease, *Laws* (*I. H. C.*, 17), 125-126. It fixed the qualification for councillors at a freehold of 500 acres. See statement by Governor Hull and Judge Woodward regarding the similar suffrage requirements in Michigan, *Amer. State Papers: Pub. Lands,* 1: 249. The two squatter petitions of December 2 and 3, 1805, cited *post,* lxxvi, n. 4, include the names of Shadrach Bond Jr., James Lemen, William and Uel Whiteside, David Badgley, James Bankson, and Thomas Kirkpatrick—all of them county judges of St. Clair; and also the names of various other officers and leading citizens, including George Blair (one-time sheriff), James Gilbreath (*post,* app. n. 63), and John Messinger.

[2] For the Vincennes resolutions, Ind. Hist. Soc. *Pub.,* 2: 461-468; the legislative memorial, of August 19, 1805, presented in Congress on December 18, 1805—*ibid.,* 478. The Congressional proceedings are in the *Annals,* 7 Congress, 2 session, (H. R.) 1353-1354—rep. of March 2, 1803; 8 Congress, 1 session (H. R.) 1023-1024—February 17, 1804; 9 Congress, 1 session (H. R.) 293—December 18, 1805; 466-468—February 14, 1806.

[3] *Annals,* 10 Congress, 1 session (H. R.) 1434, 1463, 1615, 1617, (Sen.) 129, 131, 132; (the act of February 26, 1808), 2834. These qualifications were more liberal as to residence than those for suffrage in territorial elections under the law of 1807—*post,* 175, 393, 570. A large proportion of the inhabitants of the territory, of course, were squatters. In one settlement, for example, there were 22 squatters and only 11 land claimants: *Amer. State Papers: Pub. Lands,* 1: 591.

---

censes for trade with the Indians (which, he alleged, had yielded St. Clair $1,000 annually). See correspondence with Jefferson, Ind. Hist. Soc. *Pub.,* 4: 288-289; *U. S. Stat. at Large,* 2: 58, or *Annals,* 6 Congress, 1 session, 1499—act creating Indiana Territory. He also superintended sales of the public lands (act of May 18, 1796, *U. S. Stat. at Large,* 1: 467, 468; *Annals,* 4 Congress, 2 session, 2908), and received $5 per diem "whilst engaged in that business" (act of May 10, 1800—*U. S. Stat. at Large,* 2: 78; *Annals,* 6 Congress, 1 session, 1521).

Congress to make that body elective by voters qualified to vote for representatives, and likewise to vest in them the power to elect the delegates to Congress. Both of these changes, "congenial"—in the Council's words—"to the rights or interests of the Citizens of a free Government," were introduced by an act of 1809. The same act also transferred from the governor to the Assembly the power to apportion representatives among the counties. The term of councillors was made four years.[1]

The election statutes of the territory are elaborate, but few election records are preserved in Randolph and St. Clair. It is quite evident that elections were held with nonchalant disregard for legal formalities. December 11, 1802 was the date set by proclamation for the election of delegates to the Vincennes convention; the election was apparently held in St. Clair County on December 7. The exceedingly important special elections of 1808 to elect representatives to succeed Shadrach Bond Jr. and George Fisher (promoted to the Legislative Council) were set for July 25; but the Randolph election seems to have been held on August 13.[2] The elections of representatives in the first General Assembly of the territory were ordered held on January 3, 1805, and Governor Harrison later referred to its having been held on that

[1] The resolutions of the House of Representatives were of October 11, 1808. On the prayers of this petition relating to other matters than suffrage see *ante*, xxx, n. 2. Those of the Council seem to have been passed on October 17, 1808 (Webster, Ind. Hist. Soc. *Pub.*, 4: 237-238); and those of the House apparently still earlier (Jesse B. Thomas, speaker, forwarded copy on October 12) but the official copies, for both houses, were signed and attested and forwarded on October 26. Photostatic copies from the originals in the files of the House are in the Illinois Historical Survey. For the proceedings in Congress see the *Annals,* 10 Congress, 2 session, (H. R.) 501, 856, 909, 1433, 1434; (Sen.) 20, 388, 410, 411, 412; (H. R.)—petition from citizens of Harrison County—1329; (act of February 27, 1809), 1821. A petition of the House of Representatives of 1809 is also cited in Goebel, *Harrison,* 80. All the legislation cited in this and the preceding note was in response to representations from the territorial legislature, and due to the activity of the territory's delegate. It certainly shows no indifference to self-government. As regards purely local government it is true, however, as has been pointed out by the editors of Gibson's *Executive Journal* (78), that the Assembly, even after both branches became elective, showed no inclination to extend the principle of local self-government. (On p. 71 they misdate the statute last cited, confusing it with the law affecting Mississippi Territory).
[2] Gibson, *Exec. Journal,* 113, 147; Brink, McDonough, *Hist. of St. Clair County,* 71, 73; *post,* xlviii, n. 3; li, n. 1.

date in St. Clair County; but in fact it was apparently held on the
5th. It was broken up by "disorderly citizens"—a mob of opponents of the second grade of government; and being declared null
and void by the Assembly a second election was ordered on May
20. This seems to have been held on May 21. No doubt there
were other such examples. Of course, in the last two cases the
different dates were probably due to the fact that elections habitually lasted two or three days.[1] Mr. Esarey says that "all through
this period, from 1804 to 1811, there was outspoken hostility toward
the control of the elections. . . . The common pleas justices really
controlled the sheriff, but, as the sheriff did the actual work, he got
all the blame. The justices in turn were controlled largely by the
tavern keepers whom they created. The influential politicians then

[1] *Post,* 651-652; Gibson, *op. cit.,* 125, 126-127; Brink, McDonough,
Hist. of St. Clair County, 71, 72; Dunn, *Indiana,* 325. Shadrach Bond Sr.
and William Biggs were the successful candidates. Information regarding
other elections than those mentioned in the text is limited. See letter to
St. Clair, October 20, 1800, on a stormy election in Detroit, *St. Clair Papers,*
2: 499: "Many artifices have been used, and many promises made." Mc-
Donough, *Hist. of Randolph, Monroe, and Perry Counties,* 102, states that
no election records of Randolph between 1795 and 1809 were then (1883)
discoverable, nor have any been now found. For elections in St. Clair,
records apparently existed in 1881—Brink, McDonough, *Hist. of St. Clair
County,* 70, 71, 73; but these have not been sought in connection with the
present volume. According to the latter history, at an election held January
5, 1799 to elect a representative in the General Assembly, Shadrach Bond
Sr. received 113 votes (54 American, 58 French, and 1 German name) and
Isaac Darneille 72 (36 American, 33 French, 2 German, and 1 Irish name).
May Allinson classifies the voters differently: 58 "old French inhabitants,"
25 "recent French settlers," 102 Americans. Ill. Hist. Soc., *Trans.* (1907),
292. The votes cast in the election held—supposedly on September 11,
1804, the day set by the Governor—to pass on adoption of representative
government are given *ante,* xxvi. In 1806 Shadrach Bond Jr. was elected
a representative to fill the vacancy created in the lower house when his
uncle was appointed to the Council; but the proclamation for this election
(if a special one) is not to be found in Harrison's *Messages,* nor does its
date seem elsewhere to be found. William Biggs was reëlected to the lower
house in 1807. The summer elections of 1808 are discussed *post,* 1. In
the national House of Representatives, December 15, 1808 (*Annals,* 10
Congress, 2 session, 857), Eppes presented "certain returns or statements" regarding the number of free males and votes at elections in Randolph and St. Clair, and "depositions of sundry persons . . . relative
thereto"; for these documents—so far at least as they are still existent—
see *post* xlviii, n. 3 (end); li, n. 1. Elections were viva voce: see
Pease, *Laws* (*I. H. C.,* 17), 410-411; *post,* 393, § 4. Also Burnet, *Notes,*
323; I have noted no contemporary statement on Indiana Territory.

were the sheriffs, justices and tavern keepers."[1] An act of the second legislature provided that judges of the Common Pleas should no longer act as judges of election; limited elections to one day, to be held in all townships simultaneously; and forbade "repeating."[2]

The first legislature of the territory made ineligible for election to the Assembly any person "holding a commission during pleasure, directly," under the United States or the territory, excepting justices of the peace and militia officers.[3] Multiple office-holding (inescapable in these early days when competent men were not abundant) continued, however, to characterize generally the judicial and administrative branches of the government.

The early proslavery petitions from the Illinois counties have already been referred to. The legalistic arguments in favor of slavery were rather weak: slavery had existed for generations under the pre-American régimes; George Rogers Clark had conquered the territory for Virginia; and Congress could not by the Ordinance of 1787 abolish slavery in the territory because the Treaty of 1763 and the Virginia cession of 1784 had guaranteed to the inhabitants of these lands their property. Such arguments did service until in 1824 the question was, for Illinois, forever settled. In fact the treaty of 1763 did no more than grant to former French subjects the privilege of either removing with their property or selling it to British subjects; and that of 1783 contained no reference to the western country.[4] Congress was there-

[1] Esarey, *History,* 1: 176. He refers to Indiana, but as the system was the same in the Illinois country so doubtless were the results and complaints. There was no newspaper, as there was at Vincennes. In 1811 the Indiana legislature petitioned for popular election of sheriffs (Goebel, *Harrison,* 80).

[2] Law of September 16, 1807, §§ 5, 6—*post,* 572. It is not clear what was gained by entrusting to a deputy sheriff plus a justice of the peace or a freeholder, by him selected, the duty formerly exercised by a judge.

[3] Law of December 4, 1806, § 3—*post,* 175. On multiple office-holding compare Esarey, *History,* 1: 156; also the biographical notes at the end of this introduction.

[4] It is evident that even if the treaty of 1763 were interpreted as recognizing as "property" what had theretofore been so considered, and even if the provision had been that the French inhabitants might remain "with their property," this would not have bound the government for the future. On the other hand the Virginia cession of 1784 (see *post,* ccxviii, n. 1) did guarantee them "their possessions and titles"; but the Ordinance

fore clearly free to abolish slavery, aside from the argument that abolition was illegal without consultation of the inhabitants affected (an argument by no means overlooked in the early petitions). Indeed, the Ordinance itself, if literally interpreted, had abolished slavery—leaving Congress nothing to do but give legislative effect to the abolition. That a literal interpretation was not to be applied was at first apparent to no one. The contrary construction was simply silently adopted by Congress. It will be noted later that at least one of the judges of the territory was seemingly of a contrary view. The literal construction was apparently assumed by everyone, at first, in the Illinois country; and it ultimately prevailed in the courts.[1]

The extralegal arguments appeared in 1796 much as they persisted down to 1861. "Your petitioners"—said Edgar and his fellows to Congress—"do not wish to increase the number of slaves already in the dominions of the United States; all they hope for or desire is, that they may be permitted to introduce from any of the United States such persons, and such only, as by the laws of such States are slaves therein." Article six—they said—was "contrary not only to the interest, but almost to the existence of the country they inhabit, where laborers cannot be procured to assist in cultivating the grounds under one dollar per day, exclusive of washing, lodging, and boarding; and where every kind of

---

[1] *Post,* lxxv, n. 2. See E. B. Washburne, *Sketch of Edward Coles,* 70. On the doubts of St. Clair, Tardiveau, and Hamtramck in 1788-1789 regarding the effect of the clause, see Alvord, *Kaskaskia Records* (*I. H. C.,* 5), 488, 493, 503, 508-509; *St. Clair Papers,* 2: 117-120. On doubts still persistent in 1793, *ibid.,* 318-319. Various courts ultimately held slavery illegal under the Ordinance: Jarrot *v.* Jarrot (1845), 7 Ill. 1; Merry *v.* Chexnaider, 20 Martin (La.) 699; Winney *v.* Whitesides, 1 Mo. 472; Merry *v.* Tiffin & Menard, 1 Mo. 725; Menard *v.* Aspasia, 5 Peters (U. S.) 510. Like decisions were made by other courts under constitutions containing provisions similar to that of the Ordinance of 1787, or much more general declarations, merely, of "equality": Harry *v.* Decker, Walker (Miss.) 36; Spotts *v.* Gillaspie, 6 Rand. (Va.), 566; Commonwealth *v.* Aves, 18 Pick. (Mass.) 210.

---

of 1787 did not. Clearly Virginia might (and did) renounce under the Ordinance the conditions set in her deed of cession. And various state courts eventually held (next note) that that instrument did abolish slavery. The statement is inaccurate that "the Illinois people were protected in their land titles by the treaty of peace of 1763, that of 1783, and by the cession of Virginia in 1784"—Alvord, *Illinois Country,* 417 n.

tradesmen are paid from a dollar and a half to two dollars per day; neither is there, at these exorbitant prices, a sufficiency of hands to be got for the exigencies of the inhabitants, who, attached to their native soil, have rather chose to encounter these and many other difficulties, than, by avoiding them, remove to the Spanish dominions where slavery is permitted, and consequently the price of labor much lower."[1]

In November 1802 Harrison ordered elections for a convention to consider the admission of slavery. The delegates from St. Clair were J. F. Perrey, Shadrach Bond Sr. and John Moredock; those from Randolph were Robert Morrison, Pierre Menard, and Robert Reynolds. The resolutions and petition of this convention[2] in favor of temporarily suspending the antislavery article of the Ordinance were before Congress for several years. A strong adverse report by John Randolph of Virginia, then the Republican leader of the House, was made early in 1803.[3] By recommitment a contrary report was secured a year later.[4] In the interim, however, another proslavery petition had been received from "sundry inhabitants" of the territory;[5] and the Governor and judges, by a statute which in form merely regulated the relation to their masters of "negroes and mulattoes (and other persons not being citizens of the United States of America)" brought into the territory,[6] had established a system of servitude that was substantially equivalent to slavery. For this citizens of Clark County had promptly at-

---

[1] Compare *post*, clxxvi, n. 5; *ante*, xxi, n. 1. This argument that diffusion would weaken slavery appears in a letter of Barthélemi Tardiveau written in 1789 to Governor St. Clair, *St. Clair Papers*, 2: 119-120 n.

[2] Congressional proceedings in *Annals*, 7 Congress, 2 session, 473 (February 8, 1803), and as further indicated in the following notes. Proclamation, November 22, election set for December 11, meeting set for December 20-28. The proclamation, resolutions and petitions, and some of the related documents, are reprinted in Harrison, *Messages*, 1: 60-67, 73-76, 91-93, 187-190. Collected also by Dunn in Ind. Hist. Soc. *Pub.*, 2: 461-476, 494-497.

[3] March 2, 1803—that the growth of Ohio clearly showed that slave labor was not necessary for the settlement of that region, and that to grant the prayer would be highly inexpedient and dangerous. *Annals*, 7 Congress, 2 session, 473, 1353; *Amer. State Papers: Pub. Lands*, 1: 160.

[4] February 17, 1804, by Caesar Rodney's committee—*Annals*, 8 Congress, 1 session, 1023; *Amer. State Papers: Misc.* 1: 387.

[5] *Annals*, 8 Congress, 1 session (H. R.) 783—December 20, 1803. This petition seems to be nowhere in print.

[6] Act of September 22, 1803, *post*, 42.

tacked the Governor in another petition in which they charged that his principles were "repugnant to Republicanism," and prayed the appointment of another governor, with principles "of liberty" and "more congenial with those of the people." This was the first declaration of antislavery sentiment.[1]

Although the influence of the slavery issue was certainly given excessive weight by Dunn in his consideration of the advance to government of the second grade, legislative declarations were of course immediately utilized as official expressions of the popular will. Sometime in 1805 an elaborate petition from the inhabitants of Randolph and St. Clair signed by some three hundred and fifty names was forwarded to Congress—by far the most representative in its signatures of all those presented on the subjects of slavery or division. It prayed that Article six of the Ordinance might be "so modified as to admit of slavery . . . either unconditional, or under such restrictions or limitations" as Congress might see fit to impose.[2] With this there was presented to Congress a petition, of August 19, 1805, by seven members of the Legislature (constituting a majority of each house) who submitted "the propriety" of the introduction of slaves "upon principles of Justice and policy—Justice in relation to slaves and policy as it regards the Southern states." That dispersal would increase the comforts of plantation slaves by their transfer to small farms in a land of plenty and increase the tranquillity of states where the negro population was disquietingly dense, and that it offered "the only means by which a gradual emancipation can ever be effected,"

[1] Petition of February 1803, Goebel, *Harrison,* 78. Presumably this was received by Congress, but there is no record in the *Annals* of its presentation or commitment. Harrison was reappointed on February 8, 1803, *ibid.,* 56. This petition, also, seems to be nowhere in print.

[2] Printed by Dunn, Ind. Hist. Soc. *Pub.,* 2: 483-492. The Randolph signers included John Edgar, William and Robert Morrison (and three other Morrisons), John and Parker Grosvenor, James Edgar, James Gilbreath, Miles Hotchkiss, William Kelly, John Reynolds, William Wilson, Robert Robinson, Henry Jones, John and Henry O'Hara; those from St. Clair included William Arundel, Shadrach Bond (Sr.), John Dumoulin, John Francis Perrey, Antoine Girardin, William and George Biggs, William Atcheson, George Atchison, John Hay, John Hays, John Moredock, and seven of the Whiteside family. There are 354 names, but at least one of them is a duplicate. As the signatures are certified by Robert Reynolds there were probably irregularities. One name is "A. Whyskey."

were philanthropic arguments which did valiant service in the
years following. It was always assumed that "the population
west of the Ohio must chiefly be derived from the Southern and
Western States."[1] The inaccuracy of this assumption was
to shatter the hopes of the proslavery party. Another memorial
soon followed, which purported to be the work of a convention of
citizens "appointed to form a Committee from the Several Townships in the Counties of St. Clair and Randolph, to take into Consideration and Represent to the General Government the Grievances of these Counties, the 25th day of November, 1805." Remarkably enough, however, the minutes of the committee condemned the statute of 1805 by which the territorial legislature
authorized slave immigration "and involuntary servitude for a
term of years," a violation of the Ordinance to which they declared
they would never consent, notwithstanding they were persuaded
that it would stimulate the settlement of the territory; whereas
the memorial to Congress which purported to be their handiwork
pronounced slavery a necessity and prayed its legalization. Aside
from this there are other details which discredit it as a reliable
expression of general opinion.[2] All three of these petitions were

[1] Printed by Dunn, Ind. Hist. Soc. *Pub.*, 2: 476-483.
[2] This memorial (which has only twenty signatures) pronounced
slavery an evil, but one "immovably established," which should therefore
be converted, "if possible, to some use"; repeated the allegation of the
petition of 1796 that in the Illinois country "among whites health and labor
are almost incompatible"; and suggested that the legalization of slavery
"would probably bring back the principal settlers of Upper Louisiana,
since they have been driven from home [Illinois] by the fear of losing their
servants." Printed *ibid.*, 498-502; a photostatic copy of the original signatures is in the Ill. Hist. Survey. The "minutes" order a memorial to "be
prepared"; in the next paragraph refer to "reasons stated in the Memorial
signed"; and at the end order that the memorial "now before this Committee
be . . . signed." Despite the condemnation of the territorial statute,
they stated: "When Congress shall deem a Change of the Ordinance expedient, they will Cheerfully agree to the measure." *Ibid.*, 503-505. It is
possible that these inconsistencies were due to a desire to secure the joinder
of James Lemen, who appears as a member of the Committee and—despite
his later family-canonization as an antislavery apostle—also apparently
signed the memorial (the only other signature of his name in the petitions
of the time is an obvious forgery, whatever this may be). See W. C.
MacNaul, *The Jefferson-Lemen Compact* (1915), 29-30, notes under 1805-
1806. The signature of Robert Lemen appears to the proslavery petition of
October 1, 1800, Ind. Hist. Soc. *Pub.*, 2: 460. It may be noted that the
signatures to all the petitions show clearly that either friend signed for

considered by a committee of the House which again reported, in 1806, in favor of suspending the Ordinance's prohibition.[1] There was a difference in detail between this report and that of 1804. The earlier report, though recommending the suspension of Article six to permit of the interstate migration of slaves, provided that their descendants should become free automatically at a certain age; the later report omitted this ameliorative feature.

New and unanimous resolutions of both houses of the legislature, praying the suspension of the sixth article of the Ordinance for ten years, and repeating the arguments advanced in those of 1805, were forwarded late in 1806,[2] and upon this a third favorable report in the House of Representatives (by a committee of which Benjamin Parke was chairman) was made early in 1807.[3] Both documents were admirably succinct statements of the pro-

[1] *Some* memorial from the inhabitants of Indiana Territory and a petition of the legislature were committed on December 18, 1805—*Annals,* 9 Congress, 1 session, (H. R.) 293. The original of the first of the above petitions is indorsed as committed on December 18, and the third as committed on January 17, 1806 (Ind. Hist. Soc. *Pub.,* 2: 491, 502), but the description in the *Annals,* 342, clearly refers to the *first* petition as committed January 17, 1806. The error is probably in the *Annals.* The Committee's report, of February 14, 1806 (by Garnett), is in the *Annals,* 9 Congress, 1 session, (H. R.) 466-468, the *Amer. State Papers: Misc.,* 1: 450-451, and Harrison, *Messages,* 1: 187-190.

[2] They were forwarded by Harrison on December 20, 1806, and were received in Congress on January 21 (Senate) and 20 (H. R.). *Annals,* 9 Congress, 2 session, 37-38, 375-376. The memorial is printed in *Amer. State Papers: Misc.,* 1: 467; Ind. Hist. Soc. *Pub.,* 2: 507-509. They deemed that the territory was deserving of indulgence by Congress because in 1787 slaves were "generally" held by its citizens, amounting to half the present population of the territory. See *post,* xli, n. 2.

[3] February 12, 1807, *Annals,* 9 Congress, 2 session, 482-483; *Amer. State Papers: Misc.,* 1: 477-478; Ind. Hist. Soc. *Pub.,* 2: 509-510; Harrison, *Messages,* 1: 202-203. The report was referred to the Committee of the Whole (*Annals, loc. cit.,* 483), and there the matter ended.

friends, and one member of a family for others or there is an abundance of forgery. Dozens of errors occur in the transcription of names as printed by Dunn. In an antidivision petition of 1807 (*post,* xlvi, n. 1) signed among others by five judges or former judges of Randolph County, it is said of this "sham convention" that its "presumptious proceedings . . . turns the name convention into contempt and ridicule . . . No election was holden in Mitchi Township, nor that of Priara du Rocher—in Kaskaskia there was a sham election of a few persons, it is believed the Deputies chosen comprised one half of those present & indeed of those who had any notice of it." The conventionists replied (*post,* xlvi, n. 2) that their memorial "was duly authorised by the Voice of the People, taken by Vote in most if not all of the Towships."

slavery arguments. They marked the high tide of the proslavery effort, but all these reports were of no avail.

Still another petition by the legislature followed late in 1807, asking for suspension of Article six of the Ordinance "for a given number of years."[1] But a great change suddenly became apparent in the situation. Up to this time only petitions—public or private—favorable to slave immigration, with the single exception above noted, had been received. But in October 1807 a second protest was received against slavery from Clark County. This remonstrance declared that the clause of the petition of the Vincennes convention (1802) regarding slavery was decidedly opposed by the representatives of all the territory east of Vincennes; that the memorial presented to Congress in 1805, allegedly the voice of a majority of each house of the legislature, was in fact rejected in the lower house; so that those of each house who joined therein did so only as private citizens; that the legislative petition of 1807 had been passed in the Council when but three members were present; and that it was "certainly doubtful" whether a majority of the territory's inhabitants were proslavery. These allegations gave great weight to their very measured suggestion that in view of the great movement of immigration into the territory, including many settlers of antislavery convictions, they felt "satisfied" that Congress would suspend legislation until, upon admission to statehood, the inhabitants might determine the matter for themselves. This remarkable memorial brushed aside the sophistry of the Edgar petition with an allegation of the indisputable facts that even in the slave states slavery was very generally regarded only as an inescapable evil, and that many immigrants into Indiana Territory were leaving such states to escape slavery.[2] The petition gave

[1] Voted September 19, 1807. *Amer. State Papers: Misc.*, 1: 484-485; Ind. Hist. Soc. *Pub.*, 2: 515-517; Harrison, *Messages*, 1: 253-255. Echoing the old arguments, it points to Kentucky and Tennessee as evidence that slaves could never so increase as to endanger Indiana Territory. See the next note.

[2] *Annals*, 10 Congress, 1 session (Sen.), 26-27; *Amer. State Papers: Misc.*, 1: 485-486; Ind. Hist. Soc. *Pub.*, 2: 518-520; Harrison, *Messages*, 1: 263-266. According to the petitioners "a number of citizens thought proper to sign" the memorial of 1805, "and, amongst the rest, the Speaker of the House of Representatives and the President of the Council, (though the President of the Council denies ever having signed the same) and, by some

final repose to the efforts of the proslavery party of the territory in Congress. A Senate committee appointed to consider it, together with the last memorial of the legislature, reported that legislation would be inexpedient.[1]

Events moved toward a climax in 1808, alike with reference to slavery and to division of the territory. In the autumn of the year, after elections in the Illinois counties in which the anti-Harrison divisionists triumphed, and a combination in the legislature between them and the anti-Harrison antislavery men of the eastern counties, the House of Representatives approved (October 19, 1808) an antislavery committee report of truly remarkable power by General Washington Johnston, later speaker of the House. Its conclusions were three: that it was "inexpedient" to petition Congress for a modification of the Ordinance; that slavery "cannot and ought not to be admitted"; and that the territorial statute of 1807 legalizing the introduction of negroes and mulattoes should be forthwith repealed.[2] With this report there was forwarded to Congress an equally remarkable popular petition in which "sundry inhabitants of the . . . Territory" attacked the indenture law, declared that the repeated proslavery petition of the past had expressed merely the wishes of a minority, and expressed "in the most unequivocal manner their . . . determination to resist henceforward by every lawful means every attempt to introduce into this infant Country a system so calamitous in its effects."[3] Both documents were tabled in Congress, without further action.[4]

[1] November 13, 1807--*Amer. State Papers: Misc.*, 1: 484; *Annals*, 10 Congress, 1 session, (Sen.) 22, 23-27, 31; (H. R.) 816, 920; Ind. Hist. Soc. *Pub.*, 2: 521; Harrison, *Messages*, 1: 274-275.

[2] Printed by Dunn in Ind. Hist. Soc. *Pub.*, 2: 522-527; photostatic copy of original MS in Ill. Hist. Survey. Dunn characterizes it as perhaps the ablest of all Indiana State Papers. On the negro statute (of September 17, 1807) see *post*, 523.

[3] Not printed by Dunn; photostatic copy in Ill. Hist. Survey. It was forwarded to Congress October 24, 1808. Its language is highly impassioned. Its points are in large part embodied in Johnston's report.

[4] November 18, 1808—*Annals*, 10 Congress, 2 session, (H. R.) 501.

———

legislative legerdemain, it found its way into the Congress of the United States, as the legislative act of the Territory." The matter again came up in 1807, and proslavery resolutions were, they state, passed by a vote of 2 to 1. But it is impossible to say whether the petitioners referred to the legislative resolutions presented January 21, 1807, or to those of September 19, 1807—cited *ante*, xl, n. 2; xli, n. 1, respectively.

However, this closed the struggle under the Indiana Territory, although it was still to perplex the politics of Illinois for more than two decades. Another antislavery petition of the next year was primarily an attack upon Governor Harrison.[1] Despite this, and the attacks in divisionist petitions soon to be noted, he was reappointed in 1809, though his fast lessening prestige was evident.

The memorial of the Vincennes convention (December 1802), as well as various of the petitions, legislative and private, which have just been referred to, were not confined to the question of repealing the antislavery clause of the Ordinance. They dealt at the same time with the demand by actual settlers on the public lands for preëmption rights, with the extension of suffrage, land claims, and all the other matters which were occupying public interest in the territory. The agitation over slavery has been referred to as a matter separate and distinct. In reality it was, of course, bound up at every step with the issue of division.

Looking backward, the eventual division of the territory seems inescapable. Aside from its size, disharmony and sectionalism were necessities within it. As the Gore was bound to Cincinnati, the Illinois country seemed, at that day, united to the future of the Mississippi outlet. The sympathies of the French and southerners in the west were very different from those of the easterners who controlled the government of the original northwest, who dominated Ohio when it was formed, and who—despite large southern immigration from Kentucky and elsewhere—were powerful in the Indiana counties of the territory. With reference to slavery these

---

[1] Goebel, *Harrison,* 81, abstracts this petition of February 3, 1809. Harrison was reappointed for his last term of three years on December 20, 1809, *ibid.,* 56. The attack on Harrison in the Clark County petition of 1803 (*ante,* xxxviii, n. 1) was a strong one. The memorial presented with Johnston's report of 1808 did no more, after characterizing the indenture law as "in evasion if not in manifest violation" of the Ordinance, than to add: "and such a law has received the sanction of the Executive, the appointed guardian of that same Ordinance." The attack in the petition of February 1809 was evidently more direct and sustained. But this is as nothing to the venom of the petitions of 1808 from the Illinois country. Presumably it was hoped to prevent reappointment in 1809. That Harrison was fearful of the outcome (his appointment was months delayed) is evident from Gallatin's letter to him—answering a letter which betrayed doubt of Badollet's influence: see *post,* app. n. 8. In November the legislature urged his reappointment (Harrison, *Messages,* 1: 391-392) by a vote stated as unanimous in the House and 3 to 1 in the Council.

differences proved to be momentous, and they were not less so in their relation to the issue of division.

The efforts to that end began with the petitions for annexation to Louisiana, prepared in the Illinois country in 1803, which have already been referred to. Early in 1805 the lower house of the legislature expressed its "lively regret that certain discontented factious men" were endeavoring to effect division and attach the Illinois country to Louisiana. "It is understood" they said, " . . . that very improper means have been employed to obtain signatures to their memorials; and that to augment their numbers, small boys and the most worthless characters in the Country are permitted to subscribe to them"—charges certainly true of some, and probably to some extent of all, the petitions of the time. Their arguments on the merits of the issue were certainly not promising of successful resistance; they were partly weakly defensive, partly of hope, partly of fear. They denied that any peculiar advantage accrued to the eastern counties from proximity to the seat of government (indeed, claimed that it was approximately equidistant from all settlements except Detroit—ignoring Knox!); expressed the hope that, with the Indian titles cleared and land offices open, the whole territory would soon be unified; and protested that the east could not alone support the new burdens of the second grade of government.[1] The supposed joint memorial of the two houses of the Assembly in December 1805, referred to above, which asked suspension of Article six, also prayed that no division of the territory be made, but that a state government be permitted so soon as population should warrant this. A private petition from the settlers in the Gore prayed annexation to Ohio.[2] Two others, from the Illinois

---

[1] Harrison, *Messages*, 1: 173-174; *Annals*, 9 Congress, 1 session, (H. R. December 19, 1805) 297. The resolution (that division was inexpedient, and adverse to the interests of the territory) was of February 7, 1805; Harrison did not forward it until November 15.

[2] *Ante*, xxxix, n. 1; *Annals* (December 18), 293, 294. "No measure whatever will have a more serious and pernicious influence on the interests and future prosperity of the Territory"; they could discover "no plausible reason in favor of it"; Vincennes was "as near the center . . . as convenience and propriety will admit"; a journey thither was "in very few instances necessary"; the east could not alone bear the expense of government of the second grade. The Gore petition is printed by Dunn, Ind. Hist. Soc. *Pub.*, 2: 492-494.

counties—the petition-of-350[1] and the "convention" petition,[2] both already referred to—prayed division, as well as suspension of Article six. All of these memorials were referred to one committee, which reported in 1806 adversely, on the ground that division, so soon after the adoption of the second grade of government, would throw the whole expense of this upon the eastern section and would be unjust. The committee also advised against admission of the whole territory, so soon as population warranted, as one state; which would violate the plan of the Ordinance, since such a state could not be later divided without its consent.[3] But petitions continued; most of them praying both division and slave immigration, but one from Randolph (with 102 signers—a significant declaration) opposing division. A committee headed by Ben-

[1] *Ante,* xxxviii, n. 2; according to this petition (received, according to the *Annals,* on January 17, 1806, p. 342, but in reality probably on December 18, 1805, p. 293; see *ante,* xl, n. 1) the distance of Vincennes was a "ruinous inconvenience." The intervening prairies were always impassable—flooded in wet seasons, overdry in others, affording water hardly sufficient to sustain life—and their destitution of wood and water "utterly precludes the possibility of settlement to any extent worthy of notice." Communication or union, therefore, between the Illinois and the eastern settlements, whether with respect to private or to political interests, could not "for centuries yet to come . . . be of the least moment to either of them."

[2] *Ante,* xxxix, n. 2. This "convention" petition repeated all the arguments of the petition cited in the preceding note, urging in addition the advantage of giving tranquility to the Illinois counties, stimulating their settlement, and building a bulwark along the east bank of the Mississippi. It also deplored a resolution "attempted to be passed" at the last legislative session "for continuing the union between the middle and the western state . . . till each shall have a sufficient population to form an independent one." Ind. Hist. Soc. *Pub.,* 2: 499-500. This must refer to the supposed joint memorial of August 19, 1805 (*ante,* xxxix, n. 1; xliv, n. 2), the exact proposal of which was "to connect the two divisions in one State Government, until they severally obtain a population that will authorise a division into two States" (Ind. Hist. Soc. *Pub.,* 2: 481); and therefore this supports the allegation of the Clark County memorialists (*ante,* xli) that that memorial was not in reality a legislative act. Depositions which they forwarded, showing the history of the measure, have disappeared. As to its merits they would only say "that its effect would have been to continue the seat of government at Vincennes, *where some of our principal characters have ample possessions.*" Ind. Hist. Soc. *Pub.,* 2: 500. This last (italics added) was a slap at Harrison; cp. Goebel, *Harrison,* 58, 61; *ante,* xi, n. 2; and letter of Jonathan Jennings in *Ind. Hist. Bulletin,* February, 1924, p. 59-60. "The landowners" of the Wabash country, the memorialists declared, had "already begun to feel, or to fancy, an interest" in preventing the population of the Mississippi counties.

[3] Garnett report, of February 14, 1806. *Ante,* xl, n. 1.

jamin Parke considered all these and reported that division was expedient; and the House of Representatives so resolved.[1]

The report was in plain contradiction of the apparent weight of public opinion as manifested in the petitions. After some months the divisionists forwarded their attack upon the petition of their Randolph opponents—which, they said, had been "circulated in Private to obtain Signatures of the Ignorant and ungarded citizens . . . Principally" illiterate Frenchmen, and was opposed "to the full Expression of the Public Voice in committee" which had been forwarded late in 1805. They mustered a few more signers than the antidivisionists and a few less illiterate Frenchmen.[2] Two other divisionist petitions went forward about the same time. One was of little importance except as a partial expression of St. Clair sentiment.[3] The other repeated the stock

[1] Two petitions were presented on March 26, 1806, both favoring division and slavery—*Annals,* 9 Congress, 1 session, 848. One of these appears to have been identical with the "convention" memorial. *Ante,* xxxix, n. 2. See Dunn's note, Ind. Hist. Soc. *Pub.,* 2: 502. The other was presumably the accompanying "minutes" of the "Committee." On February 20, 1807 two more petitions from Randolph and St. Clair were presented; one favoring and one opposing division. The first (*ibid.,* 510-512) was signed by eighteen, including John Edgar, John Beaird, and Robert Robinson of Randolph; J. F. Perrey, N. Jarrot, John Messinger, and James Lemen of St. Clair. They asked for a government like that "proposed" for Michigan Territory; held up the importance, in view of European affairs (!), of union and energy on the Mississippi; and under this emotion could not but "shudder at the horrors which may arise from a *disaffection in the West*" (original italics). This was an attempt to draw profit from the uneasiness roused by Burr. The second petition (printed *ibid.,* 512-515) carried the signatures of J. Bpte. Barbau, Antoine Louviere, George Fisher, Samuel Cochran, Jas. Finney, James Gilbreath, two brothers of Pierre Menard, and forty illiterate French who signed with marks. A photostatic copy of the signatures is in the Ill. Hist. Survey. They opposed division because it would leave the Illinois counties worse off. "A Representative government has been secured to the country; no taxes have yet been paid by the Mississippi settlements, & from the measures of the last session of the Legislature your petitioners . . . believe that a system of prudence and economy will be pursued by that body. As yet there has been no cause to complain. No reason . . . renders the project at least plausible." *Annals,* 9 Congress, 2 session, 624 (February 26, 1807).

[2] Photostatic copy in Ill. Hist. Survey; unprinted. There are 167 signatures, twenty-three of Frenchmen who signed by mark. The only names of much note are those of Robert McMahon, Robert Reynolds, N. Jarrot, John Reynolds, Antoine Girardin, J. F. Perrey, Wm. Atcheson, John Hays, David Badgley, William L. and John J. Whiteside, and (but cp. *supra,* n. 1) James Gilbrath. See *ante,* xxxix, n. 2.

[3] Unprinted; photostatic copy in Ill. Hist. Survey. There are only forty-two signatures, of which those of Wm. Biggs, William Kinney, Uel Whiteside, and James Bankson are most important.

arguments of the party, but in the main it was a passionate attack upon Harrison[1] for conduct "unworthy of his office and disgraceful to the Nation."

The charges against him were nine. Firstly, that he had precipitated the territory into the second grade "without being legally, or in fact, satisfied that a majority of the Inhabitants wished for it . . . in order to increase his influence and lesson his responsibility." And though as American citizens they held dear "even an approximation to liberty," yet "alas! the only liberty which the people of the Illinois have acquired by this change is the liberty of submitting to the will of a part of the Territory more populous . . . a District . . . able . . . to drain off our money to erect it's public buildings." Secondly, that in order to gain their money he had approved the territorial law requiring the United States land commissioners, contrary to their duty and their positive instructions (to report to the national administration only), to remit to the territorial auditor, under penalty, transcripts of confirmed claims, for taxation.[2] "Thirdly, That not being able by this mockery of Legislation either to intimidate or coerce, he has given his sanction to a Law providing, that not only every holder of real property but that every claimant to land whose claim had not been decided on by the said Commissioners should pay a specific tax on every acre thus holden or claimed or that in default

[1] An earlier attack upon Harrison based upon his land interests is noted above in *ante*, xlv, n. 2. In the petition cited *ante*, xlvi, n. 2, it is remarked: "his Excellency is opposed to the measure of cortailing his Domains, and has hitherto exerted every effort to prevent it." These charges were wholly incidental. The memorial now referred to is an elaborate impugnment of Harrison's administration. Its exact date cannot be determined without access to the journals of the General Assembly. A photostatic copy is in the Ill. Hist. Survey, which also contains such copies of four depositions (all of September-October 1808) by inhabitants whose signatures were forged to the memorial. These involve 12 names. In addition John Kidd, well acquainted with the families of Robert Reynolds and William Kelly (*post*, lxxxviii) showed that a son of the latter who signed was only 19, and two sons of the former only 12 and 14. Another deponent declared that though there were many signatures from Goshen settlement (Robert Reynolds had removed thither in 1807—Reynolds, *My Own Times*, 64), the petition was never brought into that settlement.

[2] *Post*, 147—act of August 26, 1805. For penalty, *post*, 174, § 9. No evidence is in print which shows that the instructions of the commissioners were as here stated; but of course there could be no compulsion by the territorial government upon them.

of such payment the property or the claim should be sold at public auction by the Sheriff, which measure it was well known would, in a vast number of instances, amount to nothing more nor less than a forced loan repayable at the pleasure of those who had forced it." "Fourthly, That knowing all involuntary servitude to be forbidden in the Territory by the solemn Ordinance of 1787," he had nevertheless sanctioned an indenture law which, said the petitioners—and no one better than they, at whose behest and in whose interest it was passed, could more fittingly judge it!—might "properly be entitled 'A Law for the Establishment of disguised slavery in opposition to the National Will.'" Fifthly, that he had sanctioned the establishment of a court of chancery[1] "independent of and superior to the National Court [established in the] Territory—a measure which has for it's effect the wounding and weakening of the great ligature which was intended to bind the Colony to the Nation."[2] Sixthly, that though he had sanctioned a resolution of the legislature in favor of a census and a reapportionment, yet notwithstanding the census had been duly taken he had not given Randolph and Clark counties the additional representative each to which they were entitled in the last session of the legislature.[3] Seventhly, that he had arbitrarily vetoed several bills of the legislature "calculated for the impartial administration of Justice and the general good of the Territory."[4] All of which acts, said the memorialists,

[1] See *post,* cxv, on the attempts to enforce the taxation statutes. See also *post,* 108, 136.

[2] The document is torn; the words in brackets are almost certainly the original words.

[3] This must have been the session of August-September, 1807. Accompanying the "convention" memorial of late 1805 (*ante,* xxxix, n. 2; xlv, n. 2) was the following census: population by the census of April 1, 1801—2,361; at Prairie du Chien and on the Illinois River, "at least" an additional—550; immigrants since 1801, "at least"—750; Ohio River settlements from the Wabash to and including Ft. Massac—650; total—4,311. In the debate of 1808-1809 on division the Thomas committee estimated the population of the eastern counties at 17,000, that of the western at 11,000, souls; the number of persons in the latter of 16 to 21 years of age was put at 2,700. *Annals,* 10 Congress, 2 session, 972-973, 1093. In the course of the same debate Eppes presented statements regarding the number of free males, and also of actual voters at certain elections (*ibid.,* 857). Photostatic copies of these are in the Ill. Hist. Survey. The former, certified by Secretary Gibson (November 2, 1808), gave the number of such males as 676. For the votes see *post,* li, n. 1.

[4] *Ante,* xxx; *post,* clxviii and n. 1.

"destructive of the National Authority, are displeasing to the people of this Country, and we cannot but ask ourselves if the American Government has yet to learn how to hold it's Colonies."

So far as regards Harrison's acts (apart from the conclusions which the petitioners attached thereto and apart from their own hypocrisy), every one of these charges was either wholly true or contained much of truth. Two other charges were made. Eighthly, that the Governor had not only joined in a combination of speculators to reduce the price of public lands by stifling competition at the public sales, although bound by his duty as superintendent thereof to secure to the government the best possible prices therefor, but had "publicly avowed his right to carry this combination to any length he pleased."[1] Ninthly, and lastly, it was charged that Davis Floyd, condemned to punishment for participation in the Burr conspiracy and "come to Vincennes hot and fresh from his punishment," had been appointed through Harrison's instrumentality clerk to the House of Representatives. As regards these last two charges, what truth there was in the first cannot be today determined, while in the second case Harrison probably showed merely a decent (though politically indiscreet) humanity.[2]

[1] The petition says: although "receiving [si]x dollars per day for protecting this property, at the very time when he was taking measures for cheating the Nation out of it—We offer here no other document than his own statement annexed." This has apparently disappeared. Mrs. Goebel says of these charges that "no real evidence was ever produced against Harrison"—certainly a rash statement in the absence of the document forwarded by the petitioners. Gallatin, in the next spring (1808), sent a circular letter to all the territorial governors warning them against joining companies for land speculation. The receiver of the Vincennes office was individually warned. Goebel, *Harrison*, 70-71. Harrison was, however, a land speculator, like everybody else. See *ibid.*, 46-47, 57, 70, 197, 237; *post*, lxxxvii, n. 2.

[2] Floyd was elected in the autumn session of 1807, while under indictment. He was found guilty and sentenced to imprisonment for three hours. At public meetings held in Vincennes on January 4, 1808, and in Kaskaskia on February 18, resolutions were passed denouncing the action of the legislature, and disclaiming—for Indiana Territory—any sympathy for Burr. The Kaskaskia resolutions declared that the Randolph representatives were absent when Floyd was elected. According to Dunn these meetings were attempts by Harrison's opponents to discredit him. See his *Indiana*, 363-364. For Harrison's opinion of Floyd see his letter of April 3, 1807 (in *Messages*, 1: 205) to Governor Williams and that of April 13 to Jefferson (W. F. McCaleb, *The Aaron Burr Conspiracy*, 282). For his treatment of certain unimportant Burr refugees see *Messages*, 1:

These three memorials were received and committed together to a committee of which Parke was a member but Matthew Lyon chairman. In its report the committee sympathetically reproduced the oft repeated plaints of the Randolph and St. Clair petitioners, against the "many hardships, inconveniences, and privations" resulting from the "unnatural" union with the eastern counties. Particularly they stressed discontent with dependence upon the distant General Court at Vincennes,[1] and the monopoly of administrative officers of federal appointment enjoyed by the eastern counties. The eastern portion of the territory having also three-fifths of the representation in the legislature, the inhabitants of the western portion were "oppressed with taxes," the avails whereof were expended "in the country which is to form the Eastern State, and at the discretion of those over whom they can have no control." At the same time, the press of the embargo question and the condition of the public treasury, "and particularly the impolicy of increasing the number of Territorial Governments without its being manifestly necessary," made it inexpedient, in the opinion of the committee, then to deal with the matter.[2]

The elections which took place in Randolph and St. Clair in the summer of 1808 made certain, however, that the triumph of division was near. Shadrach Bond Sr. and Pierre Menard having resigned in 1807 from the Legislative Council, two members of the House—Shadrach Bond Jr. and George Fisher—were appointed to take their places, and to fill the resulting vacancies an election was ordered held in the Illinois counties on July 25, 1808.[3] These elections (only one of which, rather characteristically, was held on the day officially set therefor) were preceded by a contest of extraordinary passion. The issue was one between

[1] The Michigan separatists had done the same with respect to this—*Annals,* 8 Congress, 1 session, 29-30. *Ante,* xlvi, notes 2 and 3; xlvii, n. 1.

[2] *Annals,* 10 Congress, 1 session, (H. R. April 6, 1808) 1976, (report, April 11) 2067-2068; *Amer. State Papers: Misc.,* 1: 922; Harrison, *Messages,* 1: 288-289.

[3] Harrison, *Messages,* 1: 245-246, 247, 253, 295.

205, 228. The letters do him credit. But in July 1808 Harrison revoked Floyd's commissions as major of militia and pilot at the Ohio rapids—Gibson, *Exec. Journal,* 147.

divisionists and antidivisionists, which was the same as between those pro- and anti-Harrison. In both counties the divisionists were successful, John Messinger being elected by them in St. Clair and Rice Jones in Randolph.[1]

It had become apparent that so long as the legislature asked for slavery but rejected the division which the west desired (as it did in its petition of 1805), or asked for both despite the anti-slavery sentiment of the east (as the private petitions from the west persisted in doing), no success was possible. It was evident by this time that Congress could not annul or modify Article six, because the Senate would not. The Illinois representatives in the legislature of 1808 accordingly subordinated slavery to division and combined with the antislavery men from the easternmost counties, and the lower house voted prodivision and antislavery. It unanimously adopted (October 19, 1808) resolutions against slavery; unanimously passed a bill—which, however, the Council defeated—for the repeal of the black-indenture law; and voted (October 11)—the Council also opposing this—in favor of division. The action of the House was contrary on both issues to Harrison's position, and also to that of the Council.[2]

Jesse B. Thomas was elected delegate to Congress (another defeat for Harrison), not only pledged but under bond to act for division.[3]

[1] See *ante,* xlviii, n. 3. Secretary Gibson's certified statement of votes cast shows that at the St. Clair election of July 25 the number was 171; at the Randolph election of August 13, 151. See app. n. 24 on Rice Jones, whose murder grew out of the bitterness of this campaign. For discussions of this election see Dunn, *Indiana,* 365-367; Buck, *Illinois in 1818,* 191.

[2] For the antislavery resolutions, *ante,* xlii, n. 2; on the resolutions demanding division (presented, not printed), *Annals,* 10 Congress, 2 session, 18. A photostatic copy of the resolutions is in the Ill. Hist. Survey. See Dunn, *Indiana,* 369, 375; Webster, citing journals of the two houses, Ind. Hist. Soc. *Pub.,* 4: 220-221.

[3] T. Ford, *History of Illinois,* 30; Dunn, *Indiana,* 376; Webster, Ind. Hist. Soc. *Pub.,* 4: 221. Division was supported in the House by a three-fifths vote. The House having resolved that the delegate to Congress be instructed to procure division, and the Council that he oppose it, and Jesse B. Thomas—who was elected delegate by a vote of 6 (including his own) in 10—being of a doubtful dependability, John Rice Jones, of the Council minority and Harrison's bitterest opponent, put Thomas under bond.

The time for arguments had long since passed. The resolutions for division were a mere reallegation of existing discontents, a mere reiteration of the demand for separation.[1] Congress could only come, in time, to agreement with the petitioners that division was "the only means now left of restoring harmony." The grand jury of St. Clair County took similar action in the same, and that of Randolph in the following,[2] month; while sundry inhabitants of Knox County opposed the petitions from the Illinois country—they did not wish to have the capital moved, nor to bear alone the burden of representative government.[3] The representations went to friendly hands. A committee of which Jesse B. Thomas was chairman reported in favor of separation,[4] and presented a bill for the purpose.

This committee, of course, was bound to make the most of the more plausible arguments of the divisionists. It stressed the maladjustment of the judicial system to the needs of the western counties, and also expressed the opinion that the thin and scattered distribution of the population enervated the executive power in administration. Only one argument, they thought, existed against division—the increased expense of government; and that would be far more than balanced by the increase in land values "arising from the public institutions which would be permanently fixed" in the new territory, and from the increased immigration which division would stimulate. What a "large majority" of the inhabitants desired, it was a "just and wise policy to grant." Opposition to di-

[1] They did not repeat the causes, but urged the policy of self-government, and expressed the belief (certainly a venturesome one) that the western counties contributed in taxes "considerably more than the expences of the Government they pray for would draw from the publick Treasury."

[2] *Annals,* 10 Congress, 2 session, 633, 901. These are nowhere printed.

[3] *Annals,* 10 Congress, 2 session, (H. R. December 16, 1808) 862. A photostatic copy is in the Ill. Hist. Survey. The most important names are those of Henry Hurst, John Johnson, and Benjamin Parke. Rather disingenuously the petitioners declared that the territory's population was "spread across the country from the Miami River to the Mississippi—and on the Mississippi from the Ohio to Wood creek opposite the Missouri."

[4] December 31, 1808—*Amer. State Papers: Misc.,* 1: 945-946; Harrison, *Messages,* 1: 324-327; *Annals,* 10 Congress, 2 session, 971-973. In the Senate the committee, headed by Pope of Kentucky, made no independent report on the memorials, but eventually reported the House bill.

vision was not lacking.[1] Nevertheless, the bill became a law[2] on February 3, and took effect on March 1, 1809. Kaskaskia became the capital of Illinois Territory.

One is left, at the end, doubting whether in truth "a large majority of the citizens of the said Territory" desired division. It is probable that the divisionists were in a decided minority.[3] The petitions prove nothing even as regards the Illinois counties. It is doubtful whether a hundred genuine signatures could be found on all of them. It is certain, however, that a very large part of the leading men of the Illinois country (of the judges of the county courts, for example) signed petitions for division;[4] and presum-

[1] The arguments—The new government would cost $6950 for no more people than lived in Washington. It would involve a useless multiplication of offices (no more a begging of the question than the usual arguments of the divisionists). The inconveniences complained of were nowise peculiar to Indiana Territory. "There was no other part of the United States in which the same inconvenience was not felt as that complained of . . . that there were many places in different States whence the people had to go two or three hundred miles to the courts; that a compliance with this petition would but serve to foster their factions, and produce more petitions." (*Annals, loc. cit.,* 1094). This was probably true. In *Hist. of St. Clair County* (Brink, McDonough), 81, the figures are given for the entire cost of county government in 1809; which was $663.54, plus a ten per cent disbursement fee. The judges of the Common Pleas cost $142.67, the farmers of the poor $122.42; the other items were $104 for wolf-scalps; fees in criminal cases wherein conviction failed, $98.93; the clerk, $95; sheriff, $32.50; justices of the peace, $23.02; constables, $18; courthouse fixtures, $15; clerks of elections, $12.

[2] *Annals*, 10 Congress, 2 session, (H. R.) 815, 971-973, 1077-1078, 1093-1095—bill passed (January 18, 1809) by 69 to 37; (Sen.) 326, 327, 330, 335, 338, 339 (passed unamended, January 31); (the act of February 3, 1809) 1808-1810.

[3] In the Knox petition presented December 16, 1808 (*ante*, lii, n. 3), presumably written after the Illinois elections, and signed by John Johnson and Benjamin Parke (among others), they characterized the divisionists as "a small section of the people." In Harrison's address to the legislature of the new eastern territory in October 1809, he declared that division "could only have been effected by a total misrepresentation of the interests and wishes of four fifths of our citizens." *Messages*, 1: 378.

[4] *Ante*, xlvii, n. 1. In Randolph: John Beaird (signed 2 petitions), John Edgar (5), John Grosvenor (3), Nathaniel Hull (1, that for annexation to Louisiana, only) and Pierre Menard (1, same), Robert McMahon (2), William Morrison (3), Robert Reynolds (4). In St. Clair: George Atchison (3), David Badgley (2), James Bankson (2), William Biggs (3), Shadrach Bond Sr. (2), John Dumoulin (2), Nicholas Jarrot (4), James Lemen (3), John F. Perrey (5), Uel Whiteside (3), William Whiteside (3). These are all judges who sat in one court or another, at one time or another, during the years 1800-1809. In Randolph James McRoberts signed no petitions; to him, as undeclared, might well be added Nathaniel Hull

ably we may safely, in this case, attribute to "the people" the sentiments of their leaders.

Similar doubts must assail one who seeks to identify the cohesive forces in such party grouping as appears in the petitions and elections of the time. It is not contended by anyone that national party differences had any influence. Certainly, also, slavery was not—could not be—a subject of party difference. If there was any antislavery sentiment worth mentioning in the Illinois country it was wholly inarticulate.[1] Slavery sentiment and divisionist sentiment, of course, went more or less together; but it is inadmissible to assume with Dunn that the demand for division was no more than a proslavery maneuver. To do so is to ignore the greatest force of the frontier—unbridled individualism; which, as backwoodsmen were forced into communities, necessarily assumed in the political sphere the demand for local self-government. It involves the wholesale attribution to men who were quite capable of independent thought of the very naïve assumptions— of whose unsoundness each year gave proof—that if Congress would not grant slavery on popular petition it would nevertheless do so on legislative petition, and that though it would not do so for the legislature of Indiana Territory it would do so for the legislature of another territory. It ignores the known fact that some leading men who owned slaves and favored relaxation of

[1] On the claims for James Lemen as an antislavery apostle see *ante,* xxxix, n. 2; MacNaul, *The Jefferson-Lemen Compact, passim;* Buck, *Illinois in 1818,* 261 n., 280, 319. It is said that not later than January 1806 he started antislavery petitions in the eastern counties—MacNaul, 15, and cp. his diary, 30, where he says that he was circulating petitions in Illinois. The signatures of the judges to the proslavery petitions were as follows. In Randolph—Beaird (1), Edgar (4), Grosvenor (1), Menard (1), W. Morrison (3), Barbau (1), Fisher (1). In St. Clair—G. Atchison (2), Bond Sr. (2), Bankson (1), W. Biggs (2), Dumoulin (3), Jarrot (1), Lemen (1, but see xxxix, n. 2), Perrey (3), Uel Whiteside (1), W. Whiteside (2). Mr. Esarey, in the *Ind. Hist. Bulletin,* February, 1924, p. 57, gives various convincing reasons why political lines could not have been drawn on the slavery issue in Indiana; but he assumes, quite gratuitously, that therefore there was no "division of territorial Indiana into a Harrison and an anti-Harrison party."

and Pierre Menard, from the above list. Jean Bpte. Barbau, Samuel Cochran, James Finney, Antoine Louviere and George Fisher signed the antidivision petition of 1807 (as did also two of Menard's brothers). In St. Clair, out of fifteen active judges only three were undeclared: Shadrach Bond Jr., Thomas Kirkpatrick, Benjamin Ogle.

the Ordinance (and probably many others regarding whose property and whose opinions information is lacking) were opposed to division—such as, among the judges, Jean Baptiste Barbau, George Fisher, and Pierre Menard, all of whom signed not only the petitions for annexation to Louisiana but some of the later petitions in which slavery and division were joined, and who joined in the antidivision memorial of 1807. So far as regards political agitation proslavery sentiment was less, not more, intense than the sentiment for division.[1]

It has been customary to refer to the anti-Harrison or divisionist party of the Illinois country as the "Edgar-Morrison party." The name is not inappropriate, but it requires qualifications. That there was in Randolph County an Edgar-Morrison dominance one local expression of which was an anti-Harrison party is indubitable. But John Edgar and the Morrisons most certainly did not dominate St. Clair; yet that county was at least as uncompromisingly divisionist as was the other. Clearly, then, causes purely personal to Edgar and the Morrisons cannot explain the divisionist movement.

Utterly trivial and negligible, of course, was the expenditure of money at Vincennes for public buildings, notwithstanding the references to this in the petitions and in the report of the Thomas committee.[2]

Of real importance was the issue of transition to the second grade of government. This was at first not a sectional issue nor even a party issue. It became both when Harrison espoused the change as a means of strengthening his control of the territory, and the Illinois leaders sought to defeat him in that plan. Thus, when the change was made it was opposition to it, not support of it, which he felt called upon to pardon in Shadrach Bond and others. Harrison's success, and his political finesse in gaining it,

---

[1] Compare the greater number of signatures by the judges to divisionist petitions: 30 signatures by 17 judges for slavery and 53 by 19 for division. And if it be admitted that in 1803 a signature of the petitions for annexation to Louisiana was indistinguishably one for division and for slavery, and omit divisionist signatures of those petitions only, the number would still be 51.

[2] Citations *ante*, xlvii, n. 1; lii, n. 4. On the courthouses of several counties see *post*, ccx, n. 2.

undoubtedly left irritations in the Illinois country. The matter really amounted to no more. The constantly repeated charge of its citizens that he forced representative government upon them against their will would have been, in itself, a sorry reason for appeal to Congress. Back of it lay the real cause of complaint, the fear of control by the eastern counties. This, and not either desire for or opposition to representative government, exercised cohesive force upon sentiment in the Illinois counties. It has been seen that Harrison himself attributed to the fears of the "land-jobbers" the opposition to adoption of government of the second grade.

Somewhat more impressive, on its face, is the suggestion that Harrison, in his use of his appointing power, was unfair to the western counties, and that he used it to build up a party headed by his friends.[1] His appointments to territorial offices were indeed made exclusively from his intimates of Knox County. But as such officers were extremely few it is difficult to imagine that these appointments could have had consequences either wide or profound; nor would it be easy to show, as regards the charge of unfairness, that men equally fit for choice were available in the western counties. Other appointments—to county offices, and to the Council so far as Harrison acted for or influenced the President—were necessarily distributed. There is abundant evidence that in the Illinois country he used this patronage politically. There is rarely evidence which could justify one in attributing to him purely personal motives for his action; and certainly, whatever may have been his motives, it cannot be denied that most of those whom he barred from office were unworthy.

"Ever since Clark's Conquest [1778], office-holding"—says Mr. Esarey—"had been an attractive occupation in the Illinois and Wabash countries. For ten years dishonest men had had control and called their system of plunder a government . . . The arrival of Harrison was awaited in fear by these men. Their fears were justified, for they soon learned that he came to govern. Some

[1] This was one charge in the *Letters of Decius* of Isaac Darneille (*post*, app. n. 81); cp. Webster, Ind. Hist. Soc. *Pub.*, 4: 220; Dunn, *Indiana*, 328; Goebel, *Harrison*, 63; Alvord, *Illinois Country*, 423.

of the better men of this clique received offices from him, in which they rendered faithful service. The others formed an opposition which attacked the Harrison administration at every opportunity. As early as 1801 these malcontents were trying to create a party in favor of a representative government. They succeeded in arousing some interest, both at Vincennes and in Illinois."[1]

The evidence falls short of fully sustaining this eulogistic estimate of Harrison's strength and judgment.[2] His later enemies in Randolph had not in 1801 been refused honors and emoluments; Secretary Gibson had appointed John Edgar and William Morrison, inter alios, judges of Quarter Sessions and Common Pleas (presumably, as in later cases, during good behavior) and Harrison, after his arrival in the territory, made no change. He himself, late in 1801, appointed Robert Reynolds; and still later John Beaird and John Grosvenor. In St. Clair, Secretary Gibson had similarly filled the courts, and for some reason Harrison reappointed all the judges (with one change) early in 1801, but his appointees included all the later prominent divisionists—George Atchison, William Biggs, Shadrach Bond Sr., John Dumoulin, Nicholas Jarrot, and J. F. Perrey; and he later appointed David Badgley and James Bankson. It is true however that the first

---

[1] Esarey, *History,* 1: 160.

[2] Harrison might, in political irritation, regard as undesirable malcontents those who desired representative government; but Mr. Esarey seems, somewhat naïvely, to adopt the same view. To his *Messages* of Harrison there is prefixed a rhetorical passage from Lew Wallace expressive of the Indiana Harrison-complex; of its eight allegations one only is true and acceptable; the others are either evidently absurd or open to grave doubt, or require great qualifications based upon notorious facts. Mrs. Goebel's characterization of Harrison is acceptable: "As governor, Harrison was a good administrator; had it been otherwise, he would probably have failed to secure three reappointments. That he did not distinguish himself by a 'noble stand' on any specific issue—for example, opposition to slavery, or an attempt to extend the people's powers, or a stand for the sale of land at a cheaper price—is true. Politics was his business, however, for the time being . . . A study of this period must change somewhat the legendary conception of Harrison as the 'father of the Northwest' and replace it by an infinitely more real person, struggling in the limited field of territorial politics to maintain his power and place." Goebel, *Harrison,* 87-88, cp. 378-380. Harrison was an affable man (see the characterization by Isaac Darneille, quoted by Mrs. Goebel, 87), of mediocre ability and weak character; but his rare political prescience is very evident in his administration of Indiana Territory.

petition for division of Indiana Territory itself, as distinguished
from the earlier petitions for annexation to Louisiana—the peti-
tion-of-350—was not presented in Congress until late in 1805.
But that Harrison may have had knowledge of its character before
that date seems not an unreasonable assumption; and it happened
that the reorganization of the county courts—which he may very
well have brought about for political reasons—gave him at this same
time an opportunity to be rid of his enemies. In his mind these
would certainly have included advocates of either the second grade
or of division. It would also be good to believe that in his action he
treated as undesirable the officials known to be involved in the land
frauds, if we can assume that these had been revealed so early.[1]
Not a one of the above Randolph judges was recommissioned;
and only Shadrach Bond Sr. and Perrey of the St. Clair group.
Not a one of either county ever received thereafter a civil appointment at Harrison's hands; although he later had good words for
Bond—when he could favor only him or Perrey—in advising the
President on appointments to the Council (and great honors for
Shadrach Bond Jr., who however never signed any petitions).[2]
A few minor civil appointments were given to divisionists, and some
military also;[3] but these are doubtless of little significance. Nor

[1] The commissioners were required by the statute to begin their
work not later than January 1, 1805; reappointments to the county courts
were made in April and December, 1805. *Post,* app. n. 27. Michael Jones
was named to the Randolph Common Pleas in the latter month. This indicates certainly that Jones had gained the Governor's confidence. How,
if not by revealing the truth about Randolph conditions? However, there
is no evidence that the implication of John Rice Jones in charges of land
frauds (*post,* lxxxvii, xcix) was the cause of Harrison's break with the
former (*post,* app. n. 10), and James Gilbreath's implication did not lessen
the honors awarded him (*post,* lix and n. 2). All such judgments, however,
are speculative; the commissioners published no reports until 1809. The
perpetrators of fraud, however, certainly knew, from their examinations
before the commissioners, what to expect. Probably the drift of things
was common knowledge in the Illinois country.

[2] One of the charges by Isaac Darneille against Harrison in the
Letters of Decius was that he was holding an office as surveyor for the
younger Bond—Goebel, *Harrison,* 63-64. See *post,* app. n. 19.

[3] John Hay, notary in 1808; John Hays, justice of the peace in 1807;
Henry Levens, same in 1806; military honors to Parker Grosvenor, son
of John, in 1806, and to Robert Robinson in 1807 (Gibson, *Exec. Journal,*
146, 139, 137, 143 respectively). Darneille charged that Harrison gave office to
three of the Whiteside family, all of them justices of Quarter Sessions, two
of them captains of militia, though all were under indictments for horse

is it especially significant that John Hay was retained as clerk of the St. Clair courts, recorder, and treasurer throughout the territorial period, and was appointed by Harrison (acting for the President) to the Council in 1805; for he was an excellent man, has always been regarded as a personal friend of the Governor, and had signed no more than the 350-petition of that year.[1] But it is a striking fact that James Edgar was retained as sheriff of Randolph until he resigned, in 1806; John Edgar as head of the Randolph militia until he resigned, in 1806; Robert Morrison as clerk of the Randolph courts throughout the territorial period; George Atchison as head of the St. Clair militia until his death, in 1808; and John Whiteside as coroner of St. Clair throughout the same period. John Edgar was also retained as county treasurer. All of these men were pronounced divisionists and enemies of Harrison, and the gravest charges of corruption and official misconduct could easily have been sustained against the first three. Every man appointed to high civil office in Randolph after the date of the petition-of-350 is found among the signers of the Randolph antidivision petition of 1807.[2] Every prominent signer of the petition of 1808 attacking Harrison had reason for personal animus.[3] This record is precisely what one could expect. Harrison was not at all the man of power or principles suggested by

---

[1] *Post,* app. n. 17.

[2] Samuel Cochran, James Finney, George Fisher, and James Gilbreath. Pierre Menard did not sign, but his two brothers did. James Gilbreath signed the Louisiana petition of 1803: appears in Dunn's reprint as a signer of the prodivision petition-of-350; his name appears (as "Gilbrath") on the prodivision "remonstrance" of April, 1808; and on the antidivision memorial of 1807. Of these the first and fourth (seen in MS) agree and are undoubtedly genuine; the third (MS) is evidently not his autograph.

[3] William Wilson, surveyor of Randolph, had had his commission revoked outright by Harrison for good cause (*post,* clxxvi, n. 4). John Edgar and William Morrison, lords of Kaskaskia, had been ignored in civil offices, were deeply mired in the land scandals, their nemesis—Michael

---

stealing—Goebel, *Harrison,* 64. William Whiteside and his son William Bolin probably held captaincies when Darneille wrote, but the latter was never a judge. William and his son Uel sat occasionally in the St. Clair Orphans' Court—see *post,* app. n. 40. The former received military appointments in 1802 and (of major) in November 1805; the latter was made a justice of the peace in 1803; and William Bolin received his captaincy in 1802 (Gibson, *Exec. Journal,* 111, 116, 130). The third Whiteside referred to by Darneille was probably John. All were extreme divisionists.

Mr. Esarey. He was of the type of administrator who preserves
the conventions, depriving his enemies of favors, loading favors
upon his friends, replacing the former with the latter as deaths or
resignations give opportunities. But that he could act with judgment and despatch in creating opportunities is shown by his coup
de main in proclaiming adoption of representative government,
and probably by the legislation which reorganized the county
courts, and[1] which to a large extent stripped Edgar of his duties
as county treasurer.

Quite evidently Harrison's exercise of his appointing power,
far from gaining him support, could only have irritated and consolidated his enemies. Emphasis has therefore rightly been placed
upon it. But its results reduce to personal animosities. It was
an age (not less on the Mississippi than the Atlantic) when politics
were envenomed, slanderously and malignantly personal, to a degree beyond the comprehension of today. The ambitions of individuals, together with personal hatreds and personal loyalties,
were the real cohesive force of such "political" grouping as existed.
And more important by far than resentments aroused by the distribution of patronage were, undoubtedly, those which originated
in the land problem.

There is no doubt that Harrison endeavored to derive political
credit from his land policy. He deserved to do so, for he sought
throughout his governorship to secure to immigrants the cheap
and abundant land which they desired. That the government ex-
tinguished the Indian titles at a rate vastly in excess of the actual
economic needs of immigrants cannot be denied. Only about a
quarter of the area of the present state of Illinois had been surveyed in 1819, and of that surveyed not a sixth had been sold; in
1834 nine-tenths of the whole area was still unsold (and two-thirds

---

[1] See the discussion of the taxation statutes, *post*, cxvii *et seq.*, and *ante*,
xxvi, n. 3.

Jones—had been appointed to their court, given Harrison's marked confidence. Robert Reynolds was hopelessly besmirched by the land commissioners. John Grosvenor was always likely to stand with Reynolds. William and Uel Whiteside were extremely prominent in St. Clair and may
well have resented neglect. James Lemen's signature ("Laman") was
not his own.

of Indiana).[1] The one result was to encourage scattered settlement and the early picking of the richest land, leaving the government under difficulties in later sales;[2] a policy very different from, and less wise than, that pursued in Louisiana under the Spanish rule. Another result, ultimately, was war; whether or not that also was consciously sought by Harrison to hold his waning popularity. Most of the lands were bought almost for nothing. An area almost as great as the total of all land sold in Illinois to the end of 1819 cost absolutely nothing; and what is worse, it was secured by insistence upon Indian cessions to the Wabash and Illinois companies which our government had repeatedly pronounced illegal and worthless.[3] Of his treaties in general it is said by the highest authority that "he made no pretense of extinguishing the title of all the claimants, but held treaties with factions, with isolated bands; in short, with any Indians over whom he could exert a temporary influence, quite in defiance of Indian usage, which required the consent of a general council." In addition, he bribed, and threatened starvation, in order to bring to terms the chiefs who were his tools. This was the cause of Tecumthe's effort to restore a confederate authority, and end the wastage of the hunting grounds by recreant and unrepresentative tribal chiefs. He did, indeed, secure a verdict for libel against William McIntosh, who charged him with cheating the Indians of their lands and arousing their hostility, but the case is not one from which his apologists can derive great comfort.[4] Whether Harrison was principal in this

[1] See particularly *Amer. State Papers: Pub. Lands,* 3: 456-462; 7: 530. Also, for other years—3: 497 (1821), 533 (1821) ; 4: 770, 909 (1825). Memorial of Illinois legislature, January 12, 1827, *ibid.,* 4: 871.

[2] Compare memorial of the Illinois legislature, February 8, 1825, in *Amer. State Papers: Pub. Lands,* 4: 148.

[3] H. Adams, *History of the United States,* 6: 83-84. The costs are ascertainable from the above sources. Harrison was disappointed in a price of one cent per acre and expressed to Jefferson the hope that he could make the average lower (letter of August 29, 1805, unprinted, cited in Webster, Ind. Hist. Soc. *Pub.,* 4: 260). Mrs. Goebel states that for none of the lands in the three great cessions of 1803-1804 (*ante,* xii, n. 4) did the government pay "more than one or two cents an acre . . . although at this time the minimum price accepted by the United States for public land was two dollars an acre." *Harrison,* 105. On the Ft. Wayne Treaty of 1803, referred to in the text, see *ibid.,* 100-104.

[4] The quotation is from A. H. Abel, "The History of Events resulting in Indian Consolidation West of the Mississippi," Amer. Hist. Associa-

general policy, or only the hand of Jefferson, is a question which little affects the fact that his execution of it was wholehearted and unscrupulous. That he sought to counteract by a popular Indian policy the dissatisfaction created by his civil administration was a charge made at the time which historians have generally endorsed.[1]

Mrs. Goebel, in her recent monograph upon Harrison, does all that can be done to show that he did no more than carry out policies that were Jefferson's. It is evident that in regard to this matter, as in regard to many others, there are contradictions between Jefferson's principles and his practice. It was inevitable that he should seek to secure the western lands, for cheap land, widely owned, was the very basis of his political philosophy. It is also indubitable that Jefferson (at any rate his Secretary of War) instructed Harrison "to ask the Indians if they did not consider . . . valid" their old cessions to the Illinois and Wabash companies, "and if not, what were their reasons. Secondly, he was told to try to persuade the Indians to transfer these cessions to the United States. If Harrison failed to accomplish this, he should at least assert a claim *to the whole tract which he considered to have been ceded to the French.*"[2] And though this was not an absolute insistence upon those utterly discredited grants, nevertheless, acting under this authority, Harrison did insist upon them (and bribe and threaten), and secured a great cession on the basis of these claims. Jefferson also personally ordered Harrison to involve the tribal

---

[1] McMaster, *History of the United States,* 3: 137, 528-529; H. Adams, *History of the United States,* 6: 82-84; Abel, "Indian Consolidation," 267; Alvord, *Illinois Country,* 416. Mrs. Goebel admits this, *Harrison,* 94. Her position is that Harrison merely carried out Jefferson's instructions (*ibid.,* 94 and note, 97, 100, 104), and that "in following this policy Harrison pleased the president"—citing no evidence—"and the settlers" (97). Henry Adams also says, "during eight years of Harrison's government Jefferson guided the Indian policy"; and that "his greed for land equalled that of any settler on the border." *Op. cit.,* 69, 74.

[2] *Ante,* xxvi, n. 3; Goebel, *op. cit.,* 100, citing MS sources. See further on these grants, *post,* lxvii, n. 1.

---

tion, *Report* for 1906, I, 267, 388. Although Mrs. Goebel is an apologist for Harrison her account fully sustains the quotation, *op. cit.,* 100-107, *passim.* On his acts in relation to Tecumthe's policy see H. Adams, *op. cit.,* 6: 78-83, 87. On the McIntosh libel compare Dunn, *Indiana,* 413; Goebel, *op cit.,* 125.

chiefs in debt in order to oblige them to sell the tribal lands; a policy which Henry Adams scathingly, and of course justly, denounced.
There is, nevertheless, something to be said on the other side, both
in criticism of Harrison and in defence of Jefferson. Mrs. Goebel
asserts that Jefferson "disapproved no land acquisitions."[1] It may
be noted, however, that when a land office was established at Kaskaskia in 1804 it was only "for so much of the lands included
within . . . the treaty . . . with the Kaskaskia tribe . . .
as is not claimed by any other Indian tribe"; and this was apparently the only treaty with reference to which such reservation was
made, and also the only one which did not give rise to discontent.[2]
And there was a special reason for the form of that statute. It
appears in orders given to Harrison in 1805—in view of rumors of
an Indian conspiracy—"to make explanations to dissenting chiefs
and to counteract the effect of his own questionable methods." In
1809, similarly, he was ordered to make a certain treaty provided
the chiefs of "all the Nations who have or pretend a right to these
lands should be present." Finally, when Harrison wanted to ne-
gotiate for still more land in 1811 he was told it was inexpedient
until "the discontents occasioned by the one lately concluded" had
been quieted.[3]

There is also a little to be said in defence of Jefferson.
Granted that a political philosophy in favor of small landowners
is not superior morally, as a reason for taking lands, to the frontiersman's unphilosophical attitude, it remains true that from the
time of the Louisiana acquisition onward, acquisition of lands east
of the Mississippi was associated in Jefferson's mind with the plan
of removing the Indians onto reserved lands west of the river,
which he believed would put an end to wars. He believed that as
game became scarce the Indians would necessarily either become
citizens or remove to the west.

[1] Letter of February 27, 1803, Harrison, *Messages*, 71; see H. Adams,
History of the United States, 6: 74-75; Goebel, *Harrison*, 94 n.
[2] Law of March 26, 1804, *U. S. Stat. at Large*, 2: 278, § 2; Goebel,
op. cit., 105.
[3] Quotations from Abel, "Indian Consolidation," 267, citing MS
sources of 1805; compare Goebel, 106; *Amer. State Papers: Ind. Aff.*
1: 761; Goebel, 113-115. Harrison disregarded the instructions, and, as
Mrs. Goebel says (115), "the sequel of this treaty was the Battle of Tippecanoe."

In all other matters than land cessions the attitude of both
Jefferson and Harrison was one of genuine sympathy for the Indians.[1] There is no reason to suspect that the humanitarianism
of either was tainted by hypocrisy.

Harrison's use of his land policy in the attempt to hold his
position against his gathering enemies was unsuccessful. A general policy does not often placate men with individual grievances.
And so it was in this case. The judges and other county officers—
with but very few others—were the landed magnates of the Illinois
country. Nowhere could a local gentry ever more completely have
dominated local society and government. They feared, since the
territorial taxes fell almost exclusively upon land, exploitation by
the populous eastern counties so long as the territory should remain undivided. They resisted to the utmost the enforcement of
the tax laws. These grievances, we have seen, were prominent in
the petition of 1808 which listed Harrison's misdeeds. Finally,
there was the matter of disputed land claims. No evidence of
friendliness to particular individuals or factions can be found in
Harrison's action upon claims presented to him. Scores of thousands of acres of land claimed by the above named men were, however, pronounced invalid by the land commissioners for lack of
evidence to support their claims, for perjury, and for forgery.
And the commissioner who for almost thirty years dominated the
proof of titles and the sales of land, Michael Jones, the man most
hated and feared in these early years by the Illinois potentates,
was supported and confided in by Harrison; appointed to the
Randolph Court, put forward as the Harrison candidate for delegate to Congress in the legislature of that year in which division
triumphed.[2] Division was the only real political issue of the
time. The desire for self-government—after division, but not
through representative government within the Indiana Territory—
and the complications of the land problem were the chief contribu-
tors to its vitality.

[1] Abel, *loc. cit.*, 241, 244, 252, 268; *post,* cxxx, n. 1; clxxxiv, n. 3.
[2] Biographical note, app. n. 13. On governors' confirmations see *post,*
lxxix, n. 3.

Though tedious in its details the land problem must therefore be considered, for the light it throws upon the character and policies of the men who managed the affairs of the Illinois country.

Under the French régime crown grants were originally uniformly made, apparently, en franc alleu—roughly equivalent to a fee simple.[1] But such grants did not include all the land; indeed, only a small part, the rest being reserved to the king. The commandants seem always to have assumed a right to grant lands. It is open to question whether their concessions were made, not in fee simple but in usufruct; the land reverting to the crown upon abandonment. The British had to some extent regranted confiscated French concessions, possibly on this theory; and St. Clair favored its application to the French settlers who had migrated across the Mississippi into Louisiana, but who—very naturally—asserted, under ancient grants, a continuing claim to lands formerly occupied. The policy adopted by the government in favor of their claims was generous, but the opportunity to simplify the problem was lost.[2] It was further complicated by the prevalence of fraud in Spanish and French grants throughout the Mississippi valley, and by the custom of making individual transfers of land—naturally enough under the Custom of Paris, which was the law of the valley —by simple delivery of seisin, or by paper grants of the most in-

---

[1] Alvord, *Illinois Country*, 203-207. On the French feudal system generally in America see the works of W. B. Munro: *The Seigniorial System in Canada*, ch. 4-5; *Documents Relating to the Seigniorial Tenure in Canada 1598-1854*, lxxxiv-xc; brief summary in his *Canada and British North America*, 137-143.

[2] St. Clair to Jefferson, February 10, 1791, *Amer. State Papers: Pub. Lands*, 1: 19; *St. Clair Papers*, 2: 400; S. Breese, *The Early History of Illinois*, 297-299 (important example of 1762); Louis Houck, *History of Missouri*, 2: 199 (citing Charleville v. Chouteau, 18 Mo. at 505—but this relates to lots in common fields), 214. See Alvord, *Cahokia Records (I. H. C., 2)*, xxii note 2. The provisions of the Laws of the Indies are inconsistent. Compare, in *Amer. State Papers: Pub. Lands*, 5: 631 *et seq.* (White's Compilation): Lib. IV, Tit. 12, ley 2 (p. 649), IV-12-3 (p. 650), IV-12-14 (651), Royal Regulation of October 15, 1754 (p. 656, § 4), all of which express the usufructuary theory, with III-5-1 (p. 669—of the *Novissima Recopilacion*, 1805) and IV-12-4 (p. 650). Some examples of British regrants are given in McDonough, *Hist. of Randolph, Monroe and Perry Counties*, 98. In the petition by Edgar et al. cited *ante*, xxi, n. 1, it is repeatedly alleged that the French grants were made in fee.

formal character, which of course were unrecorded.[1] Following
the French, the local British authorities after 1763 made extensive
grants in violation of royal proclamation, and frequently (if not
always) for personal gain.[2] Following Clark's conquest came
Colonel John Todd, Virginia's lieutenant of the county of Illinois,
who made other grants; and after him Timothé de Monbreun made
grants "without number."[3] A court set up by Todd at Vincennes,
and claiming authority under him to do so, granted lands in the
Wabash country for eight years (1779-1787) "to every applicant,"
and ended by dividing among themselves—each sensitively absenting himself on his own day of good fortune—the whole of the vast
remainder supposedly cleared of Indian titles.[4] Finally, claims

[1] Harrison to Gallatin, from Kaskaskia, October 18, 1803—Webster.
in Ind. Hist. Soc. *Pub.*, 4: 248; Gallatin, *Amer. State Papers: Pub. Lands,*
1: 187, evidence 187-189; compare 1: 610 (Miss. Ter. 1807), 6: 6-7 (Ark.
1829), 7: 732 (Ala. 1835). Secretary Sargent, in *Amer. State Papers:
Pub. Lands,* 1: 10; Judge Woodward, 282, compare 250, 599— "Abstract
(C)"; *St. Clair Papers,* 2: 166 n., 171-172; H. S. Cauthorn, *History
of the City of Vincennes,* 46. See Judge Law's account of conditions at
Vincennes—John Law, *The Colonial History of Vincennes, under the
French, British and American Governments* (ed. 1858), 107-108.
[2] *Amer. State Papers: Pub. Lands,* 2: 121, 206-209, 139 (claims 1591,
1593, 1594, 1595, 1969, 1971). On the corruption of Lieutenant-colonel
Wilkins, illustrated in some of these grants, see Alvord, *Illinois Country,*
266, 282, 283, 297; *post,* lxxix, n. 1. General Gage, it seems, "always
declined to participate in a colonizing project"—Albert T. Volwiler, *George
Croghan and the Westward Movement, 1741-1782,* 263.
[3] In St. Clair's words, which seem to evidence an extraordinary
vagueness of knowledge regarding events in the Illinois country only seven
to eleven years before his own arrival there, "a gentleman of the name of
Todd" and "a person of the name of De Numbrun"—*Amer. State Papers:
Pub. Lands,* 1: 19. See Alvord, *Cahokia Records* (*I. H. C.,* 2), index,
"land." Of course all settlement north of the Ohio was contrary to the
Virginia statute; but it was nevertheless favored by George Rogers Clark
and John Todd as a means of garrisoning the country, and they had made
grants accordingly—*ibid.,* lxix-lxx, lxxxiv. See also Alvord, *Kaskaskia
Records,* (*I. H. C.,* 5), 446 and citations.
[4] *Amer. State Papers: Pub. Lands,* 1: 10—Secretary Sargent to the
President, July 31, 1790; 16—members of the "court of the district of Post
Vincennes, under the jurisdiction of the State of Virginia" to Winthrop
Sargent; 123—Harrison to Secretary of State, January 19, 1802 (Harrison,
Messages, 1: 36—same); 41—Harrison to Secretary of War, February 26,
1802. John Law, *The Colonial History of Vincennes,* 117-118, gives one of
the old deeds. The total grants by this court are stated in *St. Clair Papers,*
2: 166 n. to have been about 48,000 acres; this is doubtless based (what
purports to be Sargent's journal is mixed with the editor's paraphrases and
additions) upon *Amer. State Papers: Pub. Lands,* 1: 10, where Acting-
governor Sargent gives the same figures, but adds: "The court has also

to immense areas were asserted by land companies upon the basis of alleged Indian grants made during the British period,[1] as against which the United States denied the validity of such titles, and also set up later quitclaims of the Indian titles allegedly so gained.[2] In this there was no inconsistency; but later our land-hunger led our government to demand recognition of these same titles, already repeatedly officially pronounced invalid!

By a resolution of the old Congress, in 1788, the claims were immediately confirmed of all "French and Canadian inhabitants, and other settlers . . . who on or before the year 1783 had professed themselves citizens of the United States, or any of them"; and a donation of 400 acres "for each of the families now living" in villages of the Illinois country.[3] As a result of

---

[1] The Illinois Land Company of 1773 was organized to exploit a decision rendered in 1757 by Pratt later Lord Camden and Charles Yorke (and adapted for their own purposes by the land speculators about 1773), that a title deriving from the grant of an East Indian potentate was complete without a royal patent. Virginia, in her battle with the various western land companies, repudiated this doctrine in 1776; as did, later (1823), the United States Supreme Court in Johnson *v.* McIntosh, 1823, 8 Wheat. 543; cp. Commonwealth *v.* Roxbury, 1857, 9 Gray (Mass.) 451, 478. And see T. M. Marshall, *The Life and Papers of Frederick Bates,* 1: 72; Volwiler, *George Croghan,* 295-296, 298, 309, 319-320; Alvord, *Illinois Country,* 300-301, 341. On the use made by Jefferson and Harrison of these claims of the Illinois and Wabash companies see *ante,* lxii.

[2] In 1787 ("We solemnly surrender our charter whatever it is")— Madison to Congress, December 1, 1803, in Harrison, *Messages,* 1: 90-91. Only bare reference to fundamental legal points involved in these controversies can here be made.

[3] In a committee report to Congress made on June 20, 1788, which report was approved, it was resolved: (1) that "the antient settlers . . . should be confirmed in the possession of such lands as they may have had at the beginning of the late revolution, which may have been allotted to them according to the laws or usages of the governments under which they have respectively settled"; and that *"separate tracts"* should be reserved to satisfy such claims. (2) "That measures be immediately taken for confirming in their possessions and titles, the French and Canadian inhabitants, and other settlers on those lands, who on or before the year 1783 had professed themselves citizens of the United States, or any of them, . . . and [3] for laying off for the benefit of said inhabitants three *additional tracts* adjoining the several villages, Kaskaskies, la Prarie du Rochers, and Kahokia, in the form of a parallelogram, . . . and of such extent as shall contain four hundred acres for each of the families

---

granted to individuals, in some instances, tracts of many leagues square." etc. The 48,000 acres, as a total, would be absurd; cp. *post,* lxxii-lxxiii. Alvord, *Illinois Country,* 418, erroneously applied Sargent's report to the Illinois country; see also 347.

petitions from various classes of settlers not included within the provisions of these resolutions (in particular, no doubt, late comers of English speech), Congress passed an act of March 3, 1791. By this act the family donation was extended to include every person who in 1783 was head of a family in either "Vincennes" (which was construed to mean the Wabash country) or the Illinois country and who had since removed from one to the other; and also to such family heads of 1783 who had afterwards left the territory, provided they should return within five years after passage of this act. Subject to the same proviso they were also confirmed (the language included only such heads of families) in all grants made to them before 1783 "according to the laws and usages of the government under which they had respectively settled." In addition, with regard to lands "actually improved and cultivated" under any "supposed grant of the same by any commandant or court claiming authority to make such grant," the governor was empowered to "confirm to the persons who made such improvements, their heirs or assigns, the lands supposed to have been granted as aforesaid, or such parts thereof as he . . . judge reasonable, not exceeding to any one person four hundred acres"; and likewise to grant not over 100 acres to each man, not having received a family or improvement donation, who was enrolled in the militia on August 1, 1790, and had done militia duty.[1]

[1] *U. S. Stat. at Large*, 1: 221; *Annals*, 1 Congress, 3 session, 2348-2350. For lists of early Illinois inhabitants compiled for Governor St. Clair (1796-1797) under the several provisions of this law see *Chicago Historical Collections*, 4: 192-229. Similar lists could of course be far more accurately compiled from the claims affirmed by the commissioners; such lists, the accuracy of which has not been tested, are given on pp. 424-425 of Reynolds, *Pioneer History*. Compare *ibid.*, 130-131. See *post*, lxxv, n. 2; ccxx, n. 8.

This act of 1791 also confirmed (§ 5) the Vincennes commons, and "a tract of land including the villages of Cohos and Prairie du Pont, and

now living at either of the villages of Kaskaskies, la Prarie du Rochers, Kahokias, fort Chartres or St. Phillips." Alvord, *Kaskaskia Records* (*I. H. C.*, 5), 479-482—italics added. The limitation (later abandoned) to settlers who had become citizens followed a condition imposed by Virginia when she made her cession in 1784 (*ibid.*, 412-413).

Resolutions (1) and (2) covered the confirmation of ancient grants, (3) was the basis of "future donations" based on family rights or head-rights. Many difficulties inherent in the phraseology of these resolves disappeared when the act of 1791 replaced them.

These powers of the governor were transferred in 1804 to the land commissioners within their respective districts.[1] Thus most—but if the statute be literally construed, not all—former grants were recognized, subject to proof of good faith in the claimants; and new bounties from the United States were added.

There was rarely a grant that could be certainly located on the land. Descriptions such as "on the Kaskaskia, seven or eight miles above the village," "on the Okaw, six miles below Horse Prairie," "adjoining the Jesuits' land," "on the road to fort Charters, opposite the village of Kaskia," "situation unknown," "ten leagues up the Ohio River," "on the Mississippi some thirty miles above the mouth of the Ohio," "right below Tower Rock," "on Clark's trail to Vincennes," "seven arpents front from the Mississippi to the hills and back on the hills eighty arpents," "a large tract of land on the Illinois river," "a large tract near Fort Chartres," "five arpents front by sixty in depth, east of the Kaskaskia river, and below the village," "about three thousand acres lying within the Renault grant," "in the Big Wood above Kaskaskia," "in the Indian Prairie," "in the Grand Prairie,"[2]—were not unique, nor even exceptional: they are ordinary descriptions of

---

[1] Statute of 1804 cited *post*, lxxx, n. 1.
[2] These are taken from McDonough, *Hist. of Randolph, Monroe and Perry Counties*, 98; *Amer. State Papers: Pub. Lands*, Vol. 2, *passim* in the reports on ancient grants, 138-139, 157-161, 211-212.

---

heretofore used by the inhabitants of the said villages as a common" (see *Amer. State Papers: Pub. Lands*, 3: 432; McDonough, *Hist. of Randolph, Monroe and Perry Counties*, 97). No express confirmation of the Kaskaskia commons was made; the commissioners confirmed the lots within it under the head of ancient grants. Governor St. Clair, in 1796, referred to claimants as being unwilling to pay for the surveying of lands "which they could not cultivate, and were restrained from selling till five years after possession had been given them"—*St. Clair Papers*, 2: 399. There was no such provision in the statute, and the basis of his statement does not appear.

The three parallelograms for donation lands, provided by the resolutions of Congress of June 20, 1788 (preceding note) were to be located west of "the ridge of rocks," the bluffs bordering the flood plain of the Mississippi. They would have fallen largely in "the American Bottom." Three squares east of the ridge were substituted (unacceptably to the inhabitants of Cahokia—*Amer. State Papers: Pub. Lands*, 1: 19-20) by another resolution of August 28, 1788—*ibid.*, 32; and Alvord, *Kaskaskia Records* (*I. H. C.*, 5), 490. The act of March 3, 1791 repealed the alteration. But the original location areas remained likewise unsatisfactory.

locality, bounds being rare and metes unknown. The descriptions in the governors' patents were equally vague. The same is true of those of town lots in Vincennes.[1] The territorial laws on surveying were merely an invitation, or—one might say, considering the state of titles,—a longing. There were no surveys because there were no surveyors. To be one was to be a highly educated man.[2] St. Clair in 1790, could find only one man around Cahokia who knew anything of the subject; but neither there nor at Kaskaskia would claimants pay the fees, which he agreed they were ill able to afford.[3] Secretary Sargent agreed with the citizens of Cahokia and Prairie du Pont, in 1797, upon two tracts for their common lands supposedly containing 5,400 acres: it turned out that one alone contained 20,000.[4] Undoubtedly, too, French and American measures were confused.[5]

[1] In the land commissioners' report of 1807, *ibid.*, 1: 592, they refer to the great vagueness in the patents, "no topographical description being ever given by which it may be known in what part of the country the lands lie." See also Law, *Colonial Hist. of Vincennes*, 59-61.

[2] *Post*, 25 (1802), 459 (1807). The law (copied from Virginia) unfortunately required the surveyor to be a resident of the county. It forbade any survey without chain carriers. Compare Governor Reynolds, *Pioneer History*, 330, 331. There are various such passages in this book and in *My Own Times*. On the surveying problem compare *St. Clair Papers*, 2: 166 n., 168, 171, 173, 399.

[3] St. Clair in *Amer. State Papers: Pub. Lands*, 1: 19-20. According to him the Kaskaskia surveyor was paid $2.50 per mile, $2 for a village lot. By territorial statute of 1802 (*post*, 27) the charge was fixed at $5.25 for not over 400 acres (plainly bounded with plats), per mile (and 30 cents per mile for more than 10 miles), $1 for a village lot. See, on the poverty of the inhabitants, *Amer. State Papers: Pub. Lands*, 1: 20, (petition by James Piggott and 45 others), 21 (Father Gibault's picture of the misery of the Illinois country, the absolute impossibility of bearing the surveying costs); *St. Clair Papers*, 2: 148-149, 168 (St. Clair's concurrence with Gibault), 399; Alvord, *Kaskaskia Records* (*I. H. C.*, 5), 513.

[4] Instead of 4,000—*Amer. State Papers: Pub. Lands*, 2: 194; the area was given as 5,400 in the statute of March 3, 1791—*ante*, lxviii, n. 1.

[5] "Arpent" was doubtless popularly used as the equivalent of "acre," as by Secretary Sargent in *Amer. State Papers: Pub. Lands*, 1: 84. As Judge Woodward in one place gives the values of the arpent of Paris ("universally" used in the French colonies of North America, according to him) it amounted to .848 American acres (*ibid.*, 264). An average of all instances in the reports of the Kaskaskia commissioners where comparison is possible (*ibid.*, 2: 213, 214, 219, 225) gives .846. The value of the arpent of length is likewise nowhere explicitly stated. Judge Woodward gives it as 192.25 feet, and this I have used. The commissioners twice give 84 arpents as the value of a league (*ibid.*, 192, 212; though this cannot be reconciled with the details of claim 2641, p. 139, and the map at p. 183). General Harmar used 22 leagues as about 50 miles (*St. Clair Papers*, 2: 31).

The titles in the Wabash country were certainly less confused than those in the Illinois counties. Yet Judge Symmes wrote of the former: "The confusion of title here is a labyrinth of perplexity which requires the utmost care nay tenderness to set right—they have been called on to aduce their titles—they have a variety; prescription, bare possession—fraudulent deeds from those who had no right to sell, but mere American imposters who came among them after the subjugation of this country, pretending authority to convey lands & rights to take up lands—no records are preserved—they sometimes have had a notary public, but when ever one died or removed all his papers & entries were lost."[1]

The chaotic uncertainty of titles, the cheapness of land even aside from such uncertainty, offered irresistible incentives to speculation. Furs were the chief item of trade in the pre-American period; land was the chief concern of the Americans. Such speculation "was the only outlet for any considerable amount of capital. But it was more than that—it was practically the only activity in which men could give free scope to their business ability." Speculators in continental currency and in land had long since found their way into the Illinois country. In order to understand conditions there it is essential to remember that, as John Adams said, land speculation has been endemic in this country since William Penn (or earlier); to recall the notorious fact that the Ordinance of 1787 was born, as Alvord has said, in "a rare combination of New England settlers and New York land speculators"; and to remember that a very large part of the public men of the time were quite as active in land-jobbing as in statesmanship—by no means least so Franklin, despite the preachments of Poor Richard in favor of prudence and frugality.[2] All our history until very

[1] June 22, 1790, to Robert Morris—Bond, *John Cleves Symmes*, 291. In an official report by Secretary Sargent, of the same year, he wrote: "There is scarcely one case in twenty where the title is complete, owing to the desultory manner in which public business has been transacted, *and some other unfortunate causes*" (italics added)—*Amer. State Papers: Pub. Lands*, 1: 10. See *post*, xciii, n. 2 on Michigan titles.

[2] Buck, *Illinois in 1818*, 152; Alvord, *Cahokia Records* (I. H. C., 2), lxix, lxx, lxxi; *Illinois Country*, 392, 393; Beard, *Economic Origins of Jeffersonian Democracy*, 320.

The activities of Franklin and Washington can best be seen in Volwiler, *George Croghan*, index; likewise those of William Franklin, Sir William

recent times has been dominated and colored by this presence of cheap land. It has played a part of universality, yet of paradox: the hope of democracy, the spur to individual initiative, the greatest cause of family instability, it has also been a powerful contributor to our national conservatism; the strongest pillar of prosperity, it has also been the greatest single impulse to economic debauchery. It first infected us with the fever for sudden wealth. From the days when our forefathers began to strip the Indian of his hunting-grounds with beads and gallons of New England rum down to Teapot Dome it has tempted and corrupted us. The venality uncovered by the land commissioners in the Illinois country is a mere example, nothing more.

Under the resolves of Congress in 1788 some claims would have been inalienable for three years. The Spanish authorities in upper Louisiana seem effectually to have barred speculation under their grants.[1] But the statute of 1791 placed no impediments in its way. The amount of the traffic in the claims to be confirmed under that act was immense. Claims originally held by hundreds passed within a few years into the hands of a few score individuals.[2] In the Wabash country "court" grants of two and

[1] Compare Houck, *Missouri*, 2: 215, 216, 223-224; but see 220—unperfected titles were evidently to some extent transferable. See also *Amer. State Papers: Pub. Lands*, 5: 735.

[2] Brink, McDonough, *Hist. of St. Clair County*, 74-75, summarizes the original record book of John Hay, recorder; still preserved at Belleville.

Johnson, and the firm of Baynton, Wharton & Morgan, who were active in Illinois. See, for interests in the early land companies, Alvord, *Illinois Country*, 289, 302, 381, 392-395. Also, for the years around 1787, Beard, *Economic Interpretation of the Constitution of the United States*, 23, 27, 49, 151, and details in the sketches of the men (Jonathan Dayton, Franklin, Hamilton, Washington, etc.) named on the page last cited. As for the interests of Patrick Henry and Gallatin—the latter lost much of his patrimony in land deals—H. Adams, *Life of Albert Gallatin*, 67; and when George Rogers Clark was commissioned for the conquest of the Illinois country Governor Henry and he seem to have formed a land partnership—Alvord, *Illinois Country*, 341-342. The act of Congress of March 3, 1791 (*ante*, lxviii) confirmed to P. Gibault a lot formerly in the occupation of the priests at Cahokia. Cp. Law, *Colonial Hist. of Vincennes*, 55-59. Query whether this land confirmed to Gibault was not the same which Gibault had tried to pass to Clark. See further on these claims *Amer. State Papers: Pub. Lands*, 2: 139, claim 336; and on Clark's land claims in general, J. A. James, *George Rogers Clark Papers* (*I. H. C.*, 19), xxxiv. On Hamilton's involvements see also *Lectures on Legal Topics 1921-22* before the Association of the Bar of the City of New York, 117.

three hundred thousand acres were taken by speculators, who took them to the east and sold them to the ignorant. Plans for colonization by innocent settlers became imminent. Subgrants of a thousand acres could be had "for an indifferent horse or a rifle gun."[1] In the Illinois country smaller grants, but practically the entire country, were involved. When St. Clair and Randolph counties were organized the donation claims under the Congressional statutes, together with the French, British, Virginian, and Company claims, called for hundreds of thousands of acres. All of the Mississippi bottom lands and the adjoining bluffs for many miles were plastered with conflicting claims. There also the traffic in claims had scattered them over the United States. Headrights are said to have sold (presumably for the higher prices in later years) at from seven to fifty cents per acre; militia rights for from six to fourteen cents; improvement rights for seldom less than fifty cents.[2] The improvement claims would naturally be to better lands. Variations in the other claims, unlocated, must have reflected popular appraisals of their validity. The largest sale recorded, of 9,233 1/3 acres (21 1/3 headrights and seven militia

---

[1] Harrison, *Amer. State Papers: Pub. Lands,* 1: 123. Matthew Lyon stated in Congress that he knew of 200,000 acres on the Wabash offered for sale at 20 cents per acre—*Annals,* 9 Congress, 1 session, 469.

[2] St. Clair, *Amer. State Papers: Pub. Lands,* 1: 90; *Hist. of Randolph, Monroe and Perry Counties,* 101. Governor Reynolds (*My Own Times,* 156) says the militia rights sold for about 75 cents; Brink, McDonough, *Hist. of St. Clair County,* 75-76, gives examples (chiefly of 1793-1796) of farm lands sold for 30 to 50 cents; militia rights, 12 to 17 cents; family rights, averaging about 20 cents. Mr. Boggess, *The Settlement of Illinois* (*Chic. Hist. Colls.,* 5), 92, says that in 1806 $3 was the maximum price even in settled parts of the territory; this must have been for clear titles.

In less than seven years claims held by about 400 individuals passed into the hands of 89, of whom only a dozen were French! Of the total of over 96,000 acres fifteen judges (fourteen of the Illinois country and John Cleves Symmes) held almost 63,000. With three exceptions all the men who claimed 1,000 or more acres, (fifteen in number) were either county or territorial officials. John Edgar claimed 39,700 acres; Pierre Menard 10,300; William McIntosh 3,800; John Rice Jones 2,340; George Atchison 2,100; John Dumoulin 1,826; John F. Perrey 1,520; Henry O'Hara 1,400; Nicholas Jarrot 1,298; John Cleves Symmes 1,200; Shadrach Bond Sr. 1,190; William Biggs 1,100; James Piggott 1,120; two others, 1,000 each— a total of 70,894 acres. The Randolph County figures cannot be segregated in the commissioners' reports—their district included both counties and there is no Randolph record giving the precise data for that county alone; but see *post,* lxxiv for the general situation.

rights), was for $9,000 to parties in Baltimore.[1] The profit is evident. The Quarter Sessions of Randolph, in 1807, valued the improvement rights and headrights of various of the largest land-owners along the Kaskaskia—who "applicated this"—at seventy-five cents, and those in the Mississippi bottom at twice as much. Unlocated claims, confirmed, were of course of much less value.[2]

We shall see the obstinacy with which assessment was resisted. In what appears to be the first one regularly made in Randolph, in 1808, 435,800 acres were taxed to less than 300 individuals, successors to more than 1,000 original claimants. The largest holders were John Edgar, 130,400 acres; Robert Morrison, 34,000; William Morrison, 24,800; John Rice Jones, 16,400; James O'Hara, 15,200; Pierre Menard, 12,600; Richard Lord, 11,200.[3] Much, perhaps most, of Robert Morrison's land was acquired at sheriff's sales.[4] Add to the above names those of Nicholas Jarrot, George Atchison, J. F. Perrey, and John Dumoulin of St. Clair, and of Henry O'Hara, William Kelly and Robert Reynolds, of Randolph, and the list includes the leading land traders of the Illinois country. All of those above named were, or had been, judges or other high officials except the O'Haras and Lord. Dumoulin died bankrupt; the land commissioners swept away large portions of the claims of all the others; perhaps Edgar and Jarrot alone died, in some sense for that time, wealthy. Governor Rey-

[1] Sale by Pierre Menard and wife, February 22, 1799—McDonough, *Hist. of Randolph, Monroe and Perry Counties,* 101.

[2] *Post,* cxviii, n. 5; McDonough, *Hist. of Randolph, Monroe and Perry Counties,* 104, gives the tax valuations (per 100 acres): $1, first class, river bottom) lands; $0.75, second class (uplands); $0.37½, unlocated but confirmed claims. They give the rates of 1808 (p. 98) as: $2.00, "cultivated" land; $1.50, "improved" land; $1, "wild" but located; $0.75, wild and unlocated; $2, on "fields"—i. e. doubtless, common fields—mainly around Kaskaskia and Prairie du Rocher; and one 3-acre tract (owned in London and Philadelphia), $2.

[3] McDonough, *op. cit.,* 98. The conveyance record there referred to (101), in which deeds to Edgar fill 172 consecutive pages, still exists at Chester. The number of original grantees might be approximately determined by counting those indicated in the reports of the land commissioners, which I have not done. The number 1,000 is approximately accurate. Mr. Webster (Ind. Hist. Soc. *Pub.,* 4: 249) states the number of fraudulent claims rejected in the reports of the commissioners in 1810 as 890. This agrees with Davidson and Stuvé, *History of Illinois,* 237.

[4] A large part of Randolph *Deed Record L,* 1805, consists of such deeds to him. It was characteristic of his caution.

nolds—whose father was ruined, and own name smirched, by the temptations that surrounded Randolph titles—invariably refers with respect to the few, like John Hay, who never engaged in the traffic, "altho the whole country, almost, were engaged in it."[1]

Some of these speculators concealed from those entitled under the acts of 1788 and 1791 their rights thereunder, with the result that many Americans, becoming discouraged, left the country; and assured the French Catholic slaveowners that their slaves would be confiscated, with the result that "most" of these migrated to Louisiana; the speculators buying up the rights of both.[2]

Even before the resolutions of Congress in 1788 petitions had been received praying a settlement of land titles, and Congress had voted in 1785 to send a commission to investigate them.[3] The action of 1788 only increased difficulties, for it was found that the

[1] See app. n. 33. It is extremely doubtful whether any, unless Edgar and William Morrison, retained much wealth. The absence of Robert Reynolds from this assessment roll of 1808 is significant; see *post*, cxvii; *Pioneer History*, 229.

[2] *Amer. State Papers: Pub. Lands*, 2: 124. The ruse had been used before. George Morgan had made use of it to draw settlers from Illinois to his colony at New Madrid—Hamtramck to General Harmar, March 28, 1789: Alvord, *Kaskaskia Records (I. H. C.,* 5), 503. Barthélemi Tardiveau wrote to Governor St. Clair that Article six of the Ordinance had been "translated and circulated" by "some designing characters"; "it was designedly represented to them, and with many aggravating circumstances rumored that the very moment your Excellency landed at the Illinois all their slaves would be set free. A panic seized upon their minds, and all the wealthiest among them, having but the wreck of once affluent fortunes, have gone to seek from the Spanish Government that security which they conceived was refused to them. The plot has succeeded to a miracle. Imposition has reaped the fruits of her cunning, and obtained for a paltry consideration very valuable estates." *St. Clair Papers*, 2: 118-119. See also St. Clair's report to the President after his visit to the Illinois country in 1790, *ibid.*, 175-176, 400. He mentions Morgan "particularly"; but it is evident that Tardiveau had the resident Illinois land-jobbers in mind. The population of Illinois by 1800 had fallen to about the same as in 1750. The greatest decrease was in the late 1780's. In 1783 there were in Kaskaskia 194 heads of families (39 of these American); in 1790 only 44, a decrease of 77 per cent. By 1800 the population of Illinois had again risen to about 2500, of which perhaps 900 or 1000 were Americans; and of these about 150 had arrived before 1787. See Alvord, *Illinois Country*, 359, 373, 407-408; *Cahokia Records (I. H. C.,* 2), cxliii.

[3] In 1784 such petitions were presented by Carbonneaux, former clerk of the Kaskaskia court, and by John Dodge, as a result of which the resolution referred to was passed in 1785— Alvord, *Illinois Country*, 363. In June, 1786, seventy-one Americans at Vincennes made a similar petition—Boggess, *The Settlement of Illinois*, 47.

lands provided for the location of headrights were nearly, if not entirely, covered by ancient grants of earlier governments or by irregular grants whose validity must be determined under the statute of 1791. Many claims, also, fell outside the location areas. It was also objected that these were in part rocky and of little value.[1] John Edgar, William Morrison, William St. Clair (cousin of the Governor), and John Dumoulin, therefore, prayed in 1796 a relocation of donation lands.[2] The Vincennes convention of 1802 urged that claims under the acts of 1788 and 1891 should be definitely estimated.[3] Five popular petitions and one from the General Assembly gave expression to discontent in 1805. The gist of these petitions was a prayer that claimants might locate their claims in the land offices at some fixed rate per acre, upon such public lands as they might select.[4] But this was impossible. Though seventeen years had passed, and almost nothing had been done, eight more were to pass before titles would be sufficiently settled to determine what lands belonged to the government, and permit the sales of public land to begin. In the meantime more

[1] St. Clair to U. S. Senate, January 7, 1799—*Amer. State Papers: Pub. Lands,* 1: 90; report of committee of the House of Representatives, *ibid.,* 68-69; land commissioners to Gallatin, February 24, 1806—*ibid.,* 286; Governor St. Clair to President, *St. Clair Papers,* 2: 400-401.

[2] On any public lands, of equal value with the donation tracts, in the vicinity of the respective villages. Petition of January 12, 1796, cited *ante,* xxi, n. 1.

[3] Dunn, Ind. Hist. Soc. *Pub.,* 2: 472; *Annals,* 8 Congress, 1 session, 1024; report to House of Representatives in favor of such action.

[4] The commissioners approved of this in their report of February 24, 1806—*Amer. State Papers: Pub. Lands,* 1: 285. Two of these petitions, dated December 2 and 3, 1805, and a third undated petition, were presented in Congress on January 13, 1806—*Annals,* 9 Congress, 1 session, 339. Photostatic copies of the originals are in the Illinois Historical Survey. The legislative petition, presented December 18, 1805, is included in Dunn's "Slavery Petitions" (Ind. Hist. Soc. *Pub.,* 2: 479-480). A fourth popular memorial, committed in the national House on January 17, 1806, is also given by Dunn, *ibid.,* 501, 504. For the fifth, from Peoria, see *post,* xcv, n. 4. The first two petitions were from squatters, who wished bounty grants of the land upon which they had settled (prayer rejected, *Annals, loc. cit.,* 352, January 21, 1806) and held up the generous policy of the Spanish authorities in Louisiana. See *ante,* xxxii, n. 1, for signers. The third petition referred to prayed that the claimants of Indiana Territory, under the law of 1791, be put on an equality with settlers in Louisiana Territory prior to December 20, 1803, who had been given, the petitioners believed, more generous treatment (by a law of March 2, 1805, *U. S. Stat. at Large,* 2: 324). See also the report of March 3, 1800 (House of Representatives), *Amer. State Papers: Misc.,* 1: 206.

and more claimants and new immigrants became squatters on government land.

Governors St. Clair[1] and Harrison made some attempt to deal with the claims. St. Clair, when in the Illinois country in 1790, directed the inhabitants to exhibit their titles. "A great many claims and title deeds were accordingly exhibited, examined, and decided upon, and orders of survey, for such as were found authentic, were issued; which was necessary to be done before patents of confirmation could be made out." But no locations were made in view of the objections to the lands provided for that purpose.[2] As St. Clair rejected at this time all Virginia grants (by Todd, De Monbreun, and the Vincennes court—though these last did not affect the Illinois lands), and as the statute of 1791 conditionally recognized all of these, it became necessary to reëxamine many claims, which he did on a second visit to the west in 1795; also passing upon many before then unpresented. But still no locations were made; nor did he decide in any case upon the quantity of land to be granted in cases of improvement rights and headrights. With respect to militia rights alone did he feel safe in taking final action. Finally, twenty-one claims (of other classes, apparently) had progressed to patents in 1799.[3]

It is interesting to observe how the laws were administered by those charged with their execution. Secretary Sargent, following the law, confirmed the whole or portions of improvement claims, both in the Wabash and the Illinois countries, at his discretion;[4] but ignored the law in assigning locations other than those

[1] Acting-governor Sargent, in 1797, appointed a board to investigate titles in the Vincennes district. *Amer. State Papers: Pub. Lands,* 1: 576, 579.

[2] *Amer. State Papers: Pub. Lands,* 1: 90; *ante,* lxviii, n. 1; lxxvi, n. 1. The first surveyor for Vincennes left the country, the first for the Illinois country did nothing—probably the pressure on them was strong. In 1795 new surveyors were appointed.

[3] *Amer. State Papers: Pub. Lands,* 1: 90; *St. Clair Papers,* 2: 398-400, 412. Governor St. Clair, in 1796, misinterpreting the statute of 1791, instructed his surveyor outright, with regard to the court grants in the Vincennes country, "all those will stand"! And in fact they did—*Amer. State Papers: Pub. Lands,* 1: 298, 559; act of March 3, 1807, *U. S. Stat. at Large,* 2: 446, § 1. See *post,* xcvi, n. 2.

[4] *Amer. State Papers: Pub. Lands,* 1: 91; see also representation of the Illinois legislature to Congress, January 14, 1831—*Amer. State Papers: Pub. Lands,* 8: 335. The law of 1791 (*ante,* lxviii, n. 1) per-

assigned by Congress. St. Clair observed law in the latter respect, but agreed with Pickering to ignore it in the other—granting 400 acres for any honest improvement (without regard to value), or none at all.[1] Harrison ignored the statutory provisions with respect both to militia and family donations. St. Clair complained that Sargent left only "some rough minutes of his transactions"; Harrison, that St. Clair would not deliver records to him; the Kaskaskia commissioners, that neither governor supplied them with a list of patents issued (leaving to claimants to suppress or present them as their interests dictated), and that St. Clair communicated to them the evidence upon which he acted in but a single case— a case, as it happened, of most manifest fraud, which he had overlooked.[2] Apparently St. Clair submitted very scanty memoranda of his confirmations, Harrison somewhat fuller.[3] One record of the former, cited by the commissioners as "a specimen," was a page from his minute book in which (in thirty-one printed lines) he disposed of twenty-eight claims by bundles of evidence ("bundles of papers given in by Mr. Edgar")—with almost no names, no dates, no mention of specific deeds, no descriptions that identified any particular land; involving a total of some 13,000 acres! He confirmed the same claim to different persons; the same claim twice over (for duplicated acreage) to the same person.[4] To John Edgar and John Murray St. Clair, his son, he confirmed a claim the patent for which called for 13,986 acres but the bounds for 30,000, and which rested upon a British grant that on its face— aside from its invalidity because violating crown orders—was con-

[1] *Amer. State Papers: Pub. Lands,* 1: 91 (St. Clair's official report of January 7, 1799; compare his draft of 1796 in *St. Clair Papers,* 2: 398).
[2] *Amer. State Papers: Pub. Lands,* 1: 91, 286; 2: 204, top; *Messages,* 1: 50.
[3] The commissioners' comments upon the former are elaborate and caustic; but a mere reference (*Amer. State Papers: Pub. Lands,* 1: 286), in the case of Harrison, to "the Governor's records sent us in November last," 1805.
[4] Details on these claims, *ibid.,* 2: 203-240; see especially 203, cl. 2009—taking it in its least unfavorable aspect as one of inadvertence; 205, 219 (Geo. Atchison, Jas. Ogle); 147, 218 (claims 1903 and 521); 235 (claim 1407).

mitted the governor to confirm family claims in his discretion, not exceeding 400 acres per person; but Secretary Sargent's action caused endless complaints. To these the legislature in 1831 still gave voice.

ditioned upon approval by higher authority (never given) and was made speculatively by the grantor for a share reserved to himself in the grant. One-half of this claim had been assigned to the Governor's son before the confirmation, and the patent was issued "after the powers of Governor St. Clair had ceased to exist in the Indiana Territory."[1] Another claim of precisely the same kind covered only 1,105 acres; and a third—save that Edgar assigned a moiety of this to Arthur St. Clair, another of the Governor's sons—was for 5,969 acres. Other egregious errors of official judgment seem ordinary only by comparison with these.[2] Harrison's record is similar, but better. In dealing with individual claims his carelessness or errors of judgment were equal to those of St. Clair,[3] but no cases of nepotism are recorded against him.

This hasty action by St. Clair and Harrison, whose time was hopelessly inadequate to deal with the interminable intricacies of

[1] *Ibid.*, 204, 208, 216, 239-240 (cl. 2208). The original grant was made by Lieutenant-colonel Wilkins in 1769 to the firm of Baynton, Wharton, and Morgan (with whom Wilkins had general and corrupt connections), he to receive one-sixth in case of confirmation, and he himself signed the statement: "For form's sake I have registered the above; but the grants therein alluded to"—of which the one here in question was but one of six—"are null and void until confirmed by the General's approbation." On Wilkins' corruption see *ante*, lxvi, n. 2; also C. E. Carter, *Great Britain and the Illinois Country, 1763-1774,* 155-156. General Gage and the British government never confirmed these grants; they were flagrant violations of crown proclamations. It is doubtless this land the deed of which by Edgar to John Murray St. Clair (on June 11, 1790) is printed in Brink, McDonough, *Hist. of St. Clair County,* 86; it is described as between Kaskaskia and Prairie du Rocher, and as "purchased by me at public sale, by order of the syndic of Kaskaskias, as the estate of Richard Winston." The consideration given by the Governor's son was one phaeton and harness valued at $200. See *post,* lxxxix, n. 1.

[2] *Amer. State Papers: Pub. Lands,* 2: 203 (claim 2009); 204, 211 (claim 2207—exact acreage 1104.8); 214 (claim 2209).

[3] Confirmations to Wm. Atcheson, Wm. Biggs, Wm. McIntosh, Wm. Morrison, Wm. St. Clair, and Robert Morrison were made exclusively, or almost so, by Governor St. Clair; to Jean Bte. Barbau, Geo. Fisher, Nicholas Jarrot, J. Rice Jones, Jas. O'Hara, John F. Perrey, Robert Reynolds, John Reynolds, by Governor Harrison; to George Atchison, Shadrach Bond Sr. and Shadrach Bond Jr., Jas. Dunn, John Edgar, Nathaniel Hull, and Pierre Menard by both governors. Probably those who began early used St. Clair, and him exclusively if they had few claims; and those who began late used Harrison. If the question of territorial division is taken as a party test it is impossible to find politics in these confirmations. See *ante,* liii, n. 4. It was charged by Isaac Darneille in his *Letters of Decius* (quoted in Goebel, *Harrison,* 67) that Harrison had confirmed claims of favorites and rejected claims of equal merit presented by Darneille. On Darneille see *post,* app. n. 81.

the problem, had no other effect than to add new snarls to the title of great portions of the country.

Finally, in 1804, Michael Jones and Elijah Backus were appointed a board of federal land commissioners to examine into all claims in the Illinois country. Their final reports were submitted, after six years of arduous labor, early in 1810. A second board (Michael Jones, John Caldwell and Thomas Sloo) was appointed in 1812 to deal with the governors' confirmations, and concluded its work in 1813. All the reports of both boards in favor of claimants; also all claims reported specially by the second board, without rejections; and certain exceptional claims recommended by Michael Jones were confirmed by Congress.[1]

[1] The first board acted under Congressional statutes of March 26, 1804 and March 3, 1805 (similar boards operating in Vincennes, Michigan, Mississippi, and Louisiana). The second board acted under a statute of February 20, 1812. For these statutes—*U. S. Stat. at Large*, 2: 277 (1804), 343 (1805), 677 (1812); *Annals*, 8 Congress, 1 session, 1285-1293 (1804); 8 Congress, 2 session, 1699-1702 (1805); 12 Congress, 1 session, 2237-2238 (1812). For the reports of the commissioners—*Amer. State Papers: Pub. Lands*, 1: 285-286 (1806); 590-591 (1807); 2: 123-241, 740-741 (reports of December 31, 1809, February 24, 1810, and January 4, 1813); 3: 1-5 (1815). For Congressional action—*U. S. Stat. at Large*, 2: 517 or *Annals*, 10 Congress, 2 session, 1811 (act of February 15, 1809, prolonging powers of the board to end of 1809); *U. S. Stat. at Large*, 2: 548, or *Annals*, 11 Congress, 1 session, 2506 (act of June 15, 1809, salaries for 1808); *U. S. Stat. at Large*, 590 (act of April 30, 1810, giving minors additional time to present claims); *ibid.*, 607, or *Annals*, 11 Congress, 2 session, 2584 (act of May 1, 1810, confirming all decisions reported December 31, 1809, in favor of claimants); *Amer. State Papers: Pub. Lands*, 2: 254-255, 257-258 (Congressional reports, 1811); *U. S. Stat. at Large*, 677, or *Annals*, 12 Congress, 1 session 2237-2238 (act of February 20, 1812; confirming all decisions reported December 31, 1809, in favor of claimants to town lots, commons, and rights in common, subject to the right to try titles in the courts; also authorizing revision, by a second board, of governor's confirmations); act of April 16, 1814— *U. S. Stat. at Large*, 3: 125—confirming (a) all confirmations by the second board, (b) all cases of that board "where the commissioners have reported specially and have not rejected the claims" in their general reports of January 4, 1813 and (c) claims specially reported favorably, left-overs from the work of the second board, by Michael Jones on January 18, 1813 (*Amer. State Papers: Pub. Lands*, 2: 741-743); *Annals*, 13 Congress, 1 session, 112, 127 (no action); *Amer. State Papers: Pub. Lands*, 3: 384-385 (report of February 24, 1818, upon a petition by certain disgruntled claimants, favoring confirmation of governor's confirmations except in "cases dependent upon grants of the Governors, founded on 'ancient grants,'"), 421 (report of January 27, 1820, to same effect—no action on either). It is generally stated that *all* of the findings and recommendations of the commissioners were approved—Alvord, *Illinois Country*, 422. This is correct; but it would be extremely difficult to say, in various of the cases reported specially, whether the commissioners "reported specially and have not rejected the claims," their comments being unfavorable.

The principles that guided both boards were generous. Under a literal interpretation of the statute of 1791 it was only grants to heads of families who were such before 1783 that were confirmed, and subject to the proviso that if they had left the territory they must return within five years after the date of the statute. The commissioners ignored both restrictions; acting, as respects the second, upon the liberal assumption that anyone who came forward to support a claim not manifestly dishonest had complied with all the requisitions of the law.[1] No more was required than honest proof of an actual improvement. Headrights were allowed by the first board to all who had been *"settlers in the country, and heads of families, become citizens of the United States, or some one of them, on* [in] *or before 1783."*[2] The second board—following the view acted upon by St. Clair and Harrison, and by the board at Vincennes—went even farther, and confirmed donations to the heirs of those who died as heads of families between Clark's conquest (1779) and 1783.[3] Militia rights were restricted by the first board to those who were residents, whether or not on the rolls, on the statutory date, no matter how recently arrived. The second board made donations to all who proved militia service after the country came under the dominion of the United States, treating the enrollment merely as evidence of the performance of that duty, but not as a condition.[4] Claims confirmed by the governors presented the most perplexing question.

---

[1] *Amer. State Papers: Pub. Lands*, 2: 124-125; *ante*, lxxv, n. 2 gives their reasons.

[2] *Amer. State Papers: Pub. Lands*, 2: 124 and 229-230; the language is that of the second board. This was probably because the resolutions of 1788 made the grant to those "now living" in the Illinois villages; but the statute of 1791, perhaps by oversight—and, it might be argued, in disregard of vested rights—adopted the date 1783.

[3] *Ibid.*, 2: 229-230—on the theory that the intent of Congress was to provide "a remuneration for the probable loss they would sustain by the introduction of the new Government, and consequent failure of Indian trade." These reasons were advanced in the resolutions of June 20, 1788—*ante*, lxvii, n. 3.

[4] *Amer. State Papers: Pub. Lands*, 7: 708. No such militia rolls as the statute required were to be found. Some were compiled for St. Clair in 1796-1797 *ad hoc*, on the testimony of selected and respectable inhabitants and were certified by them. See the citations in lxviii, n. 1. The second board accepted these lists as the best evidence available—*Amer. State Papers: Pub. Lands*, 2: 237.

With regard to these great anxiety existed from the moment the commissioners were appointed. The board followed the generous policy of excluding confirmed claims from their findings until the evidences of fraud incidentally revealed in such cases forced a change of policy. The passage of the act of 1812, already referred to, ordered the revision of all confirmations.[1]

[1] Claims were traced up to confirmation; it was then assumed that patents had always been issued and recorded, and that the territorial law "might" provide rules to regulate subsequent conveyances. But no list of patents was supplied to them; many confirmees had in fact no patent; others might suppress it, if narrower than their hopes. Not only were there scores of cases in which parties (sometimes three or four) claimed adversely to the conveyances upon which confirmations were obtained, but the rights of confirmees had been split and portions were claimed by different assignees. To deal with the problem fully, therefore, presented a very difficult problem; yet, until so dealt with, no final and secure titles could be recorded. *Amer. State Papers: Pub. Lands*, 1: 285-286. The statute of 1804 which defined the duties of the commissioners was very broad in its terms. It provided that every person claiming land under any legal grant from the French or British government, or under any resolution or act of Congress, should present his claim, and the commissioners should examine "the claims" and "decide thereon according to justice and equity," subject to approval by Congress (*U. S. Stat. at Large*, 2: 278, §§ 3, 4). It would therefore seem that the powers of the board were ample to deal with confirmed claims (*Amer. State Papers: Pub. Lands*, 2: 255, report of a House committee so holding). It was contended, however, by the confirmees that the act of the governors, by authority of Congress, conferred an absolute title. But as it appeared that they had confirmed claims resting upon ancient grants manifestly illegal, thus exceeding any possible interpretation of their powers, and had confirmed scores of claims supported by perjury and fraud, the government was forced to the position that they were only its agents, and it could revise its own acts. Claims under ancient grants rested upon a preëxisting legal title; under improvement rights, upon an equity; under family and militia donations, upon the statutes that expressed the bounty of Congress. So in all cases the right of the claimant was in no case derived from the Governor who was the instrument of the execution of the law, but antedated in existence that agency. "Viewing the Governors as agents, with limited and defined powers, the right to inquire into the performance of the duties assigned them cannot be doubted." *Ibid.*, 2: 254-255, 257-258 (Congressional reports). Under the act of 1812 the second board, empowered to review confirmations by Governors St. Clair and Harrison, did not stop with passing upon the validity of the original right (under ancient grant, improvement, etc.), but carried its finding forward in the chain of title to the governor's confirmation, rejecting or approving the right of the confirmee. But the confirmee might still appeal to the courts against adverse decisions, as might also claimants adverse to a successful confirmee. *Ibid.*, 2: 210. The headings to the various lists of the second board (except that on p. 215) are ambiguous, but the details of their actions clearly reveal their effect to have been as stated (e. g. 213-214, claims 2049, 2209; 219-220, claims 322, 2047, 2066, etc.).

More than 2,500 claims were considered by the boards.[1] Nothing but a prolonged examination of their reports, which would fill several volumes such as this, can convey an idea of the stupendous difficulties of their task and the painstaking scrutiny with which they discharged it. Within a small margin of error[2] the results, as they affected the leading claimants, can be presented in figures.

KASKASKIA LAND CLAIMS[3]

CLAIMANTS	CLAIMS AFFIRMED	CLAIMS DISAPPROVED because of—			TOTALS
		FORGERY	PERJURY	INADEQUATE PROOF	
Arundel, William.	1500				
Atchison, George..	*1100*				
Barbau, J. Bte.....	*400*				
Beaird, John......	400			500	
Biggs, William...	800			1300	
	1600			*100*	
Bond, Shadrach, Sr.	400				
	1290.4			*400*	
Bond, Shadrach, Jr.	400			800	
	400				
Dumoulin, John...	900				
	800				
Dunn, James......					
	1200				
Edgar, John.......	9651.8	7249	49246.7	42465.3	98961
	57881.8			*31225.4*	*31225.4*
Fisher, George....	1300			700	700
	100				

[1] The highest number noted is 2759.

[2] Due partly to obscurities inevitable in the board's summary presentation of such a vast mass of detail, and partly to the fact that no acreage can be discovered of various tracts of vague description.

[3] Compiled from the lists showing the action taken upon individual claims, listed under various heads in the commissioners' reports. The figures italicized represent claims which St. Clair or Harrison had confirmed. For

KASKASKIA LAND CLAIMS—*Continued*

CLAIMANTS	CLAIMS AFFIRMED	CLAIMS DISAPPROVED because of—			TOTALS
		FORGERY	PERJURY	INADEQUATE PROOF	
Gilbreath, James..			1200	1600	1600
Grosvenor, John...				400	400
Harrison, Wm. H..	800			400	400
Hay, John........	400				
Hull, Nathaniel...	400				
	900				
Jarrot, Nicholas...	31597.7			8321.8	8321.8
	2000			*1000*	*1000*
Jones, John Rice..	10637.3			1918	1918
	5294.6	*2030.4*		*1967.2*	*3997.6*
Kelly, William....		9200	5000	2800	17000
Lord, Richard.....	400	11300	5800	4200	21300
McIntosh, William.	1881.7			400	400
	10266.7			900	900

lists of claims confirmed see: common fields, *Amer. State Papers: Pub. Lands,* 2: 174-202; ancient grants, 157-158, 211-212; and 213-214 (claims neither approved nor confirmed by the commissioners but reported specially to Congress, though clearly disfavored by them; but confirmed by the act of April 16, 1814; family headrights, 162-165, 227-230; improvement rights, 158-161, 217-220; (including, p. 219, two claims by Shadrach Bond Sr. and John Edgar, specially reported, confirmed by act of April 16, 1814; militia rights, 166-174, 235-238. Claims rejected: ancient grants, 138-139, 215-217; family headrights, 148-154, 230-235 (unsupported before board—therefore, in effect rejected); improvement rights, 140-148, 220-226 (unsupported); militia rights, 155-156, 238. Rejected claims of Edgar, unclassified, 203-205 (none included in the other lists). See also *ibid.*, 2: 741-743, donation claims of all three types, confirmed by act of April 16, 1814.

The varying policies of the two boards of commissioners resulted in scarcely any contradictory action—in the main the second board merely dealing with cases left unsettled by the first board. A claim for 135.4 acres by Edgar—p. 203, cl. 2056—on which the first board had no power to act, but in which it reported extraordinary evidences of fraud and forgery was seemingly nevertheless affirmed by the second board—p. 212; but the descriptions are variant, and evidently there is in one case a misprint of the claim number. No final action is to be found on a few claims; namely, on Edgar's claim No. 2078 (p. 203) for 400 acres, nor on 6 out of the 90

INTRODUCTION lxxxv

KASKASKIA LAND CLAIMS—*Concluded*

CLAIMANTS	CLAIMS AFFIRMED	CLAIMS DISAPPROVED because of—			TOTALS
		FORGERY	PERJURY	INADEQUATE PROOF	
Menard, Pierre...	8557.4			8221.3	8221.3
	1300			*2710.6*	*2710.6*
Morrison, James..	400		400	2100	2500
Morrison, Joseph..	5112	1600	1200	2000	
Morrison, Robert..	1200	1600	34800	7700	44100
				400	*400*
Morrison, William.	19907.8	2800	8400	15372	26572
	2500			*900*	*900*
O'Hara, James....					
	6700			5561.4	
Perrey, J. F.......	4232			3501.5	3501.5
	951.5			4550	4550
Reynolds, John....				1600	1600
		800			*800*
Reynolds, Robert..	477.5	7400	10800	5800	24000
				1850	*1850*
Whiteside, William.			1200	400	1600

family rights for 400 acres each, covered by his claim No. 2055 (p. 204; 71 approved in pp. 227-229, 13 disapproved in 230-235). No other examples were discovered. See also *ante,* lxx, n. 5.

In the commissioners' "remarks" upon each claim one finds various characterizations. Classed under forgery are cases with the annotations "forgery," "deed fraudulent," "deed forged"—perjury being, of course, also usually present; and the same is true of claims carrying the annotation "deed suspicious," "supposed forgery," and "no such man" (as the claimant's supposed grantor). Classed under perjury are cases carrying the remarks "perjury," "subornation and perjury"; and also those labeled "fraud," "transaction fraudulent"; although the ambiguity of the latter cases is manifest. Classed under insufficient proof are cases labeled "proof insufficient," "entered more than once," or without any label.

Rejected claims in the last column omit three ancient grants presented by Edgar (*Amer. State Papers: Pub. Lands,* 2: 214, cl. 2107), Jones (p. 138, cl. 1738—"a large tract") and R. Reynolds (p. 138, cl. 35) which are of indeterminable area. The affirmed claims of Edgar include one for 1116.8 acres, and half of another (totalling 5968.8 acres) claimed jointly by Edgar and Arthur St. Clair (p. 214, half of cl. 2209), which were disfavored by the commissioners, but referred to Congress, and by it approved in the law of April 16, 1814. (Not included are two tracts of indeterminable area claimed by Jones (p. 144, cl. 1292 and 1293) and "a large tract" of unknown area claimed by Wm. Morrison (p. 143, cl. 471), all three as improvement rights.

Many of the Kaskaskia claimants were also claimants in Missouri, and some of them also in the Vincennes district. One must therefore supplement the above table in order to show completely how well each fared at the hands of the government.[1]

| | VINCENNES | | MISSOURI | |
	CONFIRMED	REJECTED	CONFIRMED	REJECTED
J. Edgar	1200			
Jas. Gilbreath		400 (perjury)		
Wm. H. Harrison	3185.7			
N. Jarrot				1600
J. R. Jones	2710	680		
Wm. McIntosh	7732	800		
P. Menard				3000
Jas. Morrison				2350
R. Morrison				2992
Wm. Morrison	938.3	440		1222
Jas. O'Hara	400			
J. F. Perrey		680	("Jean" and "John" Perry)	3177
R. Reynolds		1600 (perjury)		
H. Vander Burgh	7049			

Many men prominent as officials (judges, sheriffs, clerks, etc.) or otherwise in the Illinois counties do not appear at all in the lists of the commissioners, or only appear in a way that casts no possi-

[1] The Missouri reports (unalphabetized, and without reasons given) are in *Amer. State Papers: Pub. Lands,* 2: 463-729; see also Marshall, *Life and Papers of Frederick Bates,* index s. v., "Board of Land Commissioners"; Scharf, *History of Saint Louis,* 1: 316 *et seq.* It appears however from Marshall, *op. cit.,* 2: 293, that the Perry of the table was very likely not John Francis Perrey. For the Vincennes reports, see *Amer. State Papers: Pub. Lands,* 1: 288-303, 558-581 (duplicates in 7: 675 *et seq.*); 2: 455-463; 7: 700. An act of March 3, 1807 (*U. S. Stat. at Large,* 2: 447, § 4; *Annals, 9.* Congress, 2 session, 1290-1292) required location of all Vincennes confirmed claims by July 1, 1808; otherwise they should be void. Another act, of February 13, 1813 (*U. S. Stat. at Large,* 2: 800; *Annals, 12* Congress, 2 session, 1329) extended the time to October 1, 1813. Curiously enough, the only ones who made locations were J. Rice Jones, for only 722 acres (under 1807 act, *Amer. State Papers: Pub. Lands,* 7: 709-727, nos. 2, 119, 149, 150); Wm. McIntosh, for only 2427 acres (under 1807 act, *ibid.,* nos. 85, 86, 87, 125, 127, 129, 139, 140, 141, 143, 147, 148); William Morrison, for 1619 acres (under both acts, *ibid.,* nos. 134, 135, 142, 158, 170, 203, 229, 232). These facts seem to be inexplicable. Some of the Vincennes confirmations to "William Morrison," however, cannot be to him of Kaskaskia, who died in 1837, for they are to his heirs.

ble discredit upon them.[1] None of the judicial and administrative
officers of the territory except William McIntosh, John Rice Jones
and Henry Vander Burgh were charged with improprieties in
either the Illinois or the Wabash districts.[2]

The incredible forgeries, fraud, subornation and perjuries
which the commissioners uncovered are explainable only by attributing to the land-jobbers an assumption of immunity that led to
carelessness or a stupidity of which it is difficult to believe them
capable. The discovery of more than seven hundred perjured
depositions given before one magistrate in upper Louisiana led to
the uncovering of hundreds more. The board, in its own words,
struggled "in the very mire and filth of corruption." Almost all
of the claims rejected for perjury rested upon the supposed original
title or improvements of fifteen persons, attributed to them either
by themselves or by others who assumed their names. Some of
these fifteen were respectable citizens who disavowed hundreds
of their alleged depositions. One tool of the land-jobbers confessed
to the wholesale use of another's name. The rest of the fifteen were
wholesale perjurers bought and sold by the speculators. Depositions were bought outright, or signatures obtained from drunken
men to blank depositions. Among those who gave as many as two
hundred depositions each, one was characterized by the commissioners as "a kind of straggling blacksmith," another as a "poor

[1] Of the judges of Randolph County, James Finney, Samuel Cochran,
Robert McMahon, and Michael Jones do not appear at all. There is nothing
discreditable in the cases of Jean Baptiste Barbau, a judge of earlier years,
and a justice of the peace in the years dealt with in this volume (his
testimony frequently enabled the commissioners to defeat fraud), John
Grosvenor, Nathaniel Hull, John Beaird, and George Fisher. Of the
sheriffs James Edgar (1803-1806) appears not at all, and James Dunn (1795-
1800) not discreditably.

Of the St. Clair judges James Bankson does not appear. In the records
of Jean Bte. Saucier, a judge of earlier times who was heavily interested in
ancient titles, David Badgley, George Atchison, Shadrach Bond Sr., and
Shadrach Bond Jr., there was nothing unworthy. Nor was there in the
records of William Arundel, prominent justice of the peace; John Hay,
clerk and recorder; and Wm. St. Clair, former clerk and recorder.

[2] Governor Harrison received two family rights, and failed to sustain
claim to a third. In the Vincennes district, as the above table shows, he
was confirmed in 3186 acres (*Amer. State Papers: Pub. Lands*, 1: 290, 559
et seq., 573). He speculated more or less in land despite his animadversions
against land-jobbers (*ante*, xxvi, n. 3; xlv, n. 2; xlvii, n. 1; xlix, n. 1; lviii,
n. 1; *post*, clxxxiv, n. 3).

wandering wretch, equally destitute of morality or character," several as men "of no education, property, or character." Two gave sworn and written confessions. Almost all of the depositions in these fifteen names were given to support claims of John Edgar, Robert and William Morrison, Robert Reynolds, William Kelly— three judges, the clerk, and a former coroner of Randolph—and Richard Lord, a mere (land) privateer. The depositions of one prolific deponent, proved to be false, were signed and sworn to exactly as written in the hand of John Edgar.[1]

Claims were made under family heads who died or left the country before 1783 (the second board validated some of these) or who entered it—sometimes long—thereafter; under supposed family heads proved never to have had a family; under militiamen who came to the country after 1790, or were living elsewhere in that year; by inheritance from men proved still to be living; under improvements that must have been made by the original right-holders, and under soldiers who must have served their country, in tender infancy. To be concrete, and confining attention to a few of those highest in station, it was found that John Edgar forged the signatures of many deponents. He presented a deed on the paper of a mill erected years after its date, with names of the witnesses forged thereto; and another deed, on paper of the same future mill, whose grantor swore he did not give it, made by the latter as the heir of a man whose death the parish records showed to have occurred some months later. He presented a deed acknowledged (before William Morrison) five months before its date, with the name of a witness forged; and to prove bona fides produced a letter signed by the grantor in a good hand, although to the deed he affixed his mark. Another of his deeds was by a grantor whose brother swore he had never been in the country, signed in fact by a son and the father's name later substituted; witnessed by John Grosvenor (who repudiated the signature) and William Morrison, and acknowledged before the latter; the grant being based upon improvements of the grantor—made, therefore, in absentia! He forged, then, the name of his follow judge, Gros-

---

[1] *Amer. State Papers: Pub. Lands*, 2: 125-127; for the confession of one of William Morrison's liquor-deponents, 137.

venor; and also that of Barbau (both men untainted by the land scandals). He interpolated a document in a book of records. He claimed one tract on evidence that A was illegitimate and not the heir of X, and an adjoining tract on the contrary evidence. He claimed the family right of one of his unmarried clerks who lived in his own house.[1]

Robert Reynolds was the first man to file claims with the commissioners; which proved his effrontery, for his record is as bad as Edgar's—perhaps worse, since it reveals no stupidity. He forged the names of witnesses, deponents and grantors; even the

[1] *Ibid.*, 2: 127 (cl. 2044), 128 (cl. 1997, 2046, 2068, 2094), 131 (cl. 751, 2017), 203 (cl. 2056), 204 (cl. 1392—compare p. 234), 205 (cl. 2068), 213 (cl. 2049). St. Clair confirmed some of these claims; the commissioners remarked of Edgar—"This man has been either weak enough or honest enough to give us a clearer view of the grounds on which the Governor has acted, by producing many of his documents, than others who have withheld them" (*ibid.*, 205). See Alvord, *Illinois Country*, 420-421; Davidson and Stuvé, *History of Illinois*, 237-238 Mr. James H. Roberts has stated—in the *Transactions* of the Ill. State Hist. Society, 1907, p. 64— that "authentic contemporary documents show conclusively that in all his vast transactions in land he acted with strict integrity"; and also that by a report of a committee of the United States Senate of which Judge Jacob Burnet was chairman Edgar was "exonerated from all blame." In fact this report (*U. S. Sen. Documents*, 21 Congress, 1 session, Sen. rep. 10, of January 5, 1830), made by the Committee on Private Land Claims upon a memorial by Edgar, did recommend the confirmation of thirteen family rights (5200 acres), originally confirmed by Governor St. Clair but adversely reported upon by the Board of 1812. At the same time it rejected Edgar's joint claim with Murray St. Clair, cited *ante*, lxxix, n. 1 (for 24,000 acres according to a survey made for Edgar), on the grounds that it violated the royal proclamation; was in terms subject to confirmation by the Crown, never given; was on its face fraudulent on the part of John Wilkins; was so vague that "neither its situation, quantity, nor limits" could be ascertained with any reasonable certainty; and that the governors were never empowered to confirm British grants, as such, but only for actual improvement (here not asserted). The Committee offered no judgment whatever on Edgar's general record. Judge Burnet had known Edgar for more than thirty years. One may perhaps attribute to friendship—for no extant evidence in any way confirms them—the assumptions that St. Clair acted on "evidence" and "testimony" of "witnesses examined," which evidence was not preserved; and that the witnesses had removed from the territory or died before the examination made by the commissioners in 1812. The committee therefore regarded the revision by the latter as made unreasonably late, and "more liable to error than the original decision" by St. Clair. All existing evidence discredits such a judgment; *ante*, lxxviii. When this report was made Congress had still never acted upon the reports of the second board. Actually, however, Edgar had been allowed three of the thirteen headright claims; which must have been through the later action of Michael Jones. The other lands had been sold, and Edgar claimed an equivalent.

names of fellow judges, Menard and Hull—again two honest men; himself gave depositions under an assumed name, and appeared before a magistrate with deponents who deposed under false names for his benefit.[1] He forged a grant to himself from a slave woman.[2] Not even against Edgar—or Lord or Kelly, whose records (statistically speaking) were worse—were the commissioners so bitter and contemptuous as against Reynolds.[3] Needless to say the statutes in this volume provide ample penalties against acts of perjury and forgery; yet for all those revealed in the land cases Robert Reynolds alone was indicted. Unfortunately, the result of the seventeen indictments brought against him has not yet been discovered in the records. Robert Morrison's record was also bad.[4]

The cases of forgery and perjury listed by the commissioners do not begin to exhaust the cases of reprehensible character. The record of John Francis Perrey is, for example, almost clear of the graver charges; yet among his claims to family rights which the commissioners reported merely as "unsupported" were five in which it appeared that the original claimant never married; another in which he left the Illinois country at a date which barred the claim. In each case Perrey was the first assignee. Of such cases there are scores in the reports. Again, there are dozens of cases of double entry of the same claim by the same claimant—for example John Edgar secured two patents from St. Clair for the same piece of land, made alterations in one in his own hand, then filed both with the board.[5] It is difficult to reconcile these cases with good faith.

[1] Either he or Wm. Kelly or both: *Amer. State Papers: Pub. Lands,* 2: 136.

[2] *Ibid.,* 2: 152 (cl. 23). See also 129 (cl. 38, 10), 142 (cl. 6), 153 (cl. 311), 155 (cl. 12, 14), 156 (cl. 1018).

[3] Characterizations "as forger and perjurer" on *ibid.,* pp. 128, 129, 136.

[4] On the Reynolds' indictments see *post,* clxxix, n. 1. As to Morrison, *Amer. State Papers: Pub. Lands,* 2: 130 (cl. 2492), 132 (cl. 2410, 2411—judge's name forged). Richard Lord used unwisely, like Edgar, paper of an unbuilt mill (129, cl. 1362). William Kelly had unsigned depositions taken before a notary of upper Louisiana (136), and presented depositions purporting to be given before Jean Bte. Barbau when the latter was not a magistrate (130, cl. 887).

[5] *Amer. State Papers: Pub. Lands,* 2: 206. Twenty-one double entries by Edgar were noted. For Perrey, 230-235.

The relations of the county grandees with each other are curious. Edgar, Reynolds, Kelly, and Robert Morrison forged the names of judges. Reynolds claimed, resorting to forgery in doing so, against John Rice Jones and against John Edgar.[1] Pierre Menard addressed to the second board, in 1812, a remarkable protest that throws light on these cases:

"The subscriber having . . . understood . . . that, where it should appear that any fraud had been practised by the confirmees or patentees. . . . upon proof being adduced to the Board, they would . . . decide thereon according to justice and equity of title; or . . . would leave the parties to determine the legality of their titles in a court of law:

"Therefore the subscriber respectfully states, that having . . . presented several counter claims to fraudulent conveyances and confirmations obtained by surprise of the Governors; and in some cases produced, and in others offered proof of fraud and surprise, on the part of the confirmees or their agents, in obtaining confirmations of such claims; he therefore is driven to the necessity of protesting, and doth hereby most solemnly protest, against all confirmations . . . which may be made to John Edgar, or any other person or persons claiming, by fraudulent and pretence titles [5 certain family rights and 3 improvement rights enumerated; or to Nicholas Jarrot etc., 3 certain improvement rights; or to William Morrison etc., 2 certain family rights] . . .

"However limited the equitable and judicial powers of your Board may be . . . your protestant only means to lay the groundwork of an appeal to a higher tribunal; and he doth hereby aver, that he is in possession of the legal titles to the above-mentioned tracts of land, and therefore protests against any patent or confirmation being made either to the said John Edgar, Nicholas Jarrot, or William Morrison, or any other person or persons, except to your protestant, or those whom he represents, or his or their assignee . . ."

This was a protest after action taken.[2] It was made by a man whose record was clear, and who was honored later by the

---

[1] *Ibid.*, 149 (cl. 20, 22); 151 (cl. 24, 61).
[2] *Ibid.*, 238-239. The second board affirmed 5 of Edgar's claims, 2 of Jarrot's, 2 of Morrison's. There were 5,200 acres involved.

state. During the Indiana Territory period, however,—the later records have not been examined—no suits were brought by Menard to contest title.

In but one of these thirteen important cases does Menard appear in the commissioners' reports as an adverse claimant. With titles confused and fraud unrestrained such conflicting claims were numerous. In one case William Morrison, John Rice Jones, John Grosvenor, Nicholas Jarrot, and John Edgar all claimed the same land. Claims by two or three grandees were common. Imperfectly as these facts are revealed by the lists of the commissioners—who did not deal at all with the rights of adverse claimants inter sese—it nevertheless incidentally appears that Edgar disputed at least 21,356 acres with fellow claimants included in the table above printed.[1]

A charge was made against Henry Vander Burgh by the Vincennes commissioners which the full panoply of legal documents cannot make more than comic. The charge was that he, a federal judge of otherwise good although not unchallenged record, risked his name in order surreptitiously to obtain for his mother-in-law an extra allowance of 136 acres of land (which the judge's wife must have shared with seven other children!) by juggling with the improvement right and nickname of her grandfather on the maternal side, who died thirty years before the judge became acquainted with the family, and whose name the judge swore he had not known until the charge was made against him. Although the latter's inconsistent defences were no credit to his astuteness, and the balance of factual evidence was against him, it is impossible to believe him guilty.[2]

The case is worth citing only because it is the single one in the whole record that suggests a possibility of personal or political maneuvering. At least with regard to the Kaskaskia district it can be said with confidence that there is no trace, in the reports of the

---

[1] Of these 7,869 were disputed with William Morrison. Excluding disputes with Edgar, Morrison's conflicts with others in the table amounted to 5,144 acres, Jarrot's to 4,400. Menard tried to hold 3,822 acres against Edgar, 3,804 against William Morrison, 1,200 against Jarrot, and disputed 1,500 with others (including the data revealed by his protest).

[2] *Amer. State Papers: Pub. Lands*, 1: 301-303, 575-581; 7: 716 (cf. 97) for final outcome.

commissioners, of political or personal influence or prejudice. For reasons easily to be surmised Governor Reynolds sought to give a contrary idea. It is indeed doubtless true as he says, that as years passed and investigations proceeded, without any reports by the board, "this delay excited the people and a very bitter and rancorous feeling was engendered between the commissioners and many of the inhabitants." He is also, doubtless, correct in stating that these feelings were embittered by the political activity of Michael Jones,[1] which was certainly most unfortunate, quite irreconcilable with his earlier hope of leaving the Illinois country, "by way of exception, in a state of quietude";[2] and indeed—in view of the conditions of the time—reprehensible. The land question necessarily became involved in "politics" when the commissioners uncovered the frauds of the leading members of the Edgar-Morrison faction. And the members of that faction—presumably in a desperate effort to drive Michael Jones from office—aggravated the situation by attempting to make him responsible for the murder of Rice Jones following the embittered election of 1808.

[1] *Pioneer History*, 351-352.
[2] *Amer. State Papers: Pub. Lands*, 1: 590. The hope was expressed in 1807, by which time it was quite clear that in Missouri and Michigan content would not follow the work of the commissioners. Frederick Bates wrote in 1807 of conditions in Missouri: "The public sentiment has acquired an astonishing degree of ferocity, and God knows where it will end.—One of the Land Commissioners was reminded a few days ago, that the board had very extensive powers . . . and that they must gratify the expectations of the People or expect to feel their resentments. The Commissioner who was Judge Lucas, replied: 'I shall do my duty; and my Fate, should I die at my Post will be preferable to that of my murderer, who must suffer on a Gibbet'"—Marshall, *Life and Papers of Frederick Bates*, 1: 136-137. The thousands of findings of the Missouri board are summarily stated, without reasons (*ante*, lxxxvi, n. 1). On fraud and speculation see Marshall, *op. cit.*, 1: 29, 221, 282; 2: 10. According to Scharf, *History of Saint Louis*, 1: 323, the board of 1808-1812 confirmed 1,342 claims; apparently out of a total of about 3,000, Marshall, *op. cit.*, 2: 70 n. Under later acts of Congress covering other claims Bates confirmed 1,746 claims out of 2,555—Scharf, *op. cit.*, 325. On Michigan see Judge Woodward's several letters, *Mich. Pioneer and Hist. Colls.* 12: 507; *Amer. State Papers: Pub. Lands*, 1: 248, 283; *ibid.*, *Misc.*, 1: 461. As he says in one of these, "in a country nearly a century and a half old, and nearly a quarter of a century the property of the United States," there existed "only *eight legal titles to land.*" *Ibid.*, *Pub. Lands*, 1: 283. In fact the board approved *only 6*, totaling 600 acres, out of more than 700 claims—*ibid.*, *Pub. Lands*, 1: 305-557. Naturally "the anxiety, confusion, and distress of the country is . . . impossible to describe or to conceive" (April, 1806). *Ibid.*, *Misc.*, 1: 461.

It may also safely be said that if the land question was not originally involved in politics the Edgar-Morrison faction party did their best to involve it.   In a letter written by John Rice Jones, before the murder of his son, to Judge Backus, he charged the latter with reported threats against his son's life if he should remain in the country; and Edgar and the Morrisons, after the murder, not only sent these reports to Washington[1] but caused the indictment, for instigating the crime, of Michael Jones—who was acquitted and sued his accusers successfully for libel.[2]   It is important to re-

[1] McDonough, *Hist. of Randolph, Monroe and Perry Counties*, 105. In the Miscellanies Box, Chester, there is a deposition given on August 3, 1811 in Kentucky by Matthew Lyon, part of the evidence used in the suit of Michael Jones against Robert Morrison, from which it appears that he received a letter in Washington from William Morrison, Robert Morrison, and John Edgar, in May or June, 1809, which he showed "to Squire Backus to read—in order to know how he could defend himself against the charges." Lyon says the original was lost, and he set out its substance in a separate paper which is also lacking. Alvord, *Illinois Country*, 426, says that letters were published by John Edgar to Gallatin and by William Morrison to Matthew Lyon, attributing the murder to the machinations of the two commissioners.

[2] A certified copy of the indictment against Dunlap is also in the Miscellanies Box at Chester. The murder was on December 7, 1808, by pistol. Contrary to published reports, it is not charged that Jones was shot in the back, but in the right breast. And it charged that Michael Jones on December 6, "did excite move abet council command and procure" Dunlap to commit the murder. In an account (apparently contemporary) of the details of the murder written by someone of the Edgar-Morrison party Judge Backus, Robert Robinson, James Gilbreath, James Finney, Michael Jones and —— Langlois were named as coconspirators of Dunlap—*Chic. Hist. Colls.*, 4: 278-279. The charge is of no importance; the party grouping is more important. On the case of U. S. *v.* Michael Jones see Alvord, *Illinois Country*, 426-427 and W. A. Burt Jones, *Chic. Hist. Colls.*, 4: 280-281. He was indicted on July 20, 1809, and acquitted April 10, 1810. The writer has not yet examined the judicial records of the Illinois Territory. Jones emphasizes the fact (McDonough, *Hist. of Randolph, Monroe, and Perry Counties*, 105) that two of the defendant's bondsmen (one of the *other* bondsmen was Shadrach Bond Jr.) were on the trial jury. Such irregularities were not uncommon (*post*, clxxx), but most regrettable in a case of importance. The relief of the prosecutor from costs, allowed under statute when the court found there were "probable grounds" for indicting, proves little; it was very freely allowed. The plea of William Morrison in the libel suit brought against him by Michael Jones is in the Miscellanies Box at Chester—the words complained of were spoken the day of the murder; and in Canvas Envelope II is a bill of costs for continuance at the September term, 1811, in the case of Michael Jones against John Edgar. The plaintiff sued Wm. Morrison for $15,000, and recovered $200 and costs; Robert Morrison for $9,000, but had the case dismissed; John Edgar for $11,000. In 1813 Edgar compromised by paying costs and $300, and making a public declaration "that Michael Jones was entirely innocent of any part in the murder of Rice Jones" (Alvord, *loc. cit.*).

member, in this connection, that Judge Backus was not an opponent, but a supporter, of the Edgar group, politically.[1] It is not surprising that Governor Reynolds, in view of his father's fate, presents Michael Jones as moved by "excited feelings against his political enemies" in branding as forgers, defrauders, and perjurers "many of the best citizens in the country," who—according to him—"had no means or manner of defending themselves." No one but those ignorant of the commissioners' reports can be so naïve as to give weight to such charges. The courts were open to try their titles and their character. No recourse was ever had to them; but, as will be seen, success was achieved, by political means, in nullifying a few of the commissioners' decisions.

The work of both of the land boards was mainly due to the infinite pertinacity and capacity for detail of Michael Jones. The object of Congress was to determine what was public land.[2] The land office at Kaskaskia was opened in 1804 by the act which created the first board, but the first sales were made in 1814. The uncertainty of titles meanwhile seriously hampered taxation, and also undoubtedly retarded the settlement of the country. Preemption rights were accorded in 1813 to settlers on government land up to that time.[3] This, and the opening of government sales, marked the end, substantially, of difficulties. Michael Jones remained register at Kaskaskia until his death in 1822.[4]

[1] See *post*, app. n. 14.

[2] *Amer. State Papers: Pub. Lands*, 1: 285; 2: 182, 254. It was for this reason that claims in the common were simply confirmed en masse "to the legal representatives of the original concedees": the United States could have no interest to protect, since it was certain that the French crown had divested itself of all claims, and therefore the claimants could settle in the courts their disputes inter sese.

[3] *U. S. Stat. at Large*, 2: 797; Buck, *Illinois in 1818*, 47-49. As to uncertainty of titles, see *My Own Times*, 156; convincing data in Buck, map at 52-53. The reason appears, partly, in § 5 of the law of March 3, 1805— *Annals*, 8 Congress, 2 session, 1701— which prohibited further alienations, even of lands the claims to which were confirmed by the commissioners, until final action by Congress.

[4] On Michael Jones see *post*, app. n. 13. Peoria was not originally within the district of the Kaskaskia commissioners (*Amer. State Papers: Pub. Lands*, 1: 285) but was included upon petition of its inhabitants (photostatic copy in Ill. Hist. Survey; proceedings in the *Annals*, 9 Congress, 2 session, 624; 10 Congress, 1 session, 1600-1601, 1846. A report by Edward Coles, register at Edwardsville, in 1820 leaves one wondering how effective were the labors of the commissioners, for he states that possession was the only title to the lands in that community. *Amer. State Papers: Pub. Lands*, 3: 477.

One important question remained open. It has been noted that all the reported decisions of the commissioners in favor of claimants were confirmed except those of the second board revising confirmations by the governors. It was understood by both Gallatin and Harrison in 1804 that confirmations would not stand if proved to have been "surreptitiously and fraudulently obtained," and Harrison published notice to that effect at Vincennes.[1] The Vincennes board, accordingly, from the beginning dealt with the claims of confirmees; although evidently with little scrutiny, confirming all with but a single exception.[2] Although no orders seem to have been given to the Kaskaskia board to do so, it is clear that Gallatin assumed they were likewise dealing with such claims.[3] The magnitude of the task, and its political dangers, undoubtedly caused the first board to abstain from making final findings; but the bases for such were abundantly revealed in its evidence. The claims summarized in the first of the tables printed above included some, confirmed by the governors, which the commissioners condemned for fraud; but most of the confirmed claims which were rejected by the board were rejected for lack of proofs sustaining them.[4]

[1] Correspondence of July 10, 1804—*Messages,* 1: 101-102. But see St. Clair's view, *ante,* lxxvii, n. 3.

[2] *Amer. State Papers: Pub. Lands,* 1: 289. In the case of the Vincennes confirmation cases § 2 of the act of March 3, 1807 (*U. S. Stat. at Large,* 2: 447; *Annals,* 9 Congress, 2 session, 1291), which confirmed all such "unless when actually rejected by the said commissioners," might seem upon casual reading impliedly to confirm such rejections. Anyway, there was only one rejection—*ante,* xcii, n. 2. In Kaskaskia there were many such condemned (although—for supposed lack of power—no final rejections). See *ante,* lxxxii, n. 1.

[3] From his reference in *Amer. State Papers: Pub. Lands,* 2: 123, to his letter to them of May 23, 1810. Their reports however had made the contrary clear, *ibid.,* 1: 285 (1806).

[4] The acreage of confirmed claims rejected by the commissioners for forgery was 2,030 in the case of John Rice Jones; 800 in the case of John Reynolds. There were no perjury cases. Such claims rejected for lack of supporting evidence amounted to: 400 acres in the case of William Biggs; 186, John Dumoulin; 31,225, John Edgar; 1,000, Nicholas Jarrot; 1,967, John Rice Jones; 900, William McIntosh; 2,711, Pierre Menard; 400, Robert Morrison; 900, William Morrison; 4,550, J. F. Perrey; 1,850, Robert Reynolds. The confirmed claims approved by the commissioners, for these same men, were: Biggs, 1,600; Dumoulin, 800; Edgar, 57,882; Jarrot, 2,000; Jones, 5,295; McIntosh, 10,267; Menard, 1,300; William Morrison, 2,500; Perrey, 951.

Politics alone could explain the failure of Congress to approve the findings of the second board.[1] The natural inference from such inaction would be that the speculators kept the fruits of their perjuries and forgeries, and likewise the vast illegal British grants which St. Clair confirmed to Edgar after the latter shared them with the Governor's sons. As regards the worse of these two cases which were on their face totally illegal, nothing was ever done affirmatively by Congress to recognize its validity, but the other was confirmed.[2] As regards the other confirmations, its mere inaction prolonged uncertainties.

In 1818 (and again in the same terms in 1820) a Congressional committee, upon petition by sundry inhabitants of the Illinois

[1] In a letter in which he recommended for approval various claims submitted too late for action by the second board, Michael Jones wrote to Gallatin (January 18, 1813—*Amer. State Papers: Pub. Lands,* 2: 741-742):

If confirmed "there will be an end to this perplexing business; unless, indeed, the Government should indulge the speculators with the privilege of a re-investigation of claims rejected by the former [second] Board. On this subject I can only observe, that I am wearied with these painful duties, which, for eight years past, it has fallen to my lot to discharge. Nor do I believe that the Government would be doing justice to itself, or its officers, by extending this indulgence. When witnesses have been suborned, when the ancient records have been recently interpolated, and when the officers who dared to discharge their solemn duty have been attempted to be made the victims of this corruption, it is time to close the doors against the admission of new frauds.

"My objection to the re-organization of a Board of Commissioners for the purpose of reviewing claims rejected by the former Board, does not arise from any apprehension that the former commissioners could be in the least degree implicated; on the contrary, could I reconcile it to my feelings to stoop to the drugery of wading again through this sea of corruption, I would anxiously solicit it, fully persuaded that such an investigation would forever silence our declaimers, and raise us in the estimation of our Government. But the task is too laborious and painful; besides, I am convinced that none but speculators desire it, and that they can have no claim on the Government for this indulgence. So far from this, it is my impression that they have had too much justice done them; and I am inclined to think that if a review of decisions made by the former Boards could now take place they would be still further curtailed. However, I am perfectly reconciled to any course my Government may think proper to adopt, provided it does not deprive me of the means of justifying my official conduct."

[2] On the worse claim (2208) see *ante,* lxxix, n. 1; lxxxix, n. 1; also *Amer. State Papers: Pub. Lands,* 2: 254-255, 257-258. The claim (No. 2209) made jointly with Arthur St. Clair Jr.—see *ante,* lxxix, n. 2— was reported specially by the second board—*Amer. State Papers: Pub. Lands,* 2: 214), and therefore confirmed by the act of April 16, 1814—see *ante,* lxxx, n. 1.

Territory whose names are unfortunately not given, reported in favor of confirming all governors' confirmations of grants dependent on family, improvement, and militia rights; on the truly phenomenal ground that these rights created by Congress in 1788 and 1791 had "accrued" respectively twenty-nine or twenty-two years before the act of 1812 that provided for their revision! The committee thus intimated, without explicitly asserting, that the statute of limitations could run against the government, and even in favor of fraud and corruption; and they urged the injustice of requiring claimants "at so distant a period, after the death or removal of their witnesses, to prove again their claims"![1] It is evident that under this extraordinary doctrine any claimant, with or without a governor's confirmation, might have been held safe in 1810 or 1805. Congress did not stultify itself by acting as recommended.

A Congressional committee acted on a petition of James Hughes who claimed as assignee of John Reynolds, who had purchased the improvement right of an alleged John Fowler. The first board had rejected the claim and the second had listed it unsupported. Deponents before the second board had testified that "they know no such man" as John Fowler.[2] The Congressional committee reported that it could "not conceive how it would be possible to support a claim with much stronger evidence" than attended this, supported as it was by "upwards of twenty years actual possession, and a patent issued by competent authority . . . It does not appear to the committee that there is any foundation for a belief that the patent was obtained by fraud or collusion, *or that it has ever been supposed or alleged to have been so obtained* (italics added)"![3] Now it may be said of this that inasmuch as the commissioners lived for seven years in a community of but a few thousand souls, all the time studying names and relation-

[1] Of course they also utterly misstated the procedure of the board. They say no presumption of the validity of a confirmed claim was indulged, "but, where the witnesses called by that Board had no knowledge of the claim, it was condemned"—*Amer. State Papers: Pub. Lands*, 3: 384 (February 24, 1818) and 421 (January 27, 1820). On the contrary, notice was then served upon the claimant to come forward with evidence. Claims vouched by the "respectable inhabitants" first consulted were accepted as good, others were regarded merely as impeached—*ibid.*, 2: 210.

[2] *Ibid.*, 2: 223 (cl. 314), 232 (cl. 913).

[3] *Ibid.*, 3: 412-413 (February 3, 1819).

ships, and quite evidently uncovered the truth (of the nonexistence, married or single state, time of arrival in or departure from the territory, present whereabouts in any of the United States if still living though alleged dead, and so on) with regard to scores of individuals, there is not the least reason to doubt their conclusion that "John Fowler" was a man of ideal existence created merely for the purpose of the title. And this committee did not suggest that a defrauder was included within the bounty of Congress, or safe against attack in twenty years.[1] Upon this report, also, no action was taken.

One more illustration of the attempts of the governors' confirmees to secure political favor beyond the generous action of the second board, appears in a petition of 1818 (when he was holding high office in Missouri) by John Rice Jones. The commissioners had rejected for forgery two of his claims confirmed by Harrison, one of them for making interpolations in the records of ancient grants.[2] In his petition to Congress in 1818 he stated that part of the land had recently been sold by the United States, and that the rest was up for sale. On the basis of evidence in his favor given, after inspection of the ancient records, by Ninian Edwards (then United States Senator, who had for years been a political enemy of Michael Jones), the committee reported that "every position taken by the commissioners in support of their opinion is indefensible," that every charge was "explained satisfactorily by the . . . petition, which is abundantly confirmed by Mr. Edwards."[3] Congress did not at that time give the relief recom-

---

[1] In the absence of fraud, of course the position would be maintainable. It is pointed out *ante*, xciii, n. 2 that in Michigan only a half-dozen titles were pronounced valid. Yet, as Judge Woodward wrote to Jefferson (October 10, 1805, *ibid.*, 1: 248), "However defective . . . the class of original proprietors may be with respect to the *evidence* of title according to the American forms, it is conceived their *rights* are extremely strong." The argument is inapplicable to intruders on the public lands, and to persons seeking by fraud to bring themselves within the bounty of the government.

[2] *Ibid.*, 2: 215-216 (cl. 1285, 1286).

[3] *Ibid.*, 3: 394 (December 14, 1818). When Edwards became governor the Edgar group presented him with an address, in which they asked him to make appointments exclusively from their party; and also—having been informed (or for effect saying so) that Edwards was authorized to inquire into the conduct of the Kaskaskia land office—they besought him,

mended, but in 1854 the two claims rejected by the commissioners were satisfied.[1]

The government land office (Michael Jones was the register) was apparently slow in selling lands of governors' confirmees the claims to which fell outside the confirmations made by Congress in 1810-1814. Doubtless all were ultimately sold, and it does not appear that any claimant dared to go into court in defence of his alleged rights.

The law of Indiana Territory was constituted of the English law, adopted by statute of 1795 as of 4 James the First,[2] of all the enactments of the Northwest Territory, and of the additional legislation of the Indiana Territory under both the first and second grade of government.

The statute of 1795 originated in Virginia's statutes of adoption and in turn is the origin of the present Illinois statute. The common law had been earlier extended over the Northwest, of course without restriction, by British proclamation; but this was purely theoretical. St. Clair's favorite topic was the perfection of the common law. He favored, very sensibly, adoption as of the beginning of the Revolution; and to the first Assembly of the Northwest Territory he pointed out that adoption as of the earlier date deprived the people of many improvements,[3] such as the writ of habeas corpus and the statute of frauds. In this he showed his habitual intelligence, and superiority to his fellow judges; in

[1] By act of August 4, 1854, *U. S. Stat. at Large*, 10: 96. At that time his son, George Wallace Jones, was U. S. Senator from Iowa—*Chic. Hist. Colls.*, 4: 264. Nicholas Jarrot also received a favor in 1821—*U. S. Stat. at Large*, 6: 258.

[2] Pease, *Laws* (*I. H. C.*, 17), 253; *post*, 323.

[3] Cp. *post*, clxxii, n. 1. *St. Clair Papers*, 1: 210; 2: 456.

"as a precautionary measure for the security of our titles," to seal meanwhile all the books and papers of the office. Edwards, *History of Illinois*, 28-29. Edwards soon aligned himself against Jones; why is not clear. See Washburne, *Edwards Papers*, 39-40, and *post*, app. n. 70. "There was bitter feeling between him [Michael Jones] and the governor over the settlement of land claims." The two were rival candidates for the U. S. Senate (but see *post*, app. n. 13) in October 1818 and again in February 1819, Edwards being victor both times. For a dozen years they had been members of opposing political groups—Buck, *Illinois in 1818*, 201, 303. Mrs. Goebel states that charges against Jones and Backus "were made by Governor Edwards soon after his arrival in the newly created Illinois Territory"—*Harrison*, 67, citing MS records.

this case Parsons and Varnum, who shared the aversion, common enough at that time, to an institution deemed to have "entered essentially into the principles of monarchical government."[1]

Virginia had first given legislative recognition to the common law in 1662. The act of 1795 adopted literally the Virginia act of 1776; but so far as this gave force to English statutes it was repealed by an act of December 27, 1792. It was therefore the opinion of Salmon P. Chase that the act of 1776, being "so far as the English statutes were concerned" not a law of Virginia but only a dead form, it could not, as to them, be adopted.[2] The point is of little moment, for there were various other state statutes adoptive of the English law that could have been chosen had this objection been foreseen.

How far the adoptive act of 1795, in view of the admitted vitality of the Virginia act with respect to the unenacted English law, enlarged the field theretofore accorded to the common law, in the territory is a question of greater importance. It would seem, considerably; for the Ordinance of 1787 guaranteed to the inhabitants merely "the benefit . . . of judicial proceedings according to the course of the common law." Chase ignored this point. He disposed of the whole matter by arguing that the legislative power conferred by the Ordinance was intended to extend merely "to the selection of single acts . . . with reference to the adaptation of each act, to the circumstances of a new country. It was plainly the intention of congress, also, that each law adopted should be published, that every citizen might know the extent and nature of his social obligations. Neither of these purposes could be answered by the adoption of the English law, written and unwritten, in the mass . . . It appears, therefore, that the adoption of this law, if in conformity with the terms, was in violation of the spirit of the ordinance." This argument, albeit of a future chief justice of the nation, is not convincing. It was a single act, believed to be proper for the territory, that was adopted and was published. It is pure assumption that Congress expected the laws

[1] See their discussions in *ibid.*, 2: 71, 76; and cp. Charles Warren, *A History of the American Bar*, 224-239.
[2] Warren, *op. cit.*, 39; Chase, *The Statutes of Ohio and of the Northwestern Territory from 1788 to 1833*, 1: 190 n.

of the territory to be more accessible than those of the original
states; and, as to those, it is admitted that in the original states
very few lawyers had complete sets of the local statutes, much less
of English statutes.

But for Chase's opinion it would hardly be worth while to
discuss the question whether the common law was, legally and au-
thoritatively adopted.[1] It is evident that even if "judicial proceedings according to the course of the common law" be construed
to cover procedure only, that would certainly include common law
pleading, which necessarily involved adoption of great masses of
substantive law. And the statute-book of 1795, which Chase
lauded, would have been in truth miserably deficient without a
common law background; as Judge Burnet and others undoubtedly
realized at the time. In the Indiana and Illinois territories such
questions regarding the adoption of the common law were never
seriously mooted.[2]

One misapprehension has also existed with reference to the
statutes of the Northwest Territory. It has been stated that "the
laws passed by the first session of the General Assembly [of the
Northwest Territory, September 23 to December 19, 1799] did
not generally go into force in Indiana Territory on account of the
separation occurring so soon afterward (May 7, 1800)." Doubtless these statutes did not go into practical effect. It is true that
the General Assembly did reënact a few of the Northwestern
laws; and all of these were laws of 1799; and it gave, in one case as
the reason for doing so the opinion that without revival the law
was "of very doubtful authority and of uncertain obligation." The
treatment of the elaborate taxation laws of 1799 (not reënacted,

[1] The Ohio Court, in 1806 (Thompson's Lessee *v.* Gibson, 2 Oh. R.
339), divided equally on the question whether the statute of uses was law
of the state. In 1819 there was published at Steubenville, Ohio, a volume
by Milton Goodnow which is described (in Warren, *Hist. of the Amer.
Bar,* 235-236) as "a learned and elaborate work . . . in which it was
endeavored to prove . . . that the Common Law . . . had no
authority in any of the States that had been formed out of the old Northwestern Territory." Chase must have known this book. In 1833 he regarded the question as "still unsettled."

[2] See Burnet's remarks in his *Notes,* 303-304. The Revision Act of
September 17, 1807 (*post,* 323), reënacting the law of 1795, excepted the
usury statutes of 13th Eliz. c. 8 and 37th Hen. 8: c. 9.

but immediately supplanted by others of Indiana Territory), suggests the existence of the same doubt. On the other hand all the statutes were necessarily, on principle, part of the law of the new territory. Moreover some statutes of 1799 were specifically repealed; others were not reënacted, yet were clearly treated as the operative law. And others were neither reënacted nor regarded as operative.[1] Dunn's statement that the Northwestern laws were "always treated as in force" in Indiana Territory[2] is substantially accurate.

The terms of the legislatures were as follows:[3]

Gov'r and judges:
1st session, January 12—January 26, 1801.
2nd session, January 30—February 3, 1802.
3rd session, February 16—March 24, 1803.
4th session, September 20, 1803—September 22, 1804.

First General Assembly:
1st session, July 29, 1805—August 26, 1805.[4]
2nd session, November 3, 1806—December 6, 1806.

Second General Assembly:
1st session, August 16, 1807—September 19, 1807.[5]
2nd session, September 26, 1808—October 26, 1808.

[1] Monks, *Courts*, 1: 5; *post*, cxiv, cxxiii, notes 1, 2, 4 and 5; cxxiv, n. 2; cxxvii, n. 1; cxxviii, n. 3; cxxxi, n. 1; cxxxiv, n. 1; cxlix, n. 5.
[2] *Indiana*, 294. See also the introduction to Gibson, *Exec. Journal*, 68-69.
[3] For the adjournment dates under government of the first grade (not necessarily identical with the dates of the latest statutes) I rely upon Howe, Ind. Hist. Soc. *Pub.*, 2: 17, 144; of the fourth he says, "doubtless with several intermediate adjournments." The dates on which the sessions of the Assembly began are likewise taken from Howe—*loc. cit.*, 144. The adjournment dates are unfortunately nowhere stated by Dunn, Mr. Esarey, and Mr. Webster; though all were familiar with the journals of both houses of the General Assembly, printed in the *Western Sun* of Vincennes, which I have not seen. I therefore give the dates of the last legislative acts.
[4] On August 26, 1805 Governor Harrison prorogued the Assembly, "to meet again on the last Monday in Oct. 1806"—*Messages*, 1: 164. That would be October 27.
[5] Judge Gross indicated later sessions, but this seems doubtful.

It is difficult to compare quantitatively—though it has several times been attempted—the legislative activity of the governor and judges with that of the Assembly of either territory; or of one territory, under either grade of government, with the other territory. Much legislation was wholly or substantial reënactment; and some laws were more fundamental or more original or more complicated than others. One thing is certain, however: that the task of St. Clair and the judges of the old territory under the first grade was heaviest.[1] For the Northwest Territory a statute-book had to be created de novo; the work of the legislators of the younger territory was supplementary only. Division caused no break in the administration of justice or other machinery of government—as was true likewise when Indiana Territory was later divided, and true of the other territories for which the Ordinance was the basic law. The code of the older territory persisted as the law of the newer. Thus the latter started with a statute-book relatively complete, and supposedly adjusted by careful selection of laws from the original states to the needs of frontier conditions. When the Assembly appointed revisers to "reduce into one code the laws in force in this territory" it was understood that this included the legislation of the Northwest Territory; and the revision reported, described as "comprising those Acts formerly in force," as revised and again enacted, in fact included almost the total of the earlier code. Never, until the revised code was enacted and all earlier laws repealed in 1807, had there ever been—save of statutes of 1799, as above indicated—reënactment of statutes of the Northwest Territory.

It was not in the least by mere choice, however, that these were adopted.[2] True, no act of Congress, and no general statute

---

[1] See for statute lists, Smith, *St. Clair Papers,* 1: 147, 188-189, 211; 2: 80 n., 167 n., 275 n., 311-312 n., 355-356 n., 438 n., 452-453 n., 523-524 n., 543-544 n.

[2] Judge Banta says (*Ind. Mag. of Hist.,* 9: 240) that "it would seem as if" the old laws continued to be enforced. And apparently he regarded this as without legal justification. "The judges who had passed the laws stood ready to enforce them and from their decision there was no appeal, and Congress could only disapprove, not repeal." This would be less inaccurate if confined to laws independently enacted by governor and judges, excluding those properly "adopted" from laws of the original thirteen states; for to these, at least, the references to government under the Ordi-

of Indiana Territory (such as that by which the statutes of the latter were later adopted for Illinois Territory) explicitly so provided. But the act which divided the Northwest Territory declared that a portion thereof should, "for the purposes of temporary government" constitute Indiana Territory; and its effect was limited to the establishment in the portions thus separated of "two distinct and separate governments." So also when Indiana Territory was later divided it was by an act captioned "for dividing the Indiana Territory into two separate Governments," and it was provided therein that that part of Indiana Territory west of the Wabash should constitute a separate territory, "for the purpose of temporary government." These words were interpreted by everybody in their natural sense: "the theory adopted was that the division . . . was merely for administrative purposes; that the laws were as much in force in one division as in the other"[1]—that is, so far

[1] Dunn, *Indiana*, 294; D. W. Howe, in Ind. Hist. Soc. *Pub.*, 2: 14; the creative acts, *Annals*, 6 Congress, 1 session, 1498 (May 7, 1800), and 10 Congress, 2 session, 1808 (February 3, 1809). Dunn is in error in referring to this as a unique example. It was in harmony with general principles of international law. The District of Louisiana was treated in the same way by explicit provision of Congress. When Harrison planned (under the duty laid upon him and the judges of Indiana Territory by the act of March 26, 1804) to enact a complete code of laws for the District, Madison reminded him of the statutory provision (§ 13) which continued in force the former French and Spanish laws "until altered, modified, or repealed by the Governor and judges of the Indiana Territory." Madison to Harrison, June 14, 1804, Harrison, *Messages*, 1: 96; *Annals*, 8 Congress, 1 session, 1298. Similar examples, without express statutory provision, are to be found in the history of states included in the later Mexican cession. In certain "deliberations" of freeholders of the Northeast Coast of Detroit, December 8, 1806 (*Mich. Pioneer and Hist. Colls.*, 8: 582), they say that "agreeable to the sentence rendered in the Supreme Court in September last, it has been decided that the Indiana laws were in force in this Territory." The dissenting views of Judge Bates, embodied in a memorandum addressed to his colleagues, are in Marshall, *Life and Papers of Frederick Bates*, 1: 84-86. Mr. Webster (in Ind. Hist. Soc. *Pub.*, 4: 188 n., citing Thornton, *Bench and Bar*—which I have not seen) states that in 1803 the Territorial court decided that a law of the Northwest Territory, passed after 1800, was in force in Wayne County after its annexation to Indiana Territory, although a different law prevailed in the rest of that territory. Neither of these decisions was noted by me in a somewhat hurried examina-

nance, quoted *post*, cix and n. 1, would clearly apply. But the view is unacceptable with reference even to laws improperly enacted; they were part of the government de facto. Monks, *Courts*, 1: 22—referring to the courts of Indiana Territory as "accepting" the laws of the mother territory, and characterizing this action as an "assumption"—reflects the view of Judge Banta.

as those of the old territory, already advanced to second grade, were applicable to those of the new while still in the first grade.

The statutes in this volume abound with examples, aside from that of the Revision of 1807, in which acts of the old territory were repealed or amended by legislation of the new territory.[1]   In fact large portions of the latter's administrative system operated for years solely upon the authority of laws of the Northwest Territory.   The governor and judges of Indiana Territory did not even amend the statutes of 1799 and earlier years relative to justices of the peace; they passed no laws establishing or regulating orphans' courts or probate courts.   But justices of the peace and judges of probate (until abolished in 1805) were continually appointed.   The same is true of coroners until the Revision of 1807. As for the regular county courts, it is true that their organization was repeatedly overhauled by legislation during both the first and second grade of government, but this legislation was purely emendatory.   Although acting Governor Gibson's first official act was to make appointments to all the local courts and other county offices, this amounted merely to a renewal of personel: the continued operation of the administrative system was nowise dependent on such action.

Mr. Pease has referred, in his introduction to the preceding volume of this series,[2] to the serious problem that arose from the clause of the Ordinance of 1787 which required the governor and judges to "adopt" laws from the original thirteen states.   St. Clair and his fellows acted from necessity.[3]   The disapproval of Con-

---

[1] E. g. the very first law is entitled, "A Law supplemental to a law [of the Northwest Territory] to regulate county levies" (*post*, 1) ; the sixth law passed is entitled, "An Act repealing certain laws and acts and parts of certain laws and acts" of the Northwest Territory; and so on.

[2] Pease, *Laws* (*I. H. C.*, 17), xx-xxii, xxiii-xxx, giving remarkable examples of "adoption."

[3] See for their views *St. Clair Papers*, 2: 67-68, 69, 71, 356 *et seq.*, 363 *et seq.*, 439-440, 446 *et seq.*, 453.

---

tion of the Order Book of the General Court.   If the cause of action, in the second case, arose after annexation to Indiana Territory the decision would be wrong.   The effect of the act of March 2, 1801, which provided that suits initiated in Indiana, and of which the territorial court had taken jurisdiction *before* division, should proceed therein to final judgment as if no division had occurred, is somewhat misstated in Monks, *Courts*, 1: 22.

gress[1] did not end what was unavoidable. The officials of the
Indiana Territory, Mississippi Territory, and the Territory of
Michigan all followed the same latitudinarian practice. A state-
ment of the difficulty by Governor Hull and Presiding Judge A. B.
Woodward of the last named territory is worth quoting.

"On all the subjects requiring legislation, the present Government act with difficulty, and, on many, cannot act at all. All laws
will be found to operate on particular *places, times,* and *persons;*
and in no State . . . will an abstract code of principles be
discovered free from a connexion, and that a very close one, with
the *places, times,* and *persons* affected by them. Hence the strict
adoption of any code, or even of any one law, becomes impossible.
To make it applicable, it must be adapted to the geography of the
country, to its temporary circumstances and exigencies, and to the
particular character of the persons over whom it is to operate.
Hitherto it has been religiously the object to follow what has been
deemed the substance of the law, whatever modifications the form
of it was obliged to undergo. But different minds will not always
correspond in sentiment on what is *substance,* and what is *form;*
and in all the litigations which arise under laws, those affecting
the validity of the law itself are the most intricate and difficult.
Hence, in a country whose administration ought to be marked with
simplicity, intricacy, procrastination, and uncertainty in affairs, result. To adopt laws from all the original States, the laws of all

[1] *Amer. State Papers: Misc.,* 1: 82, committee report of May 24,
1794, to the House of Representatives. The committee reported, of the
thirteen acts passed by Acting-governor Sargent and Judges Putnam and
Symmes on August 1, 1792, that many provisions thereof were objection-
able, but that to enumerate these was superfluous, since the laws were
invalid in toto: "These laws appear to have been passed by the Secretary
and judges on the idea that they were possessed generally of legislative
power, and have not, either in whole or in part, been adopted from laws
of the original States." The House prepared and passed a joint-resolu-
tion invalidating all the laws except one—*Annals,* 3 Congress, 601, 1214,
1223, 1227; but the Senate did not concur—*ibid.,* 37, 84, 825, 830. As to
law excepted—Pease, *Laws (I. H. C.,* 17), 87. By act of May 8, 1792—
U. S. Stat. at Large, 1: 286, § 6—Congress had disapproved of the statute
of limitations passed on December 28, 1788—Pease, *Laws (I. H. C.,* 17),
25; hence the new law passed in 1795, *ibid.,* 161. The territory would have
been in a curious condition if all the laws of 1792 had been invalidated. See
for the views of St. Clair and Symmes, *St. Clair Papers,* 2: 339, 350, 356-
362, 364-366, 439-440, 450-453.

the original States ought to be furnished; and, waiving the difficulty and expense of procuring them, what body of men, under the pressure of immediate business, can acquire a complete acquaintance with them? The possession of all the codes, if it were possible, and a complete acquaintance with their contents, would still prove an abortive cure; for, in many very simple cases, a strict precedent will be searched for in vain. Is the object to establish a ferry, to regulate the affairs of any district, to erect a courthouse, or to institute a school, however urgent the call, however obvious the means, it must often be abandoned for want of a precedent that will apply; and often, when attempted, may be defeated, from the want of a strict correspondence between the law made and the precedent from which it professes to be adopted? The real security for the prevalence of republican principles rests not in a provision of this awkward kind: for, even in the codes of the States, the disciple of aristocracy may sometimes find a weapon. . . . It rests in the parental control of Congress."[1]

When an act was needed to compensate the clerk of the Assembly (a certain reward to an individual occupying a particular office), or to establish a ferry at a certain place on an Indiana or Illinois river, or to authorize payments for sending pony expresses on public business across the prairies[2]—in such cases, chosen merely as examples to point Judge Woodward's argument, how could the law of some other state be "adopted"?

[1] Letter to President Jefferson, October 10, 1805—*Amer. State Papers: Pub. Lands*, 1: 249. Compare the statement of Governor Sargent and judges of Mississippi Territory, *Annals*, 6 Congress, 1 session, 717. A committee of Michigan citizens stated quite correctly in a representation of October 16, 1809 (asking for government of the second grade) that "the inconvenience of a legislative power under so extraordinary and so awkward a modification have been perpetuated after reason had proved its inconsistency, and transplanted to other governments when experience had demonstrated its inadequacy"—*Mich. Pioneer and Hist. Colls.*, 12: 547. Judge Woodward drafted a code that ignored the restriction of the Ordinance; for caustic comments upon "Woodward's Code" see *ibid.*, 8: 617-619. The question long continued a thorny one. When the British, after having conquered that territory in 1812, regulated its civil government they provided that legislative provisions need *not* be adopted from any American state (*ibid.*, 8: 634-635). This was doubtless intended as a grant of complete legislative power.

[2] Pease, *Laws* (*I. H. C.*, 17), 287 (August 13, 1795); also *post*, 18, 20, 87.

Although the governor and judges of Indiana Territory, in using the words "law," "act," and "resolution" to describe their legislation, might be assumed to have used those words with exact discrimination, in fact they did not do so. They sometimes referred to "acts" of their predecessors as "laws." Their own "laws"—even one amending or supplementing earlier statutes—are justified as "adopted from the code" of a designated state. When they repealed a statute by an "act" it is described as "made . . . conformably to" the Ordinance. But neither formula is used to justify a resolution—even one repealing a statute. On the whole the terminology means nothing except that they resolved when they doubted their authority to enact; but, again, in various cases a "resolution" is at its end "declared to be a law of the Territory."

Considering that in all the territories that started with the Ordinance as their basic law its "adoption" clause was of necessity evaded, that almost nothing was actually done by Congress to invalidate such legislation and that all of it was locally enforced as law of the land, it would be a puerile technicality to insist that such "resolutions" lacked legality. Considering that power was assumed to repeal in toto any laws, whether of the Indiana or of the Northwest Territory,[1] it seems an equally empty technicality to deny validity to partial repeals.[2] But very many of the laws adopted ·by the governor and judges were taken from Kentucky,[3] and such

[1] The statute of May 8, 1792 (*U. S. Stat. at Large,* 1: 286, § 2) gave the governor and judges of the old territory authority to repeal "their laws by them made," with no explicit reference to partial repeals. The act creating Indiana Territory provided that its government should be that provided by "the ordinance"; but it also contained the language quoted in the text, *ante,* cv. It seems, therefore, that Indiana Territory was to enjoy government under the Ordinance as the Northwest Territory had enjoyed it from 1792 to 1799, i. e. with the interpretation or modification established by Congress through the statute cited at the beginning of this note. The governor and judges of Indiana Territory, as a matter of fact, exercised unchallenged the power of repeal, total and partial, and with respect equally to their own statutes and laws of the older territory.

[2] Monks, *Courts,* 1: 25, characterizes as illegal all "resolutions," also all partial repeals of laws of the Northwest Territory. The larger question referred to in the preceding note is overlooked.

[3] Adoptions from southern states (especially Kentucky and Virginia) greatly preponderated, whereas the laws of the Northwest Territory had come very largely from northern states. There is no reason to believe

action was manifestly a violation of the literal terms of the Ordinance. It has therefore, probably generally, been assumed that the statutes thence derived were necessarily illegal.[1] Whether such adoptions violated the spirit of the Ordinance, as a matter of statutory construction, is a difficult question. If the purpose of the provision was that stated above in Judge Woodward's opinion, could it be contended that the society or statutes of the original thirteen states contained more of republicanism than did those of Kentucky's frontier democracy? The question was formally considered in Michigan in 1805, and the position was taken by the judges that, inasmuch as that territory was by its creative act merely given a government "similar" to that provided by the Ordinance, and inasmuch as the Ordinance, with respect to Michigan, derived its effect from the creative statute of 1805, every state then existing and participating in the creation of the territory was one whose laws might, "conformable to the strict letter" of the Ordinance be adopted; and inasmuch as the obvious general intent of the Ordinance's restriction was merely to apply to incipient states "the laws which societies further advanced under the same *principles of government,* have found convenient and advantageous," the same liberty of choice was sanctioned by the spirit of the Ordinance.[2] These arguments seem convincing.

As has been said above, such was Harrison's political finesse that no trouble arose in Indiana Territory over what under St. Clair had raised a storm. But when an autocrat like Winthrop

---

[1] E. g. by Judge William L. Gross, Ill. State Bar Assoc. *Proc.* (1881), pp. 76, 81; Monks, *Courts,* 1: 25.

[2] Report by Judges Woodward and Bates to their fellows, *Mich. Pioneer and Hist. Colls.,* 8: 603-604.

---

that slavery had anything to do with this. Immigration into Indiana Territory was in these years very largely from the south. This, and the different origins of the governors and other leaders of the two territories, are a sufficient explanation. On the Kentucky influence see J. R. Robertson in Ind. Hist. Soc. *Pub.,* 6: 82 *et seq.* The connection of the Illinois country with Nashville was close from 1782 onward—Alvord, *Illinois Country,* 359. The extraordinary number of Pennsylvania statutes adopted in the Northwest Territory—Pease, *Laws* (*I. H. C.,* 17), xxvi—is partly explainable by the fact that the judges did not have statute books of the other states (*St. Clair Papers,* 2: 334), but doubtless also by St. Clair's years of experience in administering Pennsylvania law (Pease, *op. cit.,* xvii), and to his greater ability and force in comparison with his fellows.

Sargent did the same things in Mississippi, remonstrance against unconstitutional laws again reverberated in Congress, and he was denounced by a champion of the people, with the fervor of that age of romanticism, as "a tyrant, who has trampled on their rights with a tiger's stride; and plucked from them, by voracious and disgraceful laws, their hard earnings" (to wit—precisely as in Indiana Territory—in ferry tolls, tavern licenses, and court fees).[1]

Salmon P. Chase gave high praise to the statutes of the Northwest Territory.[2] For their precise (but also cumbersome) terminology many of them might indeed be praised. But as a system they were recognized by the judges themselves, and by Judge Burnet, who was mainly to be credited with their revision in 1799,[3] as extremely incomplete. In fact they covered only a few subjects. The additions and amendments which they suffered at the hands of the legislators of Indiana Territory amply illustrate their deficiencies. In his address to the first legislature Governor Harrison suggested that there was "much room for alteration and improvement," and that at least the organization of the lower courts must be reformed; but he ventured the opinion that "the formation of a new code would be attended with an expense which our citizens are at present ill able to supply; and the advantages which would result from it would be probably, more than counterbalanced by the many embarrassments which it might occasion."[4]

[1] See *Annals*, 6 Congress, 1 session, 717-718 (May 14, 1800); 2 session, 837, 838-840 (December 19, 22, 1800). "It is a fact well known, that at the time this man was appointed Governor of the Mississippi Territory, he was hated and despised by the people of the Western country" (Davis, of Kentucky: *ibid.*, 840). The specifications against him and the judges related to laws regarding ferries, treason, taverns, and court fees.

[2] Namely, that the system was "not without many imperfections and blemishes; but it may be doubted whether any colony, at so early a period after its first establishment, ever had one so good"—*Statutes of Ohio*, 1: 27.

[3] Symmes and Turner to St. Clair, May, 1795, pronouncing the statute book "by far too inadequate, at present, to answer the ends of good government." *St. Clair Papers*, 2: 365. Mr. Esarey says that the burden fell "on the lawyers of the eastern [Ohio] counties," *History*, 1: 150. Burnet lists the laws of which he was the author in his *Notes*, 310-311. He was a graduate of Princeton, well trained in law.

[4] July 29, 1805—Harrison, *Messages*, 1: 155-156. In Michigan the variety of governments and laws successively in force was even greater, including—in addition to those which entered into the law of Indiana Ter-

But the legislature resolved, nevertheless, that John Johnson[1] and John Rice Jones should "reduce into one code" the laws in force in the territory and report to the next session.[2] The power was evidently found inadequate, for at the next session it was resolved that they "revise and reduce," with authority to "make the said laws . . . as complete as the nature of the case will admit of."[3] The result of their revision, and of "several alterations, additions and amendments" made by the Assembly,[4] was the "Revision" of 1807, included in the present volume. All other laws theretofore of authority were repealed, and the "revisal" was declared to be of exclusive authority. Competent judges have given the work of the revisers high praise.[5] Praise it undoubtedly deserves, notwithstanding that it was with few and slight exceptions mechanical in character.[6]

In one respect, however, the Revision is greatly superior to the statutes of the Northwest Territory: its phraseology is far

[1] A leading lawyer of the Wabash country. Mr. Esarey (Harrison, *Messages*, 1: 317; Monks, *Courts*, 1: 184) gives 1804 as the date of his appearance in Indiana. The *Order Book* of the General Court (copy of the original volume), 1: 56, shows that on January 10, 1803, he produced a Kentucky license as attorney and was ordered examined as a counsellor (by John Rice Jones and Robert Hamilton); and on March 1 he and Jones were the examiners of Isaac Darneille. One of his opinions in a slavery case is given in Ind. Hist. Soc. *Pub.*, 2: 528; cp. *ibid.*, 482. For details of his career see Monks, *op. cit.*, 175, 184.

[2] August 26, 1805, *post*, 153.

[3] December 4, 1806, *post*, 217. Jones and Gen. W. Johnston indexed the Revision, prepared the errata, and superintended the printing, and were paid therefor $30 and $50 respectively—*post*, 605, 656, 674. The revisers received $350 for their labors: *post*, 208, 607. Nine copyists (including Jonathan Jennings) were paid $2.50 per diem.

[4] *Post*, 608.

[5] E. g. Judge William L. Gross, in Ill. State Bar Assoc. *Proc.* (1881), 86: "The work they did in bringing together the large number of acts that had been in force in the Territory since 1788, and the erudition and judgment they displayed in framing the new legislation, was, considering the times and circumstances under which they worked, very remarkable."

[6] Howe seems correct, Ind. Hist. Soc. *Pub.*, 2: 23-24. Nevertheless, considering the qualities of statutory revision in this country, generally (see Frederic J. Stimson, *Popular Law-Making*, 354 *et seq.*), even mechanical rearrangements, if accompanied by omissions of obsolete matter, are notable merits.

ritory—royal ordinances of France, the Custom of Paris (not theoretically, but in actuality), and the statutes of Indiana Territory. The problem of revision was therefore correspondingly greater. *Mich. Pioneer and Hist. Colls.*, 12: 464-465 (No. x), 466.

more direct and less cumbersome. Referring to the difference in this respect between the laws of the first legislature of the younger territory and the enactments by St. Clair and his judges, a commentator has justly characterized it as "the difference between the parlance of the lawyer and layman."[1]

A great embarrassment in the administration of justice was the difficulty of making the laws known to the people, or even to the judges. Governor St. Clair had no way to make the laws known except through reading in the courts, which few attended. "Even the magistrates who are to carry them into execution"—he wrote—"are strangers to them, for the secretary does not conceive it to be his duty to furnish them with copies. Indeed the business of his office increases so fast, that it would be impossible to do it; besides, they are in English, and the greatest part of the inhabitants do not understand a word of it; the translation of them, therefore, seems to be necessary, and that a sufficient number of them should be printed in both languages; and that can only be done in the territory where the original rolls are deposited. Every public act and communication, of what kind soever, I was myself obliged [when in the Illinois country in 1790] to translate into French; and having no person to assist me, it made the business extremely troublesome and laborious."[2] A few months later an act was passed creating the office of clerk of the legislature, and making it his duty to publish the laws in every county, and furnish copies to the governor and to the territorial and county judges; and by another act a penalty (strangely enough, of only three dollars) was imposed for tearing down or defacing a posted statute.[3] But the former law (the federal government having made provision for publishing the territorial laws) was repealed in 1792. It has already been noted that John Rice Jones, two years after St. Clair's visit in the west, translated the statutes for the use of the French-speaking judges.[4]

[1] Monks, *Courts,* 1: 25.
[2] Letter of Secretary of State, February 10, 1791—*Amer. State Papers: Pub. Lands,* 1: 20.
[3] Pease, *Laws* (*I. H. C.,* 17), 43 (law as to clerk); (law as to posted statutes) 42, 332, and *post,* 374, § 14.
[4] See *ante,* xvii, n. 3.

No similar provision was made for publication of the laws of the Indiana Territory. Harrison urged similarly the great inconvenience that resulted from the want of printed laws, and he and the judges authorized the copying of the law on county levies, and such other laws as might be deemed necessary, "for the use of the territory."[1] The opening of the printing establishment of Elihu Stout in Vincennes, in 1804, relieved the situation. A moderate number of the statutes passed by both sessions of the first Assembly, and of the Revision printed with the laws of the first session of the second Assembly, were ordered sent to each county for official use.[2] Wayne County, while still a part of Indiana Territory, never had any copies of the statutes, and after it became the Territory of Michigan, though the statutes of the older territory were a portion of its law, apparently never saw any of the printed copies.[3]

Among the statutes most elaborately devised, yet repeatedly amended, were those on taxation. Three times in as many years the Assembly overhauled the territorial land tax, constantly improving it in definiteness—though starting with an elaborate law of 1799 under which the government operated until 1805. Twice by the governor and judges and four times by the Assembly the law

[1] *Messages*, 1: 50—Harrison's letter of July 7, 1802, to Secretary Madison. Resolution of November 7, 1803—*post*, 85.

[2] Twenty copies of the laws of the second (and probably of the first) session of the first Assembly; 45 copies of the Revision of 1807 and of the laws of the first and second sessions of the second Assembly—to each county. *Post*, 153, 217, 578, 604, 656, 672. The act of Congress of May 8, 1792, cited *ante*, cix, n. 1, provided (§ 1) that the United States government should print 200 copies of the laws of the Northwest Territory for distribution therein. No similar statute, apparently, was passed with reference to the Indiana Territory.

[3] In October, 1804 it was stated in a petition to Congress that of the laws passed by the governor and judges in September, 1803 (but see *ante*, cv, n. 1) not one had, in a year, been seen in Wayne County, nor of course been in actual operation—see petition in *Hist. Public. of Wayne County Michigan*, Nos. 1-2, p. 30. Judge Woodward stated in 1807 that "of the northwestern and Indiana laws there is not a complete copy in the Territory"—*Mich. Pioneer and Hist. Colls.*, 12: 505. And in a statute of 1810, repealing British and other statutes theoretically theretofore in force, through unavoidable ignorance of which the people might be ensnared, it was stated that the laws of the two territories did not exist in manuscript or print in Michigan, and also were out of print—*ibid.*, 8: 612 (§ 3).

on county levies was amended or restated[1]—starting again with the elaborate law of 1799, of which manuscript copies were distributed to the counties. The territory relied upon land, the counties mainly upon personalty and license taxes.

To one unable to read between the lines, the operation of the territorial tax would seem a veritable opera bouffe. The act of 1805 required the courts of Common Pleas to appoint assessors and collectors; empowered the territorial auditor to "apply for and procure from the proper officers" abstracts of "all entries and locations" of land, which lists he should forward to the county assessors;[2] required the assessors thereupon to list every tract claimed in his county ("either by entry, patent, deed of conveyance, bond for conveyance, or any other evidence of claim"), and return valuations thereon to the auditor; who should then levy such assessment as would produce the revenue required. Provision was made for the sale of lands for taxes, and bonds were required of assessors and collectors ($500 and $2000 respectively). Now it appears that assessors and collectors were not appointed in St. Clair, Randolph, and Dearborn counties, nor valuation lists supplied to the auditor; wherefore the latter was ordered nevertheless to assess upon said counties "their proportion of the taxes" for 1806, and in default of full abstracts to act "from the best information he can collect." Heavy penalties were put upon the county courts for future failure to name assessors and collectors; and likewise upon *"any register,* surveyor, or other person in whose possession the records and proofs of the grant and confirmation of land may be" (italics added), who should, "upon being thereunto lawfully required," withhold abstracts from such records.[3] Farther, it appears that the territorial auditor did not transmit the land entries for Randolph County until after the day of appeal, in consequence of which the assessments were void; yet the collector had collected some of the taxes, and sold lands for nonpayment of others; wherefore a special session of the Common

[1] For land tax 1805, '06, '07—*post,* 147, 171, 592; for law regulating county levies 1801, '03, '06, '07, '08—*post,* 1, 68, 186, 196, 481, 664.
[2] *Post,* 147, §§ 1-5, 11, 14, 18, 24, 25. See *ante,* lxxiv.
[3] Act of November 29, 1806, *post,* 171 §§ 5, 7, 8, 9.

Pleas was ordered to hear appeals, and subject thereto the assessments and collections were validated.[1]   Again, it appears that the sheriffs "of several counties," though under penalty of $500 to do so under the act of 1805, had not taken lists of the free male inhabitants of their counties; wherefore they were ordered to do so, under renewed threat of said penalty[2]—but it does not appear that the first penalty was collected.   Finally, the act of 1805 required certain publication "in some public newspaper in this territory"; but "the public newspaper for this territory,"—there was only one—"was for some time suspended"—nevertheless taxes were declared to have been legally collected in Knox and Clark counties.[3]   In short the law of 1805 was punctually observed in not a single county.

The act of 1806 was likewise ineffective.   The assessor of St. Clair "refused to make an assessment and return"; wherefore it was ordered that said assessor, "being furnished" with entry lists, which the auditor was again ordered to supply, "and having taken such oath as is required by law" should proceed to do his duty; and a special session of the Common Pleas was ordered, to examine his returns.   It does not appear that $300 was collected for his first default, but the penalty of default under the corrective act was to be personal liability for the taxes.   The collector and assessor of Knox had violated the law, and being conscious thereof the collector did not collect until by special act he was ordered to do so.   The collector of Dearborn, on the other hand, did collect taxes wrongfully assessed, and was ordered to make reimbursement.[4]

With this accumulation of experience the Assembly attempted in 1807 to frame a law that should be proof against all officials. In the main the system it provided was that of the statute of 1805, though the new law was much more precisely and clearly framed.   A novelty was a prohibition against the appointment of sheriffs or deputy sheriffs as assessors.   Another was provision for

[1] Act of September 14, 1807, *post*, 558.
[2] "Resolution" of December 6, 1806, *post*, 177.
[3] Act of November 29, 1806 (§§ 5, 6), *post*, 172-173.
[4] Acts of September 3, 1807, and September 16, 1807, *post*, 553, 574; resolution of September 19, 1807, *post*, 602.

redemption from tax sales. It would be difficult to say how the statute could have been better drafted.[1] But despite all precautions the law was disobeyed. The assessors of St. Clair and Randolph failed to make and return assessments for 1808, thereby making impossible a valid collection for 1808 or 1809. For remedy whereof they were by special act "hereby directed immediately to proceed" to do their duty.[2] And by resolution "proper officers" were directed to take speedy and effectual measures to compel tax collectors to pay their arrearages.[3]

Such examples (for the above is not a unique presentment of territorial administration) make very clear the weakness of the executive branch of government, which was one argument for division of the territory in 1800 and in 1809. The situation was in part due to the state of land titles in the Illinois counties; in truth it would have been impossible to furnish reasonably exact abstracts or to assess a just tax. In part, also, the difficulty was simply recalcitrancy on the part of the Illinois officers.[4]

And back of this lay politics. In the formal charges against Harrison forwarded to Congress by the Illinois divisionists in 1808 the use made of the records of the federal land registers to secure the names of all claimants, and the imposition of a tax upon mere claims, were given precedence over all others except precipitation into government of the second grade. It seems clear that Harrison used the legislature to put pressure on the Illinois dissidents; and it seems probable that in this Michael Jones willingly coöperated—

[1] Act of September 19, 1807, *post*, 592. Mere formalism, copied from earlier statutes, survived in the provision that notice of tax sales should be advertised "in some publick news-paper, either in the Territory, or in the states of Kentucky, and Ohio." The act cited *ante*, cxv, n. 3 provided for advertisements set up at two or more public places in the county of location, in case there should be no newspaper in the Territory. The history of the *Western Sun* (1804-1845; known for the first year and a half as the *Indiana Gazette*) is given in Law, *Colonial Hist. of Vincennes*, 137-140.

[2] Act of October 26, 1808, *post*, 669.

[3] Resolution of same date, *post*, 673. In the *Order Book* of the General Court, 1 (copy), 84, is a judgment of September 8, 1803, against the collector of Knox for arrearages of 1802. All the collectors (sheriffs) were constantly in arrears.

[4] Section 2 of the law of October 26, 1808, *post*, 664 (appropriating the land tax exclusively to local building purposes) undoubtedly illustrates this attitude. Compare *ante*, lxxiv and *post*, cxix, n. 2.

for certainly both he—and Harrison[1] realized that the territory had no control over the records of the former's office.

The specific provisions of the statutes on county levies, except as mentioned in connection with other subjects, require little comment. In the main the Court of Quarter Sessions merely voted the rates prescribed by the statute; but it had some independent power of importance, such as fixing the rate of tavern and ferry licenses.[2] More criminal prosecutions originated under the provision for a retail license tax, which imposed a fine for the sale without license of merchandise other than the produce or manufacture of the territory, than from any other cause. Where the territorial statute fixed a maximum, naturally the Quarter Sessions fixed the rate considerably lower;[3] and for the protection of bachelors they cut in half the minimum set by the statute.[4] Needless to say, the court of tax appeals reduced assessments, and low valuations were set upon lands (on petition of the leading landholders).[5]

[1] *Ante*, xlvii, lxiv.

[2] These were politically, even more than financially, important. Recommendation by the Quarter Sessions had been since 1795—Pease, *Laws* (*I. H. C.*, 17), 193—a prerequisite to a tavern license. See *post*, cxxvii, n. 3. The act of November 5, 1803 (*post*, 68) refers in § 12 to the tavern tax, but § 1 merely refers to all "houses in town" (as real estate), and no other section provides for such a tax. The maximum ferry tax set by this statute (§ 14—unchanged by later laws) was $10.

[3] Same act (§ 13). The maximum on slaves and bond servants was $1, but the Quarter Sessions of Randolph (where most of the slaves were held) fixed the rate at $0.50; on mills, $0.25 (in 1803, p. 43, $0.50) per $100 valuation; on town houses and lots, $0.25; mansion houses in the country, $0.25. Randolph, *Court Record 1802-06*, 62 (term of May, 1804). Similar taxes, *ibid.*, 86, 92, 10.

[4] The minimum set (*post*, 73, § 9) was $0.50; the rate laid, $0.25—Randolph, *Court Record 1802-06*, 1. c. The maximum of $2 was lowered in 1806 to $1, and the taxable property possession of which gave release from the tax was lowered from $400 to $200 (*post*, 187, § 2); in 1808 (*post*, 664, § 1) the tax was abolished.

[5] E. g. a sawmill of Henry Levins, valued at $500, was reduced in valuation to $300—Randolph, *Court Record 1802-06*, 43 (December, 1803). These values are of some interest. The tax on town lots and houses, "outlots" (which may have meant strips in the commons), and country mansion houses, was restricted to those worth at least $200 (*post*, 69, § 1; unamended). Compare *post*, cxxiv on mills. On the petition of John Edgar, William Morrison, Robert Morrison, John Rice Jones, Pierre Menard, John Beaird, Robert Reynolds, William Whiteside, and George Belsha the "Court of Appeals" (i. e. the Common Pleas so acting in tax questions) fixed the value of all improvement and family concessions at 75 cents per

It is difficult, today, to realize which taxes were at that time most significant. Governor Harrison displayed great concern over the taxes upon cattle and horses. The Quarter Sessions laid taxes on horses and neat cattle under three years,[1] which the legislature left untaxed. The difficulty of finding objects of taxation, the impolicy of such heavy taxation as would discourage immigration, and the injustice of taxing "the incipient exertions of the settlers with more than they could conveniently pay," were repeatedly urged by Governor Harrison upon the Assembly. According to his message of 1808 there was very general and just complaint against the weight of the county levies. Particularly bad, he considered, was the tax on neat cattle and working horses. At his behest the fees to road surveyors and the taxes on neat cattle and on bachelors were abolished; but he protested in vain against the heavy tax on horses as compared with that on land.[2]

The difficulties already noted in collection of the territorial taxes were not absent in the administration of the local levies. It is noteworthy that four very well known Americans in Randolph were fined one dollar each for refusing to give lists of their tax-

---

[1] Horses at 25, cattle at 6¼ cents—Randolph, *Court Record 1802-06,* 62 (May 1, 1804). The Assembly had fixed maxima of 50 and 10 cents on horses and neat cattle, respectively, 3 years and upwards—*post,* 73, § 9.

[2] *Messages,* 1: 157, 230, 304, 305-306, 321, 380. For the taxes abolished there was substituted the tax on land for county purposes referred to, *ante,* cxvii, n. 4. "The average price of all the horses . . . in any county will not, I am confident, exceed forty dollars, and for that forty dollars of capital fifty cents per annum is exacted,"—as a maximum, plus the independent county tax on younger horses—"whilst a capital of one hundred dollars in land pays only twenty cents to the Territory and five cents to the counties. The tax on horses in the State of Kentucky is fixed, as I am told, at nine cents. Let us imitate this wise example of our neighbors, and relieve the poorer class of our fellow citizens from the intolerable burden that oppresses them."

---

acre, in favor of the persons named, who had "applicated this." *Ante,* lxxiv. Also they fixed the value of "all the lands belonging to the following persons lying in the Mississippi Bottom"—to wit John Edgar, William Morrison, William McIntosh, John Rice Jones, Pierre Menard, Robert Morrison, John Beaird, Robert Reynolds, and Robert Robinson—at $1.50 per acre; "except" when such lands might have been assessed at less, in which case the lower value should stand—Randolph, *Court Record 1802-06,* 111 (October 15, 1807). Be it noted that Edgar, Menard, Beaird, and Reynolds were members of the court; Robert Morrison was its clerk; Robinson was the lawyer who represented several of those who were not members, also Menard.

able property, whereas one American and four French citizens who
are raised solely in this connection out of obscurity were fined
five times as much.[1] In 1805 the court ordered a report on delinquent taxpayers and debtors.[2] It is hardly necessary to say that
they were all of the county magnates:

William Morrison (richest merchant), retail licenses.........$60

    on purchase of old courthouse...................... 25

Pierre Menard (judge of both county courts), retail licenses.. 60

George Fisher (judge of both county courts), retail licenses.. 30

    for stones of old courthouse........................ 40

    2 tavern licenses................................... 24

Ephraim Carpenter, 2 tavern licenses...................... 24

Miles Hotchkiss, 3 tavern licenses......................... 36

    fines for contempt of court......................... 10

John Grosvenor (judge of both county courts), 2 tavern

    licenses 24

Joseph Archambeau, 2 tavern licenses..................... 24

    1 retail license.................................... 15

John Edgar (judge of both courts, richest landowner), 2 retail

    licenses 30

    Five years later the debts remained the same. They were
left to the county, as a part of Illinois Territory, to collect.[3]

    The same was true of the various other claims, notably against
Robert Morrison, as clerk of the Common Pleas, and against James
Gilbreath, last sheriff of Randolph under the preceding régime.[4]
It is noteworthy that claims against the county, unpaid before,
were promptly allowed by the new government.[5]

[1] Randolph, *Court Record 1802-06*, 35 (September 6, 1803). And
the $1 fine was in one case later remitted.

[2] *Ibid.*, (December 3, 1805) 101.

[3] *County Court Record 1810*, of Illinois Territory, 37 (April 18,
1810)..

[4] *Ibid.*, (Morrison) 15, 94-98; (Gilbreath) 104, 107. Also (Morrison)
County Commissioners volume, 124.

[5] Randolph *County Commissioners*, 89—July 3, 1809, first session of
the new court under Illinois Territory; 141, fees allowed Benj. Stephenson
for services as sheriff in Indiana Territory period. *County Court Record
1810*, 6, 11, 12, various allowances to judges and clerks of elections in
1805-1808; 133, George Fisher "allowed the sum of $154 for his services as
sheriff from the first day of August 1800 to the twentieth of August 1803
and his Extra Services as sheriff during this period as per his account

Noteworthy in the field of commercial law are the statutes permitting some assignees to sue in their own name.[1] The principle of the statute of 1799 ruling bills and notes was extended by that of 1805 to "bonds or other writings obligatory for the payment of money, or any specific article"; the assignee being subject to set-offs and equitable defences against himself and against the assignor before notice had by defendant. The narrowness of these statutes, however, which was apparently characteristic of the time, leaves them less noteworthy than the contemporary judicial developments in the alienability of choses in action.[2] The general corporation law adopted in 1798 for the Northwest Territory (the adoption of which was in itself remarkable)[3] was not altered or supplanted under the Indiana Territory. The examples in this volume (a borough, two towns, a canal company, a university, a library, and a church) are all of corporations public or quasi-public in nature. This was typical of conditions throughout the country.[4]

[1] Law of November 15, 1799, Pease, *Laws* (*I. H. C.*, 17), 361 (on promissory notes and inland bills of exchange); of August 15, 1805, *post,* 98 (as quoted in the text); of 1807, *post,* 355—which is a reënactment of the two preceding laws.

[2] Compare W. W. Cook, "The Alienability of Choses in Action," *Harvard Law Review,* 29: 826-834. The Virginia statutes went back at least to 1748 (Lewis *v.* Harwood, 6 Cranch, 82), and were probably the source of the Indiana Territory act of 1805 (cp. Stewart *v.* Anderson, *ibid.,* 203), directly or through the Kentucky act of 1798 (cp. Hard. 8 and 5 J. J. Marsh, 43). However liberally interpreted (e. g. to include bonds for conveyance of land, 2 Litt. 167) such statutes necessarily left most choses in action under common law rules. Various other assignment statutes were passed about this time by S. C. in 1798, Vt. in 1798, etc. No cases were found in which the Indiana Territory statute was applied.

[3] Pease, *Laws* (*I. H. C.*, 17), 293. It was taken from Pennsylvania, whose statute of 1791 was the third (all American) "since the days of Queen Elizabeth"—S. E. Baldwin, in *Two Centuries' Growth of American Law,* 281.

[4] *Post,* 112, 196, 513 (Vincennes); 564 (Jeffersonville); 568 (Kaskaskia); 154 (canal); 572 (church); 178, 184, 532 (university); 202, 547 (library). It seems probable that Detroit was incorporated in 1798 or 1799

rendered and approved"; 9, Jas. Gilbreath, late sheriff, allowed $244 for fees in various criminal prosecutions, for holding elections, and for taking the census; 132, Henry Hurst, clerk of the General Court of Indiana Territory, allowed $160 "for his salary due from this county while a part of the Indiana Territory at the rate of fourty dollars per year for the years 1803 1804 1805 and 1806 ending in the month of September 1807." There are various other examples.

The statutes on land are in one feature remarkable. In addition to special acts authorizing guardians to sell the ward's unproductive estate and make conveyances,[1] and a partition law (in this respect unchanged from an act of the Northwest Territory) authorizing the commissioners, when the property was incapable of division, to sell, and give conveyances which should be good at law and in equity, there is a private act in which the administrators of a decedent are authorized to convey lands already conveyed by the decedent to trustees who had not acted on their trust;[2] and, what is more remarkable, a general act of 1805 authorizing the Common Pleas to appoint commissioners to make conveyance of land in fulfillment of a contract made by a deceased vendor, in case the heirs were infants or the executor (if any) lacked authority.[3] This enactment, moreover, was actually applied.[4] This last territorial act was one of the earliest ones, of the kind, of this country. Regulation of the partition of estates held by tenancy in common was at first, because of the scattered residence of the owners in all parts of the country, of especial importance; by 1795 the principles adopted were substantially in accord with present law.[5]

There are many statutes which are of no great interest individually but which are significant when considered together as an attempt to adjust the statute-book to the special situation of the territory. First, there is a group that bear an evident relation to frontier conditions. Such are the acts aimed against acquisition by Indians of arms and ammunition; the elaborate militia laws—failures, despite Harrison's attempts to make the people take them

[1] *Post,* 106, 575 (in the second case Governor Harrison was the guardian, and the wards were children of Major Hamtramck).
[2] Pease, *Laws* (*I. H. C.,* 17), 267-268 (law of 1795); *post,* 124, 521, 576 (Major Hamtramck the decedent).
[3] Act of August 15, 1805, *post,* 93. With this and the preceding laws compare C. A. Huston, *The Enforcement of Decrees in Equity,* 66, and citations; also the appendix of statutes, under Maryland, etc.
[4] St. Clair, *Orphans' Court* 47C (March, 1809); a bond for conveyance given by George Atchison to Aaron Badgley was so enforced after the obligator's death.
[5] See *St. Clair Papers,* 2: 64.

under the act of the Northwest Territory—*Mich. Pioneer and Hist. Colls.,* 8: 507. See Baldwin, *op. cit.,* 276, 311.

seriously; the acts dealing with enclosures and trespassing animals;[1] granting wolf bounties;[2] requiring the registration of marks and brands;[3] fixing penalties for cutting timber from private or public lands.[4] A few acts were framed still more specifically to meet the peculiar circumstances of the territory: laws which, as the governor and judges had found, could not be "adopted" from the statute-books of the original states. Such were the laws on common fields, recognizing the traditions of the French villages, the laws regulating ferries,[5] and pilots for the

[1] *Post,* 213, 294, 344, 399—based mainly on the law of 1799, Pease, *Laws* (*I. H. C.,* 17), 418—590. All the legislation regarding enclosures and trespassing animals followed precedents of the southern states. A law of 1791 (Pease, *op. cit.,* 46) specified with great exactness a lawful fence, and gave the landowner damages for trespass only when such a lawful enclosure had been broken. This has always been a common rule in the southern states. A statute of June 25, 1795 (Pease, *op. cit.,* 235) made the landowner liable for harm done to animals driven away, unless his land was lawfully enclosed; but was less stringent than the earlier law in defining a lawful fence. A statute of 1799 (Pease, 347) restated the rule of damages due the landowner, but not the reverse rule. A lawful fence, as specified by the law of 1799 (even more stringently than in that of 1791) must have been rare. This statute of 1799 was embodied in the Revision of 1807— *post,* 344; but, unlike some of the statutes of 1799 referred to *ante,* ciii, n. 1, without having been previously reënacted. Yet it was enforced by the courts, before 1807, as the operative law of Indiana Territory.

[2] By resolution of February 16, 1803, the general Northwestern law on wolf bounties (Pease, *op. cit.,* 503) was repealed—*post,* 30. A statute of 1807—*post,* 562—reënacted the same law.

[3] *Post,* 210. Also ordering the gelding of ordinary stallions running wild—*post,* 205. The St. Clair book of brands, 1807-1809, is preserved in the Belleville Museum; the Randolph record begins at a later date.

[4] *Post,* 357, a substantial reënactment of the law of 1799—Pease, *Laws* (I. H. C., 17), 362, displacing 254. Mr. J. J. Thompson (Ill. State Hist. Soc. *Trans.,* 22: 69), says that the act allowed recovery in one action for repeated trespass; but the statute does nothing more than fix a certain penalty for each tree cut.

[5] The governor and judges, in 1795, resolved that "public convenience requires, that the Governour should cause Public Ferries to be established. And whereas no laws concerning Ferries can be found for adoption, but such as are of a local, not general nature." They further resolved that the governor should by proclamation locate ferries and that the Quarter Sessions should fix the rates—Pease, *Laws* (*I. H. C.,* 17), 287-288. In 1799, when untrammeled legislation was possible, the subject was fully regulated— *ibid.,* 357. The governor and judges of Indiana Territory recited by way of preamble the complaint of their predecessors, but then "resolved" that ferries should be governed by the regulations of the statute of 1799!—and then ended: "The foregoing is hereby declared to be a law of the Territory." They did not need to adopt a law that already bound them; but if they wished to do so would the Ordinance bar them from adopting a law framed precisely for them, to fit their very own needs? See *ante,* ciii, n. 1. The Revision of 1807 (*post,* 352) again reënacted the law of 1799.

rapids of the Ohio.[1] Not peculiar to the territory, and yet quite especially important to it, were the statutes regulating mills;[2] for it was Governor Reynolds' opinion that the want of mills "retarded the improvement of the country in early times more than all other considerations."[3] A similar importance is presumably to be attributed to the road laws. Few were more carefully considered, and they illustrate the difficulty of making provisions theoretically excellent fit the actual conditions of the territory.[4]

Mixed with these enactments of prosaic ends there are others in this volume which show our forefathers, no less true Americans than we today, engaged in the task of exorcising original sin with preamble and command. The preamble to all their efforts might well have run somewhat like this: "Whereas this Territory contains many citizens of French origin and traditions who, though characterized by their friends as 'quiet and inoffensive' and 'an innocent and happy people,' and though in truth rarely guilty of serious crimes and less addicted than their American fellow citizens to

[1] *Post,* 63 (September 24, 1803), 480 (Revision, 1807). Cp. *ante,* cviii. (See *Annals,* 9 Congress, 1 session, 827-828, on canal around the rapids).

[2] The act of 1799—Pease, *Laws* (*I. H. C.,* 17), 366—was not reenacted. *Post,* 133 (August 24, 1805), 361 (Revision of 1807, based on both sets). The laws of 1799 and 1805 did not overlap; the former was regarded as operative—indeed it was referred to (§ 9) as existing law.

[3] *Pioneer History,* 315. He repeatedly recurs to the subject. John Edgar manufactured flour for the New Orleans market; John Francis Perrey was also a miller, and John Dumoulin bankrupted himself in a mill enterprise. This activity of three such prominent men and capitalists goes to confirm Reynolds' statement.

[4] Two Northwestern laws, of 1792 and 1799, were inherited—Pease, *Laws* (*I. H. C.,* 17), 74, 257, 339, 452. Of the latter it is said by Judge Gross that "modern road legislation has evolved no principle or practice not found in the Act; while in perspicuity, brevity, and simplicity it is a model"—Ill. State Bar Assoc. *Proc.* (1881), 78. Nevertheless it was considerably amended, and large portions repealed in 1805—*post,* 108; and these were not (with a trivial exception) reinstated by the Revision of 1807—*post,* 427. With these changes, then, the governor and judges, the revisers, and the Assembly found the law satisfactory. And yet, in 1808, upon the urging of Governor Harrison it was enacted that whereas "the expence of laying out public roads in the different counties, is found, not only burdensome, and a great means of draining the county treasuries of their funds, but is altogether useless and unnecessary," there should thenceforth be no surveying. *Post,* 646. This was an echo of Harrison: as he said, "The opening of roads is certainly a matter of considerable consequence; but as this is always done by the labor of each individual citizen, and not by contract, I could never learn what public advantage has ever resulted from surveying them"—*Messages,* 1: 305.

rough and brutal vices, do nevertheless lend themselves to frivolous pleasures and also are peculiarly susceptible to the detestable
vice of gambling:[1]   And Whereas there also live among us many
Indians, to whom we have from the beginning taught our vices
in exchange for their possessions, and upon whom our Indian
agents (in the words of our Governor) continue to prey, and
who, in consequence and in particular have sunk to the utmost
degradation and misery through indulgence in liquor, for which
they will sell their lands, their clothes from their body, yea even
their children:[2]   And Whereas, among our American fellow citizens there are many who likewise, men and women, drink over-
much of whiskey—even running for the bottle at weddings,—use
profane language, indulge in brutal fighting, and in horse and
foot-racing and all kinds of gaming for money, and even take each
other's lives in duels, and otherwise, in their habits of exaggerated
and unbridled individuality and independence, are forgetful of
their social duties:[3]   And Whereas all these sinners, French and

[1] The land commissioners, Michael Jones and Judge Backus, characterized them as "the most quiet and inoffensive part of this community"
(Randolph County)—*Amer. State Papers: Pub. Lands*, 2: 124. Governor
Reynolds, whose first wife was French and who lived among them for
many years and was familiar with their language and customs, used the
second characterization quoted in the text. According to him they "seldom
indulged in drinking liquor," "were never an intemperate people in the use
of liquor," "a spurious offspring was almost unknown among them," and
they were never guilty of crimes more serious than violations of the Sunday
laws and the like misdemeanors, *My Own Times*, 37, 39, 49, 51 (but 139
is somewhat inconsistent). The court records generally bear out these
statements, but the "nevers" must of course be changed to "rarely" and the
"almost unknown" is much exaggerated. See citations on *post*, clxxxiv, n. 1,
also clxxvi, n. 4. A priest's judgment would naturally be less lenient:
see Father Gibault's words, *Kaskaskia Records* (*I. H. C.*, 5), xlvii—1786;
also Volney's, in Dunn, *Indiana*, 118—1796.
[2] Dunn, *Indiana*, 124-125, quotes Volney's description of them in Vincennes. Harrison's statement is to quite the same effect, *Messages*, 1: 28—
1801.
[3] Reynolds, *Pioneer History*, 316, 324, 345; *My Own Times*, 40, 48,
51. An early duel is noted by Mr. Esarey, Harrison, *Messages*, 1: 301.
See app. n. 24. John Mason Peck, distinguished missionary and minister, contributed to Reynolds' *Pioneer History* a chapter of twenty-three
pages on "the religion and morals of Illinois prior to 1818"; of these less
than two are devoted to other matters than the arrival and activities of
fellow ministers. The godless he dismisses in a fraction of a page as a
class who, "they and their posterity," were in 1850 "unknown." Considering Governor Reynolds himself, this lapse of memory was remarkable;
not less so than the "strange" friendship between him and Dr. Peck—cp.

American and Godless Indians, pay no regard to the Sabbath:
Now Therefore be it enacted . . ."

A fearsome law was passed for the prevention of vice and
immorality, making many common habits of the people crimes
punishable by fine or imprisonment; but it cannot be said that the
act amounted to more than the ethical preachments with no penalties attached with which the Marietta legislators began, more
sensibly, in 1788. Except as a joke between one judge and lawyers
with him on the circuit[1] no trace appears of the prohibition
against profanity; no trace of fines imposed for drunkenness
(could it be otherwise when failure of a taverner to keep "ordinary
liquors of a good and salutary quality" was cause for summary
revocation of his license?);[2] nor of fines for tavern sales of
liquor to slaves and bond servants; nor of fines imposed, or contracts voided, for gaming in any of the forms—of cards, dice,
"bullet playing," shovel-board, "bowls," cock-fighting, horse-rac-
ing, etc.—elaborately interdicted by the statutes. Though undoubtedly gouging and like incidents of frontier fighting were
common, and though civil actions for batteries (how trivial or
how serious cannot, of course, be distinguished through the con-
ventional verbiage of a trespass declaration) are common, and
prosecutions for the same are fairly illustrated in the records,[3]
no prosecution was ever made under the mayhem statute. Private
lotteries were outlawed from 1795 onward; but the act creating
Vincennes University provided for the raising of money by a
public lottery.[4] Billiard playing, a vice which curiously enough

[1] *Post,* 367; Pease, *Laws* (*I. H. C.,* 17), 21; Smith, *Early Indiana
Trials,* 53-54.
[2] Law of 1792, Pease, *op. cit.,* 64.
[3] The mayhem law of 1798—Pease, *Laws* (*I. H. C.,* 17), 296—was
taken, most appropriately, from Kentucky.
[4] *Post,* 183, § 15 (Nov. 29, 1806), 538. On the University see *Annals,*
7 Congress, 1 session, 497 (Feb. 12, 1802), 949-950 (petition from Wayne
County) ; *Annals,* 10 Congress, 1 session, 1206-1208 (House report, Dec. 17,
1807), or *Amer. State Papers: Misc.,* 1: 654. On the Vincennes Library
Company see *post,* 202 (Dec. 3, 1806), 547. An attempt to exercise the
lottery privileges conferred upon the University by the act of 1807 was
made in 1879; but—the Supreme Court of the United States having held
in Stone *v.* Mississippi, 101 U. S. 814, that a constitutional abrogation of

J. F. Snyder, *Adam W. Snyder and His Period in Illinois History, 1817-
1842,* p. 323.

laid hold upon denizens of Vincennes as far back as 1778, was at once banned as a gambling device and lucratively taxed.[1]

Taverns were as essential, for safety and regalement along the wilderness traces, as the medieval inn on the king's highway; so much so that the Vincennes convention petitioned for federal aid to them.[2] The statutes elaborately regulated them. From the beginning it was required that licensees be recommended by the county court, and by a later law they were bonded to observe all regulations. Yet it is a fact that men who were repeatedly indicted for violations of these were as repeatedly again recommended and relicensed.[3] Invalidation of credits beyond a trivial sum,[4] prohibition of sales to minors, Indians, servants, "bond-servant or slave,"[5] were other attempts at social control. Rates were established by the county court.[6]

More significant than the statutes that consciously expressed moralistic ideals are those which unconsciously embodied the habits and accepted standards of the time with regard to the family, the dependent, the stranger, the ignorant, the poor and weak and unfortunate. One rises from a study of the statute-book somewhat surprised that the supposed liberative and regenerative influence

[1] Dunn, *Indiana,* 109. The law of 1799—Pease, *Laws* (*I. H. C.,* 17), 380—forbade any to continue after May 1, 1802. The territorial tax law of 1807, *post,* 601-602 (§ 34-36), taxed each table $50 annually; as much as one hundred horses or fifty slaves. This is apparently another instance of a statute of 1799 which was not regarded as in force in Indiana Territory—*ante,* ciii, n. 1.

[2] Adverse report in *Annals,* 8 Congress, 1 session, 1023 (H. R. Feb. 17, 1804).

[3] Pease, *Laws* (*I. H. C.,* 17), 63 (of 1792), 193 (1795); *post,* 114, § 1 (1805), 284 (1807); *post,* clxxx, n. 1; clxxxi, n. 1.

[4] This provision of the laws of 1792 ($2—Pease, *op. cit.,* 66) and 1795 (*ibid.,* 196) was repealed in 1805 (*post,* 115, § 5).

[5] These prohibitions dated from 1795—Pease, *Laws* (*I. H. C.,* 17), 195, 196; *post,* 286-287, §§ 7-8 (1807).

[6] *Ante,* cxviii. Randolph rates set in November 1806 were: breakfast, 25 cents; dinner, 33⅓; supper, 25; lodging, 6; horse at hay 24 hours, 12½; whiskey per half-pint, 12½; brandy ditto, 37½; taffia (Monongahela whiskey), 25. *Court Record 1802-06,* 109. The rates set in June 1803 were somewhat lower—*ibid.,* 24. The St. Clair rates were about the same— *Orphans' Court,* 47B ("bedding," 12½).

lottery privileges was not an impairment of contracts within the prohibition of the Federal constitution—it was held that the Indiana constitution of 1851 (Thorpe, *Federal and State Constitutions,* 2: 1091) had abrogated the territorial statute. See State *v.* Woodwan, 89 Ind. 110.

of the frontier seems totally lacking, and that the legislators, with the statutes of all the older states to choose from, should have done no better. The statutes are typical of the time.

Few states could match in 1805 the law permitting aliens to purchase and hold realty.[1]

Bachelors were, as has been seen, subjected to a county tax;[2] possibly because they were a factor of disorder, but more probably out of regard for family life. In any event the Randolph Court thought the penalty severe, for it violated the statute outright by making the tax half the minimum set by the legislature. The fundamental safeguards over marriage banns, parental consent for minors, civil or ecclesiastical celebration, and registration of certificates were established in 1788, and aside from alterations of the provisions concerning licenses the Northwestern statutes were left unaltered.[3] In 1803, however, a startling law was passed "to prevent forcible and stolen marriages." The vindicatory statement that "women, as well maidens as widows, and wives having substances . . ., for the lucre of such substances, have been oftentimes taken by misdoers, contrary to their will; and afterwards married to such misdoers, or to others by their consent, or defiled," is suggestive of a state of society vastly worse, doubtless, than the reality. It is impossible to believe that such conditions characterized our territorial society; rather, we must assume that the statute was responsive to sporadic abuses. In fact the law was taken bodily from Virginia, whose law in turn goes back to one of 3 Henry VII. Bigamy, by the same act, was made a felony.[4] No prosecutions under the statute appear in Randolph

---

[1] *Post,* 94, 500.

[2] *Ante,* cxviii, n. 4. The tax was remitted to Andrew Barbau, as he proved property taxed in the name of his father, the judge—Randolph *Court Record 1802-06,* 43 (December 17, 1803).

[3] Pease, *Laws* (*I. H. C.,* 17), 22, 88, 330; *post,* 205, 251. The marriage certificate records of Randolph and St. Clair have for the most part disappeared; some original certificates remain in Chester, Miscellanies Box. On dower the law of 1795 stood until embodied in the Revision of 1807—Pease, *op. cit.,* 244; *post,* 306-307.

[4] *Post,* 66; further, to "take any woman, so against her will unlawfully . . . and the procuring and abetting to the same and also receiving wittingly the same woman so taken" was made a felony. The meaning of this is not beyond doubt. Section 3 covers abduction; 4, abduction and rape; 2, possibly to rape alone. Section 1 was taken from a Virginia statute

or St. Clair. Nothing in the Ordinance or in the statutes on wills denies married women the power to devise their lands, but it has been stated that in fact the right was denied.[1] Separate examination of the wife in acknowledgments of joint conveyances by husband and wife was law from 1795 onward.[2]

A divorce law adopted in 1795 from Massachusetts had allowed absolute divorce for attempted bigamy (annulment), impotence, or adultery; and separation from bed and board for extreme cruelty. This act assumed throughout a chancery procedure, though no court of equity existed. It also optimistically required service by publication, when defendant was out of the county of suit or the territory, "in one of the Territorial News Papers." Only the General Court and circuit courts had jurisdiction. The act was repealed in 1801, then reëstablished in 1803—prophetically—"until the end of the first session of the general assembly of the Indiana Territory." The first Assembly did no more than restrict publication to cases of respondents absent from the territory.[3] Governor Harrison attempted, in his message to the Assembly of 1807, to prevent the inclusion of the statute in the revised laws,[4] but it was nevertheless adopted.[5] No records of divorces before this date, in the Illinois counties, seem to exist; but some of later date do. A legislative divorce appears in the present volume.[6]

---

[1] Judge W. L. Gross says so, Ill. State Bar Assoc. *Proc.* (1881), 75. The writer has not yet examined the probate records. If Judge Gross is correct such denial was an outright violation of the Ordinance—Pease, *Laws* (*I. H. C.,* 17), 123.

[2] Pease, *op. cit.,* 242; *post,* 292, § 11.

[3] Pease, *Laws* (*I. H. C.,* 17), 258; *post,* 15 (January 26, 1801), 65 (September 26, 1803), 107.

[4] *Messages,* 1: 232. He favored reservation to the legislature, exclusively, of power to grant divorces.

[5] *Post,* 323.

[6] Belleville Museum, Francois Arenousse (undated, probably late 1808 or 1809, since John Rice Jones was his attorney); Gilbreath, Atchison (undated, but of the same circuit term). No divorce bills were discovered in Randolph. Brink, McDonough, *Hist. of St. Clair County,* 83, gives instances of 1811, 1817. *Post,* 648, for a legislative divorce.

---

of December 8, 1788, Hening, *Statutes,* 12: 691 (reproduced almost verbatim); sections 2-4 are a reproduction of a statute of November 19, 1789, Hening, *Statutes,* 13: 7. The wording of the Virginia statute copies that of 3 Hen. VII Cap. 2.

All the statutes for the protection of the Indians against the ruin of liquor were idle words, and even as such they are not particularly creditable.[1]

The statutory provisions protecting minors, the poor, and the mentally incompetent were in theory good enough. The Northwestern statutes relating to guardians, minors, and orphans were left unaltered.[2] What really happened may better be judged from the record of the Orphans' Court of St. Clair:

> July, 1807—"Ordered that the Insane Boy (Lemay) be put in the hands of J. F. Perrey"—a member of the Court— "for boarding and clothing—for the same sum as last year —beginning last March."
>
> March, 1808—"The Insane Boy Lemay was cried down to Francois Turcotte for sixty-nine dollars for one year from that date."
>
> Nov., 1808—"Ordered that the Overseers of the Poor of Eagle Township do give out to the lowest bidder the keeping of one McNeal a pauper now sick in the care of John Scott, untill our next March term—proviso that he do getted better before that time. The purchaser to begin on the day the said pauper came to the said J. Scott's 'house.' "[3]

Of course the statutes required bonds and accountings. It is true that the court was only "empowered" to name guardians

---

[1] Jefferson's fine but unattainable humanism appears in a letter to Harrison, in the latter's *Messages*, 1: 69-73. Harrison's attitude also does him some credit—*ibid.*, 199-200. A statute of 1790—Pease, *Laws* (*I. H. C.*, 17), 26—a good beginning, was repealed in 1795 (*ibid.*, 256); in 1799 protection was given to Indian towns only (*ibid.*, 415). Harrison and the judges did nothing. The Assembly, in 1805, empowered the Governor to establish prohibition during treaty meetings (*post*, 91); another, of 1806, established prohibition for forty miles around Vincennes (*post*, 216). The Revision of 1807 retained only the first of these acts. *Post*, 497. In 1805 a general and stringent law was passed to go into effect when like statutes should be passed, by the states of Ohio and Kentucky and the territories of Louisiana and Michigan (*post*, 97). This was also embodied in the Revision of 1807. Proclamations by Harrison, before the empowering act of 1805; Gibson, *Exec. Journal*, 102, 103, 112-113; *Messages*, 1: 31, 32, 59-60.

[2] An act of 1792 protected even prodigal minors—Pease, *Laws* (*I. H. C.*, 17), 92, § 6. This was omitted in the act of 1795 (*ibid.*, 181). This second act (§ 7) authorized the Orphans' Court, at the request of guardians, to bind minors out as apprentices.

[3] St. Clair, *Orphans' Court*, 35, 41, 46.

for lunatics and minors (but also the judges of Quarter Sessions were merely "empowered" to hold an Orphans' Court) : they sometimes acted under the law for the relief of "poor, old, blind, impotent and lame persons"[1] which permitted the farming out of paupers "at public vendue, or out-cry"; but wards were perhaps usually indentured.[2]

Gamesters, wife deserters, and "other idle, vagrant and dissolute persons, rambling about without any visible means of subsistence," must be apprenticed if minors, hired out if adults (earnings going to creditors, then to family) ; but if nobody would hire—though only for food and clothing during "his servitude," he must be lashed.[3] Notwithstanding that all justices, sheriffs, constables, and grand juries were commanded to be zealous in enforcing this law it does not appear that any vagrants were discovered.

Imprisonment for debt existed from the beginning under the laws of the Northwest Territory. Debtors occupied, indeed, an apartment in the jail separate from that for other prisoners, but they received bread and water alone, and for that became indebted

---

[1] The law of 1795—Pease, *Laws* (*I. H. C.*, 17), 216—provided for a poor rate, assessable by the township overseers, and for poor houses; though also permitting (§ 5) the contracting out of any or all their wards. The law of 1799 (*ibid.*, 510) substituted the system of farming out. The two are embodied in the Revision of 1807 (*post*, 308) with no great change except in greatly elaborating the provisions regulating the overseers' records, certificates and accounts. Apparently no trace of these remains for either St. Clair or Randolph. In both of these counties French citizens are prominent—indeed greatly predominant among the overseers appointed. It is quite impossible to suppose that the extremely elaborate provisions of the statute regarding pauper settlements were living law.

[2] Bateman and Selby, *Hist. of St. Clair County*, 2 : 699, quotes a Cahokia indenture (undated) binding out "a poor child, named Philis, aged six years, with Joseph Buelle, for twelve years from this date; to learn the arts, trade and mystery of a spinster." In the St. Clair *Orphans' Court 1797-1809*, 19 (March, 1803) is an indenture of three orphans, one to Shadrach Bond. In the Chester Miscellanies Box is an indenture of two boys, by Nathaniel Hull, chairman of the Randolph Orphans' Court, to his fellow judge John Beaird. In the *County Court Record, 1810* (Ill. Territory), 5 (March 6, 1810), it is "Ordered that John Grosvenor be allowed the sum of twenty eight dollars for keeping Branham a Blind man four months previous to the April Court of Common pleas in the year 1808 in conformity to an order of the said court"—which order is not recorded. Other allowances, pp. 22, 47.

[3] *Post*, 566. This is one of the very few original statutes of the 1807 Revision. Similarly, *post*, cxxxiii, n. 2.

to the sheriff (this was not true of "the expense of furnishing meat, drink and fire-wood to a prisoner in jail for a crime"!— such as murder)—who might jail them again for nonpayment. Indeed imprisonment was originally a positive requirement, even for debts under five dollars, collectible before a single justice with final jurisdiction and on allegations of a creditor alone; but Governor St. Clair induced his fellow judges so to change the law as not to compel a humane creditor to take advantage of it. All these statutes continued law throughout the Indiana Territory period. The harshness of the early statutes was mitigated by the first Assembly of the older territory, which introduced a usury act and a bankruptcy discharge (though judgments remained in force against property later acquired) ; and also by allowing the prisoners the liberty of prison bounds, by day only, under bond.[1] These two statutes were substantially reënacted, with slight ameliorations, by the first Assembly of Indiana Territory[2]—again the governor and judges had done nothing.

The Pennsylvania constitution of 1776, first in this country, pronounced for the abolishment of imprisonment for debt, but the declaration was evidently long a dead letter. The gross disparity between judgment sum—for tort or debt—and the costs added by legal procedure (often added in a revengeful spirit, especially when the creditor split a larger claim into smaller claims that gave him the advantage of the summary procedure of a justice's court) was characteristic of conditions throughout the country. In some ways conditions in Indiana Territory were, after 1795, very much less harsh than in the older communities of the east; for by a statute passed in that year it was provided that imprisonment

[1] Single-justice courts for small causes were created in 1788—Pease, *Laws* (*I. H. C.*, 17), 8; and the statutes of 1792, though not directly enacting imprisonment for debt, assumed it with reference even to debts collected in these courts—*ibid.*, 77-78 (separate room), 83 (food—cp. §§ 9 and 10; of course other prisoners, able to do so, could buy better fare), 98 (form of final execution). For proceedings for debts under $5, *ibid.*, 143-144; the change—*St. Clair Papers*, 2: 366; Pease, *op. cit.*, 286. Duration of imprisonment, *ibid.*, 286 (1795). Usury law, *ibid.*, 352 (*post*, 347—Revision of 1807) ; bankruptcy statute, Pease, *op. cit.*, 448; prison bounds, 494.

[2] *Post*, 99. It saved to the prisoner "his or her necessary apparel and utensils of trade," and gave the freedom of the prison bounds by night. It was taken into the Revision without this last generosity—*post*, 502.

should not extend beyond the second day of the next session of the court unless the plaintiff should show that the defendant was concealing assets. This was a law truly remarkable for its time. Nevertheless, if guilty of hiding assets, and those found were insufficient to satisfy the creditor, the debtor was required to make satisfaction "by personal and reasonable servitude"; and—with some concessions to age and to men with families—this might extend to seven years. However, no matter what the statute-book permitted, the practical nonexistence of jails must have involved substantial abolishment of imprisonment. The generous spirit expressed by Pennsylvania in her Revolutionary constitution gradually spread, and debtors' prisons disappeared under the influence of Jeffersonian and Jacksonian democracy. From a few records remaining of very humble creditors who "scheduled out" under the bankruptcy law one infers that it must have been freely applied.[1]

The first legislature (1805) also passed an act on exoneration of sureties which, naturally, is still (in part) embodied in the statute-book of Illinois. The Revisers added an attachment statute against absconding debtors.[2]

The slavery statutes of the territory cannot be understood apart from the social legislation that accompanied them. All were part of a state of mind now disappeared. A thief who could not restore the value of the thing stolen and pay the fine set by law was lashed, and could be sold to labor for not exceeding seven years to "any suitable person" who would discharge the sentence.[3] A defendant convicted under the mayhem law (1798) was imprisoned and fined, and for want of means to pay was "sold to service . . . for any time not exceeding five years the purchaser finding him food and raiment during the term." The debtor who had no estate was bound to "make satisfaction, by personal and reasonable servitude." The vagrant was similarly sold to

[1] Two were found in the St. Clair records; that of Benj. Hagerman, Belleville Museum; of François Paillet, *Orphans' Court*, 42 (June, 1808). Brink, McDonough, *Hist. of St. Clair County*, 70 gives another example of 1801 (Baptiste Mercier). The Randolph records seem to be gone.
[2] *Post*, 120, 517, 555.
[3] Pease, *Laws* (*I. H. C.*, 17), 18, law of September 6, 1788.

labor, and apprentices and indentured servants—as will be seen—performed service much on the same terms. The road acts contained language of compulsion, and at best a defaulter could not escape imprisonment for debt.[1] From 1788 onward imprisonment was the penalty for disobedience by servants or children, and whipping the penalty for striking a master or a parent.[2] The revised statutes of 1807 introduced the general provision that any person convicted of any crime punishable by fine—and this included mayhem, bigamy after 1807, sodomy, larceny (except of horses), obtaining goods by false pretenses, altering brands, misbranding, perjury, forgery, and assault and battery—might be "sold or hired" to anybody paying the fine and costs for any term judged reasonable by the court.[3] The jail, the lash, and compulsory labor, far from being confined to the criminal law, were part and parcel of family government, of township government, and even of the law's charity for the weak and poor. The social conscience—though perhaps no more in Indiana Territory than in Virginia or Massachusetts—was calloused by ideas of class and force.

While the fruitless efforts, already detailed, were being made in Congress to secure the legalization of slave immigration, the proslavery party had turned with greater success to the territorial legislature. It did what was possible to legalize slavery. Some of the antislavery members of the Assembly must have joined in adopting what they regarded as compromise measures. And only one private petition seems to have been made against these extraordinary statutes.[4]

[1] *Ante,* cxxvi, n. 3. By the acts of 1792 and 1799—Pease, *Laws* (*I. H. C.,* 17), 76, § 6 and 458, § 10—the recalcitrant or idle forfeited a fixed sum daily to the supervisor, recoverable before a justice of the peace; *ante,* cxxxii, n. 1. The same (1799, § 14) for asking money or drink or other reward of any passerby! The act of 1805 authorized the supervisor to "compel" men to work (*post,* 108, § 1); which could have been interpreted to mean by subjecting them to the danger of imprisonment for debt upon such forfeitures, but the revisers omitted it from the law of 1807 (*post,* 427). Persons might also, by authority of law, be committed to the supervisors for labor on the roads, in which case, the labor "being performed," they should be "discharged" (1799, § 30; 1807, *post,* 438, § 23).

[2] Pease, *op. cit.,* 20, law of September 6, 1788.

[3] *Post,* 250.

[4] In 1807, from Dearborn County (presented to Congress in January, 1808). *Annals,* 10 Congress, 1 session, 1331. This is, of course, aside from

A law of 1803 "concerning servants," borrowed from Virginia,—a law which in fact referred only to black servants—was the first of the "black laws" of Indiana (and by later adoption of Illinois) Territory. This law provided that negroes and mulattoes —"and other persons not being citizens of the United States"!— who should "come" into the territory "under contract" to serve "in any trade or occupation" should "be compelled to perform such contract specifically during the term thereof." A second act, of 1805, dealt with white apprenticeship, which had existed under the legislation of the Northwest Territory.[1] Similarly to the servant act, this provided that apprentices, bound of their own will or by their guardians (to serve, if males, until twenty-one, and if females until eighteen) "shall serve accordingly." Another act of 1805 authorized the master to "hold . . . to service and labour" his registered servant, and declared that the latter "shall serve."[2] It was not until 1821, in Indiana, that the Supreme Court found occasion to make the self-evident holding that such a contract could not be specifically enforced.[3] Meanwhile extralegal enforcement doubtless almost always sufficed; yet at least as regards a white indentured servant, an Illinois court assumed to order

[1] The highway law of 1792—Pease, *Laws* (*I. H. C.*, 17), 76—refers to apprentices. The statutes of 1795 regulating poor relief and orphans' courts authorized indenturing in particular cases. In general, such service must have been treated as existing under the common law. *Post*, 42, § 1 (September 22, 1803) ; 95, § 1 (August 15, 1805) ; 500 (reënactment in 1807).

[2] *Post*, 136 (August 26, 1805), §§ 2, 5, 6; 523 (reënactment in 1807).

[3] *Case of Mary Clark* (1821), 1 Blackf. 122; specific performance asked of an indenture for 20 years entered into in 1816. Application was made for discharge under a writ of habeas corpus. This sufficiently proved the service to be involuntary; and the constitution of 1816 prohibited involuntary servitude. The court might therefore have rested its holding on this ground—as in later cases under the 13th amendment of the federal constitution. It held also, however, that even if considered as a contract voluntarily made, "neither the common law nor the statutes in force in this state recognize the coercion of a specific performance of contracts." This loose statement necessarily had to be restricted later, as the equitable jurisdiction developed. The general question was a relatively novel one in 1821. In 1808 a writ of habeas corpus sued out by a mulatto girl was dismissed by the General Court of the Territory—Hannah *v.* Benj. Beckes, Jr., *Order Book,* 281, 290, September 12-13, 1808.

the disingenuous and purely political attack upon Harrison for favoring these acts made by his Illinois opponents in 1808, various of them slaveholders, and many, undoubtedly, of proslavery sentiments. See *ante*, xlviii.

performance—and without the legal basis which, in the case of
negroes and mulattoes, was later afforded by the constitution of
1818.[1]

The law of 1803 made void all other contracts between master
and servant during the term of service; made the benefit of the
"contract" assignable by a master if the servant should "freely
consent" thereto in the presence of any justice of the peace; and
made it pass to legatees and personal representatives.[2]

Under the first act of 1805, complaints by either party might
be made to "some Justice of the Peace, unconnected with either
of the parties within the county" (certainly none such could have
been found in Randolph or St. Clair), who should discharge the
apprentice or administer "due correction" according to the equities
—with an appeal to the Common Pleas. This statute was taken
over unaltered into the Revision of 1807. The second act of 1805,
dealing with the introduction of negroes and mulattoes provided
that such, being under fifteen years of age and "owing service"

[1] St. Clair, *Orphans' Court 1797-1809*, 14 (June, 1801); "Ordered
that Mr. Baptiste Saucier inquire if Miss Baudré was right in leaving Mrs.
Pinconneaus, if so, for Mrs. Pinconneaus to return her cloaths, if not, the
girl to return." The later territorial act of September 17, 1807 (*post*,
cxxxviii, n. 2) was adopted for the Illinois Territory June 13, 1809.
It contained no express provision for specific performance, but only the
general language of the second act of 1805. The Constitution of December
3, 1818, prohibited slavery and "involuntary servitude," but it provided
that: "Each and every person . . . bound to service by contract or
indenture in virtue of the laws of the Illinois Territory heretofore existing,
and in conformity to the provisions of the same, without fraud or collusion,
shall be held to a specific performance of their contracts or indentures;
and such negroes and mulattoes as have been registered in conformity with
the aforesaid laws shall serve out the time appointed by said laws: *Provided,
however*, That the children hereafter born of such person, negroes, or
mulattoes, shall become free, the males at the age of twenty-one years, the
females at the age of eighteen years." Under this constitutional provision
specific performance of indentures was enforced Nance *v.* Howard, 1. Ill.
242; Phoebe *v.* Jay, *ibid.*, 268; Boon *v.* Juliet, 2, Ill. 258; Choisser *v.* Hargrave, *ibid.*, 317; Sarah *v.* Borders, 5 Ill. 341.

[2] Act of September 22, 1803, *post*, 42. No appeal by a servant to the
court was found in the St. Clair or Randolph records—who would make
the motion (§§ 5, 7)? The provisions for the whipping of lazy and disorderly servants, as pointed out in the text, merit no special comment if
regarded in the setting of their time. And the phraseology of the provisions that under laws fining "free persons" servants should be whipped,
and that at the end of his term a servant should receive a certificate of
"freedom," has been overemphasized by laymen unacquainted with the ageold phraseology of indentures.

as slaves in other states or territories might be brought into the territory and there held to labor until thirty-five if males or thirty-two if females. If over fifteen their "owner or possessor" must take them before the clerk of Common Pleas, register them, and there "agree" with them upon the term of years that their service should continue; giving bond that they should not, after expiration of such term, become public charges. The master might remove them from the territory, and must do so (or forfeit all his rights over them) should they refuse to bind themselves to service! Heavy penalties were laid upon persons kidnapping and removing from the territories negroes bound to others. The children of "a parent" so bound were themselves bound to serve the master of the parent, with the same protection against ill-usage as was given to apprentices under the first act of 1805, above referred to. But there was no similar provision for the protection of those, under or over fifteen years of age, who immigrated into the territory. This act was altered scarcely at all in the Revision of 1807.[1]

These two acts of 1805 were passed by the first session of the first legislature. The second session added a fourth act "concerning Slaves and Servants" (of color) which contained characteristic slave-code provisions for punishing the unauthorized wandering of slaves from home, their assembling, and the harboring of them. These were made more stringent by a fifth act of the second legislature in 1808.[2] Such provisions are intelligible in states of the lower south, with great populations of blacks, but were mere imitations, quite unresponsive to local conditions, in a territory which in 1800, according to the census, contained only 135 slaves, and in 1810 contained 168 (and 613 free persons, other than whites and untaxed Indians, who must have been mainly blacks).[3] The General Assembly in a proslavery memorial addressed to Congress in the very month in which they passed the fourth statute solemnly argued that slavery could never be a

---

[1] *Post,* 95, 136 (1805), 523 (1807).

[2] *Post,* 203 (December 3, 1806) ; 657 (October 25, 1808).

[3] Dunn, (*Indiana,* 296) estimated the slaves in 1800 as 175, five-sixths in Randolph, and the free negroes at 123. See *ante,* xiii, n. 2.

danger in the territory.[1] The fourth act and the first were consolidated by the revisers of 1807 into one act "concerning Servants."[2]

"The law of the Territory entitled an act concerning the introduction of negroes and mulattoes into the Territory,"—wrote General Washington Johnston in his legislative report of 1808—"makes it lawful for an holder of slaves to bring them into the Territory and to keep them therein during sixty days, during which period the negroe is offered the alternative of either signing an indenture by which he binds himself for a numbr of years, or of being sent to a slave state or Territory there to be sold. The natural inference from this statement forces itself upon the mind that the slave thus circumstanced is held in involuntary servitude, and that the law permitting such proceedings is contrary both to the spirit and letter of the ordinance and that therefore it is unconstitutional—your committee might add that the most flagitous abuse is made of that law; that negroes brought here are commonly forced to bind themselves for a number of years reaching or extending the natural term of their lives, so that the condition of those unfortunate persons is not only involuntary servitude but downright slavery—it is perhaps unnecessary to advert to the novel circumstances of a person under extreme duress of a slave becoming a party to a contract, parting with himself and receiving nothing." It has already been noted that some of the greatest slave owners of the territory themselves characterized the law as one "for the Establishment of disguised slavery."[3] The Ordinance of 1787 declared that there should be "neither slavery nor involuntary servitude" in the Northwest; the thirteenth amendment to the federal constitution later adopted the same terminology; the modern cases under that amendment denying specific performance of contracts to do manual labor—like those (already cited)[4]

[1] *Amer. State Papers: Misc.*, 1: 467.
[2] September 17, 1807, *post,* 463; combining the laws of 1803 and 1806 cited *ante,* cxxxv, n. 1 and cxxxvii, n. 2.
[3] December 17, 1808—Ind. Hist. Soc. *Pub.*, 2: 522-523; *ante,* xlviii. Compare Buck, *Illinois in 1818,* 140; Howe, in Ind. Hist. Soc. *Pub.*, 2: 20, 29; Goebel, *Harrison,* 77, 81; Dunn, *Indiana,* 315.
[4] *Ante,* cxxxv, n. 3; cxxxvi, n. 1. Early cases holding "slavery" illegal after the adoption of the Ordinance, see *ante,* xxxvi, n. 1.

decided under the Ordinance—have never attempted to distinguish between "slavery" and "involuntary servitude." To stress the point seems foolishly superfluous; yet the existence of slavery in Indiana Territory has been denied by casuists.[1]

These statutes did not require free blacks to register and secure passes, but such was probably at this time the practice—as it was later; for otherwise—in the words of Blackstone's jejune definition of liberty—they could have enjoyed no freedom of motion and locomotion whatever. They sometimes appeared by their next friends in litigation.[2]

Various indentures of white servants still exist in the records of St. Clair and Randolph counties. They follow the prescriptions of the statutes, and save for their oddity have little interest. Sometimes they paint a picture of the local magistrates. For example:[3]

[1] In an article by Mr. Esarey upon unsolved problems of early Indiana history we find the following: "Slavery never existed in Indiana. The term is not used in American history except in the legal sense. It is sharply defined from all phases of indenture. The latter condition was generally in use in the states in 1800 and recognized by the codes of most of the states. The Ordinance of 1787 is older than Indiana either as a territory or state. It is an unfortunate mistake to represent even in a title"—referring to Dunn's *Indiana: a Redemption from Slavery*—"that Indiana was redeemed from what never existed. The only way to open Indiana either as territory or state to slavery was by a law of congress, by constitutional provision or by judicial decision. None of these was ever done. Colored persons remained with masters in both territory and state of Indiana, some for love of their masters, some for fear of kidnapping and others because it was the safest way to procure a living. Colored persons had few if any legal rights in Indiana which they could enforce." (*Ind. Hist. Bulletin,* February 1924, p. 57). This naïve argument is Mr. Esarey's answer to "special pleading on the slavery question." In confirmation of the last lines, however, there are apparently "instances of colored men selling themselves to masters" in St. Clair County in 1794—that is before any indenture acts were passed; see Brink, McDonough, *Hist. of St. Clair County,* 88. And Governor Reynolds says: "Although this proceeding"—i. e. introduction of the indenture system—"was intended by the legislature to introduce a species of slavery, yet I knew many slaves and their families who were manumitted by the operation, and are now free. This act of the legislature operated as a kind of gradual emancipation of slavery in the Territory"—*My Own Times,* 133. Governor Ford says: "Such slaves"—those registered—"were then called indentured and registered servants; the French negroes were called slaves"—*History,* 32. See *ante,* xxxvi, n. 1.

[2] John, a free negro, by John Edgar his next friend, sued Robert Patton for assault in the Randolph County Court, October 1809. Chester Miscellanies Box. On the treatment of free blacks, from 1800 onward, in Ohio and elsewhere see F. N. Thorpe, *A Constitutional History of the American People,* 1: ch. 12 (especially 360 *et seq.* and 375); 2: 326-327 n., 404, 447-448.

[3] 1808, Belleville Museum.

"Indeana   (this indenter witnesseth that on
S^te   County   (the 9th Day of June 1808 Isaak Gilham
and James Cirkpetrick two of the overseers of the poor hath put
John Henderson Soposed to be 14 years oald, in the County of
St Clere Goshen township and by these presence Doth bind the
S^d John Henderson a prentis to James Downing of S^d County
to Larn the art of farming and after the manner of anaprentis
to Serve him from the Day and Date hereof for and During the
whoale terme of time untill he arives to the age of one and twenty
During all which time he the S^d aprentis his master shall feath-
fully Serve his Secrets keep his Lawfully comand Gladly obey he
shlal Do No Damage to his S^d master. Nor Se it Dun by others
without Letting his master know he Shall. Not Sell his S^d
masters Goods. Nor lend them without his Leve he shall Not
Comit any misdemener Nor by nor Sell without his Leve he Shall
Not absent him Self Day nor Night without Leve he Shall Not
Contract marrag Nor Comit furnecation but in all things beheve
him Self. Asafethfull aprentis ought to Do. During the S^d term—
And he the S^d master Doth oblegate him Self to give the S^d
apprentis one yares Scooling if S^d apprentis Can be Conformed
to the Rueels of the Scool and instruct the S^d aprentis in the art
of farming and provid Sefisent meet Drink aperrell lodging and
washing and a Soot on and a Soot of at the End of S^d term—
And for all and Every porformence of the S^d Covenant we asign
our hand^s ad Seels in presents of D White one of the Acting
Justis of S^d County

          "Isaak Gilham (seel)
          "James Kirkpatrick (seel)
          "James Jones (seel)   "

The St. Clair records under the act of 1805 show the registration of various colored boys and girls of sixteen to eighteen
years of age who "agreed" to terms of eighteen to forty-seven
years. The average term for three registered by Shadrach Bond
Jr. was twenty-one years.[1] To permit the continued introduction

[1] The examples are from the period 1805 to 1809. In addition he
registered one boy of 13 years. There is one free woman, aged 23, who
bound herself for 12 years. Various bonds to the territory still exist at
Chester and at Belleville.

into the territory of slaves under the guise of indentured servants was a subterfuge so bold and transparent that—once it was seen to go unchallenged—we may confidently assume that slaves whose term of "contract" bondage had expired were not always released and furnished with their certificates of freedom.[1] The very record book of the St. Clair Court was labeled "indentured slaves." In a bond given to Governor Harrison by John Beaird, a judge of the Randolph Common Pleas, the condition stated was that Beaird should indemnify county and territory against all charges for the support of his mulatto boy Berry after the expiration of the term for which he was bound "as a slave."[2] Bills of sale of negroes, with warranty of title, were recorded in the records of the courts.[3] Sheriffs were authorized by statute to collect fees by distraint upon "slaves, or goods and chattles";[4] taxes were levied upon each "bond servant and slave"; the "time" due from indentured blacks was subject to execution and sale.[5] Trover was brought in Randolph for a negro woman.[6] Negroes, mulattoes and Indians were not permitted to testify except in federal indictments against, or in civil pleas the parties to which were exclusively, persons of one or other of those classes.[7]

One or two cases that got into the courts[8] caused much excitement. In 1794 two negroes held by Judge Vander Burgh as slaves, but who in Judge Turner's opinion were "free by the

[1] McDonough, *Hist. of Randolph, Monroe and Perry Counties,* 109, gives an example of a servant indentured to John Edgar in 1794 for eleven years whose certificate was granted in 1819.

[2] Chester, Miscellanies Box, bond of September 20, 1807 (with William Morrison).

[3] E. g. by James Jordan to George Belsha, December 14, 1804, *loc. cit.*

[4] *Post,* 61 (§ 27 of law of September 24, 1803) ; see also *post,* 478, § 29 ; 542.

[5] *Post,* 73, § 9 (November 5, 1803). *Post,* 189, § 7 (November 26, 1806), 541, § 7 (Revision of 1807).

[6] Chester, Miscellanies Box, docket papers of 1809. I cannot state the outcome of the case, but the chances are very heavy that plaintiff succeeded.

[7] *Post,* 40, § 21 (1803).

[8] Cockrum, *Pioneer History of Indiana,* 131-132, states that "the questions that came principally before the courts . . . were land speculation, the adjustment and settling of land titles and the perplexing question of slavery," and that the last "was one of the most stubbornly contested questions before the courts." Hardly a trace of the three questions appears in the judicial records up to 1810.

Constitution of the Territory," applied to the latter for a writ of habeas corpus, but—again according to Judge Turner—were seized and forcibly abducted by persons in the employ of Judge Vander Burgh. This was one time Governor St. Clair, whose interpretation of the Ordinance did not accord with that of Judge Turner, gave him no encouragement, and the matter was dropped.[1] Judge Symmes, when on circuit in the Illinois country in 1798, held that a former slave and his wife, brought into the territory by their master, were citizens of the United States, entitled "to enjoy all and every privilege and franchise with relation to their personal liberty and protection of property, unmolested, subject only to the laws of the land. And all persons are hereby"—his judgment ran —"advised and forewarned not to invade or annoy the entire freedom of the said Guy and Abigail, *which by this record is absolute.*"[2] The influence of such a case is not to be forgotten in connection with the slavery petitions and agitation already discussed. Another and more sensational case was that of United States *v.* Simon Vannorsdall, which in its varied aspects runs through the record of the General Court for more than four years. It involved the question whether George and Peggy, colored, were fugitives from service within the meaning of the federal fugitive slave act of 1793;[3] and unfortunately the issue turned in part upon the sufficiency of proof of a foreign record. In substance nothing more was decided than the fact that Peggy was not proved to be a fugitive, and therefore Vannorsdall's

[1] Turner wrote to the Governor, June 14, 1794: "I have caused several of the offenders to be apprehended, but others of them were encouraged by Vanderburgh to resist the execution of process, and in one instance this was actually done by drawing a knife upon the sheriff. Such of the offenders, however, as were not taken have since surrendered themselves, and, full of contrition for their misconduct, have amply exposed the machinations of Judge Vanderburgh in this nefarious business"—*St. Clair Papers,* 2: 325-326. For St. Clair's attitude, *ibid.,* 331 (a letter after six months of delay, to Turner) and citations *ante,* xxxvi, n. 1. The negroes were kidnapped pendente lite, and sold into slavery in the south.

[2] McDonough, *Hist. of Randolph, Monroe and Perry Counties,* 107-108. Various important records, seen by the authors of the county histories of St. Clair and Randolph cited in this introduction, are apparently no longer in the archives.

[3] This act, together with the Ordinance of 1787, which commanded the return of fugitive slaves—Pease, *Laws (I. H. C.,* 17), 130—and the Constitution, was printed with the Northwestern laws of 1799 in an edition of 400 copies and distributed among all the counties (*ibid.,* 519, 546).

writ of habeas corpus was dismissed, without prejudice to "the right that Vannorsdall or any other person shall have to the said negro girl Peggy provided he Vannorsdall or any other person can prove said Peggy to be a slave, nor shall this order impair the right of said Peggy to her freedom provided the said Peggy shall establish her right to the same." She was permitted to sue Vannorsdall in forma pauperis, with time to take advice of counsel and summon witnesses; and in this suit (represented by Thomas Randolph, attorney-general of the territory) she failed.[1] The interest of the case lies partly in the fact that the judges of the court when the first decision was rendered were Vander Burgh (who had brought slaves with him to the territory)[2] and Davis, a Virginian, Benjamin Parke being also a member of the court when the second case was decided; and partly in the circumstance that the negroes were for a time in the custody of Governor Harrison.

More numerous and more intricately wrought than any others in this volume are the statutes regulating courts.[3] At the head of the judicial system was the General Court, which met twice yearly. Its judges were, of course, appointed by the President— to serve during good behavior; and its writs ran in the name of the United States. It could be held by any two judges, and had both original and appellate jurisdiction, with power to issue writs of habeas corpus, certiorari, and of error. Its jurisdiction under the last writ was unrestricted, except that this must be brought within five years; but its original jurisdiction and its jurisdiction in cases on appeal were limited in 1806 to causes that might involve more than fifty dollars (omitting the alternative of earlier laws, "or relate to a franchise or freehold"); and so great did the demands on it continue that in 1808 it was provided that no suit should be

[1] General Court, *Order Book*, 1: 203 (April 10, 1806), 290 (September 16, 1808). Dunn gives an abstract of the proceedings and a full discussion—*Indiana*, 237-239. See Cockrum, *Pioneer History*, 133-134. There seems to be little ground for criticism of the court.

[2] Monks, *Courts*, 1: 13.

[3] Of the thirty-eight laws in the Maxwell Code of 1795 thirty dealt primarily with this subject. The statutes in the present volume are mainly revisions or readoptions, but they fill a large part of it. The whole system was of colonial origin; compare, for example, C. L. Raper, *North Carolina. A Study in English Colonial Government*, ch. 7.

removable to it (or other court) after issue joined in the court where such suit was begun. It also had jurisdiction over capital crimes, and (with the circuit courts) exclusive jurisdiction of divorce cases. Finally, it was empowered to punish "contempts, omissions and neglects, favours, corruptions, and defaults" of all judges and judicial-administrative officers of the territory.[1]

Below the General Court were the circuit courts, held in each county by a judge of the former once yearly.[2] Not only was the jurisdiction of the General Court in capital crimes and in divorce exercised largely on the circuit, but "an issue" in a cause pending in the General Court was tried by the circuit judge in the county whence such cause was removed; a final decision being possible only in the General Court. The Revision of 1807 provided that the Circuit Court might order new trials, and should render final judgment and issue execution unless a bill of exceptions should be filed, or some other good cause appear for taking the opinion of the General Court.[3]

[1] Pease, *Laws* (*I. H. C.*, 17), 156-158, §§ 8-12 (1795); 259, § 5 (divorce). *Post*, 3-5, § 5 and 454, § 34 ($50 lower limit); 10-12 §§ 8-12 (Jan. 23, 1801); 215 (Dec. 5, 1806); 551; 662 (Oct. 25, 1808). By this last act the session was restricted to a maximum of twenty days. Appeal to the Supreme Court in cases involving a freehold goes back to § 5 of *post*, 3-4 (1801).

[2] Under the law of 1788 it sat four times yearly, in such places as were judged "most conducive to the general good"; in 1790 an annual session in each county was introduced. Pease, *op. cit.*, 11, (repealed, 255), 35.

[3] *Post*, 10-11, 12, §§ 9, 12; 215, § 1; 230-231, § 2. The "issues" made in the General Court, but triable on circuit, were of fact only; they are erroneously stated in Monks, *Courts*, 1: 27, to have been "both of the fact and law." The law (*post*, 10-11, § 9) did not provide that only one judge should go on circuit in each county, but this was doubtless the invariable practice (and compare *post*, 215, § 1). The circuit courts of Randolph and St. Clair opened on the first and third Mondays in October respectively, but as it was found that these times "interfere with the General court of the Louisiana Territory, to the great detriment of several suiters in the said courts," they were changed to the last Monday of October for St. Clair and the first Monday of November for Randolph—*post*, 555 (Sept. 8, 1807). The interference was undoubtedly more with counsel, several attorneys of St. Louis being among the most prominent practitioners in these counties. The name Oyer and Terminer was apparently often applied to the Circuit Court, and sometimes (even statutory terminology being obscure—*post*, 8-9, 12, §§ 3, 4, 13) to the General Court. Monks states that the latter was "usually" so called—Monks, *Courts*, 1: 26. The Circuit Court was frequently called the Court of Oyer and Terminer and General Jail Delivery.

In addition to the civil session the circuit judge held a jail delivery whenever necessary. As a court of jail delivery the jurisdiction of the Circuit Court was not, of course, restricted to the capital cases in which the General Court had exclusive original jurisdiction.[1] Whenever officially informed that a prisoner was held in a county for a capital crime the Governor was empowered to issue a commission to one or more judges of the General Court to hold a special court of oyer and terminer.[2] In practice no more than one was ever commissioned; but commissions were simultaneously sent to one or more local judges to sit with the circuit judge.[3]

It is evident that the Circuit Court was the hub of the judicial system. "Upon it," as Mr. Esarey says, "fell the burden of upholding the power of the government and teaching the people its supreme value."[4] The life of the circuit-rider—lawyer or missionary—was one of rough romance. In the coming of the circuit judge, attended by a retinue of leading lawyers who spellbound local political meetings and social gatherings with their eloquence and made the court itself a thing of wonder through the countryside, the law revealed its picturesque aspect. The courts were the theater of the backwoods. Indiana Territory, in this respect, merely reproduced the experience of colonial times and of all the

[1] The statement in Monks, *Courts*, 1: 27, that "as a matter of fact, courts were held much oftener for jail delivery" is correct if the special courts of oyer and terminer are included. But even so these were not frequent.

[2] *Post*, 215, § 3 (Dec. 5, 1806).

[3] Gibson, *Exec. Journal*, 104, shows such commissions (Sept. 28, 1801) to Judge Vander Burgh for Randolph and St. Clair, with John Edgar and Pierre Menard as his associates in the first, and John Dumoulin and Shadrach Bond [Sr.] in the second, county. Commissions for another court in Randolph were issued only a few weeks later (*ibid.*, 105, Nov. 3, 1801) to the three judges of the General Court—Vander Burgh, Clarke, and Griffin; on March 24, 1802 (*ibid.*, 107) to Clarke for Clark County, with two local associates. Commissions of September 24, 1802, to Edgar and Menard as associates of Judge Griffin are preserved in the *Chic. Hist. Colls.*, 4: 168-171; Harrison, *Messages*, 1: 57-59. It is highly probable that such courts were associated every year with the regular circuit courts, and that Secretary Gibson's record is incomplete.

The reference in *Exec. Journal*, 112, to an oyer and terminer in Knox is presumably to a special court (*post*, 10-11, § 9, and 215, § 1, do not set the date of the Knox circuits).

[4] *History*, 1: 167.

older states. The emphasis placed by the frontier upon eloquence and cleverness has exercised an abiding and pernicious influence upon the legal profession of the country.[1]

Circuit-riding greatly weakened the General Court. Judge Symmes complained in 1790 that the judges must employ the whole year in traveling, snatching a little time for legislating when a quorum could be brought together. In 1795 he seems to have left Marietta at the end of March in order to hold the General Court at Vincennes in May. This is somewhat difficult to understand, for Governor Reynolds says—with reference, indeed to travel sixteen years later, but modes of travel had not changed—that by "exceedingly fast" travel one could go from Vincennes to his home near St. Louis in two and a half days.[2] At the best, however, it was exhausting and time consuming work,[3] so much so that as counties increased in number it became necessary, in 1803, to authorize the holding of a General Court by a single member; a change that had bad results and caused great dissatisfaction.

Until 1805 the county system was extremely elaborate. The Court of General Quarter Sessions of the Peace, in addition to its quarterly regular sessions, held "special and private sessions when

[1] Senator Smith's *Early Trials* (e. g. 168-169) gives interesting views of circuit-riding of somewhat later years; conditions, however, evidently could not greatly have changed. See also Warren, *Hist. of the Amer. Bar*, 124, 204-206. "At a court in Cahokia, in olden times, a great crowd of people remained there all night"—Reynolds, *My Own Times;* 103. Governor Ford describes, not unkindly, the old-time ministers, who "made up in loud hallooing and violent action what they lacked in information" (*History*, 38-40), and adds: "In course of time their style became the standard of popular eloquence. It was adopted by lawyers at the bar, and by politicians in their public harangues; and to this day [1854], in some of the old settled parts of the State, no one is accounted an orator unless he can somewhat imitate thunder in his style of public speaking. From hence, also, comes the vulgar notion that any bellowing fellow, with a profusion of flowery bombast, is a 'smart man,' a man of talents, fit to make laws, govern the country, and originate its policy" (*ibid.*, 40). Dean Roscoe Pound has emphasized the importance, in the development of our law, of the frontier attitude toward the court as a theater (*The Spirit of the Common Law*, 124-125, 137).

[2] Smith, *St. Clair Papers*, 2: 187, 339-340; Reynolds, *My Own Times*, 77.

[3] Compare Burnet, *Notes*, 65-67; Smith, *Early Trials*, 116-117. Even in 1820, on the first circuit of Indiana there was only one tavern, though the judge was fourteen weeks on circuit—Ind. Hist. Soc. *Pub.*, 6: 119-121. Judge Parsons, of the first General Court, was drowned in crossing a stream when on circuit in 1789—Pease, *Laws* (*I. H. C.*, 17), xxii.

and as often as occasion shall require," and had cognizance of crimes, except the capital cases reserved to the General Court.[1] The Court of Common Pleas met at the same time, and with few exceptions was composed of the same judges. Its jurisdiction was unrestricted, and concurrent with that of the General Court.[2] Each court could be held by three judges, and each judge had certain powers (later, in both civil and criminal cases) which he could exercise out of court. Any judge of any court—county or general—could issue writs and other process, which ran throughout the territory.[3]

An Orphans' Court was established in 1795 by a law which remained unchanged so long as the court existed. Its judges were likewise those of the Quarter Sessions.[4] It had jurisdiction over

[1] *Post*, 8-10, § 1-7. It is stated in various places (e. g. by Mr. Esarey *Indiana*, 1: 168) that the court tried "petty" crimes and misdemeanors, and that "felonies" were reserved to the territorial courts. Of course the Quarter Sessions did try petty crimes primarily, and it is also true that the penalties prescribed by the law of 1788 (continued in force in 1799, Pease, *op. cit.*, 13, 338)—when jails were practically non-existent—make the crimes seem less serious. But from 1795 onward it was only felonies of death that were reserved to the General (or Circuit) Court—*ibid.*, 158, § 12; law of 1801, *post*, 12, § 12.

[2] *Post*, 13, § 14. It is said in Monks, *Courts*, 1: 14, that "three Common Pleas Justices usually sat together, one of whom should be a lawyer, though one of them, the lawyer, frequently held court alone." Even the law of 1788 (Pease, *Laws* (*I. H. C.*, 17), 4, 7) required three judges to hold the Common Pleas. There is no trace in the records of St. Clair and Randolph of action such as that stated. It is also stated in Monks, *op. cit.*, 2: 807-808, that "according to the federal statute, two courts were provided for the territory. The so-called General court exercised jurisdiction throughout the whole territory, while the Common Pleas court was restricted in its jurisdiction to the county where it was organized. The latter court exercised civil and criminal jurisdiction, and also had charge of all probate matters. These two courts were in existence during the sixteen years [1800-16] Indiana was a territory, the Federal Judges having charge of the General court and the Associate Judges presiding over the Common Pleas courts in the respective counties."

[3] *Post*, 8, §§ 2, 6, 14-17. In 1790, when the county of St. Clair was organized, three judicial districts and courts were established—at Cahokia, Kaskaskia, and Prairie du Rocher (John Dumoulin, John Edgar, and Jean Bte. Barbau being the respective judges); and writs ran in each district only. Governor Reynolds relates John Rice Jones' plea to the jurisdiction of one of these courts—*Pioneer History*, 180; Washburne's note, *Edwards Papers*, 73-74. Doubtless this early experience sufficed.

[4] Under the creative act of June 16, 1795—Pease, *Laws* (*I. H. C.*, 17), 181—an Orphans' Court was proclaimed open for St. Clair County on August 5, 1796: St. Clair *Orphans' Court 1797-1809*, p. 1. See *post*, app. notes, 17, 28. No records of a court in Randolph County seem to exist.

all persons who, "as guardians, trustees, tutors, executors, administrators or otherwise" were anywise accountable for property belonging to an infant.   It controlled investments, bound minors as apprentices, controlled the Probate Court in matters pertaining to their estates.   Appeals lay to the Circuit or General Court.[1]

A Probate Court—ordinarily consisting of one judge—had been established earlier, in 1788, in each county; and this law also remained unaltered.   In deciding upon contested points, and in his final decrees the probate judge was required to join with him two judges of the Common Pleas as members of the court.[2]   A statute of 1792 conferred temporarily upon the judge of probate the powers given three years later to the Orphans' Court; indeed more, for his powers extended to persons mentally incompetent.[3] The subject of probate, and also the court, were first dealt with, in the legislation of Indiana Territory, by the Revision of 1807, and very considerably modified.   A provision of 1808, that no judge of the county court should be administrator of an estate unless entitled thereto as decedent's next of kin,[4] would—had it been earlier in effect—most radically have altered the business of the Probate Court.   Administration by the judges had been exceedingly common.   The Executive Journal of the territory does

---

[1] Pease, *Laws* (*I. H. C.,* 17), 181.

[2] *Ibid.,* 9; reënacted in 1799, 338. This act of 1788, as finally adopted, was largely due, in essentials, to Governor St. Clair. His comments upon the original draft of the judges (Parsons and Varnum, *St. Clair Papers,* 2: 67-68) is a fair illustration of his sound judgment and ability. The Probate Court was abolished by the statute of August 24, 1805—*post,* 117, § 10.

[3] Pease, *Laws* (*I. H. C.,* 17), 89. This act was repealed after the creation of the Orphans' Court (*ibid.,* 257).

[4] *Post,* 270, 652, 662, § 3. See *post,* ccvii, n. 6, as to Perrey. Other instances: *Orphans' Court 1797-1809,* p. 21 (Perrey), 22 (George Atchison).

The orphans' courts were abolished by statute of August 24, 1805—*post,* 115. In the records of the St. Clair Court there is an order of February 23, 1797, giving the clerk of the Orphans' Court the same fees as allowed "in the former fee bill to the Judge of Probate" (p. 2). The statute referred to must be that of 1795, Pease, *op. cit.,* 179: this law, unlike the laws of 1792 and 1798 (*ibid.,* 104, 305), did not regulate fees in the Orphans' Court. In Monks, *Courts,* 1: 33, it is suggested that "since the prothonotary of the Common Pleas was always clerk of the Orphans' court, it seems the Common Pleas Justices presided." But the creative statute required the court to be held by justices of the Quarter Sessions—Pease, *op. cit.,* 181-182.

not show many appointments to these last two courts, but it does show some,[1] and the local records indicate that both courts were in regular operation.[2]

The same obscurity surrounds the boards of county commissioners. The statutes of the Northwest Territory provided for their appointment by the Quarter Sessions, and for their performance of important duties, and maintenance of distinct records.[3] The Quarter Sessions, like its prototype developed in all the southern colonies (where tendencies far advanced in the English Quarter Sessions before the seventeenth century had simply been carried farther),[4] exercised large powers of self-government; indeed, in it were gathered most of the functions of civil administration. The township system, elaborate in its statutory form, in reality probably scarcely existed.[5] The county

[1] Secretary Gibson appointed clerks of the orphans' courts of Knox, Randolph, St. Clair, and Clark (*Exec. Journal*, 92, July 28, 1800; 93, 94, August 1, 1800—Robert Morrison for Randolph, John Hay for St. Clair; 101, February 4, 1801). The place of meeting of the Clark County Court was changed in 1802 (*ibid.*, 109); appointments were made to the court for Dearborn County in 1803 (*ibid.*, 117, March 7, 1803). No other appointments appear.

On the same days just noted some appointments were also made of probate judges—including John Edgar for Randolph. No appointment for St. Clair anywhere appears; nevertheless the court was there in operation. Shadrach Bond was judge in 1805 (*Orphans' Court 1797-1809*, 27). William St. Clair was judge in 1796 (*ibid.*, 1). In the Miscellanies Box at Chester are some probate records, e. g. letters of administration issued December 1, 1802, to John Edgar by Robert Morrison.

[2] See list of estates administered by the St. Clair judge of probate from 1790 onward in Brink, McDonough, *Hist. of St. Clair County*, 83. In the records of that court (St. Clair *Orphans' Court 1797-1809*) we find a resolution (p. 21, February 6, 1804): "It is the opinion of the Court that the Adm^r shall be paid in preference to all other creditors."

[3] Pease, *Laws* (*I. H. C.*, 17), 201 (1795), 483 (1799), and index. The justices evidently sat, themselves (at least generally) as commissioners. In the Randolph record of the *County Commissioners 1809-10* those attending are usually referred to simply as "Justices of the Peace," sometimes (p. 148) as "the Worshipful—[naming them], Justices of the Peace." The earlier records do not furnish similar evidence.

[4] Compare G. E. Howard, *An Introduction to the Local Constitutional History of the United States*, 406-407, 416; G. W. Prothero, *Select Statutes and other Constitutional Documents*, index, *s. v.* "Justices."

[5] The editors of Secretary Gibson's *Executive Journal* (p. 77) correctly state that the elaborate law of 1790 (Pease, *Laws*, 37) was "never carried out, nor was any similar act adopted in the Indiana Territory." Cp. *ante*, ciii. "Indeed, the township as a political organization seems to have attained very little importance during the territorial period. The existence of townships

commissioners, unlike those of present-day officers of the same name, had relatively limited, though very important, powers relative to the assessment and collection of taxes and the auditing and settlement of county claims and debts. Substantially, their powers appear in the records as powers of the Quarter Sessions. In Randolph County their proceedings, inextricably mixed with proceedings of the Quarter Sessions, are recorded in a court record of the latter; in St. Clair their proceedings are similarly mixed with records of the Orphans' Court—which themselves, for reasons elsewhere set out, were confused with acts of the Quarter Sessions.[1] That court (until absorbed in 1805 into the Common Pleas) created and bounded townships and appointed their officers; controlled all public improvements—the purchase or erection of county buildings, the authorization and building of bridges and roads, the appointment of road-viewers and surveyors and of superintendents of highways; it licensed ferries and fixed their rates; licensed taverns and fixed their rates; exercised large powers

[1] The Randolph *Court Record 1802-06,* and the St. Clair *Orphans' Court 1797-1809.* In McDonough, *Hist. of Randolph, Monroe and Perry Counties,* 101, it is stated that after January 13, 1804 "the administrative functions of the county were next performed by a court, styled orphans' court . . . from 1804 to 1808." Rather, it seems that in both periods the court was, in substance and reality, the same; that is, the justices of the Quarter Sessions. This Randolph record of the Orphans' Court seems to have disappeared. In the St. Clair *Orphans' Court 1797-1809,* p. 31, a road is ordered laid out; 31, 36, 40 constables are appointed; 40, overseers of the poor and supervisors of the road appointed; 41, county levy list delivered to sheriff for collection; 42, petition granted for division of a township. And on 43 (July, 1808) the record very properly refers—this being after the absorption of the Sessions in the Common Pleas—to "this County Court of Common Pleas."

was recognized in the law for appointing overseers of the poor, and also in the laws governing elections, but as a distinct political organization the township was scarcely known in the laws or"—but of course it had no place here—"in the appointments made by the governor." Overseers of the poor were regularly appointed—and here alone French names are common after 1800; but what they did does not appear. Constables and supervisors of highways were also more or less regularly appointed; and township appraisers of personalty. In remarks to the St. Clair Quarter Sessions made in October 1791 by the presiding judge, we read: "It is a long time since the publication of an act for laying off our county into townships, and appointing clerks and overseers of the poor to each, and nothing is done in that yet." Bateman and Selby, *Hist. of St. Clair County,* 2: 699. From 1802 onward, at least, such appointments were regular in Randolph County.

in taxation—appointing assessors, fixing basic land valuations, remitting taxes.[1]   Except in the control of elections—which, for historical reasons, fell more naturally to the Common Pleas[2] —it might assume to act for the community in any way.   The St. Clair Court, for example, corresponded (in 1797) with the Spanish authorities of St. Louis, protesting against competition with the ferry between that village and Cahokia;[3] established local liquor prohibition in Cahokia after the law of 1790, under which it might have claimed authority, had been repealed;[4] and took measures (1801) to exclude the smallpox, when prevalent in upper Louisiana.   The office of county commissioner has had a long development.   A century ago its differentiation from the quarter sessions was new and insecure.   To this is due the vagueness that envelops it in the records.

A little group of men controlled the entire local government, judicial and administrative.   They recommended each other, and a few friends, to the governor as fit to keep the taverns; and it will be seen that repeated indictments for violations of the laws did not affect either recommendations or appointments.   Similarly, they and a few others held the ferry licenses.   As county commissioners—for with rare exceptions they acted as such themselves—

[1] Ferries: the record of the commissioners' proceedings in the Randolph *Court Record 1802-06* is incomplete.   George Fisher (p. 6, September, 1802) and Pierre Menard (*ibid.*, 57, March, 1804) appear as filing bonds when they presented the Governor's license; also a Mrs. Sally Lusk (*ibid.*, 76, December 1804).   The taxes in 1803 were $7 on John Edgar's ferry across the Kaskaskia; $5 on George Fisher's across the Mississippi; $1 on James Edgar's across the Mississippi (*ibid.*, 27, July 1803).   In 1805 Fisher, John Edgar, James Edgar, Pierre Menard, paid $5; William Goings, $1.50; Paul Herlston, $1 (*ibid.*, 91, June, 1805).   The ferry rates fixed in March 1804 were: for single man, 6¼ cents; children under 8 years, 3; horse, 6¼; man and horse, 12½; full-grown cattle, 6½; cattle 2 years old or younger, 3⅛; cart and 2 oxen, or 2 horses, 25; 4 horses or oxen, 50; sheep or hog, 3⅛ (*ibid.*, 57).

Roads: the Randolph *Court Record 1802-06* contains a few examples, pp. 17, 33, 41.   See *ante*, cxxiv, n. 4 for Harrison's attitude.

[2] Compare Howard, *Local Const. Hist.*, 407, and Pease, *Laws (I. H. C.*, 17), 409, etc.

[3] Bateman and Selby, *Hist. of St. Clair County*, 2: 700; Brink, McDonough, *Hist. of St. Clair County*, 70.   Grand juries have always acted in much the same way; see *ibid.*, 85, the recommendations of the grand jury in 1791 relative to the Indian trade.

[4] Bateman and Selby, *Hist. of St. Clair County*, 2: 700, and *ante*, cxxx, n. 1.

they appointed the tax collectors, and assessors if none were elected; supposedly pursued delinquent collectors and taxpayers (we have seen that half of the delinquent taxpayers—delinquent over five years—were judges themselves); and supposedly pursued themselves as delinquent commissioners. They tried each other for misdemeanors and nonpayment of debts. Two hundred names would more than include, a hundred names would come near to including, all the judges, clerks, sheriffs, assessors, collectors, notaries, constables, coroners, court-criers, grand jurymen, petit jurymen, road supervisors, fence viewers, county commissioners, large landowners, tavern-keepers, ferrymen, mill-owners, store-keepers, and even wolf-killers who appear in the Randolph records. And these would include also a very large share of the civil litigants and criminal defendants.

In 1805 all powers theretofore vested in the Common Pleas, Quarter Sessions, and Orphans' Court, and judge of probate were vested in a new Court of Common Pleas of three judges, two of whom constituted a court. There were six sessions annually, three reserved excusively for the business of the former courts of Common Pleas and Quarter Sessions. The act took effect on January 1, 1806. The jurisdiction of the former courts passed unaltered to the new.[1]

Even after this simplification of the judicial system its expense was burdensome, and statutory limits were placed upon sessions of both the General Court and the county courts.[2]

Below all these courts were those of the justices of the peace. It has been seen, in discussing imprisonment for debt, that the second law established for the Northwest Territory empowered any judge of Common Pleas to hear and finally determine claims for debt under five dollars.[3] The law of 1795 gave exclusive and final jurisdiction in these cases to any judge of Common Pleas and any justice of the peace; and extended it to claims between five and

[1] *Post*, 115 (Aug. 24, 1805), 225 (Revision of 1807), 661 (fees).
[2] *Post*, 663, § 2 (1808).
[3] Pease, *Laws* (*I. H. C.*, 17), 8. As is suggested in Monks, *Courts*, 1: 30, the act of 1788 could not have been conveniently used until townships were created and constables appointed in 1790 (Pease, *op. cit.*, 37), for the sheriff lived at the county court, and (the counties being immense), his services were expensive.

twelve dollars, with appeal to the Common Pleas. It excluded in all cases claims for rent, and those where the title to land "comes into question"; and in the second class of cases, also, actions in covenant, "or upon any real contract," replevin, trover, case for slander, and trespass to the person.[1] Some hardships or abuses that became apparent under these laws were corrected by a statute of 1799, which in turn was amended by the General Assembly of Indiana Territory, no changes having been made by the governor and judges. This emendatory legislation points plainly to hardships which it was found difficult to correct. The law of 1795 required the action to be brought within the county where defendant resided or should be found; that of 1799 within the township of defendant's residence, and the justice must also there reside; a law of 1806 made it available where the debt was contracted, or where the plaintiff resided, or where the defendant might be found (if brought elsewhere, and the magistrate should find "vexatiously," the suit must be dismissed), and the justice was not required to be a resident thereof. Monetary jurisdiction was raised to eighteen dollars in 1799, and in 1806 jurisdiction was extended to causes for personal property. Stay laws began in 1799. One great abuse under the act of 1788, that of splitting demands into five-dollar claims, in order to recover them summarily and without appeal, was cured by penalties from 1799 onward. Reference to arbitrators, upon whose findings judgment must be given, was introduced in 1795 and preserved thereafter. Set-off was introduced in 1799, and likewise continued. Appeals, except for very trivial claims, were allowed in all cases after 1799. The laws of the territory after 1806 made no important changes except in raising the monetary jurisdiction to forty dollars; and in repealing the power, in view of the abuses that had arisen therefrom, to sue where the plaintiff resided.[2]

[1] Pease, *op. cit.,* 143 (1795), §§ 1, 4 (jurisdiction); 2, 15 (whether exclusive); 3, 16 (excepted cases).

[2] *Ibid.,* §§ 4 and 9 (referees); 389 (1799), §§ 1 and 4 (jurisdiction), 8 (set-off in small causes), 9 and 4 (referees), 10 (stay laws), 14 (appeals), 18 (splitting causes), 21 ($18 jurisdiction); 354 (November 15, 1799, general arbitration act, not confined to small causes). *Post,* 184-185 (Dec. 6, 1806), §§ 1, 2 (jurisdiction); 223-224 (1807), §§ 2, 3 (petty crimes, batteries); 351, § 6 (1807, extending set-off to higher courts); 375 (1807,

Maintenance of the peace, with power to take recognizances
or commit, and also jurisdiction to try petty crimes, had been entrusted to the justices under another line of statutes from the
beginning, but they were brought together in 1807 in the statutes
regulating the trial of small causes.[1]

All the justices and county judges were, of course, appointed
by the governor; and all the latter, apparently, were appointed
to serve during good behavior.[2]

The abundance of legislation on the topic is in itself evidence
that trouble in regard to the courts was experienced from the beginning.

Dissatisfaction was felt by the bar with the combination in
the General Court of broad original and appellate jurisdiction.[3]

[1] Pease, *Laws* (*I. H. C.*, 17), 5, 6, 20 (1788); 328 (same, revised
1792); 297 (1798). Puzzlement is expressed in Monks, *Courts,* 1: 31-32,
over the fact that the earlier statutes regulating the trial of small causes
conferred no such jurisdiction. The other line of statutes, here cited, was
overlooked. Confusion was caused by an unhappy statutory terminology.
In 1788 civil jurisdiction was conferred upon judges of the Common Pleas,
and criminal upon justices of the peace, in the same statute (Pease, *op. cit.*,
5, 6, 8). But the latter were inseparably united in men's minds with the
justices of the General Quarter Sessions of the Peace, which could be held,
under this statute of 1788, by any three justices of the peace in the county.
Moreover, justices of the peace were in 1795 added to the "justices" (in
later years consistently called "judges") of the Common Pleas in the civil
jurisdiction (*ibid.*, 143, §§ 1, 3), and in 1799 part of the criminal jurisdiction
was conferred upon both (*ibid.*, 378); but then it became necessary to enact,
first that no judge of Common Pleas should hear on appeal such cases
decided by himself below (*ibid.*, 148, § 14; 397, § 15), and later that no
such judge (this was after the Quarter Sessions was abolished) should
hear the cases originally (*post*, 185, § 4; 388, § 22). This restored the
original division of jurisdictions; and meanwhile, in 1805, the Quarter
Sessions were abolished. It was therefore evidently felt desirable to em-
phasize in the statute of 1807 the fact that the two jurisdictions belonged
to the justices of the peace. See *post*, 223.

[2] See *ante*, xix, notes 2 and 3. Secretary Sargent, while acting
governor in 1793—ignoring with characteristic arrogance the troubles over
this question between England and the colonies only thirty years before—
had commissioned county judges to hold at the pleasure of the governor,
and this had raised a storm in the territory. Compare *St. Clair Papers*,
2: 312 n., 323 n., 366; G. E. Howard, *Preliminaries of the Revolution*, 86.

[3] See *ante*, x and n. 3; Monks, *Courts,* 1: 175-177. See Mr. Esarey's
account of the Indiana constitutional convention of 1816, Ind. Hist. Soc.
Pub., 6: 105-108.

general revision of Pease, 389), §§ 1, 4, 8, 9, 10, 14, 18, 21, 22, corresponding
to above §§ of 1799; 443 (1807), practice in the General Court and County
Common Pleas; 658 (1808), § 1 (no suit merely where plaintiff resides),
660, § 3 (monetary jurisdiction $40, $100 in Prairie du Chien).

The increasing burden of circuit duties made it necessary as early as 1792 (as already noted) to permit the holding of a General Court by a single judge; and the law had never required more for the Circuit Court and the Court of Oyer and Terminer. The combination of the two provisions was not a happy one. It was not acceptable to one judge on circuit to be overruled by one at Vincennes.[1] Nor were litigants content, apparently, with final decisions by a single judge in the General Court. It seems probable that there must have been few such cases, of either class. Nevertheless, the connection of the Northwestern judges with the great land companies made the last law, in the opinion of Governor St. Clair, actually dangerous. Many representations were made to him against it. He favored its repeal, and the establishment of appeals, from a fuller court, to the Supreme Court of the United States. By an act of the Indiana Territory passed in 1801 two judges were declared necessary—as the Ordinance had provided—to hold the General Court or (as to which the Ordinance contained no provision) courts of oyer and terminer and general jail delivery. By another act of 1803—whose validity is no more doubtful than that of the Congressional act of 1792 which had similarly modified the "compact" of 1787—one judge was declared sufficient. Experience evidently showed that a court of one was better than no court at all.[2]

There was also dissatisfaction with the circuit courts held by one judge. A bill passed by the General Assembly in 1808, forbidding the same judge to hold the circuit courts successively in

[1] This seems to have been the case in one of the clashes between Judges Turner and Symmes in 1795; see *St. Clair Papers*, 2: 397-398.

[2] The Ordinance—Pease, *Laws* (*I. H. C.*, 17), 522—had required two judges to hold a General Court; this had been violated in Michigan— see the protest of December 8, 1806 in *Mich. Pioneer and Hist. Colls.*, 8: 581, and that of December 12, 1806 in the same, 12: 647. For act of May 8, 1792, declaring one judge sufficient: *U. S. Stat. at Large*, 1: 285. For St. Clair's comments upon the evil effects of this law see *Amer. State Papers: Misc.*, 1: 116 (December 15, 1794, to Edmund Randolph; given erroneously in *St. Clair Papers*, 2: 333 as of December 14 to Thomas Jefferson). The editor of the *St. Clair Papers* (1: 194) says that "the act"—of Congress, of 1792—"which permitted the holding of the Supreme Court by a single judge was productive of many unpleasant complications, which taxed the address and patience of the Governor sorely to adjust." For the laws of 1801 and 1803 see *post*, 8, 85. The latter appears as a "resolution" of the governor and judges "assembled as a legislature"!

the same county, was necessarily vetoed by Governor Harrison. The difficulty persisted in Indiana until it became a state.[1]

Great discontent was necessarily incident, also, to the inconvenience and expense of litigation in the General Court.[2] This difficulty was unavoidable; it was mainly due to the great size of the territory. The expense of litigation in the county courts was high for the same reason; and this had caused Governor St. Clair in 1790, when St. Clair County was created, to divide it into three judicial districts. Grand juries were organized in each; writs ran only within each; separate sessions of the various county courts were held in each, and under arrangements that made them almost independent courts; a defendant could be sued only in the district of his residence; although the judges, sheriff, and clerk had jurisdiction throughout the county. For these arrangements there was no authority in the Ordinance or statutes. St. Clair, always a strict constructionist in defending his own authority against encroachments by his fellow judges, himself acted in this instance upon latitudinarian principles, under a plea of necessity. As this division of the county did not "give that ease and facility to the administration of justice which was expected, and the great extent of the county would render it almost impracticable were the courts

[1] *Messages*, 1: 319. See, on the interesting conflict which arose in 1814 between the legislature and the federal territorial judges, Smith, *Hist. of Indiana*, 2: 575-579; and *Mich. Pioneer and Hist. Colls.*, 12: 642 for a parallel case. Compare Dillon, *Indiana*, 543.

[2] In the report by a committee to the House of Representatives in 1808, Jesse Thomas, chairman, they say that "the great difficulty of travelling through an extensive and loathsome wilderness, the want of food, and other necessary accommodations on the road, often presents an insurmountable barrier to the attendance of witnesses; and even when their attendance is obtained, the accumulated expense of prosecuting suits where the evidence is at so remote a distance, is a cause of much embarrassment to a due and impartial administration of justice, and a proper execution of the laws for the redress of private wrongs." *Amer. State Papers: Misc.*, 1: 945 (Dec. 31, 1808). Similarly, *Annals*, 8 Congress, 1 session, 29 (November 1, 1803); 10 Congress, 1 session, 2067 (April 11, 1808). In a memorial of 1805 from the Illinois country committed January 17, 1806 (Ind. Hist. Soc. *Pub.*, 2: 499), the petitioners declared: "the poor man is often deeply oppressed by the appeal of a wealthy antagonist to a court so distant." And again: "a considerable portion of the inhabitants of the Illinois are obliged, several times a year, to travel as officers, as jurors, as witnesses, as suitors in the National Court holden at Vincennes" over the 150 miles of dreary waste separating them from that town. The colossal exaggeration of the second statement somewhat discredits the first.

to be held at one place only," Randolph County was created in 1795.[1]

A cause of dissatisfaction probably more important than any of the preceding—although less emphasized than the last as a reason for the division of the territory in 1800—was the impossibility of carrying the burden that rested on the circuit courts. Here lay the true "inconveniences and embarrassments" of continued connection with the Wabash country. Governor St. Clair was never able to visit Michigan and in six years only two circuit courts were held there.[2] It was stated by a Congressional com-

[1] The quotation is from St. Clair's proclamation of October 5, 1795 creating Randolph County—*St. Clair Papers,* 2: 345 n. See St. Clair to President Washington, November 21, 1790, *ibid.,* 172, giving his reasons for ignoring legal requirements; also 371. Reynolds, *Pioneer History,* 180; Davidson and Stuvé, *History,* 213; May Allinson, "The Government of Illinois, 1790-99," Ill. State Hist. Soc. *Trans.* (1907), p. 284-285. Mr. Alvord's statement (*Illinois Country,* 404) that "the courts established in each district . . . were those of common pleas, general quarter sessions, the justices of the peace, and the probate court," is technically wrong. Practically, however, since the prothonotary of the common pleas, the "clerk of the peace" (i. e. of the Quarter Sessions), and the judge of probate were ordered to elect deputies and open offices in each district, and since a "chief justice" was appointed (or at least acted) for each district, the result must have been substantial decentralization. Compare *St. Clair Papers,* 2: 172, with Miss Allinson, *loc. cit.,* 284-285. It should be remembered that under the law of 1788, there being no substantial distinction between justices of the peace and justices of the Court of General Quarter Sessions of the Peace (*ante,* cliv, n. 1), that court could readily have been held in any district, and probably was. It was different with the Common Pleas, if the statute was observed; for it required—Pease, *Laws* (*I. H. C.,* 17), 7— the appointment of from 3 to 5 judges, a majority of whom were alone competent to hold the court anywhere. St. Clair's action, according to Miss Allinson (*loc. cit.,* 285) and the editor of the *St. Clair Papers* (2: 198 n. 2), was condemned by Jefferson and Washington. In truth the sections of St. Clair's journal of his proceedings in the Illinois country upon which Jefferson animadverted (*The Writings of Thomas Jefferson* (Ford ed.), 5: 260) did not include that—of April 27, *St. Clair Papers,* 2: 165 n.—which referred to the creation of the three judicial districts. However, St. Clair frankly excused it solely on the ground of necessity, and the strictures of Jefferson and Washington (*ibid.,* 198), were directed against similar irregularities under a like plea.

[2] *Mich. Pioneer and Hist. Colls.,* 8: 512. In *Hist. Publications of Wayne County Michigan,* Nos. 1-2: "Documents relating to the Erection of Wayne County and Michigan Territory" various memorials to Congress are given. In one of March 20, 1803 the petitioners complain that the defective administration of justice under the Northwest Territory was aggravated by the attachment of Wayne County to Indiana Territory: "Experience has already taught us the various consequences which a procrastination in judicial proceedings, produces to Commerce; for a term of more

clviii   *ILLINOIS HISTORICAL COLLECTIONS*

mittee in March, 1800 that in the five preceding years only one
court of criminal jurisdiction had been held in the three western
counties, including Knox. If this is correct it must have been the
court held in the Illinois country in 1795.[1] After 1800 the courts
seem to have been held annually, but these sessions were inade-

---

[1] *Amer. State Papers: Misc.*, 1: 206. Compare *St. Clair Papers*,
2: 483. St. Clair spent considerable time—March 5 to June 11—in Illinois
in 1790; his official report is in *St. Clair Papers*, 2: 164-180 (see also 129,
130., 131), but contains little on legal matters and nothing regarding courts.
Judges Symmes and Turner were apparently on their way to Illinois in
May and June of 1790, and Mr. Bond says that the former met the Governor
"at Kaskaskia early in the summer"; it seems rather that both judges
joined him at Vincennes in June after his return from the Illinois country
(B. Bond, *John Cleves Symmes*, 83 n., 128, 130 and n., 287), and apparently
did not go farther west. In January 1792 Symmes thought that he "must"
hold the Illinois courts in June, unless the President should grant him leave
of absence, in which case he would feel "justified in neglecting the western
circuit" (*ibid.*, 161-162). There is no evidence that he went either east or
to the Illinois; but he was in the east from February 1793 to September
1794 (*ibid.*, 163 n.). His land interests were primary, and allowed only
slight attention to his official duties: *ibid.*, 22-23, 140-141. In the meantime
Judge Turner held Circuit Court in Illinois—apparently early in 1795, though
the time fixed by law was June! He was, therefore, as Miss Allinson says,
"the first territorial judge to hold court in Illinois," at least "so far as
present records reveal to us" (Ill. State Hist. Soc. *Trans.* (1907) p. 287. She
says he reached Kaskaskia in October 1794; *St. Clair Papers*, 2: 345-346 and
373 indicate that court was held in late winter or early spring). Apparently
he held court at Kaskaskia only, wherefore the complaints of Cahokia:
ibid., and *Amer. State Papers: Misc.*, 1: 151. See *post*, ccvi for troubles
he stirred up. Later in 1795—again at a time not provided by law (September)—Judge Symmes, who had gone to the Illinois with the Governor to
allay the excitement aroused by Judge Turner, held court in both Kaskaskia
and Cahokia (*St. Clair Papers*, 2: 345 n., 396; Bateman and Selby, *Hist.
of St. Clair County*, 699). St. Clair's health prevented him from going
again in 1796. Apparently there were no more courts until 1801.

---

than Six Years, whilst under the Government of the North Western Territory, but Two Superior-Courts were held in the County of Wayne; notwithstanding the many Actions removed into the General Court by error
& ca—Several of which still remain undecided, altho' pending for Three
or Four years." The distance which the judges must travel on circuit under
the Indiana Territory was "at least double the distance the late Judges
had to travel" and would increase earlier inconveniences (pp. 13-15). In
another memorial, perhaps of 1805, after commenting upon the practical
immunity of criminals, it is stated: "In Civil matters, too, the delay and
the expense are equally fatal.—During the last eight years, we have had
but two Circuit Courts.—The Creditor is deterred from an appeal to the
laws, under the painful assurance, that altho' justice is not *sold*, it costs
more than, some among us are, able to pay" (p. 34).

quate. An increase of the judges of the General Court would
have remedied this difficulty.[1]

   Agitation began early to secure an appeal from the General
Court to the Supreme Court of the United States. Governor St.
Clair had favored this change in 1794; mainly because the
large interests of all the judges of the first court in land
speculation weakened the independence of the court.[2]   There
was probably no reason to doubt the impartiality of the court in
later years, and it was obvious that, whatever the advantages of
such appeals, they were open to all the objections urged at the
same time against appeals from the Illinois county courts to the
General Court.[3]   Nor could the magnitude of the issues involved

[1] Petition of the General Assembly in 1805, Dunn, *Indiana,* 338;
Bateman and Selby, *Hist. of St. Clair County,* 699. No records of the
circuit courts remain in Randolph except a few scrappy sheets of 1808;
and none in St. Clair except a few undated sheets, apparently also of 1808.
The General Court, on September 5, 1809, ordered them sent to the clerk
of that court (*Order Book,* 1: 328). Possibly they now exist at Vincennes
or in Indianapolis.

[2] Writing to the Secretary of State, December 14, 1794, of the provision that one judge might hold the General Court, without appeal, he
says: "Many representations have been made to me on this subject. The
people very generally think it an unsafe situation which they are in . . .
Circumstances exist at present that render it dangerous. The principal
settlements have been made in tracts of land purchased by . . . the Ohio
Company, and . . . the Miami Company. In both these associations
the management of the directors and agents are thought to have laid the
foundation of endless disputes. General Putnam has been the active director
in the first association, and Mr. Symmes the principal, if not the sole, agent
in the second; and they are both judges of the Supreme Court. Every land
dispute will be traced to some transaction of the one or of the other of those
gentlemen, and they are to sit in judgment upon them. It must, I think, be
acknowledged that . . . the people have but a slender security for the
impartiality of their decision"—*St. Clair Papers,* 2: 332-333; *Amer. State
Papers: Misc.,* 1: 116. See *ante,* clv, n. 2, and *post,* cxcix, n. 4.
Dunn, *Indiana,* 276-277, says that "nearly all of the litigation of the territory
grew out of transactions" with the land companies in which the judges
were interested. This is a vast exaggeration. My examination of the
Order Book of the General Court and records of the Illinois county courts
has revealed nothing to support the statement.

[3] A committee of the House of Representatives, December 29, 1803,
reported adversely to the change on the ground of delay and expense.
Such appeals, they said, would certainly sometimes be made "an instrument
of vexation and oppression." Again: "The committee are not informed,
nor do they believe, that there is any unusual want of confidence in the
courts of the Territories." *Annals,* 8 Congress, 2 session, 1577-1579.

well justify appeal.[1] Appeals were granted, however, in cases involving federal questions, in 1805.[2]

Some irritation arose from employment of the attorney-general of the territory in causes of the United States, for which he was not at first compensated.[3]

The county courts were held with considerable irregularity under the government of Northwestern Territory, but this was less noticeable under that of the Indiana Territory.[4] Another difficulty arose from the fact that the county judges were paid from fees, and so inadequately that Governor Harrison finally urged, in 1808, that their compensation be assumed by the territory.[5] This difficulty existed throughout the territorial period. The judges derived little or no emolument from their commissions, and in consequence it was necessary, in order to assure the attendance of a sufficient number to hold the regular sessions of the courts,

[1] Mr. Webster, in Ind. Hist. Soc. *Pub.*, 4: 212, cites a letter by Thomas Terry Davis relative to a verdict for $13,000 given in the General Court in a case involving a doubtful point of law. And some of the verdicts in the Randolph County Court were very large; see *post*, cxci.

[2] *Annals*, 8 Congress, 2 session, 1693 (March 3, 1805). No debates whatever are reported. By act of April 18, 1806, the Judiciary Act of February 28, 1799, was extended to the territories. Probably the strongest reason for desiring the change was that Kentucky had been given a United States District Court. The act gave to the superior courts of the several territories in which no federal District Court had been established the same jurisdiction and powers, in cases involving a federal question, as were possessed by the District Court of Kentucky Territory.

[3] See reports to the House of Representatives in *Annals* (1803), 7 Congress, 2 session, 1354, and (1804) 8 Congress, 1 session, 1024. Also *post*, app. n. 9.

[4] William St. Clair wrote to the Governor on June 2, 1793 from Kaskaskia: "Our courts are in a deplorable state; no order is kept in the interior, and many times not held. Prairie du Rocher has had no court this sometime, and Kaskaskia has failed before. The magistrates, however, have taken upon themselves to set it going again"—*St. Clair Papers*, 2: 317; cp. resolution of August 20, 1795 in Pease, *Laws* (*I. H. C.*, 17), 288. The prothonotary and clerk of Knox County absented himself for a long period in 1794—*St. Clair Papers*, 2: 326, 332. The Hamilton County Court met illegally and invalidated its proceedings (1795)—*ibid.*, 348. In Adams County the justices—apparently for reasons connected with land speculations—removed the courts from the place appointed by law for their meetings (1798)—*ibid.*, 425 n. The Knox Court was not held in August, 1805 "by reason of the non attendance of a sufficient number of Justices to form a court"—*post*, 98. The court of Dearborn County was held by mistake a week early—*post*. 201.

[5] *Messages*, 1: 305.

to multiply their number, as Governor Harrison pointed out in his message of 1805, "to an extent which precludes all hope of a uniformity of decision. It is, indeed, not infrequent that the judges who determine the question are not those who have presided at its discussion." It was in accordance with his insistence that it was "indispensably necessary that an evil should be corrected which strikes at the roots of one of the first objects of civil society" that the Assembly reconstituted the county courts in 1805.[1] The effects of that act were probably very slight indeed. The abolition of separate courts of criminal, probate, and orphan jurisdiction would have effected a great saving had the judges of each been paid independent salaries. But as almost the same individuals were actually appointed to serve in these various courts (presumably because of the considerations just stated), the only effect of the reduction in the number of courts was that the same fees were thenceforth collected for services performed in one court that had previously been performed in several. For the same reason the number of variant opinions cannot have been lessened; the slight difference in personnel between the old Common Pleas and Quarter Sessions being unimportant, since the jurisdictions were distinct. The reconstitution of the courts was therefore a mere administrative simplification, notwithstanding that the Assembly doubtless believed its statute to be responsive to the Governor's criticisms. The real improvement was made by Harrison himself, in appointing fewer and better men to the reconstituted courts.

Confusion between justices of the peace—of whom, though seemingly numerous, there were apparently never enough[2]—and judges of the county courts, particularly justices of the Quarter Sessions, leaves plain traces in the records. In England it was

---

[1] *Ibid.*, 1: 156, July 29, 1805.

[2] See the petition of 69 inhabitants of Randolph County to the Governor, of March 23, 1807, in *Messages*, 1: 204, as to the need; and 105—Dearborn County, 1804—as to the quality that was frequently the best available. Note that in the second case the petitioners, as a matter of course, recommended that a man, of whom the best that they could say was that he would be better "than none," be appointed justice of the peace and justice of the Quarter Sessions of the Peace. Compare also *St. Clair Papers*, 2: 424 on Jefferson County in 1798.

easy to maintain a distinction between ordinary justices of the peace and those of the "quorum"—the law members—who were members of the Court of General Quarter Sessions of the Peace. Some traces of the distinction, but only the barest traces, are discernible in the records of the Northwest Territory: General Rufus Putnam, for example, was appointed by Governor St. Clair in 1788 a "Justice of the Peace and Quorum." But this is almost a unique example.[1] And Secretary Sargent, at least, did not keep the distinction plain, for on April 29, 1790, he tells us that St. Clair made appointments for St. Clair County of—first, "Judges of the Court of Common Pleas"; secondly, "Justices of the Court of General Quarter-Sessions of the Peace, *and* Justices of Peace and Quorum"; thirdly, "Justices *of the Court* of St. Clair County." But these last were simply justices of the peace, none of them included in the first lists and none of them ever members of the courts.[2] The confusion was unavoidable, because of provisions in a law of 1788 already discussed. In fact the confusion went back before the creation of the Northwest Territory.[3] No commissions of this period, seemingly, survive. As Secretary Gibson kept the Executive Journal there is no distinction indicated between ordinary justices of the peace and those of the Quarter Sessions. Thus, John Beaird was named "Judge of the Court of

[1] *St. Clair Papers,* 2: 79 n.

[2] Italics added. See *ante,* cliv, n. 1. *St. Clair Papers,* 2: 165 n. These appointees were five: François Janis, Bte. Saucier, François Trottier, James Piggott, and Nicholas Smith. The first seems to have left no significant mark in contemporary records. The other two Frenchmen were distinguished, had been judges in Todd's Virginia court of 1779—and Trottier also in that of Clark of 1788 [Alvord, *Cahokia Records,* (I. H. C., 2), index]—but were advanced in years. Of the two Americans, Nicholas Smith had been a justice of the peace in Grand Ruisseau but Piggott had not. He was however soon to become, in 1795, a judge of the county courts. In stating that none of these five sat in either court I am relying (the judicial records are missing) upon the fact that I have nowhere found any indication that they served as judges.

[3] Jean Bte. Barbau, when deputy county-lieutenant of Illinois in 1787, issued commissions to various persons as "Justices of the peace for the District of KasKasKias and judges of the Court of the said District in cases *both civil and criminal*" (italics added.)—Alvord, *Kaskaskia Records* (I. H. C., 5), 402. In McDonough, *Hist. of Randolph, Monroe and Perry Counties,* 100, it is said—after naming the judges under the Indiana Territory (incorrectly, confusing the two courts): "These gentlemen were territorial or United States justices of the peace, and as such members of the court of common pleas." Cp. Reynolds, *Pioneer History,* 302.

Common Pleas and Justice of the peace for the County of Randolph," and we find him sitting regularly in the Quarter Sessions;[1] but he had been recommended for appointment to the court and the appointment was so intended.[2] "Judge" was the usual designation for members of the civil, and "justice" that for members of the criminal, court. But the latter was also used, even in the judicial records and statutes, to designate members of the Common Pleas. That can perhaps not be properly called a confusion; but there are examples in the statutes of positive confusion.[3] The failure to discriminate between ordinary justices and those of the quorum, and between "judges" and "justices," had the result of blurring the line between the Common Pleas and the criminal-and-administrative sessions. There was some confusion of jurisdiction; and there are curious cases of judges sitting in the civil court who had no authority to do so unless by virtue of commissions as justices of the peace—or appointment (presumably for good behavior) to the court in the Virginia period, before the creation of the Northwest Territory.[4] Finally, in 1806, judges of the Common Pleas were forbidden to act as justices of the peace.[5]

More important than most of these questions, intrinsically, was that of the introduction of courts of equity jurisdiction. The Ordinance of 1787—which in this respect reflected the strange misunderstanding and distrust of chancery procedure which prevailed generally at that time—conferred upon the General Court

[1] December 25, 1802—Gibson, *Exec. Journal,* 114. Thus in appointing Henry Fisher and Charles Reaume, ostensibly, as justices of the *Court* for St. Clair County, there is also the statement regarding Reaume: "appointed to the same office at *LaBay* in St. Clair County" (italics added. *ibid.,* 122). Neither ever sat as a member of the court. Mr. Esarey has expressed doubts regarding the status of certain appointees, by St. Clair in 1790, for Clark County (Monks, *Courts,* 1 : 31)—due to the same vagueness in commissions.

[2] See *ante,* xix, n. 2.

[3] Compare *post,* 389, paragraph 3 of § 2, with Pease, *Laws (I. H. C.,* 17), 402, § 2; also *post,* 426, § 3 ("and the Justices of the several courts of Common Pleas, of the Peace," etc.) with Pease, 444, § 3. And this was in 1807. The revisers must have left their work to an assistant, or failed to revise the work of a presumptuous copyist.

[4] See *post,* cci. "There must have resulted considerable confusion from the lack of a clear boundary between the Common Pleas and Justice of the Peace courts"—Monks, *Courts,* 1 : 32.

[5] Act of December 6, 1806, *post,* 185.

merely a common law jurisdiction. Appeals to the Supreme Court of the United States could not, of course, alone have remedied this.[1] In 1802 James Johnson, for most of the time since 1790 and for years later the presiding judge of the Knox Common Pleas, joined with his fellow judges in a petition to Congress praying that the Ordinance should be amended and chancery powers conferred. The petition was referred to a committee then engaged in a revision of the federal judicial system, but nothing further was done.[2] The next year, however, the same committee which reported appeals to the Supreme Court to be inexpedient urged with understanding words the conferment of equity powers,[3] and the act of 1805 already referred to introduced this change with the other.

Equity might have been introduced into the local courts (subject to Congressional approval during the continuance of government of the "first grade") at any time, if we assume that the mention of the common law in the Ordinance did not impliedly and as matter of principle exclude the other. This assumption the legislature later (under the second grade) made and acted upon—that is, by assuming concession of the power under the Ordinance's grant of "authority to make laws, in all cases, for the good government of the district, not repugnant to the principles and articles in this Ordinance established and declared." Until that step was taken hardly a trace of equity parlance occurs in the statutes.[4] This was quite proper. It is curious that although Pennsylvania, which affords our most notable example of a state without equity courts where equity principles were slowly insinuated through common law actions, was the source of the basic legislation of the Northwest Territory, the only statute that avowedly introduced equity was taken from Massachusetts—though, to

[1] Pease, *Laws* (*I. H. C.*, 17), 522; Monks, *Courts,* 1: 36, erroneously assumes the contrary.

[2] *Annals,* 7 Congress, 1 session, 1131 (April 3, 1802). The district courts of the United States were given the power to issue injunctions by an act of February 13, 1807—*ibid.,* 9 Congress, 2 session, 1258.

[3] *Ante,* clix, n. 3.

[4] Notable is the reference, above quoted, to the accountability of "trustees" to the Orphans' Court. And testimony *de bene esse* (*post,* 6) was not common law of 1607.

be sure, her experience in attempting to do without equity was almost as notable as that of Pennsylvania.[1] The choice of this statute (which limited recoveries in forfeitures to so much as should be due "in equity and good conscience") presumably responded to some special local need.[2] An attempt to give other equitable relief was, however, inevitable. "The Courts of Common Law," says Judge Burnet, "as far as their forms and modes of administering justice would permit, assumed those powers from necessity, by which partial relief was obtained." An attentive examination of even the scanty existing records of the General Court would doubtless yield various interesting examples of the judicial application of equity principles. Debt was allowed, for example, on an equity decree of one of the United States.[3]

In the county courts conditions were very different. The unschooled judges of those courts undoubtedly would not have known when they crossed the border of equity, or of any recondite province of the common law. What, for example, could a court untrained in equity and future interests make of a "deed of gift" of livestock, household furnishings and utensils, and a "crop" of corn and oats given by William Chribbs to his daughter[4] in these terms?—

"The total of these items . . . I do freely & of my own accord grant & convey unto the said Mary Chribbs under the following restrictions to wit the said property or at least the use of the said property is to be & remain subject to the control & direction of my wife Eliz^a Chribbs during her natural life or untill by & with the free consent of the parties concerned it might or may be thought proper to revoke the within given under my hand & seal this 22^d day of September 1804
"Witnesses present
      W. King
      Mathew Adams."

[1] S. G. Fisher, "The Administration of Equity through Common Law Forms," *Law Quart. Rev.*, 1: 455-465; E. H. Woodruff, "Chancery in Massachusetts," *Law Quart. Rev.*, 5: 370-386.
[2] Pease, *Laws (I. H. C.*, 17), 246 (1795); *post*, 307 (Revision of 1807).
[3] Burnet, *Notes*, 305; and see *post*, cxcvii, n. 1.
[4] Randolph, *Deed Record K, 35*.

What William Chribbs wanted done, undoubtedly they tried to do; and that was equity. The bar did not know enough to litigate such matters.

A few months after Congress conferred equity jurisdiction upon the General Court the General Assembly set up a territorial court of chancery (of a single judge) under the rules and practice of the English courts. The statute contained, doubtless by way of quieting apprehensions, a provision that no injunction should issue against proceedings at law, before judgment, unless the court should "be satisfied of the complainants Equity"; but this provision—which was evidently put in to quiet the fears of some opponent—the Revision of 1807 omitted.[1] Its provisions for sequestration, execution, and enforcement generally of decrees were ample in the extreme. In case respondent should not obey a decree, fieri facias against his property could be had to satisfy the complainant's demand, or a capias ad satisfaciendum under the same rules as at law, or an injunction for the delivery of property. And a decree for a conveyance, release, or acquittance not actually given should have in all courts of law and equity the same effect as the act decreed but unperformed. The local need which more than anything else had led to the creation of the court was satisfied by the provision that the court should always be open for the granting of ne exeats.[2] Procedure was fully regulated by another statute.[3] In view of the abolishment by the legislature, in this same session, of superfluous common courts, it is somewhat surprising that it should have created a separate court of chancery, instead of imitating the federal statute which had just conferred double jurisdiction on the General Court.

The chancellors successively appointed have already been referred to. The creative act had fixed no salary, and the legislature provided none. No doubt in part this was due to repentance over the creation of a new court. It seems evident from the messages of Governor Harrison, who ardently favored it, that doubts continued regarding the looseness of equitable discretion, and the

[1] *Post,* 110 (August 22, 1805), 507.
[2] A statute passed four days later (August 26, 1805) taxed lands claimed under a bond for conveyance—*post,* 147.
[3] *Post,* 193.

desirability otherwise of the court. As regards the first objection, there is no evidence that such distrust of magisterial power was any greater in the frontier community of Indiana Territory than in various of the old states of the east. The Governor first reminded the Assembly, merely, that no appropriation had been made; then he argued the issue, assuring them that equity is "bound down by rules and laws as well defined, and as well understood, as those of any other court," and urging its peculiar value "to protect the simple and ignorant against the artful and designing," and to meet the special needs of the territory; finally he could only again remind them that without appropriation there could be no court.[1] His words are worth quoting:

"If ever there was a country where a court of Chancery was necessary, ours is the one; because in no other (as I believe) has there ever been so much valuable property transferred without the observance of the legal forms of conveyance, or where the evasion of the specific performance of contracts would produce so much confusion, injustice, and ruin. It is not many years since a bare assignment of title to lands upon a bit of paper, without any of those peculiar phrases which our laws require in the transfer of real property, was deemed both by the buyer and seller a sufficient conveyance. Indeed, there have been instances where the delivery of possession has been considered and accepted as sufficient evidence of purchase. To enforce the observance of *bona fide* contracts made in this manner it is believed a court of Chancery is alone competent; nor is it by any means that loose and fluctuating tribunal which some have considered it, where will and not law presides, and where the arbitrary opinion of the judge is the only rule of decision."

In a memorial to Congress drawn up in the Illinois counties in 1805 the petitioners declared: "altho your Memorialists can sufficiently appreciate the advantage of having a Court acting with Chancery powers, yet they wish to see these powers vested in the Supreme Court of the territory. It was with pain therefore that

---

[1] Messages of August 18, 1807 (*Messages*, 1: 231); September 27, 1808 (*ibid.*, 307); October 17, 1809 (*ibid.*, 382); the quotation is from the second message. Cp. Baldwin (ed.), *Two Centuries' Growth of American Law*, 130.

they saw a law passed by the last territorial assembly vesting these powers in a single judge appointable by the Governor." The memorial of 1808 which directly attacked Harrison included among its nine complaints two based upon his advocacy of a court of chancery and his veto of bills designed to obviate the conferment of equitable powers upon the ordinary courts of law.[1] Both memorials affected a concern for the continued control of the territory which properly pertained to Congress; their real motives were doubtless enmity to Harrison, and, very likely, fear for the land claims of the petitioners.[2] Their gross exaggerations reveal their political motive. Illinois was a separate territory before a chancery court became a reality. That it was needed appears in the records of Illinois Territory from the moment of its introduction.[3]

Not a few things in the practice acts evidence a liberalism that is modern. Practically all of these laws came from Virginia, directly or by way of Kentucky, and reflect Virginian experience. Not only was the English statute of jeofails (as of 1752) adopted

[1] This petition is described *ante,* xlvii, n. 1 and xlviii. The charges were: "Fifthly, That he has given his sanction to a Law establishing a Court of Chancery, independent of and superior to the National Court [established in the] Territory—a measure which has for its effect the wounding and weakening of the great ligature which was intended to bind the Colony to the Nation. This Court has already granted a number of Injunctions; the causes are hung up to be tried, when a salary (which has not yet been done) shall be granted, For this Court, impressed with the force of the old French Maxim, that the 'point d'Argent' is the 'point de Suisse,' is at present in a torpid state. . . .
"Seventhly, That he has in an arbitrary manner put his veto on several bills passed by both Houses of the Legislature, which were calculated for the impartial administration of Justice and the general good of the Territory—and among many others the following, A Bill for the selection and [MS torn: appointment of judges and a bill vesting certain] equitable powers in the several Courts of Law, which would supercede the necessity of a Court of Chancery, relieve the Inhabitants from an oppressive burthen and the Suitors from the delays and expences attendant on such Courts."
On the "many" acts vetoed see *ante,* xxx.
[2] Memorial cited *ante,* clvi, at end of n. 2. "It is with pain"— they also declared, "they are now told that it is in proposition, at the next session, to create a court of appeals. Where will this end? Is it in contemplation to deprive the present Government of its control over its colony?"
[3] The governor and judges of the territory of Michigan (though the United States statute of 1805 clearly made this unnecessary) conferred equity powers upon their Supreme Court in 1812—*Mich. Pioneer and Hist. Colls.,* 8: 617.

by the first statute passed in the field of procedure, but a very full and explicit statement was made of defects that should not be substantial.[1] Rather broad power was given to the General Court to adopt its own rules of procedure, though it did not go far in exercising this.[2] Not more than two new trials were granted to the same party in one cause; where less than all of several defendants were served, judgment was taken against those served and a scire facias against the others; in case of several counts, one defective, and verdict for entire damages, this was good. The jury might take any papers read in evidence, even though unsealed. A scroll was given the effect of a seal. The provision that "after issue joined in an ejectment on the title only, no exception of form or substance shall be taken to the declaration in any court whatsoever," presumably was intended to exclude pleadings to the fictions in the form of action; but may possibly, in view of the state of land titles in the territory, have embodied an expression of broader public policy. Extremely modern is the rule that if the verdict in detinue omit the value it might be ascertained by writ of inquiry; and that if several things were claimed and the verdict given only for part, it should be good as to those.[3] The capias ad respondendum was generally used instead of a summons. The statute of 1795 regulating small causes provided that it should not be used against a freeholder, but there was no such restriction in actions generally.[4] There are scores of suits in the Randolph records in which a capias was employed against judges and other leading members of the community.

[1] *Post,* 7, and 40, § 24.
[2] *Post,* 3. Rules of Court appear in its *Order Book,* 1: 1, 19— these deal only with return days and delivery of the record, on appeal to the presiding judge; 26—motions in arrest to be argued the same term unless put over at request of plaintiff.
[3] *Post,* 39, § 18 (1803)—new trials; Pease, *Laws* (*I. H. C.,* 17), 351 (1799)—unserved defendants; *post,* 39, § 19—seal; § 20—defective count: 41, § 25—evidence; § 26—ejectment; § 27—detinue.
[4] Pease, *op. cit.,* 94 (1792), 143, 145 (1795) simply assume it as a regular procedure; the statute of 1799 on small causes—*ibid.,* 390—was the first to define the special circumstances in which it might be used. This was law throughout the territorial period—*post,* 376, § 2; 377, § 4. Out of 47 pleas in the St. Clair *Order Book 1801-03* the capias was used in 26. In Randolph it was at least as common. A protest against the use of the capias in Michigan is printed in *Mich. Pioneer and Hist. Colls.,* 8: 579 (1806).

The capias ad satisfaciendum was also, at least in statute theory, in common use.[1]

The statutes of the Northwest Territory did not subject real estate to execution if the rents and profits were reported, by inquest of twelve men, sufficient to pay the debt in seven years; and this remained the law until 1806.[2] Right to redeem from the sale, during one year, the tenement "upon which the defendant is chiefly seated" was also recognized in 1795; and both the homestead and the redemption rights were extended by the legislation

[1] "A writ of *capias ad satisfaciendum* upon which the judgment debtor was committed to prison till the debt was paid was as common a remedy one hundred years ago as an ordinary writ of execution to sell the debtor's goods"—J. F. Dillon, *The Laws and Jurisprudence of England and America*, 359. The writ has gradually disappeared in this country; as a result of statutes prohibiting its use unless in specified cases, and of other statutes facilitating the discharge of debtors.

"Statutes abolishing imprisonment for debt have been generally held not to affect the right to take the body in execution in actions of tort. It may be laid down as a proposition, generally true, that except where by statute this right has been expressly taken away, it exists [in the U. S.] as it did in the time of Henry VIII, subject to the defendant's right of freedom upon taking the 'Poor Debtor's Oath' "—Baldwin (ed.), *Two Centuries' Growth of American Law* (1901), 112. The law of 1795 (Pease, *Laws (I.H. C.,* 17), 145, § 6) assumes the c. a. s. as always available in default of goods and chattels to satisfy the judgment. In the Randolph judicial records the execution returns are not generally available. The absence of adequate jails must have made c. a. s. more theoretical than real: *post,* clxxxi, n. 4. Preference for a c. a. s. over a summons was presumably shown with a view to making easily available execution against the body. In the Michigan protest cited *ante,* clxix, n. 4, the petitioners say: "We find it very lamentable to us that now a freeholder, for the smallest sum under twenty dollars, is taken by a capias as a criminal, and that execution follows immediately; whereas by our ancient laws we were all summoned, and execution could not be had but three or six months after judgement."

[2] Pease, *op. cit.,* 132, §§ 3, 4; *post,* 188, § 6 (1806). See *St. Clair Papers,* 2: 353-354 n. on this law of 1795; also, on its application in the territorial period see the dissenting opinion of Judge Burnet in McArthur *v.* Porter, 1 Ohio R. 99. The policy of Major Hamtramck in October, 1789, before the new governor and judges had reached the territory, was stated in a letter to John Edgar thus: "I mean that the authority of such magistrates shall extend to the internal policy of your country, & prevent debtors from absconding from their creditors; but my intentions are that for the present, no execution shall take place in favor of a creditor, but as the people are daily moving on the Spanish side without paying their debts, it is my wish that against such people attachments may be granted, provided the plaintiff gives bond & security, & *not otherwise."* Alvord, *Kaskaskia Records (I. H. C.,* 5), 511. There was no statute until 1795. What was the law, and the practice? See *post,* ccxvii, n. 3.

of Indiana Territory.[1] The right of the debtor to offer particular
lands for either execution or foreclosure sale was recognized in
1805, but not until 1808[2] was it expressly provided that the
officer must first take what the execution debtor should designate,
realty or personalty, and sell in the order of his preference. This
statute of 1805 is far more notable, however, for its stay law provisions. Not only must the officer take what the debtor tendered,
but if the property (real or personal) would not sell for two-
thirds of its value, ascertained by inquest, enough thereof, chosen
by the creditor, to satisfy the judgment, exclusive of costs, was
"adjudged to be purchased by the creditor" at the two-thirds
valuation. After the "sale or valuation" the debtor could be discharged. And if the creditor refused to take the lands the sheriff
should repeatedly offer them for sale, until they should sell for
two-thirds of the appraised value or the creditor should become
willing to accept them.[3] Such valuation-and-stay laws, which
practically suspended the collection of debts, have had a large
history since colonial times, the final chapter in which was written
by the Supreme Court of the United States in holding unconstitutional a later statute of Illinois of this type.[4]

The Northwest Territory started with a criminal law[5]
(1788) which was evidently regarded as satisfactory so far as it
went, since its actual provisions were altered only in details; but it
was very inadequate. As has been said; "This code is more remarkable, if possible, for what it does not contain than for what
it does. There is not an act of turbulence or injury to the person
of another that is forbidden either by way of admonition or fine,
save those of murder and robbery. The citizens of the new territory might fight, engage in riots, slit noses, perpetrate mayhem,

[1] Nothing further appears on this in the law of 1805 (*post,* 126), but
a two-year redemption (half per year) was allowed in 1806 (*post,* 171, § 1;
554, § 4—Revision of 1807).
[2] *Post,* 665.
[3] *Post,* 126 (August 24, 1805).
[4] See I. N. Arnold's reminiscences in Ill. State Bar Assoc. *Proc.*
(1881), 110-111; citing Bronson *v.* Kinzie, 1 How. 311, and McCracken *v.*
Hayward, 2 How. 608.
[5] Pease, *Laws* (*I. H. C.,* 17), 13.

gamble, commit rape, but they must not get drunk, and they ought not to swear nor fail to keep the sabbath."[1]   Though this is much exaggerated, the law was in truth a mere beginning.

Treason, murder, and arson resulting in a death were the original capital crimes.   All arson was made such in 1799;[2] forgery (of public securities) in 1799;[3] horse stealing, for a second offence, in 1805, and for a first—and equally for knowingly receiving the stolen animal—in 1808; bigamy and abduction of women, in 1803; rape in 1807.   No statute of limitations existed in the case of capital offences until 1807, when a bar of three years was established for all except murder; and for lesser offences two years.[4]

To the original felonies of 1788—arson not resulting in death, manslaughter, burglary and robbery by one armed with dangerous weapons—mayhem was added (substantially) in 1798;[5] rape was substantially so treated before 1807;[6] bigamy and abduction of women (now reduced in gravity) were added in 1807; sodomy in 1807.[7]

Hanging was the penalty imposed for capital crimes.   For all others the punishments varied.   The construction of jails,

[1] Judge D. D. Banta, "The Criminal Code of the Northwest Territory," *Indiana Quarterly Magazine History,* 9: 236, 241-242.   The statute punished riots and assaults and batteries (Pease, *op. cit.,* 16, 19).   Moreover, it specifically adopted the common law with respect to one crime, and since the Ordinance of 1787 had guaranteed the territory some of the common law guaranties of personal liberty, that law must therefore be regarded as partially in force even before its formal and general adoption in 1795 (Pease, *op. cit.,* 253).

[2] Pease, *Laws (I. H. C.,* 17), 505; *post,* 243, § 15.   The law against treason was, of course, open to the general objection that it exceeded the powers of the legislators under the Ordinance; but the definition came apparently within that of the Constitution (the adoption of which was proclaimed on July 2, 1788), and seems to be substantially descriptive of acts that were taking place, or might well take place, in the western country at the time.   Compare *post,* 246-247, § 20.

[3] Pease, *op. cit.,* 388, § 17.

[4] *Post,* 66, 118, 120, § 5; 243, § 16; 247, § 21; 249, § 28; 667.

[5] Pease, *Laws (I. H. C.,* 17), 296.   There was no state's prison; a jail sentence was imposed by the territory.   The first penitentiary of Indiana was established in 1820; in Illinois there was none until considerably later.

[6] Note case of 1802, *post,* clxxvi.   Perhaps § 3 of the bigamy act of 1803 (*post,* 67) means rape; § 4 includes it.

[7] *Post,* 247, §§ 23, 24; 248, § 25.

whipping posts, pillories, and stocks was first ordered by statute
in 1792.[1] No reference to stocks is found in the records of
the courts. But the noose, whip, pillory, and branding iron
were statutory realities.[2] In the Virginia period, never later,
the stake and fire—and some other extralegal punishments
—were not wholly absent. On the other hand there is no
trace of the ducking stool, cropping knife, cage, wheel or
stocks; all of which had been, and to a varying degree still were,
used in the Atlantic states. From them the statutes of Northwestern Territory were taken, but with moderation in the number
of capital offences; and the governor and judges of the Indiana
Territory, in their continued borrowings from the older states and
from Kentucky, mitigated the ferocity of their criminal codes.
Nobody acquainted with the history of the criminal law could
regard the statutes in the present volume barbarous for their time.

[1] Pease, *Laws* (*I. H. C.*, 17), 77.

[2] The statute of 1788 provided for imprisonment up to 40 years in
punishment of burglary or robbery with violence. The longest terms imposed by any other laws were those under the statute against forcible and
stolen marriages (1803, 1807—*post*, 68, § 4; 249, § 27), 5 years, and for
sodomy (1807); this being only 1 to 5 years. This extraordinary fact is
probably associated with the lack of jails. See *post*, clxxxi, n. 4.

The lash was alternative with fine in larceny of less than $1.50 (up to
15 lashes), in larceny generally if the first offence (up to 31 stripes), and
in perjury (up to 39). It was prescribed for arson before 1799 (not exceeding 39 stripes); burglary or robbery without violence or carrying deadly
weapons (up to 39); bigamy and forcible marriage after 1807 (100 to 300);
sodomy after 1807 (100 to 500); larceny, second offence (not exceeding 39
stripes); horse stealing, first offence, until 1808 (50 to 200); hog stealing, or
alteration of brand with larcenous intent (25 to 39); altering brands, first
offence (40); striking of parent or master by child or servant (up to 10).

The pillory was prescribed in arson until 1799; perjury, forgery, and for
altering brands (second offence). Three hours for forgery was the maximum pillory penalty possible. Brink, McDonough, *Hist. of St. Clair County*,
61, and Bateman and Selby, *Hist. of St. Clair County*, 2: 679, say that the
only case of actual use of the pillory was one of 1822, for forgery.

Branding was a penalty for the second offence of altering brands.

Forfeiture was part of the penalty for arson (until 1799), burglary
with violence, robbery with violence. (The statute attempted impossible
distinctions between violence and violent intention).

Disability as witness, juror, or office holder was included in the penalties for bigamy after 1807, perjury, and forgery.

In general fines, if not paid, were followed by imprisonment: see
ante, cxxxiii-cxxxiv.

On the startlingly variant penalties imposed today in different states
for the same offence—some of them reminiscent of details of the legislation
of Indiana Territory—see Baldwin (ed.), *Two Centuries' Growth of American Law*, 375, 377-378.

Indeed, as regards their list of capital offences they were strikingly humane.[1]

The records of the courts reveal illustrations of most of the crimes provided for in the statutes. None, however, have been discovered of arson, robbery, riot, obtaining of property by false pretences (treated as larceny), mayhem, bigamy, dueling, or perjury. At least two murderers were ordered hung by the General Court, of whom Governor Harrison pardoned one;[2] and at least two in Randolph County (both Indians) and one in St. Clair.[3]

[1] A. translation of Beccaria was printed in 1793 in Philadelphia, with Voltaire's commentary. Note, *post,* cxcv, presence of a Beccaria in a frontier lawyer's library. On the general character of criminal punishments in the older states in the period 1776-1820 see J. B. McMaster, *Rights of Man in America,* 36-40, 48-49. Also Baldwin, *op. cit.,* 354-356, 360-361; Howard, *Local Const. History,* 416-423. Judge Banta's article, cited *ante,* clxxii, n. 1, is a defence of the Northwest (and Indiana) Territory code against Howard's characterization of it as "barbarous."

[2] Robert Slaughter (*Order Book,* 1: 107, 133, 134, 145; hung October 25, 1804); Abraham Hiley, indicted with three others (*ibid.,* 291, 293-296, ordered hung October 29, 1808; pardoned—Gibson, *Exec. Journal,* 150). Defendant's counsel (whose name does not appear) moved an arrest of judgment because: (1) the indictment named no township where defendant resided or the crime was committed; (2) did not state which hand held the rifle; (3) alleged four shots, but that the victim received three wounds; (4) did not allege the length or depth of the wounds; (5) omitted "then and there"; (6) was argumentative; (7) charged all defendants as principals both in the first and second degree; (8) concluded "against the statute," whereas there was none in the territory against the crime as alleged; (9) some jurors were not freeholders; (10) "Speir" Spencer was summoned as juror, but "Pierre" was sworn as such; (11) the indictment was not properly signed by the foreman and indorsed as a true bill.

[3] Governor Reynolds says (*Pioneer History,* 304) that in 1802, late autumn, a Delaware Indian was hung for the murder of a white man. The existing records of the Quarter Sessions (*Court Record 1802-06*) begin September 7, 1802, and show (p. 101, December 1805) an allowance to James Edgar, sheriff, of $37.50 "for expenses of 25 soldiers in attending the execution of the Delaware Indians." Edgar was sheriff 1803-1806. At a Circuit Court of Oyer and Terminer held at Kaskaskia by Judge Vander Burgh in November 1808 (Canvas Envelope No. 2) the Indian Marangoin was ordered hung for the murder of John Russell, gentleman. This may be the Piankashaw chief "Le Maringouin or Mosquito" (signature "Maringoin"—*Amer. State Papers: Pub. Lands,* 2: 119, 120). There are references to the murderer in the record of *County Commissioners* (Illinois Territory July, 1809-January 1810), 117, 118. Governor Reynolds also says (*Pioneer History,* 304; *My Own Times,* 49) that Emsley Jones was hung at Kaskaskia in 1804 for killing a man named Reed, and that the two executions were the last in Illinois until 1821. Both statements are apparently erroneous. An Emsley Jones was indicted for assault and battery in 1806 (Randolph *Common Pleas,* 5: 257) and the action abated by death of

A man indicted for murder in the General Court was found guilty
of manslaughter, and was sentenced to be branded with an M in
his left hand—"which sentence," says the record, "was executed
by the sheriff in open court, and proclamation being made as the
manner is" he was then discharged.[1] Sentence was similarly
executed upon a defendant in Cahokia.[2] Such punishment was
wholly extralegal.[3] As further illustrations of extralegal punishment it may be mentioned that in 1779 a negro was ordered
burned at the stake in Kaskaskia, though the order was super-
seded by one for hanging;[4] and that when a man was convicted
(with his wife) of a "statutory offense" at Cahokia in 1794 it was
"Ordered that . . . he be mounted on horseback with his face
to the tail, and conducted through the town from the jail to the
church door and then back to jail and then to be liberated," and

[1] Nelson Johnson (John Johnson his attorney, and James Johnson one
of his witnesses)—*Order Book*, 1: 297, 299-305; convicted April 6, 1809.
For another similar case from Harrison County in 1811 see Gibson,
Exec. Journal, 176 n. In Baldwin (ed.), *Two Centuries' Growth of
American Law*, 381, it is suggested that burning and branding would come
within the constitutional prohibition of "cruel and unusual punishments."
No doubt they might, today, be held to do so; but there were undoubtedly
many instances of both after 1789. Branding was recognized in the statutes
of Illinois Territory. See E. J. White, *Legal Antiquities*, 239-240, 242.

[2] *Ante*, clxxiv, n. 3. The other defendant there involved, and here
referred to, was a white.

[3] The statutes of 1788, 1799, and 1807 punished manslaughter simply
as at common law.

[4] McDonough, *Hist. of Randolph, Monroe and Perry Counties*, 94,
gives Colonel John Todd's written order of June 13, 1779 to Richard Winston,
sheriff of the District of Kaskaskia, in the case of Negro Manuel, slave:
"after having made honorable fine at the door of the church, to be chained
to a post at the waterside, and there to be burnt alive and his ashes scattered, as appears to me by record." And another slave, Moreau, was
ordered to be executed about the same time at Cahokia (*ibid.*, 94). The
two orders for execution are also given in *Chic. Hist. Colls.*, 4: 302-303,
where the name of the second convict is given as "Morace." But Governor
Todd changed his order in Manuel's case to death by hanging—Alvord,
Kaskaskia Records (I. H. C., 5), 97 and note. See also Alvord, *Cahokia
Records (I. H. C.*, 2), 12-21; cp. Reynolds, *Pioneer History*, 175, who
dates these events as of 1790, and states that Moreau was hung, "Emanuel"
shot.

the defendant. I find no reference evidence of a capital crime by any such
man. Mr. Webster, in Ind. Hist. Soc. *Pub.*, 4: 232 quotes from the *Western Sun* an account of two indictments at Cahokia for murder in 1808;
the defendant in one was an Indian, who was executed. The records of the
St. Clair courts for this time are lost.

"Ordered that she lead the horse."[1] This was medieval practice, English as well as French, persisting on the Mississippi.

Of crimes against the person, other than homicide, the only ones largely represented in the records are assaults and batteries. One rapist, convicted in the General Court, was fined $15 and sentenced to "stand in and upon the pillory at Vincennes" for two hours on each of two days, and lie in jail six weeks.[2] But Governor Harrison pardoned him.[3] Indictments were brought in the Illinois county courts for adultery, bastardy, and other sex offences;[4] but it would be difficult to find legal basis for these proceedings. Indictments for assault and battery were more numerous than civil suits. Both were distinctly discouraged by the statutes; so much so in criminal prosecutions that the complainant was made responsible for the errors of the state's attorney and grand jury, and equally for the leniency of the former in discharging defendants.[5] It seems reasonably safe to assume, considering the manners and customs of the southwest at that time, that the

[1] François Quintett—Bateman and Selby, *Hist. of St. Clair County,* 699-700. This passage is probably translated from the French. The authors presumably mean buggery. There was no statutory law governing this in 1794.

[2] Joseph Michel—*Order Book,* 1: 8, 10, 13, 21, 34-35, 37, 41-44; convicted September 11, 1802. The jury included John Edgar, Shadrach Bond, and John Hays, of the Illinois country.

[3] Gibson, *Exec. Journal,* 112 (September 16, 1802).

[4] William Wilson (the surveyor) and Cole Beatt were indicted in the Randolph Quarter Sessions (*Court Record 1802-06,* 24, 31—June 7 and September 6, 1803) for bastardy. The former was discharged; the latter was found guilty, and ordered to pay $40 to the complainant, $8 for "Lying Inn," and $8 quarterly for one year. The women were French. An indictment of William Goings for adultery (*ibid.,* 22, June, 1803) was quashed. Goings was a picturesque old reprobate (Reynolds, *Pioneer History,* 182-183), quite prominent in the court records. As far back as 1797 he and George Adams were indicted for stealing Indian women (Bateman and Selby, *Hist. of St. Clair County,* 2: 700; compare *post,* ccx, n. 3). Ephraim Connor was indicted in St. Clair in 1799 "for being a nuisance in living with" another's wife (Bateman and Selby, *op. cit.,* 701). In St. Clair, in addition to the conviction in 1794 for "statutory offences" referred to *ante,* clxxv, there were other indictments in 1797. Bateman and Selby, *op. cit.,* 700.

[5] *Order Book,* 1: 76, 91, 92, 94 (1803 Anthony Campbell, assault and battery upon a woman, but nothing to indicate a more serious offence) ; 62, 72, 93 (1803, Joseph Scaffen, battery upon Pierre Gamelin, a leading citizen) ; 149, 151, 164 (1805, Josias Carrico) ; 181, 193 (1806, Benjamin D. Price) ; 268 (1808, John Glass). In the Belleville Museum is a paper of a Circuit Court of October 31, 1808, showing a fine of 25 cents upon Guillaume Vaudry for a battery committed in 1806. Mr. Webster, "Harrison's Admin-

cases in court were not trivial, yet we find even the General Court imposing fines of $3.11, $2, $1, 25 cents, 1 cent—and costs— upon the guilty defendant.[1] It was quite the same, of course, in the county courts, with the remarkable exception that in Randolph the heavy fine of $20 was imposed upon a woman for an assault upon another, apparently in a quarrel over the affections of a man.[2]

The only defendant charged with burglary,[3] and most of those indicted for larceny, were acquitted. One Philip Catt, indicted for theft, possibly turned upon the informant, for we find

[1] Costs could not be recovered in the civil action unless the verdict exceeded $16.66 in the General Court or $6.66 in a county court (*post,* 41). By act of 1805 (*post,* 141) by which the cost of prosecuting in the past persons discharged or unable to pay was ordered paid by the counties, it was provided that thereafter the name of the prosecutor, indorsed on the indictment, was essential to its validity, and if defendant should be acquitted or otherwise lawfully discharged the prosecutor should pay all costs, unless the court should think there had been reasonable cause for the indictment. See *ante,* xciv, n. 2. The prosecuting officer constantly dismissed or failed to prosecute. There was no attempt to control him. Compare, for example, *post,* cc, n. 6; Gilbreath paid $24.66 in costs.

[2] Randolph *Court Record 1802-06*—30 (1803, Mary Adams, assault on Mary Dunn; defendant and Wm. Chaffin each bound in $100 to keep the peace) ; 60, 66 (1804, Miles Hotchkiss—see app. n. 74—fined $5) ; Randolph *Common Pleas,* 5: 107 (1807, Henry Levens "Esq"—see app. n. 67—fined 50 cents and costs ; *ibid.,* 4: 131 (1807, Jas. Henderson, for assault and battery upon a woman in her home, fined 25 cents and costs) ; 177 (a second assault by Henry Levens upon the same victim, Charles Hulsey, plea guilty, fine 25 cents and costs. The cause of these two assaults is clear : contemporaneous with the first Levens was defendant in a civil action brought by Hulsey, discontinued, defendant paying costs (*ibid.,* 4 : 179). In St. Clair County—1796, Marianna Arnouse, fined $1.50 and costs (Bateman and Selby, *Hist. St. Clair County,* 2: 701).

Elizabeth Chribbs was indicted in 1806 for battery upon her husband, but the charge was dismissed. Daniel Bissel, Stephen Rumsey, and Elizabeth Chribbs were indicted in December 1804 for attempting the life of William Chribbs—this must have been at common law, since the statutes did not cover the case; the men defendants could not be found. They had blown up the house with gunpowder (Randolph *Court Record 1802-06,* 71, 94; *Common Pleas,* 5 : 304, 306). The deed of gift quoted *ante,* clxv was made in September 1804.

[3] John Jessup—Randolph *Common Pleas,* 5: 308 (1805).

istration," 214, cites various cases. It should be remembered that prices were high (see *St. Clair Papers,* 2: 317 n., figures for Kaskaskia in 1793) as compared with the east. Nevertheless, compared with those prices, or with the cost of tavern lodging (*ante,* cxxvii, n. 6), or with the rate of current wages (men were paid 25 cents daily to guard prisoners—but see *ante,* xxxvi; and the regular witness fee was 25 cents daily) fines laid were absurdly and stultifyingly low.

Joseph Buchanan indicted soon thereafter for theft of corn from
Catt, and the verdict was, "guilty of stealing corn to the amount
of five cents"! In accordance with the statute, not being able to
make restitution of the corn, he paid ten cents to Catt, ten cents
to the territory, and costs, thereby avoiding an alternative penalty
of twenty lashes.[1] This is the only case found in which, for any
offence whatever, whipping was included in the penalty, even
alternatively.[2] Horse stealing is supposed to have been a common crime—and probably it was, as on all frontiers; but the only
conviction mentioned was followed by a pardon from the governor.[3] Hog thieves have left but a trace of their wrongdoing in
the records of the courts. In the only case where the defendant
was convicted the statute was not observed in the penalty imposed.[4] Evidence of the operation of the misbranding statute is
even scantier.[5]

[1] General Court, Order Book, 1: 233 (April 1807). There are several
other indictments in the General Court; one for stealing a cotton shirt
worth $1.50, and one pound of tea worth $2.50 (ibid., 113, 120). In Randolph only two indictments were found, both defendants found not guilty
(Court Record 1802-06, 68, 69).
[2] In 1794, however, in St. Clair Auguste Bellecoure was given fifteen
lashes for the nonpayment of a debt—Bateman and Selby, Hist. of St. Clair
County, 2: 700. Brink, McDonough, Hist. of St. Clair County, 61, intimate
that whipping was common. This is extremely doubtful.
[3] In his message to the General Assembly in September 1808 (Messages, 1: 306) Governor Harrison refers to horse stealing as frequent on
the southeast boundary of the territory. It was there, in Clark County,
that one Ingram was condemned to death for the offence in 1807, but pardoned on the scaffold; this being the only sentence in that county under
the statute—Ind. Mag. of Hist., 4: 17. There were no cases in Randolph
from 1802 to 1809. The records in St. Clair do not exist that would give
an answer for that county. Apparently the law was ineffective. Monks,
Courts, 1: 145, 151, throws no light from the records of the Indiana counties. (Houck, Missouri, 2: 203, cites a whipping imposed by the Spanish
commandant at Cape Girardeau in 1799 upon a well-known inhabitant of
Horse Prairie, near Kaskaskia, for horse stealing; restitution of the animals, payment of costs, and 30 lashes—and 500 every time he should return).
[4] Thomas Drinnen, tried in the General Court, was found not guilty
(Order Book, 1: 100, 101, 104, 115, 163; 1803-1805, including one jury disagreement). John and Benjamin Vermillion were found not guilty in Randolph (Common Pleas, 5: 318—1806). Joseph Barns was convicted in Randolph in 1806 of stealing a sow worth $10. The penalty was: payment of $20
to the owner, and a fine of $50. If the first offence, the court should have
imposed a fine of not more than $20 or not exceeding 39 lashes; if a second
offence, a fine of not exceeding $40 and a whipping (ibid., 316).
[5] One indictment only (Randolph Common Pleas, 4: 405—December
1808). Defendants misbranded a bull (worth $4), and unwisely chose

Despite the scores of perjuries of which leading citizens were guilty, and likewise forgeries, according to the land commissioners, no indictments were brought except eighteen against Robert Reynolds; and neither in those, nor in the other cases of forgery discovered, was there a conviction.[1]   Practically, therefore, the statutes on perjury and forgery were as empty homilies as the preachments of the Marietta code—without penalty attached—against profanity and sabbath breaking.

The almost total ineffectiveness of the moralistic legislation of the territory—as to gambling, drunkenness, sabbath breaking, and profanity—has been already pointed out.[2]

Statutes under which indictments were relatively numerous were those forbidding purchases from Indians[3] without special

[1] Solomon Hays was indicted in the General Court for forgery of a deed; a capias and an alias were issued but apparently defendant got safely away. This transaction involved one of the Vincennes court grants referred to *ante*, lxvi. Hays sold 3,000 acres for $55; he had himself bought 66,000 acres for a price unspecified (*Order Book,* 1: 60, 74, 75). Wilson Buttel was indicted in the Randolph Quarter Sessions (*Court Record 1802-06,* 83—March, 1805), and found not guilty. There was an indictment for forgery in St. Clair in 1796—Bateman and Selby, *Hist. of St. Clair County,* 2: 700. Seventeen indictments against Reynolds were brought in the Randolph Common Pleas in August 1806 (5: 261-301) and one in December 1807 (*ibid.,* 1). John Grosvenor was foreman of the grand jury, Robert Robinson state's attorney. The last in date was for forgery of the name of Pierre Menard; two others were for forging the names of John Beaird and Nathaniel Huil. All were taken up by certiorari to the General Court, the seventeen in August 1807 and the other in December 1808. Under the law they must have been tried in the Circuit Court in Randolph; and as nothing of them appears in the *Order Book* of the General Court such proceedings must have been final. But there are no records left of proceedings in these cases on circuit. However the penalty of conviction would have included the pillory and civil disability; and it is inconceivable that, if there was a conviction, no report of it should have survived. The files of the *Western Sun* have not been examined, but as Dunn, Mr. Webster, and others have examined them, and cite them on various subjects, it may be assumed that they contain no information.

[2] *Ante,* cxxiv *et seq.*

[3] James Gilbreath, before he became sheriff, was indicted for buying a cloth "called stroud" (Randolph, *Court Record 1802-06,* 59, 60, 66) in 1804, but was found not guilty. Another indictment, with the same result, occurred in the General Court (John Small, 1800—*Order Book,* 1: 9, 13, 26, 31).

one belonging to the sheriff, James Gilbreath. The action was quashed, since the county court lacked jurisdiction to try felonies. Robert Robinson, as state's attorney, made the error.

license, forbidding the sale of whiskey to Indians,[1] and prohibiting the sale of merchandise without license.[2] Add a few indictments for entering upon Indian lands, for not properly serving a ferry, and for counterfeiting, and one has a complete view of the work of the courts in enforcement of the criminal statutes.[3] The only object of indictments under the license statute was to compel the taking out of licenses.[4]

On the whole, whatever might be thought of punishments theoretically possible under the statutes, it is impossible to find in their application anything of brutality. It might have been otherwise in an older community whose government was capable of enforcing its laws. In Indiana Territory their enforcement was imperfect in the extreme. It is merely characteristic, for example, that when—in one of the cases above cited—a prominent citizen was indicted for illegally selling liquor without a license, an equally prominent citizen and tavern-keeper, twice indicted in the preceding year for sales of liquor to Indians (indictments quashed), was on the jury. It is no more surprising that in the very term when the latter was indicted for the second time he was again recommended to the Governor as a fit and proper person to conduct a public house. It is necessarily unusual, but otherwise not surprising, that a few months later he should have been named

[1] Drusilla Turcotte, John Grosvenor, Miles Hotchkiss, and Joseph Archambeau—all tavern-keepers at one time or another, and presumably at the times when indicted—were defendants under this statute in Randolph (Court Record 1802-06, 21, 22, 23, 32, June and September 1803), and only Hotchkiss was found guilty. He was fined $5.
[2] In General Court—Joseph Barron, discharged (1803, Order Book, 1: 80, 89) Ephraim Doolittle, fined 50 cents and costs (1803, ibid., 82, 88); Antoine Marchal, not guilty (1803, ibid., 81, 102). In Randolph James Gilbreath was found not guilty (Court Record 1802-06, 59, 60, 66); Joseph Benoke pleaded guilty, and was fined $1 and costs, and required to take out a license.
[3] Only one indictment for each of these crimes was noted in the General Court (Order Book, 1: 5, 13, 18—Joshua Fleehart, 1801, plea of guilty, fined $30; 64, 91—John Small, guilty, fined $6; 230, 241, 242—outcome not discovered). But it should be noted that the cause of indictment frequently does not appear in the Order Book. It is therefore impossible to make conclusive statements.
[4] Thus in the above case of Joseph Benoke the costs were $9.83, the license could have been had in the beginning for $12. Had there been any other purpose, the fine of 50 cents—when taffia brought in 25 cents and brandy 37½ per half pint—would have been ridiculous.

a judge of the Common Pleas.[1] As for the penalties imposed
for minor offences it can only be said that then, as today, no less
and no more, the courts made the statute-book ridiculous by the
fines which they imposed.

Lynchings, and private vengeance less extreme in form, must
have been more or less common, but the evidences of it seem to be
scanty.[2] It is worthy of remark that in 1809 it was moved in a
special court of oyer and terminer at Vincennes that the court
"instruct the grand jury to find according to the truth of the case,
as well in regard to the fact as the law arising on it." The court
followed English authorities in rejecting the motion.[3]

The lack of secure jails was a cause of early complaint.[4]
Undoubtedly it largely explains the severity of the criminal code.

[1] Gilbreath case, ante, clxxx, n. 2. The juror was John Grosvenor,
his indictments—Randolph Court Record 1802-06, 21, 32, 38. Several cases
were noted of men who served on juries while themselves under indictment.

[2] Mr. Esarey says that such cases "often" occurred, particularly
lynching of horse thieves—Indiana, 1: 167. According to Bateman and Selby,
Hist. of St. Clair County, 679, the people "often took the law into their
own hands." Governor Reynolds says that the action of the regulators
who put down counterfeiters in St. Clair County after the war of 1812
(ibid., 737) was the first instance of lynch law in Illinois—My Own Times,
113. Private vengeance, of which he gives earlier instances, was evidently
not regarded by him as lynch law—e. g. Pioneer History, 286. Cp. Burnet,
Notes, 57.

[3] General Court, Order Book, 1: 298. Vander Burgh and Parke
were the judges. They cited 2 Hale P. C. b. 157-159; 2 Ld. Raym. 1485,
1574; 2 Stra. 166, 882; Foster, 255. Their argument was a careful one.

[4] In 1780 the military authorities at Kaskaskia gave the court leave
to use the military prison "in case of necessity"; but later in the same year
Richard Winston wrote to John Todd from Kaskaskia: "as to our Civil
department it is in but an indifferent way ever [since] the Military have
refused us their Prison for which we off[ered to] Pay very handsomely"
Alvord, Kaskaskia Records (I. H. C., 5), 152, 195. In 1782 various inhabitants petitioned the court to erect a jail, and the court ordered a general
assembly of "all the French and American citizens . . . to consider the
erection of a jail, at which meeting none should be absent"—ibid., 286,
290-291. Evidently nothing was done. The difficulty continued for years,
and involved some problems of great gravity. It was one of the various
subjects over which Judge Turner quarreled with Governor St. Clair and
his other colleagues—St. Clair Papers, 2: 218-222; their correspondence
shows that in 1791 there was still no jail at or near Ft. Washington, and
that the military guard-house had been used more or less as a jail for civil
prisoners up to that time. While St. Clair was in the Illinois country in
1790 "orders were issued for erecting prisons and an assignment of lots
to build them upon"—ibid., 2: 177. If these orders were the Governor's
they were extra-legal; but any way they were not observed. "Genteel
Men":—said James Piggott, presiding judge to his colleagues of the St.

A penitentiary was beyond the means of the territory: in the meantime, therefore, "adequate punishment" was relied upon.[1] The frequency of escapes from such jails as existed is reflected in the early law fining negligent jailers, and making those who connived at escapes subject to the same penalties as the fugitive[2]—

[1] Harrison, *Messages,* 1: 306.

[2] 1792—Pease, *Laws* (*I. H. C.,* 17), 80, § 1 (civil prisoners), 82, § 5 (criminals); *post,* 259, § 5. It was modified by later law as regarded prisoners who gave bonds and were allowed the freedom of prison bounds (Pease, *op. cit.,* 495; *post,* 258, § 3). Monks, *Courts,* 1: 18, 29, assumes that the sheriffs actually aided escapes, being out of sympathy with the judges; and states that the sheriffs, in the absence of jails, "often" accepted bail on their own authority, which bail "frequently" was worthless. The law above cited of 1799 (Pease, *op. cit.,* 495) was passed in December. In September Governor St. Clair stated to the legislature: "As the law now stands, the sheriffs are not answerable for the escapes of prisoners"—*St. Clair Papers,* 2: 456. This is inexplicable. St. Clair seems to have been personally responsible) cp. his views in 1791, *ibid.,* 2: 220, 221, with the law of 1792, Pease, 80) for the liability imposed upon sheriffs for escapes.

Clair County Quarter Sessions in October, 1791—"It is now one year and six months since this court set under an established constitution. And as yet we have not a prison in our county, for want of which the transgressors of the law pass unpunished . . . It is now about one year since I understood that there was a collection of money or property for buliding or repairing a house for a prison, and nothing further is done in that yet"—Bateman and Selby, *Hist. of St. Clair County,* 2: 699. The first grand jury of St. Clair accordingly reported "that for the support of the laws and government of our county the speediest means be taken to have a proper jail in this village" (Cahokia—*ibid.,* 699). A statute of 1792 ordered the erection in each county of a courthouse (*post,* ccx, n. 2) and a jail—Pease, *Laws* (*I. H. C.,* 17), 77. McDonough, *Hist. of Randolph, Monroe and Perry Counties,* 101, says that James Dunn, sheriff "prior to 1803" (really 1795-1800), built the first jail of Randolph County, which it bought for $270.35 on July 12, 1803. In the records, from 1802 onward, I have noted no such transaction. Of course the sheriff's own house was ordinarily the jail. In petitioning Congress in 1803 for authority to tax Indian traders Harrison declared: "Every [other] object which would bear a Tax, and for [which] legal precedent could be found, has been sufficiently burthened to raise County Levies for the Erection of Jails, Court Houses, &c."—*Messages,* 1: 88. Stories of the use of rail fences by resourceful judges, for short but effective confinement of prisoners (confined with their necks under the bottom rail) appear in various books on Indiana. That the jails were still of little account in 1799 is apparent from Governor St. Clair's legislative address, *St. Clair Papers,* 2: 456. "It would be proper," he concluded ". . . to pass laws to compel the inhabitants of every county to erect proper jails and convenient court-houses." In Wayne County there seem, strangely enough, to have been jails; for petitioners to Congress, about 1805, stated that, "persons *capitally punishable* are seldom prosecuted to conviction. They remain in confinement for the want of competent authority to try them,"—*ante,* clvii, n. 2—"until they are forgotten, when, with the assistance of their associates in guilt, they break their bonds, and deride from the opposite bank"—of the Detroit River—"the impotence of our magistrates"—*Hist. Public. of Wayne Co. Mich.,* Nos. 1-2, p. 35.

surely a statute of tremendous theoretical difficulties! Another
aid to criminals was the poverty of the territory, which, according
to a statement to Congress by Governor Harrison in 1803, made
impossible "the Apprehension and prosecution of the most notorious offenders against the laws."[1] The uncertainty of boundaries,[2] and questions of the competence of a Territory in matters
of extradition,[3] were further hindrances.

A committee of which Governor Harrison himself, when a
delegate in Congress in 1800, was a member, in a report on defects
in the administration of justice, declared that the territory was
an asylum for "the most vile and abandoned criminals."[4] Others
have repeated and exaggerated the statement.[5] The unbridled
independence of frontier life is possibly more productive of lesser
crimes of violence than are the concentrated irritations and covet-
ousness of more densely settled communities. This has never,
however, been proved; and the idea rests upon more than one
doubtful assumption.[6] But serious crimes of violence were certainly not common, and crimes of the myriad forms assumed by
fraud and cunning in cities were almost unknown. On the whole

[1] *Messages,* 1: 88.
[2] Dawson, *Harrison,* 8 (Harrison to Secretary of War, 1801); Burnet, *Notes,* 308-310. There was also a question of jurisdiction over roads
leading through Indian lands: Harrison, *Messages,* 37-38, 43.
[3] Harrison, *Messages,* 1: 318. Monks, *Courts,* 1: 42, gives three
instances of extradition. One of them is from Randolph, 1806: that of
Michael Squires charged with the murder of Abraham Stanley. *Post,* 83-84,
is a special appropriation in a case of extradition.
[4] Report of March 3, 1800, *Annals,* 6 Congress, 1 session, 1321.
[5] Thus, Mr. Esarey speaks of "the great numbers of vicious men who
came from the east to the borders to gratify their criminal natures"—
History, 1: 148. And Monks, *Courts,* 1: 12, 19, speaking of the rarity of
circuit courts, says: "Such a country, of course, soon became a rendezvous
for criminals of the worst type . . ."
"The West at that time was full of desperate criminals . . . Every
frontier is largely a dumping ground for the social misfits of settled society.
In the history of crime there are few worse criminals to be found than the
professional horsethief. The Northwest was full of them . . . Counterfeiters . . . deluged the back country with their spurious products."
The horse thief was, of course, no more than a frontier annoyance, though
the penalty he suffered was often extreme, in proportion to the annoyance.
[6] Namely, that criminal impulses are rarer in "settled" communities;
that their expression is restrained by the mere presence of more numerous
punitive agencies; or at least by punishment. The penalties actually imposed
upon lesser offenders in Indiana Territory could not have restrained anybody.

the records would not support a contention that criminals were either numerous or active.

The French were unquestionably more law-abiding than the Americans.[1]

The criminal law broke down completely where Indians were either defendants or complainants. Governor Reynolds says that it was "rather common" for the whites to hire Indians to kill persons they wished to get rid of.[2] But if one wished to kill an Indian it could be done without such roundabout proceedings, and with impunity. Both Governor St. Clair and Governor Harrison[3] deplored the situation, but it was irremediable. The rather considerable legislation[4] designed to protect them against the horrible ravages caused among them by whiskey[5] was equally ineffective. Harrison's denunciation of the Indian traders,[6] his own exemplary conduct as superintendent of Indian affairs, and his repeated efforts to secure justice to the Indians in the courts do him the greatest credit. An Indian accused was as much as convicted,

[1] Governor Reynolds says that the records of the courts "do not exhibit an indictment of a creole Frenchman for any crime higher than keeping his grocery open on a prohibited day of the week" (*Pioneer History,* 126). This is an exaggeration; see *ante,* cxxv, n. 1; clxxvi, notes 1 and 2; also Alvord, *Kaskaskia Records* (*I. H. C.,* 5), 543. There were, presumably, very few non-Creole Frenchmen—J. F. Perrey and Pierre Menard being the most notable exceptions; and the latter was a Creole, though of Quebec. It is barely possible that various French defendants indicted at different times were not Creoles.

[2] *Pioneer History,* 285.

[3] Smith, *St. Clair Papers,* 2: 396-397, 503. See also Harrison, *Messages,* 1: 25, 199, 515, and *post,* clxxxv, n. 1; also Dillon, *Indiana,* 424 n. Mrs. Goebel's discussion, *Harrison,* 96-97, is excellent; she says, and apparently with entire justice, that "aside from the question of land policy Harrison tried to treat the Indians fairly" (95). The land policy—the encroachment of white settlement, the extinction of Indian title to old hunting grounds—was, however, absolutely the crux of all difficulties, as Harrison himself at times recognized; cp. his *Messages,* 1: 179 and 26-27.

[4] *Ante,* cxxx, n. 1.

[5] Harrison, *Messages,* 1: 29, 154, 155 n.; Dunn, *Indiana,* 124-125.

[6] Writing in 1802 to the Secretary of War he says that the trade, "with a few exceptions, is in the hands of the greatest villains in the world"—*Messages,* 1: 44; also 32. "An act to regulate trade and intercourse with the Indian tribes, and to preserve peace on the frontiers" (March 3, 1795), *Annals,* 5 Congress, 3 session, 3956-3963, gives a view of many abuses sought to be corrected.

but the juries would not convict a white murderer of an Indian.[1] Of course there were indictments in such cases, but the first convictions—perhaps the first ever secured in the United States—were obtained in Indiana in 1824.[2] Such legal subtleties were naturally beyond the comprehension of the Indians. Their delivery of every Indian murderer of a white was rigorously exacted, but "no consideration on earth," as Governor Harrison confessed, would move them to deliver to our courts an Indian who killed another Indian.[3]

If one is left somewhat in doubt with regard to the criminal propensities of the pioneers, the records leave no room whatever for doubt with reference to their tastes for litigation. They make it abundantly evident that the general arbitration law,[4] the taxes

[1] Reynolds, *Pioneer History*, 304. "The Indian always suffers, and the white man never"—Harrison to the General Assembly, 1806: *Messages*, 1: 199. See Dawson, *Harrison*, 31, for the statement that throughout the territory it was "the prevailing opinion that a white man ought not in justice to suffer for killing an Indian"; *St. Clair Papers*, 2: 327-329 for references to a mob attack upon Choctaws at Cincinnati in 1794; also a "Public Notice" issued in the Miami purchase territory in the same year by a committee acting for "many good citizens," offering rewards for Indian scalps. The county court at Cincinnati ignored the mob. When Judge Turner was in Illinois in 1795 two Indians were murdered in the presence of a militia guard, and in the custody of the sheriff to whom the guard had just delivered them. According to the Governor the Judge took no steps to cause the arrest of the murderers, and although Judge Symmes later endeavored to secure the indictment of two inhabitants of St. Clair County whom "the most positive testimony" showed to be the murderers, no indictment even for manslaughter could be secured. Governor St. Clair proposed that fines should be levied upon the counties that failed to bring wrongdoers "to justice." See *St. Clair Papers*, 2: 344 n., 351, 374, 376, 386 n., 396-397. Compare Houck, *Missouri*, 2: 209-214.

[2] On a case that arose in 1802 in Clark County, see Harrison, *Messages*, 60; Monks, *Courts*, 1: 43-44 (possibly not the same case). James Red was indicted in the General Court in 1806 for killing Indian Rob (May 26, 1806, *Order Book*, 1: 206—no further entries noted). Harrison felt that a conviction was so important that he brought a lawyer from St. Louis to prosecute, but Red escaped before trial. A reward of $300 was offered for his capture, and $100 for the discovery of any accomplice, but in vain (Dawson, *Harrison*, 85-86; Gibson, *Exec. Journal*, June 21, 1806, 134). Smith, *Early Trials*, 51-53, 55-57, 176-179.

[3] Compare *Messages*, 1: 131, 199, 223.

[4] Pease, *Laws* (*I. H. C.*, 17), 354; *post*, 349 (1807 Revision). The provisions for arbitration in the justices' courts have been referred to *ante*, cliii, n. 2. Arbitration was very characteristic of procedure under the French law; see Alvord, *Kaskaskia Records* (*I. H. C.*, 5), 40, 384 n., and index s. v. "Arbiters"; *Illinois Country*, 266. There is nothing whatever to indicate that the territorial statutes were a concession to French tradition.

on process,[1] and the court fees taxed as costs (which in general were small) were all insufficient to curb the litigious character of the people.[2] Nor were the trivial damages recovered—trivial not only from our standpoint but judged by the conditions of that time—any more effective.[3]

The fees of the sheriff and of the clerk however caused much trouble. A law of 1808 recites that "whereas, numerous, and in some cases, just complaints do still exist among our citizens with respect to the exorbitancy of the Clerks' fees of the courts of record in this territory; and likewise that they are compellable by execution, to pay large sums of money for fees, without knowing for what services they do pay: for remedy whereof" the

[1] *Post,* 31, 32, 201, 496 (1807 Revision), 649. For the early fee statutes: Pease, *op. cit.,* 102 (1792), 170 (1795), 302 (1798); but these are taxed costs. The later laws are county taxes. The taxed costs in the Randolph County fees in 15 sample cases run between extremes of $8.35 in an action for $18 to $42.97 in one for $600. The clerk's fees were almost always the largest item; very rarely the sheriff's. In these sample cases the largest costs were: for the judges $3.34; clerk, $26.97; sheriff, $11.10; jurors, $3; witnesses, $0.75; attorneys, $5. Randolph *Common Pleas,* 4: (3), 263, 265, 274, 303, 326, 335, 339, 353, 405, 413, 416, 432, 436, 438. For the fees prevailing in 1807 in all the states see *Amer. State Papers: Misc.,* 1: 656-700.
[2] Smith, *Early Trials,* gives some extraordinary examples, probably from the 1820's—pp. 11, 13, 19-21, 27-28, 59-60. Among them: action for sale of beef worth $0.25, final costs over $1100; for sale of a hoe, final verdict for plaintiff for $7, costs over $300. There are many cases in Randolph and St. Clair that were carried to the General Court, but in no case, probably, could the costs be calculated; many passed through the Circuit Court, for which no data exist. The litigiousness of the Illinois communities is clearly indicated by other facts mentioned in the text. The fee system was open to many abuses. In the Randolph *County Court Record 1810* the account is given of Robert Morrison (94-98) as clerk of the Common Pleas under Indiana Territory. His salary from December 31, 1807 to March 1809 was $35; his claim for fees, $193.26. He made a claim "for swearing witnesses to the Grand Jury"; denied, "it is an ex officio." In the same volume (99-100) are allowances, under Illinois Territory, for bringing a prisoner to jail, "keeping" him in jail, and paying jail guards *to* keep him there. There are various such instances in older records.
[3] *Ante,* clxxvi, n. 5; clxxvii, n. 2.

Such statutes, in various states, were associated with the contemporary prejudice against lawyers—cp. Warren, *Hist. of the Amer. Bar,* 221, 223, etc. There are fairly numerous examples of arbitration in the records: e. g.—Randolph *Common Pleas* 4: 162 (Rebecca Shanklin *v.* John Beaird Sr., December, 1808). This was submitted to the award of five—three of them fellow judges of Beaird (John Grosvenor and Robert Reynolds, his close friends, for him; John Edgar and Paul Herlston for plaintiff); later, Edgar and Grosvenor, and William Morrison as umpire, were ordered to make a final award, upon which judgment was given.

clerks were ordered to deliver to the sheriff with the execution "a detailed bill of the costs in the said suit, from its commencement to its termination," and the sheriff must deliver the same to the debtor, and also a receipt when he paid.[1]

The same persons occur over and over, litigating debts until one wonders who ever paid voluntarily, and torts until one wonders more over the relation of neighbor with neighbor—for such they were in their little community, and nowhere more closely than in the records of the court. The French were far more prominent in the St. Clair than in the Randolph Court.[2]

With some remarkable exceptions all the common law actions are abundantly illustrated in the records. Trespass in assault or battery is far less frequent than one would expect (evidently self-help was the usual and sufficient redress),[3] and one therefore regrets the more that the verbiage of the action makes it impossible to distinguish the trivial from the grave;[4] the usual charge being of a battery "with swords, staves, sticks, and fists" at the least, with feet, knives, hammers, sledges, chisels, and guns not infrequently, and sometimes "tomahaks," added for good measure. Nor are the damages given of much help, since—as already noted— damages for serious offences were often quite illusory. Trespass quare clausum fregit is decidedly rare. Trespass on the case in tort also occurs rather rarely, though instances of it occur for negligent performance, for conversion, for consequential harm in

---

[1] October 22, 1808—*post*, 649-650; compare 31, 32.

[2] In the St. Clair *Order Book 1801-03* there are 36 litigants with French and 32 with British names (in some cases it is difficult to be sure, of course); 49 names occur more than once as plaintiff or defendant. In the index to volume 3 of the Randolph *Common Pleas* out of 109 names I should classify 20 as French. Of these 109 there are only 72 that occur but once as a party; the other 37 occur 114 times.

[3] Three cases in St. Clair in three years; three (doubtless not an exhaustive count) in Randolph, 1798-1808.

[4] Judge Hoover (*Ind. Quart. Mag. Hist.*, 2: 22), who settled in Indiana in 1806, describes a case of 1811 in which a juryman thought unduly harsh the charge of force and arms in an indictment for stealing a pocket knife; the defendant, a boy, was found guilty, however. This case was remarkable in that Judge Parke traveled several hundred miles to try it, it being the only case on the circuit docket. (Smith, *Indiana*, 1: 200; Webster, Ind. Hist. Soc. *Pub.*, 4: 214; and others mention this case).

battery and in damming a stream, and for slander.[1] Case was almost invariably used for trover or assumpsit. Exceedingly few instances were noted of their use as independent actions; evidently the attorney who dared so to use them was one both of sure knowledge and of courage.[2] By far the most common action was case on promises; and general assumpsit was very many times more common than special assumpsit.[3] The latter was rarely used, even when perfectly applicable, as where the declaration was on a note. Debt is less abundantly, but still well, illustrated—on for-

[1] Every case of trespass q. c. f. noted in Randolph was for entering and taking crops—only half a dozen; though probably the count was not exhaustive it indicates the rarity of the action. Not a case occurred in three years in St. Clair. No instance of trespass by cattle was noted in either county. Distribution of trespass on the case: for slander—half a dozen in Randolph, three in St. Clair; for obstructing a stream, one in St. Clair; for negligent performance of an undertaking, two in Randolph (I, pl. 5; III, pl. 66—the latter against an attorney); for consequential harm in battery, one in Randolph (II, pl. 9). Notes below as to conversion and assumpsit. In the mill case John Dumoulin alleged an expenditure of $6000 in 1800 in building a grist mill on a rivulet in St. Clair, and of $6000 more in 1801 in building and furnishing "a mill house, race and tail race and all and singular the wheels and other running works of the said water grist mill." Negligence cases were probably everywhere rare at this time. C. Warren, *History of the Harvard Law School and of Early Legal Conditions in America,* 1: 248—the first in New York being of 1810. See also on the distribution of actions Baldwin (ed.), *Two Centuries' Growth of American Law,* 84; Brink, McDonough, *Hist. of St. Clair County,* 88.

[2] Only two instances were noted of assumpsit as an independent action, and one of trover, in Randolph; none of either in St. Clair. The first instances occurred in 1807, and Robert Robinson was the innovating attorney (IV, pp. 215, 254). His opponent, Rufus Easton (215), demurred on the ground that no such action was known.

[3] Trespass on the case on promises occurs in scores of cases. In St. Clair, 1801-1803, out of a total of 47 pleas, 39 were in case. In 12 of these the exact nature is not identifiable (the declaration is often omitted from the record in both counties). Two of the others are indicated in the preceding note. The other 25 included three for conversion; one on a note, the form of assumpsit not appearing; two on notes in special assumpsit; five on notes in general assumpsit; fourteen others in general assumpsit on common counts. (The other 9 of the 47 pleas were 5 in ejectment and 3 in trespass for battery, noted elsewhere). In Randolph the figures would not be different in their general nature. Only 13 cases of case in special assumpsit were noticed there, but not all declarations were read with care. In the St. Clair Common Pleas (*Order Book 1801-03,* pl. 30) is an action in general assumpsit by John Lyle *v.* Dennis Valentin for "divers medicaments Ointments fomentations and other necessaries by him the said John at the special instance and request of him the sd Dennis and his family [for the cure] of a certain Malady called . . . small Pox of which the said Dennis and his family as afsd languished, found, provided applied and Administered."

eign judgments, writings obligatory, accounts stated, notes, and (but more rarely) for goods sold and work done. Notes payable in peltries, lead, or other merchandise were of course very common, the rarity of money being a matter of considerable moment;[1] and they involved nice distinctions between debt and assumpsit of which in our moneyed age pleaders are safely ignorant.[2]

Not that the pleaders whom we are discussing were less so. Even the ignorant, armed with a form book that is the precipitate of centuries of practice, may seem learned, but they often slipped;[3] and there was usually no one to take advantage of their fault. A statute of 1805 repealed the practice provision which required the true species of action to be indorsed upon the original writ or subsequent process.[4]

As might be expected such complicated matters as partnership scarcely leave a trace in the records.[5] What is truly remarkable

[1] Compare Harrison, *Messages,* 1: 88.

[2] Typical notes: for "150 dollars in receiptable peltries"; for "18 bushels good merchantable salt"; for "32 dollars in lead or merchantable peltries at current price"; for "157 dollars to be paid in good merchantable salt at 3 dollars per bushel"; for "50 dollars in peltry at 2-1-2 pounds per dollar." In one note sued in St. Clair, for 4,585 livres and 14 sols ($917.14) in peltry, these prices are given: deerskins, 25 cents per pound; raccoon, 15; wildcat, fox, mink, wolf, 30; bear, $1.00; otter, $1.60. Notes for cash were also very common; perhaps more so. Only one action was noted in Randolph upon a bill—against the acceptor; there may be others, but evidently bills were rare.

[3] For example—3: pl. 75, entitled Trespass on the Case, is really debt (not indebitatus assumpsit) on a note—Rufus Easton was plaintiff's attorney; 3: pl. 81, 82, 83, all labeled debt, on sealed notes, were really framed in indebitatus assumpsit, and common counts were added in each declaration for goods sold—Wm. C. Carr was plaintiff's attorney; 4: 348, entitled debt, is really special assumpsit on a note; 4: 243, entitled trespass on the case, really trespass q. c. f.—Rufus Easton was plaintiff's (John Edgar's) attorney, John Scott demurred for defendant correctly, and action was discontinued: 4: 348, 350—actions on notes entitled simply "Trespass," even by Robert Robinson (in 4: 348, though in 346 he used special assumpsit).

[4] *Post.* 104, repealing matter on 33.

[5] In Randolph one action of covenant was brought on a partnership agreement (for dealings in buffalo hides at $4 each—*Common Pleas,* 2: pl. 71). A case of partnership accounting between John Singleton and Isaac Darneille appears in the St. Clair Circuit Court of October 1808 as continued from 1807 (Belleville Museum); it had been in the General Court—presumably was there begun—and was sent down for an accounting, the auditors to report in September 1807; later proceedings in the General

cxc ILLINOIS HISTORICAL COLLECTIONS

is that no single instance was noted, in Randolph County, of replevin, detinue, or ejectment. It is curious, considering the elaborate legislation of the territory regarding fences and branding
of cattle and estrays, that no cases in trespass quare clausum
fregit, detinue, or replevin should reflect the frontier conditions
to which this legislation must have been responsive. The nonuse
of replevin is, indeed, understandable, since the territory took its
practice acts from states where that action had not been liberalized. But detinue, which has always been used in the southern
states, whence so many of the immigrants and (at least some of
the leading) lawyers came, one would have expected to find.
Trover was used instead. As for ejectment, the explanation of
its absence must be due to a wise wariness against judicial tests
of the land titles. Quite aside from their almost universal inse-
curity, there could scarcely have arisen any case in which members
of the court would not have been, directly or indirectly, immediately or remotely interested. In St. Clair Isaac Darneille used
the weapon of Richard Smith and William Stiles effectively to
secure several lots in Peoria. One of these suits was apparently
against J. F. Perrey—who, if so, sat on his own case; and there
was notice by the casual ejector and writ of restitution in proper
form.[1] In the other four cases, however, all recovered on defaults against simple French citizens unrepresented by counsel—
to whom an ejectment action would have been legal acroamatics
beyond possibility of comprehension—the record causes one to
suspect that Darneille may have gone back to the practice of Tudor
times, recovering against Stiles without notice to the actual occupant.[2] He would undoubtedly have been capable of such clever-

[1] *Order Book 1801-03*, pl. 14. Rich. Smith dem. Isaac Darneille *v.*
Wm. Stiles dem. J. F. Perrey. Stiles' notice is to "Mr. Francois La Pierre"
the index is "Perrey"; the writ of restitution (in the Belleville Museum)
has "Francis La Pierre." This confusion is doubtless due to the copyist
of the *Order Book*. Perrey's name occurs constantly in the records of the
St. Clair courts.
[2] Unlike the case against Judge Perrey they do not show (pleas
33-36) any notice to the actual occupant. On the other hand the writ in
pleas 33 and 34, at least, ran in the names of the true parties, and the writ

Court continued into 1809 (*Order Book*, 1: 246, 307, 322, 331). Equity
bills for partnership accountings appear in the Randolph records of the
beginning of Illinois Territory.

ness.[1] Two other ejectment actions were litigated in the General Court.[2]

Some judgments were for large sums. James O'Hara recovered one for $43,086, and another for $5,481, against Pierre Menard on foreign judgments.[3] But actions for above a thousand dollars were rare. The work of the General Court being mostly appellate, the sums involved in its cases were not greater.

In the juries, petit and grand, there is a constant reappearance of prominent citizens. One day they litigated with a friend, the next day they gave a verdict on his quarrel with another. Lawyers appeared on the juries not infrequently. So, it may be added, did past sheriffs and future judges[4]—and in the Circuit Court the judges of the county court sat on the grand jury.[5] Few French names occur in the jury lists of Randolph; a much larger number in St. Clair.[6]

As for the attorneys who practiced in the courts of the territory, it would be difficult to find a law of any place or time more admirably expressing the qualifications proper to members of the

[1] See *post,* app. n. 81.

[2] Elliot ex. d. F. Vigo *v.* Buntin (*Order Book,* 29, 32-33, 71—1802-1803) is a complicated case. Judge Edgar was sued by Bartholomew Richard; the case was continued six times, through three years, and was then settled out of court (*ibid.,* 48, 74, 89, 102, 143, 153, 163, 174, 211). Reynolds (*Pioneer History,* 181) says, apparently of years even before 1800, "Ejectment suits were common."

[3] Randolph *Common Pleas,* 1: pl. 7 (1802), 71 (1801).

[4] James Finney and John Grosvenor, in particular, frequently served as jurymen in Randolph County. See *ante,* clxxxi, n. 1.

[5] In the Circuit Court held in St. Clair County in October 1808, the grand jury included James Lemen, William Whiteside, Nicholas Jarrot and Benjamin Ogle (Belleville Museum). The record of the Common Pleas does not exist beyond 1803; one cannot be certain which judges actually sat in 1808.

[6] In eleven lists from three volumes of the Randolph Common Pleas there are 62 different names, only 3 French; if twenty lists were taken the total number of names would be little increased. In three lists of 1801 in St. Clair there are 31 names, 15 being French.

of restitution in the Perrey case (unfortunately the only one preserved) was "against William Stiles and Francis La Pierre the supposed tenant in possession." The statutes of 1795 contained the usual modern enactment requiring notice by the tenant to his landlord—Pease, *Laws* (*I. H. C.,* 17), 281. The remark by Judge Gross upon this statute, Ill. State Bar Assoc. *Proc.* (1881), 76, is curious.

bar than a statute of the Northwest Territory of 1792:[1]
". . . .no person shall be admitted or practise as an attorney in
any of the courts of this territory unless he is a person of good
moral character and well affected to the government of the United
States and of this territory and shall pass an examination of his
professional abilities before one or more of the territorial judges
and obtain from him or them before whom he may be examined
a certificate of possessing the proper abilities and qualifications
to render him useful in the office of an attorney. And further
shall in open court have taken and subscribed the oath prescribed
to all officers by an act of the United States and an oath in tenor
following

" 'I swear that I will do no falsehood nor consent to the
doing of any in the courts of justice and if I know of an intention
to commit any I will give knowledge thereof to the justices of
the said courts or some of them that it may be prevented. I will
not wittingly or willingly promote or sue any false groundless or
unlawful suit nor give aid or consent to the same and I will conduct
myself in the office of an attorney within the said courts according to the best of my knowledge and discretion and with all good
fidelity as well to the courts as my clients. So help me God.' "

This law was repealed in 1795, and attorneys left unregulated
until 1799. A law of that year provided that a practising attorney
of the territory, in whose office the candidate should have studied
for four years, should give the certificate of his ability; that not
less than two judges of the General Court should then examine
him; and only thereafter might he be licensed. Only "counsellors"
could practice before the General Court, after being for two years
an attorney and passing a second examination "on the theory of

---

[1] Pease, *Laws* (*I. H. C.*, 17), 88-89 (August 1, 1792); repealed in
1795, *ibid.*, 257. No party was permitted to employ more than two attorneys,
and only one if there should be only two attorneys available, and in no
case might the fees of more than one be taxed. As the number of lawyers
increased this provision against "cornering" legal talents became unnecessary. There were various old colonial precedents for these statutes—
Warren, *Hist. of the Amer. Bar,* 78, 218 (Mass. Statutes of 1715, 1785,
1786); 52, 107 (same problem in Maryland, 1669, and Pennsylvania, 1709,
but no statute; equitable relief—an injunction against the rich adversary—
sought in the Pennsylvania case).

law."[1] Members of the bar elsewhere in the United States were not excused from these examinations.[2]

The legislation of the Indiana Territory considerably weakened these provisions. Office study ceased to be prescribed; likewise all examinations. A shorter residence, moral character, an oath, and a license became the requirements for admission.[3] The requirements of the older law were ignored by Governor Harrison before their repeal or modification. Some good lawyers were unquestionably needed, but it cannot be possible, in view of the great number of attorneys admitted to practice, that the low admission requirements were necessitated by the circumstances of the territory. It is certain that few were well prepared, and of course some proved to be disreputable.[4]

[1] Judge Gross, overlooking this statute, could not discover the distinction between attorneys and counsellors, Ill. State Bar Assoc. *Proc.* (1881), 74. In colonial times the distinction between attorneys and counsellors (or "barristers" in Massachusetts) existed in New York, New Jersey and Massachusetts; in the latter sergeants existed from 1755-1859; and the United States Circuit Court, First Circuit, recognized for a time after 1789 the classes of attorneys, counsellors, barristers and sergeants. See Warren, *Hist. of the Amer. Bar,* 85, 113, 202, 242-244. For the requirements for admission to the bar in Massachusetts about 1800 see *ibid.,* 196-200 and in other states, 200-202.

[2] Pease, *Laws (I. H. C.,* 17), 340 (October 29, 1799). The admirable oath of 1792 was replaced by one shorter to mumble.

[3] *Post,* 2 (January 20, 1801); 86 (undated—September 1803); 141 (August 26, 1805); 340 (1807 Revision). Both Monks, *Courts,* 1: 20, and Webster, in Ind. Hist. Soc. *Pub.,* 4: 192-193, misstate the act of 1799: it required four years of resident office study. That of 1803 permitted a single judge to examine and license. This was in turn repealed in 1805. The Revision of 1807 reënacted in part the law of 1799. It retained the requirement of good moral character which was present in both the earlier statutes, but abandoned the requirement of examination. Under the act of 1799 (§ 11) an attorney of any court of record in the United States could be examined at any time after a residence of one year in the territory for the degree of attorney, and could be examined for the degree of counsellor without prior residence. It was the former requirement that was repealed in 1801.

[4] The following admissions were noted in the *Order Book* of the General Court, volume one. George Bullitt (101, 105). William C. Carr (105); see *post,* app. n. 80. James Clark (101, 105). Isaac Darneille (59, already admitted as an attorney in the territory; 68); see *post,* app. n. 81. Rufus Easton (105); see *post,* app. n. 83. Rodominck Gilmore (39, 46). James Haggin (17, 22, examination ordered; 25, license produced, oath taken; 26, examination ordered); see *post,* app. n. 84. Robert Hamilton (2, exam. ordered; appears later in practice): see *post,* app. n. 85. Edward Hempstead (101, 105): see *post,* app. n. 87. John Johnson (56, produced license before examinations; 59); see *ante,* cxii, n. 1. General Washington

Whether the statutes of the Northwest Territory regulating fees were intended merely to regulate attorneys' fees taxable with costs, or to control the contract between lawyer and client, is not entirely clear;[1] but it would seem that both purposes were in-

[1] The statute of 1792—Pease, *Laws* (I. H. C., 17), 110—reads: "Attornies fees to be allowed to the party recovering costs"; that of 1795 (170, 176) says, "No officer or person shall, at any time, exact or demand, for services hereafter to be rendered, any larger, or other fee than as hereinafter provided"; that of 1798 (302, 305) was "in addition to" the last-named act, and its own language indicates nothing. Limitation of contract fees was common in the colonies during the 1600's—Warren, *Hist. of the Amer. Bar,* 41-42, 53, 72, 121, 143. As fixed in 1795 and 1798 the fees were—in the General Court: retaining fees, $3.50; term fee, $0.75; arguing special motion, $1.25; trial fee, $1.50; brief (and copy or copies), $1.12; examining witness, $0.50; selecting jury, $0.62½; and lesser charges for every process, entry, bond, affidavit, service, motion, copy, notice, etc. In the county courts: retaining fee, $1; pleading ("where issue or demurrer"), $1.50; term fee, $0.50; the other fees in General Court applying. The statutes of Indiana Territory began with modifications of the act of 1795 (*post,* 19, 31, 32); but in 1803 all the prior statutes of both the Northwest and Indiana Territories were repealed (*post,* 64) and a new and complete schedule established, under which attorneys' fees were very considerably raised (September 24, 1803; *post,* 46-63). This statute was substantially unchanged in the 1807 Revision (*post,* 467-80); but by act of September 14, 1807 attorneys' fees in the General Court were again considerably reduced (*post,* 560-562).

Johnston, John Rice Jones (2—exam. ordered; 22, took oath); see *ante,* cxii, n. 3, and *post,* app. n. 10. Benjamin Parke (22, produced license as "counsellor" and took oath; 23, exam. ordered as "attorney"); see *post,* app. n. 7. John Scott (105); see *post,* app. n. 93. Daniel Symmes (35, admitted upon prior admission to bar of Northwest Territory; 43, admitted later as attorney!). John Taylor (105, exam. ordered); he later practiced in Illinois; see *post,* app. n. 94. Beyond this point few names were noted. Among those later occurring are James Boyle (229, 241); Jonathan Jennings (232, 242).

These citations reveal various cases in which the Governor gave licenses without heed to the law. They certainly show, also, an excess of men ready to act as lawyers and accepted as such. John Rice Jones, Washington Johnston, Benjamin Parke, Hamilton, Haggin, and Darneille were particularly active in the General Court.

Attorneys especially prominent in Randolph and St. Clair in the earlier years of Indiana Territory were: J. Rice Jones, before his removal to Vincennes; Isaac Darneille, James Haggin and Rufus Easton. Those most active in its later years were: Easton, Robert Robinson, John Scott and Nathaniel Pope. (Of these four Easton was least effective). Less prominent were John Rector, John Taylor, Henry Jones, Wm. C. Carr, William Hamilton, Robert Hamilton. None of these save the last was a strong lawyer (at that time in their careers, at least).

All of the above appeared in Randolph. In St. Clair a far greater proportion of litigants appeared for themselves, but in almost all cases in which any lawyer appeared, between 1801 and 1803, it was Darneille or Haggin, or both.

cluded. The fees established, seemingly extremely low, were not
so when judged by the circumstances of the time. A few dollars
as surveying fees sufficed to hold up for years the survey and
patenting of lands, so poor were most of the citizens; and taxes
seemingly trivial were deemed by Governor Harrison to be a crush-
ing burden. There is no doubt that attorneys' fees, unlimited by
law, would have been a great impediment to the administration
of justice. Even those fixed by the statute, assuming them to
exclude all untaxed remuneration, would have mounted high in a
protracted cause.[1]

In Illinois the lawyers seem to have relied almost wholly on
local business, including the occasional circuit courts; though some
practiced also in the courts of upper Louisiana. Rarely did attorneys resident in the eastern counties ride circuit in the Illinois
country. Doubtless almost all were self-made; apparently very
few possessed a classical education, and probably only in rare cases
legal training.[2] Few textbooks, and fewer reports, were available
in the territory. We have the list of books owned by Samuel
H. I. Young of Ste. Genevieve, left at his death in 1810, with their
values as estimated by the clerk of the Randolph County Court
and the actual prices which they brought when sold, and the names
of the buyers.[3] The list of law books is worth reproduction:

	Appraised at—	Sold for—	Buyer
Burns' Law Dictionary	$2.50	....	
Criminal Law of Kentucky	2.00	....	
Beccaria on Crimes	1.00	$ 1.50	Andrew Scott
Barton's Equity	1.00	....	
Powell on Contracts	2.00	4.00	Henry Breckinridge
Graydon's Digest	2.00	2.25	Andrew Scott

[1] See *ante,* clxxxvi, n. 1.
[2] Compare *ante,* cxciii, n. 4. Possibly conditions in Indiana were
better; see Smith, *Early Trials,* 117-119, 122, 130. Woollen, *Sketches,* gives
details regarding such men as Jonathan Jennings, James Noble, J. Brown
Ray (pp. 29, 178, 56).
[3] Randolph *Execution Docket,* 1813-1822, at end, entered in reverse.

In fourteen actions picked at random from volume four of the Randolph
Common Pleas the fees for attorney were $2.50 in twelve; $5.00 in one;
$0.50 in one.

	Appraised at—	Sold for—	Buyer
Little's Law & Equity	.25	....	
Clerk's Magazine	.75	.75	Hempstead
Blackstone's Commentaries	4.00	8.00	Thomas F. Crittenden
Dec. of the Court of Appeals	.50	1.75	John Rice Jones
Espinasse's Nisi Prius	5.00	8.00	Thomas F. Crittenden
Comyn's Digest (6 vol.)	18.00	25.00	Nathaniel Pope
Gilbert's Law of Evidence	2.50	....	Rufus Easton
Chitty on Bills	1.50	3.00	Andrew Scott
Laws of Ohio	.25	....	William C. Allen
Laws of Louisiana	1.50	....	
Laws of U. S. (6 vol.)	1.00	....	
Pleader's Assistant	2.00	3.25	Rufus Easton
Compton's Practice (2 vol.)	3.00	5.00	Rufus Easton
Caine's Prin. of Equity	2.00	5.25	Andrew Scott
Morgan's Vademecum	2.00	3.25	Rufus Easton

That the library was unusual is shown by the purchasers. In 1805, when James Haggin's career as a leading attorney collapsed, the sheriff levied on "twenty two law books" which he owned—evidently a large collection for the time.[1]

A law of 1808 required written opinions in the General Court,[2] and in two opinions rendered soon thereafter the court cited various English and two United States (federal) decisions, and one colonial Connecticut case; but whether at first hand cannot be known.[3] It is regrettable that so little remains of the

[1] Randolph *Common Pleas,* 4: 291. Smith, *Early Trials,* writing of Indiana about 1824-1826 when he was a circuit prosecuting attorney, says that Espinasse's *Nisi Prius,* Peak's *Evidence,* Phillips' *Evidence,* and Breckenridge's *Miscellanies* were extensively used (pp. 19, 170). Fifty to a hundred volumes was, for that time, a very considerable collection. Warren, *Hist. of the Amer. Bar,* 161-164.

[2] *Post,* 663 (October 25, 1808). It was not obeyed—only a few opinions are given. Connecticut had made the same requirement by statute of 1785—Warren, *op. cit.,* 328 ("the first move towards the establishment of a record of American law").

[3] *Order Book,* 313-316 (Ewing *v.* Hurst, Ap. 10, 1809), 316-319 (Hill *v.* Robert Morrison, same date). Copies of Blackstone were probably fairly common, for John Edgar and fellow petitioners cited Blackstone (1: 424-425) in their proslavery petition of January 12, 1796—*ante,* xxi, n. 1. The Connecticut case cited was Kibbe *v.* Kibbe, 1786 (Kirby, 119).

records of the court, for in one of these cases, the decision is not only an important one in the field of conflict of laws but refers to an earlier decision in the same cause which is of extraordinary interest.[1]

The idea prevails that the proceedings of the territorial courts were characterized by technicality.[2] Possibly this was so in Indiana—at least the stories told by Senator Oliver H. Smith of Indiana practice of a few years later, as compared with the practice then prevalent in Kentucky and Ohio, support such views regarding Indiana special pleaders.[3] So far as the court records of the Illinois country show, there is little visible basis for such generalizations. Doubtless litigants disliked the cost and delay of procedure—they always will; but both were apparently low. Doubtless there were shysters; and—among self-educated practitioners who learned a few books more or less by heart—there were inevitably pettifoggers. But the truth is, evidently, that lawyers and judges did not know enough law, in most fields, to be technical. Relatively speaking, pleading is an exception; form books are easily copied, and there is some good pleading.[4] But

[1] Namely: "This court decided at the last term that an action of debt would lie on the decree of the Court of Chancery" of New Jersey. See W. W. Cook, "Powers of Courts of Equity," *Columbia Law Rev.,* 15: 116-118, 237-242. The final decision (Hill *v.* R. Morrison, *ante,* cxcvi, n. 3) was that the New Jersey decree was not to be treated as a foreign judgment in regard to an inquiry into the original merits of the New Jersey proceedings.

[2] Esarey, *Indiana,* refers (1) to "the delays and expenses of procedure" as wearing out the patience of the pioneers; and says (2) that "the courts, then even more than now, were hide-bound by precedents and technicalities. [3] Juries, under the influence of eloquent lawyers, were disposed to do substantial justice. But [4] there were plenty of pettyfogging shysters who took advantage of the technicalities and delay of the law to rob the unwary or evade justice" (pp. 167, 171). And again, in Monks, *Courts,* 1: 15: "These minor courts,"—the county courts—"which ought to have been as free as possible in their action, were limited [5] by all the formalities of the Common Law and many to which the Common Law was a stranger." Statements (2) and (5) are certainly quite wrong; (3) seems naïve; I know of no special evidence supporting (1) and (4)—they would be more or less true of any period of law.

[3] *Early Trials,* 43, 46, 47, 160-161, 170-171.

[4] The appearance of John Scott, Robert Robinson, Nathaniel Pope, and Rufus Easton immediately changed the appearance of the Randolph records. Before them there was no pleading worth the name. In St. Clair James Haggin and Isaac Darneille were adroit but far less sound. Important clients, like Bryan and Morrison, took these younger men up immed-

even there countless openings for technical wrangles were over-looked. Some of the stock stories used to illustrate the technical pedantry of the courts could only have been true, in civil cases, of later times when the territorial statutes had been abandoned, since they directly contradict these.[1] There are no records of the evidence admitted.

Of the members of the territorial General Court something has already been said. In the main they seem to have attended zealously to their duties. Thomas T. Davis, however, was censured in 1807 by the grand jury of Knox County for his failure to attend the court during two successive terms.[2] It was also necessary, at least once, to adjourn a session of the court,[3] presumably in order to secure the attendance of two judges.

Their salaries were very meager. Under the Northwest Territory, and at first under the Indiana Territory,[4] they received $800. With good reason Judges Symmes and Turner had complained to Governor St. Clair, when their circuits extended from Marietta to Kaskaskia and from Cincinnati to Detroit, that the allowance was not "of that ample nature which the duties of the office and the expenses, fatigues, and danger unavoidable on these wide-extended circuits, seem in our opinion to require."[5] The

[1] Senator Smith, *op. cit.*, 160-161, and Monks, *Courts*, 1: 151-152 relate a story of a judge who discouraged technical objections such as these: that the defendant was indicted as "John" but was really "John H.," that the animal involved and described as a "horse" was really a "gelding," and that no value was laid. So far as regards criminal cases even laymen probably know that such cases do not show more technicality than existed almost yesterday in Illinois (and others of the United States) in the cause of saving criminals. But as regards civil causes most of such obstructionism was curbed by the very liberal statute of jeofails already referred to (*ante,* clxviii-clxix).

[2] General Court, *Order Book,* 1: 232, April 8, 1807—terms of September, 1806 and March, 1807.

[3] *Post,* 551.

[4] *Amer. State Papers: Misc.,* 1: 260, 305.

[5] Smith, *St. Clair Papers,* 2: 188 (1790).

iately, and shifted from one to the other as any one seemingly established his superiority. The earliest recorded deeds have the swollen verbosity of Anglo-American tradition; see e. g. Brink, McDonough, *Hist. of St. Clair County,* 86-87, for examples. Compare, too, a French manumission by B. Tardiveau (a very prominent citizen) in four lines, with one in English (of which John Rice Jones was witness, and probably draftsman) in twenty! *Ibid.,* 87, 88.

circuits, though somewhat shorter later, were more regularly traveled, and the situation was not eased. Efforts made to raise the salary were vain until 1807,[1] when the salaries of judges in all the territories were raised to $1200.[2] Special remuneration (of $300 each) was also given them for their services in drafting— "after a lengthy and laborious Session, under many difficulties"— a half dozen laws for the District of Louisiana, organizing the government, and holding a court therein.[3]

The judges under the Northwest Territory were all heavily and—at least to one who looks back upon them—embarrassingly involved in land speculation.[4] In considering the smirch left by land deals upon the county judges of the Illinois country it is necessary to remember this fact; as also, indeed, the fact that the first settlement of the Northwest Territory was accompanied by— or perhaps one should say, more properly, initiated by—contributions to the financial needs of land speculators in Congress.[5] It

---

[1] *Annals*, 8 Congress, 1 session (1803-1804) ; 9 Congress, 1 session (1806).

[2] Mississippi, Indiana, Michigan, and Louisiana—*Annals,* 9 Congress, 2 session, 1272, act of March 3, 1807; for proceedings, index *s. v.* Mississippi Territory.

[3] Harrison, *Messages,* 1: 170-171, gives their petition to Congress of November 10, 1805. Not only Governor Harrison but Judges Vander Burgh, Griffin, and Davis all went to the District—Houck, *Missouri,* 2: 382. Proceedings in *Annals,* 9 Congress, 2 session. Harrison's claim was for services up to October 1, 1804. On that day he arrived at St. Louis as Governor (*Messages,* 1: 113 n.). Presumably, then, he received thereafter $2000 as governor of each territory. Houck, *op. cit.,* 379-381, gives a summary of these laws.

[4] See *ante,* clv, n. 2; clix, n. 2. Judges Parsons and Symmes were directors in the Ohio Company which held some 900,000 acres. Symmes was the purchaser for the Miami Company* (holding about 250,000 acres). *Amer. State Papers: Public Lands,* 3: 459; 4: 909. Harrison was a son-in-law of Symmes, but apparently not involved in his land deals. See Hulbert, *Records of the Ohio Company,* introduction. General Putnam, General Parsons, and Secretary Sargent were all active; indeed, leaders in the company. Mr. Bond says of the appointments of Symmes and Putnam: "As the judges exercised final jurisdiction in land disputes, these two appointments caused much criticism. *Journals of Cont. Congress,* February 19, 1788 [MSS], vol. 38; *Annals of Congress,* I, 64; *Proceedings,* New Jersey Historical Society, 2d Series, V. 23, 26, 43 (note VI)"—B. Bond, *John Cleves Symmes,* 38 n. 26.

[5] St. Clair became governor, Winthrop Sargent secretary, and General Parsons chief-judge as a result of arrangements growing out of the land speculation in which members of the Continental Congress and their friends were interested. The sources can be found through Dunn, *Indiana,* 216-218.

has already been noted that the court was distrusted because of
their entanglements with the great land companies of the territory.
Governor St. Clair complained, but he too speculated.[1] Judge
Turner had to be ordered off of a military reservation, and warned
that a judge of a federal court should set an example of respect
for government.[2]

Whatever the weaknesses of the court under the daughter
territory, its members were not similarly tied to any special "interest." Some shadow seems to hang about Judge Vander Burgh
in regard to liquor sales to Indians.[3] He was also the only member who engaged heavily in the land trade.[4] And he was guilty
of some slight administrative irregularities.[5] John Rice Jones,
after he had ceased to be attorney-general but while a member of
the Legislative Council, was indicted at least twice, once for malfeasance as attorney-general; although found not guilty.[6] Henry
Hurst, clerk of the court throughout the territorial period, was
indicted for accepting from a prisoner in the county jail a fee for
serving him as an attorney, although he was also then retained
as prosecutor for the government; and for having failed to prosecute the prisoner. He was found not guilty.[7] But we may note
again the statute which specifically forbade the clerk of the General Court to practice as an attorney.[8]

Of the judges of the Randolph County Courts of Common
Pleas and Quarter Sessions who were appointed upon the creation

[1] *St. Clair Papers,* 1: 194.
[2] *Ibid.,* 2: 212 n.
[3] See *post,* app. n. 3.
[4] *Ante,* lxxxvi, lxxxvii.
[5] He acted as the deputy of the deputy of the clerk of the Knox
County Court; see *St. Clair Papers,* 2: 326, 330.
[6] *Post,* app. n. 10, for the latter case. In the Belleville Museum is
an undated record of the Circuit Court, almost certainly of 1808, in which
a case of U. S. *v.* John Rice Jones was dismissed, "by reason that the
prosecutor N. Jarrot will not farther prosecute." In the other case (General
Court, *Order Book,* 1: 270, April 6, 1808) he was found not guilty. It
was upon statements by Henry Hurst (next note) that Judge Parke relied
in joining with Harrison and others in the petition to the President to have
Jones removed from the Legislative Council.
[7] General Court, *Order Book,* 1: 44, 52, September 1802. The prisoner
was taken for larceny from John Small—ferry keeper and local politician
and former sheriff (Monks, *Courts,* 1: 11); and after the trial Hurst was
put under bonds to keep the peace with Small for three months.
[8] Pease, *Laws* (*I. H. C.,* 17), 343-344; *post,* 342, § 6.

of Indiana Territory, four—John Edgar, William Morrison, Pierre Menard, and Nathaniel Hull—had been members in the preceding period of the Northwest Territory. Morrison rarely sat after 1801, nor Hull after 1803. Edgar was active until 1805. Of these men Nathaniel Hull was probably the most valuable. None were reappointed to the new Common Pleas created in 1805, when the other county courts were abolished, except Menard; but Hull was then near death. Of the other judges appointed under the first grade of government but not recommissioned when the county courts were reconstituted in 1805, John Beaird and Robert Mc-Mahon were certainly men of better character than John Grosvenor and (most decidedly) Robert Reynolds. Reynolds was much the most active in the court. The term of appointments made by Governor Harrison in 1800 and in 1805 was presumably in all cases for good behavior.[1]

Somewhat difficult to explain is the fact that two judges frequently sat after the creation of Indiana Territory who were not commissioned by Governor Harrison in 1800 in the reconstitution of either the Quarter Sessions or the Common Pleas: Antoine Louviere and Jean Baptiste Barbau. The former does not appear after the spring of 1801, but the latter frequently sat down into the summer of 1803. The probable explanation of this is the confusion, already referred to, between the jurisdiction of justices of the peace and that of justices of the county courts.[2] Both

[1] See Harrison, *Messages*, 1: 23, 182 (or *Chic. Hist. Colls.*, 4: 168, 171-172) for the commissions of Pierre Menard of 1801 and 1805. It was resolved by the governor and judges of the Northwest Territory in 1795 "that where persons sufficiently learned in the law can be found to fill the benches of the courts of Common Pleas, it would be the safer way to commission them during good behaviour." Pease, *Laws* (*I. H. C.*, 17), 288. Apparently it was assumed that all commissioned met this test, and Governor Harrison followed the example of St. Clair. See *ante*, xix, notes 2 and 3; cp. Reynolds, *My Own Times*, 67.

[2] See *ante*, cliv, n. 1; clxi. We find Barbau sitting in both county courts—in Quarter Sessions down through 1805 at least. In fact he was appointed justice of the peace on October 27, 1801; though it does not appear whether one of the quorum. When the Quarter Sessions were abolished in 1805, new appointments must have been made to the Common Pleas; but evidently no commissions theretofore issued to justices of the peace were withdrawn. Louviere was not even commissioned a justice of the peace under the Indiana Territory. Similarly we find James Finney, who was appointed a judge of the Common Pleas on October 7, 1807, acting also as "Justice of the Peace" (*Common Pleas*, 4: p. 118, 120, 285); al-

of them, however, had rendered judicial service in the period of Virginian supremacy; and it is barely possible that such appointments, during good behavior, may have been regarded as entitling them to sit in the courts of the Northwest and Indiana Territories. It is also a curious fact, and even more difficult to explain, that months before John Grosvenor and George Fisher were appointed to the Common Pleas or Quarter Sessions under the Indiana Territory, and without any appointment thereunder as justice of the peace, they sat as judges of the Common Pleas;[1] which might be due either to an appointment as justice of the peace (under the Northwest or the Indiana Territory)—of which there is no trace—or to a judicial appointment by Harrison unnoted in the Executive Journal—which seems improbable.

In St. Clair County, similarly, William and Uel Whiteside sat in the Orphans' Court, which only justices of the Quarter Sessions had authority to do. But they were never appointed such, nor is there any evidence that William was even commissioned as justice of the peace.

In the new Common Pleas after 1805 only two judges were at first appointed—Menard and Michael Jones. The latter, however, apparently never sat; undoubtedly he resigned because he

---

[1] Fisher was appointed to both courts January 7, 1804 (Gibson, *Exec. Journal*, 122); his first appearance noted in the Quarter Sessions is on April 10, 1804 (Randolph *Court Record 1802-06*, 54); but he was sitting in the Common Pleas in 1803 (e. g. 2: pl. 3, June, 1803; 5, September, 1803). Yet if sitting simply as a justice of the peace one would have expected him to sit, more certainly, in the Quarter Sessions. Hence it is possible that there is an omission in the *Executive Journal*. Similarly, Grosvenor was appointed to both courts on February 16, 1805; but we find him sitting in 1803 and 1804 in the Common Pleas (4: p. 267—September 1803; 2: pl. 35—March, 1804).

---

though the *Executive Journal* does not show that he was so commissioned, and although acting as such after 1806 would have been in violation of a statute. In an action of Charles Gratiot v. John Rice Jones in 1800 (*ibid.*, 2: pl. 41), defendant craved oyer of the writ which concluded, "Witness John Edgar Esquire first Justice of our said court at Kaskaskia aforesaid the fifteenth day of July in the year . . . one thousand eight hundred." He then prayed judgment, pleading that Edgar—who was appointed to both courts of the county on August 1, 1800—"was not at that day a Justice of the said court of common pleas," etc. The Court gave defendant time "to imparle herein" until the next term; the cause was then continued to a third term; and, the plaintiff not appearing, he was nonsuited. Edgar's judicial status under the Northwest Territory was regarded, doubtless, as continuing until appointment of a new court actually displaced the old.

had already discovered how deeply members of the court had been involved in the land frauds. To this involvement one also naturally attributes the nonreappointment of Edgar, Morrison, and Reynolds. George Fisher was promptly named in place of Michael Jones, and also Samuel Cochran. Later James Finney replaced Cochran. All three of these judges were active in performance of their duties. There are blemishes upon the record of Fisher,[1] but none upon that of the others. Rarely, judges of the pre-1805 court apparently sat in the court of later years.[2]

In the courts of both Randolph and St. Clair counties the judges were the most persistent litigants. In one volume of the Randolph pleas ten of them occur as plaintiff or defendant forty-two times; the sheriff, a former sheriff, the coroner and the clerk of court appeared—this was decidedly below their usual showing—only once each.[3] In the forty-one pleas of another volume sixteen of the parties come from the same list.[4] In another volume all except Menard and Jarrot appear, and seven of them appear a total of twenty-six times.[5] Two only of the Randolph judges never appear as litigants: James Finney and Samuel Cochran.[6] The statutes forbade any judge or other officer of court to practice as an attorney in the county of his office.[7] But they some-

[1] *Ante,* cxx.
[2] E. g. in *Common Pleas,* 5: p. 77 (March, 1806), John Beaird, Robert Reynolds, and John Grosvenor all sat. An easy—and presumably the correct—explanation of such cases is that the case began in the old court, and that the record is not made up to show this fact.
[3] Randolph *Common Pleas,* vol. 3; Judges William Morrison (12 times—11 as a member of his firm), R. Reynolds (9), G. Fisher (5), N. Jarrot (5), J. Grosvenor (3), P. Menard (3), J. B. Barbau (2), J. Dumoulin, J. Edgar, J. F. Perrey (1 each). Other officers: Jas. Gilbreath, Jas. Dunn, W. Kelly, R. Morrison.
[4] Vol. 2: G. Fisher (4), W. Morrison (3), R. Morrison (2), W. Kelly (2), R. Reynolds, J. Dumoulin, J. Grosvenor, J. B. Barbau, J. Gilbreath.
[5] Vol. 5: W. Morrison, 6; R. Reynolds, 7 (not counting 18 indictments against him); G. Fisher, 3; J. Grosvenor, 2; J. B. Barbau, 2; J. Edgar, 4; R. Morrison, 2. In addition there appear J. Beaird (2) and R. McMahon (2). The number of appearances of the other judges was not noted, nor those of any judges in volumes one and four. But all would tell the same story. In St. Clair, in 47 pleas of 1801-1803, J. Dumoulin appears 6 times; N. Jarrot, 2; J. F. Perrey, 1.
[6] Also Michael Jones, but apparently he never sat with the court.
[7] Pease, *Laws (I. H. C.,* 17), 344, § 7 (1799); *post,* 342, § 6 (1807 Revision).

times practiced in another county, and in the St. Clair Common
Pleas several of the judges appeared for themselves, both as plaintiffs and defendants, before the court of which they were members![1]   The Randolph judges were eternally litigious but they
invariably hired lawyers to appear for them.   However, lest their
lawyers make a mistake, some of them frequently sat as judges in
their own cases.[2]   The same thing also happened in St.
Clair.[3]

Judged by present-day standards of spelling, of course most,
if not all, of the county judges seem but semi-literate.[4]   No evi-

[1] In the St. Clair *Order Book 1801-03*, George Fisher appears in plea
No. 3 for himself and John Fisher.   John Dumoulin appeared for himself
in pleas 4, 5, 16, 18 (semble)—but not in 23.   J. F. Perrey appeared for
self in plea 7, and defaulted in plea 14; Nicholas Jarrot appeared for himself in plea 16.   The statute of 1799 (then governing) read: "No person
shall . . . practice as an attorney at law, by instituting, conducting or
defending any action . . . who is not a citizen . . . (of the territory)
or who holds a commission as a judge of the general court; nor shall . . .
a judge of any court of common pleas . . . practice as an attorney or
counsellor at law in the county in which he is commissioned or appointed."
In the St. Clair *Orphans' Court,* Perrey, George Atchison, and Shadrach
Bond appear as administrators of estates before their own court—"off the
Bench," then "back on the bench" (pp. 21, 22, 30, 43).

[2] *Ante,* cciii, notes 3, 4 and 5, include all of the cases (in the
volumes cited) to which the persons named—judges at one time or
another between 1801 and 1809—were parties.   The present note, of course,
refers solely to cases brought or determined when they were actually members of the court.   Out of 13 cases to which W. Morrison was a party he
sat in 12 not at all—neither during the hearings nor when judgment was
rendered; in 1 he was on the bench only when hearings were in progress;
in none did he join in judgment.   The corresponding figures for other judges
were: J. Edgar—8, 1, 0; J. B. Barbau (if he is to be regarded as a member
of the court in March, 1805)—1, 0, 0; J. Grosvenor (if he is to be so
regarded in December 1806 and August 1807)—3, 0, 0; P. Menard—5, 1, 2—
with two additional doubtful cases; G. Fisher—0, 2 (once plaintiff, once
defendant, both discontinued), 3 (judgment for Fisher in all three cases)—
also one doubtful case; R. Reynolds—1, 3 (once plaintiff, twice defendant,
all discontinued), 6—with two additional doubtful cases.   The doubtful
cases are where the clerk started to write in the name of the judge in
question, then stopped; or wrote it but it is marked out.

[3] In the three cases of 1795 against John Dumoulin (*post,* ccvi), Jean
Baptiste Barbau presided, coming from Prairie du Rocher for the purpose—
May Allinson, Ill. State Hist. Soc. *Trans.* (1907), 291.   N. Jarrot sat in
one case in which he was defendant; it was continued to another term.
St. Clair *Order Book,* 120.   In another case "Nicholas Jarrot Esquire comes
down the bench and was admitted to enter special bail" for the defendant.
Ibid., 60.   William Biggs did the same. *Ibid.,* 76.   As for J. F. Perrey
see *supra,* n. 1.

[4] For example, in the Randolph Miscellanies Box is this note by
George Fisher—leading physician, legislator, and judge:

dence has been seen that any of them had schooling, or owned or read books. They made, as Governor Reynolds said, "no pretention to law-learning; but were about similar to the best of our Justices of the Peace" seventy-five years ago, when he wrote.[1] It was, of course, difficult to find good men. Governor St. Clair's utmost hope was that there should be one lawyer on the bench "where their decisions are final." He complained of the ignorance of courts and juries.[2]

The same complaint might have been made—of the same judges and the same juries, speaking generally—under the Indiana Territory. Necessarily few illustrations of monumental ignorance or extravagantly bad law have been preserved. Senator Oliver H. Smith's stories are from somewhat later years. He tells of an indictment for theft of a log-chain quashed because the words "then and there being found" showed that the remedy should have been trover; of a defence under the statute of frauds overcome by reading the constitutional provision that no state shall pass a statute impairing the obligation of contracts; of a day of adverse British authorities overcome by reading the Declaration of Independence.[3] Governor Reynolds' story of an indictment brought in Prairie du Rocher for the murder of a hog[4] is not at all surprising, for we have seen that even in later years the French judges could not understand the statutes until translated.

[1] *My Own Times,* 66. Doubtless this has a special reference to the Quarter Sessions, and justices of the peace who were or were not of the quorum—*ante,* clxi.
[2] *St. Clair Papers,* 2: 415.
[3] *Early Trials,* 46, 62, 122-123. Also 55 (on habeas corpus). As regards the British authorities, see Warren, *Hist. of the Amer. Bar,* 224-239 on the post-Revolution prejudice against them. New Jersey (1799), Kentucky (1807), and Pennsylvania (1810-1836) passed statutes forbidding the citation in their courts of British decisions made after July 4, 1776 (*ibid.,* 232-233).
[4] *Pioneer History,* 181. The case evidently arose when Prairie du Rocher was a separate judicial district, *ante,* cxlvii, n. 3.

"Sir Pleas to let the bearer Henry Conner have a Coppy of the Laws which will be the one that I am intiteled to as one of the Members of the Legislator.
August 26th 1808   **George Fisher**
Rob Morrison Esq."
See John Edgar's letters in Alvord, *Kaskaskia Records* (*I. H. C.,* 5), 376, 395 (but compare 513); letter of Shadrach Bond Jr. quoted *post,* app. n. 19.

A justice of the peace, whom a widow petitioned in 1784 to restrain an intruder from working her sugar-claim, offering evidence by old inhabitants of her prior rights, rejected the petition, "it being the intention of the State that all persons may seek after their own happiness."[1]

Judge Turner's visit to the Illinois country in 1794 was so stormy that one might discount his reports of improprieties on the part of the local judges if the evidence of later years did not confirm him.[2] His personality is a guaranty that his charges were piquant, but unfortunately they are not preserved. We only know that they gave pain to Governor St. Clair, who fondly hoped that any improprieties of which the judges might have been guilty had proceeded "from a mistaken judgment, and not a perverted will . . . You must be sensible, . . ." he wrote in reply, "that to find persons in that country who are capable of performing the duties of judges in a strictly legal manner, is impossible."[3]

It has been noted that various judges, in violation of the statute's explicit prohibition, acted as attorneys—and, if it be said that they merely represented themselves, as any citizen might, though before their own court, it was at least an impropriety; and that some of them sat as judges of their own causes. There are other evidences of their judicial unfitness. John Dumoulin, of the St. Clair Court, was defendant in three suits in 1795; one of them brought, successfully, by a fellow Frenchman for depriving him of a cow.[4] "In February of 1796, three of the judges, Dumoulin, William St. Clair and James Piggott, were involved

---

[1] *Amer. State Papers: Pub. Lands,* 2: 206.

[2] *Ante,* clviii, n. 1. The charges against him will be found in the *Amer. State Papers: Misc.,* 1: 151, 157; *St. Clair Papers,* 2: 372-374. Governor St. Clair's bitterness against the Judge is unpleasantly clear; he even proposed to William St. Clair (clerk of the St. Clair Court, with whom Turner had quarreled) the circulation of a petition to Congress embodying charges against him. See also *ibid.,* 2: 342, 345-347, 348-349. Some of the judges were too inactive to suit St. Clair; Judge Turner was too active and officious, the Governor resenting his encroachment upon executive functions. See also, on trouble between Judges Turner and Vander Burgh, *ibid.,* 2: 353 n.; Monks, *Courts,* 1: 13. See also *St. Clair Papers,* 2: 354 n., for some legislative motions by Turner that certainly reflected popular desire, tabled by his fellows.

[3] *St. Clair Papers,* 2: 348, letter of May 2, 1795 to Judge Turner.

[4] Allinson, Ill. State Hist. Soc. *Trans.* (1907), 291; Bateman and Selby, *Hist. of St. Clair County,* 2: 700.

in law suits, which came before the court of this session and which would seem to undermine the efficiency and even the justice of the court."[1]   Notwithstanding these faults Dumoulin was recommissioned by Harrison in 1800 and 1801.   In 1803 he was indicted for an assault and battery.[2]   Meanwhile, in 1801, the grand jury found a presentment against him in the Circuit Court for having in several instances acted tyrannically, corruptly, and illegally in the conduct of his office.   A commission headed by Shadrach Bond Sr., his fellow judge, was appointed to take testimony and report to the Governor,[3] but their report has disappeared.   However, he was continued in office.   In 1802 two informations issued against him for "malpractice" in his office as justice of the peace and "malpractices" as judge of the Common Pleas.   As he made oath in both cases that he could not expect a fair and impartial trial in St. Clair County the venue was changed to Knox.   He was found not guilty in one case; the outcome in the other does not appear.[4]   Nicholas Jarrot was indicted in 1802, for what offence does not appear; apparently he was found not guilty.[5]   J. F. Perrey seems to have taken a special and an undue interest in the administration of estates.   Presumably they were profitable, and there is evidence that he was guilty of some of the improprieties—in addition to that of being an executor de son tort, which would seem to be an impropriety of conduct in case of a judge—that occurred in this field of the law.[6]   He

[1] Allinson, *loc. cit.,* 291; *ante, cciv,* n. 3.

[2] Battery upon John Porter, General Court, 1803, *Order Book,* 1: 72, 76, 86.   Quashed.

[3] Gibson, *Exec. Journal,* 105-106.

[4] General Court, *Order Book,* 1: 23, 24, 45, 49, 50, 69, 70, 72.   No later entry in second case noted.

[5] *Ibid.,* 25 (March 25, 1802) 37, 46, 132; to the country, on plea of not guilty; later entry not noted, but presumably overlooked—it is practically certain that he got the verdict.

[6] See *ante,* cxlviii, n. 4.   In the record of the *Orphans' Court 1797-1809,* p. 1, it appears that on August 5, 1796 the Probate Judge, William St. Clair, represented that several cases had arisen in which the security given did not satisfy the law, but "great inconveniences would arise (as also Great loss to several persons) should the administration heretofore granted to them be declared void"; wherefore it was ordered that all administrators be cited to lodge sufficient security.   The first appearance of William Mears (see Reynolds, *Pioneer History,* 361) in the records is in ousting an administrator not qualified to act as such—*Orphans' Court,*

too was indicted, in the Circuit Court, for what offence does not appear, but found not guilty.[1] Sam S. Kennedy, a justice of the peace in St. Clair County and later a county judge under the Illinois Territory, was sued in the Common Pleas in 1808 for assault and battery.[2]

In Randolph the record is similar. The several indictments against John Grosvenor[3] and Robert Reynolds[4] have already been referred to. In 1808 an attempt was made to impeach Robert Morrison, a clerk of the Common Pleas.[5] It appears from a record of the General Court of earlier years that Morrison had been permitted by the court to appear before it as attorney, but the grounds for the impeachment in 1808 do not appear.[6]

The fundamental trouble, of course, was that the courts were political; as they are today in the main. Beyond a doubt there were some (and very likely many) better men available than those appointed.[7] Several of the attorneys who practiced in

---

[1] Records in the Belleville Museum, of October 1808.

[2] Belleville Museum, recognizance of April 17, 1808 (of Kennedy, Robert Reynolds, and William Bolin Whiteside).

[3] *Ante,* clxxx, n. 1; clxxxi, n. 1.

[4] *Ante,* clxxix, n. 1.

[5] Webster, Ind. Hist. Soc. *Pub.,* 4: 238. He says "Mr. Morrison, a Judge in Randolph county." William Morrison had not for several years been a judge; Robert Morrison never was, but the reference must be to him. See *post,* app. n. 70.

[6] They may appear in the journal of the Assembly in the *Western Sun,* which I have not seen. On March 9, 1803 in the General Court (*Order Book* 1: 74), on motion of James Haggin, it was ordered that the Randolph Court seal a bill of exceptions tendered to them at the trial (if tendered—this showing the court's distrust of Haggin), objecting to the appearance of Robert Morrison as attorney. It is significant that the objections were merely that he was neither a licensed attorney nor held a power of attorney; the violation of statute involved was not mentioned! See *ante,* cciii.

[7] In Harrison's *Messages,* 1: 221, appears the complaint of some inhabitants of Knox County that "by means of rong or Pertial Information Given" to Harrison he had appointed as justice of the peace one Captain

---

47 (1808). Perrey was the administrator of John Dumoulin—*ibid.,* 29 (March 1806); there are many references to this administration in the *Order Book* of the General Court—1: 153 *et seq.* In the Belleville Museum are papers of a circuit court of October 1808 which show a suit against him by Nicholas Jarrot as executor de son tort. The record of the *Orphans' Court 1797-1809,* 48 (March 20, 1809) shows that he had taken the administration of two estates, which he declared "trifling," on condition that Shadrach Bond Sr. "would charge half the Costs of the letters"; and Bond testified (the bonds were already lost!) that he thought this was done.

Randolph were vastly superior to the judges of the county court. So undoubtedly were some of the justices of the peace: however poor the quality of some of the justices of the peace that of others was excellent. The judges were largely the economic and political magnates of their counties, the "county gentry"; they had no other qualifications, educational or moral, in any noticeable degree.

The governor had power, of course, to dismiss undesirable judges, but apparently the power was never exercised. In 1805 the General Assembly passed an impeachment statute.[1] No provision for impeachment had, until this, existed. No removal was accomplished under the statute, although several impeachments were made.[2] A bill passed by the Assembly in 1808 was vetoed by Governor Harrison because it provided that the executive should remove any clerk of court upon application of the court. It seems proper to assume that the bill was due to dissatisfaction with the qualities or conduct of the clerks. The veto was based on the ground that the executive discretion could not be subordinated to the wishes of the judges.[3]

Some irregularities of procedure in the county court of Randolph, corrected in the General Court, appear in the records of the latter. Thus, in a case of 1801, on motion of John Rice Jones,

[1] *Post*, 123, 520.

[2] Monks, *Courts*, 1: 42. Governor Reynolds says that the governor "scarcely ever exercised his power in dismissing any [judges] from office"— *Pioneer History*, 179; he gives no instances, and none have been discovered.

[3] It is natural to connect this with the impeachment (or attempted impeachment) of Robert Morrison this same year. We have seen, also, that the record of Henry Hurst, clerk of the General Court was far from impeccable: *ante*, cc. The bill also provided that the clerks of the Common Pleas should be ex officio clerks of the "district" (i. e. circuit) courts in their respective counties "where the emoluments of each are not sufficient to induce a properly qualified person to undertake the discharge of them." Harrison, *Messages*, 1: 319. The Governor, naturally, refused to renounce his power of unrestrained appointment. For a third provision of the bill see *ante*, clv. Another bill, concerning the office of attorney-general, was vetoed by the Governor at the same time on the ground that it violated his appointing power and interfered with a federal office. Harrison, *Messages*, 1: 320. Apparently the bill proposed election of the attorney-general by the Assembly. Mr. Esarey says (*ibid.*, 320 n.) that the second bill was political, inspired by the antislavery and prodivision coalition in the Assembly (*ante*, xlii).

Jacob Winemiller, who according to his critics "Cannot or at least does not speak or Write any language so as to be understood." On the other hand, see *post*, app. n. 65.

counsel for appellant, writs were issued commanding that court to sign and seal a bill of exceptions as tendered to them at the trial below, and correcting deficiencies in the record. And this was not the only instance.[1]

Unlike jails, courthouses, of a kind, seem to have existed at both Kaskaskia and Cahokia at an early date. That at Kaskaskia was sold before 1802, and during the remainder of the period of Indiana Territory rooms were rented in private houses or (usually) taverns.[2] There was no need, as in some of the wilderness counties, to hold courts in the forest clearings, with logs and stumps for seats. It is most probable that all the county courts were conducted with extreme informality.[3] But the judges seem to have received the deference to which in their own opinion they were entitled, for only one case of contempt appears in the

[1] General Court, *Order Book,* 1: 18 (September 8, 1801), 25, 29. And see *ante,* ccviii, n. 6.

[2] County-lieutenant Todd seems to have built what was used as a courthouse at Kaskaskia, in 1779; and this was, apparently (McDonough, *Hist. of Randolph, Monroe and Perry Counties,* 100) the one sold to William Morrison and George Fisher, and for which they were, in 1805, still indebted to the county—*ante,* cxx. Construction of another was contemplated in 1804, Randolph *Court Record 1802-06,* 6, 52. The rate allowed John Grosvenor for use of his house (which was a tavern) was $1.50 a day; the houses of Philip Fouke, Robert Morrison, Drusilla Turcotte (a tavern), and others were also used as meeting places. (Randolph *Court Record 1802-06,* passim; bills by Grosvenor for 1806, 1807 in Chester Miscellanies Box; allowances to Grosvenor and Fouke for 1808, in Randolph *County Commissioners* volume of Illinois Territory, 1809-1810, pp. 110, 116; McDonough, *Hist. of Randolph, Monroe and Perry Counties,* 101).

[3] "It is said, that at that time," when Judge Symmes held Circuit Court in St. Clair under the Northwest Territory in 1796 (Governor St. Clair was with him), "courts were . . . disorderly and indecorous": Bateman and Selby, *Hist. of St. Clair County,* 2: 699; see McDonough, *Hist. of Randolph, Monroe and Perry Counties,* 66, on William Goings' bell-dance in Judge Symmes' Circuit Court. For John Reynolds' manner of holding court, in somewhat later years, see Governor Ford's *History of Illinois,* 82-85, and Reynolds' *My Own Times* (Fergus ed.), 138, 139-140. C. Warren, *History of the Harvard Law School and of Early Legal Conditions in America,* 1: 81, says that: "Anthony Stokes, Chief Justice of Georgia, in 1783, in his *View of the Constitution of the British Colonies of North America and the West Indies,* states that in the Colonies where a system of County Courts prevailed and where there were a large number of judges in general unacquainted with the law, little decorum was observed: in Colonies where judges went on circuit there was more impartial administration of justice." This, of course, anybody would have expected. For one illustration of the greater dignity of the circuit courts in Illinois compare *ante,* cxci, on juries.

Randolph records. In that case a fine of five dollars was imposed "for an insult to the State's attorney" and an equal sum for an insult "to the Court while on the bench." But the fines were not paid, and after six years were remitted.[1] John Dumoulin was sued in St. Clair County for assault; but the evidence showed that he had only ordered the plaintiff imprisoned for insultingly and contemptuously obstructing him in the performance of his duties as a justice of the peace, the officer having apparently found considerable force necessary in executing the order; and the court sustained Dumoulin in maintaining the dignity of his office.[2] A harassed witness, who attacked a judge in court and broke his arm, in Dearborn County, was imprisoned for a few hours beneath a heavy worm fence.[3]

Apparently many contempts were shown for the General Court. In the unique ejectment suit against John Edgar (already referred to), taken up from Randolph County, William Wilson, county surveyor, was twice ordered attached for contempt in failing to survey the land, as ordered; but there is nothing to show that he was actually punished.[4] In 1805 James Edgar, sheriff of Randolph, was ordered to show cause why an attachment should not issue against him for not executing a ca. sa. against Robert Morrison, "and for making an improper and untrue return" to the General Court; also for not bringing in one "William Williams" (probably William Wilson) as ordered. He appeared, and —being of course a powerful politician—he was fined in each case twenty-five cents and costs,[5] for thus flouting the Supreme Court

[1] Miles Hotchkiss was so fined on June 5, 1804—*Court Record 1802-06*, 60. See *ante*, cxx, on the nonpayment of the fines. They were remitted by the county court of Illinois Territory in 1810 on "satisfactory proof being adduced to the Court that the said Court of Common Pleas [of Indiana Territory] had ordered the same to be remitted but had omitted to be entered on their records"—*County Court Record 1810*, 62 (July 7, 1810).

[2] Miss Allinson quotes the record in Ill. State Hist. Soc. *Trans.* (1907) 291 n.

[3] About 1803—Monks, *Courts*, 1: 44-45 (2: 629 for proper date). This is given among incidents vouched for (1: 41) as "of unquestioned historical standing." Compare *ibid.*, 1: 151, and *ante*, clxxxi, n. 4.

[4] General Court, *Order Book*, 1, 89 (September 10, 1803), 143 (September 26, 1804): *post*, app. n. 75.

[5] *Order Book* 1: 157 (June 14, 1805), 159 (June 15, 1805), 165 (September 15, 1805).

of the territory. The next year he was again ordered to show cause why he should not be punished for failing to return execution in three cases—two of them again against Robert Morrison.[1] The next year shows two attachments for contempt against him— whether or not in the same causes not appearing—that were continued.[2] No punishment appears in any of these cases. One wonders why he should have felt he could show contempt for such a court. It is to be remembered that the Edgar-Morrison party had for years been dominant in the county. In 1805 attachments were issued against William Morrison (then a judge of the Randolph Common Pleas), James Gilbreath (a former sheriff), and others, for contempt of the process of the General Court.[3] No punishment appears. Absent jurymen or officers of the court were usually excused or fined in petty sums (and the same in the county courts) for nonattendance.[4]

It is hardly necessary to add, however, that the efforts of the General Court to punish contempts, contemptibly feeble as they were, were made the basis of political charges and maneuvers.[5]

Casual references have been made to the French inhabitants in connection with certain laws and administrative details: the part played by them in the legal history of Indiana Territory was very small. Their submergence beneath the flood of American immigrants is unintelligible apart from the incidents of earlier years. The story is essentially one of the clash of two noncoalescible cultures. Except illiteracy there was nothing common to the two classes. Self-sufficient in their traditional isolation, the French did

[1] *Ibid.*, 202 (April 10, 1806).
[2] *Ibid.*, 234 (April 8, 1807, continued to the September term).
[3] *Ibid.*, 156 (June 5, 1805).
[4] *Ibid.*, 7 (constable fined 50 cents); 11 (three grand jurymen excused); 35 (grand jurymen fined $4 and costs); 61 (same, $1); 63 (same, $1); 69 (petit jurymen put under $100 bond to appear next day and regularly). Except the last, which is most extraordinary, these are fair samples.
[5] In the Illinois-country petition to Congress of 1805 (Ind. Hist. Soc. *Pub.*, 2: 488; *ante*, xxxviii, n. 2) the memorialists stigmatize "the practice of issuing attachments for contempt of court, against witnesses for non-attendance, and public officers, upon pretexts, in the opinion of your memorialists, resting upon the slightest grounds, a vexatious practice, which has a great tendency to sour the minds of the citizens of this remote part of the territory, from the hardships, as already described, to which they must be exposed from these proceedings." For fees allowed witnesses, see *post*, 51, 58, 473, 475.

not use the word "America" as including the Illinois country.[1]
Also, as Governor Reynolds says, they had lived so long in villages
that they could not conceive of existence otherwise.[2] Very different was the spirit of the American backwoodsmen, whose rule
was: "When you hear the sound of a neighbor's gun, it is time
to move away."[3] The attitude of the two peoples toward religion,
the Indians, law, and mode of life was sharply distinct. A splen-
did, had it not been a licentious, independence, a hard nature, a
general indulgence in liquor and in boisterous and brutal contests,
an utter intolerance of law and other social restraints, characterized
the Americans. A gentler and indolent nature, a greater temper-
ance, dependence upon authority, devotion to community life, and
a taste for at least some refinements, characterized the French.
Small differences of life—in industry, in farming, in amusements,
in social attitudes— were numerous, and such matters are always
irritating.[4] Variant opinions regarding Indian relations caused,

[1] Reynolds, *Pioneer History,* 297. French was for many years the
language used in Governor Reynolds' home.

[2] Reynolds, *Pioneer History,* 229. Count Volney says: "Visiting
and talking are so indispensably necessary to a Frenchman from habit, that
throughout the whole frontier of Canada and Louisiana there is not one
settler of that nation to be found, whose house is not within reach or within
sight of some other"—*View of the Climate and Soil of the United States*
(ed. London, 1804), 386. "The French People for the most part live in
villages and cultivate a Common Field. They cannot bear the idea of
separation. To live in the country without a neighbour in less than half a
mile is worse than death, and almost as bad as Purgatory"—letter of Frederick Bates in 1807 from St. Louis, Marshall, *Life and Papers of Frederick
Bates,* 1: 243. These quotations show how profoundly this characteristic
of the French impressed all observers.

[3] Mr. Buck, *Illinois in 1818,* 99, quotes this from George Flower.

[4] For descriptions, men who wrote from personal observation, see:
Volney, *op. cit.,* appendix IV, especially 369-375, 385-389; Governor St. Clair,
in *St. Clair Papers,* 2: 137; V. Collot, *A Journey in North America,* 1:
232-233; "Invitation Sérieuse aux Habitants des Illinois," Ill. State Hist.
Soc. *Trans.* (1908), 294, 338-339; Reynolds, *My Own Times,* 23, ch. 12-13,
15-18, and *Pioneer History,* 61, 67-73, 125-126; Judge Symmes, in B. Bond,
John Cleves Symmes, 287-290; Marshall, *Life and Papers of Frederick
Bates,* 1: 241-244; Ford, *History of Illinois,* 35-38. See also Alvord, *Cahokia
Records (I. H. C.,* 2), xxi n., xxii-xxv, lxiv-lxvi; Houck, *Missouri,* 2: 267-
283; Buck, *Illinois in 1818,* ch. 4. Governor Reynolds says of his arrival at
Kaskaskia in 1800: "In fact, the people, their dress, language, houses, manner
of living and doing business were so different from the Americans in the
States that it almost made us believe we had traveled out of America."
Pioneer History, 297. He says of the Illinois French that they "scarcely
ever troubled themselves with milking cows . . . and made little or no

in the beginning, intense feeling. The French enjoyed an immunity from Indian attacks, and wished free association and open trade; the Americans deserved no immunity, enjoyed none except through war and fear, and of course were opposed to the free intercourse which had existed before the establishment of American dominion.[1] From the time of Clark's conquest onward, first from necessity and later without excuse, the French were plundered by American troops. As early as 1779 they prayed their court to relieve them from this "brigandage and tyranny" and to bestow upon them "some glimmer of that liberty which has been so often announced"; but for years, it continued as a monstrous abuse.[2] The land donations to the French were largely intended as a recompense for the loss of the Indian trade, and for their sacrifices due to the long military occupation of their country.[3] The inevitable result of all these irritations was that the French came to regard the Americans as intruders upon an idyllic past; and very much could be said to support them.[4] In return they were, by the Americans—as Alvord has said—"held in contempt and regarded as aliens settled on American soil."[5]

In these conflicts and animosities questions of law and courts played a large part. The British commandants of the country had

[1] Boggess, *Settlement of Illinois,* 48-49, referring to the Wabash country. Governor Reynolds says that, about 1800, great numbers of Indians camped most of the year around Kaskaskia; perhaps two Indians to one white.
[2] Alvord: *Cahokia Records* (I. H. C., 2), lxxx-i; cp. li, lxvii-viii, lxix, lxxv-lxxxii, xcvii, xcix, cxxi; *Illinois Country,* 346, 352-353.
[3] Alvord: *Cahokia Records* (I. H. C., 2), cxxi; *Kaskaskia Records* (I. H. C., 5), 445-449, 479.
[4] Compare Reynolds, *Pioneer History,* 66, and Alvord, *Illinois Country,* 202, 373, 375. Count Volney, *op. cit.,* 370, records in his diary the story as told by the French of Vincennes.
[5] Alvord, *Illinois Country,* 360.

butter. They scarcely ever used a churn, a loom, or a wheel."—*My Own Times,* 57. So Count Volney, recording in his diary the opinions voiced of each other by the French and Americans of Vincennes, includes in the charges against the former this: "The women can neither sew, nor spin, nor make butter; but spend their time in gossipping, and leave their houses dirty and in disorder. The men . . . know neither how to cure salt or hung pork or venison, make small beer or sour crout, or distil spirits from corn or peaches; all *capital* things for a farmer"—*op. cit.,* 373-374. Such matters, far from being trivialities, were doubtless of very exceptional importance in their effect upon the relations of the two races.

assumed—though the proclamation of 1763 gave them no explicit warrant for so doing—to introduce English law; but there was a British court for only a brief time,[1] and it is certain that not much could have been done in displacing the old customs. Under Virginian rule there was greater displacement of that law; but the judges remained almost wholly French and in the main it was French law that was applied, slightly modified by Virginian statutes.[2] The French inhabitants clung to the court throughout

---

[1] *Ibid.*, 266-268.

[2] Alvord, *Cahokia Records* (*I. H. C.*, 2), cxii. The whole Virginia tradition was one of generous adjustment to the French tradition. The statute of December 1778 which established government for the "county of Illinois" provided for administration of the Custom of Paris—*ibid.*, lii-iii. In February 1785 Congress adopted a committee report which recommended that a commissioner be sent to Illinois "to suppress those disorders and irregularities of which the said Inhabitants complain. And that in the exercise of his Authority and the administration of justice he pursue the mode which he may judge the best calculated to quiet the Minds of those peop[l]e and secure their attachment to the fœderal government"—Alvord, *Kaskaskia Records* (*I. H. C.*, 5), 370. A committee of Congress, reporting on the powers of such commissioner, recommended that he cause the election, by districts, of "three or more magistrates, who shall be invested with power and authority to hear and determine all civil Controversies not relative to the property in lands, *agreeably to the laws, usages and customs that prevail in such districts*"; though in criminal cases no penalty might extend to "loss of life, limb or member," unless sanctioned by Virginia law. Substantially the same recognition of former laws and customs was provided for in cases involving "titles and possessions." (March 14, 1785, *ibid.*, 371-372; italics added). Another committee made similar recommendations two years later (May 7, 1787, *ibid.*, 399-400). No such commissioners were appointed. Much less liberal concessions were made by the Ordinance of 1787. These two committee reports substantially described, apparently, the practice under Virginian administration: the law enforced was the French custom modified by the Virginia bill of rights, and perhaps some Virginian statutes relative to courts or procedure—Alvord, *Cahokia Records* (*I. H. C.*, 2), lxii-iii; cp. Alvord, *Kaskaskia Records* (*I. H. C.*, 5), 383-384, note on 384. The French judges, in July 1787, protested against the addition to the court of English judges; and the consequent agreement among the citizens which excluded those judges referred to them as "not understanding the French language in order to . . . follow the law to which we are accustomed which has been granted us by the General Assembly of Virginia" —*ibid.*, 405, 409, to the same effect, 286-287.

The Custom of Paris was, apparently, often not observed even in Canada, that of Normandy—whence came a very large proportion of the population—being followed instead. Moreover, it had been modified by vast numbers of royal orders etc., that remained in manuscript and inaccessible. Its enforcement, especially by the British courts set up after 1763, was very difficult, and they had resort to evidence of local—unenacted—custom, instead until a digest of the law was published in London in 1772-1774; moreover, in 1772-1773, elaborate reports were made, by competent law officers of the British crown, upon the legal situation of the colony. See W. B.

the period of Virginia's rule, because it was their sole protection against military rule and pillage.[1]

It goes without saying that the American authorities, as befitted the special guardians of liberty, held toward their French subjects a patronizing attitude. When Patrick Henry sent John Todd out as county lieutenant-commandant of the County of Illinois he instructed him: "You are on all Accatons to inculcate on the people the value of liberty and the Difference between the State of free Citizens of the Commonwelth and that Slavery to which Ilinois was Destined."[2] "All these people"—wrote General Harmar nine years later—"are entirely unacquainted with what Americans call liberty. Trial by jury, etc., they are strangers to. A commandant with a few troops to give them orders is the best form of government for them; it is what they have been accustomed to."[3] "The are worse," wrote John Edgar, "then the Indians and ought to be ruled by a rod of Iron."[4] And Judge Symmes had barely reached Vincennes in 1790 when he expressed similar opinions: "We have an arduous task before us to form the government & put the laws in operation here—from appearances the people will not relish a free government, they say our laws are too complex, not to be understood, and tedious in their operation[5]—the command or order of the Military commandant is better law and spedier justice for them & what they prefer to all the legal systems found in Littleton and Blackstone. it is a language which they say they can understand, it is cheap

[1] Alvord, *Cahokia Records* (*I. H. C.*, 2), lxvi, lxvii, lxxv.
[2] December 12, 1778—*ibid.*, liii, liv, lv.
[3] November 24, 1787—*St. Clair Papers*, 2: 32. Compare the court order quoted *ante*, clxxxi, n. 4. Harmar merely voiced the contempt felt by John Dodge for the Kaskaskia French, who permitted him to insult and bully them. See Alvord, *Kaskaskia Records* (*I. H. C.*, 5), 425, and *Illinois Country*, 369-371.
[4] November 7, 1785, to George Rogers Clark—Alvord, *Kaskaskia Records* (*I. H. C.*, 5), 376.
[5] Only the statutes of 1788 had at this time been passed. For every one of these criticisms there was much justification. The statutes were exaggeratedly legalistic in form (*ante*, cxi), the system of local government was extremely cumbersome, and nothing had been done to make the laws known to the French population.

Munro: *The Seigniorial System in Canada*, 10, 100, 195-196, 198 n., 205-208, 209 and n.; *Documents Relating to the Seigniorial Tenure in Canada, 1598-1854*, c-ciii, 154 n.

and expeditious & they wish for no other—Indeed I am of opinion that the establishing of law in this extremity of the United States will be the means of driving to the Spanish government, multitudes of those who remain—very many having already gone. Indeed they went away because they had no government—and they will still go away because the government they now are like to have is not on the foot of an absolute Government like france."[1] There is nothing to support the idea that the establishment "of law" caused migration from the territory; but it is certain that toward the system established the French population was unsympathetic. Even trial by jury was not acceptable to all.[2] Of the French in Missouri Frederick Bates (who had known them also in Michigan) wrote, a few years later:

"The very name of *liberty* deranges their intellects, and it appears absolutely impossible for them to form accurate conceptions of the rights which Justice creates on the one hand, and the obligations which it imposes on the other.

"The summary decree of a military officer however tyrannical or absurd is much better suited to their ideas of the fitness of things, than the dilatory trial by jury and 'the glorious uncertainty of the Common Law.' "[3]

Small concession was made to their traditions by Congress. Virginia's deed of cession confirmed to them their "possessions and titles," "rights and liberties." The Ordinance of 1787, however, merely saved to them "their laws and customs . . . relative to the descent and conveyance of property." Yet the system

[1] June 22, 1790—B. Bond, *John Cleves Symmes*, 290-291.

[2] The British court of 1768-1770 had not attempted to apply trial by jury; although the reasons given ("on account of its Small number of Inhabitants as Well as their Want of Knowledge of the Laws and Customs of England") seem meaningless—Alvord, *Illinois Country*, 267-268. In a petition of 1810 from Michigan inhabitants to their governor and judges they asked that it should be merely permitted in the higher courts, and to those desiring it—*Mich. Pioneer and Hist. Colls.*, 8: 619. See Houck, *Missouri*, 2: 394 on distrust of jury trial among the inhabitants of upper Louisiana (report by Rufus Easton to President Jefferson, January 7, 1805). Alvord's statement, already referred to—*Cahokia Records* (*I. H. C.*, 2), lxiii—is based upon the court proceedings.

[3] Marshall, *Life and Papers of Frederick Bates*, 1: 242-243. On government by a military commandant, see the American instance *ante*, clxx, n. 2.

to which they were immediately subjected did not protect them, even within the Ordinance's narrow guaranty.[1] They had, for example, retained in their isolation, like their fellows in Louisiana and Quebec, the political and economic traditions of the France of Louis XIV, of common fields and manorial organization; yet their American rulers forced upon them the elaborate county and township organization which had been developed in the British colonies.[2] Although the displacement of the French custom by Anglo-American law was general, it was of course somewhat gradual. This was probably especially true in the field of family relations.[3]

As the service of the courts improved the government became more acceptable. In early years—under the Northwest Territory

[1] The Virginia legislative act tendering cession, of December 20, 1783, included the guarantees quoted; the deed of cession of 1784, was "on the conditions of the said recited act"—Thorpe, *Federal and State Constitutions,* 2: 955-957. The Ordinance of 1787—*ibid.,* 958; Pease, *Laws (I.H.C.,* 17), 124— was less generous, but more practicable. Neither instrument could easily be construed to guarantee slavery. Governor St. Clair, when in Illinois in 1790, commissioned notaries in order to enable them to make their conveyances as in the past, in accordance with the guaranty of the Ordinance— *St. Clair Papers,* 2: 172-173. But the American system seems to have displaced very quickly the old practices. The absence of ejectment suits makes it impossible to say whether it was *forced* upon French claimants.

[2] Mr. Esarey (*History,* 1: 137) and Dunn (*Indiana,* 271) have both pointed out this anachronism. Count Volney, comparing the French of Vincennes with the recent immigrants at Gallipolis, attributes to the former the feudal sentiments of the subjects of Louis XIV and XV—*op. cit.,* 391. Tocqueville, after similar opportunities for observation of Canadian institutions, declared that the qualities of the old régime—social, economic, and political—could best be studied in the colonies (cited in Munro, *The Seigniorial System in Canada,* 15). Governor Reynolds says that the Cahokia inhabitants were predominantly from Canada, and those of Kaskaskia from Louisiana, and that their speech and customs were slightly different— *My Own Times,* 37.

[3] Nothing like the sources mentioned, *ante,* ccxv, n. 2, exist for the study of the Custom of Paris in the Illinois country. Nor is there anything comparable to the study, for Michigan, by Justice W. R. Riddell, *Michigan Under British Rule. Law and Law Courts 1760-1796* (Mich. Hist. Commission), 35 *et seq.* and *passim.* In editing the records of Cahokia and Kaskaskia Alvord omitted documents "of a private character, such as marriage contracts, settlements of estates, petitions to the Court in private law suits, etc."—*Kaskaskia Records (I. H. C.,* 5), iv. Doubtless a great mass of such material remains to be garnered. An example of the persistent vitality of the old customs in the period of the Northwest Territory—a prenuptial property contract between Pierre Menard and his wife—is printed in *Chic. Hist. Colls.,* 4: 145, 162-165. See also *Amer. State Papers: Pub. Lands,* 2: 83; Houck, *Missouri,* 2: 195-197.

—when the executive branch of government was wholly autocratic, judicial service in the western counties practically non-
existent, and legislation was imposing a political system totally
alien and unintelligible, the feelings of the French population
were undoubtedly identical with those of their countrymen in
upper Louisiana (many of their leaders emigrants from Illinois)
who remonstrated in 1804 against the illiberal characteristics of
the government first accorded them—to wit: "A single magistrate,
vested with civil and military, with executive and judiciary powers,
upon whose laws we had no check, over whose acts we had no
control, and from whose decrees there is no appeal: the sudden
suspension of all those forms to which we had been accustomed;
the total want of any permanent system to replace them; the introduction of a new language into the administration of justice; the
perplexing necessity of using an interpreter for every communication with the officers placed over us; the involuntarry errors, of
necessity committed by judges uncertain by what code they are
to decide, wavering between the civil and the common law, . . .
and with the best intentions unable to expound laws of which they
are ignorant, or to acquire them in a language they do not understand."[1]

So far as regards administration of the new government, in
the first county organizations (both in the Wabash and the Illinois
counties) the French element was preponderantly represented;
but the courts, and all the rest of the system above the townships
(at least in Illinois), were speedily and completely given over to
Americans. The change was made by Governor St. Clair in 1795.[2]
It has been said of the beginnings of the judiciary under the

---

[1] *Annals*, 8 Congress, 2 session, 1598. See *ante*, cv, n. 1 as to
the status of French and Spanish law in Louisiana, after cession to the
United States. The situation in Illinois was simpler, and occasions for the
application of foreign law were less numerous.

[2] Of his appointees to the two St. Clair courts in 1790 (there was
then but one county) five—including Philip Engel—were French; only
one, John Edgar, was an American. *St. Clair Papers*, 2: 165 n. In 1795 only
two Frenchmen were appointed, and six Americans, in St. Clair County.
Allinson, Ill. State Hist. Soc. *Trans.* (1907), p. 290. In Randolph County
three French judges—Menard, Barbau, and Louviere—may possibly have
been appointed. For the period following 1800 see the court lists in Appendix.

Northwest Territory that "the majority of the first court officers were French and showed no capacity for political affairs. The government soon fell into the hands of the Americans, where it remained."[1]   The estimate is both ungenerous and inadequate. The contrasting history of the older courts at Kaskaskia and at Cahokia is significant. Of the French court of the former village during the Virginian era Alvord has said that "it is probably true that the leaders of the party were ignorant, . . .   and incapable under the existing conditions of fulfilling the duties which the accidents of war and geographical position had thrust upon them";[2] that they made money out of their offices, illegally retained them, and did little to relieve the sufferings of their countrymen.[3] But the failure of the British court of 1768-1770,[4] and of Todd himself[5] were equally complete; the former, too, was characterized by corruption, and the latter not unstained by self-interest.[6]   On the other hand the courts at Cahokia were annually elected, functioned regularly, enforced order with decision; and in every way their record challenges a judgment that denies to the French element capacity for self-government.[7] The cause for the difference seems plain. In Cahokia, up to about 1790 there had been, aside from British merchants, only four immigrants of non-French race, and three of these were connected by marriage with their French fellows. In Kaskaskia, on the other hand, the American element had steadily increased from 1779, at least, onward.[8] It would not submit to be ruled by the French; and the court—unlike the court at Cahokia—lacked the

[1] Monks, *Courts*, 1: 12.

[2] Alvord, *Cahokia Records* (*I. H. C.*, 2), cxii.

[3] Alvord, *Illinois Country*, 347. For a picture of the appalling conditions at Kaskaskia in 1786 see Father Gibault's letter in Alvord, *Kaskaskia Records* (*I. H. C.*, 5), xlvii, 542-544. Also John Edgar to Major Hamtramck, October 28, 1789, and John Rice Jones to the same—*ibid.*, 513-514, 514-517.

[4] Alvord: *Illinois Country*, 267-268, 293; *Cahokia Records* (*I. H. C.*, 2), lvii.

[5] Alvord, *Cahokia Records* (*I. H. C.*, 2), lxvii-viii, lxxiii-iv, lxxviii.

[6] *Ibid.*, lxix and (as to Wilkins) *ante*, lxvi, n 2: lxxix, n. 1; Alvord, *Illinois Country*, 282-283.

[7] Alvord: *Cahokia Records* (*I. H. C.*, 2), cxlvii-cl, 589-591; *Illinois Country*, 374-378.

[8] Alvord: *Illinois Country*, 373, 375, 376; *Cahokia Records* (*I. H. C.*, 2), xxxi, n., cxxii, cxlviii; *ante*, lxviii, n. 1; lxxv, n. 2.

strength to compel obedience. The French, too, influenced by the example of the Americans ceased to give obedience to their own court.[1] Most of their leaders, at Kaskaskia, left them and migrated to Louisiana. They left, as Judge Symmes said, because there was no government. Not, however, because of their own political incapacity but for lack of support by the government that owed them thanks and protection. They were ruined by generous loans to the cause of the Revolution, and by the maintenance and pillage of troops; they were neglected in their ruin for years by Congress; the title to their slaves was threatened by the Ordinance; the lands promised them in recompense for their sufferings were long withheld, until speculators beguiled them into parting, almost for nothing, with their claims; in place of the political system which—if not through institutions of self-government at least in spirit—had been their own, another was established over them that did not preserve to them the privileges which the Ordinance had guaranteed; and they were crowded out of its administration. They left, in short, because they were ruined, hoping to retrieve their fortunes under a more friendly government beyond the Mis-

[1] "The difference in the destinies of the two villages can only be ascribed to the presence of the turbulent frontiersmen in the southern village; for the inhabitants of the villages were of the same origin, and their experience had been practically identical except for the few years of the Virginia period"—Alvord, *Cahokia Records* (*I. H. C.*, 2), cxxi-ii; cp. cl. "Influenced by the example of the Americans, the French themselves gave no obedience to the court which they had established" at Kaskaskia—*ibid.*, cxl. John Edgar's explanation was of course different: "You know better than I, the dispositions of a people who have ever been subject to a military power, & are unacquainted with the blessings of a free government by the voice of their equals"—*ibid.*, cxl; *Kaskaskia Records* (*I. H. C.*, 5), 513 as above cited. It is true that the record of the French court at Vincennes preceding 1790 was both corrupt and inefficient—see *ante*, lxvi; Major Hamtramck to General Harmar, November 11. 1789—Alvord, *Kaskaskia Records* (*I. H. C.*, 5), 512; same, August 14, 1789, *ibid.*, 508; and that before that time there was little American immigration. Monks says that "no higher tribute can be paid to the early lawyers of Indiana than is involved in a comparison of Vincennes at the time of the visit of Count Volney, with it in 1810 after an American court had been in power ten years." *Courts,* 1: 12. It was twenty years, however, instead of ten. There were great improvements, also, in Kaskaskia. But these, to which Governor Reynolds testifies, are not by him attributed to the courts. There is no evidence that the courts made any appreciable contribution to the punishment of crime and the betterment of public order. Besides, various distinctions might be pointed out, if the state of the Illinois country were not here primarily in question, between conditions at Vincennes and at Kaskaskia.

sissippi. They "gave way before the egoism"—though in justice one must add, the steady energy—"of the Americans."[1]

The institutions of the old Illinois country have now been passed somewhat elaborately in review. Some dozens of its characters, in some aspects of their life, have been shown in the high relief of administrative and judicial process. If the doubt at times (somewhat belatedly) assails one whether it is worth while to lift them out of the flatness and obscurity of their village communities, and subject them to such minute attention, the answer must be that at least it should be; for their manner of life was unquestionably typical of the American frontier of the time.[2] One is impelled, too, to offer one or two conclusions; adequately grounded, it is hoped, in the evidence already stated.

The first is that the statutes in this volume cannot support the theory, of which lawyers are vainly and inordinately fond, that the laws of a community are unique memorials of its history.[3]

[1] Alvord, *Cahokia Records* (*I. H. C.*, 2), lxv. "The French villagers gave freely to the cause of independence and were rewarded with destitution"—Alvord, *Illinois Country*, 397. "We are well convinced that all these misfortunes have befallen us for want of some Superior or commanding authority; for ever since the cession of this Territory to Congress we have been neglected as an abandoned people, to encounter all the difficulties that are always attendant upon anarchy & confusion; neither did we know from authority until latterly, to what power we were subject. The greater part of our citizens have left the country on this account to reside in the Spanish dominions"—Le Dru (curate), in the name of the inhabitants of Kaskaskia, to Major Hamtramck at Vincennes, September 14, 1789; Alvord, *Kaskaskia Records* (*I. H. C.*, 5), 510.

[2] It is not, however, such a pioneer community as Dean Pound, for example, has repeatedly assumed. Dozens of times he has contrasted the problem of administering justice in our present urbanized population with courts designed to do justice "in a homogeneous pioneer or rural community of the first half of the nineteenth century," "a homogeneous community, of vigorous pioneer race, restrained already for the most part by deep religious conviction and strict moral training" (R. Pound, *The Spirit of the Common Law*, 114, 115; cp. 71, 117). Even with the French subtracted the Illinois of 1790-1810 could not be brought within such a description.

[3] "The legislation of a community is the exponent of its needs and the measure of its attainments, and the laws of *any given period* become the best memorial of its history . . . They not only tell what our predecessors needed—they show what they were. They faithfully exhibit the state of society, the successive steps of change and progress, and the gradual but sure advance in civilization"—W. L. Gross, Ill. State Bar Assoc. *Proc.* (1881), 57. "Law . . . arises from what is being done in the community and is the final record of the community mind. It is, therefore, the most reliable historical criteria" (sic)—J. J. Thompson, Ill. State Hist. Soc. *Trans.*, 22: 70.

These statutes were not an indigenous product, slowly developed, responsive and nicely adjusted to the peculiar needs of the territory. Some, indeed, do represent a rough attempt at such adjustment. The rest are the foreign system of older states, imposed upon the scattered villages of the territory. They did not embody the attainments, and only in a very partial sense did they express the traditions and the spirit of the territory—even of the American element. It is not in the statute-book, but outside of it, that one must seek for a view of the real life of the territory. Far from representing accurately what was being done in the community, we have seen that the laws most fundamental and most painfully drafted were very indifferently observed; and it is almost certain that the same was true of all the statutes. They were commands to live in a certain way that was an unfamiliar way, awkwardly and slowly learned. Despite the legislative mandates in this volume, to a large extent the people undoubtedly lived quite otherwise than commanded. To imagine that such things—merely for example— as the law of pauper settlements were a reality in the Illinois country would be absurd. The whole system was overwrought, too complicated for application—or even, as regards the French inhabitants, for understanding; it could actually have worked only where it had been long familiar. It was not alone, but only in a greater degree than of the American, that all this was true of the French population.

Lawyers are prone to believe that a society is civilized in proportion as its law is elaborated. By this test, in view of the bulky legislation of the Northwest and Indiana territories dealing with the administration of justice, there must have been a prodigious forward step in civilization between 1787 and 1809. Yet anyone who reflects upon the life which was led, before the American period, in the French villages of Illinois, may recall the other doctrine, implicit in our national political professions, that "civilization consists in teaching men to govern themselves by letting them do it," and must harbor doubts as to the progress.

The truth is, of course, that the bulk of the statute-book is no test at all. The legislation on the courts in the book before us is bulky precisely because most of it was ineffective and had no adjusted relation to the social life that it supposedly served. The true test—one true test—is the actual administration of justice.[1] How was it with that? When the first court was opened with pomp and circumstance at Marietta in 1788 the sheriff naturally proclaimed with the three solemn "Oyes" of tradition that it was open "for the administration of even handed justice to the poor and the rich, to the guilty and the innocent, without respect of persons, none to be punished without a trial by their peers, and then in pursuance of the laws and evidence in the case."[2] It is quite evident from the preceding pages that this ideal was most imperfectly realized. This is not, as we have seen, primarily because it was lacking in equity procedure, or in equity in a broader sense. The inexpertness of the bar and bench, though involving what we today would regard as miscarriages of justice, fell impartially upon all litigants; and besides, from a nontechnical viewpoint, must often have been the more just for its ignorance. We might well apply to both judges and attorneys what Governor Reynolds said of Judge George Fisher as a physician: "His practice was bold and fearless and he succeeded well." On the other hand the courts of the Northwest and Indiana territories, as little as those of the Virginia period, were capable of controlling the society of which they were a part, thrown together by the accidents of war and the advance of the backwoodsmen. They did little to punish even violent crime; nothing to punish crime more recondite in nature, or fraud; nothing to restrain the barbarous personal combats and license characteristic of a frontier. Of course as much might be said of the frontier courts of later times; self-help has always had wide freedom under like conditions.[3] Finally, when judges were so corrupt in their personal affairs, it is impossible to

---

[1] "The administration of justice is a good test of the civilization of the people where it exists; it shows their interest in equity, their freedom to adapt themselves to new conditions and their courage in protecting the weak and controlling the rapacious. It measures the point they have reached in education and in virtue, and how far they are serious in the formal expression of their will"—Judge Learned Hand, in *Lectures on Legal Topics 1921-22* of the Association of the Bar of the City of New York, 105. The test is one which evidently requires a considerable past and development of law before it can be well applied: a frontier system is necessarily imperfect even in substance, much more in operation.

[2] Ind. Hist. Soc. *Pub.*, 2: 7.

[3] See *ante*, clxxxvii.

suppose that embracery was absent from their official practice. Nevertheless, great as the shortcomings of the profession may have been it seems certain that so far as there was any learned profession in the territory it was that of the lawyers; that—as Mr. Esarey has said—"by far the most vigorous part of the early government with the judiciary";[1] and that on the whole theirs was the greatest social contribution to their time.

[1] Ind. Hist. Soc. *Pub.*, 6: 121.

APPENDIX

TERRITORIAL AND COUNTY OFFICERS AND PROMINENT ILLINOIS ATTORNEYS OF 1800-1809.[1]

GOVERNOR

William Henry Harrison—July 4, 1800-March 3, 1813.

SECRETARY

John Gibson—July 4, 1800-November 22, 1816.

JUDGES OF THE GENERAL COURT OF INDIANA TERRITORY

William Clarke[2]—July 4, 1800-November 11, 1802. Died.
Henry Vander Burgh[3]—July 4, 1800-April 12, 1812. Died.
John Griffin[4]—July 4, 1800-[?].
Thomas Terry Davis[5]—February 8, 1803-November 15, 1807.
Waller Taylor[6]—April 17, 1806-December 11, 1816 [?].
Benjamin Parke[7]—April 22, 1808-December 11, 1816 [?].

TERRITORIAL CHANCELLORS

John Badollet[8]—September 2, 1805-March 1, 1806 [?].
Thomas Terry Davis—March 1, 1806-November 15, 1807.
Waller Taylor—November 24, 1807-March 11, 1813.

ATTORNEYS-GENERAL OF THE TERRITORY[9]

John Rice Jones[10]—January 29, 1801-[?].
Benjamin Parke—August 4, 1804-[?].
Thomas Randolph[11]—June 2, 1808-November 7, 1811. Died.

CLERK OF THE GENERAL COURT
Henry Hurst[12]—January 14, 1801-December 11, 1816 [?].

FEDERAL LAND COMMISSIONERS

Michael Jones[13]—November 20, 1804-[?].
Elijah Backus[14]—November 20, 1804-[?].
John Caldwell[15]—April 1, 1812-[?].
Thomas Sloo[16]—1812-[?].

REPRESENTATIVES AND LEGISLATIVE COUNCILLORS IN THE GENERAL ASSEMBLY

St. Clair County

LEGISLATIVE COUNCILLORS

John Hay[17]—May [?], 1805-January 9, 1806 [?]. Resigned.
Shadrach Bond Sr.[18]—January 9, 1806. Resigned before August 31, 1807.
Shadrach Bond Jr.[19]—February 1, 1808-March 1, 1809.

REPRESENTATIVES

Shadrach Bond Sr.[?]—May 21, 1805 [?]-January 9, 1806 [?]
William Biggs[20]—May 21, 1805-March 1, 1809.
Shadrach Bond Jr.—1806 [?]-1808 [?].
John Messinger[21]—July 25, 1808-March 1, 1809.

Randolph County

LEGISLATIVE COUNCILLORS

Pierre Menard[22]—January 6, 1806-September 19, 1807. Resigned.
George Fisher[23]—February 1, 1808-March 1, 1809.

REPRESENTATIVES

George Fisher—May 20, 1805-February 1, 1808 [?].
Rice Jones[24]—August 13, 1808-December 7, 1808. Died.

DELEGATES IN CONGRESS

Benjamin Parke—December 12, 1805-April 22, 1808.
Jesse B. Thomas[25]—December 1, 1808-March 3, 1809.

COUNTY COURTS[26]—ST. CLAIR COUNTY

GENERAL QUARTER SESSIONS[27]

John Dumoulin[28]—August 1, 1800-1802 [?].
George Atchison[29]—August 1, 1800-January 1, 1806.
Shadrach Bond Sr.—August 1, 1800-January 1, 1806.
John Francis Perrey[30]—August 1, 1800-January 1, 1806.
James Lemen[31]—August 1, 1800-January 1, 1806.
William Biggs—August 1, 1800-January 1, 1806.
Benjamin Ogle[32]—August 1, 1800-February 3, 1801.
Nicholas Jarrot[33]—February 3, 1801-January 1, 1806.
David Badgley Sr.[34]—April 22, 1805- January 1, 1806.
James Bankson[35]—April 22, 1805-January 1, 1806.

COMMON PLEAS[36]

John Dumoulin—August 1, 1800-1802 [?].
George Atchison—August 1, 1800-January 1, 1806.
Shadrach Bond Sr.—August 1, 1800-May 12, 1808 [?]. Resigned.
John Francis Perrey—August 1, 1800-March 1, 1809.
James Lemen—August 1, 1800-January 1, 1806.
William Biggs—August 1, 1800-January 1, 1806.
Benjamin Ogle—August 1, 1800-February 3, 1801.
Thomas Kirkpatrick[37]—December 10, 1805-March 1, 1809.
Shadrach Bond Jr.—May 12, 1808-March 1, 1809.

ORPHANS' COURT—1795-1806[38]

John Dumoulin—August 5, 1796-1802 [?].
Shadrach Bond Sr.—August 5, 1796-January 1, 1806.
James Piggott[39]—August 5, 1796-February 20, 1799. Died.
George Atchison—August 5, 1796-January 1, 1806.
James Lemen—August 5, 1796-January 1, 1806.
Wm. Biggs—August 5, 1796-January 1, 1806.
John Francis Perrey—August 1, 1801-January 1, 1806.
Nicholas Jarrot—February 3, 1801-January 1, 1806.
William Whiteside[40]—1803-1805 [?].
Uel Whiteside—1803-1805 [?].

David Badgley—April 22, 1805 [?]-January 1, 1806.
James Bankson—April 22, 1805 [?]-January 1, 1806.

Probate Court

William St. Clair[41]—1797-January or February 1799. Died.
Shadrach Bond Sr.—1799-January 1, 1806 [?].

COUNTY COURTS—RANDOLPH COUNTY

General Quarter Sessions[42]

John Edgar[43]—August 1, 1800-January 1, 1806.
William Morrison[44]—August 1, 1800. Resigned before November 28, 1801.
Antoine Pierre Menard—August 1, 1800-January 1, 1806.
Nathaniel Hull[45]—August 1, 1800-January 1, 1806.
Robert McMahon[46]—August 1, 1800-January 1, 1806.
Robert Reynolds[47]—November 28, 1801-January 1, 1806.
John Beaird[48]—December 25, 1802-January 1, 1806.
George Fisher—January 7, 1804-January 1, 1806.
James McRoberts[49]—April 4, 1804-January 1, 1806.
John Grosvenor[50]—February 16, 1805-January 1, 1806.
Jean Baptiste Barbau[51]—1800-1805.
Ant. Duchaufour de Louviere[52]—1800-1801 [?].

Common Pleas

John Edgar—August 1, 1800-January 1, 1806.
William Morrison—August 1, 1800. Resigned before November 28, 1801.
Ant. Pierre Menard—August 1, 1800-March 1, 1809.
Nathaniel Hull—August 1, 1800-January 1, 1806.
Robert McMahon—August 1, 1800-January 1, 1806.
Robert Reynolds—November 28, 1801-January 1, 1806.
John Beaird—December 25, 1802-January 1, 1806.
George Fisher—January 7, 1804-January 1, 1806.
John Grosvenor—February 16, 1805-January 1, 1806.
Michael Jones—December 28, 1805. Resigned before February 28, 1806.

APPENDIX ccxxxi

George Fisher—February 28, 1806-March 1, 1809.
Samuel Cochran[53]—February 28, 1806. Resigned before October 7, 1807.
James Finney[54]—October 7, 1807-March 1, 1809.

PROBATE COURT
John Edgar—August 1, 1800-January 1, 1806.

JUSTICES OF THE PEACE[55]
(All the Justices of Quarter Sessions were also Justices of the Peace.)

ST. CLAIR COUNTY
Dr. [Peter?] Mitchell[56]—September 1, 1801.
Adehemar St. Martin—September 1, 1801.
Lewis Labosierre [Labuxiere]—October 29, 1801.
Antoine Champs—October 30, 1801.
John Campbell—August 19, 1802.
Robert Dickson—August 19, 1802.
Uel Whiteside—March 2, 1803.
Henry Fisher—November 26, 1803.
Charles Reaume—November 26, 1803.
Richard Rue[57]—April 11, 1806.
Robert Elliot—April 11, 1806.
John Hays[58]—March 14, 1807.
Caldwell Cairns[59]—March 14, 1807.
John Boon—March 24, 1807.
James Long—March 24, 1807.
Charles Jouvet—April 11, 1807.
John Kinzey[60]—April 11, 1807.
David White—June 1, 1807.
Sam. Simpson Kennedy[61]—August 28, 1807.
Nicholas Bole—October 27, 1808.

RANDOLPH COUNTY
Jean Bte. Barbau[62]—October 27, 1801.
Pierre Compte—October 29, 1801.

James Ford—December 14, 1805.
Robert Hays—December 14, 1805.
James Gilbreath[63]—April 19, 1806.
Paul Herlston[64]—April 19, 1806.
William Rogers—July 28, 1806.
Frederick Graeter[65]—August 15, 1806.
Audrien Langlois[66]—November 18, 1806.
Henry Levens[67]—November 18, 1806.
Joseph Evermaull—November 18, 1806.
Hamlet Ferguson[68]—April 11, 1806.
Thomas Ferguson—April 11, 1806.
Sam. Omelvany[69]—July 30, 1807.
Jonathan Taylor—March 3, 1808.
Isaac White—March 3, 1808.
Archibald Thompson—September 7, 1808.
William Fouk—October 3, 1808.
David Anderson—October 5, 1808.
William Alexander—January 16, 1809.

CLERKS OF THE COUNTY COURTS
St. Clair County

John Hay—August 1, 1800-March 1, 1809.

Randolph County

Robert Morrison[70]—August 1, 1800-March 1, 1809.

SHERIFFS
St. Clair County

George Blair[71]—August 1, 1800. Resigned before May 5, 1802.
John Hays—May 5, 1802-1809.

Randolph County

George Fisher—August 1, 1800. Resigned before August 30, 1803.
James Edgar[72]—August 30, 1803. Resigned before October 11, 1806.
James Gilbreath—October 11, 1806-March 1, 1809.

CORONERS

St. Clair County

J. Whiteside[73]—August 1, 1800-March 1, 1809.

Randolph County

Giles Hull—January 28, 1801-August 19, 1802 [?].
Miles Hotchkiss[74]—August 19, 1802. Resigned before June 26, 1804.
Thos. Newbery—June 26, 1804-July 26, 1806 [?].
James Gilbreath—July 26, 1806. Resigned before November 19, 1806.
James Finney—November 19, 1806-March 23, 1808 [?].
David Robi[n]son—March 23, 1808-March 1, 1809.

RECORDERS OF DEEDS

St. Clair County

John Hay—August 1, 1800-March 1, 1809.

Randolph County

Robert Morrison—August 1, 1800-March 1, 1809.

TREASURERS

St. Clair County

John Hay—August 1, 1800-March 1, 1809.

Randolph County

John Edgar—August 1, 1800-March 1, 1809.

SURVEYORS

William Wilson[75]—March 10, 1802. Commission revoked before September 5, 1805.
David C. Robinson[76]—September 5, 1805-March 1, 1809.
Elias Rector[77]—Acting in May, 1808.
William Rector[78]—Acting in May, 1808; June, 1809.

LAWYERS WHO PRACTICED IN ILLINOIS COURTS

George Bullitt[79]
William C. Carr[80]
Isaac Darneille[81]
Benjamin H. Doyle[82]
Rufus Easton[83]
James Haggin[84]
Robert Hamilton[85]
William Hamilton[86]
Edward Hempstead[87]
Henry Jones[88]
John Rice Jones
William Mears[89]
Nathaniel Pope[90]
John Rector[91]
Robert Robinson[92]
John Scott[93]
John Taylor[94]

NOTES TO APPENDIX

1. The act of Congress (of May 7, 1800) creating Indiana Territory took effect on July 4, 1800; on that day, also, the government became a reality, Secretary Gibson taking charge. Gibson, *Exec. Journal*, 65. The act (of February 3, 1809) creating Illinois Territory took effect on March 1, 1809. The state of Indiana came into existence on December 11, 1816. *Ibid.*, 68, 69.

2. This William Clarke is often confused with two other men of the same name, a brother and a cousin of George Rogers Clark, who were for a time resident in the territory—W. H. English, *Conquest of the Country Northwest of the Ohio*, 1015-1016. His appointment as "Chief Justice of the Indiana Territory" was confirmed on December 10, 1800—U. S. Senate, *Exec. Journal*, 1:357. He died very suddenly on November 11, 1802— English, *op. cit.*, 1017, 1018; according to the editors of Gibson's *Exec. Journal* (91 n. 3) after attending two sessions of the governor and judges.

3. He was born in 1760 in Troy, New York. Apparently in November, 1806 he wrote of himself as 47 years of age, of which 30 had been spent in public service—*Amer. State Papers: Pub. Lands*, 1: 578. He entered the Revolutionary War as a lieutenant in 1776, and served until the close of the war, becoming a captain. Sometime before February, 1790, when he was married to a young French woman of Vincennes, he had removed to that village. J. P. Elliott, *A History of Evansville and Vanderburgh County, Indiana*, 66. On June 26, 1790 he was appointed a major in the militia—*St. Clair Papers*, 2: 166 n. On August 12, 1791 he was appointed by Governor St. Clair judge of probate and "Justice of the Peace"—*i. e.* doubtless a judge of the Quarter Sessions—of Knox County; and possibly also a judge of the Common Pleas—*ibid.*, 2: 275 n.; compare 167 n. and 275 n.—the tangle is inextricable, but at least he was appointed to the Quarter Sessions. On August 13, 1792 he was named one of the two commissioners for that county, "to license merchants, traders, and tavern-keepers"—*ibid.*, 2: 311 n. And on July 23, 1793, the judges of Knox being charged with the enforcement of the law (*ante*, xviii) prohibiting the sale of liquor to Indians, he was appointed one of "a committee to take charge of the business, and to supply Indians visiting Vincennes such quantity of spirits as should seem to them proper"—*St. Clair Papers*, 2: 323 n. Out of this last office sprang some of the charges made against him by Judge Turner of the General Court, who threatened to impeach him before the governor and judges; see *ibid.*, 325, 330, 397; Monks, *Courts*, 1:13; *ante*, cc. The other charges had to do with two negroes, "who"— according to Turner—"were free by the Constitution of the Territory," i. e. the Ordinance of 1787 (*ante*, xxxvi), and who, being held by Vander Burgh as slaves, had applied to Turner for a writ of habeas corpus. *Ante*, cxli-ii. He was presumably that "one of the principal proprietors, by birth a Dutchman, who spoke very good French" who entertained Count Volney during the latter's visit to Vincennes in August, 1796: according to the

latter "with all the kind offices of simple, frank, and easy hospitality"—Volney, *View of the United States,* 369. The next year he was a member of a commission appointed to investigate land titles in the Wabash country, and acted as secretary of the board—*Amer. State Papers: Pub. Lands,* 1: 577, 580. Though not elected to the lower house of the first General Assembly of the Northwest Territory (1799) he was among those nominated by it for the Legislative Council, and was appointed by the President. U. S. Senate, *Exec. Journal,* 1: 323 (March 3, 1799). He was the only member from all the western country, outside the Ohio counties. Judge Burnet speaks of him in this connection as "an intelligent citizen of Vincennes, engaged in the Indian trade," and Governor St. Clair as having "been in trade"; so that he probably had never studied law. He was chosen president of the Council when it was organized—Burnet, *Notes,* 289, 296; *St. Clair Papers,* 2: 441. See the signatures to the laws of 1799 in Pease, *Laws* (*I. H. C.,* 17), 337 *et seq.* When the Indiana Territory was created he was appointed probate judge of Knox on July 28, 1800—Gibson, *Exec. Journal,* 92—and acted as such until (his successor was appointed on January 14, 1801: *ibid.,* 95) he took office as a judge of the General Court, to which office he had been confirmed on December 10, 1800—U. S. Senate, *Exec. Journal,* 1: 357 and in which he served until his death. References to this service will be found *ante,* xv. The editors of Secretary Gibson's *Executive Journal,* 71, say that "Davis, Vanderburgh and Griffin served until the Territory passed to second grade"; which is correct, though transition to the second grade had nothing to do with their judicial tenure. In Monks, *Courts,* 2: 404, it is stated that Vander Burgh was again appointed to the Legislative Council—this time of Indiana Territory—in 1805, and "continued to serve until the state was admitted to the Union in 1816;" but·this is erroneous. He was never a member of Indiana Council; and in Harrison, *Messages,* 1: 21 n., Mr. Esarey states that he died at Vincennes on April 12, 1812. His career amply indicates his ability and the confidence which he inspired in those who knew him.

4. See *ante,* xvi. He was a son—Harrison, *Messages,* 1: 24 n.—of Cyrus Griffin, last president of the Continental Congress, president of the admiralty court of the Confederation, and a district federal judge in Virginia from 1789 until his death in 1810—*Biog. Congressional Directory, 1774-1911,* 61 Congress, 2 session, Sen. Doc. 654, p. 686. His birth is given as in "1799" (possibly 1769) in the *Michigan Biographies* (Mich. Hist. Commission, 1924), 1: 354, and his death as "between 1842 and 1845," probably in Philadelphia; Mr. Esarey, however, gives 1840—Harrison, *Messages,* 1: 24 n. According to the former authority "he made a tour of Europe and when he returned he was appointed" to the territorial court of Michigan. Presumably this tour preceded his appointment to the Indiana court—U. S. Senate, *Exec. Journal,* 1: 357. He was nominated for the Michigan court on December 23, 1805 ("agreeably to his own desire, as is represented"), and confirmed on March 29, 1806—*ibid.,* 2: 11, 30. According to Judge Campbell and Judge Cooley he was wholly dominated by his imperious colleague, Chief-justice Augustus B. Woodward, and was a mischief-maker in the court—J. V. Campbell, *Political History of Michigan,* 238, 239, 245, 411; T. M. Cooley, *Michigan,* 150. His own letters and those of his colleagues show that he was fond of social pleasures; and according to Governor Bates he was the life of the circles in which he moved—*Mich. Pioneer and Hist. Colls.,* 8: 559-560, 12: 472-473; Marshall, *Life and Papers of Frederick Bates,* 1: 172, 174-175, 192-193, and 2: 113.

5. Thomas Terry Davis represented Mercer County in the Kentucky legislature in 1795-1797 (Lewis Collins, *Hist. of Kentucky,* ed. 1877, 603) ; and represented Kentucky in the U. S. House of Representatives from 1797 to 1803 (*Biog. Congressional Directory, 1774-1911,* 596). See his denunciation of Winthrop Sargent, *ante,* cxi, n. 1, which doubtless endeared him to Indiana Territory. Davis was named judge of Indiana Territory on February 8, 1803, in succession to William Clarke—U. S. Senate, *Exec. Journal,* 1: 441, 442. On March 1, 1806 he was appointed chancellor of the territorial Court of Chancery—Gibson, *op. cit.,* 132. According to Monks, *Courts,* 2: 404, he served in both offices, until his death, which occurred on November 15, 1807—Dunn, *Indiana,* 361.

6. He was born in Virginia, probably in 1785; was educated in the law and practiced in Virginia; served as a representative in the Virginia legislature; removed to Vincennes in 1804; was appointed to the General Court on April 17, 1806—U. S. Senate, *Exec. Journal,* 2: 32, 33, 34; and as chancellor (vice Davis) on November 24, 1807—Gibson, *Exec. Journal,* 144. He seems to have served in the General Court until Indiana became a state, and as chancellor until the court was abolished in 1813. Monks, *Courts,* 1: 39; 2: 404. In 1812, he was an unsuccessful candidate against Jonathan Jennings for the office of delegate to Congress. He was one of Indiana's first two United States Senators (a Democrat), serving from December 12, 1816 to March 3, 1825. Died in Virginia, August 26, 1826. The preceding statements, if other authority is not cited, are based upon the *Biog. Congressional Directory, 1774-1911,* 1046; *Nat. Cycl. Amer. Biog.,* 4: 531; Lamb, *Biog. Dict. of the U. S.,* 7: 295.

7. See *ante,* xvi. Born in New Jersey in 1777 (Gibson, *Exec. Journal,* 109 n., has it 1787), he moved to Kentucky in 1797. He studied law at Lexington in the office of James Brown (minister to France in 1823-1829, G. W. Ranck, *History of Lexington,* 151). According to Dunn—*Indiana,* 322—he began to practice law at Vincennes in 1801 but he was licensed by the General Court as a counsellor, with no earlier action on him as an attorney, on March 2, 1802—*Order Book,* 1: 22—and by the Governor to practice as an attorney, on May 26, 1802—Gibson, *Exec. Journal,* 109. He became attorney-general on August 4, 1804—Gibson, *op. cit.,* 124. He was a member of the first House of Representatives of Indiana Territory, 1805, was elected delegate to Congress in September, 1805, was reëlected in August, 1807, and resigned to accept appointment to the territorial court—Dunn, *op. cit.,* 327, 328, 357; Harrison, *Messages,* 1: 21 n., 304. His nomination to the General Court was confirmed on April 22, 1808— U. S. Senate, *Exec. Journal,* 2: 81. He served as a circuit judge of the state of Indiana from December 21, 1816 to February 8, 1817—Monks, *Courts,* 2: 812; and as a federal district judge from March 6, 1817 (U. S. Senate, *Exec. Journal,* 3: 73, 92, 93) until his death on July 12, 1835. See Woollen, *Sketches,* 384-390. He founded the Indiana (State) Law Library and the Indiana Historical Society—Dunn, *op. cit.,* 329.

8. He was born in Geneva in 1758, the son of a Lutheran minister— Cauthorn, *A History of the City of Vincennes,* 184; but H. Adams, *The Life of Albert Gallatin,* 646, would indicate 1759. A college mate of Gallatin at the Academy in Geneva (1775-1779), he was urged by the latter to come to America, and arrived in 1786. For a time they lived together in western Pennsylvania, and they remained affectionate friends throughout life. Gallatin secured his appointment as register of the land office at Vincennes, 1804-1835 (confirmed on November 20, 1804—U. S. Senate, *Exec. Journal,* 1: 472, 473), and as such was one of the commissioners who investigated

land claims in the district of Vincennes, 1804-1806. He was one of the original trustees of Vincennes University in 1807—*post*, 178. Unlike Gallatin, he seems not to have engaged at all in land speculation. He was characterized by his friend as one of the purest of men; too honest and too simple to win material success—H. Adams, *op. cit.* 645-646 (see also 15, 51, 60, 63, 404-405). Henry Adams refers to him as "carrying on"—evidently in 1808 or 1809—"a fierce and passionate struggle with General W. H. Harrison, the governor, to prevent the introduction of negro slavery." And Harrison evidently feared his influence, for Gallatin judged it well to assure him that Badollet would not seek his displacement as governor—H. Adams, the *Writings of Albert Gallatin*, 1: 463. In 1835 he resigned his office as register (his son Albert succeeding him—U. S. Senate, *Exec. Journal*, 4: 504—on January 13, 1836). In 1816 he served as a member of the first constitutional convention of Indiana—Dunn, *Indiana*, 425. He died on July 29, 1837—Cauthorn, *op. cit.*, 185. There is no evidence that he studied law, but he studied and taught theology in Geneva—J. A. Stevens, *Albert Gallatin*, 26. He was a very critical man, and it is evident that he reported to Gallatin that vice and intrigue were triumphant in Indiana Territory—H. Adams, *Life*, 133, 404. See also *ibid.*, 15, 51, 60, 62.

9. There were some peculiarities about this office. The attorney-general was a territorial, and therefore a federal, officer; yet the earlier holders of the office were appointed by the governor—there is no evidence of presidential appointment. In later years, after Illinois became an independent territory, it seems that the president appointed—Monks, *Courts*, 2: 405. On claims by the territory because the attorney-general was called upon to do work for the United States see *ante*, clx.

Appointments of special prosecuting attorneys, or deputy attorneys-general, were numerous. Thus, on May 21, 1808, John Johnson "was appointed Attorney General of this Territory to Prosecute in behalf of the United States, Abigail Rough," etc. (Gibson, *Exec. Journal*, 146); but on June 2, Thomas Randolph "was appointed Attorney General of the Indiana Territory, vice Benjamin Parke Esqr." (146). This was especially true in Randolph's term during which both he, and others after his resignation, were also appointed "prosecuting attorney" for individual counties—Clark, Dearborn, Franklin, Harrison, Jefferson, and Knox—(*ibid.*, 169, 176, 179; also index under counties, civil appointments). Though none appear in the *Journal* for Randolph and St. Clair counties, at any time, it is a fact that various attorneys (Robert Hamilton, Robert Robinson, Benjamin Doyle, Edward Hempstead, George Bullitt, and perhaps others) so served in the circuit courts in Illinois.

10. The chief authorities are *Chic. Hist. Colls.*, 4: 230-270 (an uncritical sketch by W. A. Burt Jones); Reynolds, *Pioneer History*, 170-172, 179-181, and *My Own Times*, 128; Monks, *Courts*, 2: 404-405. There are important inconsistencies in dates between these authorities. The first is followed in such cases, and for statements when no other authority is cited.

He was born in Wales on February 10, 1759; is said to have been educated at Oxford in letters, and afterwards to have taken "a regular course" in both law and medicine. He "came" to this country in February, 1784, practiced law for two years in Philadelphia, and then removed to the west.

In September, 1786, at Louisville, Kentucky, he joined the army under George Rogers Clark which that autumn campaigned against the Indians of the Wabash country. For this army (perhaps as a lieutenant in rank) Jones bought supplies in the Illinois country; on this "depredation and plunder," as viewed by Governor St. Clair (Clark was invading territory of the United States), see *St. Clair Papers,* 2: 168. Jones acted at great danger to himself both then and later in opposing John Dodge, Connecticut bully of Kaskaskia, and the courage he displayed was evidently the only thing needed to break Dodge's prestige, for he soon was forced to remove to the Spanish side of the Mississippi: Alvord, *Kaskaskia Records (I. H. C.,* 5), 426, 430, and *Illinois Country,* 367-368, 372: compare St. Clair to Jefferson—*St. Clair Papers,* 2: 168, 399. He was made commissary of the garrison established by Clark at Vincennes in October, 1786—Boggess, *Settlement of Illinois,* 54, citing secret *Journals of Congress,* at which time, or soon after, his family were also there—Dunn, *Indiana,* 164, 167-168. He was not awarded, and did not claim, a donation as head of a family in Illinois before 1788—*Amer. State Papers: Pub. Lands,* 2: 151, 163, 288.

His residence during the next decade, contrary to various statements, was in Illinois. In October, 1789, we find him writing from Kaskaskia as a resident thereof—Alvord, *Kaskaskia Records (I. H. C.,* 5), 517; in July 1790, he is listed as one of the effectives in Pierre Gamelin's militia company at Vincennes—Law, *Colonial Hist. of Vincennes,* 157; but also on the Kaskaskia roll of August 1, 1790—*Chic. Hist. Colls.,* 4: 210 (and his militia right was affirmed by the land commissioners, *Amer. State Papers: Pub. Lands,* 2: 170); in 1792 the court at Cahokia employed him to translate the laws into French for the French judges—*ante,* xvii, n. 3; in 1793 he was licensed as a merchant at Kaskaskia—Brink, McDonough, *Hist. of St. Clair County,* 83; sometime in the 1790's he seems to have practiced law in both St. Louis (Missouri) and the Illinois courts— Billon, *Annals 1804-21,* 161, 162 (as of 1796) and Reynolds, *Pioneer History,* 181 (before 1794); and in 1795 he was appointed by Judge Turner deputy clerk of the St. Clair Court. St. Clair maintained that this was illegal; but it would hardly seem so under his own orders—*St. Clair Papers,* 1: 195; 2: 165 n., 172—regarding William St. Clair's plural offices; the Governor also referred to Jones as of "known bad character," *ibid.,* 372—the reason, almost certainly, being his acts for "the Wabash Regiment" above referred to. In 1798 he was prothonotary of Common Pleas of Randolph County (*Court Record* 1: 269—April 1798), and a deed in *Deed Record J,* of that county (p. 148) shows that he was still in Illinois in January, 1800. He was still there in the following spring—Reynolds, *My Own Times,* 17. He must have returned shortly thereafter to Vincennes; if W. A. Burt Jones, *op. cit.,* 235 is correct in saying that Secretary Gibson found him resident there in July, 1800; but the only case noted in the records of the Randolph courts in which Jones appeared as counsel was one of the November term of 1800 in which he was defendant—Charles Gratiot *v.* John Rice Jones, Randolph *Common Pleas,* 2: 120; *ante,* cci-ccii, n. 2.

On January 29, 1801, he was appointed attorney-general of the territory—J. Gibson, *Exec. Journal,* 95. His examination for license as counsellor was set, however, by the General Court (at its first session on March 3, 1801) for September 7, 1801—*Order Book,* 2. He was secretary of the Vincennes slavery convention of December, 1802—Ind. Hist. Soc. *Pub.,* 2: 468, 469; although not a delegate thereto—Dunn, *Indiana,* 305; and the convention recommended him for appointment as chief-justice of the territory— *ibid.,* 307. He resigned the attorney-generalship some time before August 4, 1804, when his successor was appointed—Gibson, *Exec. Journal,* 124.

It is barely possible that he went to the Illinois country temporarily after the appointment in 1804 of the commissioners to investigate land titles in the same, for by special act of Congress passed in 1819 he was given compensation, not to exceed $281, for services rendered to them "as an interpreter and translator of the French language"—*U. S. Stat. at Large, Private Acts 1789-1845,* p. 229, act of March 3, 1819; *Annals,* 15 Congress, 2 session, index. See *ante,* c, n. 1. He was not clerk or deputy clerk of the first board (Robert Robinson and James Finney held those positions); moreover we know from his deposition given years later that he was in attendance with the second board, which was the one which rejected on the ground of fraud a claim whose confirmation he later sought from Congress. It was therefore the second board, almost certainly (the first board is assumed in *Chic. Hist. Colls.,* 4: 248), which he aided as translator—cp. *Amer. State Papers: Pub. Lands,* 2: 216-217; 3: 394. On the other hand the General Court in September, 1804, ordered several lawyers (William C. Carr, Rufus Easton, John Taylor) to be examined by him and Benjamin Parke at the opening of the autumn Randolph circuit; and as Parke, who had just become attorney-general would properly be on circuit, it is plain that Jones expected to be in Illinois—General Court *Order Book,* 1: 105.

Selected in April, 1805 for appointment by the President to the Legislative Council (Harrison, *Messages,* 1: 126-128), his appointment was confirmed on January 6, 1806 (U. S. Senate, *Exec. Journal,* 2: 9, 10, 13). He served as president pro tem. of that body in the second session of the first Assembly (this volume, *post,* 175 *et seq.,* Dec. 1806), and as president in the second session of the second Assembly (*post,* 646 *et seq.,* Sept.-Oct. 1808). Meanwhile he had served as "Clerk to the Commissioners of the Land Office at Vincennes District"—at least in 1806, *Amer. State Papers: Pub. Lands,* 1: 579. Meanwhile, also, he had quarreled with Harrison; which was one of several causes that prevented his election as delegate of the territory to Congress, although he evidently held the balance of power—Dunn, *op. cit.,* 368, 376.

This quarrel was of momentous consequences to both men. Mr. Esarey—(in Harrison, *Messages,* 1: 296 n.) says that they "parted when Jones became interested in land speculation." But he had then for many years been speculating in lands, as the Governor perfectly well knew. The excuse for their final break in 1808 is shown by the documents printed by Mr. Esarey (*ibid.,* 296-299); namely his indictment for corrupt practices while attorney-general several years before (*ante,* cc, n. 6). Though Harrison had in the meantime (1805) recommended him to Jefferson for appointment to the Legislative Council, his excuse was that Jones had conducted himself with such "art" as to deceive everybody. He was, the Governor assured the President in 1808, "really one of the most abandoned men I ever knew" (letter of July 16, 1808, Harrison, *Messages,* 297). Mr. Esarey interprets this statement morally, and takes it seriously—*Ind. Hist. Bulletin,* February, 1924, p. 54. So interpreted, there is apparently no shred of evidence to support it. It should evidently be read politically. The underlying difficulty was perhaps, as Dunn suggested, that Jones was not appointed to the territorial court. Dunn, *Indiana,* 361. Although recommended by the convention of 1802 for appointment as chief-justice (*ibid.,* 307), he was not appointed, and he was supplanted in Harrison's counsels by Parke and the Governor's fellow Virginians, and doubtless this rankled. Supervening upon, though possibly deriving from, this difficulty was one undoubtedly even more important; namely, Jones's activity, and that of his son Rice Jones in Randolph, in advocating division of the territory. This is the view taken by W. A. Burt Jones, *Chic. Hist. Colls.,* 4: 244-246. The triumph of the separatists, or anti-Harrisonians, in Randolph County in the election of August 13, 1808—

Rice Jones being returned to the House of Representatives (*ante,* li) was coincident with Harrison's denunciation of Jones. Read politically one can make sense of Harrison's statement that "his whole conduct" after appointment to the Council had manifested "a total absence of moral & Political virtue & a most rancorous enmity, both to the administration of the General Government & that of the Territory." Harrison, *Messages,* 1: 298. There is no independent evidence whatever to support such charges. They evidently sprang from Harrison's political intemperance. Yet Harrison should have anticipated independence of action, for Jones had shown it in the past. In further explaining his earlier recommendation of him for the Council Harrison says: "His talents are unquestionable—And he had taken so decided a part in favor of the second Government altho one of the largest landholders in the Territory, & altho a professed Federalist had manifested so much Moderation that it appeared to me that he could not with Justice be neglected in the arrangement of officers consequent upon the change of System." Harrison, *Messages,* 1: 297. Jefferson showed acumen and good sense in not removing him.

After this quarrel Jones "formed an alliance with William McIntosh and Elijah Backus for newspaper work against the opposition, and their bitter articles goaded their enemies almost to madness." Dunn, *Indiana,* 362. It is hinted by Mr. Esarey that he had earlier aided Isaac Darneille in composing the *Letters of Decius—post,* app. n. 81; *Ind. Hist. Bulletin,* February, 1924, p. 58. His bitterness against Harrison, perhaps as much as or more than distrust of Jesse B. Thomas, explains his requiring that the latter sign a bond to work for division before permitting his election—*ante,* li, n. 3. After Harrison's dissolution of the General Assembly in October, 1808, he immediately (W. A. Burt Jones, *op. cit.,* 238) removed once more to Kaskaskia. Mr. Esarey, referring to Jones (apparently) as co-author with Isaac Darneille of the *Letters of Decius,* says that the former "when charged with bribery fled the jurisdiction"—*loc. cit.* This is wide of the facts. He retained his office in the Council; he was elected its president (see signatures to the laws of 1808, *post* 646 *et seq.*) for the session following Harrison's vitriolic denunciation of him—we may certainly assume, despite Harrison's opposition. After that he did leave the Territory.

In Kaskaskia his eldest son was murdered in December, 1808—*ante,* xciii. He finally, in 1810, removed to Louisiana Territory (Missouri), where he practiced law, and mined lead at Potosi. He was appointed to the Legislative Council of Missouri Territory—nominated January 7, confirmed January 11, 1815: U. S. Senate, *Exec. Journal,* 2: 601, 602 (though according to Houck he took his seat in December, 1814); holding the office, apparently, for but two years; was named by the legislature a trustee of an academy at Potosi incorporated in 1817; and was one of the most conspicuous members of the Missouri constitutional convention in 1820. Although an unsuccessful candidate for election by the first legislature to the U. S. Senate (1820), this was after his appointment as a justice of the first Supreme Court of the state, in which position he served for four years. He died on February 18, 1824. Houck, *Missouri,* 3: 6-8, 69, 249, 256-257, 266, 267. According to Houck he established his home in Ste. Genevieve in 1804, "but continued the practice of law both at Kaskaskia and Vincennes" (*ibid.,* 257). This seems impossible. Houck gives the death-date as above, and as he quotes from a contemporary newspaper this date is adopted; although February 1 is the date given by W. A. Burt Jones, *op cit.,* 254. Billon, *Annals 1804-21,* 30, gives him as elected to the Council in 1816.

On his land claims (and a forgery charge against Jones) see *ante,* xcix. Governor Reynolds is certainly not an impeccable character witness, but on the whole his characterization of Jones (*My Own Times,* 128)—as having "sustained his professional, official, and private character and standing, as a gentleman and scholar, during his long and eventful life in the Valley of the Mississippi"—is unquestionably much truer than Harrison's. His family was also remarkable. One son held high office in Texas during its era of independence, another was a senator of the United States. See W. A. Burt Jones, *John Rice Jones* (*Chic. Hist. Colls.,* 4), 260 *et seq.*

11. According to Woollen, *Sketches,* 391-398 (which is followed except where other authority is cited), he was born in Virginia in 1771, was graduated from William and Mary, subsequently studied law, served one term in the Virginia legislature, and arrived in Indiana Territory by May, 1808. He was appointed attorney-general on June 2, 1808—Gibson, *Exec. Journal,* 146; and held the office until killed at Tippecanoe, November 7, 1811. It was on September 6, 1808, that he produced his commission and took the oath of office before the General Court—*Order Book,* 1: 264. A report by him upon John Rice Jones's alleged corruptions (so soon after his arrival in the territory that it arouses suspicion of politics) was the basis of Harrison's charges against Jones discussed in app. n. 10. As Mr. Esarey does not print this report in Harrison's *Messages* it is presumably lost. Like other prominent Virginians in the territory he followed Harrison and was close in his councils. In 1809 he was the candidate of the pro-slavery or Harrison party for delegate to Congress, but was defeated (May 22, 1809) by Jonathan Jennings. He was counsel, with General Washington Johnston, for Harrison in his successful libel suit against William McIntosh—*ante,* lxi. McIntosh and John Johnson (*ante,* cxii, n. 1) were numbered among his special enemies.

12. According to Monks, *Courts,* 2: 808, he was clerk both of the General Court and of the Knox County Common Pleas from 1801 to 1816; presumably also of the Quarter Sessions 1801-1805—cp. *post,* app. n. 36. A charge against him of corruption in office is mentioned *ante,* cc.

13. Michael Jones was born, according to Reynolds, in Pennsylvania. In nominating him for the office of register of the land office at Kaskaskia the President described him as "of Ohio"; he was confirmed on November 20, 1804—U. S. Senate, *Exec. Journal,* 1: 472-473. This was his first federal position. He held the office for many years; apparently continuously until his death. He was appointed a last time on March 2, 1821—U. S. Senate, *Exec. Journal,* 3: 251, 254. The Senate's Journal shows no appointments between 1804 and 1821; but the continuity of his service is indicated by the various statutes extending the powers of the first board of commissioners (Jones and Elijah Backus) until 1810—*ante,* lxxx, n. 1: then, by the form of the reports of the second board of commissioners, 1812-1813 (Jones, John Caldwell, and Thomas Sloo)—cp. *Annals,* 12 Congress, 1 session, 2237 (act of February 20, 1812) with reports in *Amer. State Papers: Pub. Lands,* in *ibid.,* 3: 2, 385; 4: 9,—in later years. The date of his last report clearing up unfinished business of the second board was January 18, 1813.

It is clear enough that Harrison supported him against the clamor that rose when he uncovered the land frauds; as well he might, not only for moral but also for political reasons, for all the chief offenders were members of the Edgar-Morrison divisionist group (they were united only as Masons—Bateman and Selby, *Hist. Ency. of Illinois,* 1: 176). In Febru-

ary 1805—the commissioners apparently began their work on January 1—
Harrison, in a letter introducing him to August Choteau, spoke of him as
"a gentleman of worth and integrity & one who possesses my entire confidence"—*Messages,* 1: 116. In December, 1805, the Governor appointed
him to the reorganized Common Pleas—Gibson, *Exec. Journal,* 131; but
he never sat, and in February, 1806, George Fisher was appointed to the
court, "vice Michael Jones Resigned"—*ibid.,* 132. In May, 1807, in a
letter to Pierre Menard Harrison refers to having "hitherto entrusted
the management of the Indian business in the Illinois country" to Jones—
Messages, 1: 214. Finally, he was the candidate of the Harrisonians for
delegate to Congress, against Jesse B. Thomas, in October 1808; receiving,
however, only three out of ten votes—Alvord, *Illinois Country,* 425; Dunn,
Indiana, 368, 376-377. Undoubtedly his decided ability was generally recognized, and no doubt he was generally respected (note e. g. that he was one
of the trustees of Kaskaskia chosen by the legislature in September, 1807—
post, 568); it is difficult, however, to understand the strategy of such a
candidacy—whether it was simply an appeal to the sentiments of decent
men, or particularly one to Indiana prejudices against the Illinois divisionists.

It is very plain that Jones did indeed possess the governor's entire
confidence. Nevertheless, the statement of Alvord that "the members
of the Edgar-Morrison faction were *fighting for* property and *honor in
their effort to overthrow the governor's ring*" (*Illinois Country,* 424; italics
added) embodies, aside from the "property," nothing but regrettable mis-
apprehensions; it implies a full acceptance of the only argument that the
defrauders could use in appealing to localism in the Illinois counties,
making themselves out defenders of and sufferers for the community of
which in truth they were despoilers (as Alvord knew—*ibid.,* 421).
Alvord also says that "there was an element of politics in the whole *process
of investigation* which should have been avoided by referring the questions
at issue to United States courts" (*Illinois Country,* 421; italics added).
No evidence whatever has been discovered that supports the phrase italicized;
and the statement misses the point that only favorable reports were confirmed by Congress, leaving claimants free to assert in the courts claims
reported on by the commissioners adversely. It also overlooks the fact that
the primary duty and object of the statute was to protect the claim of the
United States to public land (*ante,* xcv, n. 2); this could not be settled
in private lawsuits. He also says (*Illinois Country,* 427) of Jones that
"his passion and that of his opponents had involved the question of the
land titles in a partisan strife," and (*ibid.,* 424) that "the infusion of this
question . . . into politics weakened the effect of the commissioners'
report and *strengthened the suspicion of the judicial character of their decisions*" (italics added). This italicized matter seems to the writer
unfair to Michael Jones. It rests, probably, upon Reynolds' statement
(*Pioneer History,* 352) that Jones was sometimes overwhelmed by passion,
and upon a desire to compromise which was uncorrected by a careful
study of the commissioners' reports. But of course Alvord is correct in
stating that the discrediting and banishment of Jones became a chief purpose of the defrauders. That they failed is evident from their own political
fate—*ante,* lix, n. 3. The drift of popular opinion is only apparent in the
election of Jones to the lieutenant-colonelcy in the Randolph militia—
Alvord, *op. cit.,* 426; Edgar himself being colonel all these years since
1800—*ante,* lix. (Elections were sometimes held to guide the governor in

appointments—cp. app. n. 19; but in this case the appointment of Jones does not appear in Gibson's *Journal*). The bitterness that accompanied and followed the election of 1808, the murder of Rice Jones, the charges made by the Edgar faction against Michael Jones of complicity therein, and the result of his libel suits against Edgar and William and Robert Morrison, are discussed *ante*, xciii-iv. The career of Michael Jones after 1812 is obscure. The opposing faction sought the confidence of Ninian Edwards immediately upon his accession to the governorship of Illinois Territory—Ninian W. Edwards, *Hist. of Illinois*, 28-30); Washburne, *Edwards Papers*, 40. That they gained it is manifest from his favors to Robert Morrison (*post*, app. n. 70), his removal of Michael Jones from his militia command in 1811 (Buck, *Illinois in 1818*, 201), and his later aid to John Rice Jones in attempting to reverse one galling decision of the second board commissioners— *ante*, xcix-c. Whether the Michael Jones named by Reynolds—*My Own Times*, 134—as a leader of the anti-Edwards party was the land commissioner, or was the Shawneetown politician is a question still obscure. According to Mr. Buck it was the land commissioner who was an unsuccessful rival of Ninian Edwards for the United States senatorship in October, 1818— *op. cit.*, 303 (though the index states—erroneously in that case—"of Gallatin" County). This is presumably correct; although no evidence survives of political activity, popularity or ambition on his part in the years 1808-1818. On the other hand the other Michael Jones, although young, had already been a member of the constitutional convention (Ill. State Hist. Society *Journal*, 6: 358), was a senator in this first General Assembly (*The Illinois Intelligencer* October 7, 1818, p. 2), with a prominent career ahead of him, and, being a half-brother of Jesse B. Thomas and a brother-in-law of another enemy of Edwards (Buck, *op. cit.*, 201), might well have been the candidate—as it is stated in J. M. Palmer, *Bench and Bar of Illinois*, 2: 852, that he was in 1820. Although it is surprising that Reynolds (and others) should not have noted such a fact in the life of the land commissioner, it would be more surprising that no comments should survive had Edwards' ambitions been challenged simultaneously by two brothers. He died on November 26, 1822—Buck, *op. cit.*, 201 n.

14. Elijah Backus was receiver in the land office at Marietta when appointed to the same office at Kaskaskia on November 20, 1804—U. S. Senate, *Exec. Journal*, 1: 353, 354, 472, 473. He signed with John Edgar and others the proslavery, prodivision petition-of-20, January 17, 1806: Ind. Hist. Soc. *Pub.*, 2: 502 (Dunn's transcriber made the name "Barker"). He is named as one of the "convention" that framed the preceding—*ibid.*, 503. It was doubtless this petition which he himself took to Washington, whither he was sent by the Edgar-Morrison party to urge division upon Congress—Dunn, *Indiana*, 350. He coöperated with John Rice Jones and William McIntosh, after the former's break with Harrison in 1808, in bitter newspaper writing against the Harrisonians—*ibid.*, 362. In the land matters it pleased the Edgar group to regard Backus as the tool of his colleague. The utterly silly nature, from the legal standpoint, of the charges against Judge Backus and others can best be judged by the passages from a Morrison record printed in *Chic. Hist. Colls.*, 4: 278-279. The date of the last report by the first board of land commissioners—*Amer. State Papers: Pub. Lands*, 2: 239—was January 5, 1811.

15. John Caldwell was appointed receiver of the Kaskaskia land office on April 1, 1812, and to the same office at Shawneetown on October 3, 1814—U. S. Senate, *Exec. Journal*, 2: 242, 531, 532. In nominating him

in 1812 the President described him as of Indiana, and in 1814 as of Illinois Territory. The date of the final report of the second board was January 4, 1813.

16. Thomas Sloo was chosen, with Michael Jones and John Caldwell, as the third member of the second board of land commissioners—*Annals*, 12 Congress, 1 session, 2237, § 1. On October 3, 1814, he was made register at Shawneetown—U. S. Senate, *Exec. Journal, 2*: 531, 532. The date of the final reports made by the second board was January 4, 1813.

17. According to Governor Reynolds, whose sketch of Hay was based upon long personal acquaintance and is suffused with admiration and affection, Hay's father was a Pennsylvanian, the last British governor of Upper Canada; his mother was a French native of Detroit. He himself married a French creole of Cahokia. Born at Detroit, 1769; settled in Cahokia, 1793; died at Belleville, 1843—*Pioneer History*, 225-230. He received a good schooling, used French and English with equal ease, and in addition possessed in eminent degree the ability and honesty that made him an invaluable public servant. In 1793 he was licensed as a merchant at Cahokia—Brink, McDonough, *Hist. of St. Clair County*, 83. But he soon drifted into political life. He was, it is said, appointed by Governor St. Clair on February 15, 1799, clerk of the Quarter Sessions, the Common Pleas and the Orphans' Court, and also treasurer—Brink, McDonough, *Hist. of St. Clair County*, 46. But he was clearly clerk of the Common Pleas earlier, for cp. *ibid.*, 71; and it is extremely probable that he held these offices, all or some of them, from at the latest 1795 onward. The record of the *Orphans' Court: 1797-1809* refers (p. 11) to William Arundel, "late Clerk of the Orphans' Court," as having on May 9, 1799, given up all papers thereto pertaining "according to the receipt given him by John Hay." (Arundel was also "clerk to the *Qt* Sessions from 1795 to 1799," *ibid.*, 40: account disallowed). He was sworn into office (*ibid.*, 13) on October 9, 1800. On August 1, 1800 Governor Harrison made him treasurer, recorder, and clerk of the Quarter Sessions and Orphans' Court; and on December 10, 1805 clerk of the new Common Pleas—Gibson, *Exec. Journal*, 94, 130. He accompanied Harrison and the judges of the General Court to St. Louis in 1804—Reynolds, *Pioneer History*, 229; Dunn, *Indiana*, 326. In 1805 President Jefferson gave him a recess appointment to the Legislative Council, probably about May or June; but although a friend, and in general apparently a political supporter of Harrison, he resigned, so that his appointment did not come before the Senate in December for confirmation—U. S. Senate, *Exec. Journal, 2*: 9, 11; Harrison, *Messages, 1*: 127, 174, 187. He was therefore actually a Councillor for some months, but whether he actually sat (I have not seen the journals of the Council) is doubtful. As it is not known when his resignation was accepted his term is indicated as ending with the appointment of his successor. Michael Jones employed him in taking depositions relative to land claims; which, as Governor Reynolds says, was "a very delicate trust"—*Pioneer History*, 228—and a marked proof of confidence by one who gave no confidence lightly. He served as clerk of various county courts of St. Clair County from 1809 to 1836; circuit clerk, 1818-1841; probate judge, 1825-1842. He was also a member of the temporary county Court of Justices of 1818—Bateman and Selby, *Hist. of St. Clair County*, 2: 689, 690; Brink, McDonough, *Hist. of St. Clair County*, 76, but compare E. B. Greene and C. W. Alvord, *The Governors' Letter-Books 1818-1834 (I. H. C.*, 4), 8 n. According to Governor Reynolds he made "a bare living" out of all his offices, and he notes with an emphasis that was merited

the fact that he never speculated in land—*Pioneer History,* 228. See also Brink, McDonough, *Hist. of St. Clair County,* 46-47.

18. Much confusion exists between Shadrach Bond "Sr." ("Judge" Bond) and Shadrach Bond "Jr." ("Captain" or "Governor" Bond); cp. the index of Buck, *Illinois in 1818, s. v.* "Bond, Shadrach." The former was by birth a Virginian. Reynolds gives 1781 as the date of his arrival in Illinois—*Pioneer History,* 113; but according to his own testimony in court in 1781 (when he was, he said, about 30 years old) he had come with Clark (in 1779), and after his discharge was a day laborer for the inhabitants—May Allinson, "A Trial Scene in Kaskaskia in 1781," *Transactions* of Ill. State Hist. Society, 1906, p. 267; English, *Conquest of the Northwest,* 1060. He signed B. Tardiveau's contract with the Americans in 1787—Alvord, *Kaskaskia Records (I. H. C.,* 5), 444; and the land commissioners affirmed his claim to a family right as a resident head of a family before 1788—*Amer. State Papers: Pub. Lands,* 2: 162; see also 217, cl. 321, and 219, cl. 322. On September 28, 1795 he was appointed a justice of the Common Pleas—see letter patent in Brink, McDonough, *Hist. of St. Clair County,* 69. And doubtless he was also made a justice of the Quarter Sessions, for he was one of the four judges who on August 5, 1796 proclaimed the opening of the Orphans' Court, whose record shows him sitting regularly in 1797-1799, in one term of 1803, 1804, and 1806, and regularly again in 1807-1808. His last appearance was in July, 1808, when, having resigned, he was succeeded by Shadrach Bond Jr. (*Orphans' Court: 1797-1809,* 43). He also succeeded William St. Clair as probate judge when the latter died (*post,* app. n. 41, and Brink, McDonough, *Hist. of St. Clair County,* 83), and was still serving as such in 1805 (September, 1805—*Orphans' Court: 1797-1809,* 27; doubtless he served until January 1, 1806), although no such appointment under Indiana Territory is recorded in the *Executive Journal.* Meanwhile he represented his county in the first legislature of the Northwest Territory, which met at Cincinnati on September 23, 1799—*St. Clair Papers,* 2: 439 n. and 446-447 n.; Burnet, *Notes,* 289. Washburne, *Edwards Papers,* 44 n., erroneously states that Shadrach Bond Jr. was the delegate (and gives the date as 1789). He signed the proslavery petition forwarded to Congress under date of October 1, 1800—Ind. Hist. Soc. *Pub.,* 2: 460. As the election was held on January 5, 1799—Brink, McDonough, *Hist. of St. Clair County,* 70-71—it is improbable that Bond attended the preliminary meeting of the House of Representatives on February 4 to nominate members of the Legislative Council; he was absent, however, from the February session of the Orphans' Court, present at the May session, and absent thereafter until September 1803. At an election held on December 7, 1802 he was chosen a delegate to the Vincennes slavery convention—Brink, McDonough, *Hist. of St. Clair County,* 71, 73; and doubtless voted for the petition of that body to Congress asking suspension of the antislavery article of the Ordinance—Ind. Hist. Soc. *Pub.,* 2: 462. The index (to p. 304) of Dunn's *Indiana* errs in making Shadrach Bond Jr. the delegate to this convention. He was named in this as the third judge, but he headed the commission appointed on December 26, 1801 to try charges made against John Dumoulin—Gibson, *Exec. Journal,* 105-106. Both Bond and Perrey signed the petition-of-350 which in 1805 attacked Harrison for adoption of government of the second grade and demanded division of the territory—Ind. Hist. Soc. *Pub.,* 2: 489, 491; Perrey's greater activity than Bond in land speculation seems primarily to have influenced Harrison in recommending the latter to the president in preference to the former (after having earlier given preference

over Perrey to John Hay, who resigned the office—*ante,* app. n. 17, and Dunn, *Indiana,* 326), for appointment to the Legislative Council in 1805. The appointment was confirmed on January 9, 1806—Harrison, *Messages,* 1: 174-175, 186, 187; U. S. Senate, *Exec. Journal,* 2: 11, 13. (He was recommended, November 20, 1805; nominated, December 23; confirmed, January 9, 1806; and his commission forwarded, February 2, 1806—these dates illustrate the time then consumed in such changes, even when there was no opposition). He offered his resignation from the Council before August 31, 1807—Harrison, *Messages,* 1: 245-247. It is not absolutely clear whether Shadrach Bond Sr. was a member of the House of Representatives when nominated for the Council. The confusion on this point is immense—see e. g. Buck, *Illinois in 1818,* 187, 191; McDonough, *Hist. of Randolph, Monroe and Perry Counties,* 112; Harrison, *Messages,* 1: 230, note by Mr. Esarey. Most books (including Dillon) name the two men simply as "Shadrach Bond," without attempting to distinguish them. The journal of the Assembly in the *Indiana Gazette* (which Miss Nellie C. Armstrong of the Indiana State Library kindly examined for me) gives no aid. According to Brink, McDonough, *Hist. of St. Clair County,* 71, 73, it was the elder Bond who on May 21, 1805 was elected; his later elevation to the Council creating a vacancy in the House which was filled in 1806 (at a special election of which there is seemingly no printed evidence) by the choice of the younger Bond; the latter subsequently succeeding his uncle, similarly, in the Council, thereby creating a second vacancy in the lower house that was filled by the election of John Messinger. These are the facts assumed in the table of members of the General Assembly as given above. But according to Dunn, who was acquainted with the Journals of the Assembly—*Indiana,* 327, 355—it was Shadrach Bond Jr. who was elected in 1805 to the House of Representatives (giving the date May 20, on which the election should indeed have been held, but apparently was not). If this be so the table is incorrect in including the elder Bond as a representative; and there was no need for an election in 1806. After 1807 he held no other offices. His death occurred in 1812, and he left a personal estate valued at $2879—Brink, McDonough, *op. cit.,* 83; *Amer. State Papers: Pub. Lands,* 2: 219, cl. 322. Governor Reynolds' characterization of him is apparently well deserved: "Judge Bond in his neighborhood possessed a standing for integrity and honesty that could not be surpassed . . . and when he acted for the public it was to accommodate them, not himself. He possessed a strong mind and an excellent heart. He had a very limited education"—*Pioneer History,* 114-115; cp. his letter, Harrison, *Messages,* 1: 177. Governor Harrison's judgment of him was very similar: "altho' he has had little advantage from education he posses[ses] a very strong natural capacity & his character for honesty has never been impeached. He is withall a staunch republican & much more popular than any other man in his County"—*Messages,* 1: 175. On his land record see *ante,* lxxxiii.

19. Shadrach Bond "Jr.", nephew of Shadrach Bond "Sr.", was born in 1773 in Maryland, and arrived in 1794 in Illinois. Apparently he held no public office before 1805. Examples of confusion between him and his uncle—by Washburne in making him a representative in the first legislature of the Northwest Territory (1799), and by Dunn in making him a delegate to the Vincennes convention (1802)—have been referred to in the preceding note; and the question which was the representative of St. Clair County elected on May 21, 1805 to the first legislature of Indiana Territory is also there discussed. It is believed that he was first elected in

1806 to fill his uncle's unexpired term (to June 30, 1807), and reëlected on February 2, 1807 for a second term (to June 30, 1809)—Brink, McDonough, *Hist. of St. Clair County,* 71, 73; McDonough, *Hist. of Randolph, Monroe and Perry Counties,* 102; Dunn, *Indiana,* 355. Harrison's favoritism toward him at this time was one of the "charges" against the former made by Isaac Darneille in his *Letters of Decius* (1805—Goebel, *Harrison,* 63-64). When his uncle resigned from the Council, he was nominated to fill the vacancy, and was appointed by the President—Harrison, *Messages,* 1: 245-247, 295; U. S. Senate *Exec. Journal,* 2: 68 (nominated January 28, confirmed February 1, 1808). It was after this, apparently, that he resigned his seat in the lower house—Gibson, *Exec. Journal,* 147, entry of July 6, 1808 stating that July 25 was the date proclaimed for election of Bond's successor as representative. On May 12, 1808 he was made judge of the Common Pleas of St. Clair County; again vice the elder Bond, who had resigned—*ibid.,* 145. In the July term of the record of the *Orphans' Court 1797-1809* is the entry: "Shadrach Bond Junr came into court and was sworn in as a presiding Judge of this County Court of Common Pleas, and took his seat accordingly—Sharach Bon Senr resigning—Shadrach Bon Senr off the bench"—*loc. cit.,* 43. His second appearance was on March 20, 1809, after Illinois Territory was independent. His duel with Rice Jones in 1808—presumably shortly before or after the bitter election of August in Randolph County,—followed as it was by the murder of Jones by Bond's second, did not of course, injure him with Harrison, but it probably did hurt him with Ninian Edwards. On July 7, 1806 Harrison had appointed him adjutant in the St. Clair militia, and on October 26, 1808 lieutenant-colonel, vice George Atchison, deceased—Gibson, *Exec. Journal,* 134, 149. This office Secretary Pope had continued under the Illinois Territory (May 3, 1809). There is some evidence, however, and there was a contemporary feeling, that Governor Edwards leaned toward the Edgar-Morrison faction of Randolph—*ante,* xcix, n. 3; Bond, on the other hand, was more or less of the anti-Edwards group—Washburne, *Edwards Papers,* 150; Buck, *Illinois in 1818,* 201-202; T. C. Pease, *Illinois Election Returns 1818-1848* (*I. H. C.,* 18). Probably for political reasons Edwards displaced him in the militia by William B. Whiteside, Bond refusing to submit their rivalry to a popular election. "I shall send you the Certificate"—he wrote on July 2, 1809 to Governor Edwards—"of Thomas Todd Esqr which will enable you to judge wheather or not Whiteside has been that terror to Disorganisors as represented in his Potition. he has been indited for horse stealing"—see *ante,* lviii-ix, n. 3—"and now lies under an inditement in this County Court for harboring runaway Negroes. these with other reasons I believe induced governor Harrison to give me the appointment over Whiteside—as I never wrote to brake on the Corrector of anyman, I am sorry to be compeled to Do it now nor would I but to show your Excelency the Corrector of the man which you Propose for me to go into an election with . . . . I cannot condesend to put myself on a level with such a character as Major Whiteside"—Chic. Hist. Society, MSS; cp. Washburne, *Edwards Papers,* 45-46; Buck, *Illinois in 1818,* 202, says it was William *B.* Whiteside. He was made a justice of the peace by Edwards, December 9, 1809; and on April 4, 1812 a judge of the St. Clair Common Pleas—Greene and Alvord, *The Governors' Letter-Books 1818-1834* (*I. H. C.,* 4), 4 n. He served as the first delegate in Congress of Illinois Territory, October 10, 1812 (taking his seat December 3) to October 3, 1814 when his appointment was confirmed as receiver of public money for lands at Kaskaskia—Brink, McDonough, *Hist. of St. Clair County,* 74;

U. S. Senate, *Exec. Journal, 2*: 531, 532. His correspondence while delegate in Congress is in Washburne's *Edwards Papers,* but contains practically nothing of interest. He was elected on September 19, 1818 the
first governor of Illinois (1818-1822) almost without opposition; probably
because his rivals for election to Congress induced him to take the governorship and leave them unmolested—Buck, *Illinois in 1818,* 296, 299. On
October 3, 1814 he was appointed receiver of public moneys in the Kaskaskia land office—U. S. Senate, *Exec. Journal, 2*: 531, 532; which office
presumably he resigned when elected governor (although seemingly his successor—Edward Humphreys—was not named until February 23, 1821—
ibid., 3: 218, 246). On January 28, 1823 he was appointed register, vice
Michael Jones, deceased—*ibid., 3*: 325, 328; and on January 5, 1827 was
reappointed—*ibid.,* 551, 555. He was defeated in 1824 by Daniel P. Cook
in his candidacy for election to Congress—T. C. Pease, *Election Returns*
(I. H. C., 18), 24. His death took place on April 11, 1830 according to
Reynolds—*Pioneer History,* 327; on the 14th according to Washburne—
Edwards Papers, 44 n.; and in 1832 according to Greene and Alvord,
op. cit., 4 n. Against a man of Daniel Cook's charm and force Bond's
popularity, in earlier years sufficient to give him any elective office for
the asking, was of no avail (though neither was the strength of anybody
else in Illinois). In that later period, too, real political issues had come
to exist; whereas in the territorial period there was little more than personal groups. Both of the Bonds were seemingly plain and simple men,
with nothing colorful in their personality—although Governor Bond seems
to have possessed a certain bonhomie—yet they were the most popular men,
each in his generation, in St. Clair County. Sound practical judgment and
indubitable integrity were apparently the basis of their popular appeal. See
a curious marriage item in McDonough, *Hist. of Randolph, Monroe and*
Perry Counties, 140.

20. William Biggs, according to Governor Reynolds, was born in
Maryland in 1755, was a subaltern officer under George Rogers Clark in
1778-1779, returned after the Revolution to western Virginia, and before 1788
to Illinois—*Pioneer History,* 341-342. There is no evidence in the *Clark*
Papers (I. H. C., 8 and 19), or in English's *Conquest of the Northwest*
(see e. g. 1067) that he actually served under Clark. Nevertheless, by act
of May 22, 1826 and "in consideration of his services as lieutenant in the
regiment of the late General George Rogers Clark, which marched against,
and subdued, the posts of Kaskaskias and Vincennes," Congress granted
him three sections of land—*U. S. Stat. at Large,* 6: 353. According to the
lists prepared in 1796 and 1797 by William St. Clair he was a head of
family in 1783 and as such entitled to a land donation—*Chic. Hist. Colls.,*
4: 205, 208; and his claim was confirmed to him by the land commissioners—*Amer. State Papers: Pub. Lands,* 2: 162 (though they recognized
claims for residence to 1788, *ante,* lxxxi). He signed the Tardiveau contract of 1787—Alvord, *Kaskaskia Records (I. H. C.,* 5), 445. After the
French court at Cahokia had suppressed the attempt of Americans at
Bellefontaine and Grand Ruisseau to set up an independent magistracy, in
August or September of 1787, they were permitted to elect justices of the
peace, and on November 2 Biggs took the oath of office before the Cahokia
court—Alvord, *Cahokia Records (I. H. C.,* 2), cxlix, 307. Governor
St. Clair appointed him sheriff of St. Clair County on April 29, 1790—*St.*
Clair Papers, 2: 165 n.; and according to May Allinson he was made a
judge of the Quarter Sessions (but not of Common Pleas) in 1795—
Ill. State Hist. Soc. *Trans.* (1907), p. 290. There is some evidence that he

continued to act also as sheriff until 1798—Brink, McDonough, *Hist. of St. Clair County,* 51, 71 (George Blair appearing as sheriff on January 5, 1799), 77, 86-87; Bateman and Selby, *Hist. of St. Clair County,* 2: 690. Although not one of the judges who opened the Orphans' Court in August, 1796, he sat in it fairly regularly—in 1797, 1800-1802, and again in 1804 and 1805—until the reorganization of the county courts in the last year, having been reappointed to the Quarter Sessions, and also appointed to the Common Pleas, by Governor Harrison in 1800—Gibson, *Exec. Journal,* 94. He was not reappointed to the new Common Pleas in 1805. In 1802 he was an unsuccessful candidate for election to the Vincennes convention. Contrary to the statement of Governor Reynolds, *Pioneer History,* 343, he never served in the legislature of the older territory (1799), but he was elected on May 21, 1805 to the first General Assembly of Indiana Territory, and was reëlected in 1807—Brink, McDonough, *Hist. of St. Clair County,* 71, 73. He was not of the Harrison party, signing various of the Illinois petitions for division of the territory that were sent to Congress—*ante,* liii, n. 4; lvii. His integrity, however, was unquestioned. For his land record—*ante,* lxxxiii. He took proofs of land claims for the first board of land commissioners in St. Clair County—see *Amer. State Papers: Pub. Lands,* 2: 133; and his evidence (along with that of Jean Bte. Barbau and others) was relied upon to disprove fraudulent claims—e. g. see *ibid.,* 134. From 1812 to 1816 he represented St. Clair County in the Legislative Council of Illinois Territory. At the same time he was a member, from October 1813 onward, of the first county court of St. Clair; and again of the reorganized county court from February 1816 to January 12, 1818. Brink, McDonough, *Hist. of St. Clair County,* 76. He was defeated in 1818 as a candidate for the state Senate. He signed an antislavery address to the "friends of Freedom" in Illinois while the constitutional convention was sitting in 1818. He died in 1827. Brink, McDonough, *Hist. of St. Clair County,* 51, 72; Buck, *Illinois in 1818,* 261, 301.

21. John Messinger (he wrote well, and always used the *i*) was born in Massachusetts in 1771; migrated in 1799 to Kentucky with Matthew Lyon, who was his father-in-law; and in 1802 removed to Illinois. He is more important as a surveyor and an educator than in political life. He surveyed large portions of the public domain in southern Illinois, participated in the official demarcation of its northern boundary, and published in 1821 a manual on practical surveying which must have been one of the earliest scientific books of the middle west. As an educator he was a man of importance. In evening schools and in private instruction he taught young and old, and according to Governor Reynolds many adults—including Governor Kinney—learned of him their letters. In 1827 he became professor of mathematics in the Rock Spring Theological Seminary and High School. See Reynolds, *Pioneer History,* index. In the election of July 25, 1808, in which Rice Jones (on August 13 *post,* app. n. 24) was elected by the prodivisionists as their representative in the lower house of the Assembly from Randolph County, Messinger was elected by them in St. Clair in succession to Shadrach Bond Jr.—Gibson, *Exec. Journal,* 147; Harrison, *Messages,* 1: 295; Brink, McDonough, *Hist. of St. Clair County,* 53; Dunn, *Indiana,* 366-367; *ante,* li. He was appointed county surveyor by Governor Edwards on June 22, 1809; was clerk pro tem of the lower house of the first legislature of Illinois Territory, November, 1812; was appointed county treasurer on December 24, 1814. In 1818 he was a member of the Illinois constitutional convention, and voted with the proslavery party and land speculators. Buck, *Illinois in 1818,* 279-280,

289-292; Ill. State Hist. Society, *Journal,* 6: 358, 380, 401-402. It is interesting to observe that he was president of an antislavery convention held at Belleville on March 22, 1823, at which was formed the "St. Clair Society for the prevention of slavery in the State of Illinois"—Alvord, *Governor Edward Coles* (*I. H. C.,* 15), 333-334. The explanation of this strange inconsistency does not appear; though it is possible that Messinger was a man whose opinions could be changed by argument. The same year he represented St. Clair County in, and served as speaker of, the first House of Representatives of the state. Buck, *op. cit.,* 300; Greene and Alvord, *Governors' Letter-Books 1818-1834* (*I. H. C.,* 4), 47 n.; Brink, McDonough, *op. cit.,* 52-53. He died in 1846.

22. Antoine Pierre Menard was a native of Quebec, born on October 7, 1766; son of a Frenchman who fought for the American cause in the Revolution. As early as 1788 (Reynolds says 1786) he was working in the Indian trade for Francis Vigo at Vincennes. He removed in 1790 to Kaskaskia, and in 1792 became related by his first marriage to the Bauvais family; as he did by his second, in 1806, to the Saucier family of Cahokia. (Cp. *post,* app. n. 30). His militia claim, for service in or before 1790, was affirmed by the first board of land commissioners—*Amer. State Papers: Pub. Lands,* 2: 172. He was licensed as merchant at Kaskaskia in 1793—Brink, McDonough, *Hist. of St. Clair County,* 83. He was doubtless appointed by Governor St. Clair in 1795 to the county courts of Randolph County. He sat before 1800 in the Common Pleas, as appears from the scanty records of that court—*Common Pleas,* 1: 73, of July 1798. He also appears as a notary in the records of the time—e. g. in *Deed Record J,* of 1799. On August 1, 1800 Governor Harrison appointed him to both the Quarter Sessions and Common Pleas—Gibson, *Exec. Journal,* 92, 93; the commission for the latter court is printed in the *Chic. Hist. Colls.,* 4: 168, and is dated February 5, 1801; also in Harrison, *Messages,* 1: 23. He was reappointed in 1805 to the new Common Pleas—Gibson, *Exec. Journal,* 131, under date of December 28; the commission, dated the 27th, is printed in *Chic. Hist. Colls.,* 4: 171-172, and in Harrison, *Messages,* 1: 182; it was effective January 1, 1806 but he took the oath of office on July 18. He was notably regular in attendance during his eight years of service. On his land record see *ante,* lxxxv, lxxxvi, xc. He was county commissioner from 1803 to 1809— McDonough, *Hist. of Randolph, Monroe and Perry Counties,* 125. He was one of the Randolph delegates to the Vincennes convention of 1802—Dunn, *Indiana,* 304; see also *ante,* liv, n. 1. His commission of that year (September 24) to sit with John Edgar and Judge Griffin of the General Court in a court of general jail delivery is printed by Mason, *Chic. Hist. Colls.,* 168-171, and in Harrison, *Messages,* 1: 57-58. When the territory passed to representative government it was he and George Fisher who carried Randolph County for the change, against the efforts of the Edgar-Morrison party—*ante,* xxvi. The lower house of the Assembly—Fisher was the Randolph representative—nominated Menard for the Legislative Council and he was appointed by Jefferson—U. S. Senate, *Exec. Journal,* 2: 9, 10, 13 (nominated December 20, 1805; confirmed January 6, 1806); serving as president pro tem. in both sessions of the first Assembly—*post,* for signatures to laws in this volume. He resigned on September 19, 1807—Harrison, *Messages,* 1: 256 *and* 253, 263. The reasons are disputed; but whether or not one attribute to Menard disaffection with Harrison, it is clear that the resignations of Bond (Sr.) and Menard had great political significance in their effect, inasmuch as the elections thereby caused (see *ante,* 1) were the beginning of Harrison's loss of control over

the territory. When Illinois Territory attained in turn to representative
government, Menard was elected to the Legislative Council in all three of
the territorial legislatures, and served as president in all six sessions—
McDonough, *Hist. of Randolph, Monroe and Perry Counties,* 40-41. In
the struggle over slavery in December 1817 in the third territorial legislature he voted against the repeal of the indenture laws—Buck, *Illinois in
1818,* 217. He stood aloof from the political factions of the period—Buck,
Illinois in 1818, 202; his honors were due to his universal popularity. He
served as first lieutenant-governor of the state, October 6, 1818 to December
5, 1822. His election to this office was for one reason most remarkable.
He was naturalized only in 1816; but the constitution (art. III, §§ 3, 13)
required a lieutenant-governor to have been thirty years a citizen of the
United States. The constitutional convention, to make Menard eligible,
provided in the schedule for transition to the new régime (§ 14) merely
that the candidate must *be* a citizen. Certainly a remarkable tribute!—
H. S. Baker, in *Chic. Hist. Colls.,* 4 : 153. This was the end of his service
in state politics. In addition, like all the local gentry of that time, he held
offices in the militia. St. Clair made him a major in 1795; Secretary Gibson
renewed the office in 1801—August 1: Gibson, *Exec. Journal,* 93 ; Harrison
made him lieutenant-colonel of the Randolph regiment in 1806 when John
Edgar resigned—July 12: *ibid.,* 135; and Nathaniel Pope continued him
in the office in 1809 (May 6). In addition to thus serving the three territories of his successive allegiance, he received in 1809 (April 1) from
Governor Meriwether Lewis of the Territory of Louisiana a commission
as "Captain of Infantry in a Detachmt. of Militia, on special service"—
the nature of which seems to be indeterminable. All these commissions
are printed in *Chic. Hist. Colls.,* 4 : 166, 167, 172, 173-174, 175. Meanwhile
he had continued all these years his trading ventures. Reynolds states that
he spent 1808 in the Rocky Mountains in the interest of "the mammoth
company of Emanuel Liza and others"—*Pioneer History,* 294. He was on
the bench frequently through 1807 and down to April, at least, of 1808;
but may have gone thereafter. On April 2, 1813 he was appointed by the
Secretary of War a subagent of Indian Affairs, and held the office many
years—*Chic. Hist. Colls.,* 4 : 176; cp. Buck, *Illinois in 1818,* 13. With Lewis
Cass he served as a commissioner in the negotiation of Indian treaties in
1828—*Chic. Hist. Colls.,* 4 : 176. U. S. Senate, *Exec. Journal,* 3 : 618
(confirmed May 24, 1828). He died on June 13, 1844. His education was
slight, but his career sufficiently evidences his reputation for public spirit,
fair mindedness, and judgment. Nothing could speak more highly for his
character than Reynolds' statement that "the Indians almost worshiped
him"—*Pioneer History,* 292. In his very large dealings in lands the Kaskaskia commissioners discovered nothing discreditable—*ante,* lxxxv, xci ;
the Vincennes commissioners did him the signal honor of empowering him
to take depositions and examine witnesses in his county relative to land
claims of the Vincennes district—*Chic. Hist. Colls.,* 4 : 171 (commission of
December 14, 1805). The forgery of his name by fellow judges and land-
jobbers—*ante,* lxxxix-xc—bears out Reynolds' statement that there
was no guile or cunning in him. "Menard," he also says, "was first in
almost every enterprise in pioneer times in Illinois." He was particularly
interested in schools. See Reynolds, *Pioneer History,* 291-294; *My Own
Times,* 67, 113; E. G. Mason, "Pierre Menard," *Chic. Hist. Colls.,* 4 : 142-
148; H. S. Baker, "The First Lieutenant-Governor of Illinois," *ibid.,* 149-
161; the "Pierre Menard Papers," *ibid.,* 162-180, most of which are cited

above; Greene and Alvord, *Governors' Letter-Books 1818-1834* (*I. H. C.,* 4), 10-11 n.

23. *Ante,* ccii, n. 1. George Fisher, who settled in Kaskaskia in 1798, was the most prominent physician of the Illinois country in the early 1800's. In September 1802 he was licensed to keep a ferry across the Mississippi, six miles below Kaskaskia; the tax upon it in 1803 and in 1805 was $5—Randolph *Court Record, 1802-06,* 6, 27 (June 1803), 91 (June 1805). In the December term, 1803 he was licensed to keep an inn in Kaskaskia—*ibid.,* 42; and no doubt he continued to do so for years. He was also a merchant; for it appears that in 1805 he was delinquent on one retail license as well as for two tavern licenses—*ante,* cxx. To keep a ferry or a tavern was a certain sign of political favor. To be sheriff was to control politics. He had been made sheriff of Randolph County on August 1, 1800—Gibson, *Exec. Journal,* 93; from which office he resigned, however, before August 30, 1803, when James Edgar became his successor—*ibid.,* 121. The county commissioners of Illinois Territory in 1810 allowed him $154 for his services, regular and "extra," from August 1, 1800 to August 20, 1803, "as per his account rendered and approved"—*County Commissioners* (1810), 133. He was a county commissioner himself between 1803 and 1809—McDonough, *Hist. of Randolph, Monroe and Perry Counties,* 125. On January 7, 1804 he was made a judge of both county courts—J. Gibson, *Exec. Journal,* 122. Before this he had acquired extraordinary popularity. It was his influence and Menard's that carried Randolph County in 1805 in favor of (whereas St. Clair opposed) transition to government of the second grade—*ante,* xxvi. In the election called for the first House of Representatives of Indiana Territory Fisher was chosen (on May 20, 1805) as representative of Randolph County. He was reëlected on February 2, 1807—Gibson, *Exec. Journal,* 72; Dunn, *Indiana,* 277, 325, 327, 355, 365. When Pierre Menard resigned (*ante,* app. n. 22) from the Legislative Council, and he and James Finney were nominated by the House to fill the vacancy, Harrison favored him in his recommendations to the President, and he was appointed on February 1, 1808—Harrison, *Messages,* 1: 253, 263; U. S. Senate, *Exec. Journal,* 2: 68 (nominated January 28, confirmed February 1). When Illinois Territory passed to the second grade he was the representative of Randolph County and speaker of the House in both the first and the third Assemblies (Nov. 25-Dec. 26, 1812 and Nov. 8, 1813; Dec. 2, 1816-Jan. 14, 1817 and Dec. 1, 1817-Jan. 12, 1818)—McDonough, *History of Randolph, Monroe and Perry Counties,* 40-41. In 1814 he was also a member of the reconstituted Common Pleas of Randolph County—*ibid.,* 181. He had always joined with the proslavery party in their petitions to Congress—*ante,* xxi, n. 1. The third legislature closed with an important debate on slavery, in which Fisher took a leading part in defence of the indenture law. Slavery became the dominant issue in the campaign for delegates to the constitutional convention. Fisher was elected, and again stood with the proslavery party—Buck, *Illinois in 1818,* 215-218, 257, 280; Ill. State Hist. Society, *Journal,* 6: 358, 380, 401. But he was defeated as a candidate for election to the first state Senate, in 1818—Buck, *op. cit.,* 300. He died in 1820. Reynolds' sketch of him is inadequate and evidently not based on close acquaintance—*Pioneer History,* 358.

24. Rice Jones, the eldest son of John Rice Jones, was born in Wales September 28, 1781. He is said to have graduated from Transylvania University, from Judge Reeve's famous law school at Litchfield, Connecticut, and—in medicine—from the University of Pennsylvania; to have opened a law office at Kaskaskia in 1806; and to have been a young man of bril-

liant abilities and promise. See Reynolds, *Pioneer History*, 172-174; *Chic. Hist. Colls.*, 4: 271-284—an uncritical memoir by W. A. Burt Jones. No trace whatever of his activity as a lawyer appears in the Randolph archives. The existing records of Transylvania University merely contain the name "Jones" in a list of "tuition monies, 1802," but presumably he was graduated. He certainly did not graduate in medicine at Pennsylvania, and there is no evidence that he attended any classes; he certainly did not attend those of Dr. Benjamin Rush, said to have been his father's friend. (*Chic. Hist. Colls.*, 4: 231), whose class books are intact. Nor is there any evidence that he completed a course of study at Litchfield, although the catalogs do list him as an attendant in 1807 (from Louisiana). It is therefore most improbable that he opened an office at Kaskaskia in 1806. His name is not upon a single one of the petitions to Congress of 1806 to 1808. Of his abilities and personality there is, however, ample evidence in one field, that of politics. He joined the Edgar-Morrison faction—the division:st or anti-Harrison party—in Randolph, and if he did not become its leader (as the two authors last cited state, although it is impossible to believe that he was more than a useful instrument of Edgar and the Morrisons), he did become one of its passionately ardent and prominent members when only 26 years old. To what extent this factional grouping was affected by opposition to the local land commissioners, Michael Jones and Elijah Backus—whose later reports, after these events, involved in charges of forgery John Rice Jones, Edgar, both Morrisons, and others of their group— is not clear; Alvord says (*Illinois Country*, 424) that he "had thrown himself whole-heartedly" into their defence—although as yet there were no public reports of the commissioners' findings; *ante*, lviii, n. 1. According to Dunn Judge Backus was ardently anti-Harrison (*ante*, app. n. 14), yet it was he by whom John Rice Jones considered the life of his son to be threatened—see his letter in McDonough, *Hist. of Randolph, Monroe and Perry Counties*, 105. On the other hand Michael Jones was most certainly and decidedly pro-Harrison—*ante*, app. n. 13—yet he was generally charged with inciting Dunlap in his attacks upon Rice Jones. The order of events was probably thus: First, the break between John Rice Jones and Governor Harrison, for reasons no longer precisely determinable (*ante*, app. n. 10), probably much antedating the division campaign of 1808, but doubtless aggravated thereby, and possibly also by Jones's anticipation of the report of the commissioners; second, the open conflict between Jones and Harrison with division as the immediate occasion; third, the consequent candidacy of Rice Jones at the election of August 13, 1808, resulting in his election by the divisionists to the lower house of the Assembly. See *ante*, l-li. Before the election he had engaged in a duel, seconded by William Morrison, against Shadrach Bond Jr. The principals settled their differences amicably on the field; but the circumstance that Jones's pistol was prematurely discharged gave rise to a bitter controversy between him and Bond's second, Dr. James Dunlap, the end of which was the murder of the former by the latter on December 7, 1808. (The original indictment— Miscellanies Box, Chester—does not allege that he was shot down from behind as stated by Governor Reynolds). Dunlap escaped and was never brought to trial. See *ante*, xciv, n. 2. The extremely uncritical statements of W. A. Burt Jones, save one, are there sufficiently discussed. That one is a reference to "the interests" of Rice Jones which the land commissioners deliberately attacked. No evidence has been found that he owned a foot of land (or anything else); his name does not occur in the land commissioners' reports.

25. Jesse Burgess Thomas was born in Maryland in 1777, but grew to manhood in Kentucky, whither his family removed in 1779. There he studied and began the practice of law. In 1803 he removed to Indiana Territory. Dearborn County elected him on January 3, 1805 a representative in the first General Assembly and reëlected him on February 2, 1807. He was elected speaker of the lower house in both legislatures, and served as such in all four sessions, from July 29, 1805 to October 24, 1808. His signature is on practically all the laws in this volume. The struggle over territorial division in the summer of 1808, and the circumstances under which Thomas was picked by the anti-Harrison party—the prodivisionists of Illinois and the antislavery men of eastern Indiana—as a compromise candidate against the Harrison forces have been stated. See *ante,* li, and n. 3; app. n. 10. He was elected on October 24, 1808—see Dunn, *Indiana,* 376—and in his brief term of service from December 1, 1808 to March 3, 1809 fulfilled his obligations to those who elected him by securing passage of the act of February 3, 1809 which made Illinois an independent territory. That act became effective on March 1, 1809. On March 7, 1809, he was appointed by President Madison one of the judges of the Illinois territorial court—U. S. Senate, *Exec. Journal, 2*: 119, 120. The President described him in his nomination to the Senate as "of the Illinois Territory." It was of course his knowledge that he could have no further political future in Indiana which prompted him to secure the judgeship. "The citizens of Vincennes were so incensed at what they considered his perfidy that they hung him in effigy, and heaped upon him, upon his return from Washington, the vilest abuse and reproach"—J. F. Snyder, *Adam W. Snyder,* 12. He settled first in the country near Kaskaskia, later at Cahokia. He served as judge throughout the territorial period of Illinois. Elected on July 8, 1818 one of the St. Clair delegates to the constitutional convention, and was elected its president (August 3-24, 1818)—Ill. State Hist. Society, *Journal, 6*: 356, 358. On October 4 he was elected by the first legislature United States senator, and reëlected by the third, serving for ten years (December 4, 1818-March 3, 1829)—Buck, *Illinois in 1818,* 303, 316; Pease, *The Frontier State,* 95-98. The amendment that is the gist of the Missouri Compromise of 1820 was introduced by him and bears his name. In 1829 he again changed his residence, this time to Ohio, and thereafter acted with the Whig party, although up to that time his record had been strongly proslavery. Aside from being a delegate to the Whig national convention of 1840, and activity in advancing the candidacy of Harrison his political career ended, substantially in 1829. From August 6, 1843 to December 4, 1848 he was a justice of the Supreme Court of Ohio. He died, by suicide, on May 4, 1853. Friendly sketches by J. F. Snyder, in *Adam W. Snyder,* 9-18, and Ill. Hist. Soc. *Trans.,* (1904), pp. 514-523; Thomas was a benefactor of Adam W. Snyder. See also Reynolds, *Pioneer History,* 401-402; Greene and Alvord, *Governors' Letter-Books 1818-1834 (I. H. C.,* 4), 4 n.

26. The law creating Indiana Territory went into effect on July 4, 1800. The first appointments of August 1st, could not have been officially known for some little time, nor the appointees sworn into office until the October sessions. It seems best, therefore, to use the date of appointment. It appears from *ante,* app. n. 17, that some officers may possibly have had unofficial information in advance. As no sessions of the courts were held between July and October there was no need to act under old commissions; though doubtless as justices of the peace they did so.

27. The first seven named justices were appointed on August 1, 1800—Gibson, *Exec. Journal,* 94. On February 3, 1801 all except Benjamin Ogle were reappointed—*ibid.,* 97—December 10, 1805 and December 28, 1805, were the dates on which, for St. Clair and Randolph counties respectively, the judges of the new Common Pleas, in which the Quarter Sessions and other courts were merged, were appointed; but the act creating the new court (*post,* 115) did not go into effect until January 1, 1806. The terms of the old judges are therefore indicated as continuing to this date.

28. According to Governor Reynolds, Dumoulin was Swiss by birth and came to Illinois from Canada, had enjoyed an education in the sciences and classics, and knew the civil law—*Pioneer History,* 209. He is mentioned first in Alvord's *Cahokia Records* in January, 1786, and frequently thereafter in the judicial records of the years 1786-1789. He was at this time evidently employed in miscellaneous mercantile ventures—*op. cit.,* index. His militia claim, for services up to 1790, was affirmed by the second board of land commissioners—*Amer. State Papers: Pub. Lands,* 2: 236. Apparently he held no judicial office, even as a justice of the peace, until 1790. Governor St. Clair appointed him in that year a judge of the Common Pleas; and apparently he acted as the chief-judge of the Cahokia district (*ante,* cxlvii, n. 3), though order of appointments would not have indicated such precedence—cp. *St. Clair Papers,* 2: 165 n. (April 29, 1790) and Allinson, Ill. State Hist. Soc. *Trans.* (1907), p. 285; Reynolds, *op. cit.,* 180, 209. On September 28, 1795, he was named by Governor St. Clair, who was then at Cahokia, a judge of the Common Pleas—see letter patent in Brink, McDonough, *Hist. of St. Clair County,* 69. He was also evidently, made a justice of Quarter Sessions, presumably at the same time, for he was one of the four judges who proclaimed the opening of the Orphans' Court on August 5, 1796; and the *Orphans' Court 1797-1809* record shows him in regular attendance thereafter. On February 23, 1797 he was ordered to surrender to the Judge of Probate all records in his possession relating to "succession business & Estates"—St. Clair *Orphans' Court 1797-1809,* 2. Why such should have been in his custody does not appear. No evidence seems to support the statement of Reynolds, *Pioneer History,* 209, that he was judge of probate. He was at some time appointed by Governor St. Clair lieutenant-colonel in the militia—not in 1790: *St. Clair Papers,* 2: 165— for in March, 1800 he was the county commandant—*ibid.,* 495; and Governor Harrison recommissioned him on August 19, 1802—Gibson, *Exec. Journal,* 110. He seems to have been both decorative and efficient in this position—Reynolds, *Pioneer History,* 209, 210. He ceased to sit in the Orphans' Court (and presumably in other courts) after the end of 1802. On December 26, 1801 Governor Harrison commissioned Shadrach Bond Sr. and the six other colleagues of Dumoulin in the Court of Quarter Sessions to inquire into charges against him made by the grand jury of St. Clair to the Circuit Court "for having in several instances therein enumerated, acted tyrannically corruptedly and Illegally whilst in the Execution of the duties of his said offices"—Gibson, *Exec. Journal,* 105-106, and *ante,* ccvii. Although the findings of the commission are apparently lost, they presumably forced his retirement. He lived until 1805. (Alvord gives 1808—*Cahokia Records* (*I. H. C.,* 2), 230 n.; and Governor Reynolds, 1808—*op. cit.,* 210). He left a personal estate, according to the Brink, McDonough, *Hist. of St. Clair County,* 83, of $7307.67. But his fellow judge, John Francis Perrey, who was his administrator, secured an order from the Orphans' Court in March, 1806 for the sale of his house, "it being going to ruin, and the yearly rent will not pay the

repairs"—*Orphans' Court 1797-1809*, 29; and another order a year later "to sell the real Property of said dec'd as the said estate is insolvent"—*ibid.*, 33. After more than another year John Edgar was still granted time to settle his account with decedent—July, 1808, *ibid.*, 44. Governor St. Clair, stating his military qualifications, characterized him as "a very good man, of fair character"—*St. Clair Papers*, 2: 495; cp. Reynolds, *loc. cit.* He was a large speculator in lands, buying up the claims of his fellow Frenchmen, and was supposed to be wealthy until death revealed the truth. "His virtues of benevolence, kindness, and generosity," says Reynolds, "were not questioned, and he lived and died very popular. . . . Altho he speculated in lands, he was honest and correct"—*op. cit.*, 210, 211. There is nothing discreditable to him in records of the land commissioners. *Ante*, lxxxiii.

29. George Atchison is said by J. M. Peck to have settled in the Illinois country in 1786—Reynolds, *Pioneer History, 255-256*; which may well be correct, notwithstanding that he does not appear (for neither does John Dumoulin) in the 1787 census of Cahokia—Alvord, *Cahokia Records, (I. H. C., 2)*, 624 *et seq.*; and that Governor Reynolds names two other persons as the only non-French residents in Cahokia before 1788—*Pioneer History*, 128. He may have been living in the Kaskaskia district, or in Grand Ruisseau, which was but barely organized and of disputed jurisdiction—Alvord, *Cahokia Records (I. H. C., 2)*. At any rate he signed Tardiveau's contract of August 1787 with the American land claimants— Alvord, *Kaskaskia Records (I. H. C., 5)*, 444. See also English, *Conquest of the Northwest*, 1067. In 1790 he was appointed a lieutenant of militia—*St. Clair Papers*, 2: 165 n. On September 28, 1795, he was commissioned judge of the Common Pleas of St. Clair County—see letter patent in Brink, McDonough, *Hist. of St. Clair County*, 69. Presumably he was named at the same time a justice of the Quarter Sessions, for he was one of the four judges who on August 5, 1796, proclaimed the opening of the Orphans' Court, in which (*Orphans' Court 1797-1809*, passim) he sat very regularly down into 1805. In August 1802 he was made a major by Harrison—Gibson, *Exec. Journal*, 111; became a lieutenant-colonel on the death of Dumoulin; and died sometime before October 26, 1808, when Shadrach Bond succeeded him in this command—*ibid.*, 149. His name is spelled variously, and not always in one way by himself, but his habitual signature was "Atchison."

30. The main source of information regarding his purely personal characteristics is a sketch by his grandson, J. F. Snyder, in *Adam W. Snyder*, 426-434. Although he always wrote his name "Perrey" (usually in the French style, without initials), and it uniformly so appears in the judicial records, he was doubtless generally known as Perry; Governor Reynolds calls him "Jean Francis." He was born in France in 1766, of a middle-class family (Mr. Esarey's statement—Harrison, *Messages*, 1: 175 n.—that he was "an emigre noble" is erroneous), educated and well to do, and had himself been rather well schooled, including some study of law, when in 1792 he left France, "well supplied with money" which enabled him to begin business in Illinois. According to Snyder, "his polished manners and polite, courteous deportment testified to the refined social conditions in which he was reared." In 1797 he married a daughter of Jean Baptiste Saucier, who had been a member of Todd's Virginia court created in 1779, and altogether a leading citizen; named by Governor St. Clair in 1790 only a justice of the peace, but in 1795 a judge of Common Pleas and presumably also of Quarter Sessions—*post*, app. n. 38. On August 1, 1800, he was appointed by Governor Harrison to the two county courts, but he was not sworn in as a judge

of Quarter Sessions until April of 1801—Bateman and Selby, *Hist. of St. Clair County,* 701; and his attendance in the Orphans' Court began with the June term. He continued a rather regular attendance to the end of the Indiana Territory. In 1802 he was one of the three St. Clair County delegates to the Vincennes slavery convention—Brink, McDonough, *Hist. of St. Clair County,* 71, 73; and he signed various of the proslavery conventions of the time—*ante,* liv, n. 1. According to his grandson, however, so far as can be ascertained he was not a slaveholder—Snyder, *op cit.,* 430. He was twice nominated by the lower house of the Assembly, in 1805, for appointment to the Legislative Council; first with John Hay—Dunn, *Indiana,* 325—and then, after Hay declined the office, with Shadrach Bond—Harrison, *Messages,* 1: 174; but in both cases Harrison gave the preference to the other nominee. Unlike Bond he was not a member of the nominating body. Harrison's criticism of him, certainly disingenuous (*ante,* xxvi, n. 3), was that he had speculated heavily in the French land claims—*Messages,* 1: 175. His record therein is relatively honorable—*ante,* lxxxv, lxxxvi, xc. On a fondness for administration of estates, *ante,* ccvii, n. 6. His signature to prodivision petitions *ante,* liii, n. 4, was assuredly distasteful to Harrison; though Bond was very likely for other reasons the better man. He died at Cahokia in 1812. According to Snyder, "He was popular with all people, and distinguished for his kindness, charity and unstinted hospitality. Honor with him was instinctive, not the bantling of policy, and he recoiled from everything suggestive of deceit, vulgarity or immorality"—*op. cit.,* 432. As Snyder's characterizations of his relatives are very impersonally critical this judgment deserves especial weight. Although some typically generous exaggerations in Governor Reynolds' *Pioneer History,* 287-291, are pointed out by him, he adds and alters little in the way of facts, and leaves uncorrected his statement that Perrey had served with Bond and John Moredock in the territorial assembly; it was in the Vincennes convention, Brink, McDonough, *op. cit.,* 71.

31. James Lemen was born in 1761 and came to Illinois in 1786—Brink, McDonough, *Hist. of St. Clair County,* 163; Alvord, *Kaskaskia Records* (*I. H. C.,* 5), 445 n.; Reynolds, *Pioneer History,* 271 (where J. M. Peck says he reached Kaskaskia on July 10, 1786). He signed B. Tardiveau's land contract with American land claimants in August, 1787—*Kaskaskia Records* (*I. H. C.,* 5), 445; and the land commissioners affirmed his claim as a resident head of family before 1788, and also his militia claim—*Amer. State Papers: Pub. Lands,* 2: 164, 236 (the confirmation in each case was to James "Lemon," but such confusion was very common; cp. for example Governor Ford's *History,* 42). He was not appointed to the Common Pleas in 1795—see Brink, McDonough, *op. cit.,* 69. But he must have been named then or later a justice of the Quarter Sessions; for although he was not one of the justices who opened the Orphans' Court in August 1796, he attended sessions in February, 1797, one in 1800, 1801 and 1803, two in 1802, and three in 1804, after which his name appears no more—St. Clair *Orphans' Court 1797-1809,* 2, 13, 15, 17, 18, 20, 23, 24. His record on slavery is of particular interest inasmuch as family tradition has made him an antislavery apostle of early Illinois. Such he very likely was; for although his signature on at least one proslavery petition appears to be genuine, on others it clearly is not—*ante,* xxxix, n. 2; and assuming one to be in fact his own, he might have been in some way deceived. He was a defeated candidate in the election, on December 7, 1802, of delegates to the Vincennes slavery convention—Brink, McDonough, *op. cit.,* 71. In the early history of the Baptist church in Illinois, he was a very important figure—Reynolds,

Pioneer History, 256, 259, 272; Brink, McDonough, *op. cit.,* 163. Whether he was actually a friend of Jefferson, who sent him west to fight slavery in the Northwest Territory, and of what value the "Lemen Notes," had they been preserved in their alleged original form, might have been for the student of early Illinois history, are mysteries of historiography. See *ante,* liv, n. 1; Ill. State Hist. Soc. *Trans.* (1908), pp. 74-84; Alvord, *Kaskaskia Records (I. H. C.,* 5), 445 n. His later leadership against slavery is clear. He joined in an antislavery address to "the friends of Freedom in the state of Illinois" published on the day on which the constitutional convention was called, Buck, *Illinois in 1818,* 260-261, 280. (Although Mr. Buck and many others do not so indicate it was James Lemen Jr. who was a member of the convention, and voted with the antislavery members—J. F. Snyder, *Adam W. Snyder,* 309). He died on January 8, 1822—Brink, McDonough, *op. cit.,* 163. For sketches of him and other members of his family see Reynolds, *Pioneer History,* 271-272, 411-413.

32. There seems to be little information regarding him. Governor Reynolds refers to him principally as an Indian fighter—*Pioneer History,* 153, 175. Likewise Brink, McDonough, *Hist. of St. Clair County,* 50. He signed the Tardiveau contract in 1787—Alvord, *Kaskaskia Records (I. H. C.,* 5), 445, and the second board of land commissioners allowed him his militia claim—*Amer. State Papers: Pub. Lands,* 2: 237; cp. McDonough, *Hist. of Randolph, Monroe and Perry Counties,* 137. He was therefore still living in 1813. Just why he was so pointedly omitted in the recommissions of February 3, 1801 does not appear; but Nicholas Jarrot, who took his place, was doubtless a better man for the position.

33. Most that is known of Nicholas Jarrot is found in Governor Reynolds' sketch—*Pioneer History,* 211-215—which is evidently based upon personal acquaintance; and this is followed or quoted when other authority is not cited. He was born in France, whence he emigrated in 1790, arriving in Cahokia in 1794 after stops in Baltimore and New Orleans. (On statements that he came to Illinois with George Rogers Clark—statements made of nearly everybody who achieved prominence in early Illinois—cp. English, *Conquest of the Northwest,* 1067). The fact that he was an emigré of 1790 gives color to Reynolds' statement that he came of "a highly respectable family." "He received a liberal education and was, withal, a gentleman of elegant and accomplished manners." To these qualities were added the impulses of poverty and an extraordinary energy, which was directed into the extravagantly profitable trade with the Indians of the upper Mississippi, a retail store in Cahokia, and traffic in land claims. No doubt he was aided by his marriages, first to a daughter of Jean Baptiste Barbau, and later into the Bauvais family, which in the early years of the Virginian period was the richest and most influential of the Illinois country, and three of whose members had been justices of the Cahokia court—see Alvord, *Cahokia Records (I. H. C.,* 2), index. In 1798 he was a county assessor—Allinson, Ill. State Hist. Soc. *Trans.* (1907), p. 291. He was appointed a judge of Quarter Sessions on February 3, 1801—Gibson, *Exec. Journal,* 97; and took the oath of office in March—Bateman and Selby, *Hist. of St. Clair County,* 701; but his attendance in the Orphans' Court began only in June, 1802, and was rather occasional (at 7 sessions out of 12 in 3 years), *Orphans' Court 1797-1809,* 16, 17, 18, 20, 23, 24, 27. According to Reynolds "his decisions on the bench were prompt and quick"—*Pioneer History,* 214. He was appointed on February 3, 1801 to the Common Pleas and sat somewhat irregularly in that court—e. g. *Order Book,* 54 and 60 (1801), 120 (Dec. 1802), etc. He was also commissioned by Harrison

as a major in the militia on February 6, 1801—Gibson, *op. cit.*, 101. He
was a very ardent Catholic, according to Reynolds. He gave to the Monks
of La Trappe the Cahokia (or Monks') Mound, where they made their
home from 1807 to 1816, then returning to France. Brink, *Hist. of Madison
County*, 80. Although he at one time held what Governor Reynolds calls
"an immense fortune in real estate . . . . the best selection of land in
the country"—*op. cit.*, 213—a large part of his claims were disallowed by the
land commissioners—*ante*, lxxxiv, lxxxvi; he dissipated much of his means,
like John Dumoulin, in milling enterprises. His record in the reports of
the land commissioners was relatively honorable; see, however, the protest
by Pierre Menard, *ante*, xci-xcii. He died at Cahokia in 1823.

34. David Badgley was a Baptist minister who was born in New
Jersey in 1748 or 1749, and settled in Illinois in 1797, after having helped
to organize in 1796 the first Baptist church in Illinois. His appointment
to the Quarter Sessions—Gibson, *Exec. Journal*, 127—was of course accompanied by service as a justice of the peace, probably for many years.
He died on December 16, 1824. In order to secure some idea of his
knowledge of the English language consult Rufus Babcock, *Memoir of
John Mason Peck*, 157, and cp. Ford, *History*, 38-41. See Brink, McDonough, *Hist. of St. Clair County*, 53, 282; Bateman and Selby, *Hist. of St.
Clair County*, 1: 35, 445; Reynolds, *Pioneer History*, 236, 259-260, 269;
and *My Own Times*, 123; Chapman, *Portrait and Biographical Record of
St. Clair County*, 211.

35. James Bankson is not mentioned in Alvord's *Cahokia Records*
(*I. H. C.*, 2) up to 1790. Nor does he seem to have appeared again in
public life after holding the judgeship in the Quarter Sessions—Gibson,
Exec. Journal, 127. He appears at but one session in the record of the
Orphans' Court 1797-1809, namely in November, 1805, p. 28.

36. The first seven named judges were appointed to this court at the
same time as to the Quarter Sessions—Gibson, *Exec. Journal*, 94; and, with
the exception of Benjamin Ogle, were reappointed on February 3, 1801—
ibid., 97. Bond and Perrey were reappointed, and Thomas Kirkpatrick
added, on December 10, 1805 to the new Common Pleas—*ibid.*, 130. The last
two served until Illinois became a separate territory on March 1, 1809.
Shadrach Bond Jr. was appointed presiding judge, vice Shadrach Bond Sr.,
who had resigned, on May 12, 1808—*ibid.*, 145 and likewise served until
Illinois became independent.

37. The appointment of Thomas Kirkpatrick to the St. Clair Common
Pleas on December 10, 1805—Gibson, *Exec. Journal*, 130—is the earliest
definite record regarding him. He sat regularly in every term in the Orphans' Court, beginning in August, 1806, through the rest of the Indiana
territory period—St. Clair *Orphans' Court 1797-1809*, 30, 32, 34, 37, 41, 43,
45, 47. At this time he was a miller—Reynolds, *Pioneer History*, 315; on
June 2, 1817 he took the oath as a judge of the county court of Bond County,
newly created, and was such at least through 1818—W. H. Perrin, *Hist. of
Bond and Montgomery Counties*, 31, 73, 74. He was a delegate from Bond
County to the constitutional convention, and voted therein with the antislavery group—Ill. State Hist. Society, *Journal*, 6: 358, 380, 401; Buck,
Illinois in 1818, 280-281.

38. The St. Clair judges of the Quarter Sessions appointed in 1790
were John Edgar, Ant. Girardin, Philip Engel, and Ant. Louviere—*St.
Clair Papers*, 2: 165 n. When Randolph County was created out of
St. Clair—on October 5, 1795: *St. Clair Papers*, 2: 345—new appointments for St. Clair were necessarily made, although they are not recorded

in the *St. Clair Papers.* We know otherwise, however, that on September 28, 1795 Governor St. Clair, then at Cahokia issued his letter patent naming as judges of the Common Pleas: William St. Clair, John Dumoulin, James Piggott, Shadrach Bond Sr., Jean Baptiste Saucier, and George Atchison—see Brink, McDonough, *Hist. of St. Clair County,* 69. Presumably the same men were made justices of the Quarter Sessions, but no record evidence exists to prove this. At any rate when an Orphans' Court was proclaimed open on August 5, 1796 it was by Dumoulin, Bond, Piggott, and Atchison—*Orphans' Court 1797-1809,* p. 1. And neither St. Clair nor Saucier ever sat in that court (which was held by justices of the Quarter Sessions—*ante,* cxlvii, n. 4). Those sitting are indicated in the table.

39. James Piggott, according to Reynolds, was born in Connecticut, and served in the privateering service in the Revolution—*My Own Times,* 33. His commissions as captain in the Pennsylvania infantry in 1776 are still preserved, and he served under General St. Clair in 1776-1777—Alvord, *Cahokia Records (I. H. C., 2),* 190 n. There is no evidence to support Reynolds' statement that he served with George Rogers Clark— no more than in the cases of William Biggs, George Atchison, and Nicholas Jarrot—English, *Conquest of the Northwest,* 1067. Piggott himself declared that he settled in Illinois in 1780—Alvord, *op. cit.,* 191 n., citing *Pap. of Old Congress.* His various appearances in the Cahokia Records are never favorable. He was leader in 1787 of the movement by disgruntled Americans to make Grand Ruisseau independent of the French court at Cahokia, which that court promptly and decisively checked, holding him for 24 hours in irons at Cahokia by way of giving meaning to orders that he cease from further insubordination on pain of expulsion from the district and confiscation of his property. See Alvord, *op. cit.,* cxlix, 599 *et seq.,* and index. He signed the Tardiveau land contract of 1787—Alvord, *Kaskaskia Records (I. H. C., 5),* 444; the first board of land commissioners confirmed to his heirs his claim as a head of family before 1788—*Amer. State Papers: Pub Lands,* 2: 164; list compiled by William St. Clair in 1796—*Chic. Hist. Colls.,* 4: 208; cp. Alvord, *Cahokia Records (I. H. C., 2),* 289 *et seq.* When Governor St. Clair, his old commander, came to the Illinois country in 1790 he appointed Piggott a captain of militia and a justice of the peace of St. Clair County on April 29, 1790—*St. Clair Papers,* 2: 165 n., and *ante,* clxii, n. 2. September 28, 1795, he was made a judge of the Common Pleas— commission in Brink, McDonough, *Hist. of St. Clair County,* 69; and presumably also a justice of the peace and of the Quarter Sessions, for he was one of the justices of the latter court who on August 5, 1796 proclaimed the opening of the Orphans' Court. He attended thereafter in February 1797 and in February 1799—St. Clair *Orphans' Court 1797-1809,* 1, 2, 9. In 1795 he established what was later famous as Wiggins Ferry to St. Louis. He died on February 20, 1799, leaving only $409 in personal property— Reynolds, *My Own Times,* 36; Bateman and Selby, *Hist. of St. Clair County,* 2: 761; Brink, McDonough, *Hist. of St. Clair County,* 83.

40. William Whiteside was the head of the numerous Whiteside family, which came from the frontier of North Carolina through Kentucky to Illinois. According to Governor Reynolds (whose brother Robert married a daughter of William Bolin Whiteside, son of William), he was a soldier in the Revolution, fought at King's Mountain, and settled in Illinois in 1792 (*My Own Times,* 109) or 1793 (*Pioneer History,* 185, 416). The whole family was conspicuous in Indian warfare, and William preeminently so— *ibid.,* 186-189. He is called both "captain" and "colonel"; the latter appar-

ently by courtesy only. He is stated by Reynolds to have been "a justice-of-the-peace and judge of the court of common-pleas"—*ibid.,* 190. Neither he nor Uel ever appears sitting in the latter court according to its *Order Book 1801-03* (January, 1801-March, 1803). They both did sit in the Orphans' Court—which they could do only as justices of the peace and of the Quarter Sessions in December, 1803, February 1804, and in May and June, 1805—*Orphans' Court 1797-1809,* 20, 21, 25, 27. No evidence exists to show an appointment of either to the Quarter Sessions, by Harrison; but Uel was made a justice of the peace in 1803 (Gibson, *Exec. Journal,* 116), and it is possible that St. Clair had given William some appointment. It is elsewhere stated—Brink, *Hist. of Madison County,* 76—that the latter was "justice of the peace, and judge of the court of common pleas of Monroe county" (created in 1816), and this may be true. William Whiteside died in 1815— Reynolds, *Pioneer History,* 190. Of Uel, who was also his son (*ibid.,* 188, 189 n.) practically nothing is known. (Washburne, *Edwards Papers,* 45, speaks of some Uel as the son of William Bolin). In Isaac Darneille's *Letters of Decius* he charged that Harrison made three of the Whiteside family justices of Quarter Sessions in order to curry popularity in St. Clair County, notwithstanding that all three had been indicted for horse stealing, though the trial had been continually deferred. Goebel, *Harrison,* 64. The third was doubtless William Bolin; but in the Orphans' Court, at least, he never sat. When Shadrach Bond Jr. was asked by Governor Edwards in 1809 to enter an election with William Bolin to settle their rivalry for the lieutenant-colonelcy of the St. Clair militia he refused, and protested in a letter which is quoted *ante,* app. n. 19. The matter is puzzling; for though the charges might possibly have been no more than a bit of the rancorous personal politics of the time, such charges were not likely to be made with impunity on the frontier, certainly not against a family like the Whitesides. Bolin Whiteside later took a prominent part in Illinois' participation in the War of 1812. See Reynolds, *My Own Times,* 84, 91, 94, 97; *Pioneer History,* 416-417. In 1822 a "William B. Whiteside" who, by the description, appears to have been William Bolin, was tried for burglary in Greene County, but the jury disagreed (he had a friend on it), and after the death of the complaining witness the case was dismissed; a fellow defendant—the complainant had testified that he recognized both—was, however, convicted. *Hist. of Greene and Jersey Counties* (Contin. Hist. Company, 1885), 599-600. William Whiteside was also the father of John D. Whiteside (1794-1850; state treasurer, 1837-1841) who had a distinguished political career. Some other William Whiteside signed an address to the "friends of Freedom" in Illinois when the constitutional convention had just assembled. He was from Madison County—Buck, *Illinois in 1818,* 261 n.—to which the home of William Bolin Whiteside and Samuel Whiteside (cousin of William Bolin) had moved in 1802—Reynolds, *Pioneer History,* 416; Brink, *Hist. of Madison County,* 76.

41. William St Clair was a younger son of the Earl of Roslin and cousin of Governor St. Clair—Alvord, *Illinois Country,* 404 n.—who wrote of him in 1799: "He was formerly a resident at Detroit, and was obliged to leave it, for refusing to serve in the militia to aid the savages against this part of the country, and threw himself on my protection." He had but very recently settled in Cahokia (if indeed he had already gone there)— *St. Clair Papers,* 2: 441—when, on April 29, 1790, he was appointed pro-thonotary and clerk of the Common Pleas of St. Clair County, and on May 7 recorder of deeds—*St. Clair Papers,* 2: 165 n., 166 n. His difficulties with Judge Turner in connection with the territorial records are referred to *ante,* ccvi, n. 2. September 28, 1795 he was named chief judge of the

Common Pleas—Brink, McDonough, *Hist. of St. Clair County,* 69. He must have been made, also, at this time or shortly thereafter, judge of probate, for he appears as such when the Orphans' Court was proclaimed open on August 5, 1796—St. Clair *Orphans' Court 1797-1809,* 1; John Dumoulin being ordered on February 23, 1797 to surrender to him the records of that office—*ibid.,* 2. He appears acting as the probate judge in April, 1797—Brink, McDonough, *op. cit.,* 82. Miss Allinson states that he was also named in 1795 a justice of Quarter Sessions—Ill. State Hist. Soc. *Trans.* (1907), p. 290; but, inasmuch as he never sat in the Orphans' Court, this seems improbable. In February, 1799 Governor St. Clair wrote of him and Jacob Burnet to President Adams as "two young gentlemen of the bar, and of handsome abilities," and of the former as then "in trade"—*St. Clair Papers,* 2: 441. His will, of January 12, 1799, is printed in Brink, McDonough, *op. cit.,* 82-83. John Hay was one of the subscribing witnesses and an executor. In fact he was dead when Governor St. Clair wrote his letter. On February 8, 1799 George Wallis presented letters granted by "the deceased William St. Clair, Judge of Probate"—*Orphans' Court 1797-1809,* 9. In December 1801 his property was sold to satisfy creditors, and in the following June John Hay rendered his final account—*ibid.,* 15, 16. See also the *Order Book* of the Common Pleas, 13 (September 7, 1801).

42. The first five judges named were appointed on August 1, 1800—Gibson, *Exec. Journal,* 92. There were no reappointments, such as were made in St. Clair County, during the further existence of the Quarter Sessions. Further details appear in the biographical memoranda below.

43. John Edgar was born in Ireland; according to his first wife, in 1733, though he claimed greater youth when he remarried. When he came to America, and whether he married his first wife in Boston before or after 1781, does not appear—J. H. Roberts, "The Life and Times of General John Edgar," Ill. State Hist. Soc. *Trans.* (1907), p. 68. According to his own affidavit he commanded from 1772 to 1775 a British public vessel on Lakes Huron and Erie, engaged then in trade, was arrested in Detroit in August 1779 for correspondence with Americans (other documents in the Draper Collection show that he aided American prisoners to escape), was imprisoned for about two years, and escaped in September 1781—*ibid.,* 66-67. Roberts could find no evidence in Canada, England or this country to substantiate Edgar's naval service either for Great Britain or the United States—*ibid.,* 65-66, 68, 70; cp. Alvord, *Cahokia Records (I. H. C., 2),* cxxxiii, n. 3—repeating the story as to 1772-1775, though citing the Roberts' study. His name does not appear in Edward W. Callahan's *List of Officers of the Navy of the United States and of the Marine Corps from 1775 to 1900,* compiled from the official records of the Navy Department. Congress, however, on May 26, 1830 granted him a pension as "an acting Captain in the Navy, during the revolutionary war"—*U. S. Stat. at Large,* 6: 427 and 4: 269-270. His administrators collected the full amount, $2291.33, after his death—McDonough, *Hist. of Randolph, Monroe and Perry Counties,* 117 n. He made known upon escaping to this country the correspondence (which he supposed treasonable) between Vermonters and the British in Canada—Roberts, *loc. cit.,* 66-67, 69. This was not, however, a novelty. Congress had received full information from the Vermont negotiators nine months earlier; indeed most of Edgar's details were matters of public suspicion six months earlier. Hiland Hall, *The History of Vermont,* 347-349, 363-364; S. Williams, *The Natural and Civil History of Vermont*—1809 ed.—2: 204 *et seq.,* and 214 n. Edgar's affidavit left no trace in either the regular or the secret *Journals of Congress.* He immediately began pressing upon Congress relief for the losses he had suffered through his attachment to the American cause; and,

upon a committee report "that his peculiar sufferings . . . requires the particular attention of Congress," it was resolved that the Superintendent of Finance should give him "assistance . . . for his support," not exceeding one year, until he should secure employment—W. C. Ford, *Journals of the Continental Congress*, 22: 61 (January 29, 1782), 201 (April 20, 1782). After Congress had on April 23, 1783 and again on June 30, 1786 resolved to aid the Canadian refugees as soon as possible—*ibid.*, 24: 268-269; *Journals of Congress* (Folwell ed.), 8: 144; 11: 95—by act of April 7, 1798 relief was provided, and by supplementary act of February 18, 1801—which provided more generous relief—Edgar received 2,240 acres of land; which was the largest amount granted, and only to five persons. *U. S. Stat. at Large*, 1: 547; 2: 101. (Roberts' quotation, *loc. cit.*, 69, is not in the statute he indicates, nor in any of the other sources here cited). By no means all of Edgar's fortune was confiscated. He came to Kaskaskia in 1784 with a stock of goods, and money that enabled him to begin business in a large way—*Amer. State Papers: Pub. Lands*, 2: 132 n.; Reynolds, *op. cit.*, 116; Roberts, *loc. cit.*, 70. His donation claims both under his militia right and a head of family before 1788 were affirmed by the land commissioners— *Amer. State Papers: Pub. Lands*, 2: 168, 227. He engaged in the local and Indian trade; operated the largest—and one of the few—flour mill in Illinois, shipping great quantities of flour to New Orleans; and engaged in land speculation on a vast scale. For many years he was the wealthiest man in Illinois—Reynolds, *op. cit.*, 116-117. His trading practices did not meet with the approval of Father St. Pierre, minister at Kaskaskia, who denounced them repeatedly (1785) as stealing; no doubt judging him by unworldly standards. Alvord, *Kaskaskia Records (I. H. C.*, 5), 522-532. When John Rice Jones came to Illinois in 1786 to purchase provisions for George Rogers Clark's Wabash expedition Edgar guaranteed his purchases— Alvord, *Cahokia Records (I. H. C.*, 2) cxxxiii. In other ways he proved his patriotism. When the Kaskaskians prayed Major Hamtramck in 1789 to send 21 soldiers to relieve them from anarchy, Edgar offered to provision them, taking in payment bills on Congress—Alvord, *Kaskaskia Records (I. H. C.*, 5), 511; though he knew that such advances to George Rogers Clark, a few years earlier, had ruined the richest French families of Illinois. The Spanish authorities across the Mississippi were making strenuous efforts to attract population from the Illinois villages; offering free land, and to Edgar freedom in addition to work the lead and salt mines, all untaxed. These offers he refused—*ibid.*, 516. In 1785 he wrote to George Rogers Clark: "it is impossoble to live here if we have not ragluer Justice very Soon." Alvord, *Kaskaskia Records (I. H. C.*, 2), 376. It is very much to his credit that he gave no countenance to John Dodge, and that on the whole he stood for the French party and upheld the French court against the subversive tendencies of the restless American squatters. Alvord, *Cahokia Records (I. H. C.*, 2), cxxxv, cxlii; *Kaskaskia Records (I. H. C.*, 5), 376 n., 430. In 1789 he wrote to Major Hamtramck: "I have waited five years in hopes of a Government; I shall wait until March . . . but if no succour nor government should then arrive, I shall be compelled to abandon the country, & I shall go to live at St. Louis. Inclination, interest & love for the country prompt me to reside here, but when in so doing it is ten to one but both my life & property will fall a sacrifice, you nor any impartial mind can blame me for the part I shall take." *Ibid.*, 514. There is no reason to doubt the sincerity of his assurance to George Rogers Clark: "There is Nothing that I would not do to Serve General Clark, & my Country"— *ibid.*, 395. It must be said, however, that remaining behind when his French neighbors crossed the Mississippi did not serve him ill. The claim lists of the land commissioners show that the wealth of the Bauvais and other once-dominant French families passed to Edgar and fellow land-jobbers. Indeed the commissioners declared that the speculators (and, though unnamed, Edgar was the greatest) stimulated the terror of the emigrants—*ante,* lxxv. Be that as it may, Governor St. Clair came to. Kaskaskia in March, 1790 and Edgar stayed. On April 29, 1790 he was appointed a captain of militia, judge of the Common Pleas, and justice of Quarter Sessions—*St. Clair Papers,* 2: 165 n. He was chief-justice of the Kaskaskia district—*ante,* cxlvii, n. 3. August 13, 1792 he was appointed, with Antoine Girardin of Cahokia, a county commissioner, "to license merchants, traders, and tavern-keepers"— *St. Clair Papers,* 2: 311 n.; cp. Brink, McDonough, *Hist. of St. Clair County,* 83. No doubt (the records seem lost) he was reappointed to both courts in 1795 when Randolph County was created. We find him acting as a justice of the peace (e.g. *Chic. Hist. Colls.,* 4: 204, 222, both of 1797); and a man so prominent, if a justice, would undoubtedy have been of the "quorum," i.e. of the court—*ante,* clxi-iii, cci. We find him sitting, too, in the Common Pleas—Randolph *Common Pleas,* 1: 32 (April, 1798), 67 (January, 1800), etc. In an action recorded in the Randolph *Common Pleas,* 2: 120, Charles Gratiot *v.* John Rice Jones, the defendant craved oyer of the writ, which concluded: "Witness John Edgar Esquire first Justice of our said court . . . the fifteenth day of July . . . one thousand eight hundred." Defendant pleaded (in part) that Edgar "was not at that day a Justice of the said court of common pleas." The plea was in effect overruled, but— coming from Jones—it leaves one doubting whether Edgar had in fact received an appointment before Harrison's, of August 1, 1800. Edgar was also, apparently, one of the "notaries" (the Randolph *Deed Record J.* shows him acting as such) whom Governor St. Clair appointed to give effect to the Ordinance's guaranty to the French inhabitants of their ancient forms of conveyance—*St. Clair Papers,* 2: 172-173. For this he was unfitted; an Anglo-American deed seems to exercise a peculiar fascination upon non-legal minds—Edgar used it even to manumit a slave. The Northwest Territory passed under representative government in 1799 and Edgar represented Randolph County in the first House of Representatives—Burnet, *Notes,* 289; *St. Clair Papers,* 2: 439 n. In 1800 he was made first judge of both the county courts and judge of probate—Gibson, *Exec. Journal,* 92, 93. He had already risen to the chief command of the Randolph militia—St. Clair to President Adams, March 30, 1800, *St. Clair Papers,* 2: 495 (compare the words with which he characterized Edgar and Dumoulin). He held his judicial offices until the creation of the new Common Pleas became effective with the beginning of 1806: i.e., for fifteen years—not twenty-five, as stated by Roberts, *loc. cit.,* 71, and by Alvord, *Cahokia Records,* (*I. H. C.,* 2), cxxxiii n. He was not then reappointed. In this politics of course played a part; no man, certainly not another politician like Harrison, could have overlooked Edgar's political activity—*ante,* xxv, n. 1. Neither could his moral deficiencies be ignored. It is lamentable that a record on the whole good should have been ruined by the temptations of the land donations; but Edgar's record is beyond explanation or palliation; it was full of fraud on an immense scale—*ante,* lxxxiii, lxxxvi, lxxxviii, lxxxix, n. 1, xc. It is said that after the creation of Illinois Territory he again served as a member of the county court—McDonough, *Hist. of Randolph, Monroe and Perry Counties,* 125. On December 16, 1817 he was appointed, as from October 10, 1816, brigadier-general of the first regiment of militia of Illinois Territory—U. S. Senate, *Exec. Journal,* 3: 98, 99. He died on December 19, 1830—McDonough, *Hist. of Randolph, Monroe and Perry Counties,* 117 n.

44. William Morrison, the leading merchant of early Illinois, was a Pennsylvanian who settled at Kaskaskia in 1790—Reynolds, *Pioneer History,* 160, *My Own Times,* 112; *Amer. State Papers: Pub. Lands,* 2: 132 n. In 1793 he was licensed as a merchant—Brink, McDonough, *Hist. of St. Clair County,* 83; but presumably he had entered trade immediately upon his arrival. In partnership with his uncle, Guy Bryan (not "Bryant"), of Philadelphia, he maintained stores in both Kaskaskia and Cahokia which were wholesale providers for the Indian trade and for all the nearby settlements across the Mississippi, and shipped to the east and south the furs, lead, and flour of Illinois and Missouri. The law reports of Randolph and St. Clair counties are full of their law suits. Their business extended to Pittsburgh, New Orleans, Prairie du Chien, and the Rocky Mountains. They entered the last field in 1804 (though from the beginning they had doubtless sold to the trans-Mississippi Indians). Reynolds is apparently correct in stating that Morrison (Bryan remained in the east) "was the first who laid the foundation of the commerce across the plains from the Mississippi Valley to New Mexico"—*My Own Times,* 112; *Pioneer History,* 161-163; Elliott Coues, *The Expeditions of Zebulon Montgomery Pike,* 2: 500-502, 602-603. His militia right—for enrollment in August, 1790, and actual service—was recognized by the first board of land commissioners— *Amer. State Papers: Pub. Lands,* 2: 171; however, on the Kaskaskia militia roll compiled by Governor St. Clair when there in October 1795, he appears as "Etable Depuis 1790"—*Chic. Hist. Colls.,* 4: 213; while in another sworn to before John Edgar and William Morrison in 1797 the latter appears with no such comment—*ibid.,* 221. He must have been appointed by Governor St. Clair a justice of Quarter Sessions in 1795; at least he acted in this period as a justice of the peace (e.g. *Chic. Hist. Colls.,* 4: 204, 222, in 1797), and he was too important to be omitted from the quorum. He also sat in the Common Pleas—*Common Pleas,* 1: 67 (January, 1800), 73 (July, 1798), etc. Governor Harrison appointed him on August 1, 1800 to both the county courts—Gibson, *Exec. Journal,* 92, 93; before November 28, 1801, when his successor was appointed—*ibid.,* 105. He and John Edgar were chief of the "Edgar-Morrison" faction, which stood for slavery and division of the territory, and was unfriendly to Harrison. This alone is doubtless sufficient to explain his omission from the reconstituted county court of 1806—see *ante,* cci. But his land record was also decidedly bad—*ante,* lxxxv. A William Morrison (possibly his son) is stated to have been a member of the Randolph Common Pleas as reestablished in 1814—McDonough, *Hist. of Randolph, Monroe and Perry Counties,* 181. In later years he devoted himself mainly to his commercial enterprises. In 1827 and 1830 he appears in the federal statutes as an army contractor—*U. S. Stat. at Large,* 6: 361, 442. He died in April, 1837.

45. Nathaniel Hull was born in Massachusetts, and according to Reynolds came to Illinois in 1780—*Pioneer History,* 207. His only appearance in the *Kaskaskia Records* is in 1787—Alvord (*I. H. C.,* 5), 444— when he signed the Tardiveau contract. In 1790 he was listed, most reliably, as having been a head of family in Prairie du Rocher on or before 1783, and as an ensign in James Piggott's militia company—*Chic. Hist. Colls.,* 4: 204, 214. His family right was confirmed (to John Edgar) by the first board of land commissioners—*Amer. State Papers: Pub. Lands,* 2: 163; Governor St. Clair must have appointed him in 1795 to the Common Pleas, since he is found on its bench—Randolph *Common Pleas,* 1: 32, 73, 67 (April 1798, July 1798, January 1800) ; and it is a safe prediction that he was also a justice of the Quarter Sessions. On August 1, 1800 Governor Harrison made him a judge of both courts—Gibson, *Exec. Journal,* 92,

93. According to Governor Reynolds "he possessed a character for probity and integrity that was recognized by all," and "was for many years the main pillar of the Randolph-County court"—*Pioneer History*, 208. It is believed that both these statements are just. On his showing with the land commissioners see *ante*, xc. He rarely sat in court after 1803. He was active as an Indian fighter, but his military career was not exceptional. St. Clair made him an ensign in 1790—*St. Clair Papers, 2*: 166 n.; and Harrison, in 1802, a captain—Gibson, *Exec. Journal*, 110. According to Reynolds—*op. cit.*, 208—he lived until 1806. As late as 1810 Shadrach Bond Sr. appeared as his surviving executor—Randolph *County Court Record, 1810,* 116 (November 5, 1810). See also McDonough, *Hist. of Randolph, Monroe and Perry Counties*, 76.

46. Robert McMahon was born in Virginia, removed to Kentucky, and thence in 1793 or 1794 to Illinois. In 1795 his wife and six children were killed or captured by the Indians; he himself was also made prisoner, but escaped—such instances explain of course the treatment of the Indians in the courts: *ante*, clxxxv, n. 1. On August 1, 1800 he was made a judge of both county courts of Randolph— Gibson, *Exec. Journal*, 92, 93. There is no evidence that discredits Governor Reynolds' statement that he "executed the duties of these offices with punctuality and honesty"; nor does he seem to have been active in politics. Nevertheless he was not reappointed in 1805. He died in 1822. See Reynolds, *Pioneer History*, 193-197; McDonough, *Hist. of Randolph, Monroe and Perry Counties*, 67. In *My Own Times*, 103-104, Reynolds tells a bedroom story of "backwoods' merriment" of which McMahon was the butt, and which illustrates not only the coarse humor of the time but also the little respect which a judge, even "rather a dignified character," inspired in a pioneer community.

47. Robert Reynolds, father of Governor Reynolds, was born in Ireland. In 1788 the family moved to eastern Tennessee, and in 1800 to Illinois, settling first in Randolph and in 1807 in St. Clair County. According to the Governor he was induced to stay at Kaskaskia, in part (instead of going on into upper Louisiana), by John Edgar, Robert Morrison and other leading men of that community. It must have been due to them that he was appointed a judge of the two county courts—November 28, 1801: Gibson, *Exec. Journal,* 105. He attended very regularly to his duties. Some minor irregularities of judicial decorum are referred to *ante*, ccx, n. 3. In December, 1802 he was chosen one of Randolph's delegates to the Vincennes slavery convention—Reynolds, *My Own Times,* 67; Dunn, *Indiana*, 304. He was not reappointed to the reorganized and united county court of 1806. This was doubtless in part due to his affiliation with the anti-Harrison party. He was very ardent in politics, and various details in the records show that his friends were of the Edgar-Morrison, not of the Menard-Fisher, group; also, he signed most of the prodivision petitions—note list of signatures, *ante*, liii, n. 4 (and apparently was responsible for some of their irregularities—*ante*, xlvii, n. 1). But his land frauds also barred his reappointment. The boldness displayed in these, in their maintenance as much as their commission, and very likely politics in addition—for in all those cases prosecuted there were forgeries of the name of Pierre Menard (which, however, was equally true of some of Edgar's deeds)—presumably explain why he alone was indicted under the perjury and forgery statutes; for his operations were small as compared with John Edgar's. *Ante*, lxxxv, lxxxvi, xc, xci, clxxix and n. 1. Besides, by 1803 or 1804 he had begun to drink to excess—Reynolds, *My Own Times,* 49-50; J. F. Snyder, *Adam W. Snyder*, 300, 314 n. He was pensioned as a Revolutionary soldier by act of Congress of June 30, 1834—*U. S. Stat. at*

Large, 6: 585. He was living in 1814 (Snyder, *op. cit.,* 314 n.) but his son nowhere gives the date of his death. According to the Governor he "possessed a good English education," though no library in the Governor's youth; and, in his later years "read much and wrote essays for the papers" *Pioneer History,* 300. Most of Governor Reynolds' excellent traits of character—his complete abstinence from liquor and gambling after his early manhood, his discretions in land speculation (for a forgery case in which his name was involved, *ante,* xcviii), and complete cessation therein when he assumed judicial duties, his rigid financial probity in public office, and very likely too the admirable character of his home life—were evidently due to the warnings of his father's career. Cp. *My Own Times,* 52, 110; *Pioneer History,* 352; J. F. Snyder, *Adam W. Snyder,* 312, 314 and n. The rarity of his references to his father, amid the vast reminiscences of his contemporaries is extremely noticeable.

48. John Beaird was born in Virginia, removed in 1787 to Tennessee, and later to Kentucky, and finally to Randolph County in 1801. While in Tennessee he had been a representative in the legislature, and very prominent in Indian warfare. In 1793, when in command of a punitive expedition against some Indian raiders, he precipitated border war by killing indiscriminately a group of principal chiefs who had assembled at the express order of the President. He was court martialed, but not punished. J. G. M. Ramsey, *The Annals of Tennessee,* 577-578, 624, 626; James Phelan, *Hist. of Tennessee,* 157. On December 25, 1802, upon the recommendation of the court of Quarter Sessions—*ante,* xix, n. 2—he was appointed a member of both county courts; the governor preferring him to James Morrison (brother of William and Robert) and Thomas Todd (one of the very early pioneers)—*Court Record, 1802-06,* 8, and Gibson, *Exec. Journal,* 114. A peculiarity in his appointment is noted, *ante,* clxii. He was faithful in his attendance, and there is nothing to indicate that he was other than a satisfactory judge. He was not reappointed to the reorganized court in 1805. One judges from the statements of Governor Reynolds, who was intimately associated for years with his son, that he was of less education than several of his fellow judges. He died in the second half of 1809—Randolph *County Commissioners, 1809-10,* 122; *County Court Record 1810,* 9. He was connected by marriage with Robert Reynolds. See Reynolds, *Pioneer History,* 310-312.

49. James McRoberts was born on May 22, 1760 in Scotland, and came with his family in 1772 to Pennsylvania. He fought in the Revolution from 1777-1781, and continued in the army until 1783. He removed to Kentucky in 1788, thence to Illinois in 1797, according to Reynolds. But the second board of land commissioners confirmed his donation claim under a militia right (as it had been confirmed by the governor the first board did not deal with it)—*Amer. State Papers: Pub. Lands,* 2: 236; which required militia service before August 1, 1790. He appears on the general militia list of St. Clair—*Chic. Hist. Colls.,* 4: 225. On April 4, 1804 he was appointed a judge of the Quarter Sessions (but not of the Common Pleas)—Gibson, *Exec. Journal,* 123. He was not reappointed in 1805. He died in September, 1846. Two of his sons had distinguished political careers. The fact that both were graduates of Transylvania University throws light upon the father. See Reynolds, *Pioneer History,* 300-303. There is a James McRoberts on two lists of American residents in the Illinois country prepared in 1787—Alvord, *Kaskaskia Records (I. H. C.,* 5), 423, 444. As Reynolds states that McRoberts visited Kaskaskia in 1789 (but returned to Kentucky after exploring "the Northwest and the Spanish country west of the Mississippi"), it is probable that his visit was actually in

1787. The confirmation of his militia claim must have been connected with his visit. He seems to have served again as a county judge under the Illinois Territory—McDonough, *Hist. of Randolph, Monroe and Perry Counties,* 125; Reynolds says that he was "elected to the office of county-judge under the State government." He was a slaveholder—McDonough, *op. cit.,* 133.

50. John Grosvenor (who signed his name both with and without, but more often with, the *s*) went from Connecticut to Illinois at least as early as 1799—under circumstances which, Governor Reynolds hints, would today be a violation of the Mann Act, but were then still a matter of individual liberty, and which left him, in the Governor's habitually generous judgment "an honest, correct man, moral in all things." Reynolds, *Pioneer History,* 184. Appointed to both of the county courts on February 16, 1805—Gibson, *Exec. Journal,* 126—and not reappointed the same year to the reorganized Common Pleas, he served for but a few months. He was fairly regular in attendance in the courts, but some of his professional shortcomings, and violations of the law as an innkeeper, are noted *ante,* clxxx, n. 1; clxxxi, n. 1. On his land record, *ante,* lxxxviii. He was of the Edgar-Morrison political faction, signing various prodivision (and proslavery) petitions— *ante,* liii, n. 4; liv, n. 1; and seems, in personal relations to have been near to Robert Reynolds and John Beaird.

51. Jean Baptiste Barbau's is one of the most honorable names in the early history of Illinois. He was probably born in New Orleans, whither his parents had emigrated from France, about 1720. Alvord, *Cahokia Records (I. H. C.,* 2), lvi and n., cxxxii and n. He was a member of the British court created at Kaskaskia in 1768 by Lieutenant-colonel Wilkins (abolished in 1770), at which time he was a captain of militia—*ibid.,* lxi; *Kaskaskia Records (I. H. C.,* 5), 18, 69. On May 19, 1779 he was elected from Prairie du Rocher—under the description "captain of the militia and commandant of this village"—as a member and first-judge of the Virginia court set up at Kaskaskia by County-lieutenant John Todd—*ibid.,* 85, 86. He was not reëlected on June 18, 1782, as the policy of rotation was adopted—*ibid.,* 291-292. One of the fraudulent land claims of William Kelly, *ante,* xc, n. 4, included an acknowledgment before Barbau in 1782 when he was not a magistrate—*Amer. State Papers: Pub. Lands,* 2: 130, cl. 887. He was the undisputed leader of the French party throughout the chaotic maladministration, pillage, and disorder of the years 1782-1790—Alvord, *Kaskaskia Records (I. H. C.,* 5), index *s. v.* Barbau. It was he who was "called upon to lead the French in their struggle for political liberty"— Alvord, *Illinois Country,* 367; and when Timothé de Monbreun was forced to resign on August 14, 1786 he commissioned Barbau to take his place as deputy lieutenant and commandant of the County of Illinois—Alvord, *Kaskaskia Records (I. H. C.,* 5), 232, 390, 396, 580. His powers nominally ceased, necessarily, when Congress created a government for the Northwest Territory, theoretically, in 1787, but the long delay in actually extending administration to the Illinois country only increased the anarchy of the last years preceding 1790; cp. John Edgar's letters quoted above in app. n. 43. Governor St. Clair named him on April 29, 1790 as a judge of the Common Pleas, but not of the Quarter Sessions, the criminal court—*St. Clair Papers,* 2: 165 n.; *ante,* app. n. 38. It is indicated *ante,* cxlvii, n. 3— the vast extent of the county rendering administration according to the letter of the statute impossible—the Governor divided it into three districts, one with Prairie du Rocher as its center, over the courts of which Barbau presided. He is described in this period as "judge and president of the district of Prairie du Rocher"—Alvord, *Kaskaskia Records (I. H. C.,* 5), 322 n.; Reynolds, *Pioneer History,* 180. According to Miss Allinson he was not

included in the appointments to the St. Clair courts in 1795—Ill. State Hist. Soc. *Trans.* (1907), p. 290; and this—which is as it should be, for Prairie du Rocher fell within the new county of Randolph whose creation necessitated new appointments—is confirmed by his absence from the St. Clair *Orphans' Court: 1797-1809* record. On the other hand he sat in the Randolph Common Pleas before 1800. Similar facts regarding Dumoulin and various other personages of St. Clair County have been treated as sufficient evidence of their appointment in 1795 to the Quarter Sessions of that county—since they sat in the Orphans' Court : *ante,* app. notes 18, 28, 29, 31, 38, 39. But such an assumption proves unfounded in the case of Barbau and Louviere; for they continued to sit in the court after 1800, notwithstanding that Harrison gave them no appointments as judges, though he did appoint Barbau (if it was not his son) a justice of the peace on October 27, 1801—Gibson, *Exec. Journal,* 104. Louviere had no appointment whatever. That the explanation is probably to be found in their old commissions as justices of the peace is suggested *ante,* cci, n. 2. Barbau sat in the Quarter Sessions as late as March 1805 (*Court Record: 1802-06,* 10, June, 1803; 39, December, 1803; 77, March 5, 1805). The extraordinary omission of honorable and distinguished Frenchmen from Governor St. Clair's appointments in 1795 is noted *ante,* ccxix, n. 2. No instance is more remarkable than Barbau's. In 1802 Harrison appointed him captain in the Randolph militia—Gibson, *Exec. Journal,* 110. Barbau died in 1810—Alvord, *Cahokia Records* (*I. H. C.,* 2), lvi, n.; cxxxii. On April 17, 1810 letters of administration were granted to his widow—Randolph *County Court Record 1810,* 28. His record as a judge, citizen and man is apparently stainless. The first board of land commissioners—*ante,* lxxxvii, n. 1—frequently used his testimony to disprove fraudulent claims. Strange to say, there do not seem to have been presented, by him or others, any donation claims based upon his militia right; but his family right was affirmed by the first board—*Amer. State Papers: Pub. Lands,* 2: 162. He wrote an educated French style—see for example Alvord, *Kaskaskia Records* (*I. H. C.,* 5), 398; and his written English was decidedly superior to that of John Edgar and various others of the American leaders of the time—cp. Alvord, *Cahokia Records* (*I. H. C.,* 2), cxxxiv and *ante,* app. n. 43.

52. Of Antoine Duchaufour de Louviere less is known than of Barbau. He was also a resident of Prairie du Rocher. Though not an original member of the court established in 1768 under the British régime by Lieutenant-colonel Wilkins, he became a member in the winter of 1769-1770—Alvord, *Illinois Country,* 267. With Barbau he was elected on May 19, 1779 as a member of Todd's court at Kaskaskia—Alvord, *Cahokia Records* (*I. H. C.,* 2), lxi; *Kaskaskia Records* (*I. H. C.,* 5), 85, 86; and served the full term of three years, but was not reëlected—*ibid.,* 291-292, 419 n. On April 29, 1790 Governor St. Clair appointed him one of the judges of the Quarter Sessions, but not of the Common Pleas—*St. Clair Papers,* 2: 165 n. Thus, according to the record, Barbau should have presided over the civil, and Louviere over the criminal, courts in the district of Prairie du Rocher. With respect to his status after 1795 what is said in the preceding note of Barbau applies also to Louviere. He died some time before March 1802, for a sheriff's return on a writ of that date is found in a suit by his administrator in the Randolph *Common Pleas*—4: pl. 27 (June, 1803).

53. Of Samuel Cochran nothing seems to be known save his service in the court—Gibson, *Exec. Journal,* 132, 143. He was conspicuously conscientious in his attendance. There are two Cochrans who left traces in the *Kaskaskia Records* (*I. H. C.,* 5)—see index—and he was probably of the same family.

54. The earliest appearance of James Finney noted in the records is as foreman of a petty jury in the June term, 1803—Randolph *Court Record 1802-06, 23.* Various documents in the *Amer. State Papers: Pub. Lands,* vol. 2 (pp. 132, 134, 136-137, 205-208) show a "J." Finney acting as the deputy-clerk of the first board of land commiss.oners in 1805 to 1809. He was appointed by the board (*Annals,* 8 Congress, 1 session, 1287). It is assumed that the jury foreman and the clerk of the land board are the same James Finney (no "John" anywhere appears) whom Harrison appointed coroner of Randolph County in November, 1806 and judge of the Common Pleas a year later—Gibson, *Exec. Journal,* 137, 143. Like Cochran he was extremely faithful in attendance. In 1807 he was the second choice of the House of Representatives (George Fisher being the first) for appointment to the Council—Harrison, *Messages,* 1: 253, 263. A record made by one of the Morrisons of the events connected with the murder of Rice Jones quotes Finney as declaring that "if Dunlap was to go to heaven, he would get a higher seat in heaven than Jesus Christ, and be set at the right hand of God for killing Rice Jones"—*Chic. Hist. Colls.,* 4: 279. Whether he did or not say just this, it conveys a significant reflection of the incredibly bitter personalities which made up the "politics" of the day. Beginning in 1813 a James Finney served for many years as clerk of the county court of Johnson County—Palmer, *Bench and Bar,* 2: 872; and this might well be the Randolph County judge. On the other hand it is stated that—after serving from 1803 to 1809 as a county commissioner—James Finney was a member of the Common Pleas Court of Randolph County as reëstablished in 1814— McDonough, *Hist. of Randolph, Monroe and Perry Counties,* 125, 181.

55. See *ante,* app. notes 27, 42. Dates for appointments are taken from Gibson, *Exec. Journal.*

56. Among the many Mitchells of St. Clair County the only one possibly identifiable as this appointee is Peter Mitchell. He was an immigrant of 1797—Reynolds, *Pioneer History,* 237, 337; Brink, McDonough, *Hist. of St. Clair County,* 269. He is on the election roll of 1799—*ibid.,* 70; and is described as having served as justice of the peace—*ibid.,* 53. He was an unsuccessful candidate for the first General Assembly in 1818—*ibid.,* 72; a member of the temporary "court of justices" of St. Clair County in 1818— *ibid.,* 76; a county commissioner from 1826 to 1830—*ibid.,* 77. But Peter Mitchell is nowhere referred to as "Dr."

57. It is impossible to tell, because of the punctuation in Gibson's *Journal,* 132-133, whether Rue was an appo:ntee in Dearborn County or in St. Clair. The French name makes St. Clair probable. In Monks, *Courts,* 2: 632, he is assigned to Dearborn County.

58. John Hays was born in 1770 in New York City; was employed in the Indian trade of the Northwest while a youth; in 1793 settled in Cahokia and after acting for a time as clerk in John Hay's commerc:al house entered the Indian trade independently—Reynolds, *Pioneer History,* 223-225. On May 5, 1802 he was appointed by Harrison sheriff of St. Clair County— Gibson, *Exec. Journal,* 109; in which office he continued until after the inauguration of state government in 1818—Brink, McDonough, *Hist. of St. Clair County,* 72, 73, 76, 77. He was acting as sheriff as early as June, 1802—*Order Book* of Common Pleas, 120. In January 1814 he was made collector of direct taxes and internal revenue for Illinois Territory—U. S. Senate, *Exec. Journal,* 2: 457, 461 (confirmed January 22); on March 3, 1821 was confirmed as Indian agent at Fort Wayne, Indiana—*ibid.,* 3: 235, 255; on May 12, 1824, on January 21, 1828, and on April 26, 1832 was confirmed as receiver of public moneys at Jackson, Missouri (this is assumed to be the same John Hays)—*ibid.,* 3: 375-376, 586, 594; 4: 236, 242. Ac-

cording to Reynolds he was also, in early times, for many years postmaster in Cahokia. The same authority states that he died there, an old man. This is consistent with the statement in Brink, McDonough, *op. cit.,* 46, that he was a resident of Cahokia from 1798 to 1822 and again later, and died there.

59.   Caldwell Cairns was later one of the three judges of the first county court of St. Clair County under Illinois Territory, 1813 to 1816—Brink, McDonough, *Hist. of St. Clair County,* 76.

60.   This John "Kinzey" was not the John Kinzie of Chicago history—see A. T. Andreas, *History of Chicago,* 1: 72-75. And although the latter early established trading posts on the Kankakee, Rock, and Illinois rivers it seems that he could hardly have been the J. "Kinzie," described as "merchant," who was sued in the St. Clair Court, by John Lyle, administrator of Jean Baptiste Maillet (commandant at Peoria—Alvord, *Cahokia Records (I. H. C.,* 2), lvi, 230 n.; *St. Clair Papers,* 2: 138, 167 n. and *ante,* xii, n. 4.) for conversion in August 1801 of a stock of trading goods—*Order Book: 1801-03* of Common Pleas, 92. Accordingly, it seems probable that the defendant in that suit and the justice of the peace were one person. Nothing else appears regarding any John Kinzie in Illinois at this time. The stock of goods converted has some general interest: 33 3-4 yards of blue cloth, 1 1-4 do. of fine cloth, 10 3-4 do. molton, 9 1-2 do. spotted Kersey, 2 pair of 3-point blankets, 7 1-2 pr. of 2 1-2-point blankets, 3 pr. of 1 1-2-point blankets, 2 1-2 yd. striped cloth, 2 1-4 yd. scarletts, 3 black silk handkerchiefs, 4 1-2 yd. calico, 1 roll red teritan, 2 dowgaines, and 10 butcher knives, 4 "paper looking-glasses," 5 black ostrich feathers, 18 1-2 pr. large ear bobs, 19 1-2 pr. common ditto, 8 steels to strike fire, 168 large silver brooches, 129 common ditto, 4 screws for fusils, 10 oz. small beads, 9 boxes of combs, 1-4 lb. vermillion, 3-4 lb. white thread, 3-4 piece ribband, 59 needles, 1 spur, 5 doz. buttons, 13 gun flints, 13 3-4 lb. ball, 104 doe, 4 buck, 3 raccoon, and 1 muskrat skin. Declared value, $1000; verdict that "the goods were worth $393 according to the Value of the same."

61.   See *ante,* ccviii.

62.   Probably this was Jean Baptiste Barbau Sr.—*ante,* app. n. 51. Possibly it was his son. Three generations of the same name appear as early as in the census of Prairie du Rocher in 1787—Alvord, *Kaskaskia Records (I. H. C.,* 5), 419: the "Mr. Barbau pere" of that census is the noted French leader, the "Mr. barbau fils" is the son now referred to. He appears infrequently in the records—*ibid.,* 292, 442.

63.   The Gilbreath family, according to Reynolds, came to Illinois in 1804—*Pioneer History,* 398. If this be correct it is rather remarkable that James Gilbreath should have been made a justice of the peace in April, coroner in July, and sheriff in October, 1806 of Randolph County—Gibson, *Exec. Journal,* 133, 135, 137. The first appointment might well have been made upon petition of his neighbors; the others would seemingly require some extraordinary qualities. Of these, and of his antecedents, we have no knowledge. He signed the petition of 1807 opposing division—see *ante,* xlvi, notes 1 and 2; and probably signed no prodivision petition except that of 1803 for annexation to Louisiana—*ante,* lix, n. 2. His record before the land commissioners was not creditable—*ante,* lxxxiv. Yet he held the very important office of sheriff through the remainder of the Indiana Territory period. On his alleged complicity in the Rice Jones murder, and party affiliations, see *ante,* xciv, n. 2 and see also *ante,* clxxix, n. 3. He served as a county commissioner of Randolph County from 1803 to 1809—McDonough, *Hist. of Randolph, Monroe and Perry Counties,* 125. He was a member of the second territorial General Assembly (November 14-

December 24, 1814), from which he was expelled, the reasons not appearing—McDonough, *op. cit.*, 40, 112. It is said that he built the first cotton gin in Illinois—Brink, McDonough, *Hist. of St. Clair County*, 53.

64. Paul Herlston (Harolson, etc.—the name was spelled with the most careless freedom—but he sometimes spelled it very plainly as Herlston) appears frequently in the early records. He served as a county commissioner in the period 1803-1809; and, as a justice of the peace, was a member of the first county court of Randolph as organized under the Illinois Territory, 1809—McDonough, *Hist. of Randolph, Monroe and Perry Counties*, 125, 181.

65. Frederick Graeter wrote a beautiful and cultivated hand. A Franz Graeter was licensed as a merchant at Cahokia in 1793—Brink, McDonough, *Hist. of St. Clair County*, 84. Frederick appears in land transactions in 1793 and 1794—*ibid.*, 87. The name does not appear in Alvord's *Cahokia and Kaskaskia Records*, as occurring before 1790.

66. The Langlois family was very numerous and important in Kaskaskia—see Alvord, *Kaskaskia Records* (*I. H. C.*, 5), index; but the identity and relationship of Audrien Langlois does not appear. He is presumably the Langlois charged by the Edgar-Morrison faction with complicity in the murder of Rice Jones—*ante*, xciv, n. 2.

67. Henry Levens is very prominent in the early records of Randolph County. He signed his own name variantly, and very plainly—"Levens" and "Leavens"; but the former more commonly. Some Henry Levens was in Illinois at least as early as 1787—Alvord, *Kaskaskia Records* (*I. H. C.*, 5), 444. Governor Reynolds, however, says that the well-known pioneer of that name immigrated from Pennsylvania in 1797. His grist and saw-mills were important in the economy of the territory; the latter was the only one in the country about 1800—Reynolds, *My Own Times*, 23; compare *ante*, cxxiv. As justice of the peace he was a member of the first county court under Illinois Territory in 1809—McDonough, *Hist. of Randolph, Monroe and Perry Counties*, 181. In 1818, a true pioneer, he moved to the frontier of Missouri—cp. Houck, *Missouri*, 3: 83. To Reynolds' sketch, which gives the character of the man well—*Pioneer History*, 157-159—it may be added that he was decidedly litigious. See *ante*, clxxvii, n. 2.

68. Hamlet Ferguson, as a justice of the peace, was a member of the new county court of Illinois Territory in 1809—McDonough, *Hist. of Randolph, Monroe and Perry Counties*, 125, later appears as a member of the first county court of Johnson County under the Illinois Territory, in July, 1813—Palmer, *Bench and Bar*, 2: 872; also as a delegate to the constitutional convention of 1818 from Pope County—Ill. State Hist. Society, *Journal*, 6: 358.

69. Samuel Omelvany, as a justice of the peace, was a member of the first county court of Randolph County under Illinois Territory—McDonough, *Hist. of Randolph, Monroe and Perry Counties*, 181. He was also a delegate from Pope County to the constitutional convention of 1818—Ill. State Hist. Society, *Journal*, 6: 358.

70. Robert Morrison was a brother of William Morrison, whom he followed to Kaskaskia from Pennsylvania in 1798—Reynolds, *Pioneer History*, 165. He was one of the three delegates of the county to the Vincennes convention in December, 1802—Reynolds, *My Own Times*, 67; Buck, *Illinois in 1818*, 186. He was a county commissioner from 1803 to 1809—McDonough, *Hist. of Randolph, Monroe and Perry Counties*, 125. He served as clerk of the Randolph courts of Indiana Territory from 1800 to 1809—Gibson, *Exec. Journal*, 93, 131 (though the appointment does not appear he served as clerk of the Common Pleas before 1805). After 1809 he was clerk of the General Court of Illinois Territory. On his land record see

ante, lxxxv, lxxxvi, xc, xci. For attempt to impeach him in 1808—*ante,* ccviii. He seems to have gained the confidence of Ninian Edwards soon after the latter came to Illinois. It was of his appointment to the office of adjutant-general of Illinois Territory (he served from July 18, 1809 to May 28, 1810—McDonough, *Hist. of Randolph, Monroe and Perry Counties,* 40) that Senator John Pope of Kentucky (brother of Nathaniel Pope) on November 9, 1809 wrote to Edwards: "I am sorry you removed Rector and appointed Morrison . . . The Rectors are honest men and would have been your firm friends. Morrison I know to be a scoundrel and will not be your friend unless you do the hundredth good turn and is identified with a party which will require more of you than you can do for them. Robert Morrison professed to be a friend to Nat. Pope, although Nat. would not speak to his brother, and clandestinely signed a petition to the executive containing some very strong representations against him . . . I saw the paper with his signature"—Washburne, *Edwards Papers,* 40. Alvord, *Illinois Country,* 431 n. refers to this letter as directed against Edwards' refusal to remove Morrison from the clerkship of the General Court; but no Rector held that position, whereas Elias Rector was adjutant-general from May 3 to July 18, 1809, and again from May 28, 1810 to October 25, 1813. McDonough, *op cit.,* 40. It looks as though the governor came to accept Senator Pope's views. And see *post,* app. n. 77, on Elias Rector. In 1818 he was an unsuccessful candidate for a United States senatorship—Buck, *Illinois in 1818,* 303. He died in Kaskaskia in 1842.

71. George Blair came to Illinois in 1796—Brink, McDonough, *Hist. of St. Clair County,* 51; Reynolds, *Pioneer History,* 377. Belleville was located on his land in 1814. Governor Reynolds' picture of him—in Brink, McDonough, *op. cit.,* 183-184—is unflattering. In 1818 he was one of a few signers of an address "to the friends of Freedom in the state of Illinois"—Buck, *Illinois in 1818,* 260-261; presumably, therefore, well-known for anti-slavery sentiments (as certainly various of the other signers were).

72. James Edgar was a brother of John. Aside from his service as sheriff—and that unsatisfactorily: see *ante,* lix—he left no traces in the records.

73. John Whiteside was a brother of William Whiteside (*ante,* app. n. 40), and, like him, had served in the Revolutionary War—Reynolds, *Pioneer History,* 185, 190. He was active as an Indian fighter—*ibid.,* 186. Otherwise his service as coroner gives him his only place in history. General Samuel Whiteside, of the Winnebago and Black Hawk wars, was his son.

74. Miles Hotchkiss was a prominent citizen, an innkeeper; repeatedly in trouble for violation of the liquor laws, and once for insulting the court; all of which—as pointed out *ante,* clxxx, n. 1; ccxi, n. 1—in the end involved no punishment at all. It is said that he was a member of the reorganized Common Pleas in 1814—McDonough, *Hist. of Randolph, Monroe and Perry Counties,* 181.

75. William Wilson was appointed, according to Gibson's *Exec. Journal,* 107, for St. Clair County; but "—Robinson" was appointed for Randolph County, "vice William Wilson whose commission is Revocked"—*ibid.,* 145. The reason for the revocation is shown *ante,* clxxvi, n. 4. For the reason indicated no attempt is made to distinguish between the two counties.

76. A general map of Kaskaskia's situation, made "agreeably to a request of the Board of Commissioners for the District of Kaskaskia," dated September 21, 1807 and signed by him as "County Surveyor," appears in *Amer. State Papers: Pub. Lands,* 2: between pages 182 and 183.

77. Elias Rector's name is signed to map of Prairie du Pont dated May 23, 1808, and printed in *ibid.*, 2: at 194-195. Another map, undated—*ibid.*, 182-183—of the Kaskaskia common field is signed by "Elias Rector D. S.," i.e. Deputy Surveyor; as deputy of the then surveyor of public lands in Illinois. Wilson and Robinson were probably the only county surveyors. The whole Rector family moved to St. Louis with William Rector about 1816. Elias Rector was postmaster of the city from 1819 to 1822. Houck, *Missouri,* 3: 184, 255.

78. William Rector was the oldest of the large Rector family. Four maps, all signed by him as "D. S.," of dates 1808-1810, are found in *Amer. State Papers: Pub. Lands,* 2: at 182-183, 186-187, 192-193, 194-195. He was appointed surveyor of the public lands of Illinois and Missouri in 1816, and reappointed—and his jurisdiction extended over Arkansas—in 1823—U. S. Senate, *Exec. Journal,* 3: 51, 52, 329, 334. On February 7, 1811 he was appointed brigadier-general of the territorial militia of Illinois—U. S. Senate, *Exec. Journal,* 2: 165, 166. He commanded a regiment in 1812 in operations against the Indians in Illinois, and was known as "colonel" Rector—Reynolds, *Pioneer History,* 354. After his removal to Missouri in 1816, he was prominent in the politics of that territory sitting in the constitutional convention of 1820 as a representative of St. Louis County. His brother Thomas killed Joshua Barton, U. S. attorney of Missouri, in one of the famous duels of Missouri annals (June 30, 1823), which grew out of a dispute over William Rector's conduct as surveyor-general—Houck, *Missouri,* 3: 17, 249, 255-256; and cp. U. S. Senate, *Exec. Journal,* 3: 329, 331 (the instructions to the committee indicate the charges against him) He died in Illinois on June 6, 1826.

79. George Bullitt was admitted by the General Court on September 4, 1804 to examination by Benjamin Parke and John Rice Jones for the degree of attorney and counsellor, and on the 6th produced his license as counsellor and took the oath—*Order Book,* 1: 101, 105. In December 1805 he served as deputy attorney-general in Kaskaskia—Randolph *Common Pleas,* 5: 308. He practiced very little in Illinois. He had a distinguished career later in other fields. On February 9, 1814, and again on February 19, 1818 he was appointed a judge of Missouri Territory, at which times the President, in nominating him, described him as of that territory—U. S. Senate, *Exec. Journal,* 2: 470; 3: 122, 124. He was a member (from Ste. Genevieve) of the first territorial House of Representatives, elected in November, 1812, and acted as speaker in its second session, in December 1813—Houck, *Missouri,* 3: 3, 5. On April 6, 1820—being now described as "of Arkansas," he was made register of the land office at Cape Girardeau. To this office he was reappointed on April 19, 1824 and on January 21, 1828, and on April 26, 1832 he was appointed to the same office at Jackson—*ibid.,* 3: 205, 206, 368, 372, 585, 594; 4: 236, 237, 242.

80. William C. Carr was born on April 15, 1783 in Virginia, where he was educated and studied law before coming west. According to Billon he was one of the first Americans to arrive in St. Louis (March 31, 1804) after its transfer to the United States, and the first American lawyer after John Rice Jones. It was only on September 6, 1804 that the General Court set the first day of the next Randolph circuit for his examination by Benjamin Parke and John Rice Jones (subject to his producing a license as attorney from some one of the United States and a certificate of moral character)—*Order Book,* 1: 105. Perhaps, however, he was not present in the court. He acted as U. S. attorney for the district of Ste. Genevieve (where he settled for one year immediately after reaching the territory) when its first courts were organized by the governor and judges of Indiana

Territory in December 1804. On his practice in the Kaskaskia courts see
ante, clxxxix, n. 3 and cxciii, n. 4. Apparently from December 1805 until
1810 he served as agent of the United States (clerk) before the board of
land commissioners to examine the land titles of the territory—Houck,
Missouri, 3: 44; Marshall, *Life and Papers of Frederick Bates,* 1:
127-128, 278, 280; 2: 151. He was in Kentucky much of 1810-1812—*ibid.,* 2:
151, 227, 229. He was strongly opposed to General Wilkinson when governor of the territory, and an intimate friend and executor of his successor,
Governor Meriwether Lewis. In November 1812 he was elected from St.
Louis as a representative in the first territorial General Assembly, was
chosen speaker (presiding over the first session, in December of that year,
but not over the second); and was a member of the second legislature, of
1814-1816. In 1817 he was one of seven men, including Governor William
Clark and Thomas Hart Benton, named by the legislature as the first trustees of the St. Louis public schools. From 1826 to 1834 he served as state
circuit judge. He was impeached, 1832, for neglect of duty, incapacity, and
favoritism, but was acquitted. His death occurred on March 31, 1851. He
was of great prominence and influence in St. Louis throughout his life.
See Billon, *Annals of St. Louis, 1804-21,* index; Scharf, *Hist. of St.
Louis City and County,* 1: 340; 2: 1453-1454; Houck, *Missouri,* index, adding 2: 383.

81. Isaac Darneille, according to Governor Reynolds, was the second
resident lawyer of Illinois; he settled in Cahokia in 1794 (*Pioneer History,*
181) or 1796 (*My Own Times,* 128). The latter date is probably correct, for
Darneille was doubtless the "Isaac Daxueille" appointed by Governor St.
Clair United States attorney for Hamilton County on November 27, 1794—
St. Clair Papers, 2: 337 n. There were good lawyers in Ohio, and Darneille
would not have lasted long. On March 1, 1804 the General Court appointed
John Rice Jones and John Johnson to examine him for admission as counsellor (it is stated that he had already been admitted as an attorney), and
on the 4th he took the oath—*Order Book,* 1: 59, 68. In 1798 he was clerk
of a Court of Commissioners and Assessors of St. Clair County—
Allinson, Ill. State Hist. Soc. *Trans.* (1907), p. 291. He was very active
for a time in law at Cahokia, appearing in almost every case (in which the
parties employed counsel) in the years 1801-1803; and not infrequently in
Kaskaskia. See *ante,* cxc and n. 2; cxciii and n. 4; cxcvii and n. 4. As
early as 1797, however, "for several contempts and disorders in this court,
and by reason of his horrid moral character" the Common Pleas of St.
Clair County had barred him from appearing before it—Bateman and Selby,
Hist. of St. Clair County, 2: 701, quoting the entry; possibly "1797" is a
misprint for 1807. He was also active in the General Court. His legal
attainments were shallow, but sometimes effective in offering obstructions
to opponents in common law pleading. As Governor Reynolds says (*Pioneer
History,* 222), "The courts and juries at that day were not remarkably well
versed in the technical learning and therefore Darneille could figure with
ease and safety before these tribunals." An example of his resourcefulness:
in the General Court he made a motion which the court overruled; he then
moved that the plaintiff show cause why it should not be allowed!—the
court finally overruled this—*Order Book.* He was also active in politics.
He was defeated by Shadrach Bond, Sr. on January 5, 1799 as a candidate
for the office of representative in the General Assembly of the Northwest
Territory—Brink, McDonough, *Hist. of St. Clair County,* 71 (the vote was
72 to 113; the list of those supporting each candidate is interesting); and
he was again unsuccessful in 1802 as a candidate for delegate to the Vincennes proslavery convention—*ibid.,* 71, 73. Whether he again tried his

political fortunes does not appear. He was the author of the *Letters of Decius* (1805); cleverly written and barbed attacks upon Harrison which caused the latter much anguish of mind. According to Harrison Darneilie made a retraction under threat of violence, by "12 of the Citizens of Kentucky" (*Messages*, 1: 195; but cp. Mrs. Goebel's sensible comments, *Harrison*, 63-64, 67, and Dunn, *Indiana*, 302 n., 328. Possibly he had, thus early, some special connection with Kentucky. His adventures of gallantry included an elopement with a Cahokian matron to Peoria, where, according to Governor Reynolds, he lived "many years." He was living there in 1812—Bateman and Selby, *op. cit.*, 1: 418. He owned various claims to land in Prairie du Pont—(*Amer. State Papers: Pub. Lands*, 2: 200-202; also in Peoria—note *ante*, cxc. Rejection of his claims by Harrison (*ante*, lxxix, n. 3) was one point of bitterness in the *Letters of Decius*. He seems also to have puttered in the fur trade—*Wis. Hist. Colls.*, 19: 301-303. He fell out with John Singleton, his partner (in what business does not appear). See *ante*, clxxxix, n. 5. In later years he removed to Kentucky, taught school, and died there, "rather humbled and neglected," in 1830. It is said that he was trained for the ministry. He was well educated, of polished appearance and impressive address, facile in speech, and abundant in talent. He was for some time very conspicuous. See Reynolds, *Pioneer History*, 221-223. General Wilkinson, writing to Jefferson, referred to him as "that rascal Darnielle whose name is mentioned only in the same breath as 'libel on integrity!'"—Houck, *Missouri*, 3: 14.

82. Benjamin H. Doyle came to Illinois from Tennessee (Brink, McDonough, *Hist. of St. Clair County*, 89, say Knox County, Kentucky), and settled at Kaskaskia in 1804 or 1805—Reynolds, *My Own Times*, 129; *Pioneer History*, 360. The date of his admission by the General Court was not noted in examining its *Order Book*. He was appointed attorney-general of Illinois Territory, and served as such from July 24 to December, 1809—McDonough, *Hist. of Randolph, Monroe and Perry Counties*, 40. Why he resigned, and why he left the territory, does not appear.

83. Rufus Easton was born on May 4, 1774 in Litchfield, Connecticut. He was well educated before studying law, 1791-1793, in the office of Ephraim Kirby of Litchfield, of repertorial fame. At the beginning of the century he was practicing in Rome, New York. While there, and during two winters in Washington (1803-1804 and 1804-1805) he established political relationships with Gideon Granger, De Witt Clinton, Aaron Burr and other influential men. Burr seems to have shown him many courtesies. He traveled from Vincennes to Louisiana with Harrison and the Indiana Territory judges in the autumn of 1804. Just before starting west, evidently, he— and several others who were ready to start for St. Louis (George Bullitt, Edward Hempstead and John Scott)—produced to the General Court licenses as counsellors and took the oath on September 6, 1804. John Rice Jones and Benjamin Parke were appointed to examine him for admission as attorney and as counsellor on the first day of the next Randolph circuit. *Order Book*, 1: 105. Thenceforth he practiced actively in the Kaskaskia courts and in the General Court of Indiana Territory; see *ante*, clxxxix, n. 3; cxciii, n. 4; and cxcvii, n. 4. He was prothonotary of the St. Louis district Quarter Sessions in 1804; U. S. attorney for the St. Louis district of the District of Louisiana from March 19 to June 18 (between two terms of Edward Hempstead), 1805; and judge of the territorial General Court from March 1805 to April 21, 1806. The termination of this last service is the peculiar incident above referred to. When not reappointed, venturing to request an explanation, he received from Jefferson the reply (of February 22, 1806): "Your commission as Judge of Louisiana,

according to its own terms and those of the Constitution, is to expire at the end of the present session of the Senate . . . Every one must be sensible what kind of altercation I should be involved in, on every nomination, were I to specify the grounds of passing over a candidate, as you desire in your letter. However, if you think proper to call on me I will verbally state to you two or three facts and hear anything you may wish to say respecting them. It is the first time it has ever been asked, and it is most probable that it is the last time it will ever be yielded to." Houck, *Missouri,* 2: 401-402 n. Burr seems to have procured this judgeship for Easton, and to have endeavored to establish confidence between him and Wilkinson, doubtless judging both fit material for tools—Scharf, *Hist. of St. Louis City and County,* 2: 1455. Before he came west Easton had applied for a position as one of the land commissioners for the District of Louisiana: Gallatin found him: "an amphibious character"—Houck, *Missouri,* 3: 40 n. Easton and Wilkinson did their best to discredit each other—*ibid.,* 2: 402-403 and n., 405. Scharf attributes Easton's failure to be reappointed as judge to Wilkinson's charges of his official corruption; says he saw Jefferson, cleared himself, and was appointed U. S. attorney. But there was no appointment after the president's letter. He continued to serve, however, as the first postmaster of St. Louis, 1805-1814. On September 17, 1814 he was elected delegate of Missouri Territory in Congress, holding office from November 16, 1814 to March 3, 1817. From 1821 to 1826 he served also as U. S. district attorney for the state. His death occurred July 5, 1834. Scharf characterizes him as "indisputably the leading lawyer of the territory": his early efforts certainly contained no promise of such attainments. Alton, Illinois (named after his son) was laid out by him in 1817. See Scharf, *op. cit.,* 1: 334; 2: 1454-1456; Billon, *Annals of St. Louis, 1804-21,* index; Houck, *Missouri,* 2: 384, 401-402; Brink, *Hist. of Madison County, Illinois,* 375; *Biog. Congressional Directory, 1774-1911,* 80, 85, 622. Cp. Frederick Bates's characterizations of Easton to William C. Carr and of Carr to Easton—Marshall, *Life and Papers of Frederick Bates,* 2: 231, 292; rather characteristic of Bates.

84. James Haggin settled at Kaskaskia in 1803. Beginning in September 1801 the General Court three times set a date for his examination as attorney; in the meantime—a not uncommon occurrence (present e. g. also in the case of Benjamin Parke)—he produced a license as, and took the oath of, a counsellor on March 6, 1802. General Court, *Order Book,* 1: 17, 22, 25, 26. He practiced in both Randolph and St. Clair counties and in the General Court; for some years he and Darneille almost monopolized practice at Cahokia. *Ante,* cxciii, n. 4 and cxcvii, n. 4. In shiftiness of character they were well matched. In 1803 and 1804 we find five suits against him in the Randolph Common Pleas: to recover a retainer fee, services not performed; for fees collected for services not performed; to recover the statutory penalty imposed for selling without a license goods from without the territory; for negligence in services rendered as attorney; and for breach of promise to pay $70 if the General Court should reverse a judgment recovered by plaintiff in the county court, Haggin his attorney. Randolph *Common Pleas,* 1: pl. 55; 3: pl. 57, 58, 66, 67. We also find this, in the General Court—*Order Book,* 1: 94, I. Darneille *v.* J. Haggin, September 16, 1803: "The sheriff having this day returned the writ of Habeas Corpus not executed, for a want of time, and it appearing to the satisfaction of the Court that the execution thereof was entirely owing to the Defendant, Ordered that the clk do not issue a second writ for the same cause." See also *ante,* ccviii, n. 6. In a paper analyzing political conditions in the territory, supposedly written by Benjamin Parke, Haggin

was characterized as an adherent of the Edgar-Morrison party, and as "an attorney, notorious for his avarice, impudence and cowardice"—Woollen, *Sketches,* 5. In March, 1805 Bryan and Morrison recovered a judgment against him under which the sheriff attached on house, 200 acres of land, "and 22 law books"—Randolph, *Common Pleas,* 4: p. 291. *My Own Times,* 128; *Pioneer History,* 360. In the Miscellanies Box at Chester there is a petition of Haggin to the Mercer Circuit Court, Kentucky, probably of 1807, in some proceeding against Robert Morrison. In this Haggin says he was "about to leave that country"—Randolph County—"in December 1804 or January 1805," and complains of money collected for and withheld from him by Morrison (clerk of the court), and of an unjust settlement which he was forced to make with him, "being anxious to set off for this country." He was an associate judge of the short-lived "new court" of appeals (January 15, 1825-December 30, 1826) which was the storm-center of Kentucky politics for two years. See Collins, *Hist. of Kentucky,* 1: 31, 321-323, 494-497.

85. Robert Hamilton seems to have acted as prosecuting attorney for the U. S. in the Circuit Court of St. Clair County in October, 1800—Brink, McDonough, *Hist. of St. Clair County,* 70. He appeared in a private action in the St. Clair Court on October 9, 1800—*Orphans' Court 1797-1809,* 13. On the first day that the General Court met, March 3, 1801, his examination (and that of General Washington Johnston and John Rice Jones) for a counsellor's license was set by the General Court for September 7, 1801—*Order Book,* 2. He was very active in practice before the General Court, but appeared—after 1800—very rarely, if ever, in the Illinois courts. He was a representative of Pope County (if indeed it be the same man) in the first General Assembly of the state, 1818-1820.

86. William Hamilton appeared as attorney in some cases of the Randolph *Common Pleas,* vol. 2; but their dates were not noted. Nor was any action noted in the *Order Book* of the General Court admitting him to practice.

87. Edward Hempstead was born on June 3, 1780 at New London, Connecticut. He received an academic education, read law, was admitted to the bar in 1801, and practiced somewhat in Rhode Island, before coming west. He was one of those who hurried to Louisiana upon its transfer to the United States. According to Houck he walked from Vincennes to that territory. It must have been in the autumn, for on September 4, 1804 his examination for admission as an attorney and for counsellor (by Benjamin Parke and John Rice Jones) was ordered by the General Court; and on the 6th he—together with John Scott and George Bullitt—produced his license and took the oath as counsellor. *Order Book,* 1: 101, 105. According to Washburne, however, he accompanied Governor Harrison and the judges of the Indiana Territory (address cited below). He was several times between 1804 and 1809 deputy attorney-general of the districts of St. Louis and St. Charles, in the District of Louisiana and Louisiana Territory (first by appointment of Governor Harrison in December, 1804); clerk of the court of the St. Charles district, 1805; clerk of the Legislative Council, 1805; clerk of the legislature (of governor and judges), 1806; and on May 29, 1809 became attorney-general of the Territory of Louisiana, serving as such until October 31, 1810 (when his successor—Thomas T. Crittenden took office upon his resignation); curious questions are suggested by the note in Washburne, *Edwards Papers,* 56. On November 9, 1812 he was elected the delegate of Missouri Territory in Congress, serving from January 4, 1813 to November 16, 1814—the first representative in Congress of the trans-Mississippi west. He was a member of the third territorial

General Assembly, and speaker of the House of Representatives, when he was killed in an accident on August 9, 1817. See Billon, *Annals of St. Louis 1804-21,* index; Houck, *Missouri,* index; Scharf, *Hist. of St. Louis City and County,* 1: 331 *et seq.* (quoting address of Washburne before Missouri legislature); Marshall, *The Life and Papers of Frederick Bates,* index (unfriendly to Hempstead); *Biog. Congressional Directory, 1774-1911,* 75, 80, 718.

88. Of Henry Jones nothing is known. He appears in the Randolph records only; as attorney and as litigant in various cases. The action by the General Court with respect to his license was not noted.

89. William Mears was the first attorney after Isaac Darneille to make his permanent home in Cahokia. The action of the General Court upon his license was not noted. According to Reynolds he was born in Ireland in 1768, and had taught school and studied law in Pennsylvania before coming to Cahokia, where he arrived in 1808 "as if he had dropped down from the clouds—without horse, clothes, books, letters, or anything except himself— a rather singular and uncouth-looking Irishman." *Pioneer History,* 361; *My Own Times,* 129. His first appearance noted in the St. Clair records was in that year—*Orphans' Court: 1797-1809,* 47A. He was attorney-general of Illinois Territory, from August 1, 1813—U. S. Senate, *Exec. Journal,* 2: 400, 418, 436 (he was nominated on July 26)—to February 17, 1818; circuit judge, of the eastern circuit of the Territory, from that date onward; and attorney-general of the state from December 14, 1819 until February 26, 1821. McDonough, *Hist. of Randolph, Monroe and Perry Counties,* 40, 42; Brink, McDonough, *Hist. of St. Clair County,* 77, 89, 186. He died at Belleville, of which he became a resident in 1816, in 1826.

90. Nathaniel Pope was born at Louisville, Kentucky on January 5, 1784. He was educated at Transylvania University. He is said to have emigrated from Kentucky to New Orleans in 1804, but evidently went almost immediately to upper Louisiana, where he remained for some years, making Ste. Genevieve his home—Reynolds, *Pioneer History,* 393. He was a resident of Ste. Genevieve when the first court was opened there in December 1804; and was resident there when made a trustee of the Ste. Genevieve Academy, organized in 1808. It was in these years that he attended court at Kaskaskia. No action of the General Court upon his license was noted. His eminence, with John Scott, among those there practicing has been noted *ante,* cxcvii, n. 4. He does not appear in the St. Clair records. He studied law with his brother John Pope, later senator from Kentucky; evidently before leaving Kentucky. Alvord says that when he became secretary he "had been living in the country for about a year, during which time he had associated himself in politics with his relative, Michael Jones, by whom he had been put forward as a rival of Rice Jones"—*Illinois Country,* 428; which partly explains his opposition to the Edgar-Morrison party. Why he would not speak to William Morrison—*ante,* app. n. 70—does not appear. He was appointed secretary of Illinois Territory on March 7, 1809 and reappointed on June 1, 1813—U. S. Senate, *Exec. Journal,* 2: 119, 120, 347, 348; serving until he was elected delegate of the territory in Congress in the summer of 1816—Washburne, *Edwards Papers,* 126. He took his seat December 2, 1816. (According to McDonough, *Hist. of Randolph, Monroe and Perry Counties,* 40, he served as secretary until December 17). On November 30, 1818 he was appointed register of the land office at Edwardsville—U. S. Senate, *Exec. Journal,* 3: 143, 150. When nominated as secretary of the territory in 1809 he was described as "of Louisiana Territory," and in 1813 as "of Kentucky": he was now, in 1818, described as "of Illinois." March 3, 1819 he was nominated and confirmed as U. S.

district judge for Illinois—*ibid.,* 184. In this position he served until his death (at St. Louis) on January 23, 1850. In 1826 he was an unsuccessful candidate for appointment to the U. S. Supreme Court, when the creation of a new circuit was in contemplation. See Reynolds, *Pioneer History,* 393-395; *My Own Times,* 86, 104, 106, 128-129, 134, 154; Bateman and Selby, *Hist. of St. Clair County,* 1: 428; McDonough, *op. cit.,* 40; Washburne, *Edwards Papers,* 122-123 n., 245, 249; Buck, *Illinois in 1818,* index; *Biog. Congressional Directory, 1774-1911,* 85, 90, 930; Houck, *Missouri,* 3: 13, 67 n. On his judicial career, in which he displayed rare talents and legal knowledge see Judge John M. Scott, *Supreme Court of Illinois 1818,* 266; and General Alfred Orendorff's address at the unveiling of Judge Pope's portrait in the rooms of the federal courts at Springfield on June 2, 1903. His brother, John Pope, 1770-1845, was U. S. senator from Kentucky, 1807-1813; governor of Arkansas Territory, 1829-1835; and representative in Congress, 1837-1843. Nathaniel was the father of Majorgeneral John Pope, of the Civil War.

91. John Rector, according to Governor Reynolds, was a Virginian, who came to Kaskaskia in 1804 (*My Own Times,* 129) or 1806 (*Pioneer History,* 360), and after practicing a few years at that town and Cahokia "left the country." The action in the *Order Book* of the General Court upon his license, and the date when he first appeared in the Randolph courts —*Common Pleas,* vol. 4—were not noted. He did not begin practice in Cahokia until 1808. In July of that year "John Rector was admitted as a Practicing attorney for this County Court," the Common Pleas—St. Clair *Orphans' Court: 1797-1809,* 43, 44. His family and presumably he, went to Missouri—Houck, *Missouri,* 3: 255-256. Reynolds characterizes his family in *Pioneer History,* 353-354. He was a brother of Elias Rector and William Rector, *ante,* app. notes 77, 78.

92. Of Robert Robinson little is known. He was clerk of the first board of land commissioners, 1805-1809—*Amer. State Papers: Pub. Lands,* 2: 133, 134, 135, 137 (the date "1803" in the first document so signed is a misprint); and sometimes signed and was referred to by the commissioners as "agent"—*ibid.,* 132, 239. The fact that he was named by the legislature one of the trustees of Kaskaskia in 1807—*post,* 568—(the name "Robertson" is almost certainly a misprint: Robeson, Robinson, Robertson are often confused in the county records where the identity seems plain)—indicates his high standing. No action upon his license to practice was noted in the *Order Book* of the General Court. He was active as an attorney, and ranked with Nathaniel Pope and John Scott in the high quality of his work. *Ante,* clxxviii-ix, n. 5; clxxxviii, n. 2; clxxxix, n. 3; cxciii-iv, n. 4; cxcvii, n. 4. He served more than once as prosecuting attorney for the U. S. in the Kaskaskia courts. He was of course closely associated with Michael Jones. Whether he was active in politics does not appear, but he was one of those whom the Edgar-Morrison faction named as implicated in the murder of Rice Jones—*Chic. Hist. Colls.,* 4: 278-279; which, of course, only shows that he was prominent, and honored by their enmity.

93. John Scott was a Virginian, born about 1782, a graduate (1802) of Princeton College. He probably came to Vincennes and on to Louisiana in 1804 (Billon; though Houck says he stopped in Vincennes, studied law there, and moved to Ste. Genevieve in 1805). He remained all his life in Ste. Genevieve, from 1806 onward. In early years he was active in practice in the Illinois courts, and his work was of strikingly good quality. *Ante,* cxciii-iv, n. 4: cxcvii, n. 4. For a time he was in partnership with Nathaniel Pope, before the latter left Missouri. Governor Reynolds says, quite justly, of Scott and Nathaniel Pope: "These two young gentlemen

were the choice fruits of nature, possessing great strength of intellect and much energy. They rose fast in the profession, and stood deservedly at the head of the bar in their day in Missouri and Illinois." *My Own Times,* 128-129. On February 16, 1813 he was appointed to the Legislative Council of Missouri Territory—U. S. Senate, *Exec. Journal,* 2: 318, 324. He was nominated U. S. attorney for Missouri Territory in July, 1813, but the nomination not being acted upon, he was renominated, and confirmed on February 9, 1814—*ibid.,* 2: 401, 418, 470. On August 5, 1816 he was elected delegate to Congress over Rufus Easton, the then incumbent, and sat from December 2, 1816 to January 13, 1817, when, his election being voided for irregularities, he was again elected and repeatedly reëlected under the territory and the state, sitting from December 1, 1817 until March 3, 1827 (Missouri having meanwhile become a state, in 1821). His vote for Adams as President in 1825, resulted in his relegation to private life. He was thereafter absorbed in the practice of law, in which he won great distinction. He died on October 1, 1861. See Billon, *Annals of St. Louis 1804-21,* index; Houck, *Missouri,* 3: 3, 13, 67, 77, 243, 245, index; Reynolds, *My Own Times,* 53, 128; *Biog. Congressional Directory, 1774-1911,* 85, 90, 96, 99, 105, 110, 981.

94. The examination of John Taylor (by Benjamin Parke and John Rice Jones) for admission as an attorney and counsellor was ordered by the General Court to be held on the first day of the Randolph circuit in the autumn of 1804—*Order Book,* 105. He appears almost exclusively in the second volume of the Randolph *Common Pleas.* Little more can be definitely stated. (There was a John Taylor who was nominated in 1813 as a collector in Massachusetts, but was not confirmed; was (if the same) later nominated and confirmed to a similar office in Mississippi Territory, in 1814; and served as a legislative councillor of that territory in 1816. A John Taylor, also,—now described as "of South Carolina"—was next, in 1817, made receiver of public moneys at a land office in Mississippi; and in 1821 at another in Alabama; having meanwhile, in 1820, served as a commissioner to treat with the Creek Indians. U. S. Senate, *Exec. Journal,* 2: 438, 443, 444, 457, 473; 3: 24, 25, 92, 93, 213, 251, 254. It would not be in the least extraordinary if but one man, and not three individuals, was here involved. Cases of service in two territories in these years were numerous; of three by no means unknown.

LAWS

ADOPTED BY THE

GOVERNOR AND JUDGES

OF THE

INDIANA TERRITORY,

AT THEIR FIRST SESSIONS HELD AT

SAINT VINCENNES,

JANUARY 12th, 1801.

———   ———

Published By Authority.

———   ———

FRANFORT, (K.)

PRINTED BY WILLIAM HUNTER.

———

1802.

TABLE

OF

CONTENTS.

———*———

LAWS

FOR THE GOVERNMENT OF THE

INDIANA TERRITORY.

I.

A Law supplemental to a law to regulate county levies,

INDIANA TERRITORY.

* * * * * *
*   L. S.   *
* * * * * *

WILLM. HENRY HARRISON,
WM. CLARKE,
HENRY VANDER BURGH,
JOHN GRIFFIN.

Adopted from the Pennsylvania code, and published at Saint Vincennes the nineteenth day of January, one thousand eight hundred and one, by William Henry Harrison, g o v e r n o r, William Clarke, Henry Vander Burgh, and John Griffin, judges in and over said territory.

THE commissioners, or any two of them, in every county shall within three weeks after their annual appointments, issue forth their precepts directed to the constables of every township, requiring them to make, within six weeks next after the date of such precepts, fair and true certificates and lists in writing, upon their oaths or affirmations, of all persons and property declared to be objects of taxation by the law to which this is a supplement. And the said constables are hereby vested with the same powers, are to perform the same duties, be

B

[6]

subject to the same penalties, and are to receive the same emoluments as are by the said recited law given to, or imposed upon persons therein denominated listers of land.

The foregoing is hereby declared to be a law of the territory, to take effect accordingly. In testimony whereof, we, William Henry Harrison, William Clarke, Henry Vander Burgh, and John

1

Griffin, have caused the seal of the territory to be thereunto affixed, and signed the same with our names.

Willm. Henry Harrison,
Wm. Clarke,
Henry Vander Burgh,
John Griffin.

INDIANA TERRITORY.
* * * * * *
* L. S. *.
* * * * * *
WILLM. HENRY HARRISON,
WM. CLARKE,
HENRY VANDER BURGH,
JOHN GRIFFIN.

II.

A Resolution

Entered into the twentieth day of January, one thousand eight hundred and one, by William Henry Harrison, governor, and William Clarke, Henry Vander Burgh, & John Griffin, judges in and over the said territory.

R ESOLVED, that so much of the act passed at the first session of the general assembly of the territory of the United States north-west of the Ohio, entitled 'an act regulating the admission and practice of attornies and counsellors at law,' as makes a residence of one year in the territory necessary to persons desirous of obtaining licenses

[7]

to practice as attorneys, previously to the issuing such licenses; and so much of the second section of the said act as makes it necessary for an applicant to the general court for a license, to produce to the court a certificate of his having studied law for the space of four years, shall be, and the same is hereby repealed.

Published at Vincennes the day and year above written, by William Henry Harrison, governor, and William Clarke, Henry Vander Burgh, and John Griffin.

Willm. Henry Harrison,
Wm. Clarke,
Henry Vander Burgh,
John Griffin.

III.

INDIANA TERRITORY.

* * * * * *

*   L. S.   *

* * * * * *

WILLM. HENRY HARRISON,

WM. CLARKE,

HENRY VANDER BURGH,

JOHN GRIFFIN.

A Law to regulate the practice of the General Court upon Appeals and Writs of Error, and for other purposes,

Adopted from the Kentucky code, and published at Saint Vincennes the twentieth day of January, one thousand eight hundred and one, by William Henry Harrison, governor, and William Clarke, Henry Vander Burgh, and John Griffin, judges in and over the said territory.

§ 1.   THE general court shall annually appoint one of the judges thereof, to inspect the clerk's office of the said

[8]

court, and to report to the next session of the said court the condition in which he shall find the papers and records, which report shall be recorded.

§ 2.   There shall be no discontinuance of any suit, process, matter or thing returned to, or depending in the general court, although a quorum of judges shall fail to attend at the commencement, or any other day of any session; but if a majority of them shall fail to attend at the commencement of any session, any judge of the said court, or the sheriff attending the same, may adjourn the said court from day to day, for three days successively; and if a quorum shall not attend on the fourth, or having attended one day, shall fail to attend on a subsequent day of a session, the court shall stand adjourned 'till the court in course.

§ 3.   Execution shall be issued from the general court according to law; and the returns shall be appointed by the said court.

§ 4.   The general court shall have power to direct the writs, summonses, process, forms and modes of proceedings to be issued, observed and pursued by the said general court.

§ 5.   In appeals and writs of error the following rules shall be observed:—No appeal shall be granted from the judgment or decree of an inferior court to the general court, unless such judgment or decree be final, and amount, exclusive of costs, to fifty dollars, or relate to a franchise or freehold.

[9]

Every appeal shall be prayed at the time of rendering the judgment, sentence or decree.

The person appealing shall, by himself or a responsible person on his behalf, in the office of the clerk of the court from whence the appeal is prayed, give bond and sufficient security, to be approved by the court, and within a time to be fixed by the court to the appellee, for the due prosecution of his appeal. The penalty of the said bond shall be in a reasonable sum in the direction of the court.

It shall be the duty of the appellant to lodge an authenticated copy of the record, in the clerk's office of the general court before the expiration of the next succeeding term thereof; provided there be thirty days between the time of making such appeal and the commencement of the said term; and if there be not thirty days between the making the appeal and the sitting of the first term of the general court, then the record shall be lodged as aforesaid, at or before the commencement of the second term of said court; or else it shall stand dismissed, unless further time shall be granted by the court before the end of the term to which the same should have been returned.

If the judgment or decree be affirmed in the whole, the appellant shall pay to the appellee a sum not exceeding ten per centum, at the discretion of the court, on the sum due thereby, besides the costs upon the original suit and appeal.

[10]

If the judgment or decree shall be reversed in the whole, the appellee shall pay to the appellant such costs as the court in their discretion may award. Where the judgment or decree shall be reversed in part, and affirmed in part, the costs of the original suit and appeal shall be apportioned between the appellant and appellee in the discretion of the court. The general court shall in case of a partial reversal, give such judgment or decree as the inferior court ought to have given.

On appeals or writs of error it shall be lawful for the general court to issue execution, or remit the cause to the inferior court, in order that an execution may be there issued, or that other proceedings may be had thereupon.

No writ of error shall be a supersedeas, unless the general court, or some judge thereof in vacation (as the case may be) after inspecting a copy of the record, shall order the same to be made a supersedeas, in which case, the clerk issuing the said writ, shall endorse on the said writ of error "that it shall be a supersedeas, and it shall be obeyed as such accordingly;" and it shall also be necessary before a writ of error shall operate as a supersedeas, that bond, to be approved by the clerk of the court issuing the said writ, shall be given in the same manner and under the like penalty as in the case of appeals. And the plaintiff in error shall lodge an authenticated copy of the record, under the

[11]

same regulations, and the parties in error shall be subject to the same judgment and mode of execution as is already directed in the case of appeals.

A writ of error shall not be brought after the expiration of five years from the passing the judgment complained of; but where a person thinking himself aggrieved by any decree or judgment, which may be reversed in the general court, shall be an infant, feme covert, non compos mentis, or imprisoned when the same was passed, the time of such disability shall be excluded from the computation of the said five years.

Whensoever the said general court shall be divided in opinion on hearing any appeal or writ of error, the judgment or decree appealed from, shall be affirmed.

§ 6. The clerk of the general court shall carefully preserve the transcript of records certified to his court, with the bonds for prosecution, and all papers relating to them, and other suits depending therein, docketing them in the order he shall receive them, that they may be heard in the same course; unless the court for good cause to them shewn, direct any to be heard out of its turn.

The proceedings of every day during the term, shall be drawn at full length by the clerk, against the next sitting of the court, and such corrections as are necessary being first made therein, they shall be signed by the presiding judge.

When any cause shall be finally deter-

[12]

mined, the clerk shall make a complete record thereof. And all writs, processes and summonses, issuing from the general court, shall be signed by the clerk of the same, and shall bear test in the name of the chief justice, or presiding judge for the time being.

§ 7. For good cause the general court, or any judge thereof, may grant commissions for the examination of witnesses; and the clerk of the said court, when any witness is about to depart from the said territory, or shall by age, sickness or otherwise, be unable to attend the court, or where the claim or defence of any party, or a material part thereof, shall depend on a single witness, may upon affidavit thereof, issue a commission for taking the deposition of such witness *de bene esse,* to be read as evidence at the trial, in case the witness be then unable to attend; but the party obtaining such commission shall give reasonable notice to the other party of the time and place of taking the deposition.

The foregoing is hereby declared to be a law of the territory, to take effect accordingly. In testimony whereof, we, William Henry Harrison, William Clarke, Henry Vander Burgh, and John Griffin, have caused the seal of the territory to be thereunto affixed, and signed the same with our names.

Willm. Henry Harrison,
Wm. Clarke,
Henry Vander Burgh,
John Griffin.

[13]

IV.

A Law respecting amendment and jeofail,

INDIANA TERRITORY.
* * * * * *
*   L. S.   *
* * * * * *
WILLM. HENRY HARRISON,
WM. CLARKE,
HENRY VANDER BURGH,
JOHN GRIFFIN.

Adopted from the Kentucky and Virginia codes, and published at Saint Vincennes the twenty second day of January, one thousand eight hundred and one, by William Henry Harrison, governor, and William Clarke, Henry Vander Burgh, and John Griffin, judges in and over the said territory.

WHEN a demurrer shall be joined in any action, the court shall not regard any other defect or imperfection in the writ, return, declaration or pleading, than what shall be specially alledged in the demurrer as causes thereof, unless something so essential to the action or defence, as that judgment according to law and the very right of the cause cannot be given, shall be omitted. And. for prevention of delay, by arresting judgments, and vexatious appeals, the several acts of parliament commonly called the statutes of jeofails, which were in force and use in England on the seventh day of February, one thousand seven hundred and fifty-two, shall be and are hereby declared to be, for so much thereof as relates to mispleading, jeofail and amendment. in full force in this territory.

The foregoing is hereby declared to be a law of the territory, to take effect accordingly. In testimony whereof, we, William Henry Harrison, William Clarke, Henry Vander Burgh and John Griffin, have caused

C

[14]

the seal of the territory to be thereunto affixed, and signed the same with our names.

Willm. Henry Harrison,
Wm. Clarke,
Henry Vander Burgh,
John Griffin.

V.

A Law establishing courts of judicature,

INDIANA TERRITORY.

* * * * * *
*   L. S.   *
* * * * * *

WILLM. HENRY HARRISON,
WM. CLARKE,
HENRY VANDER BURGH,
JOHN GRIFFIN.

Adopted from the Pennsylvania code, and published at Saint Vincennes the twenty third day of January, one thousand eight hundred and one, by William Henry Harrison, g o v e r n o r, William Clarke, Henry Vander Burgh and John Griffin, judges in and over the said territory.

§ 1. THERE shall be a court styled the general quarter-sessions of the peace, holden and kept four times in every year in every county, viz.—In the county of Knox, on the first Tuesdays of February, May, August, and November, yearly and every year;—in the county of Randolph, on the first Tuesdays of June, September, December and March, yearly and every year;—and in the county of Saint Clair, on the last Tuesdays in the same months, yearly and every year.

§ 2. There shall be a competent number of justices in every county, nominated and authorised by the governor, by commission under the seal of the territory; which said

[15]

justices, or any three of them, shall and may hold the said general sessions of the peace according to law.

§ 3. The said justices of the peace or any three of them, may, pursuant to their said commissions, hold special and private sessions when and as often as occasion shall require. And the said justices and every of them, shall have full power and authority in or out of sessions, to take all matter of recognizances and obligations, as any justice of the peace in any of the United States may, can, or usually do; which said recognizances and obligations shall be made to the United States. And all recognizances for the peace, behaviour, or for appearance, which shall be taken by any of the said justices out of sessions, shall be certified into their said general sessions of the peace, to be holden next after the taking thereof: and every recognizance taken before any of them for suspicions of any manner of felony or other crime, not triable in the said court of quarter-sessions of the peace, shall be certified before the judges of the general court, or court of oyer and terminer, at their next succeeding court to be holden next after the taking thereof, without concealment of, or detaining or embezzeling the same; but in case any person or persons shall forfeit his or their recognizances of the peace, behaviour or appearance for any cause whatsoever, then the recognizance so forfeited, with the record of the default, or cause of the forfeiture,

[16]

shall be sent and certified without delay by the justices of the peace, into the said general court or court of oyer and terminer, as the case may require, that thence process may issue against the said parties according to law; all which forfeitures shall be levied by the proper officers, and go to the territory.

§ 4. All fines and amerciaments which shall be laid before the justices of the said courts of general quarter-sessions of the peace, shall be taxed, affeered and set, duly and truly, according to the quality of the offence, without partiality or affection; and shall be yearly estreated by the clerks of the said courts respectively, into the said general court or court of oyer and terminer: to the intent that process may be awarded to the sheriff of every county, as the case may require, for levying such of their fines and amerciaments as shall be unpaid to the uses for which they are or shall be appropriated.

§ 5. Provided always, that the said courts of the general quarter-sessions of the peace, may be kept and continued for the space of three legal days, or seventy-two hours, in every of the said counties respectively, at any of the said times herein before appointed to hold and keep the said court and session there.

§ 6. To the end that persons indicted or outlawed, for felonies or other offences, in one county or town corporate, who dwell, remove or be received into another county

[17]

or town corporate, may be brought to justice, it is hereby directed that the justices, or any of them, shall and may direct their writs or precepts to all or any of the sheriffs or other officers of the said counties, (where need shall .be) to take such persons indicted or outlawed; and it shall and may be lawful to and for the said justices, and every of them, to issue forth subpœnas and other warrants under their respective hands and seal of the county, into any county or place of this territory, for summoning or bringing any person or persons to give evidence in & upon any matter or cause whatsoever, now or hereafter examinable or in any ways triablebyor before them, or any of them, under such pains and penalties as subpœnas or warrants of that kind usually are or ought by law to be granted or awarded.

§ 7. If any person or persons shall find him or themselves aggrieved by the judgment of any of the said courts of general quarter-sesons of the peace, or of anyother court of record within this territory, it shall and may be lawful to and for the party or parties so aggrieved to appeal from the said judgment, under the restrictions and regulations of the law 'to regulate the practice of the general court upon appeals and writs of error,' or to have his or their writ or writs of error which shall be granted of course, in manner as other writs are to be granted and made returnable to the general court.

§ 8. There shall be holden and kept

[18]

twice in every year, a supreme court of record, which shall be called and styled the general court; the sittings of which court to commence at Saint Vincennes, in the county of Knox, on the first Tuesday in March and September, yearly and every year, and the judges of the said court, and every of them, shall have power when as often as there may be occasion, to issue forth writs of habeas corpus, certiorari, and writs of error, and all remedial and other writs and process returnable to the said court and grantable by the said judges by virtue of their office.

§ 9. Provided always, that upon any issue joined in the said general court, such issue shall be tried in the county whence the cause was removed, before the judges aforesaid, or any one

of them, as a circuit court, who are hereby empowered and required to go the circuit once in every year in each county in this
territory; the said circuit courts for the counties of Randolph
and St. Clair, shall be held, in the former on the first Monday in
October, and in the latter on the third Monday of the same month,
to try such issues in fact as shall be depending in the said general
court, and removed out of either of the counties aforesaid, when
and where they may try all issues joined or to be joined in the
same general court, and to do generally, all those things that shall
be necessary for the trial of any issue, as fully as justices of nisi
prius in any of the United States may or can do,

[19]

§ 10.   The said judges, or any two of them, shall in their
said court hear and determine all causes, matters and things
cognizable in the said court; and also hear and determine all and
all manner of pleas, plaints and causes which shall be removed or
brought there from the respective general quarter-sessions of the
peace, and courts of common pleas, or from any other court to be
holden for the respective counties, and to examine and correct all
and all manner of errors of the justices of the inferior courts in
their judgments, process and proceedings in the said courts, as
well in all pleas of the United States, as in all pleas real, personal
and mixed; and thereupon to reverse or affirm the said judgments
as the law doth or shall direct; and also to examine, correct and
punish the contempts, omissions and neglects, favours, corruptions
and defaults of all or any of the justices of the peace, sheriffs,
coroners, clerks and other officers within the said respective counties; and also shall award process for levying as well of such fines,
forfeitures and amerciaments as shall be estreated into the general court, as of the fines, forfeitures and amerciaments
which shall be lost, taxed and set there, and not paid to the uses
to which they are or shall be appropriated; and generally shall
minister ample justice to all persons, and amply exercise the
jurisdictions and powers herein mentioned, concerning all and
singular the premises according to law.

[20]

§ 11. All the said writs shall run in the name and style of the United States of America, and bear test in the name of the chief justice; but if he be plaintiff or defendant, then in the name of one of the other judges; and shall be sealed with the judicial seal of the said court, and made returnable to the next court after the date of such writs.

§ 12. The judges of the general court, have power from time to time, to deliver the jails of all persons who now are, or hereafter, shall be committed for treasons, murders and such other crimes, as by the laws of this Territory now are, or hereafter shall be made capital, or felonies of death, as aforesaid; and for that end, from time to time, to issue forth such necessary precepts and process, and force obedience thereto, as justices of the assize, justices of oyer and terminer, and of jail delivery, may or can do, within the United States.

§ 13. In order to compel the due attendance of jurymen on the said circuit and nisi prius courts, and all other courts within this Territory;—it is hereby declared, that if any person shall be duly summoned to attend any court of judicature, to serve on a jury, or on any inquest required by law; and shall neglect or refuse to give his attendance on the day, and during the time his service is necessary,— every such person so offending, shall be fined for every such offence in the general court, and court of oyer and terminer, by the judges thereof, any sum not exceeding

[21]

eight dollars; and for every such offence in in the court of common pleas, or court of quarter-sessions of the peace, for any county of the Territory, by the justices thereof, any sum not exceeding five dollars, unless such delinquent shall at the same, or next succeeding court, render to the judges or justices thereof, a reasonable excuse for such neglect or refusal, to be allowed by such of them as shall be present; which said judges or justices are hereby empowered and required on failure of such delinquent to render such reasonable excuse, to issue a writ to the sheriff of the county, to levy the said fines on the goods and chattels of

every such delinquent, to be paid to the clerks of the several courts
of quarter-sessions, common pleas, and general court respectively,
and by the said clerks to the Territorial treasurer, for the use of
the Territory.

§ 14. A competent number of persons shall be commissioned by the governor, under the seal of the Territory, as justices of the common pleas, who shall hold and keep a court of
record in every county, and which shall be styled and called the
court of common pleas, of [naming the particular county] and
shall be holden four times in every year, in each county, at the
place where the general quarter-sessions of the peace shall be
respectively kept; which said justices, or any three of them, according to the tenor or directions of their commissions, shall hold
pleas of assize, scire facias, replevins, and

D

[22]

hear and determine all and all manner of pleas, suits, actions and
causes, civil, personal, real and mixed, according to law.

§ 15. Every of the said justices shall, and are hereby empowered to grant, under the seal of their respective courts, replevins, writs of partition, writs of view, and all other writs and
process upon the said pleas and actions, cognizable in the said
respective courts, as occasion may require.

§ 16. The said justices of the said respective courts last
mentioned, shall and are hereby empowered to issue forth subpœnas under their respective hands and seal of the court, into any
county or place within this Territory, for summoning or bringing
any person or persons, to give evidence in, or upon the trial of
any matter or cause whatsoever, depending before them, or any
of them, under such pains and penalties, as by the rules of the
common law, and course of the practice of the general court, are
usually appointed.

§ 17. Upon any judgment obtained in any of the said courts
of common pleas, and execution returned by the sheriff or coroner
of the proper county where such judgment was obtained, that the
party is not to be found, or hath no lands and tenements, goods or

chattels in that county; and thereupon it is testified, that the party
skulks, or lies hid, or hath lands, tenements, goods or chattels in
another county, in this Territory; it shall and may be lawful to,
and for the court that

[23]

issued out such execution, to grant, and they are hereby required
to grant an alias execution, with a testatum, directed to the sheriff
or coroner of the county or place where such person lies hid, or
where his lands or effects are; commanding him to execute the
same, according to the tenor of such writ or writs, and make
return thereof to the court of common pleas, where such recovery
is had, or judgment given; and if the sheriff, or coroner to whom
such writ or writs, shall be directed, shall refuse or neglect to
execute and return the same accordingly; he shall be amerced in
the county where he ought to return it, and be liable to the action
of the party grieved; and the said amerciament shall be truly and
duly set, according to the quality of the offence, and estreated by
the prothonotaries of the respective courts of common pleas into
the next succeeding general court, or court of oyer and terminer,
in course, that thence process may issue against the offenders, for
levying such fines and amerciaments as shall be unpaid, to the uses
for which they are, or shall be appropriated.

§ 18.   All suits, actions, and causes before the general court,
or the courts of common pleas, & general quarter-session of the
peace, that shall remain undetermined, shall be continued over to
the next respective term ensuing, under the authority of this law.

§ 19.   The courts of common pleas in each county, shall
commence their term, on the

[24]

same day as is herein directed for the commencement of the courts
of general quarter-sessions of the peace.

The foregoing is hereby declared to be a law of the territory,
to take effect accordingly. In testimony whereof, we, William
Henry Harrison, William Clarke, Henry Vander Burgh and John

Griffin, have caused the seal of the Territory, to be thereunto affixed, and signed the same with our names.

Willm. Henry Harrison,
Wm. Clarke,
Henry Vander Burgh,
John Griffin.

VI.

An Act repealing certain laws and acts and parts of certain laws and acts,

INDIANA TERRITORY.
* * * * * *
*   L. S.   *
* * * * * *

WILLM. HENRY HARRISON,
WM. CLARKE,
HENRY VANDER BURGH,
JOHN GRIFFIN.

Made and published conformably to the act of the United States, entitled 'an act respecting the government of the Territories north-west and south of the river Ohio,' at Saint Vincennes the twenty sixth day of January, one thousand eight hundred and one, by William Henry Harrison, governor, & William Clarke, Henry Vander Burgh, and John Griffin, judges in and over said territory.

B E it enacted that the laws and acts and parts of laws and acts, herein after particularly enumerated and expressed, be and the same are hereby repealed, to wit:—The '   act to create the offices of territorial

[25]

treasurer and auditor of public accounts,' passed by the general assembly of the territory of the United States north-west of the Ohio, on the second day of December, one thousand seven hundred and ninety-nine, excepting the fifth section of said law;— the 'law respecting divorces,' adopted and published by the governor and judges, the fifteenth day of July, one thousand seven hundred and ninety-five;—the 'act for allowing compensation to the attorney general of the territory, and to the persons prosecuting the pleas in behalf of the territory in the several counties,' passed by the general assembly of the territory north-west of the Ohio, the nineteenth day of December, one thousand seven hundred & ninety-nine.

The foregoing is hereby declared to be a law of the territory, to take effect accordingly. In testimony whereof, we, William Henry Harrison, William Clarke, Henry Vander Burgh, and John Griffin, have caused the seal of the territory to be thereunto affixed, and signed the same with our names.

Willm. Henry Harrison,
Wm. Clarke,
Henry Vander Burgh,
John Griffin.

[26]

INDIANA TERRITORY.
* * * * * *
*   L. S.   *
* * * * * *
WILLM. HENRY HARRISON,
WM. CLARKE,
HENRY VANDER BURGH.

VII.

A Law appointing a Territorial Treasurer,

Adopted from the Kentucky code, and published at Saint Vincennes the twenty sixth day of January, one thousand eight hundred and one, by William Henry Harrison, governor, and William C l a r k e, and Henry Vander Burgh, judges in and over the said territory.

§ 1.   THAT the governor be authorised and required to appoint and commission during pleasure, a treasurer for the said territory, who shall keep his office at the seat of government thereof; that the said treasurer shall not be capable of executing the said office until he hath given bond with two sufficient securities, to be approved by the governor, in the sum of three thousand dollars, payable to the governor and his successors, for the use of the territory, and conditioned for the faithful accounting for and paying according to law, all such sums of money as shall be received by him from time to time, by virtue of any law of the territory, to be recovered upon the breach thereof, on motion of the attorney general in the general court for public use; provided, ten days previous notice be given in writing of such motion. And moreover, the said treasurer before he enters on his said office, shall take the following oath before the governor:—I *A. B.* do swear or

[27]

affirm that I will faithfully and truly execute the office of treasurer in all things relating to the said office to the best of my skill and judgment according to law. So help me God.

§ 2. And the said treasurer is hereby authorised, empowered & required to receive of the several clerks & prothonotaries of this territory, all fines & other monies by them, or any of them received for the use of the territory; and all other public money payable, or that may become payable into the treasury by virtue of any law of the territory.

§ 3. And the said treasurer shall keep in a book or books, to be provided for that purpose at the public charge, true, faithful and just accounts of all the money received by him from time to time, by virtue of any law of the territory; and also of all such sum and sums of money as he shall pay out of the treasury pursuant to law; and he shall lay a statement thereof before the legislature annually.

§ 4. And if the said treasurer divert or misapply any of the money paid into the treasury for public use, contrary to the direction of law, the said treasurer for such offence shall forfeit his office; and moreover shall be liable to pay double the value of any sum or sums so misapplied, to be recovered for the public use, by motion of the attorney general in the general court, provided ten days previous notice be given in writing of such motion, to the said treasurer so offending.

[28]

§ 5. The said treasurer shall be allowed a commission of six per centum on the sums by him received, as a compensation for his services.

The foregoing is hereby declared to be a law of the territory, to take effect accordingly. In testimony whereof, we, William Henry Harrison, William Clarke and Henry Vander Burgh, have caused the seal of the territory to be thereunto affixed, and signed the same with our names.

Willm. Henry Harrison,
Wm. Clarke,
Henry Vander Burgh.

VIII.

INDIANA TERRITORY.

* * * * * *

*   L. S.   *

* * * * * *

WILLM. HENRY HARRISON,
WM. CLARKE,
HENRY VANDER BURGH.

A Resolution respecting the establishment of Ferries,

Published at Saint Vincennes the twenty-sixth day of January, one thousand eight hundred and one, by William Henry Harrison, governor, and William Clarke, & Henry Vander Burgh, judges in and over the said territory.

WHEREAS it is provided by the first section of the law, to establish & regulate ferries, that application shall be made to the general assembly, for leave to erect ferries over any river or creek in the Territory; and whereas no general assembly has yet been organized in this Territory, and as public convenience requires that ferries

[29]

should be erected, other than those which have been established by the said law; and as no laws can be found for adoption on the subject of ferries, but such as are of a local, not a general nature:

Resolved, therefore, that the governor be requested, and he is hereby authorized and empowered to declare by proclamation or otherwise, from time to time, what ferries shall be erected, by whom to be kept, and where. And the ferries so erected, shall be subject to the same rules, regulations and restrictions, as are provided by the said recited law, for ferries intended to have been established by the general assembly.

The foregoing is hereby declared to be a law of the Territory, to take effect accordingly. In testimony whereof, we, William Henry Harrison, William Clarke and Henry Vander Burgh, have caused the seal of the Territory to be thereunto affixed, and signed the same with our names.

Willm. Henry Harrison,
Wm. Clarke,
Henry Vander Burgh.

E

[30]

IX.

INDIANA TERRITORY.
* * * * * *
*   L. S.   *
* * * * * *
WILLM. HENRY HARRISON,
WM. CLARKE,
HENRY VANDER BURGH,
JOHN GRIFFIN.

A Law in addition to a law, entitled 'a law ascertaining and regulating the fees of the several officers and persons therein named,' Adopted from the Virginia code, and published at Saint Vincennes the twenty sixth day of January, one thousand eight hundred and one, by William Henry Harrison, governor, & William Clarke, Henry Vander Burgh and John Griffin, judges in and over the said territory.

THE clerk of the general court's fees, for taking bond on issuing a writ of error or supersedeas—forty three cents; for making a complete record of every cause, inserting a case agreed on special verdict, at large from the notes, and all deeds and other evidences at large, for every twenty words—two cents; for issuing a dedimus potestatum—thirty-five cents.

The foregoing is hereby declared to be a law of the Territory, to take effect accordingly. In testimony whereof, we, William Henry Harrison, William Clarke, Henry Vander Burgh and John Griffin, have caused the seal of the Territory to be thereunto affixed, and signed the same with our names.

Willm. Henry Harrison,
Wm. Clarke,
Henry Vander Burgh,
John Griffin.

[31]

X.

INDIANA TERRITORY.

* * * * * *

*   L. S.   *

* * * * * *

WILLM. HENRY HARRISON,
WM. CLARKE,
HENRY VANDER BURGH.

A Resolution respecting the compensation of the clerk to the legislature,
Published at Saint Vincennes on the twenty sixth, day of January, one thousand eight hundred and one, by William Henry Harrison, governor, and William Clarke, and Henry Vander Burgh, judges in and over the said territory.

R ESOLVED, that Henry Hurst, clerk to the legislature, shall receive as a compensation for his services—four dollars per day, for each and every day that he may have officiated as clerk; and the governor is hereby authorized to draw by warrant, from the treasury, the sum which may be found due to the said Hurst, upon the settlement of his accounts, for services as aforesaid; and a reasonable allowance for stationary, which may have been expended in the service of the legislature.

The foregoing is hereby declared to be a law of the Territory, to take effect accordingly. In testimony whereof, we, William Henry Harrison, William Clarke and Henry Vander Burgh, have caused the seal of the Territory to be thereunto affixed, and signed the same with our names.

William Henry Harrison,
Wm. Clarke,
Henry Vander Burgh.

INDIANA TERRITORY, *ss*.

I hereby certify, that the foregoing 'copy of Laws, passed in the Indiana Territory, in January 1801,' has been carefully collated with, and rendered literally conformable to the original on file, in the office of the Secretary of the Territory.

JOHN GIBSON, *Secretary.*

LAWS

ADOPTED BY THE

GOVERNOR AND JUDGES

OF THE

INDIANA TERRITORY,

AT THEIR SECOND AND THIRD SESSI-

ONS, BEGUN AND HELD AT SAINT

VINCENNES,

30th JANUARY, 1802, & FEBRUARY 16th,

1803.

Published by Authority.

VINCENNES, (I. T.)

PRINTED BY E. STOUT.

1804.

LAWS

FOR THE GOVERNMENT OF THE

INDIANA TERRITORY.

I.

INDIANA TERRITORY.   *A Law for the appointment of Surveyors and their deputies,*

(L. S.)   Adopted from the Virginia code, and published at Vincennes the thirtieth day of January, one thousand eight hundred and two, by William Henry Harrison, governor, and William Clarke, Henry Vander Burgh, and John Griffin, judges in and over said territory.

§ 1.   A SURVEYOR shall be appointed in every county and commissioned by the governor, with reservation in such commission for one sixth part of the legal fees for the use of the Territory, for the yearly payment of which he shall give bond with sufficient security to the governor, shall reside within his county, and before he shall be capable of entering upon the execution of his office, shall, before the court of quarter sessions of said county take an oath, and give bond with two sufficient sureties to the governor and his successors, in such sum as he shall direct for the faithful execution of his office.

§ 2. All deputy surveyors shall be nominated by their principals, who shall be an-

(4)

swerable for them, and if of good character commissioned by the governor, and shall thereupon be entitled to one half of all fees received for services performed by them respectively, after deducting the proportion thereof due to the territory.

§ 3.   If any principal surveyor shall fail to nominate a suffi-cient number of deputies to perform the services of his office in due time, the court of quarter sessions of the county shall direct what number he shall nominate, and in case of failure, shall nom-inate for him, and if any deputy surveyor, or any other on his behalf and with his privity shall pay, or agree to pay any greater part of the profits of his office, sum of money in gross, or other valuable considerations to his principal for his recommendation or interest in procuring the deputation, such principal and his deputy shall be thereby rendered incapable of serving in such office.

§ 4.   That no survey shall be made without chain carriers, to be paid by the person demanding the same, and sworn to measure justly and exactly to the best of their knowledge, and to deliver a true account thereof to the surveyor, which oath every surveyor is hereby empowered and required to administer.

The foregoing is hereby declared to be a law of the terri-tory, to take effect from the adoption thereof.   In testimony whereof, we, William Henry Harrison, William Clarke, Henry

(5)

Vander Burgh, and John Griffin, have caused the seal of the territory to be hereunto affixed, and signed the same with our names.

WIILLIAM HENRY HARRISON.
Wm. CLARKE.
HENRY VANDER BURG,
JOHN GRIFFIN.

II.

INDIANA TERRITORY.   *A Law allowing fees to the Surveyors.*

Adopted from the Virginia code, and published at Vin-cennes, the third day of February, one thousand eight hundred and two, by William Henry Harrison, governor, and William Clarke, Henry Vander Burgh, and John Griffin, judges in and over said Territory.

(L. S.)

D C

§ 1.   FOR every survey by him plainly bounded, as the law directs, and for a platt of such survey after the delivery of such platt, where the survey shall not exceed four hundred acres of land,   5 25

For every hundred acres contained in one survey above four hundred   25

For surveying a lot in town.   1

And where a surveyor shall be stopped or hindred from finishing a survey by him begun, to be paid by the party who required the same to be surveyed   2 62

For running a dividing line.   2 10

For surveying an acre of land for a mill.   1 5

(6)   D C

For every survey of land formerly patented, and which shall be required to be surveyed, and for a platt thereof delivered as aforesaid the same fee as for land not before surveyed, and where a survey shall be made of any lands which are to be added to other lands in an inclusive patent, the surveyor shall not be paid a second fee for the land first surveyed, but shall only receive what the survey of the additional land shall amount to.

And where any surveys have been actually made of several parcels of land adjoining, and several platts delivered, if the party shall desire one inclusive platt thereof, the surveyor shall make out such platt for, ·   1 5

For running a dividing line between any county or township, to be paid by such counties or townships in proportion to the number of taxable inhabitants, if ten miles or under,   10 50

And for every mile above ten   30

For receiving a warrant of survey, and giving a receipt therefor,   17

For a copy of a platt of land, or a certificate of survey,   25

Provided always, That where any person shall employ a surveyor, and shall have received a platt of land surveyed, and afterwards shall assign the platt of land to any o-

[7]

ther, either before or after obtaining a patent for the same, if such person for whom the land was first surveyed shall not have paid for the said survey, it shall and may be lawful for the sheriff or other officer of the county or corporation where such assignee shall reside, at the instance of such surveyor, to make distress upon the slaves, goods and chattels of such assignee, in like manner as is herein after provided for surveyors fees refused, or delayed to be paid.

The surveyor of every county shall annually before the twentieth day of January, deliver, or cause to be delivered to the sheriff of every county, his account of fees due from any person or persons residing therein, which shall be signed by the said surveyor.

And the said sheriffs are hereby required and empowered to receive such accounts, and to collect, levy and receive the several sums of money therein charged of the persons chargeable therewith, and if such person or persons after the said fees shall be demanded, shall refuse or delay to pay the same till after the tenth day of April in every year, the sheriff of every county wherein such person resides, or of the county in which such fees became due, shall have full power, and he is hereby required to make distress of the slaves, or goods and chattels of the party so refusing or delaying payment, either in that county where such person inhabits, or where the same fees became due.

[8]

Every sheriff of every county, shall, on or before the last day of May in every year, account with the respective surveyors for all fees put into his hands pursuant to this act, and pay the same abating six per centum for collecting. And if any sheriff shall refuse to account or pay the whole amount of fees put into his hands, after the deductions aforesaid made, together with an allowance of what is charged to persons not dwelling or having no visible estate in his county, it shall and may be lawful for the surveyors, their executors or administrators, upon a motion made in the next succeeding general or circuit court, or in the court of common pleas of the county, to demand judgment against such sheriff, for all fees wherewith he shall be chargeable by virtue of this act, and such court is hereby authorized and required to give judgment accordingly, and to award execution thereupon provided the sheriff have ten days previous notice of such motion.

The executors or administrators of any such sheriff or under sheriff shall be liable to judgment as aforesaid, for the fees received to be collected by their testator or intestate and accounted for. Every receipt for fees produced in evidence on any such motion shall be deemed to be the act of the person subscribing it, unless he shall deny the same upon oath.

· The foregoing is hereby declared to be a law of the territory, to take effect from the

(9)

adoption thereof. In testimony whereof, we, William Henry Harrison, William Clarke, Henry Vander Burgh, and John Griffin have caused the seal of the territory to be hereunto affixed, and signed the same with our names.

> WILLIAM HENRY HARRISON,
> WILLIAM CLARKE,
> HENRY VANDER BURGH,
> JOHN GRIFFIN.

LAWS

FOR THE GOVERNMENT OF THE

INDIANA TERRITORY.

ADOPTED AT THEIR THIRD SESSION.

I.

R ESOLVED by the governor and judges of the Indiana Territory in their legislative capacity, that the act passed by the general assembly of the North Western Territory, on the nineteenth day of December, one thousand seven hundred and ninety-nine, "entitled an act to encourage the killing of Wolves" be, and the same is hereby repealed.

The foregoing is hereby declared to be a law of the territory, to take effect accord-

B

(10)

ingly. In testimony whereof, we, William Henry Harrison, governor, and Henry Vander Burgh, and John Griffin, judges in and over said territory, have caused the seal of the territory to be hereunto affixed, and signed the same with our names, at Vinceenes, this sixteenth day of February, one thousand eight hundred and three.

> WIILLIAM HENRY HARRISON,
> HENRY VANDER BURG,
> JOHN GRIFFIN.

II.

INDIANA TERRITORY. *A Resolution,*

(L. S.) Repealing certain parts of the law entitled a law ascertaining and regulating the fees of the several officers and persons therein named. Published at St. Vincennes, on the twenty fourth day of March, one thousand eight hundred and three, by William Henry Harrison, governor, and Henry Vander Burgh, and John Griffin, judges in and over said territory.

R ESOLVED that so much of the law entitled a law ascertaining and regulating the fees of the several officers and persons therein named, adopted from the New-York & Pennsylvania codes, and published at Cincinnati the sixteenth day of June, one thousand seven hundred and ninety-five, as relates to sheriffs fees in serving executions out of any court of record of this territory, and also so much thereof as relates to mileage payable to the sheriff on service of writs out of

(11)

the general court, be, and the same are hereby repealed.

The foregoing is hereby declared to be a law of the territory, to take effect accordingly. In testimony whereof, we, William Henry Harrison, Henry Vander Burgh, and John Griffin, have caused the seal of the territory to be thereunto affixed, and signed the same with our names.

WILLIAM HENRY HARRISON.
HENRY VANDER BURGH,
JOHN GRIFFIN.

III.

INDIANA TERRITORY. *A Law in addition to a Law regulating certain Fees.*

(L. S.)   Adopted from the Virginia and Pennsylvania codes, and published at Saint Vincennes, the twenty-fourth day of March, one thousand eight hundred and three, by William Henry Harrison, governor, and Henry Vander Burgh, and John Griffin, judges in and over said Territory.

FOR proceeding to sell on any execution on behalf of the United States, or of any individual of this territory, if the property be actually sold, or the debt paid, the commission to the sheriff shall be five per centum on the first three hundred dollars, and two per centum on all sums above that, and one half of such commission, where the land or goods seized or taken shall not be sold, and no other fee or reward shall be allowed upon a-

(12)

ny execution except for the expence of removing and keeping the property taken.

And sheriffs on service of writs issuing out of the general court, shall be entitled to a mileage fee of six cents a mile.

The foregoing is hereby declared to be a law of the territory, to take effect accordingly.—In testimony whereof, we, William Henry Harrison, Henry Vander Burgh, and John Griffin, have caused the seal of the territory to be thereunto affixed, and signed the same with our names.

WILLIAM HENRY HARRISON.
HENRY VANDER BURGH,
JOHN GRIFFIN.

LAWS

FOR THE GOVERNMENT OF THE

INDIANA TERRITORY,

ADOPTED AT THEIR FOURTH SESSION.

INDIANA TERRITORY. *A Law in addition to a law intitled a law to regulate the practice of the General Court upon Appeals and Writs of Error, and other purposes.*

(L. S.)   Adopted from the Virginia and Kentucky codes, and published at Vincennes the twentieth day of September, one thousand eight hundred and three, by William Henry Harrison, governor,

(13)

and Thomas T. Davis, and Henry Vander Burgh, judges in and over said territory.

§ 1 st.   IN all actions hereafter brought to recover the penalty for the breach of any penal law not particularly directing special bail to be given, in actions for slander, trespass, assault and battery, actions on the case for trover or other wrongs, and all personal actions except such as shall be hereinafter particularly mentioned, the plaintiff or his attorney shall on pain of having his suit dismissed with costs, indorse on the original writ, or subsequent process, the true species of action that the sheriff to whom the same is directed, may be thereby informed whether bail is to be demanded on the execution thereof, and in the cases before mentioned, the sheriff may take the engagement of an attorney practising in the general court, and the courts of common pleas endorsed on the writ, that he will appear for the defendant or defendants, and such appearance shall be entered with the clerk in the office, on the first day after the end of the

court to which such process is returnable, which is hereby declared
to be the appearance day in all process returnable to any day of
the court next proceeding. And although no such engagement of
an attorney shall be offered to the sheriff he shall nevertheless be
restrained from committing the defendant to prison, or detaining
him in his custody for want of appearance bail, but the sheriff shall
in such case

[14]

return the writ executed, and if the defendant shall fail to appear
thereto there shall be the like proceeding against him only as is
herein after directed against defendants and their appearance bail,
where such is taken.—*Provided always,* That any judge of the
general court, or justice of the common pleas, in actions of trespass, assault and battery, trover and conversion, and in actions on
the case where upon proper affidavit or affirmation, it shall appear
to him proper that the defendant or defendants should give
appearance bail, may, and he is hereby authorized to direct such
bail to be taken, by indorsement on the original writ, or subsequent process, and every sheriff shall govern himself accordingly.

§ 2d. In all actions of debt founded upon any writing obligatory bill or note in writing for the payment of money, all actions
of covenant & detinue, in which cases the true species of action
shall be indorsed on the writ as before directed, and that appearance bail is to be required, the sheriff shall return on the writ the
name of the bail by him taken, and a copy of the bail bond to the
clerks office before the day of appearance; and if the defendant
shall fail to appear accordingly, or shall not give special being
ruled thereto by the court, the bail for appearance may defend the
suit and shall be subject to the same judgment and recovery as the
defendant might or would be subject to, if he had appeared and
given special bail; and in actions of de-

[15]

tinue the bail piece shall be so changed as to subject the bail to
the restitution of the thing whether animate or inanimate sued for,
or the alternative value, as the court may adjudge.

§ 3d. And if the sheriff shall not return bail, and the copy of the bail bond, or the bail returned shall be adjudged insufficient by the court, and the defendant shall fail to appear and give special bail if ruled thereto in such case the sheriff may have like liberty of defence, and shall be subject to the same recovery as is provided in the case of appearance bail, and if the sheriff depart this life before judgment be confirmed against him, in such case the judgment shall be confirmed against his executors or administrators, or if there shall not be a certificate of probat, or administration granted, then it may be confirmed against his estate, and a writ of *Ficri Facias* may in either case be issued. But the plaintiff shall object to the sufficiency of the bail during the sitting of the court next succeeding that to which the writ is returnable, or in the office on the first or second rule day and at no time thereafter. And all questions concerning the sufficiency of bail so objected to in the office, shall be determined by the court at their next succeeding term; and in all cases where the bail shall be adjudged insufficient, and judgment entered against the sheriff, he shall have the same remedy against

[16]

the estate of the bail, as against the estate of the defendant.

§ 4th. And every judgment entered in the office against a defendant and bail, or against a defendant and sheriff, shall be set aside, if the defendant at the succeeding court shall be allowed to appear without bail put in good bail, being ruled so to do, or surrender himself in custody, and shall plead to issue immediately. The court shall regulate all other proceedings in the office during the preceding vcaation, and rectify any mistakes or errors which may have happened therein.

§ 5th. Any Judge of the General Court, or Justice of the court of Common Pleas may take recognizance of special bail in any action in either of the said Courts depending which shall be transmitted by the person taking the same before the next succeeding Court to the Clerk of the said Court to to be filed with the papers in such action.—And if the plalntiff or his attorney shall except to the sufficiency of the bail so taken, notice of such exception shall be given to the defendant or his attorney at least ten days previous to the day on which such exception shall be taken, and if such bail shall be adjudged insufficient by the Court, the recognizance thereof shall be discharged, and such proceedings shall be had as if no such bail had been taken. The form of which recognizance shall be in the following words, to wit,

(17)

County to wit: Memorandum, that upon the   day of in the year   E. F. of the county of   personally appeared before me (one of the Judges of the General Court, or Justices of the Court of Common Pleas of the county aforesaid, as the case may be) and undertook for C. D. at the suit of A. B. in an action of   now depending in the (naming the court where the suit is depending) that in case the said C. D. shall be cast in the said suit, he the said C. D. will pay and satisfy the condemnation of the court; or render his body to prison, in execution for the same, or that he the said E. F. will do it for him.

§ 6th.   The person taking such bail as aforesaid, shall if required, at the same, deliver to the person or persons acknowledging the recognizance afore mentioned, a bail piece in the words & form, following, to wit: county to wit: C. D. of the county of   aforesaid is delivered to bail on a *Cepi Corpus* unto E. F. of the county aforesaid, at the suit of A. B. the   day of in the year

§ 7th.   Rules shall be held monthly in the clerks office of the general court, and each court of common pleas beginning the day after the rising of such court: the plaintiff shall file his declaration in the clerks office at the next succeeding rule day after the defendant shall have entered his appearance, or the

C

(18)

defendant may then enter a rule for the plaintiff to declare, which if he fails or neglects to do, at the succeeding rule day, or shall at any time fail to prosecute his suit, he shall be nonsuited, and pay to the defendant or tenant, besides his costs, three dollars, where his place of abode is at the distance of twenty-five miles or under from the place of holding the said general court, or court of common pleas, and where it is more, ten cents for every mile above twenty.

§ 8th. One month after the plaintiff hath filed his declaration, he may give a rule to plead, with the clerk, and if the defendant shall not plead accordingly at the expiration of such rule the plaintiff may enter judgment for his debt or damages and costs.

§ 9th. All rules to declare, plead, reply, rejoin, or for other proceedings, shall be given regularly from month to month, shall be entered in a book to be kept for that purpose, and shall expire on the succeeding rule day.

§ 10th. No plea in abatement shall be admitted or received unless the party offering the same, shall prove the truth thereof by oath or affirmation as the case may require, and no plea of *non est factum* offered by the person charged as the obligor or grantor of a deed, shall be admitted or received unless the truth thereof shall in like manner be proved by oath or affirmation.

§ 11th. And where any person other than

(19)

the obligor shall be defendant, such defendant shall prove by oath or affirmation, that he or she verily believes that the deed on which the action is founded, is not the deed of the person charged as the obligor or grantor thereof; in which last mentioned case the plea of *non est factum* shall not be admitted or received without such oath or affirmation.—And where a plea in abatement shall upon argument be adjudged insufficient, the plaintiff shall recover full costs to the time of over ruling such plea, a lawyers fee only excepted.

§ 12th. The plaintiff in replevin and the defendant in all other actions may plead as many several matters whether of law or fact as he shall think necessary for his defence.

§ 13th. The clerk shall proportion the causes upon the docket from the first day of the court to the twentieth both inclusive if in his opinion so many days will be expended in trying the causes ready for trial, and issue *subpœnas* for witnesses to attend the days to which the causes stand for trial. He shall docket the causes in order as they are put to issue, and no cause shall be removed from its place on the docket, unless where the plaintiff at the calling of the same, be unprepared for trial, in which case, and no other shall the cause be put at the end of the docket.

§ 14th.   All actions of trespass quare clausum fregit, all actions of trespass detinue, actions sur trover, and replevin for taking away goods and chattles, all actions of ac-

[20]

count, and upon the case, other than such accounts as concern the trade of merchandise between merchant and merchant, their factors, or servents, all actions of debt grounded upon any lending or contract without specialty; all actions of debt for arrearages of rent; all actions of assault, manace, battery, wounding and imprisonment, or any of them, which shall be sued or brought hereafter shall be commenced and sued within the time and limitation hereafter expressed, and not after, that is to say; the said actions upon the case other than for slander, and the said actions for account, and the said actions for trespass, debt detinue and replevin, for goods and chattles, and the said action of trespass quare clausum fregit, within five years next after the cause of such action or suit, and not after; and the said actions of trespass, of assault, battery, wounding, imprisonment, or any of them within three years next after the cause of such actions or suits and not after, and the said action upon the case for words within one year next after the words spoken, and not after.

§ 15th.   In all actions upon any bond, or on any penal sum, for nonperformance of covenants or agreements, in any indenture, deed or writing contained, the plaintiff or plaintiffs may assign as many breeches as he or they shall think fit; and the jury upon trial of such action or actions, shall and may assess damages for such of the breaches as the plaintiff

[21]

shall prove to have been broken, and on such verdict the like judgment shall be entered as heretofore has been usually done in such actions; and where judgment on a demurer, or by confession, or *nihil dicet,* shall be given for the plaintiff he may assign as may breaches of the covenants or agreements as he shall think fit, upon which a jury shall be summoned to enquire of the truth of every one of those breaches and to assess the damage the plaintiff shall have sustained thereby & execution shall issue for so much, & judgment shall remain as a security to the plaintiff, his executors & administrators for any other breaches which may afterwards happen, and he or they may have a *sciera facias* against the defendant, and assign any other breach, and thereupon damages shall be assessed and execution issued as aforesaid. And in all actions which shall be brought upon any bond or bonds, for the payment of money, wherein the plaintiff shall recover, judgment shall be entered for the penalty of such bond, to be discharged by payment of the principal and the interest due thereon, and the other costs of suit, and execution shall issue accordingly, or if before judgment the defendant shall bring into court the principal and interest due upon such bond, he shall be discharged, and in that case judgment shall be entered for the costs only. And in any action of debt on single bill, or in debt, or *sciera facias* upon a judgment, or in debt upon bond

[22]

if before action brought the defendant hath paid the principal and interest due by the *defeasance* or condition he may plead payment in bar.

§ 16th. Interpreters may be sworn truly to interpret when necessary.

§ 17th. Every person desirous of suffering a nonsuit on trial, shall be barred threfrom unless he do so before the jury retire from the bar.

§ 18th. Not more than two new trials shall be granted to the same party in the same cause.

§ 19th. Any instrument to which the person making the same shall affix a scrall by way of seal, shall be adjudged and holden to be of the same force and obligation as if it were actually sealed.

§ 20th. Where there are several counts, one of which is faulty, and entire damages are given, the verdict shall be good; but the defendant may apply to the court to instruct the jury to discharge such faulty count.

§ 21st. No negro, mulatto or Indian shall be a witness except in the pleas of the United States against negroes, mulattoes or Indians, or in civil pleas where negroes, mulattoes or Indians, alone shall be parties.

22nd. Every person other than a negro, of whose grand fathers or grand mothers any one is, or shall have been a negro, altho' all his other progenitors, except that descending from a negro, shall have been white

[23]

persons, shall be deemed a mulatto, and so every such person who shall have one fourth part or more of negro blood shall in like manner be deemed a mulatto.

§ 23rd. No suit shall hereafter be commenced in any court within the territory by a non-resident until he shall file in the clerks office of such court, a bond with a proved security, who shall be a resident of this territory, conditioned for the payment of all costs that may accrue in consequence thereof, either to the opposite party or to any of the officers of such court, and the same may be put in suit by any of the persons aforesaid for the nonpayment of the sums that may respectively become due to them.

§ 24th. No judgment after a verdict of twelve men, shall be stayed or reversed for any defect or default in the writ original, or judicial, or for a variance in the writ from the delaration or other proceedings, or for any mispleading, insufficient pleading, discontinuance, misjoining of the issue, or lack of a warrant of attorney, or for the appearance of either party, being under the age of twenty-one years, by attorney, if the verdict be for him and not to his prejudice; or for not alledging any deed, letters testamentary, or commission of administration, to be brot' into court, or for omission of the words 'with force and arms' or 'against the peace' or for mistake of the christian name, or surname of either party, sum of money, quantity of mer-

[24]

chandize, day, month or year, in the declaration or pleading, (the name, sum, quantity, or time being right in any part of the record or proceeding) or for omission of the averment 'this he is ready to verify' or 'this he is ready to verify by the record,' for not alledging 'as appeareth by the record,' or for omitting the averment of any matter, without proving which, the jury ought not to have given such verdict, or for not alledging that the suit or action is within the jurisdiction of the court, or for any informality in entering up the judgment by the clerk, neither shall any judgment entered upon confession, or by *nil dicit,* or *non sum informatus,* be reversed, nor a judgment after enquiry of damages be stayed or reversed for any omission or fault, which would not have been a good cause to stay or reverse the judgment if there had been a verdict.

§ 25th.   Papers read in evidence, though not under seal may be carried from the bar by the jury.

§ 26th.   After issue joined in an ejectment on the title only, no exception of form or substance shall be taken to the declaration in any court whatsoever.

§ 27th.   If in *detinue* the verdict shall omit price or value the court may at any time award a writ of enquiry to ascertain the same.   If on an issue concerning several things in one count in *detinue,* no verdict be found for part of them, it shall not be error, but the

(25)

plaintiff shall be barred of his title to things omitted.

§ 28th.   A judgment on confession shall be equal to a release of errors.

§ 29th.   In all actions of assault and battery and slander, commenced and prosecuted in the general court, if the jury find under the sum of sixteen dollars and sixty-six cents, and in the like actions commenced and prosecuted in any county court, if the jury find under six dollars and sixty-six cents, the plaintiff in either case, shall not recover any costs.

§ 30th.   This law shall commence and be in force from and after the first day of January next.

Published at Vincennes the day and year above written, by, William Henry Harrison, governor, and Thomas T. Davis, and Henry Vander Burgh, judges in and over said territory. ·

WILLIAM HENRY HARRISON.
THOMAS TERRY DAVIS,
HENRY VANDER BURG,

D

(26)

II.

INDIANA TERRITORY. *A Law concerning Servants.*

(L. S.)   Adopted from the Virginia code, and published at Vincennes, the twenty-second day of September one thousand eight hundred and three, by William Henry Harrison, governor, and Thomas T. Davis, and Henry Vander Burgh, judges in and over said Territory.

§ 1st.   A LL negroes and mulattoes (and other persons not being citizens of the United States of America,) who shall come into this territory under contract to serve another in any trade or occupation, shall be compelled to perform such contract specifically during the term thereof.

§ 2nd. The said servants shall be provided by the master with wholesome and sufficient food, cloathing and lodging, and at the end of their service if they shall not have contracted for any reward, food, cloathing and lodging, shall receive from him one new and complete suit of cloathing, suited to the season of the year, to wit: a coat, waistcoat, pair of breeches and shoes, two pair of stockings, two shirts, a hat and blanket.

§ 3rd. The benefit of the said contract of service, shall be assignable by the master to any person being a citizen of this territory, to whom the servant shall in the presence of a justice of the peace freely consent that it shall be assigned, the said justice attesting such free consent in writing, and shall also pass to the executors, administrators and legatees of the master.

(27)

§ 4th. Any such servant being lazy, disorderly, guilty of misbehavior to his master or his masters family shall be corrected by stripes on order from a justice of the county wherein he resides; or refusing to work, shall be compelled thereto in like manner, and moreover shall serve two days for every one he shall have so refused to serve, or shall otherwise have lost without sufficient justification. All necessary expences incurred by any masters for apprehending and bringing home any absconding servant, shall be repaid by further service after such rates as the court of the county shall direct; unless such servant shall give security to be approved of by the court for repayment in money, within six months after he shall be free from service, and shall accordingly pay the same.

§ 5th. If any master shall fail in the duties prescribed by this act, or shall be guilty of injurious demeanor towards his servant, it shall be redressed on motion, by the court of the county wherein the servant resides, who may hear and determine such cases in a summary way, making such orders thereupon as in their judgment will relieve the party injured in future.

§ 6th. All contracts between master and servant during the time of service, shall be void.

§ 7th. The court of every county shall at all times receive the complaints of servants, being citizens of any one of the Unit-

(28)

ed States of America, who reside within the jurisdiction of such court, against their masters or mistresses, alledging undeserved or immoderate correction, insufficient allowance of food, raiment or lodging, and may hear and determine such cases in a summary way, making such orders thereupon, as in their judgment will relive the party injured in future; and may also in the same manner hear and determine complaints of masters or mistresses against their servants for desertion without good cause, and may oblige the latter for loss thereby occasioned, to make retribution, by further services, after the expiration of the times for which they had been bound.

§ 8th. If any servant, shall at any time, bring in goods or money, or during the time of their service, shall, by gift or other lawful means acquire goods or money, they shall have the property and benefit thereof, to their own use. And if any servant shall be sick or lame, and so become useless or chargeable, his or her master or owner, shall maintain such servant until his or her whole time of service shall be expired. And if any master or owner shall put away or lame or sick servant under pretence of freedom, and such servant becomes chargeable to the county, such master or owner shall forfeit and pay thirty dollars to the overseers of the poor of the county wherein such offence shall be committed to the use of the poor of the

(29)

county, recoverable with costs, by action of debt in any court of common pleas of this territory; and moreover shall be liable to the action of the said overseers of the poor, at the common law for damages.

§ 9th. No negro, mulatto or Indian shall at any time purchase any servant, other than of their own complexion; and if any of the persons aforesaid, shall nevertheless presume to purchase a white servant, such servant shall immediately become free, and shall be so held deemed and taken.

§ 10th. No person whatsoever shall buy, sell, or receive of, to, or from any servant, any coin or commodity whatsoever, without the leave or consent of the master or owner of such servant; and if any person shall presume to deal with any servant without such leave or consent, he or she so offending, shall forfeit and pay to the master or owner of such servant four times the value of the thing so bought, sold or received; to be recovered with costs by an action upon the case in any court of common pleas of this territory; and shall also forfeit and pay the further sum of twenty dollars to any person who will sue for the same; or receive on his or her bare back, thirty nine lashes, well laid on, at the public whipping post, but shall nevertheless be liable to pay the costs of such suit.

§ 11th. In all cases of penal laws, where free persons are punishable by fine, servants shall be punished by whipping, after the rate

[30]

of twenty lashes for every eight dollars, so that no servant shall receive more than forty lashes at any one time, unless such offender can procure some person to pay the fine.

§ 12th. Every servant upon the expiration of his or her time, and proof thereof made before the court of the county where he or she last served, shall have his or her freedom recorded, and a certificate thereof under the hand of the Prothonotary, which shall be sufficient to indemnify any person for entertaining or hiring such servant; and if such certificate shall happen to be torn or lost, the Prothonotary, upon request shall issue another, reciting therein the loss of the former. And if any person shall harbour or entertain a servant, not having and producing such certificate, he or she, shall pay to the master or owner of such servant, one dollar for every natural day he or she shall so harbour or entertain such runaway; recoverable with costs, by action of debt, in any court of common pleas of this territory. And if any runaway shall make use of a forged certificate, or after delivery of a true certificate to the person hiring him or her, shall steal the same, and thereby procure other entertainment, the person entertaining or hiring shall not be liable to the said penalty, but such runaway besides making reparation for loss of time, and charges of recovery, shall stand two hours in the pillory, on a court day, for making use of such forged or stolen certificate,

[31]

and the person forging the same shall forfeit and pay thirty dollars; one moiety to the territory, and the other moiety to the owner of such runaway, or the informer, recoverable with costs, in any court of common pleas of this territory; and on failure of present payment, or security for the same within six months such offender shall receive thirty-nine lashes on his or her bare back, well laid on, at the common whipping post. And where a runaway shall happen to be hired upon a forged certificate, and afterwards denies the delivery thereof the *ownus probandi* shall lie upon the party hiring such runaway.

§ 13th. This law shall commence and be in force from and after the first day of November next.

Published at Vincennes, the day and year above written, by, William Henry Harrison, governor, and Thomas T, Davis, and Henry Vander Burgh, judges in and over the said territory.

WILLIAM HENRY HARRISON:
THOMAS TERRY DAVIS,
HENRY VANDER BURGH,

[32]

III.

INDIANA TERRITORY. *A Law ascertaining and regulating the fees of the several officers and persons therein named.*

(L. S.) Adopted from the New-York, Pennsylvania, and Virginia codes, and published at Vincennes the twenty-fourth day of September, one thousand eight hundred and three, by William Henry Harrison, governor, and Thomas T. Davis, and Henry Vander Burgh, judges in and over said territory.

§ 1st. NO officer or person shall at any time exact or demand for services hereafter to be rendered, any larger or other fee to be taxed in the bill of costs, than as herein after is provided.

§ 2nd. The attorney general or his deputy's fees, where the duty is performed by them.

	D	C	M
Entering *nolo prosequi,* for each defendant,		62	5
Every process or indictment,		75	
Every information per sheet of seventy two words,		18	
Drawing all special indictments and pleadings per sheet of seventy-two words		18	
A copy thereof per sheet as aforesaid		18	
Every motion in court,		62	5
Fee on trial, demurrer, special verdict, or in error, or in pleas confessed.	3		
For trial of every capital cause where life is concerned,	10		

(33)

	D	C	M
For the whole prosecution, except for drawing of the indictment or information, for the trial of every other matter by bill of indictment or information,	5		

Term fee,	75	
Arguing every special motion,	1 50	
Making up judgment,	75	
Examining a witness,	50	
Taxing bill,	75	
Copy of cost bill if before issue joined	37	5
If after issue joined,	75	

And to the attorney general in lieu of such fees as hereafter may be chargeable to the territory, the annual
sum of   60

§ 3rd. *Counsellors and Attorneys fees in the General court.*

In all civil actions where the title of lands do not come
in question,   7

In all civil actions where the title of lands comes in
question.   10

For advice where the suit is not pending,   3 50

§ 4th. *The Clerk of the General court in civil causes.*

For drawing, sealing and entering a writ,	8	2
Filing a declaration,	12	5
Entering an appearance,	12	5
Filing all other pleadings each,	12	5
Entering every rule,	18	

D

(34)

	D	C	M
Swearing and entering a jury,		28	
The return of a writ and filing the same		12	5
Swearing each witness,		6	
Swearing a constable,		6	
Taking the jurys verdict and entering the same in the minutes,		18	
Special verdict drawing or engrossing per sheet of seventy-two words,		12	5
Entering judgment,		28	
A retraxit, or discontinuance,		12	5

Copies of records or pleadings per sheet of seventy-two
  words,   12 5
Attending and striking a special jury, and delivering a
  copy thereof to each party,   75
Filing an affidavit or other paper on request,   9
Entering satisfaction of record.   18
Searching the record within a year,   18
And for every year back,   6
Drawing recognizance of bail,   25
Every continuance,   40
Entering issue joined,   50
Venire Facias,   50
Every trial,   50
Every rule of reference, for trial, to shew cause, to take
  depositions, give security for costs, for persons out of
  the territory,   17
Copy of the same if demanded,   25
Entering default of either party,   26
Commissions to take depositions,   82

(35)

                                                              D C M
Taking bond on issuing writ of error or supersedeas,   43
For making a complete record of every cause, intering a
  case agreed on special verdict at large from the notes,
  and all deeds and other evidences at large, for every
  sheet of seventy two words,   18
Certificate and seal,   .   75
Entering lease, entry and ouster,   25
For entering each suit on the judges docket,   6
  § 5th. In Criminal cases.
For every appearance,   12 5
Discharge any person on bail,   12 5
Every imparlance to an indictment.   12 5
Drawing process against any person upon information
  or other process,   44
The plea to an indictment or information,   6
Reading the indictment, information or record,   6

Swearing every witness on trial,	6	
Engrossing judgment or information.	18	
Respecting every recognizance	9	
Taking a recognizance, and entering thereof,	56	
Copies of all indictments, informations, and pleadings per sheet of seventy-two words,	12	5
Relinquishing a plea,	12	5
A submission,	**12**	**5**

(36)

	D	C	M
Judgment thereon,		12	5
Copy of the traverse,		12	5
Every subpœna with seal for four witnesses or under		50	
Every witness more		6	
Every order or rule of court,		18	
Taking copy of every special verdict per sheet of seventy-two words,		18	
For the allowance and recording a warrant of *nolo prosequi,*		50	
And to the clerk of of the general court in lieu of such fees in the general court as hereafter may be chargeable to the territory, the annual sum of	40		

§ 6th. To the clerk of the circuit court,

For entering in the judges book every cause to be tried,	6	
Filing every nisi prius record,	25	
Entering every rule	18	
Swearing and impannelling a jury,	28	
Swearing each witness	6	
Swearing a constable,	6	
Reading every deed or piece of evidence,	12	5
Filing a bill of exceptions or demurrer,	12	5
Copies thereof per sheet of seventy-two words,	12	5
Taking verdict and entering it on the minutes,	28	
Entering every nonsuit.	18	

[37]

	D	C	M
Entering default of a juror, and the discharge of others,		18	

§ 7th. Sheriffs fees in the general court,

Serving a writ,   75
Every mile to be computed from the court house of the
  county to the place of defendants residence   6
Taking bail bond and copy or same,   50
Returning a writ   12 5
    Milage for returning writs to the general court from
any county other than the one from which the writ issued,
for the first forty miles,   4
And for every mile over forty   2
Summoning a jury,   1 25
    For proceeding to sell on any execution on behalf of the
United States, or of any individual of this territory if the property be actually sold, the commission to the sheriff shall be five
per centum on the first three hundred dollars, and two percentum
on all sums above that; and one half of such commission where
the money is paid to the sheriff without seizure, or where the
land or goods seized or taken, shall not be sold, and no other fee
or reward shall be allowed on any execution, except for the expence of removing and keeping the property taken.

[38]   D C M

Serving a writ of possession without the aid of the posse
comitatus   1 25
With the aid of the posse comitatus,   3 75
Every mile from the court house   6
Executing a criminal,   7 50
Calling a verdict,   9
Discharging every person by proclamation,   9
Calling plaintiff on nonsuit,   9
Calling a defendant on recognizance,   9
Calling a defendant,   9
§ 8th. Jurys fees in the general court,
Every juryman in each action on which he is sworn   25
Every juror in coming to and attending a view and re-
  turning per day   75
Every juror attending court from a foregn county, com-
  ing and returning per day   56

§ 9th.   Witnesses fees in the general court.

Each witness attending in his own county on trial per day.   37 5

Attending from a foregn county, and coming and returning per   56

Each witness subpœnaed in the county and detained
from a foreign county per day.   56

To a witness on a *duces tecum* coming from a foreign
county attending and returning per day   56

Except for the judge of probat, a clerk

(39)

	D	C. M
of a court, attending in a foreign county with wills, records, and other paper evidence, on subpœna, per day.		1 66
Making a list of freeholders to strike a jury,		2
Serving a *scire facias* and returning,		75
Every person committed to prison,		37 5
Discharging of every person out of prison,		37 5
Bringing up a prisoner by habeas corpus in civil case		1 50
Where the prisoner is actually brought, for every mile from the place of taking him,		6
Executing a writ of enquiry and returning the same		2 50
Attending a view in the same county per day,		1 87 5
The like in a foreign county per day		1 87 5
Attending with a prisoner before a judge on his being surrendered by his bail		1
Summoning a jury on forcible entry and detainer		3 75
Besides a milage fee for every mile from the place of holding court		6
Copy of every writ		18
Serving warrant of attachment so much as the judge issuing the same shall certify		
serving subpœna on each witness		37 5
Calling every action		9

[40]

	D	C	M
Calling every jury		12 5	
swearing a witness.		6	

For dieting a prisoner per day	25
For making a deed for the sale of land, and which deed it is hereby made the duty of the sheriff to make.	2
And to the sheriff for such fees as hereafter may become chargeable to the territory, the annual sum of	50

§ 10th. surveyors fees.

For going to and returning from a view per day, and thirty miles per day	1 25
His actual service on the view per day	1 50
For going to, attending the court on trial and returning per day,	1 25

§ 11th. Justices fees in the court of common pleas.

For all actions in the court of common pleas,	37 5
signing every judgment of court,	12 5
Taking bail,	25
Acknowledging satisfaction on record,	9
Taxing and signing bill of cost,	25
Proof or acknowledgement of a deed before a justice of the court of common pleas,	37 5
For every issue joined,	50
For every trial,	1
Allowing writ of error, habeas corpus,	
Certiorari when presented from the judges of the general court,	50
Granting reference,	25

[41]

	D C M
Approving report of referrees	30
On surrender of principal in court,	20
Hearing petition and making order thereon,	25

§ 12th. Justices of the peace, their fees.

For every warrant in a crimical case.	18
On every trial for forcible entry and detainer,	2 50
Every precept in forcible entry and detainer,	37 5
Every bond or recognizance,	25
Administering an oath,	12 5
Every certificate or order upon act of relief of insolvent debtors.	37 5

Every warrant, order, report or certificate upon an absconding act,   37 5
Every appointment of trustees,   37 5
For summons or capias on debt,   10
For every subpœna,   10
For every name inserted after,   3
Entering every judgment for debt when trial,   20
Every judgment by confession of defendant,   10
Every execution,   20
Certified copy of all proceedings on appeals or certiorari,   33
Writing, signing and sealing every attachment,   13
Entering rule of reference on docket,   10
Every recognizance of bail in civil causes,   10

F

[42]

	D	C	M
Issuing special bail piece,		13	
Swearing a witness,		6	
Administering oath on deposition,		10	
Acknowledgment of a deed and power of attorney by every justice of the peace,		25	
Order for removing a pauper,		50	
Order for relieving a pauper,		25	
Issuing *scira facias* against special bail,		20	
Issuing *scire facias* to revive a judgment after a year and a day,		20	
Or to appraise damages in trespass,		20	
Publishing banns of matrimony.		67	

§ 13th. Prothonotarys fees.

Every writ of capias, entering action and seal,   50
A bond given by the plaintiff when he is not a resident
   of the territory,   37 5
Filing declaration,   6
Copy of declaration or other pleading if required per
   sheet, each sheet containing seventy two words,   6
Discontinuance or retraxit,   12 5

Altering declaration in ejectment and admitting a de-
fendant,   15
Entering every motion & rule thereon,   12 5
Copy of every rule when required,   12 5
Bringing a particular record into court,   25
Entering satisfaction of record,   12 5
Receiving and entering verdict,   12 5
Entering judgment,   15
Reading and entering allowance of e-

(43)

                                                              D C M
very *habias corpus* writ of orror or *certiorari,* and
the return,   25
An execution,   20
Transcript of the record in error, and returning it with
the writ, every sheet of seventy-two words,   6
Entering a defendants appearance,   6
Drawing and filing special bail in or out of court,   18
Every writ of enquiry per sheet,   6
Filing every plea, replication, or rejoinder or other
pleading,   6
A Venire,   28
Receiving and entering the panel and swearing the jury,   18
A *habeas corpora juratorum*   28
Subpœna for four witnesses or under,   37 5
Swearing each witness,   6
Swearing constable,   6
Making up and entering a record of a judgment per
sheet of seventy-two words,   12
Engrossing,   6
Copy of a record of a judgment when required per sheet
of 72 words,   6
Searching the record within one year,   12 5
Every year back,   6
Copy records per sheet of seventy-two words each,   6
Entering report of referrees,   15
On confession of judgment, default, joinder or demurrer,   25

[44]

	D	C	M
Entering rule of court on appointing referrees,	15		
Continuing each cause,	20		
On surrender of principal in court by sureties,	15		
On every issue joined,	25		
On entering every principal motion,	10		
On every trial,	25		
On drawing special list of jury, attending and striking and making copies of jury list for plaintiff and defendant,	50		
Issuing commission to take depositions,	50		

§ 14th. Clerk of the sessions fees.

	D	C	M
For taking recognizance and drawing it up in form to be paid to the clerk or other person who does the service,	37	5	
For engrossing every indictment and filing and reading the same,	56		
Subpœna for four witnesses or under,	37	5	
A venire or other writ,	50		
Entering defendants appearance,	6		
An execution,	25		
Making up the record per sheet of seventy-two words,	12	5	
Copy of same,	6		
Every order or rule of court,	9		
Entering a *nolo prosequi* or *cessat processus,*	18		
A venire for a jury to enquire of riots, forcible entries, detainers, &c.	25		

[45]

	D	C	M
Drawing and engrossing inquisition, and returning same,	6		
Filing record,	12	5	
Entering the panel and swearing the jury,	25		
Swearing witness and constable each,	6		
Reading each evidence or petition in court,	6		
Taking and entering verdict.	12	5	
Entering judgment and the fine,	15		

Entering defendants confession,	15
Copies of indictments and pleadings if required each sheet of seventy-two words,	6
Receiving, reading and filing every order brought to be allowed at the court of sessions, and entering the confirmation, and recording the same as in other cases per sheet of seventy-two words.	12 5
For discharging a recognizance,	10
Each order on recommendation for license including record,	25
Reading petition and entering order of court thereon,	20
For examining every account in court,	10
On entering appeal allowing *habias corpus* and writ of *certiorari* when presented from the judges of the general court.	12 5
Every trial,	25
Continuing a cause,	20

(46)

	D	C M
Entering *nolo prosequi*,		12 5
Certificate and seal,		75
To the clerk of Quarter sessions in lieu of all fees hereafter chargeable to the county, the annual sum of		25

§ 15th.   Sheriffs fees in the Common Pleas in civil matters.

For serving a writ and taking into custody,		50
For every mile as fixed by law,		6
Every bail bond and copy of the same,		50 5
Returning writ,		9
Summoning jury,		75
Attending on view per day,		1
Going and returning,		1
Serving and returning sciera facias,		37 5

For proceeding to sell on any execution on behalf of the United States, or of any individual of this territory if the property be actually sold or the debt paid, the commission to the sheriff shall be five per centum on the first three hundred dollars, and

two per centum on all sums above that, and one half of such
commission where the money is paid to the sheriff without
seizure, or where the lands or goods seized or taken shall not
be sold, and no other fee or reward shall be allowed upon any
execution except for the expence of removing and keeping the
property taken,

(47)

	D	C	M
Serving a writ of possession with the aid of the *posse commitatus*,		2	50
Every mile from the place of holding court,			6
Serving such writ without the aid of the *posse commitatus*,		1	25
For calling a jury on each cause,		12	5
Every person committed to the common jail,		37	5
Calling every witness,			6
Discharging of every person out of the common jail,		37	5
Calling every action,			9
Executing a writ of inquiry, drawing inquisition and returning the same,		1	50
Discharging every person by proclamation,			9
Serving a summons,		37	5
For attending with a prisoner before a judge when surrendered by his bail and receiving the prisoner into custody			50

In criminal cases the like fees in the respective courts
as for the like services in civil cases to be allowed
where the defendant enters a *nolo coutendere* or on
voluntary composition, hath his fine mitigaged, or
where the services are done at the request of, or for
the ease or advantage of the defendant or prisoner,
or by order of court,

(48)

	D	C	M
For dieting a prisoner per day,			25
To the sheriff in lieu of all fees that may be hereafter chargeable to the county the annual sum of,		50	

§ 6th.   jurors fees in the common pleas.

EVERY juryman sworn in each action,   25
EVERY juror attending a view per day.   50

    § 17th.   Coronors fees.

For the view of each body,   3
EACH juryman that sets on the body,   12 5
FOR witnesses the same allowance as in the general
    court, serving writs in all cases the same as is before
    allowed to the sheriff for like services.   The fees of
    the coroners inquest shall be certified by the coroner
    and paid by the treasurer of the county.

    § 18th.   FEES of the probate.

FOR administering an oath,   18
FOR all copies for each folio of one hundred and twenty-
    eight words,   18
FOR seal,   75
FOR filing,   18
FOR a citation exclusive of seal,   50
FOR a letter of administration,   2 50
Taking and filing a renunciation, and taking proof of a
    renunciation, and which proof the judge of probate
    is hereby authorised and required to take,   50
Where a will or administration is contested for hearing
    and determining,   2

(49)

                                                                D C M

For proving a will, endorsing certificate thereon, record-
    ing the same and filing it.   2 50
For qualifying administrator, taking bond and writing
    certificate.   1 50
For a citation when issued,   50
For filing caveat,   18
For proving codicil, if proved seperately, endorsing cer-
    tificate, recording the same and filing it,   1 50
For examining and proving an inventory or account,   1
For granting administration with the will annexed,   2 50
For a search.   18

§ 19th.   Recorders fees.

For recording mortgages per sheet of one hundred words,   16
And the like fees for recording all other deeds and instruments.

For copies of records and deeds per sheet.   12 5

§ 20th.   Attornies fees in the common pleas and quarter
   sessions.

In all civil actions where the title of lands do not come
   in question,   2 50
In all civil actions where the title of lands do come in
   question.   5
For advice where suit is not pending,   1 27

§ 21st.   Secretary's fees.

For copies or exemplifications of re-

G

(50)   D C M

cords per sheet of 72 words, twelve and one half cents,   12 5
And for seal and certificate thereto when required
   seventy-five cents,   75
For affixing the seal to any patent, seventy-five cents, 75
For recording an extract of every patent for land, where
   the same is not recorded at full length.   25
For recording at full length any such patent, on the
   application of the patentee, requesting the same, but
   not otherwise, for every 100 words,   16

§ 22nd.   Clerk of the Orphans court,

Entering every judgment order or rule of court,   20
For reading and filing every petition and report,   13
Entering report,   25
Certificate with seal annexed to a copy for parties use, 50
Every citation,   33
Entering settlement of accounts of executors and ad-
   ministrators,   50
For every copy of said accounts not exceeding one hun-
   dred items with certificate and seal of office,   1 50
Reading and filing petition to sell land swearing admin-
   istrator to the truth of the statement made, and enter-

ing the necessary order thereon,   67
Giving notice by order of court for sale of land for
every advertisement not exceeding three,   25

[51]

Sec, 23.   And to the end all persons chargeable with any
of the fees aforesaid, may certainly know for what the same
are charged, none of the fees herein before mentioned, shall be
payable by any person whatsoever, until there shall be produced, or ready to be produced unto the person owing or
chargeable with the same, a bill or account in writing containing the particulars of such fees, signed by the clerk or officer
to whom such fees shall be due, or by whom the same shall be
chargeable respectively; in which said bill or account, shall
be expressed in words at length, and in the same manner as
the fees aforesaid are allowed by this law, every fee for which
any money is or shall be demanded.

Sec. 24th.   The clerks of the general and circuit courts,
clerks of the quarter sessions and prothonotaries of the courts
of common pleas of this territory shall cause to be set up in
some public place in their offices and there constantly kept,
a fair table of their fees herein before mentioned, on pain of
forfeiting forty dollars for every court day the same shall be
missing through their neglect.   Which penalty shall be to the
use of the person or persons who shall inform or sue for the
same, and shall and may be recovered in any court of record
within this territory, by action of debt or information.

§ 25th.   If any officer hereafter shall claim, charge, demand, exact or take any more or

(52)

greater fees for any writing, or other business by him done,
within the purview of this act, than herein before set down
and ascertained, or if any officer whatsoever shall charge or
demand and take any of the fees herein before mentioned
where the business for which such fees are chargeable, shall
not have been actually done and performed, (to be proved by

the fee book of such officer upon his corporeal oath) such officer for every such offence shall forfeit and pay to the party injured, besides such fee or fees, six dollars for every particular article or fee so unjustly charged or demanded or taken; to be recovered with costs, in any court of record in this territory, by action of debt or information: Provided the same be sued for within twelve months after the offence shall be committed.

§ 26. And for the better collection of the said fees, the clerks and prothonotaries of every court respectively, shall annually before the first day of March deliver or cause to be delivered to the sheriff of every county in this territory, their accounts of fees due from any person or persons residing therein which shall be signed by the clerks or prothonotaries respectively.

§ 27. And the said sheriffs are hereby required and empowered to receive such accounts & to collect, levy and receive the several sums of money therein charged of the persons chargeable therewith, and if such person

[53]

or persons, after the said fees shall be demanded, shall refuse or delay to pay the same 'till after the tenth day of April in every year, the sheriff of that county wherein such person resides, or of the county in which such fees became due, shall have full power and are hereby required, to make distress of the slaves, or goods & chattles of the party so refusing or delaying payment, either in that county where such person inhabits or where the same fees became due. And the sheriff of any county for all fees which shall remain due and unpaid after the said tenth day of April in any year, either to themselves or the sheriffs of another county, which shall be put into his hands to collect as aforesaid is hereby authorised and empowered to make distress and sale of the goods and chattles of the party refusing or delaying payment, in the same manner as for other fees due to any of the officers herein before mentioned, but no action, suit or warrant from a justice shall be had or maintained for clerks or prothonotaries fees,

unless the sheriff shall return that the person owing or chargeable with such fees hath not sufficient within his bailiwick,
whereon to make distress, except where the clerk or prothonotary as aforesaid shall have lost his fee book by fire or other
misfortune, so that he be hindered from putting his fees into
the sheriffs hands to collect; and in that case any suit or warrant may be had and maintained for the recovery there-

[54]

of. And if any sheriff shall be sued for any thing by him done,
in pursuance of this law he may plead the general issue and
give this law in evidence.

§ 28th. Every sheriff of every county, shall on or before
the last day of May in every year account with the clerks and
prothonotaries respectively, for all fees put into his hands pursuant to this law, and pay the same abating ten per centum
for collecting. And if any sheriff shall refuse to account or
pay the whole amount of fees put into his hands, after the
deductions aforesaid made, together with an allowance of what
is charged to persons not dwelling, or having no visible estate
in his county, it shall and may be lawful for the clerks or
prothonotaries, their executors or administrators upon a
motion made in the next succeeding general court, circuit
court, or in the court of common pleas of the county of such
sheriff, to demand judgment against such sheriff, for all fees
wherewith he shall be chargeable by virtue of this law, and
such court is hereby authorised and required to give judgment
accordingly, and to award execution thereupon; provided the
sheriff have ten days previous notice of such motion.

§ 29th. The executors or administrators of any such
sheriff or under sheriff shall be liable to a judgment as aforesaid, for fees received to be collected by their testator or
intestate, and accounted for. Every receipt

(55)

for fees produced in evidence on any such motion, shall be
deemed to be the act of the person subscribing it unless he

shall deny the same upon oath.

§ 30. Sheriff's poundage and all other legal fees in a suit from final judgment to execution, shall, by the sheriff, be levied out of the estate and effects of the person against whom such execution shall be issued.

The foregoing is hereby declared to be a law of the territory, to take effect accordingly. In testimony whereof, we, William Henry Harrison, Thomas T. Davis, and Henry Vander Burgh, have caused the seal of the territory to be thereunto affixed, and signed the same with our names:

WILLIAM HENRY HARRISON.
THOMAS TERRY DAVIS,
HENRY VANDER BURG,

IV.

INDIANA TERRITORY. *A Law authorising the appointment of a Pilot.*

Adopted from the Kentucky code, and published at Vincennes, the twenty-fourth day of September one thousand eight hundred and three, by William Henry Harrison, governor, and Thomas T. Davis, and Henry Vander Burgh, judges in and over said Territory.

(L. S.)

WHEREAS great inconveniences have been experienced, and many boats have been lost in attempting to pass the rapids of the Ohio for want of a pilot, and from persons offering their services to strangers to

[56]

act as pilots by no means qualified for the business for remedy whereof the Governor of this territory is hereby authorised and directed to appoint such person or persons for pilots as to him shall seem best qualified for that purpose, taking bond and security of the person so appointed payable to the governor and his successors in the sum of eight hundred dollars for the due and faithful performance of his office; and the pilot so appointed shall receive for each boat he pilots through the rapids two dollars. And any other person acting as pilot without being duly authorised as by this law directed, shall for every such offence forfeit and pay ten dollars to the use of the territory to be recovered before any justice of the peace of the county of Clark, at the suit of the pilot, whose duty it is hereby made to prosecute for the same, and collected by the sheriff or constable of the said county in the same manner that other fines are by law directed to be collected; and the sheriff or constable shall pay the money so collected to the treasurer of the Territory taking his receipt for the same and the sheriff or constable shall have the same fees for their services as they are entitled to by law for collecting fines and forfeitures in other cases, but nothing herein contained is meant to compel any owner or skipper of a boat to employ said pilot or pilots, but they shall be at liberty to pilot their own boats thro the said rapids.

(57)

The foregoing is hereby declared to be a law of the territory, to take effect accordingly. In testimony whereof, we, William Henry Harrison, Thomas T. Davis, and Henry Vander Burgh, have caused the seal of the territory to be thereunto affixed, and signed the same with our names.

WILLIAM HENRY HARRISON.
THOMAS TERRY DAVIS.
HENRY VANDER BURGH,

V.

INDIANA TERRITORY. *An act repealing certain laws and acts and parts of certain laws and acts.*

Made and published conformably to the act of the United States, entitled "an act respecting the government of the territories north west and south of the river Ohio," at Saint Vincennes, the (L. S.) twenty-sixth day of September one thousand eight hundred and three by William Henry Harrison, governor, and Thomas T. Davis and Henry Vander Burgh, judges in and over said Territory.

BE it enacted that the laws and acts and parts of laws and acts herein after particularly enumerated and expressed be and the same are hereby repealed, to wit, the law ascertaining and regulating the fees of the several officers therein named adopted from the New-York and Pennsylvania codes and published at Cincinnati the sixteenth day of June one thousand seven hundred and ninety five; the law in addition to a law entitled a

H

[58]

law ascertaining the fees of the several officers and persons therein named published at Cincinnatti the first day of May one thousand seven hundred and ninety eight. The law respecting amendment and jeofail adopted from the Kentucky and Virginia codes and published at Saint Vincennes the twenty second day of January one thousand eight hundred and one. The law in addition to the law entitled a law ascertaining and regulating the fees of the several officers and persons there in named adopted from the Virginia code and published at Vincennes the twenty sixth day of January one thousand eight hundred and one. The law in addition to a law regulating certain fees, adopted from the Virginia and Pennsylvania codes, and published at Saint Vincennes the twenty fourth day of March one thousand eight hundred and three. The Resolution repealing certain parts of the law entitled a law ascertaing and regulating the fees of the several officers and persons therein named published at Saint Vincennes the twenty-fourth of March one thousand eight hundred and three. So much of the act intitled an act repealing certain laws and acts and part of certain laws and acts published at Vincennes the twenty sixth day of January one thousand eight hundred and one, as repeals the law entitled a law respecting divorce adopted from the Massachusetts code and published at Cincinnatti the fifteenth day of July one thousand seven hundred and ninety five.

[59]

And the said law respecting divorce is hereby declared to be
and continue in full force until the end of the first session of
the general assembly of the Indiana Territory.

The foregoing is hereby declared to be a law of the territory to take effect accordingly. In testimony whereof we
William Henry Harrison, Thomas T. Davis and Henry
Vander Burgh have caused the seal of the territory to be
thereunto affixed and signed the same with our names.

WILLIAM HENRY HARRISON,
THOMAS TERRY DAVIS,
HENRY VANDER BURGH.

VI.

INDIANA TERRITORY. *A Law to prevent forcible and stolen marriages; and for punishment of the crime of Bigomy,*

Adopted from the Virginia code, and published at
Vincennes the fourth day of November, one
thousand eight hundred and three, by William
(L. S.) Henry Harrison, governor, and Thomas T.
Davis and Henry Vander Burgh, judges in and
over the said territory.

§ 1st.   IF any person or persons within this territory,
being married, or who shall hereafter marry,
do at any time after the commencement of this law. marry any
person or persons, the former husband or wife being alive,
every such offence shall be felony, and the person or persons
so offending, shall suffer death, as in cases of felony; and the
party and parties so offendinding,

[60]

shall receive such and like proceedings, trial, and execution
within this territory, as if the offence had been committed in
the county where such person shall be taken or apprehended.
Provided, that nothing here in contained, shall extend to any
person or persons whose husband or wife shall be continually
remaining beyond the seas, by the space of seven years to-

gether, or whose husband or wife shall absent him or herself, the one from the other, by the space of seven years together, in any part within the United States of America or elsewhare the one of them not knowing the other to be living within that time. *Provided also,* that nothing herein contained, shall extend to any person or persons, that are or shall be at the time of such marriage divorced by lawful authority, or to any person or persons where the former marriage hath been, or hereafter shall be by lawful authority, declared to be void and of no effect, nor to any person or persons for or by reason of any marriage, had or made, or hereafter to be had or made within age of consent, *And provided also,* that no attainder for the offence made felony by this law, shall make or work any corruption of blood, or forfeiture of estate whatsoever.

§ 2nd. And whereas women, as well maidens as widoms, and wives having substances, some in goods moveable, and some in lands and tenements, and some being heirs apparent unto their ancestors, for the lucre of such substances, have been oftentimes tak-

(61)

en by misdoers, contrary to their will; and afterwards married to such misdoers, or to others by their consent, or defiled: Be it further enacted, that whatsoever person or persons shall take any woman, so against her will unlawfully, that is to say, maid, widow or wife; such taking, and the procuring and abetting to the same, and also receiving wittingly the same woman so taken, against her will, shall be felony, and that such misdoers, takers, and procurers to the same, and receivers, knowing the said offence in form aforesaid, shall be reputed and judged as principal felons. Provided always, that this law shall not extend to any person taking any woman, only claiming her as his ward or bond-woman.

§ 3rd. If any person above the age of fourteen years, shall unlawfully take and convey away or shall cause to be unlawfully taken or conveyed away, any maiden or woman child unmarried, being within the age of sixteen years, out of, or from the possession, and against the will of such person or persons as then shall happen to have by any lawful ways or means, the order, keeping, education or governance of any such maiden, or woman child, and being thereof duly convicted, shall suffer imprisonment, without bail or mainprize, for any term not exceeding two years, as shall be adjudged against him.

§ 4th. If any person or persons shall so take away, or cause to be taken away, as is

[62]

aforesaid, and deflower any such maid, or woman child, as is aforesaid, or shall against the will or knowledge of the father of any such maid or woman child, if the father be in life, or against the will or knowledge of the mother of any such maid or woman child, having the custody and governance of such child, if the father be dead, by secret letters messages or otherwise, contract matrimony with any such maiden or woman child, every person so offending and being thereof lawfully convicted, shall suffer imprisonment of his body, by the space of five years, without bail or mainprize.

The foregoing is hereby declared to be a law of the territory; and to take effect accordingly. In testimony whereof, we, William Henry Harrison, Thomas T. Davis, and Henry Vander Burgh, have caused the seal of the territory, to be thereunto affixed and signed the same with our names.

WILLIAM HENRY, HARRISON,
THOMAS TERRY DAVIS,
HENRY VANDER BURGH.

(63)

VII.

INDIANA TERRITORY. *A Law to regulate county levies.*

(L. S.)   Taken from the law heretofore in force in the territory on that subject, and from the Virginia code published at Vincennes the fifth day of November one thousand eight hundred and three by William Henry Harrison governor, and Thomas T. Davis and Henry Vander Burgh judges in and over the same.

§ 1st.   T HAT all houses in town, town lots, out lots, and mansion houses in the country, which shall be valued at two hundred dollars and upwards, and all able bodied single men, who shall not have taxable property to the amount of four hundred dollars, all water and windmills and ferries, all stud horses and other horses, mares, mules and asses, three years old and upwards, all neat cattle three years old and upwards, all bond servants and slaves, except such as the court of quarter sessions shall exempt for infirmities, between sixteen and forty years of age, within this territory, are hereby declared to be chargeable for defraying the county expences, in which they may respectively be found, to be taxed and collected in such manner and proportion as herein after directed.

§ 2d. That the sheriffs in the several counties within this territory shall and are hereby empowered and required as herein after mentioned to receive from each and every person or persons chargeable with taxes, under this law, a written list under oath con-

(64)

taining a just and true account of all and every species of property in his or her possession or care, subject to taxation under this law, and the said sheriffs respectively are hereby empowered and directed to administer the following oach or affirmation to such persons, I A. B. do solemnly swear or affirm, as the case may be, that this list signed by me contains a just and true account of all persons and of every species of property in my possession or care within this county, and that no contract change or removal has been made or entered into or any other method devised practised or used by me in order to evade the payment of taxes.

§ 3rd. That the said sheriff shall advertise at the county town, and also in each and every township in their counties that he will attend at a convinent place, therein to be mentioned, not within five days of such advertisement in each township to receive of each person a list of all the taxable property, which they possess as above mentioned, and the said persons are hereby required to attend at such time and place in their respective townships therefor accordingly.

§ 4th.   If any person or persons shall give or deliver to a sheriff a false or fraudulent list of persons or property, subject to taxation, or shall refuse to give a list on oath or affirmation at such time and place, to the sheriff, the person or persons so refusing shall be liable to a fine, of fifteen dollars, and the sheriff shall proceed to list such person or per-

[65]

sons property agreeable to the best information he can procure, and all such property so ascertained shall be moreover subject to a triple tax to be collected and destrained for by the sheriff of the county as in other cases, and in the case of an imperfect false or fraudulent list the person or persons giving the same shall be subject to pay a fine of fifteen dollars, and the property subject to a triple tax, which fines and triple tax shall be recovered in the county court of common pleas, by the following mode of proceeding and applied as herein after directed.

§ 5th.   The sheriff shall give information thereof personally, or if unable to attend, in writing under his hand to the next court of common pleas held for his county, which court shall forthwith direct the prothonotary to issue a summons requiring the party to appear at the next court, to be held for the county, to shew cause, if any he can, why he should not be fined and triply taxed for giving an imperfect or fraudulent list of his or her taxable property, and the person or persons upon being served therewith by the coroner, and appearing shall immediately plead to issue, and the matter thereof shall be enquired into by a jury or the court, at the defendants option, and on conviction, or the person not appearing, being summoned, the fine and triple tax shall be established by the judgement of the court, who un-

I

[66]

less good cause shewn to the next succeeding court for such failure, shall award execution for the fine and costs and certify the amount of the tax to the sheriff for collection, the amount of which fine, after deducting thereout such allowance as the court may think reasonable to make the coroner for his extraordinary trouble on the occasion, shall be applied towards lessening the county levy, and the triple tax shall be charged to the sheriff, and accounted for in like manner as other taxes.

§ 6th. Every person or persons having knowledge of any incorrect false or fraudulent list being given a sheriff shall give information thereof either to a sheriff or the county court of common pleas, in like manner as the sheriff is directed, and thereupon the same mode of proceedings shall be had, as if the sheriff gave information, and the person informing, shall be entitled to receive one half of the fine imposed on the offender or offenders to his own use, and the other half to be applied towards lessening the county levy.

§ 7th. In case any person taxable, should not attend at the time and place notified by the sheriff to give in a list of his taxable propty, and it should appear to the sheriff that such absence was not intentional or done with a view of avoiding the delivery of such list it shall be lawful for the sheriff to receive his or her list at any time at the dwelling house

[67]

of the sheriff, provided such person tenders his or her list to the sheriff and makes oath to the justness of it, on or before the twentieth of March annually, and in case of failure, the sheriff shall proceed in like manner, as is before directed in cases of refusal to give in lists and the courts shall determine upon the circumstances of the case, whether to inflict or remit the fine and triple taxes.

§ 8th. That the sheriffs in the several counties, throughout this territory shall and they are hereby required to make two fair and complete lists of the persons and property so taken in, and arranged in alphabetical order in manner following, to wit:

Names of persons.	Number of bond servants & slaves	Number of horses, &c. above 3 years old.	Number of neat cattle above 3 years old.	Number of stud horses.	Rate the season.

one of which he shall keep, and the other together with the vouchers, taken by him as aforesaid shall deliver to the clerk of the court of quarter sessions, on or before the

[68]

last day of March yearly. Which lists and vouchers the clerk shall file in his office, and the clerk of the said court shall make thereof a true transcript, which he shall lay before the court at the same term at which they audit the public accounts for their examination and allowance. The bill of tax being allowed by the said court, they shall annex thereto their warrant, under the hand and seal of the presiding justice, and the clerk of the said court, shall, ten days thereafter deliver the same to the sheriff for collection, for which, and for all other services, rendered under this law, the said clerk shall receive from the county ten dollars. Every sheriff so charged shall collect all sums for which he is accountable within four months after he is charged with the collection of the same, and shall be allowed in full compensation for his trouble in taking in the property and collecting the levy ten percentum on all sums by him collected. And the said sheriff shall previously to his entering on those duties take and subscribe before any justice of the peace the following oath or affirmation "I   do solemnly swear or affirm (as the case may be,) that I will faithfully and impartially execute the office of collector of   county, according to the best of my abilities," which oath shall be filed by the said justice with the clerk of the court of quarter sessions, and the said sheriff shall enter into a bond in the penalty of two thousand

[69]

dollars payable to the governor of the territory and his successors in office with two or more responsible sureties, and bonnd for the faithful collection, accounting for and paying the sums wherewith he shall be chargeable as collector of the county, in manner directed by law : and every sheriff so charged to collect the county taxes and levies, may appoint one or more deputies to assist him as well in taking in the property as in the collection of the levy, for whose conduct he shall be answerable, which deputies shall have the same power as the sheriff himself, and such sheriff shall have the same remedy and mode of recovery against his deputies, or either of them, and their sureties respectively for any sums of money which by virtue of this law such sheriff may be subject to the payment of on account of the transactions of any of his deputies, as he himself is subject to by law. And all monies collected by the sheriff as aforesaid shall remain in his hands subject to the orders of the court of quarter sessions of each county respectively for the payment of the debts of the county.

§ 9th. That the following rate of taxation be observed by the court of quarter sessions, in levying the county tax, viz. on each horse, mare, mule or ass, a sum not exceeding fifty cents, on all neat cattle as aforesaid a sum not exceeding ten cents, on every stud horse a sum not exceeding the rate for which he stands at the season. E-

[70]

very bond servant and slave as aforesaid, a sum not exceeding one hundred cents, and every able bodied single man of the age of twenty one years and upwards, who shall not have taxable property to the amount of four hundred dollars, a sum not exceeding two dollars nor less than fifty cents.

§ 10th. That it shall be the duty of the courts of quarter sessions throughout this territory at the first term next after the last day of March annually, and at such other special sessions as they shall appoint to proceed to audit and adjust all claims and demands against their counties, allowing all just claims and demands which now are, or hereafter shall be chargeable upon the said counties respectively.

§ 11th. That the several courts of quarter sessions through-out this territory at their court preceding the thirty first day of March annually, appoint two discreet freeholders in each township who shall proceed to appraise and value each house in town, town lot, town out lot, and mansion house in the country of the value aforesaid, and also shall appraise and value all water and wind-mills, situate on such tract of the country as may be assigned to them respectively by the court of quarter sessions, taking into view the situation and value of the same, and the said freeholders, after having fixed such valuation shall proceed and make out two fair alphabetical lists thereof, stating the proprie-

[71]

tors or occupiers of such lots and mills, with the valuation of each annexed to the same in form following, viz.

Proprietors, owners, or occupiers names.	Town lots and out lots.	Wind and water-mills.	Houses, &c.	Valuation in dollars.

of which lists of valuation the said freeholders shall keep, and deliver the other to the quarter sessions at the next court to be held for said county, which list shall be filed by the clerks in their respective offices, and the said quarter sessions shall at the same time when they lay the county tax, levy a sum not exceeding thirty cents on each hundred dollars of such appraised value.

§ 12th. It shall be the duty of the courts of quarter sessions throughout the territory at the same term at which they audit the public accounts of the sheriff for monies collected **and paid** by him as aforesaid, and having allowed all such

claims and demands against the county as are just and reasonable, to proceed to ascertain the probable expen-

[72]

ces of the county, the aggregate amount of claims allowed, and
also such sum or sums of money as will be necessary to carry
into effect any contract that shall have been made for building
or repairing any county jail, court-house, or bridges, adding
thereto the expence of collection, and such other sum or sums
of money, as the said court of quarter sessions shall conceive
needful to make good deficiencies in collections, insolvencies,
delinquencies and other contingencies. And the said court
shall take into view the money [if any there be] in the treasury, the probable amount that will be received from licences,
to vend and retail merchandise, tavern licences, and taxes on
ferries, and other sources of county revenue, such as fines,
forfeitures &c. after which the said court shall proceed to levy
a tax upon the owners, proprietors or occupiers of all and
singular the objects of taxation pointed out by this or any
other law, having due reference to the returns of the sheriffs
and freeholders aforesaid, and the rule of taxation, truly apportioning such tax upon all objects taxable by this law, so
as to raise a sum of money sufficient to answer and satisfy all
demands then existing against the said county, or which shall
afterwards become due by virtue of any contract or contracts
by the said courts of quarter sessions in behalf of the county
as aforesaid, previously made and entered into, and to answer
such other con-

[73]

tingent county expences, as the necessities of said counties
may require.

§ 13th. That from and after the first day of March next,
every person within this territory, being owner occupier, or
possessor of merchandize, other than the produce or manufacture of this territory, shall previously to offering the same
for sale, by himself or agent, within the territory, or on any

of the waters within or bounding the same pay to the sheriff, for the use of the county in which he or she resides, or offers such merchandize for sale, the sum of fifteen dollars for each store or stand, in which he or she may vend any such merchandize, and the sheriff on receipt thereof, shall give such person paying as aforesaid, a certificate in the words following, viz.   Indiana territory,   county,   the day of
this certifies that A. B. is authorised to vend merchandize within this territory for one year from the date hereof, the said A. B, having this day paid to me, C. D. sheriff of the said county of   the sum of fifteen dollars, it being the annual tax imposed on the retailers of merchandize by a law of this territory.

C. D. sheriff of the county of

Any person obtaining a certificate as aforesaid shall be authorised to vend and sell merchandize by retail in this territory, for one whole year from the date of the same,

K

[74]

and no longer. And if any person or persons shall, after the first day of March next, presume by himself or his agent, to vend or sell, any kind of merchandize within this territory, or on any of the waters aforesaid, not the growth or manufacture of said territory, not having first obtained a certificate as aforesaid he, she or they so offending, shall for every such offence forfeit and pay a sum not exceeding eighteen dollars, to and for the use of the county in which the offence was committed, to be recovered at the suit of the sheriff, whose duty it is hereby made to prosecute therefor, before any court proper to try the same. And the sheriff is hereby required to keep a fair account of all monies received as aforesaid, and also a regular account of the dates of all the certificates by him given to retailers or venders of merchandize under this law. And it shall be the further duty of the sheriffs respectively to lay the same before the county courts of quarter sessions at the same term at which they audit the public accounts annually.

§ 14th. That it shall be the duty of the court of quarter sessions in each and every county at their session next after the thirty-first day of March annually to fix and establish a reasonable tax or duty upon each ferry within their respective counties, the said court in fixing said tax, to take into consideration the value and income of said ferries,

[75]

provided that no one ferry shall be taxed in one year more than ten dollars. And it shall be the duty of the courts of general quarter sessions, when they lay the county levy, to tax the owners or proprietors of such ferries accordingly.

§ 15th. That if any sheriff shall take, demand or receive of any person from whom taxes are due more than his her, or their proper taxes, or shall in any sale of property taken for taxes act contrary to the true intent and meaning of this act or shall neglect or refuse to render a just and true account of all such sales to the county courts of quarter sessions he shall forfeit and pay any sum, not exceeding one hundred dollars to be recovered by action of debt, qui tam, or by indictment before any court having jurisdiction, the one half to the person suing for the same, the other half to the use of the county, and moreover be subject to the suit of the the party injured for damages.

§ 16th. That all sheriffs shall settle and close their accounts annually with the county courts of quarter sessions, at the second term after the period at which they are obliged by this law to finish the collection of the taxes, and shall in their settlements be credited for all the orders of the said court by them produced, and by such deficiencies arising from delinquencies and insolvencies as the said court shall allow, together with the commission, and paying the monies by them

[76]

received. But should any such sheriff fail or neglect to settle his accounts in manner aforesaid, it shall be the duty of the attorney prosecuting the pleas in the respective counties on giving such delinquent sheriff and his security their executors or administrators, ten days notice thereof in writing delivered personally or left at their usual place of abode, on motion to obtain a judgement against them before any court having competent jurisdiction for the amount due such county, with an interest of twelve per cent thereon from the time the same became due. Provided always that if any such delinquent sheriff shall produce his account authenticated as aforesaid to the court to which he is notified, judgement shall not be taken for more than the balance due the county with interest as aforesaid.

§ 17th. That the several courts of quarter sessions shall have power, and they are hereby authorised to make and enter into contracts, in the name and in behalf of their said counties for building anew, or repairing county jails, court houses, pillories, stocks & whipping-posts, and county-bridges when and so often as the courts of quarter sessions may conceive the interest or convenience of said counties may require. And the better to carry such contract into operation the said courts respectively may appoint one or more persons to superintend such building or repairs, and to see that the same is done agreeably to

[77]

the conditions of such contracts, and to make reasonable allowances to such person or persons for his or their services therein. The original contracts so by the said courts to be made for the purposes aforesaid shall be filed in the office of the clerk of the said court.—And the said courts are hereby authorised and required to pass, audit, and allow, the accounts and demands arising under such contracts made by said court, the same being certified by three justices of said court, and to draw orders in favor of such creditors in like manner as they draw other orders on the treasury. Provided always that no such contracts by the said courts to be made shall be of any force or authority to warrant the said court to allow or pass any accounts or demands arising thereon unless the person contracting with the said court shall enter into bond with one or more sufficient surety or sureties to be approved of by the said court in double the sum of said contract payable to the justices of said courts for said county or their successors in office, conditioned for the faithful performance of such contract which bond when executed, shall be lodged with the clerk of said court in trust for said county.

§ 18th. That if any justice of the peace, sheriff as colector, coroner, clerk of the sessions, lister or freeholder shall neglect or refuse to do or perform any of the duties required of them or either of them by this law, he, she,

[78]

or they so offending shall forfeit and pay any sum not exceeding one hundred dollars to be recovered before any court having jurisdiction, by action of debt qui tam or indictment, one moiety to the person suing for the same, the other to the use of the county.

§ 19th. That if any person charged with county taxes or levies, by virtue of this act shall neglect or refuse to pay the same to the collector, or his deputy, within three months next after the court of quarter sessions at which the county tax or levy is or shall be approved, the collector or his deputy shall have power to take the property of such delinquent (he first having demanded the same, and furnished such person with the sum of his or her tax ten days before such distress made, or having left a copy of such tax, ten days as aforesaid, at the usual place of abode of such delinquent) and may proceed to sell the same to the highest bidder. Provided always, that ten days previous notice of such sale be given, by advertising the same in the most public place of the township where such delinquent resides; and provided also that the delinquent may, at any time before the property destrained be sold, ask for, demand and receive the same on tendering his or her taxes then due, and the expences of keeping the property destrained.

And in case the property taken sells for more than the taxes that are due, the collector shall pay the overplus [after deducting reasona-

[79]

ble expences for keeping and taking care of such property] to the person from whom the same was taken. And the said collector shall keep a fair & regular account of all such sales, stating particularly what he detained for his trouble in keeping the property, &c. and lay the same before the court of quarter sessions, who shall examine the same, and if they find the collector has acted in any wise improper they shall forthwith see justice done to the party injured.

§ 20th. And if any person shall think him or herself aggrieved by the valuation of his or her house by the freeholders to be appointed for that purpose, he or she may appeal to the court of quarter sessions of the county, who shall in a summary way, hear and determine upon the case, and shall confirm or alter the assessment of the said freeholders, as to them shall appear just and reasonable. Provided always, that the appeal shall be made before the bill of taxation shall be put into the hands of the sheriff for collection.

§ 21st. It shall be the duty of all the house holders in their respective townships to give in to the sheriff, at the same time that they deliver in a list of their taxable, property and under the like penalties, the names of all single men, (above the age of twenty one years, & who have not taxable property to the amount of four hundred dollars) who lodge or dwell in their respective houses, and if any

[80]

such single man &c. as above mentioned, shall neglect or refuse, on application being made to him, for the purpose by the sheriff or his deputy to pay his tax, it shall be lawful for such sheriff or deputy, to commit such delinquent to the county jail, where he shall remain, until the said tax shall be paid, unless some responsible person, in the opinion of the sheriff shall be forthcoming threfor.

§ 22nd. The office of county treasury in each of the counties, within this territory, shall be abolished from and after the first day of February next, from which period, all the duties of the county treasurer, in each of the counties respectively, shall be performed by the sheriffs, who shall be allowed two per centum on all the monies by them paid upon the orders of the courts of quarter sessions or otherwise conformably to law.

§ 23rd. That the act entitled an act to regulate county levies [excepting the proviso contained in the twenty fifth section thereof, which provides for the collection of the taxes then due and unpaid under the former law of the territory] subjecting lands to taxation, shall be and the same is hereby repealed, provided nevertheless that all penalties and forfeitures that have been incurred may be recovered, and prosecutions and suits, that may have been commenced, may be prosecuted to final judgment, under the said act, as if the said act was continued and in full force.

[81]

The foregoing is hereby declared to be a law of the Territory, to take effect on and from the first of January next. In testimony whereof, we, William Henry Harrison, Thomas Terry Davis, and Henry Vander Burgh, have caused the seal of the territory to be thereunto affixed, and signed the same with our names.

WILLIAM HENRY HARRISON,
THOMAS TERRY DAVIS,
HENRY VANDER BURGH.

VIII

INDIANA TERRITORY—*A Law laying a tax upon law process.*

Adopted from the Virginia code, and published at Vincennes the fifth day of November, one thousand eight hundred and three, by William Henry

L. S.   Harrison governor and Thomas T. Davis and Henry Vander Burgh, judges in and over the said territory.

§ 1st. The following tax on law process shall be paid for the use of the territory:

D C

On each writ or declaration in ejectment, instituting a suit in the general court, the sum of — 1

On each writ of error, supersedeas and habeas corpus, cum causa, or certiorari, issued from the general court — 1

On each appeal from any court of common pleas, or quarter sessions, to the general court — 1

On each writ or declaration in eject-

L

[82]

D C

ment instituting a suit in any court of common pleas, the sum of — 50

On each certificate under the seal of any court, the sum of — 50

which taxes shall by the respective clerks be taxed in the bill of costs.

§ 2d. No writ, supersedeas, certiorari, habeas corpus cum causa, or writ of error shall be issued, or declaration in ejectment, filed by any clerk, unless the taxes hereby imposed be paid down. And in all appeals and writs of error, no transcript of the record shall be delivered to the appellant, or plaintiff in error, by the clerk of the court, or forwarded by him to the general court, before the tax thereon be paid, nor shall any certificate under the seal of any court be granted, until the tax thereon shall have been first paid to the clerk keeping such seal.

§ 3d. The clerks of the said several courts respectively shall keep regular accounts of all the monies which they may or ought to have received, in pursuance of this law, and shall on every the first Tuesdays of March and September account with, on oath, and duly pay to the treasurer of the territory, for the public uses thereof, the said several sums of money by them so received, under the penalty of paying to the use of the territory for every default or neglect, the sum of one hundred dollars, to be recovered with costs, on motion of the treasurer, in the general

[83]

court on giving ten days previous notice of such motion.

The foregoing is hereby declared to be a law of the territory; to take effect on and from the first day of December next ensuing. In testimony whereof, we, William Henry Harrison, Thomas T. Davis and Henry Vander Burg have caused the seal of the Territory to be thereunto affixed and signed the same with our names.

WILLIAM HENRY HARRISON,
THOMAS TERRY DAVIS,
HENRY VANDER BURGH.

IX.

INDIANA TERRITORY—*A Resolution authorising the Governor to draw money from the territorial treasury, for the purposes therein mentioned.*

(L. S.) Published at Vincenns the fifth day of November, one thousand eight hundred and three, by William Henry Harrison, governor, and Thomas T. Davis, and Henry Vander Burgh, judges in and over the said territory.

Resolved, that the governor be, and he is hereby authorised to draw from the territorial treasury, for such sum or sums of money as shall be sufficient to pay and discharge the expences incurred by the territory in demanding and obtaining from the governor of the state of Tennessee, Robert Slaughter, a fugitive from justice, charged with having committed a felony in this territory.

Also that the clerks to the legislature, shall

[84]

receive as a compensation for their services, four dollars per day, for each and every day that they may, respectively have officiated as such—and the governor is hereby authorised, to draw by warrant, from the treasury, the sums which may respectively be found due to them, upon the settlement of their services as aforesaid.

The foregoing is hereby declared to be a law of the territory, to take effect accordingly. In testimony whereof, we, William Henry Harrison, Thomas Terry Davis, and Henry Vander Burgh, have caused the seal of the territory to be thereunto affixed, and signed the same with our names.

WILLIAM HENRY HARRISON,
THOMAS TERRY DAVIS,
HENRY VANDER BURGH.

X

INDIANA TERRITORY—*A Resolution requesting the governor to make application to Congress, for the purposes therein mentioned.*

(L. S.)   Published at Vincennes, the seventh day of November, one thousand eight hundred and three, by William Henry Harrison, governor, and Thomas T. Davis, and Henry Vander Burgh, judges in and over the said territory.

Whereas in the present circumstances of this territory, the revenue is inadequate to the necessary expences thereof. And whereas the territory frequently incurs expences by reason of prosecutions on behalf

[85]

of the United States, to defray which there is no provision by any law of the United States.

Resolved, that the governor be, and is hereby requested to make application to Congress for leave to impose a reasonable tax, yearly, on all persons trading with the Indian tribes within this territory, to and for the use thereof.

The foregoing is hereby declared to be a law of the territory, & to take effect accordingly. In testimony whereof, we, William Henry Harrison, Thomas Terry Davis, and Henry Vander Burgh, have caused the seal of the territory to be thereunto affixed, and signed the same with our names.

WILLIAM HENRY HARRISON,
THOMAS TERRY DAVIS,
HENRY VANDER BURGH.

XI.

INDIANA TERRITORY—*A Resolution authorising the governor to contract for making copies of certain laws.*

Published at Vincennes the seventh day of November one thousand eight hundred and three, by William Henry Harrison governor, and Thomas T. Davis and Henry Vander Burgh judges in and over the said territory.

L. S.

Resolved, that the governor be, and he is hereby authorised and empowered to contract for copying such number of the law adopted the fifth day of this instant, for laying and collecting county levies, or other laws, as he may deem necessary, for the use

[86]

of the territory, and to order the expence thereof to be paid out of the territorial treasury.

The foregoing is hereby declared to be a law of the territory and to take effect accordingly. In testimony whereof, we William Henry Harrison, Thomas T. Davis & Henry Vander Burgh, have caused the seal of the territory to be thereunto affixed and signed the same with our names.

WILLIAM HENRY HARRISON,
THOMAS TERRY DAVIS,
HENRY VANDER BURGH.

XII.

INDIANA TERRITORY,

Resolved by the governor and judges of the Indiana Territory duly assembled as a legislature for the said territory,

That so much of the law entitled a law "establishing courts of judicature adopted from the Prensylvania code and published at Vincennes the twenty third day of January one thousand eight hundred and one, and so much of the law to regulate the practice of the general court upon appeals and writs of error and for other purposes adopted from the Kentucky code and published at Vincennes the twentieth day of January one thousand eight hundred and one, as directs that the attendance of two judges shall be necessary to hold a general court, or court of

[87]

oyer and terminer and general jail delivery be and the same is hereby repealed.

Resolved, that the spring session of the general court heretofore held at Vincennes on the first Tuesday in March in every year shall hereafter be held on the first Tuesday in April of every year, and that all process returnable to the March term is hereby made returnable to the said April term.

INDIANA TERRITORY.

Resolved that so much of the law entitled a law regulating the admission and practice of attornies and counsellors at law passed by the general assembly of the North Western Territory the twenty ninth day of October one thousand seven hundred and ninety nine as requires the applicant to obtain a rule in the general court previous to his examination, and so much of the law as requires the presence of two of the judges at the said examination and also so much as empowers the governor of the territory to grant a licence to attornies be and the same is hereby repealed, and that any one of the said judges be and is hereby authorised to examine and licence any person apllying to be admitted to practice law in the territory either as counsellor or attorney.

[88]

XIII.
INDIANA TERRITORY.

Resolved, that a circuit court shall be held in the counties of Clark, Dearborne and Wayne, and the judges of the general court or any one of them are hereby empowered and required to go the circuit once in every year if necessary into the counties aforesaid when and where they may try all issues in fact in the same manner and under the same regulations as is provided by a law entitled a law establishing courts of judicature.

The foregoing is hereby declared to be a law of the territory to take effect from and after the twenty second day of September one thousand eight hundred and four. In testimony whereof, we,

William Henry Harrison governor, and Thomas T. Davis, Henry Vander Burgh and John Griffin judges in and over said territory have hereunto set our hands and affixed the seal of the said territory the day and year above written.

WILLIAM HENRY HARRISON,
THOMAS TERRY DAVIS,
HENRY VANDER BURGH,
JOHN GRIFFIN.

XIV.
INDIANA TERRITORY.

Resolved by the governor and judges of the Indiana territory, duly assembled, as a legislature for the said territory,
Resolved that the governor be, and he is

[89]

hereby authorised to draw from time to time upon the Treasury of the Territory for all sums of money that may be necessary to defray any expence that is or may hereafter be incurred by sending any express or expresses on public service.

The foregoing is hereby declared to be a law of the territory; to take effect from and after the twenty-second day of September, 1804. In testimony whereof, we, William Henry Harrison, Governor, and Thomas T. Davis and Henry Vander Burgh Judges in and over said Territory, have hereunto set our hands and affixed the seal of the said Territory the day and year above written.

WILLM. HENRY HARRISON,
THO: TERRY DAVIS,
HENRY VANDER BURGH.

William Henry Harrison governor, and Thomas T. Davis, Henry
Vander Burgh, and John Griffin judges in and over said territory
have hereunto set our hands and affixed the seal of the said territory the day and year above written.

WILLIAM HENRY HARRISON,
THOMAS TERRY DAVIS,
HENRY VANDER BURGH,
JOHN GRIFFIN.

XIX.

INDIANA TERRITORY.

Resolved by the governor and judges of the Indiana territory,
duly assembled as a legislature for the said territory.

Resolved that the governor be, and he is

[81]

hereby authorised to draw from time to time upon the Treasury
of the Territory for all sums of money that may be necessary to
defray any expence that is or may hereafter be incurred by sending any express or expresses on public service.

The foregoing is hereby declared to be a law of the territory;
to take effect from and after the twenty-second day of September,
1804. In testimony whereof, we, William Henry Harrison, Governor, and Thomas T. Davis and Henry Vander Burgh judges in
and over said Territory, have hereunto set our hands and affixed
the seal of the said Territory the day and year above written.

WILLIAM HENRY HARRISON,
THOMAS TERRY DAVIS,
HENRY VANDER BURGH.

LAWS

PASSED

AT THE FIRST SESSION

OF THE

General Assembly

OF THE

INDIANA TERRITORY,

BEGUN AND HELD

AT THE BOROUGH OF VINCEENNES,

ON MONDAY THE TWENTY-NINTH OF JULY,

In the Year 1805.

By Authority.

VINCENNES,

PRINTED BY ELIHU STOUT.

ACTS

Passed at the first Session of the Legislature.

CHAPTER I.

AN ACT *for prohibiting the sale of ardent spirits, or other intoxicating liquors to Indians.*

§ 1. Be it enacted by the Legislative Council and House of Representatives, and it is hereby enacted by the authority of the same, That from the date hereof, it shall and may be lawful for the Governor of this territory, and he is hereby authorised and empowered during the sitting of any council or holding any public treaty or conference with any Indian nation or tribe, to prohibit by proclamation, the sale, or other disposition of any ardent spirits or other intoxicating liquors, to any Indian or Indians, by any person or persons, for any purpose, or under any pretence whatsoever, within thirty miles of the place of holding such council, treaty or conference. **Governor to issue proclamation,**

§ 2. Be it enacted, That if any person shall not strictly observe whatever restrictions may be imposed under the authority aforesaid, he, she or they so offending, shall, on conviction by indictment or presentment, be fined in a sum not exceeding five hundred dollars, nor less than fifty dollars; and in case of inability to pay the fine with costs, shall be imprisoned not more than six months, nor less than three months. **Penalty.**

JESSE B. THOMAS, Speaker of the House
of Representatives.

P. MENARD, President pro tempore of the
Legislative Council.

Approved 6th August, 1805.

William Henry Harrison.

CHAPTER II.

AN ACT *to amend an act entitled an act establishing courts for the trial of small causes.*

§ 1. Be it enacted by the Legislative Council and House of Representatives, and it is hereby enacted by the authority of the same, That from and after the passage of this act the jurisdiction **Justices jurisdiction.**

of all and every the Justices of the peace in the territory for the trial of small causes, shall be co-extensive with the limits of his or their county, any law to the contrary thereof notwithstanding.

Constables.

§ 2.   And be it further enacted, That the constable of every township in the territory to whom any warrant shall be directed for service by any Justice of the peace of the proper county, shall have power and authority to execute the same in any township in the county any law to the contrary notwithstanding.

§ 3.   And be it further enacted, That when any judgment is obtained before any Justice of the peace for the sum of twelve

Stay of execution.

dollars and under, there shall be a stay of execution for fifteen days, and when the judgment may be for a sum above twelve dollars, there shall be a stay of execution for thirty days, but in both cases the person or persons against whom such judgment may be rendered shall be subject to the same laws and regulations respecting securities as heretofore, any law or usage to the contrary notwithstanding.

JESSE B THOMAS Speaker of the House
of Representatives.
P. MENARD, President pro tempore of the
Legislative Council.

Approved August 12th, 1805.

William Henry Harrison.

CHAPTER III.
AN ACT *regulating notaries public.*

Governor to commission notaries public

§ 1.   Be it enacted by the Legislative Council and House of Representatives, and it is hereby enacted by the authority of the same, That the Governor shall commission so many notaries public in this territory as to him shall seem necessary, who shall hold their offices during good behavior.

Duty and fees.

§ 2.   And be it further enacted, That they shall make all attestations, protestations and other things which are by law directed relative to their offices,

[4]

and it shall and may be lawful for every notary public to demand and receive the following fees to wit.   For every attestation, protestation, and other instrument of publication under his proper seal relative to foreign bills of exchange, one dollar, and for recording the same in a book to be kept for that purpose if thereunto required by the holder of such bill or note 75 cents; and for every attestation, protestation and other instrument of publication under his proper seal relative to inland bills of exchange or promissary notes the sum of 50 cents, and for recording the same in a book to be kept for that purpose if thereunto required by the holder of such bill or note twenty five cents.

§ 3. And be it further enacted, That it shall be the duty of the Governor to take bond with sufficient security from each notary **To give** public before he enters on the duties of his office in the sum of **bond.** five hundred dollars, conditioned for the due performance of the duties of his office, which bond if forfeited, shall be sued for in the name of the territory and for its use.

JESSE B. THOMAS, Speaker of the House of Representatives.

P. MENARD, President protempore of the Council.

Approved August 15th, 1805.

William Henry Harrison.

CHAPTER IV.

AN ACT authorising the court of common pleas to appoint commissioners for the conveyance of land in certain cases.

§ 1. Whereas many persons die intestate, having previous to their death made sales of land without executing deeds of con- **Proviso,** veyance for transferring the same, or having made a will shall not in such will have authorised their executors or some other person to make such deeds in performance of their contract, for which if suits in law or equity should be instituted by the person or persons possessing from such contract an equitable claim in such lands, it would tend greatly to the injury of the estate of such decedent.

§ 2. Be it enacted, That where any person has died or hereafter shall die intestate leaving his or her heirs or any of them infants, or having made a will, shall not in said will have authorised his or

Executors or admini strators to apply to court of common pleas to apPoint commissio ner..

her executors or some fit persons to make deeds of conveyance, and having previous to his or her death executed bonds or any instrument of writing binding him or her to convey any tract of land or lot of ground in such case the administrator or executor shall apply to the court of common pleas where the land lies to appoint three fit persons as commissioners who shall have full power and authority to convey any tract of land or lot of ground to the person entitled to the same which the decedent bound him or herself and his or her heirs by any instrument of writing to convey agreeably to the tenor of such instrument, and such conveyance so made shall be as valid and obligatory upon the heirs as if made by the ancestor in his life time; Provided however, that nothing in this act shall be so construed as to prevent the infant representatives of such decedent from instituting suits to recover such land or a compensation in damages from the person or persons to whom it shall have been conveyed if any fraud shall have been practised in obtaining the same; Provided always, that the bond or instrument on which said conveyance is prayed shall be filed with the records of the said court. This act shall commence and be in force from the passage thereof.

JESSE B. THOMAS, Speaker of the House
of Representatives.

P. MENARD, President pro tempore of the
Council.

Approved August 15th, 1805.

William Henry Harrison.

CHAPTER V.

AN ACT *to authorise aliens to purchase and hold real estates within the Territory.*

Be it enacted by the Legislative Council and House of Representatives, and it is hereby enacted by the authority of the same, That from and after the passage of this act it shall and may be lawful for any foreigner or foreigners, alien or

[5]

aliens, not being the legal subject or subjects of any foreign state or power, which is or shall be at the time or times of such purchase at war with the United States of America, to purchase lands tenements and hereditaments within this territory, and to have and to hold the same to them, their heirs and assigns forever as fully to all intents and purposes as any natural born citizen or citizens may or could do

JESSE B. THOMAS, Speaker of the House
of Representatives:

P. MENARD, President pro tempore of the
Council.

Approved August 15th, 1805.

William Henry Harrison.

CHAPTER VI.
AN ACT *respecting Apprentices.*

§ 1. Be it enacted by the Legislative council and house of representatives and it is hereby enacted by the authority of the same, That if any white person within the age of twenty one years who now is or hereafter shall be bound by indenture, of his or her own free will and accord and by and with the consent of his or her father or in case of the death of his or her father with the consent of his or her mother or guardian to be expressed in such indenture and signified by such parent or guardian sealing and signing the said indenture and not otherwise to serve as apprentice in any art, craft, mystery, service, trade, employment manual occupation or labor until he or she arrives, males 'till the age of twenty one and females 'till the age of eighteen years (as the case may be) or for any shorter time, then the said apprentice so bound as aforesaid shall serve accordingly.

Bound apprentices to serve,

§ 2. And be it further enacted that if any master or mistress shall be guilty of any misuage, refusal of necessary provision, or cloathing, unreasonable correction, cruelty or other ill treatment, so that his or her said apprentice shall have any just cause to complain, or if the said apprentice shall absent himself or herself from the service of his or her master or mistress, or be guilty of any misdemeanor, miscarriage or ill behavior, then the said master or mistress, or apprentice being aggrieved and having just cause of complaint shall repair to some Justice of the Peace, unconnected with either of the parties within the county where the said master

Master mistress or apprentice guilty ill treatment their remedy

or mistress dwells, who having heard the matters in difference shall have authority to discharge if he thinks proper, by writing under his hand and seal the said apprentice of and from his or her apprenticeship, and such writing as aforesaid shall be a sufficient discharge for the said apprentice against his or her master or mistress, and his or her executors or administrators, the said indenture or any law to the contrary notwithstanding. And if default shall be found to be in the said apprentice then the said Justice shall cause such due correction to be administered unto him or her as he shall deem to be just and reasonable, and if any person shall think himself or herself aggrieved by such adjudication of the said Justice, he or she may appeal to the next court of common pleas in and for the county where such adjudication shall have been made, such person giving ten days notice of his or her intention of bringing such appeal, and of the cause and matter thereof to the adverse party, and entering into a recognizance within five days after such notice before some Justice of the peace of the county, with sufficient surety, condition to try such appeal at, and abide the order or judgment of, and pay such costs as shall be awarded by the said court, which said court, at their said sessions, upon due proof upon oath or affirmation of such notice being given, and of entering into such recognizance as aforesaid, shall be, and are hereby empowered and directed to proceed in and hear and determine the cause and matter of such appeal, and give and award such judgment therein with costs to either party appellant or respondent as they in their discretion shall judge proper and reasonable.

§ 3.   And be it enacted, that no writ of certiorari or other process shall issue

[6]

or be issuable to remove into the general court any proceeding had in pursuance of this act before any justice of the peace, or before any court of common pleas.

JESSE B. THOMAS, Speaker of the House
of Representatives.

P. MENARD, President protempore of the
Council.

Approved August 15th, 1805.

William Henry Harrison.

CHAPTER VII.

AN ACT *to prohibit the giving or selling intoxicating liquors to Indians.*

WHEREAS many abuses dangerous to the lives, peace and property of the good citizens of this territory, and derogatory to the dignity of the United States, have arisen by reason of traders and other persons furnishing spirituous and other intoxicating liquors to the Indians inhabiting or coming into this territory, for remedy whereof,

Proviso.

§ 1. Be it enacted by the Legislative Council and House of Representatives, and it is hereby enacted by the authority of the same, That if any trader or other person whomsoever residing in, coming into, or passing through the said territory or any part thereof, shall presume to furnish, vend, sell or give, or shall direct or procure to be furnished, vended, sold or given upon any account whatever to any Indian or Indians, or nation or tribe of Indians being within the territory, or waters adjoining to, or bounding the same, any rum, brandy, whiskey or other intoxicating liquor or drink, he she or they so offending shall on conviction by present-ment or indictment, forfeit and pay for every such offence any sum not exceeding one hundred dollars nor less than five dollars to the use of the territory   Provided, that nothing herein contained shall be taken or construed to impair or weaken the powers and authority that now are, or at any time hereafter may be vested in the Governor or other person as superintendant or agent of Indian affairs, or commissioner plenipotentiary for treating with Indians. This act shall commence and be in force, when, and as soon as the governor of this territory shall be officially notified that the states of Kentucky and Ohio, and the territories of Louisiana and Michi-gan have passed, or shall pass laws for prohibiting the sale or gift of intoxicating liquors to Indians within their respective states and territories; and it shall continue in force so long as the said acts made or to be made in the said states and territories shall continue in force therein.   The governor of the territory is re-

No ixtoxi cating li quors to be sold or given to Indians.

When in force.

quested to transmit copies of this law to the governors of the several above mentioned states and territories.

JESSE B. THOMAS, Speaker of the House of Representatives.

P. MENARD, President pro tempore of the Council.

Approved August 15th, 1805.

William Henry Harrison.

CHAPTER VIII.

AN ACT making bonds for the payment of money or property assignable.

§ 1. Be it enacted by the Legislative council and House of Representatives, and it is hereby enacted by the authority of the same, That the assignments of bills, bonds or other writings obligatory for the payment of money, or any specific article, shall be good and effectual in law, and an assignee of such may thereupon maintain an action in his own name, but shall allow all just sett offs, discounts and equitable defence, not only against himself but against the assignor, before notice of such assignment shall have been given to the defendant.

JESSE B. THOMAS, Speaker of the House of Representatives.

P. MENARD, President pro tempore of the Council.

Approved August 15th, 1805.

William Henry Harrison.

[7]

CHAPTER IX.

AN ACT *reviving and continuing suits in the Court of Common Pleas of Knox county, and regulating the teste of writs.*

§ 1. WHEREAS the court of common pleas for the county of Knox, which ought to have been held on the first Tuesday of this month of August was not held by reason of the non attendance of a sufficient number of Justices to form a court, whereby all suits and process which were depending therein were discontinued.

Proviso.

§ 2. Be it therefore enacted, That the said suits and process which were commenced for the said court and returnable thereto, and also all suits and process which were depending in the said court be, and the same are hereby revived, and the same proceedings may be had in all the suits and precess aforesaid, as if the said court of common pleas had been regularly opened and adjourned.

Suits continued,

§ 3. And be it further enacted, That all writs and process issuing out of any court of record in this territory shall bear teste in the name of the clerks of the respective courts and be dated on the days on which they issue, any law, usage or custom to the contrary notwithstanding. This act to be in force from and after the passage thereof.

Teste of writs.

> JESSE B. THOMAS, Speaker of the House
> of Representatives.
> P. MENARD, President pro tempore of the
> Legislative Council.

Approved August 22d, 1805.

> *William Henry Harrison.*

CHAPTER x.
AN ACT *for the relief of persons imprisoned for debt.*

§ 1. Be it enacted by the Legislative Council and House of Representatives, and it is hereby enacted by the authority of the same, That any person who now is, or hereafter may be in actual confinement in any of the gaols of this territory, and is willing to deliver up to his or her creditors all his or her estate, both real and personal towards the payment of his or her creditor or creditors shall have leave to present a petition to the court of common pleas in and for the county wherein he or she is so imprisoned, setting forth the cause or causes of his or her imprisonment together also with a list of all his or her creditors with the money due and arising to each of them, to the best of his or her knowledge.

Persons in confinement for debt to petion,

§ 2. And be it further enacted, That the court to whom such application is made, are required to name the time and place at which they will attend to hear what can be alledged for or against

Court shal name the day for hearing.

Debtor to cause noti ce to be given to his credi tors,
the liberation of such debtor, of which time and place so appointed by the court, the debtor shall cause notice thereof in writing at least thirty days previous thereto, to be served or left at the usual place of residence of each of his or her creditor or creditors if residing within this territory, and have the same inserted in one of the newspapers of this territory most contiguous to the place of his or her confinement, if any such creditor or creditors should not reside in the territory.

§ 3 And be it enacted, That at such time and place as aforesaid the debtor so applying to the court as aforesaid shall subscribe and deliver a schedule of his or her whole estate, and make oath and swear to the effect following, that is to say, "I, A B, in the presence of Almighty God, do solemnly swear or affirm [as **To give a schedule and make oath,** the case may be] that the schedule now delivered and by me subscribed doth contain to the best of my knowledge and remembrance a full, true, just and perfect account and discovery of all the estate, goods and effects unto me any-wise belonging, and such debts as are to me owing or to any persons in trust for me, and of all securities and contracts whereby any money may hereafter become payable, or any benefit or advantage accrue to me, or to my use, or to any other person or persons in trust for me, and that I or any other person or persons in trust for me have not land, money, stock, or any other estate real or personal, in possession, reversion or remainder of the value of the debt or debts by me due, and that I have not since the commencement of the suits for which I am imprisoned, or at any day or time directly or indirectly sold, lessened or otherwise dis-

B

[8]

posed of in trust, or concealed all or any part of my lands, money, goods, stock, debts, securities, contracts or estate, whereby to secure the same, or receive or expect any profit or advantage therefrom, or to defraud any creditor or creditors to whom I am indebted in anywise howsoever." Which schedule being so sub**Schedule when sign ed to be returned to the clerk,** scribed in open court shall be returned to the clerk of the court there to remain for the benefit of the creditors, and after delivering in such schedule, and taking such oath, such prisoner shall be discharged by warrant from such court, which warrant shall be sufficient to indemnify such sheriff or officer against any escape or escapes action or actions whatsoever which shall or may be brought or prosecuted against him or them by reason thereof : and if any such action should be commenced for performing his duty in pursuance of this act, he may plead the general issue and give this act in evidence, *Provided always*: that notwithstanding such discharge it shall be lawful for any creditor or creditors by judgement at any time afterwards to sue out a writ of scirefacias to have execution against the lands or tenements, goods or chattels, which such insolvent person shall thereafter acquire, or be possessed of. But no person delivering in such schedule, and having taken the oath, and been liberated from prison by the provisions of this act, shall be subject to imprisonment on final process, for any debts contracted or for damages acrued for the breach of any contract entered into prior to such liberation unless such liberation be fraudulently obtained.

§.4. All the estate which shall be contained in such schedule and any other estate which may be discovered shall be vested in such person as the court of common pleas of the county where such prisoner was discharged shall appoint as assignee, and such assignee is hereby authorised and empowered and required, within sixty days after the taking the said oath, ten days previous notice of the time and place of sale being given to sell and convey the same to any person whomsoever for the best price that can be got for the same, and the money arising by such sale, shall by such assignee, within thirty days thereafter be paid to the creditor or creditors of such insolvent debtor pro rata according to their respective debts, saving however to every such prisoner his or her necessary apparel and utensils of trade, and when any debts are by such schedule said to be due to such insolvent debtor, the said assignee shall sue for and recover the same in his own name as assignee of such debtor in any court proper to try the same, and such assignee shall be allowed to retain out of the effects of such insolvent debtor, before the distribution thereof all reasonable expences in recovering such money and disposing of such estate as shall be adjudged reasonable by the court.

All the e state to be vested in an assig nee.

Prisoner guilty of perjury

§ 5. And be it further enacted, That if any such prisoner as aforesaid shall be convicted of having sold, leased or otherwise conveyed, concealed or otherwise disposed of, or intrusted his or her estate, or any part thereof, directly or indirectly, contrary to his or her foregoing oath or affirmation, he or she shall not only be liable to the pains and penalties of wilful perjury, but shall receive no benefit from the said oath or affirmation. And in case such prisoner at the time of such intended caption, shall not take the said oath or affirmation, or be admitted thereto by the said court, he or she shall be remanded back to prison, and shall not be entitled to the benefit of this act, unless a new notification be made out and served in manner aforesaid.

Prison bo unds,

§ 6. And be it further enacted, That so much of the law regulating prison bounds, as requires persons giving security for prison bounds to stay within the walls of the prison during the night, be, and the same is hereby repealed. This act shall commence and be in force from the first day of September next.

JESSE B THOMAS Speaker of the House
of Representatives,

B. CHAMBERS, President of the Council.
Approved August 22d, 1805.

William Henry Harrison.

CHAPTER xi.
AN ACT *to regulate weights and measures.*

§ 1. Be it enacted by the Legislative Council and House of Representatives,

[9]

Court au thorised to get weights & measures

and it is hereby enacted by the authority of the same, That the several courts of common pleas within this territory, be, and they are hereby authorised whenever they may think it necessary to procure for their respective counties and at the expence of the same, a set of the following measures and weights for the use of their county, that is, one measure of one foot or twelve inches English measure (so called) also one measure of three feet or thirty six inches, English measure as aforesaid, also one half bushel measure for dry measure which shall contain one thousand seventy five and one fifth solid inches, also one gallon measure which shall contain two hundred and thirty one solid inches, which measures are to be of wood or any metal the court may think proper, also one set of weights commonly called averdupoise weight, and seal with the name or initial letters of the county inscribed on it, which weights and measures shall be kept by the clerks of each court for the purpose of trying and sealing the weights and measures used in their county.

§ 2. And be it further enacted, That as soon as the court shall have furnished the weights and measures as aforesaid they shall cause notice thereof to be given at the court house door for one month and any person who shall knowingly buy or sell any commodity whatever by measures or weights that shall not correspond with the county weights and measures shall for every such offence being legally convicted thereof forfeit and pay the sum of twenty dollars for the use of the county where such offence shall have been committed, and also the costs, to be recovered before any Justice of the peace for said county. Every person desirous of having their measures or weights tried by the county standard, shall apply to the clerk of the county, and if he find it correspond with the county standard, shall seal them with the seal provided for that purpose. This act shall commence and be in force from the passage thereof, and shall continue in force until Congress shall pass a law on the subject of this act.

shall notify when got,
penalty for buying or selling by false weight or measure,
May have them sealed,

> JESSE B. THOMAS, Speaker of the House
> of Representatives.
> B. CHAMBERS, President of the Council.

Approved August 22d, 1805.

> *William Henry Harrison.*

CHAPTER xii.

AN ACT *respecting bail in certain cases.*

§ 1. Be it enacted by the Legislative Council and House of Representatives, and it is hereby enacted by the authority of the same, That in all actions where, by the laws of the territory appearance bail is not required such bail shall be required where an affidavit shall be made and filed by the plaintiff or any person

Where appearance bail shall be taken,

in his behalf of an existing debt then due from the defendant to the plaintiff, which affidavit shall be made before any Judge or commissioner authorised to take special bail, or any Justice of the peace in this territory, or if the plaintiff be out of the territory before any Judge of any court of judicature, or notary public of the state, kingdom or nation in which he resides or happens to be, and the sum so specified in such affidavit shall be endorsed on the writ or process by the clerk or prothonotary, for which sum so endorsed the sheriff or other officer to whom such writ or process shall be directed, shall take bail and for no more, and if the party making such affidavit swear to the best of his knowledge or belief the same to be deemed to be sufficient, and when no such affidavit shall be filed and endorsement made as above mentioned, it shall be the duty of the clerk or prothonotary to endorse on the back of the original writ or subsequent process whether appearance bail is to be required or not.

Qualifica tion of bail,

§ 2. And be it enacted, That no person shall be permitted to be special bail in any such action unless he be a householder and resident within this territory, and of sufficient property, if the writ or process issue out of the general court, or if it issue out of any of the courts of common pleas unless he be a house holder of sufficient property, and resident in the county where such court is held.

shall not be admit ted as bail

§ 3. And be it enacted, That no counsellor or attorney at law, sheriff, under sheriff, bailiff or other person concerned in the execution of process shall be permitted to be special bail in any action.

[10]

Practice in general court,

§ 4. And be it enacted, That so much of the first and second sections of a law of the territory entitled, 'A law in addition to a law to regulate the practice of the general court upon appeals and writs of error and other purposes,' adopted and published the twentieth day of September, one thousand eight hundred and three, as requires the true species of action to be endorsed on the original writ or subsequent process be, and the same is hereby repealed.

§ 5. Provided always and be it enacted, That nothing in this act shall prevent any of the said courts or any Judge thereof from ordering as heretofore the defendant in any action, to be held to special bail in such sum as the said court or Judge under all the circumstances of the case shall think proper to direct, which sum shall be endorsed on the process, and the sheriff or officer shall take bail for the said sum and no more. **Special bail,**

§ 6. And whereas by the present laws of the territory the appearance day to all writs and process issuing out of any court of record is declared to be on the rule day after the rising of the several courts to which the said writs are returnable which has been found to be inconvenient and in several cases injurious to the interest of the suitors, for remedy whereof, Be it further enacted, That it shall and may be lawful for the plaintiff or plaintiffs in any action or suit, to file his her or their declaration at and in the term to which such writ or writs are returnable, to which the defendant or defendants may if he she or they think proper appear at the said term and such proceedings may be had therein at the same term to final judgment as the parties in the suit may mutually agree on. Provided however, that no defendant or defendants shall by any thing herein contained be compelable unless he she or they may think proper to enter his her or their appearance before the rule day established by the said law of the territory. **Parties may file declaration**

§ 7. And be it further enacted, That the sheriffs shall return all writs to them directed on the first day of the next succeeding term, any law to the contrary notwithstanding, **Return day**

§ 8. And be it further enacted, That all writs issued during the term of any court may be executed and returned to any day of the same term. This act shall commence and be in force from and after the first day of November next.

JESSE B. THOMAS, Speaker of the House of Representatives.

B. CHAMBERS, President of the Council.

Approved August 22d, 1805.

William Henry Harrison.

CHAPTER XIII.

AN ACT *to authorise guardians of minors to sell houses and lots in towns and villages in certain cases.*

Guardians may sell houses & lots.

§ 1. Be it enacted by the Legislative Council and House of Representatives, and it is hereby enacted by the authority of the same, That whenever it shall appear to the several courts of common pleas of any county in this territory on petition of any guardian or guardians of any minor or minors, being owner or owners, and proprietor or proprietors of any houses and lots in any town or village in this territory that the yearly rents, issues and profits beyond all reprisals of the same are not sufficient to keep them in repair, it shall and may be lawful for such court to authorise the said guardian or guardians to sell and dispose of the said house and lot or houses and lots by public anction to the highest bidder on giving thirty days previous notice of the time and place of such sale which shall be on such credit as the court shall direct payable with lawful interest.

To take bond,

§ 2. And be it further enacted, That the said guardian or guardians on the said sales being made shall take bond from such purchaser or purchasers with sufficient security to be approved of by the court for the payment of such consideration money who shall thereupon by proper deeds convey to such purchaser or purchasers his or her heirs all the estate, right, title and interest of such minor or minors of, in and to the said house and lot or houses and lots which conveyance so made shall be as valid and effectual, as if the same had been made by such minor or minors when of full age.

[11]

To accou nt forsuch sales.

§ 3. And be it further enacted, That the said guardian or guardians shall account for the consideration money received for such house and lot or houses and lots in the same manner as for the other estate of such minor or minors.

JESSE B. THOMAS, Speaker of the House of Representatives.

P. MENARD, President pro tempore of the Council.

Approved August 22d, 1805.

William Henry Harrison.

CHAPTER XIV.

AN ACT *to amend and continue in force a law entitled, 'a law respecting divorce.'*

§ 1. Be it enacted by the Legislative Council and House of Representatives, and it is hereby enacted by the authority of the same, That so much of the said law as requires advertisements to be inserted in some newspaper for the several times therein mentioned in case the party libelled shall not reside within the county of his or her usual residence, or within this territory, shall be, and the same is hereby repealed. **To be repealed.**

§ 2. And be it enacted, That where the party libelled shall not be within the limits of this territory, then the summons by the said law directed to be served upon him or her shall be published at least once a week in some public newspaper in this territory nearest to the usual residence of the parties for at least eight weeks. **Sommons to be served.**

§ 3. And be it further enacted, That with the foregoing amendments the said law, entitled "a law respecting divorce," shall be, and the same is hereby revived and continued in force.

JESSE B. THOMAS, Speaker of the House of Representatives:

P. MENARD, President pro tempore of the Council.

Approved August 22d, 1805.

William Henry Harrison.

CHAPTER xv.

AN ACT *to amend an act entitled an act for opening and repairing Public Roads and Highways.*

To work on roads.

§ 1.   Be it enacted by the Legislative Council and House of Representatives, and it is hereby enacted by the authority of the same, That all persons who by law are bound to work on public roads shall be compelled to work on the same for any number of days not exceeding twelve in each year whenever the supervisor of the district in which he resides shall deem it necessary, under

Penalty

the penalty specified in the said law, that it shall be the duty of the court of common pleas, at the same time that they appoint supervisors to apportion to each one his part of the roads and hands to assist in opening and keeping the same in repair.

To be re pealed,

§ 2.   That so much of the law to which this is an amendment as is contained in the fifteenth, sixteenth, seventeenth, eighteenth, nineteenth, twentieth, twenty first and twenty ninth sections be and the same is hereby repealed.

§ 3.   And be it further enacted, That all and every supervisor or supervisors of the public roads and highways of this territory, who shall refuse or neglect to do and perform his or their duty

Penalty for neg lect or re fusal,

as directed by this act shall on conviction by presentment or indictment before any court of record be fined in any sum not more than forty nor less than five dollars at the discretion of the court and stand committed until payment thereof.   This act shall commence and be in force from and after the passage thereof.

JESSE B. THOMAS, Speaker of the House
of Representatives.

P. MENARD, President pro tempore of the
Legislative Council.

Approved August 22d, 1805.

William Henry Harrison.

CHAPTER xvi.

AN ACT *for organizing a Court of Chancery.*

§ 1.   Be it enacted by the Legislative Council and House of Representatives, and it is hereby enacted by the authority of the same, That there shall be a court

C

[12]

established in this territory under the name and style of the court
of chancery which shall be vested with, and is hereby empowered
and authorised to exercise all the powers and authority usually
exercised by courts of equity.

§. 2.   And be it further enacted, That the said court shall consist of one judge to be appointed and commissioned by the governor of the territory, for, and during good behavior, and the said
judge shall receive such compensation as shall be allowed by law.

§. 3.   And be it further enacted, That the said Judge shall
hold annually at Vincennes two stated terms commencing the last
Monday in March, and last Monday in August, and such special
terms at the same place as the said court shall from time to time
appoint.

§ 4.   And be it further enacted, That in all suits in the said
court the rules and methods which regulate the practice of the
high court of chancery in England so far as shall be deemed by
the Chancellor applicable to this court, shall be observed except,
as is herein after excepted.

§ 5.   And be it further enacted, That if the said court shall
not sit or be opened at any of the said terms whether stated or special the writs and process then returnable, and the bills, suits,
pleadings and proceedings before the said court shall be continued
of course 'til the next term and from term to term until the court
shall sit.

§ 6th.   And be it further enacted, That the said court shall be
always considered as open so as to grant writs of *ne exeat,* injunctions, certiorari and other process usually granted by a court
of Equity in vacation.

§ 7.   And be it further enacted, Tnat if the complainant resides out of the territory, he shall before the issuing of process to
appear, cause a bond to be executed by at least one sufficient person being a freeholder and resident within the territory to the
defendant in the penal sum of   dollars conditioned to prosecute
the suit with effect, and to pay costs if he should be intitled there
unto, and to have the same filed with the clerk, or in default
thereof that the complainants counsellor or attorney, who shall

Court of
Chancery

To consist
of one
Judge,

Hold two
sessions,

Rules,

Proceed
ings contin
ued,

Always
open,

Complai
nant to
give bond

file the said bill, and issue the process thereon, shall be responsible to pay the defendant such costs as he may be entitled to by the order of the court.

§ 8. And be it further enacted, That any complainant residing within the territory shall at the discretion of the court, give security in the manner and form as is required in the case of nonresidents.

May grant a stay,

§ 9. And be it further enacted, That no injunction shall be granted to stay any proceedings in any suit at law before verdict or judgment. unless the court in term time, or the Judge in vacation, be satisfied of the complainants Equity, either by affidavit, certified at the foot, or on the back of the bill, that the allegations thereof are true, or by other means.

Duty of Clerk,

§ 10. And be it further enacted, That every subpena, process of sequestration, writ of execution, or other writ or process shall be issued by the clerk at the instance of the party, and the service or execution thereof, shall be signed and sealed by the clerk.

Rule days

§ 11. And be it further enacted, That rules to plead, answer, reply, rejoin, or other proceedings whan necessary, shall be given on the first Saturday in the months of January, April, July and October, with the clerk in his office, and shall be entered in a rule book for the information of all parties, attornies or counsellors therein concerned.

Clerk to advertise,

§ 12. And be it further enacted, That when any defendant resides out of the territory, or cannot be found to be served with process of subpena, or absconds to avoid being served therewith, public notice shall be given by the clerk to the defendant, in any newspaper printed in the territory as the court shall direct, that unless he appear and file his answer by a day given him by the court, the bill shall be taken pro confesso.

On failure, of defend ant,

§ 13. And be it further enacted, That if the defendant does not file his answer in the time prescribed by the rules of the court, having also been served with process of subpena, or notice given as prescribed by the preceding section hereof, the plaintiff may have a general commission to take depositions, and

[13]

proceed on to hearing, as if the **answer had** been filed and **the** cause was at issue, Provided however that the court for good cause shewn may allow the answer to be filed and grant a further day for such hearing.

§. 14. And be it further enacted, That every defendant may swear to his answer before any judge of this or of the general court or any justice of the peace.

defendant mayswear

§. 15. And be it further enacted, That if the defendant resides out of the territory, he may swear to his answer before any justice of the peace of a county, city, or town corporate; the common seal of any court of record of such county city or town corporate being thereunto annexed.

§ 16. And be it further enacted, That commissions for taking depositions shall be issued, and written notice shall be given of the time and place of taking the same, in such manner as the court in their discretion shall direct.

Depositions,

§ 17. And be it further enacted, That the complainant having obtained a decree, and the defendant not having complied therewith by the time appointed, it shall be lawful for the said court to issue a writ of fieri facias against the goods and chattels, lands, tenements and hereditaments, and real estate of the defendant, upon which sufficient property shall be taken and sold, to satisfy said demand, with costs, or to issue a capias ad satisfaciendum, against the defendant: upon writs of ficri facias, and capias ad satisfaciendum, there shall be the same proceedings as at law, or to cause by injunction, the possession of effects and estate, demanded by the bill, and whereof the possession, or sale, is decreed to be delivered to the complainant or otherwise, according to such decree, and as the nature of the case may require.

defendant failing to comply fi era facias or other process issue.

§ 18. And be it further enacted, That when a decree of the court of chancery shall be made for a conveyance, release, or acquittance, and the party against whom the decree shall pass, shall not comply therewith by the time appointed, then such decree shall be taken and considered in all courts of law and equity, to have the same operation and effect, and be as available as if the conveyance, release, or acquittance, had been executed conformably to such decree.

Decree of court.

§ 19. And be it further enacted, That a decree of the court of Chancery, shall from the time of its being signed, have the form, opperation and effect of a judgment at law in the General Court of this territory, from the time of the actual entry of such judgment.

Fiera faci as,

§ 20 And be it further enacted, That a writ of fieri facias shall bind the goods of the person against whom it is issued, from the time it was delivered to the sheriff or officer to be executed, as at law.

To appoi nt a clerk

§ 21. And be it further enacted, That the said court or the Judge thereof, shall have power to appoint a clerk, who shall hold his office during good behaviour, and be entitled to such fees as shall be authorised by law.

JESSE B THOMAS Speaker of the House of Representatives,

B. CHAMBERS, President of the Council.

Approved August 22d, 1805.

William Henry Harrison.

CHAPTER XVII.

AN ACT *for incorporating the Borough of Vincennes.*

§ 1. Be it enacted by the Legislative Council and House of Representatives, and it is hereby enacted by the authority of the same, That such parts of the township of Vincennes as are contained within the following limits and boundaries, that is to say: beginning on the Wabash on the line that divides the Vincennes lotts and the plantation of William Henry Harrison, thence along the said line to the outer boundary line of the common, thence along the said line to the outer boundary line of the common, thence along the said line to the southern extreme of the Cathrenette Prairie, thence by a line northwest to the Wabash, thence along the said river to the place of beginning, shall be, and the same is hereby erected into a Borough, which shall henceforth be distinguished, known and called by the name of the Borough of Vincennes.

Bounda ry and name,

§ 2. And be it further enacted, That for the better ordering, ruling and governing the said Borough of Vincennes, and the inhabitants thereof, there shall

[14]

henceforth be in the said Borough, a Chairman and nine assistants, which said chairman and assistants, shall be a body corporate, in deed, fact and name, by the name and style of the "Chairman and Assistants of the Borough of Vincennes," and by the same name shall have perpetual succession, and they and their successors at all times hereafter, by the name of "The Chairman and Assistants of the Borough of Vincennes" shall be persons able and capable in law to sue and be sued, implead and be impleaded, in any court of justice whatever and to make and use one common seal, and the same to alter and change at pleasure. **Ordering ruling & govern ing the bo rough,**

§ 3. And be it further enacted, That the said chairman and assistants shall on the first day of November annually be chosen and elected by such persons as may be possessed of any lotts or other lands within the Borough, and being resident therein, Provided always, that the said officers before they proceed to execute their respective offices, shall take an oath or affirmation that they will faithfully discharge and execute such office according to the best of their knowledge and understanding. **To take an oath.**

§ 4. And be it further enacted, That the chairman and assistants or a majority of them, of which the chairman is always to be one, shall have full power from time to time, and at all times hereafter to hold a common council within the said Borough, as the chairman shall appoint, and to make such bye laws, ordinances and regulations in writing not inconsistant with the laws of this territory or of the United States as to them shall appear necessary for the good government of the said Borough and the inhabitants thereof, and the same to put in execution, revoke, alter and make anew, as to them shall appear necessary and convenient, and to appoint such subordinate officers as they may think necessary for the police of the said Borough, and for carrying this law in effect. And by ordinance to require such sureties from the several officers, and to annex such fees to the several officers of the corporation, and to impose such fines for a neglect of duty, or misconduct in office, as to them shall appear necessary, and to make, limit, impose and tax reasonable fines against all, and upon all persons who shall offend against the laws, ordinances and regulations of **Their du ty.**

the corporation made as aforesaid, and all and every such fines to take, demand, require and levy of the goods and chattels, of such defender, to be appropriated to the use and benefit of the inhabitants thereof.

§ 5. And be it further enacted, That it shall and may be lawful for the said chairman and assistants to commit every person or persons, offender or offenders, who by law they are or shall be authorised to commit to jail, or imprison to and in the jail of the county of Knox, and the keeper of the said jail is hereby authorised to receive such person so committed and him her or them to keep in close and safe custody, until thence discharged by due course of law. This act to be in force from and after the passage thereof.

JESSE B THOMAS Speaker of the House
of Representatives,

B. CHAMBERS, President of the Council.

Approved August 24th, 1805.

William Henry Harrison.

CHAPTER XVIII.
AN ACT *to amend an act respecting Tavern License.*

Court of common pleas to grant tavernlicense

§ 1. Be it enacted by the Legislative Council and House of Representatives, and it is hereby enacted by the authority of the same, That the powers heretofore vested in the court of general quarter sessions of the peace, under an act of this territory, entitled 'An act respecting tavern license,' shall be hereafter vested in the several courts of common pleas of each county, that permission granted by said court to any person for keeping a tavern shall be sufficient to authorise the same without a license from the governor for the term of one year thereafter.

Court to impose a tax on li cense,

§ 2. And be it further enacted, That the said court shall at the time of granting any license under this act demand of and from the person obtaining the same any sum not exceeding twelve dollars, which they may deem reasonable, taking into consideration the stand where such tavern is to be opened, which sum so received, shall, by the said court be paid to the county treasurer, for the

[15]

use of the county, and the said court shall also demand of such applicant, one dollar for the use of the clerk.

§ 3. And be it further enacted, That the courts of common pleas respectively at the time of granting any license, or permission under this act, shall make out a list of rates for the government of the tavern keepers applying for the same, and it shall be the duty of the clerk of the common pleas at the time of granting such license or permission under the direction of the court aforesaid, to make out a copy of the said rates, and deliver the same to the person applying for permission or license to keep a tavern, who shall set the same up in the most public room in his or her house, and any person who shall presume to sell at any higher rates than those made by the court or without having first set up his rates as aforesaid, for every such offence, shall forfeit and pay twenty dollars for the use of the person suing for the same, before any justice within this territory.

Court to make out a list of rates,

Penalty,

§ 4. And be it further enacted, That all laws and parts of laws which come within the purview of this act, be, and the same are hereby repealed.

Repealed

§ 5. And be it further enacted, That so much of the law aforesaid, as prevents the keepers of taverns within this territory from keeping accounts with any customer for any other or greater sum than three dollars, be, and as to any tavern accounts hereafter to be contracted, the same is hereby repealed. This law shall commence and be in force from and after the passage thereof.

Allowing tavern ke epers to keep ac counts.

JESSE B THOMAS Speaker of the House of Representatives,

B. CHAMBERS, President of the Council.

Approved August 24th, 1805.

William Henry Harrison.

CHAPTER XIX.

AN ACT *Organizing Inferior Courts.*

Powers of the sever al courts

§ 1. Be it enacted by the Legislative Council and House of Representatives, and it is hereby enacted by the authority of the

vested in a
court of
common
pleas.
same, That from and after the first day of January next, all the
powers vested in and exercised by the courts of common pleas,
courts of general quarter sessions of the peace, and the orphans
courts in this territory shall be, and they are hereby invested in a
court to be established in each county under the name and style
of the court of common pleas.

To consist
of three
judges.
§ 2.   And be it further enacted, That the said court shall consist of three judges, any two of whom shall form a quorum, to be
appointed and commissioned by the governor, for and during
good behaviour.

Shall hold
six sessions
annually.
§ 3.   And be it further enacted, That the said court shall hold
annually six sessions, at three of which business properly belonging to the common pleas and quarter sessions, only shall be transacted, but the said court at all the said terms shall be open for
any other kind of business usually transacted in either of the said
courts.

At what
times,
§ 4.   And be it further enacted, That the terms of the said
court for business heretofore cognizable in the court of common
pleas, and such as has been and is now cognizable in the court of
general quarter sessions of the peace of a criminal nature, shall
commence at the following periods, to wit: for the county of Dearborn, on the second Mondays in January, May & September; for
the county of Clark, on the first Mondays of January, May and
September; for the county of Knox, on the last Mondays of
March, July and November; for the county of Randolph, on the
third Mondays in April, August and December; and for the
county of St. Clair, on the last Mondays in April, August and
December, yearly, and every year.

§ 5.   And be it further enacted, That the three other annual
sessions of the said courts shall be holden for the county of
Dearborn, on the first Tuesdays in March, August and November;
for the county of Clark, on the first Mondays in March, July and
November; for the county of Knox on the first Tuesdays in
February, May and September; for the county of Randolph, on
the first Mondays in March, July and November; and for the
county of St. Clair, on the third Mondays in March, July and
November, yearly and every year.

§ 6, And be it further enacted, That if the said courts shall not be opened at

D

[16]

the periods aforesaid, it shall be lawful for the sheriff to adjourn the said court from day to day for two days, and if the said court shall not then be opened, he shall, and is hereby authorised to adjourn the said court 'til court in course.

Sheriff to adjourn court from day today

§ 7. And be it further enacted, That the judges of the said court shall respectively receive two huudred and fifty cents for every day they shall sit, to be paid out of the county levy.

Judges salary.

§ 8. And be it further enacted, That the fees which are now allowed to the judges and justices of the courts of common pleas, general quarter sessions and orphans court, and which may hereafter accrue on any prosecutions or suits, which may, or shall be instituted in any of the said courts, shall be collected by the sheriff, and by him be accounted for on the first day of January, and the first day of June, annually; to and for the use of the county.

Sheriff to collect & account for fees.

§ 9. And be it further enacted, That a clerk of the said court shall be appointed and commissioned by the governor for and during good behavior, who shall be entitled to, and authorised to receive such fees as are now allowed to clerks in either the common pleas, quarter sessions or orphans court.

To be a clerk and his fees,

§ 10. And be it further enacted, That from and after the said first day of January next, all powers and authority, now vested in, and exercised by the judges of probate in the respective counties, shall be invested in the said courts of common pleas, and the clerks thereof shall severally be entitled to such fees as are allowed to the judges of probate.

Powers of the court of probate vested in a court of common pleas.

§ 11. And be it further enacted, That all prosecutions, suits, pleadings & other proceedings which may be pending in either of the said courts of common pleas quarter sessions of the peace or orphans court on the said first day of January next, shall be and the same are hereby continued to the said court of common pleas.

§ 12. And be it further enacted, That from and after the said first day of January next, all laws, and parts of laws, which come within the purview of this act, be, and the same are hereby repealed.

JESSE B. THOMAS, Speaker of the House
of Representatives.

B. CHAMBERS, President of the Council.

Approved August 24th, 1805.

William Henry Harrison.

CHAPTER xx.

AN ACT *respecting certain Crimes and Punishments.*

proviso,

WHEREAS by the existing penal laws of this territory, the punishment in certain cases is not proportioned to the crime, for remedy whereof,

§ 1. Be it enacted by the Legislative Council and House of Representatives, and it is hereby enacted by the authority of the same, That if any person or persons shall steal or purloin, from

Persons guilty to be punish ed

another person or persons any Horse Mare Gelding Mule or Ass, he she or they so offending shall for the first offence pay to the owner of such horse mare gelding mule or ass the value thereof and receive not less than fifty nor more than two hundred stripes, and shall moreover be committed to the jail of the county until such value be paid with the costs of prosecution. Upon the second conviction the offender shall suffer the pains of death.

§ 2. And be it further enacted, That any person who shall steal any hog, shoat or pig, or mark or alter the mark of any hog,

Stealing or mark ing a hog, shoat or pig shall be punish ed

shoat or pig with an intention of stealing the same, for every such offence, upon being thereof lawfully convicted shall be fined in any sum not exceeding 100 dollars nor less than fifty dollars, and moreover receive on his or her bare back any number of lashes not exceeding 39 nor less than twenty five; Provided nevertheless, that nothing herein contained shall be so construed as to prevent any person from marking or killing his own unmarked hogs which may be running at large with others in his own mark.

Profane swearing

§ 3. And be it further enacted, That if any person shall presume to appear before any court of justice within this territory, before any judge or justice of the peace when acting as such, or before any congregation assembled for public worship, and there make use of profane swearing or other disorderly behaviour the effect of which would have an evident tendency to disturb that good order to be observed on those occasions; if before a court of justice he shall be fined in any

(margin note: or disord- erly beha viour.)

[17]

sum not exceeding fifty nor less than five dollars; if before a judge or justice of the peace he or she shall be fined in any sum not exceeding ten nor less than three dollars; if before any congregation assembled for divine service he or she so offending shall be fined in any sum not exceeding ten nor less than three dollars; and it shall be the duty of any justice of the peace within this territory the same coming within his own knowledge or upon information by one or more respectable witnesses to issue his warrant and have the offender brought forthwith before him and shall immediately assess his fine and for want of sufficient goods and chattles belonging to the defender to be by him shewn to satisfy the fine and costs aforesaid, the said justice shall commit the said offender to the jail of the proper county where the offence shall have been committed; Provided, that nothing herein contained, shall be so construed, as to prevent any court of justice from punishing the like offenders in the manner herein before mentioned.

§ 4. And be it further enacted, That if any person shall hereafter presume to erect or keep any billiard table within this territory without having first entered the same with the collector of the county in which he or she shall wish to erect such billiard table, to be by the said collector returned to the auditor of the territory, to be by him listed as other objects of taxation, he or she so offending, shall on conviction thereof by presentment or indictment be fined in any sum not less than fifty nor more than one hundred dollars, and it shall be the duty of the said auditor at the same time at which he transmits to the collector respectively the lists of lands within their respective counties, to send also a list of all billiard tables entered with him agreeably to the pro-

(margin note: Owners of billiard ta bles to list them.)

visions of this law, and it shall be the duty of each collector respectively within this territory at the same time and in the same manner as is pointed out by the law to collect the revenue of this territory to collect from each person having entered a billiard table the sum of 50 dollars to be paid and accounted for by the said collector in the same manner that other revenue taxes are accounted for, any law, usage or custom to the contrary notwithstanding.

Evidence in case of a rape.

§ 5. And be it further enacted, That so much of the law regulating the evidence in case of a rape, as makes emission necessary is hereby repealed; Provided nevertheless, That the court, before whom any offender may be brought for trial for said offence, shall have other satisfactory proof of evident violence on the person of the woman reported to have been ravished.

§ 6. And be it further enacted, That all laws and parts of laws which come within the meaning and purview of this law be and the same are hereby repealed.

JESSE B. THOMAS, Speaker of the House of Representatives:

B. CHAMBERS, President of the Council.

Approved August 24th, 1805.

William Henry Harrison.

CHAPTER xxi.

AN ACT *concerning Debtors and their Securities, and to empower Securities to recover damages in a summary way.*

Persons bound as securities to give notice to creditors.

§ 1. Be it enacted by the Legislative Council and House of Representatives, and it is hereby enacted by the authority of the same, That when any person or persons shall hereafter become bound as security or securities by bond, bill or note for the payment of money or other property, shall apprehend that his or their principal debtor or debtors is or are likely to become insolvent, or to migrate from this territory without previously discharging such bond, bill or note so that it will be impossible, or extremely difficult for such security or securities after being compelled to pay the money or other property due by such bond bill or note to recover the same back from such principal debtor or debtors, it shall and may be lawful for such security or securities, in every such case, provided an action shall have accrued on such bond, bill or note, to require by notice in writing of his, her or their creditor or creditors, or his or their assignee, forthwith to put the bond, bill or note, by which he she or they may be bound as security or securities as aforesaid in suit; and unless such creditor or creditors, or assignee so required to put such bond, bill or note in suit, shall in a reasonable time com-

[18]

mence an action on such bond, bill or note, and proceed with due diligence in the ordinary course of law to recover a judgement for, and by execution to make the amount due by such bond, bill or note, the creditor or creditors or assignee so failing to comply with the requisition of such security or securities shall thereby forfeit the right which he or they would otherwise have to demand and receive of such security or securities, the amount which may be due by such bond, bill or note.

§ 2. Any security or securities, or in case of his or their death, then his or their heirs executors or administrators may in like manner and for the same cause make such requisition of the executors or administrators or assignee of the creditor or creditors of such security or securities, as it is herein before enacted may be made by a security or securities of his or their creditor or creditors, and in case of failure of the executors or administrators so to proceed such requisition as aforesaid being duly made, the security or securities his or their executors or administrators making the same, shall have the same relief that is herein before provided for a security or securities when his or their creditors shall be guilty of a similar failure. *Executors or administrators how to proceed,*

§ 3. Provided always, That nothing in this act contained shall be so construed as to effect bond with collateral conditions, or the bonds which may be entered into by guardians, executors, administrators or public officers. *with guardians and public officers.*

§ 4. And provided also, That the rights and remedies of any creditor or creditors, against any principal debtor or debtors shall be in no wise effected by this act any thing herein to the contrary or seeming to the contrary notwithstanding.

§ 3. And be it further enacted, That in all cases where judgment hath been or shall hereafter be entered up in any of the courts of record within this territory, against any person or persons as security or securities, their heirs, executors or administrators, upon any note, bill, bond or obligation, and the amount of such judgment or any part thereof hath been paid or discharged by such security or securities, his her or their heirs, executors or administrators, it shall and may be lawful for such security or securities, his, her or their heirs, executors or administrators to obtain judgment by motion against such principal obligor or obligors, his, her or their heirs, executors or administrators for the full amount of what shall have been paid with interest by the security or securities, his, her or their heirs, executors or administrators in any court where such judgment may have been entered up against such security or securities, his, her or their heirs, executors or administrators.

§ 6. And be it further enacted, That where the principal obligor or obligors have, or hereafter shall become insolvent, and there have been or shall be two or more securities, jointly bound with the said principal obligor or obligors in any bond, bill, note or other obligation for the payment of money or other thing, and judgment hath been or hereafter shall be obtained against one or more of such securities, it shall and may be lawful for the court before whom such judgment was or shall be obtained upon the motion of the party or parties against whom judgment hath been entered up as securities as aforesaid to grant judgment and award execution against all and every of the obligors and their legal representatives, for their, and each of their respective shares, and proportions of the said debt, with the damages and costs of the former suit.

§ 7. And be it further enacted, That no security or securities, his, her or their heirs, executors or administrators shall be suffered to confess judgment, or suffer judgment to go by default, so as to distress his, her or their principal or principals, if such principal or principals will enter him, her or themselves a defendant or defendants to the suit and tender to the said security or securities, his, her or their heirs, executors or administrators

(marginal notes)
may ob tain a jud gment by motion,

Each per son equal ly bouud,

shall not confess or suffer a judgment by de fault,

other good and sufficient collateral security to be approved of by the court before whom the suit shall be depending.

§ 8. And be it further enacted, That in all cases where judg- *when jud ment may be had on motion,* ment hath been or hereafter shall be entered up in any of the courts of record in this territory, against any person as appearance or special bail for the appearance of another to defend any suit depending in such court, and the amount of such judgment or any part thereof hath been paid or discharged by such bail, his, her or their heirs, executors or administrators it shall and may be lawful for such bail, his,

[19]

her or their heirs, executors or administrators to obtain judgment by motion against the person or persons for whose appearance they were bound, his, her or their heirs, executors or administrators for the full amount of what may have been paid by the said bail, his, her or their heirs, executors or administrators, together with interest and costs, in any court where judgment may have been entered up against such special bail.

§ 9. Provided always, That no judgment shall be obtained by motion in any of the cases aforesaid, unless the party or parties, against whom the same is prayed, shall have ten days previous notice thereof. *Ten days notice.*

§ 10. This act shall commence and be in force from and after the passing thereof.

JESSE B THOMAS Speaker of the House
of Representatives,

B. CHAMBERS, President of the Council.

Approved August 24th, 1805.

William Henry Harrison.

CHAPTER XXII.

AN ACT *directing the manner of proceeding in cases of Impeachment.*

§ 1. Be it enacted by the Legislative Council and House of Representatives, and it is hereby enacted by the authority of the same, That all civil officers, holding any commission under the authority of this territory shall be impeachable by the house of *House of represent atives to impeach civil offi cers.*

representatives, either for mal administration or corruption in his office. Such impeachment shall be prosecuted by the attorney general, or such other person or persons as the house may appoint.

Impeach ments.

§ 2.   The legislative council, shall have the sole power to try all impeachments, when sitting for that purpose, they shall be on oath or affirmation, and no person shall be convicted without the concurrence of two thirds of the members present.

§ 3.   Judgment in cases of impeachment shall not extend further than to removal from office, and to disqualification to hold and enjoy any office of honor, trust or profit under this territory; but the party convicted shall nevertheless be liable and subject to indictment, trial, judgment and punishment according to law. This act shall commence and be in force from the passage thereof.

> JESSE B. THOMAS, Speaker of the House
> of Representatives:
> B. CHAMBERS, President of the Council.

Approved August 24th, 1805.

> *William Henry Harrison.*

CHAPTER XXIII.
AN ACT *for the partition of Land.*

§ 1.   Be it enacted by the Legislative Council and House of Representatives, and it is hereby enacted by the authority of the same, That where any one or more persons, proprietors of any tract or tracts, lot or lots of land within this territory, and are desirous of having the same divided, it shall and may be lawful for the court of common pleas of the county where such lands or lots may lie, on the application of either party (notice of such application having been previously given by the party so applying, for at least 4 weeks, in some one of the public newspapers in this territory, and in the state of Kentucky) to appoint three reputable freeholders residents of said county, not related to either of the parties as commissioners for dividing the said tract or lot of land; and having previously taken an oath before any Judge of the general court, or of the court of common pleas of said

Court of common pleas to appoint commissi oners to partition land,

county, honestly and impartially to execute the trust reposed in them as commissioners aforesaid, shall proceed to make division of the said lands, lots, tenements and hereditaments as directed by the court, among the owners and proprietors thereof according to their respective rights. Which partition being made by the said commissioners, or any two of them, and return thereof being made in writing under their hands and seals to the said court, particularly describing the lots or portions allowed to each respective owner or proprietor, mentioning which of the owner or owners, proprietor or proprietors are minors if any such there shall be, which return being acknowledged by the

E

[20]

commissioners making the same, before any one of the Judges of the court of common pleas for the said county and accepted by the court and entered of record in the clerks office, shall be a partition of such lands, lots and tenements therein mentioned.

§ 2. That where any houses and lots, are so circumstanced, that a division thereof cannot be had without great prejudice to the proprietors of the same, and the commissioners appointed to divide the same shall so report to the court, the court shall thereupon give orders to the said commissioners to sell such house and lot or houses and lots, at public vendue, and shall make and execute good and sufficient conveyance or conveyances to the purchaser or purchasers thereof, which shall operate as an effectual bar both in law and equity, against such owners or proprietors, and all persons claiming under them, and the monies arising therefrom to pay to the owners or proprietors of such houses and lots, their guardians or legal representatives, as shall be directed in the said order.

In case a devision cannot be made without injury the commissi oners to report.

§ 3. That the said commissioners so appointed shall be entitled to receive from the person making the application the sum of one dollar and fifty cents for every day they shall be employed in effecting said division.

Commissi oners fees

§ 4. And the guardians of all minors shall be, and hereby are respectively authorised and empowered on behalf of the respec-

acts of the
guardian
binding on
minors.

tive minors whose guardians they are, to do and perform any matter or thing respecting the division of any lands, tenements and hereditaments as is herein directed, which shall be binding on such minor, and be deemed as valid to every purpose as if the same had been done by such minor after he had arrived at full age.

no divis
ion to be
made con
trary to in
tention of
testator

§ 5. Provided always, That no division or sale shall be made by order of the said court as above directed, contrary to the intention of any testator, as expressed in his last will and testament.

§ 6. This act shall commence and be in force from the passage thereof.

JESSE B. THOMAS, Speaker of the House
of Representatives.

B. CHAMBERS, President of the Council.

Approved August 24th, 1805.

William Henry Harrison.

CHAPTER xxiv.

AN ACT *for the Sale and Conveyance of Land under Executions.*

§ 1. Whereas it is represented to the general assembly that great injury has been sustained as well by the debtors as creditors within this territory, by the operation of the present laws, and the mode of selling real estate under execution, for remedy whereof,

Proviso

Lands ta
ken under
execution
the credi
tor may
tender
lands to
the sheriff

§ 2. Be it enacted by the Legislative Council and House of Representatives, and it is hereby enacted by the authority of the same, That where any writ of execution shall be issued against the property or estate of any debtor or debtors, it shall and may be lawful for such debtor or debtors, to tender to the sheriff or other officer serving the same, any freehold lands in his county, to the value of the debt, damages and costs, to be ascertained as hereafter is mentioned, for which such execution may have issued, at which time, or within ten days thereafter the said debtor or debtors, shall make out a good title [to be approved of as hereafter is mentioned] to the said lands, and shall deliver the deeds and evidences relating thereto to the sheriff, and shall also by a writing signed by him, her or them, notify the sheriff of the situation of the said land, and the number of acres contained in each separate tract if more than one.

§ 3. And be it enacted, That the said sheriff or other officer on such tender being made as above mentioned, shall advertise the said lands for sale in the manner and for the time required by the laws of the territory for the sale of real estates, and shall thereupon proceed to sell the same, or so much thereof as will satisfy the judgment or decree [exclusive of costs as hereafter mentioned] as the case may be for the best price thas can be got for the same, and execute deeds therefor to the purchaser or purchasers; Provided always, that if such lands cannot be sold for two thirds of their value in the least, in the opinion of the persons hereafter directed to be appointed for that purpose, then, and in such case

Sheriff to advertise such lands for sale,

[21]

the said lands, or so much thereof as will be sufficient to satisfy the said judgment or decree exclusive of costs, and such parts thereof as the execution creditor shall give notice he will chose to accept of, shall be adjudged to be purchased by the creditor or creditors, at the said two thirds of their value, and the said sheriff or other officer shall thereupon execute to him, her, or them, sufficient deeds in fee simple therefor: Provided always nevertheless, that if such creditor or creditors, his her or their agent or attorney, shall neglect to notify the said sheriff or other officer, of the time of the said sale what tracts or parts of tracts of land, he she or they would make choice of sufficient to satisfy the said judgment or decree, exclusive of costs, then the said sheriff or other officer shall convey to the said creditor or creditors, such tract or tracts or part or parts thereof, as the said debtor or debtors shall require him so to do, and sufficient to satisfy the same, and in case neither creditor nor debtor or any agent or attorney on their behalf shall neglect or refuse to notify the sheriff of such their choice, then the said sheriff or other officer, shall convey to the said creditor or creditors such or so much of the said lands as he may think proper, sufficient to satisfy such judgment or decree exclusive of costs, agreeably to such valuation.

Creditors may take the lands at two thirds of its valuation,

§ 4. And be it further enacted, That when any writ of capias ad satisfaciendum shall hereafter be served on any debtor or debtors, it shall be lawful such debtor or debtors, on making the title, delivering the deeds, and making the notifications to the sheriff directed to be made in regard to the execution against the property or estate of debtors, to tender to the sheriff or other officer serving the same, any freehold lands as before mentioned sufficient to satisfy the said judgment or decree, exclusive of costs, the value of which said lands shall be ascertained as hereafter is mentioned, and on such tender being made, the said sheriff shall proceed to have the said lands valued, sold and disposed of, in the manner herein before mentioned, in the third section of this law.

§ 5. And be it further enacted, That the said sheriff shall not on such tender made discharge or release the person or property of such debtor, until sale or valuation of the lands as before mentioned, at which time if the said lands at such sale or at such valuation will amount to the debt and damages, exclusive of costs, due by such judgment or decree, he shall discharge the person or property of such debtor, if not, he shall detain such person or property until satisfaction made for such deficiency which may be discharged in manner before mentioned.

§ 6. Provided always nevertheless, That the person or property, as the case may be, of such debtor or debtors, shall not be released or discharged by such sheriff, nor shall such tender of lands be legal or accepted of to discharge such execution, until such debtor or debtors shall enter into bond to the creditor or creditors when the said land shall be adjudged to him or them at the said two thirds of the value with sufficient surety, to be approved of the appraisers hereafter directed to be appointed, in double the sum of such valuation, with condition, that if the said creditor or creditors being such purchasers, his, her or their heirs or assigns shall be lawfully evicted of the said lands or any part thereof so adjudged to him, her or them by any prior title or incumbrance, that then and in such case the said debtor or debtors, his, her or their heirs, executors or admistrators shall pay to the said creditor or creditors, his, her or their heirs or assigns, the value of the said lands at the time of such eviction, of which he, she or they

Marginal notes: Creditor after notification may tender land to sheriff

Such tender not to release the person or property until valuation and sale,

Not to release person or property nor such tender to be legal until the debtor enters into bond with security to creditor.

shall be so evicted of, which bonds shall be assignable and recovered by the assignee or assignees in his and their own name or names; And provided also, that no such tender shall be accepted of by the sheriff, or such release made until such debtor or debtors shall pay to the sheriff all the fees due to the several officers of the court as well in prosecuting or defending the suits on which the said judgments or decree was obtained, as the fees due to the said sheriff and valuers, which shall be deducted from the total amount of such judgment or decree; And provided also, That nothing in this act shall be construed to extend to any proceedings made, or to be made for the recovery of any debts or taxes due to the United States, or this territory, or any county therein, or for any distress for rent, or to sheriffs as such, or as collector of clerks or other officers fees, any thing herein before contained to the contrary notwithstanding: And provided

[22]

also, That no such creditor shall be obliged to become the purchaser of any such land to a greater amount than the balance due of such judgment or decree.

§ 7. And be it further enacted, That where any freehold estate in this territory shall be taken in execution, to satisfy a judgment or decree obtained on any mortgage or mortgages, the sheriff or other officer shall advertise the same for sale for the time, and in the manner required by law and if upon such sale the same shall not fetch at least two thirds of the value, to be estimated by the persons hereafter directed to be appointed, the said sheriff or other officer shall in such case convey to the mortgagee or mortgagees or their executors administrators or assigns, the whole or such part of the said mortgaged premises (at the choice of such creditor) if he should give notice of such choice to the sheriff, as will be sufficient to satisfy the said judgment or decree, exclusive of costs, at the said two thirds of the appraised value, and in case the said mortgaged premises, or any part thereof, will on such sale or valuation, exceed the amount of such judgment or decree, then the said creditor or creditors, shall acknowledge satisfaction on record for the said mortgage; Provided always nevertheless,

In case of mortgages the sheriff to advertise for sale,

mortgagor to give a title,

That no such conveyance shall be made until the mortgagor shall make out a title, deliver the deeds and execute the like bond and surety as are herein before mentioned and directed in cases of other executions, nor until the fees due to the several officers of the court or courts shall have been paid by the mortgagor as is herein before mentioned, the amount of which fees shall be deducted from the total amount of such judgment or decree.

Creditor to ac knowledge satisfacti on.

§ 8. And be it further enacted, That if the said creditor or creditors, mortgagee or mortgagees, his, her or their heirs executors administrators or assigns shall on such conveyance being executed, or within six months thereafter, neglect or refuse to acknowledge satisfaction on record for the said judgment or decree, in the manner by law required, then such judgment or decree shall be taken and considered and be as available in any court of law or equity as if such person had acknowledged satisfaction on record for the said judgment or decree as is by law required.

Convey ances by the sheriff to vest all right of debtor in purchaser

§ 9. And be it further enacted, That all conveyances to be executed by the sheriff or other officer in pursuance of this law shall vest in the purchaser or purchasers, creditor or creditors, and his, her and their heirs, all the estate, right, title and interest of such debtor or mortgagor, of, in and to, all and singular, the lands and premises in such deeds mentioned to be conveyed, which deeds shall by such sheriff or other officer be acknowledged in the court of common pleas of the county in which such lands lie, who shall thereupon deliver the same, together with the title deeds deposited with him in pursuance of the first section of this act, to the creditor or creditors, purchaser or purchasers, his, her or their agent, attorney in fact, or on record, and if none such to be found therein, or he, she or they shall refuse to receive the said deed or deeds, he shall deposit the same in the office of the clerk of the court from which such execution issued, who shall when required, deliver the same to the creditor or creditors, his, her or their agent or attorney.

In cese the credi tor shall refuse to take land

§ 10. Provided always and be it further enacted, That if any creditor as aforesaid shall refuse to take lands of any defendant, upon the valuation made in manner and form as is herein authorised and required, and give notice thereof in writing to the defendant at or before the said valuation takes place, the said lands shall remain in the hands of the sheriff, and be by him once in four months upon giving notice as is herein required, exposed to sale, until the said lands shall sell for two thirds of their appraised value, or until the creditor agrees to take the same as is aforesaid provided for.

§ 11. Provided always and be it further enacted, That nothing herein contained shall be so construed as to exempt personal property from being taken in execution in the same manner as is herein authorised in case of land, and it is hereby further provided that if the said personal property will not sell for two thirds of its value, upon an appraisment and valuation made as is herein required in case of land and the creditor shall signify his refusal to take the same; then it shall and may be lawful for the defendant to replevy the same by giving bond with one or more sureties, to be taken and approved of by the sheriff of the proper county, **Personal property may be taken.**

[23]

which said replevin shall continue for the term of six months and no longer, and provided further, that no replevin herein authorised shall be taken to extend to any judgment entered by a justice of the peace.

§ 12. Provided always and be it further enacted, that it is hereby fully understood, that nothing contained in this act shall be construed to impair any contract, or to have either an expost facto, or retrospective operation. **Not have expost fac to opera tion**

§ 13. And be it further enacted, that the court of common pleas of every county in this Territory shall appoint five persons to act as commissioners to value such lands and of the validity of titles thereto and the sufficiency of sureties that may be offered or tendered under this act; and no sale under execution shall be made but in the presence of at least three of the said commissioners who shall value the lands then offered for sale, but who shall not be interested in the suit or related to either of the parties: Provided always, that in case where the creditor shall be dissatisfied with the sufficiency of the sureties or the title admitted and approved of by the said commissioners, it shall be lawful for such creditor **Five per sons to be appointed as commis sioners,** to appeal to the next court of common pleas, to be held for the said county giving five days notice thereof to the debtor or his attorney, and if such court shall be of opinion that the sureties or title so admitted was insufficient, the execution upon which such security was admitted shall be deemed and taken as a lien upon the real and personal estate of such debtor, and shall not be discharged but upon render of other sufficient security satisfactory to the court; and moreover, the bond and security given by such debtor shall remain valid until such security given. There shall be paid to each of the appraisers appointed by virtue of this act, one dollar for each days attendance at any sale to be taxed in the bill of costs, and where any lands shall be sold or tendered and given up to the creditor, at two thirds of their value under this act, such appraisers shall give to the sheriff or other officer a certificate that the said valuation was made by them, that the security so taken was sufficient and the title to the said lands valid and good, and such certificate shall be by the said sheriff or other officer returned with the execution and shall be a full indemnity for him therein. And such sheriff or other officer shall be allowed seventy five cents exclusive of his other fees for taking such bond and no more. Every person appointed by the court to judge of the title and value of lands and of the sufficiency of sureties offered agreeably to the directions of this law, shall before he proceeds to act under such appointment take an oath or affirmation before the said court or any justice of the peace of the county, that he will truly and impartially execute the trust reposed in him by this act.

Valuers to be amean able to court,

§ 14. And be it further enacted, That the valuers shall be ameanable to the respective courts of common pleas of the said county, and may be deprived of their office for neglect of duty or malfeasance therein, and upon the death, resignation or removal from office of any such valuer, the vacancy shall be supplied by new appointment, of the said court of common pleas of the county, in which it shall happen.

officers to give this act in evi dence repealing clause.

§ 15, And be it further enacted, That if any action or suit shall be brought against any sheriff or other officer, by reason of performing the duties enjoined on him by this act he may plead the general issue, and give this act in evidence.

§ 16. And be it further enacted, That all laws, and parts of laws coming within the purview of this act shall be, and the same are hereby repealed. This act shall commence and be in force from and after the 1st day of September next.

JESSE B. THOMAS, Speaker of the House
of Representatives.

B. CHAMBERS, President of the Council.
Approved August 24th, 1805.

William Henry Harrison.

CHAPTER xxv.
AN ACT *concerning mills and millers.*

§ 1. Be it enacted by the Legislative Council and House of Representatives, and it is hereby enacted by the authority of the same, That when any person

F

[24]

owning lands on one side of a water course, the bed whereof belongs to himself, and desiring to build a water grist mill on such lands, and to erect a dam across the same, shall not himself have the fee simple property in the lands on the opposite side thereof against which he would abut his said dam, he shall make application for a writ of *ad quod damnum* to the court of common pleas of the county where such lands may lie, and having given ten days previous notice to the proprietor thereof if he be to be found in the county, and if not, then to his agent if any he hath in the county, or if no agent, to be advertised at the door of the court house of the proper county for two terms, which court shall thereupon order their clerk to issue such writ to be directed to the sheriff, commanding him to summon and empannel twelve fit persons to meet on the land so proposed for the abutment, on a certain day to be named by the court and inserted in the said writ, of which notice shall be given by the sheriff, to the said proprietor or his agent if any he hath. *(marginal: a writ of ad quod damnum)*

§ 2. The jury so summoned and impannelled, shall be charged by the sheriff impartially and to the best of their skill and judgment *(marginal: the jury when met their duty)* to view the land proposed for an abutment, and to locate and circumscribe by metes and bounds one acre thereof, having due regard therein to the interest of both parties, and to appraise the same according to its true value, to examine the lands above and below, the property of others which may probably overflow, and say what damage it will be to the several proprietors, and whether the mansion house of any such proprietor or proprietors or the offices, courtelages or gardens thereunto immediately belonging will be overflowed, to enquire whether and in what degree fish of passage, or ordinary navigation will be obstructed, whether by any, and what means such obstruction may be prevented, and whether in their opinion, the health of the neighbors will be annoyed by the stagnation of the waters.

Inquest when made with the writ to be re turned

§ 3. The inquest so made and sealed by the said jurors together with the writ shall be returned by the said sheriff, to the next succeeding court, who shall thereupon order summonses to be issued to the several persons proprietors or tenants of the land so located or found liable to damage, if they be to be found within the county where the land so to be condemned or overflowed do lie, and if not then to their agent if any they have, to shew cause, if any they have, why the party so applying should not have leave to build his said mill dam.

§ 4. And be it further enacted, That where any person may have built a mill or other dam whereby the water of any river, creek, run or spring may be rendered thereby stagnant, it may be lawful for any person interested therein, or who may be damaged by the overflowing of said water, to obtain a writ of *ad puod damnum* in the same manner as is directed in case of a person wishing to build a new mill, and the jury so summoned &c. shall

persons who may have built mills may apply for writ of ad quod dam num

ascertain the damage which any individual may sustain in consequence of the continuance of said mill dam, and whether the said mill is of public utility, and after the jury aforesaid shall have made their return, it shall be the duty of the owner or owners of said mill to pay to any and every individual, the sum assessed by the jury aforesaid, and upon payment of said assessment, the said owner or owners, shall be clear of all damages to the person interested as foresaid, any law, usage or custom to the contrary notwithstanding.

§ 5. In like manner if the person proposing to build such mill and dam have the fee simple property in the lands on both sides of the stream, yet application shall be made to the court of the county where the mill house will stand for a writ to examine as aforesaid, what lands may be overflowed, and to make the same examination and report, as in the case last mentioned, which writ shall be directed, executed and returned, as prescribed in the former case.

where the person is owner of both sides

§ 6. If on such inquest or other evidence it shall appear to the court that the mansion house of any proprietor, curtelage or garden thereunto immediately belonging will be overflowed or the health of the neighborhood annoyed, shall not give leave to build such mill and dam, but if none of these injuries are likely to ensue, they are then to proceed to adjudge whether all circumstances weighed, it be reasonable that such leave should be given or not given accordingly.

The court may, or may not give leave

§ 7. And if the party applying shall obtain leave to build the said mill and

[25]

dam, he shall upon paying respectively to the several proprietors entitled, the value of the acre so located, and the damage which the jurors find will be by overflowing the lands above or below, become seized in fee simple of the said acre of land But if he shall not within one year thereafter begin to build the said mill, and finish the same within three years, and afterwards continue it in good repair for public use, or in case the said mill and dam be destroyed, if he shall not begin to rebuild it within one year after such destruction and finish it within three years thereafter, the said acre of land shall revert to the former proprietor and his heirs, unless at the time of such destruction the owner thereof be a feme covert, infant, imprisoned or of unsound mind, in which case the same time shall be allowed, after such disability removed.

where leave may be obtained the mill shall be built and kept in repair.

§ 8. The inquest of the said jurors nevertheless, or opinion of the court shall not bar any prosecution or action which any person would have had in law had this act never been made, other than for such injuries as were actually foreseen and estimated by the jury.

action may be brought,

§ 9. All millers whose mills shall be established under this law shall well and sufficiently grind the grain brought to their mills, and in due time as the same shall be brought, and may take for **To grind well and in turn,** toll such rates as are established by a law of this territory, entitled 'An act regulating grist mills and millers,' and every miller failing to grind as aforesaid, as the same shall come in turn, or shall take or exact more toll, shall for every such offence, forfeit and pay to the person injured the sum of two dollars and fifty cents, recoverable before any magistrate within the county where the offence was committed.

§ 10. Every owner or occupyer of a mill, shall keep therein a **Sealed measures,** sealed half bushel Peck and toll dish, and measure all grain by striking measure, under the penalty, as is mentioned for exacting more grain then is allowed by law, and if a miller be a servant his master shall pay the same.

§ 11. The owner of every dam over which a public road passes shall constantly keep such dam in repair, at least twelve feet wide, under the penalty of one dollar for every twenty four hours, but where a mill dam shall be carried away or destroyed by tempest, the owner or occupier shall not be liable to the said penalty, Provided the same be repaired within six months.

§ 12. That all acts and parts of acts that come within the purview of this law, shall be, and the same is hereby repealed.

JESSE B THOMAS, Speaker of the House
of Representatives

B. CHAMBERS, President of the Council.
Approved August 24th, 1805.

William Henry Harrison.

CHAPTER xxvi.
AN ACT *concerning the introduction of Negroes and Mulattoes into this Territory.*

§ 1. Be it enacted by the Legislative Council and House of Representatives, and it is hereby enacted by the authority of the **Slave may be brot in to this ter ritory.** same, That it shall and may be lawful for any person being the owner or possessor of any negroes or mulattoes of and above the age of fifteen years, and owing service and labour as slaves in

either of the states or territories of the United States, or for any
citizen of the said states or territories purchasing the same, to
bring the said negroes or mulattoes into this territory.

§ 2. That the owner or possessor of any negroes or mulattoes,
as aforesaid, and bringing the same into this territory, shall within **Slaves to**
thirty days after such removal, go with the same before the clerk **be indent**
of the court of common pleas of the proper county, and in the **ed**
presence of the said clerk the said owner or possessor shall determine and agree to and with his or her negro or mulatto upon
the term of years which the said negro or mulatto will and shall
serve his or her said owner or possessor, and the said clerk is
hereby authorised and required to make a record thereof, in a
book which he shall keep for the purpose.

§ 3. That if any negro or mulatto removed into this territory
as aforesaid, shall refuse to serve his or her owner as aforesaid, it
shall and may be lawful for such person within sixty days thereafter, to remove the said negro or mulatto to

[26]

any place, which by the laws of the United States, or territory
from whence such owner or possessor may or shall be authorised
to remove the same.

§ 4. That if any person or persons shall neglect or refuse to
perform the duty required in the second, or to take advantage of **Persons**
the benefit of the preceding section hereof, within the time therein **failing to**
respectively prescribed, such person or persons, shall forfeit all **comply,**
claim and right whatever, to the service and labour, of such
negroes or mulattoes.

§ 5, That any person removing into this territory, and being
the owner or possessor of any negro or mulatto as aforesaid, under **under the**
the age of fifteen years, or if any person shall hereafter acquire a **age of fif**
property in any negro or mulatto under the age aforesaid, and **teen**
who shall bring them into this territory, it shall and may be lawful
for such person, owner or possessor, to hold the said negro or
mulatto to service and labour, the males, until they arrive at the
age of thirty five, and the females, until they arrive at the age of
thirty two years.

§ 6. Any person removing any negro or mulatto into this territory under the authority of the preceding sections, it shall be incumbent on such person within thirty days thereafter, to register the name and age of such negro or mulatto, with the clerk of the court of common pleas of the proper county.

to be registered

§ 7. That if any person shall remove any negro or mulatto from one county to another county within this territory, who may or shall be brought into the same under the authority of either the first or fifth sections hereof, it shall be incumbent on such person to register the same, and also the name and age of the said negro or mulatto with the said clerk of the county from whence, and to which such negro or mulatto may be removed within thirty days after such removal.

if removed

§ 8. That if any person shall neglect or refuse to perform the duty required by the two preceding sections hereof, such person for such offence, shall be fined in the sum of fifty dollars, to be recovered by indictment or information, and for the use of the proper county.

penalty on failure

§ 9. That if any clerk shall neglect or refuse to perform the duty and service herein required, he shall for every such neglect or refusal be fined in the sum of 50 dollars to be recovered by information or indictment & for the use of the county.

penalty on clerk for neglect

§ 10. And be it further enacted, That is shall be the duty of the clerk of the court of common pleas aforesaid, when any person shall apply to him to register any mulatto or negro agreeably to the preceding section to demand and receive the said applicant's bond with sufficient security in the penalty of five hundred dollars, payable to the governor or his successor in office, conditioned that the said mulatto or negro, or mullattoes or negroes as the case may be, shall not after the expiration of his or her time of service become a county charge, which bond shall be lodged with the county treasurers respectively, for the use of the said counties; provided always, that no such bond shall be required or requireable in case the time of service of such negro or mulatto shall expire before he or she arrives at the age of forty years, if such negro or mulatto, be at that time capable, him or herself, by his or her own labour.

to give bond,

§ 11. Any person who shall forcibly take or carry out of this territory, or who shall be aiding or assisting therein, any person or persons, owing, or having owed service or labour, without the consent of such person or persons, previously obtained before any judge of the court of common pleas, of the county where such person owing, or having owed such service or labour resides, which consent shall be certified by said judge of the common pleas, to the clerk of the court of common pleas where he resides, at, or before the next court, any person so offending, upon conviction thereof, shall forfeit and pay one thousand dollars, one third to the use of the county, and two thirds to the use of the person so taken or carried away, to be recovered by action of debt, or on the case; Provided, That there shall be nothing in this section so construed, as to prevent any master or mistress from removing any person owing service or labour from this territory, as described in the third section of this act. *in what manner slaves may be re moved*

§ 12. That the said clerk, for every registry made in manner aforesaid, shall receive seventy five cents from the applicant therefor. *Clerks fees,*

§ 13. And be it further enacted, That the children born in this territory of

[27]

a parent of colour, owing service or labour by indenture according to law, shall serve the master or mistress of such parent, the males, until the age of thirty, and the females, until the age of twenty eight years. *Children of colour born in the terri tory,*

§ 14. And be it further enacted, That the provisions contained in a law of this territory respecting apprentices, and passed at this session of the legislature, shall be in force as to such children in case of the misbehaviour of the master or mistress, or for cruelty or ill usage. This act shall be in force from the passage thereof.

JESSE B. THOMAS, Speaker of the House of Representatives.

B. CHAMBERS, President of the Council.

Approved August 26th, 1805.

William Henry Harrison.

CHAPTER XXVII.

AN ACT *to authorise the Courts of the Counties within this Territory, to draw on the county Treasurer for the services and expenses therein mentioned.*

Sheriffs as treasurers to pay or ders from court.

§ 1. Be it enacted by the Legislative Council and House of Representatives, and it is hereby enacted by the authority of the same, That the sheriffs as treasurers of the several counties in this territory, shall pay to the sheriffs, clerks and judges of the polls in taking the sense of the good people of this territory, whether they would wish to enter into the second grade of government, such sum as the court of common pleas of the said respective counties shall think reasonable, which order the said several courts are hereby required to make.

Courts to order pay ment for certain services

§ 2. And be it further enacted, That the said several courts are empowered and are hereby required to order the sheriffs as treasurers of their respective counties, to pay to all and every person or persons having any claims or demands as well for attending the several courts of record in the said counties as constables or otherwise, for fire wood and court house rent, and the fees due to witnesses, and the several officers of the courts in the public prosecution of those persons who were either acquitted of the charges brought against them, or discharged or unable to pay the fees, all of which shall be certified by the said courts in which such prosecutions were had, attendance given or expenses accrued, which orders shall be by said sheriffs as treasurers, paid accordingly, out of any county monies in his hands.

in cases of public prosecuti on.

§ 3. And be it further enacted, That all costs fees and charges to which the officers of the counties are now or may hereafter be entitled for or on account of any public prosecution in either the superior or inferior courts shall be paid out of the county funds respectively, on an order attested by the clerks of either court as the case may be, and it is further provided, that the salaries that are now or which may hereafter be due to any county sheriff or to the clerk of the general court, shall be paid out of the county funds on an order of the court of common pleas, attested by the clerks thereof, of the counties respectively.

§ 4. And be it further enacted, that on all presentments or indictments hereafter to be found in this territory the name or names of a prosecutor or prosecutors, shall be endorsed on every indictment or presentment, in default whereof the said indictment or presentment shall be immediately quashed by the court.

§ 5. And be it further enacted, That in case the defendant or defendants in any indictment hereafter to be found against him or them, shall be acquitted of the charges brought against him, her or them, or shall otherwise be lawfully discharged, the person or persons whose name or names are endorsed on the said indictment or presentment, as prosecutor or prosecutors shall be obliged to pay all the costs of the prosecution of such indictment or presentment, unless the court in their opinion shall think there were probable grounds for prefering the same, for which costs, execution may issue against the said prosecutor or prosecutors, his, her or their bodies or estates.

JESSE B. THOMAS, Speaker of the House
of Representatives.

B. CHAMBERS, President of the Council.
Approved August 26th, 1805.

William Henry Harrison.

G

[28]

CHAPTER xxviii.

AN ACT repealing a part of an act, entitled "An act for the admission of Attornies and Counsellors at Law."

BE it enacted by the Legislative Council and House of Representatives of this territory, and it is hereby enacted by the authority of the same, That the resolution adopted by the Governor and Judges at their session of September, eighteen hundred and three, regulating the admission and practice of Attornies and

Marginal notes:
name of prosecut or to be endorsed on Indictments.

In case of acquittal

Counsellors at law, be, and the same is hereby repealed. This act shall be in force from and after the passage thereof.

JESSE B. THOMAS, Speaker of the House
of Representatives.

B. CHAMBERS, President of the Council.

Approved August 26th, 1805.

William Henry Harrison.

CHAPTER xxix.
AN ACT for the more easy acknowledgment of deeds.

May be acknow ledged or proved in any coun ty

§ 1.   Be it enacted by the Legislative Council and House of Representatives, and it is hereby enacted by the authority of the same, That it shall and may be lawful for any judge of the court of common pleas, or justice of the peace of any county in this territory, within the limits of their respective counties, to take the acknowledgment or proof of the execution of any deeds or conveyances, or release of dower of lands, tenements, lying and being in any other county in this territory, which acknowledgments, or proofs, or release so taken and made, the same being duly certified by the clerk under the county seal, shall be valid and effectual, and have the same force and effect, as if the same were taken before any judge or justice of the peace in the county in which the said lands or tenements are situate.

recorders to keep their offi ces at the seat of jus tice

§ 2.   And be it further enacted, That the recorders of the several counties within this territory shall hereafter keep their offices at the county seats of justice, and on failure thereof, the governor of this territory shall appoint and commission others in their stead, who will conform thereto. This act shall commence and be in force from and after the first day of November next.

JESSE B. THOMAS, Speaker of the House
of Representatives.

B. CHAMBERS, President of the Council.

Approved August 26th, 1805.

William Henry Harrison.

CHAPTER xxx.

AN ACT making appropriations for the ensuing year.

§ 1. Be it enacted by the Legislative Council and House of Representatives, and it is hereby enacted by the authority of the same, That the sum of five hundred dollars shall be and the same is hereby appropriated for contingent expenses and that all the monies which shall be received into the territorial treasury, except as above appropriated for contingent expenses, shall be a general fund for all monies allowed by law, which shall not be directed to be paid out of contingent expenses.

Contin gent fund

§ 2. And be it further enacted, that there shall be allowed and paid to E. Stout, Printer of this territory, for printing two hundred copies of the laws of this territory, at this present session, a sum not exceeding three hundred dollars, to be paid out of the contingent expences; the residue of the monies allowed for contingent expences, or so much thereof as may be necessary, shall be subject to the payment of monies on the order of the governor, for expresses and other incidents which may be necessary and cannot be foreseen by the legislature, a statement of which shall be laid before the legislature at their next session.

allow ance to the public

§ 3. And be it further enacted, That there shall be allowed and paid out of the general fund, to the following persons, the following sums of money, to wit: To the territorial treasurer, one hundred dollars; to the auditor of public accounts, one hundred and fifty dollars; to A. Marchal, for house rent to the end of the present session, fifty dollars; to the members of

specific appropriati ons,

[29]

the legislative council and house of representatives, and their secretary & clerks, their several allowances established by law, not exceeding nine hundred and fifty dollars; to Toussaint Dubois, for stationary furnished to both houses of the legislature, sixty nine dollars and seventy five cents; to Abraham Defrance, for chairs and other articles by him furnished for the legislature, fourteen dollars and fifty cents; to the assessors and collectors of land, and the clerks of the courts for their services under the act entitled 'an act for levying and collecting a tax on land,' a sum not exceeding six hundred dollars; to the attorney general, one hundred and fifty dollars.

JESSE B. THOMAS, Speaker of the House
of Representatives.

B. CHAMBERS, President of the Council.

Approved August 26th, 1805.

William Henry Harrison.

CHAPTER xxxi.

AN ACT *for the appointment of an auditor and territorial treasurer.*

BE it enacted by the Legislative council and house of Representatives, and it is hereby enacted by the authority of the same, That the governor shall appoint an auditor who shall continue in office during pleasure, whose duty it shall be to keep the accounts of this territory with any state or territory, and with the United States, or any individual, to audit all accounts of the civil officers of this territory, who are paid out of the treasury, of the members of both branches of the legislature, and of all other persons authorised to draw money out of the treasury; but nothing herein contained shall be so construed as to authorise the auditor under any pretext whatever, to audit any account, or give any certificate which would enable any person or persons to receive any sum or sums of money, unless in cases particularly authorised by law.

Governor to appoint an auditor

§ 2. And be it further enacted, That it shall be the duty of said auditor as soon as he shall have ascertained the balance due any individual, to give such person or persons, a certificate, certifying that there is a balance (mentioning the sum) due to the person applying for the same.

Auditor to give certificate

§ 3. And be it further enacted, That the said auditor before he enters on the duties of his office, shall give bond with approved security to the governor of this territory or his successor in office, in the penal sum of 8000 dollars, conditioned as follows, that he shall justly and honestly audit, and fairly keep the accounts between this territory and any state or territory, the United States or any individual as the case may be, and that he will deliver to his successor in office all books and other vouchers which shall be

give bond and make oath.

by him kept by virtue of this law, and moreover take the following oath or affirmation, 'I, A B do solemnly swear or affirm (as the case may be) that I will justly and honestly perform the duties of auditor of this territory to the best of my skill and judgment, so help me God.'

§ 4. And be it further enacted, That the said auditor shall make a fair list of all accounts by him audited in a book to be kept by him for that purpose, as also an account of all taxes and other monies which may be due to any from this territory, and it shall be the duty of such auditor, to make out and present to the legislature a transcript of said accounts, shewing the amount of all certificates by him given, as also the amount of all taxes which have been received, or are still due the said territory, on the first week of their session, or as often as the legislature may require. *shall make out a list of all ac counts of the terri tory and lay them before the legisla ture*

§ 5. And be it further enacted, That the said auditor shall keep a fair record of all warrants and certificates by him drawn, numbering the same in a book by him kept for that purpose. *keep a re cord of all warants & certifi cates.*

§ 6. And be it further enacted, That when the said auditor shall have made out abstracts of all sums due in the respective counties, and sent them to the different collectors, he shall make out in a book for said purpose, a fair account against each collector a copy of which shall be sufficient for the attorney general to proceed by motion in a summary way against all delinquent collectors, before the general court, or court of common pleas, provided the said collector shall have ten days previous notice of such motion, and the said auditor shall *In case of default in collector*

[30]

upon receiving the treasurers receipt give to said collector a quietus which shall after receiving the same, prevent the auditor or attorney general from motioning against him for the sum mentioned in said receipt.

§ 7. And be it further enacted, that the governor shall appoint a treasurer, who shall continue in office during pleasure, who shall prior to the entering upon the duties of his office, give and execute a bond with sufficient security in the sum of 8000 dollars, to be approved of by the governor, conditioned for the due and *governor to ap point a treasurer* faithful performance of the duties of his office, the said bond shall be given to the governor payable to him or his successors in office for the use of the territory.

§ 8. And be it further enacted, That the governor may when he suspects the obligors in said bond to be insufficient require the treasurer to give other bond with sufficient security, to be approved of as aforesaid, which said bond shall be deposited in the office of the secretary of this territory.

§ 9. And be it further enacted, That if said treasurer die, resign or be displaced, or cease to hold his office, then such treasurer, or if he be dead, his heirs executors or administrators shall fairly and regularly state the amount and deliver the monies, together with all instruments of writing, book and papers of the territory in his, her or their possession to the succeeding treasurer, who shall make report thereon to the legislature, and the said report if confirmed by the legislature shall be a discharge of the said bond, which in such case shall be delivered to the said treasurer, his heirs, executors or administrators.

§ 10. And be it further enacted, That it shall be the duty of the treasurer to receive the proceeds of all taxes and other public monies of this territory.

§ 11. And be it further enacted, That he shall not pay any money but on a warrant or certificate from the auditor, except the auditors salary.

§ 12. And be it further enacted, That he shall keep a regular account of all monies he receives and pays agreeably to law, stating therein on what account each particular sum was paid or received, and the time when, and lay a fair statement of said accounts before the legislature on the first week in every session, or as often as the legislature may require.

§ 13. And be it further enacted, That it shall be the duty of the treasurer to deliver monthly to the auditor an account of his payments and of the warrants on which they were made, & the auditor shall copy it in a book kept for that purpose.

§ 14. And be it further enacted, That the treasurer on receiving any sum of money shall receipt for it to the person paying the same.

Margin notes:

may re quire new bond

In case of vacancy in the of fice of tre surer,

receive all territo rial mo nies

on what he shall pay mo ney.

keep reg ular ac counts

§ 15. And be it further enacted, That the present treasurer shall deliver to the auditor all paper, books and other things appertaining to his office, in a convenient time after said auditor shall have been appointed.

§ 16. And be it further enacted, That the present treasurer shall deliver all public monies in his possession to the succeeding treasurer, in a convenient time after said treasurer shall have been appointed.

§ 17. And be it further enacted, That it shall be the duty of the auditor to direct the attorney general to motion against all delinquents for the payment of public monies, which have heretofore accrued to the territory.

§ 18. And be it further enacted, That this law shall be in force from and after the passage thereof.

JESSE B THOMAS, Speaker of the House
of Representatives.

B. CHAMBERS, President of the Council.

Approved August 26th, 1805.

William Henry Harrison.

CHAPTER XXXII.

AN ACT *for levying and collecting a tax on Land and for other purposes*

§ 1. Be it enacted by the Legislative Council and House of Representatives, and it is hereby enacted by the authority of the same, That on or before the first day of January next the courts of common pleas of the several counties within this territory be empowered, and they are hereby authorised and required to appoint an assessor and collector for the purposes herein after mentioned, each assessor or collector before they begin the exercise of the duties of their respective

courts to appoint an assessor & collec tor

[31]

offices shall take and subscribe the following oath or affirmation, before any judge of the court aforesaid of the county viz. I do solemnly swear or affirm (as the case may be) that as collector, or assessor, for the county of   I will to the best of my skill and judgment, diligently and faithfully execute the duties of the office, without favor, affection or partiallity, and that I will do equal right and justice to the best of my knowledge and understanding in every case in which I shall act as collector (or assessor) so help me God. A certificate of which oath or affirmation shall be delivered to the assessor or collector, and a copy thereof transmitted without delay to the auditor of the territory to be by him filed in his office.

Duty of auditor

§ 2. And be it further enacted, That it shall be the duty of the auditor and he is hereby authorised and impowered to apply for and procure from the proper officers an abstract of all entries and locations of lands of this territory noting the quality of, where, and on what creeks, water courses &c. such entries and locations have been made, with the names of the persons to whom entered, and it shall be the duty of the auditor to transmit complete lists of such entries and location of lands to the assessors of the respective counties by the first day of January annually, any expense incurred by the performance of the services and duty required by this section, shall be paid out of the territory treasury.

Duty of assessor,

§ 3. And be it further enacted, That the assessor of each county respectively on or before the tenth day of February, having taken the oath or affirmation prescribed by this act, shall take a true account, and make out an exact list of each and every tract of land claimed by the inhabitants of his county, and every inhabitant of the county shall on application of the assessor forthwith render on oath, which the assessor is hereby empowered and authorised to administer the same, a full and true account of his, her or their name or names, and of the lands which he, she or they claim within this territory either by entry, patent, deed of conveyance, bond for conveyance, or any other evidence of claim, which the assessor shall set down in writing; and it shall be the duty of the assessor to attend at the court house of his county from nine o'clock in the morning until four o'clock in the afternoon of the twelfth day of February, to receive the returns of such inhabitants as may be delinquent.

penalty for frau dulent list

§ 4. And be it further enacted, That if any inhabitant shall neglect or refuse to render such account, or shall render a false or fraudulent account, he shall be fined in the sum of fifty dollars, or refusal togiveany with costs, to be recovered by information, or indictment, in any court having competent jurisdiction.

§ 5. Be it enacted, That the assessor at the time he takes a list assessor to make a valuation, of lands as aforesaid, shall make a valuation of each tract per hundred acres, according to the quality of soil and its relative situation, which he at the same time shall signify to the land holders, but in making such assessment and valuation, houses, barns, and other improvements, shall be excluded.

§ 6. Be it enacted, That if any non resident, claiming lands in nonresident land holders, this territory either by entry, patent, deed of conveyance, bond for the conveyance, or any other evidence of claim, his or her agent or attorney shall neglect or refuse to list his or her lands with the assessor of the county where such lands may have been entered or located between the first day of January, and the twelfth day of February, agreeably to the requisitions of the third section hereof, then the assessor shall immediately proceed to list the lands of such non resident, that may be in his county, and shall also make a valuation thereof, in the manner required by the preceding section of this act.

§ 7, That the judges of the common pleas shall assemble at the court house of their proper county on the 15th day of February annually, and the assessor shall lay before them an abstract of assessor to lay an abstract before the judges of common pleas, assessment and valuation of lands, made by him in manner and form aforesaid, fairly and correctly stated, and the said judges are hereby empowered and authorised to hear any complaints of an improper or partial assessment or valuation of lands, which may have been made by the said assessor, and to make such alterations in the estimate, as they, or a majority of them, shall think reasonable and just.

H

[32]

§ 8. Be it enacted, That when the abstract of assessment for abstracts when revised to be returned to the assessors the respective counties shall be thus revised and corrected, the clerks of the said court shall make out two fair and correct transcrips thereof, one of which shall be forwarded to the auditor of the territory by the 20th day of March, the other shall be filed by the said clerks in their respective offices, a copy whereof they shall regularly transmit to the house of representatives, on the first week of their annual meeting, and the original abstract, with such alterations and corrections as may have been made by the said judges, certified by the said clerks, shall by them be returned to the assessors respectively.

penalty on clerk for neg lect of du ty

§ 9. Be it further enacted, That if any clerk shall neglect or refuse to perform the service and duty required by this act, he shall, for every such neglect or refusal, be fined in the sum of fifty dollars, to be recovered with costs, by information or indictment, and for the use of the territory.

his salary

§ 10. Be it further enacted, That the said clerks shall receive for the performance of the duty required herein the annual salary of twenty dollars, to be paid out of the territorial treasury.

auditors duty

§ 11. Be it enacted, That the auditor, on receipt of the said abstracts, shall make an assessment on each tract of land according to the aforesaid valuations at such rate per dollar as will be sufficient to produce the sum required.

§ 12. Be it further enacted, that the auditor shall make out fair and correct abstracts for each county, containing the names of possessors, the qantity of land respectively claimed, and the assessment made on each tract in manner aforesaid, and on or before the first day of May, transmit the same to the collectors of the proper counties.

collector to dc mand pay ment

§ 13. Be it enacted, That the collector of each county by the 25th day of May shall demand payment of the tax or sum assessed on each inhabitant in his county in person, or by notice in writing left at his or her usual place of residence.

in case of non-pay ment col lector to advertise and sell,

§ 14. Be it enacted, That in case of non payment of taxes at the time appointed, it shall be the duty of the collector to levy and collect the tax so in arrear, with costs, by a sale at the court house of his county, of the lands of such delinquent, whether resident or non resident, giving at least forty days notice by advertisement at the county seat, and in some public newspaper in this territory of the time and place of such sale.

§ 15. Be it enacted, That it shall be the duty of the collector to receive any arrearage taxes at any time before the sale commences, provided such delinquent pays him the additional sum of fifty cents for his own use.

§ 16. Be it enacted, That when any tract of land is not sold as aforesaid, for the want of buyers, it shall be the duty of the collector to advertise as aforesaid, and to expose the same to sale, at each successive court of common pleas, until the land be sold, or the tax thereon, with costs, be paid.

§ 17. Be it enacted, That when any lands are sold as aforesaid, it shall be the duty of the collector to convey the same to the purchasers by deed in due form of law executed, which conveyance shall vest in the purchaser all right, title and interest of the proprietor, and it shall not be lawful for the collector or his deputies, directly or indirectly to purchase any land or lands sold under the authority of this act.

when lands are sold collector to make a title

§ 18. Be it enacted, That from the time of assessment the territory shall have a *lein* on any tract of land for the amount of taxes due thereon, which shall remain until the taxes be paid.

§ 19. Be it enacted, That when any non resident may have transferred, or may hereafter transfer his or her claim to land in this territory, it shall be lawful for his or her sub claimant, agent or attorney to enter the same within the time prescribed for listing lands by this act with the assessor of the county where the lands lie, who shall keep a book for the purpose, and such person shall be chargeable with the taxes on such land thereafter. Each person having such transfer made shall pay the assessor fifty cents for his own use.

in cases of transfer

§ 20. Be it enacted, That it shall be the duty of the collector to pay the tax money which he shall have received to the treasurer of the territory by the 31st day of July, in every year, and for the monies so paid, the treasurer shall give a

collector to pay in to the treasury tax money.

[33]

receipt, which shall be a sufficient voucher, and exonerate and discharge the said collector of the amount therein contained.

§ 21. Be it enacted, That the collector shall have six percent upon all monies which he shall collect under the authority of this act, to be discounted with him by the treasurer of the territory.

§ 22 Be it enacted, That the assessor shall, for the name of each person whose lands he may list, receive ten cents to be paid out of the territorial treasury.

auditor to
publish ex
tracts

§ 23. Be it enacted, That it shall be the duty of the auditor to publish such extracts from this law as relates to the time and manner of listing lands in this territory belonging to, or claimed by non residents, and also the time and manner of paying and collecting the taxes in one newspaper within this territory, eight weeks, and also in one at the city of Washington for the term of three weeks to commence on the first week in November next, and the expences thereof shall be defrayed out of the treasury of the territory.

assessor to
give bond

§ 24. Be it enacted, That the assessor of each county shall give bond to the court of common pleas with one or more sureties to be approved of by the said court, in the sum of five hundred dollars for the use of the territory conditioned for the faithful performance of the service and duty of assessor, as required by this act, which bond, the due execution thereof being proved before, and certified by a judge of the county, wherein it may be executed, shall be recorded in the office of the secretary of the territory, and copies thereof legally exemplified by the said secretary shall be legal evidence in any court of law in any suit against such assessor, and his sureties.

collector
to give
bond,

§ 25. Be it enacted, That each collector shall give bond in the sum of two thousand dollars with similar sureties for the same purposes, and in like manner as is provided for and in case of assessors in the preceding section, and the said bond shall be authenticated in the same manner, and for similar purposes as is before provided for in case of assessors.

§ 26. Be itenacted, That if any, or either of the days mentioned as aforesaid shall fall on a Sunday, the duties required to be performed as aforesaid, on any, or either of the said days, shall commence on the day following.

sheriffs to
take a list
of inhabi
tants.

§ 27. Be it enacted, That the sheriffs of the counties respectively at the time they take a list of the taxable property under the county levy act, take an exact account of all free male inhabitants in the same, and by the first day of April next, transmit the same to the secretary of the territory, and for performing the service and duty herein required, the said sheriff shall receive three cents for each name, to be paid out of the counties funds, in manner, and in form, as is required in other cases.

§ 28. And be it further enacted, That if any such sheriff shall neglect or refuse to take such account of the free male inhabitants **Penalty** in his county, or to transmit the same to the secretary of the terri- **on failure** tory by the said first day of April next he shall forfeit 500 dollar, to, and for the use of the territory, to be recovered with costs by action of debt, in the name of the auditor, or by indictment or information.

JESSE B. THOMAS, Speaker of the House
of Representatives.

B. CHAMBERS, President of the Council.
Approved August 26th, 1805.

William Henry Harrison.

A RESOLUTION *for revising the Laws of this Territory, and for other purposes.*

R ESOLVED, by the Legislative Council and House of Representatives, That John Johnson and John Rice Jones, be appointed to reduce into one code, the Laws now in force in this territory, and make report thereof to the next session of the legislature. And that the same persons do superintend

[34]

the printing of the laws passed at this session, and be authorised to take the inrolled bills out of the territorial secretary's office [and return the same] to make out an index for the same, as also marginal notes.

JESSE B. THOMAS, Speaker of the House
of Representatives.

B. CHAMBERS, President of the Council.
Approved August 26th, 1805.

William Henry Harrison.

A RESOLUTION *allowing compensation to*
A. Defrance, Door keeper.

RESOLVED, by the Legislative Council and House of Representatives, That Abraham Defrance be allowed one dollar per day, as door keeper to both houses of the Legislature, to be paid out of any monies in the territorial treasury.

JESSE B. THOMAS, Speaker of the House
of Representatives.

B. CHAMBERS, President of the Council.

Approved August 26th, 1805.

William Henry Harrison.

[35]

AN ACT *to Incorporate the Indiana Canal Company.*

WHEREAS it has been represented to this General Assembly, that Benjamin Hovey, and Josiah Stephens, and sundry other persons have associated for the purpose of making a canal at the falls of the Ohio, on the north west side thereof, and with a view to further this laudable design, have actually subscribed considerable sums of money thereto, upon condition that the Legislature shall deem it expedient to grant them support and encouragement by giving them, and such others as shall hereafter subscribe and join their association, a suitable charter of incorporation, as doth appear by their memorial to the legislature; And whereas, it is highly interesting to the commerce and agriculture of this territory, that the object of the said association should be carried into effect, and the legislature being disposed to give every suitable aid thereto,

BE it therefore enacted by the Legislative Council and House of Representatives of the Indiana territory, That the said Benjamin Hovey and Josiah Stephens and their present and future associates; their successors, and assigns, be, and they are hereby created a body corporate and politic, by the name of the "President and directors of the Indiana Canal Company," and are hereby ordained, constituted and declared to be forever hereafter a body politic and corporate, in fact and in name, and by that name they and their successors shall and may have continual succession, and shall be persons in law capable of suing and being sued, pleading and being impleaded, answering and being answered unto, defending and being defended in all courts and places whatsoever, in all manner of actions, suits, complaints, matters and causes whatsoever, and that they and their successors may have a common seal, and make and alter the same at their pleasure, & also that their successors by the same name & style shall be in law capable of purchasing, holding & conveying any estate real & personal for the use of the said corporation.

§ 2. And be it further enacted, That the capital stock of said company shall consist of twenty thousand shares of fifty dollars each, and that subscriptions to the capital stock of said company may be received by such person and persons, and under such regulations as the directors for the time being or a majority of them shall prescribe and ordain.

§ 3. And be it futher enacted, That the stock property and concerns of the said company shall, until the first Monday in May next, be conducted by twelve directors hereafter named, and after that day the same shall be conducted and managed by seven directors, being stockholders, who shall hold their offices for one year from the said first Monday in May next, and the said directors shall be elected by ballot annually, on the first Monday in May, at such hour of the day and at such place within the said territory, as the said president and directors for the time being shall appoint and public notice shall be given by the said directors, not less than 30 days previous to the time of holding said election by an advertisement to be inserted in some one or more newspapers printed in the territory, and in the state of Kentucky, and the said election shall be made by such of the stockholders as shall attend for that purpose, or by proxy, each share having one vote for every share as far as ten shares, and one vote for every five shares above ten; and the directors so to be chosen, shall at their first meeting elect by ballot, one of their members to be their president.

§ 4. And be it further enacted, That George Rogers Clark, John Brown, Johnathan Dayton, Aaron Burr, Benjamin Hovey, Davis Floyd, Josiah Stephens, William Croghan, John Gwathmey,

John Harrison, Marston G. Clark, and Samuel C. Vance, shall be the first directors, and shall hold their offices untll the first Monday in May next, and that at their first meeting they shall by ballot, elect one of their members to be their president, and that the said president and directors, and the president and directors hereafter to be chosen, a majority of whom being assembled shall constitute a board, shall have power to appoint the time and place of all meetings for the dispatch of business, to appoint such superintendants, engineers, clerks and other officers, agents and servants and exact from them such security for the performance of the duties assigned them, as they, the said directors shall judge requisite and proper and necessary, for carrying into effect the purposes of this act, and to agree for, and settle their respective wages, and all allowances, and to pass and sign their accounts, and also to make and establish rules of proceedings, and to make such bye-laws, rules and regulations not inconsistant with the constitution and laws of the United States, nor the laws of this territory, as may appear to them most conducive to the ends proposed by this act, and to conduct all other business and concerns of the said company.

[36]

§ 5. And be it further enacted, That in case of the death, resignation or refusal to act of any director or directors chosen as aforesaid, it shall and may be lawful for the remaining directors, upon public notice being given at least fifteen days for that purpose, to proceed to elect a director or directors, to fill such vacancy or vacancies.

§ 6. And be it further enacted, That in case of the death, resignation or refusal to act of the president, it shall and may be lawful for said directors to choose a president pro tem. and for the meeting only, for which he shall be chosen.

§ 7. And be it further enacted, That it shall and may be lawful for the said company, by its president and directors, or by any superintendant, agent or engineer, appointed under the seal of the said company, to enter into and upon, and to take possession of any land, whether covered with water or not, which the said company may deem necessary for the prosecution of the works and improvements contemplated by this act, or whereon, or whereby to construct any canal, locke, dyke, embankment, pond, dam or other work intended or permitted by this act, and that without the lease and permission of the owner or owners, proprietor or proprietors, of such land first had and obtained, but the land so to be taken and appropriated, shall be valued and paid for in the manner herein after provided. Provided always, and it is hereby fully understood, That for the purposes aforesaid it shall not be lawful for the said company to condemn a greater quanty of land than one hundred acres.

§ 8. And be it further enacted, That it shall be lawful for the said company hereby incorporated, and for all and every other person or persons, employed by or under them for the purposes contemplated by this act, from time to time, to enter upon any lands contiguous or near to the intended canal or other works, or the places which may be selected for, or intended to be used or employed for the same, with carts, waggons and other carriages, and beasts of draught and burthen, and all necessary tools and implements, both for executing and making, and for altering and repairing the said works, or any of them, and to take and carry away any timber, stone, clay, gravel, sand or earth, from the same, for the making, altering or repairing of the said works, or any of them, subject always to the making of compensation for all damages thereby occasioned, either by agreement of parties, or in the mode hereafter prescribed: Provided, That the said company shall not take, or carry away any timber, stone, clay, gravel, sand or earth, after the said canal and other works hereby contemplated are completed, until they shall pay the damages assessed as aforesaid.

§ 9. And be it further enacted, That the said president and directors for the time being, may agree with the owners of any lands so taken or appropriated, or injured as aforesaid, for the purchase of the said lands, or for compensation for the said injury and damages, as the case may be, but in case of disagreement, or in case of the owner or owners of such lands shall be *feme covert,* under age, *non compos mentis,* or out of the territory, then it shall be lawful for the Judges of this territory, or the Judges of the supreme court when this territory shall become a state, or any one of them not being interested in the said company, or in the said lands, upon the application of either party to nominate and appoint seven indifferent persons, to view and survey the said lands, and to estimate the injury sustained as aforesaid, or the value of the said lands, as the case may require, and to report thereupon, to the said court without delay, and upon the coming in of such report, and the confirmation thereof by the said court, the said president, directors and company, shall pay to the said owners, respectively, the sum mentioned in such report, in full compensation for the said lands, or for the injury done as aforesaid, as the case may be, and upon such payment, the said president, directors and company, shall be, and become seized in fee, of all such lands, hereditaments and tenements, as they shall have taken possession of, appropriated, and paid for as aforesaid, and they, and all those who have acted under them, shall be acquitted and exonerated, of and from all claim and demand, on account of such injury or damage.

§ 10. And be it further enacted, That whenever the said canal shall cross any public or private laid out road or highway, or shall divide the grounds of any person into two parts, so as to require a bridge to cross the same, the referees who shall enquire of the damages to be sustained in manner herein directed, shall find and ascertain whether a passage across the same shall be admitted and maintained by a bridge, and on such finding, the said directors shall cause a bridge fit for the passage of carts and waggons to be built, and forever hereafter maintained and kept in repair, at all and every the places so ascer-

[37]

tained by the said referees, at the costs and charges of the said company; but nothing herein contained shall prevent any person from erecting and keeping in repair any foot, or other bridge across the said canal, at his or her own expense, when the same shall pass through his or her ground: *Provided,* the same shall be of such height above the water as shall be usual in the bridges **erected by the company.** *And provided also,* that such foot or other bridges to be erected by the owner or owners of such land, shall not interfere with any of the locks, buildings, passage of vessels, boats, rafts or other works of the company.

§ 11. And be it further enacted, That the said president and directors and their successors, a majority of them being assembled, shall have full power and authority to agree with any persons on behalf of the said company to cut such canal from such place above, to such place below the falls, on the north west side of the river Ohio, & to erect such locks, and to perform such other works as they shall judge necessary, for opening, improving and extending the navigation of said river, and for the other purposes authorised by this law, and for repairing and keeping in order the said canal, locks & other works.

§ 12. And be it further enacted, That it shall be lawful for the said company to receive from the United States, or from any state, or from any body corporate or politic, donations of lands, money or other chattels for the use of the said company, and to receive for the same use and purpose, voluntary subscriptions and donations from any individuals who may be disposed to encourage and promote the objects of this act, and it shall and may be lawful for the said company, in case of refusal or neglect of payment, in the name of the company aforesaid, to sue for, and recover of all such subscribers, their heirs, executors or administrators, the sums by them respectively subscribed, by action of debt, or upon the case, in any court of record having competent jurisdiction.

§ 13. And be it further enacted, That if at any time, it shall, in the opinion of the said company, become necessary in order to effect the purposes authorised by this act, to increase the said capital stock, and number of shares, it shall and may be lawful for the said company, in their discretion from time to time to increase the said capital, by the addition of so many whole shares, as shall be judged necessary by the said proprietors, or a majority of them in interest, and that subscriptions for the said shares shall be received at such time and place, and in such manner, as the directors for the time being, shall think proper to order and prescribe.

§ 14. And be it further enacted, That it shall be lawful for the said directors to call for, and demand from the stockholders, respectively, all such sums of money by them subscribed, or to be subscribed, at such times, and in such proportions, as they shall see fit, under pain of forfeiture of their shares, and all previous payments thereon to the said president, directors and company.

§ 15. And be it further enacted, That in consideration of the expenses the said proprietors shall be at in opening and completing the said canal, and in keeping the works in repair, and in effecting the objects authorised by this act, the said works and canal, and other property which the said company shall acquire, with all profits and appurtenances, shall be, and the same are hereby vested in the said company, and their successors forever, and the canal, and the water works erected thereon, or adjoining thereto, shall be exempt from the payment of any tax, imposition or assessment whatsoever, until the said works shall be in operation, and that the shares in the stock of the said company, shall be deemed, and are hereby declared to be personal, and not real estate, and that the same may be transferred and assigned, so as to convey the absolute property thereof, in such manner and form as by the said president and directors, shall by, bye laws to be made for that purpose ordain and prescribe.

§ 16. And be it further enacted, That it shall and may be lawful for the said president and directors at all times, forever, to demand and receive at such time and place, or places on the said canal, as they shall adjudge and determine to be most convenient for all boats, vessels and rafts conveyed through the said canal, or any part thereof, according to the following table and rates to wit: For each boat not more than 14 feet wide, and 30 feet long, three dollars; For each boat not more than 14 feet wide, and 45 feet long, four dollars; For each boat not more than 14 feet wide, and 60 feet long, five dollars; And every foot over and above 14 feet wide and 60 feet long, nine cents;—For each keel boat, perogue or canoe, not more than 35 feet long, two dollars; For each keel boat, perogue or canoe, not more than 45 feet long, three dollars; For each keel boat, perogue or canoe, not more than 60 feet long, four dollars; And

[38]

for every foot over and above sixty feet long, nine cents; And for all rafts or lumber, not laden on board a boat or vessel such sum as shall be agreed by and between the owner or supercargo and the said company or their agent.

§ 17. And be it further enacted, That the collector of the toll duly appointed and authorised by the president and directors of the said corporation, may stop and detain all boats and vessels using the canal until the owner or commander or supercargo of the same shall pay the toll so as aforesaid fixed, or may distrain part of the cargo therein contained, sufficient by the appraisement of two indifferent persons to satisfy the same, which distress shall be kept by the collector of tolls taking the same, for the space of eight days, and afterwards be sold by public vendue, in any public place in the neighborhood, to the highest bidder, in the same manner and form, as goods distrained for rent, are by law sold, rendering the surplus, on demand, if any there be, after the payment of the said toll, and costs of distress and sale, to the owner, or owners thereof.

§ 18. And be it further enacted, That the said company may vest any part of their capital, or of the profits thereof, as to the directors for the time being shall deem expedient, in the public debt of the United States, or of any particular state, or in the stock of any incorporate monied institution, or may employ the same in commercial operations, or in any other monied transactions, not inconsistent with the constitution and laws of the United States, or laws of this territory, and for the sole benefit of the said company.

§ 19. And be it further enacted, That as soon as one hundred thousand dollars in gold or silver shall have been actually received, or the value thereof in lands actually acquired in fee simple, on account of the subscription for the said stock, it shall and may be lawful for the said company to issue promissary notes, payable to any person or persons, his, her or their order, or to bearer, which being signed by the president, and countersigned by the treasurer or clerk, although not under the seal of the corporation, or having been issued pursuant to any resolution, or bye law of the said company, though not so signed, shall be binding and obligatory on the same, and shall be negotiable & assignable by endorsement, or if payable to bearer, by delivery; Provided, That the said company shall make a fair statement of all the lands which they possess, to the Legislature, yearly, if thereto required, who will estimate the value of the same.

§ 20. And be it further enacted, That the total amount of the notes issued in manner and form aforesaid, shall not at any time exceed double the amount of cash in fund, and the value of the lands belonging to said company, in case of excess, the president and directors under whose administration it may happen, shall be liable for the same in their natural and private capacities, and an action of debt, or on the case, may be brought against them, or any of them, or any of their heirs, executors or administrators, in any court of record in the United States, having competent jurisdiction, by any crediror or creditors of the said company, and may be prosecuted to judgment and execution; But this shall not be construed to extend, to exempt the said company, or the lands, tenements, hereditaments, goods or chattels of the same, from being also chargeable with the said excess.

§ 21. And be it further enacted, That the books of the said company shall always be open for the inspection of the Legislature of this territory, or any person or persons to be appointed by them for that purpose.

§ 22. And be it further enacted, That in case the said company shall not begin the said canal within nine months from the passing of this act, or shall not, on or before the first day of December, which will be in the year eighteen hundred and eleven, so far complete the said canal, as to admit of the passage of boats drawing not more than three feeet water, then, and in either of those cases, or on such defrult being ascertained, all the preference, privileges and powers, given and granted by this act, shall thenceforth cease, determine, and be absolutely void.

§ 23. Provided always nevertheless, and it is hereby enacted and declared, That it shall and may be lawful for any future Legislature of this territory, or any state to be formed therein, at any time or times hereafter, after the expiration of fifteen years from the passage hereof, to alter, abridge, limit, extend, annul or destroy all, or any of the powers, privileges and immunities hereby given, so as the said canal, and the tolls thereof, and the buildings and works erected thereon, or on the waters taken therefrom, shall remain to the said company, their heirs and successors.

§ 24. And be it further enacted, That the directors herein appointed to act as such, until the first day of May next shall be entitled to have and receive three dollars per day, for every day they shall attend or expend from their several places of abode, in, and about the execution of the trust hereby reposed in them, which shall be paid to such director or directors, from the funds of the company. Provided always, and it is further enacted and declared, That it shall and may be lawful for this territory, or any state to be formed therein, in that part thereof in which the said canal is situate, at any time or times hereafter, to subscribe for such, and so many shares of the said capital stock, as may be then unsubscribed for, and in case the same shall be so subscribed, then for so many shares of additional stock, as they may think proper, not exceeding in the whole, one thousand shares.

§ 25. And be it further enacted, That it shall be incumbent on the said president and directors, to keep open their books of subscription for the space of four months from the passage hereof, at the town of Jeffersonville, in the Indiana territory. This act shall commence and be in force from and after the passage thereof.

JESSE B. THOMAS, Speaker of the House
of Representatives.

B. CHAMBERS, President of the Council.
Approved, August 24th, 1805.

William Henry Harrison.

INDEX,

LAWS

PASSED

AT THE SECOND SESSION

OF THE

First General Assembly

OF THE

INDIANA TERRITORY,

BEGUN AND HELD

AT THE BOROUGH OF VINCENNES,

ON MONDAY THE THIRD DAY OF NOVEMBER,

In the Year Eighteen Hundred & Six.

By Authority.

VINCENNES,

PRINTED BY ELIHU STOUT.

ACTS

Passed at the second session of the first General Assembly of the Indiana Territory.

CHAPTER I.

AN ACT *supplemental to an act, entitled "An act for levying and collecting a tax on land and for other purposes."*

§ 1st. Be it enacted by the Legislative Council and House of Representatives, and it is hereby enacted by the authority of the same, That when any lands may in future be sold for the non payment of taxes, whether belonging to a resident or non resident; it shall be lawful for any of said persons within the period of two years from the sale of the said land, to redeem the same by paying the purchase money with fifty per cent. interest, per annum, thereon, and upon tender of said purchase money and interest, within the aforesaid period to the said purchaser, or his agent, if either of them live within the county in which the land lies; but if not, then he or they shall by advertisement in some public newspaper in this territory, if one is published therein, if not, in some newspaper published the nearest to the place where the land lies, at least for the space of three weeks, appoint a time when he or they will attend at the clerks office of the county in which the said land lies, where the said purchase money and interest will be tendered and paid, if the purchaser or his agent will attend to receive it, the said advertisement to be published at least six months before the aforesaid two years expires, and if neither the purchaser nor his agent will attend at the time and place mentioned in the aforesaid advertisement, then his title shall be vacated and become void. *(Land sold by collector may be redeemed.)*

§ 2nd. Be it further enacted, That when any tract of land is to be sold for the non payment of taxes, the collector shall sell the tract, or so much thereof, as will bring the tax and costs due thereon, to be laid off in the form of a square, or a parellelogram, in some corner of the tract, disignated by the collector at the time of sale. *(Duty of Collector in selling land for taxes.)*

§ 3rd. Be it further enacted, That it shall be the duty of the collector to give notice of the time and place of the sales of lands *(Collector to notify)*

one of the
Judges of
the court
of Com-
mon pleas
of the
time and
place of
sale.

for the non payment of taxes, to one of the Judges of the court of
Common Pleas, of the county in which the land lies, at least ten
days before said sales; and it shall be the duty of the said Judge
to superintend the said sales, and prevent any fraud or collusion in
the same; the said Judge shall receive for each days attendance,
two hundred cents, to be laid on the land sold by the collector, and
collected by him and paid to the said Judge.

Collector
to make
report of
such sale.

§ 4th.   Be it further enacted, That every collector making such
sale as aforesaid, shall make return thereof to the clerk of the
court of Common Pleas, of the county where the said lands may
lie, within twenty days after the said sale shall, or may take place,
in which return he shall particularly state every circumstance and
expence attending the same.   And if any collector shall fail to
make said return, or shall charge other or greater fees, either for
himself, or the said Judge, than allowed by law, he shall be liable
to be fined the sum of thirty dollars, to be recovered by motion
in said court by the party grieved.

§ 5th.   Whereas, The courts of Common Pleas in the counties
of St. Clair, Randolph, and Dearborne, failed to appoint an assessor and collector in each of the aforesaid counties, for the purpose
mentioned in the act to which this is a supplement; and whereas,
the assessors mentioned in the said act, thereby are directed to lay
an abstract of assessment and valuation of land by them made,
before the said courts; and the clerks thereof are required
after the

(4)

Proviso.

said abstracts are received and corrected, to forward a fair transcript thereof to the Auditor of the Territory; and whereas, the
Auditor is required by the said act, on the receipt of the said
abstracts, to make an assessment upon each tract of land, according
to the aforesaid valuation, at such rate per dollar, as will produce
the sum required.   That in consequence of the failure of the receipt of the said abstracts from the aforesaid counties, the Auditor
could not make the assessment agreeably to the aforesaid act; but
he made the assessment upon the returns of the abstracts of lands
in the counties of Knox and Clarke, and the taxes according to
said assessment, have been collected in said last mentioned coun-

ties. And whereas, the public newspaper for this territory, was for some time suspended in its operation, and it therefore became impossible for the collectors, respectively, to comply with that part of the act, to which this is a supplement, which made it necessary before any sale of land, for the tax due thereon, that an advertisement should be published in said paper for forty days previous to said sale. Be it therefore enacted, That the assessment as made by the Auditor for the last mentioned counties, and the taxes collected by the several collectors in consequence thereof, be, and the same is hereby considered as legal, and the said Auditor, and the several collectors and assessors concerned in the collection of the taxes in the said two counties, are hereby indemnified for any acts by them done in the collection of the above taxes, in consequence of the before mentioned failures, or incomplete assessments; Provided always, That nothing herein contained shall be so construed as to affect, or legalize any sale of land for taxes made by said collector, contrary to the requisitions of the said act. **Proceedings of Auditor collectors made legal.**

§ 6th. And whereas by the act to which this is a supplement it is provided, that the sale of lands upon which the taxes have not been, or are not paid, at the time required by said act, shall be advertised in some public newspaper in this territory. Be it therefore enacted, that if no newspaper be printed therein, then the said advertisement shall be set up at two or more different public places in the several counties in which the land lies, under the same regulations as to time, as is provided in the said act. **Time of sale to be made public.**

§ 7th. Be it further enacted, That the auditor is hereby authorised and required to assess, and lay on the counties of Randolph, St. Clair, and Dearborne, their proportion of the taxes for the year eighteen hundred and six, which they have failed to discharge, owing to an abstract not being made and returned to the Auditor from the said counties, respectively. The collectors for the ensuing year, for the several last mentioned counties, are hereby required to collect, and shall have the same power to enforce the payment of the assessment so made, as he shall by law have to enforce the payment of taxes for the ensuing year, and he shall pay the same to the treasurer of the Territory, at the time that he is by law required to pay the taxes collected for the said ensuing year. And that so much of the second section as makes **Duty of auditor & collector** it necessary for the Auditor to designate the quality of the land, be, and the same is hereby repealed.

§ 8th. Be it further enacted, That if the Auditor does not receive the whole abstracts, as mentioned in the eleventh section of the aforesaid act from the several counties, that in such case he shall proceed to make an assessment from the best information he can collect.

Duty of auditor.

§ 9th. Be it further enacted, that the said courts of Common Pleas, mentioned in the first section of the law to which this is a supplement, shall annually appoint an assessor and collector, for the purpose mentioned in said act. And if the Judges of the said courts, or any of them, shall neglect or refuse to attend and appoint the said assessors and collectors, at the time mentioned in said act, they shall be fined a sum not exceeding two hundred dollars, to be recovered by indictment or information, for the use of the ter-

Courts of common pleas to appoint an assessor and collector.

(5)

ritory. And in case of the refusal or neglect of any register, surveyor, or other person in whose possession the records and proofs of the grant and confirmation of land may be, to give an abstract from their books and records, upon being thereunto lawfully required, he or they so offending shall be fined in the sum of five hundred dollars, to be recovered by action of debt, in the name of the Attorney General. whose duty it is hereby made to sue for the same in any court having competent jurisdiction, for the use of the Territory.

§ 10th. And be it further enacted, That all laws, and parts of laws which come within the purview of this act, be, and the same are hereby repealed.—This act to take effect from the passage thereof.

JESSE B. THOMAS, Speaker of the House of Representatives.

P. MENARD, President pro tem. of the Legislative Council.

Approved—November 29th, 1806.

William Henry Harrison.

CHAPTER II.

AN ACT *to regulate Elections of Representatives to the General Assembly.*

§ 1st. Be it enacted by the Legislative Council and House of Representatives, and it is hereby enacted by the authority of the same, That so much of an act passed by the General Assembly of the North Western Territory, on the sixth day of December, one thousand seven hundred and ninety nine, entitled "An act ascertaining the number of free male inhabitants of the age of twenty one, in the Territory of the United States, north west of the river Ohio, and to regulate the elections of representatives for the same," as is contained in the ninth, tenth, eleventh, twelfth, thirteenth, fifteenth, sixteenth, seventeenth, eighteenth, nineteenth, twentieth, twenty first, and twenty second sections, except as it relates to the time of holding elections, be, and the same is hereby continued in force in this territory.

Parts of an act continued in force.

§ 2nd. Be it further enacted, That all general elections for representatives to serve in the general assembly, shall invariably be began on the first Monday in February, in the year one thousand eight hundred and seven, and afterwards on the first Monday in April, bi annually.

Time of elections

§ 3rd. Be it further enacted, That no sheriff, under sheriff, clerk of any court, or person holding a commission during pleasure, directly, under the United States or this territory, except Justices of the Peace and Militia officers, shall be eligible to a seat in either branches of the Legislature.—This act to take effect from and after the passage thereof.

JESSE B. THOMAS, Speaker of the House of Representatives.

JOHN RICE JONES, President pro tem. of the Legislative Council.

Approved—December 4th, 1806.

William Henry Harrison.

CHAPTER III.

AN ACT *to establish Election Districts in the county of Dearborne.*

Election districts.

§ 1st.   Be it enacted by the Legislative Council and House of Representatives, and it is hereby enacted by the authority of the same, That there shall be four election districts established in the county of Dearborne, to wit: all that part of the said county lying north of the south line of the twelfth township, first and second ranges, shall be one district; the second district

(6)

Different ranges.

shall commence at the south line of the twelfth township, and to extend down White water to the centre of the ninth township, of the said first and second ranges; the third district shall commence at the south line of the second district, and to extend to the place where the meredian line between the state of Ohio and this territory crosses White water; and all that part of the said county lying west of a line drawn a due north course from the mouth of Grants creek, shall make the fourth district.

Sheriff to appoint deputies.

§ 2nd.   And be it further enacted, That for the purpose of carrying this act into more complete operation and effect, the high sheriff of the county shall appoint his deputies and assistants, to act in the said several election districts, who shall severally have the same power in opening and closing the election in their said districts, as is given to the sheriff of the county by the tenth section of the act to which this act is an amendment, and the returns from the said deputies shall be severally made by them to the said high sheriff within fifteen days after holding the said election.—This act shall take effect from and after the passage thereof, and shall continue in force for one year and no longer.

JESSE B. THOMAS, Speaker of the House
of Representatives.

JOHN RICE JONES, President pro tem. of
the Legislative Council.

Approved—December 6th, 1806.

William Henry Harrison.

CHAPTER IV.
A RESOLUTION.

WHEREAS the sheriffs of several counties in this territory failed to take in lists of the free male inhabitants of the counties as required by the twenty seventh section of the act passed last session, for levying and collecting a tax on land, and for other purposes. **Proviso.**

Resolved therefore by the Legislative Council, and House of Representatives, The better to enable the Governor of this territory, equally to apportion the additional representation to the general assembly, that the sheriffs of the counties of Dearborne, Clarke, Knox, and Randolph, shall take in a list of all the free male inhabitants of their respective counties, of the age of twenty one years and upwards, and return a list thereof to the secretary of this territory, on or before the first day of June next, and for failure thereof shall be liable to the same fine as mentioned in the above recited law, and shall be entitled to, and receive the sum of three cents per man, to be paid in the manner therein mentioned. And that the Governor be authorised at any time after receiving said returns, to issue his writ of election to such counties as may be entitled to an additional member any law to the contrary notwithstanding. **Sheriffs to take census.**

Resolved also, That there shall be paid out of the Territorial Treasury, to the several counties where the censuses have been taken the amount of the sums by them paid to the sheriffs for taking the same, in pursuance of the law passed at the last sessions of the Legislature.

JESSE B. THOMAS, Speaker of the House
of Representatives,
JOHN RICE JONES, President pro tem. of
the Legislative Council.
Approved—December 6th, 1806.

William Henry Harrison.

(6)

CHAPTER V.

AN ACT *to Incorporate an University in the Indiana Territory.*

Proviso.

WHEREAS the independence, happiness and energy of every republic depends (under the influence of the destinies of Heaven) upon the wisdom, virtue, talents and energy, of its citizens and rulers.

And whereas, science, literature, and the liberal arts, contribute in an eminent degree, to improve those qualities and acquirements.

And whereas, learning hath ever been found the ablest advocate of genuine liberty, the best supporter of rational religion, and the source of the only solid and imperishable glory, which nations can acquire.

And forasmuch, as literature, and philosophy, furnish the most useful and pleasing occupations, improveing and varying the enjoyments of prosperity, affording relief under the pressure of misfortune, and hope and consolation in the hour of death. And considering that in a commonwealth, where the humblest citizen may be elected to the highest public office, and where the Heaven born prerogative of the right to elect, and to reject, is retained, and secured to the citizens, the knowledge which is requisite for a magistrate and elector, should be widely diffused.

University incorporated & trustees appointed.

§ 1st. Be it therefore enacted by the Legislative Council and House of Representatives, That an University be, and is hereby instituted and incorporated within this Territory, to be called and known by the name, or style of the "Vincennes University," That William Henry Harrison, John Gibson, Thomas T. Davis, Henry Vander Burgh, Waller Taylor, Benjamin Parke, Peter Jones, James Johnson, John Badolett, John Rice Jones, George Wallace, William Bullitt, Elias M'Namee, Henry Hurst, Genl. W. Johnston, Francis Vigo, Jacob Kuykendoll, Samuel M'Kee, Nathaniel Ewing, George Leach, Luke Decker, Samuel Gwathmey, and John Johnson, are hereby declared to be Trustees of the said University; that the said Trustees, and their successors, be, and they are hereby created a body corporate and politic, by the name of the "Board of Trustees for the Vincennes University," and are hereby ordained, constituted and declared to be forever hereafter, a body politic and corporate, in fact and in name, and by that name, they, and their successors, shall and may have continual succession, and shall be persons in law capable of suing, and being sued, pleading, and being impleaded, answering, and being answered unto, defending, and being defended, in all courts and places whatsoever, in all manner of actions, suits, complaints, matters and causes whatsoever, and that they, and their successors, may have a common seal, and make, and alter the same at their pleasure, and also that they, and their successors, by the same name and style, shall be in law capable of purchasing, holding, leasing and conveying, any estate, real or personal, for the use of the said corporation, except as is herein after mentioned, so that the said Trustees shall not at any one time, hold or possess, more than one hundred thousand acres of land.

§ 2nd. And whereas, Congress has appropriated a township of land of twenty three thousand and forty acres, for the use and support of the University, or a public school in the district of **May sell** Vincennes, and whereas, the township is now located, and the **or trans-** boundaries designated. Be it therefore enacted, That the Trus- **fer a part** tees in their corporate capacity, or a majority of them, be, and **of their** they are hereby authorised to sell, transfer, convey and dispose **land.** of any quantity, not exceeding four thousand acres of the said land, for the purpose of putting into immediate operation the said institution, or University, and to lease, or rent the remaining part of the said township, to the best advantage, for the use of the said public school, or University.

§ 3rd. Be it enacted, That the places of any of the said trustees, who shall

B

(8)

resign, remove from the territory, die, or wilfully absent himself, **Vacancies,** or themselves, from three stated meetings, shall from time to time, **how filled** be supplied by the board of trustees, at their stated meetings, which shall be held on the first Monday, of April and October, yearly, and every year, and at such other times as the said board of trustees shall direct, by electing one for every two whose seats may be so vacated, so that the whole number shall not be less than fifteen; after which time one trustee shall be elected at the stated meetings, as above mentioned, to supply every vacancy that may so happen.—Extraordinary meetings of the said board may be had by the President, or any three of the trustees, giving at least ten days notice thereof, either in writing, or in some public newspaper most convenient to said University.

Extraord inary mee tings.

§ 4th.   Be it enacted, That the trustees or a majority of them, shall have full power from time to time, to make such bye laws, ordinances and regulations in writing, not inconsistent with the charter, with the laws of this territory, or of the United States, as to them shall appear necessary for the good government of the said University, and the students thereof, and the same to put in execution, revoke, alter and make anew, as to them shall appear necessary, and to appoint such subordinate officers as they may think convenient for the police of the said University, and for carrying this law into effect and by ordinance to require such sureties from the several officers, and to annex such fees to the several officers of the corporation, and to impose such fines for a neglect of duty, or misconduct in office as to them shall appear proper.

Trustees to make bye laws.

§ 5th.   Be it further enacted, That the trustees at their first stated meeting shall elect a President out of their own body, and in case of his absence at any future stated or extraordinary meeting, the said trustees shall elect a President pro tem.

To elect a president.

§ 6th.   And be it further enacted, That the said trustees shall as speedily as may be, establish and erect an Uuniversity within the limits of the Borough of Vincennes, and shall appoint to preside over and govern the said University, a President and not exceeding four professors for the instruction of youth in the Latin, Greek, French and English languages, Mathematics, Natural Philosophy, Antient and Modern History, Moral Philosophy, Logic, Rhetoric and the Law of Nature and Nations; that it shall be the duty of the said president and professors to instruct and give lectures to the students of the said university, according to such plan of education as the said trustees may approve and direct in the branches of learning above mentioned; that the said president and professors or a majority of them, shall be called

Establish an univer sity ap- point a president and four professors and their duty.

and styled the faculty of the university, which faculty shall have the power of enforcing the rules and regulations adopted by the said trustees for the government and discipline of the said university, and for granting and confirming by and with the consent of the said trustees such degrees in the liberal arts and sciences to such students of the said university who by their proficiency in learning the said professors shall think entitled to them, as are usually granted and conferred in other universities in the United States, and to grant to such graduates deplomas under the common seal of the said university to authenticate and perpetuate the memory of such graduations, and that the said president and professors shall hold their offices during the pleasure of the trustees, and that the President of the university, ex-officio for the time being, shall be considered as one of the trustees of said university.

§ 7th. Be it further enacted, That it shall be the duty of the said Trustees and they are hereby authorised and required as soon as may be, to erect, purchase or hire as they may deem most expedient for carrying the said institution into effect, suitable buildings for the said university, to make ordinances for the government and discipline thereof, to establish plans of education therefor, which plans shall embrace each and every of the languages,

Duty of trustees.

(9)

sciences and branches of learning herein mentioned or directed to be taught in the said university, to regulate the admission of students and pupils into the same, to elect and appoint persons of suitable learning and talents to be president and professors of the said university, to agree with them for their salaries and emoluments, to visit and inspect the said university, and examine into the state of education and discipline therein and make a yearly report thereof to the Legislature, and generally to do all lawful matters and things whatsoever necessary for the maintaining and supporting the institution aforesaid, and for the more extensive communication of useful knowledge.

§ 8th. Be it further enacted, That as soon as may be after the establishment of the said university, the said Trustees shall establish a Library in and for the use of the students, professors

To establish a library.

and other members of the said institution, to consist of such books and experimental apparatus as they may deem proper for said institution, to be provided in such manner and by such ways and means as they or a majority of them shall by ordinance direct, and by ordinance to regulate the terms upon which books &c. may be taken out of said Library and returned to the same.

Appoint other pro fessors.

§ 9th.   Be it enacted, That the said Trustees shall from time to time elect and appoint a professor of Divinity, of Law and of Physic, whenever they may deem it necessary for the good of the institution, or when the progressed state of education in the said university may require it, to agree with them for their salaries, to point out the duties of said professors, the said professors shall be considered as members of the faculty of said university, to hold their appointments during the pleasure of the board of Trustees.

§ 10th.   Be it enacted, That no particular tenets of religion shall be taught in said university by the president and professors mentioned in the sixth section of this act.

Proviso.

§ 11th.   And whereas the establishment of an institution of this kind in the neighborhood of the aborigines of the country, may tend to the gradual civilization of the rising generation, and if properly conducted be of essential service to themselves, and contribute greatly to the cause of humanity and brotherly love which all men ought to bear to each other of whatever colour, and tend also to preserve that friendship and harmony which ought to exist between the government and the Indians.

Indians supported & taught gratis.

Be it therefore enacted, and it is hereby enjoined on the said Trustees to use their utmost endeavours to induce the said aborigines to send their children to the said university for education, who when sent, shall be maintained, clothed and educated at the expense of the said institution; and be it further enacted, That the students, whenever the funds of the institution shall in the opinion of the Trustees permit it, be educated gratis at the said university in all or any of the branches of education which they may require.

§ 12th,   And be it further enacted, That the professors during their professorship, and the students while at college shall be exempt from militia duty.

§ 13th. Be it enacted, That the said Trustees as soon as in their opinion the funds of the said institution will admit are hereby required to establish an institution for the education of females, and to make such bye laws and ordinances for the said institution and the government thereof, as they may think proper. **Education of females**

§ 14th. Be it further enacted, That the said Trustees shall have the power to establish a Grammar school connected with, and dependant upon the said university, for the purpose of teaching the rudiments of the languages, and that they may employ a master and ushers specially for this purpose, or employ the professor of languages to superintend the same, as the one or the other may be found most convenient and œconomical. **To establish a grammar school.**

§ 15th. And be it further enacted, That for the support of the aforesaid institution, and for the purpose of procuring a library and the necessary phi-

(10)

losophical and experimental apparatus, agreeably to the eighth section of this bill; there shall be raised a sum not exceeding twenty thousand dollars, by a Lottery to be carried into operation as speedily as may be after the passage of this act; and that the Trustees of the said university shall appoint five discreet persons, either of their own body, or other persons, to be managers of the said lotteries, each of whom shall give security, to be approved of by the said Trustees, in such sum as they shall direct, conditioned for the faithful discharge of the duty required of said managers: and the said managers shall have power to adopt such schemes as they may deem proper, to sell the said tickets, and to superintend the drawing of the same, and the payment of the prizes; and that as often as the said managers shall receive one thousand dollars, they shall deposit the same in the hands of the Treasurer of the said board of Trustees; and the said managers and Trustees shall render an account of their proceedings therein at the next session **To raise a sum of money by lottery.**

of the legislature after the drawing of said lottery.—This act to take effect from and after the first day of January next.

JESSE B. THOMAS, Speaker of the House of Representatives.

P. MENARD, President pro tem. of the Legislative Council.

Approved—November 29th, 1806.

William Henry Harrison.

CHAPTER VI.

AN ACT *supplemental to an act to Incorporate an University in the Indiana Territory.*

Be it enacted by the Legislative Council and House of Representatives, and it is hereby enacted by the authority of the same, That the act to incorporate an University in the Indiana Territory, shall take effect from and after the passage of the same, and that a special meeting of the Trustees of the said University shall be held on the first Saturday in December next, for the election of officers, and to commence their operations to carry the said law into effect, any thing in the said law to the contrary notwithstanding.

JESSE B. THOMAS, Speaker of the House of Representatives.

P, MENARD, President pro tem. of the Legislative Council.

Approved—November 29th, 1806.

William Henry Harrison.

CHAPTER VII.

AN ACT *to amend an act, entitled "An act establishing Courts for the trial of Small Causes.*

Where suit shall be brot' § 1st. Be it enacted by the Legislative Council and House of Representatives, and it is hereby enacted by the authority of the same, That it shall be the duty of the plaintiff to bring his suit before any Magistrate in the township where the debt was contracted, or where the plaintiff resides, or where the defendant may be found; and if the plaintiff brings his suit in any other township, for the purposes of harrassing the defendant, which shall be determined by the Magistrate before whom the suit is commenced, and it appears to the said Magistrate, that the said suit was vexatiously commenced, then he shall dismiss the said suit, with costs to the defendant.

§ 2nd.   Be it further enacted, That the jurisdiction of a Magistrate shall

(11)

extend to all causes for personal property, where the value of the property does not exceed eighteen dollars.

§ 3rd.   Be it further enacted, That when any judgment is **Stay of** obtained before any Justice of the Peace, for the sum of six dol- **execution** lars and under, that there shall be a stay of execution for thirty days; and for any sum over six, and under twelve dollars, sixty days; and if the judgment shall be for the sum of twelve dollars and upwards, there shall be a stay of execution for ninety days. But in either case, the person or persons against whom such judgment may be rendered, shall be subject to the same laws and regulations respecting securities as heretofore, any law or usage to the contrary notwithstanding.

§ 4th.   Be it further enacted, That no Judge of a Court of Common Pleas, of any county in this Territory, shall act as a Justice of the Peace, for the trial of small causes.

§ 5th.   And be it further enacted, That all laws and parts of **Repeal-** laws coming within the perview of this law, be, and the same **ing clause** are hereby repealed.—This act shall commence and be in force from and after the first day of February next.

JESSE B. THOMAS, Speaker of the House
of Representatives,

JOHN RICE JONES, President pro tem. of
the Legislative Council.

Approved—December 6th 1806.

William Henry Harrison.

CHAPTER VIII.

AN ACT *for the relief of the Territorial Treasurer, and for other purposes.*

§ 1st. Be it enacted by the Legislative Council and House of Representatives, and it is hereby enacted by the authority of the same, That James Johnson, Esquire, Treasurer of the Territory, be allowed the sum of nine dollars and fifty cents, being the amount by him expended for necessaries furnished for the office of the Treasurer.

§ 2nd. And be it further enacted by the authority aforesaid, That the sum of two hundred dollars, be appropriated out of any money in the Treasury, except the contingent fund, for the purpose of purchasing stationery, and a chest, the better to secure the funds of the Territory from fire and robbery; and that Jacob Kuykendoll, and James Johnson, Esquire, be appointed to purchase said articles.—This act to take effect from and after the first day of February next.

> JESSE B. THOMAS, Speaker of the House of Representatives.
> P, MENARD, President pro tem. of the Legislative Council.

Approved—November 24th, 1806.

> *William Henry Harrison.*

CHAPTER vix.

AN ACT *to amend an act respecting County Levies.*

§ 1st. Be it enacted by the Legislative Council and House of Representatives, and it is hereby enacted by the authority of the same, That from and after the first day of February next, all sheriffs within the Indiana Ter-

C

(12)

Sheriffs as treasurers
ritory, (as Treasurers of the counties respectively) at the same term at which by law they are directed to settle their accounts, make out a fair copy of the accounts aforesaid, and set it up at

the court house door, which account shall state the monies received, as also the monies paid out of the Treasury, that year, and shall shew the amount that said county may be in arrears, or the amount remaining in the Treasury, [for which they shall be severally allowed the sum of six dollars, out of the county funds] and any sheriff, as Treasurer aforesaid, who shall fail to comply with the requisite of this act, shall be fined in the sum of one hundred dollars, to be recovered at the suit of the attorney general, by action of debt, whose duty it shall be to institute said suit, when he receives information of the non complyance with this act, in any court having competent jurisdiction, for the use of the county.

to make out their accounts and set them up at the court house door.

§ 2nd. Be it further enacted, That so much of the law to which this is an amendment, as imposes a tax of two dollars on able bodied single men, who have not taxable property to the amount of four hundred dollars, be repealed; And from and after the first day of February, each able bodied single man, who has not taxable property to the amount of two hundred dollars, shall be taxed in a sum not exceeding one dollar.—This act to take effect from and after the first day of February next.

Part of a law repealed.

JESSE B. THOMAS, Speaker of the House
of Representatives.

P. MENARD, President pro tem. of the Legislative Council.

Approved—November 24th, 1806.

William Henry Harrison.

CHAPTER x.
AN ACT *concerning Executions.*

§ 1st. Be it enacted by the Legislative Council and House of Representatives, and it is hereby enacted by the authority of the same, That when any writ of fieri facias, issuing out of the General court, or any court of Common Pleas within the Territory, shall be levied on any real or personal estate of the defendant or defendants, it shall and may be lawful for such defendant or defendants, to release the same, by tendering to the sheriff, or other officer, bond, with sufficient security, to pay the amount of such

How property taken on execution may be released

execution, including all costs, with lawful interest thereon, from the date of said bond, within five months; and on such bond being given, the said sheriff, or other officer, shall restore to the defendant or defendants, such personal or real estate. And where no bond shall be tendered by such defendant or defendants, or any person for him or them, the sheriff, or other officer, shall proceed to sell the said estate, for whatever it will bring in cash, ten days previous notice having been given of such sale.

The body may be released,

§ 2nd. Be it further enacted, That any defendant or defendants, on any writ of capias ad satisfaciendum, may in like manner release his, her or their body, or bodies, from execution, by tendering bond and security, as required in the foregoing section.

Bons shall have the force of judgments.

§ 3rd. All and every bond so taken, in pursuance of this act, shall have the force of judgments, and such sheriff, or other officer, taking such bonds, shall return the same to the office from which the execution issued, within twenty days thereafter.

Creditor may have execution issued.

§ 4th. If the amount of said bond shall not be paid agreeably to the condition thereof, it shall and may be lawful for the creditor or creditors, his her or their executors or administrators, at any time thereafter, to sue out of the clerks office of said court, his execution, against the real and personal estate

(13)

of the said defendant, or obligors in said bond, their executors or administrators; and the clerk issuing such execution, shall endorse on the back thereof, that no security of any kind is to be taken.

Replevy bonds.

§ 5th. If any replevy bond be quashed, or the security adjudged insufficient at the time of receiving the bond; the sheriff taking the same, and his securities shall at all times be liable to the party injured, or his representatives.

Return of writs.

§ 6th That all executions issuing out of any of the courts of this Territory, shall be returnable to the clerks office on the second rule day, next after the test of the writ. That the law passed at the last session of the General Assembly, entitled "An act for the sale and conveyance of land under execution," and so much of the act entitled "An act subjecting real estate to execution for debt," adopted by the Governor and Judges of the North Western territory, on the first day of June, one thousand seven hundred

Parts of acts repealed.

and ninety five, as provides that before the sale of real estate taken under execution, the sheriff shall enquire by jury, whether the same will yield the yearly rents and profits, beyond all reprisals, sufficient within the space of seven years, to pay the debt or damages, be, and the same are hereby repealed.

§ 7th. And whereas doubts have arisen whether the time of service of negroes and mulattoes, bound to service in this territory may be sold under execution; Be it therefore enacted, That the time of service of such negroes or mulattoes may be sold on execution against the master, in the same manner as personal estate; immediately from which sale, the said negroes or mulattoes, shall serve the purchasor or purchasors, for the residue of their time of service; and the said purchasors, and negroes and mulattoes, shall have the same remedies against each other, as by the laws of the territory, are mutually given them in the several cases therein mentioned, and the purchasors shall be obliged to fulfil to the said servants, the contracts they made with the masters, as expressed in the indenture, or agreement of servitude, and shall for want of such contract, be obliged to give him or them their freedom dues, at the end of the time of service as expressed in the second section of a law of the territory entitled, 'A law concerning servants', adopted the twenty second day of September, eighteen hundred and three.—This act shall commence and be in force from and after the first day of February next.

Servants may be taken and sold as personal estate.

JESSE B. THOMAS, Speaker of the House
of Representatives.
PIERRE MENARD, President pro tem. of
the Legislative Council.
Approved—November 26th, 1806.

William Henry Harrison.

CHAPTER xi.

AN ACT *relating to the duties of Sheriffs, and for other purposes.*

§ 1st. Be it enacted by the Legislative Council and House of Representatives, and it is hereby enacted by the authority of the same, That every sheriff or coroner, himself, or his lawful officer or deputies, shall from time to time, execute all writs and process

Sheriffs & Coroners or their

legal de-
puties to
execute
all pro-
cess to
them di-
rected.
to him legally issued and directed within his county, or upon any river or creek adjoining thereto; and shall make due returns under the penalty of forfeiting one hundred dollars for every failure, one moiety to the use of the territory, and the contingent expenses thereof, and the other moiety to the party grieved, to be recovered with costs by action of debt, or information, in any court of record of this territory, out of which such process may have issued; and such sheriff or coroner shall be further liable to the action of the party grieved at common law, for his or

(14)

her damages; and for every false return the sheriff or coroner shall forfeit and pay one hundred dollars, to be recovered, devided and applied in the manner last mentioned, and shall also be liable in like manner to the party grieved for damages.

Death of a prisoner
§ 2nd. If any person being a prisoner charged in execution shall happen to die in execution, the party or parties at whose suit, or to whom such person shall stand charged in execution, for any debt or damages recovered, his or their executors or administrators, may after the death of the person so dying in execution, lawfully sue forth and have new execution against the lands and tenements, goods and chattels of the person so deceased.

In case of goods remaining in the sheriff's hands unsold the clerk to issue venditioni exponas
§ 3rd. If the lands, tenements or hereditaments, or goods and chattels taken by any sheriff or other officer, or any part thereof shall remain in his hands unsold, he shall make return accordingly, and thereupon the clerk of the court from whence such execution issued, shall and may, and he is hereby required to issue a *Venditioni Exponas* to such sheriff or other officer directed, whereupon the like proceedings shall be had, as might and ought to have been had on the first execution, which writ of *Venditioni Exponas* shall be in the form following.

Form.
The United States &c. greeting: We command you that you expose to sale the lands or goods and chattels (as the case may be) of A B, to the value of   which according to our command you have taken, and which remain in your hands unsold as you have certified to our Judges (or Justices) of our court, to satisfy C D, the sum of   whereof in our said

court he hath recovered execution against the said A B, by virtue of a judgment in the said court and that you have &c.

§ 4th. If any sheriff shall levy an execution on property, and a doubt shall arise whether the right of such property shall be in the debtor or not, such sheriff may, and it is hereby declared to be his duty to empannel twelve freeholders, each of whom shall be disinterested in the event, to try the right of property aforesaid; and after hearing the evidence, the said jury shall determine whether the property belongs to the defendant or the person claiming it, and the verdict of the said jury shall be a sufficient justification for said sheriff to sell the said property or deliver it to the person claiming the same, as the case may be; and in case of any action being brought against any sheriff for his conduct herein, he may plead the general issue and give this act in evidence.

In case of uncertainty as to right of property

§ 5th. If any sheriff or other officer shall make return upon any writ of *Fieri Facias* or *Venditioni Exponas* that he hath levied the debt, damages or costs, as in such writ is required, or any part thereof, and shall not immediately pay the same to the party to whom the same is payable, or his attorney; or shall return upon any writ of *Capias ad satisfaciendum,* or attachment for not performing a decree in chancery for the payment of any sum of money, that he hath taken the body or bodies of the defendant or defendants, and hath the same ready to satisfy the sum in such writ mentioned, and shall have actually received such money of the defendant or defendants, or have suffered him or them to escape with the consent or negligence of such sheriff or other officer, and shall not immediately pay such money to the party to whom the same is payable or his attorney, then, and in either of the said cases, it shall and may be lawful for the creditor at whose suit such writ of *Fieri Facias, Venditioni Exponas, Capias ad satisfaciendum* or *Attachment* shall issue, upon a motion made in the next succeeding General court, òr other court from whence such process issued, to demand judgment against such sheriff or other officer, and the securities of such sheriff or other officer for the money mentioned in such writ, or so much as shall be returned levied on such writs of *Fieri Facias* or *Venditioni Exponas,* **with interest thereon at the rate of fifteen**

Sheriff to make return of writs.

(15)

per centum, per annum from the return day of the execution until the judgment shall be discharged and such court is hereby authorised and required to give judgment accordingly, and to award execution thereon, provided such sheriff or other officer have ten days previous notice of such motion.

How judg ments shall be rendered against sheriffs.

§ 6th.   And whereas doubts have arisen in what manner judgment should be rendered against any sheriff or coronor, who shall fail to return an execution to the office from whence it issued on or before the return day thereof; Be it enacted, That where any writ of *Execution* or *Attachment* for not performing a decree in Chnncery, shall come into the possession of any sheriff or coronor, and he shall wilfully or negligently fail to return the same to the office from whence it was issued, on or before the return day thereof, it shall be lawful for the court, ten days previous notice being given, upon motion of the party injured, to fine such sheriff or coroner at their discretion, in any sum not exceeding five dollars, nor less than two dollars per month, for every hundred dollars contained in such judgment or decree, on which the execution or attachment so by him detained was founded, and so on in proportion for any greater or lesser sum, counting the aforesaid months from the return day of the execution or attachment, to the day of rendering the judgment for the said fine; which fine shall be for the benefit of the party grieved.

Execution maybe renewed.

§ 7th.   Be it further enacted, That when any writ of *Capias ad satisfaciendum,* is issued against any person or persons, out of any court of record within this Territory, and he or they are taken by virtue of the same, and if the party at whose suit the said writ was issued, after issuing of the same, shall by request of the prisoner, release said prisoner, for the purpose of giving him or them further time to make the money thereon, it shall and may be lawful for the party at whose suit the execution was issued, at any time thereafter, to issue forth his or their writ of *Capias ad satisfaciendum* or *Fieri facias* on the said judgment, notwithstanding the release of the said prisoner or prisoners.—

This act shall commence and be in force from and after the first day of February next.

JESSE B. THOMAS, Speaker of the House
of Representatives.

PIERRE MENARD, President pro tem. of
the Legislative Council.

Approved—November 29th, 1806.

William Henry Harrison.

CHAPTER xii.

AN ACT *concerning writs of ne exeat and other proceedings in the court of Chancery.*

§ 1st. Be it enacted by the Legislative Council and House of Representatives, and it is hereby enacted by the authority of the same, That no subpœna in Chancery shall issue until the bill is filed with the clerk, whose duty it shall be to copy the same and deliver the copy to the person applying for the subpœna, which copy shall be delivered to the defendant if in the Territory, by the officer or person serving the subpœna, which shall be endorsed on the back thereof; and if there be more than one defendant, the said copy shall be delivered to the one first named in the subpœna, if he be resident within this Territory, if not, the next one named in the subpœna, that is a resident. *Respecting subpoenas.*

§ 2nd. And be it further enacted, That where a bill is amended, a copy of the amendatory bill shall in like manner be delivered to the defendant or

D

(16)

defendants. It shall not be necessary that an attachment to procure an appearance or answer shall issue, but in all cases where the subpœna is returned executed, and a copy of the bill left with the defendant or defendants, conformably to this act, the complainant may proceed to take his bill *pro confesso,* as in cases of attachments heretofore returned executed.

§ 3rd. And be it further enacted, That no injunction shall be granted to stay any proceedings at law, unless the party *Respecting injunctions* praying the injunction, have by the affidavit of at least one witness, proved that the opposite party had at least ten, and not more than fifteen days notice of the time and place of applying for such injunction, from the time of which notice given all proceedings at law shall be stayed, until the Chancellor's decision shall be made, whether an injunction shall, or shall not be granted; But if the complainant shall not make application to the Chancellor for such injunction, on the day specified in such notice, then the plaintiff below may proceed at law as if none had been given, nor shall any injunction be granted to stay any judgment at law, for a greater sum, than that the plaintiff shall shew himself equitably bound not to pay, and so much as shall be sufficient to cover the cost, and every injunction when granted, shall operate as a release to all errors in the proceedings at law, that are prayed to be enjoined.

Nor shall any injunction be granted unless the complainant shall have previously executed a bond to the defendant, with sufficient surety to be approved of by the Chancellor, in double the sum prayed to be enjoined, conditioned for the payment of all money and costs due, or to be due, to the plaintiff in the action of law, and also all such costs and damages as shall be awarded against him or her, in case the injunction shall be dissolved. If the injunction be dissolved in whole, or in part, the complainant shall pay six per cent, exclusive of legal interest, besides costs, and the clerk shall issue an execution for the same, when he issues an execution upon said judgment, on the dissolution of an injunction, judgment shall be given by the court against the securities as well as the plaintiff in the injunction bond.

§ 4th. And be it further enacted, That whereever affidavits are taken either to support, or dissolve an injunction, the party taking the same shall give the adverse party reasonable notice of the time and place of taking the same, and the clerk shall issue to either of the parties, subpœnas to procure the attendance of witnesses at the time and place appointed, and such affidavits taken as aforesaid, shall be read on the final hearing

Respecting affidavits.

of the cause, in which they may be taken, under the same restrictions as depositions taken according to law.

§ 5th.   No notice shall be necessary in any case where application is made for an injunction in term time, nor in vacations, where the title, or bonds for land come in question.

§ 6th.   And be it further enacted, That writs of *ne exeat,* shall not be granted, but upon bill filed, and affidavit to the allegations, which being produced to the Chancellor, in term time, or in vacation, may grant or refuse, such writ, as to him shall seem just, and if granted, he shall endorse thereon, in what penalty, bond and security be required of the defendant.

Respecting writs of ne exeat.

No writ of *ne exeat,* shall issue until the complainant shall give bond and security in the clerks office, to be approved of by the Chancellor, and in such penalty as he shall adjudge necessary, to be endorsed on the bill, and in case any person stayed by such bill of *ne exeat,* shall think himself or themselves aggrieved, he or she may bring suit on such bond, and if on the trial it shall appear that the writ of *ne exeat,* was prayed without a just cause, the person injured shall recover damages.

§ 7th.   And be it further enacted, That if the defendant or defendants to the bill, shall go out of the Territory, but shall return before a personal ap-

(17)

pearance shall be necessary to perform any order or decree of the court, such his or her temporary departure, shall not be considered a breach of the condition of the bond.

§ 8th.   Whereever the defendant to the bill, shall give security that he will not depart the Territory, the security shall have leave at any time before the bond shall be forfeited, to secure his principal in the same manner that special bail may surrender by principal, and obtain the same discharge.

Security may surrender principal

§ 9th.   In suits in Chancery, the complainant may take depositions in one month after he shall have filed his bill, and the defendant may do the like as soon as he has filed his answer, which may be done without a dedimus, unless the witness live without the Territory, provided that reasonable notice

Parties may take depositions.

be given of the time and place of taking such depositions.—
This act shall commence and be in force from and after the
first day of January next.

JESSE B. THOMAS, Speaker of the House
of Representatives.

P. MENARD, President pro tem. of the Legislative Council.

Approved—November 29th, 1806.

William Henry Harrison.

CHAPTER XIII.

AN ACT *supplemental to an act regulating County Levies.*

§ 1st. Be it enacted by the Legislative Council and House
of Representatives, and it is hereby enacted by the authority of
the same, That it shall be the duty of the sheriffs of the respective
counties in the Territory, previous to the time of advertising for
taking the list of taxable property, under the above recited act to
apply personally, or by deputy, to every person subject to taxation
within his county, for a list of their taxable property, as is required by said act; and every sheriff failing to perform the duties
required by this act, without good cause shewn, shall be fined in
any sum not exceeding five hundred, nor less than twenty five
dollars, at the discretion of the court of Common Pleas of the
county, to and for the use of the county.—This act shall commence and be in force from and after the first day of January
next.

JESSE B. THOMAS, Speaker of the House
of Representatives,

PIERRE MENARD, President pro tem. of
the Legislative Council.

Approved—November 29th 1806.

William Henry Harrison.

CHAPTER XIV.

AN ACT *to alter and amend an act, entitled "An act for Incorporating the Borough of Vincennes.*

§ 1st. Be it enacted by the Legislative Council and House
of Representatives of the Indiana Territory, and it is hereby

enacted by the authority of the same, That the Borough of Vincennes shall hereafter be bounded by the plantation of William **How**
Henry Harrison on the north east, the Church lands on the south **bounded.**
west, the river Wabash on the north west, and the lines of the
common as laid out for the inhabitants of Vincennes in pursuance
of an act of Congress on all the other parts and sides thereof,
excluding thereout the Cathrenette, and Lower Prairie lands, any
thing in in the said act contained to the contrary notwithstanding.

(18)

§ 2nd. And be it further enaacted, That so much of the **Certain**
second section of the said act as requires that there should be **sections re**
a chairman and nine assistants, and so much of the third section **pealed.**
thereof as requires that said charman and assistants, should annually be chosen and elected in the manner and by the persons
therein mentioned, be, and the same are hereby repealed.

§ 3rd. And be it further enacted, That there shall be nine
Trustees in the said Borough, a majority of whom shall form a
quorum, who shall exercise the same powers, and shall have the **Number**
same perpetual succession, as by the said act is given to the said **of trustees**
chairman and nine assistants, and that Robert Buntin, Joshua
Bond, William Bullitt, Henry Hurst, Charles Smith, Jacob Kuykendoll, Hyacinthe Lasselle, Touissaint Dubois and Peter Jones,
be, and they are hereby appointed the first Trustees of the said
Borough, who shall hold their offices from the first day of January
next, for three years.

§ 4th. The said Trustees at the first sitting after their
appointment, shall be divided into three classes, the seats of those **To be**
of the first class shall be vacated at the end of the first year, those **classed.**
of the second class at the end of the second year, and those of
the third at the end of the third year, so that one third may
be chosen every year; that the said Trustees or a majority of
them shall annually between the first day of February, and the
first day of March, choose and elect three members in the room
of those whose seats shall be vacated at the expiration of every
year as before mentioned, and in case such election shall not be
made between the said days, then the court of Common pleas of

the county shall at the next court name three Trustees in the room of those whose seats shall be so vacated.

§ 5th.   That the said Trustees shall elect their own chairman, and also elect their own clerk, either out of their own body or otherwise, and they shall have, use and exercise the same rights, powers, privileges and authority as by the fourth and fifth sections of the said act are given to the said chairman and nine assistants, and they shall have power and authority to purchase ground, and erect a market house in the said Borough, and make bye laws for the government and regulation thereof, and they shall also have power and authority to make such bye laws as they may think necessary for widening, extending, repairing and cleansing of the streets of the said Borough, and shall have further power and authority to cause a survey to be made of the said streets, and to ordain as well what width or breadth they shall hereafter be of, not exceeding sixty feet, as to prevent any person or persons from erecting any kinds of buildings within the limits of the said streets, as so ordered to be widened or extended, and from inclosing any part or parts thereof; Provided, that no buildings now actually erected shall during the existence of such buildings be demolished or pulled down without the consent of the owner, or paying an adequate compensation therefor, to be estimated in such manner as by the said bye laws shall be declared.

Their powers.

§ 6th.   That it shall be the duty of the Trustees to give publicity to their bye laws, and all persons inhabitants of said Borough, shall have free access to the said bye laws, and shall have full liberty to peruse the same, and take copies, or such extracts therefrom as they may think proper.

Give publicity to their laws

§ 7th   And be it enacted, That the bye laws so to be made, and the proceedings of the said Trustees, together with an account of the receipts and expenditures in detail, shall whenever thereto required, be laid before either branch of the Legislature of the Territory, requiring the same.

Lay their proceedings before the legislature.

§ 8th.   And be it further enacted, That the said late chairman and nine assistants, shall deliver all the books, papers, and monies in their hands, or the hands of their officers, belonging to the said Borough, to the above named

(19)

Trustees, whenever they shall be thereto required.—This act to commence and be in force from and after the first day of January next.

> JESSE B. THOMAS, Speaker of the House of Representatives.
>
> P, MENARD, President pro tem. of the Legislative Council.

Approved—November 29th, 1806.

> *William Henry Harrison.*

CHAPTER xv.

AN ACT *concerning Clerks of Courts.*

§ 1st. Be it enacted by the Legislative Council and House of Representatives, and it is hereby enacted by the authority of the same, That it shall be the duty of the General court of this Territory, and the several courts of Common Pleas of the counties at their first session after the first day of January next, to receive of their respective Clerks, bonds with approved security, in the penalty of one thousand dollars, payable to the Governor of the Territory, for the time being, and his successors in office, conditioned for the faithful discharge of the duties of their respective offices. And all Clerks hereafter to be appointed to said courts, shall, previous to their exercising the duties of their office, enter into bond in the like manner, which bonds shall by said Clerks, be lodged in the office of the Secretary of the Territory, within three months thereafter.

Clerks to give security.

§ 2nd. And be it further enacted, That it shall be the duty of the presiding Judge of the several courts of Common Pleas in this Territory, and of the first Judge of the General Court, to examine the respective Clerks books in open court, and see what fines are due thereon to the Territory, or to the county, and make out a fair list thereof, and report those due to the Territory to the Auditor thereof, who shall report the same to the Legislature at the same time he makes his annual report; and if the said Clerks fail to pay the said fines to the treasurer of the territory, or the county, as the case may be, on or before the first day of

Judges to examine their clerks book in open court

March, annually, the Auditor shall direct the Attorney General to obtain judgment by motion, against said Clerks in their respective courts, upon giving ten days notice thereof, and immediately collect the same and pay it into the treasury of the territory, or the county, as the case may be, and the said Judges shall further report to the sheriffs, as treasurers of their respective counties, the amount of fines due to said counties on or before the first day of March, and the sheriffs as treasurers, if the said fines are not paid to them on or before the first day of May, by the said Clerks, then the said sheriffs, as treasurers, shall proceed to collect the same in manner and form as is directed in the foregoing part of this section.—This act to commence and be in force from and after the passage thereof.

JESSE B. THOMAS, Speaker of the House
of Representatives.

P. MENARD, President pro tem. of the Legislative Council.

Approved—December 2nd, 1806.

William Henry Harrison.

E

(20)

CHAPTER xvi

AN ACT *altering the time of holding the Courts of Common Pleas, of the counties therein mentioned.*

§ 1st.   Be it enacted by the Legislative Council and House of Representatives, and it is hereby enacted by the authority of the same, That the courts of Common Pleas heretofore held in the county of Dearborn, on the second Monday in the months of January, May and September, shall hereafter be held on the first Monday in the months of April, August and December; that the terms heretofore held in the months of March, August and November, be hereafter held in the months of February, June and October, in every year.

That the court heretofore held in the county of Clark, on the first Monday in September, be hereafter held on the second Monday of said month in every year.

Marginal notes:

Times of holding courts in Dearborn

In Clark

That the court heretofore held in the county of Knox, on the last Monday in March, and the first Monday in September, be hereafter held on the third Monday in said months. **In Knox.**

§ 2nd. Whereas it has been represented to this General Assembly, that the court of Common Pleas for the county of Dearborn, which ought to have been held on the second Monday of January last, was, through mistake, held on the first Monday of said month; Be it enacted, that the proceedings had and made in the said court as so held, shall be, and the same are hereby legalized in as full a manner, as if the said court had been held on the proper day.—This act shall commence and be in force from and after the first day of February next. **Legalizing the proceedings in the court of Dearborn**

> JESSE B. THOMAS, Speaker of the House of Representatives.
>
> P. MENARD, President pro tem. of the Legislative Council.

Approved—December 2nd, 1806.

> *William Henry Harrison.*

CHAPTER XVII.

AN ACT *directing the Taxes on Law process, &c. in the different counties, to be paid into the county Treasuries.*

§ 1st. Be it enacted by the Legislative Council and House of Representatives, and it is hereby enacted by the authority of the same, That the taxes hereafter collected on law process, &c. in the different counties in this territory, now payable into the territorial treasury, shall be payable into the treasuries of the respective counties, and the clerks of the courts of Common Pleas, shall account for the same, with the said courts in the same manner and times, as they are now bound by law to account with the treasurer of the territory.

§ 2nd. Be it further enacted, That so much of the law laying a tax upon law process, adopted by the Governor and Judges, on the fifth day of November, one thousand eight hundred and three, as lays a tax on law process in the General court, be, and the same is hereby repealed.—This act to commence from the passage thereof.

JESSE B. THOMAS, Speaker of the House
of Representatives.
JOHN RICE JONES, President pro tem. of
the Legislative Council.

Approved—December 3rd, 1806.

William Henry Harrison.

(21)

CHAPTER xviii.

AN ACT *to Incorporate the Vincennes Library Company.*

Proviso.

WHEREAS it has been represented to the General Assembly, that sundry citizens of Vincennes and its neighborhood, have associated themselves together for the purpose of establishing a Circulating Library; and in order to establish the said institution more permanently, they pray that a suitable charter may be granted, organizing said institution.

To be a President and directors,

§ 1st. Be it enacted by the Legislative Council and House of Representatives, and it is hereby enacted by the authority of the same, That for the better ruling and governing the said institution, and the share holders in the said Library, there shall be appointed a President and seven Directors, said President and seven Directors shall be a body corporate, in deed, fact and name, by the name and style of the "President and Directors of the Vincennes Library," and by the same name shall have perpetual succession, and they, and their successors at all times hereafter, by the name of the President and Directors of the Vincennes Library, shall be persons able and capable in law to sue, and be sued, implead and be impleaded, answer, and being answered unto, in any court of Justice whatever, and to make and use one common seal, and the same to alter and change at pleasure.

§ 2nd. Be it further enacted, That the President and seven Directors shall be appointed annually, at a meeting of the shareholders in said Library.

§ 3rd. Be it further enacted, That the President and **Their powers.**
seven Directors or a majority of them, shall have power from
time to time, and at all times, hereafter, to meet and to make
such bye laws, ordinances and regulations in writing, not inconsistent with the laws of the United States, or of this territory, as may be necessary for the government of the said institution; which bye laws shall be in force until the next annual meeting, and afterwards, unless disagreed to at such
meeting, for which purpose all the bye laws made by such
President and directors, shall be laid before the succeeding
meeting for their approbation or rejection.

§ 4th. Be it further enacted, That there shall be a gen- **General**
eral meeting of the share holders on the first Monday in Feb- **meetings of share**
ruary, yearly, when they shall take into consideration the gen- **holders.**
eral interest of the said institution, and elect a President and
seven Directors, and all other necessary officers, and exact
such security from the said officers as they may deem proper,
and in case a general meeting shall not be had on the stated
day, the officers then acting shall continue their functions until
the next general meeting.

§ 5th. Be it further enacted, That no determinate number of share holders shall be necessary to form a quorum to
business.

JESSE B. THOMAS, Speaker of the House
of Representatives,

JOHN RICE JONES, President pro tem. of
the Legislative Council.

Approved—December 3rd, 1806.

William Henry Harrison.

CHAPTER xix.
AN ACT *concerning Slaves and Servants.*

§ 1st. Be it enacted by the Legislative Council and House
of Representatives, and it is hereby enacted by the authority **Servants**
of the same, That if any slave or servant shall be found at the **to have a pass or to-**
distance of ten miles from the tenement of his or her master, **ken.**
or other person with whom he or she lives, without a pass,

or some letter or token whereby it may appear that he or she is proceeding

(22)

by authority from his or her master, employer or overseer, it shall and may be lawful for any person to apprehend and carry him or her before any Justice of the Peace, to be by his order punished with stripes, not exceeding twenty five, at his discretion.

Not to be about the dwelling houses of other persons than their owner.

§ 2nd.   If any slave or servant shall presume to come and be upon the plantation, or at the dwelling house of any person whatsoever, without leave from his or her owner, not being sent upon lawful business, it shall be lawful for the owner of such plantation, or dwelling house, to give, or order such slave or servant, ten lashes on his or her bare back.

§ 3rd.   Riots, routs, unlawful assemblies, trespasses and seditious speeches by any slave or slaves, servant or servants, shall be punished with stripes, at the discretion of a Justice of the Peace, not exceeding thirty nine, and he who will, may apprehend and carry him, her or them before such Justice.

Penalty for harboring a servant.

§ 4th.   If any person shall harbour any servant or slave of color, who is bound to service, without the consent of his or her master first obtained, he or she so offending, shall be fined in any sum not exceeding one hundred dollars, at the discretion of the court, to be recovered by indictment or information; and if any person shall aid and assist any servant or slave to abscond from his or her master, upon conviction thereof, he or she so offending shall be fined in any sum not exceeding five hundred dollars, at the discretion of the court, for the use of the party aggrieved, to be recovered as aforesaid.—This act shall take effect, and be in force from and after the first day of January next.

JESSE B. THOMAS, Speaker of the House
of Representatives.

JOHN RICE JONES, President pro tem. of
the Legislative Council.

Approved—December 3rd, 1806.

William Henry Harrison.

CHAPTER xx.
AN ACT *to regulate Marriages.*

§ 1st. Be it enacted by the Legislative Council and House of Representatives, and it is hereby enacted by the authority of the same, That so much of the laws now in force in this Territory as authorises the Governor to grant marriage licences, be, and the same are hereby repealed.

Parts of a law repealed.

§ 2nd, Be it further enacted, That the clerks of the courts of the Common Pleas of the respective counties, shall issue Marriage Licenses for which they shall be entitled to have and receive the sum of one dollar: and the said clerks shall keep a record of all such licenses by them issued.

Clerks to issue licenses.

§ 3rd. And be it further enacted, That the certificates of the solemnization of marriage, which by law are required to be transmitted to the register's office, shall hereafter be transmitted to the clerks of the said courts of Common Pleas, and not to the Register's; which clerk shall keep a record thereof, and receive the same fees for so doing as the register's or recorder's are by law entitled to.—This act shall take effect from and after the first day of February next.

To keep a record

JESSE B. THOMAS, Speaker of the House
of Representatives,
JOHN RICE JONES, President pro tem. of
the Legislative Council.
Approved—December 3rd, 1806.
William Henry Harrison.
(23)

CHAPTER xxi.
AN ACT *for improveing the breed of Horses.*

§ 1st. Be it enacted by the Legislative Council and House of Representatives, and it is hereby enacted by the authority of the same, That it shall and may be lawful for any person or persons, to take up and cut or geld, at the risk of the owner, any stone horse of the age of eighteen months and upwards, that may be found running at large out of the inclosed ground of the owner or keeper, and if the said horse

Stud horses running at large may be cut.

should happen to die, he shall have no recourse against the person or persons who shall have so taken up or gelded the said horse; and the owner of the said horse shall moreover pay to the person who has so taken up and cut or gelded the said horse, or caused it to be done, the sum of three dollars, to be recovered before any Justice of the Peace of the county.

§ 2nd. Be it further enacted, That it shall not be lawful for any person to cut or geld any horse above fourteen and one half hands high, that is known to be kept for covering mares; but if any owner or keeper of a covering horse, shall wilfully or negligently suffer said horse to run at large, out of the inclosed lands of said owner or keeper, any person may take up said horse, and carry him to his owner or keeper, for which he shall receive two dollars, recoverable before any Justice of the Peace of the county, for a second offence, double the sum, and for a third offence, the said horse may be taken and cut or gelded, as is provided in the first section hereof.

§ 3rd. Be it further enacted, That all and every act and acts within the perview of this act, shall be, and the same are hereby repealed.

JESSE B. THOMAS, Speaker of the House
of Representatives,

JOHN RICE JONES, President pro tem. of
the Legislative Council.

Approved—December 3rd, 1806.

William Henry Harrison.

CHAPTER XXII.

AN ACT *for making Appropriations for the ensuing year.*

**Conting-
ent fund.**
§ 1st. Be it enacted by the Legislative Council and House of Representatives, That the sum of five hundred dollars shall be, and the same is hereby appropriated for contingent expences; and that all the monies which shall be received into the territorial treasury, except as above appropriated for contingent expences, shall be a general fund, for all monies allowed by law, which shall not be directed to be paid out of the contingent expences.

§ 2nd. Be it further enacted, That there shall be allowed and paid to the printer for this territory for printing two hundred copies of the laws of this territory, passed at this session, a sum not exceeding three hundred dollars, to be paid out of the monies allowed for contingent expences. The residue of the monies allowed for contingent expences, or so much thereof as may be necessary, shall be subject to payment of monies on the order of the Governor, for expresses and other incidents which may be necessary, and cannot be foreseen by the legislature; a statement of which shall be laid before the legislature at the next session.

§ 3rd. And be it further enacted, That there shall be allowed and paid

F

(24)

out of the general fund, to the following persons, the following sums of money, to wit:

To the territorial treasurer, one hundred dollars;

To the auditor of public accounts, one hundred and fifty dollars;

To the county of Knox, for house rent to the end of the present session, fifty dollars;

To the Legislative Council and House of Representatives, and their secretary and clerk, their several allowances established by law, not exceeding fourteen hundred dollars;

To George Wallace, junior, for stationery, furnished to both houses of the legislature, twenty one dollars fifty eight and one third cents;

To Samuel Hays, for fuel, and other articles by him furnished for the legislature, twenty dollars;

To the assessors and collectors of land, and the clerks of the courts for their services, under the act "for levying and collecting a tax on land," a sum not exceeding six hundred dollars;

To the attorney general, one hundred dollars;

Specific appropriations.

To William Bullitt, for his services in going under the warrant of the Governor, after Wm. Briscoe, jr. a fugitive from justice, thirty six dollars;

To Henry Hurst, for books purchased by him for the use of the general court, twenty two dollars;

To John Harbin, for his services in going under the warrant of the Governor, after Robt. Slaughter, a fugitive from justice, one hundred dollars;

To John Johnson and John Rice Jones, for superintending the printing of the laws passed at the last session, making marginal notes to the same, and revising the laws of the territory, agreeably to a resolution of the last assembly one hundred dollars;

To Peter Jones, for his expences in obtaining abstracts of land lying in the county of Dearborn, and for stationery, and other purposs, seventy eight dollars and eighty seven cents.

To James Edgar, for his services in going after Michael Squires a fugitive from justice, under the warrant of the governor, eighteen dollars;

JESSE B. THOMAS, Speaker of the House of Representatives.

JOHN RICE JONES, President pro tem. of the Legislative Council.

Approved—December 4th, 1806.

William Henry Harrison.

CHAPTER XXIII.

AN ACT *for allowing compensation to the members of the Legislative Council and House of Representatives of the Indiana Territory, and to the officers of both houses, for the last and the present session.*

Appropriations.

§ 1st. Be it enacted by the Legislative Council and House of Representatives, and it is hereby enacted by the authority of the same, That each and every member of the Legislative Council and House of Representatives, shall be entitled to, and receive for each and every days attendance on Legislative business, at the present session, the sum of two dollars, and shall moreover, be allowed the sum of two dollars for every twenty miles travel, to, and from

(25)

the seat of government, to their places of residence, by the most usual road.

§ 2nd. And be it further enacted, That the members of the last session of the Legislature shall be allowed the sum of one dollar, for each days attendance, and two dollars, for every twenty miles travel, as aforesaid.

§ 3rd. And be it further enacted, That the secretary of the Council, and clerk of the House of Representatives, for the last and present sessions, shall be allowed the sum of three dollars each, per day, for their services. *To the secretary & clerk.*

That the door keeper of both houses, at this session, be allowed the sum of one dollar and fifty cents per day. *The doorkeeper.*

§ 4th. And be it further enacted, That each and every member of the House of Representatives, who attended pursuant to the Governor's proclamation, to put in nomination the members of the Legislative Council, are entitled to, and shall receive the sum of one dollar, for each, and every days attendance on the foregoing business, and shall moreover, receive the same milage, as is allowed to the members of the last session of the Legislature. *To the members of the first session.*

§ 5th. And be it further enacted, That Henry Hurst, clerk to the House of Representatives, when met to nominate the Council, shall receive the sum of two dollars, for each days services, on the business of said House. *To their clerk.*

§ 6th. And be it further enacted, That the compensation which shall be due to the members and officers of the Legislative Council, shall be certified by the President thereof; and that which shall be due to the members and officers of the House of Representatives, shall be certified by the Speaker, which certificates shall be to the auditor sufficient evidence of claim, and he shall thereupon issue certificates to the several *The President and Speaker to give certificate* members, and other officers thereof, payable at the treasury of the territory, as in other cases.

JESSE B. THOMAS, Speaker of the House of Representatives.

JOHN RICE JONES, President pro tem. of the Legislative Council.

Approved—December 4th, 1806.

William Henry Harrison.

CHAPTER xxiv.

AN ACT *to prevent altering and defacing marks and brands, and mismarking and misbranding Horses, cattle and hogs, unmarked and unbranded.*

§ 1st. Be it enacted by the Legislative Council and House of Representatives, and it is hereby enacted by the authority of the same, That if any person or persons, shall alter or deface the mark or brand of any other person or persons, horse, neat cattle, or hog, such person being thereof lawfully convicted by indictment or presentment, shall for every horse, mare, colt, neat cattle, or hog, whose mark or brand he or she shall alter or deface, forfeit and pay the sum of five dollars, over and above the value of such horse, mare or colt, neat cattle, or hog, to the person whose mark or marks, brand or brands, shall be so altered or defaced; Provided, he prosecute for the same within six months after discovery of the fact committed, and the offender, shall, over and above the said fine, receive forty lashes, on his or her bare back, well laid on; and for the second offence shall pay the fine aforesaid, stand in the pillory two hours, and be branded in the left hand with a red hot iron, with the letter T, and if any person or persons shall mismark, or misbrand, any unbranded or unmarked, horse, mare or colt, neat cattle, or hog, not properly his or their own, he or they, shall forfeit and pay the sum

Penalty for misbranding or mismarking.

(26)

of five dollars, over and above the value thereof, for every such horse, mare, colt, neat cattle, or hog, so mismarked, or misbranded, which fines, shall be recovered by indictment, or action of debt, in any court of record within this territory.

§ 2nd. And to prevent the concealing of such offences; Be it further enacted, That if any person or persons, shall see any other person or persons, committing any of the crimes aforesaid, and shall not discover the same in ten days to some magistrate, then, and in such case, such person or persons, for not discovering the said crimes, or any of them committed, shall forfeit and pay the sum of ten dollars, to the use of the county, to be recovered by any person or persons who will sue for the same, by action of debt, or by indictment or information, in any court of record in this territory.

Persons knowing any of the crimes to be committed to give information

§ 3rd. And because it is difficult to convict any person who has seen such crime committed, if he will deny the same, Be it further enacted, That it shall be sufficient evidence to convict any person, that he has seen such crime committed, if it be proven, that he has told any other person that he did see the said crimes, or any of them committed.

Evidence of the crime.

§ 4th. And whereas, the common custom in this territory, of killing of cattle and hogs in the woods, give great opportunities to steal the cattle and hogs of other people; Be it therefore enacted, That if any person or persons, shall kill any one or more neat cattle, or hogs, in the woods, he shall within three days, shew the head and ears of such hog, or hogs, and the hide, with the ears on, of such neat beast, or cattle, to the next magistrate, or to two substantial freeholders under the penalty of ten dollars, to be recovered by any person who will sue for the same, by action of debt, information or indictment, in any court of record in this territory.

Persons killing hogs or cattle in the woods to shew the mark

§ 5th. And be it further enacted, That every person in this territory who hath any horses, cattle or hogs, shall have an ear mark or brand different from the ear mark of all his neighbours, which ear mark and brand he shall record with the clerk of the county where his horses, cattle or hogs are, for recording of which ear mark and brand, the clerk shall be entitled to demand and receive the sum of twelve and a half cents. And every person shall brand horses with the said

The mark or brand to be recorded.

brand, from eighteen months old and upwards, and ear mark all his hogs from six months old and upwards, with the said ear mark; and ear mark or brand all his cattle from twelve months old and upwards with the said ear mark or brand; and if any dispute shall arise about any ear mark or brand, the same shall be decided by the book of the clerk of the county where such cattle, hogs or horses are.

The mark or brand of acquired property may be altered,

§ 6th.   And be it further enacted, That where any person shall buy any neat cattle from an other person, or come to the same by gift, will, or any other lawful means, that then, and in such case, the person who has gained the same by any of the ways aforesaid, shall within eight months, brand the said neat cattle with his own proper brand, in the presence of two credible witnesses, a certificate of which shall be signed by the said witnesses.

§ 7th.   And be it further enacted, That if any person shall cause to be brought to his own house, or any other house, or on board any boat or vessel, any hog, shoat or pig, without ears, he or she so offending shall be adjudged a hog stealer: Provided nevertheless, That any person may bring, or cause to be brought, to his or her own or any other house, or on board any boat or boats, or other vessel, his or her own swine, though without ears, he or she proving the same to be his or her property.

§ 8th.   The Judges of the several courts of record in this territory shall give this act in charge to the grand jury, at each and every court in which

(27)

a grand jury shall be sworn.—This act shall commence and be in force from and after the first day of February next.

JESSE B. THOMAS, Speaker of the
House of Representatives.

JOHN RICE JONES, President pro tem.
of the Legislative Council.

Approved—December 5th, 1806.

William Henry Harrison.

CHAPTER xxv.

AN ACT *to revive and amend an act establishing and regulating the militia.*

WHEREAS the law passed the thirteenth day of December, one thousand seven hundred and ninety nine, entitled 'An act establishing and regulating the militia,' is in the opinion of this assembly of very doubtful authority, and of uncertain obligation.

§ 1st. Be it therefore enacted by the Legislative Council and House of Representatives, That the sections herein mentioned in the said act, be, and the same are hereby declared to be in force within this Territory, as fully and completely as though they were herein recited at length, and re-enacted that is to say: first, second, third, fourth, fifth, sixth, seventh, eighth, ninth, tenth, eleventh, twelfth, thirteenth, fourteenth, fifteenth, sixteenth, seventeenth, eighteenth, nineteenth, twenty first, twenty second, twenty third, twenty fourth, twenty fifth, twenty sixth, and such parts of the twenty seventh section as relates to the method of collecting fines; twenty eighth, thirtieth, thirty first, thirty third, thirty fourth, thirty fifth, thirty sixth, thirty seven, thirty eight, thirty ninth, fortieth, forty first, forty second, and the articles mentioned in the latter part of said act except such parts as are hereby altered.

§ 2nd. Be it further enacted, That the division of the Militia by divisions and brigades, as mentioned in the twentieth section of said act is hereby left to the discretion of the commander in chief of the militia.

§ 3rd. Be it further enacted, That the commandant of each regiment shall appoint a judge advocate and a provost martial for his regiment, who shall hold their appointment during the pleasure of said commandant, and allowed such compensation as the court martial may direct, to be paid out of the fines, and it shall be the duty of said judge advocate and provost martial, to attend any court of enquiry or court martial, when thereto required by the said commandant.

[Marginal notes:] Proviso. Sections in force. Divisions To be a judge advocate & provost martial

**To be u-
niformed**

§ 4th. Be it further enacted, That it shall be the duty of each officer, non commissioned officer and each militia man whenever they shall meet for the purpose of mustering to appear in some cheap uniform, the color and form of which shall be determined by a board composed of the commissioned officers of each regiment, who shall meet for that purpose on or before the first day of March next, or at any time thereafter when the colonel of each regiment shall direct; and that the officers and men of said regiment shall within six months after said meeting, provide themselves with the uniform as directed by said board.

G

(28)

**Duty of
judge ad-
vocate &
provost
martial.**

§ 5th. Be it further enacted, That the judge advocate shall exercise the duties of clerk to the regiment, and the provost martial of each regiment shall exercise the duties of collector of fines and forfeitures, and it shall be the duty of the president of the court martial which hears and determines upon the fines and forfeitures which may accrue under the said act, to issue his warrant to the provost martial to collect said fines by distress or otherwise.

**Repeal-
ing clause**

§ 6th. Be it further enacted, That so much of the fourteenth section as directs the brigadier general to call a meeting of the commissioned and non commissioned officers for the purpose of disciplining them, be, and the same is hereby repealed; and the same power is hereby vested in the colonel of each regiment.—This act to take effect from and after the first day of January next.

JESSE B. THOMAS, Speaker of the House
of Representatives,

JOHN RICE JONES, President pro tem. of
the Legislative Council.

Approved—December 5th, 1806.

William Henry Harrison.

CHAPTER xxvi.

AN ACT *relative to the General Court, and the better to promote the impartial administration of Justice.*

§ 1st. Be it enacted by the Legislative Council and House of Representatives, and it is hereby enacted by the authority of the same, That the Chief Justice, or one of the Judges of the General court, shall hold a Circuit court and court of Oyer and Terminer and General Jail Delivery, once a year in the counties of Clark and Dearborn, in the same places where the courts of Common Pleas are held; the court for the county of Clark, shall be held on the first Monday of June, and that for the county of Dearborn, on the third Monday of June yearly. **Courts to be held.**

§ 2nd. And be it further enacted, That the General court, shall not be held by less than two Judges.

§ 3rd. And be it further enacted, That it shall and may be lawful for the Governor of the Territory, and he is hereby authorised and empowered, whenever he is officially informed that a capital offence has been committed in any county of this Territory, and the offender or offenders is or are confined, or likely to be confined for the same, to issue a commission for holding a special court of Oyer and Terminer, in any county in this Territory, at such time or times as he may think proper or necessary, which commission shall be directed to the Judges of the General court, or any one of them, who shall hold the said court accordingly. **Governor to issue a commission to the judges to hold a court.**

§ 4th. Be it further enacted, That no suit shall hereafter be commenced in the General court, or be removed into the said court from any of the inferior courts, by appeal or otherwise, except by writ of error, unless the matter in controversy between the parties shall exceed the sum of fifty dollars. **Respecting suits.**

In all actions of assault and battery, and slander, commenced and prosecuted in the General court, if the jury find under twenty dollars, the

(29)

plaintiff shall not recover any costs.—This act shall be in force from its passage.

> JESSE B. THOMAS, Speaker of the House
> of Representatives.
> JOHN RICE JONES, President pro tem. of
> the Legislative Council.

Approved—December 5th, 1806.

> *William Henry Harrison.*

CHAPTER XXVII.

AN ACT *to prohibit the giving or selling intoxicating liquors to Indians within forty miles of Vincennes, in the county of Knox.*

Proviso.

WHEREAS many abuses dangerous to the lives, peace and property of the citizens of the said county, and derogatory to the dignity of the United States, have arisen by reason of traders and others furnishing speritous and other intoxicating liquors to Indians within the settled parts of the county of Knox, for remedy whereof,

Penalty

§ 1st. Be it enacted by the Legislative Council and House of Representatives, and it is hereby enacted by the authority of the same, That if any trader or other person whomsoever, residing, coming into, or passing within the distance of forty miles from Vincennes, in the county of Knox, in this Territory, shall presume to vend, sell or give, or direct or procure to be vended, sold or given, upon any account, to any Indian or Indians, or nation or tribe of Indians, any rum, brandy, whiskey, or other intoxicating liquor or drink, he, she or they so offending, shall on conviction by presentment or indictment, forfeit and pay for every such offence, any sum not exceeding one hundred dollars, nor less than five dollars, with costs, to the use of the county.

Provided, That nothing herein contained shall be taken or construed to impair or weaken the powers and authority that now are, or hereafter may be vested in the governor or other person as superintendant or agent of Indian affairs, or commissioner plenipotentiary for trading with Indians.—This act shall be in force from and after the first day of January next.

JESSE B. THOMAS, Speaker of the House
of Representatives.
JOHN RICE JONES, President pro tem. of
the Legislative Council.

Approved—December 6th, 1806.

William Henry Harrison.

CHAPTER xxviii.

A RESOLUTION *for revising of the laws of this Territory, and for other purposes.*

R ESOLVED by the Legislative Council and House of Representatives, That John Rice Jones, and John Johnson, be appointed to revise and reduce into one code the laws in force in this territory at the end of this session of the Legislature, by bringing all laws and parts of laws on one subject

(30)

under one head, where ever the different parts of laws comport with each other, and where they do not, then the said committee are authorised to make the said laws, and parts of laws, as complete as the nature of the case will admit of, and report the same to the next session of the Legislature.

Resolved also, That the same persons contract for the printing of the laws passed at this sessions, upon the most reasonable terms they can, and that they be authorised to take the enrolled bills out of the secretary's office and return the same; and that they make out an index to the said laws, and also marginal notes; and that the said committee be authorised to send twenty copies of the laws to the Clerks of the courts of Common Pleas of the different counties, to be by them given to the several officers of said counties, the expences of which shall be paid out of that part of the contingent fund subject to the order of the Governor.

JESSE B. THOMAS, Speaker of the House of Representatives.

JOHN RICE JONES, President pro tem. of the Legislative Council.

Approved—December 4th, 1806.

William Henry Harrison.

Table of Contents.

LAWS

OF THE

INDIANA TERRITORY;

Comprising those Acts formerly in force, and as Revised by

Messrs. *John Rice Jones,* and *John*

Johnson, and passed (after amendments) by

the Legislature; and the Original Acts

Passed at the First Session of the

Second General Assembly of

the said Territory.

Begun and held at the Borough of Vincennes, on the

sixteenth day of August, Anno Domini

eighteen hundred and seven.

————:********:————

*Printed by Authority, and under the inspection of
the Committee.*

————:********:————

VINCENNES,

PRINTED BY STOUT & SMOOT,

Printers to the Territory.

— — — — —

1807.

LAWS

OF

THE INDIANA TERRITORY.

CHAPTER I.

An act for the appointment of Justices of the Peace within the several counties of the Territory, and therein of their duties and powers.

§ 1. THERE shall be a competent number of Justices in every county, nominated and commissioned by the Governor, under the seal of the Territory, who shall have power and authority to take all manner of recognizances and obligations, as any Justices of the Peace in any of the U. States may, can or usually do, which said recognizances and obligations shall be made to the United States; and all recognizances for the peace, behavior or for appearance, which shall be taken by any of the said Justices, shall be certified into the Court of Common Pleas, to be holden next after the taking thereof; and any recognizances taken before any of them for suspicions of any manner of felony, or other crime not triable in the said court of Common Pleas, shall be certified before the Judges of the General court, or court of Oyer and Terminer, at their next succeeding court to be holden, after the taking thereof, without concealment of, or detaining, or embezzeling the same.

§ 2. One or more Justices of the Peace shall and may hear and determine according

(4)

to the course of common law petit crimes and misdemeanors, wherein the punishment shall be by fine only, and not exceeding three dollars, and to assess and tax costs.

Marginal notes:

Justices of the peace.

To take recognizances, &c.

To whom payable.

To be certified to court of common pleas.

or General court or court of Oyer & terminer.

May hear petit crimes the punishment whereof shall be by fine only.

In cases of refusal to commit to prison.

And in case any person or persons, shall refuse to obey, fulfil and perform the sentence or sentences, given against him or them by the Justice or Justices herein, it shall and may be lawful for such Justice or Justices to commit the delinquent

Crimes committed in justices presence.

or delinquents to jail there to remain until sentence be performed; and it shall be lawful for such Justice or Justices, whenever the crime shall be committed in his or their presence, or view, to sentence as aforesaid without further examination, and which fines shall be by such Justice or Justices

Fines to whom payable

paid to the clerk of the county court of Common Pleas, and by him paid into the county treasury; all warrants issued by a Justice or Justices of the Peace, either for apprehending,

warrants to be under hand & seal directed to an officer who shall obey the same

searching or committing to jail persons suspected, or convicted of crimes shall be under the hand and seal of such Justice or Justices, and directed to an officer or officers, whose duty it shall be to execute criminal process, and such officer or officers shall obey the warrant or warrants, issued as aforesaid.

Further power and duty of magistrates to cause offenders to be arrested and give recognizance for appearance at court, also for the peace

§ 3. It shall be within the power, and be the duty of every Justice of the Peace, within his county, to punish by such fine, as is by the statute law of the Territory provided; All assaults and batteries, that are not of a high and aggravated nature, and to cause to be stayed and arrested, all affrayers, rioters and disturbers of the peace, and to bind them by recognizance, to appear at the next General court, Circuit court, or court of

(5)

and good behaviour in cases of refusal to commit.

Common Pleas, to be held within or for the same county, at the discretion of the Justice, and also to require such persons to find sureties for their keeping the peace, and being of good behavior until the sitting of the court they are to appear before, and to commit such person as shall refuse, or delay to recognize and find such surety or sureties; and the Justices of the Peace shall examine into all homicides, murders, treasons and felonies done and committed in their respective counties, and commit to prison

To commit capital offenders, and

all persons guilty, or suspected to be guilty of manslaughter, murder, treason, or other capital offence, and to hold to bail all persons guilty or suspected to be guilty of lesser offences, which are not cognizable by a Justice of the Peace; And require sureties for the good behavior of idle, vagrant and disorderly characters, swindlers and gamblers, as well as of dangerous and disorderly persons; and shall take cognizance of, and examine into all other crimes, matters and offences, which by particular laws, are put within their jurisdiction.

to bail for lesser offences.

To require securities of vagrants.

Their further power.

JESSE B. THOMAS,

Speaker of the House of Representatives.

B. CHAMBERS,

President of the Council.

Approved—September 17th, 1807.

WILLIAM HENRY HARRISON.

(6)

CHAPTER II.

An act organizing courts of Common Pleas.

§ 1. THERE shall be a court of record in each county in the Territory, to be styled and called the court of Common Pleas of   county, to consist of three Judges, any two of whom shall form a quorum, to be appointed and commissioned by the Governor, for and during good behavior; the said courts shall and may hear and determine and sentence according to the course of the common law, all crimes and misdemeanors, of whatever nature or kind, committed within their respective counties, the punishment whereof doth not extend to life, limb, imprisonment for more than one year, or forfeiture of goods and chattels, or lands and tenements, and they shall also hold pleas of *Assize, Scirefacias, Replevins,* and hear and determine all manner of pleas, suits, actions and causes, real personal and mixed, according to law.

Courts of common pleas authorised in each county—to consist of 3 judges—by whom to be appointed—their power and duties.

§ 2. The said court shall hold annually six sessions, at three of which no proceedings shall be had in suits, or process of a civil or criminal nature.

To hold six sessions annually.

§ 3. The terms of the said court, wherein suits of a civil and criminal nature may be transacted shall commence at the

Terms of the court for ci-

vil and criminal proceedings. Dearborn, Clark, Knox Randolph and St. Clair.

following periods, to wit: For the county of Dearborn, on the first Mondays in the months of April, August, and December; For the county of Clark, on the first Mondays of January, and May, and the second Monday of September; For the county of Knox, on the last Mondays of July, and

(7)

November, and the third Monday of Márch; For the county of Randolph, on the third Mondays in April, August, and December; and for the county of St. Clair, on the last Mondays in April, August, and December, yearly and every year.

Other terms of the court.

§ 4.   The three other annual sessions of the said court shall be holden for the county of Dearborn, on the first Tuesdays in February, June, and October; For the county of Clark, on the first Mondays of March, July, and November; For the county of Knox, on the first Tuesdays of February, May, and September; For the county of Randolph, on the first Mondays of March, July, and November; and for the county of St. Clair, on the third Mondays in March, July and November.

In case not opened, sheriff to adjourn.

§ 5.   If the said court shall not be opened at the period aforesaid, it shall be lawful for the Sheriff to adjourn the said court from day to day, for two days, and if the said court shall not then be opened, he shall, and is hereby authorised, to adjourn the said court 'till court in course.

Judges, their pay.

§ 6.   The Judges of the said court shall respectively receive two hundred and fifty cents for every day they shall sit, to be paid out of the county levy.

Judges to take recognizances &c. payable to the U. S. to whom to be certified— forfeited recognizances, how & to what court to be certified.

§ 7.   The said Judges, and every of them, shall have full power and authority, in, and out of court, to take all manner of recognizances, and obligations, which said recognizances and obligations, shall be made to the United States; and all recognizances for the peace, behavior, or for appearance, which shall be taken by any of the said Judg-

(8)

es, out of court, shall be certified to the next court of Common Pleas, to be holden after the taking thereof, and every recognizance taken before any of them for suspicions of any manner of felony, or other crime, not triable in the said court, shall be certified before the Judges of the General court, or court of Oyer and Terminer, at their next succeeding court, to be holden next after the taking thereof, without concealment of, or detaining or embezzelling the same; but in case any person or persons shall forfeit his or their recognizance of the peace, behavior, or appearance, for any cause whatsoever, then the recognizance so forfeited, with the record of the default, or cause of forfeiture, shall be sent and certified without delay by the Judges of the said court, into the General court, or court of Oyer and Terminer, as the case may require; that thence process may issue against the said parties according to law, all which forfeitures shall be levied by the proper officers, and go to the Territory.

§ 8. All fines and amercements which shall be laid before the Judges of the said court of Common Pleas, shall be taxed, offered and set, duly and truly, according to the quality of the offence, without partiality or affection; and shall be yearly estreated by the clerks of the said courts respectively into the General court, or court of Oyer and Terminer, to the intent that process may be awarded to the sheriff of every county, as the case may require, for levying such of their fines and amercements as shall

Fines to be truly taxed, and how to be yearly estreated, judges to issue their writs or precepts to arrest persons indicted in one county to another.

(9)

be unpaid, to the uses for which they are or shall be appropriated.

§ 9. To the end that persons indicted, or out-lawed for felonies or other offences, in one county, who remove into, or dwell in another county, may be brought to justice; it is hereby directed that the Judges, or any of them, shall, and may direct their writs or precepts, to all, or any of the Sheriffs, or other officers of said counties (where need shall be) to take such persons indicted or out-lawed; and it shall and may be lawful to and for the said court to issue forth *subpœnas* and other warrants, (under the seal of the court, and signed by the Clerk) into any county or place of this Territory, for sum-

Judges to issue their warrants or precepts to arrest persons indicted in one county & fleeing to another.

To issue subpoenas for witnesses to any county

in the territory.

moning or bringing any person or persons to give evidence in, and upon any matter or cause whatsoever, now or hereafter, examinable, or in any ways triable by, or before them, or any of them, under such pains and penalties as *subpœnas* or *warrants* of that kind usually are, or ought by law to be granted or awarded; They shall have further power and authority when, and as often as necessity may require, to issue dedi-

To issue dedimuses.

muses for the examination of witnesses, living in, or moving to a different county, under the like rules and regulations as dedimuses issuing from the General court.

Appeals how made.

§ 10. If any person or persons shall find him or themselves aggrieved by the judgment of any of the said courts of Common Pleas, it shall and may be lawful to, and for the party or parties so aggrieved, to appeal from the said judgment, under the restrictions and regulations of the law to regulate

(10)

the practice of the General court upon appeals and writs of error, or to have his or their writ or writs of error, which shall be granted of course, in manner as other writs are to be granted, and made returnable to the General court.

Writs to run in name U. S. how tested and dated under seal of the court.

§ 11. All writs issuing out of the said courts, shall run in the name and style of the United States, and bear teste in the name of the Clerk, and be dated when they issue, and shall be sealed with the judicial seal of the said court, and made returnable according to law.

What writs to be issued by the courts

§ 12. The Judges of the said respective courts, shall and are hereby empowered to grant under the seal of the said court, *replevins, writs of partition, writs of view,* and all other writs and process upon the said pleas and actions, cognizable in the said court, as occasion may require.

Power of the court to issue subpœnas, &c.

§ 13. The said courts of Common Pleas shall, and are hereby empowered to issue forth *subpœnas,* under the seal of the said court, and signed by the Clerk, into any county or place within this Territory, for summoning or bringing any person or persons to give evidence in, or upon the trial of any matter or cause, whatsoever depending before them, or any of them, under such pains and penalties as by the rules of the common law and course of the practice of the General court are usually appointed.

§ 14. Upon any judgment obtained in any of the said courts of Common Pleas, and execution returned by the Sheriff or Coroner of the proper county, where such judgment was obtained, that the party was

(11)

not to be found, or hath no lands and tenements, goods or chattels in that county; and thereupon it is testified that the party skulks or lies hid, or hath lands and tenements, goods and chattels in another county in this Territory, it shall and may be lawful to and for the court that issued out such execution, to grant, and they are hereby required to grant an *alias Execution,* with a *Testatum,* directed to the Sheriff or Coroner, of the county or place where such person lies hid, or where his lands or effects are, commanding him to execute the same according to the tenor of such writ or writs, and make return thereof to the court of Common Pleas, where such recovery is had, or judgment given, and if the Sheriff or Coroner, to whom such writ or writs shall be directed, shall refuse or neglect to execute and return the same accordingly, he shall be amerced in the county where he ought to return it, and be liable to the action of the party grieved, and the said amercement shall be truly and duly set according to the quality of the offence, and estreated by the Clerks of the respective courts of Common Pleas, into the next succeeding General court, or court of Oyer and Terminer in course, that thence process may issue against the offenders for levying such fines and amercements as shall be unpaid, to the use for which they are or shall be appropriated.

§ 15. The Clerk of the said court shall be appointed and commissioned by the Governor for and during good behavior, who shall be entitled to and authorised to re-

B

(12)

ceive such fees as are now allowed, or hereafter may be by law.

.JESSE B. THOMAS,
Speaker of the House of Representatives.

B. CHAMBERS,
President of the Council.

Approved--September 17th, 1807.

WILLIAM HENRY HARRISON.

CHAPTER III.
An act regulating the General Courts.

General court to be held twice a year at Vincennes.

§ 1. THERE shall be holden and kept twice in every year, a Supreme court of Record, which shall be called and styled the General court, the sittings of which court shall be at Vincennes, in the county of Knox, in the first Tuesdays of April, and September, yearly and every year; and the Judges of the said court,

Powers and duties of the judges.

and every of them, shall have power and authority, and as often as there may be occasion, to issue forth writs of *Habeas Corpus, Certiorari,* and writs of *Error,* and all remedial and other writs and process returnable to the said court, and grantable by the said Judges by virtue of their office.

On removal of causes, issue to be tried in proper county,

§ 2. *Provided always,* That upon any issue joined in the said General court, such issue shall be tried in the county whence the cause was removed, before the Judges aforesaid, or any one of them, as a Circuit

(13)

Circuitcourts where, and when to be held.

court, who are hereby required to hold a Circuit once a year, in each of the following counties: that for the county of Dearborn, on the third Monday in June, yearly; for the county of Clark, on the first Monday of June, for the county of Randolph, on the first Monday of October; and for the county of St. Clair, on the third Monday of October, annually and every year, to try such issues in fact as shall be depending in the said general court, and removed out of either of the counties aforesaid, (when and where they may try all issues joined) or to be joined in the same General court, and to do generally, all those things that shall be necessary for the trial of any issue, as fully as Justices of *nisi prius* in any of the United States, may or could do; *Provided always,* That the Circuit court shall render a final judgment, and issue execution upon verdict found in the said Circuit court, in the same manner that the General court has power to do, unless a bill of exceptions shall be filed to the opinion of the said Judge, or some other good cause shewn, which in the opinion of the said Judge holding such Circuit court, may render it necessary that the determination of the General court should be taken thereon; and the said Circuit court shall have power to grant and order new trials. *In certain cases circuit courts to render final judgment and issue execution.* *May grant new trials.*

§ 3. The said court shall hear and determine all causes, matters and things, cognizable in the said court, and also to hear and determine all, and all manner of pleas, plaints and causes, which shall be removed or brought there from the respective Com- *Further powers of the court.*

(14)

mon Pleas, or from any other court to be holden for the respective counties, and to examine and correct all, and all manner of errors of the Judges of the inferior courts in their judgments, process and proceedings in the said courts, as well in all pleas of the United States, as in all pleas real, personal and mixed, and thereupon to reverse or affirm the said judgments, as the law shall or doth direct, and also to examine, correct, and punish the contempts, omissions, and neglects, favors, corruptions and defaults, of all, or any of the Justices of the Peace, Sheriffs, Coroners, Clerks, and other officers within the said respective counties. *To examine and correct errors of inferior courts.* *To examine and punish contempts &c. of certain officers.*

§ 4. And also shall award process for levying, as well of such fines, forfeitures and amercements, as shall be estreated into the said General court, as of the fines, forfeitures and amercements which shall be lost, taxed, and set there, and not paid to the uses to which they are or shall be appropriated, and generally shall minister ample justice to all persons, and amply exercise the jurisdictions and powers herein mentioned, concerning all and singular the premises according to law. *To award process for levying fines &c.*

§ 5. All the said writs shall run in the name and style of the United States of America, and bear teste in the name of the Clerk of the General court, on the days in which the said writs *Style teste & date of writs.*

How returnable.

shall be issued, and shall be sealed with the judicial seal of the said court, and made returnable according to law.

To deliver jails and issue process

§ 6.   The Judges of the said General court shall have power from time to time, to de-

(15)

liver the jails of all persons who now are, or hereafter shall be committed, for treasons, murders, or such other crimes as by the laws of the Territory now are, or hereafter shall be made capital, or felonies of death, as aforesaid, and for that end, from time to time, to issue forth such necessary precepts and process, and force obedience thereto, as Justices of Assize, Justices of Oyer and Terminer, and of jail delivery, may or can do within the United

In what cases governor to issue a special commission.

States; *Provided always,* That it shall and may be lawful for the Governor of the Territory, and he is hereby authorised and empowered whenever he is officially informed that a capital offence has been committed in any county of this Territory, and the offender or offenders is or are confined, or likely to be confined for the same, to issue a commission for holding a special court of Oyer and Terminer in any county in this Territory, at such time or times as he may think proper or necessary, which

To whom directed.

commission shall be directed to the Judges of the General court, or any one of them, who shall hold the said court accordingly.

Jurors summoned and not attending to be fined in the general and circuit courts any sum not exceeding 8 dollars in the courts of common pleas not exceeding five dollars, unless excused, & when and how.

§ 7.   In order to compel the due attendance of jurymen in the said Circuit and *Nisi Prius* courts, and all other courts within this Territory; it is hereby declared, that if any person shall be duly summoned to attend any court of Judicature, to serve on a jury, or on any inquest required by law, and shall neglect or refuse to give his attendance on the day, and during the time his service is necessary, every such person, so offending, shall be fined for every such offence in the

(16)

General court and court of Oyer and Terminer, by the Judges thereof, any sum not exceeding eight dollars; and for every such offence in the court of Common Pleas, for any county of the Territory, by the Judges thereof, any sum not exceeding five dollars, unless the delinquent shall at the same, or next succeeding court, render to the Judges or Justices thereof, a reasonable excuse for such neglect or refusal, to be allowed by such of them as shall be present; which said Judges or Justices are hereby required and empowered, on failure of such delinquent, to render such reasonable excuse, to issue a writ to the Sheriff of the county, to levy the said fines on the goods and chattels of every such delinquent, to be paid to the Clerks of the several courts of Common Pleas and General court, and by the said Clerks to the Territorial Treasurer, for the use of the Territory. *In default of rendering excuse, how the fines are to be levied and collected & to whom paid.*

§ 8. All suits and causes before the General court, and courts of Common Pleas, that shall remain undetermined, shall be continued over to the next respective term, ensuing, under the authority of this act. *Suits undetermined to be continued to the next succeedingcourt*

JESSE B. THOMAS,
Speaker of the House of Representatives.
B. CHAMBERS,
President of the Council.

Approved—September 17th, 1807.
WILLIAM HENRY HARRISON.

(17)

CHAPTER IV.
An act for the establishing of the Office of Sheriff, and for the appointment of Sheriffs,

§ 1. THERE shall be appointed and commissioned by the Governor, under the seal of the Territory, a Sheriff, who shall give bond with two sufficient sureties, in the penal sum of four thousand dollars, for the faithful discharge of the duties of his office. *Sheriffs, how to be appointed, to give bond with sureties.*

The duties of each Sheriff shall be, to keep the peace, by causing all offenders against law, in his view, to enter into recognizances, with sureties, for keeping the peace, and appearing at the next court of Common Pleas in the same county, and to commit in case of refusal; and which recognizances, shall by the said Sheriff, be returned and certified to the said court of Common Pleas. *His duty to keep the peace &c. take recognizances in certain cases to commit in case of refusal. Recognizances, how taken.*

To quell affrays, &c.

It shall also be his duty to quell and suppress all affrays, routs, riots, and insurrections; and for which end, he shall, and is hereby empowered, to call to his aid the power of the county.

To pursue, apprehend & commit felons &c. execute writs & process.

He shall pursue, apprehend, and commit to jail all felons and traitors; he shall execute all warrants, writs, and other process, which by law shall appertain to the duties of his office, and which shall be directed to him by legal authority.

To attend upon courts have custody of the jail.

He shall duly attend upon all courts of record, at their respective terms or sessions in his county, (and shall have the custody of the jail of the county) and shall do, and per-

(18)

form, such other duties, as are, or shall be enjoined on him by law.

JESSE B. THOMAS,
Speaker of the House of Representatives.
B. CHAMBERS,
President of the Council.

Approved—September 17th, 1807.
WILLIAM HENRY HARRISON.

CHAPTER V.
An act respecting Oaths of Office.

Civil officers commissioned by the governor, to take oaths of office or affirmation.

§ 1. EVERY person appointed to any civil office in the Territory, and commissioned by the Governor shall previously to his entering upon the exercise of his office take the following oath, to wit: I, A B being appointed to the office of   do solemnly swear, that I will well and truly execute the duties of my said office, according to the best of my skill and understanding, without fraud or partiality, so help me God. Any person appointed as aforesaid, conscientiously scrupulous of taking an oath, shall make the following affirmation previously to his entering upon the duties of his office, viz. I, A B being appointed to the office of   do solemnly, sincerely, and truly declare, and affirm, that I will well and truly execute the duties of my said office, according to the best of my skill and understanding,

[19]

without fraud or partiality, and this I declare and affirm under the pains and penalties of perjury; and that all oaths of office, or declarations and affirmations prescribed as aforesaid, shall be taken before the Governor, or such person or persons, as shall, by him be appointed and commissioned for that purpose, and certifyed upon the commission of the person taking the same; and in case of the absence of the Governor, the said oath, or declaration and affirmation may be taken before, and certified by either of the Judges of the Territory.

Before whom taken and how certified.

JESSE B. THOMAS,
Speaker of the House of Representatives.
B. CHAMBERS,
President of the Council.

Approved—September 17th, 1807.
WILLIAM HENRY HARRISON.

CHAPTER VI.
An act respecting Crimes and Punishments.

TREASON.

§ 1.   IF any person residing in, belonging to, or protected by the laws of this Territory, shall levy war against the United States, or against this Territory, or shall knowingly or wilfully aid or assist any enemies at war against the United States or this

What offences shall be deemed treasonable.

C
[20]

Territory, by joining the armies or fleets of such enemies, or by inlisting, persuading or procuring others to join said fleets or armies, or by furnishing such enemies with arms, ammunition, or provisions, or any other article for their aid or comfort, or by carrying on a treasonable or treacherous correspondence with them, or shall form, or be any way concerned in forming any combination, plot or conspiracy, for betraying the United States or this Territory into the hands or power of any foreign enemy, or shall give, or attempt to give or send any intelligence to any such enemy, for said purpose, the person or persons so offending, shall be deemed guilty of treason, and upon conviction thereof shall suffer the pains of death.

How punished,

MURDER.

Murder and how punished.

§ 2. If any person or persons shall with malice aforethought, kill or slay another person, he, she, or they, so offending shall be deemed guilty of murder, and upon conviction thereof, shall suffer the pains of death.

MAN-SLAUGHTER.

Manslaughter, how punished.

§ 3. If any person or persons shall wilfully kill or slay another person, without malice aforethought, he, she, or they, so offending shall be deemed guilty of man-slaughter, and upon conviction thereof shall be punished as the common law hath heretofore been used and accustomed; *Provided nevertheless,* That if any person in the just and necessary defence of his own life, or the life of any other person, shall kill or

(21)

proviso.

slay another person, attempting to rob or murder in the field or high way, or to break into a dwelling house, if he cannot with safety to himself otherwise take the felon, or assailant, or bring him to justice, he shall be holden guiltless.

BURGLARY.

Burglary, what crimes deemed.

§ 4. If any person or persons shall in the night season, break open and enter any dwelling house, shop, store, or vessel, in which any person or persons dwell or reside, with a view and intention of stealing and purloining therefrom, he, she, or they, so offending, shall be deemed guilty of Burglary, and upon conviction

How punished & fined.

thereof, shall be whipped not exceeding thirty-nine stripes, and find sureties for good behavior, for a term not exceeding three years, and upon default of sureties shall be committed to jail for a term not exceeding three years, or until sentence be performed.

Forfeiture on breaking houses and stealing there from.

If any person or persons, so breaking and entering any dwelling house, shop, store, or vessel, as aforesaid, shall actually steal and purloin therefrom, he, she, or they, so offending, upon conviction thereof, shall moreover be fined in treble the value of the articles stolen, one third of such fine to be to the Territory, and the other two thirds to the party injured.

If the person or persons so breaking and entering any dwelling house, shop, store, or vessel, as aforesaid, shall commit, or attempt to commit any personal abuse, force or violence, or shall be armed with any dangerous weapon or weapons, as clearly to indicate a

If with personal abuse how punished.

(22)

violent intention, he, she, or they, so offending, upon conviction thereof, shall moreover, forfeit all his, her, or their estate, real and personal, to this Territory, out of which the party injured shall be recompensed, as aforesaid, and the offender shall also be committed to any jail in the Territory for a term not exceeding forty years.

And if the death of any innocent person should ensue, from the breaking and entering any dwelling house, shop, store, or vessel, as aforesaid, in any of the instances as aforesaid, the person or persons so breaking and entering, shall be deemed guilty of wilful murder, and all persons aiding and assisting in breaking and entering any dwelling house, shop, store, or vessel, as aforesaid, or in any of the crimes consequent thereupon, as before pointed out, shall be deemed principals.

In what cases deemed wilful murder.

ROBBERY,

§ 5. If any person or persons shall unlawfully and forcibly take from the person of another, in the field or highway, any money, goods or chattels, he, she, or they, so offeding, shall be deemed guilty of robbery, and upon conviction thereof shall suffer as in the first instance of burglary.

What crimes deemed robbery & how punished.

Whoever shall commit such robbery with personal abuse or violence, or be armed at the time with any dangerous weapons so as clearly to indicate an intention of violence, he, she, or they, so offending, upon conviction thereof, shall moreover suffer as in the second instance of burglary. And in case any person or persons robbing, or attempting

If with abuse or violence how punished.

(23)

to rob as aforesaid, shall kill or slay any person or persons, defending him her, or themselves, or others, or his, her or their property, against such robber or robbers, or person or persons attempting to rob, or in pursuing and endeavoring to apprehend and secure such person or persons so robbing or attempting to rob, he, she, or they, so offending shall be deemed guilty of wilful murder, and all aiders and abettors in any robbery as aforesaid, and in any of the crimes consequent thereupon, as before pointed out, shall be deemed principals.

RIOTS and UNLAWFUL ASSEMBLIES.

Fines on un-lawful assem-blies.

§ 6. If three or more persons shall assemble together with intention to do any unlawful act with force and violence, against the person or property of another, or to do any other unlawful act against the peace and to the terror of the people, or being lawfully assembled, shall agree with each other to do any unlawful act as aforesaid, and shall make any movements and preperation there-for, the persons so offending, and upon conviction thereof, shall

How fined.

pay as a fine, each, to this Territory, the sum of sixteen dollars, and find surety for their good behavior, respectively, for the space of six months, and stand committed until sentence be performed.

Duty of jud ges &c. on unlawful as-semblies.

Whenever three or more persons shall be assembled as afore-said, and proceeding to commit any of the offences as aforesaid, it shall be the duty of all Judges, Justices of the Peace, and Sheriffs, and all ministerial

(24)

officers immediately upon actual view, or as soon as may be, upon information, to make proclamation in the hearing of such offend-ers, if silence can be obtained, commanding them in the name of the United States immediately to disperse, and depart to their

If rioters do not disperse how punish-ed.

several homes, or lawful employments, and if upon such proclama-tion, or when silence cannot be obtained, such persons so assém-bled, shall not disperse, and depart as aforesaid, it shall then be the duty of such Judges, Justices of the Peace Sheriffs and other ministerial officers respectively, to call upon all persons near, and of abilities, and throughout the county if necessary, to be aiding and assisting in dispersing and taking into custody all persons assembled as aforesaid, and all military officers, and others called upon as aforesaid, are hereby ordered and directed to render instant and full obedience in this behalf, upon the penalty of ten dollars, each, for every neglect or refusal herein, and commitment in case of non-payment.

If any of the persons so unlawfully assembled, shall be killed, maimed, or otherwise injured, in consequence of resisting the Judges, or others in dispersing and apprehending, or in attemping to disperse and apprehend them, the said Judges, Justices of the Peace and Sheriffs, and other ministerial officers, and others, acting by their authority, or the authority of any of them, shall be holden guiltless. *Rioters &c. killed holden guiltless*

If any person or persons shall forcibly obstruct, any of the authority, aforesaid, or, if any three, or more persons shall continue together, after proclamation, as aforesaid, *Fine on obstructing authority &c.*

[25]

made, or attempted to be made, and prevented by such rioters, or in case of no proclamation, and three or more persons being assembled, as aforesaid, shall commit any unlawful act, as aforesaid, every offender upon conviction thereof, shall be fined in a sum, not exceeding three hundred dollars, or to be whipped not exceeding thirty-nine stripes, and find surety for good behavior, for a time not more than one year, at the discretion of the court, before whom the conviction may be had; and upon a second conviction, each, and every offender, shall be whipped and fined as aforesaid, and find surety for good behavior, and the peace, for a time not exceeding ten years; and may be committed to any jail in the Territory, 'till sentence be fully performed. *How punished.*

PERJURY.

§ 7. If any person lawfully called upon to give evidence, before any court of record or other authority, in this Territory, qualified to administer oaths, and solemn declarations and affirmations, shall wilfully depose, affirm or declare, any matter to be fact, knowing the same to be false, or shall in like manner deny any fact, knowing the same to be true, or shall refuse to depose to affirm, or declare fact knowing the same to be true; the person so offending shall be deemed guilty of perjury, and upon conviction *Perjury, what cases deemed & how punished,* thereof, shall be fined in a sum not exceeding sixty dollars, or be whipped not exceeding thirty nine stripes, and shall moreover be set in the pilory, for a space of time not exceeding two hours, and be ever after incapable of

(26)

giving testimony; being a juror, and of sustaining any office, civil or military, in this Territory; and if any person or persons shall

Subornation of perjury, how punished.

corruptly procure any other person to commit the crime of perjury, as before defined, he, she or they, so offending, shall upon conviction thereof, suffer the same punishments and disabilities as in the case of actual perjury.

LARCENY.

Larceny what deemed

§ 8. If any person or persons shall steal or purloin from another person or persons, any money, goods, wares or merchandize, or any other personal property, or thing whatever; he, she, or they, so offending, shall be deemed guilty of larceny, and upon

How punished.

conviction thereof, shall for the first offence, restore to the owner the thing stolen, and pay to him the value thereof, or two-fold the value thereof, if the thing stolen be not restored, and shall be fined in a sum not exceeding two-fold the value of the thing or goods stolen, or shall be whipped not exceeding thirty one stripes, at the discretion of the court. Upon a second conviction, restitution, and payment shall be made to the owner as aforesaid, and a fine shall be set, and paid to the Territory, not exceding four-fold the value, as aforesaid; and the offender shall be whipped not exceeding thirty nine stripes, and in like manner upon every succeeding conviction; and in case such convict shall not have property real or personal wherewith to discharge and satisfy the sentence of the court, it shall be lawful for the Sheriff by direction of the court, to

(27)

bind such person to labor, for any term not exceeding seven years, to any suitable person, who will discharge such sentence.

Receiving stolen goods

If any person or persons shall receive any goods, or other things, as aforesaid, knowing the same to be stolen, he, she, or they, so offending, shall be deemed principly guilty, and upon conviction thereof, shall be punished accordingly.

And if any person or persons shall agree to compound, or take satisfaction for any stealing, or goods stolen, such person or persons upon conviction thereof, shall forfeit twice the value of the sums or things agreed for, or taken; but no person shall be debarred from taking his goods again, *provided* he prosecute the thief; *Provided also,* That nothing herein shall be construed so as to oblige a parent to prosecute a child, being an infant, or in a state of minority.

&c., how pun ished.

Compound-ing felony, how fined.

Proviso.

FORGERY,

§ 9. Whoever shall forge, deface, corrupt, or embezzle any charters, gifts, grants, bonds, bills, conveyances, wills, testaments, or written contracts of any nature or kind, or shall deface, or falsify any enrollment or registry, or record, or matter or instrument recorded, or shall counterfeit the seal or hand writing of another, with intent to defraud; every person so offending shall upon conviction thereof, be fined in double the sum he shall thereby have defrauded or attempted to defraud another, one half thereof to the party injured, or intended to be injured, and shall moreover forever after be

Forgery what cases deemed

How punish-ed.

D

(28)

rendered incabable of giving testimony, being a juror, or sustaining any office of trust, and be set in the pillory not exceeding the space of three hours, and all persons wilfully aiding and assisting in the commission of these crimes, or who shall cause, or procure the same, or any of them to be perpetrated, shall be deemed principals.

Persons aid-ing & assist-ing, how pun ished.

USURPATION.

§ 10. No person shall take upon himself, or exercise or officiate in any office, or place of authority in this Territory, without being lawfully authorised thereto: and if any person shall presume so to do, he shall, upon conviction thereof, be fined in a sum not exceeding one hundred dollars.

Usurpation, what deem'd

How fined.

ASSAULT and BATTERY.

Assault and battery what deemed.

How fined & punished.

§ 11. If any person shall unlawfully assault or threaten another, in any menacing manner, or shall strike or wound another, he shall, upon conviction thereof, be fined in a sum not exceeding one hundred dollars, and the court before whom such conviction shall be had, may in their discretion, cause the offender to enter into recognizance with surety, for the peace and good behavior, for a term not exceeding one year.

FRAUDULENT DEEDS.

Fiaudulent deeds and per sons making them how fined.

§ 12. All bonds, bills, deeds of sale, gifts grants, or other conveyances or obligations whatever, made with intent to deceive and defraud others, or to defeat creditors of their just debts or demands, shall be null and

(29)

void, and the person or persons so offending, shall, upon conviction thereof, be fined in a sum not exceeding three hundred dollars, and pay double damages to the party or parties injured.

DISOBEDIENCE of CHILDREN and SERVANTS.

Power of justice in cases ofdisobedient children &c.

§ 13. If any children or servants shall contrary to the obedience due to their parents or masters, resist, or refuse to obey their lawful commands, upon complaint thereof to any Justice of the Peace, it shall be lawful for such Justice, to send him or them so offending to the jail, or house of correction, there to remain until he or they shall humble themselves to the said parents or masters satisfaction, and if any child or servant, shall, contrary to his bounded duty, presume to assault or strike his parent or master, upon complaint and conviction thereof, before two or more Justices of the Peace, the offender shall be whipped not exceeding ten stripes.

How punished.

OBTAINING GOODS BY FRAUDULENT PRETENCES.

Obtaining goodsby frau dulent preten tions.

§ 14. If any person or persons, shall knowingly and designedly by any false pretence or pretences, obtain from any other person or persons, any monies, goods or merchandize, or other effects whatever, with intent to cheat or defraud such person or persons of the same, he, she, or they so

(30)

offending, shall, on conviction thereof, by verdict or confession, on judgment, suffer such punishment as in case of larceny is provided to be inflicted.

How punished.

ARSON.

Arson, what deemed.

§ 15. If any person or persons shall wilfully and maliciously burn, or cause to be burned, or shall willingly or knowingly aid or assist in burning, or causing to be burned, any dwelling-house, store-house, barn, stable, or other building adjoining thereto, or if any person or persons shall wilfully attempt to burn, by setting fire to any dwelling-house, store-house, barn, stable, or other building adjoining thereto, every person or persons so offending, shall, on conviction thereof, suffer death.

How punished.

HORSE STEALING.

Horse stealing, what deemed.

§ 16. If any person or persons shall steal or purloin from any other person or persons, any horse, mare, gelding, mule, or ass, he, she, or they, so offending, shall for the first offence pay to the owner of such horse, mare or gelding, mule or ass, the value thereof, and receive not less than fifty, nor more than two hundred stripes, and shall moreover be committed to the jail of the county, until such value be paid, with the costs of prosecution; Upon the second conviction, the offender shall suffer the pains of death.

How punished,

HOG STEALING.

Hog stealing, what deem'd

§ 17. Any person or persons who shall steal any hog, shoat or pig, or mark, or alter

(31)

the mark of any hog, shoat or pig, with an intention of stealing the same, for every such offence, upon being thereof lawfully convicted, shall be fined in any sum not exceeding one hundred dollars, nor less than fifty dollars, and moreover receive on his or her bare back, any number of lashes not exceeding thirty nine, nor

How punished,

Proviso. less than twenty five; *Provided nevertheless,* That nothing herein contained shall be so construed as to prevent any person from marking or killing his own unmarked hogs, which may be running at large, with others in his own mark.

Altering & defacing &c. marksbrands &c. § 18. A law to prevent altering and defacing marks and brands, and mismarking, and misbranding, horses, cattle and hogs, unmarked and unbranded.

How punished. If any person or persons, shall alter or deface the mark or brand, of any other person or persons, horse, neat cattle, or hog, such person being thereof lawfully convicted by indictment or presentment, shall for every horse, mare, colt, neat cattle, or hog, whose mark or brand, he or she shall alter or deface, forfeit and pay the sum of five dollars, over and above the value of such horse, mare, colt, neat cattle, or hog, to the person whose mark or marks, brand or brands, shall be so altered or defaced: *Provided,* He prosecute for the same within six months after discovery of the fact committed; and the offender shall over and above the said fine receive forty lashes, on his or her bare back, well laid on; and for the second offence, shall pay the fine aforesaid, stand in the pillory two hours, and be branded in the left hand, with a red hot iron, with the letter T, and if any person or persons, shall

How to be prosecuted.

Further punishment.

(32)

mismark, or misbrand, any unmarked or unbranded horse, mare or colt, neat cattle, or hog, not properly his or their own, he, or they, shall forfeit and pay the sum of five dollars over and above the value thereof, for every such horse, mare, colt, neat cattle or hog, so mismarked or misbranded, which fines shall be recovered by indictment or action of debt in any court of record within this Territory.

Persons seing said crimes commited & not discovering, how punished. And to prevent the concealing of such offences, if any person or persons, shall see any other person or persons committing any of the crimes aforesaid, and shall not discover the same, in ten days, to some magistrate, then, and in such case, such person or persons, for not discovering the said crimes, or any of them committed, shall forfeit and pay the sum of ten dollars, to the use of the county; to be recovered by any person or persons who will sue for the same by action of debt, or by indictment or information in any court of record in this Territory.

And because it is difficult to convict any person who has seen such crime committed, if he will deny the same, it shall be sufficient evidence to convict any person that he has seen such crime committed, if it be proven that he has told any other person that he did see the said crimes or any of them committed: *And whereas,* the common custom in this Territory, of killing of cattle and hogs in the woods, give great opportunities to stealing the cattle and hogs of other people: *Be it therefore enacted,* That if any person or persons, shall kill any one or more neat cattle, or hogs in the woods, he shall within three days shew the head

Evidence, what sufficient.

Persons kiling cattle & hogs in the woods, how to proced,

(33)

and ears, of such hog or hogs, and the hide with the ears on, of such neat beast or cattle to the next magistrate, or two substantial freeholders, under the penalty of ten dollars, to be recovered by any person who will sue for the same, by action of debt, information, or indictment in any court of record in this Territory

On neglect how punished,

Every person in this Territory who hath horses, cattle or hogs, shall have an ear mark or brand, different from the ear mark or brand of all his neighbors, which ear mark and brand, he shall record with the clerk of the county, where his horses, cattle or hogs are; for recording of which ear mark, and brand, the clerk shall be entitled to demand and receive the sum of twelve and half cents, and every person shall brand horses with the said brand from eighteen months old, and upwards, and ear mark all his hogs from six months old, and upwards, with the said ear mark, and ear mark or brand all his cattle from twelve months old and upwards with said ear mark or brand; and if any dispute should arise about any ear mark or brand, the same shall be decided by the book of the clerk of the county where such cattle horses or hogs are.

Owners to recordbrands with theclerk

Clerks fee.

At what age to brand and mark.

Disputeshow settled,

Where any person shall buy any neat cattle from any other person, or come to the same by gift, will, or any other lawful means, then, and in such case, the person who has gained the same by any of the ways aforesaid, shall within eight months, brand the said neat cattle, with his own proper brand in the presence of two

Purchasers how to proceed.

credible witnesses, a certificate of which shall be signed by the said witnesses.

(34)

Selling hogs without ears. How punished.

Proviso.

If any person shall cause to be brought to his own house, or any other house, or on board any vessel, any hog, shoat or pig, without ears, he or she so offending, shall be adjuded a hog stealer: *Povided nevertheless,* That any person may bring or cause to be brought to his or her own, or any other house, or on board any boat or boats, or other vessel, his or her own swine, though without ears, he or she, proving the same to be his or her property.

MAIMING or DISFIGURING.

Maiming or disfiguring.

§ 19. Whoever on purpose, and malice aforethought, by lying in wait, shall unlawfully cut out or disable the tongue, put out an eye, slit or bite the nose, ear, or lip, or cut off or disable any limb, or member, with intention in so doing, to maim or disfigure such person, or shall voluntarily, maliciously, and of purpose, pull or put out an eye, while fighting or otherwise, every such offender, his or her aiders, abettors and counsellors shall be

How punished.

sentenced to undergo a confinement in the jail of the county in which the offence was committed, for any time not less than one month, nor more than six months; and shall also pay a fine, not less than fifty dollars and not exceeding one thousand dollars, one fourth of which, shall be to the use of the Territory, and three fourths thereof to the use of the party grieved, and for the want of the means of payment, the offender shall be sold to service by the court, before which he is convicted, for any time not exceeding five years, the purchaser finding him food and raiment during the time.

(35)

ANNULLING DISTINCTION between PETIT TREASON and MURDER.

Petit treason deemed murder & pun-

§ 20. In all cases wherein hereintofore any person would have been deemed and taken to have committed the crime of petit treason, such person shall be deemed and taken to have committed the crime of murder only, and be indicted, and prosecuted to final judgment accordingly, and the same punishment only shall be inflicted as in the case of murder.

ished accordingly–

RAPE.

§ 21.   Any person or persons who shall have carnal knowledge of a woman forcibly and against her will, or who shall aid and abet, counsel, hire, or cause or procure any person or persons to commit the said offence, being of the age of fourteen years, shall unlawfully and carnally know and abuse any woman child, under the age of ten years, with, or without her consent, shall on conviction suffer death.

Rape what deemed.

How punished.

§ 22.   So much of the law regulating the evidence in case of a rape, as makes emission necessary, is hereby repealed: *Provided nevertheless,* That the court before whom any offender may be brought for trial, for said offence, shall have other satisfactory proof or evidence of violence on the person of the woman reported to have been ravished.

Evidence in case of rape.

E

(36)

SODOMY.

§ 23.   Any person committing sodomy, or the infamous crime against nature, with mankind or beast, shall, on conviction thereof, be fined not exceeding five hundred dollars, nor less than fifty dollars, be imprisoned for any term not less than one year, nor more than five years, and be whipped not less than one hundred nor more than five hundred stripes, well laid on, on his or her bare back, and shall moreover be rendered infamous, and incapable of giving testimony, or holding any civil or military commission in this Territory.

Sodomy what deemed.

How punished.

BIGAMY and FORCIBLE and STOLEN MARRIAGES.

§ 24.   If any person or persons within this Territory, being married, or who shall hereafter marry, do at any time marry any person or persons, the former husband or wife, being alive, upon conviction thereof, shall be whipped on his or her bare back, not

Bigamy what deemed.

**How punish-
ed.**

less than one hundred, nor more than three hundred stripes, well laid on, be fined in not less than one hundred, nor more than five hundred dollars, to, and for the use of the party injured, and imprisoned not less than six, nor more than twelve months, and thereafter be rendered infamous, be incapable of giving testimony, or holding any commission civil or military, in this Territory. And the party and parties so offending, shall receive such like proceedings, trial and execution within this Territory, as if the offence had been committed in the county

(37)

Where tried.

where such person shall be taken or apprehended: *Provided,* That nothing herein contained shall extend to any person or persons, whose husband or wife shall be continually remaining beyond the seas, for the space of seven years together, or whose husband or

**Proviso. in
case of ab-
sence for sev
en years.**

wife, shall absent him or herself, the one from the other, for the space of seven years together, in any part within the United States of America, or elsewhere, the one of them not knowing the other to be living within that time: *Provided also,* That nothing

**In case of di
vorce.**

herein contained shall extend to any person or persons, that are, or shall be at the time of such marriage, divorced by lawful authority, or to any person or persons where the former marriage hath been, or hereafter shall be by lawful authority declared to be void, and of no effect, nor to any person or persons, for, or by reason of any marriage had or made, or hereafter to be had or made within the

**or withinage
of consent.**

age of consent: And *provided also,* That no attainder for the offence made fellony, by this law, shall make, or work any corruption of blood, or forfeiture of estate whatsoever.

**forcible and
stolenmarria-
ges.**

§ 25. *And whereas,* Women, as well maidens as widows and wives, having substance, some in goods moveable, and some in land and tenements, and some being heirs apparent to their ancestors, for the lucre of such substances have been often times taken by misdoers, contrary to their will, and afterwards married to such misdoers, or to others by their consent, or defiled: *Be it further enacted,* That whatsoever person or persons shall take any woman so against her will unlawfully, that is to say, maid, widow, or

(38)

wife, such taking, and the procuring and abetting to the same, and also receiving willingly the same woman so taken, against her will, shall be fellony, and that such misdoers, takers and procurers to the same, and receivers, knowing the said offence in form aforesaid, shall be reputed and judged as principal fellons: *Provided always*, That this law shall not extend to any person taking any woman, only claiming her as his ward, or bond woman. **How punished,**

Proviso.

§ 26. If any person above the age of fourteen years, shall unlawfully take and carry away, or shall cause to be unlawfully taken and conveyed away, any maiden, or woman child, unmarried, being within the age of sixteen years, out of, or from the possession, and against the will of such person or persons, as then shall happen to have, by any lawful ways or means, the order, keeping, education, or governance of any such maiden, or woman child, and being thereof duly convicted, shall suffer imprisonment, without bail or mainprize, for any time not exceeding two years, as shall be adjudged against him. **Stealing women under 14 years of age.**

How punished.

§ 27. If any person or persons, shall so take away, or cause to be taken away, as is aforesaid, and deflower any such maid, or woman child, as is aforesaid, or shall against the will, or knowledge of the father of any such maiden, or woman child, if the father be in life, or against the will and knowledge of the mother of any such maiden, or woman child, having the custody and governance of such child, if the father be dead, by secret letters, messages or otherwise contract matrimony, with any such maiden, or wo- **Stealing and marrying them.**

(39)

man child, every person so offending, and being thereof lawfully convicted, shall suffer imprisonment of his body, for the space of five years, without bail or mainprize. **How punished.**

§ 28. No person or persons shall be prosecuted, tried or punished, for treason or other offence, punishable with death, (murder excepted) unless the indictment for the same, shall be found by a Grand Jury, within three years, next, after the treason, **Limitation of prosecutions for crimes.**

or other offence, punishable with death, shall be done or committed, nor shall any person be prosecuted or punished for any offence not punishable with death, unless the indictment for the same shall be found within two years from the time of committing the offence, or incurring the fine or forfeiture aforesaid; *Prvided,* That nothing herein contained, shall extend to any person or persons fleeing from justice.

Death how punishment of inflicted.

§ 29.   The manner of inflicting the punishment of death, shall be by hanging the person convicted, by the neck, until dead.

Persons convicted of crimes to be sold for fines & costs how & for what time.

§ 30.   When any person or persons shall on conviction of any crime or breach of any penal law, be sentenced to pay a fine or fines, with or without the costs of prosecution, it shall and may be lawful for the court before whom such conviction shall be had to order the Sheriff to sell or hire the person or persons so convicted, to service, to any person or persons who will pay the said fine and costs for such term of time, as the said court shall judge reasonable.

Punishment in case of absenting from service.

And if such person or persons, so sentenced and hired or sold, shall abscond from the service of his or her master or mistress, be-

(40)

fore the term of such servitude shall be expired, he or she so absconding, shall on conviction before a justice of the Peace, be whipped with thirty nine stripes, and shall moreover serve two days for every one so lost.

Courtstogive this act in charge to grand juries.

§ 31.   The Judges of the several courts of record in this Territory, shall give this act in charge to the Grand Jury, at each and every court, in which a Grand Jury shall be sworn.

JESSE B. THOMAS,
Speaker of the House of Representatives.
B. CHAMBERS,
President of the Council.

Approved—September 17th, 1807.
WILLIAM HENRY HARRISON.

CHAPTER VII.
An act regulating Marriages.

§ 1. MALE persons of the age of seventeen years, and female persons of the age of fourteen years, and not prohibited by the laws of God, may be joined in marriage.

At what age persons may marry.

It shall be lawful for any of the Judges of the General court, or the court of Common Pleas, or any of the Justices of the peace in their respective counties, ministers of any religious society, or congregation, within the district in which they are settled, and the society of Christians, called Quakers,

By whom.

(41)

in their public meetings, to join together as husband and wife, all persons of the above description, who may apply to them, agreeably to the rules and usages of the respective societies, to which the parties belong.

§ 2. Previously to persons being joined in marriage, as aforesaid, the intention of the parties shall be made known, by publishing the same for the space of fifteen days at least, either by the same being publicly and openly declared, three several Sundays, Holydays, or other days of public worship, in the meeting in the towns where the parties respectively belong, or by publication in writing, under the hand and seal of one of the Judges before mentioned, or of the justices of the Peace within the county, to be affixed in some public place in the town wherein the parties respectively dwell, or a license shall be obtained from the Clerks of the courts of Common Pleas, of their respective counties, which said license shall authorise the marriage of the parties, without publication, as is herein required, for which license the Clerk shall be entitled to have and receive the sum of one dollar, and the said Clerk shall keep a record of such licenses by them issued.

In what manner intention of the parties to be published &c.

Licence how obtained & from whom.

Fee.

§ 3. Male persons, under the age of twenty one years, and females under the age of eighteen, shall not be joined in marriage, without first obtaining the consent of their fathers, respectively, or in case of the death or incapacity of their fathers, or their mothers, or guardians: *Provided,* Such parents or guardians

under what age toobtain previous consent of parents &c.

live within the Territory; where persons not resident within the Territory, apply to be joined in mar-

(42)

riage, the consent of fathers, mothers and guardians shall be obtained in like manner as if they were citizens of the Territory.

Certificates of marriage by whom given, &c.

§ 4. A certificate of every marriage solemnized as aforesaid, signed by the judge or justice, or minister, solemnizing the same, or in case of Quakers, by the Clerk of the meeting, shall be by such Judge, Justice, Minister or Clerk, respectively transmitted to the Clerk of the court of Common Pleas, in their respective counties, wherein the marriage has been solemnized, within three months thereafter, to be entered on record by the said Clerk, an exemplification of which shall be evidence of such marriage.

Exemplification thereof to be deemed evidence.

GENl. W. JOHNSTON.
Speaker pro tem. of the House of Representatives.

B. CHAMBERS,
President of the Council.

Approved—September 17th, 1807.
WILLIAM HENRY HARRISON.

CHAPTER VIII.
An act for the appointment of Coroners, their duty and power.

Coroners to be appointed

§ 1. A Coroner shall be appointed in each county in this Territory.

Their duty & powers.

§ 2. Every Coroner within the county for which he is appointed, shall serve all writs and precepts, when the Sheriff or any of his deputies shall be a party to the

(43)

same, and shall return jurors in all causes where the Sheriff shall be interested, or related to either party. The Coroners, or in case of their absence, any Justice of the Peace of the respective counties, shall take inquests of violent deaths, and casual deaths happening within their respective counties, and shall before they enter

To take oath or affirmati-

upon the duties of their respective offices, be severally sworn or affirmed, to the faithful discharge thereof and give security in the same manner as sheriffs are obliged to do. **on and give security.**

§ 3. Every Coroner shall, as soon as he shall be certified of the dead body of any person supposed to have come to his or her death by violence, or casuality, found or lying within his county, make out his warrant, directed to the constable of the Township, where the dead body is found, or lying, requiring him forthwith to summon a jury of good and lawful men, of the same Township, not less than eighteen in all (so that twelve may be present) to appear before such Coroner, at the time and place in his warrant expressed, and to enquire upon a view of the body of (name here the person deceased, if known) there lying dead, how, in what manner, and by whom, he or she, came by his or her death; and every constable, to whom such warrant, shall be directed and delivered, shall forthwith execute the same, and shall repair to the place where the dead body is, at the time mentioned, and make return of the warrant with the proceedings thereon, unto the Coroner who granted the same. **To issue warrant for jury of inquest.**
To whom directed.
Number of jury.
When Jury to appear.
Duty of Constable.

Every Constable, failing unnecessarily, of

F

(44)

executing such warrant, or of returning the same, as aforesaid, shall forfeit and pay the sum of eight dollars; and every person summoned as a Juror, as aforesaid, that shall fail of appearance, without having a reasonable excuse, shall forfeit five dollars: which fines shall be recovered by action of debt, before any jurisdiction that can take cognizance of the same, and be applied to the use of the county. **Fine on failure by constable.**
How recoverable.

§ 4. The Coroner or Justice shall administer an oath, or affirmation, to twelve of the Jurors, that shall appear, to the foreman first; in the following manner: **Jurors to be sworn &c.**

"You do solemnly swear, [or solemnly, sincerely, and truly declare and affirm as the case is] that you will diligently enquire, and true presentment make, how, in what manner, and by whom, A B, who here lies dead, came to his death, and you shall deliver **Foreman's oath.**

to me the coroner of this county a true inquest thereof, according to such evidence as shall be laid before you, and according to your knowledge, so help you God."

§ 5. The other jurors shall swear or affirm, as the case may be, in the following form:

Oath of o-ther jurors. "Such oath or, affirmation, as your foreman hath taken, you, and each and every of you, shall well and truly observe and keep so help you God."

Charge to ju rors. § 6. The Jurors being sworn, the Coroner, or Justice shall give them a charge upon their oaths to declare of the death of the person; whether he, or she died of felony, or mischance, or accident; and if of felony, who were principals, and who were accesa-

(45)

ries, with what instrument, he or she was struck or wounded; and so of all prevailing circumstances which may come by presumption, and if by mischance or accident, whether by the act of man, and whether by hurt, fall, stroke, drowning or otherwise; also, to enquire of the persons who (if any) were present, the finders of the body, his, or her relations and neighbors; whether he or she was killed in the same place where the body was found; and if elsewhere, by whom, and how the body was brought thence, and of all other circumstances relating to the said death: and if he or she died of his or her own felony, then to enquire of the manner, means or instrument, and of all circumstances concerning it.

Proclamati-on for evi-dence when and how to be made. § 7. The Jury being charged, shall stand together, and proclamation shall be made for any persons who can give evidence, to draw near, and they shall be heard.

Coroner to issue warrant for witnesses. § 8. Every Coroner or Justice, is further impowered to send out his warrant for witnesses, commanding them to come before him to be examined, and to declare their knowledge concerning the matter in question. He shall administer an oath, or affirmation, to them in the following form:

Form of oath "You do solemnly swear, or solemnly, sincerly, and truly declare and affirm, that the evidence you shall give to this inquest concerning the death of A B, here lying dead, shall be the truth, the whole truth and nothing but the truth, so help you God."

§ 9. The evidence of such witnesses shall be in writing, subscribed by them; and if it relate to the trial of any person concerned in the death, then shall the Coroner or Justice

(46)

bind such witness, by recognizance in a reasonable sum, for their personal appearance at the next General or Circuit court, to be holden within the same county, there to give evidence accordingly: and commit to the common jail of the county, any witness or witnesses, refusing to enter into such recognizance; and shall return to the same court, the inquisition, written evidence, and recognizance by him taken; and the jury having viewed the body, heard the evidence, and made all the enquiry within their power, shall draw up and deliver unto the Coroner, their verdict upon the death under consideration, in writing, under their hands and seals.

§ 10. Upon an inquisition found before any Coroner, of the death of any person, by the felony or misfortune of another, he shall speedily inform one or more of the Justices of the same county thereof, to the intent, that the person killing, or being any way instrumental to the death, may be apprehended, examined, and secured, in order for trial.

JESSE B. THOMAS,
Speaker of the House of Representatives.
B. CHAMBERS,
President of the Council.

Approved—September 17th, 1807.

WILLIAM HENRY HARRISON.

(47)

CHAPTER IX.

An act to authorise and require the Courts of Common Pleas to divide the counties into Towhships, and to alter the boundaries of the same, when necessary.

§ 1 The Judges of the court of Common Pleas in the several counties within this Territory, shall in their terms respectively, proceed to divide the said counties into Townships, assigning to such Townships respectively, such limits and bounds, natural or

Marginal notes:

Evidence to be in writing and subscribed by witnesses.

Witnesses when to be bound in recognizance and when & where.

To commit in case of refusal,

Jurors verdict to be in writing under theirhands and seals.

When and in what cases coroner to give information to Justices. To what intent.

Courts of C. P. to divide counties into townships.

imaginary, as shall appear to be most proper, having due regard to the extent of country and number of inhabitants residing

Power to subdivide them. within the same; and the said Townships or any of them to subdivide from time to time, whenever the interest and convenience of the inhabitants thereof may seem to require it; and the said

Clerks their duty. court of Common Pleas, shall cause their Clerk to enter of record on the docket of the same court, the particular time when each Township is set off and the specific boundaries assigned thereto.

JESSE B. THOMAS,

Speaker of the House of Representatives.

B. CHAMBERS,

President of the Council.

Approved—September 17th, 1807.

WILLIAM HENRY HARRISON.

(48)

CHAPTER X.

An act for rendering authentic as Evidence in the courts of this Territory, the public acts, records and Judicial proceedings of Courts in the United States.

Legislative acts how authenticated. § 1. Every act of the Legislature of any one of the United States, having the seal of such state affixed thereto, shall be deemed authentic, and receive full faith and credit when offered in evidence, in any court of justice within this Territory.

Judicial acts how authenticated. § 2. And the records and judicial proceedings of the several courts of, or within the United States, shall be proved and admitted in the courts of justice in this Territory, by the attestation or certificate of the Clerk or Prothonotary, and the seal of the court annexed, together with the certificate of the Chief Justice, or one, or more of the Judges, or of the presiding Magistrate of every such court, as the case may be, that the person who signed such attestation or certificate was, at the time of subscrib

When to be read in evidence. ing it, the Clerk or Prothonotary of such court; and the said records, and judicial proceedings, authenticated as aforesaid, shall have full faith and credit given to them in every court within this Territory, as by law or usage they have in the courts of the United

States, or of any one of the states, whence the said records are, or shall be taken; anything in

(49)

this, or any other act contained, to the contrary notwithstanding.

JESSE B. THOMAS,
Speaker of the House of Representatives.
B. CHAMBERS,
President of the Council.

Approved—September 17th, 1807.
WILLIAM HENRY HARRISON.

CHAPTER XI.
An act regulating Prisons, and Prison bounds.

§ 1. The several courts of Common Pleas within this Territory, shall lay off and assign by metes and bounds, around and adjoining each county jail, a certain and determinate space of land, to be termed prison bounds: *Provided,* That such prison bounds in no instance, extend in any direction from said jail more than two hundred yards, which prison bounds when fixed and assigned, shall be recorded amongst the public records of said courts, a copy of which shall be delivered to the jailor, to be by him fixed up in some conspicuous place in the debtors room, for the government of such of them, as shall be entitled to the benefit of such prison bounds. *(Courts to lay out prison bounds, and recorded copies in debtors room.)*

§ 2. Any person imprisoned for debt either upon *mesne* process or an execution, shall be permitted and allowed, the priviledge and benefit of the prison bounds, but in no instance to pass over or without said limits: *Provided,* That such prisoner before he shall be entitled to such priviledge, shall give bond with sufficient surety or sureties, living within the county, to the creditor or creditors, in double the sum for which such prisoner stands committed, conditioned, that from the executing such bond he or she will continue a true prisoner, in the custody of the jailer, or person keeper, and within the limits of the said prison bounds, *(debtors allowed benefit of bounds)* *(Giving bond & security in double the debt for keeping within the bounds.)*

(50)

until discharged by law, without committing any manner of escape; and in order to prevent any oppression under pretence of the surety or sureties being insufficient, two disinterested Justices of the Peace for said county, shall be called to approve of the surety or sureties, and the same being approved of by them shall be deemed sufficient, and if the creditor or creditors, shall refuse to take and accept the bond, the same shall be lodged with the sheriff, to be by him kept, until the creditor, or creditors, shall demand the same; and upon putting such bond in suit, when the condition shall be broken, judgment shall be entered up for the penalty, and no relief in chancery shall be allowed therein.

§ 3.   If any action or suit shall be brought or instituted, against any Sheriff or jailor, for any manner of escape committed by any prisoner, allowed the benefit and priviledge of prison bounds, having first given bond as by this law required, such Sheriff or jailor shall have the liberty of pleading the general issue, and giving this act in evidence.

§ 4.   If any person or persons shall direct-

(51)

ly or indirectly, by any way or means, howsoever, without the knowledge or privity of the keeper, convey any instrument, tool, or other thing whatsoever, to any prisoner, or into any prison, whereby any prisoner might break the prison, or work himself, or herself unlawfully out of the same, every person so offending, shall forfeit and pay, such fine, as by the direction of the court shall be imposed, not exceeding one hundred dollars, according to the nature of the cause of the prisoners committment, or suffer such corporeal punishment, not exceeding forty stripes, as the court shall inflict, and if it shall so happen that the prisoner shall make his or her escape, by means of any instrument, tool, or other thing so conveyed, without the knowledge and privity of the keeper, the person so conveying the same, shall be liable to pay all such sums of money as the prisoner stood committed for, if on civil process, and shall also have inflicted on him or her, all such punishment, as the escaped prisoner would be liable unto if a criminal; and had been convicted of the charge for which he or she had been com-

Two justices of the peace to approve of the surities.

If bonds forfeited judgment to be for penalty withont relief.

Sheriffs sued for allowing P B. may plead the g. issue.

Persons conveying tools &c. into any prison, where by prisoners might break out.

To be fined or whipped.

If prisoner actually escape the persons so conveying tools &c. to what punishment liable.

mitted, unless such prisoner would be liable to capital punishment, in which case, the person assisting in such escape, shall be punished by fine, imprisonment, whipping, pillory, or setting on the gallows with a rope about his or her neck, or any one or more of said punishments, as the court having cognizance thereof shall think proper to inflict.

§ 5. If any jailor or prison keeper, shall voluntarily suffer a prisoner committed un-

Jailor suffering voluntary escape of prisoners, punishment of.

G

(52)

to him, to escape, he shall suffer and undergo the like pains, punishments and penalties, as the prisoner so escaping, should, or ought by law to have suffered and undergone for the crime or crimes, wherewith he stood charged, if he had been convicted thereof, and if any jailor or prison keeper, shall through negligence, suffer any prisoner accused of any crime to escape, he shall pay such fine, as the Judges of the court before whom he is convicted, shall in their discretion inflict, according to the nature of the offence, for which the escaped prisoner stood convicted.

Suffering negligent escape, punishment of.

§ 6. *Provided nevertheless,* That if any person who may be committed for debt, shall violently escape from prison, without connivance of the Sheriff, or keeper, and the sheriff, jailor or prison keeper, shall within three months, next after such escape, recover the prisoner so escaped, and recommit him to prison again, then the Sheriff shall be liable to nothing further than the costs of such action or actions, as may have been commenced against him for such escape.

On violent escape of prisoner for debt if sheriff or jailor retake him in three months there after sheriff only liable to costs.

§ 7. All warrants, mittimusses, writs and instruments of writing of any kind, or the attested copies of them, by which any prisoner may be committed, enlarged or liberated, shall be safely kept (regularly filed in their order of time) in a suitable box for the purpose, provided by the keeper o the jail, under the Sheriffs' direction, and upon the death, or removal of any Sheriff, the box, with the contents thereof, shall be delivered to his successor in office, under the penalty of one hundred and fifty

Warrants &c. to be regularly filed in a box provided by the jailor, & delivered over to succeding sheriff under penalty of 150 dollars.

(53)

dollars, to be paid by the Sheriff removed, or his executors or administrators, in case of the death of the Sheriff, to be recovered by any person who shall prosecute therefor to effect, in any court having jurisdiction to try the same.

Judges of the court of common pleas at every term to enquire into the state of prisons &c.

§ 8. It shall be the duty of the Judges at the begining of every court of Common Pleas, to enquire into the state of the prisons in their respective counties, with regard to the sufficiency of such prisons, the condition and accommodation of the prisoners, and shall, from time to time, take such legal measures, as may best tend to secure the prisoners from escape, sickness and infection, and to have the jails cleansed from filth and vermin.

Seperate rooms for the sexes.

Sheriff to provide meat &c to certain criminals.

§ 9. The Sheriffs shall keep seperate rooms for the sexes, except where they are lawfully married, and be responsible that his jailor at all times provide proper meat and drink, for all criminals committed to the prison of the county, if such prisoners have no other convenient way of supplying themselves with provisions, which shall always pass to them through the keepers hands, and in every case when the Sheriff or jailor shall be at the expense of furnishing meat, drink or fire-wood, to a prisoner in jail for a crime or at the suit of the United States, who is not of sufficient ability in point of property, to re-pay or indemnify such

Sheriff is to make out his account on oath before judges of commonpleas who shall make allowance out of county charges.

Sheriff or jailor, their reasonable expence and charges for supplying such prisoner; in every such case the Sheriff or jailor shall make out his account thereof, and on oath shall testify the truth of the same before the Judges of the court of Common Pleas, who shall tax the same as

(54)

they shall think just and reasonable, and lay the amount thereof in the yearly estimate of the county charges.

Certain persons on civil process to be furnished by sheriff with bread & water.

§ 10. In every case, where any person is committed to prison in a civil action, either on *mense process,* or an execution for debt, trespass, slander, or other cause of action, at the suit of one citizen against another, or at the suit of an alien against a citizen, or at the suit of a citizen, against an alien ally, in every such case, it shall be the duty of the Sheriff to provide only the daily bread and water of such prisoner, and he is hereby directed to furnish the same regularly to every such prisoner, who is not of sufficient ability in point of property, to provide for his or her own support, while in prison, and the expence and charges occurring to the Sheriff or jailor, herein, shall be repaid to him by the prisoner, so soon as the prisoner shall be liberated from the jail; for the recovery of which the Sheriff or jailor shall have his action at law, against the prisoner, in any court where the same may be cognizable, and when any prisoner shall be committed to jail in a civil action as aforesaid, and shall provide for his or her own support, in a way wherein the Sheriff or jailor, shall have no concern, it shall be the duty of the jailor or prison keeper to admit to the wicket grate, or small window of the prison, in which such prisoner shall be confined, any person who may come to administer to the wants of such prisoner, by furnishing him or her with meat and drink, which shall be conveyed through such small window or grate, that the security of the prison be not too fre-

Sheriffs remedy for recovery of costs and charges for keeping such prisoner

Prisoners right to furnish themselves with necessaries admitted thro' wicket grate or small window of the prison.

(55)

quently exposed by opening the doors thereof.

§ 11.   All fines and penalties, arising upon the breach of this act, shall be for the use of the county, where the offence is committed, or the duty neglected; and the same remedy shall be had for the recovery thereof, as in other cases, where duties are enjoined by statute, and no particular mode of prosecution directed; in case of default, it shall be the duty of the attorney, prosecuting the pleas of the United States, to prosecute for the same, either by writ or indictment, and the fine when recovered, shall be paid to the Sheriff or Treasurer, for the use of the county.

Fines to be for the use of the county.

How recovered & paid to the sheriff or the county treasurer,

JESSE B. THOMAS,
Speaker of the House of Representatives.
B. CHAMBERS,
President of the Council.

Approved—September 17th, 1807.
WILLIAM HENRY HARRISON.

CHAPTER XII.

An act subjecting Real Estates to Execution for Debt.

Real estate liable to be seized & sold upon judgment & execution. § 1. TO the end, that no creditors may be defrauded of debts justly due to them, from persons who have sufficient real, if not personal estates to satisfy the same; all lands, tenements and hereditaments, whatsoever,

(56)

where no sufficient personal estate can be found, shall be liable to be seized and sold, upon judgment and execution obtained.

If lands seized do not sell for amount of execution, sheriff on an other writ to seize any other lands &c in execntion, and sell by public sale. § 2. In case the lands, tenements and hereditaments, seized and taken in execution, shall not on a sale thereof, produce the amount of the debt, damages and costs due thereon, it shall and may be lawful for the Sheriff, or other officer, by another writ, to seize and take, any other lands, tenements, and hereditaments, in execution, and thereupon, with all convenient speed, with, or without any writ of *venditioni exponas,* to make public sale thereof, for the most they will yield, and pay the price or value of the same, to the party towards satisfaction of his debt, damages and cost.

Sheriffs duty before sale to advertise the time & place of sale at least 10 days But before any such sale be made, the Sheriff or other officer, shall cause so many writings to be made upon parchment, or good paper, as the debtor or defendant shall reasonably desire or request, or so many without such request as may be sufficient to signify and give notice of such sales or vendues and of the day and hour when, and the place where the same will be, and what lands or tenements, are to be sold, and where they lie; which notice shall be given to the defendant, and the parchments or papers, fixed by the Sheriff or other officer, in the most public places of the county, at least ten days before sale; and upon such sale the **Sheriff to give the buyer a deed therefor.** Sheriff, or other officer, shall make return thereof, endorsed or annexed to the said writ of execution, and give the buyer a deed duly executed, and acknowledged in court for what is sold; but in case the said lands and hereditaments, so to be exposed

(57)

Proceedings in case lands do not sell. cannot be sold, then the officer shall make return upon the writ, that he exposed such lands or tenements to sale, and the same

remained in his hands unsold for want of buyers, which return
shall not make the officer liable to answer the debt or damages
contained in such writ, but the writ of *levari facias* shall forthwith   **Levari facias**
be awarded, and directed to the proper officer, commanding him
to deliver to the party, such part or parts of those lands, tenements and hereditaments, as shall satisfy his debt, damages and
interest, from the time of the judgment given, with costs of suit,
according to the valuation of twelve men; to hold to him, as his
free tenement, in satisfaction of the debt, damages and costs, or
so much thereof, as those lands by the valuation thereof, as aforesaid, shall amount unto, and if it shall fall short, the party may
afterwards have execution for the residue, against the defendant's
body, lands or goods, as the laws of this Territory shall direct and
appoint, from time to time, concerning other executions; all which
said lands, tenements, hereditaments and premises, so as aforesaid   **Purchasers to**
to be sold or delivered, by the Sheriff, or officer aforesaid, with all   **hold for such**
their appurtinances, shall or may be quietly or peaceably held, and   **estate &c. as**
debtors had
enjoyed by the person or persons, or bodies politic, to whom the   **at the time**
same shall be sold or delivered, and by his and their heirs, success-   **of taking in**
execution.
ors and assigns, as fully and amply, and for such estate or estates,
and under such rents and services, as he or they, for whose debt
or duty, the same shall be sold or de-

(58)

livered, might, could or ought to do, at or before the taking
thereof in execution.

§ 3. *Provided always,* That the messuage, or lands or tene-   **Proviso as to**
ments, upon which the defendant is chiefly seated, shall be the last   **defts. chief**
seat.
taken and sold on execution, before the expiration of one whole
year after judgment is given, to the intent, that the defendant, or
any other for him, may redeem the same.

§ 4. Where default or defaults have been, or shall be made   **Proceedings**
or suffered, by any mortgagor or mortgagors of land, tenements,   **on mortga-**
ges.
or other hereditaments within this Territory, or by his, her or
their heirs, executors, administrators and assigns, of, or in payment of the mortgage money, or performance of the condition or
conditions, which they, or any of them, should have paid or performed, or ought to pay or perform, in such manner and form,

and according to the purport, tenor and effect of the respective provisoes, conditions or covenants, comprised in their deeds of mortgage or defeasance, and at the days times and places in the same deeds respectively mentioned and contained, in every such case, it shall and may be lawful, to, and for the mortgagee or mortgagees, and him, her or them, that grant the said deed of defeasance, and his, her or their heirs, executors, administrators or assigns, any time after the expiration of twelve months, next ensuing, the last day whereon the said mortgage money ought to be paid, or other conditions performed as aforesaid; to sue forth a writ or writs of *scire facias,* which the Clerk of the court of Common Pleas for the county where the said mortgaged lands or hereditaments lie, is hereby empowered

Mortgagee in 12 months after default, of payment, may issue fi-rafacias from the court of common pleas of the proper coun. ty.

(59)

and required to make out and dispatch, directed to the proper officer; requiring him by honest and lawful men of the neighbour-hood, to make known to the mortgagor or mortgagors, his, her or their heirs, executors or administrators, that he, or they, be and appear before the Judges or Justices of the said court or courts, to shew if any thing he or they have to say, wherefore the said mortgaged premises ought not to be seized and taken in execution for payment of the said mortgage money with interest, or to satisfy the damages which such plaintiff in such *scire facias* shall upon the record suggest, for the breach, or non-performance of the said conditions. And if the defendant in such *scire facias,* appear, he or she may plead satisfaction or payment of part, or all the mortgage money, or any such other lawful plea, in avoidance of the deed or debt, as the case may require, but if the defendant in such *scire facias,* will not appear on the day whereon the writ shall be made returnable, then if the case be such, damages only, are to be recovered, an inquest shall be forthwith charged to enquire thereof; and the definitive judgment therein, as well as all other judgments to be given upon such *scire facias,* shall be entered, that the plaintiff in the *scire facias* shall have execution by *levari facias,* directed to the proper officer; by virtue whereof the said mortgaged premises shall be taken in execution, and exposed to sale in manner aforesaid, and, upon sale, conveyed to the

Defdt. may appear and plead.

On judgment against mortgagor &c. the mortgaged premises to be sold on execution, and conveyed to the buyer.

buyer or buyers thereof, and the money or price of the same rendered to the mortgagee or creditor, but

H

(60)

for want of buyers, to be delivered to the mortgagee, or creditor, in manner and form as is herein above directed, concerning other lands and hereditaments to be sold, and delivered upon executions, for other debts or damages. And when the said lands and hereditaments shall be sold, or delivered as aforesaid, the person or persons, to whom they shall be sold or delivered, shall and may hold and enjoy the same, with their appurtenances, for such estate or estates as they were sold or delivered, clearly discharged and freed from all equity and benefit of redemption, and all other incumbrances made or suffered by the mortgagors, their heirs or assigns; and such sales shall be available in law; and the respective vendees, mortgagees, or creditors, their heirs and assigns, shall hold and enjoy the same, freed and discharged, as aforesaid. But before such sales be made, notice shall be given in writing, in manner and form as is herein above directed, concerning the sales of lands upon executions, any law or usage to the contrary notwithstanding.

Sheriffs duty before sale.

§ 5. *Provided also,* That when any of the said lands, tenements or hereditaments, which, by the direction and authority of this law, are to be sold for the payment of debts and damages, in manner aforesaid, shall be sold for more than will satisfy the same debts, or damages, and reasonable costs; then the sheriff or other officer who shall make the sale, must render the overplus to the debtor or defendant; and then, and not before, the said officer shall be discharged thereof, upon record, in the same

Overplus of sales, if any, to be by sheriff rendered to the debtor and then, & not before the sheriff or officer shall be discharged therefrom upon record.

(61)

court where he shall make return of his proceedings concerning the said sales.

§ 6. *Provided also,* That no sale or delivery which shall be made, by virtue of this law, shall be extended to create any further term or estate, to the vendees, mortgagees, or creditors, than the lands or hereditaments, so sold, or delivered, shall appear to be mortgaged for, by the said respective mortgages, or defeazible deeds.

In case judgment reversed, the premises sold shall not be restored, nor sale avoided, but restitution shall be made only of the price for which sold.

§ 7. *Provided also,* That if any of the said judgments which do or shall warrant the awarding of the said writ of execution, whereupon any lands, tenements or hereditaments, have been, or shall be sold, shall, at any time hereafter be reversed for any error or errors; then, and in every such case, none of the said lands, tenements or hereditaments, so as aforesaid taken, or sold, or to be taken or sold upon executions, nor any part thereof shall be restored, nor the sheriff's sale or delivery thereof avoided; but restitution in such cases shall be made only of the money or price for which such lands were or shall be sold.

JESSE B. THOMAS,
Speaker of the House of Representatives.
B. CHAMBERS,
President of the Council.

Approved—September 17th, 1807.
WILLIAM HENRY HARRISON.

(62)

CHAPTER XIII.
An act allowing Foreign Attachments.

Real & personal estate of non residents may be attached for debt or other demand.

§ 1. THE lands and tenements, goods, chattels and effects, rights and credits, of every person or persons, non-residents in this Territory, shall, and may be attached, for the payment of any just debt, or other demand, by a writ or writs, to be issued out of the General court, or any Circuit court, or court of Common Pleas, and, as early as may be, shall and may be proceeded against in the same manner as is directed against the lands, tenements, hereditaments and estates of absconding debtors, except where otherwise herein directed.

Party applying for writ of attachmt. to make oath &c. that defendant is not

§ 2. *Provided,* That every person or persons, applying for such writ or writs of attachment, shall, before the issuing thereof, make oath or affirmation (and which shall be filed in the proper clerk's office,) that he, she or they, verily believe, that the person or persons, against whose estate or estates, the application is made, is, or are not, at that time resident within the Territory, and that such person or persons, is, or are, justly indebted unto the said plaintiff or plaintiffs, in a certain sum or sums of money, as nearly as may be, to the amount of the debt, or other demand, of such plaintiff or plaintiffs, as the case may admit, and as he, she or they can lawfully swear or affirm to. to his belief a resident of the territory, and to amt. of demand as nearly as may be,

§ 3.   Where two or more persons are jointly indebted, either as joint obligors, partners, or otherwise, then the writ or writs of attachment, shall and may be issued a- Where joint obligors or partners &c. attachment may issue a-gainst joint and seperate estate of such joint debtors, and in what manner, or against heirs, executors or administra-tors.

(63)

gainst the seperate and joint estate of such joint debtors, or any of them, either by their proper names, or by, or in the name or style of the partnership, or by whatsoever other name or names such joint debtors shall be generally reputed, known, or distinguished within this Territory, or against the heirs, or executors, or administrators of them, or either or any of them.   And the lands, tenements, goods, chattels and effects, or any of them, shall be liable to be seized and taken, for the satisfaction of any just debt or other demand, and may be sold to satisfy the same.

§ 4.   No judgment shall be entered in any attachment, hereby directed to be issued, until the expiration of twelve months, during which term the party suing out the attachment, shall, and he hereby is required, to cause notice thereof to be advertised in one of the public news-papers of this Territory, at least three times, which advertisement shall set forth, that a foreign attachment or attachments, have been issued, at whose suit, and against whose estate or estates, the same so issued.   And that unless the debtor or debtors, whose estate or estates are so seized, shall appear by himself or attorney, to give special bail, to answer such suit, that then judgment will be entered against such debtor or debtors by default, and the estate or estates attached, be sold for the satisfaction of the plaintiff; *Provided always,* That where any goods or chattels of a perishable nature shall be so seized, it shall and may be lawful for the court, from which such attachment issued, to order the said perishable property, so attached, to be No judgt. to be entered in less than 12 months, dur-ing which time, notice thereof to be advertised, how & in what manner Courts power to order sale of perishable property pro-ceeds of sale to remain in

(64)

sheriffs hands
until judg-
ment &c.

Creditors not
to receive a-
ny share of
estates sold,
until they
give bond
with security
to be approv-
ed of by the
court in dou-
ble the sum
conditioned
to refund in
12 months,
such sums as
on trial shall
appear to
have been re-
ceived & not
justly due to
such creditor
together
with costs.

sold by the sheriff, by auction, who shall detain the proceeds of
the sale thereof in his hands, subject to the order of the court,
until final judgment and execution.

§ 5.   No creditor or creditors entitled to any share of estates,
sold under this law, shall receive the same, until he, she or they,
shall enter into bond, to the defendant or defendants, with good
and sufficient security, to be approved of by the court, and also to
be filed in the office aforesaid, in double the sum to be received,
with condition thereunder written, that the party so receiving,
shall appear to any suit or suits, that shall or may be brought, by
such defendant or defendants, within the space of twelve months,
then next ensuing, and shall pay unto such defendant or defendants, all such sums of money, which on trial to be had thereon,
shall appear to have been received, and not justly due and owing
to such creditor or creditors, together with costs of suit.

JESSE B. THOMAS,
Speaker of the House of Representatives.
B. CHAMBERS,
President of the Council.

Approved—September 17th, 1807.

WILLIAM HENRY HARRISON.

(65)

CHAPTER XIV.
An act to prevent unnecessary delays in causes after issue joined.

If pltffs. aft-
er issue join-
ed delay the
trial the crts.
upon motion
& notice giv-
en in open
court the pre
ceeding term
to give jdmt.
of non-suit,
unless upon
cause shewn,
further time

§ 1.   WHERE any issue is, or shall be joined, in any action
or suit at law, in any of the courts of this Territory, and the
plaintiff or plaintiffs in any such action or suit, hath, or have
neglected, or shall neglect to bring such issue on, to be tried according to the course and practice of the said courts, respectively;
it shall and may be lawful for the Judges, or Justices, of the said
courts, respectively, at any time after such neglect, upon motion
made in open court, (due notice thereof having been given, in
open court the preceeding term) to give the like judgment for the
defendant or defendants, in every such action or suit, as in cases

of non-suit, unless the said Judges or Justices, shall upon just cause, and reasonable terms, allow any further time or times, for the trial of such issue, and if the plaintiff or plaintiffs shall neglect to try such issue, within the time or times so allowed, then, and in every such case, the said Judges or Justices, shall proceed to give judgment, as aforesaid.

§ 2. *Provided always,* That all judgments given by virtue of this law, shall be of the like force and effect as judgment upon non-suits, and of no other force or effect.

§ 3. *Provided also,* That the defendant or defendants, shall, upon such judgment, be awarded his, her or their costs, in any action or suit, where he, she or they would

(66)

upon non-suit, be entitled to the same, and in no other action or suit whatsoever.

JESSE B. THOMAS,
Speaker of the House of Representatives.
B. CHAMBERS,
President of the Council.

Approved—September 17th, 1807.
WILLIAM HENRY HARRISON.

CHAPTER XV.
An act concerning persons Conscientiously scrupulous to take an Oath in the common form.

§ 1. ALL and all manner of crimes, offences, matters, causes and things, to be enquired of, heard, tried and determined, or done, or performed by virtue of any law or otherwise, shall and may be enquired of, heard, tried and determined by Judges, Justices, witnesses and inquest. And all other persons, qualifying themselves according to their conscientious persuasions, respectively; those of the people commonly called Quakers, by taking the solemn affirmation, and those of the persuasions who swear with uplifted hand or hands, by taking an oath in the following words: 'I, A B, do swear or affirm (as the case may be) that I will, (and so forth)⠀⠀⠀⠀and that as I shall answer to God at the great day.'—Which oath, so taken, by persons who conscienti-

Marginal notes:

be allowed if after such further time allowed pltffs. neglect to try such issues, the like judgment to be given. Judgmts. given to be judgmts. of non-suit only Upon such jdgmts. dfts. to recover costs &c.

Persons scrupulous to take an oath may take an affirmation &c.

Form of an oath or affirmation.

(67)

Affirmation to have the same effect in law as an oath. ously refuse to take an oath, in the common form, shall be deemed and taken, in law, to have the same effect with an oath taken in the common form.

Punhishment for false affirmation same as for perjury. § 2. If any person shall be legally convicted of taking a false affirmation or of falsely swearing, under the form herein particularly prescribed, he or she, shall incur, and suffer the same pains, penalties, disabilities, and forfeitures, as persons convicted of wilful, and corrupt perjury, do incur and suffer by law.

No person enabled to exercise an office before he takes oath, &c. to the government of the U. S. and oath &c. of office. § 3. *Provided always,* That nothing herein contained, shall be held, deemed, or construed, to enable any such person to receive, take, or exercise, any office, judicial or ministerial, before he shall take the oath or oaths to the government, according to his conscience, and agreeably to the directions of an act of the United States, entitled "An act prescribing the time and manner of administering certain oaths," and also the oaths of office.

JESSE B. THOMAS,
Speaker of the House of Representatives.
B. CHAMBERS,
President of the Council.

Approved—September 17th, 1807.
WILLIAM HENRY HARRISON.

I

(68)

CHAPTER XVI.

An act authorising the granting of letters Testamentary, and letters of Administration, for the settlement of intestate's estates, and for other purposes.

The duty of clerks respecting wills &c. and power of court. § 1. THE Clerks of the courts of Common Pleas, of each county in this Territory, shall take proofs of last wills and testaments, and grant letters of testamentary, and letters of administration: *Provided however,* That the said letters testamentary, and letters of administration, granted by such Clerk in the vacation, may be repealed by sentence of the court of Common Pleas for the county at their term, next after the granting of such letters, and other letters may, by the same court, be granted to any person applying therefor, and having legal right thereto, in which cases, all acts and proceedings, done and made, by the former executor or administrator, shall be legal and valid, and such further proceedings may be had and made, in the name or names of the succeeding executor or administrator, as though the original suits, or proofs had been commenced in his, her or their name or names.

§ 2. The said Clerks shall record last wills and testaments, and make entries of the granting of letters testamentary, and letters of administration, and shall receive, put on file, and carefully preserve all bonds, inventories, accounts, and other documents necessary to be perpetuated in their office.

Clerk to record and put on file all papers &c.

§ 3. All bonds that under, or by authority of this law, are directed to be taken,

(69)

shall be made to the Judges of the respective courts of Common Pleas.

To whom bonds to be made payable

§ 4. The courts of Common Pleas of each county of this Territory, shall have full power to award process, and cause to come before them, all, and every such person and persons, who, as guardians, trustees, tutors, executors, administrators, or otherwise, are, or shall be intrusted with, or in any wise accountable for any lands, tenements, goods, chattels or estates, belonging, or which shall belong, to any orphan, or person under age, and cause them to make and exhibit, within a reasonable time, true and perfect inventories and accounts of the said estates.

Courts power to award process & cause to come before them all guardians &c and cause themto make inventories and accounts &c.

§ 5. When any complaint is made to the said court, that an executrix, having minors of her own, or being concerned for others, is married, or likely to be espoused to another husband, without securing the minors portions, or estates, or that an executor, or other person, having the care and trust of minors estates, is likely to prove insolvent, or shall refuse, or neglect to exhibit, true and perfect inventories, or give full and just accounts of the said estates, come to their hands or knowledge, then, and in every such case, the said court is hereby required to call all, and every such executors and trustees, and also such guardians or tutors of orphans or minors, as have been formerly appointed, or shall at

How minors estates are to be secured on complaint of an executrix married or likely to marry, where executor is likely to become insolvent.

any time hereafter be appointed, to give security to the orphans
or minors, by mortgage or bond, in such sums, and with such
securities, as the said court shall think reasonable, conditioned for
the performance of their respective

(70)

trusts, and for the true payment and delivery, to, and for the use
and behoof of such orphans as they are concerned for, or such as
shall legally represent them, the legacies, portions, shares and divi-
dends of estates, real and personal, belonging to such orphans or
minors, so far as they have assest; as also for their maintenance
and education, as the said court shall think fit to order, for the
benefit and best advantage of such orphans, as is usual in such
cases.

**Executor &c
by leave of
court placing
minors mon-
ey at interest
not to be ac-
countable in
case of loss,
but otherwise
while in their
own hands.**

§ 6. Any of the said executors, administrators, guardians,
or trustees, may, by the leave, and direction of the said court, put
out their minors money to interest, upon such security as the court
shall allow of ; and if such security to taken, *bona fide,* and without
fraud, shall happen to prove insufficient, it shall be the minor's
loss. But if no person who may be willing to take the said money
at interest, with such security, as can be found by the person, so
as aforesaid, concerned for the minors, nor by any others, then the
said executors, administrators, guardians or trustees, shall in such
cases be responsible for the principal money only, until it can be
put out at interest, as aforesaid.

**Term of pay-
ment of mi-
nors money
so lent not to
exceed 12
months.**

§ 7. *Provided always,* That the day of payment of the
money, so to be put out to interest, at any one time, shall not
exceed twelve months, from the date of the obligation, or other
security taken for the same, and so *toties quoties,* when and so
often as the said money shall be paid in, or come to the hands of
the said executors, guardians or trustees.

§ 8. *Provided also,* That no executors,

[71]

administrators or guardians, shall be liable to pay interest, for the
surplusage of the decedent's estate, remaining in their hands or
power, and belonging to the minors, when the accounts of their

**Executors
&c. how lia-
ble to interest**

administration are, or ought to be settled, and adjusted before the said courts.

§ 9. The said courts shall have full power and authority, to admit orphans or minors, when, and as often as there may be occasion, to make choice of guardians, or tutors, and to appoint guardians, next friends, or tutors, over such as the said court shall judge too young, or incapable, according to the rules of the common law, to make choice themselves, and at the instance and request of the said executors, administrators, guardians or tutors, to order and direct the binding, or putting out of minors, apprentices to trades, husbandry, or other employments, as shall be thought fit. And all guardians and *prochein amies,* who shall be appointed, by any of the said courts, shall be allowed and received, without further admittance, to prosecute and defend all actions and suits, relating to the orphans or minors, as the case may require, in any court or courts of this Territory.

Courts to admit minors to make choice of guardians &c. and to appoint guardians &c. to such as are too young to choose for themselves and order the binding of minors to trades &c. guardians so appointed to prosecute & defend their minors.

§ 10. If any person or persons, being duly summoned to appear in any of the said courts of Common Pleas, relating to any matter or thing, by this law made cognizable in the said court, ten days before the time appointed for their appearance, shall make default, the said courts may send their attachment, for contempts, and force obedience to their warrants, sentences and orders, concerning any matters or things, cog-

Power of the court in case of contempts &c:

(72)

nizable in the same courts, by imprisonment of body, or sequestration of lands or goods.

§ 11. *Provided always,* That if any person or persons, shall be agrieved, by any definitive sentence, or judgment of the said court, it shall be lawful for them to appeal from the same, to the General, or Circuit courts, which appeal, upon security given, as is usual in such cases, shall be granted accordingly.

Appeal to the general and circuit courts

§ 12. If any of the said executors, administrators, guardians, or trustees, did, or shall receive and give discharges, for any sums of money, debts, rents, or duties, belonging to any orphan or minor, for whom they are, or were interested, it is hereby declared, that all such discharges, or receipts, shall be binding, to, and upon the orphan or minor, when he, or she, attains to full age,

Discharges or receipts given by executor &shall bind minors or orphans.

and shall be effectual in law, to discharge the person or persons that take the same.

Minors attaining full, age how they shall act, on refusal how the court shall act.

§ 13. When any of the said minors attain to the full age, and the person or persons, so, as aforesaid, intrusted or concerned for them, having rendered their accounts to the court of Common Pleas, according to law, and paid the minors their full due, then such minors shall acknowledge satisfaction in the said court; but in case any of them refuse so to do, then the said court shall certify how the said persons concerned have accounted and paid, which shall be a sufficient discharge to the guardians or tutors, and to the trustees, executors or administrators, who shall so account and pay, and thereupon all bonds entered into, for

(73)

payment of such orphans portions, shall be delivered up and cancelled.

No minor or orphan to be put under the Control of those of different religgion.

§ 14. *Provided always,* That none of the said courts of Common Pleas, shall have any power to order or commit the tuition or guardianship of any orphans or minors, or bind them apprentices, to any person or persons, whose religious persuasion shall be different from what the parents of such orphan or minor professed, at the time of their decease; or against the minors own mind, or inclination, so far as he or she has discretion and capacity to express or signify the same; or to persons that are not of good repute, where others of good credit, and of the same persuasion may, or can be found.

The courts to have due regard to the direction of all last wills

§ 15. *Provided also,* That the said courts of Common Pleas, and all others concerned in the execution of this law, shall have due regard to the direction of all last wills, and to the true intent and meaning of the testators, in all matters and things that shall be brought before them concerning the same.

All Bonds given relating to minors or decendents estates, how to whom liable,

§ 16. All such bonds or obligations, as are by this, or any other law of the Territory, directed, or required to be given to the said courts, relating to minors, or decedents estates, and all such bonds as by any law are directed to be given by any Judge or other officers or persons in office, for the due execution of his or their respective offices or employments, are hereby declared to be to, and for the use of, and in trust for, the person or persons concerned;

and the benefit thereof shall be extended, from time to time, for the relief and advantage of the party grieved, by the misfeazance, or non-

(74)

feazance of the officers that did, or shall give the same.

§ 17. And when any of the said bonds shall be put in suit, and judgment thereupon obtained, the judgment shall remain in the same nature the bonds were; and no execution shall issue thereupon, before the party grieved shall, by writ of *scire facias,* summon the person or persons against whom the said judgment is obtained, to appear and shew cause, why execution shall not issue upon the said judgment. And if the party grieved shall prove what damages he sustained, and thereupon a verdict be found for him, the court where such suit is, shall award execution for so much as the jury shall then find, with costs, and no more—and the former judgment is hereby declared still to remain cautionary, for the satisfaction of such others as shall legally prove themselves damnified, and recover their damages in manner aforesaid.

§ 18. The Clerks of the said courts of Common Pleas, and all others, in whose hands the said bonds shall be deposited or lodged, are hereby required to give any person injured and requesting the same, a true copy of any of the said bonds, he paying thirty seven and a half cents, for the same, and to produce the original in court, upon any trial that shall be had for the breach of any of them, if required by the court. And if the person in whose hands the said bonds shall be lodged, or come to, shall refuse, or delay to give copies thereof, and produce the original in court, as aforesaid, he or they, shall forfeit and pay to the party grieved, treble damages; to be reco-

(75)

vered against the officer who gave such bonds and his sureties, by action of debt, *bill, plaint,* or information, in any court in the Territory, where no *essoin,* protection or *wager* of law, or any more than one *imparlance* shall be allowed.

§ 19. The Clerks of the courts of Common Pleas, shall, upon granting letters of administration of the goods and chattels

Side notes:

When such bonds are sued and judgment had, no extn. to issue before a scire facias sent out—damages and costs how to be awarded on verdict, former judgment tostand cautionary.

Clerks to give copies on demand of such bonds,

Fee thereon,

To produce the original in court if required,

Clerk refusing or delaying to give such copies,

or produce the original in court, to pay treble damages.

Administrators to give

bond with two or more sureties &c.

of persons dying intestate within this Territory, take sufficient bonds, with two or more able sureties, (respect being had to the value of the estate) in the name of the Judges of the said court, with the conditions in manner and form following, *mutatis mutandis,* viz.

Condition thereof. Such bonds valid and pleadable in any court.

§ 20. The condition of this obligation is such, that if the within bounden A B, administrator of all and singular, the goods, chattels, and credits of C D, deceased, do make, or cause to be made, a true and perfect inventory, of all and singular, the goods, chattels and credits of the said deceased, which have, or shall come to the hands, possession, or knowledge of him the said A B, or into the hands and possession of any other person or persons for him, and the same so made, do exhibit, or cause to be exhibited in the court of Common Pleas of the county of   at or before the   day of   next ensuing, and the same goods, chattels and credits, and all other the goods, chattels and credits, of the said deceased, at the time of his death, which at any time hereafter, shall come to the hands, or possession of the said A B, or

K

(76)

into the hands and possession of any other person or persons for him, do well and truly administer according to law, and further do make, or cause to be made, a true and just account of his said administration, at or before the   day of   and all the rest and residue of the said goods, chattels and credits, which shall be found remaining upon the said administrator's account (the same being first examined and allowed of by the court of Common Pleas, of the county where the said administration is granted) shall deliver and pay unto such person or persons, respectively, as the said court of Common Pleas (in the respective county) by their decree or sentence, pursuant to the true intent and meaning of law, shall limit and appoint.—And if it shall hereafter appear, that any last will and testament was made by the said deceased, and the executor or executors therein named, do exhibit the same, into the said court of Common Pleas, making request to have it allowed and approved accordingly, if the said A B, within bound, being thereunto required, do render and deliver the said letters of administration, approbation of such testament being first had and made, in the said court of Common Pleas, then this obligation to be void, and of none effect, or else to remain in full force and virtue.'

§ 21. Which bonds are hereby declared, to be good to all intents and purposes, and pleadable in any court of Justice, and also the said courts of Common Pleas, in the respective counties, shall, and may, and are hereby enabled, to proceed and call such

Courts may oblige administrators to account. Further power and duty of the court.

(77)

administrators to account for, and touching the goods of any person dying intestate, and upon hearing, and due consideration thereof, to order and make just and equal distribution of what remaineth clear, after all debts, funeral, and just expences of every sort, first allowed and deducted, according to the ordinance of Congress for the government of the Territory, and to the rules and limitations hereafter set down, and the same distributions to declare and settle, and to compel such administrators to observe and pay the same, by the due course of the laws of this Territory, saving to every one supposing him, or themselves aggrieved, their right of appeal, to the General or Circuit courts.

§ 22. *Provided always,* That in case any child who shall have any estate by settlement, from the intestate, or shall be advanced by the said intestate in his life time, by portion, not equal to the share which will be due to the other children by such distribution as aforesaid, then, so much of the surplusage of the said estate of such intestate, to be distributed to such child, or children as shall have any land by settlement from the intestate, or were advanced in the life time of the intestate, as shall make the estate of all the said children to be equal, as nearly as can be estimated. And in case there be no children, or any legal representatives of them, then one moiety of the said estate, to be allotted to the wife of the intestate, and the residue of the said estate to be distributed, equally, to every of the next kindred of the intestate, who are in

Children of intestate to share the estate, equally.

Where no representatives, wife to have one half the other to the next of kindred.

[78]

Concerning collateral branches. When no wife, children to take the whole, when no wife nor child how distribution to be made.

equal degree, and those who legally represent them: *Provided,* That there be no representatives admitted among collaterals, after brother's and sister's children; and in case there be no wife, then all the said estate to be distributed equally to, and among the children: and in case there be no child, then to the next of kin, in equal degree, of, or unto the intestate, and their legal representatives, as aforesaid, and in no other manner whatsoever.

Distribution of personal estate not to be made with in the year. Party sharing estate to give bond to refund & in the court of com mon pleas

§ 23. *Provided also, and to the end,* That a due regard be had to creditors, that no such distribution of the goods of any person dying intestate be made, till after one year be fully expired, after the intestate's death; and that such, and every one, to whom any distribution and share shall be allotted, shall give bond, with sufficient sureties, in the said court of Common Pleas, that if any debt or debts, truly owing by the intestate, shall be afterwards sued for, and recovered, or otherwise duly made to appear, that then, and in every such case, he or she, shall respectively refund and pay back to the administrator, his or her ratable part of that debt, or debts, and of the costs of suit, and charges of the administrator, by reason of such debts, out of the part and share, so, as aforesaid, allotted to him or her; thereby to enable the said administrator to pay and satisfy the said debt or debts, so discovered, after the distribution made as aforesaid.

Administration with the will annexed, how grantable.

§ 24. *Provided always,* That in all cases where by law, administration with the will annexed, ought to be granted, the said

(79)

Clerk, or the court of Common Pleas, shall grant administration accordingly, as before directed.

Letters administration granted with out justices, to be void,

The officers so granting them, to be liable to the damages ar-

§ 25. Where any letters of administration shall be granted, and no bond with sureties given, as the law in that case requires, such letters of administration shall be, and are hereby declared to be void, and of none effect, and the Clerk, or Judges of the court that grant the same, shall be *ipso facto,* liable to pay all such damages as shall accrue to any person or persons, by occasion of granting such administration. And the party to whom the same shall be so granted, may be sued as executor in his own wrong, and shall be so taken and deemed, in any suit to be brought against him, for, or by reason of his said administration; or if upon such examination it appears that the said court have not taken sufficient sureties, where the administrators may not be of ability, to answer or make good the value of what the decedent's estate doth, or shall amount unto, then the said court of Common Pleas, are hereby required and empowered to cause all such administrators to give better security to the said court, by bonds, in manner and form as the law prescribes, and under such penalties, and with such sureties as the said court shall approve of, after they have heard the objections of creditors, or persons concerned, if any such be made, during the sitting of the court.—And if it appear that any of the said administrators have embezzled, wasted, or misapplied, or suffered so to be, any part of the decedent's estates, or shall neglect, or re-

(80)

fuse to give bonds, with sureties, as aforesaid, then, and in every such case, the said court shall forthwith, by their sentence, revoke, or repeal the letters of administration granted by them, and thereupon, where such occasion happens, they are hereby required to grant letters of administration to such person or persons, having right thereunto, as will give bonds in manner and form, aforesaid, who may have their actions of *trover* or *detinue,* for such goods or chattels, as came to the possession of the former administrators; and shall be detained, wasted, embezzled, or misapplied, by any of them, and no satisfaction made for the same.

§ 26. If any person or persons, shall die intestate, being owner of lands or tenements within this Territory, at the time of their death, and leave lawful issue to survive them, but not a sufficient personal estate to pay their just debts, and maintain their children, in such case it shall be lawful for the administrator or administrators of such deceased, to sell and convey such part or parts of their said lands or tenements for paying their just debts, maintenance of their children, and for putting them apprentices, and teaching them to read and write, and for improvement of the residue of the estate, if any be, to their advantage, as the

[Margin notes:]

rising therefrom, and the party under them deemed executor in his own wrong.

Power of the court where insufficient security is taken, also in case of waste or embezzlement, when other letters shall be granted and bond taken, former administrator liable to suit.

Where personal estate is insufficient, the common pleas may order the real to be sold for the payment of debts, education & maintenance of the children.

court of Common Pleas of the county, where such estate lies, shall think fit to allow, order and direct from time to time.

Except under marriage settlement.

§ 27. *Provided always,* That no lands or tenements, contained in any marriage settlement, shall, by virtue of this law, be sold or disposed of, contrary to the form and ef-

[81]

fect of such settlement, nor shall any court of Common Pleas, allow, or order any intestates lands or tenements to be sold, before the administrator requesting the same, doth exhibit a true and

Inventory to be first exhibited and other proceedings had,

perfect inventory, and conscionable appraisement of all the intestate's personal estate whatsoever, as also a just and true account, upon his or her solemn oath or affirmation, of all the intestate's debts which shall be then come to his or her knowledge. And if thereupon it shall appear to the court that the intestate's personal estate will not be sufficient to pay the debts, and maintain the children, until the oldest of them attains the age of twenty-one years, or to put them out to be apprentices, and teach them to read and write, then, and in every such case, and not otherwise, the court shall allow such administrator to make public sale of so much of the said lands belonging to any minor, as the court, upon the best computation they can make of the value thereof, shall judge necessary for the purposes aforesaid, reserv-

Mansion house & most profitable part of the estate to be reserved to the last,

Advertisements to be put up of time & place of sale,

ing the mansion house, and most profitable part of the estate till the last. But before any such sale be made, the court shall order so many writings to be made by the Clerk, upon parchment, or good paper, as the court shall think fit, to signify and give notice of such sales, and of the day and hour when, and the place where the same will be, and what lands are to be sold, and where they lie; which notice shall be delivered to the Sheriff or Constables, in order to be fixed in the most public places of the county, or city or town, at least twenty days before sale: and the

(82)

Administrator to report his proceedings therein to the next court,

Sheriffs or Constables are hereby required to make publication accordingly; and the administrator that makes such sale, shall bring his or her proceedings therein, to the next court of Common

Pleas, after the sale made. And if it shall happen that any lands be sold by virtue of this law, for more than the courts computation of the value thereof, then the administrator shall be accountable for the same, as by this law is required for intestate's personal estates.

§ 28. Where any person has died, or hereafter shall die intestate, leaving his or her heirs, or any of them infants, or having made a will, shall not in said will have authorised his or her executors, or some fit persons to make deeds of conveyance, and having previous to his or her death, executed bonds or any other instrument of writing, binding him or her to convey any tract of land, or lot of ground, in such case, the administrator, or executor shall apply to the court of Common Pleas, where the land lies, to appoint three fit persons as commissioners, who shall have full power and authority to convey any tract of land, or lot of ground, to the person entitled to the same, which the decedent bound him or herself, and his or her heirs, by any instrument of writing to convey, agreeably to the tenor of such instrument; and such conveyance so made, shall be as valid, and obligatory, upon the heris, as if made by the ancestor in his life time: *Provided however,* That nothing in this act shall be so construed, as to prevent the infant representatives of such decedent, from instituting suits to

(83)

recover such land, or a compensation in damages from the person or persons, to whom it shall have been conveyed, if any fraud shall have been practised in obtaining the same: *Provided always,* That the bond or instrument on which said conveyance is prayed, shall be filed with the records of the said court.

§ 29. Whenever it shall appear to the several courts of Common Pleas, of any county in this Territory, on petition of any guardian or guardians, of any minor or minors, being owner or owners, and proprietor or proprietors, of any houses and lots, in any town or village, in this Territory, that the yearly rents, issues and profits, beyond all reprisals of the same, are not sufficient to keep them in repair; it shall and may be lawful for such court to authorise the said guardian or guardians to sell and dispose of the

---

Side notes:

Where lands sell for more than the computed valuation, administrator to account for excess.

Where testators or intestates leave infants, having given bonds &c to convey any real estate, the court on application of executor or administrator to appoint 3 commissioners to convey the said estate, which shall bind the heirs

In case of fraud practiced, infant representatives may recover the land or compensation in damages, Bond &c. to be filed among the records of the court.

Where the rents of houses & lots in town belonging to minors are not sufficient to keep them in repair, The court on petition of guardianmay authorise him to sell the same by auction, on giving 30 days notice of sale and on such credit as the court shall direct. Guardians on such sale to take bond with sureties to be approved of by the court, And thereupon convey to the purchasors.

said house and lot, or houses and lots, by public auction, to the highest bidder, on giving thirty days previous notice of the time and place of such sale, which shall be on such credit as the court shall direct, payable with lawful interest.

§ 30. The said guardian or guardians, on the said sale's being made, shall take bond from such purchasor or purchasors, with sufficient security, to be approved of by the court, for the payment of such consideration money, who shall thereupon by proper deeds, convey to such purchasor or purchasors, his or her heirs, all the estate, right, title and interest, of such minor or minors, of, in, and to the said house and lot,

L

(84)

or houses and lots; which conveyance so made, shall be as valid and effectual, as if the same had been made by such minor or · minors, when of full age.

Guardians to account for the consideration money.

§ 31. The said guardian or guardians, shall account for the consideration money received for such house and lot, or houses and lots, in the same manner as for the other estate of such minor or minors.

Written wills duly proved, are declared good conveyances of the estates devised and bequeathed, How proof to be made of such wills,

§ 32. All wills in writing, wherein, or whereby, any lands, tenements or hereditaments, have been, are, or shall be devised (being proved by two or more credible witnesses, upon their solemn oath or affirmation, or by other legal proof, in this Territory, or being proved before such as have, or shall have power in any of the United States, or elsewhere, to take probates of wills, and grant letters of administration, and a copy of such will, with the probate thereof annexed, or endorsed, being transmitted hither under the public or common seal of the courts, or offices where the same have been, or shall be taken or granted, and recorded or entered in the office of the Clerk of the court of Common Pleas in this Territory) shall be good and available in law, for the granting, conveying and assuring of the lands or hereditaments, thereby given or devised, as well as of the goods and chattels thereby bequeathed; and the copies of all wills and probates, under the public seals of the courts, or offices, where the same have been,

Probate of wills declared matter af re

or shall be taken or granted, respectively, other than copies, or probates of such wills as shall appear to be annulled, disapproved or revoked, shall be

(85)

judged and deemed, and are hereby declared to be matter of record, and shall be good evidence to prove the gift or devise thereby made. And all such probates, as well as all letters of administration, granted out of this Territory, being produced here, under the seals of the courts, or offices, granting the same, shall be as sufficient to enable the executors or administrators, by themselves or attornies, to bring their actions in any court within this Territory, as if the same probates, or letters testamentary, or administrations were granted here, and produced under the seal of the court of Common Pleas, in any county of this Territory.

§ 33. *Provided always,* That if any of the wills whereof copies or probates, shall be so as aforesaid, produced and given in evidence, shall, within seven years after the testators death, appear to be disproved, or annulled, before any Judge or officer having cognizance thereof, or shall appear to be revoked or altered, by the testator, either by a latter will, or codicil in writing, duly proved as aforesaid, then, and in every such case, it shall and may be lawful for the party aggrieved, or his or their heirs, executors or assigns, to have their action for what shall be taken, or detained from them, by occasion of such wills, or have their writ or writs of error, for reversing the judicial proceedings thereon, (as the case shall require) any thing herein contained, to the contrary notwithstanding.

§ 34. No *nuncupative* will, shall be good, where the estate thereby bequeathed shall

(86)

exceed the value of eighty dollars, that is not proved by two or more witnesses, who were present at the making thereof, nor unless it be proved, that the testator at the time of pronouncing the same, did bid the persons present, or some of them, bear witness that such was his will, or to that effect; nor unless such nuncupative will, be made in the time of the last sickness of the

Marginal notes:

cord and may be given in evidence,

Probates & letters of administration granted out of the Territory, to have full force within it.

Should a will be disproved within 7 years remedy given to the party aggrieved.

Nuncupative will bequeathing more than 80 dollars value declared void, unless proved and how.

Further requisites to make such will valid. deceased, and in the house of his or their habitation, or dwelling, or where he or they have, or hath been resident, for the space of ten days or more, next before the making of such will; except where such person was surprised, or taken sick, being from his own house, and died before he returned to the place of his or her dwelling.

Limitation of proof as to such nuncupative wills. § 35. When six months have passed, after speaking of the pretended testamentary words, no testimony shall be received to prove any will nuncupative, except the said testimony, or the substance thereof was committed to writing within six days after the making of the said will.

No brobate of wills nuncupative to issue, till 14 days after the death, nor till the widow or next of kin, be summoned to contest the same. § 36. No letters testamentary, or probate of any nuncupative will, shall pass the seal of the court of Common Pleas in the respective counties, till fourteen days at least after the death of the testator, be fully expired, nor shall any nuncupative will, be at any time received to be proved, unless process have first issued out, to call in the widow, or next of kindred to the deceased, to the end, that they may contest the same, if they please.

This law not to effect mariners, persons at sea and soldiers in actual service. § 37. Notwithstanding this law, any mariner, or person being at sea, or soldier, be-

(87)

ing in actual military service, may dispose of his moveables, wages and personal estate, as he might have done before the making hereof.

JESSE B. THOMAS,
Speaker of the House of Representatives.
B. CHAMBERS,
President of the Council.

Approved—September 17th, 1807.
WILLIAM HENRY HARRISON.

CHAPTER XVII.
An act to License and Regulate Taverns.

Publicans to be licensed by the courts of common pleas. § 1. FOR preventing disorders, and the mischiefs that may happen by multiplicity of public houses of entertainment, no person or persons shall in future have or keep any public inn or tavern, ale house or dram shop, or public house of entertainment, in any county, town or place within this Territory, unless such person or persons, shall first obtain permission or license from the court of Common Pleas, which shall continue for one year and no longer, under the penalty of one dollar per day, for every day on which the party offending, shall keep such public inn, tavern, ale house, dram shop, or public house of entertainment, to be recovered with costs, before any Justice of the Peace, in an action *qui tam,* two thirds whereof shall go to

Under what penalties.

(88)

the use of the poor of the county, where the offence may be committed, and the other third to the prosecutor suing for the same, to effect,

§ 2. No person licensed as aforesaid, shall, knowingly suffer any disorder, as drunkenness, or unlawful games, whatever, in such his, her, or their houses, under the penalty of five dollars for the first offence, to be recovered as aforesaid, and for the second offence to be suppressed by the Judges of the several courts; and no such inn-keeper, tavern-keeper, or other person as aforesaid, shall presume to continue such house of entertainment, of his own accord, after such suppression, or the expiration of his license, without new license, as aforesaid, under the penalty of one dollar per day as aforesaid, to be recovered in manner aforesaid, two third parts whereof shall go the use of the poor of the county, where the offence shall be committed, and the remaining third to the party prosecuting,

No disorderly conduct or unlawful Games, under pain of suppression and fine.

§ 3, All tavern-keepers, and inn-keepers, as aforesaid, shall provide and furnish good entertainment and accommodations for man and horse, under penalty of five dollars, to be recovered in manner and for the use aforesaid.

Good entertainment to be provided under a penalty of 5 dollars.

§ 4. The said court shall at the time of granting any license under this act, demand of, and from the person obtaining the same, any sum not exceeding twelve dollars, which they may deem reasonable, taking into consideration the stand, where such tavern is to be opened, which sum so receiv-

Fee on every license to the county and to the clerk.

(89)

ed, shall, by the said court be paid to the county Treasurer, for the use of the county, and the said court shall also demand of such applicant, one dollar, for the use of the Clerk.

No license to be given, unless bond with surety, if required, executed to the governor under a penalty,

§ 5.   No license shall be given, unless the person requiring the same, shall first become bound to the Governor of the Territory, with security if required, in any sum not exceeding three hundred dollars, that he, she, or they, on obtaining such license, shall at all times, be of good behaviour, and observe all the laws and ordinances, which are, or shall be made, or be in force relating to inn-keepers, or tavern-keepers, within the Territory, and whoever shall keep a tavern, inn, or public house of entertainment, before he or she has given bond as aforesaid, such person shall suffer the same penalty, as if the same had been done without license.

No person unless qualified by this law to sell liquors under certain quantities.

§ 6.   No person or persons, other than such as are, or shall be qualified so to do by this law, shall presume, under any colour or pretence, to sell, barter with, or deliver any Wine, Rum, Brandy, or other spirits, or strong water, Beer, Cider, or any mixed, or strong liquors, to be used, or within his, her, or their houses, yards, or sheds, or to be with his, her, or their knowledge, privity, or consent, used or drank, in any shelters, places or woods, near, or adjacent to them, by companies of servants, slaves, or others, nor to retail, or sell, to any person or persons, any Rum, Brandy, or other spirits, or strong water, by less quantity or measure, than one quart, nor any Wine by less

(90)

quantity or measure than one quart, nor any Beer, Ale or Cider, by any quantity less than two gallons, the same liquors being respectively delivered to one person, and at one time, without any collusion or fraud, contrary to the true intent and meaning of this law, every person offending herein, shall pay a fine of twelve

Penalty thereon.

dollars, on conviction, by indictment, to the use of the proper county.

Retailers & publicans not to harbor or trust minors servants &c. on forfeiture &c.

§ 7,   If any inn-holder, or keeper of public house, or any retailer of liquors, shall receive, harbour, entertain or trust any minor under the age of twenty one years, or any servant, knowing them, or either of them to be such, or after having been cautioned or warned to the contrary, by the present guardian, master or mistress, of such minor or servant, in the presence of one or more credible witnesses, such inn-holder, keeper of public house, or retailer of liquors, so offending, shall, for the first or second offence, being duly convicted thereof, forfeit and pay the sum of three dollars, for every such offence, over and above the loss and forfeiture of any debt such minor or servant, shall or may contract for liquors or entertainment, and upon conviction for the third offence, the license obtained by such offender, is hereby declared null and void; and the person so repeatedly offending, shall forfeit and pay the sum of twelve dollars, on conviction by indictment to the use of the county, and be forever after incapable of keeping a public house, or inn, within the Territory.

§ 8. No person shall, by any means, pre-

(91)

sume to furnish, supply, or sell to any bond servant or slave, any rum, brandy, spirits, or any other strong liquors, or strong water, mixed, or unmixed, either within or without doors; nor shall receive, harbor or entertain any slave or servant, in or about his, her, or their houses without special license had and obtained under the hand of such master or mistress, of such slave or bond servant respectively, under the penalty for the first offence of three dollars, and for every succeeding offence four dollars, to be recovered before any one Justice of the Peace of the county where the offence is committed, on the proof of one or more credible witnesses, or upon the view of any Justice within the respective Counties where the fact shall be committed.

Not to sell &c. to bond servants or slaves, or harbor or entertain them withhoutconsent of master &c. on forfeiture. &c.

§ 9. The several fines imposed by this law, shall on conviction be levied by execution on the offenders goods, or his, her, or their persons shall be committed to the County Jail until the same be paid, and all fines and forfeitures recovered by virtue hereof, which are not otherwise appropriated by law shall be applied in manner following that is to say; one moiety thereof shall be paid to the father, mother, guardian, master or mistress of the minor or servant entertained as aforesaid, or to the servant himself as the Justice of the Peace may direct; the other moiety shall be paid

Fines &c. how levied & disposed of.

to the Sheriff as Treasurer, for the county where the offence was committed.

§ 10.   The courts of Common Pleas respectively at the time of granting any license

M

(92)

Courttomake out a list of rates,

Publicans to set up a copy thereof in the most public room of his house, Penalty on neglect or selling at higher rates and how recoverable.

or permission, under this act, shall make out a list of rates for the government of the Tavern-Keepers applying for the same, and it shall be the duty of the Clerk of the Common Pleas, at the time of granting such license or permission under the direction of the court aforesaid, to make out a copy of the rates and deliver the same to the person applying for permission or license to keep a tavern, who shall set the same up in the most public room in his, or her house, and any person who shall presume to sell at any higher rates than those made by the court or without having first set up his rates, as aforesaid, for every such offence shall forfeit and pay twenty dollars, for the use of the person suing for the same, before any Justice within this Territory.

JESSE B. THOMAS,
Speaker of the House of Representatives.

B. CHAMBERS,
President of the Council.

Approved—September 17th, 1807.
WILLIAM HENRY HARRISON.

CHAPTER XVIII.
A Law establishing the Recorders Office, and for other purposes.

§ 1.   THERE shall be an office of Record in each and every county; which shall

(93)

Recorders office established, Where to be kept,

be called and styled the Recorder's Office, and shall be kept in some convenient place, at the county seat of Justice, in the respective counties; and the Recorder shall duly attend the service of the same, and at his own proper costs and charges, shall provide parchment, or good large books of royal, or other large paper, well bound and covered, wherein he shall record, in a fair and legible hand, all deeds, and conveyances, which shall be brought to him for that purpose, according to the true intent and meaning of this law.

§ 2.   All deeds to be recorded in pursuance of this law, whereby any estate of inheritance in fee simple; shall hereafter be limitted to the grantor and his heirs; the words, grant, bargain, sell, shall be adjudged an express covenant, to the grantee, his heirs and assigns, to wit: That the grantor was seized of an indefeasible estate, in fee simple, freed from incumbrances, done, or suffered from the grantor, except the rents and services that may be reserved; as also for quiet enjoyment against the grantor, his heirs and assigns, unless limitted by express words contained in such deed, and that the grantee, his heirs, executors and administrators and assigns, may in any action, assign breaches, as if such covenants were expressly inserted: *Provided always,* That this law shall not extend to leases at rack rent, or to leases not exceeding one and twenty years; where the actual possession goes with the lease.

What words in deeds shall pass a fee & amount to certain covenants, on which grantee may in any action assign breaches.

Proviso.

§ 3.   If any person shall forge any entry of the acknowledgements, certificates, or

Forging acknowledgments &c. How punished.

(94)

endorsements, whereby the freehold or inheritance of any man may be charged, he shall be liable to the penalties against forgers of false deeds; and if any person shall perjure himself in any of the cases herein above mentioned, he shall incur the like penalties as if the oath or affirmation had been in any court of record.

Punishment on perjury.

§ 4.   Every mortgagee of any real or personal estate in this Territory, having received full satisfaction and payment of all such sum and sums of money as are really due to him by such mortgage, shall at the request of the mortgagor, enter satisfaction upon the margin of the record of such mortgage, recorded in said office, which shall forever thereafter discharge, defeat, and release the same, and shall likewise bar all actions brought, or to be brought thereupon.

Satisfaction on mortgages how to be entered by mortgagees

§ 5.   And if such mortgagee, by himself or his attorney, shall not within three months after request, and tender made for

Penalty on mortgagees,

his reasonable charges, repair to said office, and there make acknowledgment as aforesaid, he, she or they, neglecting so to do, shall for every such offence, forfeit and pay unto the party or parties aggrieved, any sum not exceeding the mortgage money—to be recovered in any court of record, by bill, plaint or information.

§ 6. There shall be appointed a recorder in every county, now or hereafter to be erected. But before any of the recorders enter upon their respective offices, they shall become bound to the Governor and his successors in office, with one or more sufficient sureties, in a bond for fifteen hun-

(95)

dred dollars; conditioned for the true and faithful execution of his office, and for delivering up the records, and other writings belonging to the said office, whole, safe and undefaced, to his successor in said office. Which said respective bonds, shall be filed in the Secretaries office, and there safely kept, in order to be made use of, for making satisfaction to the parties, that shall be damnified, or aggrieved, as is or shall be in such case directed by law.

§ 7. And no recorder whatsoever, now or hereafter appointed, as aforesaid, shall enter upon, or officiate in his said office, before he hath given such security as aforesaid, upon pain of forfeiting the sum of three hundred dollars; one half to the Territory, and the other half to him or them, that shall sue for the same to be recovered as aforesaid.

§ 8. All deeds and conveyances, which shall be made and executed within this Territory, of, or concerning any lands, tenements, or hereditaments, therein, or whereby the same may be in any way effected in law or equity, shall be acknowledged by one of the grantors or bargainors, or proved by one or more of the subscribing witnesses to such deed, before one of the Judges of the General court, or before one of the Judges of the court of Common Pleas, or before one of the Justices of the Peace of the county where the land conveyed do lie; and shall be recorded in the recorder's office of the county where such lands or hereditaments are lying and being, within twelve months after the execution of such

(96)

deeds, or conveyances: and every such deed or conveyance, that shall at any time after the publication hereof be made and executed, and which shall not be proved and recorded as aforesaid, shall be adjudged fraudulent, and void against any subsequent purchaser, or mortgagee for valuable consideration; unless such deed or conveyance be recorded as aforesaid; before the proving and recording of the deed or conveyance under which such subsequent purchaser or mortgagee, shall claim. *if not recorded within a year, may be avoided.*

§ 9. Where the grantors and witnesses of any deed or conveyance are deceased or cannot be had, it shall and may be lawful to and for the Judges of the General court, or court of Common Pleas, or any Justice of the Peace, of the county where the lands lie, to take the examination of any witness, or witnesses, on oath, or affirmation to prove the hand writing of such deceased witness or witnesses; or where such proof cannot be had then to prove the hand writing of the grantor or grantors, which shall be certified by the Judge or Justice before whom such proof shall be made; and such deed or conveyance, being so proved shall be recorded as is usual in other cases, directed above by this law. *How proved, where grantors or witnesses are dead.*

§ 10. Every recorder shall keep a fair book in which he shall immediately make an entry of every deed or writing brought into his office to be recorded; mentioning therein the date, the parties, and the place where the lands, tenements or hereditaments granted or conveyed by the said deed or writing, are situate; dating the *Recorders duty,*

(97)

same entry, on the day in which such deed or writing was brought into his office; and shall record all such deeds and writings, in regular succession, according to their priority or time in being brought into said office; and shall also immediately give a receipt to the person bringing such deed or writing to be recorded, bearing date on the same day with the entry, and containing the abstract aforesaid; for which entry and receipt he shall take or receive no fee or reward whatever. And if any recorder shall record any deed or writing before another first brought into his *How recovered and by whom.*

office to be recorded; or in any other manner than is herein directed, or shall neglect or refuse to make such an entry, or give such a receipt as is herein before directed; or shall directly or indirectly take or receive any fee, or reward for such entry and receipt, or either of them, he shall forfeit and pay for every such offence a sum not exceeding three hundred nor less than one hundred dollars; one half to the use of the Territory, and the other half to him or them, that shall sue for the same, to be recovered in any court of record by action of debt, bill or plaint, wherein no essoin, protection or wager of law or more than one imparlance shall be granted.

How husband & wife may convey real estates

§ 11.   Where any husband and wife shall hereafter incline to dispose of and convey the estate of the wife, or her right of, in or to any lands, tenements or hereditaments, whatsoever, it shall and may be lawful, to, and for the said husband and wife, the wife not being less than twenty one years of age, to make seal, deliver and execute, any grant

(98)

bargain and sale, lease, release, feoffment, deed, conveyance, or assurance in the law, whatsoever, for the lands, tenements, and hereditaments, intended to be by them passed and conveyed; and after such execution to appear before one of the Judges of the General court, or court of Common Pleas, or before a Justice of the Peace, of, and for the county, where such lands, tenements and hereditaments shall lie, and to acknowledge the said deed or conveyance, which Judge of the General court, or court of Common Pleas, or Justice of the Peace, shall, and he is hereby authorized and required to take such acknowledgement; in doing whereof he shall examine the wife separate and apart from her husband, and shall read, or otherwise make known the full contents of such deed or conveyance to the said wife; and if upon such separate examination, she shall declare that she did voluntarily, and of her own free will and accord, seal, and as her act and deed deliver the said deed or conveyance, without any coercion, or com-

Duty of magistrates taking acknow ledgment,

pulsion of her said husband every such deed or conveyance shall be, and the same is hereby declared to be good and valid in law, to all intents and purposes, as if the said wife had been sole, and not covert at the time of such sealing and delivery, any law, usage or custom to the contrary in any wise, notwithstanding; *Provided,* That the Judge or Justice, taking such acknowledgement, shall under his hand and seal, certify the same upon the back of such deed or conveyance.

§ 12.   It shall and may be lawful for any

(99)

Judge of the court of Common Pleas, or Justice of the Peace of any county in this Territory, within the limits of their respective counties, to take the acknowledgment or proof of the execution of any deeds or conveyances, or release of dower of any lands or tenements, lying and being in any other county in this Territory; which acknowledgments or proofs, or release so taken and made, the same being duly certified by the Clerk, under the county seal, shall be valid and effectual, and have the same force and effect, as if the same were taken before any Judge, or Justice of the Peace of the county, in which the said lands or tenements are situate.

§ 13.   All deeds and conveyances, made and executed by any persons not residing within this Territory, and brought hither to be recorded in the county where the lands lie, the acknowledgment thereof being taken and made in manner herein before directed, before any mayor or chief magistrate, or officer of the cities, towns or places, where such deeds or conveyances are, or shall be made, or executed, and certified under the common or public seal of such cities, towns or places shall be as valid and effectual in law, as if the same had been made and acknowledged in manner aforesaid, before any Judge of the General court of this Territory, or before any Judge of the court of Common Pleas, or Justice of the Peace, for the county where the lands

the said acknowledgment to be certified.

Justices &c in one county may take acknowledgment or proof of the execution of deeds of lands in another county in the territory.

Deeds for lands executed out of the territory, How to be acknowledged &certified

N

(100)

lie; any thing herein contained to the contrary notwithstanding.

JESSE B. THOMAS,
Speaker of the House of Representatives.
B. CHAMBERS,
President of the Council.

Approved—September 17th, 1807.
WILLIAM HENRY HARRISON.

CHAPTER XIX.
An act concerning Trespassing Animals.

Trespassing animals may be detained till damages &c paid,

§ 1. IF any horse, mare, colt, cattle, sheep or hogs, shall trespass, by breaking into the lawful enclosure of any person or persons; every such person being injured by such trespass, may seize and distrain such trespassing creature, and the same so seized, and distrained, may retain, until he, she or they, shall recover and receive the damages sustained by such trespass, together with the costs of advertising, and reasonable charges for keeping such distress, in manner hereinafter directed.

Notice of Distress to be given and how.

Proceedings after notice,

§ 2. Every person or persons, making such distress, shall, within the space of forty eight hours after the same shall be made, give notice thereof to the owner or owners, of such horse, mare, colt, cattle, sheep, lamb, or hog, if he, she or they can be conveniently found; but if not, then such per-

(101)

son or persons, seizing or distraining such creature, shall, within three days after the distress taken, as aforesaid, cause an advertisement of the marks, brands, stature and colour thereof, and of the place where the same may be found, to be affixed in a conspicuous manner, at the most public place of his, her or their townships; and if, upon such notice, or advertisement, such owner or owners shall appear, but neglect, or refuse to make, or tender a reasonable satisfaction to the party injured, for the damages sustained by such trespass, and in keeping the said creature; or if the said person or persons, so making the distress, shall not accept the said satisfaction, it shall and may be lawful for either of the parties aforesaid, to complain and apply to any Justice of the Peace, of the county, where such creature shall be seized and distrained, as aforesaid, who shall upon such complaint, and application, issue his warrant, directed to any two honest and reputable freeholders of the neighbourhood, commanding and enjoining them forthwith, to view the said trespass, and to value, appraise, and ascertain the injury or damage done to, or within the enclosure aforesaid, having regard to the lawfulness of said fence, with the expense and cost of keeping the said creature, and to make report thereof to him the said Justice, with all convenient speed, which said valuation and appraisement, and return, they, the said freeholders, are hereby required, and enjoined, to make accordingly—and if the said valuation and appraisement, shall not amount to more than the sum of How satisfaction to be made.

(102)

money tendered to the party injured, as a recompence for the damage done as aforesaid, before such complaint made, then the said Justice shall give judgment for the same only, to the party refusing such tender, and award reasonable costs and charges to the other party, for the unjust vexation; but if the said valuation shall amount to more than the sum tendered, or if no such tender be made, then, and in that case, the said Justice shall award and give judgment for the valuation aforesaid, to the party injured, with reasonable costs and charges, for keeping the said creature, so trespassing against the other party, and shall award execution upon every such judgment, with costs of suit accordingly.

§ 3. Whoever shall hurt, kill or do damage, to any horse, mare, colt, cattle, sheep, lamb, or hog, by hunting or driving them out of, or from the said enclosure, or by neglecting to provide them with sufficient food and water, after they may have been distrained, shall be liable to make good all damages sustained thereby, to the owner of such creature or creatures. Damages on hurting or killing animals &c or not providing them with sufficient food after distress made,

§ 4. If no owner or owners appear and make out, his or their property in the said creatures, within two weeks after such advertisements, shall be published in the township, as aforesaid, Proceedings in case no owner appears,

the person or persons making such distress, shall forthwith under the penalty of twelve dollars, cause the like advertisement to be published three times successively, in one or more news-papers or gazettes, printed and published within this Territory, provided, there is a gazette

(103)

or news-paper then printed and published within the county, wherein the trespass shall happen; But in case of no such public paper, then such advertisement shall be put up in a conspicuous manner at the court house door of the county; and the party distraining shall make application, at the expiration of two months after the publication of the same advertisements, to the said Justice of the Peace, who is hereby authorised and required, to issue his warrant to two honest and respectable freeholders, and cause them upon their oath or affirmation, which he is hereby empowered and required to administer to them, to view, value, and appraise the creature or creatures so distrained, and to ascertain the damages so done, as aforesaid, with reasonable charges for keeping the said creature, and to make return thereof, to him as aforesaid, upon which valuation and return, the property of, and in the said creatures, so valued, shall become, and be held and taken to be, and is hereby vested in the person so making such

Proviso

distress; but so nevertheless, that he shall be answerable and accountable to the owner or owners aforesaid, for the valuation

Where owner appears within one year.

money aforesaid, at any time afterwards within the space of one year, next after the publication of such advertisement, last aforesaid, having first deducted thereout, the cost of such proceedings, advertisements, and charges of keeping the said creature with the damages so ascertained. But if the said owner or owners shall not appear and demand the same, within the time limited, last aforesaid, then the said person or persons, so making the said

(104)

distress, shall, upon demand made, pay all such overplus money to the sheriff of the county, for the use of the county, under the penalty of double the sum retained in his, her or their hands, contrary to the direction of this law.

§ 5. If any such person or persons so distraining, shall neglect to give such notice, as herein before directed, or shall neglect to set up, and publish such advertisements in the most public place of his, her, or their Township, he, she, or they, shall forfeit and loose, all right or title or pretence of right, to a recovery of any sum or sums of money for such trespass, or any recompense for the same; but shall deliver up the said creature so distrained, to the owner or owners thereof, without any recompense or reward whatsoever; and that one half of all the fines imposed by virtue of this law, shall be to the use of the owner, or owners of such creature and the other half thereof to the use of the county, to be recovered by them or either of them, in a summary way, as debts not exceeding eighteen dollars, are by law directed to be recovered.

If party distraining neglects to give notice, owner to have restitution without expence.

All fines to go to the owner of certain animals & the poor. How recovered.

§ 6. If any person or persons shall knowingly, and wittingly, keep and retain any horse, mare, colt, cattle, sheep, lamb or hog, within his, her or their enclosures, for the space of forty-eight hours, without giving the notice and publishing the advertisements aforesaid, every such person or persons, shall forfeit and pay the sum of twelve

Penalty on detaining animals within enclosures for 48 hours, without giving notice &c,

(105)

dollars for every such offence, to be recovered and applied in manner aforesaid.

JESSE B. THOMAS,
Speaker of the House of Representatives.
B. CHAMBERS,
President of the Council.
Approved—September 17th, 1807.
WILLIAM HENRY HARRISON.

CHAPTER XX.
An act to regulate the disposition of Water Crafts, of certain descriptions found, gone, or going adrift, and of estray animals.

§ 1. IF any person shall take up any boat, flat, periague, canoe or other small vessel gone or going adrift, he or she, shall within five days cause the same to be viewed by some householder of the county where the same shall be taken up, and shall forth-

Persons taking up Boats &c. adrift, how to proceed,

Duty of jus-
tice,
with go with such householder, before a Justice of the Peace of
the same county and make oath when and where the same was
taken up, and that the marks thereof have not been altered or
defaced by him, or by any other person to his knowledge since the
taking up, and the Justice shall take from such householder, upon
oath, an exact description of such boat, flat, periague, canoe, or
other small vessel, and shall enter the

(106)

same in his estray book, to be by him kept for that purpose, and
shall transmit a certified copy thereof to the Clerk of the court
of Common Pleas of the county to be by him recorded in his
estray book to be kept for that purpose within fifteen days thereafter if the said Justice does not reside at a greater distance that
fifteen miles from the Clerk's office; but if the said Justice resides
at a greater distance than fifteen miles from the said office, he shall
transmit the said certificate, within the space of thirty days, and
Duty ofclerk
of the com-
mon pleas,
the Clerk shall cause a copy of such certificate to be set up at his
court house door, during the two succeeding terms to be held for
said county, for which service, he shall be entitled to take and
Allowanceto
justice and
clerk, and
how paid.
receive twenty-five cents, for every such boat, flat, periague, canoe,
or other small vessel to be deposited by the taker up in the hands
of said Justice and by him transmitted to the said Clerk with the
certified copy of such description, and the Justice for administering the oath, making the entry and granting the certificate as aforesaid, shall be entitled to twenty-five cents for his services, which
sum shall be paid by the taker up.
Persons tak-
ing up horses
&c, as estray
how to pro-
ceed,
§ 2.   Every person who shall take up a stray horse, gelding,
mare, colt, mule or ass, shall within five days advertise the same
in three different places in the neighborhood or township, and
shall also within ten days thereafter, unless it shall have been previously claimed and proved by the proper owner and a tender
made of the compensation herein after provided, take the same
before some Justice of the Peace of the coun-

(107)

ty where such stray shall be taken up, and make oath before such
Justice that the same was taken up at his or her plantation or place

of residence, in said county or otherwise, (as the case may be) and that the marks or brands have not been altered by him or any other person or persons, to his knowledge, before or since the taking up; the Justice shall then issue his warrant to three disinterested householders in the neighborhood, unless they can be otherwise had, causing them to come before him to appraise said stray, and after they, or any two of them, are sworn to appraise such stray, without partiality favor or affection, they shall forthwith proceed to appraise the same, and immediately make return thereof, in writing, together with the description of the marks, natural and accidental, brand, stature, color, and age of said horse, gelding, mare, colt, mule or ass, to said Justice, who shall enter the same in his estray book, and transmit a certified copy thereof, under his hand together with the original return of the appraisers, under their hands to the Clerk of the court of Common Pleas of said county within the time as limited in the first section of this act, who shall enter the same in his estray book, and file the aforesaid transcript, and certificate of the appraisers in his office: and the taker up shall pay unto the said justice fifty cents, and further deposit in the hands of the said Justice fifty cents, to be paid unto the Clerk aforesaid, which sum of fifty cents shall be transmitted at the same time with the aforesaid certificate of entry and

Duty of justice,

Duty of the clerk.

Fees to justice & clerk and how paid,

O

(108)

appraisement, and the said Clerk shall cause a copy of such valuation and description to be publicly affixed at the court house door of his county during three succeeding terms.

§ 3. Any person who shall take up any head of neat cattle, sheep hog or goat, shall within five days after, cause the same to be advertised in three different places in the neighborhood or township, and shall also within ten days thereafter, unless it shall have been previously claimed and proved, by the proper owner, and a tender made of the compensation herein after provided, cause the same to be viewed by some householder of the county, where the same shall be taken up, and immediately go with such

Persons taking up neat cattle, sheep &c,

How to pro-
ceed,

Duty of jus-
tice.

Duty of the
clerk,

Fees to the
justice and
clerk & how
paid.

householder before a Justice of said county, and make oath before him, as is required in taking up a stray horse, gelding, mare,
colt, mule or ass, and then such Justice, shall take from such
householder, upon oath, a particular description of the marks,
brands, colour and age of every such neat cattle, sheep, hog, or
goat; and such Justice shall cause the said stray or strays to be
appraised in like manner as is required to be done in case of stray
horse, gelding, mare, colt, mule or ass, which description and
valuation shall be entered by such Justice, in his estray book, and
by such Justice transmitted to the Clerk of the court of Common
Pleas of said county, and to be by him recorded in his estray
book, and he shall cause a copy to be publicly affixed at the court
house door of his county as before directed in taking up stray
horse, gelding,

(109)

mare, colt, mule or ass, and the taker up shall pay, the Justice
twenty-five cents for his services, and deposit with such Justice,
twenty-five cents, to be transmitted at the same time with the
certified copy to the Clerk as aforesaid, for his services: *Provided,*

Proviso,

Where two
ormorestrays
of same
species taken
up,
Not to take
up or post a-
ny neat cat-
tle &c. be-
tween 1st
Days of a-
pril & novem-
ber, unless
&c.

Reward for
taking up &c.

With charg-
es for keep-
ing &c. and
how assessed

That if two or more strays of the same species, are taken up by
the same person, at the same time, they shall be included in one
entry and one advertisement, and in such case the said Justice
and Clerk shall receive no more than for one such species: *Provided also,* That no person shall be allowed hereafter, to take up
and post any head of neat cattle, sheep, hog, or goat, between the
first day of April and the first day of November, following, unless the same may be found within the lawful enclosure of the
taker up, having broken in the same.

§ 4. As a reward for taking up, there shall be paid by the
owner to the taker up, or such other person as may be authorised
by this act to receive the same; For every boat or flat, one dollar,
for every periague, canoe, or other small vessel, fifty cents, every
horse, gelding mare, colt, mule, or ass one dollar, for every head
of neat cattle, fifty cents, for every sheep or goat, twenty-five
cents, and for every hog above six months old ten cents, together
with the fees paid by the taker up, to the Justice and Clerk aforesaid, and reasonable charges for keeping said estray or estrays

to be assessed by two disinterested householders appointed by some one Justice in the manner and form as other appraisers are to be appointed under this act, who shall in the same man-

(110)

ner, and under the same restrictions proceed to make appraisement, and return to the said Justice, as by this act in other cases is required, and on failure of the claimant to satisfy such fees and charges, the estray or estrays, shall be by the Sheriff, after giving two days notice, sold to the highest bidder to satisfy such costs and charges for keeping, and the said Sheriff after paying such costs and charges, and deducting one dollar for his fees of sale, shall pay the remainder to the claimant. *In default of payment estrays to be sold & how.*

§ 5. If no owner shall appear to prove his or her property, within one year after such publication, and when the valuation does not exceed five dollars, the property shall be vested in the taker up, but when the valuation shall exceed five dollars, and no owner appears within the time aforesaid, the property shall be vested in the Sheriff of the county to be sold to the best bidder, and the money arising from the sale thereof, after paying the fees that have accrued, and reasonable expences for keeping the same, shall be put into the county Treasury, which expences shall be ascertained in manner and form as before directed by this act, saving *nevertheless,* The right in the taker up, at the expiration of one year, to pay into the county Treasury, the appraisement value of such estray, and in that case the property of said estray shall be vested in the taker up : *Nevertheless,* The former owner may and shall at any time thereafter, by proving his or her property in the court of Common Pleas of the county, where such estray was taken up, and obtaining a certifi- *When no owner appears in one year. How to proceed in case valuation under 5 dollars,*

(111)

cate from the Clerk, receive an order from the court of Common Pleas, to the Sheriff, for the nett proceeds, after paying costs and charges, and if any person shall trade, sell, or take away any such stray, or water craft, out of the Territory, before he is vested with the right of property, agreeable to this act, for any purpose whatsoever, he or she, so offending, shall forfeit and pay double the *Penalties on persons selling, trading or taking away estrays,* value thereof, to be recovered by any person suing for the same, in any court of record within this Territory, having cognizance thereof, the one half to the informer, and the other half to the county; and it shall not be lawful for any person to take up any stray, except as shall hereafter be excepted, unless he shall have a freehold, be a tenant for three years, have bond for the land on which he resides, or be in possession of the tenement on which such estray was found trespassing.

What persons to take up estrays.

§ 6.   Any person finding any stray horse, gelding, mare, colt, mule or ass, running at large, without the settlement of this Territory, may take up the same, and shall immediately carry such stray or strays, before the nearest Justice of the Peace, and make oath, as before directed in this act, after which it may be lawful for him, if qualified as aforesaid, to post such stray, or strays, in the manner and form as herein before directed, as if the same had been taken up on his plantation or place of residence, and when the taker up shall not be qualified as aforesaid, he shall take the oath before required, and deliver up such stray to the said Justice, who shall cause the same to be dealt

Horses &c. found running at large without the settlements, how to be dealt with.

When taker up not qualified how to proceed,

(112)

with as before directed by this act, and if no owner appears to prove his or her property within one year, such Justice shall deliver such stray or strays, unto the Sheriff of the county, to be disposed of in manner before directed, and after paying the taker up all reasonable charges, and deducting the expences for keeping, which shall be ascertained as aforesaid, such Sheriff shall, within three months pay the ballance into the county treasury; *Nevertheless,* The former owner at any time after, by proving his, or her property before the court of Common Pleas, in the county where the said stray was taken up, shall receive a certificate from the Clerk of the said court to the Sheriff as Treasurer, who shall pay the ballance aforesaid: *Provided always,* That nothing in this act contained, shall be construed to authorise any person or persons to take up any horse, gelding, mare, colt, mule or ass, running at large, between the first day of April and the first day of November, so as to entitle him or them to receive the reward or compen-

when no owner appears in one year, how to proceed, No Horse &c. to be taken up between the first days of april and november, unless found within taker up's lawful enclosure.

sation herein provided, unless the same be found within the lawful enclosure of the taker up, having broken the same.

§ 7. If any stray or water craft taken up as aforesaid, shall die or get away before the owner shall claim his, or her right, the taker up shall not be answerable for the same, unless it be proven that such stray or water craft died or got away through the neglect or inattention of the taker up, and if any person shall take up any stray at any other place within the inhabitants, than his or her place of residence, or without being qualified as

(113)

required by this act, such person shall forfeit and pay ten dollars, with costs before any Justice in the county where the offence shall have been committed, or not having property sufficient to pay such fine, he shall be liable to be confined one month in the Jail of the county where he may be found, by warrant under the hand and seal of any Justice of the peace, directed to the proper officer, who shall confine such offending persons accordingly, and the prison fees of such delinquent shall be paid by the county: *Nevertheless,* Such delinquent shall be liable to repay such fees to the county, should he thereafter have property sufficient; and any person taking up a stray out of the limits of the settlements of this Territory and failing to comply with the requisitions of this act shall be subject to the same penalties.

§ 8. When any water craft or animal taken up in persuance of this act, the appraised value whereof shall exceed the sum of five dollars, may be restored to the proper owner, or when the same may be lost, it shall be the duty of the taker up, within one month afterwards to certify in writing, under the signature of the taker up, to the Clerk of the court of Common Pleas of the proper county; such restoration where the same may be restored, with the name and place of residence of the person claiming the same, or such loss (where the same may be lost) together with the time when, and the manner whereof, and if the taker up of any such water craft, or animal taken up in persuance of this act, shall neglect to make the certificate aforesaid within the time limited by

Marginal notes:

When strays die or water crafts get away, Taker up not accountable, unless for neglect &c.

Penalty on persons not qualified takiug up estrays except at his or her place of residence,

and on persons taking up estrays without the limits of a settlement.

When estrays &c. are restored or lost; certificate thereof to be by the taker up delivered to the clerk of the court within one month &c.

(114)

Penalty on neglect.

How recoverable & applied.

this act, or shall make a false statement of facts, in any such certificate, every person so offending, for every such offence, shall forfeit and pay the value of such water craft, or the appraised value of such stray animal respectively, to be recovered by action of debt, qui tam or indictment, in any court where the same may be cognizable, one half thereof to the county respectively, and the other half to whoever will sue for the same.

Court of C. P. to cause pounds to be erected,
When & of what descriptions.
What strays shall be put in the pound & how long kept.

§ 9.   The Judges of the court of Common Pleas within each county of this Territory, shall cause a pound to be made, at or near the several court houses; and in all new counties that may be formed in this Territory, within three months after the place of erecting the public building is fixed upon, with a good sufficient fence, gate, lock and key, where all stray horses, geldings, mares, colts, mules or asses, above two years old, taken up within twenty miles of the court house, shall be kept on the first day of every court of Common Pleas in said county for three succeeding terms after the same is taken up, from twelve until four o'clock on each day, that the owner may have an opportunity of claiming his or her property; and any person taking up any stray horse, gelding, mare, colt, mule or ass, not exceeding two years old, shall not be compelled to exhibit, such stray or strays at the court house, but

Persons living 20 miles from the pound taking up estray horses &c.

shall be dealt with in other respects, as is directed in this act, and when any person taking up any stray horse, gelding, mare, mule or ass, more than two years old resides twenty miles and upwards from the court

(115)

house, he shall not be compelled to exhibit such stray or strays

Proviso.

more than once in the pound, which shall be on the first day of the second term after taking up: *Provided always,* That such taker up, cause a particular description of such stray or strays to be advertised at the door of the court house at and before the term, at which the same is put in the pound, by the clerk of the court

Courts of C. P. neglect-

of Common Pleas of said county, in manner and form as before directed by this act, and the Judges of the court of Common Pleas for the said county, failing to have such pound erected, shall forfeit and pay a sum of twenty dollars for every court thereafter, until the same be erected: and until such pound is erected, no person taking up any stray horse, gelding, mare, colt, mule, or ass, shall be liable for any penalty for not exhibiting the same; and the Judges of the court of Common Pleas shall appoint some person to take care of the said pound, and keep the same in repair; whose duty it shall be to attend at the said pound on the several court days during the time such strays are directed to continue therein, with the key of the same, and the said Judges shall make such reasonable allowances for the expence of erecting and keeping of the said pound, as to them shall seem proper, to be paid out of the treasury, in like manner and form, that other county charges are liquidated and paid, and any person being appointed, and undertaking to take care of said pound, and failing to discharge his duty agreeable to the directions of this act, shall

marginal notes: ing to cause pounds to be erected forfeit &c. — Court to appoint pound keeper. — His duty. — Pound keeper failing in duty forfeiture on.

P

(116)

forfeit and pay to the informer the sum of eight dollars for every such offence, with costs, recoverable before any Justice of the county, where such offence shall be committed.

§ 10. If any person shall act contrary to the duties enjoined by this act, for which no penalty is herein before particularly pointed out, the person so offending shall on conviction thereof, forfeit and pay for every such offence, not more than one hundred dollars, nor less than five dollars, with costs, to the use of the proper county, to be prosecuted for, and recovered in like manner, as other fines and forfeitures are under this act, and moreover be liable to the action of the party injured, for such neglect.

marginal notes: How recovered. — Penalty on persons acting contrary to this act.

JESSE B. THOMAS,
Speaker of the House of Representatives.
B. CHAMBERS,
President of the Council.

Approved—September 17th, 1807.
WILLIAM HENRY HARRISON.

CHAPTER XXI.
An act for the speedy assignment of Dower.

§ 1. WHEN the heir, or other person having the next immediate estate of free-

(117)

Terre tenant to set out dower in one month, otherwise the widow may sue for it.

hold or inheritance, shall not, within one month, next after demand made, assign and set over, to the widow of the deceased, her dower, or just third part of, and in all lands, tenements and hereditaments, whereof, by law, she is, or may be, dowable, to her satisfaction, according to the true intendment of law, then such widow may sue for, and recover the same, by writ of dower, to be brought against the tenant in posses-

How suit to be brought and against whom.

sion, or such persons as have or claim right or inheritance, in the same estate, in manner and form as the law prescribes.

On judgment had a writ of seizin to issue to sheriff &c. who shall cause dower to be set forth, by whom and in what manner.

§ 2. Upon rendering judgment for any woman, to recover her dower in any lands tenements or hereditaments, reasonable damages shall also be awarded to her, from the time of the demand, and refusal to assign to her, her reasonable dower; and a writ of *seizin,* shall be directed to the Sheriff of the county, or Coroner; and the Sheriff, or Coroner, to whom such writ is directed, shall cause her dower in such estate to be set forth unto her, by three disinterested freeholders of the same county, under oath or affirmation, to be administered by any Justice of the Peace, to set forth the same, equally and impartially, without favour or affection, as conveniently as may be.

When estate is entire, how widow to take her thirds.

§ 3. Where estates, of which a woman is dowable, are entire, and where no division can be made, by metes and bounds, dower thereof shall be assigned in a special manner, as of a third part of the rents, issues, and profits, to be computed and ascertained, in manner as aforesaid. And no

(118)

woman that shall be endowed of any lands, tenements and hereditaments as aforesaid, shall, wantonly, or designedly, commit
or suffer any waste thereon, on penalty of forfeiting that part of
the estate whereupon such waste shall be made, to him, or
them that have the immediate estate of freehold, or inheritance, in remainder or reversion, (and in case of negligent and
inadvertant waste, by her done, or suffered, the damages that
may be assessed for such waste) to be recovered by action of
waste. And all tenants in dower, shall maintain the houses,
and tenements, with the fences, and appurtenances whereof
they may be endowed in as good repair as the same have been
delivered to them, during the term; and the same shall so
leave, at the expiration thereof.

Widow not to commit wiful waste &c.

On what penalty. In case of negligent waste, damages to be recovered against her & how. Tenants in dower to keep and leave the premises in good repair.

JESSE B. THOMAS,
Speaker of the House of Representatives.
B. CHAMBERS,
President of the Council.

Approved—September 17th, 1807.
WILLIAM HENRY HARRISON.

CHAPTER XXII.
An act giving remedies in Equity, in certain cases.

§ 1.   IN all causes brought before the

(119)

General or Circuit courts, or before any court of Common
Pleas, to recover the forfeiture annexed to any articles of
agreement covenant, or charter party, bond, obligation, or
other specialty; or for forfeiture of real estate, upon condition,
by deed of mortgage, or bargain and sale, with defeazance,
(when the forfeiture, breach, or non-performance, shall be
found by a jury, by the default, or the confession of the defendant, or upon demurrer) the court before whom the action is,

*When judg-
ment to re-
cover ac-
cording to e-
quity and
good co
science.*

What execution to issue on such judgment.

shall make up judgment therein, for the plaintiff to recover so much as is due in equity, and good conscience; and shall award execution for the same, by writ of *capias ad satisfaciendum, fieri facias,* or other judicial writ, as the case may require.

JESSE B. THOMAS,
Speaker of the House of Representatives.
B. CHAMBERS,
President of the Council.

Approved—September 17th, 1807.

WILLIAM HENRY HARRISON.

CHAPTER XXIII.
A Law for the relief of the Poor.

Overseers of the poor how & by whom appointed.

§ 1. THE court of Common Pleas in the several counties in this territory, at every first session of said court, yearly and every

(120)

year, after the first day of January, shall nominate and appoint two substantial inhabitants of every township within their respective jurisdictions, to be overseer of the poor of such township.

In case of death &c. of overseer, vacancy how supplied.

§ 2. And if any overseer shall die, remove or become insolvent, before the expiration of his office: two Judges of the court of Common Pleas, on due proof being thereof made before them, shall appoint another in his stead. Every overseer so nominated and appointed, shall before he enters upon the

Overseer to take oath &c.

execution of his office take an oath or affirmation, respectively, according to law; which any Judge or Justice in the counties respectively, is hereby authorised and empowered to administer, that he will discharge the office of overseer of the poor, truly, faithfully and impartially, to the best of his knowledge and ability.

Overseers to farm out paupers, when & how.

§ 3. It shall be the duty of the overseers of the poor in each and every township, yearly and every year, to cause all poor persons, who have, or shall become a public charge to be farmed out at public vendue, or out-cry, to wit; On the first Monday in May, yearly and every year, at some public

place in each township in the several counties of this Territory, respectively, to the person or persons, who shall appear
to be the lowest bidder or bidders, having given ten days previous notice of such sale, in at least three of the most public
places in their respective townships, which notices shall set
forth the name and age, as near as may be, of each person to
be farmed out as aforesaid.

§ 4. The overseers of the poor, shall

(121)

make a return into the Clerk's office of the court of Common
Pleas of the county, of the sum or sums of money, for which
the poor of their respective townships were sold, within fifteen days after every such sale shall have been made; and it
shall be the duty of such court, to levy and cause to be collected in the same manner as other county rates are levied and
collected, a sum of money equal to the amount of the several
sums for which the poor of the several townships shall have
been sold.

When to make return to the court of C. P.

Duty of the court.

§ 5. The farmers of the poor shall be entitled to receive
from the county treasury half yearly on the order of the court
aforesaid, on the certificate of the overseers of the poor, stating the sum due, the compensation which shall have been stipulated as aforesaid, in full stisfaction for their trouble, and
for all expences in keeping and supporting the poor, for the
term of one year as aforesaid, and if any person or persons,
shall become legally a town charge, after the poor of the
township shall have been sold as aforesaid, it shall be the duty
of the overseers to proceed in manner aforesaid to dispose
of such poor person or persons for the remainder of the year,
giving the same notice of such farming out.

Farmers of the, in what manner to be paid &c.

§ 6. And it shall be lawful for the farmers of the poor to
keep all poor persons under their charge, at moderate labour,
and every person who shall refuse to be lodged, kept, maintained, and employed in the house or houses of such farmers
of the poor, he or she, shall not be entitled to receive relief
from the overseers during such refusal; and

Farmers of the poor may keep them at moderate labor &c. Paupers re-fusing to la-bor, not en-titled to re-

(122)

lief during such refusal.

it shall be the duty of the overseers, on any complaint made to them, or on behalf of the poor, to examine into the ground of such complaint, and if in their opinion, the poor have not been sufficiently provided with the common necessaries of life, or have been in any respect illy treated, by the farmers aforesaid, it shall be lawful for the overseers to with-hold any part of the compensation aforesaid, not exceeding one half thereof.

When paupers are illy treated how to proceed.

Poorchildren to be by o-verseers put out apprentices.

§ 7. It shall and may be lawful for the overseers of the poor of the townships aforesaid, by the approbation and consent of two Justices of the Peace of the county to put out as apprentices, all such poor children, whose parents are dead, or shall be by the Justices found unable to maintain them, males till the age of twenty-one and females till the age of eighteen years.

How and at what ages.

No paupers to be relieved unless by order of two justices of the peace.

§ 8. No person or persons shall be admitted or entered in the poor book of any of the said townships, or receive relief, before such person or persons shall have procured an order from two Justices of the Peace, for the same. And in case the said overseers shall enter in their books, or relieve any such poor person or persons, without such order, they shall forfeit all such money or goods so paid, or distributed, unless such entry or relief shall be approved of as aforesaid.

Overseers ac counts how to be kept & settled.

§ 9. The court of Common Pleas shall annually on the day on which overseers of the poor are appointed, choose three capable and discreet freeholders in each township to settle and adjust the accounts of the overseers of the poor of the respective town-

(123)

ships for the preceeding year, and the person who shall have served the office, shall on the said day, or on any other day, which the said freeholders, so chosen, shall appoint, within fifteen days next after, deliver and render to the said freeholders, a just account in writing, entered in a book to be kept for that purpose, and signed by him, of all sums by him received; and also of all materials that have come to his hands, during his office, and of all

Controlledby three free-

money paid by such overseers, and of all other things concerning his office, which accounts when settled, shall be signed by the said freeholders, or any two of them, who shall have full power to allow such parts thereof only, as to them shall appear just and reasonable. **holders appointed by the court.**

§ 10. The said overseers shall make fair entries, in a book, of the names of all the poor within their respective townships; with the time when each of them became chargeable, and of all certificates delivered to them, and by whom, with the times when the same were delivered, for which trouble the said freeholders or any two of them shall make such allowances as they shall judge reasonable; and if any of the said overseers shall refuse or neglect to make and yield up such books and accounts, within the time as aforesaid, or if any such whose office shall expire, shall refuse, or neglect to pay over the money, and deliver up the books aforesaid, and every other thing in his hands, concerning his said office, to his successor, within thirty days after his going out of office; it shall be lawful to **The names of the poor to be entered in the overseers books &c.** **Compensation to overseers, how made.** **Delinquent overseers, how punishable.**

Q

(124)

and for any Justice of the Peace of the said county, to commit such overseer to the common jail, there to remain without bail or mainbrize, till such overseers shall give such accounts and pay and deliver up such money, books and other things, as he ought in manner aforesaid. If any overseer shall think himself aggrieved by the settlement of his account by the said freeholders, he may (having first paid over to his successor the balance found in his hands, if any such there be) appeal to the next court of Common Pleas, who shall, on petition of the party, take such order therein, and give such relief as to them shall appear just and reasonable, and the same shall conclude all parties. **Appeal.**

§ 11. And if any person appointed as overseer of the poor of any township, shall refuse, or neglect to take upon him, the said office, he shall forfeit twelve dollars, to, and for the use of the county; which forfeiture shall be levied by warrant, from any two Justices of the county, or of the townships respectively, under **Overseers neglecting to take office, forfeit 12 dollars to county.**

How recoverable. their hands and seals, on the goods and chattels of such person or persons, so neglecting or refusing, and sold within three days next after distress made; and if there happen any overplus upon sale thereof, the same shall be paid to the owner or owners, reasonable charges being first deducted, and if such person or persons, so neglecting, or refusing, as aforesaid, shall not have goods or chattels, wherewith he or they may be distrained as aforesaid, then the said Justices may commit the offender or offenders to prison, there to remain without

(125)

bail or main-prize, till the said forfeiture shall be fully satisfied and paid.

Overseers removing &c. how enjoined, and how executors &c. in case of death § 12.   If any overseer shall remove, he shall before his removal, deliver over to some other overseer of the township or place, from which he removes, all his books, papers, and other things concerning his office; and upon the death of any overseer, his executors, or administrators, shall, within forty days after his decease, deliver over, all things concerning his office, to some other overseer as aforesaid.

Propertymay be had for the poor & to what amount. § 13.   All gifts, grants, devises, and bequests, hereafter to be made of any houses, lands, tenements, rents, goods, chattels, sum or sums of money, not exceeding in the whole, the yearly value of twelve hundred dollars, to the poor of any township, or to any other person or persons, for their use, by deed, or by the last will and testament of any person or persons, or otherwise howsoever; shall be good and available in law, and shall pass such houses and lands, tenements, rents, goods and chattels, to the overseers of the poor of such township, for the use of their poor respectively.

Overseers in each township a body corporate, § 14.   The overseers of the poor for the several townships for the time being, respectively, shall forever hereafter, in name and in fact, be, and they are hereby declared to be bodies politic and corporate, in law, to all intents and purposes, and shall have perpetual succession; and may, by the name of the overseers of the poor of the said townships, sue, and be sued, and plead, and be impleaded, in all courts of judicature, and

(126)

by that name, shall and may purchase take or receive any lands, tenements or hereditaments, goods, chattels, sum or sums of money, not exceeding in the whole, including all gifts, grants, devises and bequests, heretofore made, the aforesaid yearly value of twelve hundred dollars, to and for the use and benefit of the poor of the respective townships, of the gift, alienation or devise of any person or persons whomsoever; to hold to them, the said overseers, and their successors, in the said trust, for the use of the said poor forever.

§ 15. If any person who shall come to inhabit in any county or place within this Territory, shall, for himself, and on his own account, execute any public office, being legally placed therein, in the said county or place, during one whole year; or if any person shall be charged with and pay his or her share of the public tax or levy of such county, for two years successively, or if any person shall really and bona fide, take a lease of any lands, or tenements in said county, or place of the yearly value of twenty five dollars, and shall dwell in or on the same for one whole year, and pay the said rent, or shall become seized of any freehold estate, in any lands or tenements in such county or place, and shall dwell in, and upon the same, for one whole year, such person in any of these cases, shall be adjudged and deemed to gain a legal settlement in the same county or place where such person shall so execute an office, be charged with, and pay taxes, take such lease or own any such freehold estate, and dwel-

Qualifications for a legal settlement.

Exercising public office Paying taxes

Leasing lands.

On being a freeholder.

(127)

ing thereon, as aforesaid, or being hired or bound, shall continue and inhabit in a place for one whole year as aforesaid, every indented servant legally brought into this territory, shall obtain a legal settlement in the county or place, in which such servant shall have first served, with his or her master or mistress the space of sixty days, and if afterwards such servant shall duly serve, in any other place for the space of six months, such servant shall obtain a legal settlement, in the county or place, where such service was

Hiring and service.

Being apprentices.

last performed, either with his or her first master or mistress, or on assignment.

As to married women & widows.

§ 16.   Every married woman shall be deemed during coverture, and after her husbands death, to be legally settled in the place where he was last legally settled, but if he shall have no legal settlement, then she shall be deemed; whether he is living or dead to be legally settled in the place where she was legally settled before the marriage.

Concerning strangers coming into townships.

§ 17.   If any person or persons shall come out of the United States into any county or place within this Territory, or shall come out of any county or place within this Territory, into any other county or place thereof, there to inhabit and reside, and shall at the same time procure, bring and deliver unto the overseers of the poor, of the township or place where he, she or they, shall

Certificates and their requisites to be valid.

come to inhabit, a certificate under the hands and seals of the overseers of the poor of the county, township or place from whence he, she or they removed, to be allowed by two or more credible witnesses, thereby ac-

(128)

knowledging, the person or persons mentioned in said certificate, to be inhabitant or inhabitants legally settled in that county, township or place; every such certificate having been allowed of and subscribed by one or more Justices of the peace of the proper county, where such county or township, shall oblige the said county, township or place, to provide for the persons mentioned in said certificate, together with his or her family, as inhabitants of that place, wherever he she or they happen to become chargeable, to, or be obliged to ask relief of the county township or place, to which such certificate was given, and into which he, she or they were received by virtue of the said certificate, and then and not before, it shall and may be lawful for any such person, and his, her, or their children, though born in the county, township or place, and his or her servants or apprentices, not having otherwise acquired a legal settlement there, to be removed, conveyed and settled, in the county, township or place from whence such certificate was brought, and the witnesses who attest the execution of the certificate by the overseers, or one of the witnesses, shall make oath or affirmation according to law, before the Justices who are to allow the same, that such witness or witnesses did see the overseers of the poor whose names and seals are thereunto subscribed and set, severally sign and seal the said certificate; and that the names of each witness attesting the said certificate are of their own proper handwriting; which said Justice shall also certify, that such oath or affirmation was made

(129)

before them, and every such certificate so allowed, and oath or affirmation of the execution thereof so certified, by the Justices, shall be taken and received as evidence without other proof thereof, and no person so coming by certificate into any county or place, nor an apprentice or servant to such person shall be deemed or adjudged by any law whatsoever, to have gained a legal settlement therein, unless such person shall after the date of such certificate, execute some public annual office, being legally placed therein in such county or place.

§ 18. No person whomsoever, coming into any county or place without such certificate, as aforesaid, shall gain a legal settlement therin, unless such person shall give security if required, at his or her coming into the same, for indemnifying and discharging such county or place to be allowed by any one of the Justices of the peace respectively.

No legal settlement gained by strangers without a certificate, unless security given &c

§ 19. Upon any complaint made by the overseers of the poor of the proper county or place, to any one or more of the Justices of the said county, wherein such township or place is situate, it shall and may be lawful to and for any two Justices of the said county, respectively, where any person or persons is or are likely to become chargeable to said county or place, where he, she or they shall come to inhabit, by their warrant or order, directed to the said overseers, to remove and convey such person or persons, to the county, township, place or state, where he, she or they was, or were, last legally settled, unless such person or persons shall give sufficient security to discharge and indemnify

Persons likely to become chargeable, how to be removed.

(130)

the said county or place, to which he, she or they, is, or are likely to become chargeable as aforesaid.

Appeal on removals.

§ 20.   If any person or persons shall think himself or themselves aggrieved by any order of removal made by any of the said Justices, such person or persons may appeal to the next court of Common Pleas, for the county from whence such poor person shall be removed, and not elsewhere, which said court shall determine the same; and if there be any defects of form in such order, the said court shall cause the same to be certified and amended, without any costs to the party; and after such amendment shall proceed to hear the truth and merits of the cause, but no such order of removal shall be proceeded upon unless reasonable notice be given by the overseers of the township or place, appealing unto the overseers of the township or place, from which the removal shall be, the reasonableness of which notice shall be determined by the court to which the appeal is made, and if it shall appear to said court that reasonable time of notice was not given, then the appeal shall be adjourned to the next court, and there determine the same.

Proceedings thereon.

Against vexatious removals & frivolous appeals.

§ 21.   For the more effectual prevention of vexatious removals and frivolous appeals the court in term, upon any appeal concerning the settlement of any poor person, or upon any proof before them then to be made of notice of any such appeal to have been given by the proper officer to the overseers of any township or place (though they did not afterwards prosecute such appeal) shall

(131)

at the same term, order the party in whose behalf such appeals shall be determined, or to whom such notice did appear to have been given, such costs and charges, as the said court shall think just and reasonable, to be paid by the overseers, or any other person against whom such appeal shall be determined, or by the person that did give such notice.

Costs on appeals:

How recoverable.

And if the person ordered to pay such costs and charges, shall live out of the jurisdiction of said court, any Justice where such person shall inhabit, shall, on request to him made, and a true copy of the order for payment of such costs and charges, certified under the hand of the Clerk of the court, by his warrant, cause the same to be levied by distress; and if no such distress can be had, shall commit such person to the common jail, there to remain without bail or mainprize, until he pays the said costs and charges.

§ 22. But if the said court, on such appeal, shall determine in favour of the appellant, that such poor person was unduly removed, the court shall at the same term, order and award to such appellant, so much money, as shall appear to the said court to have been reasonably paid by the county, township or place, on whose behalf such appeal was made, towards the relief of such poor person, between the time of such undue removal, and the determination of such appeal, with the costs aforesaid, the said money so awarded, and the costs to be recov- **On judgment for appellants.**

Costs &c. thereon.

R

(132)

ered in the same manner as the costs and charges awarded against an appellant, are to be recovered by virtue of this law as aforesaid. **How recoverable.**

§ 23. If any house keeper, or inhabitant of the Territory, shall take into, receive or entertain in his or her house or houses, any person or persons whatsoever, not being persons who have gained a legal settlement in some county, township, or place within this Territory, and shall not give notice thereof in writing to the proper overseers of the poor, within ten days, next after so receiving or entertaining such person or persons, such inhabitant, or house keeper, being thereof legally convicted, by the testimony of one credible witness on oath or affirmation, before any one Justice of the Peace of the county where such person dwells, shall forfeit and pay the sum of three dollars, for every such offence; the one moiety to the use of the county, and the other moiety to the informer, to be levied on the goods and chattels of the delinquents, in the manner hereinafter directed, and for want of sufficient distress, the offender to be committed to the work house of **Penalty on persons receiving others not being legally settled, without giving notice thereof overseers.**

How recoverable.

the township, or the jail of the said county, there to remain, without bail or mainprize, for the space of ten days.

Further penalty in case of paupers death.

§ 24.   And moreover, in case the person or persons, so entertained, or concealed, shall become poor, and unable to maintain him, or herself, or themselves, and cannot be removed to the place of his, or her, or their last legal settlement in any other state, if a-

(133)

ny such, he, she or they, have, or shall happen to die, and not have wherewith to defray the charges of his, her or their funeral, then, and in such case, the house keeper, or person convicted of entertaining, or concealing such poor person, against the tenor of this law, shall be obliged to provide for, and maintain such poor and indigent person or persons; and in case of such poor persons death, shall pay the overseers of the poor, so much money as shall be expended on the burying of such poor and indigent person or persons, and upon refusal so to do it shall be lawful for the overseers of the poor of said township, or place respectively, and they are hereby required to assess a sum of money, on the person or persons so convicted, from time to time by a weekly assessment for maintaining such poor and indigent person or persons, or assess a sum of money for defraying the charges of such poor

How recoverable.

persons funeral as the case may be; and in case the party convicted shall refuse to pay the sum of money so assessed or charged to the overseers of the poor for the uses aforesaid, the same shall be levied on the goods and chattels of the offender in the manner hereafter directed. But if such persons so convicted have no goods or chattels, to satisfy the sum so assessed for him or them to pay; then the said Justices shall commit the offender to prison, there to remain without bail or main-prize, until he or they, shall have paid the same; or until he or they shall be discharged by due course of law.

(134)

Overseers shall receive all poor lawfully removed.

§ 25.   If any person be removed by virtue of this law, from one county, township or place to another, by warrant or order under the hands and seals, of two Justices of the peace as aforesaid, the overseers of the poor of the township or

place, to which the said person shall be so removed, are hereby required to receive said person; and if any of the said overseers shall neglect or refuse so to do, he or they so offending, **Penalty on**
upon proof thereof by one or more credible witnesses, upon **neglect.**
oath or affirmation, before one or more of the Justices of the
peace of the county where the offender doth reside, shall forfeit
for every such offence the sum of twelve dollars, to the Sheriff
for the use of the county, to be levied by distress, and sale of
the offenders goods, by warrant under the hand and seal of **How recov-**
the said Justice of the Peace, which he is hereby required and **erable.**
empowered to make, directed to the constable of the township,
or place, where such offender or offenders dwell, returning
the overplus, if any there be, to the owner or owners; and
for want of sufficient distress, then the offender to be committed to the Jail of the county where he dwells, there to remain without bail or main-prize, for the space of forty days.

§ 26. If any poor person shall come to any township or **Proceedings**
place within this territory, and shall happen to fall sick or **when the**
poor of one
die, before he or she have gained a legal settlement in the **place sicken**
county or place, to which he or she shall come, so that such **or die in an-**
person cannot be removed, the overseers of the poor of the **other.**
town-

(135)

ship or place into which such person is come, or one of them,
shall, as soon as coveniently may be, give notice to the overseers of the poor of the township or place, where such person
had last gained a legal settlement, or to one of them, of the
name, circumstances and condition of such poor person; and
if the overseers of the poor to whom such notice shall be
given, shall neglect or refuse to pay the monies expended for
the use of such poor person, and to take order for relieving
and maintaining such poor, or in case of his or her death before
notice can be given as aforesaid; shall on request being made **Penalty on**
neglect or refuse to pay the monies expended in maintaining **overseers ne-**
and burying such poor person, then, and in every such case **glecting.**
it shall be lawful for any two Justices of the peace of the

county where such poor person was last legally settled, and they are hereby authorised and required upon complaint made to them, to cause all such sums of money as were necessarily expended for the maintenance of such poor person, during the whole time of his or her sickness, and in case he or she dies, for his or her burial, by warrant under their hands and seals, to be directed to some constable of the county respectively,

How recoverable.

to be levied by distress, and sale of the goods and chattels of the said overseer or overseers of the poor, so neglecting or refusing to be paid to the overseer or overseers of the township or place, where such poor person happened to be sick, or to die, as aforesaid, and the overplus of the monies arising by the sale of such goods,

(136)

remaining in the constables hands, after the sum of money ordered to be paid, together with the costs of distress are satisfied, shall be restored to the owner or owners of said goods; if any of the said overseers shall think him, or themselves aggrieved by any sentence of such Justices, or by their refusal

Appeal.

to make any order, as is aforesaid, he or they may appeal to the next court for the county where such Justices reside, and not elsewhere, which court is hereby authorised and required to hear, and finally determine the same,

Duties enjoined on fathers, mothers and children.

§ 27. The father and grand father, and mother and grand mother, and the children of every poor, old, blind, lame, and impotent person; or other poor person, not able to work, being of sufficient ability, shall at their own charge, relieve and maintain every such poor person, as the court at their terms, for the county where such persons resides, shall order and

Penalty on neglect.
How rocoverable.

direct, on pain of forfeiting the sum of five dollars, for every month they shall fail therein.

Men deserting their wives. and women their children, how

§ 28. Whereas it sometimes happen that men separate themselves without reasonable cause from their wives, and desert their children, and women also desert their children, leaving them a charge upon the said county or place, aforesaid,

although such person may have estates which should con- **to be dealt**
tribute to the maintenance of such wives or children; it shall **with.**
and may be lawful for the overseers of the poor of the said
township, or place, having first obtained a warrant or

(137)

order from two Justices of said county or place, where such
wife or children shall be so left or neglected; to take and seize
so much of the goods and chattels and receive so much of the
annual rents, and profits of the lands and tenements of such
husband, father or mother; as such, two Justices shall order
and direct, for providing for such wife, and for maintaining
and bringing up of such child or children; which warrant or
order being confirmed at the next court of common Pleas for
the county; it shall and may be lawful for the said court to
make an order, for the overseers to dispose of such goods and
chattels, by sale or otherwise, or so much of them for the purposes aforesaid, as the court shall think fit, and to receive the
rents and profits, or so much of them as shall be ordered by
the said court; of his or her lands and tenements, for the purposes aforesaid, and if no estate real or personal of such husband, father or mother, can be found, wherewith provision
may be made, as aforesaid, it shall and may be lawful to, and
for the said court for the county to order the payment of such
sums as they shall think reasonable, for the maintenance of
any wife or children, so neglected, and commit such husband,
father or mother, to the common jail, there to remain until he
or she comply with the said order, give security for the per-
formace thereof, or be otherwise discharged by the said court;
and on complaint made to any Justice of the peace in any
county of any wife or children being so ne-

(138)

glected, such Justice shall take security from the husband,
father or mother neglecting as aforesaid, for his or her appearance at the next court, there to abide the determination

of the said court, and for want of security to commit such person to jail.

Fines, how recoverable.

§ 29. The several fines, forfeitures and penalties, sum and sums of money, imposed or directed to be paid by this law, and not herein otherwise directed to be recovered, the same, and every of them, shall be levied and recovered by distress and sale of the goods and chattels of the delinquent, or offender by warrant under the hand and seal of any one Justice of the county, where the delinquent or offender dwells, or is to be found, and after satisfaction made of the respective forfeitures, fines, penalties, and sums of money, directed to be levied by such warrant as aforesaid, together with such legal charges as shall become due on the recovery thereof, the overplus, if any, to be returned to the owner or owners of such goods and chattels, his or her executors or administrators.

Appeas from Justices to the court of C. P. except &c. Whose decision to be final.

§ 30. And if any person or persons shall find him or themselves aggrieved with any judgment of the Justices, in pursuance of this act, such person or persons may appeal to the next court of common Pleas for the county where sentence was given, except in cases of removal, and cases of poor persons becoming chargeable in one place, who are legally settled in another, as is otherwise, provided by this law, whose decision in all such cases shall be conclusive.

(139)

Overseers of the poor how they may plead.

Judgmt. for them, to recover double costs.

§ 31. If any action shall be brought against any overseer, or other person, who, in his aid, and by his command, shall do any thing concerning his office, he may plead the general issue, and give this law, and any special matter in evidence, and if the plaintiff shall fail in his action, discontinue the same, or become nonsuit, he shall pay double costs.

JESSE B. THOMAS,
Speaker of the House of Representatives.
B. CHAMBERS,
President of the Council.

Approved—September 17th, 1807.
WILLIAM HENRY HARRISON.

CHAPTER XXIV.
An Act declaring what Laws shall be in force.

THE Common Law of England, all statutes or acts of the British Parliament, made in aid of the Common Law, prior to the fourth year of the reign of King James the first, (excepting the second section of the sixth Chapter of forty-third Elizabeth, the 8th Chapter, thirteenth, Elizabeth, and 9th Chapter, thirty-seventh, Henry eighth,)

The common law, British acts prior to 4th James, except &c. and laws of the territoryshall be the rules of decision.

S

(140)

and which are of a general nature, not local to that kingdom; and also the several laws in force in this Territory, shall be the rule of decision, and shall be considered, as of full force, until repealed by legislative authority.

JESSE B. THOMAS,
Speaker of the House of Representatives.
B. CHAMBERS,
President of the Council.

Approved—September 17th, 1807.
WILLIAM HENRY HARRISON.

CHAPTER XXV.
An Act respecting Divorce.

§ 1. DIVORCES from the banns of Matrimony shall be decreed where either of the parties had a former wife or husband alive, at the time of solemnising the second Marriage, or for impotency, or adultery in either of the parties.

Causes for divorses from the banns of matrimony.

§ 2. Divorce from bed and board shall be granted for the cause of extreme cruelty in either of the parties.

From bed & board.

§ 3. Whenever a divorce shall be decreed, on cause of aggression from the husband, the woman, if no issue of the Marriage be living at the time of the divorce,

Wifes alimony, when & how to be allowed in case divorce decreed on aggression of the husband.

(141)

shall be restored to all her lands, tenements and hereditaments, and be allowed out of the man's personal estate, such alimony as the court may think reasonable, having regard to the personal property that came to him by the Marriage, and his ability; but if there be issue living at the time of the divorce, then the court, in regard to ordering restoration, or granting alimony, may do as circumstances may seem to require, and, on application from either party, may, from time to time, make, at their discretion, such **In case of** alterations therein as may be necessary.

aggression of
the wife.
§ 4. If the divorce arise from the cause of aggression, of the wife, whether there be living issue or not, of the Marriage, the court may order to her the restoration of the whole, or part, or no part, of her lands, tenements and hereditaments, and may **Distribution** assign such alimony, as shall be thought proper, and may also **of the chil-** make such distribution between the parties of their children (if **dren.** any) as the court shall think proper.

What courts
have cogni-
§ 5. The General court, and the Circuit courts, shall have the sole cognizance of all divorces applied for, or made, and the **zance herein** Judges thereof may use such kind of process to carry their judgment into effect, as to them shall seem expedient. Whenever they **Oath of hus-** may think it proper, they may compel the husband to disclose on **band if re-** oath, what personal estate he hath received in right of his wife, **quired.** how the same hath been disposed of, and what proportion of it **Proceedings** remained in his hands at the time of the divorce.

in case of di-
vorce.
§ 6. No cause of divorce, or alimony, shall be brought before the same courts, un-

(142)

less the party suing, or complaining, shall file his or her libel in the proper Clerks office, specially setting forth therein, the cause of his or her complaint, and shall cause the other party, if in this Territory, to be served with an attested copy thereof, and with a summons commanding him or her to appear at the court where the cause is to be heard, fourteen days at the least before the sitting of the said court, otherwise in such manner as the court shall direct, And where the party libelled shall not be within the limits of this Territory, then such summons shall be published at least once a week in some public newspaper in this Territory, nearest to the usual residence of the parties, for at least eight weeks. The said courts shall have all the powers necessary, to the conducting and finally determing such causes, according to the true intent of this law.

Further powers of the court.

JESSE B. THOMAS,
Speaker of the House of Representatives.
B. CHAMBERS,
President of the Council.

Approved—17th September, 1807.
WILLIAM HENRY HARRISON.

(143)

CHAPTER XXVI.
An act for improving the breed of Horses.

§ 1. IT shall and may be lawful for any person or persons, to take up, and cut or geld, at the risk of the owner, any stone horse of the age of twelve months and upwards, that may be found running at large, out of the enclosed ground of the owner or keeper, and if the said horse should happen to die, he shall have no recourse against the person or persons who shall have so taken up or gelded the said horse; and the owner of the said horse shall moreover pay to the person who has so taken up and cut or gelded the said horse or caused it to be done, the sum of three dollars, to be recovered before any Justice of the Peace of the county.

Stone horses above a year old, running at large to be taken up & cut or gelded. Horse dying loss of owner. Who shall pay for cutting 3 dolls. How recoverable.

§ 2. It shall not be lawful for any person to cut, or geld any horse above fourteen and one half hands high, that is known to be kept for covering mares; but if any owner or keeper of a covering horse, shall wilfully or negligently suffer said horse to run at large, out of the enclosed lands of the owner or keeper, any person may take up said horse and carry him to his owner or keeper, for which he shall receive two dollars, recoverable before any Justice of the Peace of the county; for a second offence double the sum, and for a third offence the

Provision in favor of stud horses above 14½ hands high running at large, & proceedings in such cases.

(144)

said horse may be taken and cut or gelded, as is provided in the first section hereof.

JESSE B. THOMAS,
Speaker of the House of Representatives.
B. CHAMBERS,
President of the Council,

Approved—September 17th, 1807.
WILLIAM HENRY HARRISON.

CHAPTER XXVII.
An act against forcible entry and detainer.

Two justices may enquire by jury, and order restitution of lands &c. unlawfully withheld.

§ 1. TWO Justices of the peace shall have authority to enquire by jury, as is hereinafter directed, as well against those who make unlawful and forcible entry, into lands or tenements, and with a strong hand detain the same, as against those who having lawful and peaceable entry into lands or tenements, unlawfully and by force hold the same; and if it be found upon such enquiry that an unlawful and forcible entry hath been made, and that the same lands or tenements are held and detained with force and strong hands, or that the same after a lawful entry, are held unlawfully and with force and strong hand, then such Justices shall cause the party complaining to have restitution thereof.

Justices on a written complaint of unlawful detainer of lands, &c. how to proceed. Warrant to impannel a jury of freeholders.

§ 2. When complaint shall be formally made in writing to any two Justices of the

(145)

Peace of any unlawful and forcible entry into any lands or tenements and detainer as aforesaid, or if any unlawful and forcible detainer of the same after a peaceable entry, they shall make out their warrant under their hands and seals, directed to the Sheriff (or as the case may be) the Coroner of the same county, commanding him to cause to come before them, twelve good and lawful men of the same county, each one of whom having freehold lands or tenements, and they shall be impannelled to enquire into the entry, or forcible

detainer complained of, which warrant shall be in the form
following, *mutatis mutandis.*

H.   Sc.

AB, and CD, esquires two of the Justices assigned to keep
the peace within   and for the said county, to the   of H,
greeting: whereas complaint is made to us by E F, of   in
the   county aforesaid that G H, of   yeoman upon
the   day of   at   aforesaid with force and arms,
and with a strong hand, did unlawfully and forcibly enter
into and upon a tract of land of him, the said E F, in
aforesaid containing   acres, bounded as follows, viz.
[or into the messuage and tenement of him, the said E F, as
the case may be] and him the said E F, with force and a strong
hand, as aforesaid, did expel and unlawfully put out of the
possession of the same [for if it is a forcicle detainer only,
then the entry shall be described, and the detainer inserted as
follows] and the said E F, does ulawfully, unjusty, and with
a strong hand deforce

(146)

and still keep out of the possession of the same; you are
therefore commanded on behalf of the United States, to cause
to come before us upon the   day of   at the   in
the said county, twelve good and lawful men of your county,
each one of whom being a freeholder, to be impannelled and
sworn to enquire into the forcible entry, and detaier, [or for
the detainer only] before described; given under our hands and
seals the   day of   in the year

A B,) Justices of the
C D.)   Peace.

§ 3. And the said Justices shall make out their summons
to the party complained against, in the form following:

Sc.

L. S.)
L. S.)

A B, and C D, two of the Justices assigned to keep the
peace, within and for said county of   to the   of

complained of. greeting: Summons G H, of   to appear before us at   in the said county at   o'clock in the   noon then and there to answer to   and defend, against the complaint of E F, to us exhibited, wherein he complains that [here the complaint shall be recited] and you are to make to us a return of this summons with your proceedings therein, on or before the said day. Witness our hands and seals the   day of   in the year of

A B,)
C D,)   Justices.

(147)

Summonses how to be served. Which summons shall be served upon the party complained against, or a copy thereof left at his usual place of abode, seven days exclusively, before the day appointed by the Justices for the trial; and if after the service of such summons, the party do not appear to defend, the Justices shall proceed to the enquiry in the same manner as if he were present, and when the jury shall appear, the Justices shall lay before the jury the exhibited complaint, and shall administer the following oath to them, viz.

FOREMAN's OATH.

Jurors oath. You as foreman of this jury do solemnly swear (or affirm) that you will well and truly try whether the complaint of E F, now laid before you is true, according to your evidence, so help you God, [if swearing.]

THE OTHER JURORS
OATH, viz.

The same oath [or affirmation] that your foreman hath taken on his part, you, and every of you shall well and truly observe, and keep, so help you God. And if the jury shall find **Form of the verdict.** the same true, then they shall return their verdict in form following.

At a court of enquiry held before A B, and C D, esquires, two Justices assigned to keep the peace, within and for the

county of H   at   in the said county of H   upon
the   day of   in

T

(148)

the year   the jury upon their oaths do find that the
lands or tenements in   aforesaid, bounded or described
as follows   [as in the complaint] upon the   day
of   in the year   were in the lawful and
rightful possession of the said E F, and that the said G H,
did upon the same day, unlawfully with force and arms, and
with a strong hand, enter forcibly upon the same; or being
lawfully upon the same, did unlawfully with force and strong
hands, expel and drive out the said E F, and that he doth
still continue wrongfully to detain the possession from him,
the said E F, wherefore the jury find upon their oath or
affirmation, as aforesaid, that the said E F, ought to have
restitution thereof without delay.

If by accident or challenge, there shall happen not to be a
full jury, the sheriff shall fill the pannel by tales, as in other
cases; and if the jury after a full hearing of the cause, shall
find the complaint laid before them supported by evidence,
they shall all sign their verdict in form aforesaid, otherwise
the defendant shall be allowed his legal costs, and have his
execution thereof.

Where pannel is incomplete, then to be filled by a tales.
All jurors to sign verdict for complainant, otherwise costs to defendant.

If the jury shall return their verdict signed by the whole
pannel, that the complaint is supported, the justices shall enter
up judgment for the complainant to have restitution of the
premises; and shall award their writ of restitution accordingly,
and no appeal shall be allowed from the judgment of the
Justices.

On verdict for complainant judgment to be entered up & a writ of restitution.
No appeal from justices judgment.

(149)

§ 4. *Provided nevertheless,* That the proceeding may be removed by *Certiorari* into General court or Circuit court, holden in
such county, and be there quashed for irregularity, if any such

Appeal by Certiorari.

there may be, nor shall such judgment be a bar to any after action brought by either party; which writ of restitution shall be in form following;

H   Sc.

L. S.)
L. S.)

A B and C D, two of the Justices assigned to keep the Peace in, and for the said county, to the   of   H greeting:

Whereas at a court of enquiry, of forcible entry and detainer, held before us at   in the said county of   upon the   day of in the year   the jurors empannelled and sworn according to law did return their verdict in writing signed by each of them, that E F, was upon the day of   .   in the rightful possession of a certain messuage or tract of land, [as in the verdict returned] and that &c. [as in the verdict] whereupon it was considered by us, that the said E F, should have restitution of the same: We therefore require you that taking with you the force of the county, if necessary; you cause the said G H, to be forthwith removed from the premises, and the said E F, to have the peaceable restitution of the same, and also that you levy of the goods, chattels,

(150)

or lands of the said G H, the sum of   being costs taxed against him on the trial aforesaid, together with more for this writ, and your own fees, and for want of such goods, chattels or lands, of the said G H, by you found, you are commanded to take the body of the said G H, and him commit to the common jail of the said county, there to remain until he shall pay the sum aforesaid, together with all fees arising on the service of this writ, or until he be delivered by due course of law, and make return of this writ with your procedings: Witness our hands and seals at

aforesaid the   day of
in the year

$$A B,)$$
$$C D,)$$ Justices.

Provided nevertheless, That this law shall not extend unto **Priviso.**
any person who hath had the occupation, or been in the quiet
possession of any lands or tenements by the space of three **As to three**
whole years together, next before, and whose estate therein **years quiet possession.**
is not ended or determined.

JESSE B. THOMAS,
Speaker of the House of Representatives.
B. CHAMBERS,
President of the Council

Approved—September 17th, 1807.
WILLIAM HENRY HARRISON.

(151)

CHAPTER XXVIII.
An Act as to proceedings in Ejectment, Distress for Rent, and Tenants at will, holding over.

§   WHERE any goods or chattels shall be distrained
for any rent reserved and due, upon any demise, lease, or con- **Distress for**
tract whatsoever, and the tenant, or owner of the goods so **rent how made.**
distrained, shall not (within five days, next after such distress
taken, and notice thereof, with the cause of such taking, left **Owner of**
at the dwelling house, or other most notorious place on the **goods distrai-**
premises, charged with the rent distrained for) replevy the **ed, when to replevy.**
same, with sufficient security, to be given to the Sheriff according to law, that then, and in such case, after such distress
and notice, as aforesaid, and expiration of the said five days,
the person distraining, or his agent duly authorised, shall, and
may, with the Sheriff, under Sheriff, or any constable in the
county, where such distress shall be taken (who are hereby
required to be aiding and assisting therein) cause the goods
and chattels so distrained, to be appraised by two reputable **Otherwise**
freeholders, who shall have and receive for their trouble the **thedistress to be appraised.**

sum of fifty cents per diem each, and in the proportion for a

Appraisors fees.

longer, or shorter time, and shall first take the following oath or affirmation;

Oath.

"I, A B, will well and truly, according to the best of my understanding, appraise the goods and chattels of C D, distrained on for rent, by E F,"

Which oath or affirmation, such Sheriff,

(152)

under Sheriff, or Constable, is hereby empowered and required to administer; and after such appraisement, shall, and

when distress may be sold.

may, after six days public notice, lawfully sell the goods and chattels so distrained, for the best price that can be gotten for the same, for, and towards satisfaction of the rent for which the said goods and chattels shall be distrained, and of the charges of such distress, appraisement and sale, leaving the overplus, if any, in the hands of the said Sheriff, under Sheriff, or Constable, for the owners use.

Penalty on rescues of goods distrained.

§ 2. Upon any pound breach, or rescous of goods or chattels distrained for rent, the person or persons grieved thereby, shall in a special action upon the case, for the wrong thereby sustained, recover his, her, or their, treble damages,

And how recoverable.

and costs of suit, against the offender or offenders, in such rescous, or pound breach, any, or either of them, or against the owner or owners of the goods distrained, in case the same be afterwards found to have come to his or their use, or possession.

Distraining for rent, when none due, subjects distrainor to forfeit double value & costs.

§ 3. *Provided,* That in case any distress and sale shall be made by virtue of this act, for rent pretended to be in arrear, and due, when in truth no rent shall appear to be in arrear, or due, to the person or persons distraining, or to him, or them, or in whose name or names, or right, such distress shall be taken as aforesaid, then the owner of such goods and chattels, distrained and sold, as aforesaid, his executors or administrators shall, and may, by action of trespass, or upon the case, to be brought against the person

(153)

or persons so distraining, any, or either of them, his, or their executors, or administrators, recover double the value of the goods or chattels, so distrained and sold, together with full costs of suit.

§ 4. The goods and chattels, lying or being in or upon any messuage, lands or tenements, which are, or shall be leased, for life, or lives, term of years, or otherwise, taken by virtue of any execution, shall be liable to the payment of all such sum or sums of money, as are, or shall be due for rent for the premises, at the time of taking such goods and chattels by virtue of such execution, and the said Sheriff shall, after sale of the said goods and chattels, pay to the landlord, or other person empowered to receive the same, such rent so due, if so much shall be in his hands, and if not, so much as shall be in his hands, and apply the overplus, thereof, if any, towards satisfying the debt and costs, in such execution mentioned: *Provided always,* That the said rent so to be paid to the landlord, shall not exceed one years rent.

In case of execution, rent due to be first paid out of goods distrained.

Sheriff to pay it over to landlord.

But not exceeding one years rent.

§ 5. In case any lessee, or tenant for life, or lives, term of years, at will, or otherwise, of any messuage, lands or tenements, upon the demise whereof any rents, are, or shall be reserved or made payable, shall fraudulently or clandestinely convey, or carry off from such demised premises, his goods or chattels, with intent to prevent the landlord or lessor from distraining the same, for arrears of such rent, so reserved as aforesaid, it shall and may be lawful to, and for such lessor, or landlord, or any other person or

Tenant clandestinely removing his goods, landlord may distrain them, wherever found within 30 days.

(154)

persons, by him for that purpose, lawfully empowered, within the space of thirty days, next ensuing such conveying away, or carrying off such goods or chattels, as aforesaid, to take and seize such goods and chattels wherever the same may be found, as a distress for the said arrears of such rent, and the same to sell, or otherwise dispose of, in such manner as if the said goods and chattels had actually been distrained by such lessor, or landlord, in, or upon such demised premises, for such arrears of rent, any law, custom, or usage, to the contrary notwithstanding.

Provided such goods were not bona fide sold to another not privy to the fraud.

§ 6, *Provided nevertheless,* That nothing herein contained, shall extend, or be deemed or construed to extend to empower such lessor, or landlord, to take or seize any such goods or chattels, as a distress for arrears of rent, which shall be *bona fide,* and for a valuable consideration, sold before such seizure made, to any person or persons not privy to such fraud as aforesaid, any thing herein to the contrary notwithstanding,

Power to landlord or lessor to distrain cattle, stock, corn, &c.

§ 7. It shall and may be lawful, to, and for every lessor, or landlord, lessors, or landlords, or her, or their bailiffs, receivers, or other person or persons empowered by him, her, or them, to take and seize, as a distress for arrears of rent, any cattle, or stock of their respective tenant, or tenants, feeding or pasturing upon all or any part of the premises, demised or holden, and also to take and seize all sorts of corn, and grass, hops, roots, fruits, pulse, or other product whatsoever, which shall be growing on any part of the estate, or estates,

(155)

so demised or holden, as a distress for arrears of rent; and to appraise, sell, or otherwise dispose of the same, towards satisfaction of the rent for which such distress shall have been taken, and of the charges of such distress, appraisement and sale, in the same manner as other goods and chattels, may be seized, distrained and disposed of; and the purchaser of any

With liberty of ingross, e-gross & re-gross to repair fences & perfect the crop &c.

such corn, grass, hops, roots, fruits, pulse or other product, shall have free ingress, egress, and regress, to, and from the same, where growing, to repair the fences from time to time, and when ripe, to cut, gather, make, cure, and lay up, and thrash, and after to carry the same away, in the same manner as the tenant might legally have done, had such distress never been made,

Tenant concealing de-

§ 8. Whereas great inconveniencies may frequently happen to landlords by their tenants secreting declarations in ejectments, which may be delivered to them, or by refusing to appear to such ejectment, or to suffer their landlords to take upon them the defence thereof, every tenant therefore to whom any declaration in ejectment shall be delivered for any lands, tenements, or hereditaments, within the Territory, shall forthwith give notice thereof to his or her landlord, or landlords, or his or their bailiffs, receivers, agent, or attorney, under penalty of forfeiting the value of two years rent, of the premises so demised or holden in possession of such tenant, to the person of whom he or she holds, to be recovered by action of debt, to be brought in any court where the

claration in ejectment to forfeit two years rent.

U

(156)

same may be cognizable, wherein no essoin, protection, or wager of law shall be allowed, nor any more than one imparlance.

§ 9. It shall and may be lawful for the court where such ejectment shall be brought to suffer the landlord or landlords to make him, her or themselves defendant, or defendants, by joining with the tenant or tenants, to whom such declaration in ejectment shall be delivered, in case he, or they shall appear, but in case such tenant, or tenants, shall refuse or neglect to appear, judgment shall be signed against the casual ejector, for want of such appearance; but if the landlord, or landlords of any part of the lands, tenements, or hereditaments, for which such ejectment was brought, shall desire to appear by himself, or themselves, and consent to enter into the like rule, that by the course of the court, the tenant in possession, in case he, or she, had appeared, ought to have done, then the court, where such ejectment shall be brought, shall and may permit such landlords so to do, and order a stay of execution upon such judgment against the casual ejector, until they shall make further order therein.

Court may suffer landlord to become defendant in ejectment.

On non appearance of tenant, judgment to go against the casual ejector.

But landlord may appeal by himself or attorney and enterter into rule, &c. Whereupon stay of execution &c.

§ 10. Whereas great difficulties often arise in making avowries or connuzance upon distress for rent, it shall and

Defendants in replevin

may vow &
make con-
veyance gen-
erally.

may be lawful for all defendants, in replevin, to avow or make connuzance generally, that the plaintiff in replevin, or other tenant of the lands and tenements, whereon such distress was made, enjoyed the same under a grant or demise, at such a certain rent or service, during the time wherein the rent or service dis-

(157)

trained for incurred, which rent or service, was then, and still remains due, without further setting forth the grant, tenure, demise or title of such landlord or landlords, lessor or lessors,

If plaintiff be
nonsuit, dis-
continues or
loose the
cause, he for-
feits double
costs.

any law or usage to the contrary, notwithstanding, and if the plaintiff or plaintiffs, in such action shall become non-suit, discontinue his, her or their action, or have a judgment given against him, her or them, the defendant or defendants, in such replevin, shall recover double costs of suit.

Sheriff &c.
serving reple
vins, to take
pltffs. bond
with security
to prosecute
with effect.

§ 11.   And to prevent vexatious replevins, or distresses taken for rent, all Sheriffs, and other officers, having authority to serve replevins, may, and shall, in every replevin of a distress, for rent take in their own names, from the plaintiff, and one reasonable person as surety, a bond in double the value of the goods distrained, such value to be ascertained by the oath or affirmation, of one or more credible person or persons, not interested in the goods or distress; and which oath or affirmation, the person serving such replevin, is hereby authorised and required to administer, and conditioned for prosecuting the suit with effect, and without delay, and for duly returning the goods and chattels distrained, in case a return shall be awarded, before any deliverance be made of the distress, and such Sheriff, or other officer, as aforesaid, taking any such bond, shall, at the request and costs of the avowant,

Sheriff may
assign bond,
and how.

or person making connuzance, assign such bond to the avowant, or person aforesaid, by endorsing the same, and attesting it under his hand and seal, in the presence of two credible witnesses.   And if the bond

(158)

so taken and assigned, be forfeited, the avowant or person making connuzance, may bring an action and recover thereupon in his own name, and the court where such action shall be brought, may by a rule of the same court give such relief to the parties upon such bond, as may be agreeable to justice and reason, and such rules shall have the nature and effect of a defeazance to such bond.

Avowant may thereupon sue & recover in his own name. At discretion court may by rule give relief to parties to the bond.

§ 12. Where any person or persons, have leased or demised any lands or tenements, to any person ar persons, for a term of one, or more years, or at will, paying certain rents, he or they, or his or their assigns, shall be desirous, upon the determination of the lease, to have again, and repossess, his, or their estate, so demised, and for that purpose shall demand and require, his or their lessee, or tenant, to remove from, and leave the same, if the lessee or tenant, shall refuse to comply therewith, in three months after such request to him made, it shall and may be lawful to, and for such lessor, or lessors, his or their heirs and assigns, to complain thereof, to any two Justices of the Peace, in the county where the demised premises are situate, and upon due proof made before the said Justices, that the said lessor or lessors, had been quietly and peaceably possessed of the lands or tenements, so demanded to be delivered up, that he or they demised the same under certain rents, to the tenant in possession, or some person or persons under whom such tenant claims, or came in possession, and that the term for which the same was demised, is fully ended, then and in such case it shall and may be

Proceedings against tenants refusing to quit at the end of their term.

Two justices of the peace to have cognizance in such cases & how.

(159)

lawful for the said two Justices, to whom complaint shall be made as aforesaid, and they are hereby enjoined and required, forthwith to issue their warrant directed to the Sheriff of the county, thereby commanding the Sheriff to summons twelve freeholders to appear before the said Justices within four

Their power & duty and warrant to sheriff to summon 12 free holders.

days, next after issuing such warrant, and also to summons the lessee or tenant, or other person claiming or coming into possession under the said lessee or tenant, at the same time to appear before them the said Justices, and free holders to shew

Also lessee or tenant &c to appear & shew cause.

cause if any he has, why restitution of the possession of the demised premises should not be forthwith made, to such lessor or lessors, his or their heirs or assigns; and if upon hearing the parties, or in case the tenant or other person claiming, or coming into possession under the said lessee or

Further proceedings before the justices & jury.

tenant, neglect to appear, after being summoned as aforesaid, it shall appear to the said Justices and freeholders, that the lessor or lessors, had been possessed of the lands or tenements, in question, that he or they had demised the same for a term of years, or at will to the person in possession, or some other under whom he or she claims, or came into possession at a certain yearly, or other rent, and that the term is fully ended; that demand had been made of the lessee, or other person, in possession, as aforesaid, to leave the premises three months before such application to the said Justices, then, and

Justices to make record.

in every such case, it shall and may be lawful, for the said two Justices to make a record of such finding, by them the

(160)

Jury to assess damages.

said Justices and freeholders, and the said freeholders shall assess such damages as they think right, against the tenant or other person in possession as aforesaid, for the unjust detention of the demised premises, for which damages and

Judgment thereupon for damages and costs.

reasonable costs, judgment shall be entered by the said Justices, and shall be final and conclusive to the parties, and upon which the said Justices shall, and they are hereby enjoined and required to issue their warants under their hands and seals, directed to the Sheriff of the county, commanding him forthwith to deliver to the lessor or lessors, his or their heirs or assigns, full possession of the demised premises, aforesaid, and to levy the costs taxed by the Justices, and damages, so by the freeholders, aforesaid, assessed, of the goods and chattels of the lessee or tenant, or other persons in possession, as aforesaid; any law, custom or usage to the contrary, notwithstanding.

§ 13. *Provided nevertheless,* That if the tenant shall alledge, that the title to the lands and tenements in question, is disputed and claimed by some other person or persons, whom he shall name in virtue of a right or title, accrued or happening since the commencement of the lease, so as aforesaid made to him, by descent, deed, or from, or under the last will of the lessor, and if thereupon, the person so claiming, shall forthwith or upon summons, immediately to be issued by the said Justices, returnable before them in six days next following, appear, and on oath or affirmation, to be by the said Justices administered, declare that he

When title set up by lessee or tenant.

Proceedings Thereupon.

(161)

verily believes that he is entitled to the premises in dispute, and shall with one or more sufficient sureties, become bound by recognizance, in the sum of two hundred dollars, to the lessor or lessors, his or their heirs or assigns, to prosecute his claim at the next court of Common Pleas, to be held for the county where the said lands and tenements shall be, then, and in such case, and not otherwise, the said Justices shall forbear to give the said judgment.

Claimant to give bond to prosecnte his claim at the next court of C. P.

§ 14. *Provided also,* That if the said claims shall not be prosecuted according to the true intent and meaning of the said recognizance, it shall be forfeited to the use of the lessor or landlord, and the Justices aforesaid shall proceed to give judgment, and cause the lands and tenements aforesaid, to be delivered to him, in the manner herein before enjoined and directed.

But if the claim be not so prosecuted bond to be forfeited, & justice to proceed to judgment & cause possession of lands &c. to be delivered.

§ 15. It shall and may be lawful for any person or persons, having any rent in arrear, or due upon lease, for life, or lives, or for one or more years, or at will, ended or determined, to distrain for such arrears after the determination of the said respective leases, in the same manner as they might have done, if such lease or leases had not been ended or determined: *Provided,* That such distress be made during the con-

Landlords may distrain for rent in arrear after lease ended. Provided lessors title continues.

(162)

tinuance of such lessor's title or interest.

JESSE B. THOMAS,
Speaker of the House of Representatives.
B. CHAMBERS,
President of the Council.

Approved—September 17th, 1807.
WILLIAM HENRY HARRISON.

CHAPTER XXIX.
An Act regulating the admission, and practice of Attornies and Counsellors at Law.

Attornies & counsellors how admitted. § 1. NO person shall be permitted to practice as an Attorney or Counsellor at Law, or to commence, conduct, or defend any action, suit or plaint, in which he is not a party concerned, in any court of record within this Territory, either by using, or subscribing his own name, or the name of any other person, without having previously obtained a license for that purpose from any two of the Judges of the General Court, which license shall constitute the person receiving the same, an Attorney and Counsellor at Law, and shall authorise him to appear in all the courts of record within this Territory, and there to practice as an attorney and counsellor at law, according to the laws

(163)

Entitled to legal fees. and customs thereof, for, and during his good behavior in the said practice, and to demand and receive all such fees as are, or hereafter may be established, for any service which he shall, or may do, as an attorney, and counsellor at law in the said Territory.

Applicant to produce certificate of good moral character. § 2. No person shall be entitled to receive a license as aforesaid, until he hath obtained a certificate from the court of some county, of his good moral character.

Clk. of the G. C. to keep a roll of all licensed attornies and § 3. It shall be the duty of the Clerk of the General court, to make and keep a roll or record, on parchment, stating at the head or commencement thereof, that the persons, whose names are thereon written, have been regularly licensed, and admitted to practice, as attornies and counsellors at law within this Territory, and that they have duly taken the oath of allegeance to the United States, and also the oath of office, as prescribed by law; which shall be certified and endorsed on the said license.

§ 4. And no person whose name is not subscribed to, or written on, the said roll, with the day and year when the same was subscribed thereto, or written thereon, shall be suffered or admitted to practice as an attorney, or counsellor at law, within the Territory, under the penalty hereinafter mentioned, any thing in this law contained, to the contrary notwithstanding; and the Judges of the General court, in open court, shall have power at their discretion, to strike the name of any attorney or counsellor at law, from the roll, for mal conduct in his office; *Provided always,* That every

W

(164)

attorney before his name is struck off the roll, shall recive a written notice from the Clerk of the General court, stating distinctly the grounds of complaint, or the charges exhibited against him; and he shall after such notice, be heard in his defence, and be allowed reasonable time, to collect and prepare testimony for his justification.

And every attorney whose name shall be at any time, struck off the roll, by order of the court, in manner aforesaid, shall be considered as though his name had never been written thereon, until such time as the said judges in open court, shall authorise him again to sign or subscribe the same.

§ 5. The Judges of the General court, and the Judges of the several courts of Common Pleas, within the Territory, shall have power to punish in a summary way, according to the rules of law, and the usages of courts, any, and every attorney, or counsellor at law, who shall be guilty of any contempt in the execution of his office; and every attorney and counsellor at law, receiving money for the use of his client, and refusing to pay the same when demanded, may be proceeded against in a summary way on motion. And all attornies, counsellors at law, Judges, Clerks, and Sheriffs, and all other officers of the several courts within the

Margin notes:

counsellors at law.

No persons suffered to practice whose name is not written on the roll.

Judges in open court may strike attorney or counsellor's name from the roll.

Not afterwards to practice till restored.

To be punished for contempt of court.

How to be proceeded against for withholding money from clients.

Officers of court subject to arrest and held to bail.

Territory, shall be liable to be arrested and held to bail, and shall be subject to the same legal process, and may in all respects be prosecuted, and proceeded against in the same courts, and in the same manner, as other persons are; any law, usage, or

(165)

custom, or privilege to the contrary notwithstanding.

What persons prohibited to practice as attornies or counsellors.

§ 6. No person shall be permitted to practice as an attorney or counsellor at law, by instituting, conducting or defending, any action, suit, plea or plaint, in any court within the Territory, who is not a citizen thereof, or who holds a commission as a Judge, of any General or Supreme court, or court of Common Pleas, nor shall any person who holds a commission as a Justice of the Peace, Coroner or Sheriff, or who acts as a deputy Sheriff, jailor or Constable, within the Territory, be permitted to practice as an attorney or counsellor at law, in the county in which he is commissioned or appointed, nor shall any Clerk of the General court, Circuit court or court of Common Pleas, be permitted to practice as an attorney or counsellor at law in the court of which he is

Proviso. In favor of attornies heretofore licensed.

Clerk; *Provided nevertheless,* That nothing herein contained, shall prevent, any such attornies as may heretofore have obtained licenses to practice within this Territory, from continuing to practice as such, notwithstanding they may not be residents thereof.

Attornies &c to take the oath of allegeance & of office.

And no person shall be permitted or suffered to enter his name on the roll or record to be kept, as aforesaid, by the Clerk of the General court, or do any official act appertaining to the office of an attorney or counsellor at law, until he hath taken an oath to support the constitution of the United States, and the

The same to be certified on the license.

person administering such oath, shall certify the same on the license, which certificate shall be a sufficient vou-

(166)

cher to the Clerk of the General court, to enter or insert, or permit to be entered or inserted on the roll of attornies and counsellors at law, the name of the person of whom such certificate is made.

Form of oath of offices

§ 7. The following oath of office shall be administered to every attorney and counsellor at law, before they subscribe the respective rolls; to wit, "I swear (or affirm) that I will in all things faithfully execute the duties of an attorney at law (or counsellor at law, as the case may be) according to the best of my understanding and abilities."

§ 8. Any person producing a license or other satisfactory voucher, proving that he hath been regularly admitted an attorney at law in any court of record within the United States, and that he is of a good moral character, may be admitted to an examination, for the degree of an attorney and counsellor at law; and any attorney or counsellor at law, residing in any of the United States, who is of a good moral character, may at any time, on application be admitted an examination for the degree of an attorney and counsellor at law within the Territory.

Persons licensed to practice law in any court of record in the U. S. may be admited to practice in this territory

§ 9. If any person or persons, not licensed as aforesaid, shall receive any money, or any species of property, as a fee, or compensation, for services rendered, or to be rendered by him, or them, as attorney, or attornies, counsellor, or counsellors at law, within the Territory, all money so received, shall be considered as money received to the use of the person paying the same

Penalty on persons undertaking to practice law without a license.

(167)

and may be recovered back with costs of suit, by an action or actions for money had, and received; and all property delivered or conveyed for the purpose aforesaid, or the value thereof may be recovered back with costs of suit by the person conveying or delivering the same by action of *Detinue or Trover* and *Conversion;* and the person or persons receiving such money or property, shall forfeit threefold the amount or value thereof, to be recovered with costs of suit, before any magistrate, if within a magistrates jurisdiction, but if not, in any court of record within the Territory, by action of debt or qui tam, the one half to the use of the person who shall sue for or recover the same, and the other half to the use of the county, in which such suit shall be brought. And if any person or persons shall sign, or cause to be signed, the name of an attorney, or either of the Judges of the General court, to any certificate or license, provided for by this law, with an intent to deceive, such person or persons, shall be deemed guilty of forgery, and shall be prosecuted and punished accordingly.

Fraudulently signing the name of an attorney or judge to a license &c. deemed forgery.

Parties may prosecute & desent in pro per person.

§ 10.   Plaintiffs shall have the liberty of prosecuting, and defendants shall have the privilege of defending, in their proper persons, and nothing herein contained shall be construed to debar them therefrom, nor shall any thing herein contained, be construed

Not to affect counsellors or attornies heretofore admitted.

to effect any person or persons heretofore admitted to the degree of an Attorney, or Counseller at Law, according to the rules of the General court, so as to subject them

(168)

to further examination, or make it necessary for them to renew their licenses.

GENL. W. JOHNSTON.
Speaker pro tempore, of the House of Representatives.
B. CHAMBERS,
President of the Council.

Approved—September 17th, 1807.
WILLIAM HENRY HARRISON.

CHAPTER XXX.
An Act regulating Enclosures.

Fences of wood how to be made, & of what height to be sufficient in law.

§ 1.   ALL fields and grounds kept for enclosures, shall be well inclosed with a fence composed of sufficient posts and rails, posts and palings, palisadoes, or rails alone, laid up in the manner which is commonly called a worm fence; which posts shall be deep set and strongly fastened in the earth; and all fences composed of posts and rails, posts and palings, or palisadoes, shall be at least five feet in height; and all fences composed of rails, in manner which is commonly denominated a worm fence, shall be at least five feet six inches in height, the uppermost rail of each and every pannel thereof supported by strong stakes, strongly set and fastened in the earth, so as to compose what is commonly called staking and rider-

(169)

ing, otherwise the uppermost rail of every pannel of such worm fence, shall be braced with two strong rails, poles or stakes, locking each corner or angle thereof; and in all cases wherein any fence is composed of any of the foregoing materials, the aper- **Apertures be tween the rails palings or palisadoes.** tures between any of the rails, palings or palisadoes, within two feet of the surface of the earth, shall not be more than four inches; and from the distance of two feet from the earth, until the height of three feet six inches from the surface thereof, the appurtures between such rails, palings or palisadoes, shall not be more than six inches; and that in all worm fences, the worm of **Worm to be one third the length of the rails.** the same shall be at least one third of the length of the rails, which compose the respective pannels thereof.

§ 2. If any horse, gelding, mare, colt, mule, or ass, sheep, **Owners of a- nimals brea- king lawful enclosures li- able to pay damages.** lamb, goat, kid, or cattle, shall break into any person's enclosure, the fence being of the aforesaid height and strength, or if any hog, shoat or pig, shall break into any person's enclosure, the fence being of the aforesaid heighth and sufficiency, and by the view of two persons for that purpose, appointed by the court of Common Pleas, found and approved to be such, then the owner of such creature or creatures, shall be liable to make good all damages, to the owner of the enclosure; for the first offence single damages only, ever afterwards double the damages sustained.

§ 3. For the better ascertaining and regulating of parti- **Partition fen ces by whom to be kept & maintained.** tion fences, it is hereby directed, that when any neighbours shall improve lands adjacent to each other, or when any

(170)

person shall enclose any land adjoing to another's land already fenced, so that any part of the first person's fence becomes the partition fence between them, in both these cases, the charge of such division fence, (so far as enclosed on both sides) shall be equally borne and maintained by both parties, to which, and other ends in this law mentioned, each court of Common Pleas, yearly and every year, in the term next after the month of January, shall nominate, and is hereby re- **C. P. to ap- point fence viewers &c.** quired to nominate and appoint three honest able men, for each township respectively; who, being duly sworn to the faithful discharge of the duties of their appointment, shall proceed at the request of any person or persons feeling him, or

Duty of
fence view-
ers.
themselves aggrieved, to view all such fence and fences, about
which any difference may happen or arise; and the aforesaid
persons, or any two of them in each township, respectively,

Judges of the
sufficiency of
fences &c.
shall be the sole judges of the charge to be borne by the delinquent, or by both, or either party, and of the sufficiency of
all fences, whether partition fences, or others; and when they
shall judge any fence to be insufficient, they shall give notice

Owners refu-
sing to make
or repair par.
tition fences
how to pro-
ceed.
thereof to the owners or possessors; and if any one of the owners or possessors, upon request of the other, and due notice
given, by the said viewers, shall refuse, or neglect, to make,
or repair the said fence or fences, or to pay the moiety of the
charges of any fence before made, being the division or common fence, within twenty days after notice given, then, upon

Penalty on
neglect or re
fusal how to
proceed.
proof thereof, before two Justices of the Peace, of the respective county, it shall

(171)

be lawful for the said Justices, to order the person aggrieved
and suffering thereby, to make or repair the said fence or
fences, who shall be reimbursed his costs and charges, from the
person so refusing or neglecting to make or repair the partition fence or fences aforesaid, or to order the delinquent to
pay the moiety of the charge of the fence before made, being
a division, or a common fence, as the case may be; and if the
delinquent shall neglect or refuse to pay to the party injured,
the moiety of the charge of any fence before made, or to reimburse the costs and charges of making or repairing the said
fence or fences, under the order aforesaid, then the same shall
be levied upon the delinquents goods and chattels, under warrant from a Justice of the Peace, by distress and sale thereof,
the overplus, if any be, to be returned to the said delinquent:

Proviso in fa
vour of per-
sons inclos-
ing their
ground with
fences above
named.
Provided, That nothing herein contained, shall be intended to
prevent, or debar any person or persons from enclosing his or
their grounds, in any manner they please, with sufficient walls,
or fences of timber, other than those heretofore mentioned,
or by dykes, hedges and ditches; all such walls and fences to
be in heighth at least five feet from the ground; and all dykes

to be at least three feet in heighth from the bottom of the ditch, and planted and set with thorn and other quickset, so that such enclosures shall fully answer and secure the several purposes meant to be answered and secured by this law: *Provided also,* That such walls, or fences of timber, other than those here-

Y

(172)

tofore mentioned, and dykes, hedges, and ditches, shall be subject to all provisions, inspections, and restrictions respectively, to which by this law, any other enclosure or fence is made liable, according to the true intent and meaning hereof.

Subjected to the inspectors, &c.

JESSE B. THOMAS,
Speaker of the House of Representatives.

B. CHAMBERS,
President of the Council.

Approved—17th September, 1807.
WILLIAM HENRY HARRISON.

CHAPTER XXXI.
An Act for regulating the Interest of Money.

§ 1. CREDITORS (excepting as herein after excepted) shall be allowed to receive interest at the rate of six per centum, per annum, for all monies after they become due, on bond, bill, promissory note, or other instrument of writing, on any judgment recovered in any court of record, now, or hereafter to be established, within the Territory, from the day of signing judgment, until effects be sold, or satisfaction of such judgment be made; likewise on money lent; on money for the forbearance of the payment whereof an express promise hath been made for the payment of inter-

Legal interest, what &c.

(173)

est; on money due on the settlement of accounts, from the day of liquidating accounts between the parties, and ascertaining the balance; on money received to the use of another, and retained without the owners knowledge; and on money withheld by an unreasonable and vexatious delay of payment.

No person to take more than six per cent per annum interest.

§ 2. No person or persons, shall on any contract, which shall be made, directly or indirectly, take for the loan or use of money, or other commodity, above the value of six dollars, for the forbearance of one hundred dollars, or the value thereof, for one year, and so proportionably, for any greater or less sums, any law, custom or usage to the contrary notwithstanding.

Penalty for taking more than six per cent.

§ 3. If any person shall directly, or indirectly, receive any money, obligation, promise, or other commodity, by way of premium, or any other name by which the same may be called, or understood, to the end of obtaining any higher rate of interest than six per centum, per annum, for the loan or use of money, or any other commodity, on any contract which hath been made after the fifteenth November, one thousand seven hundred and ninety nine, or shall hereafter be made; and shall institute an action in law for the recovery of the money due on, or by reason of the breach of such contract, so as aforesaid made, it shall be lawful for the defendant in such action, in pleading, to set forth the special matter in bar of so much of the real sum of money, or price of the commodity, actually lent, advanced or sold, as shall be the amount of

(174)

the aforesaid premium or sum, actually received; and if the plea of the defendant is confessed, or adjudged good, on demurrer, or supported by the verdict of a jury, then and in every such case, the plaintiff shall recover no more than what remains of the aforesaid sum of money, or price of the commodity, actually lent, advanced or sold after deducting the said premium, without even any interest on the principal; and if a residue is still left, the plaintiff may enter judgment for the same, and have execution thereof with interest, and costs accruing from the signing of the judgment: *Provided always,* That if the premium or usurious interest, and costs, exceed the principal, or real sum of money, or the price of the commodity actually lent, advanced or sold, the excess shall be deemed a debt of record, and on motion of the defendant made in open court, such defendant may enter judgment for the same, with costs, at the next, or any subsequent term, within one year, and have execution accordingly.

JESSE B. THOMAS,
Speaker of the House of Representatives.
B. CHAMBERS,
President of the Council.

Approved—September 17th, 1807.
WILLIAM HENRY HARRISON.

(175)

CHAPTER XXXII.
An Act authorising and regulating arbitrations.

§ 1. ALL persons who have any controversy or controversies, for which there is no other remedy, but by personal action, or by suit in equity, and who are desirous of settling or terminating the same; may agree to submit the said controversy or controversies, to the umpirage or arbitration of any person or persons, to be by them, mutually chosen for that purpose, and that their submission, may be made a rule of any court of record within the Territory.

Persons having controvercies may submit the same to an umpire or arbitration. And that such submission may be made a rule of court.

§ 2. When any persons have agreed to submit, any matter or matters, in controversy between them, to umpirage or arbitration, as aforesaid, and that the said submission, may be made a rule of court; they shall enter into arbitration bonds, under their hands and seals, duly executed and delivered, with conditions for the faithful performance of the award or umpirage, which condition shall set forth the name or names of the umpire or arbitrators, and the matter or matters submitted to his or their determination; and shall also expressly state, their agreement that the submission may be made a rule of any court, of record within the Territory, or that may be made a rule of such particular court, as they may name or point out in their submission; and when the umpire or arbitrators, is, or are appointed, and the arbitration bonds are duly executed and delivered, as aforesaid.

parties to enter into arbitration bond conditioned &c.

(176)

Either party may appoint a time and place to meet

either party may appoint a time and place for the umpire to attend, or the arbitrators to meet, of which he shall give written notice to the opposite party, and to the umpire or arbitrators at least ten days before the time appointed for such meeting; and when the umpire or arbitrators, shall be ready to proceed to the business for which he or they, shall have been appointed, the parties may proceed to exhibit their proofs, and the umpire or arbitrators, shall have power to adjourn from time to time, until he is prepared

Umpire or arbitrators may adjourn

to make his umpirage, or they are prepared to make their awaed; *Provided,* The same be made up within the time stipulated in the submission.

§ 3. The parties shall have the benefit of legal process to compel the attendance of witnesses; which process shall be issued

Parties entitled to subpœna to compel the attendance of witnesses.

by the Clerk of the court of Common Pleas, or by the Clerk of the General court and shall be returnable before the umpire or arbitrators on a day certain; and any person disobeying such process, shall be deemed guilty of contempt to the court from

Penalty on witness not attending.

which such process issued, and shall be subject to the same penalties and forfeitures, as are provided, for disobeying writs of Subpœna in other cases; and the costs of such witnesses, shall be taxed by the umpire or arbitrators, according to the provisions contained in the law, ascertaining the fees of witnesses, which costs together with the sum hereinafter allowed to the umpire or

Witnesses to be sworn unless &c.

arbitrators, shall be stated in the award or umpirage, and shall be made a part of the rule of court, and all witnesses examined

(177)

by the umpire or arbitrators, shall be under oath, unless otherwise agreed to by the parties.

§ 4. The award or final determination of the umpire or

The award to be in writing.

arbitrators shall be drawn up in writing, and shall be signed by him or them, or so many of them as agree thereto, and a true

Copies thereof to be delivered to the parties.

copy of the said award or umpirage, shall without delay be delivered by the umpire or arbitrators, to each of the parties, and if either of the parties shall refuse or neglect to obey the said award or umpirage, the other party may return the same, together with the submission or arbitration bond to the court named in the submission, or if no court be named in the submission, then to the court of Common Pleas or to the General court, and the submission and award or umpirage so returned shall be entered on record, and filed by the Clerk, and a rule of court thereupon made; and after such rule is made, the party disobeying the same, shall be liable to be punished as for a contempt of the court; and the court on motion shall issue process accordingly; which process shall not be stayed or impeded, by order of any other court of law or equity, or by the court from whence it issued, until the parties shall in all things obey the award or umpirage, unless it shall be made to appear on oath that the umpire or arbitrators misbehaved, and that such award or umpirage, was obtained by fraud, corruption or other undue means; and no testimony shall be received to impeach or invalidate the said award or umpirage, after the second day of the term,

(178)

next after the term in which the submission was made a rule of court: *Provided always,* That before any submission be made a rule of court, the party moving for such rule, shall produce to the court satisfactory proof of the due execution of the submission or arbitration bond, and also that the party refusing or neglecting to obey the award or umpirage, hath been furnished with a true copy thereof.

§ 5. The umpire or arbitrators shall be entitled to receive each the sum of one dollar per day, for each and every day, which they shall employ in performing the duties of their appointment.

§ 6. In all cases where the plaintiff and defendant, having accounts to produce one against another, shall, by themselves, or attornies, or agents, consent to a rule of court for referring the adjustment thereof, to certain persons mutually chosen by them in open court, (the arward or report of such referrees, being made according to the submission of the parties, approved of by the court, and entered upon the record or roll) shall have the same effect, and be deemed and taken to be as available in law, as a verdict given by twelve men; and the party to whom any

Margin notes:

Award how enforced.

Award to be final.

Unless for misbehavior of umpire &c or for fraud &c.
No testimony to invalidate award &c. after the 2d day next after the term in which submission made rule of court. when award shall be made a rule of court.

Fees to umpire or arbitrators.

Where accounts between two contending parties, pltff. & deft. they may consent to a rule of court referring same to arbitrators, mutually chosen in court.

Report of re-ferrees, ap-proved of by the court & entered on record shall have the like effect as a verdict.

sum or sums of money are thereby awarded to be paid, shall have judgment, or a *scire facias,* for the recovery thereof, as the case may require, as is directed in the seventeenth section of the act entitled 'an act to regulate the practice in the General court, and court of Common Pleas

(179)

And court to enter judg-ment &c.

concerning sums found and settled by a jury.

JESSE B. THOMAS,
Speaker of the House of Representatives.
B. CHAMBERS,
President of the Council.

Approved—September 17th, 1807.
WILLIAM HENRY HARRISON.

CHAPTER XXXI.
An Act to establish and regulate Ferries.

Ferries to be established by the court of C. P.

§ 1. WHENEVER it shall be found necessary to establish a public ferry, over any river or creek within the Territory, the court of Common Pleas of the respective counties, on due application to them made by the proprietor of land, on either side, may establish and confirm the same by a special order for that pur-

How to make application for a ferry-

pose: *Provided always,* That no application shall avail the proprietor, unless his or her intentions relative thereto have been published in the public papers of the county, and if there be no public press in the county, then at least three of the most public places of the township, in which such ferry is proposed to be established, three months previous to the making of such application; and shall more-

Z

(180)

over have published his or her intention by advertisement, on the door of the court house of the proper county, for three days successively during the sitting of the court, within the time, above mentioned.

Courts to fix the rates of

§ 2. The court of Common Pleas, in every county, shall be, and they are hereby empowered, authorised, and required, to fix from time to time, the rates, which each ferry keeper shall hereafter demand, for the transportation of passengers, waggons or carriages, horses, cattle, &c. at any ferry, now or hereafter to be established in their respective counties within this Territory, having due regard to the distance, which the ferry boats have to travel, the dangers or difficulties incident to the same, and the state and condition at the river or creek, over which such ferry is established, and the owner or owners of any such ferry or ferries; shall within three months from the establishment of such ferry execute and deliver a bond, with one or more sufficient securities, to the said court, in the penalty of one hundred dollars, payable to the Sheriff, as treasurer of the county or his successor in office, with a condition that he or she will keep such ferry, or cause the same to be kept according to law; and that he or she will give passage to all public messengers and expresses when required, from time to time without any fee or reward for the same; and if the condition of the said bond, shall at any time be broken, the penalty therein contained, shall be recoverable with costs of suit, for the use of the county; and in case any such person shall neglect or refuse

ferriage in their respective counties

Owner of a ferry to give bond.

The condition.

Penalty on failure to give bond.

(181)

to give such bond, he or she shall forfeit and pay the sum of fifty dollars for every month's refusal or neglect, one half to the use of the person prosecuting for the same, the other half to the use of the county. All expresses sent on public service, by a commander in chief, colonel, lieutenant colonel, major or commandant of any military post, to the governor, or commanding officer of the militia, shall be accounted public messengers and expresses, and shall pass ferry free, within the condition and meaning of the bond aforesaid, in case the dispatch carried by such express, be endorsed on "Public Service," and signed by the person sending the same.

Expresses &c to pass ferry free.

Ferry keeper to set up rate of ferriage.

§ 3. Every ferry keeper shall set and keep up, upon the margin of the river or creek, opposite to the ferry place of every public ferry, a post or board, on which shall be written the rates of ferriage, of such ferry by law allowed; and if any ferry keeper shall demand from any person a greater sum for the ferriage,

Penalty for demanding higher rates.

than is or shall be allowed by the court of Common Pleas to such ferry keeper, such offender shall forfeit to the person so over-charged, the ferriage demanded and received, and also two dollars with costs of suit, for every such offence, recoverable before any Justice of the peace, within the township wherein the offence has been committed.

How recoverable.

§ 4. Each and every ferry keeper shall keep a good and sufficient boat, or boats, if more than one be necessary, with a sufficient number of good and skilful men to navigate the same, and to give due attendance

To keep good and sufficient boats &c.

(182)

to the said ferry or ferries, and the transportation of all persons who shall apply for the same during the day time, that is to say, from day light in the morning until dark in the evening, that no unnecessary delay may happen to persons having occasion to use the same: *Provided always,* That all ferry keepers shall be obliged at any hour of the night, if required, except in case of evident danger, to give passage to all public expresses above recited, and to all other persons requiring the same on their tendering and paying double the rate of ferriage allowed to be taken during the day time.

Ferries to be kept from day light till dark.

When in the night.

§ 5. And for encouraging ferry keepers, and in consideration of setting over public messengers and the persons exempted by this act, *Be it enacted,* That all men necessarily attending on ferries in this Territory, shall be free from militia duty, impressments, opening and repairing highways, so far as personal service is required, and from serving on juries, and if any person or persons other than ferry keepers, licensed as aforesaid, shall for reward set any person over any river or creek, where public ferries are appointed or established, at any place within five miles, of any such publiclic ferry, he she or they so offending, shall forfeit and pay a sum not exceeding twenty nor less than five dollars, for every such offence; one moiety to the person prosecuting for the same, and the other moiety to the use of the county wherein the offence shall have been committed.

Ferry men exempt from militia duty.

Penalty on keeping ferries without license.

(183)

§ 6. If any ferry or ferries, which now are, or may here-after be established, shall not be furnished with necessary boat or boats, and ferrymen, within the space of six months after the establishment thereof, or shall at any time hereafter, be wholly disused or unfrequented for the space of one year, it shall and may be lawful for the court of common Pleas for the county in which such ferry or ferries shall be, on complaint to them made, to summon the proprietor or proprietors of the same, to shew cause, why it should not be discontinued, and to decide according to the testimony adduced, which decision shall be valid in law. *Whencourts may discontinue ferries.*

§ 7. It shall and may be lawful for any ferry keeper, to take into his or her boat, or boats, any passenger or passengers, car-riages, waggons, horses, or cattle, of any kind whatsoever, to convey them over, and to receive the ferriages for the same agreeably to the rates established by the courts of Common Pleas: *Provided nevertheless;* That all ferries now kept by license from the Governor, shall be, and are hereby declared to be established ferries: *Provided,* The owner or owners of such ferries, have the license recorded in the recorders office in each county, wherein the ferry or ferries are, within three months after the taking effect of this act, subject to the same rules, *Ferries kept under license from the governor continued &c.*

(184)

regulations, and restrictions, as are herein contained.

JESSE B. THOMAS,
Speaker of the House of Representatives.

B. CHAMBERS,
President of the Council.

Approved—September 17th, 1807.

WILLIAM HENRY HARRISON.

CHAPTER XXXIV.

An Act making Promissory Notes, Bonds, and Inland Bills of Exchange, negotiable.

§ 1 All notes in writing that shall hereafter be made and signed by any person or persons, body politic, or corporate, where-by such person or persons, body politic or corporate, promise to *Notes in writing for the payment of money.*

pay any sum of money, or acknowledge any sum of money to be due, to any other person or persons, or his, her, or their order, or unto bearer, shall be taken to be due and payable, and the sum of money therein mentioned shall by virtue thereof be due and payable to the person or persons, to whom the said note is made; and every such note made payable to any person or persons, his, her, or their order, or unto bearer, shall be assignable by endorsement thereon, under the hand or

(185)

hands, of such person or persons, and of his, her, or their assignee, or assignees, so as absolutely to transfer and vest the property thereof in each and every assignee or assignees, successively; and any assignee, or assignees, to whom such sum of money is, by such endorsement, or endorsements, made payable, may, in his, her, or their own name, or names, institute or maintain an action for the recovery thereof, against the person or persons, who made and signed such note, or against him, her, or them, who endorsed the same, (having first used due diligence to obtain the money from the drawer or maker) and in every such action in which judgment is given for the plaintiff or plaintiffs, he, she, or they, shall recover his, her, or their damages and costs of suit.

Is made assignable by indorsement assignee may sue in his own name.

§ 2. If any such note shall be endorsed after the day on which the money therein contained becomes due and payable, and the endorser shall institute an action thereon, against the maker and signer of the same, the defendant being maker and signer, shall be allowed to set up the same defence that he might have done, had the said action been instituted in the name, and for the use of the person or persons to whom the said note was originally made due and payable.

When assigned after day of paymt. when before day of payment.

§ 3. If any such note shall be endorsed before the day the money therein contained becomes due and payable, and the endorsee shall institute an action thereon, the defendant may give in evidence at the trial, any

Inland bills of exchange declared negotiable.

(186)

money actually paid on the said note, before the said note was endorsed or assigned, to the plaintiff, on proving that the plaintiff had sufficient notice of the said payment, before he, or she, accepted or received such endorsement.

§ 4. And all inland bills of exchange shall be negotiable, by endorsement thereon, in the same manner as is above provided in case of promissory notes.

Bonds &c. assignable.

§ 5. The assignment of bills, bonds, or other writings obligatory for the payment of money, or any specific article, shall be good and effectual in law, and an assignee of such, may thereupon maintain an action in his own name, but shall allow all just set offs, discounts, and equitable defence, not only against himself, but against the assignor, before notice of such assignment shall have been given to the defendant.

Assigneemay sue in his own name.

JESSE B. THOMAS,

Speaker of the House of Representatives.

B. CHAMBERS,

President of the Council.

Approved—September 17th, 1807.

WILLIAM HENRY HARRISON.

(187)

CHAPTER XXXV.

An Act to prevent Trespassing by Cutting of Timber.

§ 1. Every person who shall cut, fell, box, bore or destroy any Black Walnut, Black, White, Yellow, or Red Oak, White Wood, Poplar, Wild Cherry, Blue Ash, Yellow, or Black Locust, Chesnut, Coffee, or Sugar tree, or sapling standing or growing upon land belonging to any other person or persons, without having first obtained permission so to do, from the owner or owners of such lands, shall forfeit and pay for such tree or sapling, so cut, felled, boxed, bored, or destroyed, the sum of eight dollars; and every person who shall cut, fell, box, bore, or destroy any tree, or sapling, not herein above named and enumerated, standing or growing upon land be-

Eight dollars penalty for cutting, boxing or boring certain trees &c.

Three dollars penalty for all others

longing to any other person or persons, without permission as aforesaid, shall forfeit and pay for every such tree or sapling, so cut, felled, boxed, bored, or destroyed the sum of three dollars.

Penalties how to be prosecuted for and recovered.

§ 2. The penalties herein above provided, shall be recoverable with costs of suit, either by action of debt, in the name, and for the use of the owner or owners of the land, or by action *qui tam,* in the name of any person who will first sue for, and recover the same, the one half for the use of the person so suing, and the other half for the use of the owner or owners of the land: *Provided always,* That if in any action that may be instituted by virtue of the pro-

If deft. sets up a title to the land, & give security

A2

(188)

how to proceed.

visions herein contained, before a Justice of the Peace, the defendant shall set up a title to the land on which the tree or trees, are alledged to have been cut, felled, boxed, bored, or destroyed, and shall forthwith give good and sufficient security to prosecute his claim or title to the said land to effect, within one year; or to appear and defend an action to be instituted against him within one year, by virtue of the provisions herein contained, in any court of record within the Territory, having cognizance thereof; and in either case to abide by, and satisfy the judgment that may be given in such court, then the said Justice shall proceed no further in the said cause, but shall forthwith dismiss the parties, and it shall be the duty of the said Justice thereupon to tax the bill of costs, that may have accrued before him; and so soon as the action shall be renewed, or instituted for the purpose aforesaid, to transmit the said bill, together with the recognizance to be taken as aforesaid, to the Clerk of the court, in which such action shall be instituted or renewed, which costs so taxed and transmitted, shall be made a part of the judgment, to be rendered as aforesaid.

§ 3. If the said recognizance shall be forfeited for not prosecuting as aforesaid, the Justice shall proceed to enter Judgment against the defendant, for the demand of the plaintiff, which shall be taken to be confessed, and execution shall thereupon issue against the said defendant and his security or securities; and if the said recognizance shall be forfeited for not ap-

Upon forfeiture of recognizance, how to proceed.

(189)

pearing and defending, or for not abiding by, and satisfying the judgment that shall be given in the court above, the party for whose benefit such recognizance was taken, may, by a writ, or writs of *scire facias,* proceed to judgment and execution thereon.

§ 4. If any person or persons, shall, after the passing of this act, under pretence of any lease, or otherwise, cut, fell, box, or bore, or destroy, any Black Walnut, Black, White, Yellow, or Red Oak, White Wood, Poplar, Wild Cherry, Blue Ash, Yellow or Black Locust, Chesnut, Coffee, or Sugar tree, or sapling, standing or growing upon any lands within the Territory, reserved, appropriated, or intended for the use and support of schools, or for the use and support of religion; such person or persons shall forfeit and pay, for every such tree or sapling, so cut, felled, boxed, bored, or destroyed, the sum of eight dollars; and if any person or persons, shall cut, fell, box, or bore, or destroy, any other tree or sapling, not herein above named and enumerated, standing or growing upon any lands, within the Territory, reserved, appropriated, or intended for the use aforesaid, such person or persons, shall forfeit and pay for every such tree or sapling, so cut, felled, boxed, bored, or destroyed, the sum of three dollars.

Penalty for cutting &c. certain trees on lands secured for public uses.

§ 5. The penalties provided in the preceding section of this act, shall and may be recovered with costs of suit, either by action of debt, brought by, and in the name, or names of the overseer, or overseers of

Penalties how recovered and appropriated.

(190)

the poor, of the township in which such tree or sapling, shall
have been cut, felled, boxed, bored, or destroyed, as aforesaid
for the use of the poor of the county; or by action *qui tam,*
in the name of any other person who will first sue for and recover the same; the one half for the person so suing and recovering, and the other half for the use of the poor of the
county in which such tree or sapling, shall have been cut,

Overseers of the poor's du ty to prosecute. felled, boxed, or bored or destroyed; and it shall be the duty
of the overseers of the poor, on complaint made to him or
them, against any person who may have cut, felled, boxed,
bored or destroyed, any tree or sapling, standing or growing,
upon any lands reserved for the uses aforesaid, within his or
their township, or upon his or their view or knowledge of such
trespass, forthwith to institute an action against the trespasser for the purpose aforesaid, unless an action *qui tam* shall
have been previously instituted for the said trespass, in the

To receive compensation. name of some other person, according to the provisions herein
contained; and the said overseer or overseers, in the settle-
ment of his or their accounts, shall be allowed a reasonable
credit for the trouble and expense, of such prosecution;

Proviso. Not to extend to ministers of the gospel *Provided always,* That nothing herein contained shall be construed to prevent ministers of the gospel from settling and
improving any lands reserved for the use of religion.

Nor to persons holding lands in the colege townships under lease &c. § 6.   Nothing herein contained shall be so construed as to
prevent persons now holding by lease, lands in the college
town-

(191)

ship, or other lands appropriated for schools, and religious
purposes, within this Territory, from cutting and using timber
agreeably to the tenor of such lease, nor shall it prevent the
Nor to prevent settlers thereon &c. present settlers thereon from cutting timber on such parts
thereof, as they shall enclose and improve, until after such
regulations as shall be made by the legislature, of the Territory are brought into operation.

§ 7. No part of the said recited act, shall be so construed as to affect such inhabitans in the said Territory, who may have settled on lands by mistake, or the owner or owners of which are unknown to them, so far as the said act relates to the penalties herein specified.

Not to extend to persons settling on lands by mistake, or where the owners are unknown.

JESSE B. THOMAS,
Speaker of the House of Representatives.
B. CHAMBERS,
President of the Council.

Approved—September 17th, 1807.
WILLIAM HENRY HARRISON.

(192)

CHAPTER XXXVI.
An Act regulating Grist Mills and Millers.

§ 1. EACH and every miller, or the owner or owners, or occupiers of every water and wind grist mill, now erected or which shall hereafter be built and erected, within this Territory, shall be entitled to have and receive out of the grain which be ground in his, her, or their said mills, the following rates of toll, in full compensation therefor, to wit: For grinding and bolting wheat or rye into flour, one tenth part thereof; For grinding Indian corn, oats, barley or Buckwheat, and the same bolting into flour when required to be bolted, one seventh part thereof; For grinding Indian corn, oats, bareley or buckwheat, when the same is not required to be bolted, one eighth part thereof; For grinding malt and chopping rye, one twelfth part thereof.

Toll allowed for grinding grain &c. in water & wind mills.

§ 2. Each and every miller, or the owner or owners, or occupiers, of each and every horse mill, when the miller, owner or occupier thereof, shall find and provide horses for turning the same, shall be entitled to take and receive, out of wheat to be ground and bolted in his, her or their said mills, one fifth part thereof; out of rye, Indian corn, oats, barley and buckwheat, one fourth part thereof; out of malt and for chopping rye, one sixth part thereof; *Provided always,* That when

For grinding in H. mills.

Proviso.
Where own-
er of the
grain shall
find horses.
the owner of the grain to be ground, shall provide horses to
grind the same, the miller or owner or

(193)

occupier of said horse mill shall be entitled to take and receive the same rate, as is provided and allowed, to water and
wind mills in the first section of this act, and no more.

Penalty for
taking more
than lawful
toll.
§ 3.   If any miller or the owner or owners or occupiers,
of any of the aforesaid described mills, within this Territory
shall presume to demand, receive or take any greater toll, fee
or reward, for grinding grain, or for grinding and bolting
grain into flour than as aforesaid, or shall knowingly cause
the same to be done, he, she, or they so offending, upon con-
How recov-
erable.
viction thereof, before any Justice of the Peace of the proper
county, in which the mill shall be erected, shall forfeit and
pay the sum of five dollars, with costs, for the use of the
county in which the offence shall have been committed, to
be levied on the offender's goods and chattels; and for want
of goods and chattels, the offender shall be committed to the
jail of the county, until the same shall be paid, or the offender
discharged by law; and moreover shall be liable to the action
of the person injured, for damages.

Owners of
mills to be
accountable
for grain &c.
§ 4.   Every miller the owner or owners or occupier of
every grist mill of the aforesaid description, shall be accountable to the owners of grain received to grind, for the safe
keeping of the same, whilst in his, her or their mills; and if
any grain, bag, or cask containing the same, shall be lost
or destroyed whilst intrusted in the care of any miller for
the purpose of being ground, the owner or occupier, as the
case may be, shall make

(194)

good the same to the owner thereof in damages: *Provided
always,* That in order to entitle any owner of grain so deposited and lost or destroyed, to recover the value thereof against
Provided the
bags &c are
marked.
the miller, owner or occupier of any of the above described
mills; the owner of the grain shall cause the bag or bags, cask

or casks, containing his, her or their grain to be distinctly
marked with initial letters, of his, her or their name or names.

Provided also, That nothing in this section shall be so construed as to charge any miller, owner or occupier of any mill, Millers not
with the loss of grain, bags or casks, that shall happen by accountable
robbery, fire, or any other unavoidable accident, without the robbery, fire
fault or neglect of such miller, owner or occupier thereof. &c.

§ 5. If any person owning lands on one side of a water In what ca-
course, the bed thereof belonging to himself, and desiring to ses the courts
build a water grist mill on such lands, and erect a dam across issue a writ
the same, shall not himself have the fee simple property in of ad quad
the land, on the opposite side thereof, against which he would damnum.
abut his said dam, he shall make application for a writ of
ad quad damnum, to the court of Common Pleas of the county
where such land may lie, and having given ten days previous Proceedings
notice, to the proprietor thereof if he be to be found in the thereon.
county, and if not, then to his agent, if any he hath in the
county, or if no agent, to be advertised at the door of the court
house of the proper county for two terms; which court shall
thereupon, order their Clerk to issue such writ, to be directed
to the Sheriff,

(195)

commanding him to summons and empannel twelve fit persons Sheriff to
to meet on the land so proposed for the abutment, on a certain summon a
day, to be named by the court, and inserted in the said writ, jury.
of which notice shall be given by the Sheriff to the said proprietor, or his agent, if any he hath.

§ 6. The jury so summoned and empannelled, shall be The jury
charged by the Sheriff, impartially, and to the best of their when met
skill and judgment, to view the land proposed for an abut- their duty.
ment, and to locate and circumscribe, by metes and bounds,
one acre thereof, having due regard therein, to the interest
of both parties, and to appraise the same accordingly to its
true value, to examine the land above and below, the property of others, which may probably overflow, and say what
damage it will be to the several proprietors, and whether the

mansion house of any such proprietor or proprietors, or the offices, curtilages, or gardens thereunto immediately belonging, will be overflowed, to enquire whether, and in what degree, fish of passage, or ordinary navigation will be obstructed; whether by any, and what means, such obstruction may be prevented; and whether in their opinion, the health of the neighbours will be annoyed by the stagnation of the waters.

Inquest when made to be returned to the next court with the writ.

§ 7. The inquest so made and sealed by the said jurors, together with the writ, shall be returned by the Sheriff to the next succeeding court, who shall thereupon order summonses to be issued to the several persons, proprietors or tenants, of the land so

B2

(196)

Further proceedings thereon.

located, or found liable to damage, if they be to be found, within the county where the lands so to be condemned, or overflowed, do lie; and if not, then to their agent, if any they have, to shew cause, if any they have, why the party so applying, should not have leave to build his said mill dam.

Persons who may have built mills may apply for a writ of ad quod dam num.

§ 8. Where any person may have built a mill, or other dam, whereby the water of any river, creek, run or spring, may be rendered thereby stagnant, it may be lawful for any person interested therein, or who may be damaged by the overflowing of said water, to obtain a writ of *ad quod damnum,* in the same manner as is directed in case of persons wishing to build a new mill; and the jury so summoned, &c. shall ascertain the damage which any individual may sustain in consequence of the continuance of the said mill dam, and whether the said mill is of public utility; and after the jury aforesaid, shall have made their return; it shall be the duty of the owner

And proceedings thereon.

or owners of the said mill, to pay to any, and every individual, the sum assessed by the jury aforesaid, and upon payment of said assessment the said owner or owners, shall be clear of all damages to the person interested, as aforesaid; any law, usage or custom to the contrary notwithstanding.

§ 9. In the like manner if the person proposing to build such mill and dam, have the fee simple property in the lands on both sides of the stream; yet application shall be made to the court of the county, where the mill house will stand, for a writ to examine as aforesaid; what lands may be over-flow-

Where the person is owner of lands on both sides the same proceedings.

(197)

ed, and to make the same examination and report, as in the case last mentioned; which writ shall be directed, executed and returned, as prescribed in the former case.

§ 10. If on such inquest, or other evidence, it shall appear to the court that the mansion house of any proprietor, curtilage or garden thereunto immediately belonging, will be overflowed, or the health of the neighborhood annoyed, they shall not give leave to build such mill and dam; but if none of those injuries are likely to ensue, they are then to proceed to adjudge whether all circumstances weighed, it be reasonable that such leave should be given, or not given, accordingly.

In what cases the court shall, or shall not give leave &c.

§ 11. And if the party applying shall obtain leave to build the said mill and dam, he shall upon paying respectively to the several proprietors entitled, the value of the acre so located, and the damage which the jurors find will be by overflowing, the lands above and below, become seized in fee simple of the said acre of land; but if he shall not within one year thereafter begin to build the said mill, and finish the same within three years, and afterwards continue it in good repair for public use; or in case the said mill and dam be destroyed; if he shall not begin to rebuild it within one year after such distruction, and finish it within three years thereafter; the said acre of land shall revert to the former proprietor, and his heirs, unless at the time of such destruction, the owner thereof be a feme, covert infant, imprisoned, or of unsound mind.

Where leave is obtained, the mill shall be built and kept in repair

If mill destroyed & not rebuilt, the land to revert unless &c.

(198)

in which case the same time shall be allowed after such disability removed.

When action may be brought.

§ 12. The inquest of the said jurors nevertheless, or opinion of the court, shall not bar any prosecution or action, which any person would have had in law, had this act never been made, other than for such injuries as were actually foreseen and estimated by the jury.

Millers to grind well & in turn.

§ 14. All millers whose mills shall be established under this law, shall well and sufficiently grind the grain brought to their mills, and in due time, as the same shall be brought, and may take for toll such rates as are herein before established; and every miller failing to grind as aforesaid, as the same shall come in turn, or shall take or exact more toll, shall

Ponalty on neglect and how recoverable.

for every such offence, forfeit and pay to the person injured, the sum of two dollars and fifty cents, recoverable before any magistrate within the county where the offence was committed.

Millers to keep sealed measures in their mills. Penalty on neglect.

§ 14. Every owner or occupier of a mill, shall keep therein a sealed half bushel, peck and toll dish, and measure all grain by striking measure, under the penalty as is mentioned for exacting more grain than is allowed by law, and if the miller be a servant his master shall pay the same.

Owners of dams over which a public road passes, to keep the dams in repair at least 12 feet wide.

§ 15. The owner of every dam, over which a public road passes, shall constantly keep such dam in repair, at least twelve feet wide, under the penalty of one dollar for every twenty-four hours; but where a mill dam shall be carried away, or destroyed by tempest, the owner or occupier shall not be

(199)

Penalty on neglect &c.

liable to the said penalty, provided the same be repaired within six months.

JESSE B. THOMAS,
Speaker of the House of Representatives.

B. CHAMBERS,
President of the Council.

Approved—17th September, 1807.
WILLIAM HENRY HARRISON.

CHAPTER XXXVII.

An Act for the prevention of Vice and Immorality.

§ 1. IF any person shall be found reveling, fighting or quarrelling, doing or performing any worldly employment, or business whatsoever, on the first day of the week, commonly called Sunday (works of necessity or charity only excepted) or shall use or practice any unlawful game, sport or diversion, whatsoever, or shall be found hunting or shooting, on the said day, and be convicted thereof; every such person, so offending, shall for every such offence, forfeit and pay a sum not exceeding two dollars, nor less than fifty cents, to be levied by distress; or in case such person being a male, shall refuse or neglect to pay the said sum; or goods and chattels cannot be found whereof to levy the same by distress,

Sunday or 1st day of the week how to be kept and observed under what penalties.

(200)

he shall be committed to the charge of one of the supervisors of the highways, in the township wherein the offence was committed, to be kept at hard labor for the space of two days: *Provided always,* That nothing herein contained shall be construed to hinder watermen from landing their passengers, or ferrymen from carrying over the water, travellers, or persons removing with their families, on the first day of the week, commonly called Sunday.

Proviso in favor of ferrymen.

§ 2. If any person of the age of sixteen years and upwards, shall profanely curse, damn or swear, by the name of God, Christ Jesus, or the Holy Ghost; every person so offending, being thereof convicted, shall forfeit and pay for every such profane curse, damn or oath, a sum not exceeding two dollars, nor less than fifty cents, at the discretion of the Justice, who may take cognizance thereof; and in case he shall refuse or neglect to pay the said forfeiture; or goods and chattels cannot be found, whereof to levy the same by distress, he shall be committed to the charge of one of the supervisors of the highways of the township where the offence was com-

Profane swearing what.

**And how pu-
nished.**

mitted, to be kept at hard labor for the space of two days for
every such offence, of which such person shall be convicted.

**Swearing &
disorderly be-
haviour be-
fore congre-
gations &c
what & how
punished.**

§ 3. If any person shall presume to appear before any
court of justice within this Territory, before any Judge or
Justice of the Peace, when acting as such, or before any congregation, assembled for public worship and there make use of
profane swearing, or other disorderly behavior, the

(201)

effect of which would have an evident tendency to disturb
that good order, to be observed on those occasions; if before
a court of justice, he shall be fined in any sum not exceeding
fifty nor less than five dollars; if before a Judge or Justice of
the Peace, he or she shall be fined in any sum not exceeding
ten, nor less than three dollars; if before any congregation
assembled for divine worship, he, or she so offending, shall be
fined in any sum not exceeding ten, nor less than three dollars;
and it shall be the duty of any Justice of the Peace within this
Territory, the same coming within his knowledge, or upon
information by one or more credible witnesses, to issue his
warrant and have the offender brought forthwith before him,
and shall immediately assess his fine; and for want of sufficient goods and chattels, belonging to the defendant, to be by
him shewn to satisfy the fine and costs, aforesaid, the said
Justice shall commit the offender to the jail of the proper

**Proviso in fa-
vor of courts
of justice.**

county where the offence was committed: *Provided,* That
nothing herein contained, shall be so construed, as to prevent any court of justice from punishing the like offenders, in
the manner herein before mentioned.

**Drunkenness
what, & how
punished.**

§ 4. If any person of the age of sixteen years or upwards,
shall be found in the public highway, or in any public house
of entertainment, intoxicated by excessive drinking of spiritu-

ous, vinous, or other strong liquors, and making or exciting
any noise, contention or disturbance, it shall be lawful for any
Justice of the Peace, on

(202)

complaint or view, to cause such person or persons to be committed to the common jail of the county, there to remain for
a term of time not exceeding forty eight hours; end every
person so committed, shall pay the fees arising on such commitment; and if any person shall be found offending as aforesaid, at any greater distance than five miles from the county
jail; it shall be lawful for any Justice of the peace, to commit
such person or persons to the custody of any constable within
the township, for the like term of time, to be by such constable
confined in any proper and convenient place, for the like term
of time; and the said constable shall be entitled to receive the
same fees, as are allowed to the keeper of the jail in the like
cases.

§ 5. The Judges of the Supreme court, every Judge of
the court of Common Pleas, and every Justice of the Peace,
within the limits of their several jurisdictions, are hereby empowered, authorised and required, to proceed against, and to
punish all persons offending against the preceeding sections of
the law, and for that purpose each of the said Judges or Justices, severally, may convict such offenders upon his own
view and hearing, or shall issue if need be, a warrant, summons, or capias, according to the circumstance of the case,
to bring the body of the person accused, as aforesaid, before
him: and the same Judges or Justices, shall respectively, in a
summary way, enquire into the truth of the accusation, and
upon the testimony of one or more credible witnesses, or the
confession of the party, shall convict

> Judges and justices to take cognizance.

> May convict on view.

> In a summary way.

(203)

And pronounce judgment.

the person who shall be guilty as aforesaid, and thereupon shall proceed to pronounce the forfeiture incurred by the person so convicted as herein before directed; and if the person

Failing to satisfy fine, to work on public highways

so convicted, refuse, or neglect, to satisfy such forfeiture immediately, with costs, or to produce goods and chattels, whereupon to levy the said forfeiture, together with costs, then the said Judge, or Justice, shall commit the offender to one of the supervisors of the highways, as aforesaid, during such time as is herein before directed; and every such conviction may be in the following words, to wit:

'Be it remembered, that on the day of　　　　　　in the year of　　　　　　A B,

Form of conviction and execution.

of the county　　　　　　labourer, (or otherwise, as his rank, occupation, or calling may be) is convicted before me, being one of the Judges, or Justices, &c. in the county of　　　　　　of swearing profane oath, or oaths, by the name of　　　　　　(or otherwise as the offence and case may be) and I do adjudge him to forfeit for the same, the sum of　　　　　　and for want of goods and chattels to be by the offender shewn, whereon to levy &c. you are to take his body into custody, and him forthwith convey to one of the supervisors of the highways, of the township &c. who is commanded hereby, to receive and keep him at hard labour, on the highway, for the space of two days.—Given under my hand and seal the day and year aforesaid.'

Limitation.

Provided, That every such prosecution

C2

(204)

be commenced within seventy-two hours after the offence shall be committed.

Cock fighting.

§ 6. If any person or persons, shall cause to fight any cock or cocks, for money, or any other valuable thing, or shall promote or encourage any match, or matches of cock fighting, by betting thereon, or shall play at any match of bullets, in any place, for money, or other valuable thing, or on any highway, or public road, with, or without a bet, or shall play at cards, dice, billiards, bowls, shovel board, or any game at hazard, or address, for money, or other valuable thing, every such person so offending, shall, upon conviction thereof, before any Justice or Magistrate as aforesaid, forfeit and pay three dollars, for every such offence; and if any person or persons, shall run any horse, mare or gelding, in any street, or public highway; every person so offending, shall, on conviction thereof before any Justice of the Peace, or on the view of such Justice, forfeit and pay the sum of five dollars, with costs.

§ 7. No E O table, or other device, except as hereinafter excepted, shall be set up or maintained, in any dwelling house, out house, or other place, by any person whatsoever; on pain of forfeiting every such E O table, or other device, and of forfeiting moreover, the sum of fifty dollars; and upon conviction thereof, before any court having competent jurisdiction, held for the county wherein the offence shall be committed: *Provided always,* That nothing

(205)

in this act contained, shall be construed so as to prohibit private families, from exercising their free will, within their own private houses for their amusement, in a peaceable manner: *Provided also,* That no person shall set up, or suffer to be set up, or kept in his or her house, barn, stable, or other out house, arbor, or bower, or yard, any table, or other thing reputed as a gaming table, or other device, for the purpose of encouraging gaming.

§ 8. If any person or persons shall loose any money, or valuable thing, at, or upon any match of cock fighting, bullet playing, or horse racing, or at, or upon any game of address, game of hazard, play, or game whatsoever, the person or persons who shall loose their money, or other valuable thing, shall not be compelled to pay, or make good the same. And any

Marginal notes:

Bullet playing.

Cards, dice &c. how punished.

Running horses in public roads.

How punished.

Keeping E. O. and other tables.

How punished.

Proviso in favor of private amusements.

Securities made or entered into for gaming void.

contract, note, bill, bond, judgment, mortgage, or other security or conveyance whatsoever, given, granted, drawn or entered into for the security or satisfaction of the same, or any part thereof, shall be utterly void, and of no effect.

Money &c. lost at gaming may be recevered back within 30 days,

§ 9. If any person or persons shall loose any money, or other thing of value, at, or upon any game of address, or of hazard, or other play, and shall pay, or deliver the same, or any part thereof; the person or persons, so loosing and paying, or delivering the same, shall have a right within thirty days, then next thereafter, to sue for, and recover the money or goods, so lost and

(206)

paid or delivered, or any part thereof, from the respective winner or winners thereof, with costs of suit, by action of debt, or case, founded on this act, to be prosecuted in any court of record, or where the value is within the sum cognizable by a single Justice, the same may be recovered before any Justice of the Peace within this Territory, subject to an appeal as in other cases.

Where to be prosecuted.

Boxing &c. what.

§ 10. If any person or persons, shall challenge another, to fight or box at fisticuffs, or with the intent to bring on a match at boxing, shall in words or gesture, endeavour to provoke any other person or persons to commit an affray, whether an affray ensues or not, every person so offending, on conviction thereof, shall forfeit and pay for every such offence, a sum not exceeding five dollars, nor less than one dollar; and every Magistrate of the county, where the offence shall have been committed, shall have cognizance thereof: *Provided however,* That such prosecution be commenced within four days from the time the offence was committed.

And how punished.

Limitation.

Duels what

§ 11. If any person within this Territory shall challenge by word, or in writing, the person of another, to fight at sword, rapier, pistol, or other deadly weapon, the person so challenging, shall forfeit and pay for every such offence, being thereof lawfully convicted, in any court of record within the

county wherein the offence shall be committed, having com- Prosecutions where to be brought.
petent jurisdiction, by the testimony of one or more witnesses,
or by

(207)

the confession of the party offending a sum not exceeding two
hundred and fifty dollars, nor less than fifty dollars; or shall
suffer imprisonment, for a term not exceeding twelve months,
nor less than three months, without bail or mainprize; and the How punish-ed.
person who shall accept any such challenge, shall in like manner upon conviction, forfeit and pay a sum not exceeding one
hundred dollars; or shall suffer such imprisonment, for a term
not exceeding six months, nor less than one month; and if
any person, shall willingly and knowingly, carry and deliver
any written challenge, or shall verbally deliver any message,
purporting to be a challenge, or shall consent to be a second Carriers of challenges &c.
in any such intended duel, and shall be legally convicted
thereof, as aforesaid, the person so offending, shall for every
such offence, forfeit and pay a sum not exceeding one hun- How punish-ed.
dred dollars, nor less than fifty dollars; or shall suffer imprisonment for a term not exceeding six months, nor less than
one month, as aforesaid.

§ 12. All prosecutions under this act shall be by action Nature of prosecutions under this act & where commenced.
of debt, or trespass on the case, or by indictment, where the
penalty exceeds a magistrates jurisdiction; and all fines and
penalties set or imposed, and paid by virtue of the provisions
herein contained, shall be paid into the treasury of the county,
in which such fine or penalty shall be set or imposed, for the
use of the said county: *Provided always,* That no person shall
be prosecuted for any offence against this act, except such
offences, as are enumerated in

(208)

the tenth section thereof, unless such prosecution be com- In what time to be com-menced.
menced, within thirty days after the offence has been com-
mitted.

Persons committed to supervisors refusing to labor to be imprisoned.

§ 13. If any person or persons who shall be committed to the supervisor of the highways, by virtue of any of the provisions herein contained; shall disobey the orders or directions of the said supervisor; it shall be lawful for the said supervisor, to commit such person or persons to the jail of the county, there to remain until the expiration of the time, for which such person or persons, may have been sentenced to labor on the highway; and the said supervisor shall endorse his order of commitment, on the magistrate's warrant, and transmit the same to the jailor, who is hereby directed on the receipt thereof, to receive such person or persons, and commit him or them accordingly.

For the same term for which he was sentenced to labor. Manner of committment.

Tearing down or defacing publications set up by authority.

§ 14. If any person or person shall wilfully and maliciously deface, obliterate, tear down, or destroy, in part, or in the whole, any copy or transcript of, or extract from, any act or law, passed by the legislature of this Territory, or by the legislative authority of the United States, or proclamation of the President of the United States, or of the Governor and Commander in Chief of this Territory; the same being officially fixed up in some conspicuous place by public authority, for general information; every person so offending, shall on conviction before a magistrate, forfeit, and pay to the use of the Territory, for eve-

How punished.

(209)

ry such offence, a sum not exceeding three dollars, besides costs, or be set in the stocks, at the discretion of such magistrate, for a space not exceeding three hours; or in case the offender shall be unable, or refuse to pay such fine [he being fined] then he shall be set in the stocks, for a space not exceeding three hours, and be afterwards discharged on paying costs only.

Tearing down or defacing banns of matrimony.

§ 15. If, as aforesaid, any person shall wilfully and maliciously deface, obliterate, tear down or destroy, in part, or in the whole, any publication of the banns of matrimony, or advertisement respecting estrays, or any other notification, set up in pursuance of any act or law, now, or which hereafter may be in force within this Territory; such offender shall for every such offence, of which he may be convicted, as afore- How punished. said, be set in the stocks for three hours, and pay costs, or stand committed to prison till the same are paid; any thing in this, or any other act or law, to the contrary, notwithstanding.

§ 16. No person in order to raise money, or other prop- No lotteries to be carried on. erty for himself or another shall publicly or privately put up a lottery of blanks and prizes, to be drawn or adventured for, or any prize or thing to be raffled or played for; whoever shall offend herein, shall forfeit to the use of the Territory, Under what penalty. the whole sum of money, or property proposed to be raised or gained.

§ 17. The presiding Judge or Justice in the several Courts to give this act in charge to juries. courts of law, shall at every

(210)

court, give this act in charge to the Grand Jury, as soon as sworn.

GENL. W. JOHNSTON.

Speaker pro tempore, of the House of Representatives.

B. CHAMBERS,

President of the Council.

Approved—17th September, 1807.

WILLIAM HENRY HARRISON.

CHAPTER XXXVIII.

An Act establishing Courts for the trial of Small Causes.

§ 1. EVERY action of debt or other demand (except such What actions cognizable before J. P. & where. actions as are herein after excepted) shall be, and the same is hereby made cognizable before any Justice of the Peace or magistrate in the township, either where the debt or cause of action was contracted, or arose, where the plaintiff resides, or where the defendant may be found; and the said Justices are hereby authorised to hold a court, to hear, try and determine the same, according to law; and the jurisdiction of every Justice of the Peace under this act, shall be co-extensive with the limits of his county, and his writs, precepts, and process, authorised by this

(211)

**Duty of con-
stables.**

act, shall run in, and through such county, and may be executed
therein, but not elsewhere, and the Constables of the several townships, and they only, shall be ministerial officers of the said court,
and the Constables of every township in the Territory, to whom
any warrant shall be directed for service, by any Justice of the
Peace of the proper county, shall have power and authority to
execute the same in any township in the county; and it shall be
their duty to execute and return all precepts, summons, warrants,
and other process, issuing out of the said court, and to them, or
any of them directed and delivered; and to perform all acts
appertaining to their offices aforesaid; and all such precepts, sum-

**Teste of pro-
cess**

mons, and other process, shall be tested of the day on which they
are respectively issued; and shall be under the hand and seal of
the Justice issuing the same.

**Magistrates
to dismiss
vexatious
suits.**

If the plaintiff brings his suit in any other township, than
is above directed, for the purpose of harassing the defendant,
which shall be determined by the Magistrate, before whom the
suit is commenced; and it appears to the said Magistrate, that the
said suit was vexatiously commenced, then he shall dismiss the

**If disinteres-
ted & not re-
lated to ei-
ther party.**

suit, with costs, to the defendant: *Provided always,* That if there
is not a Justice of the Peace residing in either of the townships,
(as above mentioned) of if there is not a Justice of the Peace,
residing in the said townships, who is disinterested in the event of

D 2

(212)

the suit, or who is not of kin, to either of the parties, in, or within
the second degree, it shall be lawful for the plaintiff to institute
his suit before a Justice of the Peace, in any of the adjoining
townships, in the same county; and the said Justice is hereby
authorised to take cognizance thereof, any thing herein contained
to the contrary notwithstanding.

**What shall
be the first
process.**

§ 2. The first process which shall be issued against any
defendant, by virtue of this act, shall be a summons or warrant,
in nature of a *capias ad respondendum,* as the case may require;

and the summons shall be used in every case under this act, where
the defendant is a freeholder within the county, and resides
therein; and the summons to be issued, as aforesaid, shall specify
a certain time, not less than six, nor more than ten days, from the
date of such process; and also a certain place, at which the defendant is to appear; and shall be served at least three days **How to be**
before the time of appearance mentioned therein, by reading the **served.**
same to the defendant, and serving him, or her with a copy
thereof, if required, when the said defendant may be found; but
if he, or she, cannot be found, then by leaving a copy thereof at
his or her house, or place of abode, in presence of some person
of the family, of the age of ten years, or upwards, who shall be
informed of the contents thereof; and the Constable serving such
summons, shall, on the oath of his office, endorse thereupon the
time and manner of his executing the same, and shall subscribe
his name thereto: *Provided always,* That in

(213)

every case in which a summons is made the proper process, by
this act, if it shall be sufficiently proved on oath, to the satisfac- **Justices to**
tion of the Justice, that the plaintiff will be in danger of loosing **issue war-**
his or her demand, unless the defendant be arrested, it shall be **rants in cer-**
the duty of the Justice to issue a warrant, in the nature of a **tain cases.**
capias, any thing herein contained to the contrary notwithstanding.

§ 3. If the defendant does not appear at the time and place **Justices to**
expressed in such summons, and it shall be found, by the return **hear & deter-**
thereon endorsed, that the summons was duly served, and no **mine causes**
sufficient reason be assigned to the Justice why the defendant **in the ab-**
does not appear; then the said Justice may proceed to hear and **sence of de-**
determine such cause, in the absence of the said defendant. **fendant.**

§ 4. The warrant in nature of a *capias ad respondendum,* **Against**
shall be used in all cases under this act, in which the defendant is **whom war-**
not a freeholder, within the county, and the Constable serving, or **rants are to**
executing the same, shall, according to the command thereof, **be issued, &**
forthwith convey the defendant before the Justice who issued the **the manner**
same, and the said Justice shall thereupon, either cause the said **of acting**
defendant to give bail, for his, or her appearing, and abiding the **thereon.**
event of the said suit; or on neglect or refusal to give such bail,

shall order the Constable to convey him, or her to the jail of the county, there to be kept in custody, until the time appointed for the trial of the cause, which shall not exceed three days, from the day of the return of the warrant, or the said Justice may

(214)

direct the Constable to hold the defendant in his custody, until the plaintiff shall have notice and time to attend, and proceed to trial; and the Constable, who served such warrant, shall, on the oath of his office endorse thereon the execution thereof, and sign his name thereto.

Justices to endorse summonse & warrants.

§ 5.   The Justice shall endorse on the summons or warrant, before the same is delivered to the constable, the sum demanded by the plaintiff, together with the costs that have accrued, and the defendant shall have the priviledge of paying the amount of the

Priviledge of deft. in paying amount endorsed.

said demand, and costs so endorsed, without further proceedings in the cause; and it shall be lawful for the constable to receive the same, and receipt therefor; which receipt shall be a full and complete discharge to the defendant from the said demand and costs; and if the constable shall not pay the money so received, to the

Liability of constables in with-holding money.

After 7 days

Justice who issued the process, or if he shall not pay the amount of the costs into the hands of the Justice, or the debt or demand, into the hands of the plaintiff named in such process, within the space of seven days after he may have received the same; then the said constable shall be liable to pay to the said plaintiff, or his

To pay double in action case.

or her legal representatives, double the amount of the said debt or demand, to be recovered with costs of suit, by anaction of trespass on the case, in any court having cognizance thereof.

§ 6.   The recognizance of bail to be ta-

(215)

ken as is above provided, shall be in the following form, to wit:

Township.)
) ss.
County.)

"Whereas A B, [naming the defendant] hath been arrested,

Form of recognizance of bail.

and is in custody, at the suit of C D, [naming the plaintiff,] in an action of   for the sum [or property to the value] of now therefore, you O P, [naming the bail] do acknowledge your-self special bail in the said action in the sum of   dollars, to be levied upon your goods and chattels, and for want thereof, upon your body, if default be made in the condition of your recognizance, which condition is, that the said A B, [naming the defendant] shall be and appear before   (naming the Jus-tice) on the   day of   next, and if judgment be given against him or her, that he or she, shall pay the costs and con-demnation money, or surrender his or her body in execution. Acknowledged before me   one of the Justices of the Peace in and for the said county of   the   day of   in the year of our Lord one thousand   ."

And every Justice of the Peace is hereby empowered to take such recognizance which shall remain with such Justice, for the benefit of the plaintiff in the suit; and if the defendant does not appear, after such

(216)

recognizance entered into, at the time and place specified in the said recognizance, and no sufficient reason be assigned to the said Justice, why he or she does not appear; then the said Justice may proceed to hear and determine the cause, in the absence of such defendant; and when the parties to any suit, to he instituted by virtue of this act, shall appear at the time and place appointed for trial, the said Justice shall proceed to hear and examine their respective allegations and proofs, and shall thereupon give judg-ment, with costs of suit, according to the justice and equity of the case, unless he shall think it proper, on application of either party to adjourn the trial; which adjournment shall not be made for a longer period than seven days, when moved for by the plaintiff, nor than for a longer period than fourteen days, when moved for by the defendant, except in peculiar cases, where a longer continu-ance may be necessary for either party to obtain depositions; for which end the said Justices is hereby authorised, upon good cause shewn, to issue a *Dedimus,* returnable before himself at such time thereafter, as he may think reasonably necessary.

§ 7.   When parties agree to enter, without process, before a Justice of the Peace, any action herein made cognizable before

The justices to proceed if the deft. does not appear af ter recogni-zance.

Without good cause shewn to give judgt.

When par-ties appear proceed to trial of cause upon equita-ble principles

May grant continuance 7 days for pltff. and 14 for deft.

May issue de dimuss.

When an ac-tion is enter-

ed by agreement without process, to proceed to judgt. & execution.

him, such Justice shall enter the same on his docket, and shall proceed to judgment and execution, in the same manner, as though a summons or warrant had been issued, served and returned; and in all actions institu-

(217)

Costs to be given deft. in case of non suit or dismission.

ted by virtue of the provisions herein contained, in which the plaintiff shall be nonsuited, discontinue or withdraw his or her suit, without the consent of the defendant, the said Justice shall give judgment for the defendant, for the costs which have accrued.

When a ballance appears in favour of deft.

§ 8. If in any cause instituted as aforesaid, it shall appear at the trial that there is a ballance due to the defendant from the plaintiff, then the Justice shall enter up judgment against such plaintiff, in favor of the defendant, for the sum so appearing to

To give judgment and award exon.

be due, with costs of suit; and such defendant shall be entitled to execution in the same manner, as though such plaintiff had been the defendant in the cause.

Parties may choose referrees.

§ 9. The parties in every case arising under this act, shall have the priviledge of referring the matter in controversy between them to referrees, who shall be chosen and mutually agreed on between them, and who, after having heard the proofs and

Whose report the J. shall receive & enter judgt. thereupon.

allegations of the parties, shall make their report in writing to the Justice, and the said Justice shall receive and file the same, and thereupon enter judgment accordingly.

Exon. to be granted on such judgt.

§ 10. Where judgment shall be given against the plaintiff or defendant under this act, the Justice who gave such judgment shall grant execution thereupon, returnable to such Justice within twenty days, thereafter, commanding the constable to make the debt or damages and costs, of the goods

(218)

To operate as fi fa & ca sa Constable to commit to jail.

and chattels of the party, and for want of sufficient goods and chattels whereon to levy and make the same, to take the body of such party, and to convey him or her to the common jail of the county; and the Sheriff or keeper of such jail is hereby required to receive the person or persons so taken in execution, and him,

Jailor to receive & keep

her or them safely to keep until the sum recovered, and the costs of suit be fully paid, and in default of such safe keeping, the said

Sheriff shall be answerable to the party aggrieved, who shall have **On escape** the same remedy against him as is provided by law in cases of **shff. liable.** escapes. But in case the constable cannot find goods and chattels **Remedy over** belonging to the party, against whom such execution hath issued, **Remeddy in cases where** sufficient to satisfy the judgment, it shall and may be lawful for **the C. return** the party in whose favor such judgment hath been rendered, to **nulla bona.** apply to the Justice for a transcript thereof, whose duty it shall **Transcript** be to grant the same, which being filed in the office of the Clerk **to be certified to C. P.** of the court of Common Pleas, in the county in which the recovery hath been had; execution may issue therefrom according to the rules and practice of the said court; and the amount of the said judgment, together with the costs of such removal, may be levied on the lands and tenements of the party against whom the same **And exon is-** hath been rendered: *Provided always,* That no execution shall **sued, & levi-** issue from the court of Common Pleas, in manner aforesaid, after **ed on land.** the party hath been taken in execution, and committed to jail, **Must be first** until he or she shall be discharged from imprisonment under such **released from** execution: *And provided* **jail.**

(219)

also, That when a judgment shall be obtained against executors **Exons. agst.** or administrators, execution shall issue thereon in the same manner **exrs. & adm.** as it is issued against them in the courts of record within the **to be issued as in other** Territory: *And provided also,* That when judgment shall be ren- **cases.** dered as aforesaid, against a freeholder, no execution shall issue **Exons. agst.** thereon until the expiration of thirty days, if the judgment be **freeholders** for the sum of six dollars and under, or until the expiration of **not to issue until expira-** sixty days if the judgment be for any sum over six and under **tion of 30** twelve dollars; nor until the expiration of ninety days, if the **days for 6 dollars.** judgment shall be for the sum of twelve dollars and upwards **60 days for** from the time of the render of such judgment, unless the party **12 dollars.** in whose favor such judgment hath been rendered, shall make it **90 days for 18 dollars.** appear on oath or affirmation, to the satisfaction of the Justice, **Unless par-** that he or she, is in danger of loosing his or her debt, or dam- **ty will make** ages, if such delay of execution be allowed, in which case the **oath or affir-** said Justice shall issue execution forthwith, as is herein above **mation of danger of loo** provided, unless the party against whom execution is moved for **sing debt** shall immediately give good and sufficient security to the adverse **when exon. shall issue im mediately.**

Unless deft. gives security.

party, for the payment of the debt or damages and costs, within the space of thirty, sixty, or ninety days, as the case may be: *And provided also,* That if Judgment shall be given as aforesaid, against a person who is not a freeholder, such person shall have the execution against him or her respited for the like term of thirty, sixty or ninety days,

Persons not freeholders to have stay of exon. On giving special bail.

E 2

[220]

as the case may be, on his or her entering into recognizance to the adverse party, with one sufficient security, in the nature of special bail, conditioned to deliver the body of the said party, to the Sheriff of the county, at, or before the expiration of the time so to be allowed, or to satisfy the amount of the judgment.

A deft. not a freeholder appearing at return of, or without warrant & obtaining security in confession of judgt. be entitled to stay.

§ 11.   If any defendant who is not a freeholder shall appear at the return of the warrant, or shall appear by consent without process, and procure a good and sufficient freeholder, resident in the county, to join with him or her, in a confession of judgment to the adverse party, with costs, then such defendant shall be entitled to all the benefits and priviledges which any freeholder is entitled to by virtue of this act.

Justices to keep docket. Enter parties pltff. & deft. Noting process as issued State motions and rules & decisions. And enter the judgt. & date thereof

§ 12.   Every Justice before whom an action shall be commenced according to, and by virtue of the provisions contained in this act, shall open and keep a book, to be styled his docket, in which he shall make fair entries, of the names of the parties to every suit instituted before him, distinguishing between the plaintiff and defendant, and in which he shall note all the process that may issue in the cause, in the order in which it issues, and in which he shall state every motion made by either party, and overruled, or made, objected to, and allowed, and in which he shall also enter the judgment, stating the precise amount of the debt

[221]

or damages and costs, together with the day on which the said judgment was rendered.

To make up & tax a bill of costs.

§ 13.   It shall be the duty of the Justice to make up and tax a bill of costs, in every action instituted before him, according to the provisions of the law, ascertaining the fees to be allowed in such cases, setting down in said bill, each item, separately and distinctly, a true copy of which bill, certified and signed by the said Justice, shall be delivered to the party against whom judgment hath been entered, or left at his or her usual place of abode, before such party shall be called upon to discharge or satisfy the said judgment, and every Justice who shall issue an execution on any judgment, or receive the amount thereof, without having previously tendered to the party, against whom such judgment hath been rendered, a certified bill of the costs as above provided, or without having delivered the same to the constable, to be left at his or her usual place of abode, and every Justice who shall insert in the said bill of costs any charge for services not actually performed, than is allowed by law, shall forfeit and pay to the party against whom such bill hath been made and taxed, a sum of money equal to the amount of the cost taxed in the said suit; which sum shall and may be recovered with costs, before any Justice of the Peace within the county, and the jurisdiction of every Justice, for the purpose of prosecuting for, and recovering such forfeiture, shall be co-extensive with the boundaries of the county, any thing herein contained to the contrary notwith-

[222]

standing: *Provided always,* That if the said forfeiture shall exceed the sum of eighteen dollars, then the sum may be recoverable by action of debt in any court of record within the Territory, and not elsewhere.

§ 14. If any person or persons, shall conceive him her or themselves aggrieved by any judgment rendered as aforesaid, it shall and may be lawful, for such person or persons, at any time within the space of twenty days, next, after the rendering of such judgment to appeal therefrom to the court of Common Pleas, next to be holden for the county in which such suit hath been tried, he, she, or they, first entering into recognizance, with at least one sufficient security, in a sum at least double the amount of the said judgment, and sufficient to answer all costs, to prosecute the said appeal with effect, and to abide the order which the court of

---

Marginal notes:

stating items
Making copy & certifying same, to be delivered to the deft. or left at usual place of abode.
J. issuing exon. before bill delivered or charge for services not rendered to be fined in amt. thereof.

To be recovered before any J. P.

Penalty to be recovered in a court of record if the same exceed 18 dollars.

Party aggrieved may appeal to the next court of C. P. within 20 days.

Entering into recognizance with 1 security.

Common Pleas may make therein; and upon any appeal demanded from any such judgment, the Justice who pronounced the same, shall send a transcript thereof to the Clerk of the court of Common Pleas of the county in which such appeal is made, on or before the first day of the term next following, such appeal; and all proceedings before the said Justice, or any process issued by him on the said judgment, shall be stayed from the time of demanding such appeal, unless the party demanding the same shall refuse and neglect to give the security above required: *Provided always,* that no defendant shall be allowed an appeal from a judgment rendered against him or her, unless the same

[223]

shall amount to two dollars or upwards, without costs, nor shall any plaintiff be allowed an appeal, from a judgment rendered against him or her, unless his or her original demand against the defendant amount to two dollars or upwards, or from any judgment given for him, or her, unless the original sum demanded by him or her, from the defendant, shall exceed the sum recovered, by four dollars; nor shall either party be entitled to an appeal in any case in which judgment hath been entered on the report of referrees appointed as aforesaid.

§ 15.   At the term to which such appeal shall be made, the person so appealing shall cause an entry of the suit to be made by the Clerk of such court, and the plaintiff in the court below, whether appellant or appellee, shall be plaintiff in the court above; and after such entry hath been made, the suit shall be considered in the same light, and the parties shall proceed in all respects in the same manner, as though the suit had been originally instituted in the said court, and mesne process returned to the term in which such entry is made; and referrence shall be had to the proceedings in the court below, no further than to include in the judgment to be rendered in the court above, the costs taxed in the court below: *Provided,* That the costs wich shall accrue for services in the court of Common Pleas, on such appeal, shall be two third parts only, of the costs allowed by law for the same ser-

---

Marginal notes (left column):

J. to send transcripts to the C. C. P. by 1st days term.

Proceedings to be stayed after appeal.

Provided security be given.

Pltff. not allowed to appeal, whose original demand was not 2 dollars

Appellant to enter with the C. of C.P.

Plff. in the court below to be plff. in court above.

Costs in J's court to be taxed in cost above,

[224]

vices, in suits originally instituted in the said court.

§ 16. If the plaintiff after an appeal hath been made and entered, as is above provided, shall file a declaration in an action, not cognizable by a single Justice, by virtue of this act, the defendant may thereupon file his or her plea in abatement to the jurisdiction of the court; and if it shall appear to the said court, that the said Justice had not cognizance of such suit by virtue of this act, they shall proceed to enter judgment for the defendant with costs of suit: *Provided,* That such judgment shall not bar the plaintiff from a recovery in a subsequent action for the same cause, instituted in a court having cognizance thereof. — **Plea in abt. where J. had not cognizance.** **Proviso.**

§ 17, Whenever an appeal shall be demanded in manner aforesaid, or a writ of *Certiorari* shall be presented to a Justice, requiring him to certify the proceedings had before him, in any cause arising under this act; it shall be the duty of such Justice to make a fair and accurate transcript from his docket of all the entries contained therein, relative to the said cause, and to transmit the same forthwith to the proper court; and if it shall appear that the said Justice hath not made a just and true entry on his said docket, of all the proceedings had before him in the cause, he may be compelled by a writ of mandamus, to correct and complete the said entry, and forthwith to certify the same to the proper court: and if it shall appear that any Justice hath — **Upon appeal or certiorari, J. to certify proceedings.** **And transmit to court.** **To issue writ of mandamus**

[225]

altered or changed, or caused, or suffered to be altered or changed, the entries made on his docket, in matter of substance, with an intent to injure either of the parties, he shall be deemed guilty of a high misdemeanor, and on conviction thereof, by indictment, shall be fined in a sum not more than one hundred dollars, nor less than fifty dollars, and shall moreover pay the costs of prosecution, and shall stand committed until the fine and fees are paid. — **Penalty on J. altering docket.**

§ 18. No Justice of the Peace, by virtue of the provisions contained in this act, shall institute or sustain, two, or more actions or suits between the same parties for demands which are of — **Where actions by consolidation may be brot. in C. P.**

such a nature, as by the rules of law may be consolidated in one

under what
penalty.

action, under the penalty of eighteen dollars, to be recovered for the use and in the name of any person who shall first sue for the same, in the same manner as is provided in the thirteenth section of this act; and every judgment recovered against any defendant or defendants, by virtue of the provisions herein contained, may be pleaded in bar, and such plea may be received in any court within the territory, as a complete bar to any subsequent action or suit, instituted by the same plaintiff or plaintiffs, against the same defendant, or defendants, for any demand due, and owing from the same defendant or defendants to the same plaintiff or plaintiffs, at the time of instituting the action in which such judgment shall have been obtained, if the demand on which such subsequent action or

[226]

suit shall have been commenced, shall be of such a nature, as by the rules of law, might have been consolidated and joined in one action.

When con-
stables shall
give bond.

Condition
thereof.

§ 19.   No constable who does not possess a freehold estate of the value of three hundred dollars or upwards, shall be permitted to serve or execute any process that shall or may be issued, under this act, until he hath executed and delivered a bond with one good and sufficient freeholder as his security, payable to the Sheriff as treasurer of the county in which he resides, in the penal sum of three hundred dollars, with a condition that he will faithfully perform the duties of his office, as constable, and that he will justly and fairly account for, and pay over all monies, that may come to his hands, upon or by virtue of any process issuing under this act, according to the provisions thereof, and every bond executed and delivered as aforesaid, shall be held for the benefit

To be hold-
en for the
benefit of
suitors.

When con-
ditionbroken
how to pro-
ceed.

and security of all suitors in the courts of Justices of the peace, of the respective townships or counties; and if the condition of such bond shall at any time be broken, it shall be the duty of the Sheriff on demand made for that purpose, to deliver the said bond to the party grieved, who is hereby authorised and empowered to institute an action thereon, having first indemnified the said Sheriff against all costs that may accrue on such prosecution, and after

judgment obtained on any bond, executed as aforesaid, the court
may proceed from time to time, to award

(227)

execution against the defendants for money withholden or embez-
zeled by the said constable, or for penalties recovered against him
by virtue of the provisions herein contained, until the amount of
monies levied shall equal the amount of such judgment; *Provided,*
That no execution shall issue as aforesaid, until the defendants
be served with a copy of a rule to shew cause why such execution
should not be awarded, and if any person or persons shall be
injured by the illegal conduct of any constable under a colour of
process issuing under this act, and shall thereupon obtain judgment against such constable, and goods and chattels cannot be
found sufficient to satisfy the said judgment, such person or persons shall have the same remedy against the said constable and
his security as is herein provided.

§ 20. This act shall not be construed or understood to extend to, or embrace, nor shall any thing herein contained extend
to, or embrace any action of debt on bonds for the performance
of covenants, actions for covenants, actions of replevin, or upon
any real contract, actions of trespass on the case, for trover and
conversion, or slander, or actions of trespass, viet armis, or actions
wherein the title of lands shall in any wise come in question.

§ 21. If any person or persons commence suit, or prosecute
any suit or suits, for any debt or demand for personal property,
by this act made cognizable before a Justice of

F 2

(228)

the peace in any other manner than is authorised and directed by
this act, and shall obtain a verdict or judgment therein for debt
or damages, which without costs of suit shall not amount to
eighteen dollars, or more, not having caused an oath or affirmation to be made before the suing out of the capias or summons,
and filed in the office of the Clerk of the court from whence such
process issued, that he, she or they so making oath or affirmation,

Marginal notes:

From time to time to a-ward exon.

Further remedy against C & security.

Exceptions

Actions not cognizable before a jus-tice.

When pltff shall not re-cover costs.

did truly believe the debt due, or damage sustained, amounted to the sum of eighteen dollars or more; he, she, or they so prosecuting, shall not receive any costs in such suit; any law, usage or custom, to the contrary notwithstanding.

No judge of C. P. to try small causes. § 22.   No Judge of a court of Common Pleas, of any county within this Territory, shall act as a Justice of the Peace for the trial of small causes.

GENL. W. JOHNSTON.
Speaker pro tempore, of the House of
Representatives.
B. CHAMBERS,
President of the Council.

Approved—17th September, 1807.
WILLIAM HENRY HARRISON.

(229)

CHAPTER XXXIX.
An Act providing for the appointment of Constables.

C. of C. P. to appoint constable. § 1.   IT shall be the duty of the court of Common Pleas at their term next after the first of March annually, in each and every county, to appoint one or more respectable confidential persons, in each and every township, within their respective counties, to serve as Constables; and the Constables so appointed shall continue in office by virtue of such appointment, for the term of one **Term of service.** year, and so long thereafter as may be sufficient for their successors in office to have notice of their appointments, take the oath, and enter on the duties of their offices: *Provided,* That nothing herein contained shall oblige them to serve as Constables for a longer time than three months after the expiration of the term of one year as aforesaid.

§ 2.   Every Constable before he enters upon the duties of his office, shall take the following oath or affirmation:

Oath office. "I do swear, or affirm (as the case may be) that I will faithfully discharge the duties of my office as Constable within the county of   according to the best of my understanding and abilities."

Which oath or affirmation shall be taken before the court of Common Pleas, or before any Justice of the Peace of the said

(230)

court; and the Justice administering such oath, if out of court, shall make a certificate thereof and cause the same to be filed with the Clerk of said court, by which such Constable shall have been appointed; and it shall be the duty of every Constable as far as **His powers** in him lies, to apprehend, and bring to justice, all felons, and **& duties,** disturbers of the peace, to suppress all riots and unlawful assemblies, and to keep the peace within the county to which he shall have been appointed, and also to serve and execute all warrants, writs, precepts, and other process to him lawfully directed, and generally to do and perform all things appertaining to the office of Constable within the Territory: *Provided always,* That nothing herein contained shall be construed to require any Constable not qualified as is provided in the act entitled, "An act establishing courts for the trial of small causes," to serve or execute any process that may issue by virtue of the provisions in that act contained

§ 3. Every person who shall be appointed to the office of **Failing to** Constable in manner aforesaid, and who shall not within eight **take oath or** days after notice of such appointment, take the oath herein pre-**perform du-** scribed, and every Constable who having taken the oath afore-**ties how pu-** said, shall neglect, or refuse to perform any of the duties apper-**nished & for** taining in the office shall forfeit and pay for every such neglect **what use.** or refusal, the sum of twenty dollars, to be recovered with costs of suit, before any court of record within the county in which such Con-

(231)

stable resides, in the name of any person who will sue for the same, the one half to the use of the person so suing, and the other half to the use of the county; *Provided always,* That no person **Proviso.** shall be liable to the penalty herein specified, for not accepting of the appointment of a Constable in the same county, more than once in the term of ten years.

Vacancy how supplied

§ 4. When any Constable in any township within this Territory, appointed as aforesaid, shall die, or remove out of the township, or shall be otherwise disqualified from holding such office, it shall be the duty of any Justice of the Peace in the township in which such death, removal, or disqualification shall happen,

Certified to C. P.

to appoint a Constable to fill such vacancies, and return his name to the next court of Common Pleas held for the county; who shall confirm the said appointment, or appoint another; and the Constable so appointed shall take the same oath, and be subject to the same forfeitures, for neglect of duty, as those appointed by the court: *Provided nevertheless,* That nothing in this act shall be

Magistrate may appoint special constable.

construed so as to prevent any Magistrate in the Territory from appointing any suitable person to act as Constable in a criminal case, or in case of attachments, where there is a probability that the criminal will escape, or where goods and chattels are about to be removed, if delay is made for the purpose

(232)

of applying to the Constable of the township.

JESSE B. THOMAS,
Speaker of the House of Representatives.
B. CHAMBERS,
President of the Council.

Approved—September 17th, 1807.
WILLIAM HENRY HARRISON.

CHAPTER XL.
A Law to regulate Elections.

Representatives when & where to be elected.

§ 1. ALL general elections for Representatives to serve in the General Assembly, shall invariably be begun on the first Monday in April, bi-annually, and be held at the court house, or place of holding courts, in the several counties; the poll of the

What hour.

election shall be opened between the hours of ten and eleven of the clock, in the forenoon, and shall be kept open without interruption or adjournment, until five of the clock of the afternoon

How long open each day

of the same first day of the election, when it shall be adjourned until ten of the clock of the next morning, when the poll shall again be opened, and carried on without adjournment, until five of the clock of the afternoon of the same second day, when the poll shall finally close, unless the Judges of the election deem it

May be closed 2nd day.

(233)

advisable to continue the election, or some candidate requires them to continue the same; and if the election is to be continued, it shall be adjourned until ten of the clock of the next morning, when the polls shall again be opened, and continue open without adjournment until three of the clock of the afternoon of the said third day, and no longer, when the election shall close, and the Judges of the said election, shall then proclaim the person or persons (if more than one are to be elected) highest in number of votes duly elected.

When finally closed.

Judges to proclaim persons elected.

Provided always, That when through any casualty, the governor's writ of election does not reach the Sheriff of any county, previous to the hour of opening the poll of the election, then the electors thereof shall have the right to elect the same number of representatives, which they were entitled to agreeably to their last return trasmitted to the governor.

When writ of election not in time.

§ 2. The Sheriffs of the several counties, shall and they are hereby authorised and required, each to take to his assistance two of the Judges of the court of common Pleas for their respective counties, ten days before the commencement of any general election, and two days before any occasional election, which two Judges together with the Sheriff, shall be Judges of all elections for representatives to serve for their respective counties in the general assembly; and if any Sheriff shall be absent by reason of sickness or other disability, when the poll is

Who shff. to take as assistants.

Judges of election.

In case of the absence of sheriff.

(234)

to be opened, his deputy by him specially appointed shall act in his stead; and, if the aforesaid Judges, or either of them are absent, whether wilfully, or by reason of sickness, or other disability, when the poll is to be opened, the sheriff shall supply his or their place; by chusing from among the freeholders present, one or more, who shall supply the place of such ab-

Absence of judges how supplied.

sent Judge or Judges: and if any shall refuse or neglect to discharge the duties by this act of him required; whereby any county may be deprived of its full representation in the legislature of this Territory; for every such offence, he shall forfeit and pay the sum of five hundred dollars, to the use of the county, to be recovered by indictment, in any court to be held in such county, wherein the same may be cognizable.

§ 3. The aforesaid Judges of the election, shall appoint two poll keepers, who, previous to any vote being received, shall severally take an oath or affirmation before any Justice of the peace of their respective county.

The oath or affirmation of the poll keeper shall be:

"I, A B, do solemnly swear, or affirm, that I will truly keep the poll of this election to commence here this, (here insert the day, month and year) for a member or members, as the case may be, to represent this county of

(here insert the county) in the General Assembly of this Territo-

(235)

ry, and that I will deliver fair and perfect entries thereof to the Judges of the same election, at the close thereof to the best of my abilities."

It shall be the duty of the several poll keepers raspectively to attend in the election room during the time that votes are received, and to enter the names of all voters, in columns, under the names of the person or persons, for whom they respectively vote, and at the close of the election, to number the votes which every person voted for has received, and there and then deliver their respective books of entries, with their names respectively thereto subscribed, to the Judges of the election: And whereas doubts have arisen in that part of the ordinance for the government of this Territory which relates to the qualifications of electors of Representatives; therefore for the purpose of obviating all doubts thereon, and to secure the right of suffrage to every person who according to the

Neglect or refusal to serve to be fined and to what use.

Judges to ap point 2 poll keepers. To take an oath.

Form.

Duty of poll keepers.

true intent, spirit, and meaning of the ordinance, aforesaid, is entitled thereto; *It is therefore enacted,* That every free male inhabitant of the age of twenty one years, resident in the Territory, and who hath been a citizen of any state in the union, or who hath been two years resident in this Territory, and holds a freehold in fifty acres of land within any county of the same, or any less quantity in the county in which he shall reside, which, with the improvements made there- *(Dubts respecting electors. Qualification of electors)*

G 2

(236)

on, shall be of the value of one hundred dollars, or who has paid for, and in virtue of a deed of conveyance for further assurances from a person vested with the fee, is in actual possession of fifty acres of land, subject to taxation in the county, in which he shall be resident, shall be, and are hereby declared to be duly qualified electors of representatives, for the counties in which they are respectively resident.

§ 4. Every elector shall vote once, and no more, in any election for representatives; and the manner of voting shall be by the elector at any time while the poll of the election is open, to approach the bar in the election room, and addressing the Judges of such election in his proper person, in an audable voice, to be heard by the Judges of the election, and poll keepers thereof, to mention by name the person or persons, to the number of representatives to which such county may be entitled; and the poll keepers, shall enter his vote accordingly; and then he shall withdraw. *(Each elector to vote one.)* *(By viva voice.)*

§ 5. At the time and place of holding elections, and before the poll begun, the Sheriff shall affix at the outer door of the house in which the election shall be held, a notice in writing, expressing the number of representatives to be elected at the ensuing election, and the names of the persons whom he hath selected as assistant Judges thereof; and previous to any votes being received, the assistant Judges shall *(Shff. to adv. place.)*

(237)

Assistant judges to take oath.

severally take an oath (or affirmation) before some person qualified to administer oaths. The oath or affirmation of an assistant shall be,

Form.

"I, A B, do solemnly swear (or affirm) that I will duly attend the ensuing election, throughout the continuance of the same, and that I will truly assist the other Judges thereof, to the best of my ability, according to law, and that I will endeavour to prevent all fraud, deceit, and abuse in carrying on the same."

To preserve order and receive votes.

It shall be the duty of the Judges of the election to preserve order and regularity in conducting the said election, to receive the votes of all persons who to them may appear to be duly qualified electors, and where they entertain doubts, they may interrogate such person on oath, touching his quali-

Administer oath.

fications as an elector; and it shall be their further duty to observe that the poll is fairly kept, and at the close of the

Inspect poll & proclaim.

election to proclaim the person or persons (if more than one are to be elected) highest in votes, duly elected.

In occasional elections writ towhom directed.

§ 6. When any writ of any occasional election shall be issued by the Governor, in case of the death or removal from office, of any representative, the same writ shall be directed to the Sheriff of such county respectively, for which such representative, who is dead, or removed from office, shall have been elected; and the Sheriff on re-

(238)

Notice of election.

ceiving the writ, shall forthwith give due and publick notice, throughout the county ten days before holding such election, and the same shall be holden within twenty days after the writ of election is received by the Sheriff, and conducted in like manner aforesaid.

Shff. & judges to give certificate attested by poll keepers.

§ 7. The Sheriff and other Judges of the election, shall deliver to every person proclaimed duly elected, a certificate of his election, signed with their names, and attested by the poll keepers; and the Sheriff shall cause a fair copy of the poll certified by the poll keepers, and the writ, (when it has come to his hand in due time) certified by himself, otherwise a certificate of the proceedings for want of such writ, to be forthwith transmitted to the office of the Secretary of the Territory; and shall, within twenty days from the close of the election, deliver duplicates of the poll, and writ, or other certificate to the Clerk of the court of Common Pleas, of the proper county, who shall carefully preserve the same.

Copy of polls & writ transmitted to secretary's office.

Duplicates &c to clk. of C. P. to be preserved.

§ 8. If any candidate, or elector of the proper county, who choose to contest the validity of any election, or the right of any person proclaimed duly elected in any county, to his seat in the Legislature; such person shall give notice in writing to the person whose election he means to contest, or leave a written notice thereof, at the house where such person last resided, within ten days after such election, expressing the

When elections are contested notice to be given thereof Within 10 days.

(239)

points on which the same shall be contested, and shall within the same time give notice to the coroner of the county, who shall thereupon summons two Judges of the court of Common Pleas of the same county, other than those who were Judges of the election, who shall be severally obliged to attend under the penalty of fifty dollars. The said Coroner shall appoint a place and time for the said two Judges of the pleas as aforesaid, to meet within the said county, which shall be within twenty days after the election; the said two Judges and every of them, shall have power to issue subpœnas, and compel the attendance of all persons required to give evidence, under the penalty of fifty dollars, to be levied on each and every delinquent, who hath been duly served with process; and the said two judges so met, shall hear and certify under seal all testimony relative to the said contested election, to the house of representatives at their next session.

To state points.

2 J's C. P. to attend. To appoint a place and time for meeting. Penalty on neglect. Judges to compel the attendance of witnesses

What penalty.

To certify to H. R.

No person shall contest any election unless he is an elector of that county in which the election is held, nor shall any testimony be received which does not relate to the point specified in the notice: Copies attested by the person who delivers or leaves said notices, shall be delivered to the said Judges of the pleas.

Contestors must be electors in the county. What testimony to be received.

§ 9. All persons elected, or appointed to serve in either branch of the Legislature, and

Members to attend upon

(240)

the call of
gov.

Penalty on
neglect.

Unless body
to which he
belongs re-
mits.

Members
may be ex-
pelled, for
what, and
how.
Proviso.

Treating or
bribing how
punished.

Sham con-
veyances to
be forfeited.

consenting thereto, shall be obliged to give due attendance, at such time and place as may be directed by the governor, having received previous and timely notice of their respective elections or appointments, under the penal sum of one hundred and fifty dollars, to the use of the territory: unless for good cause shewn, the house to which he is elected or appointed a member, shall remit the same or any part thereof.

§ 10. Each house or branch of the legislature, shall have the right of expelling its own members, for disorderly behavior or transgressing the rules: *Provided,* That no member shall be expelled without the concurrence of two thirds of the members present; and no member shall be questioned a second time for the same offence.

§ 11. No candidate or other person for him shall attempt to obtain votes by bribery or treating, with meat or drink; and any person so offending, shall be incapable of holding a seat in either branch of the legislature for the space of two years, next thereafter; or if any person in order to obtain votes, either for himself or any favorite candidate, shall make any sham conveyance of land, title or lease of land to any person with an intent of enabling him to vote; every person so offending, by making such sham conveyance, title, bond or lease, shall on conviction thereof, forfeit for every such offence, the land so pretended to be conveyed, sold or leased, to the Territory;

(241)

Penalty on
persons recei
ving sham
conveyance.

Shff. judges
& poll keep-
ers to receive
comption.

and every person so offending, by receiving any such sham conveyance, title, bond or lease, shall on conviction, forfeit the value of the land so pretended to be held, by such pretended conveyance, title, bond or lease to the use of the Territory.

§ 12. For all services done in pursuance of this act, in conducting the elections and making return thereof the by clerk of the court of Common Pleas, Sheriff, assistant Judges of elections, and poll keepers respectively in any county, a reasonable compensation shall be allowed by the court of Common Pleas of such county respectively, who are hereby directed at any time to make such reasonable allowance, as the said court deem proper, to be paid out of the county funds.

§ 13. No Sheriff, under Sheriff, Clerk of any court, or person holding a commission during pleasure, directly under the United States or this Territory, except Justices of the Peace, and militia officers, shall be eligible to a seat in either branches of the legislature.

Persons not eligible as a legislator.

§ 14. There shall be four election districts established in the county of Dearborn, to wit: All that part of the said county lying north of the south line of the twelfth township, first and second ranges, shall be one district; the second district shall commence at the south line of the twelfth township, and to extend down White Water to the centre of the ninth

election districts in Dearborn.

(242)

township, of the said first and second ranges; the third district shall commence at south line of the second district, and to extend to the place where the meredian line between the state of Ohio, and this Teritory crosses White Water; and all that part of the said county lying west of a line drawn a due north course from the mouth of Grants creek, shall make the fourth district.

§ 15. For the purpose of carrying the above section into more complete operation and effect, the high sheriff of the county, shall appoint his deputies and assistants, to act in the said several districts, who shall severally have the same power, in opening and closing the election, in their said districts, as is given to the Sheriff of the county by the second section of this act, and the returns from the said deputies shall be severally made by them to the said high Sheriff within fifteen days after holding the said election. The two last sections of this act shall continue in force for one year and no longer.

High Sff. to appoint deputies.

Their power and duty.

continuation

JESSE B. THOMAS,
Speaker of the House of Representatives.
B. CHAMBERS,
President of the Council.

Approved—September 17th, 1807.
WILLIAM HENRY HARRISON.

(243)

CHAPTER XLI.
An Act regulating the firing of Woods, Prairies and other Lands.

Firing woods &c. fined & in what sum. § 1. WHOSOEVER shall at any time, except as is herein after excepted, wilfully or negligently set on fire or cause to be set on fire, any woods, prairies or other grounds, whatsoever within this Territory, and being thereof legally convicted by the oath or affirmation of one or more credible witnesses, in any court having cognizance of the same, shall pay a fine not exceeding one hundred dollars, nor less than five dollars; the one half of **How paid.** which to be paid to the person prosecuting for the same and the other half to the use of the county wherein the offence shall have been committed.

To make good all damages. § 2. When any person or persons so offending, shall thereby occasion any loss, damage or injury to any othe person or persons, every person so offending, shall be, and is hereby declared liable to make good all damages to the person or persons injured, with costs of suit, in any court having cognizance of the same.

Servantshow punished. When any servant or servants shall offend against the tenor of this law, and being duly convicted of the same, except his, her or their master or mistress shall pay the fine herein above provided, with damages and

H 2

(244)

costs for said offence, then such servant or servants, so offending, shall be whipped not exceeding thirty-nine stripes, at the discretion of the court having cognizance thereof.

Proviso. § 4. Nothing in in this act shall be so construed as to prevent any person or persons from setting on fire any rubbish, leaves or brush, on his, her or their farms or plantations as often as occasion may require, if the same be done without damage to **What time to fire prairies.** the property of any other person or persons: *Provided also,* That nothing in this act shall be so construed, as to prevent any person or persons from setting on fire prairies or cleared land, between the first day of December and the tenth day of March, if the same be done without damage, as aforesaid.

JESSE B. THOMAS,
Speaker of the House of Representatives.
B. CHAMBERS,
President of the Council.

Approved—September 17th, 1807.

WILLIAM HENRY HARRISON.

(245)

CHAPTER XLII.
An Act establishing and regulating the Militia.

§ 1. EACH and every free, able bodied white male citizen of the Territory who is, or shall be of the age of eighteen years, and under the age of forty-five years, except as is herein after excepted, shall severally and respectively be enrolled in the militia by the captain or commanding officer of the company within whose bounds such citizen shall reside, within twenty days next, after such residence; and it shall at all times hereafter, be the duty of such captain or commanding officer of a company to enrol every such citizen as aforesaid, and also those who may from time to time, arrive at the age of eighteen years, or being of the age of eighteen years, and under the age of forty-five years, except, as is herein after excepted, shall come to reside within his bounds, and shall without delay notify such citizen of the said enrollment, by a proper non-commissioned officer of the company, by whom such notice may be proved; and every citizen so enrolled and notified, shall within six months thereafter, provide himself with a good musket, a sufficient bayonet and belt, or a fusee, two spare flints, a knapsack and a pouch, with a box therein, to contain not less than twenty four catridges, suited to the bore of his musket or fusee, each catridge to contain a proper quantity of powder and ball, or a good rifle, knap-

Persons liable to militia duty.

To be enrolled by commanding officers of co's.

How armed.

(246)

sack, pouch and powder horn, with twenty balls suited to the bore of his rifle, and a quarter of a pound of powder; and every enrolled person shall so appear armed, accutred and provided, when called out to muster, or into service, except when called out on company days, to exercise only, he may appear without a knapsack: The commissioned officers shall severally be armed with a sword or hanger, and espontoon; and it shall be the duty of each officer, non-commissioned officer and each militia man, when ever they shall meet for the purpose of mustering to appear in some cheap uniform, the colour and form of which shall be determined by a board composed of the commissioned officers of each regiment, who shall meet for that purpose, on or before the first day of March, next, or at any time thereafter, when the colonel of each regiment shall direct; and the officers and men of the said regiment shall within six months after the said meeting, provide themselves with the uniform, as directed by the said board.

Every citizen so enrolled, and providing himself with arms, amunition, uniform and accoutrements, required as aforesaid, shall hold the same exempted from all suits, distresses, executions or sales for debt, damages, or the payment of taxes.

§ 2. The Judges of the supreme court, the attorney general, the Clerk of the supreme court of the Territory, all ministers of the gospel, licensed to preach according to the rules of their sect, all keepers of jails, and

(247)

such other persons, as are exempted by the laws of the United States, shall be and are hereby exempted from militia duty.

§ 3. The militia of the Territory shall be divided into divisions, brigades, regiments, battalions and companies; each division, brigade and regiment shall be numbered and a record of such numbers made in the adjutant-general's office, and when in the field or in service in the Territory, each division, brigade or regiment, shall respectively take rank according to their numbers, reckoning the first or lowest number the the highest in rank; each division shall consist of two brigades; each brigade of not less than two, nor more than four regiments; each regiment of two battalions; each battalion of four companies, and each company shall consist of sixty-four privates: *Provided always,* That if local

Margin notes:

Commissioned officers how armed.

To appear in uniform.

Color, how determined.

Arms, &c. exempted from all seizures.

What persons exempt from militia duty.

Militia how divided.

circumstances should require it, a company may be formed of forty, or extended to eighty rank and file.

§ 4. The militia of the Territory, shall be officered as follows, to wit: To each division there shall be one major general, who shall be allowed two aid de camps, with the rank of major; To each brigade one brigadier general, with one brigade inspector, to serve as brigade major, with the rank of major, to be appointed by the brigadier general, from among the commissioned officers of his brigade; to each regiment one lieutenant colonel commandant; to

Andofficer'd

(248)

each battalion one major, and to each company one captain, one lieutenant, one ensign, four sergeants, four corporals, one drummer, and one fifer. The regimental staff shall consist of one adjutant, one quarter master, and one paymaster, to be chosen from among the subaltern officers, if fit persons can be found; one surgeon, one surgeon's mate, one sergeant major, one quarter master sergeant, one drum major, and one fife major.

§ 5. There shall be attached to each brigade, one company of artillery, and one troop of horse, when in the opinion of the brigadier general, the said companies, or either of them, can, with convenience, be raised and equipped within his brigade.—To every company of artillery, there shall be one captain, two lieutenants, four sergeants, four corporals, six gunners, six bombardiers, one drummer, and one fifer, and not less than twenty, nor more than thirty matrosses; the non commissioned officers, shall be armed with a sword or hanger, and each private, or matross, shall be furnished with a fusee, bayonet and belt, with a cartridge box, to contain twelve cartridges.—And to each troop of horse there shall be one captain, two lieutenants, one cornet, four sergeants, four corporals, one saddler, one farrier, one trumpeter and not less than thirty, nor more than sixty privates.

One com'ny of artillery & one troop of horse to be attached to each brigade

How armed & officered.

The commissioned officers shall furnish themselves with good horses, saddles, and holsters, and be armed with a sword, and

(249)

pair of pistols; and each dragoon, shall provide himself with a servicable horse, a good saddle, holsters, a bridle, a mail pillion, and valice, a breast plate and crupper, a pair of boots, and spurs, and be armed with a sabre, and pistol, or pair of pistols, and cartridge box, to contain twelve cartridges for pistols. Each company of artillery, and troop of horse, shall be formed of volunteers from the brigade, and be enlisted by the officers commanding them, and shall be uniformly cloathed in regimentals, furnished at their own expense, the colour and fashion to be determined by a board to be composed of the officers of each of the said companies.

To be formed by volunteer enlistments.

§ 6. And whereas it will be of great utility and advantage, in establishing a well disciplined militia, to annex to each battalion a light company, to be formed of young men, from the age of eighteen to twenty-eight years, whose ability and domestic circumstances, will admit of a frequency of training, and who will be in a state of readiness in all cases of emergency, not practicable or convenient for the militia in general, and their returning to the main body, on their arrival at the latter period, will be giving thereto a military pride, and experience from which the best of consequences must result; *Therefore it is enacted,* That the Governor shall appoint and commission one captain, one lieutenant, and one ensign, to each battalion; and the said company shall be distinguished by the denomination

Companies of light infantry grenadiers and riflemen to be raised.

(250)

of grenadier, light infantry, or rifle men, at the discretion of the commanding officer of the brigade. Every person belonging to the said light companies, shall wear, while on duty, such caps and uniforms, as the field officers of the regiment shall direct, to be purchased by such companies at their own expence. And the officers of such light companies shall after qualifying in the manner hereafter directed, proceed to raise their companies, by voluntary enlistments, any where within the bounds of the battalions, to which they may be attached, of young men, as before directed; and as the men of such light companies, shall, from time to time arrive at the age of twenty eight years, the captain shall make report thereof to the commanding officer of the battalion, who

By voluntary enlistments.

At the age of 28 to be enrolled in the district companies.

shall order them to be enrolled in the district company they may respectively live in, and the deficiency shall be supplied by a new enlistment. The companies shall, in all respects, be subject to the same regulations and orders as the rest of the militia, except as is hereinafter excepted.

Counties in what manner divided into districts

§ 7. The commanding officers of regiments, battalions, and companies, in each county, shall, on the first day of May next, meet at their respective court houses, there to divide the counties into districts, for the purpose of forming the regiments, battalions and companies, by this act established, which district so laid off, shall be designated by certain lines and bounds, to be by them established, and which shall be

When new districts shall be formed.

(251)

recorded by the Judge Advocate, as Clerk of each regiment: *Provided always,* That if emigration, into any of the company districts, shall render it necessary to form new districts, so as to affix to each district, its proper number of effective militia, it shall be the duty of the captain of each company, which shall have increased above the proper number, to notify the commandant of the battalion, to which such company belongs, thereof; who shall give the like information to the commandant of his regiment, whose duty it shall be to cause a meeting of the commanding officers of the companies of such battalion, or regiment (as the case may be) from which such new company is to be taken, at the most convenient place in the battalion, or regiment, as soon as may be; and the officers so met, shall proceed to divide such district, in case it contains a sufficient number of effective men, so as to form two companies, or otherwise to take from the several adjoining districts, such parts as they can spare, without reducing the original company, or companies, below their proper quota, and thereof form one new company.

Manner thereof.

§ 8. No person shall be eligible to a command in the militia, who is not a citizen of the United States, and has not resided twelve months in this Territory.

Requsites to a command.

§ 9. Every officer commissioned by virtue this act, shall, previous to his entering on the duties of his respective office, take the oath

Commissioned officers before they

I 2

(252)

act what necessary.

of allegiance to the United States, and the following oath or affirmation, to wit:

"I   do solemnly swear (or affirm as the case may be) that I will faithfully and justly execute the duties of a   in the militia of the Territory, according to the best of my abilities— so help me God."

Which oath or affirmation, shall be endorsed on the back of the commission by the person administering the same.

Rank of officers how determined.

§ 10.   All commissioned officers shall take according to the date of their commissions, and when two or more of the same grade be of equal date, then their rank to be determined by lot to be drawn by them before the commanding officer of the brigade, regiment, battalion, company, or detachment.

Regimental standards to be provided.

§ 11.   Each battalion and regiment, shall be provided with regimental standards, with the number of the regiment inscribed on the same, by the field officers; and each company with the regimental colours, with the number of the company in such regiment inscribed thereon; a drum and fife, by the commissioned officers of the company, in such manner as shall hereinafter be directed.

Ad. gen. his duty.

§ 12.   There shall be an adjutant general appointed in the Territory, whose duty it shall be to distribute all orders from the commander in chief of the Territory, to

(253)

the several corps; to attend all public reviews, when the commander in chief shall review the militia, or any part thereof; to obey all orders from him, relative to carrying into execution, and perfecting the system of military discipline, established by this act; to furnish blank forms of the different returns that may be required, and to explain the principles on which they should be made; to receive from the several officers of the different corps throughout the Territory, returns of the militia, under their commands, reporting the actual situation of the arms, accoutrements and ammunition, their delinquencies, and every other thing which relates to the general advancement of good order and discipline;

all which the several officers of the divisions, brigades, regiments, and battalions, are hereby required to make in the usual manner, so that the said adjutant general may be duly furnished therewith; from all which returns he shall made proper abstracts, and lay the same immediately before the commander in chief of the Territory: *Provided always,* That the adjutant general of the militia of this Territory, shall be, ex officio, inspector general of the same.

§ 13.   It shall be the duty of the brigade inspector to attend all musters of officers, within his brigade, to exercise and examine them; to note delinquencies, and return the same, forthwith to the lieutenant colonel of the regiment to which they belong; to attend the regimental and battalion meetings

Brigd. inspr. his duty.

(254)

of the militia composing their several brigades, during the time of their being under arms; to inspect their arms, ammunition, cloathing and accoutrements; superintend their exercise, and manœuvres, and introduce the system of military discipline, pointed out in the twenty fifth article for the government of the militia, described throughout the brigade, agreeable to law, and such orders as they shall from time to time, receive from the commander in chief of the Terrritory, or the commander of the brigade, for the time being; to make returns to the adjntant general of the Territory, twice in every year, the first on or before the first day of August, and the second on or before the first day of December, of all the militia of the brigade to which he belongs, reporting therein the actual situation of the arms, accoutrements, cloathing and ammunition of the several corps, and every other thing, which in his judgment may relate to their government, and the general advancement of good order and military discipline.

§ 14.   And whereas it will be productive of very considerable advantages to the disciplining of the militia to have frequent meetings of the commissioned and non commissioned officers of each regiment, or battalion, *It is therefore hereby enacted,* That the commissioned and non commissioned officers of each regiment, or battalion, at the discretion of the colonel of each regiment, shall meet at some convenient place as near

Officers to meet and ex ercise.

(255)

as may be, in the centre of each battalion or regiment, to be pointed out by the colonel thereof, as often as he may think expedient, not exceeding six days in every year, for the purpose of being trained and instructed by the brigade inspector, for the space of five hours each day.

Capts. to appoint sergents.

§ 15. It shall be the duty of each captain after having enrolled his company as directed by this law, to appoint four persons to his company as sergeants, giving each his rank of first, second, third, and fourth sergeant, and also four persons as corporals, giving to each his rank of first, second, third and fourth corporal, giving his company notice thereof, and shall report the said appointments to the commandant of the regiment, who shall thereupon make out his warrants to such non-commissioned officers accordingly, and they are to be obeyed and respected as such; and if any person or persons, on receiving due notice of any such appointment, shall refuse to perform the duties of the office to which he or they are appointed, such person or persons shall be returned to the next court of enquiry, by his or their captain, to be fined as this law directs.

Persons refusing to serve fined.

§ 16. It shall be the duty of the commanding officers of each and every company so enrolled, forthwith to divide his company into divisions by ballott, from one to eight, for the purpose of a regular rotine of duty, when called into actual service, and shall re-

Captains to divide co's.

(256)

turn a roaster of such division, with the rotative number attached to each class within fifteen days, to the commanding officer of his battalion, who shall forthwith transmit the same to the commandant of the regiment, who shall order the same to be recorded by the judge advocate as clerk thereof.

Persons moving from 1 Co. to another, what necessary.

§ 17. Every militia man removing out of the bounds of one company to another, shall apply to the commanding officer of the company he is removing from, who shall give him a discharge, certifying the class to which he belongs, which certificate the said militia man shall produce to the captain or commanding officer of the company in the district in which he shall next settle, within ten days after his settlement; and the said captain or commanding officer is hereby required to enroll him in the class specified in said certificate; and on failure of any militia man, obtaining a certificate in manner aforesaid, and presenting the same as before directed, the captain or commanding officer of the company to which he shall remove, is hereby required to enrol such delinquent the foremost in the first class for duty, notifying him thereof, and that he must hold himself in readiness to perform any duty by this act required.

§ 18. There shall be private musters of each company of cavalry, artilery, grenadiers, light infantry and reflemen, once in every two months, at such time and place **Co. musters, how often to be holden.**

(257)

as the commandant thereof shall appoint, except in the months of December, January, February and March in every year; and every other company formed by virtue of this act, once in every two months except, as before excepted, to be appointed by the commanding officer thereof, at, or as near as may be, the centre of the company district; there shall be a muster of each battalion in the month of April in every year, which shall be appointed by the commanding officers of the respective regiments, who shall fix on the most suitable place, as near as may be to the centre of the battalion district, and shall superintend the exercise, and direct the evolutions that shall be performed; and there shall be a muster of each regiment in the month of October, in every year, which shall be appointed by the brigadier general or commanding officer of the brigade to which such regiment belongs, at, or as near as may be, to the certre of the regimental district, and shall be made under the superintendance and direction of the brigadier general or commander of the regiment; which company, battalion and regimental muster, shall continue one day each, and no longer. **Batrallion musters.** **Regimental musters.**

§ 19. The brigadier generals, or commanding officers of brigades, shall cause notice in writing of the times and places of the said musters, to be given to the commanding officers of regiments, at least twenty five days; the commanding officers of regiments, shall give notice of the regi- **Notice of musters when & how given**

(258)

mental and batalion musters, to the commanding officers of the battalions at least twenty days; the commanding officers of battalions shall give notice to the rigimental and battalion musters to the commanding officer of companies at least fifteen days; and the captains or commanding officers of companies shall give notice of the regimental, battalion and private musters to the individuals of their respective companies, by themselves or sergeants, at least five days before such regimental, battalion or company muster, (as the case may be) shall be holden; the notices to be given by the commanding officers of brigades, regiments and battalions, shall be in writing, and delivered to the person or persons, or left at the usual place of his, or their abode, by such commanding officers, themselves, or such other officer, or officers as they may think fit to order; and the commanding officers of companies, shall have power to assign to each sergeant of their respective companies, his due proportion thereof, whose duty it shall be to give the notice before directed to that portion of the company to him assigned, which may be done by personal summons or by leaving notices in writing at the usual place of abode of the person so to be notified.

Divisions & brigades how made and officer'd.   § 20. The militia of the Territory shall be divided into divisions and brigades, at

(259)

the discretion of the commander in chief of the militia.

Hour of muster.   § 21. Every officer and soldier shall appear, at his respective muster field, on the day appointed by eleven o'clock; and at every muster, each captain, or commanding officer of a company, shall **Of roll call.** direct the first sergeant of his company, in his presence to call the roll, at half past eleven o'clock precisely, examine every person **Delinquents how noted & returned.** belonging thereto, and note down all delinquencies occuring therein, and make return thereof as well as of the strength of the company, number of rifles, muskets, bayonets, fusees &c. on parade, to the commanding officer of his battalion, within ten days after any such regimental, battalion, or company muster; and **Roll of commissioned of-** every commanding officer of a battalion, shall, at his regimental or battalion muster, (as the case may be) at the hour on which the battalion is to be formed, in like manner, proceed to call the names **ficers when** of the commissioned officers of his battalion, examine and note **called.** down all delinquencies, and make return thereof together with those reported from commanding officers of companies, to the commanding officers of the regiment, to which he belongs, within fifteen days next succeeding such battalion or regimental muster, (as the case may be) who shall lay the whole before the court hereafter appointed to take cognizance, and determine on them, and to

K 2

(260)

each of the said returns shall be annexed the following certificate, to wit:

"I   do certify, that the returns hereunto annexed, **Certificates** contain all the delinquencies which have occurred in my company, **to accompa-** (or battalion as the case may be) since my last return." **ny returns.**

And to the battalion returns shall be added,

"And that the reports which accompany them, are all which have been made by the commanding officers of companies within my battalion.

§ 22. The commanding officers of each regiment, within **Adjutants to** twenty days next after a muster of his regiment, or of the bat- **make returns** talions of the same, shall cause the adjutant of his regiment to **&c.** make out a complete return of the same, (agreeably to such forms as shall be furnished by the adjutant general, noting particularly its strength, and number of arms) to the inspector of the brigade.

§ 23. The commissioned officers of the first battalion in each **Court of en-** rigiment, shall meet on the second Tuesday; and the commis- **quiry and as-** sioned officers of the second battalion of each regiment shall meet **sessment how** on the second Thursday next after each regimental or battalion **formed.** muster, as near as may be in the centre of the battalion, to be appointed by the lieutenant colonel, at the battalion or regimental muster; and public notice thereof gi-

(261)

ven, to the battalion or battalions, whilst on parade; a majority of whom shall form a court of enquiry and assessment of fines; and it shall be the duty of the lieutenant colonel commandant, to preside at such board, and in case of his absence by sickness or otherwise, the next officer in rank shall preside. The said court shall take the following oath, to be administered by the senior officer present, and afterwards by any any other officer of the board to him, to wit:

Form of the oath. "I   do solemnly swear or (affirm as the case may be) that I will truly and faithfully enquire into all delinquencies which appear on the returns to be laid before me, and will assess the fines thereon, as shall seem just, without partiality, favour or affection, so help me God."

Delinquencies by whom laid before court The lieutenant colonel commandant or commanding officer of the regiment shall then lay before the said court all delinquencies, as directed by this act, whereupon they shall proceed to hear and determine on them.

§ 24. And for enforcing obedience to this act, the following forfeitures and penalties shall be incurred for delinquencies, to wit:

By a colonel. By a lieutenant colonel commandant, or commanding officer of a regiment, for failing to take any oath, to direct his adjutant to summons any court or board, to deliver any commission or commissions, to appoint

(262)

a regimental or battalion muster, to give information of the places of holding courts of enquiries, to attend the same, to report delinquencies, to attend a battalion or regimental muster, or a muster of officers, to appoint the staff officers to his regiment, not less than ten, nor more than one hundred dollars.

Major. By a major, or commanding officer of a battalion, for failing to take an oath, to attend any court or board, to give notice of any regimental or battalion muster, to examine and train his battalion, to report delinquencies, to make a return, or to attend a muster of officers, he shall forfeit and pay any sum not less than eight, nor more than eighty dollars.

Captain. By a captain or commanding officer of a company as the case may be, for failing to take an oath, to attend any court or board, to enrol his company, to appoint private musters, to give notice of a regimental or battalion muster, to attend any muster armed, to examine and exercise his company, as is by the twenty-fifth article directed for the government of the militia, to call his roll, and report delinquencies, to make any return, or appoint non commissioned officers as directed by this, act he shall forfeit and pay any sum not exceeding fifty nor less than five dollars:

For every such offence by a subaltern officer, for failing to take an oath, to attend **Subaltern.**

(263)

any court or board, to attend any muster armed, as is by this act directed, for every such offence or neglect, he shall forfeit and pay any sum not exceeding forty, nor less than four dollars:

By a non-commissioned officer, for failing or neglecting to attend any muster of officers, to attend any muster of his company, to serve if appointed as a non-commissioned officer, for the term of one year, to take charge of any part of his company, or march them as directed, for every such offence or neglect, he shall forfeit and pay any sum not exceeding twenty, nor less than two dollars:

By a private man for failing or neglecting to attend a regimental or battalion muster, armed and equipped as directed by law, shall forfeit and pay any sum not exceeding six dollars, nor less than one dollar and fifty cents; to attend a muster of his company at the time and place appointed in manner aforesaid, during the whole time the same is on parade, any sum not exceeding three dollars, nor less than one dollar. **Private.**

§ 25. The fathers shall be bound for the payment of fines, incurred by their sons under the age of twenty one; guardians for the payment of fines incurred by their wards, and masters for the payment of fines incurred by their apprentices, and be charged therewith by the collectors of fines accordingly. **Fines on persons under 21 by whom paid.**

(264)

§ 26. Any court of enquiry for good cause shewn, may remit fines assessed by the court preceding the same, and in such case, it shall be the duty of the judge advocate as clerk, to certify **How fines may be remitted.**

the same to the collector of fines, who shall thereupon not collect such fine or fines, or refund the same if collected.

By whom & in what manner collected

§ 27. All fines to be assessed by virtue of this act, shall be collected by the provost martial of each regiment, who shall exercise the duties of collector thereof; and it shall be the duty of the president of the court martial, which hears and determines upon the fines and forfeitures which may accrue under this act, to deliver to the provost martial, as collector, as aforesaid, a certified list of all the delinquencies therein, on or before the first day of January in every year, and take his receipt therefor; which shall be lodged by the said provost martial in the office of the sheriff of the county, as treasurer thereof, within twenty days after he received the same, taking his receipt therefor; and he shall deliver within ten days after receiving the sheriff's receipt, a duplicate thereof to the lieutenant colonel of his regiment; and the provost martial, as collector, as aforesaid, shall collect and account for all fines, placed in his hands as aforesaid, on or before the first day of November in the same year; and on failure, the sheriff of the county, on giving him twenty days previous notice, shall obtain judgment and execution for the same

(265)

with costs, and ten percentum interest on the amount, from the time the same became due; and should any person so charged with fines, fail to make payment on or before the fifteenth day of June in any year, the provost martial collector, as aforesaid, is hereby authorised and required, by warrant of the president of the court martial, which he is hereby authorised to issue, to make distress and sale therefor, in the same manner as is directed in the collection of taxes: *Provided always,* That any provost martial, collector, shall be credited by his list of delinquents, and insolvents to be first examined by the court or courts of enquiry within his county.

How fines shall be appropriated.

§ 28. All monies paid into the sheriff's hands, as treasurer, in manner aforesaid, shall be appropriated, first, to the purpose of procuring the necessary number of drums, fifes and colors, and secondly, the remainder, if any, to pay the different officers, directed to be paid by this law, subject to the orders of the courts of enquiry, countersigned by the lieutenant colonel.

§ 29. If any militia man shall make it appear to the satisfaction of the officers of the company to which he belongs, that he is unable to furnish or equip himself, as by this law is directed, and the said officers satisfying the succeeding court of enquiry thereof it shall be in the power of such court, to remit any fine that may have been imposed by

Persons unable to equip according to law &c.

(266)

virtue of this law, and to grant such militia man exemption from such fines, until he shall be enabled, in the opinion of the officers of his company, to furnish and equip himself agreeably to this law.

§ 30. If any bystander at a regimental, battalion or company muster, shall insult or otherwise molest, any officer or soldier whilst on parade, the commanding officer of the regiment, battalion, troop, or company, as the case may be, may order such person or persons to be put under guard, for any time not exceeding six hours, and to pay a fine not exceeding four dollars, which shall be collected as other militia fines are.

By standers on parade insulting an officer or soldier how to be proceeded with.

§ 31. When ever it may be necessary to call into actual service, any part of the militia, on an actual or threatened invasion of this Territory, or of any of the neighboring states, it shall and may be lawful for the Governor to order into actual service such part of the militia, by classes, as the exigency may require: *Provided*, That the part so called doth not exceed four classes of the militia, of the brigade or brigades so called out: *And provided also,* That such brigade or brigades shall not be again called into actual service, until an equal number of classes of the militia of the other brigade or brigades, respectively, be first called; unless the danger of an invasion from the Indians or others should make it necessary to

Gov. empowered to call forth the militia.

Not to exceed 4 classes at one time.

(267)

keep in reserve the militia of such brigade or brigades for their immediate defence.

§ 32. All orders for the militia to be called forth as aforesaid, shall be sent to the commanding officers of brigades, with a

Governor to forward his orders to the brigadier generals. notification of the place or places of rendezvous, who shall immediately take measures for detaching the same, with the necessary number and rank of officers, and if any brigadier general shall fail herein, or fail or neglect to comply with any of the duties of him required by virtue of this act, he shall forfeit and pay any sum not exceeding one thousand dollars, to be assessed by a general court martial.

Brig. gen. failing in his duty.

Militia how to be classed. § 33. Each battalion, or regiment of the Terrritory shall be divided into eight classes, (preserving to each man his original class) all troops of horse, and flank companies, whether grenadiers, light infantry, or rifle men, shall be called into service by companies, or detachments, and not by classes, and the first flank company shall make part of the first call, and the second flank company shall make part of the fifth call of the militia, and be commanded by their own proper officers.

§ 34. To the end the militia, when called by classes, shall be properly officered,

L 2

(268)

the following order is hereby directed and enjoined, that is to say:

The order of classing commissioned officers. For the 1st draft, the 1st ct. 2d. lt. & 4th en.

2d	do	2d do. 1st do.	3d do.
3d	do	3d do. 4th do.	2d do.
4th	do	4th do. 3d do.	1st do.
5th	do	5th do. 6th do.	8th do.
6th	do	6th do. 5th do.	7th do.
7th	do	7th do. 8th do.	6th do.
8th	do	8th do. 7th do.	5th do.

Field officers routine of command &c. Non-commissioned officers to take tour of duty with the commissioned officers, and the routine of the field officers shall be according to the date of their respective commissions; the first colonel of the brigade shall command the first detachment, if it amounts to a colonel's command, if it does not, the command shall

Term of service & how relieved. devolve on the first major, liable to serve three months and no longer; and to be relieved by the class next in numerical order, the relief to arrive at least two days before the expiration of the term of the class to be relieved; but nothing herein contained shall prevent the Governor, or any commanding officer of a county, from employing, or calling out a part or the whole of any class, or any companies, regiment or regiments, without respect to this rule, whenever the exigency is too sudden to allow the assembling of the militia, which compose the particular classes, and the service of the persons so called out, shall be accounted as a part of their tour of duty.

When the militia may be called into service other than by classes.

(269)

§ 35. When any detachment of the militia shall be called into service, the captain of each company shall take care that his proportion of men are assembled, and marched to the proper place of parade or rendezvous, under the care of a commissioned officer or sergeant, with a list of the men; which list shall be delivered to the adjutant of the regiment, whose duty it shall be to attend at the place appointed, to receive the detachment from the several companies of his regiment; and he shall make out a roll of the whole, mentioning the rank of the officers, and names of the non-commissioned officers and privates; and when the detachment shall be completed, and placed under the proper officer, he shall attend them to the place appointed for the meeting of the detachment of the brigade, when the several adjutants shall deliver to the brigade major, or inspector, or officer appointed to command the whole detachment, a complete roll containing the names of the commissioned, and non-commissioned officers and privates, composing the detachment from each regiment, or battalion, noting such remarks as circumstances may require; and it shall be the duty of the officer appointed to the command of said detachment, to cause two complete rolls to be made out and certified under his hand, one of which rolls he shall forthwith transmit to the adjutant general, and the other to the brigade inspector.

Capts. their duty when the militia are called into service.

Adjutant his duty.

Officer commanding a detachment his duty.

§ 36. It shall and may be lawful for any person called to do a tour of duty, to send a

When a person called ont may send substitute.

(270)

sufficient substitute, such substitute being approved of by the captain, or commanding officer of the company, which he shall be offered to serve in: *Provided always,* That persons serving by substitute as aforesaid, if said substitute be called in his own

Condition thereof. turn, into actual service, before the time expires which he was to serve for his employer, that then the person procuring such substitute, shall march or find a person to march in his substitute's turn, (to be accepted as aforesaid,) or be liable to pay his fine for neglect, which fine is to be recovered in the same manner as is directed in the case of any militia man neglecting or refusing to do a tour of duty, and that sons who are not subject to the militia law, may be admitted as substitutes for their fathers, to be accepted as aforesaid.

When impressment of articles may be mde. § 37.   The lieutenant colonel of each regiment, from which detachments are drawn shall, if not otherwise to be obtained, cause to be procured by impressment, for each company, a waggon, team, and driver, or a sufficient number of pack horses, six axes, and six camp kettles, or pots of convenient size; all which shall be delivered to the commanding officer of the company, who shall be accountable for returning the same when his tour is over; and the articles aforesaid, shall be returned to the owner, who shall be allowed for the use, damage and detention, of the same, whatever shall be adjudged by a court of enquiry of the regiment; and to the end, that if any arti-

(271)

When lost &c. indemnification to be made to the owners. cles impressed be lost, the owner may be paid for the same; the lieutenant colonel shall cause all property by him impressed, by virtue of this act, to be valued by three householders, or any two of them on oath, before the same shall be sent away; shall give such owner a receipt for the same, stating the quantity, quality and value of the property impressed, together with a certificate of the appraisers: and upon proof being made of any article being lost, the valuation thereof shall be allowed, and the said allowance shall be certified to the auditor of public accounts; the said court shall make enquiry into the cause of such loss, and if it shall appear that such loss was occasioned by the misconduct or inattention of any officer, the brigade inspector is hereby authorised and required, to prosecute a suit against such officer, to recover damages for the use of the Territory.

§ 38. If any sudden invasion shall be made, or threatened to be made, into any county or district within this Territory, by Indians, or any other power, the commanding officer of the militia of such county or district, is hereby authorised and required, to order out the whole, or such part of the militia of his county or district, as he may think necessary, in such manner as he may think best for the repelling such invasion; and shall call on the commanding officers of the adjacent counties or districts for such aid as he may conceive necessary, who shall forthwith in like manner, furnish the same,

Commanding officer of a county upon actual or threatened invsiasion how to proceed.

(272)

and for assembling the militia required upon such occasions, or by order of the executive, the same measures shall be taken to summons them as is directed in the case of musters; and it shall be the duty of every commanding officer of a county or district, on receiving information of the intended invasion of his, or any neighboring county or district, forthwith to convey information of the same by special messenger or otherwise, to the governor of the Territory for the time being, that he may make the necessary arrangements to repel the same.

§ 39. If any suit or suits shall be brought or commenced against any person or persons for any thing done in pursuance of this act, the action shall be laid in the county where the cause of such action did arise, and not elsewhere; and the defendant or defendants, in such action or actions to be brought, may plead the general issue, and give this act and the special matter in evidence; and in case the plaintiff or plaintiffs, in any such action, shall fail in supporting the same, he, she or they, so failing, shall pay to the defendant or defendants, in every such action double costs.

Persons prosecuted under this law how plead.

Pltff. failing to pay double costs.

§ 40. The following articles, rules and regulations shall govern the militia of this Territory, to wit:

Articles.

Art. 1.—If any field or other commissioned officer, at any regimental review, or on any other occasion, when the regiment,

Commissioned officers for misbehavior how pnnished.

(273)

battalion or company to which he may belong, or in which he may hold a command, is paraded in arms, shall misbehave or demean himself in an unofficer like manner, he shall for such offence be cashiered, or punished by fine, at the discretion of a general court martial as the case may require, in any sum not exceeding sixty dollars:

Non-commissioned officers & privates misbehaving &c.

And if any non-commissioned officer or private, shall on any occasion of parading the company to which he belongs, be drunk or shall disobey orders, or shall use any reproachful or abusive language, to his officers, or any of them, or shall quarrel or promote any quarrel among his fellow soldiers, he shall be disarmed and put under guard by the commanding officer, or officers present, until the company is dismissed, and shall be by a regimental court martial fined not more than twenty dollars, nor less than one dollar.

Lieut. col. refusing to give orders &c.

Art. 2.—If the lieutenant colonel or commanding officer of any regiment or battalion, shall neglect or refuse to give orders for assembling his regiment or battalion, at the direction of the commander of the brigade to which he belongs, or in case of an invasion of the county or district to which such regiment or battalion belongs, he shall be cashiered and punished by fine not exceeding six hundred dollars, at the discretion of of a general court martial:

How punished.

And if a commissioned officer of any com-

(274)

Capt. refusing &c.

pany, shall on any occasion neglect or refuse to give orders for assembling the company to which he belongs, or any part thereof, at the direction of the lieutenant colonel or commanding officer of the regiment to which such company belongs, he shall be cashiered and punished by fine not exceeding two hundred dollars, at the discretion of a brigade or general court martial:

How punished.

Non-commissioned officers &c.

And a non-commissioned officer offending in such case shall be fined at the discretion of a regimental court martial, in any sum not exceeding twenty dollars.

Penalty on capt. for neglect of duty

Art. 3.—If any captain or commanding officer of a company, shall refuse or neglect to make out a list of the persons, noticed to perform any tour of duty, and send or convey the same to the lieutenant colonel, or commanding officer of the regiment, to which such company may belong, or if he shall fail to call forth such officers and men as shall from time to time be legally called from his company, upon any call from the governor on an invasion or insurrection in the county or district, or requisition from an adjacent county or district, or failing on any such occasion to repair to the place of rendezvaus; for such neglect or refusal he shall be cashiered, or fined at the discretion of a general court martial, in any sum not exceeding one hundred dollars, nor less than five dollars.

(275)

Art. 4.—If any militia man shall desert while he is on a tour of duty, he shall be fined not exceeding fifty dollars, and be obliged to march on the next tour of duty, under the same penalties as the first. **Desertion punished.**

If a non-commissioned officer shall so desert, he shall be degraded and placed in the ranks, and shall pay a fine not exceeding seventy five dollars, and be obliged to serve another tour as a private.

Art. 5.—Every general court martial, shall consist of thirteen members exclusive of a judge advocate, all of whom shall be commissioned officers, not under the rank of captain, and the officer highest in rank shall preside. **Genl. court martial.**

Art. 6.—Every regimental court martial, shall be composed of five members, all commissioned officers, one of their number a president, not under the rank of a captain. **Regmtl. court martial.**

Art. 7.—All members of a court martial are to behave with decency and calmness, and in giving their votes are to begin with the youngest in commission. **members to vote &c.**

Art. 8.—No officer shall be tried but by a general court martial, nor by officers of an inferior rank, if it can be avoided, nor shall any proceedings or trials be carried on except between the hours of eight o'clock in **Officers how tried.**

M 2

(276)

the morning and three o'clock in the afternoon, excepting in cases which in the opinion of the officer appointing the court requires an immediate example.

Judge adv. how ro prosecute

Art. 9.—The judge advocate shall prosecute in the name of the Territory, but shall so far consider himself as counsel for the prisoner, as to object to any leading question, to any witness, or any question to the prisoner, the answer to which might lead to criminate himself.

Persons under guard.

Art. 10.—When a non-commissioned offficer, or private is confined under guard, his crime shall be lodged with the officer of the guard, within twelve hours after the prisoner's confinement, otherwise the prisoner shall be set at liberty.

Of court martials &c.

Art. 11.—In every court martial not less than two thirds of the members must agree in every sentence, for inflicting any punishment, otherwise the person charged shall be acquitted.

Art. 12.—The president of each and every court martial, whether general or regimental, shall require all witnesses in order to the trial of offenders, to declare on oath, or affirmation, that the evidence they shall give, is the truth, the whole truth, and nothing but the truth, and the members of all such courts, shall take an oath or affirmation as follows, to wit:

Members of a court martial to take an oath.

(277)

"I   do solemnly swear, or affirm, as the case may be, that I will hear and determine according to evidence, to the best of my understanding, and the custom of war in like cases, between the Indiana Territory, and   now to be tried, and that I will not disclose the opinion of this court, until approved or disapproved by the commanding officer, or commander in chief, as the case may be, and that I will not at any time discover or disclose the opinion of any particular member unless called upon to give evidence thereof by a court of justice, in due course of law."

By whom ad ministered.

Which oath shall be administered by the judge advocate to the president and members.

Judge advt. to take an oath.

Art. 13.—The judge advocate shall be appointed by the commandant of each regiment, who shall hold his appointment during the pleasure of the said commandant, and shall take the following oath, or affirmation, which shall be administered by the court martial, to wit:

"I   do swear, or affirm, as the case may be, that I will faithfully execute the office of judge advocate to this court now met for the trial of   to the best of my abilities and understanding, and the custom of war in like cases, and that I will not disclose nor discover the opinion of this court martial, until appro-

(278)

ved or disapproved of by the commanding officer, and that I will not at any time disclose or discover the vote or opinion of any member, unless called upon by a court of justice to give evidence thereof in due course of law."

It shall be the duty of the judge advocate, to prosecute for **His duty.** the Territory, and to keep a record of the whole proceedings of the court, taking into view the depositions of witnesses that may be introduced; and he shall also exercise the duties of Clerk to the regiment.

Art. 14.—The commandant of each regiment shall appoint a **Provost mar-** provost martial for his regiment, who shall hold his appointment **tial his duty.** during the pleasure of said commandant; It shall be his duty to summon all witnesses, having received process for that purpose from the president of courts martial; to execute the orders of the court, and keep bystanders from interrupting the court, while sitting, and he shall exercise the duties of collector of fines and forfeitures.

The judge advocate and provost martial, shall be allowed such compensation as the court martial may direct, to be paid out of the fines; and it shall be their duty to attend any court of enquiry, or court martial, when thereto required, by the commandant of their regiment.

(279)

And all persons called as witnesses, in any case before a **Witness re-** court martial, who shall refuse to attend and give evidence, shall **fusing to at-** be censured, or fined, at the discretion of the court, in any sum **tend how pu-** not exceeding fifty dollars. **nished.**

Officers transgressing rules &c

Art. 15.—No officer or private, being charged with transgressing these rules, shall be suffered to do duty in a regiment, company or troop, to which he belongs, until he has had his trial by a court martial, and every person so charged, shall be tried as soon as a court martial can conveniently be assembled.

Col. injuring a non-commissioned officer or private what proceedings thereon &c.

Art. 16.—If any non-commissioned officer or private, shall think himself injured by his lieutenant colonel, or the commanding officer of the regiment, and shall upon due application made to him, be refused redress, he may complain to the brigadier, who shall direct the commissioned officers to enquire into the nature of the complaint; and if they report that the person complaining in their opinion, has been injured, the brigadier general shall then direct the brigade inspector, at a certain time and place to summons a general court martial, for the purpose of doing justice to the person complaining; and shall also direct the brigade inspector, to give the person complained of, at least eight days previous notice of the time and place of the meeting of any such court martial.

Art. 17.—If any non-commissioned of-

(280)

If by a capt. how to proceed.

ficer or private, shall think himself aggrieved by his captain, or other superior in the battalion, troop or company, to which he belongs, he may complain to the commanding officer of the regiment, who shall cause his adjutant to summons a regimental court martial, for doing justice according to the nature of the case.

The person tried, entitled to a copy of sent.

Art. 18.—The party tried by any generrl court martial, shall be entitled to a copy of the sentence, and proceedings of such court martial, after the decision on the sentence, upon demand thereof made by himself, or by any other person or persons in his behalf, whether such sentence be approved of, or not.

Court martial its power.

Art. 19.—No penalty shall be inflicted at the discretion of a court martial, other than degrading, cashiering or fining.

Of pardon & mitigation of fines &c.

Art. 20. The commandiug officer for the time being, shall have full power of pardoning, or mitigating any censures or penalties so ordered to be inflicted, on any private or non-commissioned officer, for the breach of any of these articles, by a general court martial; and every offender convicted as aforesaid, by any regimental court martial, may be pardoned, or have the penalty mitigated by the lieutenant colonel, or commanding officer of the regiment, excepting only where such censures or penalties are directed as satisfaction for injuries received by an officer, or private, from another; but

(281)

in case of officers, such sentence to be approved of by the commander in chief of the militia, who is empowered to pardon or mitigate such sentence, or disapprove of the same.

Art. 21.—If any commissioned officer, shall at any time or upon any occasion, behave in an unofficer like, ungentlemanly, or disgraceful manner, the commander in chief, if the person accused be a major general; the general of division, if a brigadier general; the brigadier, if a field officer; or the lieutenant colonel, or commanding officer of a regiment, if an inferior officer as the case may be, upon the application of a commissioned officer, may appoint a board of three officers, to enquire into the matter of complaint, and if upon their report it shall appear to him deserving of trial, then, and in such case, he shall direct a court martial, whose proceedings herein, shall have the same effect as if the offence had been committed when on actual duty.

Commissioned officers misbehaving &c. how proceeded against &c.

Art. 22.—The militia on the days of training, may be detained under arms, on duty in the field, any time, not exceeding six hours: *Provided,* They are not kept above three hours under arms at any one time, without being allowed to refresh themselves.

Hours of parade.

Art. 23.—All fines that shall be incurred by any of these rules, shall be paid to the Sheriff as Treasurer of the county, in which the offender resides, (whose receipt

Fines to whom paid. militia when called into actual serv.

(282)

shall be a discharge for the same) within sixty days after they become due, bnt in case of neglect or refusal to pay any of the said fines, they shall be levied and collected in manner herein before directed.

Rules of discipline established by congress to be observed &c.

Art. 24.—The militia of this territory whilst in actual service, shall be subject to the same rules and regulations as the federal army; and shall receive the same pay and rations as is allowed by the United States, to the militia when in actual service: *Provided,* That upon any transgression or offence of a militia man whether officer or private, against the rules and regulations of the federal army, the cause shall be tried and determined by a court martial of the militia of this territory, if the same can be convened.

Art. 25.—The rules of discipline approved and established by congress in their resolution of the twenty ninth of March one thousand seven hundred and seventy nine, shall be observed by the militia throughout this territory, except such deviations from said rules, as may be rendered necessary by the requisitions of the acts of congress, or some other unavoidable circumstances: it shall be the duty of every commanding officer at every training whether by regiment, battalion or single company to cause the militia to be exercised and tained agreeably to the said rules, and the instructions laid down by

Baron Steuben's instructions &c.

the baron Steuben, and annexed to the said rules of discipline, pointing out

(283)

the respective duties of the officers, non-commissioned officers and privates, are recommended and enjoined upon the militia of this Territory, as particularly and fully as if the said instructions were repeated and expressed in this act at length; and it shall be the duty of every captain to instruct his non-commissioned officers accordingly.

On a call for a tour of duty what notice &c.

Art. 26.—If any militia man, on receiving three days previous notice thereof, shall neglect or refuse to be in readiness to march on any tour of duty, armed, cloathed, and equipped, as required by this act, he shall forfeit and pay a sum not more than one hundred dollars, nor less than eight dollars, for every month he is required by law to serve on such tour, to be assessed (on proper proof thereof made) by a regimental court martial: *Provided always,* That if any militia man shall be sick, or make any other just or satisfactory excuse to the court martial; such fine shall not be assessed but such militia man shall be obliged to perform a tour of duty, on the next call of the militia.

Art. 27.—The foregoing articles shall

N 2
(284)

be read at all regimental and battalion musters by order of the commanding officer.

Articles to read

JESSE B. THOMAS,
Speaker of the House of Representatives.
B. CHAMBERS,
President of the Council.

Approved—17th September, 1807.
WILLIAM HENRY HARRISON.

CHAPTER XLIII.
An Act defining and regulating Privileges in certain cases.

§ 1. THE members of the Legislative Council and House of Representatives, and the Secretaries, Clerks, Serjeant at Arms, Door Keeper, and messengers of either branch of the General Assembly, shall be privileged from arrest, during the sitting of the Legislature, or of the branch thereof to which they respectively belong, and also during the time necessarily employed in travelling to, and returning from the place of their meeting, allowing one day for every fifteen miles of the distance, by the road most usually travelled, and all proceedings in suits, pending in which either of the persons above mentioned is a party shall be stayed during the time aforesaid; and whoever shall arrest either of the persons above men-

Members of the legislature exempt from arrest.

Person arresting liable to a fine.

(285)

tioned during the time they are entitled to privilege as above provided, shall forfeit and pay for every such offence, the sum of one hundred dollars, to be recovered with costs of suit, by action of debt, for the use, and in the name of the person injured.—

Electors &c.   And all persons legally entitled to vote for Representatives to the General Assembly, shall be privileged from arrest during the time of their attendance at elections, and while on the way in going to, and returning from such elections.

Judges and clerk of the G. C.   § 2. The Judges and Clerks of the General Court, and Attorney General, shall be privileged from arrest, while attending at the said court, and for, and during the space of fifteen days next before the commencement, and for and during the space of ten days next after the close of any term thereof, and also during the time necessarily employed in going to, holding, and returning from any General court, Circuit court, or court of Oyer and Terminer, or General Jail Delivery, or court of Nisi Prius, in any county within this Territory.

Judges of th' C. P.   § 3. The Judges of the several courts of Common Pleas within this Territory, during the sittings of their respective courts, and during the space of forty eight hours next before the commencement, and during the like space next after the close of any term thereof, and the Justices of the several courts of Common Justices of the Q. S.   Pleas, of the Peace, during the sitting of the session, and

(286)

during the space of forty eight hours next before the opening, and next after the close of any session thereof; and the Justices of the Peace, while engaged in hearing and determining any action suit or plaint instituted before them, or either of them, and all Attos. Clks. &c.   Attorneys, Counsellors at Law, Clerks, Sheriffs, Coroners, Constables and Cryers, and all suitors, witnesses and jurors, while attending court, and while going to, and returning from court, shall be privileged from arrest.

Timesplaces &c that no arrest shall be made.   § 4. No person shall be arrested while doing militia duty under the order of his commanding officer, or while going to, or returning from the place of duty or parade; nor shall any person be arrested on the first day of the week, commonly called Sunday, or in any place of religious worship, during the performance of divine worship; or in the chamber of the Legislative Council or House of Representatives, during their sitting; or in any court of Justice during the sitting of the court; or on the fourth day of the month July, the anniversary of American Independence.

§ 5. Nothing herein contained shall be construed to extend to cases of treason, felony or breach of the peace.

Provided always, That where either of the member or officers of the general assembly, shall be arrested during the sitting of the legislature upon any charge of treason,

Proviso.

(287)

felony or breach of the peace, it shall be the duty of the person issuing the process, on which the arrest is made, forthwith to give written notice thereof to the house in which the person arrested shall be a member or officer, addressed to to the president or speaker, as the case may be.

§ 6. Nothing herein contained, shall be construed to priviledge any person herein named from being served at any time with a summons, or notice to appear; and all arrests not contrary to the provisions herein contained, made in any place, or on any river or water course, within or bounding the Territory, shall be deemed lawful, and if any person shall be arrested contrary to the provisions herein contained, such person may and shall be discharged by a writ of habeas corpus, or in a summary way by motion before the court from which the process shall have issued at the costs of the party suing out such process.

No privilge.
in case of
sums &c.

Illegal ar-
rest how to
proceed.

JESSE B. THOMAS,
Speaker of the House of Representatives.
B. CHAMBERS,
President of the Council.

Approved—September 17th, 1807.

WILLIAM HENRY HARRISON.

(288)

CHAPTER XLIV.
An Act for opening and regulating public Roads and Highways.

§ 1. ALL public roads or highways established by lawful authority, shall be opened, amended, and kept in repair, agreeable to the directions of this act, and the courts of Common Pleas in their respective counties, shall have authority, upon application, to make and enforce all orders necessary, all well for opening all

Pubc. roads
to be opened
&c.

C. of Q. S.
their power.

new roads, which may be useful and convenient, as to vacate any public road, or part of any public road, which upon enquiry shall be found useless and burthensome, within the limits of their respective counties.

When notice to be given & how.

§ 2.   That previous to any application being made to the court of Common Pleas, for an order to lay out any new road, every person through whose improved land such proposed road may be designed to run, who is known to be a resident in the same or adjoining county, shall have notice thereof, from some person about to apply for the same, or else a note in writing, expressing such intended application, under the signature of some one or more of the persons aabout to apply, shall be left at the house or last place of abode, or with the agent respectively of every such holder of improved lands, at least twenty days before the sesssion in which such application shall be

(289)

made; and further, such intended application shall be advertised in some public place in each township through which such proposed road may be designed to run, for thirty days prior to the session, as aforesaid, and similar advertisement shall be affixed and kept upon the court house door, for two days of the term in which application shall be made.

Application, how made,

§ 3.   Every application for any public road, shall be by petition, specifying particularly where such road begins, the remarkable places by which such road shall pass, and where the same shall terminate, presented to the court of Common Pleas, of the proper county, signed by at least twelve householders resident in the same county, three of whom shall be freeholders of the neighborhood, who shall be liable for the costs accruing on such petition, survey and view, unless the road so petitioned, for shall appear to the court from the report of the viewers to be of public and general utility, to the citizens of the county at large, when

Costs how paid

the costs attending the same shall be paid out of the county treasury.

§ 4.   When any petition in form aforesaid is presented to any court of Common Pleas, within any county of this Territory, praying for an order to lay out a new road, through any part of the said county, and the court be satisfied that the petitioners have given the necessary notice required by

(290)

this act, the court shall order such petition to be publicly read in open court, and thereupon shall appoint three disinterested freeholders of the county, which said freeholders, or any two of whom, shall proceed to view the ground, on which such proposed road is to run, and also to appoint a skilful surveyor to accompany the aforesaid viewers, and to survey the said road, agreeably to the view of the aforesaid freeholders. It shall be the duty of the said viewers and surveyors at some convenient time before the next session, to repair to the place where such proposed road begins, and the said viewers shall with diligence and attention, examine the ground and lay out such road as nearly to the prayer of the petitioners as a passible way can be obtained, at a moderate expence, having special regard to continue the road in the same direction, as far as circumstances will admit; and not to take the same through any persons enclosure of one years standing, without the owners consent, unless a preferable way cannot otherwise be had with convenience to the public; and the aforesaid surveyor shall take to his assistance two persons of honest reputation, as chain carriers, and he shall according to the view of the aforesaid freeholders, survey such road, conspicuously marking the same throughout, and truly noting the several courses and distance thereof, and at every mile's end, shall erect a monument expressing the number thereof, and shall

Court to appoint viewrs. & surveyor. &c.

Their duty &c.

Surevyor to take assistants.

(291)

protract a survey of the said road, which toget er with the proceedings of the aforesaid viewers, shall be certified respectively, and returned to the court of Common Pleas, next to be held for such county, and the court on receiving such return, shall cause the same to be publicly read in open court, on two different days of the same term, at which such return shall have been made; and if no objections are made to such proposed highway, on the second reading of the return aforesaid, it shall be the duty of the court, to order the said road to be opened a necessary width, not exceed-

Courts on re ceiving the returns, how to proceed.

ing sixty six feet, and made in other respects convenient for the passage of travellers; and cause a record thereof to be made, which shall thenceforth be deemed a public road.

§ 5. If any person through whose land any proposed public road may run, feels aggrieved thereby, such person may at any time before such road is recorded, and not afterwards, set forth his or her grievances, by way of remonstrance, against such proposed road, or any part thereof, presented to the court of Common Pleas of the proper county, and the court shall nominate five disinterested freeholders of the county, who shall not be related to any of the parties interested in opening or objecting against such proposed road, and shall assign a day for such freeholders to meet, where such proposed road begins; it shall be the duty of

Persons aggrieved their remedy.

O 2

(292)

such five freeholders respectively, having had five days previous notice, from either of the parties, to meet on the day, and at the place assigned by the court, and then, or on any other day, prior to the next session, to which the majority may adjourn, (having first taken an oath or affirmation before some person qualified to administer oaths, impartially to assess the damage or several damages, which any such objector or objectors may be likely to sustain by reason of such proposed road, in case the same should be opened, and continued through his her or their lands, to review such proposed road and take into their consideration, how much less valuable any tract of land, the property of such objector or objectors, will be rendered, by reason of such proposed road, should the same be opened, and continued through such tract respectively; and shall assess the damage or several damages accordingly, and report the same to the court of Common Pleas, next to be holden for the proper county; and if any three of them agree in assessing damage to the amount of the costs accruing on such remonstrance, the court may, if they consider it expedient, order the damage to be defrayed out of the county stock, or if that may be considered inexpedient, and the petitioners will defray the same, then, in either case, such road shall be ordered to be opened,

Take oath.

Assess & report damges.

and a record thereof made, and the costs and charges having
accrued in virtue of such remonstrance, shall be defrayed out of **Cost how pd.**
the county stock; but if three of such free-

(293)

holders do not agree in assessing damages to the amount of the
costs aforesaid, then such objector or objectors shall pay the costs
and such proposed road shall be ordered to be opened and recorded, in like manner as though no objections had been made.

§ 6. That objections in time and manner aforesaid, to any **Objection to**
proposed public road may be made by any twelve freeholders, or **road how &**
householders, of the neighborhood, through which the same runs, **by whom**
on account of the same being likely to be useless and burdensome **made.**
to the township respectively; and when such objections are made,
the court shall proceed in like manner, by review thereof as prescribed in the last preceding section of this act; and if the freeholders who review the same, or any three of them agree, that
the said proposed road is likely to be useless and burdensome if it
be opened and kept in repair by the public, then, unless the petitioners respectively will agree to open and keep in repair such
proposed road, at their own private expence, all the proceedings
shall be stayed, and the petitioners shall in either case pay the costs
and charges which may have accrued; but if three of the aforesaid viewers do not report against such proposed road, as likely to
be useless and burdensome, then the objectors shall pay the costs
and charges, which shall have accrued on such review, and the
said proposed road shall be ordered to be opened, and a record
thereof made, and shall thenceforth be deemed a public road.

(294)

§ 7. If any person through whose land any public road shall **Roads run-**
run, shall be desirous of cultivating such part of his land, it shall **ing through**
be lawful for such person or persons, to petition the court of **lands how**
Common Pleas, to permit him, her or them, at his, her or their **changed.**
own expences, to turn such road through any part of his, her or
their own land, on as good ground, and without increasing the
distance to the injury of the public, and upon such petition the
said court shall appoint three disinterested freeholders, who shall

Court to appoint 3 freeholders.

proceed to view the ground on which the said road is designed to be turned, and measure the respective distance of that part of the road already established, and of the proposed way, until it shall intersect the road established as aforesaid; and at the next term of the said court, shall report the several distances, with their

Who shall examine & report.

opinion respecting the ground on which such proposed road is to run; and if it shall appear to the satisfaction of the court aforesaid, that the ground on which such new part of the road is designed to run, is equally situated, and that the difference in the distance, will not materially injure the public; such court shall permit him, her or them, to turn such road, and on receiving satisfactory assurance that such petitioner or petitioners, have opened such proposed road, equally convenient for travellers, shall vacate so much of the former road as shall lie between the different points of intersection, and record such new report, which afterwards shall be public road or highway.

(295)

Useless roads may be discontinued & how.

§ 8.   When any public road, or highway, shall be considered useless, and the repairing thereof be an unreasonable burthen to the Township, and any twelve freeholders or householders of such township, may make application in writing, signed by such persons, setting forth the situation and other circumstances of the road which they wish vacated, as aforesaid, in a clear and intelligible manner, which shall on the term in which it is presented be publicly read in open court on two different days of the court, and no further or other proceedings, shall be then had thereon, but the same shall be adjourned to the next court, when the same shall again be read in open court; when if objections are not made thereto in writing, signed by twelve freeholders, or householders, such court shall on any day in the same term, other than the first day of the same, proceed to vacate such public road, or parts of public road, as aforesaid, and the costs and charges, shall be defrayed by the county; but if objections in manner aforesaid are made, the court shall proceed in like manner by viewers thereof, as they are authorised to do, in laying out of public roads and highways; and the judgment of any court of Common Pleas, as aforesaid, shall be conclusive in the premises, if the same be not appealed from in nine months after giving any such judgment.

§ 9. An appeal from the proceedings of any court of Common Pleas, of any of the counties within this Territory, as aforesaid

Appeal allowed.

(296)

shall lie and be allowed to the General court of the Territory, which court shall, if the party or parties applying for the same, enter into sufficient securities for costs and charges thereof, order and appoint another view of such road, and proceed thereon in like manner, as the courts of Common Pleas, are enabled by this act to proceed, and the determination and judgment of such General court shall be final: *Provided always,* That nothing in this act shall be understood to give authority to any court of Common Pleas, to vacate an street or highway, in any city borough, town or village in this Territory, which hath been laid out by the late proprietors thereof, or by any other person or persons, and dedicated to public use nor to vacate any road laid out by order of court, which is not repairable at public charge, nor any road or passage claimed by private right, nor to rivers, or streams of water.

No streets to be vacated.

§ 10. All male persons of the age of twenty one years and not exceeding fifty, who have resided thirty days in any Township, of any county within this Territory, and who are not a county charge, shall be liable yearly and every year, to do and perform any number of days work, not exceeding twelve, whenever the supervisor of the district, in which he resides, shall deem it necessary: and it shall be the duty of every supervisor respectively, to call out every such resident aforesaid, when in his opinion it may be expedient to work on the

Persons liable to work.

(297)

public road or highway, within the division respectively allotted to him; and if any such resident, having had three days notice thereof from the supervisor shall neglect or refuse to attend by himself or substitute to the acceptance of the supervisor, on the day and at the place appointed for working on the public road,

Supervisor to give notice.

with such necessary and common articles of husbandry, as the said supervisor shall have directed him to bring, wherewith to labor, or having attended, shall refuse to obey the direction of the supervisor, or shall spend, or waste the day in idleness, or inattention, to the duty assigned him; every such delinquent shall forfeit for every such neglect or refusal, the sum of seventy-five cents, to be recovered at the suit of the supervisor respectively, before any Justice of the Peace of the Township, wherein the delinquent shall reside, to be appropriated towards repairing the public roads within the same Township; and it shall be the duty of the court of Common Pleas, at the same time that they appoint supervisors, to apportion to each one, his part of the roads, and hands to assist in opening and keeping the same in repair.

Penalty failing to work.

Court to apportion road.

To appoint supervisors.

§ 11.   The court of Common Pleas of each and every county, at their first term to be held after the first day of January, yearly and every year shall appoint a necessary number of freeholders in each and every township, within their respective counties, to be supervisors of the highways; and the said

(298)

Their duty.

supervisors of the public roads and highways of the several Townships, shall and they are hereby required, and enjoined, as often as the said several roads and highways within their repective townships shall be out of repair, or as often as any new road shall be laid out, and directed to be opened by lawful authority, to hire and employ a sufficient number of labourers to work upon, open and amend, clear and repair the same, in the most effectual manner, and to purchase wood and all other materials necessary for that purpose, and to oversee the said laborers, keep them close to their business, and take care that the said roads and highways be effectually opened, cleared and amended, and repaired, according to the true intent and meaning of this act.

§ 12.   And in order to enable the said supervisors the more effectually to discharge their duty, *Be it further enacted.* That it shall and may be lawful for the supervisors aforesaid, or any other person or persons, by his or their order and direction, to enter upon any lands adjoining to or lying near the public roads and highways, within their respective Township, and to cut or open such drains or ditches through the same, as he or they shall judge necessary, completely to carry off and drain the water from such roads : *Provided,* The same be done with as little injury and damage as may be to the owner of such lands; which drain and ditches, so cut and opened, shall be kept open by the said supervisors, if necessary, and shall

Ditches drains &c.

(299)

not be stopped or filled up by the owner, or owners of such land, or any other person or persons, whatsoever, under the penalty of five dollars for every such offence, to be recovered before any Justice of the Peace in any county, and to be applied to the purpose of opening and repairing highways in the district wherein the offence shall have been committed.

Penalty for filling drains &c.

§ 13.   The said Supervisors shall have full power and authority, on any improved ground or lands, adjoining the said public road or highway, within their respective townships, to dig, or cause to be dug, any gravel, sand or stone, or to gather any loose stones, lying on the said lands, or to cut down any wood, or trees, growing or adjoining to the said roads or highways, as he or they shall think necessary for the purpose aforesaid; *Provided,* The same be done with as little damage as may be to the owner or owners of such land; and the same sand, gravel, stones or wood, so dug, gathered or cut, to be carried off, without the let, hindrance or control of the owner.

Supvr. to dig cut timber &c.

§ 14.   If any person or persons, working on the highways, or being with them, shall ask any money, or drink, or any other reward whatsoever, of any person passing or travelling upon the said public road or highway, he shall, for every such offence, pay the sum of one dollar, to be recovered by the Supervisor, or any other person suing for

Supvr. not to suffer, nor laborers to ask money of tra vellorr under penalty.

P 2

(300)

the same, before any Justice of the Peace, in the county, and applied for, and towards repairing the said highways, or public roads within the township wherein the offence shall have been committed; and in case any Supervisor shall connive at any person's asking and demanding any reward from any traveller as aforesaid, or shall himself extort, or endeavor to extort any money, or other thing, from any traveller as aforesaid, every Supervisor, so offending, shall forfeit and pay for each offence, the sum of five dollars, to be recovered by any person whatsoever in manner aforesaid, one half to the use of the prosecutor, and the other half to, and for the service of the said road or highway.

C. P. may order bridges built.

§ 15. The Judges of the court of Common Pleas, may cause any bridge or bridges to be built, over any creek or rivulet in the county, to which they belong, where they think such bridge of publick utility, and too expensive to be borne by the district in which it lies, for which purpose the said court shall agree with workmen for the building or repairing such bridge, or bridges, and the court shall make an allowance for the money becoming due,

How paid for

upon such agreement, and order the same to be paid out of the county Treasury.

Private cart ways may be opened and how.

§ 16. If any person or persons, shall, for the convenience of themselves, or neighbours, wish to have a cart road laid out, from, or to the plantation, or dwelling place

(301)

of any person or persons, or to any public highway, or from one highway to intersect another; the person or persons applying for the same, shall advertise their intentions, as by this law is required in case of highways, and shall petition the court of Common Pleas of the proper county, who shall cause the same to be read in open court and shall order and direct a view of the place where such road is required to be laid out, and return thereof shall be made in the same manner as before directed by this act, and if no objections be made thereto, the said court shall further order and appoint what breadth the said road shall be, so as the same shall not exceed thirty three feet.

Breadth.

§ 17. Every road or cartway, laid out in pursuance of this act, not exceeding thirty three feet in breadth, being first paid for by the petitioner or petitioners, for such road, shall be recorded, and from thence forward, shall be allowed and declared a common road, or cart way, as well for the use and convenience of the person or persons at whose request the same was laid out, as for the use and convenience of all such as have occasion to travel the same, and shall be opened and maintained by the persons petitioning therefor: *Provided nevertheless,* That if the said road shall be laid out through any person or persons improved land, then the same shall be valued as in this act is directed in case of persons objecting to public roads or highways, and on the value thereof being paid to the owner

How to proceed when going thro' improved lands.

(302)

or owners of the land, by the person or persons at whose request the same was laid out, they shall have liberty to open said road, agreeable to the order of the court.

To be recorded & how.

§ 18. If any owner or owners of any land through which such cart road may pass, shall be desirous of improving his, her or their lands, they shall be permitted to turn the same: *Provided,* The ground on which they propose turning it, is equally as good for a road, and shall not increase the distance more than one twentieth part thereof, or shall be permitted to hang swinging gates upon such cart road or roads, but shall at all times keep the said gates in good order and repair, under the penalty of one dollar for every offence to be recovered before any Justice of the Peace, in any county wherein the offence shall have been committed, by any person prosecuting for the same, one moiety thereof to the prosecutor and the other moiety towards keeping of said roads in repair.

How to proceed to improve cart way.

§ 19. It shall be the duty of each and every supervisor, within their respective districts to erect, and keep a post at the forks of every public road or highway within their respective districts, containing an inscription in legible characters, directing the way, and mentioning the most remarkable places on each road respectively; and if any person shall demolish any such post, deface or alter any inscription thereon made, with an intent to destroy the utility of such

Superv. to have posts erected.

(303)

design, he, or she so offending, shall for every such offence, forfeit and pay to the supervisor of such road respectively, the sum of ten dollars, to be recovered before any Justice of the Peace of the county, wherein the offence shall have been committed, for the use of such district respectively.

Penalty for defacing &c. § 20. If any person shall take down, obliterate or destroy, any advertisement or written notice, necessary to be put up, under the directions of this act, he, she or they so offending, shall for every such offence forfeit and pay the sum of ten dollars, to be recovered by indictment, before any court having cognizance thereof, to be held in the county where the offence shall have been committed, to the use of the county respectively.

adverts. Obstructing roads how punished. § 21. If any person shall obstruct any road laid out, or to be kept in repair under the authority of this act, and shall suffer such obstructions to remain to the hindrance of passengers; every person so offending, shall for every such offence forfeit and pay a sum not exceeding one hundred dollars nor less than one dollar, to be recovered by action of debt, qui tam, or indictment, before any court having cognizance thereof, to be held in the county in which the offence shall have been committed; one half to the county respectively, and the other half to whosoever will sue for the same. But when the prosecution shall first

(304)

be commenced in behalf of the county, the whole shall accrue to its use.

Compensation to superv. Persons adjudged to work on road how to be dealt with. § 22. Every supervisor shall be entitled to receive the sum of one dollar for each and every twenty dollars he shall collect, and one dollar and twenty-five cents, for superintending the hands, not less than ten on each day, who shall commute their assessments by labor and such further compensation for his trouble, as shall appear reasonable to the court.

§ 23. In all cases when persons shall be committed to the supervisor to labor, by the authority of the laws of this Territory, such supervisor may assign the proper portion of labor for such person to do and perform, or shall appoint a time and place for such person, so committed, to attend and perform the labor as aforesaid, and such service in either case being performed, such supervisor shall give such person his discharge accordingly.

§ 24. All and every supervisor or supervisors of the public roads and highways of this Territory, who shall refuse or neglect to do and perform his or their duty, as directed by this act, shall on conviction by presentment or indictment before any court of record, be fined in any sum, not more than forty, nor less than five dollars, at the

Supervr. neglecting or refusing to discharge duty to be fined

(305)

discretion of the court, and stand committed until payment thereof.

JESSE B. THOMAS,
Speaker of the House of Representatives.
B. CHAMBERS,
President of the Council.

Approved—September 17th, 1807.

WILLIAM HENRY HARRISON.

CHAPTER XLV.

An Act to regulate the enclosing and cultivating of Common Fields.

§ 1. THOSE who are or shall be proprietors or owners of land, in any field that is now occupied, used and declared, or that shall hereafter be occupied, used and declared to be a common field, may meet together, by themselves or agents, annually, on the first Monday in March, or on such other days, as they shall appoint, at some convenient place, by them appointed, for the purpose of making such rules and regulations as to them shall seem meet, for the well ordering of the affairs of such field, with respect to fencing and cultivation, and all other things necessary for the well managing the same, for the common interest of such proprietors; in which meeting, the proprietors of such field, shall have full

Owners to meet & make rules,

(306)

power by their major vote, to be computed by interest, to order all such affairs and make such regulations, as they shall deem proper and expedient, for the purposes aforesaid: *Provided always,* That any person, who is a proprietor in any common field, may at any time hereafter, separate his her or their land, from such common field, by fencing the same, subject only to making and keeping in repair fences in like manner as persons having enclosures adjoining to the common fields, as by this law directed.

To elect officers.

§ 2.   The better to enable them to carry on and manage the affairs of such fields, they are hereby authorised and empowered, to elect a chairman clerk and treasurer, who shall be sworn to the faithful discharge of their duties, respectively; and the clerk shall enter and record all the acts, votes and resolutions of the said proprietors relating to the management of the said common fields; and shall continue in his office until another shall be chosen and qualified to serve in his room; and that the election of chairman, clerk and treasurer, shall be annually, or otherwise as shall be determined by the said proprietors, or a majority of them in their lawful meetings assembled.

Elect a committee.

§ 3.   For the better management of their common fields, they shall chuse a committee of three persons, which shall be stiled "the field committee," who shall be sworn to a faithful discharge of their duties; the

(307)

said committee may call a meeting of the proprietors of such field, when they shall judge it needful, by giving warning to such of them as live in the town or village, verbally, where such fields lie, and to the agents, (if any) of non-resident proprietors, ten days previous to the time of such meeting, or by warning such proprietors in such other manner as they shall, in their lawful meetings agree upon.

§ 4.   The proprietors of common fields, are hereby authorised and empowered, at their lawful meetings, to grant and levy taxes, on themselves, when they shall judge it needful, according to their several interests in such fields, for the defraying the charges that may arise in setting out and designating the proportion of, or altering the fence of such fields, in making gates and bridges, or for any other public or common charge, relating to

Appoint assessor & collector.

such fields, and to appoint assessors and collectors for the making, apportioning, and collecting such taxes, which collectors shall have the same power and authority in every respect, as the collectors

of county taxes; which taxes, when collected, shall be paid into
the hands of the Treasurer, and shall be appropriated, by a majority of the proprietors for the common benefit.

§ 5. The field committee shall point out and designate the **Duty of com**
place where, and the proportion which, each proprietor shall **mittee.**
erect of

Q 2

(308)

such common fence, and every proprietor in such common field
shall duly erect and maintain, his, her or their proportion of such
common fence, according to the directions of such committee:
Provided such committee, shall not require any such fence to be
erected at a greater expence, or of better materials, than is directed
by a law of this Territory, entitled "An act establishing and
regulating enclosures," and shall attend all orders, and comply
with all regulations of the major part of the proprietors of such
common field, for the improvement thereof, for the common
benefit, under the penalties of such fines and forfeitures as shall
be lawfully annexed to the breach or neglect of such orders or
regulations.

§ 6. Any person or persons, having his, her or their part **Respecting**
or proprortion of common fence, designated by the said field com- **repairs to**
mittee, shall have liberty, in order to make or repair the same, of **fence.**
passing over any person's lot or land whatsoever, whenever it shall
be necessary, for the purpose aforesaid; and when it shall so
happen that the line of fence, ordered as aforesaid, for the enclosing, or securing any common field, shall run in upon, or intersect
the fence of any person making a particular enclosure, adjoining
the common field, the one half of the dividing fence between such
particular enclosure, and the common field, as aforesaid, shall be
made and maintained by the proprietors of such common field,
and the

(309)

other half by the owner of such particular enclosure; and if any
person, or persons, whose land shall adjoin any such common field,

shall neglect to keep in repair, and maintain his, her, or their part of such fence, after being requested thereto by the field committee, in writing, under their hands, for the space of ten days, it shall be lawful for the said committee to repair the said fence, at the proper charges of the delinquent; which expence, after being estimated by two reputable freeholders of the town or village, wherein such fields are situated, may be recovered by action of debt, before any court having competent jurisdiction, together with costs.

Penalty for opening fence.

§ 7. If any person or persons, whose lands shall adjoin such common field, shall lay open the same, without giving two months notice thereof in writing, lodged with the Clerk of such common field; such person or persons shall be liable to pay all damages that may accrue to the proprietors or to any of them, of such common fields, to be recovered in any action of damages, before any court having competent jurisdiction.

§ 8. All accounts for any services rendered any person act-

Acpts. for services how paid.

ing under the appointment of, or by the direction of the major part of the proprietors of common fields, shall be paid out of the common treasury of such proprietors, after being audited by the field committee; except the accounts of such

(310)

field committee; which last mentioned accounts, shall be audited by a special committee; and that all orders on the Treasurer, shall be signed by the chairman, and attested by the Clerk; and the Collectors, shall, for all, or any monies by them paid, to the Treasurer, demand duplicate receipts, one of which shall be held by the said Collectors, and the other lodged with the Clerk: the Treasurer shall also demand duplicate receipts for all monies paid by him, on orders, on the Treasurer, one of which receipts shall be holden by the Treasurer, and the other lodged with the Clerk.

Fines & forfeitures.

§ 9. The proprietors of common fields, shall have power, by their major votes, in lawful meetings assembled, to order all such fines and forfeitures, on either, or any of themselves, as to them shall seem reasonable, for carrying into effect, any of their rules and regulations, for the common benefit of the said proprietors: *Provided nevertheless,* The penalty does not exceed the sum of five dollars, and that the person or persons thinking himself or themselves to be unreasonably or oppressively fined, shall have the right to appeal from the judgment of said proprietors, to the next court of Common Pleas, holden for said county: *Provided,* That notice of such appeal, shall be given within ten days after the judgment be given by the said proprietors.

Proviso,

§ 10. The said common field shall be enclosed with a good and sufficient fence, ac-

(311)

cording to law, on or before the first day of May in each and every year, or such other day as the said proprietors may appoint, and no cattle, horses or other animals shall be suffered to be put into such fields, for the purpose of depasturing therein, between the first day of May, and the fifteenth day of November, in each and every year, or on such other day, and time, as the proprietors may agree upon, under the penalty of paying such fines, as shall be ordered by the said proprietors, in lawful meeting assembled.

To be enclosed with a good fence.

JESSE B. THOMAS,
Speaker of the House of Representatives.
B. CHAMBERS,
President of the Council.

Approved—September 17th, 1807.
WILLIAM HENRY HARRISON.

CHAPTER XLVI.

An Act regulating the Practice in the General Court, and Court of Common Pleas, and for other purposes.

§ 1. Appearance bail shall be required in all actions of debt, or on the case, founded upon any writing, obligatory bill, or note in writing, for the payment of money, and in all actions of covenant and detinue. And

Appearance bail when required.

(312)

appearance bail shall also be required in all actions, where an affidavit shall be made and filed by the plaintiff, or any person in his behalf, of an existing debt, then due from the defendant to the plaintiff; which affidavit shall be made before any judge or commissioner, authorised to take special bail; or any Justice of the Peace in this Territory, or if the plaintiff be out of the Territory, before any Judge of any court of Judicature, or notary public, of the state, kingdom or nation, in which he resides, or happens to be, and the sum specified in such affidavit, obligation, bill or note

When pltff. may endorse bail.

in writing shall be endorsed, on the writ or process, by the plaintiff or his attorney, for which sum, so endorsed, the Sheriff or other officer, to whom such writ or process shall be directed, shall take bail and for no more; and if the party making such affidavit, swear to the best of his knowledge or belief, the same to be deemed suffi-

Shff. to take acknowldgt. of attorney.

cient; when no appearance bail is required the sheriff may take the engagement of an attorney, practicing in the General court and courts of Common Pleas, endorsed on the writ, that he will appear for the defendant, or defendants, and such appearance shall be entered with the clerk in the office, on the first Monday after the end of the court, to which such process is returnable, which is hereby declared to be the appearance day in all process, returnable to any day of the court, next preceeding: *Provided always,* nevertheless, That it shall and may be lawful for the plaintiff, or plaintiffs, in any ac-

(313)

tion or suit, to file his or their declaration, at and in the term, to which suit writ or writs are returnable, to which the defendant or defendants may, if he, she, or they think proper, appear at the said term, and such proceedings may be had therein at the same term to the final judgment, as the parties in the suit may mutually agree on: *Provided however,* That no defendant or defendants, shall by any thing herein contained be compelable, unless he, she, or they, may think proper to enter his or their appearance before

Appearance bail.

Return day.

the rule day established by law; and all writs issued during the term of any court may be executed and returned to any day of the same term, where no such engagement of an attorney shall be offered, as is above mentioned, in cases where appearance is not required, the Sheriff shall nevertheless be restrained from committing the defendant to prison, or detaining him in his custody, for want of appearance bail; but the sheriff shall in such case, return the writ executed, and if the defendant shall fail to appear thereto, there shall be the like proceedings against him, only as is herein after directed, against defendants and their appearance bail, where such is taken: *Provided always,* That any judge of the general court, or justice of the common pleas, in actions of trespass, assault and battery, trover and conversion, and in actions on the case, whereupon proper affidavit or affirmation, it shall appear to him proper that the defendant or defendants should give appearance bail, may, and he is hereby au-

May have trial first term.

Judge may order bail.

(314)

thorised, to direct such bail to be taken, by endosement on the original writ, or subsequent process, and the sheriff shall govern himself accordingly.

§ 2. The Sheriff shall return all writs to them directed, on the days of the return thereof, and in all cases where appearance bail is required, he shall return on the writ the bail by him taken, and a copy of the bail bond to the clerk's office; and if the defendant shall fail to appear accordingly, or shall not give special bail being ruled thereto by the court, the bail for appearance may defend the suit, and shall be subject to the same judgment and recovery, as the defendant might, or would be subject to if he had appeared, and given special bail; and in actions of detinue, the bail piece shall be so changed, as to subject the bail to the restitution of the thing, whether animate or inanimate, sued for, or the alternative value.

How shff. to return.

Deft. fails to appear &c.

judgt. may be had agst. apprce. bail.

§ 3. And if the Sheriff shall not return bail, and the copy of the bail bond, or the bail returned, shall be adjudged insufficient, and the defendant shall fail to appear, and give special bail, if ruled thereto, in such case the Sheriff may have the like liberty of defence, and shall be subject to the same recovery as is provided, in the case of appearance bail; and if the Sheriff depart this life, before judgment be confirmed against him, in such case the judgment shall be confirmed against his executors or ad-

No bail retd. or insufficiet.

Proceedings vs. shff. estate.

(315)

ministrators, or if there shall not be a certificate of probate or administration granted, then it may be confirmed against his estate and a writ of *fieri facias,* may in either case be issued. But the plaintiff shall object to the sufficiency of the bail, during the sitting of the court next succeeding, to which the writ is returnable, in the office, on the first, second or third rule day, and at no time thereafter; and all questions concerning the sufficiency of bail, so objected to, in the office, shall be determined by the court, at their next succeeding term; and in all cases, where the bail shall be adjudged insufficient, and judgment entered against the Sheriff, he shall have the same remedy against the estate of the bail, as against the estate of the defendant.

Shffs. remedy over.

§ 4.   And every judgment in the office against a defendant, and bail, or against a defendant, and Sheriff, shall be set aside, if the defendant at the succeeding court, shall be allowed to appear without bail, put in good bail, being ruled so to do, or surrender himself in custody, and shall plead to issue immediately; the court shall regulate all other proceedings in the office, during the preceding vacation, and rectify any mistakes, or errors, which may have happened therein.

Office judgt. may be set aside.

Court to rectify mistakes

§ 5.   Any Judge of the General court, or Justice of the court of Common Pleas, may take recognizance of special bail, in

Judges to take bail.

R 2

(316)

any action, in either of the said courts depending, which shall be transmitted, by the person taking the same, before the next succeeding court, to the Clerk of the said court, to be filed with the papers in such action; and if the plaintiff or his attorney, shall except to the sufficiency of the bail, so taken, notice of such exception, shall be given to the defendant, or his attorney, at least ten days, previous to the day on which such exception shall be taken, and if such bail shall be adjudged insufficient by the court, the recognizance thereof shall be discharged, and such proceedings shall be had, as if no such bail had been taken; the form of which recognizance shall be in the following words, to wit:

Pltff. may except.

"   county, to wit: memorandum that upon the day of   in the year   E F, of the county of

Form of recognizance.

personally appeared before me, (one of the Judges of the General court, or Justices of the court of Common Pleas, of the county aforesaid, as the case may be) and undertook for C D, at the suit of A B, in an action of   now depending in the (naming the court where the suit is depending) that in case the said C D, shall be cast in the said suit, he, the said C D, will pay and satisfy the condemnation of the said court; or render his body to prison, in execution for the same, or that he the said E F, will do it for him."

§ 6. The person taking such bail as a-

(317)

foresaid, shall, if required at the same time, deliver to the person or persons acknowledging the recognizance aforementioned, a bail piece, in the words and form following to wit:

"   county to wit: C D, of the county of   aforesaid, is delivered to bail on a *cepi corpus,* unto E F, of the county aforesaid, at the suit of A B, the   day of   in the year   "

§ 7. No person shall be permitted to be special bail, in any action, unless he be a householder, and resident within this Territory, and of sufficient property; if the writ or process issue out of the General court, or if it issue out of any court of Common Pleas, unless he be a householder, of sufficient property, and resident in the county in which such court is held; and no counsellor or attorney at law, sheriff, under sheriff, bailiff, or other person concerned in the execution of process, shall be permitted to be special bail in any action. **Bail to be a householder.**

No civil officer to be bail

§ 8. Rules shall be held monthly in the Clerk's office of the General court, and each court of Common Pleas, beginning the first Monday after the rising of such court; the plaintiff, shall file his declaration in the Clerk's office, at the next succeeding rule day, after the defendant shall have entered his appearance, (unless the parties shall otherwise agree, as mentioned in the second section of this law) or the defendant **Rules to be held in office**

Steps when taken.

(318)

may then enter a rule for the plaintiff to declare; which if he fails or neglects to do, at the succeeding rule day; or shall at any time fail to prosecute his suit, he shall be non-suited, and pay to the defendant, or tenants, besides his costs, three dollars, where his place of abode is at the distance of twenty five miles or under, from the place of holding the said General court, or court of Common Pleas, and where it is more, ten cents for every mile above twenty.

§ 9. One month after the plaintiff shall have filed his declaration, he may give a rule to plead, with the Clerk, and if the defendant shall not plead accordingly, at the expiration of such rule, the plaintiff may enter interlocutory judgment, for his debt or damages and costs, and the court at the succeeding term, shall thereupon proceed to assess such damages, as they shall find upon examination, the plaintiff shall have really •sustained, and thereupon enter up final judgment: *Provided nevertheless,* That if the defendant shall come into court, at any time before signing of judgment, and shall pay down, to the adverse party, the costs he has been at thus far, or so much thereof, as the court shall judge reasonable, then the court may admit the defendant to have the same day in court, as if his default had never been recorded.

§ 10. All rules to declare, plead, reply, rejoin, or for other proceedings shall be given regularly, from month to month; shall be entered in a book to be kept for that

(319)

purpose, and shall expire on the succeeding rule day.

§ 11. No plea in abatement shall be admitted or received, unless the party offering the same, shall prove the truth thereof by oath or affirmation, as the case may require, and no plea of non est factum offered by the person charged as obliger, or grantor of a deed, shall be admitted or received unless the truth thereof shall in like manner be proved by oath or affirmation.

§ 12 And where any person, other than the obligor shall be defendant, such defendant shall prove by oath or affirmation that he or she verily believes, that the deed on which the action is founded, is not the deed of the person charged, as the obligor or grantor thereof, in which last mentioned case, the plea of non est

Marginalia:
Judgt. by default may be taken.

May be set aside.

Pleas in abatement to be sworn to.

By others than parties upon belief.

factum, shall not be admitted or received without such oath or affirmation, and where a plea in abatement shall upon argument be found insufficient, the plaintiff shall recover full costs, to the time of oyer or ruling such plea, a lawyers fee excepted.

§ 13. The plaintiff in replevin, and the defendant in all other actions may plead as many several matters, whether of law or fact, as he shall think necessary, for his defence.

§ 14. The clerk shall proportion the causes upon the docket, from the first day

(320)

of the court to the twentieth both inclusive, if in his opinion so many days will be expended in trying the causes ready for trial, and issue subpoenas for witnesses to attend the days, to which the causes stand for trial; he shall docket the causes in order as they are put to issue, and no cause shall be removed from its place, on the docket, unless where the plaintiff at the calling of the same, shall be unprepared for trial, in which case, and in no other, shall the cause be put at the end of the docket.

§ 15. All actions of trespass, quare clausum fregit, all actions of trespass, detinue, actions sur trover, and replevin for taking away goods and chattels, all actions of account, and upon the case, other than such accounts as concern the trade of merchandize, between merchant and merchant, their factors or servants; all actions of debt grounded upon any lending or contract, without specialty; all actions of debt, for arrearages of rent; all actions of assault, menace, battery, wounding and imprisonment, or any of them which shall be sued or brought, shall be commenced and sued within the time and limitation hereafter expressed, and not after; that is to say; the said actions upon the case, other than for slander, and the said actions for account, and the said actions for trespass, debt, detinue and replevin, for goods and chattels, and the said actions of trespass, quare clausum fregit, within five years next after the cause of such action or suit, and not after;

(321)

and the said actions of trespass, of assault, battery, wounding,

Slander. imprisonment, or any of them, within three years next after the cause of such action or suits, and not after; and the said action upon the case for words, within one year next after the words spoken, and not after.

Pltff. assign breaches. § 16. In all actions upon any bond, or any penal sum for non performance of covenants or agreements, in any indenture, deed or writing contained, the plaintiff or plaintiffs, may assign **Jury to in- quire & assess** as many breaches, as he or they may think fit; and the jury upon **damages.** the trial of such action or actions, shall and may assess damages for such of the breaches as the plaintiff shall prove to have been broken, and on such verdict, the like judgment shall be entered, as heretofore has usually been done; and where judgment on a demurrer, or by confession, or nihil dicit, shall be given for the plaintiff, he may assign as many breaches of the covenants or agreements, as he shall think fit; upon which a jury shall be sum- **Judgt. re- main as secu- rity.** moned to enquire of the truth of every one of those breaches, and to assess the damage the plaintiff shall have sustained thereby, and execution shall issue for so much, and the judgment shall re- **Sci. fa. to is- sued.** main as a security to the plaintiff his executors and administrators, for any other breaches which may afterwards happen, and he or they may have a scire facias against the defendant, and assign any other breach and thereupon damages shall be assessed, and execu- tion issue as aforesaid; and in all ac-

(322)

tions which may be brought upon any bond or bonds for the pay- ment of money, wherein the plaintiff shall recover, judgment shall be entered for the penalty of such bond, to be discharged by the payment of the principle and interest due thereon and the costs of **How judgt. to be enter'd** suit, and execution shall issue accordingly; or if before judgment, the defendant shall bring into court, the principal and interest due upon such bond, he shall be discharged, and in that case judg- ment shall be entered for the costs only.

Money may be paid into court. And in any action of debt on single bill, or in debt, or in debt, or scire facias upon a judgment, or in debt, upon bond, if before action brought, the defendant hath paid the principal and interest due by the defeazance or condition, he may plead payment in bar.

§ 17. If two or more dealing together, be indebted to each other, upon bonds, bills, bargains, promises, accounts or the like; and one of them commence an action in any court, if the defendant cannot gainsay the deed, bargain or assumption upon which he is sued; it shall be lawful for such defendant to plead payment of all, or part of the debt, or sum demanded, and give any bond, bill, receipt, account or bargain in evidence; and if it shall appear that the defendant hath fully paid or satisfied the debt, or sum demanded, the jury shall find for the defendant, and judgment shall be entered, that the plaintiff shall take nothing by his writ, and shall pay the costs. And

Deft. may plead paymt.

Special matter in evid.

Jury find for deft.

(323)

if it shall appear that any part of the sum demanded, be paid, then so much as is found to be paid, shall be defalked, and the plaintiff shall have judgment for the residue only, with costs of suit: but if it appear to the jury that the plaintiff is overpaid, then they shall give in their verdict for the defendant, and withal certify to the court how much they find the plaintiff be indebted, or in arrears to the defendant, more than will answer the debt or sum demanded; and the sum or sums so certified, shall be recorded with the verdict, and shall be deemed as a debt of record, and if the plaintiff refuses to pay the same, the defendant for the recovery thereof, shall have a scire facias against the plaintiff in the said action, and have execution for the same with the costs of that action.

For pltff. When over paid.

Judgt. to be given thereon Sci. fa. to issue.

§ 18. *Provided always,* That in all cases where a tender shall be made, and full payment be offered, by discount or otherwise, in such specie as the party by contract or agreement ought to do; and the party to whom such tender shall be made, doth refuse the same; and yet afterwards will sue for the debt or goods so tendered; the plaintiff shall not recover any costs in such suit.

When pltff. shall not recover costs.

§ 19. Interpreters may be sworn truly to interpret when necessary.

Interpretors to be sworn

§ 20. Every person desirous of suffering

(324)

a non suit on trial, shall be barred therefrom unless he do so before the jury retire from the bar.

Non suit.
New trials.

§ 21.   Not more than two new trials shall be granted to the same party, in the same cause.

§ 22.   Any instrument to which, the person making the same, shall affix a scrawl by way of seal, shall be adjudged and holden to be of the same force and obligation, as if it were actually sealed.

In faulty counts deft. may appeal to court.

§ 23.   Where there are several counts, one of which is faulty, and entire damages are given, the verdict shall be good, but the defendant may apply to the court to instruct the jury to discharge such faulty count.

Mo negro to be witness &c except &c.

§ 24.   No Negro, Mullatto or Indian shall be a witness except in pleas of the United States against Negroes, Mulattoes or Indians, or in civil pleas, where Negroes, Mulattoes or Indians alone shall be parties.

When deemed mulatto.

§ 25.   Every person other than a Negro, of whose grand fathers or grand mothers, any one is, or shall have been a Negro, although all his other progenitors, except that descending from a Negro, shall have been White persons, shall be deemed a Mulatto, and every person who shall have one fourth part or more of Negro

(325)

blood, shall in like manner be deemed a Mulatto.

Non-residts to give security for costs.

§ 26.   No suit shall hereafter be commenced in any court within the territory by a non-resident, until he shall file in the clerk's office, a bond with approved security, who shall be a resident of this territory, conditioned for the payment of all costs that may accrue in consequence thereof, either to the opposite party, or to any of the officers of such court, and the same may be put in suit by any of the persons aforesaid, for the non-payment of the sums that may respectively become due to them.

Amendment and jeofail.

§ 27.   No judgment after a verdict of twelve men, shall be stayed or reversed for any defect, or default in the writ, original

or judicial, or for a variance in the writ from the declaration, or
other proceedings, or for any mispleadings, insufficient pleadings,
discontinuance, misjoining of the issue, or back of a warrant of
attorney, or for the appearance of either party, being under the
age of twenty-one years, by attorney, if the verdict be for him,
and not to his prejudice, or for not alledging any deed, letters
testamentary, or commission of administration to be brought into
court, or for omission of the words, 'with force and arms,' or
'against the peace,' or for mistake of the christian name, or sir-
name of either party, sum of money, quantity of Merchandize, day
month or year, in the declaration or pleading, [the

(326)

name, sum, quantity or time, being right in any part of the record
or proceeding] or for omission of the averment, 'this he is ready
to verify,' or 'this he is ready to verify by the record,' for not
alledging 'as appeareth by the record,' or for omitting the averment of any matter, without proving which, the jury ought not to
have given such verdict, or for not alledging that the suit or
action, is within the jurisdiction of the court, or for any informality in entering up the judgment by the clerk; neither shall any
judgment entered upon confession or by nil dicit, or non sum
informatus, be reversed, nor a judgment after enquiry of damages,
be stayed or reversed; for any omission or fault, which would
not have been a good cause to stay or reverse the judgment, if
there had been a verdict.

§ 28 When a demurrer shall be joined in any action, the **Demurrer.**
court shall not regard any other defect or imperfection in the writ,
return, declaration or pleading, than what shall be specially
alledged in the demurrer as causes thereof, unless something so
essential to the action or defence as that judgment according to
law and the very right of the cause cannot be given, shall be
omitted, and for prevention of delay by arresting judgment and
vexatious appeals, the several acts of parliament, commonly called
the statute of Jeofails, which were in force and use in England,
on the seventh day of February one thousand seven hundred and **7 Feb. 1752.**
fifty two. shall be, and are hereby declared

(327)

to be, for so much thereof as relates to mispleading, jeofail and amendment, in full force in this territory.

Jury take papers.
§ 29. Papers read in evidence, though not under seal, may be carried from the bar by the jury.

After issue joined no exception,
§ 30. After an issue joined in an ejectment, on the title only, no exception of form or substance, shall be taken to the declaration, in any court whatsoever.

Part omitted barred.
§ 31. If in detinue, the verdict shall omit price or value, the court may at any time award a writ of enquiry, to ascertain the same. If on an issue concerning several things, in one count, in detinue, no verdict be found for part of them, it shall not be error, but the plaintiff shall be barred of his title to the things omitted.

Judgt. confess. release errors.
§ 32. A judgment on confession shall be equal to a release of errors.

Battery and slander, no costs in certain cases.
§ 33. In all actions of assault and battery, and slander, commenced and prosecuted in the General court, if the jury find under twenty dollars; and in the like actions commenced and prosecuted in any county court, if the jury find under six dollars and sixty-six cents, the plaintiff in either case shall not recover any costs;

Trespass vi et armis recocover only 2/3 costs.
and in actions of trespass vi et armis, instituted in any court of record within the Territory, if the plain- shall recover a sum less than five dollars, he

(328)

shall be allowed to recover two thirds of the costs given by law in such suit, and no more.

No suit in G. C. under 50 dollars.
§ 34. No suit shall be commenced in the General court, or removed into the said court, from any of the inferior courts, by appeal or otherwise, except by writ of error, unless the matter of controversy, between the parties shall exceed the sum of fifty dollars.

Judge to inspect record.
§ 35. The General court shall annually appoint one of the judges thereof to inspect the clerk's office of said court, and to report to the next session of the said court, the condition in which he shall find the papers and records which report shall be recorded.

No discontinuance if ct. dont' sit.
§ 36. There shall be no discontinuance of any suit, process matter or thing returned to, or depending in the General court.

although a quorum of the judges shall fail to attend at the commencement, or any other day of any session; but if a majority of them shall fail to attend at the commencement of any session, any judge of the said court, or the Sheriff, attending, the same may adjourn the said court from day to day for three days successively; and if a quorum shall not attend on the fourth; or having attended one day, shall fail to attend on a subsequent day of a session, the court shall stand adjourned till court in course.

Shff. may adjourn.

(329)

§ 37. Execution shall be issued from the General court according to law.

§ 38. The General court shall have power to direct the writs, summonses, process, forms and modes of proceedings to be issued, observed and pursued by the said General court.

G. C. to direct froms.

§ 39. In appeals and writs of error, the following rules shall be observed:

No appeal shall be granted from the judgment, or decree of an inferior court, to the General court, unless such judgment or decree be final; and amount, exclusive of costs, to fifty dollars, or relate to a franchise or freehold.

When no appeal from inferior to superior court.

Every appeal shall be prayed at the time of rendering the judgment, sentence or decree.

Appeal when prayed for.

The person appealing shall, by himself or a responsible person on his behalf, in the office of the clerk of the court from whence the appeal is prayed, give bond and sufficient security to be approved by the court, and within a time to be fixed by the court, to the appellee, for the due prosecution of the appeal; the penalty of the said bond shall be in a reasonable sum, in the discretion of the court.

Appellant to give bond.

It shall be the duty of the appellant to lodge an authenticated copy of the record in the clerks office of the General court before the expiration of the next succeeding

To lodge record in office in 30 days of 1st or 2d term or appeal dismissed,

(330)

term thereof: *Provided,* There be thirty days between the time of making such appeal, and the commencement of said term; and if there be not thirty days between the making of the appeal, and the sitting of the first term of the General court, then the record shall be lodged as aforesaid, at or before the commencement of the second term of said court, or else it shall stand dismissed, unless further time shall be granted by the court, before the end of the term, to which the same shall have been returned.

On affirm. judgt. 10 per cent. If the judgment or decree be affirmed in the whole, the appellant shall pay to the appellee, a sum not exceeding ten per centum at the discretion of the court, on the sum due thereby, besides the costs upon the original suit and appeal.

judgt. reversed appellent pay costs. If the judgment, or decree, shall be reversed in the whole, the appellee shall pay to the appellant, such costs as the court, in their discretion may award.

Reversed & affirmed in part ct. to apportion costs. Where the judgment, or decree, shall be reversed in part, and affirmed in part, the costs of the original suit and appeal, shall be apportioned between the appellant and appellee, in the discretion of the court.

The General court, shall, in case of a partial reversal, give such judgment or decree, as the inferior court ought to have given.

Ct. may issue exon. or remand cause. On appeals or writs of error, it shall be lawful for the General court, to issue exe-

(331)

cution, or remit the cause to the inferior court, in order that an execution may be there issued, or that other proceedings may be had thereupon.

Writ of error not a supersedeas unless J. endorse & bond given. No writ of error shall be a supersedeas, unless the General court, or some Judge thereof, in vacation (as the case may be) after inspecting a copy of the record, shall order the same to be made a supersedeas, in which case, the clerk issuing the said writ, shall endorse on the said writ of error, "that it shall be a supersedeas, and it shall be obeyed as such accordingly;" and it shall also be necessary before a writ of error shall operate as a supersedeas, that bond, to be approved by the clerk of the court issuing the said writ, shall be given in the same manner, and under the like penalty as in cases of appeals.

Plaintiff to file record And the plaintiff in error, shall lodge an authenticated copy of the record, under the same regulations, and the parties in error shall be subject to the same judgment and mode of execution as is already directed in the case of appeals.

A writ of error shall not be brought after the expiration of five years from the passing of the judgment complained of; but where a person thinking himself aggrieved by any decree or judgment which may be reversed in the General court, shall be an infant, *femme covert, non compis mentis,* or imprisoned when the same was passed, the time of such disability, shall be excluded from the computation of the said five years.

No writ of error after 5 years unless in cases of disability.

T 2

(332)

Whenever the said General court shall be divided in opinion, on hearing any appeal or writ of error, the judgment or decree appealed from shall be affirmed.

On division of ct. jndgt. affirmed.

§ 40. The Clerk of the General court shall carefully preserve the transcript of records, certified to his court, with the bonds for prosecution, and all papers relating to them, & other suits depending therein, docketing them in the order he receives them, that they may be heard in the same course; unless the court for good cause to them shewn direct any to be heard out of its time; the proceedings of every day during the term, shall be drawn at full length by the Clerk, against the next sitting of the court, and such corrections as are necessary, being made therein, they shall be signed by the presiding Judge; when any cause shall be finally determined, the Clerk shall make a complete record thereof; and all writs, processes and summonses, issuing from the General court, shall be signed by the Clerk of the same, shall bear teste in his name, and be dated on the days, on which they issue.

Clk. to preserve records

Draw up proceedings to be signed by judge.

Make complete record. Process in name of clk.

§ 41. For good cause the General court and courts of Common Pleas, or any judge thereof may grant commissions for the examination of witnesses; and the Clerks of the said courts, when any witness is about to depart from the said Territory, or shall by age, sickness or otherwise, be unable to attend the court, or where the claim or de-

Crts. of C. P. to grant dedimus's.

(333)

fence of any party, or a material part thereof, shall depend on a single witness, may upon affidavit thereof, issue a commission for taking the deposition of such witness, *"de bene esse,"* to be read as evidence at the trial, in case the witness be then unable to attend; but the party obtaining such commission shall give reasonable notice to the other party, of the time and place of taking the deposition.

Party to give notice.

§ 42. If any plaintiff or plaintiffs, shall sue out any writ of *capias ad respondendum* or summons against two or more defendants, directed to the Sheriff or Coroner of the proper county, or to elisors, as the case may require; and the said Sheriff, Coroner or elisors, cannot find each of the defendants named in the said writ of *capias ad respondendum,* or summons, within his or their bailiwick, it shall be the duty of the said Sheriff, Coroner, or elisors, to serve the said capias or summons, on as many of the said defendants as may be found in his or their bailiwick, either by taking their bodies or by delivering to them copies of such process, as the case may require; and the said Sheriff, Coroner, or elisors, shall make return of such process, by endorsing thereon *"cepi corpus,"* as to the defendant, or *"cepi corpora,"* as to the defendants, on whom the same hath been served, in manner aforesaid, and by also endorsing thereon, *"non est inventus,"* as to the defendant, or *"non sunt inventi,"* as to the defendants, who are not to be found in his or their bailiwick.

One or more defts. in the same process & officer can not find part he shall take those he can find & make a special return thereof.

(334)

Pltff. may declare specially & obtain judgt.

§ 43 After the capias or summons hath been served and returned as aforesaid, the plaintiff or plaintiffs may file a declaration against the defendant or defendants, on whom such service hath been made, [suggesting therein the return endorsed on the said process, as to the said defendant or defendants, on whom the same hath not been served,] and may proceed to judgment against the said defendants according to the custom and practice of the courts; and after such judgment hath been obtained, the plaintiff or plaintiffs, may by a writ or writs of *scire facias* cause the defendant or defendants, on whom such process hath not been

After which may issue a sci. fa. & ob-

served, to be made parties to the said judgment; unless such defendant or defendants, shew good and sufficient cause, why such judgment should not be entered against him, her or them, and the defendant or defendants, made parties to the judgment as aforesaid, shall be subject to the same final process, as though he, she or they had been duly served with *mesne* process, and had thereupon appeared and received a declaration and made defence, or suffered a default.

tain judgt.
vs. other par ties.

JESSE B. THOMAS,
Speaker of the House of Representatives.
B. CHAMBERS,
President of the Council.

Approved—September 17th, 1807.
WILLIAM HENRY HARRISON.

(335)

CHAPTER XLVII.

An Act for the appointment of Surveyors and their Deputies, and for allowing them Fees.

§ 1. A SURVEYOR shall be appointed in every county, and commissioned by the Governor, with reservation in such commission, for one sixth part of the legal fees, for the use of the Territory, for the yearly payment of which, he shall give bond with sufficient security to the governor, shall reside within his county, and before he shall be capable of entering upon the execution of his office, shall before the court of Common Pleas of said county, take an oath and give bond, with two sufficient securities, to the governor and his successors in such sum as he shall direct, for the faithful execution of his office.

Gov. to appoint survrs.

Take oath.

Give bond & security.

§ 2. All deputy surveyors shall be nominated by their principals, who shall be answerable for them, and if of good character commissioned by the governor, and shall thereupon be entitled to one half of all fees received for services performed by them respectively, after deducting the proportion thereof due to the Territory.

Nominate deputies.

§ 3. If any principal surveyor shall fail to nominate a sufficient number of deputies to perform the services of his office, in

When C. P. to nominate.

due time, the court of Common pleas of the

(336)

county shall direct what number he shall nominate, and in case of failure shall nominate for him: and if any deputy surveyor, or

Deputy how incapacitatd' any other on his behalf, and with his privity, shall pay or agree to pay any greater part of the profits of his office, sum of money in gross, or other valuable consideration to his principal for his recommendation, or interest in procuring the duputation, such principal and his deputy shall be thereby rendered incapable of serving in such office.

Chain carriers how paid   § 4.   No survey shall be made without chain carriers, to be paid by the person demanding the same, and sworn to measure justly and exactly to the best of their knowledge, and to deliver a

Take oath. true account thereof to the surveyor, which oath every surveyor is hereby empowered and required to administer.

Survey, platt fees for.   § 5.   For every survey by him plainly bounded, as the law   D. C.
directs, and for a platt of such survey after the delivery
of such platt, where the survey shall not exceed four hundred acres of land   5 25

For every hundred acres contained in one survey, above
four hundred   25

For surveying a lot in town   1

And where a surveyor shall be stopped or hindred from finishing a survey by him begun, to be paid by the party
who required the same to be surveyed   2 62

(337)

For running a dividing line   2 10
For surveying an acre of land for a mill   1 5
For every survey of land formally patented, and which shall
be required to be surveyed, and for a platt thereof, delivered as aforesaid, the same fee as for land not before
surveyed; and where a survey shall be made of any lands
which are to be added to other lands in an inclusive
patent, the surveyor shall not be paid a second fee for
the land first surveyed, but shall only receive what the
survey of the additional land shall amount to.

And where any surveys have been actually made of several parcels of land adjoining, and several platts delivered, if the party shall desire one inclusive platt thereof, the surveyor shall make out such for 1 5

For running a dividing line between any county or township, to be paid by such county, or township, in proportion to the number of taxable inhabitants, if ten miles or under 10 50

And for every mile above ten 30

For receiving a warrant of survey and giving a receipt therefor 17

For a copy of a plat of land or a certificate of survey 25

Provided always, That where any person shall employ a surveyor, and shall have re-

(338)

ceived a platt of land surveyed, and afterwards shall assign the platt of land to any other, either before, or after obtaining a patent for the same, if such person for whom the land was first surveyed, shall not have paid for the said survey, it shall and may be lawful for the Sheriff or other officer of the county or corporation where such assignee shall reside; at the instance of such surveyor, to make distress upon the slaves, goods and chattles of such assignee in like manner as is herein after provided for surveyors fees refused or delayed to be paid.

Surveys and platts made & delivered, & afterwards assigned, the shff. or other officer at the instance of survr. may distress as for fees delayed to be paid.

The surveyor of every county shall annually before the twentieth day of January deliver or cause to be delivered to the sheriff of every county his account of fees due from any person or persons, residing therein, which shall be signed by the said surveyor.

Fees due annually delivered to shff. to collect.

And the said sheriffs are hereby required and empowered to receive such accounts, and to collect levy and receive the several sums of money therein charged, of the persons chargeable therewith, and if such person or persons after the said fees shall be demanded, shall refuse or delay to pay the same till after the tenth day of April in every year, the sheriff of every county wherein such person resides, or of the county in which such fees

When shff. to make distress & sale.

became due, shall have full power, and he is hereby required, to make distress of the slaves, or

(339)

goods and chattles of the party so refusing or delaying payment, either in that county where such person resides or where the same fees became due.

Time when shff to acpt.

Every sheriff of every county shall on or before the last day of May in every year, account with the respective surveyors for all fees put into his hands pursuant to this act, and pay the same abating six per centum for collecting; and if any sheriff shall

Refusing to acpt. & pay how proceeded against.

refuse to account or pay the whole amount of fees put into his hands, after the deductions aforesaid made, together with an allowance of what is charged to persons not dwelling or having any visible estate in his county, it shall and may be lawful for the surveyors, their executors or administrators, upon a motion made in the next succeeding General or Circuit court, or in the court

Judgt. to be granted & exon. issued. Also vs. exrs. or adm of sheriffs. Recpts. good unless denied on oath.

of Common Pleas of the county to demand judgment against such sheriff, for all fees, wherewith he shall be chargeable by virtue of this act, and such court is hereby authorized and required to give judgment accordingly, and to award execution thereupon, *Provided* The sheriff have ten days previous notice of such motion. The executors or administrators of any such sheriff or under sheriff, shall be liable to judgment as aforesaid, for the fees received to be collected by their testator intestate, and not accounted for; every receipt for fees produced in evidence on any such motion, shall be deemed to be the act

V 2

(340)

of the person subscribing it, unless he shall deny the same upon oath,

JESSE B. THOMAS,
Speaker of the House of Representatives.
B. CHAMBERS,
President of the Council.

Approved—September, 1807.
WILLIAM HENRY HARRISON.

CHAPTER XLVIII.
An Act concerning Servants.

§ 1. ALL negroes and mulattoes, (and other persons not being citizens of the United States of America) who shall come into this Territory, under contract to serve another, in any trade or occupation, shall be compelled to perform such contract specifically during the time thereof.

§ 2. The said servants shall be provided by the master with wholesome and sufficient food, cloathing and lodging, and at the end of their service, if they shall not have contracted for any reward, food, cloathing, and lodging, shall receive from him, one new and complete suit of cloathing, suited to the season of the year, to wit: a coat, waistcoat, pair of breeches, and shoes, two

(341)

pair of stockings, two shirts, a hat and blanket.

§ 3. The benefit of the said contract of service, shall be assignable by the master to any person being a citizen of this Territory to whom the servant shall in the presence of a Justice of the Peace freely consent, that it shall be assigned; the said Justice attesting such free consent in writing, and shall also pass to the executors, administrators, and legatees of the master.

§ 4. Any such servant being lazy, disorderly, guilty of misbehaviour to his master, or master's family, shall be corrected by stripes, on order from a Justice of the county wherein he resides; or refusing to work, shall be compelled thereto in like manner, and moreover shall serve two days for every one he shall have so refused to serve, or shall otherwise have lost, without sufficient justification, all necessary expences incurred by any master for apprehending and bringing home any absconding servant, shall be repaid by further service, after such rates as the court of Common Pleas, of the county shall direct, unless such servant shall give security, to be approved of by the court for the payment in money within six months, after he shall be free from service, and shall accordingly pay the same.

§ 5. If any master shall fail in the duties prescribed by this act, or shall be guilty of injurious demeanor towards his servant it

Negroes indented &c.

Master to find servt. in food &c.

Master may transfer indenture.

Servts. lazy or disorderly to be whipped &c.

Master ill treating ser-

(342)

vant how redressed.

shall be redressed on motion, by the court of Common Pleas, of the county wherein the servant resides, who may hear and determine such cases in a summary way, making such orders thereupon as in their judgment will relieve the party injured in future.

Contract between master & servt. void

§ 6.   All contracts between masters and servants, during the time of service shall be void.

C. P. to hear complaint of servants.

§ 7.   The court of Common Pleas of every county shall at all times receive the complaints of servants, being citizens of any of the United States of America, who reside within the jurisdiction of such court, against their masters or mistresses, alledging undeserved or immoderate correction, insufficient allowances of food, raiment, or lodging, and may hear and determine such case in a summary way, making such orders thereupon as in their judgment will relieve the party injured in future, and may also in the same manner hear and determine complaints of masters and mistresses against their servants, for disertion without good cause, and may oblige the latter for loss thereby occasioned, to make restitution for further services, after the expiration of the time, for which they had been bound.

Servts. may acquire & hold goods.

§ 8.   If any servant shall at any time bring in goods or money, during the time of their service, shall by gift, or other lawful means, acquire goods or money, they shall have the property, and benefit thereof, to their own

(343)

use; and if any servant shall be sick or lame and so become useless or chargeable, his or her master or owner shall maintain such servant, until his or her whole time of service shall be expired;

Masters putting off servants how punished.

and if any master or owner shall put away any lame or sick servant, under pretence of freedom, and such servant becomes chargeable to the county, such master or owner shall forfeit and pay thirty dollars, to the overseers of the poor of the county wherein such offence shall be committed, to the use of the poor of the county, recoverable with costs, by action of debt in any court of Common Pleas of this Territory, and moreover shall be liable to the action of the said overseers of the poor at the common law for damages.

§ 9. No negro, Mulatto or Indian shall at any time purchase any servant, other than of their own complexion, and if any of the persons aforesaid shall nevertheless presume to purchase a white servant, such servant shall immediately become free, and shall be so held deemed and taken.

§ 10. No person whatsoever shall buy, sell or receive of, to or from any servant any coin or commodity whatsoever, without the leave or consent of the master or owner of such servant; and if any person shall presume to deal with any servant without such leave or consent, he or she so offending, shall forfeit and pay to the master or owner of such servant, four times the value of the thing so bought, sold or recei-

(344)

ved, to be recovered with costs by an action upon the case, in any court of Common pleas of this territory; & shall also forfeit & pay the further sum of twenty dollars to any person who will sue for the same, or receive on his or her bare back, thirty-nine lashes well laid on, at the public whipping post, but shall nevertheless be liable to pay the costs of such suit.

§ 11. In all cases of penal laws where free persons are punishable by fine, servants shall be punished by whipping, after the rate of twenty lashes for every eight dollars, so that no servant shall receive more than forty lashes at any one time, unless such offender can procure some person to pay the fine.

§ 12. Every servant upon the expiration of his or her time, and proof thereof made before the court of Common Pleas of the county, where he or she last served, shall have his or her freedom recorded and a certificate thereof, under the hand of the Clerk, which shall be sufficient to indemnify any person for entertaining or hiring such servant; and if such certificate should happen to be torn or lost, the Clerk upon request, shall issue another, reciting therein the loss of the former; and if any person shall harbor or entertain a servant not having and producing such certificate, he or she shall pay to the master or owner of such servant one dollar for every natural day he or she shall so harbor or entertain such run-

Servts. of color not to purchase whte servts.

Not trade with servts,

Penalty.

Persons fined servts. whpd. unless &c.

Servts. serving time how to proceed.

Unless &c.

How punished.

(345)

away, recoverable with costs, by action of debt, in any court of Common Pleas of this Territory; and if any runaway shall make use of a forged certificate, or after delivery of a true certificate to the person hiring him or her, shall steal the same and thereby procure other entertainment, the person entertaining or hiring shall not be liable to the said penalty, but such runaway, besides making reparation for loss of time and charges of recovery, shall stand two hours in the pillory on a court day for making use of such forged or stolen certificate, and the person forging the same **Person forging how punished.** shall forfeit and pay thirty dollars, one moiety to the Territory and the other moiety to the owner of such runaway, or the informer, recoverable with costs, in any court of Common Pleas of this Territory; and on failure of present payment, or security for the same within six months, such offender shall receive thirty-nine lashes on his or her bare back well laid on, at the common whipping post; and where a runaway shall happen to be hired upon a forged certificate and afterwards denies the delivery thereof, the *onus probandi* shall lie upon the party hiring such runaway.

Servts. traveling without pass how punished. § 13. If any slave or servant shall be found at the distance of ten miles from the tenement of his or her master, or the person with whom he or she lives, without a pass or some letter or token, whereby it may appear that he or she is proceeding by authority from his or her master, employer

(346)

or overseer, it shall and may be lawful for any person to apprehend and carry him or her before a Justice of the Peace, to be by his order punished with stripes, not exceeding thirty five, at his discretion.

Servts. being on others plantation to be punished. § 14. If any slave or servant shall presume to come and be upon the plantation or at the dwelling house of any person whatsoever, without leave from his or her owner, not being sent upon lawful business it shall be lawful for the owner of such plantation, or dwelling house to give, or order such slave or servant ten lashes on his or her bare back.

§ 15. Riots, routs, unlawful assemblies, trespass and sedi- **Riots how**
tious speeches, by any slave or slaves, servant or servants, shall be **punished.**
punished with stripes, at the discretion of a Justice of the Peace,
not exceeding thirty-nine, and he who will may apprehend and
carry him, her or them before such Justice.

§ 16. If any person shall harbor any servant or slave of **Harboring**
color, who is bound to service, without the consent of his or her **servt. finable**
master first obtained, he or she so offending, shall be fined in any
sum not exceeding one hundred dollars, at the discretion of the
court, to be recovered by indictment or information; and if any **Assisting ser-**
person shall aid and assist any servant, or slave to abscond from **vants to ab-**
his or her master, upon conviction thereof, he or she so offending, **scond finable**
shall be fined

(347)

in any sum not exceeding five hundred dollars, at the discretion
of the court, for the use of the party aggrieved, to be recovered
as aforesaid.

JESSE B. THOMAS,

Speaker of the House of Representatives.

B. CHAMBERS,

President of the Council.

Approved—September 17th, 1807.

WILLIAM HENRY HARRISON.

CHAPTER XLIX.

*An Act regulating the Fees of the several Officers and Persons
therein named.*

§ 1. NO officer shall at any time exact or demand for ser- **Fees to be**
vices hereafter to be performed any larger or other fee, to be **taxed.**
taxed in a bill of costs, than is hereinafter provided.

CLERKS FEES IN THE COMMON PLEAS.

	D.	C.	M.	
Every writ of capias and seal,		50		**Clerk C. P.**
Entering action, - - - - - - - - -		6		
Filing writ, - - - - - - - - - -		6		
A bond given by the plaintiff when he is not a freeholder				
and resident of the Territory		37	5	

W 2
(348)

	D. C. M.
Filing declaration	6
Copy of declaration or other pleading per sheet if required each sheet containing seventy two words	12 5
Discontinuance or retraxit	ditto
Altering a declaration in ejectment, and admitting defendant	25
Entering every motion and rule thereon	12 5
Copy of every rule when required	ditto
Bringing a particular record into court	25
Entering satisfaction of record	12 5
Receiving and entering verdict	ditto
Entering judgment	15
Reading and allowing every writ of habeas corpus, writ of error or certiorari and the return	25
An execution	50
Transcript of the record in error, and returning it with the writ every sheet of seventy two words	12 5
Entering defendants appearance	6
Drawing and filing special bail in or out of court	18
Every writ of enquiry per sheet	12 5
Entering on docket	ditto
Filing every plea, replication or joinder or other pleadings	6
Receiving and entering the panel and swearing the jury	18
A habeas corpora juratorum	50
Subpœna for four witnesses or under	do
Swearing each witness	6
Swearing constable	6

(349)

	D. C. M.
Making up and entering a complete record after judgment per sheet of seventy two words	18
Copy of a record, of a judgment, when required per sheet of seventy two words	12 5
Searching the record within one year	ditto

Every year back	6
Copy of a record per sheet of seventy two words	12 5
Entering report of referrees per sheet of seventy two words	ditto
On confession of judgment, default, joinder or demurrer	25
Entering rule of court on appointing referrees	15
Continuing each cause	20
On surrendering the principal in court by sureties	15
On entering every principal motion	10
Every issue joined	25
On every trial	do
On drawing special list of jury, attending and striking and making copies of jury list, for plaintiff and defendant	50
Issuing commission to take depositions	do
For recording certificate of marriage	12 5

CLERKS FEES IN CRIMINAL PROCEEDINGS.

Taking a recognizance and drawing it up in form, to be
paid to the clerk

(350)

	D. C. M.	
or other person who does the service	37 5	**Clk. C. P. in ctiminal cases.**
For engrossing every indictment and filing and reading the same	56	
Supoena for four witnesses or under	50	
A venire or other writ.	do	
Entering defendants appearance	6	
An execution	50	
Making up record per sheet of seventy two words	18	
Copy of same if required	12 5	
Every order or rule of court	9	
Entering nolo prosequi, or ceffat processus	18	
A venire for jurors to inquire of riots forcible entries and detainers &c.	50	
Drawing and engrossing inquisition and returning the same	6	

Filing record	12 5
Entering the panel and swearing the jury	25
Swearing each witness or constable	6
Reading each evidence or petition in court	6
Taking and entering verdict	12 5
Entering judgment and the fine	15
Entering defendants confession	do
Copies of indictment and pleadings if required per sheet of seventy two words	12 5
Discharging a recognizance	10
For examining every account in court	do
On entering appeal, allowing habeas corpus and writ of certiorari, when	

(351)

	D. C. M.
presented from the Judges of the General court	12 5
Every trial	25
Continuing cause	20
Entering a nolo prosequi	12 5
Certificate and seal	75
Receiving, reading and filing every order brought to be allowed at the court of Common Pleas, and entering the confirmation and recording the same as in other cases per sheet of seventy two words	12 5
Making cost bill	37 5
Copy thereof	25
To the Clerk in lieu of fees hearafter chargeable to the county the annual sum of	30
To the Clerk of the General court the same sum to be paid by the Territory	

PROBATE FEES.

Probate.

For all copies each folio of seventy two words	12 5
For administering an oath	6
For filing	18
For a citation	50
For a letter of administration	2 50

Taking and filing a renunciation and taking proof of a
renunciation, and which proof the Clerks of the court
of Common Pleas are hereby authorised and required
to take   50

(352)

D. C. M.

For proving a will, endorsing a certificate thereon, recording the same and filing it   2 50

For qualifying administrator taking bond, and writing
certificate   1 50

For filing caveat   18

For proving codicil, if proved seperately, endorsing
certificate, recording the same and filing it   1 50

For examining and proving an inventory or account   1

For granting the administration with the will annexed   2 50

For settlement of accounts of executor or administrator   50

Every copy of said account not exceeding one hundred
items, with certificate and seal of office.   1 50

Reading and filing petition, to sell land, and swearing
administrator to the truth of the statement made and
entering the necessary order thereon   67

Giving notice by order of court for sale of land, for
every advertisement not exceeding three   25

JUSTICES FEES IN THE COURT OF COMMON PLEAS FOR THE USE OF THE COUNTY.

For each action in court .   .   37 5   **Judges of C.**
Signing every judgment .   .   .   12 5   **P. use of**
Taking bail   25   **county.**

(353)

D. C. M.

Acknowledging satisfaction on record   9

Taxing and signing bill of costs   25

Proof or acknowledgment of a deed   37 5

For every issue joined .   .   50

Eor every trial .   .   .   1

Allowing writ of error, habeas corpus or certiorari, when
   presented form the judges of the General court   50
Granting reference   .   .   .   25
Approving the report of referees   30
On surrender of principal in court   20
Hearing petition and making order thereon . . . 25

SHEIFF's FEES.

Sheriff's.

For serving a writ and taking into custody	50
For every mile fixed by law	6
Every bail bond and copy of same	50
Returning writ	9
Summoning jury	75
Attending a view per day	1
Going and returning	1
Serving and returning a scire facias	37 5
Serving a writ of possession with the aid of the posse commitatus	2 50
Every mile from the place of holding Court	6
Serving such writ without the aid of the posse commitatus	1 25
For calling a jury on each cause	12 5
Every person committed to the common jail	37 5

(354)

	D. C. M.
Calling every witness	6
Discharging every person out of the common jail	37 5
Calling every action	9
Executing a writ of enquiry, drawing inquisition and returning the same	1 50
Discharging every person by proclation	9
Serving a summons	37 5
For attending a prisoner before a judge when surrendered by his bail and receiving the prisoner into custody	50
In criminal cases the like fees in the respective courts, as for the like services in civil cases	

For dieting a prisoner per day   25

For proceeding to sell on any execution, if the property
to be actually sold, the commission to the sheriff shall
be five per centum on the first three hundred dollars,
and two per centum on all sums above that; and one
half of such commissions when the money is paid to
the sheriff without seizure, or when the lands or goods
seized or taken shall not be sold, and no other fee or
reward shall be allowed upon any execution, except
for the expence of receiving and keeping the property

For making a deed on sale of real estate on execution   2

(355)

D. C. M.

To the sheriff in lieu of all fees that may hereafter be
chargeable to the county, the annual sum of   50

JURORS FEES IN THE COMMON PLEAS AND GENERAL COURT.

Every juror sworn in each action   25   **Jurors.**

Every juror attending a view   50

WITNESSES FEES IN THE COURT OF COMMON PLEAS AND GENERAL COURT.

Every witness attending in his own county on trial per day   37 5   **Witnesses.**

Attending from a foreign county and coming and returning per day   56

Each witness subpœnaed in the county & detained from
a foreign county per day   56

To a witness on a duces tecum coming from a foreign
county attending and returning per day   56

Except a clerk of a court, attending from a foreign
county with wills, records, and other evidences, on
subpœna per day   1 65

THE ATTORNEY PROSECUTING THE PLEAS OF THE UNITED STATES.

For every indictment or information for the whole
prosecution   5   **Atto. pros. pleas.**

Y 2

(356)

CORONERS FEES.

Coroners.

For the view of each body	3
Each juryman that sits on the body	12 5

For witnesses the same allowance as in the court of
Common Pleas

Serving writs in all cases, the same as is before allowed
to the sheriff for like services; the fees of the coroners
inquest shall be certified by the coroner, and paid by
the treasurer of the county

RECORDERS FEES.

Recorders.

For recording mortgages per sheet of one hundred words	16
And the like fees for recording all other deeds and instruments	
For copies of records and deeds per sheet	12 5

SECRETARYS FEES.

Secretary's.

For copies or exemplification of records per sheet of seventy-two words	12 5
And seal and certificate thereto when required	75
For affixing the seal to any patent	75
For recording an extract of every patent for land when the same is not recorded at full length	25

For recording at full length any such patent, on the
application of the

(357)

patentee requesting the same, but not otherwise, for every seventy-two words	12 5

SURVEYORS FEES.

Surveyors.

For going to and returning from a view per day, and thirty miles per day	1 25

His actual service per day, on the view per day   1 50
For going to, attending the court per trial and returning
   per day   1 25

JUSTICES OF THE PEACE THEIR FEES.

For every warrant in a criminal case	18	**Justces. peace**
On every trial for forcible entry and detainer	2 50	
Every precept for forcible entry and detainer	37 5	
Every bond or recognizance	25	
Administering an oath	12 5	
For a summons in debt, or a capias in debt or case	10	
For every subpœna	10	
For every name inserted after	3	
Entering every judgment for debt or damages when trial	20	
Every judgment by confession of defendant	10	
Every execution	20	
Certified copies of all proceedings on appeal or certiorari	33	
Writing signing and sealing every attachment	13	
Entering rule of reference on docket	10	

(358)

D. C. M.

Fntering recognizance of bail, in civil cases	10
Issuing special bail piece	13
Swearing a witness	6
Administering an oath or deposition	10
Acknowledging a deed or power of attorney by every Justice of the Peace	25
Order for removing a pauper	50
Order for relieving a pauper	25
Issuing scire facias against special bail	20
Issuing a scire facias after a year and a day	20
Or to appraise damages in trespass	20
Publishing the banns of matrimony	67

WITNESSES FEES BEFORE A MAGISTRATE
IN THE TRIAL OF SMALL CAUSES.

Each witness for attending per day   25   **Witnesses be fore J. P.**

CONSTABLES FEES.

Constables.	For serving a summons or warrant on each person therein named	25
	For travelling and going to serve the aforesaid process, four cents per mile.	
	When two or more are named in such process, milage shall be allowed to the place of actual service, the most remote to the place where such process is returnable	
	For a copy of the summons left at the place of abode	10

(359)

D. C. M.

Serving a subpœna for each person named therein, and milage as above	10
Making return of each summons or warrant	5
Bail bond	26
Serving execution on body or goods	25
Commitment to prison	25
And per mile from the place of abode to the jail	4
Sale of goods in either case when the amount does not exceed six dollars	25
On all sums above six dollars five per centum.	
Returning the same	10

CONSTABLES FEES IN CRIMINAL CASES

In criminal cases.	Serving a capias, on each one named, with milage as in civil cases	50
	Serving a subpœna, on each one named therein with milage as above	20
	Attending an examination of a person or persons charged with a crime	20
	If more than one, each	5
	Commitment of each person	25
	Milage from the place of examination to the county jail per mile	5
Constable ta-taking grea-ter fees fined	If any constable shall ask, demand or receive any more or greater fees than is above mentioned, he or they so offending, shall	

forfeit and pay any sum, not exceeding eighteen dollars, for every such offence, to be recovered before any court having

(360)

jurisdiction, the one half to the person suing for the same, the other half to the use of the proper county.

And to the end, all persons chargeable with any of the fees aforesaid, due to the several above officers (except constables) may certainly know for what the same are charged, none of the fees herein before mentioned, shall be payable to any person whatsoever, until there shall be presented unto the person owing or chargeable with the same, a bill or amount in writing, containing the particulars of such fees, signed by the Clerk, or officer to whom such fees shall be due, or by whom the same shall be chargeable respectively; on which said bill or account shall be expressed in words at full length, and in the same manner as the fees aforesaid are allowed by this law, every fee for which any money is or shall be demanded. *(Officers to mak and sign bills.)*

The Clerks of the General and Circuit courts, and Clerks of the courts of Common Pleas, in this Territory, shall cause to be set up in some public place in their offices, and there constantly kept, a fair table of their fees herein before mentioned, on pain of forfeiting forty dollars for every court day the same shall be missing, through their neglect, which penalty shall be to the use of the person or persons who shall inform or sue for the same, and shall and may be recovered in any court of record within *(Clk. to set up table of fees.)*

(361)

this territory, by action of debt or information.

§ 27. If any officer hereafter shall claim, charge, demand, exact or take any more or greater fees for any writing, or other business by him done within the purview of this act, than herein before set down and ascertained, or if any officer whatsoever shall charge or demand and take any of the fees herein before mentioned, where the business for which such fees are chargeable shall not have been actually done and peformed (to be proved by the fee book of such officer on his corporeal oath) such officer *(Officer taking other or greater fee.)*

How punished.

for every such offence, shall forfeit and pay to the party injured, besides such fee or fees six dollars for every particular article or fee so unjustly charged or demanded or taken, to be recovered with costs in any court of record in this Territory, by action of debt or information, provided the same be sued for within twelve

Limitation.

months after the offence shall be committed.

Clk. to deliver fee bill to sheriff.

§ 28. And for the better collection of the said fees, the Clerks of every court respectively, shall annually before the first day of March deliver or cause to be delivered to the Sheriff of every county in this Territory, their account of fees due from any person or persons residing therein, which shall be signed by the clerks respectively.

Shff. to collect.

§ 29. The said sheriffs are hereby required and empowered to receive such accounts

(362)

and to collect levy and receive the several sums of money therein charged of the persons chargeable therewith; and if such person or persons, after the said fees shall be demanded, shall refuse or

If paymt. delayed.

delay to pay the same, till after the tenth day of April in every year, the sheriff of that county wherein such person resides, or of the county in which such fees became due, shall have full

Shff. to distrain.

power and are hereby required, to make distress of the slaves, or goods and chattles of the party so refusing or delaying payment, either in that county where such person inhabits, or where the same fees became due; and the sheriff of any county for all fees

As also for own & other sheriffs.

which shall remain due and unpaid after the said tenth day of April in any year, either to themselves or the sheriffs of another county, which shall be put into his hands to collect, as aforesaid, is hereby authorized and empowered to make distress and sale of the goods and chattles of the party refusing or delaying payment in the same manner as for other fees due to any of the officers

No wart. for for fees except no property.

therein before mentioned, but no action, suit or warrant from a Justice, shall be had or maintained, for Clerk's fees, unless the Sheriff shall return that the person owing or chargeable with such fees, hath not sufficient within his bailiwick, whereon to make distress, except when the clerk as aforesaid shall have lost his fee book by fire or other misfortune, so that he be hindered from putting his fees into the sheriffs hands to collect; and in that case, any suit or warrant may be had and maintained for the recovery

Or fee book lost.

(363)

thereof. And if any Sheriff shall be sued, for any thing by him done in pursuance of this law, he may plead the general issue, and give this law in evidence.

Shff. pld. gl. issue.

§ 30. Every Sheriff of every county shall on or before the last day of May in every year, account with the Clerks respectively, for all fees put into his hands, pursuant to this law, and pay the same, abating ten per centum for collecting. And if any Sheriff shall refuse to account or pay the whole amount of fees, put into his hands, after the deductions aforesaid made, together with an allowance of what is charged to persons not dwelling, or having no visible estate in his county, it shall and may be lawful for the Clerks, their executors or administrators, upon a motion made in the next succeeding General court, Circuit court or court of Common Pleas, of the county of such Sheriff, to demand judgment against such Sheriff, for all fees wherewith he shall be chargeable by virtue of this law; and such court is hereby authorised and required to give judgment accordingly, and to award execution thereupon; *Provided,* The Sheriff have ten days previous notice of such motion.

Shff. to account &c.

Deduction.

Clk. may motion agst. Shff.

To give notice

§ 31. The executors or administrators of any such Sheriff, or under Sheriff, shall be liable to a judgment as aforesaid, for fees received to be collected by their testator or intestate, and not accounted for. Every

Exrs. & admrs. liable.

Z 2

(364)

receipt for fees produced in evidence, on any such motion, shall be deemed to be the act of the person subscribing it, unless he shall deny the same upon oath.

Recpt. evidence unless denied on oath,

§ 32. Sheriff's poundage, and all other legal fees in a suit, from final judgment to execution, shall, by the Sheriff, be levied out of the estate and effects of the persons against whom such execution shall be issued.

JESSE B. THOMAS,

Speaker of the House of Representatives.

B. CHAMBERS,

President of the Council.

Approved—September 17th, 1807.

WILLIAM HENRY HARRISON.

CHAPTER LXX.

An Act authorising the appointment of a Pilot.

Preamble.

Governor to appoint pilot

WHEREAS great inconveniences have been experienced, and many boats lost in attempting to pass the rapids of the Ohio for want of a Pilot, and from persons offering their service to strangers, to act as pilots by no means qualified for the business; for remedy whereof, the Governor of this Territory is hereby authorised and directed

(365)

Taking bond &c.

Pilot's fee.

Persons not licensed pilotting to be fined &c.

Officer collecting to pay treasurer.

Same fees as in other cases

to appoint such person or persons for pilots, as to him shall seem best qualified for that purpose, taking bond and security, of the person so appointed, payable to the Governor and his successors, in the sum of eight hundred dollars, for the due and faithful performance of his office; and the pilot so appointed, shall receive for each boat he pilots through the rapids two dollars; and any other person acting as pilot, without being duly authorised as by this law directed, shall, for every such offence forfeit and pay ten dollars, to the use of the Territory, to be recovered before any Justice of the Peace of the county of Clark, at the suit of pilot (whose duty it is hereby made to prosecute for the same) and collected by the Sheriff or Constable of the said county, in the same manner that other fines are by law directed to be collected; and the Sheriff or Constable shall pay the money so collected to the Treasurer of the Territory, taking his receipt for the same; and the Sheriff or Constable shall have the same fees for their services, as they are entitled to by law, for collecting fines and forfeitures in other cases; but nothing herein contained is meant to compel any owner or shipper of a boat to employ said pilot or pilots, but

Owners may pilot own boats.

(366)

they shall be at liberty to pilot their own boats, through the said rapids.

JESSE B. THOMAS,
Speaker of the House of Representatives.
B. CHAMBERS,
President of the Council.

Approved—17th September, 1807.
WILLIAM HENRY HARRISON.

CHAPTER LI.
A Law to regulate county Levies.

§ 1. ALL houses in town, town lots, out lots, and mansion houses in the country, which shall be valued at two hundred dollars and upwards, and all able bodied single men, who shall not have taxable property to the amount of two hundred dollars, all water and wind mills, and ferries, all stud horses, and other horses, mares, mules and asses, three years old and upwards, all neat cattle, three years old and upwards, all bound servants and slaves, except such as the court of Common Pleas shall exempt for infirmities, between sixteen and forty years of age, within this Territory, are hereby declared to be chargeable for defraying the county expences, in which they may respectively be found, to be taxed and

What property subject to cnty. levies.

(367)

collected in such manner and proportion as hereinafter directed.

§ 2. The Sheriffs in the several counties within this Territory shall and are hereby empowered and required as herein after mentioned, to receive from each and every person or

Sheriffs to receive written lists under oath, &c.

persons chargeable with taxes under this law, a written list under oath, containing a just and true account of all and every species of property in his or her possession or care, subject to taxation under this law, and the said Sheriffs respectively, are hereby empowered and directed to administer the following oath or affirmation to such persons:

Form of the oath

I, A B, do solemnly swear or affirm, as the case may be, that this list signed by me, contains a just and true account of all persons and of every species of property in my possession or care, within this county, and that no contract, change, or removal has been made or entered into, or any other method devised, practised or used by me, in order to evade the payment of taxes.

Shff. to adv. his attendance to take lists &c.

§ 3.   The said Sheriff shall advertise at the county town, and also in each and every township in their counties, that he will attend at a convenient place, as near as may be to the centre of population, therein to be mentioned, not within five days of such advertisement in each township, to receive of each person, a list of all the taxable property which they possess as above mentioned, and

(368)

the said persons are hereby required to attend at such time and place in their respective townships therefor, accordingly; but it shall be the duty of the Sheriffs of the respective counties in the Territory, previous to the time of advertising for taking the list of taxable property, to apply personally or by deputy, to every person subject to taxation within his county, for a list of their taxable property, as is above required by this act, and every Sheriff failing so to do, without good cause shown, shall be fined in any sum not exceeding five hundred nor less than twenty-five dollars, at the discretion of the court of Common Pleas of the county, to and for the use of the county.

Duty of shff. previous to advertising. To apply personally or by deputy for list &c.

Penalty for neglect.

Persons liable to fine for fraudulent list &c.

§ 4.   If any person or persons shall give or deliver to a sheriff a false or fraudulent list of persons or property subject

to taxation, or shall refuse to give a list on oath or affirmation
to the sheriff, the person or persons so refusing shall be liable
to a fine of fifteen dollars, and the sheriff shall proceed to list **Duty of shff.**
such person or persons property agreeable to the best informa- **in such cases**
tion he can procure; and all such property so ascertained shall
moreover be subject to a triple tax, to be collected and distrained for by the sheriff of the county, as in other cases; and
in case of an imperfect, false or fraudulent list, the person or
persons giving the same, shall be subject to pay a fine of fifteen
dollars, and the property subject to a triple tax; which fines **Fines when**
and triple tax shall be recovered in the county court of Com- **recoverable.**
mon Pleas by

(369)

the following mode of proceeding, and applied as herein after
directed.

§ 5. The sheriff shall give information thereof personally,
or if unable to attend, in writing, under his hand to the next **How such**
court, of Common Pleas, held for his county; which court **fines are re-**
shall forthwith direct the clerk to issue a summons, requiring **coverable.**
the party to appear at the next court to be held for the county
to shew cause if any he can, why he should not be fined, and
triply taxed for giving an imperfect or fraudulent list of his
or her taxable property: and the person or persons upon being
served therewith by the coroner, and appearing, shall immediately plead to issue; and the matter thereof shall be enquired
into by a jury or the court at the defendants option; and on
conviction, or the person not appearing, being summoned, the
fine and triple tax shall be established by the judgment of the
court; who, unless good cause shewn to the next succeeding
court for such failure, shall award execution for the fine and
costs, and certify the amount of the tax to the sheriff for collection; the amount of which fine after deducting thereout,
such allowances as the court may think reasonable to make
to the coroner for his extraordinary trouble on the occasion,

shall be applied towards lessening the county levy, and the triple tax shall be charged to the sheriff, and accounted for in like manner, as other taxes.

(370)

Persons having knowledge of such false or fraudulent list to give information &c.

Informer to receive half the fine.

§ 6. Every person or persons having knowledge of any incorrect, false or fraudulent list being given a sheriff, shall give information thereof, either to a sheriff or the county court of Common Pleas in like manner as the sheriff is directed, and thereupon the same mode of proceeding shall be had as if the sheriff gave information; and the person informing shall be entitled to receive one half of the fine imposed on the offender or offenders to his own use, and the other half to be applied towards lessening the county levy.

Persons taxable not giving in lists.

May deliver same to sheriff &c.

§ 7. In case any person taxable should not give in a list of his taxable property, and it should appear to the sheriff that such absence was not intentional or done with a view of avoiding the delivery of such list, it shall be lawful for the sheriff to receive his or her list at any time at the dwelling house of the sheriff; *Provided,* such person tenders his or her list to the sheriff and makes oath to the justness of it, on or before the twentieth of March annually, an in case of failure the sheriff shall proceed in like manner, as is before directed in cases for refusal to give in lists and the court shall determine upon the circumstances of the case, whether to inflict or remit the fine and triple taxes.

Shff. to make out two lists.

§ 8. The sheriff's in the several counties throughout this territory, shall, and they are hereby required to make two fair and complete lists of the persons and property

(371)

so taken in, and arranged in alphabetical order, in manner following to wit:

Names of persons.
Number of bond servants and, slaves.
Number of horses &c, above three years old.
Number of neat cattle above three years old.
Number of stud horses.
Rate the season.

Their form.

One of which he shall keep, and the other, together with the vouchers, taken by him as aforesaid, shall deliver to the Clerk of the court of Common Pleas, on or before the last day of March, yearly; which lists and vouchers the Clerk shall file in his office, and the Clerk of the said court shall make thereof a true transcript, which he shall lay before the court, at the same term at which they audit the public accounts, for their examination and allowance; the bill

One he shall keep the o- ther deliver to clk. C. P.

Duty of clk.

A a

(372)

of tax being allowed by the said court, they shall annex thereto their warrnet, under the hand and seal of the presiding Justice; & the Clerk of the said court shall ten days thereafter, deliver the same to the Sheriff for collection; for which, and for all other services rendered under this law, the said Clerk shall receive from the county ten dollars. Every Sheriff so charged shall collect all sums for which he is accountable within four months after he is charged with the collection of the same, and

When bill of tax allowed crt. to annex their warnt.

When clk. to deliver it to sheriff.

**Sheriffs. ac-
countable
within &c.**

shall be allowed in full compensation for his trouble in taking in the property, and collecting the levy ten per centum, on all sums by him collected; and the said Sheriff shall previously to his entering on those duties, take and subscribe, before any Justice of the Peace the following oath or affirmation.

Form &c.

"I   do solemnly swear, or affirm (as the case may be) that I will faithfully and impartially execute the office of collector, of   county, according to the best of my abilities."

Which oath shall be filed by the said Justice with the Clerk of the court of Common Pleas, and the said Sheriff shall enter into a bond, in the penalty of two thousand dollars, payable to the Governor of the Territory, and his successors in office, with two or more responsible sureties, and bound for the faithful collection, accounting for, and paying the sums wherewith he shall be chargeable, as collector of the county, in

(373)

**Sheriffs may
appoint de-
puties &c.**

manner directed by law; and every Sheriff so charged to collect the county taxes and levies, may appoint one or more deputies to assist him, as well in taking in the property, as in the collection of the levy, for whose conduct he shall be answerable; which deputies shall have the same power as the Sheriff himself, and such Sheriff shall have the same remedy and mode of recovery against his deputies or either of them,

**Shffs. reme-
dy vs. depty.**

and there sureties respectively for any sums of money which by virtue of this law such Sheriff may be subject to the payment of, on account of the transactions of any of his deputies, as he himself is subject to by law; and all monies collected by the Sheriff as aforesaid, shall remain in his hands, subject to the orders of the court of Common Pleas of each county respectively, for the payment of the debts of the county.

**Rate of tax-
ation &c.**

§ 9. The following rate of taxation shall be observed by the court of Common Pleas in levying the county tax, viz.

On each horse, mare, mule or ass a sum not exceeding fifty cents.

On all neat cattle as aforesaid, a sum not exceeding ten cents.

On every stud horse a sum not exceeding the rate for which he stands at the season.

Every bond servant or slave as aforesaid, a sum not exceeding one hundred cents.

(374)

And every able bodied single man of the age of twenty one years and upwards, who shall not have taxable property to the amount of two hundred dollars, a sum not exceeding one dollar, nor less than fifty cents.

§ 10. It shall be the duty of the court of Common Pleas throughout this Territory, at the firm term next after the last day of March annually, and at such other special sessions as they shall appoint, to proceed to audit and adjust all claims and demands against their counties, allowing all just claims and demands which now are, or hereafter shall be chargeable upon the said counties respectively.

C. P. to audit & adjust all claims &c.

§ 11. The several courts of Common Pleas throughout this territory at their court preceding the thirty-first day of March, annually, shall appoint two discreet freeholders in each township who shall proceed to appraise and value each house in town, town lot, town out lot & mansion house, in the county of the value aforesaid and also shall appraise and value all water and wind mills situate on such tract of the county as may be assigned to them respectively, by the court of Common Pleas, taking into view the situation and value of the same; and the said freeholders, after having fixed such valuation, shall proceed and make out two fair alphabetical lists thereof stating the proprietors or occupiers of such lots and mills, with the valuation of

C. P. to appoint valuers &c.

Water and wind mills.

Freeholders to make two alphabetical lists.

(375)

each annexed to the same in form following, viz.

Their form.

Proprietors, owners, or occupiers names,
Town lots and out lots.
Wind and water mills
Houses &c.
Valuation in dollars.

How disposed of.

one of which lists of valuation the said freeholders shall keep, and deliver, the other to the court of Common Pleas at the next term to be held for said county, which lists shall be filed by the Clerks in their respective offices; and the said court of Common Pleas, shall at the same time when they lay the county tax, levy a sum not exceeding thirty cents on each hundred dollars of such appraised value.

Duty of crt. in levying tax &c.

§ 12. It shall be the duty of the court of Common Pleas throughout the territory, at the same term at which they audit the public accounts of the sheriff, for monies collected and paid by him as aforesaid, and

(376)

When court shall ascertain expences &c.

having collected all such claims and demands against the county as are just and reasonable, to proceed to ascertain the probable expences of the county, the aggregate amount of claims allowed, and also such sum or sums of money as will be necessary to carry into effect any contract that shall have been made, for building or repairing any county jail, court house or bridges, adding thereto the expence of collection, and such other sum or sums of money as the said court of common Pleas shall conceive needful, to make good deficiencies in collections, insolvencies, delinquencies, and other contingencies; and the said court shall take into view the money (if any there be) in the treasury, and probable amount that will be received from licences to vend and retail merchandize, tavern licences and taxes on ferries, and other sources of county revenue, such as fines forfeitures, &c. After which the said court shall proceed to levy a tax upon the owners, proprietors or occupiers of all and singular the objects of taxation pointed out by this or any other law; having due reference to the returns of the sheriffs and freeholders aforesaid, and the rule of taxation; truly apportioning such tax upon all objects taxable by this law, so as to raise a sum of money sufficient to answer and satisfy all demands then existing against the said county, or which shall afterwards become due by virtue of any contract or contracts by the said court of Common pleas, in behalf of the county as aforesaid, pre-

When said court shall levy tax &c.

Court to apportion tax.

(377)

viously made and entered into and to answer such other contingent county expences as the necessities of the said counties may require.

§ 13. Every person within this Territory being owner, occupier or possessor of merchandize, other than the produce or manufacture of this Territory, shall previously to offering the same for sale by himself or agent within the Territory, or on any of the waters within or bounding the same, pay to the sheriff for the use of the county in which he or she resides, or offers such merchandize for sale, the sum of fifteen dollars for each store, or stand in which he or she may vend any such merchandize, and the sheriff on receipt thereof, shall give such person paying as aforesaid, a certificate in the words following, viz.

Shff to grant certificate for sale of goods.

"Indiana Territory   county,   the day of   this certifies that A B, is authorised to vend merchandize within this Territory, for one year from the date hereof, the said A B, having this day paid to me C D, Sheriff of the said county of   the sum of fifteen dollars, it

Form of certificate.

being the annual tax imposed on the retailers of merchandize
by a law of this Territory

C D, sheriff of the county of   "

Any person obtaining a certificate as a-

(378)

Penalty for selling without certificate.

foresaid, shall be authorised to vend and sell merchandize by
retail in this Territory for one whole year from the date of
the same, & no longer. And if any person or persons shall presume by himself or his agent to vend or sell any kind of merchandize within this Territory, or on any of the waters aforesaid, not the growth or manufacture of said Territory, not
having first obtained a certificate as aforesaid, he, she or they
so offending, shall, for every such offence forfeit and pay a sum
not exceeding eighteen dollars, to and for the use of the county, in which the offence was committed, to be recovered at the

Shff. to prosecute for same.

suit of the Sheriff, whose duty it is hereby made to prosecute
therefor, before any court proper to try the same; and the
Sheriff is hereby required to keep a fair account of all monies
received as aforesaid, and also a regular account of the dates
of all the certificates by him given to retailers or venders of

Shff. to keep account of monies received &c.

merchandize, under this law; and it shall be the further duty
of the Sheriffs respectively, to lay the same before the county
courts of Common Pleas, at the same time at which they audit
the public accounts annually.

When court shall lay tax on ferries.

§ 14.   It shall be the duty of the court of Common Pleas,
in each and every county, at their term next after the thirty
first day of March, annually, to fix & establish a reasonable
tax or duty upon each ferry within their respective counties;
the said court in fixing said tax, to take into consideration the

(379)

value and income of said ferries: *Provided,* That no one ferry
shall be taxed in one year more than ten dollars; and it shall
be the duty of the courts of Common Pleas, when they lay the
county levy, to tax the owners or proprietors of such ferries
accordingly.

§ 15. If any Sheriff shall take, demand or receive of any person from whom taxes are due, more than his, her or their proper taxes, or shall in any sale of property taken for taxes act contrary to the true intent and meaning of this act, or shall neglect or refuse to render a just and true account of all such sales to the county courts of Common Pleas, he shall forfeit and pay any sum not exceeding one hundred dollars, to be recovered by action of debt *qui tam,* or by indictment, before any court having jurisdiction; the one half to the person suing for the same, the other half to the use of the county; and moreover be subject to the suit of the party injured for damages.

Penalty on shff. for demanding more tax than by law allowed &c.

§ 16. All Sheriffs shall settle and close their accounts annually with the county courts of Common Pleas at the second term after the period at which they are obliged by this law to finish the collection of the taxes, and shall in their settlements be credited for all the orders of the said court by them produced, and by such deficiencies arising from delinquencies, and insolvencies as the said court shall allow; together with the commission on, and paying the monies

Shff. to settle account annually.

And shall be credited &c.

B b

(380)

by them received; but should any such Sheriff fail or neglect to settle his accounts in manner aforesaid, it shall be the duty of attorney prosecuting the pleas in the respective counties, on giving such delinquent Sheriff and his security their executors or admistrators, ten days notice thereof in writing, delivered personally, or left at the usual place of abode, on motion to obtain a judgment against them before any court having competent jurisdiction for the amount due such county, with an interest of twelve per cent thereon from the time the same became due: *Provided always,* That if any such delinquent Sheriff, shall produce his account, authenticated as aforesaid, to the court to which he is noticed, judgment shall not be taken for more than the ballance due the county with interest as aforesaid.

Shff. failing to settle.

Ten days notice given by atrny. &c.

Power of cts. of C. P. to contract &c.

§ 17. The several courts of Common Pleas shall have power, and they are hereby authorised to make and enter into contracts in the name and behalf of their said counties for building anew, or repairing county jails, court houses, pillories, stocks and whipping posts, and county bridges, where and so often as the courts of Common Pleas may conceive the interest or convenience of said counties may require; and the better to carry such contracts into operation, the said courts respectively may appoint one or more persons, to superintend such buildings or repairs, and to see that the same is done agreeably to the conditions of such contract; and to make reasonable allowances

(381)

to such person or persons, for his or their services therein. The original contracts so by the said courts to be made, for the purposes aforesaid, shall be filed in the office of the Clerk of the said court, and the said courts are hereby authorised and required to pass, audit and allow the accounts and demands arising under such contracts made by said court, the same being certified by three Justices of said court, and to draw orders in favor of such creditors, in like manner as they draw other orders on the treasury: *Provided always,* That no such contracts by the said courts to be made shall be of any force or authority to warrant the said court to allow or pass any accounts or demands arising thereon, unless the person contracting with the said court, shall enter into bond with one or more sufficient surety or sureties, to be approved of by the said court, in double the sum of said contract, payable to the Justices of said courts for said county, or their successors in office, conditioned for the faithful performance of such contract, which bond, when executed, shall be lodged with the Clerk of said court, in trust for said county.

Proviso.

Penalty for neglecting or refusing to perform duty

§ 18. If any Justice of the Peace, Sheriff as collector, Coroner, Clerk of the court, lister or freeholder, shall neglect or refuse to do or perform any of the duties required of them, or either of them, by this law, he, she or they so offending, shall forfeit and pay any sum not exceeding one hundred dollars, to be recovered before a-

(382)

ny court having jurisdiction, by action of debt, *qui tam,* or indictment, one moiety to the person suing for the same, the other to the use of the county.

Where and how to be recovered.

§ 19. If any person charged with county taxes or levies by virtue of this act, shall neglect or refuse to pay the same to the collector, or his deputy, within three months next after the court of common pleas at which the county tax or levy is, or shall be approved, the collector or his deputy, shall have power to take the property of such delinquent, he first having demanded the same, and furnished such person with the sum of his or her tax, ten days before such distress made, or having left a copy of such tax, ten days as aforesaid, at the usual place of abode of such delinquent, and may proceed to sell the same to the highest bidder: *Provided always,* That ten days previous notice of such sale be given by advertising the same in the most public place in the township where such delinquent resides: *And provided also,* That the delinquent may at any time before the property distrained be sold, ask for, demand, & receive the same, on tendering his or her taxes then due, and the expences of keeping the property distrained. And in case the property taken sells for more than the taxes that are due, the collector shall pay the overplus, after deducting reasonable expence for keeping and taking care of such property, to the person from whom the same was taken, and the said collector shall keep a fair and regular account of all such sales,

Persons refusing or neglecting to pay tax.

Collector or deputy to take property.

Notice given before sale.

Delinquents may redeem, property

If property overpays overplus re turned.

Keep account of sale.

(383)

stating particularly what he detained for his trouble in keeping the property &c. and lay the same before the court of Common Pleas who shall examine the same, and if they find the collector has acted in any wise improper, they shall forthwith, see justice done to the party injured.

Persons aggrieved may appeal.

§ 20. And if any person shall think himself aggrieved by the valuation of his or her house, by the freeholders to be appointed for that purpose, he or she may appeal to the court of Common Pleas of the county, who shall in a summary way, hear and determine upon the case, and shall confirm or alter the assessment of the said freeholders as to them shall appear just and reasonable: *Provided always,* That the appeal shall be made before the bill of taxation shall be put into the hands of the Sheriff for collection.

When appeal to be made.

Householders to give in young men.

§ 21. It shall be the duty of all the householders in their respective townships to give in to the Sheriff at the same time that they deliver in a list of their taxable property, and under the like penalties, the names of all single men above the age of twenty one years, and who have not taxable property to the amount of two hundred dollars, who lodge or dwell in their respective houses, and if any such single man &c. as above mentioned, shall neglect, or refuse, on application being made to him, for the purpose, by the Sheriff or his deputy, to pay his tax, it shall be lawful for such Sheriff or deputy, to commit such delinquent to the

(384)

county jail, where he shall remain, until the said taxes shall be paid, unless some responsible person in the opinion of the Sheriff shall be forthcoming therefor.

Shff. to be treasurer &c.

§ 22. All the duties of county treasurer in each of the counties respectively shall be performed by the sheriffs, who shall be allowed two per cent on all the monies by them paid, upon the orders of the courts of Common Pleas, or otherwise conformable to law.

§ 23. All taxes laid under the authority of the following mentioned laws, which have all been repealed, excepting as to the provisions contained in this section, to wit. A law of the Territory published 19th June 1795, entitled "A law for raising county rates and levies."

A law of the Territory published the first day of May 1798, entitled "A law for the purpose of including all unsettled and unimproved tracts or parcels of land, and subjecting them to taxation.

And another law of the Territory, entitled "An act to regulate county rates and levies," passed the 19th December 1799, which are now due and unpaid, and all penalties and forfeitures that have been incurred, may be recovered, and prosecution and suits, that may have been commenced, may be prosecuted to final judgment, under the said laws or acts, or either of them, as if

(385)

the said laws or acts were continued and in full force.

§ 24. All sheriffs within the territory, as treasurers of the counties respectively, at the same term at which by law they are directed to settle their accounts, shall make out a fair copy of the accounts aforesaid, and set it up at the court house door; which account shall state the monies received, as also the monies paid out of the Treasury that year and shall shew the amount that said county may be in arrears, or the amount remaining in the treasury, for which they shall severally be allowed the sum of six dollars out of the county funds; and any sheriff, as treasurer aforesaid, who shall fail to comply with the requisite of this section of this act, shall be fined in the sum of one hundred dollars, to be recovered at the suit of the attorney general, by action of debt, whose duty it shall be to institute said suit, when he receives information of the non-compliance with this section of this act, in any court having competent jurisdiction, for the use of the county.

Shff. as treasurer set up accounts at court house door.

Shffs. as treasurers for neglect fined.

JESSE B. THOMAS,
Speaker of the House of Representatives.
B. CHAMBERS,
President of the Council.

Approved—September 17th, 1807.
WILLIAM HENRY HARRISON.

(386)

CHAPTER LII.
An Act laying a Tax on Law Process.

Tax for use of couuty.

§ 1.   The following tax on law process, shall be paid for the use of the counties respectively.

Rates.

D. C.

On each appeal from any court of Common Pleas to
the General Court   1

On each writ or declaration in ejectment, instituting
a suit in any court of Common Pleas   50

On each certificate under the seal of any court of
Common Pleas.   50

Which taxes shall be by the respective clerks taxed in the bill of costs.

No decon. re ceived, &c, til tax paid.

No writ or declaration in ejectment, shall be issued or filed, by any clerk of the court of Common Pleas, unless the tax hereby imposed be paid down, and in all appeals, no transcript of the record shall be delivered to the appellant by the clerk of the court, or forwarded by him to the General Court, before the tax thereon be paid; nor shall any certificate under the

No seal until tax paid.

seal of the court of Common Pleas be granted, until the tax thereon be first paid to the clerk keeping such seal.

Clk to keep acpts.

The clerks of the several courts of Common Pleas shall keep regular accounts of all monies, which they may or ought to have

(387)

received, in pursuance of this law; and shall on every the first

When setle & pay trea- surer.

Tuesday of March and September, account with, on oath, and duly pay to the Sheriff as Treasurer of their respective counties, for the use thereof, the said several sums of money by

Under pen- alty &c.

them so received, under the penalty of paying to the use of the county, for every default or neglect the sum of one hundred dollars, to be recovered with costs of suit, on motion of the

Sheriff as Treasurer of the county; in the General court, on giving ten days previous notice of such motion.

JESSE B. THOMAS,
Speaker of the House of Representatives.
B. CHAMBERS,
President of the Council.

Approved—17th September, 1807.
WILLIAM HENRY HARRISON.

CHAPTER LIII.

An Act prohibiting the sale of Ardent Spirits, and other Intoxicating Liquors to Indians.

§ 1. IT shall and may be lawful for the Governor of this Territory, and he is hereby authorised and empowered, during the sitting of any council, or holding any public treaty or conference, with any Indian nation or tribe, to prohibit, by proclamation, the sale or other disposition of any ardent spirits, or other intoxicating liquors, to any Indian or Indians, by any person or persons, for any purpose, or under any pretence whatsoever, within thirty miles of the place of holding such council, treaty, or conference. *[clamation. Governor to issue his pro-]*

§ 2. If any person shall not strictly observe whatever restrictions may be imposed under the authority aforesaid, he, she or they so offending, shall, on conviction, by indictment or prosecution, be fined in a sum not exceeding five hundred dollars, nor less than fifty dollars, and in case of inability to pay the fine with costs, shall be imprisoned not more than six months, nor less than three months. *[Offenders to be fined &c.]*

§ 3. If any trader or other person whosoever, residing in, coming into, or passing through the said Territory, or any part thereof shall presume to furnish, vend, sell or give, or *[Mediately or immediately]*

C c

(388)

selling or gi-
ving to Indi-
ans be fined.

shall procure to be furnished, vended, sold or given, upon any account whatever to any Indian or Indians, or nation or tribe of Indians, being within the Territory, or waters adjoining to, or bounding the same, any Rum, Brandy, Whiskey, or other intoxicating liquor, or drink, he, she or they so offending, shall, on conviction, by presentment or indictment, forfeit and pay, for every such offence, any sum not exceeding one hundred nor less than

(389)

Not to im-
pair or weak-
en authority
vested in agt.
of Indian af-
fairs.

five dollars, to the use of the territory: *Provided,* That nothing herein contained shall be taken or construed to impair or weaken the powers and authority that now are, or at any time hereafter may be vested in the Governor, or other person as Superintendant, or Agent of Indian affairs, or commissioner plenipotentiary for treating with Indians.

When 3rd
sec. to be in
force.

The third section of this act shall commence and be in force, when, and as soon as the Governor of this territory shall be officially notified, that the states of Kentucky and Ohio, and the territories of Louisiana, and Michigan, have passed, or shall pass laws prohibiting the sale or gifts of intoxicating liquors to Indians, within their respective states and territories: and it shall continue in force so long as the said acts

Continue in
force same
time.

made or to be made in the said states or territories, shall continue in force therein.

Govr. to
transmit 3rd
sect. &c.

The Governor of the territory is requested to transmit copies of the third section of this law to the Governors of the several above mentioned states and territories.

GENL. W. JOHNSTON,
Speaker pro tempore, of the House of
Representatives.
B. CHAMBERS,
President of the Council.
Approved—September 17th, 1807.
WILLIAM HENRY HARRISON.

(390)

CHAPTER LIV.
An Act regulating Notaries Public.

§ 1. THE Governor shall commission so many Notaries Public in this territory as to him shall seem necessary, who shall hold their offices during good behaviour.

N. P. commissioned by governor.

§ 2. They shall make all attestations, protestations and other things which are by law directed relative to their offices, and it shall and may be lawful for every Notary Public, to demand and receive the following fees to wit:

Make attestations &c.

For every attestation, protestation, and other instrument of publication, under his proper seal relative to foreign bills of exchange, one dollar.

Fees.

And for recording the same in a book to be kept for that purpose, if thereunto required by the holder of such bill or note seventy-five cents.

And for every attestation, protestation, and other instrument of publication, under his proper seal, relative to inland bills of exchange or promissary notes fifty cents.

And for recording the same in a book kept for that purpose, if thereunto required by the holder of such bill, or note, twenty-five cents.

§ 3. It shall be the duty of the Governor to take bond with sufficient security from

Give bond.

(391)

each Notary Public, before he enters on the duties of his office in the sum of five hundred dollars, conditioned for the due performance of the duties of his office, which bond, if forfeited, shall be sued for in the name of the territory and for its use.

JESSE B. THOMAS,
Speaker of the House of Representatives.
B. CHAMBERS,
President of the Council.

Approved—September 17th, 1807.
WILLIAM HENRY HARRISON.

CHAPTER LV.

An Act to authorise Aliens to Purchase and hold real estates within this Territory.

Denizen friends may purchase and hold real pro*perty. FROM and after the passage of this act, it shall and may be lawful for any foreigner, or foreigners, alien or aliens, not being the legal subject or subjects of any foreign state or power, which is, or shall be at the time or times of such purchase at war with the United States of America, to purchase lands tenements and hereditaments within this territory, and to have and hold the same, to them, their heirs and assigns forever, as ful-

(392)

As citizens. ly, to all intents and purposes, as any natural born citizen or citizens may or could do.

JESSE B. THOMAS,
Speaker of the House of Representatives.
B. CHAMBERS,
President of the Council.

Approved—September 17th, 1807.
WILLIAM HENRY HARRISON.

CHAPTAR LVI.

An Act respecting Apprentices.

Apprentices when bonnd by father or guardian. § 1. If any white person within the age of twenty-one years, who now is, or shall hereafter be bound by an indenture of his or her own free will and accord, and by and with the consent of his or her father, or in case of the death of his father, with the consent of his or her mother or guardian, to be expressed on such indenture, and signified by such parent or guardian sealing and signing the said indenture, and not otherwise, to serve as apprentices in any art, craft mystery, service, trade employment, manual occupation or labor, until **Males 21 Females 18** he or she arrives, males till the age of twenty-one, and females till the age of eighteen years (as the case may be) or for any shorter time, then the said apprentice so bound as aforesaid, shall serve accordingly.

(393)

§ 2. If any master or mistress shall be guilty of any mis- | **Master ill u-**
usage, refusal of necessary provision or clothes, unreasonable | **sing apprent.**
correction, cruelty or other ill treatment, so that his or her
said apprentice, shall have any just cause to complain; or if
the said apprentice shall absent himself or herself from the | **Apprent. ne-**
service of his or her master or mistress, or be guilty of any | **glect service.**
misdemeanor, miscarriage or ill behaviour then the said mas-
ter or mistress or apprentice being aggrieved and having just
cause of complaint, shall repair to some Justice of the Peace, | **May com-**
unconnected with either of the parties, within the county | **plain to jus-**
tice not kin.
where the said master or mistress dwells, who having heard
the matters in difference, shall have authority to discharge, if | **Justice to**
he thinks proper, by writing under his hand and seal the said | **hear complt.**
& discharge
apprentice, of and from his or her apprenticeship; and such | **apprent.**
writing as aforesaid, shall be a sufficient discharge for the said
apprentice, against his or her master or mistress, and his or
her executors, or administrators, the said indenture, or any law
to the contrary notwithstanding. And if default shall be found | **Or order pu-**
to be in the said apprentice, then the said Justice shall cause | **nishment.**
such due correction to be administered unto him or her as he
shall deem to be just and reasonable, and if any person shall
think himself or herself aggrieved by such adjudication of the | **If aggrieved**
said Justice, he or she may appeal to the next court of Com- | **may appeal**
to C. P.
mon Pleas in, and for the county where such adjudication | **Giving no-**
shall have been made, such person giving ten days notice of | **tice of inten-**
tion &c.
his or her intention of

(394)

bringing such appeal, and of the cause and matter thereof, to
the adverse party, and entering into a recognizance, within | **Enter into re**
five days after such notice, before some Justice of the Peace | **cognizance**
within &c.
of the county, with sufficient surety, conditioned to try such
appeal, at and abide the order or judgment of, and pay such
costs as shall be awarded by the said court, which said court | **Court upon**
proof notice
at their said term, upon due proof upon oath or affirmation, | **& recog. to**

hear & decide, &c.

of such notice having been given, and of entering into such recognizance as aforesaid, shall be and are hereby empowered and directed to proceed in, and hear and determine the cause and matter of such appeal, and give and award such judgment therein with costs, to either party, appellant or respondent, as they in their discretion shall judge proper and reasonable

No certiorari to issue from G. C. procdgs. under this act,

§ 3.   No writ of *certiorari* or other process shall issue, or be issuable to remove into the General Court any proceeding had in pursuance of this act, before any Justice of the Peace, or before any court of Common Pleas.

JESSE B. THOMAS,
Speaker of the House of Representatives.
B. CHAMBERS,
President of the Council.

Approved—September 17th, 1807.
WILLIAM HENRY HARRISON.

[395]

CHAPTAR LVII.

An act for the relief of persons imprisoned for Debt.

Prisers. may give up property.

§ 1.   ANY person who now is or hereafter may be in actual confinement in any of the jails of this Territory and is willing to deliver up to his or her creditors all his or her estate both real and personal, towards the payment of his or her creditor or creditors, shall have leave to present a petition to

Petition C P

the court of Common pleas, in and for the county wherein he or she is so imprisoned, setting forth the cause or causes of his or her imprisonment, together also, with a list of all his or her creditors, with the money due and arising to each of them, to the best of his or her knowledge.

Court to set time.

§ 2.   The court to whom such application is made, are required to name the time and place, at which they will attend to hear what can be alledged for or against the liberation of such debtor; of which time and place so appointed by the

Give notice or adv. &c.

court, the debtor shall cause notice thereof in writing at least thirty days previous thereto to be served, or left at the usual place of residence of each of his or her creditor or creditors, if residing within this territory, and have the same inserted in one of the newspapers of this Territory the most contigous to the place of his or her confinement, if any such creditor or creditors should not reside in the Territory.

D d

(396)

§ 3. At such time and place as aforesaid the debtor so applying to the court as aforesaid, shall subscribe and deliver a schedule of his or her whole estate, and make oath, and swear to the effect following, that is to say:

To make & subscribe list of property & take oath.

"I, A B. in the presence of Almighty God do solemnly swear or affirm (as the case may be) that the schedule now delivered, and by me subscribed doth contain to the best of my knowledge and remembrance a full, true, just and perfect account, and discovery of all the estate, goods and effects unto me in any wise belonging, and such debts as are to me owing, or to any person in trust for me, and of all securities and contracts whereby any money may become payable, or any benefit or advantage accruing to me, or to my use, or to any other person or persons in trust for me, have not land money, stock, or any other estate real or personal in possession, reversion or remainder of the value of the debt or debts by me due, and that I have not since the commencement of the suits for which I am now imprisoned, or at any day or time, directly or indirectly, sold lessened or otherwise disposed of in trust, or concealed all, or any part of any lands, money, goods, stock, debts, securities, contracts, or estate, whereby to secure the same, or receive or expect any profit or advantage therefrom or to defraud any creditor or creditors, to whom I am indebted in any wise howsoever.

Form.

Which schedule being subscribed in o-

(397)

pen court, shall be returned to the clerk of the court, there

Schedule to remain with clerk.

Prisoner to be dischargd.

to remain for the benefit of the creditors, and after delivering in such schedule, and taking such oath, such prisoner shall be discharged by warrant from such court; which warrant shall be sufficient to indemnify such sheriff or officer against any escape or escapes, action or actions whatsoever, which shall or may be brought or prosecuted against him or them by reason thereof: and if any such action should be commenced for performing his duty in pursuance of this act, he may plead the general issue and give this act in evidence: *Provided always,* That notwithstanding such discharge, it shall be lawful for any creditor or creditors, by judgment at any time after wards,

Creditor may issue exon. & take propty.

to sue out a writ of *scire facias* to have execution against the lands or tenements, goods or chattles, which such insolvent persons shall hereafter acquire, or be possessed of, but no person delivering in such schedule, and having taken the oath and

Not again comtd. &c.

been liberated from prison, by the provisions of this act, shall be subject to imprisonment on final process, for any debts contracted or for damages accrued for the breach of any contract entered into prior to such liberation, unless such liberation be fraudulently obtained.

Estate vested in assignees appointed by C. P.

§ 4. All the estate which shall be contained in such schedule, and any other estate which may be discovered, shall be vested in such person as the court of Common Pleas of the county, where such prisoner

(398)

Their duty & power.

was discharged, shall appoint as assignee: and such assignee is hereby authorized and impowered and required within sixty days after the taking the said oath, ten days previous notice of the time and place of sale being given to sell and convey the same to any person whomsoever for the best price that can be got for the same, and the money arising by such sale shall by such assignee within thirty days thereafter be paid to the creditor or creditors of such insolvent debtor *pro rati,* according to their respective debts, saving however to every such prisoner, his or her necessary apparel, and utencils of

trade, and when any debts by such schedule, said to be due
to such insolvent debtor, the said assignee shall sue for and
recover the same in his own name as assignee of such debtor, **Recover debts.**
in any court proper to try the same; and such assignee shall
be allowed to retain out of the effects of such insolvent debtor
before the distribution thereof, all reasonable expences in re- **Retain for trouble &c.**
covering such money, and disposing of such estate as shall be
adjudged reasonable by the court.

§ 5. If any such prisoner as aforesaid shall be convicted **Prisoner for false swearing punished for perjury.**
of having sold leased or otherwise conveyed, concealed or
otherwise disposed of, or intrusted his or her estate or any part
thereof, directly or indirectly contrary to his or her foregoing
oath or affirmation, he or she shall not only be liable to the
pains and penalties of wilful perjury, but shall receive no
benefit from the said

(399)

oath or affirmation, and in case such prisoner at the time of
such intended caption, shall not take the said oath or affirmation, or shall not be admitted thereto by the said court, he or
she shall be remanded back to prison and shall not be entitled **Prisoner remanded may again give notice.**
to the benefit of this act, unless a new notification be made
out and served in manner aforesaid.

JESSE B. THOMAS,
Speaker of the House of Representatives.
B. CHAMBERS,
President of the Council.
Approved—September 17th, 1807.
WILLIAM HENRY HARRISON.

CHAPTER LVIII.
An Act regulating weights and measures.

§ 1. The several courts of Common Pleas within this **C. P. to procure weights & measures.**
Territory, be, and they are hereby authorised whenever they
may think it necessary, to procure for their respective counties, and at the expence of the same, a set of the following
measures and weights, for the use of their county, that is:—

One measure of one foot, or twelve inches, English measure, so called; also one

(400)

measure of three feet or thirty-six inches, English measure as aforesaid: also one half bushel measure for dry measure, which shall contain one thousand, seventy five and one fifth solid inches; also one gallon measure which shall contain two hundred and thirty-one solid inches, which measures are to be of wood, or any metal, the court may think proper; also one set of weights commonly called Avordupois weight, and seal with the name or initial letters of the county inscribed on it.

To be kept by clerk. Which weights and measures shall be kept by the clerk of each court, for the purpose of trying and sealing the weights and measures used in their counties.

§ 2.   As soon as the court shall have furnished the weights **When procured notice to be given.** and measures as aforesaid, they shall cause notice thereof to be given at the court house door for one month and any person who will knowingly buy or sell any commodity whatsoever, **Persons selling by other weights and measures finable.** by measures or weights that shall not correspond with the county weights and measures, shall for every such offence being legally convicted thereof, forfeit and pay the sum of twenty dollars, for the use of the county, where such offence shall have been committed, and also the costs to be recovered before any Justice of the Peace for said county. Every person desirous of having their weights and measures tried by **Clk. to seal.** the county standard, shall apply to the clerk of the county, and if he finds it correspond with

(401)

the county standard, shall seal them with the seal provided for that purpose. This act shall continue in force, until congress shall pass a law on the subject thereof.

Continue in force till &c.

JESSE B. THOMAS,

Speaker of the House of Representatives.

B. CHAMBERS,

President of the Council.

Approved—September 17th, 1807.

WILLIAM HENRY HARRISON.

CHAPTER LIX.

An Act for organizing a Court of Chancery.

§ 1, THERE shall be a court established in this territory under the name and style of the court of Chancery, which shall be vested with and is hereby empowered and authorized to exercise all the powers and authority usually exercised by courts of Equity.

Crt. established.

§ 2. The said court shall consist of one Judge to be appointed and commissioned by the Governor of the territory, for and during good behaviour, and the said Judge shall receive such compensation, as shall be allowed by law.

Holden by one judge.
Appointed by govnr.

§ 3. The said Judge shall hold annually,

(402)

at Vincennes, two stated terms, commencing the last Monday in March, and the last Monday in August, and such special terms, at the same place, as the said court shall from time to time appoint.

Hold two terms annually.
And special terms,

§ 4. In all suits in the said court, the rules and methods which regulate the practice of the high court of Chancery in England, as far as shall be deemed by the Chancellor applicable to this court, shall be observed, except, as is hereinafter excepted.

Rules to be observed &c.

§ 5. If the said court shall not sit, or be opened at any of the said terms, whether stated, or special, the writs and

Suits contd. when &c.

process then returnable, and the bills, suits, pleadings and proceedings before the said court, shall be continued of course, until the next term, and from term to term, nntil the court shall sit.

Always open for granting injucts. &c.

§ 6. The said court shall always be considered as open, so as to grant writs of *ne exeat, injunction, certiorari,* and other process, usually granted by a court of Equity in vacation.

Non residts. to give bond

§ 7. If the complainant resides out of the Territory, he shall, before the issuing of process to appear, cause a bond to be executed, by at least one sufficient person, being a freeholder, and resident within the Territory, to the defendant in the penal sum of   dollars, conditioned to prosecute the suit with effect, and to pay

To prosecute with effect &c.

(403)

costs, if he should be entitled thereunto, and to have the same filed with the Clerk, or in default thereof, that the complainants counsellor or attorney, who shall file the said bill, and issue the process thereon, shall be responsible to pay the defendant, such costs as he may be entitled unto, by order of the court.

In default at torny. liable for cost.

§ 8. Any complainant residing within the Territory, shall, at the discretion of the court, give security in the manner and form as is required in the case of non-residents.

Crt. may compel residents to give bond.

§ 9. Every subpoena, process of sequestration, writ of execution, or other writ or process, shall be issued by the Clerk, at the instance of the party, and the service or execution thereof, shall be signed and sealed by the Clerk.

Writs &c issued by clk.

§ 10. Rules to plead, answer, reply, rejoin, or other proceedings, when necessary, shall be given on the first Saturday of the months of January, April, July and October, with the Clerk in his office, and shall be entered in a rule book, for the information of all parties, attornies, or counsellors therein concerned.

Rules taken at clk. office When bill filed.

§ 11, No subpoena in Chancery shall issue until the bill is filed with the Clerk, whose duty it shall be, to copy the same, and deliver the copy to the person applying for the subpoena, which copy shall be delivered to

Clk. to make out copy &c.

E e

(404)

the defendant, if in the territory, by the officer or person serving the subpœna, which shall be endorsed on the back thereof; and if there be more than one defendant, the said copy shall be delivered to the one first named in the subpœna, if he be resident within this Territory if not the next one named in the subpœna, that is a resident.

§ 12. When any defendant, if but one, or defendants, if more than one, reside out of the Territory, or cannot be found, to be served with process of subpœna, or abscond to avoid being served therewith, public notice shall be given by the Clerk to the defendant or defendants, in any news-paper printed in the Territory, as the court shall direct, that unless he or they, appear, and file his or their answer, by a day given him or them, by the court, the bill shall be taken *pro confesso;* and where a bill is amended, a copy of the amendatory bill, shall in like manner be delivered to the defendant or defendants.

Non residnt. deft.s adv.

And unless they appear bill taken C.

§ 13. In suits in Chancery, the complainant may take depositions in one month after he shall have filed his bill, and the defendant may do the like, as soon as he has filed his answer, which may be done without a dedimus, unless the witness live without the territory: *Provided,* That reasonable notice be given of the time and place of taking such deposition.

Depons. may be taken &c.

§ 14. If the defendant does not file his

(405)

answer in the time prescribed by the rules of the court, having also been served with process of subpoena, with a copy of the bill, or notice given as required by this act, the complainant shall proceed on to hearing, as if the answer had been filed, and the cause was it issue: *Provided however,* That the court for good cause shewn, may allow the answer to be filed, and grant a further day for such hearing.

Deft. not filing answer,

Pltff. to proceed with trial.

Unless crt. grant further day.

§ 15. Every defendant may swear to his answer before any Judge of this, or the General court, or any Justice of the Peace; and if the defendant resides out of the territory, he may swear to his answer before any Justice of the Peace of a county, city, or town corporate; the common seal of any court of record of such county, city, or town corporate being thereunto annexed.

§ 16. The complainant having obtained a decree, and the defendant not having complied therewith, by the time appointed, it shall be lawful for the said court to issue a writ of *fieri facias,* against the goods and chattels, lands, tenements, and hereditaments and real estate of the defendant, upon which sufficient property shall be taken and sold, to satisfy said demand, with costs, or to issue a *capias ad satisfaciendum,* against the defendant: upon writs of *fieri facias,* and *capias ad satisfaciendum,* there shall be the same proceedings as at law, or to cause by injunction, the possession of effects and estate demanded by the bill, and whereof the

(406)

possession, or sale, is decreed to be delivered to the complainant, or otherwise, according to such decree, and as the nature of the case may require.

§ 17. When a decree of a court of Chancery, shall be made for a conveyance, release or acquittance, and the party against whom the decree shall pass, shall not comply therewith by the time appointed, then such decree shall be taken and considered in all courts of law and equity, to have the same operation and effect, and be as available as if the conveyance, release, or acquitance had been executed conformably to such decree.

§ 18. A decree of the court of Chancery, shall, from the time of its being signed, have the force, operation and effect of a judgment at law in the General court of this territory, from the time of the actual entry of such judgment.

Marginal notes:

Deft. swear to answer before judge or justice.

Defts. out of terty. may swear &c.

Complt. may issue a fifa.

Or Casa.

Same proceedings as at law.

How posession may be had

Decree not compld with

Same effect as a complie.

Decree to have force & effect of judgt. at law

§ 19. A writ of *fieri facias,* shall bind the goods of the person against whom it is issued, from the time it was delivered to the Sheriff, or officer to be executed, as at law:

§ 20. The said court, or the Judge thereof, shall have power to appoint a Clerk, who shall hold his office during good behaviour, and be entitled to such fees, as shall be authorised by law.

§ 21. No injunction shall be granted to

(407)

stay any proceedings at law, unless the party praying the injunction, have by the affidavit of at least one witness, proved that the opposite party had at least ten and not more than fifteen days notice of the time and place of applying for such injunction, from the time of which notice given, all proceedings at law shall be stayed, until the Chancellor's decision shall be made, whether an injunction shall, or shall not be granted; but if the complainant shall not make application to the Chancellor for such injunction, on the day specified in such notice, then the plaintiff at law may proceed as if none had been given; nor shall any injunction be granted to stay any judgment at law for a greater sum than that the plaintiff shall shew himself equitably not bound to pay, and so much as shall be sufficient to cover the costs, and every injunction when granted, shall operate as a release to all errors in the proceedings at law that are prayed to be injoined.

Nor shall any injunction be granted unless the complainant shall have previously executed a bond to the defendant, with sufficient surety, to be approved of by the Cancellor, in double the sum prayed to be enjoined, conditioned for the payment of all money and costs due, or to be due, to the plaintiff in the action at law, and also all such costs and damages as shall be awarded against him or her in case the injunction shall be dissolved. If the injunction be dissolved in the whole, or in part,

---

Marginal notes:

Sci fa to bind goods.

Crt. to appoint a clk.

His fees.

Party praying injunction to prove service of notice.

Notice to stay proceedings &c.

Application not being pltff. may proceed.

Injunction how far granted &c.

Act as relse.

Nor unless deft give bond to pltff. conditioned &c.

Injunc. dislv complt. to

(408)

pay interest.
Clk. to issue
exon.

the complainant shall pay six per cent exclusive of legal interest, besides costs, and the Clerk shall issue an execution for the same, when he issues an execution upon said judgment;

Judgt- vs-
sureties as
we,l as prin.
cipal.

on the dissolution of an injunction, judgment shall be given by the court against the securities as well as the plaintiff in the injunction bond.

Taking af-
fidavits no-
tic to be giv-
en.
Clk. to issue
supoenas.

§ 22. Whenever affidavits are taken either to support or dissolve an injunction, the party taking the same, shall give the adverse party reasonable notice of the time and place of taking the same, and the clerk shall issue to either of the parties, subpœnas to procure the attendance of witnesses, at

Affidavits to
be read.

the time and place appointed, and such affidavits taken as aforesaid, shall be read on the final hearing of the cause, in which they may be taken, under the same restrictions as depositions taken according to law.

When no-
tice not ne-
cessary.

§ 23. No notice shall be necessary in any case where application is made for an injunction in term time, nor in vacations, where the title or bonds for land shall come in question.

Ne exeat not
to be granted
unless &c.

§ 24. Writs of *ne exeat* shall not be granted, but upon bill filed, and affidavit to the allegations, which being produced to the Chancellor, in term time, or in vacation, may grant, or refuse such writ, as to him shall seem just, and if granted, he shall

(409)

Judge to en-
dorse &c.

endorse thereon in what penalty, bond and security be required of the defendant.

Complt. to
give bond &c
before writ
issue.

§ 25. No writ of *ne exeat* shall issue until the complainant shall give bond and security in the clerk's office, to be approved of by the chancellor, and in such penalty as he shall adjudge necessary, to be endorsed on the bill, and in case any

Persons a-
greived may
bring suit on
bond.

person stayed by such bill of *ne exeat* shall think himself or themselves aggrieved, he or she may bring suit on such bond, and if on the trial it shall appear that the writ of *ne exeat* was prayed without a just cause, the person injured shall recover damages.

§ 26. If the defendant or defendants to the bill, shall go out of the territory, but shall return before a personal appearance shall be necessary to perform any order or decree of the court, such, his or her temporary departure, shall not be considered as a breach of the condition of the bond.

§ 27. Whenever the defendant to the bill shall give security, that he will not depart the territory, the security shall have leave at any time before the bond shall be forfeited, to secure his principal in the same manner, that special bail may surren-

[410]

der their principal, and obtain the same discharge.

GENL. W. JOHNSTON,
Speaker pro tempore, of the House of Representatives.

B. CHAMBERS,
President of the Council.

Approved—September 17th, 1807.
WILLIAM HENRY HARRISON.

CHAPTER LX.
An Act to Incorporate the Borough of Vincennes.

§ 1. SUCH parts of the town of Vincennes, as are contained within the following limits and boundaries, that is to say:—by the plantation of William Henry Harrison, on the north east, the Church lands on the south west, the river Wabash, on the north west, and the lines of the commons as laid out for the inhabitants of Vincennes, in pursuance of an act of Congress, on all the other parts and sides thereof, shall be, and the same is hereby erected into a Borough, which shall henceforth, be distinguished, known and called by the name of the Borough of Vincennes.

§ 2. There shall be nine trustees in the

(411)

said Borough, a majority of whom shall form a quorum, which

To be nine
trustees.
said trustees shall be a body corporate, in deed, fact and in name, by the name and style of the trustees of the borough of Vincennes, by the same name shall have perpetual succession, and they and their successors at all times hereafter, by the name of the Trustees of the Borough of Vincennes, shall be persons able and capable in law, to sue, and be sued, plead and be impleaded, in any court of justice whatever, and to make & use one common seal, and the same to alter and change at pleasure; and Robert Buntin, Joshua Bond, William Bullitt, Henry Hurst, Charles Smith, Jacob Kuykendoll, Hyacinthe Lasselle, Touissaint Dubois, and Peter Jones, be, and they are hereby appointed the first Trustees of the said Borough, who

Remain in of
fice 3 years.
shall hold their offices from the first day of January, one thousand eight hundred and seven, for three years: *Provided always*,. That the said officers before they proceed to exercise their respective offices, shall take an oath or affirmation that they will faithfully discharge & execute such office, according to the best of their knowledge and understanding.

Divided into
classes.
§ 3.   The said Trustees, at their first sitting after their appointment, shall be divided into three classes, the seats of those of the first class, shall be vacated at the end of the first year, those of the second class, at the end of the second year, and those of the third class, at the end of the third year, so that one third

F f

(412)

may be chosen on every year; the said Trustees or a majority of them shall annually between the first day of February, and the first day of March, choose and elect three members in the room of those whose seats shall be vacated at the expiration of every year, as before mentioned, and in case such election shall not be made between the said days, then the court of Common Pleas of the county, shall at the next court, name three Trustees in room of those whose seats shall be so vacated.

§ 4. The said Trustees, or a majority of them shall have **Their power.**
full power from time to time, and at all times hereafter, to
hold a common council within the said Borough, as the chairman shall appoint, and to make such by-laws, ordinances and
regulations, in writing not inconsistent with the laws of this
territory, or of the United States, as to them shall appear necessary for the good government of the said Borough, and the inhabitants thereof; and the same to put in execution, revoke,
alter and make anew, as to them shall appear necessary for
the police of the said Borough, and for carrying this law into
effect; and by ordinance to require such sureties from the several officers and to annex such fees to the several officers of
the corporation, and to impose such fines for neglect of duty,
or misconduct in office, as to them shall appear necessary, and
to make, limit, impose, and tax reasonable fines, against all, **To impose**
and upon all persons who shall offend against the laws, or- **fines.**
dinances and regu-

(413)

lations of the corporation, made as aforesaid, and all and every
such fines, to take, demand, require, and levy, of the goods
and chattels of such offenders, to be appropriated to the use
and benefit of the inhabitants thereof.

§ 5. It shall and may be lawful for the said Trustees to **To commit**
commit every person or persons, offender or offenders, who, by **persons to**
law they are or shall be authorised to commit to jail, or im- **jail &c.**
prison, to and in the jail of the county of Knox, and the
keeper of the said jail is hereby authorised to receive such
person so committed, and him, her or them to keep in close
and safe custody, until thence discharged by due course of
law.

§ 6. The said Trustees shall elect their own chairman, **Trustees to**
and also elect their own clerk either out of their own body or **elect Cair-**
otherwise, and the said Trustees shall have further power and **man & clk.**
authority, to purchase ground, and erect a market house in
said Borough, and make by-laws for the government and regu- **Purchase**
ground & e-

rect market
house.

lation thereof, and they shall also have power and authority
to make such by-laws as they may think necessary, for widening, extending, repairing, and cleansing the streets of the said
Borough, and shall have further power and authority to cause
a survey to be made of the said streets, and to ordain as well
what width or breadth they shall hereafter be of, not exceeding
sixty feet, as to prevent any person or persons from erecting
any kind of buildings within the limits of

(414)

the said streets, as so ordered to be widened or extended, and
from enclosing any part or parts thereof: *Provided,* That no
buildings now actually erected, shall during the existence of
such building be demolished or pulled down, without the consent of the owner, or paying an adequate compensation therefor, to be estimated in such manner as by the said by-laws
shall be declared.

Trustees to
give publici-
ty to bye
laws &c.

§ 7.   It shall be the duty of the Trustees to give publicity
to their by-laws, and all persons inhabitants of said Borough
shall have free access to the said by-laws, and shall have full
liberty to peruse the same, and take copies, or such extracts
therefrom, as they may think proper.

§ 8.   The by-laws so to be made, and the proceedings of
the said Trustees, together with an account of the receipt and
expenditures in detail, shall whenever thereto required, be
laid before either branch of the Legislature of the territory
requiring the same.

JESSE B. THOMAS,
Speaker of the House of Representatives.
B. CHAMBERS,
President of the Council.

Approved—September 17th, 1807.
WILLIAM HENRY HARRISON.

(415)

CHAPTER LXI.

An Act concerning Debtors and their Securities, and to empower Securities to recover damages in a sumary way.

§ 1. When any person or persons shall hereafter become bound as security or securities, by bond, bill or note, for the payment of money or other property, shall apprehend that his or their principal debtor or debtors, is or are likely to become insolvent, or to migrate from this Territory without previously discharging such bond, bill or note, so that it will be impossible or extremely difficult for such security or securities, after being compelled to pay the money or other property, due by such bond, bill or note, to recover the same back from such principal, debtor, or debtors, it shall and may be lawful for such security or securities in every such case, provided an action shall have accrued on such bond, bill or note, to require by notice in writing, of his, her or their creditor or creditors, or his or their assignee, forthwith to put the bond, bill or note, by which he, she or they may be bound as security or securities as aforesaid in suit; and unless such creditor or creditors, or assignee so required to put such bond, bill or note in suit, shall in a reasonable time commence an action on such bond, bill or note, and proceed with due diligence in the ordinary course of law to recover a judgment for, and by execution to make the amount due by such bond,

Securities apprehensive of insolvency or absconding of principal.

If debt due notify creditor.

(416)

bill or note. The creditor or creditors, or assignee, so failing to comply with the requisitions of such security or securities, shall thereby forfeit the right which he or they otherwise have to demand and receive of such security or securities, the amount which may be due by such bond, bill or note.

Failing to prosecute &c

No reccurse on security.

§ 2. Any security or securities, or in case of his, her or their death, then his or their heirs executors or administrators may in like manner, and for the same cause make such

Securities or reprtvs. may

proceed in re gard to the representatives of creditor. requisitions of the executors, or administrators or assignee of the creditor or creditors of such security or securities as it is herein before enacted may be made by a security or securities of his or their creditor or creditors, and in case of failure of the executors or administrators so to proceed, such requisition as aforesaid, being duly made, the security or securities, his or their executors or administrators making the same, shall have the same relief, that is herein before provided for a security or securities, when his or their creditors shall be guilty of a similar failure.

The rights & remedies of principal not effected by this act. § 3. *Provided always,* That nothing in this act contained, shall be so construed as to effect bond with collateral conditions, or the bonds which may be entered into by guardians, executors, administrators or public officers.

§ 4. *And provided also,* That the rights

(417)

and remedies of any creditor or creditors against any principal debtor or debtors shall be in no wise effected by this act, any thing herein to the contrary, or seeming to the contrary notwithstanding.

§ 5. In all cases where Judgment hath been or shall here-
Securities ha ving paid mo ney &c. after be entered up in any of the courts of record within this territory, against any person or persons as security or securities, their heirs executors or administrators, upon any note, bill, bond or obligation, and the amount of such judgment or any part thereof hath been paid or discharged by such security or securities, his her or their heirs, executors or administrators, it shall & may be lawful for such security, or securities, his, her or their heirs executors or administrators, to
May obtain judgt. by motion. obtain judgment by motion, against such principal, obligor or obligors, his, her, or their heirs, executors or administrators for the full amount of what shall have been paid with interest, by the security or securities, his, her or their heirs, executors or administrators, in any court where such judgment may have been entered up against such security, or securities, his, her or their heirs, executors or administrators.

§ 6. Where the principal obligor or obligors, have or shall hereafter become insolvent, and there have been, or shall be two or more securities, jointly bound with the said principal obligor or obligors, in any bond, bill, note, or other obligation, for the

(418)

payment of money, or other things, and judgment hath been or hereafter shall be obtained, against one or more of such securities; it shall and may be lawful for the court, before whom such judgment was, or shall be obtained upon the motion of the party or parties, against whom judgment hath been entered up as securities as aforesaid, to grant judgment and award execution against all and every of the obligors and their legal representatives, for their and each of their respective shares and proportions of the said debt, with the damages and costs of the former suit.

§ 7. No security or securities, his, her or their heirs executors or administrators shall be suffered to confess judgment, or suffer judgment to go by default, so as to distress his, her or their principal or principals, if such principal or principals, will enter him her or themselves a defendant or defendants to the suit, and tender to the said security or securities, his, her or their heirs executors or administrators, other good and sufficient collateral security to be approved of by the court, before whom the suit shall be depending.

§ 8. In all cases where judgment hath been or hereafter shall be entered up in any of the courts of record in this territory, against any person as appearance or special bail for the appearance of another, to defend any suit depending in such court, and

(419)

the amount of such judgment, or any part thereof, hath been paid or discharged by such bail, his, her or their heirs, executors or administrators; it shall and may be lawful for such bail, his, her, or their heirs executors or administrators, to

Marginal notes:

Joint securities in cases of insolvency of principal.

By direction of court.

Shall pay equally.

Securities shall not confess or suffer judgt. by default if principal will enter deft. &c.

Give seccrities other surety.

Approved of by court.

Bail having paid money

may obtain
judgt. for
same.
Against the
principal &c.

obtain judgment by motion, against the person or persons, for whose appearance they were bound, his, her or their heirs, executors or admistrators, for the full amount of what may have been paid by the said bail, his, her or their heirs, executors, or administrators, together with interest and costs,

In proper ct.

in any court where judgment may have been entered up against such appearance or special bail.

Party to
have notice
in all case.

§ 9. *Provided always,* That no judgment shall be obtained by motion in any of the cases aforesaid, unless the party or parties against whom the same is prayed, shall have ten days previous notice thereof.

JESSE B. THOMAS,
Speaker of the House of Representatives.
B. CHAMBERS,
President of the Council.

Approved—September 17th, 1807.

WILLIAM HENRY HARRISON.

G g

(420)

CHAPTAR LXII.
*An Act directing the manner of proceeding in cases of
Impeachment.*

H. R. to pro
cure impeach
ments &c.

§ 1. ALL civil officers holding any commission under the authority of this territory shall be impeachable by the House of Representatives, either for mal administration or corruption in his office, such impeachment shall be prosecuted by the Attorney General, or such other person or persons as the house may appoint.

L. C. to try
impeachs. be
on oath.

§ 2. The Legislative Council shall have the sole power to try all impeachments, when sitting for that purpose, they shall be on oath or affirmation, and no person shall be convicted without the concurrence of two thirds of the members present.

Judgt. to ex
tend to remo
val &c.

§ 3. Judgment in case of impeachment, shall not extend further than to removal from office, and to disqualification to hold and enjoy any office of honor, trust or profit under this territory, but the party convicted, shall nevertheless be liable and subject to indictment, trial, judgment and punishment according to law.

JESSE B. THOMAS,
Speaker of the House of Representatives.
B. CHAMBERS,
President of the Council.

Approved—September 17th, 1807.

WILLIAM HENRY HARRISON.

(421)

CHAPTER LXIII.
An Act for the Partition of Land.

§ 1. WHERE any one or more persons, proprietors of any tract or tracts, lot or lots of land within this territory, and are desirous of having the same divided, it shall and may be lawful for the court of Common Pleas, of the county where such land or lots may lie, on the application of either party, notice of such application having been previously given by the party so applying, for at least four weeks, in some one of the public news-papers in this territory, if one is published therein, if not, at the court house door of the county where the land's lie, to appoint three reputable freeholders, residents of said county, not related to either of the parties as commissioners for dividing the said tract or lot of land, and having previously taken an oath, before any Judge of the General court, or of the court of Common Pleas, of said county, honestly and impartially to execute the trust reposed in them as commissioners aforesaid, shall proceed to make division of the said land, lots, tenements and hereditaments as directed by the court, among the owners and proprietors thereof, according to their respective rights, which partition being made by the said commissioners, or any two of them, and return thereof being made in writing under their hands and seals, to the said court, particularly describing the lots or portions allowed to each respective owner or proprietors, mentioning which of the

[marginal notes:] How real estate may be divided. / Notice being given. / Crt. to appoint comrs. / To take oath / Make division according to rights. / Make return under seal to court.

(422)

Describing partners &c. Ackgd. before judge C. P. Accepted by crt. to be recorded and serve as partition.

owner or owners, proprietor or proprietors, are minors, if any such there shall be; which return being acknowledged by the commissioners making the same, before any one of the Judges of the court of Common Pleas, for the said county, and accepted by the court, and entered and recorded in the Clerks office, shall be a partition of such lands, lots and tenements therein mentioned

In case division cant' be made comrs. to report.

§ 2. Where any houses and lots, are so circumstanced, that a division thereof cannot be had, without great prejudice to the proprietors of the same; and the commissioners appointed to divide the same, shall so report to the court, the court shall thereupon give orders to the said commissioners to

Crt. to order sale.

sell such house and lot or houses and lots, at public vendue, and shall make and execute good and sufficient conveyance

Comrs. to make deeds.

or conveyances to the purchaser or purchasers thereof, which shall operate as an effectual bar both in law and equity,

Bar vs. claimants.

against such owners or proprietors, and all persons claiming under them; and the monies arising therefrom to pay to the

Pay amount of sales to proprietors.

owners or proprietors of such houses and lots, their guardians or legal representatives, as shall be directed in the said order.

§ 3. The said commissioners so appointed shall be entitled to receive from the person making the application, the

Comrs. to receive from applicant 1¼ dollars per diem.

sum of one dollar and fifty cents for every day they shall be employed in effecting such division.

(423)

Guardians to act for minor

§ 4. And the guardians of all minors shall be and hereby are respectively authorised and empowered on behalf of the respective minors, whose guardians they are, to do and perform any matter or thing respecting the division of any lands, tenements hereditaments as is herein directed, which shall be binding on such minor, and be deemed as valid to every purpose, as if the same had been done by such minor after he had arrived at full age.

§ 5. *Provided always,* That no division or sale shall be made by order of the said court as above directed contrary to the intention of any testator, as expressed in his last will and testament.

No division or sale contrary to will.

JESSE B. THOMAS,
Speaker of the House of Representatives.
B. CHAMBERS,
President of the Council.

Approved—September 17th, 1807.
WILLIAM HENRY HARRISON.

CHAPTER LXIV.

An Act concerning the introduction of Negroes and Mullattoes into this Territory.

§ 1. IT shall and may be lawful for any

(424)

person being the owner or possessor of any negroes or mulattoes of and above the age of fifteen years, and owing service and labor as slaves in any of the states or territories of the United States, or for any citizen of the said states or territories purchasing the same, to bring the said negroes or mulattoes into this territory.

Slaves may be brot' to territory.

§ 2. The owner or possessor of any negroes or mulattoes, as aforesaid, and bringing the same into this Territory, shall within thirty days after such removal, go with the same before the clerk of the court of Common Pleas of the proper county, and in the presence of the said clerk, the said owner or possessor shall determine and agree to and with his or her negro or mulatto, upon the term of years, which the said negro or mulatto will and shall serve his or her said owner or possessor, and the said clerk is hereby authorised and required to make a record thereof in a book which he shall keep for that purpose.

Agree with slave for service before Clk C. P.

Clerk to mk. recd. thereof

§ 4. If any negro or mulatto removed into this Territory as aforesaid, shall refuse to serve his or her owner as aforesaid, it shall and may be lawful for such person, within sixty

Slaves may be removed, &c.

days thereafter to remove the said negro or mulatto to any place, which by the laws of the United States, or territory, from whence such owner or possessor may or shall be authorised to remove the same.

(425)

Penalty &c.   § 4. If any person or persons shall neglect or refuse to perform the duty required in the second, or to take advantage of the benefit of the preceding section hereof within the time therein respectively prescribed such person or persons shall forfeit all claim and right whatever, to the service and labor of such negroes or mulattoes.

Slave under 15 to be held to service &c.   § 5. Any person removing into this territory, and being the owner or possessor of any negro or mulatto, as aforesaid under the age of fifteen years, or if any person shall hereafter acquire a property in any negro or mulatto under the age aforesaid, and who shall bring them into this territory; it shall and may be lawful for such person, owner or possessor to hold the said negro or mulatto to service or labor, the male until they arrive at the age of thirty-five, and the females until they arrive at the age of thirty two years.

To register them with C. P.   § 6. Any person removing any negro or mulatto into this territory, under the authority of the preceding sections, it shall be incumbent on such person within thirty days thereafter, to register the name and age of such negro or mulatto, with the clerk of the court of Common pleas, for the proper county.

Removing, &c. how to proceed.   § 7. If any person shall remove any negro or mulatto from any one county to another county within this Territory, who may or shall be brought into the

(426)

same under the authority of either the first or fifth sections hereof it shall be incumbent on such person to register the same, and also the name and age of the said negro or mulatto, with the said Clerk of the county, from whence, and to which such negro or mulatto may be removed, within thirty days after such removal.

§ 8. If any person shall neglect, or refuse to perform the duty required by the two preceding sections hereof, such **Penalty**. person for such offence, shall be fined in the sum of fifty dollars, to be recovered by indictment or information, and for the use of the proper county.

§ 9. If any person shall neglect or refuse to perform the duty and service herein required, he shall for every such neglect or refusal, be fined in the sum of fifty dollars, to be recovered by information or indictment, and for the use of the county.

§ 10. It shall be the duty of the clerk of the court of Common Pleas aforesaid, when any person shall apply to him **Clerk to ta e** to register any negro or mulatto, agreeably to the preceding **bond &c.** section, to demand and receive the said applicants bond, with sufficient security in the penalty of five hundred dollars, payable to the governor or his successor in office, conditioned that the negro or mulatto, negroes or mulattoes, as the case may be, shall not after the expiration of his or her time of service, become a county charge,

(427)

which bond shall be lodged with the county treasurers respectively, for the use of the said counties: *Provided always,* That no such bond shall be required or requirable, in case the time of service of such negro or mulatto, shall expire before he or she arrives at the age of forty years; if such negro or mulatto, be at that time capable to support him or herself, by his or her own labor.

§ 11. Any person who shall forcibly take or carry out of **Servts. not** this territory, or who shall be aiding or assisting therein any **to be remov-** person or persons owing or having owed service or labour, **ed from terri-** without the consent of such person or persons, previously ob- **tory withont** tained, before any Judge of the court of Common Pleas of the **consent &c.** county, where such person owing, or having owed such service or labour resides, which consent shall be certified by said Judge of the Common Pleas, to the Clerk of the court of Common Pleas, where he resides, at or before the next court, any person so offending, upon conviction thereof, shall forfeit and pay one thousand dollars; one third to the use of the county, and two thirds to the use of the person so taken or carried away, to be recovered by action of debt, or on the case: *Provided,* That there shall be nothing in this section so construed as to prevent any master or mistress from removing any person owing service or labour, from this territory, as described in the third section of this act.

Except as provided in 3rd section.

H h

(428)

Clerk fees.

§ 12.   The said Clerk for every register made in manner aforesaid, shall receive seventy-five cents from the applicant therefor.

Servts. children to serve

§ 13.   The children born in this territory of a parent of colour, owing service or labour by indenture, according to law, shall serve the master or mistress of such parent, the male until the age of thirty, and the female until the age of twenty-eight years.

§ 14.   The provisions contained in a law of this territory, respecting apprentices, entitled "An act respecting apprentices," shall be in force, as to such children, in case of the misbehaviour of the master or mistress, or for cruelty or ill usage.

JESSE B. THOMAS,
Speaker of the House of Representatives.
B. CHAMBERS,
President of the Council.

Approved—September 17th, 1807.
WILLIAM HENRY HARRISON.

CHAPTER LXV.

An Act to authorise the Courts of the Counties within this Territory, to draw on the county Trersurer, for the services and expences therein mentioned.

§ 1. THE Sheriffs as Treasurers of the

(429)

several counties in this territory, shall pay to the Sheriffs, Clerks, and Judges of the polls, in taking the census of the good people of this Territory, whether they would wish to enter into the second grade of government, such sum as the court of Common Pleas, of the said respective counties shall think reasonable, which order the said several courts are hereby required to make

§ 2. The said several courts are empowered, and are hereby required to order the Sheriffs as Treasurers of their respective counties, to pay to all and every person or persons having any claims or demands, as well for attending the several courts of record in the said counties, as Constables or otherwise, for fire wood, and court house rent, and the fees due to witnesses, and the several officers of the courts in the public prosecution of those persons who were either acquitted of the charges brought against them, or discharged or unable to pay the fees, all of which shall be certified by the said court, in which such prosecutions were had, attendance given, or expences accrued; which orders shall be by said Sheriffs, as Treasurers, paid accordingly, out of any county monies in his hands.

§ 3. All costs, fees and charges to which the officers of the counties are now or may hereafter be intitled, for, or on account of any public prosecution, in either the superi-

(430)

or inferior courts, shall be paid out of the county funds respectively, on an order attested by the Clerks of either court, as the case may be; and it is further provided, That the sal-

---

Marginal notes:

Shff. to pay money on order of C. P.

C. P. to order paymt. demands vs. county for fees wood &c

Territorial expences.

How certified.

aries that are now, or which may hereafetr be due, to any county Sheriff, or to the Clerk of the General court, shall be paid out of the county funds, on an order of the court of Common Pleas, attested by the Clerks thereof, of the counties respectively.

Name of pro secutor endorsed.

§ 4. On all presentments or indictments hereafter to be found in this territory, the name or names of a prosecutor or prosecutors, shall be endorsed on every indictment or presentment, in default whereof, the said indictment or presentment, shall be immediately quashed by the court.

In case of acquittal prosecutor to pay costs.

§ 5. In case the defendant or defendants in any indictment hereafter to be found against him or them, shall be acquitted of the charges brought against him, her or them, or shall otherwise be lawfully discharged, the person or persons, whose name or names are endorsed on the said indictment, or presentment, as prosecutor, or prosecutors, shall be obliged to pay all the costs of the prosecution of such indictment or presentment, unless the court in their opinion shall think there were probable grounds for prefering the same; for which costs execution may

Unless the court certify there were probable grounds.

(431)

Exn. to issue

issue, against the said prosecutor or prosecutors, his, her or their bodies or estates.

JESSE B. THOMAS,
Speaker of the House of Representatives.
B. CHAMBERS,
President of the Council.

Approved—September 17th, 1807.
WILLIAM HENRY HARRISON.

CHAPTER LXVI.
An Act for the appointment of an Auditor and Territorial Treasurer.

Govr. to appoint audi-

§ 1. The Governor shall appoint an Auditor who shall continue in office during pleasure, whose duty it shall be to keep the accounts of this Territory with any state or Territory, and with the United States, or any individual; to audit all accounts of the civil officers of this Territory, who are paid out of the treasury of the members of both branches of the legislature, and of all other persons authorised to draw money out of the treasury; but nothing herein contained shall be so construed as to authorise the auditor under any pretext whatever, to audit any account, or give any certificate which would enable any person or persons, to receive any sum or sums of money, unless in cases particularly authorised by law.

tor during pleasure.

Keep territorial acpts.

(432)

§ 2. It shall be the duty of the said auditor, as soon as he shall have ascertained the balance due any individual, to give such person or persons a certificate, certifying that there is a ballance, mentioning the sum due to the person applying for the same.

Audit all demands autho rised by law. Give certificate of amot.

§ 3. The said auditor before he enters on the duties of his office, shall give bond with approved security, to the governor of this territory or his successor in office; in the penal sum of eight thousand dollars, conditioned as follows:

Cive bond in penalty.

"That he shall justly and honestly audit and fairly keep the accounts between this Territory and any state or territory, the United States, or any individual, as the case may be, and that he will deliver to his successor in office, all books, and other vouchers, which shall be by him kept by virtue of this law;" and moreover take the following oath or affirmation.

Take oath

"I, A B, do solemnly swear or affirm as the case may be, that I will justly and honestly perform the duties of auditor of this Territory, to the best of my skill and judgment so help me God."

Form.

§ 4. The said auditor shall make a fair list of all accounts by him audited, in a book to be kept by him for that purpose, as also an account of all taxes & other monies which may be due to any person from this territory; & it shall be the duty of such auditor to make out and present to the Legislature a

Duty of auditor.

transcript of said accounts, shewing the amount of all certificates by him given, as also the

(433)

amount of all taxes which have been received, or are still due
the said territory, on the first week of their session, or as often
as the legislature may require.

To number certificates. § 5. The said auditor shall keep a fair record of all warrants and certificates by him drawn, numbering the same in a
book by him to be kept for that purpose.

Make abstracts &c. § 6. When the said auditor, shall have made out abstracts
of all sums due in the respective counties, and sent them to
the different collectors; he shall make out in a book for said
purpose a fair account against each collector, a copy of which
shall be sufficient for the attorney general, to proceed by
Proceed by motion on gi ving notice. motion in a summary way against all delinquent collectors
before the general court or court of Common Pleas: *Pro-
vided,* The said collector shall have ten days previous notice of
such motion, and the said auditor shall upon receiving the treas-
Aud. to give acquitances. urers receipt, give to the said collector a *quietus,* which shall after
receiving the same prevent the auditor or attorney general from
motioning against him for the sum mentioned in the said receipt.

Govr. to appoint treasurer. § 7. The governor shall appoint a treasurer, who shall
continue in office during pleasure, who shall prior to the en-
tering upon the duties of his office, give and execute a bond
Give bond with sufficient security in the sum of eight thousand dollars,
to be approved of by the governor, conditioned for the due and

(434)

faithful performance of the duties of his office; the said bond
shall be given to the governor payable to him or his successors in office, for the use of the Territory.

Govr. require additional security. § 8. The governor may when he suspects the obligors in
said bond, to be insufficient, require the treasurer to give other
bond with sufficient security, to be approved of as aforesaid,
which said bond shall be deposited in the office of the secretary of this territory.

§ 9. If said treasurer die, resign, or be displaced, or cease to hold his office, then such treasurer, or if he be dead, his heirs, executors, or administrators, shall fairly and regularly state the amount, and deliver the monies, together with all instruments of writing, books and papers of the territory, in his her or their possession, to the succeeding treasurer, who shall make report thereon to the Legislature, and the said report, if confirmed by the Legislature, shall be a discharge of the said bond, which in such case shall be delivered to the said treasurer, his heirs, executors or administrators.

Treasurer going out of office, report to successor.

And him to legislature. If approved discharge bond.

§ 10. It shall be the duty of the treasurer to receive the proceeds of all taxes, and other public monies of this territory.

Duty of treasurer.

§ 11. He shall not pay any money, but on a warrant or certificate from the auditor, except the auditor's salary.

Not pay money &c.

§ 12. He shall keep a regular account of

(435)

all monies he receives, and pays agreeable to law, stating therein on what account each particular sum was paid, or received; and the time when, and lay a fair statement of said accounts, before the Legislature, on the first week in every session, or as often as the Legislature may require.

Keep acpts. and lay same before legisla ture.

§ 13. It shall be the duty of the treasurer to deliver monthly to the auditor, an account of his payments, and of the warrants on which they were made; and the auditor shall copy it in a book kept for that purpose.

Make month ly returns to auditor, who shall take copy.

§ 14. The treasurer, on receiving any sum of money, shall receipt for it to the person paying the same.

Give recpts.

§ 15. The present treasurer, shall deliver to the auditor, all paper, books, and other things appertaining to his office, in a convenient time, after said auditor shall have been appointed.

Present treasurer to deli ver books &c

§ 16. The present treasurer, shall deliver all public monies in his possession, to the succeeding treasurer, in a convenient time, after said treasurer shall have been appointed.

Also all mo nies.

Aud. to di-
rect A. G.
to motion for
monies due.

§ 17. It shall be the duty of the auditor to direct the attorney general, to motion against all delinquents for the payment of

I i

(436)

public monies, which have heretofore accrued to the territory.

JESSE B. THOMAS,
Speaker of the House of Representatives.

B. CHAMBERS,
President of the Council.

Approved—September 17th, 1807.

WILLIAM HENRY HARRISON.

CHAPTER LXVII.

Preamble.

An Act to Incorporate an University in the Indiana Territory.

WHEREAS the independence, happiness, and energy of every republic depends (under the influence of the destinies of Heaven) upon the wisdom, virtue, talents and energy of its citizens and rulers, and whereas, science, literature, and the liberal arts contribute in an eminent degree, to improve those qualities and acquirements; *And whereas,* Learning hath ever been found the ablest advocate of gunuine liberty, the best supporter of rational religion, and the source of the only solid and imperishable glory, which nations can acquire.

And forasmuch, as literature and philosophy, furnish the most useful and pleasing occupations, improving and varying the en-

[437]

joyments of prosperity, affording relief under the pressure of misfortune, and hope and consolation in the hour of death, and considering that in a commonwealth where the humblest citizen may be elected to the highest public offices, and where the Heaven born prerogative of the right to elect, and reject, is retained, and secured to the citizens; the knowledge which is requisite for a magistrate and elector, should be widely diffused.

§ 1. *Be it therefore enacted by the Legislative Council, and House of Representatives,* that an University be, & is hereby instituted & incorporated within this territory, to be called and known by the name or style of "the Vincennes University," that William Henry Harrison, John Gibson, Thomas T. Davis, Henry Vander Burgh, Waller Taylor, Benjamin Parke, Peter Jones, James Johnson, John Baddollet, John Rice Jones, George Wallace, William Bullitt, Elias M'Namee, Henry Hurst, Genl. W. Johnston, Francis Vigo, Jacob Kuykendoll, Samuel M'Kee, Nathaniel Ewing, George Leach, Luke Decker, Samuel Gwathmey, and John Johnson, are hereby declared to be Trustees of the said University, that the said Trustees and their successors, be, and they are hereby created a body corporate and politic, by the name of "the board of Trustees for the Vincennes University," and are hereby ordained, constituted and declared to be forever hereafter, a body politic and corporate, in fact and in name, and by

Incorporation of university, & appointment of trustees.

(438)

that name they and their successors, shall, and may have continual succession, and shall be persons in law capable of suing and being sued, pleading and being impleaded, answering and being answered unto, defending, and being defended, in all courts and places whatsoever, in all manner of actions, suits, complaints, matters and causes whatsoever, and that they and their successors, may have a common seal, and make and alter the same at their pleasure; also that they and their successors, by the same name and style, shall be in law capable of purchasing holding, leasing & conveying any estate, real or personal, for the use of the said corporation, except as hereinafter mentioned, so that the said Trustees, shall not at any one time, hold or possess, more than one hundred thousand acres of land.

§ 2. *And whereas,* Congress has appropriated a township of land, of twenty three thousand and forty acres, for the use and support of the University, or a public school in the district of Vincennes: *And whereas,* The township is now located, and the boundaries designated; *Be it therefore enacted,* That the trustees, in their corporate capacity, or a majority of them, be, and they are hereby authorised to sell, transfer, convey and dispose of any quantity, not exceeding four thousand acres of the said land, for the purpose of putting into immediate operation, the said institution, or University, and to lease or rent the remaining part of the said

May sell not exceeding 4000 acres of land.

(439)

township, to the best advantage, for the use of the said public school, or University.

§ 3. *Be it enacted,* That the places of any of the said trustees, who shall resign, remove from the territory, die, or wilfully absent himself, or themselves from three stated meetings, shall, from time to time be supplied by the board of trustees, at their stated meetings, which shall be held on the first Monday of April, and October, yearly and every year, and at such other times as the said board of trustees shall direct, by electing one, for every two, of whose seats may be so vacated, so that the whole number shall not be less than fifteen, after which time one trustee shall be elected at the stated meeting, as above mentioned, to supply every vacancy that may so happen. Extraordinary meetings of the said board may be had by the president, or any three of the trustees, giving at least ten days notice thereof, either in writing, or in some public news-paper, most convenient to the said University.

Vacancies how supplied

Extraordina ry meetings when & how holden.

§ 4. *Be it further enacted,* That the trustees or a majority of them, shall have full power, from time to time, to make such by-laws, ordinances and regulations in writing, not inconsistent with this charter, with the laws of this Territory, or of the United States, as to them shall appear necessary for the good government of the said University, and the Students thereof, and the same to be put in execution, revoke,

To make by-laws.

(440)

alter and make anew as to them shall appear necessary; and

to appoint such subordinate officers, as they may think convenient for the police of said University, and for carrying this law into effect, and by ordinance to require such sureties from the several officers and to annex such fees to the several officers of the corporation, and to impose such fines for a neglect of duty or misconduct in office as to them shall appear proper.

§ 5. *Be it further enacted,* That the trustees at their first stated meeting, shall elect a president out of their own body; and in case of his absence at any future stated or extraordinary meeting, the said trustees shall elect a president pro-tem. **Elect a president.**

§ 6. *And be it further enacted,* That the said trustees shall as speedily as may be establish and erect an University within the limits of the Borough of Vincennes, and shall appoint to preside over, and govern the said University, a president and not exceeding four professors, for the instruction of youth, in the Latin, Greek, French and English languages, Mathematics, Natural Philosophy, Ancient and Modern History, Moral Philosophy, Logic, Rhetoric, and the law of Nature and Nations; that it shall be the duty of the said president and professors to instruct and give lectures to the students of the said University, according to such plan of education as the said trustees may approve, and direct, in the branches **Establish university, appoint officers** **Their duty.**

(414)

of learning above mentioned; that the said president and professors, or a majority of them, shall be styled and called the "Faculty of the University;" which faculty shall have the power of enforcing the rules and regulations adopted by the said trustees for the government and discipline of the said University, and for granting and confirming by, and with the consent of the said trustees such degrees in the liberal arts and sciences to such students of the said University, who by their proficiency in learning the said professors shall think entitled to them, as are usually granted and conferred in other Universities in the United States; and to grant to such graduates diplomas, under the common seal of the said University,

to authenticate, and perpetuate the memory of such graduations: and that the said president and professors, shall hold
their offices during the pleasure of the trustees, and that the
president of the University, ex-officio for the time being, shall
be considered as one of the trustees of said University.

**Duty of trus-
tees.**

§ 7. *Be it further enacted,* That it shall be the duty of the
said trustees, and they are hereby authorised and required as
soon as may be, to erect, purchase or hire, as they may deem
most expedient, for carrying the said institution into effect,
suitable buildings for the said University, to make ordinances
for the government and discipline thereof; to establish plans
of education, which plans shall embrace each and every of the
languages, sciences and branch-

[442]

es of learning herein mentioned or directed to be taught in
the said University; to regulate the admission of students and
pupils into the same; to elect and appoint persons of suitable
learning and talents to be president and professors of the said
University: to agree with them for their salaries and emoluments, to visit and inspect the said University, and examine
into the state of education and discipline therein, and make
a yearly report thereof to the legislature; and generally to do
all lawful matters and things whatsoever, necessary for the
maintaining and supporting the institution aforesaid, and for
the more extensive communication of useful knowledge.

**Establish li-
brary.**

§ 8. *Be it further enacted,* That as soon as may be, after the
establishment of the said University, the said trustees shall
establish a Library, in and for the use of the students, professors and other members of the said institution, to consist of
such books and experimental apparatus as they may deem
proper for the said institution, to be provided in such manner
and by such ways and means as they or a majoity of them
shall by ordinance direct, and by ordinance to regulate the
terms upon which books, &c. may be taken out of the said
Library and returned to the same.

§ 9. *Be it enacted,* That the said trustees shall from time to **Appoint o-**
time elect and appoint a professor of Divinity, of Law and of **ther professor**
Physic, whenever they may deem it necessary for

[443]

the good of the institution, or when the progressed state of
education in the said University may require it: to agree with
them for their salaries, to point out the duties of said professors; the said professors shall be considered as members of the
faculty of said University; to hold their appointments during
the pleasure of the board of trustees.

§ 10. *Be it further enacted,* That no particular tenets of **No particu-**
religion shall be taught in said University, by the president **lar religion**
and professors mentioned in the sixth section of this act. **taught.**

§ 11. *And whereas,* The establishment of an institution of
this kind in the neighborhood of the aborigines of the country
may tend to the gradual civilization of the rising generation, **Civilization**
and if properly conducted be of essential service to themselves, **of savages.**
and contribute greatly to the cause of humanity and brotherly
love, which all men ought to bear to each other of whatever
colour, and tend also to preserve that friendship and harmony
which ought to exist between the government and the Indians:
Be it further enacted, And it is hereby further enjoined on the **Supported &**
said trustees to use their utmost endeavours to induce the said **taught gratis**
aborigines to send their children to the said University, for education, who when sent, shall be maintained, cloathed, and educated,
at the expence of the said institution: *And be it further enacted,*
That the students whenever the

K k

(444)

funds of the institution shall, in the opinion of the trustees permit it, be educated gratis at the said University, in all or any
of the branches of education which they may require.

§ 12. *And be it further enacted,* That the professors during **Professor &c.**
their professorship, and the students, while at the College, **exempt from**
shall be exempt from militia duty. **militia duty.**

Education of females.

§ 13. *Be it further enacted,* That the said trustees as soon as in their opinion, the funds of the said institution will admit, are hereby required to establish an institution for the education of females, and to make such by-laws and ordinances for the said institution, and the government thereof, as they may think proper.

Establish a grammer school.

§ 14. *Be it further enacted,* That the said trustees shall have the power to establish a grammer school, connected with, and dependant upon the said University, for the purpose of teaching the rudiments of the languages, and that they may employ a master and ushers specially for this purpose, or emply the professor of languages to superintend the same, as the one or the other may be found most convenient and œconomical.

§ 15. *And be it further enacted,* That for the support of the aforesaid institution, and for the purpose of procuring a library, and the necessary philosophical and experimental apparatus, agreeably to the eight sec-

(445)

Raise money by lottery for certain purposes.

tion of this law, there shall be raised a sum not exceeding twenty thousand dollars by a lottery, to be carried into operation as speedily as may be, after the passage of this act, and that the trustees of the said University, shall appoint five discreet persons, either of their body, or other persons, to be managers of the said lottery, each of whom shall give security to be approved of by said trustees, in such sum as they shall direct, conditioned for the faithful discharge of the duty required of said managers; and the said managers shall have power to adopt such schemes as they may deem proper, to sell the said tickets, and to superintend the drawing of the same, and the payment of the prizes; and that as often as the said managers shall receive one thousand dollars, they shall deposit the same in the hands of the treasurer of the said board of trustees; and the said managers and trustees, shall render an account of their proceedings therein at the next session of the Legislature, after the drawing of said lottery.

And be it further enacted, That this act shall take effect from and after the passage of the same, and that a special meeting of the trustees of the said University, shall be held on the first Saturday in December next, for the election of officers, and to commence their operations, to carry the

Take effect from passage

(446)

said law into effect, any thing in the said law to the contrary notwithstanding.

When meet.

JESSE B. THOMAS,
Speaker of the House of Representatives.
B. CHAMBERS,
President of the Council.

Approved—September 17th, 1807.
WILLIAM HENRY HARRISON.

CHAPTER LXVIII.
An Act for the relief of the Territorial Treasurer and for other purposes.

§ 1. *BE it enacted,* That the sum of two hundred dollars, be appropriated out of any money in the treasury, except the contingent fund, for the purpose of purchasing stationary and a chest, the better to secure the funds of the territory from fire and robbery, and that Jacob Kuykendall, and

Specific appropriation.

(447)

James Johnson, Esquires, be appointed to purchase said articles.

JESSE B. THOMAS,
Speaker of the House of Representatives.
B. CHAMBERS,
President of the Council.

Approved—September 17th, 1807.
WILLIAM HENRY HARRISON.

CHAPTER LXIX.

An Act concerning Executions.

Fifa levied on property.

§ 1. WHEN any writ of fieri facias issuing out of the General court, or any court of Common Pleas within this territory, shall be levied on any real or personal estate of the defendant or defendants, it shall and may be lawful for such

Deft. may replevy.

defendant or defendants, to release the same by tendering to the Sheriff or other officer, a bond with sufficient security to pay the amount of such execution, including all costs, with lawful interest thereon, from the date of said bond, within five months, and on such bond being given, the said Sheriff or

Officer to restore property.

other officer, shall restore to the defendant or defendants, such personal or real estate; and where no bond shall be tendered by such defendant or defendants, or any person for him or them,

(448)

Officer to sell.

the Sheriff or other officer shall proceed to sell the said estate for whatever it will bring in cash, ten days previous notice having been given of such sale.

Bd. to have validity.

§ 2. Any defendant or defendants, on any writ of capias ad satisfaciendum, may in like manner, release his, her or their body or bodies, from execution, by tendering bond and security, as required in the foregoing section.

Shff. to return bond.

§ 2. All and every bond so taken in pursuance of this act, shall have the force of judgments, and such sheriff or other officer taking such bonds shall return the same to the office from which the execution issued, within twenty days thereafter.

§ 4. If the amount of the said bond shall not be paid agreeably to the condition thereof, it shall and may be lawful, for the creditor or creditors, his, her, or their executors or administrators, at any time thereafter, to sue out of the clerks office of said court, his execution against the real & personal estate of the said defendant or obligors in said bond, their executors or administrators; and the clerk issuing such execution, shall endorse on the back thereof that no security of any kind is to be taken.

§ 5. If any replevy bond be quashed, or the security adjudged insufficient at the time of receiving the bond, the sheriff taking the same, and his securities shall at all

(449)

times be liable to the party injured, or his representatives.

§ 6. All executions issuing out of any of the courts of this Territory, shall be returnable to the clerks office on the second rule day next after the teste of the writ.

§ 7. *And whereas,* doubts have arisen whether the time of service of negroes and mulattoes bound to service in this Territory, may be sold under execution; *Be it threfore enacted,* That the time of service of such negroes or mulattoes, may be sold on execution against the master in the same manner as personal estate, immediately from which sale, the said negroes or mulattoes, shall serve the purchaser or purchasers for the residue of their time of service; and the said purchasers, and negroes and mulattoes shall have the same remedies against each other, as by the laws of the territory are mutually given them in the several cases therein mentioned, and the purchasers shall be obliged to fulfil to the said servants, the contracts they made with the master as expressed in the indenture or agreement of servitude, and shall for want of such contract be obliged to give him or them their freedom dues at the end of the time of service, as expressed in the second section of a

(450)

law of the Territory entitled, "A Law concerning Servants.

JESSE B. THOMAS,

Speaker of the House of Representatives.

B. CHAMBERS,

President of the Council.

Approved—September 17th, 1807.

WILLIAM HENRY HARRISON.

Marginal notes:

Bond insufficient shff. liable.

Exons. to be returned.

Time of servants may be sold.

To serve purchaser.

Remedy.

Give freedom dues.

CHAPTER LXX.

An Act regulating the duties of Sheriff's, and for other purposes.

Writs by whom served.

§ 1. EVERY Sheriff or Corroner, himself or his lawful officer or deputies, shall from time to time, execute all writs and process to him legally issued, and directed within his connty, or upon any river or creek adjoining thereto, and

Penalty.

shall make due returns under the penalty of forfeiting one hundred dollars for every failure, one moiety to the use of the Territory, and the contingent expences thereof, and the other moiety to the party grieved, to be recovered with costs by action of debt, or information in any court of record in this Territory out of which such process may have issued, and

Liable to action.

such sheriff or coroner shall be further liable to the action of the party grieved at common law, for his or her da-

(451)

For false return liable &c.

mages, and for every false return, the sheriff or coroner shall forfeit and pay one hundred dollars, to be recovered, divided and applied in the manner last mentioned, and shall also be liable in like manner to the party grieved for damages.

Persons in exon. dying how to proceed.

§ 2. If any person being a prisoner charged in execution shall happen to die in execution, the party or parties at whose suit or to whom such person shall stand charged, in execution for any debt or damages recovered, his or their executors, or administrators, may, after the death of the person so dying in execution, lawfully sue forth, and have new execution against the lands and tenements, goods and chattels of the person so deceased.

In case property not sell

§ 3. If the lands, tenements or hereditaments, or goods and chattels taken by any Sheriff or any other officer, or any part thereof shall remain in his hands unsold, he shall make return accordingly, and thereupon the Clerk of the court from whence such execution issued, shall and may, and is hereby

Vend. exponas to issue by clerk.

required to issue a *venditioni exponas,* to such Sheriff or other officer directed, whereupon the like proceedings shall be had, as

might, and ought to have been had on the first execution, which
writ of *venditioni exponas* shall be in the form following:

"The United States, &c. Greeting:

We command you, that you expose to sale   Form thereof

L l

(452)

the lands or goods and chattels, as the case may be, of A B,
to the value of   which according to our
command you have taken, and which remain in your hands
unsold, as you have certified to our Judges (or Justices) of
our   court, to satisfy C D, the sum of
                              whereof in our said court he
hath recovered execution, against the said A B, by virtue of a
judgment in the said court, and that you have &c."

§ 4. If any Sheriff shall levy an execution on property,   Right of pro
and a doubt shall arise, whether the right of such property   perty contes-
shall be in the debtor or not, such Sheriff may, and it is hereby   ted how shff.
declared to be his duty, to empannel twelve freeholders, each   to proceed.
of whom shall be disinterested in the event, to try the right
of property aforesaid, and after hearing the evidence, the said
jury shall determine whether the property belongs to the defendant or the person claiming it; and the verdict of the said   Verdict jus-
jury shall be a sufficient justification for said Sheriff to sell   tification to
the said property or deliver it to the person claiming the same,   sheriff.
as the case may be, and in case of any action being brought
against any Sheriff for his conduct herein, he may plead the
general issue, and give this act in evidence.

§ 5. If any Sheriff or other officer, shall make return upon
any writ of *fieri facias*, or *venditioni exponas,* that he hath levied   Shff. withhol
the debt damages or costs, as in such writ is   ding money,

(453)

required, or any part thereof, and shall not immediately pay
the same to the party to whom the same is payable, or his at-   Making im-
torney, or shall return upon any writ of *capias ad satisfaciendum,*   proper return

or attachment for not performing a decree in chancery, for the payment of any sum of money, that he hath taken the body or bodies of the defendant or defendants, and hath the same ready to satisfy the sum in such writ mentioned, and shall have actually received such money of the defendant or defendants, or

Or suffering escape. have suffered him or them to escape, with the consent or negligence of such Sheriff or other officer, and shall not immediately pay such money to the party to whom the same is payable, or his attorney, then and in either of the said cases, it shall and may be lawful for the creditor at whose suit such writ of *fieri facias, venditioni exponas, capias ad satisfaciendum,* or attach-

May be motioned agst. ment shall issue upon a motion made in the next succeeding General court, or other court from whence such process issued, to demand judgment against such Sheriff or other officer, and the securities of such Sheriff or other officer, for the money mentioned in such writ, or so much as shall be returned levied on such writs of *fieri facias,* or *venditioni exponas,*

And judgt. had vs. himself & sureties. with interest thereon at the rate of fifteen per centum per annum, from the return day of the execution, until the judgment

with interest shall be discharged, and such court is hereby authorised and required to give judgment accordingly, and to award execution thereon; *Provided,* Such Sheriff or

(454)

Notice given other officer, have ten days previous notice of such motion.

§ 6. *And whereas,* doubts have arrisen in what manner judg-

Failing to re turn exon. ment should be rendered against any sheriff or coroner who shall fail to return an execution to the office from whence it issued on or before the return day thereof: *Be it enacted,* That where any writ of execution or attachment for not performing a decree in chancery, shall come into the possession of any sheriff or coroner and he shall wilfully or negligently fail to return the same to the office from whence it issued, on or before the return day thereof, it shall be lawful for the court, ten days pre-

Having notice. vious notice being given, upon motion of the party injured to fine such sheriff or coroner at their discretion in any sum

not exceeding five dollars nor less than two dollars, per month, for every hundred dollars contained in such judgment or decree, on which the execution or attachment so by him detained was founded, and so on in proportion for any greater or lesser sum, counting the aforesaid month, from the return day of the execution or attachment to the day of rendering the judgment for the said fine, which fine shall be for the benefit of the party grieved. {.right-note May be fined.}

§ 7. When any writ of capias ad satisfaciendum is issued against any person or persons out of any court of record within this territory, and he or they are taken by virtue of the same, and if the party at whose suit {.right-note Time given prisoner not bar other execution.}

(455)

the said writ was issued after issuing of the same, shall by request of the prisoner, release said prisoner, for the purpose of giving him or them further time to make the money thereon, it shall and may be lawful for the party at whose suit the execution was issued, at any time thereafter, to issue forth his or her writ of capias ad satisfaciendum or fieri facias, on the said judgment notwithstanding the release of the said prisoner or prisoners.

GENNL. W. JOHNSTON,
Speaker pro tempore, of the House of Representatives.
B. CHAMBERS,
President of the Council.
Approved—September 17th, 1807.
WILLIAM HENRY HARRISON.

CHAPTER LXXI.
An Act concerning Clerks of Courts.

§ 1. IT shall be the duty of the General court of this Territory, and the several courts of Common Pleas of the counties at their first session after the first day of January next, to receive of their respective clerks, bonds with approved {.right-note Courts to take bonds &c.}

security, in the penalty of one thousand dollars, payable to the governor of the Territory, for the time be-

(456)

ing, and his successors in office, conditioned for the faithful discharge of the duties of their respective offices, and all clerks hereafter to be appointed to said courts shall previous to their exercising the duties of their office, enter into bond in like manner, which bonds shall by said clerks be lodged in the office of the Secretary of the Territory, within three months thereafter.

To be lodged in secy's office.

§ 2. It shall be the duty of the presiding judge of the several courts of Common Pleas in this Territory, and of the first judge of the General court to examine the respective clerk's books in open court, & see what fines are due thereon to the territory or to the county, and make out a fair list thereof, and report those due to the Territory to the auditor thereof, who shall report the same to the legislature at the same time he makes his annual report, and if the said clerk shall fail to pay the said fines to the treasurer of the territory, or the county as the case may be, on or before the first day of March annually, the auditor shall direct the attorney general to obtain judgment by motion against said clerks in their respective courts, upon giving ten days notice thereof, and immediately collect the same and pay it into the treasury of the territory, or the county as the case may be; and the said judges shall further report to the sheriffs as treasurers of their respective counties the amount of fines due to said counties, on or before the first day of March, and the sheriffs as treasurers, if the said fines are

Judges to examine clks books in open court.

Assess fines.

Report &c.

Clerk failing &c.

Aud. his duty.

(457)

not paid to them, on or before the first day of May by the said clerks then the said sheriffs as treasurers, shall proceed to

collect the same in manner and form as is directed in the foregoing part of this section.

JESSE B. THOMAS,
Speaker of the House of Representatives.
B. CHAMBERS,
President of the Council.

Approved—September 17th, 1807.
WILLIAM HENRY HARRISON.

CHAPTER LXXII.
An Act to Incorporate the Vincennes Library Company.

WHEREAS it has been represented to the General As- **Preamble.**
sembly, that sundry citizens of Vincennes and its neighbourhood, have associated themselves together for the purpose
of establishing a Circulating Library, and in order to establish said institution more permanently, they pray that a suitable charter may be granted, organizing said institution.

§ 1. For the better ruling and governing the said institu- **appoint Prdt**
tion and the share holders in the said Library, there shall be **& dirctrs.**
appointed

(458)

a president and seven directors, said president and seven directors, shall be a body coporate in deed fact and name, by the
name and style of "The president and directors of the Vincennes Library," and by the same name shall have perpetual
succession, and they and their successors, at all times hereafter by the name of the president and directors of the Vincennes Library shall be persons able and capable in law to
sue, and be sued, plead, and be impleaded, answer and be answered unto, in any court of justice whatsoever, and to make
and use one common seal, and the same to alter and change at **Have seal.**
pleasure.

§ 2. The president and seven directors shall be appointed **President &**
annually at the meeting of the shareholders in said Library. **directrs. ap-**
pointed an-
nually.

Have bye-laws.

§ 3,   The president and seven directors, or a majority of them, shall have power from time to time, and at all times hereafter, to meet and make such by-laws, ordinances and regulation, in writing not inconsistent with the laws of the United States or of this territory, as may be necessary for the government of the said institution; which by-laws shall be in force, until the next annual meeting, and afterwards unless disagreed to at such meeting; for which purpose all the by-laws made by such president and directors shall be laid before the succeeding meeting, for their approbation or rejection.

(459)

Meet annu-ally.

§ 4.   There shall be a general meeting of the shareholders on the first Monday in February, yearly, when they shall take into consideration the general interest of the said institution, and elect a president and seven directors, and all other neces-sary officers, and exact such security from the said officers as

How to pro-ceed.

they may deem proper; and in case a general meeting shall not be had, on the stated day, the officers then acting shall con-tinue their functions until the next general meeting.

§ 5.   No determinate number of shareholders shall be necessary to form a quorum to do business.

JESSE B. THOMAS,
Speaker of the House of Representatives.
B. CHAMBERS,
President of the Council.
Approved—September 17th, 1807.
WILLIAM HENRY HARRISON.

ACTS

ORIGINATED

AT THE FIRST SESSION

OF THE

SECOND GENERAL ASSEMBLY

OF THE

INDIANA TERRITORY,

Begun August 16th, 1807.

ACTS, &c.

CHAPTER LXXIII.

AN ACT to alter the next September Term of the Court of Common Pleas
of the County of Clark.

BE *it enacted by the Legislative Council and House of Represeniatives, and it is hereby enacted by the authority of the
same,* That the term of the court of Common Pleas of the county **Term alter-**
of Clark, which by law is ordered to be holden on the second **ed, &c.**
Monday in the month of September next, be, and the same is
hereby ordered to be holden on the second Monday in the
month of October next, that all writs and other process returnable to the second Monday in September, stand returnable
to the second Monday in October, and that thereafter, the term
of said court be on the second Monday in September, annually.

This act shall commence, and be in force from and after
the twenty-fifth instant.

JESSE B. THOMAS,
Speaker of the House of Representatives.
B. CHAMBERS,
President of the Council.
Approved—August 21st, 1807.
WILLIAM HENRY HARRISON.

(464)

CHAPTER LXXIV.

AN ACT for adjourning the next General Court of the Indiana Territory,
and for amending an act passed at this Session, entitled "An act to
alter the next September Term of the Court of Common Pleas of the
County of Clark."

§ 1. BE *it enacted by the Legislative Council and House of
Representatives, and it is hereby enacted by the authority of the
same,* That the next term of the General court of the Territory, **Term alter-**
ed &c.

which by law is appointed to be held on the first Tuesday in September next, shall be, and the same is hereby adjourned to the third Tuesday in November next, when the said court shall be opened and held accordingly.

Process continued. § 2. All suits and process which were, or shall be commenced for the said court, and all suits and process which are depending in the said court, shall be, and the same are hereby continued to the said third Tuesday in November next.

§ 3. All suits and process which are depending in the court of Common Pleas of Clark county) shall be, and the same are hereby continued to the court which by the act entitled "An act to alter the next September term of the court of Common Pleas of Clark county" is ordered to be held and opened, on the second Monday in October, instead of the second Monday in September next.

(465)

This act shall be in force from the passing thereof.

JESSE B. THOMAS,
Speaker of the House of Representatives.
B. CHAMBERS,
President of the Council.

Approved—August 23th, 1807.
WILLIAM HENRY HARRISON.

CHAPTER LXXV.

AN ACT Authorising the Collection of the Territorial Tax on Land in the Counties of St. Clair and Knox.

Preamble. WHEREAS, the assessor of the county of St. Clair, having refused to make an assessment and return as required by law, of the lands lying in said county, and subject to territorial tax: *And whereas* the collector for the county of Knox having also failed to proceed in the collection of the tax on lands in the said county, in consequence whereof, the tax will not under the existing circumstances, be collected the present year.

BE *it therefore enacted by the Legislative Council and House of Representatives, and it is hereby enacted by the authority of the same,* That the sheriff of the said county of St. Clair, as assessor for said county, being furnished with an abstract of the lands in said county, by the auditor of the territory, which he is hereby required to do, on **Shff. to assess.**

(466)

or before the twentieth day of September, next, and having taken such oath as is required by law of an assessor, shall immediately proceed and make the assessment, as required by the act entitled "An act supplemental to the act entitled an act, for levying and collecting a tax on land, and for other purposes," and the act to which the said act is a supplement, and return the same to the auditor by the fifteenth of November next, ensuing, the same having been examined and corrected by the court of Common Pleas of the said county of St. Clair; for which purpose, and for hearing complaints of improper assessments, the said court is hereby authorised and required, to hold a session at the court house of said county on the last Monday in October next; upon the receipt of which list, the auditor shall immediately make out and transmit to the said sheriff, the abstract as required by law, to enable him to proceed with the said collection, who shall thereupon proceed to collect the same by personal application or notice in writing, or by sale of the lands so taxed, by giving thirty days previous notice, by advertising at the court house door of the proper county, and by the first day of February ensuing, shall and do pay the same to the territorial treasurer agreeably to law. **Take oath.** **Court to hear complaint.** **Auditor his duty.** **Collector, how to proceed.**

§ 2. *Be it further enacted,* That the sheriff of the said county of Knox, shall in like manner, upon being furnished with the abstract by the auditor, which he is hereby directed immediately to furnish him with, to proceed to the collection of the tax in the said county in the same manner, and **Sff. of Knx. his duty.**

(467)

pay the same over to the treasurer by the said first day of February.

Penalty on neglect.

§ 3. *Be it further enacted,* That if the said Sheriff's or either of them shall refuse or neglect to discharge the duties hereby enjoined on them respectively, or shall neglect to pay over, or account for the amount of the taxes with which they may be so charged with the collection of, they shall be severally and respectively, personally liable for the amount there-

How recoverable.

of, which may and shall be recovered by the attorney general, by motion in the General court, giving ten days previous notice; and execution thereupon issued, no replevin shall be allowed: the Sheriff's of the said counties of St. Clair and Knox,

Fees.

shall respectively be allowed for their services the same compensation as assessors and collectors are entitled to.

§ 4. *Be it further enacted,* That when any lands may be sold for the payment of taxes, whether belonging to residents or

How redeemed.

non residents, the same may be redeemed in the manner, and under the same regulations as is provided in the first section of an act entitled "An act supplemental to an act entitled an act for levying and collecting a tax on land and for other purposes.

Repealing clause.

§ 5. *And be it further enacted,* That all laws and parts of laws coming within the purview of this act, be, and the same are hereby repealed.

N n

(468)

This act shall commence and be in force from and after the passing thereof.

JESSE B. THOMAS,
Speaker of the House of Representatives.
B. CHAMBERS,
President of the Council.

Approved—September 3rd, 1807.
WILLIAM HENRY HARRISON.

CHAPTER LXXVI.

AN ACT to alter the times of holding the Circuit Courts for the Counties of St. Clair and Randolph.

WHEREAS the time of holding the Circuit courts for the counties St. Clair, and Randolph, as now established by law interfere with the General court of the Louisiana Territory, to the great detriment of several suiters in the said courts. **Preamble.**

BE *it therefore enacted by the Legislative Council and House of Representatives, and it is hereby enacted by the authority of the same,* that the circuit courts for the said counties of St. Clair & Randolph, shall hereafter commence and be holden on the following days, viz. For the county of St. Clair on the last Monday of October; and for the county of Randolph on the first Monday of November, yearly and every year. **Courts when holden.**

§ 2. *And be it further enacted,* That all suits and process, returnable to, or depending in the said several Circuit courts, shall **Suits &c continued.**

(469)

be continued over to the said several days and times above mentioned.

This act shall take effect from the passing thereof.

JESSE B. THOMAS,

Speaker of the House of Representatives.

B. CHAMBERS,

President of the Council.

Approved—September 8th, 1807.

WILLIAM HENRY HARRISON.

CHAPTER LXXVII.

AN ACT prescribing the mode of proceeding against absconding Debtors.

§ 1. BE *it enacted by the Legislative Council and House of Representatives, and it is hereby enacted by the authority of the same,* That any Judge of the court of Common Pleas, or Justice

Judge C P or justice of the peace may issue atchmt. of the Peace, on complaint upon oath, stating the amount, or as near as may be, of the debt or demand, and that a debtor is privately removing out of the county, or absconds, so that process cannot be served on him, may grant an attachment against such debtors estate, or to the value of the creditors debt and costs, returnable if the demand is above eighteen dollars, to the next court of Common Pleas having competent jurisdiction, to be directed personally to the Sheriff, under Sheriff or Constable, and where the Sheriff is in-

Where returnable.

To whom directed.

(470)

terested, to the Coroner of the county, to be served on the goods and chattels, lands and tenements, of the debtor, or in the hands of any person indebted to, or having any effects of such debtor in his hands, and shall summon such garnishee to appear at such next court of Common Pleas, to answer on oath what he or they are indebted to, and what effects of such debtor, they have, or had in their hands, at the time of serving such attachment, which being returned executed, the court may compel such garnishee to appear and answer.

Summon garnishee.
To answer on oath.

Judges or justices to take bond &c. § 2. Such Judge or Justice, before granting such attachment, shall take bond and security of the party praying the same, in double the sum to be attached, payable to the defendant, for paying all costs to be awarded him, if the plaintiff be cast in the suit, and also all damages to be recovered against such plaintiff for his suing out such attachment; which bond such Judge or Justice shall return to the said court, on which the defendant may bring suit, and recover agreably to the tenor thereof; and any attachment issued without such bond taken and returned, shall be dismissed, and held illegal and void.

Deft. may bring suit.

Atcht. void without bond.

§ 3. All attachments shall be replevied by giving appearance bail, as in case of a *capias ad respondendum,* and if such bail shall be insufficient, the same remedy shall be had against the Sheriff as if taken on a *capias ad respondendum.*

§ 4. If the plaintiffs demand shall not exceed the sum of eighteen dollars, the Judge or Justice, granting such attachment, shall make it retrnable before himself, directed to

Where returnable.

(471)

the Sheriff of the county, or any Constable within his township, and shall require bond and security in like manner as if above eighteen dollrrs.

To whom di rected.
Bond &c. as before-

§ 5. If any attachment returnable to the court of Common Pleas, or before any judge or justice of the Peace, be returned executed, and the effects be not replevied by giving appearance bail, if the demand exceed eighteen dollars, or giving such security if under that sum, as would be demandable by a Justice on a capias against the defendant, the plaintiff shall be entitled to a judgment for his debt, and may take execution thereon, and the effects attached shall be sold, towards satisfying the plaintiff's judgment, as goods taken in execution on a fieri facias. But if the estate taken under an attachment be replevied as aforesaid, the like proceedings shall be taken thereon to obtain judgment, as if the suit had been instituted by *capias ad respondendum.*

Attacht. exd & no bail or security before justice.

Pltff. to have judgt. & issue fi. fa.

Bail entered how suit con ducted.

§ 6. And where any attachment is returned served in the hands of any garnishee, on his appearance and examination as aforesaid, judgment may be given and execution awarded against him for all money due from him, or property of the defendant in his possession or custody, or a sufficiency thereof to satisfy the plaintiff's debt and costs.

Garnishee ap pearing &c. judgt. & execution may issue vs. him.

§ 7. The sheriff or other officer who shall make sale of any property taken by attachment shall be allowed all reasonable charges for keeping the same by the court or justice before whom the same is tried.

Officers allowed reason able charges for keeping

All law and parts of laws coming within

[472]

the purview of this law, be and the same are hereby repealed.

Repealing clause.

This act shall commence, and be in force from and after the first day of January next.

JESSE B. THOMAS,
Speaker of the House of Representatives.
B. CHAMBERS,
President of the Council.

Approved—September 8th, 1807.
WILLIAM HENRY HARRISON.

CHAPTER LXXVIII.

AN ACT concerning the Territorial Tax, and authoirsing the collection thereof in the County of Randolph.

Preamble.   WHEREAS the auditor of the Territory did not in conformity to the second section of the act entitled "An act for levying and collecting a tax on land and for other purposes," transmit to the assessor of the said county, an abstract of the entries & locations of land in the said county, as obtained by him from the proper land office until after the day of appeal as fixed by law; in consequence whereof the assessment of lands made by the said assessor, were illegal and void: *And whereas* the collector of the said county proceeded to collect some of the taxes on land in said county on the assessment so illegally made, and in some in-

(473)

stances sold the lands of delinquents for non payment thereof: *And whereas* complaints have been made of such irregularities and especially for want of the benefit of a court of appeals.

§ 1. BE *it enacted therefore by the Legislative Council and House of Represeniatives, and it is hereby enacted by the authority of the same,* That the assessment as made by the assessor of the **Assessment** said county of Randolph, and the taxes as far as collected by **made & tax-** the collector, shall be, and the same are hereby declared to **es now col-** be legal and valid. **lected valid.**

Provided nevertheless, that the person or persons whose lands may be so assessed or taxed paid, shall have a right to appeal for any improper assessment, to the court of Appeals hereafter immediately mentioned.

§ 2. *Be it further enacted,* That the Judges or any two of them of the court of Common Pleas of the said county of Randolph shall assemble at the court house or place where the court of the said county is usually holden on the fifteenth day of October next, ensuing, and the collector is hereby required to lay before them the abstract of assessment as made by the auditor, with which he is now furnished, which said court is hereby empowered and authorised to hear any complaint of an improper or partial assessment, which may have been so made by the assessor; to make such alterations therein, as they may think just, and the same being so made by the said court, they shall certify by their clerk to the said collector, who shall thereupon refund to the person or persons entitled in ca-

When judges to meet & collector lay before them abstract of as sessment.

Crt. to hear complts. & make alterations & certi fy to col.

(474)

ses of collection already made and discount in cases where the collection have not yet been made, which certificate of the clerk, accompanied by a receipt of the person or persons receiving, or with whom the discount may be so made in favor of the said collector, shall be a sufficient voucher to entitle him to a credit in the settlement with the auditor, for the amount thereof.

Rect. suffici ent in settle ment with aud.

Provided always, Nevertheless, and it is hereby enacted, that all sales of land heretofore made by the collector of the said county for non payment of taxes, shall and the same are hereby declared to be null and void.

Sales heretofore null.

§ 3. *And be it further enacted,* That the collector shall immediately proceed to collect the taxes in arrear, in the same manner, and pay the same over to the treasurer as is provided and designated in an act passed at the present session en-

Collector to proceed &c. as in cap. 75

titled, "An act authorising the collection of the territorial tax
on land in the counties of St. Clair and Knox.

JESSE B. THOMAS,

Speaker of the House of Representatives.

B. CHAMBERS,

President of the Council.

Approved—September 14th, 1807.

WILLIAM HENRY HARRISON.

(475)

CHAPTER LXXIX.

AN ACT regulating the Fees in the General Court, and for other purposes.

§ 1.   BE *it enacted by the Legislative Council and House of
Representatives, and it is hereby enacted by the authority of the
same,* That from and after the passage hereof, the Clerk of the
General court, and Circuit courts of this Territory, shall not
have, take, ask or demand any other, or greater fee or reward
for services hereafter rendered in suits or proceedings, now
depending, or hereafter to be brought in the General or Circuit
courts, than is, or shall by law be allowed to the respective
Clerks of the courts of Common Pleas, of any county in this
territory, except as now excepted, that they shall respectively
have and receive fifty cents, for any manner, or kind of writ,
except special writs, for which he shall be allowed such additional fee, as the court in their discretion shall think reasonable, reguard being had to the length thereof, which may be severally issued by them; and the Clerk of the General court especially
shall be allowed, ask, demand, and take for taking bond, on issuing
writ of error, or supersedeas, seventy-five cents.

The better to preserve the records and proceedings of the
several courts within this territory, it shall be the duty of the
Clerk of the General court, and the Clerks of the respective
courts of Common Pleas, on the final determination of any suit
to enter on record, in a book which they shall keep for

Marginal notes:

Clks of G C same fees as clks. of C P

Except &c.

Clk. to make up record at full length.

O o

(476)

that purpose all the proceedings and papers filed therein, proceeding had, and also the judgment therein at full length, for which services the Clerk of the General court shall receive the same fee as is allowed to the Clerks of the courts of Common Pleas.

§ 2. *Be it further enacted,* That the respective Sheriffs and Coroners of the several counties in this territory, shall not in like manner, receive or take, ask, or demand, any other, or greater fee for services rendered by them respectively, in the General or circuit, court than is, or may be allowed by law for similar services in the courts of Common Pleas. **coroners fees the same in all courts.**

§ 3. *Be it further enacted,* That no attorney or counsellor at law, shall exact or demand any further or greater fees for services rendered either in the General court or court of Common Pleas, than the following, viz. **Counsellors or attos. fees**

	D C
In all civil actions where the title of land do not come in question	2 50
In all civil actions where the title of lands do come in question	5
For every verbal advice where suit is not depending,	1 25
For every written advice where suit is not depending,	2 50

§ 4. *Be it further enacted,* That the Clerk of the General court, if otherwise duly qualified and admitted according to law, shall be allowed and permitted to practice as attorney at law in the several courts of Common Pleas of this territory. **Clk. of G C practice in inferior crt.**

§ 5. *Be it further enacted,* That the attorney general, or attorney prosecuting the **Atto. gen. or atto. prosecuting pleas.**

(477)

pleas in the different counties shall not in like manner tax up, or charge any other or greater fee than hereafter immediately stated, to wit: Drawing up and attending to an indictment or presentment, five dollars; which fee may be received by the said attorney general, or attorney prosecuting the pleas of the United States, in no other cases than where the defendant shall be lawfully convicted, when it shall be taxed in the bill of costs.

Fees taxed on deft. if convicted.

Clks. of C. P act as clk. of Cir. crt.

§ 6. *Be it further enacted,* That the Clerks of the several courts of Common Pleas in their respective counties shall hereafter act as Clerks of the Circuit courts, which may be holden therein, who shall receive such fees for their services as may, or shall be allowed by law.

Repealing clause.

§ 7. *And be it further enacted,* That all laws and parts of laws coming within the purview of this act, be, and the same are hereby repealed.

JESSE B. THOMAS,
Speaker of the House of Representatives.
B. CHAMBERS,
President of the Council.

Approved—September 14th, 1807.
WILLIAM HENRY HARRISON.

(478)

CHAPTER LXXX.
AN ACT To encourage the killing of Wolves.

Preamble.

WHEREAS the raising of sheep ought to be encouraged by every possible means, and as the distruction of wolves would greatly tend to so desirable an object,

BE *it therefore enacted by the Legislative Council and House of Representatives, and it is hereby enacted by the authority of the same,* That every person within this Territory of the age of ten years and upwards, who shall kill any wolf within six miles of any of the settlements in any county within this territory, shall receive fifty cents for every wolf he shall kill not exceeding six months old, to be adjudged of by the Justice before whom the head shall be taken, and for every wolf of the age of six months and upwards, seventy five cents.

Persons above 10 years killing a wolf

What sum allowed.

§ 2. *And be it further enacted,* That every person claiming such reward, shall produce the head or heads, if more than one, with the ears entire, to a Justice of the peace of the county where such wolf was killed, who shall administer to such person the following oath, viz.

Produce the head & ears & take oath.

I do solemnly swear or affirm, as the case may be, that the head or heads, as the case may be, now produced by me, is the head of a wild wolf, taken and killed by me in the county of within six miles of some one of the settlements within the same, to the best of my knowledge, and that I have not wittingly or willingly spared the life of any bitch wolf in my pow-

Form thereof

(479)

er to kill with a design of encreasing the breed, so help me God.

And every Justice before he administers the foregoing oath shall first read it aloud to the person wishing to receive the same, and also the fourth section of this law: and every Justice before whom such head shall be produced, is hereby empowered and required to administer the foregoing oath, and thereupon grant to the killer, a certificate, reciting his name, the number of heads, and whether they be under or over six months old, the time and place they were killed; which certificate being produced to the court of Common Pleas, who are hereby authorised and required to give such person an order on the county treasurer for the amount to which he or they may be entitled.

Justice to read oath & 4th section.

Grant cert.

C P to grant order.

§ 3. *And be it further enacted,* That any Justice having wolves heads brought before him, shall have the ears cut off in his presence.

J. Have ears cut off.

§ 4. *And be it further enacted,* That if any person or persons, shall receive any reward contrary to the true intent and meaning of this act, the person or persons so offending shall forfeit and pay any sum not exceeding fifty dollars, to be recovered by action of debt, qui tam or by indictment, for the use of the county, before any court having jurisdiction.

Pesons finable.

(480)

This act shall commence and be in force from and after the passing thereof.

JESSE B. THOMAS,
Speaker of the House of Representatives.

B. CHAMBERS,
President of the Council.

Approved—September 14th, 1807.

WILLIAM HENRY HARRISON.

CHAPTER LXXXI.

AN ACT Concerning the Town of Jeffersonville.

Trustees appointed, &c. § 1. BE *it enacted by the Legislative Council and House of Representatives, and it is hereby enacted by the authority of the same,* That the following persons be, and they are hereby appointed trustees of the town of Jeffersonville, to continue in office until the first Monday in May next viz. Thomas T. Davis, James Lemon, Davis Floyd, Marston G. Clark, and Samuel Gwathmey.

Who elect trustees. § 4. *Be it further enacted,* That the holders of lots in the said town, being residents thereof, shall be and they are hereby authorised to elect five trustees annually on the said first Monday in May. That it shall be the duty of the sheriff of **Shff. to adv. election.** the county of Clark, to advertise twenty days previous thereto, at the door of the court house, that such an election will be held, and also to superintend and conduct the same, for

(481)

By who compensated. which services, compensation shall be made him by the trustees.

Trus. appoint clk. & assessr § 3. *Be it further enacted,* That the trustees shall have power to appoint a clerk to their board, and annually to appoint an assessor, whose duty it shall be to value and assess all the **Assessors duty.** lots in the said town, and make return thereof to the trustees having previously taken an oath before some Justice of the

Peace, truly and impartially to perform the same, but in the valuation of said lots, the houses and other improvements erected thereon shall not be taken into consideration. Houses not to be valued.

§ 4. That on the return of each list of taxable property by the assessor, the trustees shall levy a tax thereon, at a rate not exceeding two per centum on the valuation of such lots, for opening the commons and clearing and keeping in repair the streets, and such other improvements thereon as may be thought necessary by the trustees. Trus. lay tax For benefit of town.

§ 5. That the trustees shall annually at the time they appoint an assessor, appoint a collector, who shall, before he enters on the duties of his office, give bond and security, to the trustees, or a majority of them, in double the sum to be collected, conditioned for the faithful collection and accounting for the same according to law. Trus. appt. a collector.
Collec. give bond.

That the said collector shall, by sale of such lots or otherwise collect and account with the trustees of said town for the amount of the taxes with which he shall be charged within four months from the time of his appointment; for the collection of which the Collect tax

(482)

trustees shall allow him seven per cent on the whole amount. Before the said collector shall expose to sale any property for the taxes due thereon, he shall advertise the time and place of sale, for two weeks at the court house door of Clark county, and in one of the public news-papers either at Louisville or within the territory. Per cent allowed.
To adv. sale.

§ 6. On the death, resignation, or removal of any one of the trustees, the same shall be filled by the remaining trustees who shall appoint a successor, to continue in office until the next election. Vacancies how supplied

§ 7. That the trustees of the said town shall have the original plan recorded in the recorders office of Clark county and may, by affixing posts, or stones, at the corner of each square, perpetuate the same. Trus. have orig. plan recorded.
Perpetuate corners.

3 form a board.

§ 8.   That any three of the trustees shall be sufficient to form a board.

JESSE B. THOMAS,
Speaker of the House of Representatives.
B. CHAMBERS,
President of the Council.

Approved—September 14th, 1807.
WILLIAM HENRY HARRISON.

(483)

CHAPTER LXXXII.
AN ACT concerning Vagrants.

Vagrants gamesters & stranglers.

Dissolute life & deserting family.

§ 1.   BE *it enacted by the Legislative Council and House of Representatives, and it is hereby enacted by the authority of the same,* That every person who shall be suspected to get his livelihood by gaming, and every able bodied person who is found loitering & wandering about, not having wherewithal to maintain himself by some visible property, & who doth not betake himself to labour, or some honest calling to procure a livelihood; & all persons who may be found being, and who quit their habitations, and leave their wives and children without suitable means of subsistence, whereby they suffer, or may become chargeable to the county; and all other idle, vagrant and dissolute persons, rambling about without any visible means of subsistence, shall be deemed and considered as vagrants.

Justice to issue wart.

On exam. if a vagrant to be commited or give bond to govr. &c.

§ 2.   When any such person is found in any county, any Justice of the Peace, shall, from information, or from his own knowledge, issue his warrant, to the Sheriff or Constable, to bring such person before him; and if upon such examination it shall appear to such Justice, that he comes within the description of vagrants, agreeably to this act, he shall commit him to the jail of the county, until the next court of Common Pleas, unless he enter into bond to the Governor in the sum of fifty dollars, with sufficient security, to be adjudged of by the Justice, for his appearance before the said court, and there to abide the determination

P p

(484)

thereof. If upon examination it appears to the said court, that such person is within the description of vagrants, and is a minor, they shall direct the Sheriff to bind him to some person of useful trade, or occupation, until he shall arrive at the age of twenty-one years, and if such apprentice desert their masters, they shall be dealt with as other apprentices who leave their masters before the expiration of their apprenticeship. But if such vagrant be above the age of twenty-one years, the said court shall direct the Sheriff to hire him out for any term not exceeding nine months: *Provided however,* That if such person have a wife, or family, within the county, he shall be set at liberty on his entering into bond with approved security, by the court, payable to the Justices thereof, to return to his wife and family, and follow some useful employment, for their maintenance and support. *If minor vagrant how to proceed.* *If desert how dealt with.* *Adult vag. hired out.* *If married may be liberated giving bond &c.*

§ 3. When no person will hire a vagrant when deemed such by the court, or will not take him, only by furnishing him with such diet and clothes as may be necessary for him during his servitude, the court shall order such vagrant to receive any number of lashes not exceeding thirty-nine, on his bare back, and the Sheriff shall see the same executed accordingly. *If no person will take vag abond crt. to order stripes.* *Shff. have sentence executed.*

§ 4. The money arising from the hire of any vagrant shall be applied by the court towards the payment of his debts; but if he shall not be indebted, or owe to the amount of his hire, the same, or the balance thereof shall be paid to such vagrant at the time his service expire; unless he has a wife, or children, in which case it shall be applied to *Hire of vagabond how applied.*

(485)

their use. When any vagrant shall have entered into bond with security as last mentioned, to the Justices, and the penalty thereof shall become forfeited, the court shall direct an execution to issue thereupon against the goods, chattels, lands *Vags. bond forfeited how crt. to procd.*

and tenements of such security, and the Sheriff shall make distress, and collect the amount as on other executions, and the money arising therefrom shall be applied towards lessening the county levy.

§ 5.   All the Justices of their respective counties shall see this act executed, and all Sheriffs and Constables within the several counties shall give information to such Justices of all vagrants that may be within their knowledge, in their respective counties; and grand jurors impannelled for any county shall make presentment of all such persons within the county, as they may suspect to be vagrants agreeably to this act, and upon such presentment the court shall direct some Justice of the Peace to issue his warrant to bring such suspected person before him, and if upon examination it appears that they come within the description of vagrants, the same steps shall be taken against them, as are heretofore directed to be taken against vagrants.

(486)

This act shall commence, and be in force from and after the first day of January next.

JESSE B. THOMAS,
Speaker of the House of Representatives.
B. CHAMBERS,
President of the Council.

Approved—September 14th, 1807.
WILLIAM HENRY HARRISON.

CHAPTER LXXXIII.
AN ACT Concerning the Town of Kaskaskia.

§ 1.   BE *it enacted by the Legislative Council and House of Representatives, and it is hereby enacted by the authority of the same,* That the following persons be, and they are hereby appointed trustees of the town of Kaskaskia, to continue in office until the first Monday in May next viz. Michael Jones, Robert Robertson, George Fisher, John Edgar, and William Morrison.

Marginal notes:
Collected by shff. &c.
Jus see act executed. Shff. & Constable give information of vagrants.
Grand jury present vag.
Crt. direct J. to issue wart.
If vag. proceeded with as before stated.
Trustees appointed, &c.

§ 2. *Be it further enacted,* That the holders of lots in the said town, being residents thereof, shall be and they are hereby authorised to elect five trustees annually on the first Monday in May. That it shall be the duty of the sheriff of the county of Randolph, to advertise twenty days previous thereto, at the door of the court house, that such an election will be holden, and also to superintend and conduct the same, for

Who elect trustees.

Shff. to adv. election.

By who compensated.

(487)

which services, compensation shall be made by the trustees.

§ 3. *Be it further enacted,* That the trustees shall have power to appoint a clerk to their board, and annually to appoint an assessor, whose duty it shall be to value and assess all the lots in the said town, and make return thereof to the trustees having previously taken an oath before some Justice of the Peace, truly and impartially to perform the same, but in the valuation of said lots, the houses and other improvements erected thereon shall not be taken into consideration.

Trus. appoint clk & assessr

Assessors duty.

Houses not to be valued.

§ 4. *Be it further enacted,* That upon the return of such list of taxable property by the assessor, the trustees shall levy a tax thereon, at a rate not exceeding two per centum on the valuation of said lots, for surveying the town, paying the expence of their officers, and clearing, and keeping in repair the streets, and such other improvements thereon as may be thought necessary by the trustees.

Trus. lay tax For benefit of town.

§ 5. *Be it further enacted,* That the trustees, shall annually, at the time they appoint an assessor, appoint a collector, who shall, before he enters on the duties of his office, give bond and security, to the trustees, or a majority of them, in double the sum to be collected, conditioned for the faithful collection and accounting for the same according to law.

Trus. appt. a collector.

Collec. give bond.

That the said collector shall, by sale of said lots or otherwise collect and account with the trustees of the said town for amount of the taxes, within four months from the

Collect tax

(488)

time of his appointment; for the collection of which the trus-

Per cent allowed

tees shall allow him seven per cent on the whole amount. Before the said collector shall expose to sale any property for the taxes due thereon, he shall advertise the time and place of sale,

To adv. sale.

for two weeks at the court house door of Randolph county.

Vacancies how supplied

§ 6. *Be it futher enacted,* That on the death, resignation, or removal of any one or more of the trustees, the same shall be filled by the remaining trustees who shall appoint a successor or successors, to continue in office until the next election.

Trus. have plan recorded

§ 7. *Be it further enacted,* That the trustees of the said town shall have the same surveyed, and the plan thereof recorded in the recorder's office of Randolph county, and may, by affix-

Perpetuate corners.

ing posts, or stones, at the corner of each square, perpetuate the same.

3 form a board.

§ 8. *And be it further enacted,* That any three of the trustees shall be sufficient to form a board.

JESSE B. THOMAS,
Speaker of the House of Representatives.

B. CHAMBERS,
President of the Council.

Approved—September 16th, 1807.

WILLIAM HENRY HARRISON.

(489)

CHAPTER LXXXIV.

AN ACT To alter and amend an act to regulate elections, and an act to establish election districts, in the several counties in this Territory.

Election districts designated by C. P.

§ 1.   BE *it enacted by the Legislative Council and House of Representatives, and it is hereby enacted by the authority of the same,* That there shall be an election district established and held in each and every Township, in the several counties of this Territory, at such place or places therein, as near the centre of population, as may be, as the several courts of Common Pleas of the respective counties, shall by their order designate and appoint, and which they are hereby authorized to do.

§ 2. For the purpose of carrying this act into effect, the **Shff. to appt. deputies.** high sheriffs of their respective counties shall appoint a deputy in each of the townships, other than the one in which he resides, who shall take to their assistance a Justice of the **Take assits.** Peace in the respective counties, at least ten days before the commencement of any election; in case of the non attendance of **Assits. failing to attend others taken.** such Justice, the said sheriff shall take a freeholder of the said towonship as such assistant, which said sheriff and Justice or freeholder, shall be judges of elections in the said township and they shall appoint two poll keepers, who shall take **Appt. poll keepers.** the same oath, perform the same duties and receive the same compensation, as is, or shall be by law allowed; and no judge **Duties and compensatn.** of elections shall be entitled to demand or receive any pay or compen-

(490)

sation for his services; the said deputy sheriff and Justice of **Judges receive no compensation** the Peace or freeholder, as the case may be, shall before they commence the election take an oath, before some Judge or Justice of the Peace, faithfully and impartially to perform their **Take oath.** duties.

§ 3. The said deputy and Judge of elections in the several **Certify polls** townships, other than the one in which the sheriff resides, shall within ten days after the close of such elections, transmit to the high sheriff, the original poll, certified and attested by them, and the poll keepers in the respective townships; who shall thereupon immediately cast up the number of votes given **Shff. declare who is electd** in the whole of the respective townships, for the several candidates, and shall thereupon declare the person or persons having the greatest number of votes, duly elected, and deliver him or them, a certificate thereof, signed with his name; and the **Give certificate thereof.** said sheriff shall cause copies of the polls so taken to be delivered to the office of the secretary of the territory and clerk **copies of poll to sec. & clk. C. P.** of the court of Common Pleas as by law directed.

§ 4. The sheriff shall with one Justice of the Peace, take **Shff. take polls with 1 J. P.** the polls in the townships in which they respectively reside.

§ 5. The poll shall be open but one day in each township, and the elections shall invariably be held in every township in the county on the same day, and no voter shall vote in any other township than the one in which he resides.

§ 6. So much of the law of the territory as requires two Judges of the courts of Common Pleas of the respective counties to

(491)

act as Judges of elections, and all laws and parts of laws coming within the purview of this law, shall be and the same are hereby repealed.

JESSE B. THOMAS,
Speaker of the House of Representatives.
B. CHAMBERS,
President of the Council.

Approved—September 16th, 1807.
WILLIAM HENRY HARRISON.

CHAPTER LXXXV.
AN ACT to Incorporate the Wabash Baptist Church.

WHEREAS it has been represented to the General Assembly, that sundry citizens of Palmyra Township, in the county of Knox, and its neighbourhood have associated themselves together for the purpose of building a Church and thereby propagating the gospel of our blessed Saviour Jesus Christ and in order to establish the said institution upon a more permanent foundation, a charter of incorporation has been prayed for.

§ 1. BE *it enacted by the Legislative Council and House of Representatives, and it is hereby enacted by the authority of the same,* That for the better ordering, ruling and governing the said institution, and the members thereof, there shall be three trustees appointed, who shall continue in office for the term of three years, next succeed-

[margin notes:]
Elec. same day in every township.

Repealing clause.

Preamble.

Trus. continue in office. 3 years.

Q q

(492)

ing; and that Robert Elliot, John Alton, and William Bruce, **Their names**
be, and they are hereby appointed the first trustees of the said
institution, who shall hold their offices for and during three
years from the passing hereof; the said trustees and their successors in office, shall be a body corporate, in deed, fact and **Incorporated**
name, by name and style, of the "Trustees of the Wabash
Baptist Church" and by the same name shall have perpetual **Prosecute &**
succession, and they, and their successors, at all times here- **defend.**
after, by the name of the trustees of the Wabash Baptist
Church, shall be persons able and capable in law to sue, and
be sued, implead, and be impleaded, answer, and being answered unto, in any court of Justice whatsoever, as also to
purchase or receive in gift, for, and in the name, and to and for
the use of the said institution, any real estate, for the purpose **Purchase or**
of erecting the said Church: *Provided,* The same shall not at **receive real**
any time exceed four hundred acres of land. **estate.**

§ 2. *Be it further enacted,* That the office of the said trustees **Vacancies**
shall be supplied by election, to be holden at the said Church, **how supplid.**
by the members of the said institution, triennially, on the first
day of October, counting from the first day of October, now
ensuing.

§ 3. *And be it further enacted,* That the said trustees, or a **Make bylaws**
majority of them, shall have power from time to time, and at
all times hereafter, to meet and make such by-laws, ordinances
and regulations in writing, not inconsistent with the laws of
the United States, or of this territory, as may be necessary
for the government of the said

(493)

institution; which by-laws, shall be in force until the next **How long in**
triennial meeting, and afterwards, unless disagreed to at such **force.**
meeting; by a majority of the members of the said Church, for
which purpose all the by-laws made by such trustees, shall be

Laid before
meeting.
laid before the succeeding meeting, for their approbation or rejection.

This act shall take effect, and be in force from and after the passing thereof.

JESSE B. THOMAS,
Speaker of the House of Representatives.
B. CHAMBERS,
President of the Council.

Approved—September 16th, 1807.
WILLIAM HENRY HARRISON.

CHAPTER LXXXVI.

AN ACT authorising the Territorial Collector of Taxes on Lands in the County of Knox, for the year eighteen hundred and six, to collect the arrearages thereof.

Preamble.
WHEREAS the Assessor and Collector for the county of Knox, did fail to comply with the act of the General Assembly, entitled "An act for the collection of a tax on land, and for other purposes, for the year eighteen hundred and six," in consequence of which failure, there is still due by the said county of Knox, to the territory a considerable sum of money; And whereas, the

(494)

assessment as made in the aforesaid year of one thousand eight hundred and six, was considered illegal, in consequence of which the said Collector has failed to collect the said sum; for remedy whereof,

Assessmt. of
1806 valid.
§ 1. BE *it enacted by the Legislative Council and House of Representatives, and it is hereby enacted by the authority of the same,* That the said assessment, as made by the assessor, for the year eighteen hundred and six, be, and the same is hereby allowed legal and valid to all intents and purposes.

Collec. pro-
ceed to col-
lect arrears.
§ 2. *Be it further enacted,* That the said collector for the year one thousand eight hundred and six, shall, and he is hereby authorised and empowered to proceed immediately to col-

lect the said arrearages of taxes for the year of one thousand eight hundred and six, in the same manner that the Sheriff is directed to proceed in the county of Knox, for the collection of the taxes due in the year eighteen hundred and seven, by an act entitled "An act concerning the territorial tax on land, and authorising the collection thereof in the counties of St. Clair and Knox." As shff. of Knox for 1807 by chap. 75.

§ 3. *Be it further enacted,* That the said assessor shall be allowed the same fee or reward for assessing and collecting the said arrearages of taxes as is allowed to the Sheriff of Knox county, for collecting the taxes due for the year eighteen hundred and seven. Receive compensation.

§ 4. *Be it further enacted,* That the said collector shall pay over the said arrearages of taxes, on or before the first day of February next ensuing, under the same re- Aud pay over under penalty.

[495]

gulations and penalties that the said Sheriff is bound to do by the said act.

This act shall take effect from and after the passing thereof.

JESSE B. THOMAS,
Speaker of the House of Representatives.
B. CHAMBERS,
President of the Council.

Approved—September 16th, 1807.
WILLIAM HENRY HARRISON.

CHAPTER LXXXVII

AN ACT Authorising William Henry Harrison to to sell a tract of Land for the purposes therein mentioned.

WHEREAS, it hath been represented to the general assembly that William Henry Harrison, hath been appointed guardian of Julian and Harriet Hamtramck, the infant daughters of John Francis Hamtramck now deceased, by his first wife, Mary the widow of Nicholas Perrot and that he hath no funds from the proceeds of the estate of the said John Francis Preamble.

Hamtramck deceased to maintain and educate the said Julian and Harriet, and further that the said Julian and Harriet are entitled to a tract of land of four hundred acres, lying and being situate in the county of Knox in this Territory in right of their mother, which has been granted by the government, to the said Ma-

(496)

ry or the first husband Nicholas Perrot of the said Mary as the head of a family, at Vincennes, in the year seventeen hundred and eighty three.

§ 1.   *Therefore be it enacted by the Legislative Council and House of Representatives, and it is hereby enacted by the authority of the same,* That the said William Henry Harrison, be, and he is hereby authorised and empowered to sell and dispose of by public sale, for the best price that can be got, giving twenty days notice of such sale, of the said tract of four hundred acres of land, for the maintenance and education of the said Julian and Harriet, and to make and execute all necessary deeds of conveyance, for securing to the purchaser or purchasers of the said tract of land, the absolute fee simple in the same; *Provided always,* That no such sale shall be made at a shorter credit than six month's payments, to be made by bond and sufficient security and a mortgage on the prmises.

Guardian to sell land.

By pub. sale giving notice

Snpport of children. Execute transfer.

May credit.

Take bond.

JESSE B. THOMAS,
Speaker of the House of Representatives.

B. CHAMBERS,
President of the Council.

Approved—September 15th, 1807.
WILLIAM HENRY HARRISON

(497)

CHAPTER LXXXVIII.

AN ACT Authorising the Administrators of the estate of John Francis. Hamtramck, deceased to sell certain lands for the benefit of his Creditors, Heirs and Representatives.

WHEREAS, it hath been represented to the general assembly of this Territory, that a certain John Francis Ham-

tramck, and Rebecca his wife, by a special deed of trust, bearing date the eleventh day of March eighteen hundred and one,
amongst other things conveyed, certain lands, tenements and **Preamble.**
hereditaments, lying and being situate in the county of Knox,
in the said territory, to Edward D. Turner and Oliver Ormsby,
for the purpose of levying and raising a sum of money to pay
and discharge certain debts in a schedule annexed to the said
deed particularly set forth: *And whereas,* it hath been further
represented as aforesaid that the said Edward D. Turner and
Oliver Ormsby have refused and neglected to do, perform and
discharge the trust reposed in them as aforesaid, and further
that the said John Francis Hamtramck is now deceased.
Therefore

§ 1. BE *it enacted by the Legislative Council and House of
Representatives, and it is hereby enacted by the authority of the
same,* That the administrators of the estate rights and credits of **Adm. to sell**
the said John Francis Hamtramck, deceased, be, and they are **on giving no
tice.**
hereby authorised and empowered, to sell by public sale, for
the best price that can be got, on giving fifteen days public
notice of the time and place of such sale, and dispose of all the
lands, tenements, and heredita-

(498)

ments, belonging, or in any wise appertaining to the estate of
the said John Francis Hamtramck deceased, and lying and
being situate in the said territory, to and for the purposes in
the said deed of trust specified and that the said administrators **Execute**
make and execute all necessary deeds of conveyance to the **deeds**
purchaser or purchasers for securing to him, her or them the
absolute fee simple in the lands, tenements and hereditaments,
that may, or shall be sold and purchased, in manner aforesaid,
that the said administrators be, and they are hereby authorised, after the payment of the debts annexed to the said deed
of trust, to apply the balance of the proceeds of the sale of **After paymt.**
said lands, and also the amount of the sales of such other **of debts how
balance ap**
lands, belonging to said estate within this territory to the **plied.**

payment of the said decedent's other debts, and to and for the use of his heirs and legal representatives: Provided however, that such sale shall be made on a credit of not less than six nor more than twelve months, payable with interest, secured by bond and sufficient security, and also by a mortgage on the premises sold; the proceeds of such sales shall be accounted for by said administrators in a due course of administration.

Credit allowed on giving bond &c.

§ 2. *And be it further enacted,* That the court of Common Pleas, in and for the county of Knox, be and they are hereby authorised and empowered to settle and adjust with the said administrators, all accounts debts, dues and demands incurred by them and which belong, or in any wise appertain to the estate of the said John Francis Hamtramck, deceased.

C P of Knox to settle accounts of administrators.

(499)

This act shall commence, and be in force from and after the passing thereof.

JESSE B. THOMAS,
Speaker of the House of Representatives.
B. CHAMBERS,
President of the Council.

Approved—September 15th, 1807.
WILLIAM HENRY HARRISON.

CHAPTER LXXXIX.

A RESOLUTION for Printing the Laws of the Territory, and the Journals of both Houses of the Legislature.

RESOLVED *by the Legislative Council and House of Representatives,* That Messrs. Genl. W. Johnston, and John Rice Jones, be, and they are hereby appointed a committee, to contract with Messrs. Stout and Smoot, for the printing on the terms proposed by them five hundred copies of the Revised Code, and the Acts passed at the present session of the Legislature; and of two hundred copies of the Journals of both Houses of the Legislature at their present session; that upon making the contract the said committee take from the con-

Committee contract for printing &c.

tractors, bond with solvent security, in the sum of one thousand dollars, for the performance of said work, which bond they shall deposit in the Territorial Secretary's office; and that they be, and they are hereby authorised to take

Take bond &c.

R r

[500]

from the Clerk of the Legislative Council, and that of the House of Representatives, the Journals of their respective houses, and from the office of the Secretary of the Territory, the original Laws or Acts on file in his office, for the purpose of attending to the Printing, collating, and Binding thereof, which when they have done, they shall return the original and cause the copies to be distributed in the following manner:

Take from clks. journals, from secy. original acts.

Attend to printing, &c. & distributing laws.

To the county of Dearborne, forty-five copies.
To the county of Clark, forty-five copies.
To the county of Knox, forty-five copies.
To the county of St. Clair, forty-five copies.
To the county of Randolph, forty-five copies.

Which the said committee shall cause to be conveyed to the Clerks of the courts of Common Pleas of the said respective counties, to be by them distributed; one to each of the Judges of the court of Common Pleas, one to himself, one to the attorney prosecuting the pleas, one to each member of the House of Representatives, and Legislative Council, from his county, one to the Sheriff, one to each Justice of the Peace of his county, one to each Recorder, when not a Clerk, one to each Colonel Commandant, one to each Major, one to each Captain of a company, one to each Adjutant of a regiment and battalion, and one to the Coroner, except the Journals, which shall be distributed by the committee equally to the several counties, being forty to each county, to

Comtee. forward laws to clks. C P Clks. to distribute them

Forward journals.

(501)

the respective Clerks as aforesaid, to be distributed as aforesaid, the expences whereof shall be paid out of the territorial

Clks. distribute them.

Expenee pd. treasury, upon the order of the Auditor, under the certificate of the said committee, and the balance of the whole number thereof, to be by the said committee, deposited in the office of the Secretary of the territory, there to be kept, at the disposal of the Governor. And they are hereby further authorised and empowered to certify to the Auditor the amount to which **Certify in favor of print.** the said Printers may be entitled for doing said work, after the same shall be performed, which shall be a sufficient voucher for the Auditor to audit the same, and for the claimants to receive the amount when in the treasury: *Resolved further,* That the Governor, out of the copies put into the Secretary's office, and at his disposal, deliver one to the Attorney General, one **Govr. give out copies.** to the secretary, one to each of the Judges of the General court, one to the Clerk thereof, keep one himself, one to the Territorial Treasurer, and one to the Auditor.

JESSE B. THOMAS,

Speaker of the House of Representatives.

B. CHAMBERS,

President of the Council.

Approved—September 17th, 1807.

WILLIAM HENRY HARRISON.

(502)

CHAPTER XC.

AN ACT to authorise the Proprietors of Lands in the Lower Prairie, in the County of Knox, to inclose the same, and for other purposes.

§ 1.   BE *it enacted by the Legislative Council and House of Representatives, and it is hereby enacted by the authority of the* **Lower prairie fenced by certain lines.** *same,* That all the lands situate in the prairie below Vincennes, in the county of Knox, and comprised within a boundary line, which shall begin at a point one hundred feet from the high water mark of the river Wabash, on the line dividing the town lots of Vincennes, from the Church lands, and running therewith back from the said river, to the end of the Church lands, thence at right angles with the said line, to a point on the line

dividing the lands of Langedoe, from the land of Bray, at the
end of their concessions; thence with the said dividing line,
towards the river Wabash, until it strikes a point on the same
line, one hundred feet from the said river high water mark:
and thence at right angles with the said line, parallel with the
Wabash, and always at the distance of one hundred feet therefrom, until it strikes and terminates at the said point of beginning, shall on or before the last day of March, one thousand
eight hundred and eight, be enclosed and fenced as in this law
is prescribed.

By what time.

§ 2. *Be it further enacted,* That the said fence shall be made
of good and sufficient rails of ten feet in length, laid horizon-
tally in pannels, in what is commonly called a worm fence,
and shall be at least five feet

Of what fence consist.

(503)

in height exclusive of the rider, above the common level of
the earth.

§ 3. That the rails composing the first two feet of the
said fence from the ground, shall not be placed more than four
inches a part, and the second two feet from the earth, not more
than six inches from each other, nor at a greater distance from
the earth to the lowermost or bottom rail, than three inches:
and at every corner or angle of said fence, such angle shall be
secured by stakes strongly planted in the earth, and sur-
mounted with a rail or rider.

Manner of making.

§ 4. That each and every proprietor of land, within the
said boundary line, shall on or before the last day of March
next, make, and ever after maintain, in good and sufficient repair, a fence as herein prescribed, at both ends of his, her or
their lands, and also his, her or their part of the whole extent
of the fence aforesaid at both sides of the said boundary, which
part shall be ascertained by the Syndic of the field, by apportioning to each and every of them, his or her part thereof, in
proportion to the length of his, her or their concession, within
the said boundary line.

By whom made.

And kept in repair.

Persons refusing how their fence to be made.

§ 5. That if any proprietor or proprietors, shall refuse or neglect to make on or before the last day of March next, his, her, or their proportionate part of the said fence, as is herein provided, it shall be lawful for the said Syndic, forthwith to make, or cause to be made, the part aforesaid, of him, her or them, so failing, at the proper expence and charge of such

& remedy.

delinquent; which expence with costs of suit, may be recovered of such delinquent, by the said Syndic, in

(504)

an action of debt, before any court or magistrate in the said county.

Persons pulling down fence finable &c.

§ 6. That any proprietor or proprietors, or other person who shall pull down, or lay open any part of the said fence, except in the act of repairing the same, he, she or they so offending, shall be trespassers, and shall pay to any proprietor or other person who will sue for the same, not less than one dollar, for each pannel of the said fence such trespasser shall so lay open, and moreover be liable to make good all injury or damages occasioned thereby, to any proprietor or proprietors or other person injured, with costs, to be recovered as aforesaid.

Causing to be burnt any part of fence liable to fine &c.

§ 7. That any proprietor or proprietors, or other person or persons, who shall wilfully or negligently set on fire or cause to be set on fire, any woods, woodland, prairie, grass, leaves or herbage, within or without the said boundary line, and shall not extinguish the same, before any part of the said fence, shall thereby be burt, or otherwise damaged or injured, or any corn, wheat, or other grain, grass, hay, wood, copse, or underwood, growing or being within the said fence, shall thereby be destroyed or injured, he, she or they, so offending shall be, and are hereby declared liable to pay to the Syndic, five dollars for every such offence, and moreover make good all injury, damage or loss as aforesaid, which any proprietor or proprietors, or other person or persons shall thereby suffer, with costs of suit, in any court, or before any magistrate in the said county, as the case may be.

§ 8. That if any proprietor or proprie-

(505)

tors person or persons, who shall at any time or season of the
year, liberate or put to pasture, any horse or horses, cattle
sheep or hogs, within the said boundary line, he, she or they
so offending shall be deemed trespassers, and shall be and they
are hereby declared liable to pay to the syndic, one dollar for
each and every head or creature so liberated or depasturing;
and moreover make good all injury and damages thereby occasioned, to any proprietor or proprietors, other person or persons within the said boundary to be recovered as aforesaid.

Pasturing cattle &c finable &c.

§ 9. That any proprietor or proprietors, or other person
or persons, who shall wilfully or negligently liberate or suffer
to escape, or stray or depasture, over the land of another proprietor or proprietors within the said boundary line, any horse
or horses, ox or oxen, with which he, she or they may have
been performing any labor within the said boundary, without
the consent of such other proprietor or other person first had;
every person or proprietor so offending shall be deemed trespassers, and shall be, and they are hereby declared liable to pay
to the syndic, one dollar for each and every head or creature
so liberated and depasturing, and moreover make good all injury and damages thereby occasioned to any proprietor or proprietors, or other person or persons within the said boundary,
to be recovered as aforesaid.

Suffering creatures to trespass finable &c.

§ 10. That if any horse, mare, colt, cattle, sheep, lambs
or hogs, after this law shall be in force, shall trespass by
breaking into the said fence, the same being made as is hereby
prescribed, each proprietor or proprie-

Trespassing animals in breaking fence how dealt with.

(506)

tors, or other person or persons, being injured thereby, may
seize and distrain such trespassing animal or animals, as in
the second section of a law of the territory, entitled, "An act
concerning trespassing animals."

Lands of non cultivtg. pro prietors let out.

§ 11. That if any proprietors, resident or non resident, shall not cultivate his, her or their lands within the said boundary line or any part thereof, and no representative for him her or them, shall appear, who will undertake to, and with the Syndic, for such non cultivating proprietor or proprietors, that he will conform to the provisions and requisitions of this law, it shall be lawful for the syndic to lease the land of every such non cultivating proprietor or such part thereof for the shortest time he can, to any person or persons who may apply to him therefor, and who will undertake to conform thereto.

May be released from lessee after crop off & compensation made.

§ 12. That such non resident or non cultivating proprietor or proprjetors may enter upon his, her, or their land, at any time during the said term or lease, after the crop then prepared to be sown or planted, or growing on such land shall have been reaped or gathered by such lessee: *Provided,* that such non cultivating proprietor shall make compensation to such lessee for the time not expired of such lease, and that until such compensation shall be made, it shall be lawful for such lessee to occupy and cultivate the land for the term so leased, without the let, hindrance or molestation of such non cultivating proprietor or proprietors.

§ 13. That it shall not be lawful for any proprietor or proprietors, or other person

(507)

Riding or driving cart &c over o- ther's land prohibited.

or persons within the said boundary line, to ride on horse back, or ride or drive any ox or oxen or other cattle, or to drive any carriage, cart plough or harrow, over the land of any other proprietor or proprietors, coming to or going from his her or their land or otherwise, without the consent of such other proprietor or proprietors first obtained, and if any proprietor or proprietors or other person or persons, shall so ride or drive any or all of the horse or horses, ox or oxen, or other cattle, carriages, cart, plow or harrow, he, she or they so offending, shall be deemed trespassers, and shall be, and are hereby declared liable for all the loss, injury or damage, which thereby may be occasioned to all, and every person or persons, cultivating or possessing land within the said boundary line, who may recover the same with costs of suit as aforesaid.

§ 14. The said proprietors, or a majority of them, shall meet at the house of Madame Page, in Vincennes, on the first Monday in November next, and on the first Monday of Movember, annually thereafter, at such house, or place in Vincennes, as the Syndic shall appoint, and elect one of the said proprietors, to be Syndic of the field, for one year, from the day of the said respective elections. The president of said meeting shall within one day thereafter, notify the same to the person so elected, which notification, either verbally, or in writing, shall be deemed sufficient notice of his appointment. And if the person so notified shall refuse or neglect to accept of the appointment of Syndic, it shall be lawful for the

S s

(508)

said president, at any time after such refusal or neglect, to demand and receive from such person the sum of ten dollars, with costs of suit, in any court, or before any magistrate in the said county, which sum so recovered, shall be disposed of by the said proprietors in charitable or other uses. And the payment of such sum, with costs, shall be deemed equivalent to the occupation and service of such appointment, and exonerate the person paying the same from serving as Syndic, until by rotation it shall again become his duty to serve in the said capacity. And the president upon satisfactory evidence of the refusal of acceptance, absence or death, of the person so appointed, shall give notice thereof, as the case may be to the said proprietors, that they may as aforesaid, proceed on such a day as he shall appoint, to elect a successor, so that a vacancy may not continue longer than three days, after failure in any of the said cases.

§ 15. The Syndic shall at each and every season he exercises any of the duties enjoined, take an oath before any magis-

Marginal notes:

Penalty.

To elect syndict.

To be notified.

Penalty on neglect.

How appropriated.

In case of refusal.

Take oath.

trate in the said county, faithfully and impartially to discharge the duties enjoined him by this law.

Apportion fence. § 16.   The Syndic shall ascertain as in this law is prescribed, the proportion of the said fence, which each and every proprietor, resident or non resident, shall make and maintain, designate the place where it shall be erected, the materials of which it is to be made, and the height thereof according to this law, and notify the same to each and every of the proprietors, resident, and to the representatives, if any there be, of all

(509)

Give notice. non resident proprietor or proprietors, within three days after his appointment, as aforesaid.

To erect gates &c. § 17.   That until the proprietors, or two thirds of them shall consent, and make a line of fence on each side of the road, recently laid out through their said lands, by authority of the United States, two gates shall be made and erected, by subscription, under the direction of the first Syndic, one on the line of the said fence, where the said road enters the said enclosure, near the town of Vincennes, and the other, where the said road crosses the line of the said fence, on the southwestward boundary thereof.

Penalty on leaving gates open. § 18.   That any proprietor, or other person, who shall leave both, or either of the said gates open, shall be deemed a trespasser, and shall pay one dollar, with costs of suit, to any person who will sue for the same, before any magistrate in the county, and moreover shall be, and is hereby declared to be liable to each and every proprietor, or person cultivating or possessing land within the said fence, for any damage or injury, he she or they may suffer thereby, with costs, in any court, or before any magistrate in the said county, as the case may be.

Dike when where and how made. § 19.   That it shall be lawful for the proprietors, or a majority of them, on or before the last day of October, one thousand eight hundred and eight, to make, and ever after maintain a dike, or embankment, eight feet wide, at the base, two feet high on a level, and six feet wide on the top, as near the brink, of the high bank of the river Wabash, as may in the opinion of the supervisors thereof be most convenient, to

(510)

extant, of the said dimentions, from the boundary of the town lot of the heirs of Chapard, along the meanders or sinuosities of the bank of the said river, to the aforesaid boundary line of Bray's land; and thence over the most advantageous ground, to the nearest highland, so as to bank out the water of the said Wabash, to the southerly bend of the grand Caulee.

§ 20. That the said proprietors, or a majority of them, shall meet as aforesaid on the first Monday of October, one thousand eight hundred and eight, and on the first Monday of October, annually thereafter, and elect one or more proprietor or proprietors, to be supervisors of the dyke or embankment, for one year from the day of the said elections respectively, in the same manner, and subject to the same penalties, as are herein before prescribed, in the case of Syndics of the field.

Elect superv of dike.

§ 21. That it shall be the duty of every supervisor, to apportion the labour to be performed in making and maintaining the said dike, or embankment, among the said proprietors, in proportion to the number of acres, or parts of an acre of land, in front which each may claim within the said fence, and to notify the same; the place where, the carriages, implements, and tools, wherewith the said labor is to be performed, and the dimensions of the said embankment, or dike, to each and every of the said proprietors, at such time and times, and on such day or days, after the said last Monday in October, one thousand eight hundred and eight, as in the opinion

To apporn. dike.

(511)

of the said supervisor, such labour shall become expedient.

§ 22. That if any proprietor or proprietors, who shall refuse or neglect to perform his her or their proportion of labor in making the said dike embankment, for one day subsequent to the notification of the supervisor, it shall be lawful for the said surpervisor, forthwith to perform or cause to be performed, the part of the labor making and maintaining the said dike or embankment, which such proprietor or proprietors, neglect or refuse to perform,

Penalty on neglect.

at the proper charge and expence of such delinquent or delinquents, which expences with costs of suit the said supervisor is hereby authorised and empowered to recover of every such delinquent in any court or before any magistrate in the county aforesaid, as the case may be.

Supers. their power &c.

§ 23. That the said proprietors and supervisors shall have full power and authority on any unimproved grounds adjacent to the said dike or embankment, to dig any earth, gravel, clay, or stones, to cut down any trees, woods or copses, or bush, which may be found growing in the direction of, or near the dike or embankment, as he, she or they may find necessary for the purpose aforesaid. *Provided,* the same be done with as little damage to the owner or owners of such land as may be.

Road opend. and how.

§ 24. That on or before the first day of January one thousand eight hundred and eight, each and every proprietor of land within the said field, shall open and clear a road twenty feet wide, across his, her or their land, in front between the fence

(512)

and the embankment aforesaid; and until the said first day of January one thousand eight hundred & eight, the road leading from the town to the lower end of the said prairie now used and traveled, called the lower road, shall be and remain common, any thing in this law to the contrary notwithstanding, and if any proprietor or proprietors as aforesaid shall refuse or neglect to open and clear, his, her or their part of the road before mentioned,

Penalty on neglect.

it shall be lawful for the Syndic, to open and clear, or cause to be opened and cleared, the part of every such delinquent, at the expence of, and to recover the value thereof from each and every such delinquent as is herein in other cases mentioned.

Repealing clause.

§ 25. That all acts and parts of acts, heretofore made, and in force in the territory, which may countervene or impair this law or any section, provision or clause thereof, be, and the same is hereby declared to be repealed.

Pld. genl. issue.

§ 26. That if any action or suit shall be brought or instituted against any proprietor or other person for any act or thing done or committed, by him, her or them, in pursuance of this law, such proprietor or other person shall and may plead the general issue, and give this act, and the special matter in evidence.

§ 27. That the lands within the said boundary line of absent or resident non cultivating proprietor or proprietors who shall not by him, her or themselves or some person or persons for them, perform his her or their part of the labor in making and main- **Dike to be made and how.**

(513)

taining the said dike as herein directed, may be leased by the supervisor on the same terms, manner and conditions as are herein-before directed and prescribed in the case of the fence.

§ 28. That it shall be the further duty of the Syndic, at least once in every week, and oftener if circumstance should make it necessary, during his continuance in office, carefully to examine the state of the fence, and if he should find or learn that in any part thereof repairs ought to be made, he shall forthwith give notice to each and every proprietor, whose part of the said fence may in his opinion be out of repair, and each and every proprietor or proprietors, lessee or lesees, who shall fail after such notice, forthwith to repair his, her or their part, agreeably to this law, shall pay to the said Syndic, the charge of repairing the same, with costs of suit, which the Syndic is hereby authorised and required to perform or cause to be performed without delay; and if the Syndic for the time being refuse or neglect to perform his duty, he shall and hereby is declared to be liable to each and every proprietor or lessee for all loss, damage or injury, which he, she or they may suffer by reason of such neglect or refusal, to be recovered as in other cases is hereby provided. **Syndc to visit and repair fence.**

Penalty.

It shall be lawful for all or any of the said proprietors to erect a gate in the line of the said fence at the end of his or their land or where the United States road crosses the same for his, her or their convenience. If any horse or horses cattle or other creature shall enter into the said field by any of the **Propri. may erect gate, but liabie &c**

(514)

said gates, and damage or injury shall thereby accrue to any proprietor or other person, the owner of the gate through which

Have recourse.

such creature or creatures shall have entered shall be, and hereby is declared liable to pay therefor, to the person or persons injured, in the same manner as is herein provided in other cases of trespass. But such proprietor shall have his or her remedy, over against any person or persons, other than his, her or their own family who shall or may occasion such damage by opening the said private gates, and thereby permitting the said creature or creatures to enter into the said field.

Fines how disposed of.

§ 29. That all and every fine or sum of money which shall be levied and paid to the Syndic or supervisor by virtue of this law, not otherwise appropriated shall be accounted for by them respectively to the proprietors at the meeting first succeeding the reception thereof, and shall be disposed of as they or a majority of them who may attend shall direct.

Take oath

§ 30. That each and every supervisor appointed as aforesaid, before he enters upon the duties of his appointment; shall take an oath before any magistrate in the county,

(515)

faithfully and impartially to discharge the duties by this law enjoined.

JESSE B. THOMAS,
Speaker of the House of Representatives.
B. CHAMBERS
President of the Council.

Approved—September 17th, 1807.
WILLIAM HENRY HARRISON.

CHAPTER XCI.

AN ACT to prevent the disposing of Arms, and other Warlike Implements, and Ammunition to Indians and others.

Preamble.

WHEREAS it has been represented to the General Assembly, that there is reason to expect hostilities from some of the neighbouring tribes of Indians, whilst others, more contiguous, seem disposed to preserve the friendship of the United States: *And whereas,* The laws of the United States, do not prevent the sale of arms and ammunition to the peaceful tribes or others within the settled parts of the country, through which, those that may prove hostile, may procure the same.

§ 1. BE *it therefore enacted by the Legislative Council and House of Representatives, and it is hereby enacted by the authority of the same,* That the Executive of the Territory for the time being, be, and he is

Executive prohibit furnishing arms to Indians.

T t:

(516)

hereby authorised and empowered by proclamation to prohibit the furnishing by sale, gift, or otherwise, all, & every species of warlike weapons, and impliments; ammunition or warlike stores, to any Indian or Indians, dwelling within, or without the limits or lines of the several counties in this Territory, when in his opinion the publick welfare and safety may require such prohibition.

§ 2. *And be it further enacted,* That any person or persons, who shall directly or indirectly, by gift, present, donation, loan, sale or otherwise furnish and provide, or have furnished and provided any Indian or Indians, with any article of ammunition, such as flints, powder, lead or balls, or with any warlike impliments or deadly weapons, such as knives, spears, battle axes, tomehawks, pistols, fusils, rifles, smooth bores, or muskets, contrary to the proclamation of the Executive, as aforesaid, every person or persons, so offending, shall, upon conviction by indictment or presentment, in any court of record in this Territory, be fined in any sum not exceeding one thousand dollars, be whipped publickly, any number of stripes, not exceeding one hundred well laid on, and be imprisoned for a term not exceeding five years, at the discretion of the court before whom the same may be tried, and moreover, shall stand committed, after having received the stripes, until the fine and costs be paid.

Persons violating how punished.

This act shall take effect from and after the passing thereof, and shall continue in

How long in force.

(517)

force until the end of the next session of the General Assembly.

JESSE B. THOMAS,
Speaker of the House of Representatives,
B. CHAMBERS,
President of the Council.

Approved—September 17th, 1807.
WILLIAM HENRY HARRISON.

CHAPTER XCII.

AN ACT for Levying and Collecting a Tax on Land and for other purposes.

Crt. C. P. to appt. an assessor. § 1. BE *it enacted etc.* That the courts of Common Pleas of the several counties in this Territory, shall within fifteen days after the first day of January next, and within fifteen days after the first day of January quadrennially thereafter, or at any special court by them to be appointed for that purpose, which they are hereby authorised at any time to hold, shall appoint an Assessor for the purposes hereafter mentioned, each of whom shall, before they begin the duties of their respective office take and subscribe **Assessor to take oath.** the following oath or affirmation, before any Judge or Justice of the said county, viz.

Form. "I   do swear or affirm, as the case may be, that as Assessor for   I will to the best of my skill and judgment, deligently and faithfully execute the duties

(518)

of the office without favor, affection or partiality, and that I will do equal right and justice, to the best of my knowledge and understanding, in every case in which I shall act as Assessor,—So help me God."

Keep copy & deliver one to clk. C. P. A certificate of which oath or affirmation shall be delivered to the Assessors, respectively, and a copy thereof transmitted without delay to the Clerk of the court of Common Pleas of the county, to be by him filed in his office; in the case of the death, **Death &c of assessor supplied by C P** refusal to act, resignation, or removal from the county of the said Assessor, the said court of Common Pleas, shall, as soon as may be thereafter, at any special court to be held for that purpose, appoint a person to supply such vacancy, who shall take and subscribe the same oath or affirmation as the case may be, as by this act is directed to be taken and subscribed by each Assessor: *Provided always,* That no Sheriff, or deputy Sheriff of any county, shall be eligible to exercise the duty of Assessor under this act.

Successor to take oath.

Shff. cannot be assessor.

§ 2. It shall be the duty of the Auditor, and he is hereby authorised and empowered to apply for, and procure from the proper offices, an abstract of all the entries and locations, and purchases made by individuals from the United States of lands in the several counties in this Territory, noting where, and on what creeks, water courses, &c. such entries and locations, and purchases have been made, with the name of the persons for whom entered and located, and by whom purchased from the United States; and it shall be the duty of the Auditor to transmit the said abstracts of entries and lo-

Auditor procure abstract of entries &c

(519)

cations of lands to the Clerks of the respective counties, by the first day of January next, and the first day of January, quadrennially thereafter; which Clerks shall deliver the said abstracts to the respective Assessors, as soon as appointed.

Deliver same tg clks. C P

To be deld. to assessors.

§ 3. The said Assessors in the several counties shall, and they are hereby empowered and required as hereinafter mentioned, to receive from each and every person and persons, residing in the several counties, and owning lands in the same counties, a list under oath, which the Assessor is hereby empowered to administer, of his, her, or their name or names, and of the lands which he, she or they claim in the said county, either by patent, entry, deed of conveyance, bond for conveyance, or other evidence of claim or purchase from the United States, which the Assessor shall set down in writing, and thereupon the said Assessor shall make a valuation of each tract of land per hundred acres, according to the quality of the soil, and its relative situation, which he at the same time shall signify to the land holders, but in making such assessment and valuation houses, barns, and other improvements shall be excluded.

Assess. to receive list under oath, of lands.

Assessor set down in writing to make valuation informing owner thereof.

Assessor to adv. for meeting take list. § 4. The said Assessor shall advertise at the county town, and also in the most publick place in each and every township in their counties, that he will attend at a convenient place therein to be mentioned, and as near as may be, to the centre of population in such township, not within twenty days of such advertisement, in order to receive of each person resident in said township, a list of all the lands which such per-

(520)

son owns, by any, or either of the ways before mentioned, in the **Persons to at tend.** said county, and the said persons are hereby required to attend at such time and place in their respective townships therefor accordingly.

Assessor may receive list after. § 5. In case any such inhabitant shall not attend at the time and place notified by the assessor, to give in a list of his or her taxable lands in the said county as above mentioned, it shall and may be lawful for the assessor to receive his or her list at any time, provided such person tenders such, his or her list and makes oath to the justness of it within ten days thereafter, and in case of **Owner failing, asser. to list.** failure, the said assessor shall proceed to list such person or persons lands in the said county, agreeably to the best information he may possess.

For frandu lent list or failing to list fined. § 6. If any inhabitant shall neglect or refuse to render such account, or shall render a false or fraudulent account, he shall be fined to the use of the territory in any sum not exceeding fifty dollars, with costs, to be recovered in any court having competent jurisdiction by action of debt in the name of the assessor.

Non-residt. lands to be listed. § 7. If any non resident claiming lands in this territory, either by entry, patent, deed for conveyance, bond for conveyance, or other evidence of claim, his or her agent or attorney, shall neglect or refuse to list his or her lands with the assessor of the county where such lands may have been entered and located, before the tenth day of March next, and the tenth day of March, quadrennially **Case neglect assesr. to list.** thereafter agreeably to the requisitions of this act, then the assessor shall immediately proceed to list

(521)

and make a valuation of the lands of such non residents, that may be in his county in the manner required by the third section in this act.

§ 8. The said assessors respectively shall on or before the first day of April next and the first day of April quadrennially thereafter make a fair list of all the lands in their respective counties in the form following.

Assesr. make out list.

Persons names in alphabetical order.

Date of receiving.

Quantity.

Water course.

By what title.

Valuation per hundred acres.

Amount of tax | Total.

Form.

Which list they shall deliver to the Clerks of the respective courts of Common Pleas, on or before the last day of April, and the last day of April, quadrennially thereafter.

Deliver to clks. C P

Crt. C P to meet.

§ 9. The Judges of the court of Com-

(522)

mon Pleas, or any two of them shall assemble at the court house of their proper county on the first Tuesday of the month of May next, and the first Tuesday of the same month quadrennially

Clks. lay before them list &c.

thereafter, and the Clerks shall lay before them the said abstracts of assessment and valuation of lands so made by the said Assessors, in manner and form aforesaid; and the said Judges shall, and they are hereby empowered and authorised to hear any com-

Crt. to hear complts. &c.

plaints of improper or partial assessment or valuation of lands, which may have been made by the said Assessors, and to make such alterations therein as they, or a majority of them, shall think reasonable and just.

Abstracts being corrected clks. make 2 copies.

§ 10. When the abstract of assessment for the respective counties, shall be thus revised and corrected, the Clerks of the said courts, shall make out two fair and correct transcripts thereof,

How disposed of.

one of which they shall deliver to the Sheriffs of the respective counties as Collectors therein by the 15th day of May next, and the fifteenth day of May, quadrennially thereafter, and the

Orig. cert. by crt. kept in office.

other they shall regularly transmit to the Auditor of the Territory, within two months thereafter, and the original abstract with such alterations and corrections as may have been made by the said Judges, certified by the said Clerks, shall by them be filed in their respective offices.

Penalty on assesr. for ne glect.
Penalty on clk. for ne-glect.

§ 11. If any Assessor shall neglect or refuse to perform the service and duty required by this act, he shall for every such neglect or refusal, be fined in any sum not exceeding three hundred dollars; and if any Clerk, shall neglect or refuse to perform the

(523)

service and duty by this act required, he shall for every such neglect or refusal, be fined in the sum of one hundred dollars, which

Use of tery.

fines shall be recovered with costs, by information or indictment, to, and for the use of the territory.

Compensation to clk.

§ 12. The said Clerks shall receive for the performance of the duties required herein, the sum of twelve dollars, to be paid out of the territorial treasury.

§ 13. The Assessors respectively shall for each tract they may list or assess, receive five cents, to be paid out of the territorial treasury.

Compensation to assesr.

§ 14. The said rate or assessment so made on the lands in this territory shall continue to be the valuation thereof for four years thereafter without any other or further assessment or valuation, when a new valuation shall be made in manner before mentioned.

Quadrenl. as sessmts. and valuation.

§ 15. The Auditor shall annually, and every year, by the first day of January procure from the proper officers an abstract of the lands bought by individuals from the United States, noting therein the range, township, section or quarter sections thereof which abstract he shall without delay forward to the Sheriffs of the several counties who shall annually add such lands to their assessments of the former year, and rate the same at two dollars per acre, and the Auditor shall in his books charge the said Sheriffs respectively, with the additional amount of taxes due on such lands at the rate aforesaid.

Auditor procure list

Forward 'em to shff.

Shffs. make ann. adtons.

§ 16. All the lands in this territory, shall

V v

(524)

be assessed at the rate of twenty cents for every hundred dollars of the value thereof, estimated in the several manners before mentioned.

§ 17. The Sheriffs of each county shall, by the fifteenth day of July, annually, demand payment of the taxes, or sum assessed on each inhabitant in his county, in person, or by notice in writing, left at his or her usual place of residence.

Demand paymt. &c.

§ 18. In case of non payment of taxes by the time appointed, it shall be the duty of the Sheriff to levy and collect the tax so in arrears, by a sale at the court house door of his county, of the tract of land for which the said tax shall be in arrear, or so much thereof as will bring the tax due thereon, to be laid off in form of a square or parallelogram, in some corner of the tract designated by the Sheriff at the time of sale: *Provided always,* That if the

Sell land after adv.

How laid off

How land re deemed. owner of any tract, or tracts of land, for which the said tax shall be in arrear, or any person for him, shall on the day on which the said land shall be advertised for sale, as hereafter mentioned, tender and deliver to the Sheriff at the place of sale, as hereafter mentioned, goods and chattels sufficient to make the said tax, so in arrear, then the said Sheriff shall not sell the said land, or any part thereof, but shall make, and levy the said tax in arrear by a publick sale of such goods and chattels, rendering the overplus. if any, to the owner of such land, or such person for him.

§ 19. It shall be the duty of the Sheriff to give notice of the time and place of the

(525)

Shff. notify judge C P of sale. sales of the land for the non payment of taxes, to one of the Judges of the court of Common Pleas of the county in which the land lies, at least ten days before said sales, and it shall be the **Compensation to judge.** duty of the said Judge to superintend the said sales, and prevent any fraud or collusion in the same; the said Judge shall receive for each days attendance two hundred cents, to be laid on the land sold by the Sheriff and collected by him, and paid to the said Judge.

§ 20. Every collector making such sale as aforesaid, shall, **Shff. after sale make return to clk. C P &c.** within twenty days thereafter, make return thereof to the Clerk of the court of Common Pleas of the county, where the said lands may lie, in which return he shall particularly state every circumstance and expence attending the same, and if any Sheriff shall **Penalty for fraud or neglect.** fail to make said return, or shall charge other, or greater fees, either for himself or the Judge, than allowed by law, he shall be liable to be fined the sum of thirty dollars, to be recovered by motion, in said court, by the party grieved.

§ 21. Prior to any sales being made of the lands either of **Shff. adv. before sale.** residents or non resident delinquents, the Sheriff shall give at least forty days notice, by advertising at the county seat, and in some publick news-paper, either in the Territory, or in the states of Kentucky, and Ohio, on the most reasonable terms he can for three several times, of the time and place of such sale.

§ 22. It shall be the duty of the Sheriff to receive any arrearages of taxes, at any time before the sale commences: *Provided* such delinquent pays him the additional sum of five cents per tract for his own use.

May receive tax &c. before sale.

(526)

§ 23. Where any tract of land is not sold as aforesaid, for the want of buyers, it shall be the duty of the Sheriff to advertise as aforesaid, and expose the same to sale at each successive court of Common Pleas, until the land shall be sold, or the tax thereon with costs be paid.

Land unsold again adv.

§ 24. When any lands are sold as aforesaid, it shall be the duty of the Sheriff to give the purchaser or purchasers, a certificate of the tracts or parts of a tract of land sold, and for what sum, which certificate shall vest all right, title and interest of the proprietor, in the purchaser and his heirs, (subject to the proviso of redemption hereafter mentioned) but it shall not be lawful for the Sheriff, or his deputy, directly or indirectly, to purchase any land or lands, sold under the authority of this act.

Give purcha. ser certificte.

No shff to purchase.

§ 25. *Provided always,* And it is hereby declared and enacted, that when any lands have been or in future may be sold for the non payment of taxes, whether belonging to a resident or non resident, it shall and may be lawful for any of the said persons within the period of two years from the time of the sale, of such land to redeem the same by paying the purchase money, with one hundred per cent per annum thereon, and upon tender of the said purchase money with interest, within the aforesaid period to the said purchaser or his agent, if either of them live within the county in which the land lies, but if not, then he or she shall by advertisement in some public newspaper in this Territory, if one is published therein, if not, in some newspaper nearest to the place where the land lies, at least for the

Land sold, when & how redeemable.

If purchaser not found

(527)

space of three weeks, appoint a time, when he, she or they will attend at the clerks office of the county in which the said land lies, where the said purchase money and interest will be tendered

owner to adv Appoint time to attend.

and paid if the purchaser or his agent will attend to receive it, the said advertisement to be published at least six months before the expiration of the said two years, and if neither the purchaser nor his agent will attend at the time and place mentioned in the aforesaid advertisement, then his title shall be vacated and become void.

Provided, That if the said purchaser shall fail to attend to receive the same, it shall and may be lawful for the said owner or proprietor, his agent or attorney to deposit the same in the hands of the Clerk of the Common Pleas of the said county for the use of the said purchaser, taking a receipt from the said Clerk therefor.

§ 26. From the time of assessment the territory shall have a lien on any tract of land for the taxes due thereon, which shall remain until the taxes are paid.

§ 27. When any non resident may have transfered, or may hereafter transfer his or her claim to land in this Territory, it shall be lawful for his or her sub-claimant, agent or attorney, to enter the same within the time prescribed, for listing lands by this act with the Clerk of the court where the lands lie, who shall keep a book for that purpose, and such person shall be chargeable with the taxes on such lands thereafter; each person having such transfer made shall pay the clerk six cents for his own use.

§ 28. It shall be the duty of the sheriff to pay

(528)

the tax money which he shall have received, to the treasurer of the territory, by the thirteenth day of November every year, and for the monies so paid the treasurer shall give a receipt, which shall be a sufficient voucher, and exonerate and discharge the said sheriff for the amount therein contained.

§ 29. The sheriff shall have seven per cent upon all monies which he shall collect under the authority of this act, to be discounted with him by the treasurer of the territory.

§ 30. It shall be the duty of the auditor to publish such extracts from this law as relates to the time and manner of listing lands in this territory, belonging to, or claimed by non-residents,

and also the times and manner of paying and collecting the taxes
in one newspaper within this territory for three weeks to commence on the first week of March next, and the expences thereon,
shall be defrayed out of the treasury of the territory, provided
the same does not exceed one dollar per square.

§ 31. The several assessors of each county, shall give bond **Assessor give bond &c.**
to the court of Common Pleas, with one or more sureties to be
approved of by the said court in the sum of five hundred dollars
for the use of the territory, conditioned for the faithful perform-
ance of the service and duty of the assessors, as required by this **Certified and recorded.**
act, which bond, the due execution thereof being proved before
and certified by a Judge of the county wherein it may be executed,
shall be recorded in the office of the secretary of the territory, and
copies thereof legally exempli-

(529)

fied by the said secretary, shall be legal evidence in any court of
law, in any suit against such assessor and his securities.

§ 32. Each sheriff shall give bond in the sum of three **Shff. give bond.**
thousand dollars with similar sureties for the same purpose and in
like manner, as is provided for in case of assessors in the preceding
section, and the said bond shall be authenticated in the same manner and for similar purposes as is before provided for in case of
assessors.

§ 33. If any or either of the days before mentioned as afore- **Duty fallg. on sunday be performed next day.**
said shall fall on Sunday, the duties required to be performed as
aforesaid, on any or either of the said days, shall commence on
the day following.

§ 34. All and every person or persons in this territory, who **Billd. tables to be enterd. Taxed.**
shall erect or keep a billiard table within the same, shall annually
on the first day of January or within one week after erecting
such billiard table, enter the same with the sheriff of the respective
counties, and it shall be the duty of such collector, at the same
time and in the same manner as is pointed out by this law to collect the tax on land to receive & collect from each person having
entered such billiard table, the annual sum of fifty dollars to be

paid and accounted for by the said collector in the same manner as the other revenue taxes are accounted for.

Neglect to enter fined.

§ 35. If any person or persons who shall so keep or erect any such biliard table shall neglect or refuse to enter the same with the said sheriff in the time before mentioned, he or she so offending, shall on conviction by by presentment or indictment, be fined in

(530)

any sum not less than fifty dollars nor more than one hundred with costs.

Shff. make sale of goods &c. giving notice.

§ 36. In case of non payment of the said tax, on the day whereon the same ought to be paid, the Sheriff shall levy the same by distress and sale of the delinquents goods and chattels, having previously given ten days notice of the time and place of such sale, and the territory shall have a lien on the said Billiard table,

Lien on table

Audited accounts recd. by sheriff.

for the said taxes; all audited accounts against the territory, shall be received by the Sheriffs as Collectors in payment of taxes.

Repealing clause.

§ 37. All laws and parts of laws, coming within the purview of this act, shall be, and the same are hereby repealed.

JESSE B. THOMAS,
Speaker of the House of Representatives,
B. CHAMBERS,
President of the Council.

Approved—September 19th, 1807.
WILLIAM HENRY HARRISON.

CHAPTER XCIII.

A RESOLUTION concerning the Collection of certain Land Tax in the County of Dearborn.

Preamble.

WHEREAS the Assessor of land for the county of Dearborn, has assessed the lands of several persons in the said county, for the tax due and payable for the year one thou-

(531)

sand eight hundred and six, who at the time of such assessment made, had not purchased the same from the United States: and some of the said persons have paid the tax assessed on them, to the Collector.

RESOLVED *therefore by the Legislative Council and House of Representatives,* That the Collector of the land tax, for the said county of Dearborn, reimburse all those persons, who, (according to the abstract furnished by the Auditor to the Assessor of the said county, purchased their lands from the United States, after the twelfth day of February, one thousand eight hundred and six) have paid the taxes on such lands so improperly assessed, for the year one thousand eight hundred and six, the whole amount thereof by him received; and that the said Collector do desist from further proceeding in the collection of the tax from those persons who were not owners of their said lands prior to the said twelfth day of February of that year.

Resolved also, That the Treasurer of the Territory, in settling the accounts of the said Collector, do give him credit for the said amount, reimbursed, or defalked, in

W w

(532)

conformity to the provisions of this resolution.

JESSE B. THOMAS,
Speaker of the House of Representatives.
B. CHAMBERS,
President of the Council.

Approved—September 19th, 1807.
WILLIAM HENRY HARRISON.

CHAPTER XCIV.

AN ACT allowing Compensation to the Members of the Legislative Council and House of Representatives of the Indiana Territory, and to the Officers of both Houses for the present Session.

§ 1. BE *it enacted by the Legislative Council and House of Representatives, and it is hereby enacted by the authority of the same,* That each and every member of the Legislative Council, and House of Representatives, shall be entitled to, and receive out

Margin notes:

Collector to repay taxes, to certain persons.

And desist from collecti on of other similar taxes

Treasnrer to give credit.

Compensation to members.

of the Territorial Treasury, upon the certificate of the Auditor, for each and every days attendance on the Legislature at the present session, the sum of two dollars, and shall moreover be allowed the sum of two dollars for every twenty miles travel, to, and from the seat of Government, to their places of residence by the most usual road.

§ 2. *Be it further enacted,* That the

(533)

Clerk of the Legislative Council, and that of the House of Representatives, shall in like manner receive for their respective services at the present session, the sum of three dollars and fifty cents each per day.

Specific appropriations.

§ 3. *Be it further enacted,* That the door keeper of both houses at the present session shall in like manner receive the sum of one dollar and fifty cents per day, for each and every days attendance on the two houses as such door keeper.

Compensation on L C certified by President

To H R by speaker.

Andited by anditor.

§ 4. *And be it further enacted,* That the compensation which shall and may be due to the Members and Officers of the Legislative Council, shall be certified by the President thereof; and that which shall and may be due to the Members and Officers of the House of Representatives, as also the Door Keeper, shall be certified by the Speaker thereof, which certificate shall be to the Auditor sufficient evidence of claim, and he shall thereupon issue certificates to the several Members and Officers, aforesaid, payable at the treasury of the territory, as in other cases.

JESSE. B. THOMAS,
Speaker of the House of Representatives,
B. CHAMBERS,
President of the Council.

Approved—September 19th, 1807.
WILLIAM HENRY HARRISON.

(534)

CHAPTER XCV.

Specific appropriation.

RESOLVED *by the Legislative Council and House of Representatives,* That John Rice Jones and John Johnson, be allowed twelve dollars each, for superintending the printing of the Laws passed at the last Assembly, and distributing the same to the different counties.

JESSE B. THOMAS,
Speaker of the House of Representatives.
B. CHAMBERS,
President of the Council.

Approved—September 19th, 1807.
WILLIAM HENRY HARRISON.

CHAPTER XCVI.
A Joint *RESOLUTION* of both Houses.

RESOLVED, That John Rice Jones and Genl. W. Johnston be a Committee to make an Index to the Revised Code and the

Duty of com mittee.

(535)

Laws passed at this Session of the Legislature, and also Marginal Notes.

JESSE B. THOMAS,
Speaker of the House of Representatives.
B. CHAMBERS,
President of the Council.

Approved—September 19th, 1807.
WILLIAM HENRY HARRISON.

CHAPTER XCVII.
AN ACT Making appropriations for the ensuing year.

§ 1.   BE *it enacted by the Legislative Council and House of Representatives, and it is hereby enacted by the authority of the same,* That the sum of one thousand dollars shall be and the same is hereby appropriated for contingent expences, and that all the monies which shall be received into the territorial treasury, except as above appropriated for contingent expences, shall be a general fund for all monies allowed by law, which shall not be directed to be paid out of the contingent expences.

Contingent fund.

General fund.

§ 2.   *Be it further enacted,* That there shall be allowed and paid to the printers for the Territory for printing five hundred

Appropriation to printers, &c.

copies of the revised code, and the acts passed at the present session, and two hundred copies of the journals of both houses of the legislature of the present session, a sum not

(536)

exceeding five hundred and fifty dollars, to be paid out of monies allowed for contingent expences; the residue or so much thereof as may be necessary of monies allowed for contingent expences, shall be subject to payment of monies on the order of the governor for expresses and other incidents which may be necessary and cannot be foreseen by the legislature, and to the order of the joint committee of both houses for the distribution of the journals and laws, of the Territory, a statement whereof shall be severally by the said governor and the said committee, laid before the legislature at their next session.

Residue snbject to order of govr. & committee.

Make statement to next session.

Specific appropriations.

§ 3. *And be it further enacted,* That there shall be allowed and paid out of the general fund, to the following persons the following sums of money, to wit:

To the territorial auditor one hundred and fifty dollars:

To the said auditor for stationary seven dollars and ninety one cents, as a full compensation for his services, and for a case which he is hereby directed to procure, to contain the territorial papers and books and for the necessary stationary for the use of his office:

To the territorial treasurer one hundred dollars:

To each of the clerks employed by the territorial auditor to assist him in making out the abstracts of land for the counties of St. Clair and Randolph for the present year, twenty dollars:

To Charles Kilgore, register of the land office at Cincinnati, state of Ohio, for making out the list of lands from his office for

(537)

Specific appropriations

the present year, seventeen dollars and fifty cents:

To Michael Jones register of the land office for the district of Kaskaskia for making out the abstracts, lists, and returns of lands in the counties of St. Clair and Randolph, for the present year, one hundred and four dollars and eighty cents:

To the county of Knox for house rent to the end of the present session of the legislature, fifty dollars;

To messrs. Bullitt and Smith for stationery furnished at the present session, twenty one dollars and ninety six cents.

To messrs. John Rice Jones and John Johnson, for revising the laws of the territory agreeable to a resolution of the last session of the legislature, two hundred and fifty dollars.

To John Rice Jones for making out the lists and abstracts of land in the county of Knox for the year eighteen hundred and five and six, seventy five dollars.

To Johnathan Jennings, as an assistant to the clerk of the house of representatives at this session for copying several parts of the revised code as amended, six days, fifteen dollars.

To John D. Hay, as an additional assistant clerk, for copying as above, four days ten dollars.

To Thomas M'Giffin, as an assistant clerk to the clerk of the legislative council, at this session for copying as above, six days fifteen dollars.

To George Wallace, jr. as an additional assistant clerk, for copying as above two

(538)

days and one half six dollars and twenty five cents.

To Peter Jones, Reuben Anderson, and William Jones, as additional assistant clerks, for copying as above, six days, fifteen dollars.

Specific appropriations

To Joshua Bond, for making a table and bench for the use of the Legislative Council at this session, seven dollars.

To John D. Hay, for a bench for the use of the House of Representatives, two dollars.

To Samuel M'Connell, as an assistant clerk to the clerk of the Legislative Council, for copying as above, two days, five dollars.

To Samuel Hays, as an assistant clerk to the clerk of the House of Representatives, for copying as above, one day, two dollars and fifty cents.

JESSE B. THOMAS,
Speaker of the House of Representatives.
B. CHAMBERS,
President of the Council.

Approved—September 19th, 1807.

WILLIAM HENRY HARRISON.

(539)

CHAPTER XCVIII.

AN ACT declaring that the Laws of the Territory as Revised and Reported to the Legislature, shall, with the several additions, amendments, and alterations made to the Original Laws have force in the Territory.

Preamble.

WHERFAS The whole body of the Laws of this territory, to the beginning of this session, have in pursuance of a resolution passed at the last session of the Legislature entitled "A resolution for revising the Laws of this territory, and for other purposes," been carefully compiled and revised, and the said revisal laid before both houses of this Legislature, and approved of,

And whereas, Both houses of the Legislature having taken the original Laws, from which the said revisal was made, into consideration, have made several alterations, additions and amendments thereto,

Laws tepealed.

laws in force

§ 1.   BE *it therefore enacted by the Legislative Council and House of Representatives, and it is hereby enacted by the authority of the same,* That all the Laws and parts of Laws in force in this territory, at the beginning of this session of the Legislature, shall be, and the same are hereby repealed, and that the revisal of the said Laws as made by John Johnson and John Rice Jones, shall, with the several additions, alterations and amendments made by the present Legislature, have full force and effect in the territory; and that those laws so revised altered and amended shall, with the Laws passed at this Session of the Legislature, be

Y y

(540)

the only statute Laws in force in this territory.

Provided always, That all the officers now in commission in the territory, shall hold and exercise the duties of their several offices, under the Laws heretofore in force, in the territory, in the same manner as if this Law had not been made: *And provided also,* That all suits and prosecutions heretofore instited, under, or by authority of any of the said Laws, may be prosecuted to judgment and execution thereupon.

Officers remain in office.

Suits &c. prosecuted under former laws.

JESSE B. THOMAS,
Speaker of the House of Representatives.
B. CHAMBERS,
President of the Council.

Approved—September 19th, 1807.

WILLIAM HENRY HARRISON.

(340.)

the only statute Laws in force in the territory.

Officers remain in office.

Provided always, That all the officers now in commission in the territory, shall hold and exercise the duties of their several offices, under the Laws heretofore in force, in the territory, in the same manner as if this Law had not been made: And provided

Suits &c. prosecuted under former laws.

also, That all suits and prosecutions heretofore instituted, under, or by authority of any of the said Laws, may be prosecuted to judgment and execution thereupon.

JESSE B. THOMAS,
Speaker of the House of Representatives.

B. CHAMBERS,
President of the Council.

Approved—September 16th, 1807.
WILLIAM HENRY HARRISON

HAVING carefully Collated the foregoing Printed Laws, with the Original Laws and Acts in Manuscript, taken from, and now returned to the Territorial Secretary's Office,—we do certify that they are truly Printed.

GENL. W. JOHNSTON,
JOHN RICE JONES,   } *Comtee.*

Vincennes, May, 1808.

INDEX.

A

INDEX

INDEX

iii

B

INDEX

iv

C

Z z

INDEX

v

INDEX

INDEX

vii

INDEX

D

INDEX

E

INDEX

INDEX

A a 2

INDEX

INDEX

K

INDEX

INDEX

INDEX

xvii

INDEX

N

INDEX

INDEX

B b 2

INDEX

INDEX

INDEX

INDEX

INDEX

INDEX

INDEX

ACTS

OF

ASSEMBLY

PASSED AT THE SECOND SESSION

OF THE

SECOND GENERAL ASSEMBLY

OF THE

INDIANA TERRITORY.

Begun and held at the TOWN of VINCENNES, on
MONDAY the twenty sixth day of SEPTEMBER,
A. D. one thousand eight hundred and eight.

————: * * * * :————

*Printed by Authority, and under the Inspection of
the Committee.*

————: * * * * :————

VINCENNES,

PRINTED BY ELIHU STOUT,

Printer to the Territory.

————

1808.

ACTS

OF

ASSEMBLY

PASSED AT THE SECOND SESSION

OF THE

SECOND GENERAL ASSEMBLY

OF THE

INDIANA TERRITORY.

Begun and held at the Town of Vincennes, on
Monday the twenty-sixth day of September,
A. D. one thousand eight hundred and eight.

* * * *

Printed by Authority, and under the Inspection of
the Committee.

* * * *

VINCENNES.

Printed by ELIHU STOUT,

Printer to the Territory.

1808.

ACTS

OF

THE INDIANA TERRITORY.

CHAPTER I.

AN ACT to form a new County out of the Counties of Knox and Clark.

§ 1. BE *it enacted by the Legislative Council and House of Representatives, and it is hereby enacted by the authority of the same,* That from and after the first day of December next, all that part of the counties of Knox and Clark, which is included in the following boundaries, shall form and constitute a new county, that is to say; beginning at the point on the river Ohio, where the meredîan line from which the ranges take number, strikes the same, thence due north to the present Indian boundary line, thence with the said boundary line, to the intersection of the same by the line which divides the fourth and fifth ranges east, thence with the latter to the above mentioned boundary line, between the Jeffersonville, and Vincennes districts, and with the same to the intersection of the line dividing the fifth and sixth ranges, thence with the said range line until it strikes the Ohio River, and thence down the same, with the meanders thereof, to the place of beginning.

County established.

Boundaries.

§ 2. *Be it further enacted,* That the said county shall, from and after the said first day

(4)

of December next, be known and designated by the name and style of the county of Harrison, and it shall enjoy all the rights, privileges and jurisdictions, which to a seperate county do or may properly appertain and belong: *Provided always,* That all suits, pleas, plaints, actions and proceedings which may, before the said first day of December, have been commenced, instituted

Name and time of operation.

Not to effect suits now depending.

Nor taxes due.

and depending within the now counties of Knox and Clark, shall be prosecuted to final judgment and effect, in the same manner as if this act had never been passed: *And provided also,* That the Territorial and county levies or taxes which are now due within the bounds of the said new county, shall be collected and paid in the same manner, and by the same officers as they would have been, if the erection of said new county had not taken place.

Terms of circuit & other courts therein.

§ 3. *Be it further enacted,* That the Judges of the General court, or some one or more of them, shall hold a Circuit court in the said county, on the last Monday of May, annually; and that the terms of the court of Common Pleas of the said county wherein business of a civil and criminal nature is transacted, shall be at the following annual periods to wit: on the second Wednesdays of January and May, and the third Wednesday of September; and the three other annual sessions thereof, which are intended by law for county purposes, at the following periods, to wit: on the second Wednesdays of March, July and November.

(5)

Seat of Justice.

§ 4. *And be it further enacted,* That in compliance with the wishes of the good people within the bounds of the said new county, the seat of Justice thereof shall be, and is hereby fixed at the town of Corydon.

JESSE B. THOMAS,
Speaker of the House of Representatives.
JOHN RICE JONES,
President of the Legislative Council.

Approved—11th October, 1808.
WILLIAM HENRY HARRISON.

CHAPTER II.

AN ACT to amend an act, entitled "An Act for opening and regulating Public Roads and Highways.

§ 1. WHEREAS, the expence of laying out public roads in the different counties, is found, not only burdensome, and a great means of draining the the county treasuries of their funds, but is altogether useless and unnecessary.

BE *it thefore enacted by the Legislative Council and House of Representatives, and it is hereby enacted by the authority of the same,* That so much of the fourth section of the act to which this act is an amendment, as makes it necessary,

Expence of surveying & compensation to supervisors done away.

(6)

and authorises the court to which application is made, to appoint a surveyor for any road about to be established, or which may hereafter be established; and so much of the said act as provides for, and allows a compensation to the supervisor, shall be, and the same are hereby repealed.

§ 2. Whereas, by the act to which this is an amendment, it is, by the tenth section thereof, provided that all male persons of the age of twenty-one years, and not exceeding fifty, who have resided thirty days in any township in any county within this territory, and who are not a county charge, shall be liable, as in the said law is directed, to work on the public roads and highways: *And whereas,* Young men of the age of eighteen years, are equally able to work on the said roads and highways, as those above that age;

Be it therefore enacted, That all male persons between the ages of eighteen and fifty, years, shall be liable to work and labour on the public roads and highways, in the same manner, and for the same number of days, as persons above the age of twenty one years, are, by the said act bound to work, on pain of paying the fine in the said law mentioned, which shall be recoverable in the manner therein mentioned, notwithstanding the non-age of the said person by

Persons between 18 & 50 to work on roads.

(7)

this law made liable to work on the said roads and highways.

JESSE B. THOMAS,
Speaker of the House of Representatives.
JOHN RICE JONES,
President of the Legislative Council.

Approved—October 14, 1808.
WILLIAM HENRY HARRISON.

CHAPTER III.

AN ACT for the relief of Catherine Moore.

§ 1. WHEREAS, it has been represented to the Legislature, that Catherine Moore, of Clark county in this territory, was formerly married to one John Prince, who not only run through her property. and ill treated her, but likewise deserted her: *And whereas,* It has likewise been represented, that the said Catherine Moore, then Catherine Prince, feeling herself deserted by her said husband, and being in a forlorn and distressed situation, and being informed of the said John Prince, having contracted a second marriage, she was induced to contract on her part a marriage with one Robert K. Moore, of the said county of Clark, but now deceased, by whom she had one child, which is now living: And as some

(8)

doubts have arisen with respect to the legality of her marriage with the said Robert K. Moore, and as to the legitimacy of the birth of her said child; for quieting whereof,

BE *it enacted by the Legislative Council and House of Representatives, and it is hereby enacted by the authority of the same,* **Divorce declared and marriage legalized.** That the said Catherine, and the said John, shall be, and they are hereby divorced from the banns of matrimony contracted between them; and the marriage which was contracted by the said Catherine, with the said Robert K. Moore, is hereby legalized to all intents and purposes, and shall be so taken and esteemed, as well within, as without, all courts of judicature, and tribunals whatsoever, any law, usage or custom to the contrary hereof in any wise notwithstanding.

Birth of the child legitamised. § 2. *And be it further enacted,* That the birth of the said child of the said Catherine, by the said Robert K. Moore (by the name of Sarah Lloyd Moore) shall be, and the same is hereby legitamised, to all intents and purposes, and shall be henceforth taken, deemed, held, and considered, in all transactions whatsoever, either civil or criminal, as the legitimate offspring of the said Robert K. Moore, and Catherine his wife.

(9)

This act shall take effect and be in force from and after the passing thereof.

JESSE B. THOMAS,
Speaker of the House of Representatives.
JOHN RICE JONES,
President of the Legislative Council.

Approved—October 17, 1808.

WILLIAM HENRY HARRISON.

CHAPTER IV.

AN ACT to amend an act, entitled "An Act regulating the Fees of the several Officers and persons therein named.

§ 1. WHEREAS, numerous, and in some cases, just complaints do still exist among our citizens with respect to the exorbitancy of the Clerks fees of the courts of record in this territory; and likewise that they are compellable by execution, to pay large sums of money for fees, without knowing for what services they do pay: for remedy whereof;

BE *it enacted by the Legislative Council and House of Representatives, and it is hereby enacted by the authority of the same,* That in all cases, or judgments upon which execution may, or shall hereafter be

Clerk to make fee bill

B

(10)

issued from any court of record in this territory, the Clerk of the court from whence the same may so issue, shall, at the time of issuing thereof, make out under his signature, and deliver to the Sheriff or Coroner, as the case may be, with the execution, a detailed bill of the costs in the said suit from its commencement to its termination, in order that the party paying the same, may certainly know, with, and for what, he is chargeable; which said bill, the said officer, to whose hands the execution may so come, shall deliver to the party against whom the execution may be, so soon, and upon his replevying for, or paying the same, together

with execution.

Officer to receipt for.

with his certificate thereon, that the same was so replevied for, or paid by the said person.

Clerk or officer failing fined and to whose use.

§ 2. *And be it further enacted,* That should any officer concerned in the issuing or executing any execution hereafter to be issued as aforesaid, fail in the duty enjoined upon them, in the preceding section hereof, they shall severally, and respectively, forfeit and pay to the party, or person injured the sum of fifty dollars, with costs, to be recovered in any court of record in this territory, by indictment or information; and no imparlance or delay shall be allowed therein, any law, usage or custom to the contrary thereof, in any wise notwithstanding.

This act shall take effect, and be in force

(11)

from and after the first day of November next.

LUKE DECKER,
Speaker pro tem. House of Representatives.
JOHN RICE JONES,
President of the Council.

Approved—October 22, 1808.
WILLIAM HENRY HARRISON.

CHAPTER V.

AN ACT supplemental to an act, entitled "An Act regulating the Practice in the General Court, and Courts of Common Pleas and for other purposes.

§ 1. BE *it enacted by the Legislative Council and House of Representatives, and it is hereby enacted by the authority of the same,* That no suit shall hereafter be commenced in any court in this territory, by any person who is non-resident, or who is not a freeholder in said territory, until he shall file in the Clerk's office, a bond with security, who shall be a freeholder, and resident in the territory, conditioned for the payment of all costs that may accrue in consequence thereof, either to the opposite party, or to any of the officers of such courts; which bond shall be in the form, or to the purport following:

Non residents to give resident security for costs.

(12)

<table>
<tr><td>"</td><td></td><td></td><td rowspan="2">Form of
bond.</td></tr>
<tr><td>In the</td><td>County,
court } sct.</td><td></td></tr>
</table>

A. B. ⎱
vs.   ⎰
C. D. ⎰

I do hereby enter myself security for costs in the above cause, agreeably to the laws of the territory, the   day of   ."

§ 2. *And be it further enacted,* That in all cases where security for costs hereafter shall be entered, it shall be lawful for the Clerk to issue fee bills against such security for costs, in the same manner, and at the same time, as fee bills are by the laws of the territory directed to be issued: and it shall be the duty of the Sheriff to levy, collect, and receive, and pay over the amount of such fee bills at the several times, and in the manner in the said laws mentioned, under the pains and penalties in the same laws also mentioned.

Clerk may issue fee bills and sheriff shall collect.

This act to be in force from the passage thereof.

JESSE B. THOMAS,
Speaker of the House of Representatives.
JOHN RICE JONES,
President of the Council.

Approved—October 22, 1808.
WILLIAM HENRY HARRISON.

(13)

CHAPTER VI.
AN ACT for the relief of Nicholas Jarrot.

§ 1. WHEREAS, Nicholas Jarrot, esquire, acted as one of the Judges of the election holden in the county of St. Clair, for a member to represent the said county in the General Assembly of this territory, in the year one thousand eight hundred and five, which election it appears, was interrupted, and broken up, by a combination of disorderly citizens; upon which the said Nicholas Jarrot, by advice of his colleague, William Biggs, esquire, forwarded an express to the Executive of the territory, at the expence of twenty-four dollars: *And whereas,* It is thought unjust that the said expence should become a private burden, but that the same being a necessary expence, accruing out of the said election, that therefore the same should be remunerated the said Jarrot, by the county in which the election was holden:

BE it therefore enacted by the Legislative Council and House of Representatives, and it is hereby enacted by the authority of the same, That the county treasurer, of the county of St. Clair, be, and he is hereby authorised and directed to pay to the said Nicholas Jarrot, the said sum of twenty-four dollars, out of any monies in his hands not otherwise disposed of.

An allowance & from whence to be received.

(14)

This act shall take effect, and be in force from and after the passing thereof.

JESSE B. THOMAS,
Speaker of the House of Representatives.
JOHN RICE JONES,
President of the Council.

Approved—October 22, 1808.
WILLIAM HENRY HARRISON.

CHAPTER VII.

AN ACT to amend an act, entitled "An Act authorising the granting of Letters Testamentary, and Letters of Administration, for the settlement of Intestates estates, and for other purposes.

§ 1.   BE *it enacted by the Legislative Council and House of Representatives, and it is hereby enacted by the authority of the same,* That all the moveable property of any person or persons, dying testate or intestate, in the territory, shall, unless otherwise directed by the will of such testator, or by a rule or order of the court of Common Pleas of the county, be sold by his, her, or their executors or administrators, by public vendue, to the highest

Exors. or admors. unless prevented by will or order of court to sell property on credit.

bidder, on a credit of at least three months, the purchaser or purchasers giving bond with security, to be approved of by the executor or administrator, for the payment of their purchase mo-

(15)

ney at the time mentioned in the conditions of sale, either with, or without interest, as expressed in such conditions: *Provided however,* That the executor or administrator shall give at least ten days previous notice of such sale, by public advertisements set up in the neighbourhood of the deceased's late place of residence: *Provided also,* That executors or administrators may make it a part of the conditions of such sale, that purchases under three dollars, shall be paid down.

First advertising.

Certain sums to be paid down.

§ 2. *Be it further enacted,* That administrators in settling the accounts of their administrations, shall be charged with, and accountable for the nett proceeds of such sales, notwithstanding the same may amount to more, or less, than the appraised value.

Accountable for the amount of sale.

§ 3. *Be it further enacted,* That no action, or suit, shall hereafter be maintainable against any executor, or executors, administrator, or administrators, for debts due by the testator, intestate, at the time of his death, before the expiration of twelve months after the granting of the first letters of administration, or letters testamentary; and if any such action, or suit, shall be brought, contrary to the provisions of this act, the same shall be dismissed by the court with full costs.

No suit shall be sustained against them until expiration of 12 months.

This act shall take effect, and be in

(16)

force from and after the first day of January next.

JESSE B. THOMAS,
Speaker of the House of Representatives.
JOHN RICE JONES,
President of the Council.

Approved—October 24, 1808.
WILLIAM HENRY HARRISON.

CHAPTER VIII.

AN ACT supplementary to an act, entitled "An Act to authorise the Proprietors of Land in the Lower Prairie, in the County of Knox, to inclose the same, and for other purposes.

§ 1.   THAT WHEREAS, the rule prescribed in the twenty-first section of the act to which this is a supplement, to apportion the labour to be performed in making and maintaining the dike, or embankment, among the said proprietors, is found to be unequal and oppressive, for remedy whereof;

BE *it enacted by the Legislative Council and House of Representatives, and it is hereby enacted by the authority of the same,* **Supervisor of dike to apportion labor** That the supervisor of the dike, or embankment, shall apportion the said labour among the said proprietors, in proportion to the number of acres of land which

(17)

each of them claims within the said enclosure.

Election of supervisors valid. § 2. *Be it further enacted,* That the election of Supervisors of the dike, made by the proprietors who attended on the first Monday in October, of the present year, be, and the same is hereby declared to be as valid, in every respect, as if the same had been made by the said proprietors, or a majority of them; and that the **Majority of proprietors who attend shall elect officers.** several elections of Syndic, and Supervisor, at the times provided for by the act aforesaid, may, and shall be held and determined by a majority of the proprietors who shall attend and vote thereat; any clause, or thing, in this, or the said act, to the contrary notwithstanding.

Proprietors to carry into effect part of former act. § 3. *Be it further enacted,* That it shall be lawful for the said proprietors from and after the last day of October, one thousand eight hundred and eight, to carry into effect the nineteenth section of the act to which this is a supplement, anything in the said act to the contrary notwithstanding.

Owners of animals liable for trespasses § 4. *Be it further enacted,* That the owner of any horse, mare, colt, cattle, sheep, lambs, hogs, or pigs, which shall be found trespassing or straying within the said enclosure, shall be, and hereby are declared liable to make good all the injury or damage occasioned by such animals, to any proprietor, or cultivator of lands therein, who may sue for, and recover his, her, or their damages therefor, with costs, before any court or magistrate in the

Their remedy.

C

(18)

county; saving to every such owner, his remedy over therefor, against any proprietor or lessee, over, or through whose fence by reason of its insufficiency, such animal may have come into the said enclosure.

§ 5. *Be it further enacted,* That when any of the said animals shall be found as aforesaid, and the owner, or owners cannot be known, or found, any person may seize and distrain such animals, and thereupon proceed as is provided in an act entitled, "An act concerning trespassing animals.'

If no owner to be found how to proceed.

§ 6. *Be it further enacted,* That each and every proprietor or cultivator of land within the said enclosure, shall, on the last Monday of October, if fair, if not, on the next fair day, yearly, and every year, move and burn, or cause to be moved and burnt, all the grass and weeds growing, adjoining his, her or their fence, not exceeding fifteen feet from each side thereof, under the direction of the Syndic, whose duty it shall be, to attend and give notice thereof to every proprietor or cultivator, one day previous to the said last day of October, yearly; and if any of the said proprietors, or cultivators, shall refuse or neglect to move and burn the said grass and weeds, as aforesaid, the Syndic shall forthwith cause the same to be done, at the cost and charges of every such defaulter, and shall recover the expences thereof, with costs, as aforesaid.

Grass and weeds to be burnt from fence.

§ 7. *And be it further enacted,* That

(19)

it shall be lawful for the said proprietors, or cultivators, between the first and fifteenth day of March, yearly, to burn all the grass, weeds, and stubbles, on his, her, or their lands, within the said enclosure: *Provided always,* That any proprietor, or other per-

Cultivators may burn stubble &c.

son, who shall thereby occasion any injury, or damage, to any other person, other than in his, her, or their grass, weeds, or stubbles, shall be, and is hereby declared liable therefor, to any proprietor, or cultivater of lands within the said enclosure, to be recovered as aforesaid.

JESSE B. THOMAS,
Speaker of the House of Representatives.
JOHN RICE JONES,
President of the Council.

Approved—October 24, 1808.

WILLIAM HENRY HARRISON.

CHAPTER IX.

AN ACT for the relief of the Printers of the Revised Code, and for other purposes.

§ 1. BE *it enacted by the Legislative Council and House of Representatives, and it is hereby enacted by the authority of the same,* That there shall be allowed and paid out of the contingent fund appropriated at the last session for this purpose, and out of any other monies in the treasury, ei-

(20)

ther of the contingent, or general fund, to Elihu Stout, and George C. Smoot, the contractors for printing five hundred copies of the Revised Code, and Acts passed at the last session of the Legislature, together with the Index, and for binding the same, the sum of six hundred and ninety-five dollars; and the Auditor of public accounts, is hereby authorised and directed to audit and give one or more warrants for the same accordingly.

§ 2. *Be it further enacted,* That there shall be paid out of any monies in the treasury not otherwise appropriated, to the following persons, for the following services, the following sums of money, to wit: to General Washington Johnston, one of the committee appointed by the Legislature at the last session, for attending to the printing, collating, making marginal notes, and Index,

Marginal notes:

Allowance to Stout & Smoot what, and how to be paid.

Allowance to the committee of printing what

binding and distributing the Revised Code, and Acts of last session, the sum of fifty dollars; to John Rice Jones, the other member of the same committee, for the services performed by him in the business aforesaid, thirty dollars.

§ 3.   *And be it further enacted,* That the said printers, and their securities, shall be, and they are hereby severally, and respectively released, exonerated and   discharged from the bond given by them for the performance of the agreement entered into by the said Stout and Smoot, for the printing of the said Laws, and which is now depo-

Printers and securities released from bond.

(21)

sited in the Secretary's office of this territory.

This act shall take effect and be in force from and after the passing thereof.

JESSE B. THOMAS,

Speaker of the House of Representatives.

JOHN RICE JONES,

President of the Council.

Approved—October 24, 1808.

WILLIAM HENRY HARRISON.

CHAPTER X.

AN ACT to amend an act, entitled "An Act concerning Servants, and for other purposes."

§ 1.   BE *it enacted by the Legislative Council and House of Representatives, and it is hereby enacted by the authority of the same,* That if any person, or persons, shall permit, or suffer, any slave, or slaves, servant, or servants of colour, to the number of three, or more, to assemble in his, her, or their house, out house, yard, or shed, for the purpose of dancing, or revelling, either by night, or by day, the person, or persons so offending shall forfeit and pay the sum of twenty dollars, with costs, to any person, or persons, who shall sue for, and recover the same, by action of debt, in-

Persons suffering servants to assemble on premises for revelling fined how much & for what use.

(22)

formation, or indictment, in any court of record proper to try the same.

§ 2. *Be it further enacted,* That it shall be the duty of all Coroners, Sheriffs, Judges, and Justices of the Peace, who shall see or know of, or be informed of any such assemblage of slaves or servants, immediately to commit such slaves or servants, to the jail of the said county; and on view or proof thereof, to order each and every such slave or servant, to be whipped, not exceeding thirty nine stripes, on his or her bare back, on the day next succeeding such assemblage, unless it shall happen on a Sunday, then on the Monday following; which said stripes shall be inflicted by any Constable of the township, if there should be one therein, or otherwise by any person or persons whom the said Justices shall appoint, and who shall be willing so to inflict the same: *Provided however,* That the provisions hereof shall not apply to any persons of colour, who may assemble for the purpose of amusement, by permission of their masters first had in writing, on condition that no disorderly conduct is made use of by them in such assemblage.

Peace officers to send such revellers to jail.

And have them severally whipped.

By whom.

Exceptions when by leave & behaving well.

This act shall take effect, and be in force

(23)

from and after the first day of January next.

GENL. W. JOHNSTON,
Speaker of the House of Representatives.
JOHN RICE JONES,
President of the Council.

Approved—October 25, 1808.
WILLIAM HENRY HARRISON.

CHAPTER XI.

AN ACT to amend an act, entitled "An Act establishing Courts for the Trial of Small Causes.

§ 1. WHEREAS, abuses have arisen from the operation of that part of the law of the territory, to which this act is an amendment, which provides that actions of debt, or other demand should be made cognizable before any Justice of the Peace, or Magistrate in the township in which the plaintiff resides: for remedy whereof;

BE *it enacted by the Legislative Council and House of Representatives, and it is hereby enacted by the authority of the same,* That every action of debt, or other demand (except as in the said law is excepted) shall be, and the same is hereby made cognizable before any Justice of the Peace, or Magistrate, in the township either where

Suits to be brot' where debt contracted or defendant found.

(24)

the debt or cause of action was contracted or arose, or where the defendant resides or may be found, and not elsewhere.

§ 2. *And whereas,* doubts have arisen whether Magistrates in one township, have by law authority to compel the attendance of witnesses residing in any other township in the same county, for obviating of which doubts;

Be it further enacted, That in all actions and causes properly examinable into before any Justice of the Peace in any township in this territory, for the trial of small causes, such Justice may issue his subpœna to compel the attendance of witnesses on any trial before him, from any other township in the same county;

Justice may subpœna witnesses from any township.

and if any person being duly subpœnaed as a witness in any cause cognizable before a Magistrate for the trial of small causes, shall neglect, or refuse to attend at the day and time in such subpœna mention, he or she, so neglecting or refusing, shall be fined in any sum not exceeding the amount of the debt or demand sued for, to the use of the party on whose behalf such witness was so subpœnaed, for which fine with costs, the said Justice shall issue execution, against such witness, unless such witness within thirty days after the said fine shall be by such Justice so laid, render on oath a reasonable excuse to the satisfaction of such Magistrate for such delay: *Provided,* That no such witness shall be finable unless such subpœna shall have been served at least two days before

Failing to attend fined how much &c.

Execution to issue unless excused.

prerequisites to fining witness.

(25)

the trial, where the witness resides within thirty miles of the place of residence of the Magistrate, and one day more for every thirty miles, or less, above that distance: *Provided also,* That where any witness lives out of the county, the Magistrate may, and he is hereby authorised to issue a dedimus to take the deposition of any such witness, as is usually done in the courts of record in this territory, and which shall be taken and read in evidence, under the same rules and regulations that such depositions are usually taken upon commissions issuing from the said court.

Witness living out of county justice grant dedimus.

§ 3. *Be it further enacted,* That the jurisdiction of the Justices of the Peace in the township of Prairie du Chein, in the county of St. Clair, shall be, and the same is hereby extended to one hundred dollars: and that of the several Justices of the Peace throughout the other parts of this territory, shall be, and the same is hereby extended to forty dollars: *Provided however,* That the party or parties against whom any judgment may hereafter be rendered by such Justice of the Peace, shall be entitled to an appeal therefrom, as is provided in the law to which this act is an amendment, in all cases where the judgment, exclusive of costs, shall exceed the sum of three dollars; *And provided also,* That upon such appeal, the Clerk of the court to which such appeal may be made, shall be entitled to, and receive full costs; any law, usage or custom

Jurisdiction of justices of peace special and general how much.

From what sums appeals may be had.

Clerk to receive full costs.

D

(26)

to the contrary hereof in any wise notwithstanding.

§ 4. *And be it further enacted,* That upon any judgment which may hereafter be rendered as aforesaid, no execution shall issue thereon until the expiration of thirty days, if the judgment be for the sum of six dollars or under; or until the expiration of sixty days, if the judgment be for any sum above six, or under twelve dollars; nor until the expiration of ninety days, if the judgment be for any sum of, or under eighteen, and above twelve dollars or upwards; nor until the expiration of one hundred and

Stay of execution how long and for what sums.

twenty days, if the judgment be for any sum above eighteen dollars, and not exceeding thirty dollars; nor until the expiration of one hundred and fifty days, where the judgment is thirty dollars and upwards, not exceeding forty dollars; any thing in the said act, to which this is an amendment to the contrary contained notwithstanding.

GENL. W. JOHNSTON,
Speaker of the House of Representatives.
JOHN RICE JONES,
President of the Council.

Approved—October 25, 1808.

WILLIAM HENRY HARRISON.

(27)

CHAPTER XII.

AN ACT to alter and amend an act, entitled "An Act organizing Courts of Common Pleas, and for other purposes.

§ 1. WHEREAS, complaints have been made that the allowance given by law to Judges of the said courts is too high and expensive for the counties to bear,

BE *it therefore enacted by the Legislative Council and House of Representatives, and it is hereby enacted by the authority of the same,* That from and after the first day of January next, the Judges of the said courts shall receive two dollars per day when sitting as Judgs of the court of Common Pleas. **Compensation to judges of C. P.**

§ 2. *Be it further enacted,* That the following fees shall be allowed, collected and paid, by the proper officer into the county treasury. **Fees to judg of Common P. what.**

		D. C.
Every writ of capias and seal,		1
For each action in court,	-	75
Signing every judgment,	- -	25
Taking bail,	- - -	50
Acknowledging satisfaction on record,		25
Taxing and signing bill of costs,		50
Proof or acknowledgment of deeds,		75

For every issued joined,   -   -   1
For every trial,   -   -   -   -   1 20
Granting referees,   -   -   -   -   50
Approving report of referees,   -   70

(28)

D. C.

On surrender of principal in court,   50
Hearing petition, and making order thereon,   -   -   -   50
Allowing writ of error, habeas corpus, or certiorari,
    when presented from the Judges of the General
    Court,   -   -   -   -   -   1

Judges of C. P. not to be admrs. § 3. *Be it further enacted,* That no Judge of any court of Common Pleas within this territory, shall be appointed administrator to the estate of any deceased person, unless such Judge shall by law be entitled thereto, as next of kin, to such deceased person.

GENL. W. JOHNSTON,
Speaker of the House of Representatives.
JOHN RICE JONES,
President of the Council.

Approved—October 25, 1808.
WILLIAM HENRY HARRISON.

CHAPTER XIII.

AN ACT in addition to an act, entitled "An Act regulating the Practice in the General Court, and Courts of Common Pleas, and for other purposes."

§ 1. BE *it enacted by the Legislative Council and House of Representatives, and*

(29)

Suits not to be removed from inferior to superior court after issue joined. *it is hereby enacted by the authority of the same,* That no suit, action, or plaint now depending, or which may hereafter be brought in any inferior court of record in this territory, shall be removed by an habeas corpus, or certiorari, to the General court, or other superior court, after issue joined in the court in which the said cause was commenced; any law, usage or custom to the contrary thereof in any wise notwithstanding.

§ 2. *Be it further enacted,* That hereafter the General court of this territory may and shall continue in session for twenty days at each term (provided the business depending in the said court cannot be gone through in a shorter period) but no longer, when it shall adjourn 'till court in course; and the several courts of Common Pleas in this territory, at their sessions as described by law for county purposes, a time not exceeding three natural days; and at each term as designated by law for the decision of suits and determination of disputes, a time not exceeding eight days, when they shall severally adjourn until court in course.

§ 3. *Be it further enacted,* That the first, or presiding Judge of the General court, District court, or court of Errors and Appeals of this territory, shall collect, and he is hereby enjoined to collect, make up and deliver the opinion of the court, *seriatim,* in writing, with the reasons thereof, upon all questions and points of law, which may be decided by them; which opinion

(30)

shall be by the said Judge, delivered to the Clerk, and by him recorded at full length, upon the records of the said court; and should either of the said Judges differ in opinion, the dissenting Judge shall have the reasons of his dissent entered of record in said suit.

§ 4. *Be it further enacted,* That if the said Clerk shall fail or neglect to record the opinion of the court delivered as aforesaid, he shall be fined the sum of fifty dollars, to be recovered by indictment or information, in any court of record within this territory, the one half for the use of the informer, and the other half to and for the use of the territory; and it shall be, and it is hereby made the duty of the Attorney General of this territory, to collect the said fines, and pay the same into the proper treasury.

§ 5. *Be it further enacted,* That no declaration shall hereafter be considered deemed or taken as necessary to be filed in any *scieri facias,* to revive a judgment, or foreclose a mortgage, in any court of record in this territory, any law, usage or custom to the contrary in any wise notwithstanding.

Marginal notes:

Genrl. court may sit 20 days.

County court 3 days.

Common P. 8 days.

Presiding judge of superior court to deliver opinion in writing.

To be recorded by clerk.

Dissenting judge how to act.

Clerk failing to record, fined how much, how recovered & to what use.

No declaration necessary on sci. fa. to revive or foreclose.

(31)

This act shall take effect and be in force from and after the passing thereof.

GENL. W. JOHNSTON,
Speaker of the House of Representatives.

JOHN RICE JONES,
President of the Council.

Approved—October 25, 1808.

WILLIAM HENRY HARRISON.

CHAPTER XIV.
AN ACT to alter and repeat certain parts of an act, entitled "A Law to regulate County Levies."

Tax on Cattle & single men done away.

§ 1. BE it enacted by the Legislative Council and House of Representatives, and it is hereby enacted by the authority of the same, That so much of the said act as provides for laying, assessing, and collecting a tax on neat cattle, and able bodied single men who shall not have taxable property to the amount of two hundred dollars, shall be, and the same are hereby repealed.

C. P. lay tax on land, when, how much & how collected.

§ 2. *Be it further enacted,* That in lieu of the tax heretofore collected on neat cattle, and single men, the courts of Common Pleas, in each county respectively, shall, at the same time at which they levy the tax upon other objects of taxation, levy a tax on located lands, not exceeding ten cents in

(32)

each hundred dollars, which said tax of ten cents, shall be collected by the Sheriff's respectively at the same time and under the same regulations, conditions and provisions which are, or may be provided by law for the collection of the territorial taxes:

For what purpose.

Provided, that the whole of the tax collected under the authority of this section, shall be paid into the county treasury, and applied exclusively to county buildings.

Sheriffs commission what

§ 3. *And be it further enacted,* That the Sheriff for the assessment and collection of county levies, shall be entitled to have and receive eight per cent only, on the amount of tax by him received and paid to the county treasurer, and no more; any thing in the said law to the contrary notwithstanding.

GENL. W. JOHNSTON,
Speaker of the House of Representatives.

JOHN RICE JONES,
President of the Council.

Approved—October 26, 1808.

WILLIAM HENRY HARRISON.

CHAPTER XV.

AN ACT to amend an act, entitled "An Act concerning Executions."

§ 1.   BE *it enacted by the Legislative*

(33)

Council and House of Representatives, of the Indiana Territory, and it is hereby enacted by the authority of the same, That where any writ of execution shall hereafter issue out of any court of record within this territory, against the estate of any defendant or defendants, the Sheriff or officer shall take in execution, all, or such part or parts of the real or personal estate or estates of such defendant or defendants as such defendant or defendants, designate or shew to such Sheriff, or other officer, and as will, in the opinion of such Sheriff or other officer, be sufficient to satisfy the amount of the said execution & costs; and in case the said real and personal estate, or estates, so disignated or shewn, will not, in the opinion of such Sheriff or other officer, be sufficient to satisfy the said execution and costs, then such Sheriff or other officer shall in such case only, levy on, and seize so much only of the defendant or defendants other real or personal estate, as will, in the opinion of such Sheriff or other officer, be sufficient to satisfy the remainder of the said execution and costs; but in case such defendant or defendants, shall not shew or designate to such Sheriff or other officer, real or personal property to him belonging as will be sufficient to satisfy the said execution and costs, then such Sheriff or other officer, shall seize and levy on the whole or any part of the real or personal estate of such defendant or de-

[sidenote: Optional with defendant what estate to deliver in exon.]

[sidenote: If not sufficient sheriff to take other estate.]

[sidenote: If defendant fails to shew property sheriff to take a-]

ny he can find. fendants, as he can find in his bailiwick, and as will be sufficient to satisfy such execution and costs.

E

(34)

Sheff. in selling property dispose of parts required by deft.

§ 2. *Be it further enacted,* That when any Sheriff or other officer shall proceed to sell or dispose of any real or personal estate, by virtue of any writ of execution, he shall be obliged to sell and dispose (at the choice of the defendant or defendants,) either of the real or personal estate of such defendant or defendants, or such part or parts thereof, as he or they shall direct him so to dispose of, until the amount of the said execution and costs

Shff. failing in duty how fined and to what use.

shall be made; and if any Sheriff or other officer, shall either take, or sell and dispose of the real or personal estate of any defendant, or defendants, in any other manner than is directed by this law, such Sheriff or other officer, shall forfeit and pay to the defendant or defendants, whose property shall be so taken and sold, the full value of such real or personal estate, so taken and sold, to be recovered by bill, plaint, or information, in any court of record proper to try the same.

Property of principal to be first sold before sureties touched upon.

§ 3. *Be it further enacted,* That when it appears on the face of any writ of Fiere Facias, that any one or more of the defendant or defendants, against whom such writ is issued, are only security or securities, for any one or more of the other defendant or defendants in such writ named, the Sheriff or other officer, shall in such case, sell and dispose of all, or so much of the real or personal estate, of such principal defendant or defendants, as such Sheriff or other officer, shall be able to find in his bailiwick, as will satisfy the said execution and costs, before he shall set up or dispose of any part of the

[35]

Unless his choice.

real or personal estate of such surety, or sureties, unless the said Sheriff or other officer, shall be otherwise directed by such surety or sureties.

§ 4. This act shall commence and be in force from and after the first day of January next.

GENL. W. JOHNSTON,
Speaker of the House of Representatives.
JOHN RICE JONES,
President of the Council.

Approved—October 26, 1808.
WILLIAM HENRY HARRISON.

CHAPTER XVI.

AN ACT to amend an act, entitled "An Act respecting Crimes and Punishments."

§ 1. BE *it enacted by the Legislative Council and House of Representatives, and it is hereby enacted by the authority of the same,* That if any person or persons, shall steal or purloin from any other person or persons, any horse, mare, gelding, mule, or ass, he, she, or they, so offending, shall upon conviction thereof, suffer the pains of death: and if any person or persons shall receive any such horse, mare, gelding, mule or ass, knowing the same to be stolen, he, she, or they, shall be deemed principally

Horse stealing death.

Same punishment to receivers.

(36)

guilty, and upon conviction thereof, shall also suffer the pains of death.

This act shall take effect from its passage.

GENL. W. JOHNSTON,
Speaker of the House of Representatives.
JOHN RICE JONES,
President of the Council.

Approved—October 26, 1808.
WILLIAM HENRY HARRISON.

CHAPTER XVII.

AN ACT providing for Leasing the Sections of Land reserved for the use of Schools.

§ 1. BE *it enacted by the Legislative Council and House of Representatives, and it is hereby enacted by the authority of the*

Common P. to lease lands upon what terms.

same, That the several courts of Common Pleas, within this territory, shall be, and they are hereby invested with full power to lease the sections within their respective counties, which have been reserved for the use of schools, upon such terms and conditions, as shall appear to them best calculated to improve the same:

What lessee shall do.

Provided always, That the lessees shall bind themselves to clear at least ten acres for every quarter section they may lease; and that no lease shall be made for a longer term than five years, when the demised premises with the

(37)

fences thereon, shall be delivered up in good repair.

This act shall commence and be in force for the term of one year, and from thence to the end of the next sessions of the Legislature, and no longer.

GENl. W. JOHNSTON,
Speaker of the House of Representatives,
JOHN RICE JONES,
President of the Council.

Approved—October 26, 1808.
WILLIAM HENRY HARRISON.

CHAPTER XVIII.
AN ACT making appropriations for the ensuing year.

§ 1. BE *it enacted by the Legislative Council and House of Representatives, and it is hereby enacted by the authority of the*

Contingent & general fund what & how disposed of.

same, That the sum of one hundred dollars, be and the same is hereby appropriated for contingent expences; and that all monies received, or which shall be received into the territorial treasury, shall be a general fund, for all monies allowed by law; which contingent fund shall be subject to the order of the Governor, for expresses, and other incidents which cannot be foreseen, by the two houses, a statement where-

(38)

of shall be by him, laid before them at their next session.

§ 2. *Be it further enacted,* That there shall be allowed and paid, for printing four hundred copies of the laws of the present session, a sum not exceeding three hundred dollars, to be paid on the order of the joint committee of both houses for the distribution of the laws.

To the territorial Auditor, one hundred and fifty dollars.

To the territorial Treasurer, one hundred dollars.

To Peter Jones & Co. for stationery furnished at the present session of the Legislature, fourteen dollars and fifty cents.

To the Attorney General, one hundred dollars, for the ensuing year.

To Samuel Hayes, for fire wood, furnished at the present session of the Legislature, four dollars and fifty cents.

To the county of Knox, for house rent, to the end of the present session, fifty dollars.

To Elihu Stout, for printing in his weekly papers, the Journals of both houses of the Legislature, for the present session of the same, fifty dollars; to be paid

(39)

him when the printing of the said Journals shall have been completed.

GENL. W. JOHNSTON,
Speaker of the House of Representatives.

JOHN RICE JONES,
President of the Council.

Approved—October 26, 1808.

WILLIAM HENRY HARRISON.

CHAPTER XIX.

AN ACT concerning the collection of the Territorial Tax on Land, in the Counties of St. Clair and Randolph.

§ 1. WHEREAS, the assessors of the territorial tax on land in the said counties of St. Clair and Randolph, have failed to make and return, as the law directs, a list and assessment in their respective counties for the present year, eighteen hundred and eight, in consequence of which, no taxes can legally be collected in the said counties, either for the present, or ensuing year, for remedy whereof;

BE *it enacted by the Legislative Council and House of Representatives, and it is hereby enacted by the authority aforesaid,* **Assessors to make out list** That the respective Assessors of the said counties of St. Clair and Randolph,

(40)

heretofore appointed by the courts of Common Pleas thereof, are hereby directed immediately to proceed, and make out fair **How disposed of.** lists and valuation of all the located lands claimed in their respective counties, which lists, they shall dispose of as is required in the law of the territory, entitled "An Act for levying and collecting a tax on land, and for other purposes:" And the **Sheriffs to collect.** respective Sheriff's as Collectors, in the said counties, being furnished with a duplicate thereof, corrected by the court of Common **Proceedings heretofore had valid.** Pleas, shall proceed in the collection of the taxes thereon due, as well for the present year, as for the succeeding: And all proceedings, in any there are, heretofore had in either of the afore said counties, under the said law, so far as the same respects located lands, shall be, and the same are hereby esteemed legal, and shall be taken and deemed valid and binding; anything in the said law contained to the contrary notwithstanding.

GENL. W. JOHNSTON,
Speaker of the House of Representatives,
JOHN RICE JONES,
President of the Council.

Approved—October 26, 1808.
WILLIAM HENRY HARRISON.

(41)

CHAPTER XX.

AN ACT allowing Compensation to the Members of the Legislative Council and House of Representatives of the Indiana Territory, and to the Officers of both Houses for the present Session.

§ 1. BE *it enacted by the Legislative Council and House of Representatives, and it is hereby enacted by the authority of the same,* That each and every Member of the Legislative Council and House of Representatives, shall be entitled to, and receive out of the territorial treasury, upon the certificate of the Auditor, for each and every days attendance on the Legislature at the present session, the sum of two dollars, and shall moreover be allowed the sum of two dollars for every twenty miles travel, to, and from the seat of government, to their places of residence by the most usual road.

Compensation to members.

§ 2. *Be it further enacted,* That the secretary of the Legislative Council, and the Clerk of the House of Representatives, shall in like manner, receive for their respective services at the present session, the sum of three dollars and fifty cents, each, per day.

Secretary & clerk.

§ 3. *Be it further enacted,* That Jonathan Jennings, the assistant Clerk to the two houses at the present session, shall in like manner, receive the sum of two dollars and fifty cents per day, for his services during the present session.

Assistant clk

F

(42)

§ 4. *Be it further enacted,* That the Door-Keeper of both houses at the present session, shall, in like manner, receive the sum of one dollar and fifty cents per day, for each and every days attendance on the two houses as such Door-Keeper.

Door keeper.

§ 5. *And be it further enacted,* That the compensation which shall and may be due to the members and officers of the Legislative Council, shall be certified by the President thereof; and that those which shall and may be due to the members and officers

How to be certified and paid.

of the House of Representatives, as also to the door-keeper, shall be certified by the Speaker thereof; which certificate, shall be to the Auditor, sufficient evidence of Claim, and he shall thereupon issue certificates to the several members and officers aforesaid, payable at the treasury of the territory, as in other cases.

GENL. W. JOHNSTON,
Speaker of the House of Representatives.
JOHN RICE JONES,
President of the Council.

Approved—October 26, 1808.
WILLIAM HENRY HARRISON.

(43)

CHAPTER XXI.
A RESOLUTION allowing Compensation to the Attorney General.

Auditor to settle with A. G. how & for what.

RESOLVED *by the Legislative Council and House of Representatives,* That the Auditor be, and he is hereby authorised to settle the account of the Attorney General of the territory, for his services as such, from the date of his commission to the end of the present session of the Legislature, at the rate of one hundred dollars per annum and that the treasurer pay the same out of any monies in the treasury not otherwise appropriated.

GENL. W. JOHNSTON,
Speaker of the House of Representatives.
JOHN RICE JONES,
President of the Council.

Approved—October 26, 1808.
WILLIAM HENRY HARRISON.

CHAPTER XXII.
A RESOLUTION for Printing the Acts of the Present Session.

Laws to be printed and how.

RESOLVED *by the Legislative Council and House of Representatives,* That Messrs. John Rice Jones, and General W. Johnston, be, and they are hereby appointed a committee to contract with such per-

(44)

son or persons, as they may think proper, for printing, either here, or in Louisiana, or Kentucky, four hundred copies of the laws of the present session of the Legislature, on the most moderate terms they can; and that they make out copies of the said laws, to be delivered or forwarded, to such printer as may have contracted for the printing thereof.

Resolved also, That in making such contract, they shall provide, that the said laws shall be printed and ready for delivery to the committee, on or before the first day of January next; and that they distribute forty five copies of the said laws to each of the counties in this territory, and deliver the overplus, to the office of the secretary of the territory.

By what time.

And how disposed of.

GENL. W. JOHNSTON,
Speaker of the House of Representatives.
JOHN RICE JONES,
President of the Council.

Approved—October 26, 1808.
WILLIAM HENRY HARRISON.

CHAPTER XXIII.
A RESOLUTION for Collecting the arrearages of Taxes.

RESOLVED *by the Legislative Coun-*

(45)

cil and House of Representatives, That the proper officers be, and they are hereby required, to take speedy and effectual measures to compel payment by the collectors of the arrears by them respectively due.

Arrearage taxes to be collected and how.

GENL. W. JOHNSTON,
Speaker of the House of Representatives,
JOHN RICE JONES,
President of the Council.

Approved—October 26, 1808.
WILLIAM HENRY HARRISON.

ERRATA in the Revised Code.

Page 424 in place of § 4,—read § 3.

- - - 426 § 10, line 5, in place of 'section,' read 'sections.'

- - - 414 here the last 4, is misplaced, read 441.

In the certificate of collation, in place of 'Territo-ritorial,' read 'Territorial.'

In the Index, under the head of 'Coroner his fees.' in place of page '256,' read, '356.'

Immediately after 'Replevy see Executions,' in the Index, read 'Randolph Circuit court of, altered and to what period 468.'

GENl. W. JOHNSTON,⎫
JOHN RICE JONES,⎬ *Collators.*
                  ⎭

INDIANA TERRITORY, &c.

WE do hereby Certify, that we have Collated the foregoing Printed, with the Manuscript and Original Acts of the in the Secretary's Office of the Territory, and find them truly Printed.

GEN. W. JOHNSTON.
JOHN RICE JONES.

November, 1808.

INDIANA TERRITORY, sct.

WE do hereby Certify, that we have Collated the foregoing Printed, with the Manuscript and Original Acts of file in the Secretary,s Office of the Territory, and find them truly Printed.

GENL. W. JOHNSTON,
JOHN RICE JONES, } *Comtee.*

November, 1808.

INDEX

To the *ACTS* of 1808

INDEX.

INDEX.

INDEX.

iv

INDEX.

T

BIBLIOGRAPHY

BIBLIOGRAPHY

1801

Laws adopted by the governor and judges of the Indiana Territory, at their first sessions held at Saint Vincennes, January 12th, 1801—published by authority. Frankfort, Kentucky, Hunter, pr., 1802. 32 p.

Also in *Message from the president transmitting the laws of Indiana Territory passed from January, 1801 to February, 1802* [Washington, Duane, pr., 1803?]. 32 p. (7 CONGRESS, 2 SESSION, *Executive documents*, no. 32, February 14, 1803.) Reprinted in *Laws of the Indiana Territory, 1801-1806, inclusive* (Paoli, Throop & Clark, 1886).

1802

Laws for the government of Indiana Territory [adopted at their second session]. *Laws adopted by the governor and judges of Indiana Territory, at their second and third sessions begun and held at Saint Vincennes, 30th January, 1802 & February, 16th, 1803—published by authority, 1-9* (Vincennes, Stout, pr., 1804. 89 p.)

Also in *Message from the president transmitting the laws of Indiana Territory . . . 1801 . . . 1802.* Reprinted in *Laws of the Indiana Territory.*

1803

Laws for the government of the Indiana Territory, adopted at their third session. *Laws adopted by the governor and judges . . . 1802 . . . 1803,* pp. 9-12.

Also in *Message from the president transmitting the laws of Indiana Territory* [Washington, Duane, pr., 1803?]. 7 p. (8 CONGRESS, 1 SESSION, *Executive documents,* December 7, 1803.) Reprinted in *Laws of the Indiana Territory.*

1803-04

Laws for the government of the Indiana Territory, adopted at their fourth session. *Laws adopted by the governor and judges . . . 1802 . . . 1803,* pp. 12-89.

Reprinted in *Laws of the Indiana Territory.*

1805

Laws passed at the first session of the general assembly of the Indiana Territory, begun and held at the borough of Vincennes, on Monday the twenty-ninth of July, in the year 1805 —by authority. Vincennes, Stout, pr., n.d. 38 p.

Reprinted in *Laws of the Indiana Territory.*

1806

Laws passed at the second session of the first general assembly of the Indiana Territory, begun and held at the borough of Vincennes, on Monday the third day of November in the year eighteen hundred & six—by authority. Vincennes, Stout, pr., n.d. 30 p.

Reprinted in *Laws of the Indiana Territory*.

1807

Laws of the Indiana Territory comprising those acts formerly in force, and as revised by Messrs. John Rice Jones, and John Johnson, and passed (after amendments) by the legislature, and the original acts passed at the first session of the second general assembly of the said territory, begun and held at the borough of Vincennes, on the sixteenth day of August, Anno Domini eighteen hundred and seven—printed by authority, and under the inspection of the committee. Vincennes, Stout & Smoot, pr., 1807. 540, xxviii p.

This is known as the *Revision of 1807*.

1808

Acts of assembly passed at the second session of the second general assembly of the Indiana Territory, begun and held at the town of Vincennes, on Monday the twenty six day of September, A. D. one thousand eight hundred and eight—printed by authority, and under the inspection of the committee. Vincennes, Stout, pr., 1808. 45, v p.

INDEX

INDEX

INDEX

Abatement, plea in: 37; admitted when, 448; to jurisdiction of justice of peace, 385.

Account, action of, limitation on, 449.

Accounting, may be made on action, 451.

Acknowledgment of deeds, 142.

Action, right of reserved, 366.

Actions, limitations on, 38; what not cognizable before a justice, 387.

Ad quod damnum, writ in erecting of mills, 133-135, 363-365.

Adams, George, clxxvi, n. 4.

Adams, John, lxxi, cclxiii, cclxv.

Adams, Mary, clxxvii, n. 2.

Adams, Mathew, clxv.

Adams County, clx, n. 4.

Adjutant General, duty of: 404-405; office of, to record militia organization, 400-401.

Administration, letters of: how granted, 270-271; void without bond, 278.

Administrators, apply to Common Pleas to appoint commissioners to convey land, 94;

   bond: discharged, how, 274; to be given by, 275-277; to take of beneficiary, 278;

   for debts of deceased, no suits against, in a year, 653; duty regarding conveyances deceased has agreed to make, 281; how to account, 277; how to sell deceased's moveables, 653; letters to, when revoked, 279;

   sales: advertised, how, 280; of

Administrators (cont.)

   real estate, to exhibit inventory before, 280; report of, 280-281; securities and, 121, 517-518.

Advertisement, of foreign attachments, 267; of trespassing animals, 294-295, 296.

Affidavits in chancery, how taken, 194-195; notice of, 512.

Affirmations, 269-270; for those scrupulous of oath, 234; may not replace oaths of office, 270.

Agent of Indian affairs, powers reserved, 498.

Alexander, William, ccxxxii.

Aliens, may hold real estate, cxxviii, 94-95, 500.

Alimony, 323-324.

Allen, William C., cxcvi.

Altering docket, penalty for, 385.

Amendment and jeofail, repeal of law, 65; statute of, adopted, 7.

Amercements, how laid: by Common Pleas, 14; by Quarter Sessions, 9.

American Bottom, xii, lxviii-ix, n. 1.

Americans, lxxv, n. 2, cxxiv, clxxxiv, ccxiii, ccxiv, ccxix, ccxx, ccxxi, ccxxii.

Anderson, David, ccxxxii.

Anderson, Reuben, appropriation to, 607.

Appeals, by administrators, to General and Circuit Courts, 277;

   from: Circuit Court, 231; Common Pleas in road matters, 433; justices on removal of paupers, 316; Quarter Sessions, 10;

Chambers, B. (cont.)
608, 609; resolutions, 154, 580, 603, 605.

Champs, Antoine, ccxxxi.

Chancellors, xvi, clxvi, ccxxvii; duty, 511, 512.

Chancery, cxxix, clxiv; decree of, effect of, 111-112, 510; procedure in, 193-196. *See also* Courts.

Chapard, ———, 587.

Charleville *v.* Chouteau, lxv, n. 2.

Chase, Salmon P., xxvii, ci, cii, cxi.

Chestnut, penalty for cutting, 357, 359.

Chitty, *On Bills of Exchange,* copy in territory, cxcvi.

Choctaws, clxxxv, n. 1.

Choisser *v.* Hargrave, cxxxvi, n. 1.

Choteau, August, ccxliii.

Chribbs, Elizabeth, clxv, clxxvii, n. 2.

Chribbs, Mary, clxv.

Chribbs, William, clxv, clxvi, clxxvii, n. 2.

Church, no arrests in, 426.

Church lands, boundary of Vincennes, 513, 580.

Cider, not to be sold retail save by tavern-keepers, 286.

Cincinnati, xi, xliii, clxxxv, n. 1, cxcviii; land office in, 606.

Circuit Court, *see* Courts.

Clark, George Rogers, xii, n. 4, xxxv, lvi, lxvi, lxxi-ii, n. 2, lxxxi, clxii, n. 2, ccxiv, ccxvi, n. 4, ccxxxv, ccxxxviii, **ccxxxix, ccxlvi,** ccxlix, cclix, cclxi, cclxiv; director of Indiana Canal Company, 155-156.

Clark, James, cxciii, n. 4.

Clark, Marston G., director of Indiana Canal Company, 156.

Clark, William, cclxxvi.

Clark County, xix, n. 2, xxxvii, xli, xliii, n. 1, xlv, n. 2, xlviii, cxvi, cxlv, n. 3, cxlix, n. 1, clxiii, n. 1, clxxviii, n. 3, clxxxv, n. 2, 579; and Knox County, Harrison County formed from, 645-646;
Circuit Court in, 215, 230;
Common Pleas Court: suits continued, 552; terms altered, 200, 551; terms in, 116, 226;
sheriff of, to take census, 177; special provision for tax assessment, 172.

Clarke, William, ccxxxvii; adopts laws, 1, 3; biographical note, ccxxxv; judge, xv, xvi, cxlv, n. 3, ccxxxvii; signs laws, 2, 6, 7, 17, 18, 19, 20, 26, 29.

Clerks, 231;
of Chancery Court: appointed by judge, 112, 511; duties, 110, 193, 512;
of common fields: how chosen, duties, 440, 442;
of Common Pleas: act as circuit clerks, 562; appointed, how, 229-230; arbitration awards, recorded by, 351; bond given by, 199; compensated, how, 596-597; duties, 201, 227, 485, 592, 593, 595-596; duty in estrays, 298-300, 301, 302, 303, 304; election returns filed by, 571; failing to act, how punished, 596; fee tables, posted by, 477; fees, 117, 467-469; fees in criminal cases, 469-470; land transfers, recorded by, fee for, 600; laws sent to, 217-218; marriage licenses, issued by, 205, 251; marriages, recorded by, 252; measures, etc., sealed by, 103, 506-507; negroes to be indented with, 137, 138, 523, 524; probate fees, 470-471; probate functions, 270-271, 275-276; process to wit-

Clerks (cont.)

nesses in arbitrations, to issue, 350; to receive fines from justices of peace, 224; return of overseers of poor to, 309; scire facias, to issue, 264; tavern license fee to, 115, 286; tax abstract, to make out, 149-150; tax on law process, to collect, 496; tax sales reported to, 172; township boundaries, to record, 256;

of county: to record marks and brands, 211-212, 245; to seal measures, 103, 506-507;

of General Assembly, compensation of, 604;

of General Court: arbitration awards recorded by, 351; bond given by, 199; and disbarment of attorneys, 341; duties, 5-6, 457; exempt from arrest, when, 426; exempt from militia duty, 400; fees of, 19, 47-49; keep roll of attorneys, 340-341, 342; may practice in Common Pleas, 561; records of, inspected, 3, 454;

of General Quarter Sessions of the Peace: 9; duty in taxation, 72; fees, 55-56;

of legislature, compensation of, 20; of Orphans' Court, fees, 59-60; of Supreme Court, *see* General Court;

of territorial courts: 545-546; causes, how to docket, 37-38, 449; exempt from arrest, when, 426; fee bills, against security for costs, to issue, 651; fee bills, to make out with execution, 649-650; fee tables, to post, 60, 477; fined for neglect of duty, 663; ineligible to legislature, 175; may not practice as attorney in own court, 342; process, to authenticate by certificate, 256;

Clerks (cont.)

tax, to collect on law process, 82-83.

Clinton, DeWitt, cclxxvii.

Cochran, Samuel, lxxxvii, n. 1, cciii, cclxxi; biographical note, cclxx; judge, ccxxxi; signs petition, xlvi, n. 1, liii-iv, n. 4, lix, n. 2.

Cock fighting, how punished, 370-371.

Coffee tree, penalty for cutting, 357, 359.

Coles, Edward, xcv, n. 4.

Collectors, cxv-vii, clii; account with auditor, 145, 530; bond of, 152; of common fields, duty, 440-441; duty of, in tax sales, 150-151, 171-172, 172-174; fees, 151; to list billiard tables, 119-120.

College township, reservation in favor of lessees, 360.

Commissioners, conveyances agreed to by deceased, to execute, 281; county levies, law of 1801, and, 1; for partiton, 124-126, 521-522; real estate, to value, 131-132.

Commitment papers, filed by sheriff, 259.

Common fields, cxxiii, 439-443.

Common law, c, ci, cii; declared in force, 323.

Common law penalty, prescribed for manslaughter, 236.

Common Pleas, *see* Courts.

Commons, boundary of Vincennes, 513.

Commonwealth *v.* Aves, xxxvi, n. 1.

Commonwealth *v.* Roxbury, lxvii, n. 1.

Compounding felony, how punished, 241.

Compte, Pierre, ccxxxi.

Compton, *Practice,* copy in territory, cxcvi.

County taxation, cxiv-v, cxviii, cxix;
act amended, 186, 664-665;
laws: 1801, 1-2; 1803, 68-81;
1806, 196; 1807, 481-495; 1808, 664-665;
penalty for false tax list, 70-71;
sheriff: to list property, 71-72,
484-485; to take lists of property,
69-70, 481-483.
See also Taxation.

County treasurer, *see* T r e a s u r e r,
county.

Court martial, 213; how constituted,
419; oath of, 420; penalties inflicted by, 422; procedure, 419-420.

Courthouses, lv, n. 2, clxxxi-ii, n. 4,
ccx.

Courts, bill to reform, x, n. 3; disorderly conduct before, 368-369;
laws: 1801, 3-6, 8-15; 1803, 33-
42; 1805, 91-92, 93-94, 108-112,
115-118, 140-141; 1806, 184-185,
193-196, 200-201, 215-216; 1807,
225-230, 230-233, 375-388, 443-459,
507-513; 1808, 658-661, 661-662,
662-664;
practice in, 268-269. *See also*
special courts;
of Chancery, xlviii, clxvi-iii,
cxcvii, n. 1, 108-112, 507-513. *See
also* Chancery;
Circuit, cxxix, cxliv-vi, cxlvii,
n. 1, cxlviii, clv-vi, clvii-ix, clxxvi,
n. 5, clxxix, n. 1, clxxxvi, n. 2,
clxxxix, n. 5, cxci, cxcv, cc, n. 6,
ccvii, ccviii, ccix, n. 3, ccx, n. 3,
12, 215, 230-231;
appeals to: by administrators,
277; in probate, 273;
clerks: Common Pleas clerks to
act as, 562; fees of, 49; to post
fee tables, 477;
divorce jurisdiction of, 324;
duties, 11, 462; to issue process,

Courts (cont.)
231; recognizances to, 224, 255;
to regard equity, 307-308;
terms of: 86; altered in St. Clair
and Randolph, 555;
writs: of attachment, 266; certiorari to, in forcible entry, 329;
Common Pleas, xix, n. 2, xxvi,
xxxiv, xxxv, liii, n. 1, lvii, lviii,
n. 1, cxv, cxviii, n. 5, cxx, cxxii,
cxxxi, n. 2, cxxxvi, cxxxvii, cxli,
cxlvii, cxlviii, cli, clii-iii, cliv, n. 1,
clvii, n. 1, clxi, clxii, clxiv, clxxix,
n. 1, clxxxi, clxxxviii, n. 3, cxci,
n. 5, cc, cci, ccii, cciv, ccviii, ccix,
n. 3, ccxi, n. 1, ccxii, ccxxix,
ccxxx-xxxi, 115-118, 225-230;
appeals to: from assessments,
494; in small causes, 383-384;
appoint: assessors, 147, 174, 592-
593; assessors of damage by new
roads, 430-431; commissioners, 93-
94, 131-132; constables, 388; fence
viewers, 345-346; overseers of
poor, 308; supervisors, 434;
bail for action in, 447; bond, of
clerks, to take, 545-546;
county: buildings, to contract
for, 492; claims, to audit, 487; to
estimate expenses of, and levy tax,
488-489;
debtors, duty regarding release
of, 99-101, 502-504; duty, 310, 321,
396-397, 460, 462, 652; equity, to
regard, 307-308; false tax lists,
duty in case of, 70-71, 483-484;
fees, how altered, 661-662;
ferries: may discontinue, 355; to
establish, 352-353; to tax, 490;
indenture proceedings in, 137,
138; jurisdiction, 13, 116; payments, to order, 140-141, 527-528;
polling places, to designate, 570;
practice in, 36, 443-454, 457-459;

Courts (cont.)

prison bounds, to lay off, **257**;

probate: court merged in, 117; duties, 271-273, 274-283, 284;

real estate, minor's, to authorize sale of, 106; recognizances to, 223, 224, 233; return of partitions to, 125, 521;

roads: altering, at landholder's petition, duty on, 431-432; application for new, duty on, 428-430; duty regarding, 427-428; jurisdiction on, how limited, 433; vacating, duty on, 432-433;

school lands, to lease, 668; small causes in, 384-385; standard weights and measures, may provide, 102-103, 505-506; subpoenas, may issue, 229; suits continued, 552;

taverns: to license, 114-115, 285; to make rates, 288;

tax levy, duty on, 487-489; tax on law process in, 496;

terms: 14, 116; altered, 200-201, 551, 663;

vagrants, duty regarding, 566-568;

writs: ad quod damnum, to issue, 133, 363-365; of attachment, 266;

County, lviii, lix, lx, cvi, cxv, cxxvii, clii, clvi, clix, clx-xi, clxv, clxxvi, clxxvii, n. 1, cci, ccix, ccx, ccxi, n. 1; when costs not recovered, 41;

of Errors and Appeals, 663;

General (Indiana Territory), xv, xvi, xxvi, cxlii, cxliii-iv, cxlv, cxlvi, cxlvii, clii, cliv-v, clvi, clix, clx, n. 1, clxv, clxvi, clxvii, clxix, clxxiv, clxxv, clxxvii, clxxviii, n. 1, clxxix, n. 1, clxxx, n. 2, clxxxvi, n. 2, clxxxix, n. 5, cxci, cxcvi,

Courts (cont.)

cxcviii, cc, ccviii, n. 6, ccix, ccxi, ccxii, ccxxvii, 215-216, 229, 230-233;

appeals to: by administrators, 277; from Common Pleas on roads, 433; how limited, 662; in probate, 273;

attorneys: licensed by, 340; may disbar, 341;

bail for action in, 447; certiorari to, in forcible entry, 329;

clerks: bond, to give, 199, 545-546; duty, 663; exempt from arrest, when, 426; fees of, 560-561; issue process to witnesses in arbitrations, 350; office of, inspected, 454; to post fee tables, 477;

decision arrived at, how, 663; divorce jurisdiction, 324; duty, 462; equity, to regard, 307-308; jail delivery, power of, 12; no suit under fifty dollars, 454; practice in, 3-6, 33-42, 443-459; practice in, how altered, 104-105; recognizances to, 9, 223, 224, 227, 255; sessions, 10, 663; terms adjourned, 551-552; writs of attachment, 266;

General (Northwest Territory), **x, n. 1, cxxix, cxlviii,** clvii-iii, n. 2, clxiii, cxcii, cxciv, n. 1;

General Quarter Sessions of the Peace, xix, xxvi, n. 3, lvii, lxxiv, cxviii, cxix, cxxxi, cxlvi-vii, cxlix, cl, clii, cliv, n. 1, clvii, n. 1, clxi-iii, clxxiv, n. 3, clxxix, n. 1, clxxxi-ii, n. 4, cc, cci, ccii, ccv, n. 1, ccxxix, ccxxx, 9;

appeals: from, 10; to, from assessment, 80;

county: claims audited by, 73; expenses, estimated by, 75;

ferries, taxed by, 77; powers of, vested in Common Pleas, 116;

Hamilton, Robert, cxii, n. 1, cxciii, n. 4, ccxxxiv, ccxxxviii; biographical note, cclxxix.

Hamilton, William, cxciii-iv, n. 4, ccxxxiv; biographical note, cclxxix.

Hamilton County, clx, n. 4.

Hamtramck, Harriet, guardian of, 575.

Hamtramck, John Francis, xxxvi, n. 1, lxxv, n. 2, cxxii, n. 1, clxx, n. 2, ccxx, n. 3, ccxxi, n. 1, ccxxii, n. 1, cclxiv; lands of, sale of allowed, 575-576, 576-578.

Hamtramck, Julian, guardian of, 575.

Hanging, method of death penalty, 250.

Hannah v. Benj. Beckes, cxxxv, n. 3.

Harbin, John, appropriation for, 208.

Hard labor, penalty for larceny, 240.

Hargrave, William, xviii, n. 2.

Harmar, Josiah, xxi, n. 3, lxx, n. 5, lxxv, n. 2, ccxvi, ccxxi, n. 1.

Harrison, John, director of Indiana Canal Company, 156.

Harrison, William Henry, xi, xvi, xxx, xxxiii, xxxvii, xl, n. 2, xliv, n. 1, li, liv, n. 1, lvi, lix, lxvi, n. 1, lxxxi, xcvi, ciii, n. 4, cv, n. 1, cx, cxviii, cxxii, cxxix, cxxx, n. 1, cxli, cxliii, clx, clxxiv, clxxvi, clxxviii, n. 3, clxxxiii, clxxxv, cxciii, cxcv, cxcix, n. 3, cc, n. 6, cci, ccii, ccviii, n. 7, ccxxxvii, ccxxxviii, ccxli, ccxlv, ccxlvi, ccxlvii, ccl, ccli, ccliii, ccliv, cclv, cclvi, cclvii, cclviii, cclix, cclxv, cclxvi, cclxvii, cclxx, cclxxi, cclxxix, 197; appointment policy of, xix;

attitude on: Chancery Court, clxvi-vii; Northwest statutes, cxi; roads, cxxiv, n. 4, cli, n. 1; slavery, xxv; taxation, cxix;

biographical note, x, n. 1; char-

Harrison, William Henry (cont.)
acterized, lvii, n. 2; charges against, xlv, n. 2, xlvii-ix, lviii, n. 2, cxvii, cxxxiv-v, n. 4, ccxlviii; criticism of courts by, clxi; governor, appointment as, xiv, xxxviii, n. 1, xliii, n. 1; incorporator Vincennes University, 178, 533;

land: authorized to sell tract of, 575-576; claims delt with by, lxvii, n. 1, lxxvii, lxxviii, lxxix-xxx, lxxxii, n. 1, lxxxiii, n. 3, xcix; cleared of Indian titles by, xxv; policy of, lx-iii, lxiv; record of, lxxxiv, lxxxvi, lxxxvii, n. 2;

laws adopted by, 1, 3; opposition to, xiii, n. 3, xlii, xliii, n. 1, lv, cclxxvii; plantation of, boundary of Vincennes, 513; powers of, as governor, xxix;

relations of, with: Jefferson, xxvi-vii, n. 3; J. R. Jones, xvii, ccxl, ccxlii; M. Jones, ccxliii;

representative government, and, xx, xxii, xxiii, xxvi, xxviii-ix;

signs: laws, 2, 6, 7, 17, 18, 19, 20, 26, 29, 30, 31, 32, 42, 63, 64, 66, 68, 81, 83, 84, 85, 87, 91, 92, 93, 94, 95, 96, 98, 99, 102, 103, 105, 107, 108, 112, 114, 115, 118, 120, 123, 124, 126, 133, 136, 139, 141, 142, 144, 147, 153, 163, 174, 175, 176, 184, 185, 186, 187, 189, 193, 196, 199, 200, 201, 202, 203, 204, 205, 206, 208, 210, 212, 214, 216, 217, 225, 230, 233, 234, 235, 250, 252, 255, 256, 257, 261, 266, 268, 269, 270, 284, 288, 294, 297, 305, 307, 308, 322, 323, 325, 326, 331, 340, 344, 347, 349, 352, 355, 357, 361, 366, 375, 388, 390, 397, 399, 425, 427, 439, 443, 459, 462, 467, 480, 481, 495, 498, 499, 502, 505, 507, 513, 516, 520, 523, 526, 528,

Sheriffs (cont.)

adjourned by, 3, 455; of Dearborn County, duty, 176; debtor, to return surplus to, 265;

deputy: may not be attorney, 342; to serve in election districts, 397;

distress for rent, duty in, 331-332; duty, 10, 12-13, 189-190, 191, 200, 227, 233-234, 329, 337-338, 380, 412, 423, 444, 445, 458, 542-544, 546-547, 556, 557, 566, 568, 602, 658; election duty, 391, 393, 394-395, 571; escapes, how liable for, 258; estrays, when to sell, 301; executions, duty in, 126-133, 188, 262, 540; executions, duty in, changed, 665-667; exempt from arrest, when, 426; failure of, how dealt with, 479;

fees: 32, 50, 51-52, 56-57, 472-473, 494, 495, 561; collected, to account for, 62-63, 479-480; for collecting tax, 600; failing to pay, proceeded against, 462; liability of, for surveyor's, 28-29;

fines paid to, 261; free male inhabitants, listed by, 152-153; jury summoned by, 326, 363;

limitations on: ineligible to legislature, 175; may not be assessor, 593; may not be special bail, 104, 447;

penalty for neglect, 196, 229; provide food for criminals, when, 260; remedy against, for failure to return bail, 445-446; replevins, duty regarding, 336-337; riots, duty in case of, 238-239; special liability of, 554;

taxes: certificate of sale for, given by, 599; duty regarding, 77-78, 80-81, 491; on law process, to receive, as treasurer, 496-497;

Sheriffs (cont.)

property subject to, duty regarding lists of, 69-71, 71-72, 481-483; sale for, duty regarding, 598;

treasurer, duty as, 140-141, 186-187, 527-528; undersheriff, ineligible to legislature, 397; vagrants, to hire out, 567;

writs: failure to return, 14; returned, when, 105; of seizin, issue to, 306.

Shovel board, gambling at, 371.

Sign posts, to be set up on high roads, penalty for defacing, 437-438.

Single men, listed for taxation, 80, 494.

Singleton, John, clxxxix, n. 5, cclxxvii.

Slander, actions of: cliii; costs when barred, 454; limitation on, 450.

Slaughter, Robert, clxxiv, n. 2, 208; extradited, 83.

Slavery, xx-xxi, xxv, xxvii, xxviii, xxix, xxxv, xxxvii, xxxviii-xli, xlii, xliii, xlvi, n. 1, xlviii, liv, lv, cxxxiii, cxxxiv, cxxxviii-ix, ccix, n. 3. *See also* Negroes and mulattoes, Slaves.

Slaves, xiii, n. 2, xl, cxviii, n. 3, cxxvii, cxxxv-viii, cxli-iii, clxxv, n. 5, 136-139, 203-204, 523-526; assembling of, persons suffering, how punished, 657-658; sale of liquor to, 286; taxed, how, 73, 487. *See also* Negroes and mulattoes, Slavery.

Sloo, Thomas, biographical note, ccxlv; land commissioner, lxxx, ccxxviii, ccxlii.

Small, John, clxxix, n. 3, clxxx, n. 3, cc, n. 7.

Small causes, cxxxii, n. 1, cliv, n. 1, clxix, 375-388; act amended, 91-

SUPPLEMENT TO APPENDIX

(See pages CCXXVII-CCXXXIV)

LEGISLATIVE COUNCILLORS, REPRESENTATIVES, COUNTY OFFICERS, AND FEDERAL LAND COMMISSIONERS FOR INDIANA COUNTIES, INDIANA TERRITORY.   1800-1809.

HISTORICAL BUREAU

OF THE

INDIANA LIBRARY AND HISTORICAL DEPARTMENT

INDIANAPOLIS

1931

SUPPLEMENT

KNOX COUNTY

Knox County was formed by proclamation of the governor of the Northwest Territory on June 20, 1790.

LEGISLATIVE COUNCILLOR

John Rice Jones—May [?] 1805-May 22, 1809.

REPRESENTATIVES

John Johnson—January 3, 1805-February 1, 1807.

Benjamin Parke—January 3, 1805-February 1, 1807.

General Washington Johnston—February 2, 1807-April 5, 1812.

Luke Decker—February 2, 1807-April 2, 1809.

COURT OF GENERAL QUARTER SESSIONS

James Johnson—July 4, 1800-January 1, 1806.

Pierre Gamelin—July 4, 1800-January 1, 1806.

Luke Decker—July 4, 1800-January 1, 1806.

Abel Westfall—July 4, 1800-January 1, 1806.

Antoine Marechal—July 4, 1800-January 1, 1806.

Jonathan Purcell—July 4, 1800-January 1, 1806.

Abraham Huff—July 4, 1800-February 3, 1801.

Marston G. Clark—July 4, 1800-February 3, 1801.

John Noble Woods—July 4, 1800-February 3, 1801.

Benjamin Beckes—November 5, 1800. Resigned before February 2, 1803.

Ephraim Jordan—November 5, 1800-February 3, 1802. Resigned.

John Ochiltree—August 3, 1801-January 1, 1806.

George Leech—February 2, 1803-January 1, 1806.

George Wallace, Jr.—November 1, 1803-January 1, 1806.

Peter Jones—November 1, 1803-January 1, 1806.

Jacob Hardin—June 1, 1804-January 1, 1806.

Daniel McClure—September 22, 1804-January 1, 1806.

William V. Moorman—September 4, 1805-January 1, 1806.

COURT OF COMMON PLEAS

James Johnson—July 4, 1800. Resigned before April 16, 1813.

Pierre Gamelin—July 4, 1800-February 3, 1801; August 3, 1801-January 1, 1806.

Luke Decker—July 4, 1800-December 31, 1813.

Abel Westfall—July 4, 1800-January 1, 1806.

Antoine Marechal—July 4, 1800-January 1, 1806.

Jonathan Purcell—July 4, 1800-February 3, 1801.

Abraham Huff—July 4, 1800-February 3, 1801.

Marston G. Clark—July 4, 1800-February 3, 1801.

John Noble Woods—July 4, 1800-February 3, 1801.

Benjamin Beckes—November 5, 1800. Resigned before February 2, 1803.

Ephraim Jordan—November 5, 1800-February 3, 1802. Resigned.

George Leech—February 2, 1803. Resigned before June 21, 1810.

George Wallace, Jr.—November 1, 1803-January 1, 1806.

Peter Jones—November 1, 1803-January 1, 1806.

Daniel McClure—September 22, 1804-January 1, 1806.

Elihu Stout—November 5, 1805-January 1, 1806.

William V. Moorman—November 5, 1805-January 1, 1806.

Probate Court

Henry VanderBurgh—July 28, 1800-January 14, 1801.

Abraham Westfall—January 14, 1801-January 1, 1806.

Justices of the Peace

William Burnet—August 29, 1801.
William Wells—August 29, 1801.
David Robb—December 26, 1801.
John Kinsey—March 10, 1802.
George Hobin—June 4, 1805.
Jonathan Antony—August 8, 1805.
Isaac White—September 24, 1805.
William Prince—September 24, 1805.
Robert Gill—March 15, 1806.
Robert Evans—April 11, 1806.
Abraham Lander—July 15, 1806.
Wilson Montgomery—August 15, 1806.
Israel McGready—January 30, 1807.
Walter Wilson—February 19, 1807.
John Shively—May 2, 1807.

Jabez Jones—May 25, 1807.
Jacob Winemiller—July 1, 1807.
Henry Brinton—August 5 [15], 1807.
Jonathan Taylor—August 24, 1807.
Paul Casselberry—March 16, 1808.
Robert Warfth—May 24, 1808.
George Robinson—July 14, 1808.
Daniel Grass—August 17, 1808.
William Jones—September 24, 1808.
Benjamin D. Price—November 28, 1808.
William Polke—November 28, 1808.

Clerk of the County Court

Robert Buntin—July 28, 1800-December 31, 1813.

Sheriffs

William Prince—July 28, 1800. Resigned before September 22, 1804.

Daniel Sullivan—September 22, 1804. Resigned before December 29, 1806.

Parmenas Beckes—December 29, 1806. Resigned before April 5, 1810.

Coroners

Samuel McKee—June 10, 1801. Resigned before July 9, 1802.

Jacob Kuykendall—July 9, 1802. Resigned before April 13, 1810.

Recorders of Deeds

Robert Buntin—July 28, 1800-February 3, 1801 [?].

John Gibson, Jr.—February 3, 1801. Removed from Territory before June 2, 1807.

John D. Hay—June 2, 1807-February 3, 1817.

Treasurer

James Johnson—July 28, 1800-January 31, 1804.

SURVEYORS

Robert Buntin—July 28, 1800-September 15, 1801 [?].

John Small—September 15, 1801-[?].

CLARK COUNTY

Clark County was formed by proclamation of the governor of Indiana Territory on February 3, 1801.

LEGISLATIVE COUNCILLOR

Samuel Gwathmey—May [?], 1805-August [?], 1808. Resigned.

REPRESENTATIVES

Davis Floyd—January 3, 1805-February 2, 1807.

James Beggs—February 3, 1807-April 1, 1810.

COURT OF GENERAL QUARTER SESSIONS

John Gibson—February 4, 1801-January 1, 1806.

Charles Tuley—February 4, 1801-January 1, 1806.

William Harwood—February 4, 1801-January 1, 1806.

Marston G. Clark—February 4, 1801. Removed from Clark County before December 21, 1805.

Abraham Huff—February 4, 1801-January 1, 1806.

James Noble Woods—February 4, 1801-January 1, 1806.

Thomas Downs—February 4, 1801-January 1, 1806.

William Goodwin—February 4, 1801-January 1, 1806.

Nicholas Harrison—September 30, 1803-January 1, 1806.

George Newland—November 21, 1803-January 1, 1806.

Job Guest—September 22, 1804-January 1, 1806.

COURT OF COMMON PLEAS

Marston G. Clark—February 4, 1801. Removed from Clark County before December 21, 1805.

Abraham Huff—February 4, 1801-January 1, 1806.

James Noble Woods—February 4, 1801-January 1, 1806.

Thomas Downs—February 4, 1801. Resigned before April 29, 1811.

William Goodwin—February 4, 1801. Resigned before August 7, 1811.

Evan Shelby—December 21, 1805-December 31, 1813.

PROBATE COURT

Jesse Rowland—February 4, 1801-January 1, 1806.

JUSTICES OF THE PEACE

James Lemon—January 25, 1806.

Patrick Shields—July 19, 1806.

Aquilla Rogers—July 22, 1806.

John Douchett—De̶██████ 1806.

Robert McIntire—April 27, 1807.

John Smith—June 30, 1807.

Dennis Pennington—July 10, 1807.

John Rychart—August 22, 1807.

Charles Johnson — September 9, 1807.

James Smock—November 3, 1807.

William Vawter—May 18, 1808.

John Beggs—June 29, 1808.

Jacob Zenor—July 6, 1808.

John Vawter—July 16, 1808.

Absalom Littell — October 27, 1808.

James Brown—November 3, 1808.

CLERK OF THE COUNTY COURT

Samuel Gwathmey—February 4, 1801-January 21, 1811.

SHERIFFS

Samuel Hay—February 4, 1801-September 17, 1802 [?].

Davis Floyd—September 17, 1802. Resigned by December 12, 1806.

Willis W. Goodwin—December 12, 1806. Resigned before July 10, 1811.

CORONERS

Peter McDonald — February 4, 1801-December 24, 1802 [?].

John McClintock—December 25, 1802. Resigned before July 7, 1805.

James Ferguson—July 7, 1805-November 30, 1806 [?].

Peter Stacey—December 1, 1806. Died before July 11, 1810.

RECORDERS OF DEEDS

Davis Floyd—February 4, 1801-September 17, 1802.

Isaac Shelby—September 17, 1802. ...signed before March 8, 1806.

S.... Gwathmey—March 8, 1806-J.... ...1811.

...SURERS

Thomas Downs—February 4, 1801. Resigned before January 29, 1802.

Samuel Gwathmey—January 29, 1802-January 31, 1804.

SURVEYORS

Marston G. Clark—February 4, 1801. Removed from Clark County before December 21, 1805.

Isaac Shelby—December 21, 1805-January 4, 1811.

DEARBORN COUNTY

Dearborn County was formed by proclamation of the governor of Indiana Territory on March 7, 1803.

LEGISLATIVE COUNCILLOR

Benjamin Chambers — May [?], 1805-May 22, 1809.

REPRESENTATIVE

Jesse B. Thomas—January 3, 1805-April 2, 1809.

COURT OF GENERAL QUARTER SESSIONS

Benjamin Chambers—March 7, 1803-January 1, 1806.

John Brownson—March 7, 1803-January 1, 1806.

Jeremiah Hunt—March 7, 1803-January 1, 1806.

Jabez Percival—March 7, 1803-January 1, 1806.

Barent Hulick—March 7, 1803-January 1, 1806.

Richard Stevens—March 7, 1803-January 1, 1806.

William Cotton—September 8, 1804-January 1, 1806.

COURT OF COMMON PLEAS

Benjamin Chambers—March 7, 1803. Resigned before December 14, 1810.

John Brownson—March 7, 1803-January 1, 1806.

Jeremiah Hunt—March 7, 1803-January 1, 1806.

Jabez Percival—March 7, 1803-January 1, 1806.

Barent Hulick—March 7, 1803. Resigned before July 4, 1809.

Richard Stevens—March 7, 1803-January 1, 1806.

William Major—December 14, 1805-December 31, 1813.

ORPHANS' COURT

Benjamin Chambers—March 7, 1803-January 1, 1806.

John Brownson—March 7, 1803-January 1, 1806.

Jeremiah Hunt—March 7, 1803-January 1, 1806.

Jabez Percival—March 7, 1803-January 1, 1806.

Barent Hulick—March 7, 1803-January 1, 1806.

Richard Stevens—March 7, 1803-January 1, 1806.

Probate Court

John Brownson—March 7, 1803-January 1, 1806.

Justices of the Peace

William Major—March 7, 1803.
James McCarty—March 7, 1803.
Jonathan McCarty—August 30, 1803.
Justus Gibbs—April 11, 1806.
James Adair, Sr.—April 11, 1806.
Benjamin Drake—April 11, 1806.
John Templeton—April 11, 1806.
Richard Rue—April 11, 1806.
John Livingston—December 24, 1806.
Samuel Fulton—December 24, 1806.
Benjamin M. Piatt—September 14, 1807.
George Craig—September 15, 1807.
William Wilson—December 2, 1807.
Enoch McCarty—March 17, 1808.
Thomas T. Gayness—June 12, 1808.
Chambers Foster—June 12, 1808.
David Hoover—January 16, 1809.

Clerk of the County Court

Samuel C. Vance—March 7, 1803-September 6, 1813 [?].

Recorders of Deeds

James Dill—March 7, 1803-August 30, 1803 [?].
James Hamilton—August 30, 1803-February 14, 1817 [?].

Coroners

Jonathan White—March 7, 1803. Resigned before August 13, 1805.
Justus Gibbs—August 13, 1805-December 2, 1807 [?].
Jacob Horner—December 2, 1807-[?].

Sheriffs

David Lamphere—August 23, 1803. Removed from county before November 23, 1804.

James Hamilton—November 23, 1804-December 30, 1816 [?].

HARRISON COUNTY

Harrison County was formed by a statute of October 11, 1808, effective December 1, 1808.

Court of Common Pleas

Patrick Shields—December 8, 1808-December 31, 1813.
John George Pfrimmer—December 8, 1808-December 31, 1813.
Moses Boone—December 8, 1808-December 31, 1813.

Justices of the Peace

Dennis Pennington—November 3, 1808.
John Smith—November 3, 1808.
John Boone—November 3, 1808.
John Oatman—January 13, 1809.
Moses Hoggatt—January 16, 1809.
William D. Littell—January 17, 1809.

Clerk of the County Court

George F. Pope—January 17, 1809-February 11, 1811.

Sheriff

Spier Spencer—December 8, 1808. Killed in Battle of Tippecanoe, November 7, 1811.

Coroner

Samuel Black—December 8, 1808. Removed from county before January 4, 1811.

Recorder of Deeds

George F. Pope—January 17, 1809-February 11, 1811.

FEDERAL LAND COMMISSIONERS

John Badollet—April 17, 1804-[?].
Nathaniel Ewing—October 15 [?], 1804-[?].